STRATEGIC MANAGEMENT

Strategic Management

THIRD EDITION

ALEX MILLER

The William B. Stokely Professor of Management
University of Tennessee

Irwin
McGraw-Hill

Boston, Massachusetts   Burr Ridge, Illinois   Dubuque, Iowa
Madison, Wisconsin   New York, New York   San Francisco, California   St. Louis, Missouri

Irwin/McGraw-Hill

A Division of The McGraw·Hill Companies

Strategic Management

This book is printed on acid free paper.

2 3 4 5 6 7 8 9 0 DOC DOC 9 0 9 8

ISBN 0-07-043014-4

Publisher: Craig Beytien
Sponsoring editors: Adam Knepper and Karen Mellon
Marketing manager: Kenyetta Giles
Project managers: Curt Berkowitz and Ira C. Roberts
Production supervisors: Leroy A. Young, Richard A. Ausburn, and Scott M. Hamilton
Interior designer: Karen K. Quigley
Cover designer: Joe Zeller, Z Graphics
Compositor: Ruttle, Shaw & Wetherill, Inc.
Typeface: 10/12 Janson
Printer: R. R. Donnelley & Sons Company

Library of Congress Cataloging-in-Publication Data
Miller, Alex (date)
    Strategic management / Alex Miller. / 3rd ed.
        p.   cm.
    ISBN 0-07-043014-4
    Includes bibliographical references and indexes.
        1. Strategic planning. 2. Strategic planning—Case studies. I. Title
    HD30.28 .D474   1998
658.4/012—dc21   97-22814

http://www.mhhe.com

About the Author

Alex Miller is the William B. Stokely professor of management at the University of Tennessee at Knoxville. He earned an M.B.A. from Amos Tuck School of Business at Dartmouth College, where he was a Tuck Scholar, and a Ph.D. from the University of Washington. In 1989 he was a visiting research scholar at the Cranfield Institute of Technology in England. He is on the editorial board of the *Journal for Business Venturing*, and his research has been published in such journals as the *Academy of Management Journal, Corporate Environmental Strategy, Journal of Business Research, Journal for Business Venturing, Journal for High Technology Management Research, Journal of Management Studies*, and *Strategic Management Journal*. Professor Miller is an active consultant whose clients have included Citibank, Dover Corporation, Eastman Chemical, Freddie Mac, Internal Revenue Service, Lockheed Martin, Mercy Healthcare Systems, Navistar, Philips Consumer Electronics, Rockwell International, Sea Land, Tennessee Valley Authority, and Union Carbide, as well as a number of smaller firms. He was a member of the faculty teams responsible for designing and team-teaching Tennessee's unique M.B.A. and executive M.B.A. programs. He has received five teaching awards and was the first two-time winner of the Faculty Accomplishment Award from students in the Tennessee Organization of M.B.A.s. In addition to his academic and business careers, Professor Miller is also a professional cattleman. Alex Miller can be contacted through his home page at:

http://funnelweb.utcc.utk.edu/~amiller2

Contents in Brief

Contents

Instructor's Preface

FOR NEW ADOPTERS

What Is Different About This Book?

Welcome! Strategy textbooks abound, and the last thing you need is another book that looks just like the last three you reviewed. The following features make this strategic management book unique:

Level of Integration

In an age that stresses being politically correct, textbooks are written to avoid taking a clear stand in order to evade criticism from any sector, but this text clearly takes a stand. From its beginning to its end, this text emphasizes developing a competitive advantage for the purpose of achieving superior financial performance. This central focus forms an integrating theme throughout the book. It is demonstrated from the start by the "Architecture of Strategy" framework, used as a road map throughout the text, right through to the teaching notes that accompany the cases. Every chapter was written to explain another set of concepts critical to developing strategies that establish competitive advantages and yield superior economic performance, and every case was selected because it illustrates these concepts in practice.

Blend of Cutting Edge Versus Tried and True

As an offspring of general management and strategy, strategic management benefits from the hybrid vigor that comes from having parents with very different lineages. General management traces its roots back to the practice of organizational leadership and has provided many tools and concepts that are valuable for their ability to combine simplicity with power. Who would want to teach a course on strategic management that did not cover such tried and true concepts as SWOT analysis or did not illustrate the integration of different functional areas? Such contributions from general management nicely complement concepts produced from the study of strategy as a topic in its own right. The newest concepts that have resulted from the study of strategy as an academic discipline include hypercompetition, the resource-based view of the firm, and the learning organization. When we combine the best of the concepts from general management and strategy, the result is strategic management as it is explained in this text.

Balance Between Formulation and Implementation

No doubt about it, it's far easier to write about strategic analysis and strategy formulation than it is to write about strategy implementation. Yet, virtually any experienced manager will tell you that the real challenge in strategic management lies in implementation. This text provides the most comprehensive discussion on this difficult topic of any available text designed for a strategic management course. Four beefy chapters are devoted to the topic, with the first presenting an overview of the issues involved in strategic change, and the subsequent three detailing how three different categories of change levers can work both for and against desired changes. Students often complain that they cannot see the value of the "touchy-feely" stuff that too often makes up a discussion of strategy implementation. However, experience shows that students appreciate the practical, results-oriented material in the implementation section of this text.

"Digestibility" for Students

Given the wide range of topics to be covered, the high-level thinking required, and the blend of theory and practice entailed, strategic management typically is not an easy course for students. Two approaches are used to deal with this issue. One is to "dummy down" the text by avoiding challenging material, but this approach runs the risk of undereducating students on practices they will encounter in real-world organizations. The approach taken here is to include all concepts considered essential to a student's well-rounded understanding of strategic management as it is currently practiced, but to make these concepts as accessible as possible for students. The text uses an inviting, student-friendly style of writing. Concepts are carefully explained in a logical, classroom-tested sequence. Countless illustrations are used to drive home critical points. The goal of this text is to present all the concepts critical to your course and to do so in a manner that makes your student's study time as productive as possible.

Quality of Ancillaries

While the challenges facing students in this course are significant, so are those facing its instructors. Strategic management is arguably the most rapidly evolving business discipline, so remaining current on concepts is an unending responsibility. And beyond the concepts, every incoming class of students expects cases that are the subjects of today's headlines instead of yesterday's history books. The most common approach to addressing these challenges results in a sort of "arms race" that textbook salespeople judge using the "thud factor." This is a race to see whose ancillary package can produce the loudest thud when a salesperson plops it down on your desk. Contrary to this trend, development of the ancillary package for this text has emphasized quality, not quantity. Rather than being diverted by whistles and bells of marginal utility, development has focused on producing teaching notes and teaching aids for the chapters (Volume I) and cases (Volume II) that are genuinely useful.

Volume I, prepared by Ram Subramanian (Grand Valley State University), contains chapter outlines, teaching tips, examples and illustrations not found in the text, and a great test bank. Volume II, which I edited, contains all the case notes, presenting a case synopsis, a discussion on the case's pedagogy, suggestions on how to use the cases in conjunction with specific text chapters, thorough discussion of each discussion question, transparency masters presenting key points from the case analysis, and a case update. This material is also supplemented with sidebars highlighting the case's key features and others summarizing its central topics. Every case note also comes with a board plan and wherever applicable, they identify outside resources such as articles and videos. If you never look at teaching materials because they are never any good, I hope you will make an exception and look at the two-volume *Instructor's Manual* accompanying this text. It's different from all the rest. See for yourself.

If you are a new adopter and are interested in more details about the text, you may be interested in the following section, which offers previous adopters' discussion about changes made between the second and third editions.

FOR PREVIOUS ADOPTERS:

What Is Different About This Edition?

Welcome back. Here's what's different about the third edition:

- Based on surveys, interviews, and suggestions from a number of past users, this edition has several new learning aids for students. Each of the five major parts to the text has a concise part overview that shows how the upcoming materials are integrated and how they should be approached. Each chapter has a three-part opener presented as a two-page spread. These openers contain a chapter outline, a chapter overview, and a list of key learning points. Following these openers, students are given a strategic vignette presenting a real-world example of how the issues covered in the upcoming pages were critical to the success of a recognizable firm. Back by popular demand, the chapters still end with a bulleted list of managerial practices to adopt from this chapter. However, I have added study/discussion questions to the chapter closings.

- The former Chapter 1 is gone. Some of the material that was in it, specifically the motivational material that explains the course to students, has been moved to a Student's Preface that immediately follows this one. This is followed by two chapters that combine to form a unique two-chapter opening part, entitled Perspectives on Strategic Management. The perspectives to which this part title refers are the **content perspective** and the **process perspective** commonly used to organize our discipline's work.

- The new **Chapter 1** focuses on the content of strategy. This chapter explains the text's central premise—strategies should create competitive advantages that yield superior financial performance—and introduces the Architecture of Strategy framework that shows how topics covered in subsequent chapters contribute to building and maintaining competitive advantages. In explaining fundamental concepts such as **economic value added** (EVA) and **competitive advantage,** the focus throughout this chapter is on "the what" of strategy, that is, what works in producing desired outcomes. This makes it a good complement to the second chapter in Part I.

- The new **Chapter 2** focuses on the process of strategic management. This chapter views strategic management as a series of interlinked processes. It takes a detailed look at **strategic planning** and discusses its strengths and weaknesses. In this chapter, students are encouraged to look for descriptions of **strategic processes** that are presented alongside discussion of strategic content throughout the upcoming chapters. In keeping with this opener, I give new emphasis to covering content and process perspectives in an integrated fashion throughout all subsequent chapters.

- **Part II** of the text treats external and internal analysis as two sides of the same coin. Chapters 3 and 4 are presented as essential to understanding the sources of competitive advantage, **structural position** and **process execution,** respectively.

- **Chapter 3** on external analysis has been extensively revised. It still includes a discussion of five forces analysis, but it supplements this with coverage of newer concepts such as **hypercompetition** and **competition.** There is also more extensive discussion of how strategy is shaped by the competitive environment and vice versa.

- **Chapter 4** on internal analysis places far greater emphasis on the **resource-based view** of the firm. The **balanced scorecard** is presented as a useful way to analyze a firm from a number of important and mutually supporting perspectives.

- **Part III** of the text is devoted to exploring strategy formulation at four different levels: operations, business, corporate, and global. Because material on competitive advantage was moved to Chapter 1, I was finally able to implement a change that several of you have been requesting: The chapter on strategy formulation at the operations level has been moved to precede the chapter on business-level strategy, making a more logical sequence of coverage from the more narrow (operations) to the broadest (international). Thanks for bearing with me while I figured out a way to accomplish this change!

- **Chapter 6** now presents the material on business-level strategy. This is a major revision from the second edition. The **market life cycle model** popular with many users is still there. But, several instructors have asked for more coverage of **business positioning** and **competitive maneuvering.** Consequently, extensive new material has been added that draws on game theory but presents it in a more intuitive fashion rather than taking the traditional quantitative approach to this topic. I think you will find the new PARTS framework (for Players, Added Value, Rules, Tactics, and Scope) to be a useful addition to your repertoire of strategy models. This chapter also introduces **complementors** as an increasingly important competitive force to be added to Porter's list of five forces. It also integrates material on defining the business and the business mission into the broader subject of business positioning.

- **Part IV** of the text remains focused on organizational change and strategy implementation. The biggest change in this part of the text is that the concepts on different planning and implementation processes were moved forward to the new chapter on the process perspective, the new Chapter 2. This makes for a cleaner, more manageable set of four chapters on strategy implementation, without loss of any critical material.

- **Chapter 9** explains why strategy implementation and organizational change are more difficult than many students might expect, and it presents **organizational learning** as one of the most promising approaches to successfully altering how organizations work. This chapter also explains that successfully changing an organization requires the use of a broad variety of change levers rather than dependence on one or two "magic bullets."

- **Chapters 10, 11** and **12** present rich discussion on three broad categories of change levers: **contextual levers, system levers,** and **action levers.** I recognize that the amount of information in these chapters presents challenges for you—especially if you are teaching under the quarter schedule rather than the semester. However, the field continues to call for more meaningful teaching material on the critical topic of strategy implementation, and I see no realistic means of covering this complex topic adequately in only one or two chapters. Look at Volume 1 of the *Instructor's Manual* for some ideas on how to address this in planning your next course.

- **Part V** presents the cases for this edition. I've moved some student material on case analysis to the opener for this part, so look for it there rather than in its past location as an appendix to the first chapter. A related web site is provided at the end of each case. The case selection for this edition is the best ever thanks to input from an army of reviewers who attacked this issue. More on that later, but at this point, let me summarize their results by saying that this edition includes 36 cases, three of which are holdovers from the second edition, with the rest being updated versions of earlier cases or all new cases.

ACKNOWLEDGMENTS

A book such as this represents a tremendous group effort, and I have been fortunate to have the opportunity to work with an outstanding blend of experts from business, academe, and publishing.

Once again I am indebted to my colleagues at different colleges and universities who have made important contributions to this work. I received many helpful suggestions from a wonderfully insightful team of reviewers: Janice Black, Michigan State University; William Darrow, Towson State University; Alan Hoffman, Bentley College; Alan Krigline, University of Akron; Robert Lynch, Rowan College of New Jersey; Patricia Nemetz-Mills, Eastern Washington University; Alan Patz, University of Southern California; Abdul Rasheed, The University of Texas at Arlington; J. L. Stimpert, Michigan State Unversity; Charles Waston, Miami University.

Selecting cases is a difficult task, and I was aided in my search by the following colleagues who responded with helpful comments and useful suggestions for timely, engaging, and well-written cases for this edition:

Kamal Abouzeid, Lynchburg College
John Bates, Georgia Southwestern College
Joe Benson, New Mexico State University
Sylvia Black, University of North Carolina
Bill Bogner, Georgia State University
Richard Brandenburg, University of Vermont
Karen Byers, University of California, Riverside
Michael Camp, James Madison University
John J. Casson, Kean College
Hung Chu, West Chester University
Gary Clark, Saginaw Valley State University
John Clarry, Montclair State University
Jerilyn Coles, Arizona State University West
David Deeds, Temple University
Victor Doherty, Wayne State University
Richard Fabris, Jersey City State College
James F. Fairbank, The Smeal College of Business Administration
Renata Geurtz, Arizona State University West
Neil Humphreys, Longwood College
Helaine J. Korn, Texas Tech University
George Murphy, Fitchburg State College
Kevin O'Mara, Elon College
Michael Moch, Michigan State University
Laura Poppo, Virginia Polytechnic Institute and State University
George M. Puia, University of Tampa
Kannan Ramaswamy, Florida International University
Stanley Ross, Newbury College
Michael V. Russo, University of Oregon
Rakesh Sambharya, Rutgers University-Camden Campus
Paul Short, Montclair State University
Donald Siegel, Arizona State University West
Melanie Trevino, University of Texas at El Paso
Marion White, James Madison University
Shaker A. Zahra, Georgia State University

Case writing is a labor-intensive activity that is critical to the study and research of strategic management, and the authors who engage in it can never be adequately thanked for their vital contributions. I am absolutely delighted to be able to publish cases prepared by the following group of outstanding case authors:

Mary Ackenhusen, INSEAD
Dean Aluzio, University of Connecticut
Katherine A. Auer, Bentley College
Christopher K. Bart, McMaster University
Christopher A. Bartlett, Harvard Business School
Thomas M. Begley, Northeastern University and Nanyang Technological University,
    Singapore
Bernard A. Deitzer, University of Akron
John B. Gallagher, University of Tennessee
Donna M. Gallo, University of Massachusetts at Amherst
Gamewell Gantt, Idaho State University
Sumantra Ghoshal, INSEAD
Barbara Gottfried, Bentley College
Peter G. Goulet, University of Northern Iowa
Lynda L. Goulet, University of Northern Iowa
Jean M. Hanebury, Texas A&M University
Todd Himstead, Georgetown University Business School
Alan N. Hoffman, Bentley College
George Johnson, Idaho State University
Michael J. Keeffe, Southwest Texas State University
John Kilpatrick, Idaho State University
Raymond M. Kinnunen, Northeastern University
Daniel G. Kopp, Southwest Missouri State University
Nicholas V. Kovalenko, Brigham Young University
Alan G. Krigline, University of Akron
Jeffrey A. Krug, University of Memphis
Joseph Lampel, New York University
Sharon Ungar Lane, Bentley College
Andrew Libuser, Georgetown University Business School
Thomas L. Lyon, Rockhurst College
Michael Lubatkin, University of Connecticut and Groupe ESC Lyon
Bill J. Middlebrook, Southwest Texas State University
James F. Molloy, Jr., Northeastern University
Ashish Nanda, Harvard Business School
Charles O'Reilly, Stanford University
Lee T. Perry, Brigham Young University
Thomas C. Peterson, University of Akron
Jeffrey Pfeffer, Stanford University
Robert A. Pitts, Gettysburg College
Valerie Porciello, Bentley College
Ravi Ramamurti, Northeastern University
John K. Ross, III, Southwest Texas State University

George C. Rubenson, Salisbury State University
Marvin G. Ryder, McMaster University
John A. Seeger, Bentley College
Richard C. Scamehorn, Ohio University
Kathleen Scharf, Harvard Business School
Art Sharplin, University of Texas at Austin
Frank M. Shipper, Salisbury State University
Lois Shufeldt, Southwest Missouri State University
F. Bruce Simmons, III, University of Akron
N. Craig Smith, Georgetown University Business School
Monte R. Swain, Brigham Young University
Arieh A. Ullmann, State University of New York at Binghamton
Joan Winn, University of Denver
Michelle Wright, University of Tennessee

I owe a special debt of gratitude to Ram Subramanian, who did a wonderful job of preparing the teaching materials to accompany chapters in Volume I of the *Instructor's Manual*.

The task of the publisher is to bring all the materials provided from the variety of sources described above to you, the reader. This is a monumental effort, but it is performed every day with grace, good humor, and consummate professionalism by the tremendous team of experts in the College Division sales force at Irwin/McGraw-Hill. Faculty members already know many of these indivduals, those professionals who work closely with colleges and universities to link the needs of their faculty members to the extensive capabilities at Irwin/McGraw-Hill.

Back at the editorial offices, an exceptional team was responsible for this new third edition: Curt Berkowitz and Ira Roberts, Editing Managers; Michael Campbell, Marketing Manager; Adam Knepper and Karen Mellon, Sponsoring Editors; Karen Quigley, Designer; Terry Varveris, Associate Editor; Leroy Young, Senior Production Supervisor. The team also included the following freelancers: Susan Joseph, proofreader; Trish Taylor, developmental editor; and Gretlyn Cline, copyeditor.

Finally, I would like to give a special thanks to my wife Shannon, for her invaluable assistance and support throughout this project. I would like to dedicate this edition to our four children: Brandon, Eli, Wyndie, and Ian. Thanks for all the times you understood when we had to be working on "THE BOOK" instead of enjoying time spent with you.

Alex Miller

P.S. If you have questions, comments, or suggestions about this book or about teaching strategic management, share them in the discussion room accessed through my home page:

http://funnelweb.utcc.utk.edu/~amiller2

Student's Preface

THE STRATEGIC MANAGEMENT IMPERATIVE

Why should I be taking this course?

Anyone who expects to be a successful manager in the future should study strategic management today. The world has become such a complex and fast-moving marketplace that firms can no longer succeed if only a few managers or staff experts are involved in formulating and implementing strategies. In leading firms throughout a wide range of industries, managers and other employees across all the traditional functional areas and organizational levels are taking on new strategic responsibilities. The position taken throughout this text is that every manager should expect to be involved in using, or at least contributing to, the strategic management process. The nature of strategic management is changing in such a way that all managers, regardless of organizational level or functional specialty, are becoming more involved in helping formulate and implement strategies for the entire business.

Given the broad and integrative nature of strategic management, it is sometimes viewed as the exclusive responsibility of top executives and general managers, or perhaps that of their specialized strategic planning staffs. In our opinion, such a view is inappropriate. Top managers are, and should be, deeply involved in strategic management. Similarly, there must be staff support for strategic management, particularly in large complex organizations. However, as strategic management evolves, managers throughout the entire organization are coming to have new responsibilities and more important roles to play in the strategic management process. Strategic management is not a task, limited to elite "Strategists" or to a single staff group of "Strategic Planners," but rather, it is a set of managerial skills that can and should be used throughout the organization, in a wide variety of functions.

WHAT'S DIFFERENT ABOUT STRATEGIC MANAGEMENT?

If you are like most of the students who use this book, you have already had a fair amount of training in a functional management specialty such as operations, human resource management, marketing, accounting, finance, or others. There are several subtle, but important differences between strategic management and these management functions.

- **Strategic management integrates various functions.** Excellence in a wide range of functional specialties is considered an absolutely essential requirement for success in today's highly competitive global marketplace. But, while functional excellence is necessary for success, this alone is not sufficient. There must be some broader form of management orchestrating the contributions of the various functions: a guiding force that integrates the efforts of specialists throughout the organization. Strategic management is central to capitalizing on functional expertise, and in order for functional specialists to make the greatest possible contribution, they must understand how their functions fit into a broader strategy.

- **Strategic management is oriented toward achieving organization-wide goals.** The most effective managers are those who have a clear understanding of their organization's aims. Functional specialists who limit their outlooks to their individual functional areas run the risk of "achieving a local maximum while missing the global optimum." In other words, they may do what is best for their particular specialty, rather than what is best for the entire business. To understand how the needs of the firm differ from the needs of the single functional area, a manager must become involved in the overall organization's strategic management process, and thereby discover how his or her function can contribute to achieving organization-wide goals.

- **Strategic management considers a broad range of stakeholders.** Organizations must meet the needs of various constituencies such as customers, suppliers, employees, owners, and the public at large. For an organization to truly flourish, managers throughout its ranks must understand how their decisions affect the various stakeholders involved. But functional specialists tend to focus on serving individual stakeholders, rather than balancing the needs of all stakeholders. For example, human resource managers may focus on employees, purchasing managers on suppliers, and sales managers on customers, and so forth. The strategic perspective entails simultaneous consideration of all stakeholder groups so that reasoned tradeoffs are possible.

- **Strategic management entails multiple time horizons.** Managers cannot ignore the need to maintain the long-run viability of their organization, though pragmatically speaking, they must also be aware of the short-run ramifications of anything they do. Consequently, they must be constantly shifting back and forth between long- and short-run thinking. Managers of functional areas tend to focus on short-term issues alone, but if they can broaden their time-frame perspectives, they will understand how to position their functional discipline to make the best contribution both today and tomorrow.

- **Strategic management is concerned with both efficiency and effectiveness.** The difference between these two concepts is sometimes explained as "doing things right" (efficiency) versus "doing the right things" (effectiveness). Managers who take a narrow view of their responsibilities often end up concentrating the majority of their efforts on improving the efficiency of their own functional area, while neglecting the organization's overall operations. By working so hard at trying to do things right, they may forget to look up from their work occasionally to consider whether they are working on the right things to be effective in moving their organization toward its ultimate vision. The strategic perspective encourages a balanced emphasis on both of these dimensions of managerial work.

HOW IS THIS COURSE ORGANIZED?

We shall study strategic management as a process comprising three major types of interrelated activities: strategic analysis, strategy formulation, and strategy implementation. Basically, strategic analysis is the forethought required to develop an appropriate strategy; strategy formulation is the process that transforms this analysis into a plan—the intended strategy; and strategy implementation is the process of continually adjusting and refining the plan as it is put into action.

Of course, most managers are not able to compartmentalize their involvement with strategic management this neatly. They continually bounce between analysis, formulation, and implementation issues in no fixed pattern. However, you will find it more practical to first learn about strategic management concepts in a more orderly—if somewhat artificial—arrangement. Then, when you have the basic concepts in hand, you can see how they are interrelated by applying them to problems in the real world. Strategy cases provide a valuable opportunity to learn by providing detailed descriptions of the issues facing managers responsible for developing and implementing strategies. Analysis and discussion of several such cases will probably be a significant part of the course your instructor has designed. (If you would like some guidance on preparing cases, you will find a ten-step process for case analysis presented as the opener for Part V of this text.)

Integrating the various parts of the course while drawing on the concepts you have learned in your previous coursework will make this study challenging. However, if you meet this challenge by energetically engaging in the work required, you will find that the new concepts and insights you gain will be a valuable complement to what you have learned through study and experience elsewhere. You will also be well prepared to step forward and accept a role in shaping the strategies and the destinies of the organizations in your future. Good luck in your work in this course and beyond.

Alex Miller

Part One

PERSPECTIVES ON STRATEGIC MANAGEMENT

The first part of this text comprises two chapters that present overviews of strategic management from two different perspectives we label *content* and *process*.

The content perspective, covered in Chapter 1, addresses the "what" questions in strategic management. What is the purpose of business? What is a good strategy? What contributes to a firm's success? What should a firm or a manager do next? Answering these questions draws on technical disciplines such as economics, finance, operations, and marketing, as well as philosophical disciplines, such as ethics. As explained in Chapter 2, the process perspective complements the content perspective by addressing the "how" questions. How are strategies created? How does a firm compete? How is strategic planning best accomplished? How do organizations work? These studies draw more heavily on behavioral disciplines, such as psychology and sociology, and their more applied offspring, organizational behavior, organizational theory, and leadership. To summarize, when we speak from the content perspective, we are saying, "This is what needs to be done"; when we speak from the process perspective, we are explaining, "Here is how to do it."

To succeed in using any of the concepts covered throughout this text, you must become adept at both the "what" and the "how" of strategic management. Consequently, while we introduce these two perspectives to you in separate chapters, beyond this, you will see them overlap and merge. Parts Two, Three, and Four address the three major processes (how) that form the backbone of strategic management: strategic analysis, strategy formulation, and strategy implementation. But, within each of these parts, you will learn new concepts describing content issues (what) of sound strategies and effective strategic management.

Discussions in the chapters of this text move within the "Architecture of Strategy" framework presented on the facing page, which is designed to help you make connections and grasp relationships between various content and process-based concepts. As you study these chapters, refer to this framework and practice moving back and forth in the content and process perspectives as you study the "what" and "how" of strategy. Developing this two-part skill will prove invaluable to you in your role as a strategic manager.

The Architecture of Strategy

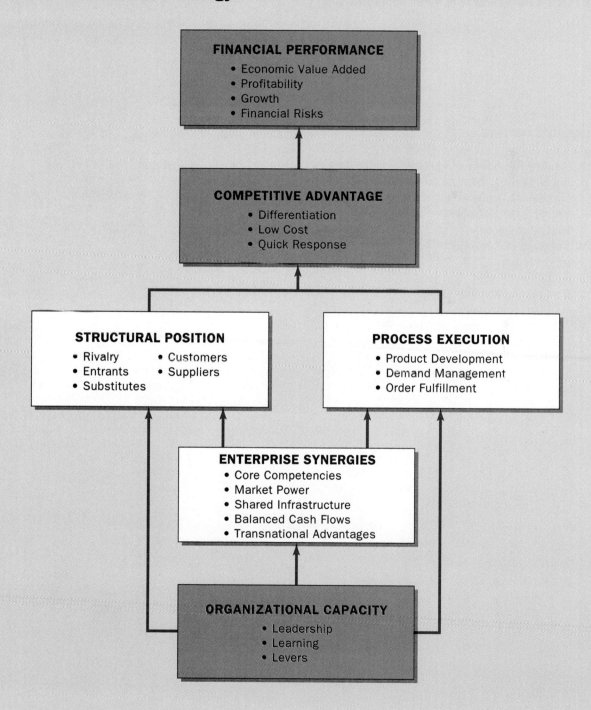

Chapter 1

The Content of Strategy

This chapter emphasizes that firms have fundamental obligations to create economic value, and that achieving this task requires development of competitive advantages. After we establish the central importance of these basic concepts, we explain and illustrate how firms create economic value by building competitive advantages. This chapter also shows how we address the remainder of the text.

The chapter comprises five parts. The first explains how the purpose of the firm is to improve the quality of life through meeting the needs of its various stakeholders. The second part explains how meeting the financial needs of stockholders is a prerequisite for meeting the needs of other stakeholders—and thus, we emphasize use of strategic management to improve financial performance throughout this text. The third part of this chapter looks at how firms create economic value for their stockholders, using a framework known as economic value added. Next, we consider different forms of competitive advantage and how they are linked to economic performance. Finally, we overview subsequent chapters, showing how they will cover topics that are critical to building competitive advantages, and consequently, to improving the financial performance of the firm.

This chapter will help you understand:

- The purpose of the firm, which is to create value that satisfies the needs of its stakeholders
- Obligations to stockholders as a prerequisite to addressing the needs of other stakeholders
- A firm's need to create economic value as a means to fulfill its obligations to stockholders
- The use of economic value added as a means for measuring and managing how firms create economic value for their stockholders
- The role that competitive advantage plays in producing superior economic returns and, consequently, its place as the focus of strategic management
- The three forms of competitive advantage, differentiation, cost leadership, and quick response, and some of the managerial issues involved in pursuing each
- The Architecture of Strategy framework as an overview of subsequent chapters in the remainder of this text

Fortune magazine has declared, "The most valuable product on this planet is not the microchip, not the automobile, not the television set. No, sir. What has produced more wealth than any other thing dreamed of by the mind of man is sugar water."[1] Of course, the writer was not referring to just any form of sugar water, but to a secret formula that yields a product known the world over as Coca-Cola. *Fortune* based its conclusion on the fact that over the last 100 years or so, the Coca-Cola company has produced more wealth for its investors than any other company in the world, increasing the value of its stockholders' investments by more than $60 billion.

In this chapter, you will learn that the most basic goal of business is increasing its stockholders' investment. Consequently, it's not surprising that in a survey of 11,000 executives, outside board members, and financial analysts, Coca-Cola was selected as the most admired business in the United States; or that Warren Buffet, the world's most highly respected financial analyst, identified Coca-Cola as "the best large business in the world."[2] But how does merely bottling and marketing sugar water for a century result in performance that can win such high praise for this company?

The central theme running through this text is that the key to financial success is to establish and sustain a strong competitive advantage. Coca-Cola's financial performance is a direct result of its ability to achieve a form of competitive advantage known as differentiation. Its curved bottle is the most widely recognized consumer products icon in the world, and Coke's brand loyalty makes it the envy of virtually every other branded-product producer. Understanding the goal of superior financial performance and understanding the connection between this and competitive advantage lies at the heart of the content of strategy, the subject of Chapter 1.

MEETING THE NEEDS OF MULTIPLE STAKEHOLDERS

To understand the content issues involved in strategically managing a firm, we begin with a basic question: What is the purpose of a business firm? If we can't answer this question, how can we hope to understand what constitutes good strategy, or successful strategic management?

This question is so broad, so fundamental, and so complex that we could spend an entire book debating different possible answers to it. However, this would not be the best means for helping you understand the overall topic of strategic management. Instead, we'll move directly to the particular answer this text is based on: *The strategic purpose of a firm is to create value that meets the needs of its stakeholders.* These *stakeholders* can include any parties that have an interest (or a stake) in the success, or performance, of a firm.[3] In other words, stakeholders are all the parties who stand to benefit from a firm's successful operation, including owners, suppliers and customers, employees, local communities, trade associations, and society at large, as shown in Exhibit 1.1.

EXHIBIT 1.1
Managers Are Responsible to a Diverse Set of Stakeholders and Have Responsibilities to All of Them

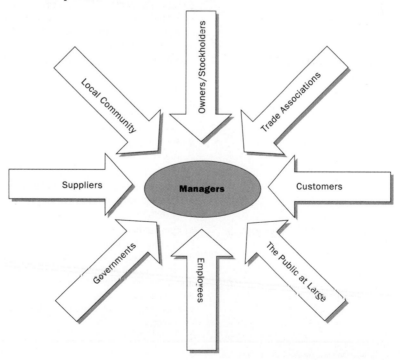

Meeting the needs of such diverse groups can be difficult as stakeholders often have polarized opinions. For example, Ford Motor Company found itself torn between meeting the conflicting needs of two stakeholder groups: the UAW and Dana Corporation, a key supplier. The UAW wanted Ford to agree to purchase parts exclusively from unionized suppliers. However, Dana had invested years of effort in developing strong employee-management relations at several of its plants and those plants had voted against becoming unionized. Ford wanted good labor relations with its employees, but it also needed low-cost suppliers such as Dana. In such situations, how can a firm meet the needs of all its stakeholders? Exhibit 1.2 notes how several leading firms identify their obligations to various stakeholders in excerpts from the firms' overall mission statements, and Exhibit 1.3 provides examples of the values firms create for different stakeholder groups.[4]

Don't confuse stakeholders with "stockholders" (also called "shareholders"). Stockholders are only one of several possible stakeholder groups. We refer to a firm's obligations to stockholders as its *fiscal responsibility*, while obligations to that same

---

EXHIBIT 1.2
Recognition of Multiple Stakeholders in Mission Statements

Company	Stakeholder Group	Relevant Portion of Mission
Du Pont	Stockholders	"Each of our businesses must deliver financial results superior to those of its leading competitors . . . for we consider ourselves successful only if we return to our shareholders a long-term financial reward comparable to the better-performing, large industrial companies."
Reynolds	Customers	"In our relationship with customers, our objectives are: ■ Offer our products for sale on the basis of competitive price, quality, service, and reliability. ■ Furnish dependable products through continuing emphasis on product design, product development, quality standards, and manufacturing performance. ■ Provide innovative leadership in product development and marketing."
Dow	Employees	"Employees are the source of Dow's success. We treat them with respect, promote teamwork, and encourage personal freedom and growth. Excellence in performance is sought and rewarded."
3M	Community at large	"3M management recognizes that 3M's business operations have broad societal impact. It will endeavor to be sensitive to public attitudes and social concerns in the workplace, the community, the environment, and within the different political and economic systems where 3M conducts business. It will strive to keep the public, employees, and investors well informed about 3M business operations."

Source: Author's correspondence with companies.

EXHIBIT 1.3
The Purpose of a Business Is to Provide Value for a Broad Range of Stakeholders

Stakeholder Group	Examples of Value Provided
Stockholders	Stock price appreciation and dividends
Customers	Products and services
Employees	Employment, wages, personal growth opportunities
Suppliers	Revenue through sales, growth opportunities
Local community	Jobs, economic development, civic involvement
Society at large	Economic health and security, environmental protection
Trade associations	Political strength, operating funds

---

firm's stakeholders are its *social responsibility*. One of management's most important roles is to strike an acceptable balance between the firm's fiscal responsibilities to its stockholders and its social responsibilities to its other stakeholders,[5] and there is an ongoing debate across business managers, business researchers, business regulators, and others about what constitutes the right balance between fiscal responsibility and social responsibility. The range of positions taken in this debate can best be seen by looking at two extremes.

At one extreme, some argue that management's only responsibility is to ensure that the firm is as profitable as possible, that is, managers should focus more or less exclusively on meeting the financial needs of stockholders and leave social issues to social institutions.[6] Given that stockholders own the business and that they have put their money at risk to create the firm in the first place, it's easy to see their logic in stressing financial returns to owners as *the* critical business goal.

However, the opposition argues that society cannot afford to let an institution as powerful as business focus narrowly on the needs of any one stakeholder group—not even its financial backers. We recognize convincing arguments here. First, many firms have had important beneficial impacts on business. Charitable giving, community programs, remedial workforce education, and programs for youth at risk are all widely supported by industry. Even beyond this, firms have no option but to be responsive to stakeholders because these groups hold tremendous power over businesses, as illustrated in Application 1.1. This application illustrates how most managers are not motivated to serve stakeholders merely from moral obligation or altruism. Self-interested managers attempt to satisfy stakeholders because otherwise they might enforce their claims on the firm with boycotts, lawsuits, government regulation, or negative publicity campaigns. With so much power so widely distributed, how can firms hope to be successful if their managers focus narrowly on the needs of any one group?[7]

As with most debates with extreme positions, a grain of truth appears in both extremes, and the most practical answer lies somewhere in the middle. The position we take throughout this text is such a middle-ground position. Although an organization clearly has obligations to a broad range of stakeholders, meeting financial obligations is a prerequisite for addressing nonfinancial goals in a serious, sustained fashion. We adopt this position for several practical reasons, as discussed in the next section.

Application 1.1

Trouble Comes When Stakeholders Are Neglected

Benetton, the Italian sportswear maker, developed a reputation as a leading innovator in the clothing industry and a darling of the market. However, the Benetton fortunes turned in the 1990s as the company angered one stakeholder group after another:

Customers

Benetton's immediate customers are the hundreds of retailers around the world who sell its clothes. These retailers launched numerous lawsuits against the company after a controversial advertising campaign addressed subjects such as homosexuality, racism, homelessness, sex abuse, AIDS, and war refugees. Retailers claimed that the ads turned shoppers away in droves and cost the shops millions in lost sales. As a result, lawsuits were brought against the company in America, Germany, France, Spain, Italy, and numerous other countries by the very parties that were to sell the company's goods. During this process, many Benetton stores closed (in the United States, the number of stores dropped from over 1,500 to under 500) and sales tumbled by as much as 15 percent in many markets.

Public at Large

Many people who were concerned with the social causes that Benetton supposedly meant to support through its controversial ads resented the company's actions. For example, in France, the gay community sued the company for exploiting AIDS and being antihomosexual in its advertising. Other critics found advertisements that portrayed sexual innuendos between Catholic nuns and priests to

be highly objectionable, and the company was regularly threatened by consumer boycotts.

Employees and Managers

These external controversies had an internal impact. The company's founding family, the Benettons, still had three of the original four siblings involved in managing the business on a day-to-day basis. However, as the company's fortunes turned for the worse, family feuding began, and key outside managers, including a well-respected managing director, left Benetton.

Owners and Stockholders

Faced with so many difficulties in the sportswear business, the Benetton family moved aggressively to diversify its holdings into outside companies, such as the makers of Rollerblades, Nordica ski boots, Prince tennis rackets, and Kastle skis, not to mention a chain of highway restaurants and a chain of superstores. Unfortunately, other stockholders saw these moves as threats to the family's ability to focus attention on the clothing business, and Benetton's stock tumbled as a result. Large institutional investors, such as Lehman Brothers and Putnam Investment Inc., were especially eager to be rid of stock in the troubled company.

By failing to meet its various stakeholders' needs, Benetton drove many of them to take action against the company. Consequently, the company is under siege from numerous fronts, and the actions taken by many of its attackers have hamstrung the company in its attempt to reclaim its former place as an industry leader.

FISCAL RESPONSIBILITY AS A PREREQUISITE FOR ADDRESSING SOCIAL RESPONSIBILITIES

First, managers take on legal obligations to make committed efforts toward fulfilling the firm's fiscal responsibility to shareholders who have invested in the firm. Stockholders may take serious legal action against a manager who fails to act with the stockholders' interests in mind. In legal terms, a firm's management team have *fiduciary* obligations, that is, they hold stockholders' investments in trust, and by so doing, they accept a legally enforceable obligation to manage those investments responsibly and in the stockholders' best interests. See Application 1.2 for examples of how stockholders enforce their legal rights as key stakeholders.

This fiduciary obligation was illustrated by a conversation concerning environmental responsibility among a group of senior managers at a semiconductor manufacturer. The managers were deeply committed to environmental stewardship on a personal level, and they also worked for companies that had made formal commitments to environmental responsibility. However, their consensus position was that they could not realistically place their desired emphasis on environmental issues until they had first fulfilled their financial obligations to stockholders. In other words, they all viewed financial success as a legally enforceable prerequisite to activism on behalf of other stakeholders. As important as the environment was to these leaders, it in no way diminished their, or the organization's, concern for profitability. As one of the managers explained, "Unless we remain a profitable firm, we will not have the option of pursuing our environmental goals. As a for-profit business, we *must* make a profit be-

---

Application 1.2

Stockholders Enforce Their Rights as Key Stakeholders

Several powerful stakeholder groups make demands on corporations, but you might be surprised to discover which particular stakeholder group most often resorts to litigation. For the United States in aggregate, the legal suits brought to court by shareholders—the owners of the corporations being sued—account for the majority of legal claims, the most expensive legal defenses, and the largest settlements. A survey of 872 such suits revealed that the average award for a successful claimant was over $3 million and the average cost of defending such a suit was $600,000.

Some industries are especially prone to stockholder suits, especially those with more volatile stock prices. In these situations, attorneys often argue that a given stock-price drop was foreseeable and that management failed to take corrective action or warn investors. Using such an argument, more than half the 150 high-tech firms in Silicon Valley have been sued by stockholders for securities fraud. Defense against such a suit is difficult and onerous, usually stretching out for over a year, during which time the firm operates under a pall. Consequently, of the suits against Silicon Valley firms, 93 percent were settled out of court, paying an average settlement of nearly $9 million.

High-tech firms are not the only businesses subject to lawsuits that protect investors. For example, shareholders sued Best Buy, an electronics retail chain, after news of lower-than-projected earnings, coupled with Whirlpool's decision to drop the chain as a distributor, sent Best Buy's stock into a tailspin. The stock fell by one-fourth immediately after the news, and continued to fall for another week. The stockholders claimed that Best Buy was being mismanaged, that managers should have known that earnings would not meet earlier forecasts, and that the firm had purposefully misrepresented its position in order to shore up stock prices.

Critics of the U.S. legal system argue that it's too easy for lawyers to instigate such shareholder suits. Some even claim that abuses of investors' legal rights have produced legal costs and disruptions that have hurt U.S. firms' competitiveness. Recently, new laws have been passed to address these concerns and to offer corporate directors and officers increased protection against legal actions from stockholders. However, these laws notwithstanding, it is still clear that stockholders have a legal right to expect firms to be managed in a manner that protects investor interests, and they are not at all hesitant to enforce this right.

fore we can devote our attention to other concerns, no matter how important those other concerns may be."

A second practical reason organizations must treat profits as a primary motive is that profits provide the cash flow that organizations usually need to address nonfinancial goals. Without cash flow, a business cannot pay for its ongoing operations, or continue to attract outside funding as a substitute for internally generated cash flow. Without internally generated or externally sourced cash flow, a firm will eventually cease to exist. Said differently, a business cannot exist without positive cash flows. Obviously, a business that does not exist will fail to meet *all* its performance standards, financial and nonfinancial alike.

Ironically, the best illustration for this point involves a *nonprofit* organization. A church-supported hospital was making a major effort to improve its operating margins by reducing its costs. As I consulted with them, they repeatedly emphasized cost reduction and operating margin improvement as critical to fulfilling the organization's mission statement. This confused me because the mission statement said nothing about costs or profits—it focused exclusively on meeting the needs of the community, especially the needs of those who could not normally afford quality health care. When I pointed out the apparent discrepancy between working to improve margins and the organization's philanthropic mission, one sister explained away the discrepancy quite directly: "No margin, no mission." In other words, cash flow from healthy operating margins provides the resources required by the hospital in order to reinvest in its future and to continue meeting its nonfinancial goals.

A third point is that we need not think of a firm's fulfilling its fiscal and social responsibilities in "either-or" terms. Many firms have profited from doing good, and many managers insist on finding strategies that do not please either stockholders alone or the firm's other stakeholders alone, but which please both.[8] In fact, it seems fair to say that financial performance is rightfully viewed as one part of a complex tangle of means and ends that address both financial accomplishments and social goals.[9] Increasingly, research and experience show that the quality of a firm's relationships with all its stakeholders—customers, employees, suppliers, communities, and so on—drive its financial performance. A survey of chief financial officers revealed that the vast majority are concerned about and even measure company performance in meeting various stakeholders' needs.[10] Kazuo Inamori, the founder of Kyocera, a company many consider to be the best-managed organization in all of Japan, stressed the interconnectedness of social and fiscal responsibilities in his book, *A Passion for Success:*

> Profit is the reward for those who serve society. This philosophical paradigm might, for many, appear to be an obstacle to success, but the opposite is true. I cannot think of a time when I had difficulty because of that ideology. Rather, I believe it is the other way around. Some companies do make money in spite of the fact that they do not serve the needs of the community. But, such companies do not remain successful very long.[11]

Thus, meeting stockholders' needs does not prevent an organization from meeting the needs of other stakeholders. If anything, we would say that meeting the needs of its other stakeholders depends on an organization's ability to first meet its stockholders' needs, and vice versa. Practicing managers understand this, and have no trouble recognizing that financial performance may not be an organization's most important accomplishment, but it is certainly a prerequisite for giving nonfinancial goals the attention and emphasis they deserve. Although the emphasis placed on various stakeholders and the respective performance dimensions differs from one firm to the next, the need to be profitable (i.e., to produce economic value for stockholders) is so basic that it is almost always stressed. Research on the details of sixty-one mission statements from *Fortune* 500 firms reveals that 90 percent mention financial soundness, profitability, or growth of the firm. Probably the only reason the other 10 percent did not mention financial goals is that their writers assumed financial integrity to be understood. With this perspective in mind, we focus on how a firm can use strategy to fulfill its fiscal responsibilities as well as its social responsibilities. Because we treat fiscal responsibility as a prerequisite, we need to consider it in more detail; therefore, we now consider how firms create economic value in order to fulfill their fiscal responsibilities.

VALUE-BASED MANAGEMENT AND CREATING ECONOMIC VALUE

The concept of creating economic value has become so central to the practice of strategic management that it has given rise to a new descriptive label, *value-based management.* This is an approach to strategic management that highlights and emphasizes a firm's fiscal responsibilities to its stockholders.[12] To understand how managers and firms fulfill their fiscal responsibilities, you must first understand the concept of *creating economic value.*[13]

Managers fulfill their fiscal responsibilities and firms build wealth for their owners by increasing the value of the owners' investments. We can measure this performance using *market value added,* or *MVA.* A firm's MVA is simply its market value less the capital tied up in the company.[14] The surest way to increase market value is to consistently garner profits in excess of the cost of the capital invested in the business.[15] We can measure a firm's ability to do this using a concept called *economic value added,* or *EVA.*[16] EVA is the spread between a firm's return on invested capital minus its weighted average cost of capital, multiplied by the amount of capital invested.[17] In other words, EVA is what's left over after a firm has covered all its factors of production, including operating and overhead expenses, interest expenses, taxes, and a fair return for investors. (For more details on EVA, refer to the appendix at the end of this chapter.) In a sense, EVA is the ultimate measure of profits, because it is the only measure that considers *all* the costs associated with the business and not just those normally reported in accounting statements, such as operating expenses, interest, and taxes. As Peter Drucker, one of the foremost gurus of business, has explained,

> We need a measure of total factor productivity. That explains the growing popularity of economic value added analysis. EVA is based on something we have known a long time: What we generally call profits, the money left to service equity, is usually no profit at all. Until a business returns a profit that is greater than its cost of capital, it operates at a loss. Never mind that it pays taxes as if it had a genuine profit. The enterprise still returns less to the economy than it devours in resources. . . . It does not create wealth; it destroys it.[18]

As Drucker points out, the concepts underlying EVA have been understood for a long time. Drucker credits economists from the last century with first discussing these concepts. Alfred Sloan, mastermind behind the creation of General Motors, used this concept as the basis for his executive compensation program, and it has regularly appeared in business finance texts for at least 3 decades. Its popularity today is probably due to the combination of increased global competition, greater access to information (discussed in Chapter 3), and the highly visible stock market successes of companies, such as Coca-Cola, that have chosen to focus on creating wealth as measured by economic value added. Those experienced with the use of EVA attribute such successes to the "four Ms," as illustrated by Application 1.3 and described below.

- *Measurement.* EVA provides more meaningful performance measures because it measures all the factors of production rather than just those normally reported in financial statements. Many organizations use much simpler accounting measures as proxies for calculating economic value added. They may use profitability measures (such as return on assets), growth measures (such as earnings growth), and risk measures (such as debt/equity ratios). These and other accounting measures will be reviewed in more detail in Chapters 4 and 11. Such accounting measures are straightforward to calculate, require less judgment than EVA,[19] and may help provide a more complete financial picture of the firm.[20] Because of their relative simplicity, they are more widely used than EVA calculations, and you may wish to use them in case analysis. However, we must recognize their limitations—specifically their failure to include the cost of owners' investment as a critical cost of doing business.

- *Motivation.* There is usually a big difference between being an owner and being a manager—how many times have you washed a rented car? (This concept is addressed in agency theory, which we'll discuss in Chapter 7.) Because EVA is so closely linked to the firm's ability to create wealth for its stockholders, by linking executive compensation to the firm's EVA or to its growth in EVA, managers are motivated to think more as business owners. Given the importance of stockholders as a key stakeholder group, this is an obvious advantage.

- *Management system.* The EVA concept applies to virtually any organizational decision, from evaluating the merit of a multimillion-dollar corporate acquisition to considering replacement of an old piece of machinery with a newer, more efficient model. In other words, managers can apply this standard to any financial alternative: What impact will it have on the economic value the firm creates for its shareholders? As such, EVA provides a unifying system for managing any organization.

- *Mindset.* This unifying system comes about as a result of developing a common mindset for managerial decision making. Obviously, detailed analysis is not warranted for decisions involving much smaller amounts of money, and even firms that most ardently support using EVA usually have a lower-dollar limit below which the full-blown analysis is neither required nor recommended. Nonetheless, EVA's *underlying* concepts help determine the financial impact of any strategic decision for managers at all organizational levels.[21]

CSX Profits from EVA

CSX, a large diversified transportation company, adopted EVA as the measure of performance for its railroad operation and realized a number of advantages:

Measurement

This operation had been using the traditional accounting measures of revenue growth and profits. Neither of these measures took into account the full cost of investing in the business. By focusing on sales growth, managers had always been willing to invest in locomotives: "You can't bill for moving freight unless you've got locomotives, so keep plenty of locomotives around to take advantage of every chance to make a sale." However, so many locomotives required a huge investment, and once managers considered the full cost of financing this investment (debt plus equity), they quickly began to understand that extra locomotives cost more than they generated.

Motivation

By tying bonuses to EVA, managers were motivated to make decisions differently. For example, in the old CSX, the saying was, "Nobody ever got fired for having too many locomotives." In other words, there was no motivation to reduce investment by maintaining a smaller fleet of locomotives. But, under an EVA-based bonus system, managers took a personal cut in pay unless every locomotive in the fleet generated more cash than it cost to finance and operate. As you might guess, the fleet shrank in a hurry!

Management System

EVA-based decision making was not limited only to capital expenditures, such as locomotives. As it became a management system, its influence spread across the organization. For example, preventive maintenance had never

been emphasized: "Who wants to take a piece of equipment out of service when it's not broken? How's that going to help us make this month's sales and profit numbers?" But preventive maintenance is a cost-effective way of ensuring that fewer locomotives and cars break down. This effectively increases fleet size without actually investing in new equipment. Consequently, focusing on EVA became the driving force behind efforts to vastly upgrade CSX's preventive maintenance program.

Mindset

As EVA became an established part of CSX's management systems, it had a profound impact on how managers understood the business and their personal accountability for its creating wealth. This change in mindset led to the development of many creative measures never previously considered. For instance, to increase its effective capacity without making heavy capital investments, managers recognized the need for better information on when customers needed to ship and receive freight. By having the right cars at the right place at the right time, fewer cars sat idle waiting on loading or unloading. CSX accessed this information by tying its computers to its customers' computers, and increased the effective number of available rail cars without actually buying the new cars.

Thus, EVA did not tell managers what to do to increase wealth; but it provided the measures, management systems, motivation, and mindset required to see what needed doing. Peter Drucker explains, "It [EVA] does not, by itself, tell us why a certain product or service does not add value or what to do about it. But, it shows us what we need to find out and whether or not we need to take remedial action."*

*Peter F. Drucker, "The Information Executives Truly Need," *Harvard Business Review, 73* (January–February 1995), 59.

Like any other measure of profits, it is not at all unusual for a firm to have a negative EVA in some years; 1 year's negative EVA may not indicate that anything is seriously amiss. For example, if a firm had just undertaken a major expansion program that had not yet begun to make a payback, a negative EVA would be quite reasonable.

But a pattern of consistently negative EVA is an indication of debilitating problems for the firm over the long run. Experts estimate that IBM produced a negative EVA for 4 out of the 5 years leading up to 1993. As investors began to realize that IBM managers were apparently not capable of investing in ways that more than paid for the cost of its capital, they stopped investing. Demand for IBM stock fell, causing the price to slide from $130 to $40 over the 5-year period, and the wealth of stockholders was destroyed by the hundreds of millions. When IBM attempted a turnaround, it could not depend on issuing new stock at the former high prices, and this limited the financing options available to managers trying to turn the firm around and greatly complicated efforts to make a comeback. Furthermore, during this time, IBM could no longer afford to make good the unwritten commitment of lifetime employment it once boasted, as it reduced its workforce by thousands. Once again, we see that meeting a firm's financial responsibilities is a prerequisite for meeting the needs of its other stakeholders.

Now that we have introduced the concept of creating economic value and explained its central importance in strategic management, we move on to a discussion of how strategic management contributes to meeting this fundamental financial responsibility. In the next section, we see how a firm's ability to create superior levels of economic value depends on its ability to create and maintain a competitive advantage.

COMPETITIVE ADVANTAGE: THE FOCAL POINT OF STRATEGY

Does the foregoing discussion imply that managers should focus directly on creating economic value and positive EVA numbers? Probably not. To focus on EVA directly would be the equivalent of a coach focusing on the scoreboard instead of the game's action. The coach is obviously interested in the score, but he or she seeks to improve it by focusing on other, more manageable aspects of the game.

Throughout this text, we take the position that managers should be committed to creating economic wealth, and that the best means to create that wealth is to focus on competitive advantage as the key. We base this position on the idea that to be financially successful over the long term, a business must hold some advantage relative to its competition. This is a theme we echo throughout this text: *Over the long run, the total amount of value a firm captures for its investors (in the form of EVA) cannot exceed the amount of value it creates for its customers (in the form of competitive advantage).* This relationship is so basic and so strong that some experts on the topic have defined competitive advantage in terms of creating profits and economic value: "[We] define competitive advantage as the ability of the firm to outperform its industry, that is, to earn a higher rate of profit than the industry norm . . . [and] for a firm to achieve a competitive advantage, it must create more value than its competitors."[22]

In the simplest terms, such a *competitive advantage* is based on excelling in providing one or more of three forms of customer value. Customers want goods and services that are (1) better and (2) cheaper, and they want them (3) faster. We refer to corresponding forms of competitive advantage as (1) differentiation, (2) cost leadership,

EXHIBIT 1.4
A Firm's Financial Performance Depends on Its Competitiveness

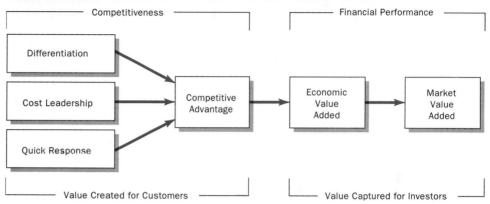

and (3) quick response, and as illustrated in Exhibit 1.4, these different forms of competitive advantage can provide critical impetus to a firm's financial performance.

Differentiation refers to the extent to which a customer finds a firm's products or services unique in some way that makes them more attractive and therefore worth a premium price: Rolls-Royce automobiles are a classic example. Alternatively, the firm may lead its competitors in terms of cost, allowing it to charge similar (or even lower) prices while realizing better-than-average margins. The Wal-Mart chain of retail stores enjoys such a cost leadership position. These two forms of competitive advantage have provided much of the basis for studying business-level strategy in the past. However, over the last decade, another form of competitive advantage has emerged: the ability to recognize, adapt to, and respond to changing customer needs faster than competitors do. We call this form of competitive advantage quick response.[23] Here, Federal Express, pioneer of the overnight package delivery service, is a good example.

Data on the relationship between competitive advantage and financial performance given in Application 1.4 suggests that a firm with more than one competitive advantage is in a particularly strong position. But a business that does not excel in at least one of these three sources of competitive advantage does not offer customers a superior option along any of the three dimensions of value, and it will consequently fare poorly in a competitive market.[24] In the long run, such businesses are probably destined to earn no more than what economists call "normal profits." Normal profits allow investors to earn an average return equal to what they would expect to receive from any other similarly risky investment, and they do not meet our goal of creating economic value. Performance that yields only normal profits is not particularly noteworthy because normal profits are only average. For-profit businesses strive to create economic value by achieving performance above the level of normal profits; consequently, the pursuit of competitive advantage has become the central theme of strategic management. The director of planning at Clark Equipment Company, the leading U.S. firm in the highly competitive forklift industry, explains:

> The process of strategic management is coming to be defined, in fact, as the management of competitive advantage—that is, as a process of identifying, developing, and taking ad-

Application 1.4

The Impact of Competitive Advantage on Business Performance

Research shows that a competitive advantage is clearly instrumental in achieving higher-than-normal levels of profitability. Exhibit 1.5 shows the importance of two forms of competitive advantage (differentiation and cost) in seven different industrial sectors. The data reported in this table are taken from the PIMS (profit impact of market strategy) database, which measures differentiation and cost, providing data from over 2,500 business units within some 200, mostly large, United States–based corporations.

Differentiation is measured as any nonprice attribute identified by customers' evaluation of competing goods and/or services. Cost advantages are measured as the direct costs of the reporting firm, expressed in percentage terms, relative to the estimated average of its leading competitors. (No comparable data are available to measure superior response time as a competitive advantage.)

The businesses within seven industrial sectors were divided into equal thirds, in terms of their differentiation and cost positions relative to the competitors in their particular markets. Data on the middle thirds were dropped, and the four combinations of high and low differentiation and cost were compared on the basis of average return on investment (ROI), perhaps the most common measure

of profitability. The value of data such as these is not in pinpointing performance targets. Rather, the data are useful primarily as a general description of what businesses in a wide range of industrial settings have done. The data are too general for use as the basis of strategy formulation, but they do indicate at least three general points:

- *Firms that hold neither form of competitive advantage (the low/low category in Exhibit 1.5) generally perform poorly in terms of their average profitability.* There was considerable variation around the overall average of 9.5 percent, but, considering that these measures of profitability are calculated before corporate overhead and taxes, not even the best of these could be expected to exceed typical costs of capital. In one industrial sector (raw or semifinished goods), this group's profitability was less than one-tenth what it was for a high-flying counterpart in the "hybrid" category, described below. Other analyses also indicated that this group performed very poorly in terms of growth, with an overall market share loss of nearly a quarter of a point per year.

EXHIBIT 1.5
Competitive Advantage Increases Profitability

		Average ROI (%)			
Industry Sector	Differentiation Advantage: Cost Advantage:	Low Low	Low High	High Low	High High
MANUFACTURING					
Consumer products:					
Durable goods		14.2	20.2	21.0	38.7
Nondurable goods		9.7	27.0	15.0	33.2
Industrial products:					
Capital goods		8.1	19.7	28.5	35.2
Raw or semifinished goods		2.9	28.8	15.1	34.9
Components for finished goods		10.5	22.8	29.0	38.8
Supplies of consumable goods		14.1	33.3	31.0	38.4
SERVICES		10.0	22.8	26.8	31.5
OVERALL		9.5	26.2	22.0	34.7

Source: Based on data gathered from author's analysis of the PIMS database.

Application 1.4 (cont.)

■ *Holding one form of competitive advantage (high/low) can lead to higher levels of profitability.* These firms typically enjoyed levels of profitability at least twice that of low/low firms in the same industrial sector. There was no consistent pattern in the kind of advantage that was most profitable, and we would advise against reading too much into any differences in the profitability levels between the two.

■ *Holding both forms of competitive advantage (high/high) most often leads to the highest possible levels of profitability.* Firms in this "hybrid" category enjoy returns on investment ranging from the mid- to high 30s, in percentage terms. With the average ROI for all business units in the database near 22 percent, such performance must be considered outstanding.

Again, this stellar performance was mirrored in terms of data on growth, with the average hybrid gaining nearly six-tenths of a point of market share per year.

In the past, managers were often advised to concentrate on a single competitive advantage, rather than run the risk of having strategic positions which were "stuck in the middle," being "neither fish nor fowl." This thinking seems especially plausible, considering the clear importance the data show for having some form of competitive advantage and the inconclusive differences among the benefits of either individual advantage. However, as Exhibit 1.5 shows, in every industrial sector, the highest performance levels are those seen by firms holding both types of competitive advantage simultaneously.

vantage of enclaves in which a tangible and preservable business advantage can be achieved.[25]

Given the central role competitive advantage plays in strategic management, let's now consider each form of competitive advantage in more detail.

Differentiation

In pursuing a competitive advantage based on *differentiation*, firms attempt to create unique bundles of products and/or services that will be highly valued by customers. Following are some attributes that can differentiate products.

■ *Product features.* A product's physical characteristics or capabilities may be an important form of differentiation. For example, Philips developed a television that can display two channels on the same screen.

■ *After-sales service.* Convenience and quality of service may be a critical factor in deciding among alternative products. Sears attracts customers who value an efficient nationwide network of repair services.

■ *Desirable image.* This is the obvious basis of virtually all fashion products, ranging from clothing and shoes to jewelry.

■ *Technological innovation.* Technology provides the basis of competitive advantage for a broad range of firms. Cambridge Speakerworks patented a stereo speaker system that gives sound quality comparable to giant loudspeakers, but is small enough to fit in any apartment.

- *Reputation.* A distinguished reputation can be an important source of sales. At one time in the computer industry, it was common to hear, "Nobody ever got fired for buying from Big Blue," in reference to IBM.

- *Manufacturing consistency.* This is especially important in making components that must mesh with others to produce a finished good. This need gave rise to greater emphasis on statistical process control (SPC) and a broad range of quality-control techniques aimed at manufacturing.

- *Status symbol.* Luxury automobiles and limited-edition sports cars are well-recognized examples. Vehicles that cost more than some houses are obviously purchased for reasons other than just transportation.

As these examples illustrate, firms can differentiate products or services in many ways. Any attribute, feature, or capability that customers value and that a particular firm is uniquely able to offer can provide a competitive advantage based on differentiation. In fact, quality is defined broadly to include anything that allows a firm to favorably differentiate its product as evidenced by an ability to bolster the price it charges for the good or service. If the firm is successful in creating some unique and desirable attribute in its goods or services, it builds brand loyalty in customers, decreases the number of alternative products the customers are willing to consider, and reduces buyers' sensitivity to prices. These results produce higher profit margins without the necessity of lowering costs. Managers who pursue this strategy must often accept lower market shares, because mass marketing is usually incompatible with the exclusive image associated with premium-priced products. Though there are many exceptions, as shown in the high/high column of the exhibit in Application 1.4, high differentiation may also limit the firm's ability to compete on cost or price, because extra research and development (R&D), higher-quality materials, more advertising, and so forth, often create the differentiation.

In summary, successful differentiation strategies require managers to (1) understand what customers value, (2) be uniquely able to provide that value, and (3) be able to extract a premium price for it. This focus on improving profitability through premium pricing is very different from the focus of firms that pursue cost leadership advantages, as explained in the following section.

Cost Leadership

Firms achieve a *cost leadership* competitive advantage by establishing a low-cost position relative to competitors. The classic cost leadership strategy often involves offering a no-frills product aimed at the most typical customer in a large target market. Because costs usually fall as a product becomes more standardized, low-cost manufacturing firms strive for long production runs, and low-cost service firms offer uniform packages. By targeting broadly defined markets with standard products, firms can use mass-production techniques to enjoy the greatest possible benefits from *economies of scale* (cost savings realized from being larger) and *learning curve effects* (cost savings realized as a result of experience). A firm aiming for low-cost production will typically spend less on R&D than will competitors who follow a differentiation strategy, and a large portion of its total R&D might be directed toward making production easier and cheaper. Advertising will often be minimal, with promotional efforts that stress price comparisons.

All this suggests that a cost leadership strategy is associated with low-end, "plain vanilla" goods or services. This is often the case, but not always. Customers care about more than just cost, or they would all drive "econo-boxes." Instead, the market for stripped-down subcompacts is actually only a small portion of the overall automobile market. Customers' willingness to pay for added features suggests that to properly appreciate the range of options for pursuit of a cost leadership strategy, we need to move beyond considering cost alone, to considering value as well. Because customers balance benefits against costs in judging value, producers can pursue a cost leadership strategy in virtually every market segment. So, for example, Lexus and Infiniti reflect Japanese automakers' pursuit of such a cost leadership strategy in the high-end luxury car market. In other words, cost leadership is a relative term; it refers to costs relative to benefits as well as costs relative to those of the competition. But, regardless of what market segment a firm chooses, success with a strategy based on cost leadership usually requires a broad-based attack on costs. It is insufficient to focus only on one or two costs, because *overall* cost leadership is required.

Eltron International, a small firm competing in the bar code label printer manufacturing business, offers a good example of how cost leadership requires simultaneously attacking costs on a variety of fronts.[26] Eltron's products are typically the lowest-priced in the industry, often costing only half as much as competitors' products. And yet, the little company is one of the most profitable in its industry, with gross margins of nearly 50 percent. To get these spectacularly high profit margins with products priced well below the competition, Eltron has had to cut every conceivable cost. Its facilities are leased for a very low cost because the company is located in an overbuilt business park in Simi Valley, California. Its furniture is secondhand, purchased from several failed financial institutions, and its tools for the plant were also bought cheap by shopping at local aerospace manufacturers who were downsizing. As a result of such thriftiness in investing, the company has been able to generate over $40 million in sales per year with less than $2 million in property and equipment. The firm also cuts its costs by offering a narrow range of simple products that are admittedly slower and less feature-laden than competitors'. The products' simplicity has several beneficial side effects. Manufacturing costs are lowered through reduced materials costs and reduced labor for assembly, and the field service organization can be kept tiny because the simple products have fewer parts to repair or replace. Focusing on a narrow product line keeps inventory costs lower and requires less managerial oversight, lowering administrative overhead costs. All this is driven by a small management team that was recruited from a range of fiercely cost-competitive industries. By taking such a broad-based approach to cost control, Eltron is able to be an industry leader in terms of low costs and low prices as well as high profits.

Quick Response

During the 1980s, managers in firms attempting to improve value for customers focused much attention on the competitive advantages of cost leadership and differentiation. In fact, during that time, firms became so successful at finding ways to combine these two forms of competitive advantage that the Japanese began referring to the situation as *atarimae hinshitsu*, which means "value is taken for granted." When value from differentiation and cost is so widespread that customers take it for granted, firms must find new forms of competitive advantage if they hope to sustain above-normal levels of profitability. During the early 1990s, many firms discovered the potential for regaining a competitive advantage by shifting focus to response time. This form of competitive superiority seeks to provide the quality and cost customers want faster than the competition does. The shift from emphasis on differentiation and cost toward competition on quick response is obvious to researchers and managers alike. One researcher has described this development by concluding, "In today's economy, the company that survives will be the one that can develop, produce, and deliver products and services to customers faster than its competitors."[27] Andrew S. Grove, CEO of Intel, the leading U.S. chip maker, agrees: "Ultimately, speed is the only weapon we have."[28]

Quick response is more than just another aspect of differentiation, although the two are obviously complementary. *Quick response* refers to the speed with which a new product, a product improvement, or even a managerial decision that affects the customer, can be made, rather than the firm's relative level of differentiation or low cost. Just as high costs or unattractive features can diminish a product's or service's desirability, slow responses to customers' needs may force them to choose alternatives. Quick response is really a way of looking at a firm's flexibility. Virtually all firms can eventually make the changes that quick responders make, but slower firms are not flexible enough to adjust what they do as rapidly as quick-response competitors. One writer has described how this flexibility translates into winning as follows:[29]

> The theory behind flexibility is simple. If you and I are competing and I can read the market quicker, manufacture many different products on the same line, switch from one to another instantly and at low cost, make as much profit on short runs as on long ones, and bring out new offerings faster than you—or do most of these things—then I win. I can parry your every thrust, attack niches in your market that you're too bulky to squeeze into, improve faster, and maintain or even fatten profits while forcing you to follow my lead on prices.

Although quick response is emerging as a source of competitive advantage in its own right, it does not require that firms ignore the competitive advantages of high differentiation or low cost. In fact, speed can actually improve performance on these other competitive dimensions. To understand how, we must first consider the concept of value-added time.

Adding value to a product consists of any activity that increases the product's worth to the customer, such as design, manufacturing, packaging, delivery, and so forth. Generally, value is being added to a product only .05 to 5 percent of the time between the customer's order and actual delivery of goods or services, although costs are being incurred more or less continuously. For instance, if you buy a custom-tailored business suit, it may well take 6 weeks (240 hours if you count business hours alone) for your order to be filled, even though a skilled tailor will require only about 12 hours to cut and sew the garment (for a value-added time of about 5 percent). The other 228 hours involve idle time, processing, scheduling, inventory, finding missing pieces, rework, shipping, waiting, and so forth—activities that do not add value but that *do* incur costs. During such nonvalue-added hours of increasing costs, the product's value may have been, in fact, *decreasing*. Most products suffer from being inventoried: parts rust or get damaged, designs become obsolete, and items are lost. Besides this, any delay forces the customer to wait, and from a quick-response perspective, this effectively decreases the value of the product. In other words, our hypothetical slow firm simultaneously drives its costs up and decreases its differentiation, as the non-value-added time slips by. On the other hand, some companies, like Atlas Door, are able to use quick response to improve cost leadership and differentiation.

Atlas produces industrial doors, a product with an almost infinite variety of specifications regarding size, material, and construction. Historically, firms in this industry took 4 months to respond to an order. Atlas entered the market determined to beat established firms by drastically reducing the time required to fill an order. It set up a just-in-time factory and greatly improved standard delivery logistics. Atlas also developed computer-assisted design capabilities so customers could describe a door to an Atlas engineer, who would then draw up the order while the customer answered questions on the phone.

Atlas became the only competitor in the industry that could consistently fill orders in weeks instead of months. With contract deadlines to meet, customers in the construction business found such availability hard to resist. The new ordering and design systems at Atlas greatly reduced mistakes, its reputation for speed allowed Atlas to charge a premium price, and its faster overall production process lowered costs.

As one would expect, the results were spectacular. In the first 10 years of operation, pretax earnings were 20 percent of sales, about five times greater than the industry average. In this short time, Atlas established itself as the number one company in the industry, replacing the former leading door suppliers in 80 percent of the distributors in the nation.[30]

The benefits Atlas Door saw from developing a quick-response strategy extend to many industries. McKinsey and Company developed an economic model showing that high-tech products that reach the market 6 months late but within the limits of their expense budgets will earn an average of 33 percent less than the profits over their first 5 years that could have been expected from an on-time launch. To put this into perspective, according to McKinsey's model, products that come to market on time, but 50 percent over development expense budget, show an average profit loss of only 4 percent compared to the 5-year profits that could be expected, had development expenses been within the budget.

By this point, it should be clear that competitive advantage, in one or more of its three forms, is the means by which firms reach the critically important end of superior financial performance. But this conclusion raises another question: What are the means by which firms establish a competitive advantage? Answering this question in detail will take the rest of this text, but the final section of this chapter provides a summary answer as it presents an overview of chapters to come.

AN OVERVIEW OF HOW COMPANIES ACHIEVE COMPETITIVE ADVANTAGE: THE ARCHITECTURE OF STRATEGY

This text is organized around the central theme of achieving superior financial performance through building a competitive advantage. That is the essence of strategic management, and in Exhibit 1.6, we summarize the various elements involved in a framework called the Architecture of Strategy. This framework links the various topics we will discuss in upcoming chapters and shows how they contribute to the firm's

EXHIBIT 1.6
The Architecture of Strategy

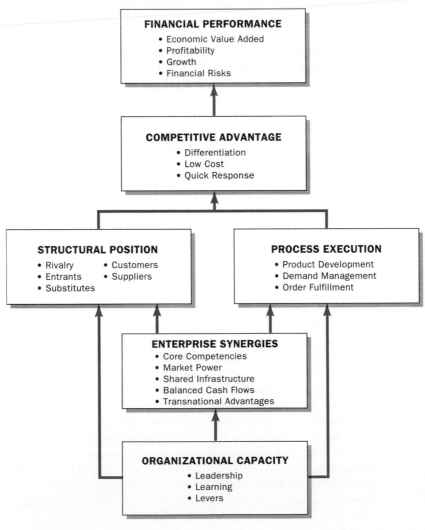

economic success. Strategic management uses each of the elements in this framework as building blocks to create a financially successful firm, and that is why the framework is called the Architecture of Strategy. You should familiarize yourself with this framework and refer back to it on a regular basis as a means of organizing and orienting your coverage of subsequent chapters. Let's look briefly at each of the elements of the framework.

As we discussed earlier in this chapter, one of the most important goals that any for-profit business has is to fulfill its fiscal responsibilities to stockholders. Because of this central importance, we have labeled the first box in the framework "Financial Performance," and the rest of the framework shows what forces contribute to a firm's success in meeting its economic goals. For example, as you have already learned, the most important determinant of a firm's ability to achieve superior financial performance is whether or not it is able to build and hold a competitive advantage, so this is the subject of the second element in the framework.

Building a competitive advantage in terms of differentiation, low cost, and/or quick response is a function of two different factors. One is the structure of a firm's competitive environment and its position within it, which we refer to as *structural position*.[31] The other deals with how well the firm executes certain core processes, and we refer to this as *process execution*.[32] Exhibit 1.6 identifies some of the topics we cover under each of these headings, but for now, it is enough for you to simply start thinking about competitive advantage as the product of both the industry's structure and the firm's ability to operate within that structure. We will take detailed looks at how managers think about and assess structural position and process execution in Chapters 3 (External Analysis) and 4 (Internal Analysis). We will then revisit these critical topics once more when we look at how managers seek to improve their firm's structural positions and process execution in Chapters 5 (Operations-Level Strategy) and 6 (Business-Level Strategy).

So far, our coverage of the Architecture of Strategy has been based on the idea of a single business unit—an organization focused on a particular product and market. However, such businesses may find benefits, called synergies, in being part of a larger enterprise, and for this reason, most corporations comprise various business units. So the next element of our framework is labeled *enterprise synergies*, and starting in Chapter 7, Corporate-Level Strategy, we will look at strategic management from the perspective of the multibusiness corporation.[33] In particular, we will look at how being part of a larger enterprise allows a business unit to achieve a stronger competitive advantage through an enhanced structural position or through improved process execution. And, because corporations are increasingly international in scope and focus, in Chapter 8, International-Level Strategy, we will look at the special challenges of developing synergies that strengthen competitive advantage across the international operations that make up a multinational enterprise.

The final element in our framework is labeled *organizational capacity*. This refers to the so-called soft issues, such as leadership, levers for organizational change, and organizational learning. The "soft" label is ironic, considering that these issues are the bedrock on which everything else in the framework rests.[34] Research yields statistics that suggest far too many firms fail to realize the greatest possible organizational capacity: some 75 percent of American workers say they could be significantly more effective at their jobs if they were better managed, while 70 percent fail to voice their feelings because of fears of repercussions from speaking out, and 78 percent are suspicious of management's motives.[35] We shall discuss means for increasing organizational capacity in terms of the leadership that fosters organizational learning and uses organizational levers to bring about needed strategic change. These interrelated topics will be presented in Chapters 9 to 12, where we will study how managers implement strategies intended to build stronger competitive advantages and more financially successful firms.

Referring back to Exhibit 1.6, the overall message suggested by this framework is that strategic management is about alignment. Reading from the bottom of the exhibit to the top, we see how managers need to develop the organizational capacity that will allow them to take advantage of enterprise synergies and to develop more favorable structural positions and/or to improve process execution. Doing so will result in the competitive advantages that can yield superior financial performance. In other words, the Architecture of Strategy is a framework for linking a series of means and ends to support superior financial performance through building strong competitive advantages. As we progress through the chapters that follow, we shall be continually moving up and down and back and forth across the Architecture of Strategy framework. Mark the page for Exhibit 1.6, and if you begin to get confused about how the chapters and concepts that follow fit together, refer back to this synopsis to get your bearings.

Careful observers may have noted that in our overview of the Architecture of Strategy, no mention was ever made of Chapter 2, The Process of Strategic Management. That is because of a fundamental difference between Chapter 2 and the issues we have begun to cover in this chapter. So far, we have looked at what elements are part of building winning strategies, and the Architecture of Strategy is the overall framework for answering this "what" question. But Chapter 2 addresses a different kind of question. It answers the "how" question of how managers and organizations build strategies. Because subsequent chapters will provide coverage of both the what and the how questions, you will want to study Chapter 2 before moving on.

Summary of Managerial Practices to Adopt from This Chapter

- Always remember that the most fundamental purpose of any firm is to provide value for its stakeholders.

- Define stakeholders broadly to include any group that has an interest in the success of the business.

- Remember that a firm must address both its fiscal responsibilities to stockholders and its social responsibilities to its other stakeholder groups.

- Do not fall into the trap of believing that a firm can meet the needs of one stakeholder group only at the expense of other stakeholders. Specifically, you should view meeting stockholders' needs as a prerequisite to meeting the needs of other stakeholder groups and you should look for opportunities whereby meeting the needs of one group supports your efforts to meet the needs of other groups.

- Do not be sidetracked by the technicalities involved in EVA. The underlying concept of producing cash flows greater than the weighted average cost of the capital employed is a simple but powerful idea that guides a wide variety of strategic decisions.

- Remember that managers should not focus on EVA measures any more than a coach should focus on the scoreboard. Instead, focus on the factors that influence a firm's ability to produce economic value. Chief among these is competitive advantage.

- Remember that, in the long run, a business continues to be successful only if it sustains a competitive advantage over its competitors. The three forms of competitive advantage are differentiation, cost leadership, and quick response.

- Look for opportunities to combine different forms of competitive advantage. Firms that simultaneously maintain more than one competitive advantage typically enjoy even greater measures of success.

- Internalize a framework, such as the Architecture of Strategy, that allows you to see the interrelations among the broad set of factors that affect a firm's ability to achieve and maintain a competitive advantage.

- Refer back to this framework in performing strategic analysis as well as when formulating or implementing strategies. Developing "fluency" in moving back and forth and across this framework is a key skill for a successful strategic manager.

Questions for Discussion and Review

1. What is the fundamental purpose of a business firm?

2. Why is meeting a firm's fiscal responsibility seen as a prerequisite for addressing its social responsibilities? How are the two types of responsibilities mutually supportive?

3. Explain what is meant by economic value added.

4. What is the relationship between economic value added and competitive advantage? What are the three major categories of competitive advantage?

5. Reconstruct the basics of the Architecture of Strategy framework and briefly explain how lower elements of the framework are linked to elements above them.

Notes

1. Terence P. Paré, "The New Champ of Wealth Creation," *Fortune* (September 18, 1995), 131–132.

2. Anne B. Fisher, "Corporate Reputations: Comebacks and Comeuppances," *Fortune* (March 6, 1996), 90–98.

3. Thomas Donaldson and Lee E. Preston, "The Stakeholder Theory of the Corporation: Concepts, Evidence, and Implications," *Academy of Management Review, 20:* 1(1995), 65–91.

4. Max B. E. Clarkson, "A Stakeholder Framework for Analyzing and Evaluating Corporate Social Performance," *Academy of Management Review, 20:* 1(January 1995), 92–117.

5. For a discussion of the critical importance of these nonfinancial considerations, see D. W. Griesinger, "The Human Side of Economic Organization," *Academy of Management Review, 15* (1990), 478–499.

6. Milton Friedman, "The Social Responsibility of Business Is to Increase Its Profits," *New York Times Magazine* (September 13, 1970), 25.

7. Dennis P. Quinn and Thomas M. Jones, "An Agent Morality View of Business Policy," *Academy of Management Review, 20:* 1(January 1995), 22–42.

8. Russell Mitchell, "Managing by Values," *Business Week* (August 1, 1994), 46–52.

9. Brad Brown and Susan Perry, "Removing the Financial Performance Halo from *Fortune*'s 'Most Admired' Companies," *Academy of Management Journal, 37:* 5(October 1994), 1347–1359; Thomas M. Jones, "Instrumental Stakeholder Theory: A Synthesis of Ethics and Economics," *Academy of Management Review, 20:* 2(April 1995), 404–437.

10. Bill Birchard, "How Many Masters Can You Serve?" *CFO: The Magazine for Senior Financial Executives* (July 1995), 48–54.

11. George Taninecz, "Kazuo Inamori: 'Respect the Divine and Love People,' " *Industry Week, 244* (June 5, 1995), 47–51.

12. See Timothy Koller, "What Is Value-Based Management?" *McKinsey Quarterly, 3*(Summer 1994), 87–101.

13. Francis V. McCrory and Peter Gerstberger, "The New Math of Performance Measurement," *Journal of Business Strategy* (March–April 1992), 33–38.

14. The worth of a business can be measured as the total value of all outstanding stock for publicly traded businesses or the fair market value of privately held businesses. See Shawn Tully, "America's Best Wealth Creators," *Fortune, 130:* 11(November 28, 1994), 143–162.

15. Joel Stern, "Management: Its Mission and Its Measure," *Director, 48:* 3(October 1994), 42–44.

16. For additional discussion and examples, see Daniel J. McConville, "All About EVA," *Industry Week, 243:* 8(April 18, 1994), 55–58; and Shawn Tully, "The Real Key to Creating

Wealth," *Fortune* (September 20, 1993), 44. For a discussion of the drawbacks and limitations of EVA, see G. Bennett Stewart III, "EVA Works—But Not If You Make These Common Mistakes," *Fortune, 131:* 8(May 1, 1995), 117–118; and Randy Myers, "Why Scott Paper Dumped EVA," *CFO: The Magazine for Senior Financial Executives, 11:* 10 (October 1995), 18.

17. Economic value added and EVA are the trademarked terms used by Stern Stewart and Co., the leading consulting firm in the application of concepts related to creating economic value. See Bennett Stewart, *The Quest for Value*, New York: Harper, 1994; Tom Copeland, Tim Koller, and Jack Murrin, *Valuation*, New York: Wiley, 1990.

18. Peter F. Drucker, "The Information Executives Truly Need," *Harvard Business Review, 73* (January–February 1995), 58–59.

19. For example, EVA requires judgmental decisions in calculating the cost of capital for investments and in what number to use for the total cost of capital invested.

20. James J. Glasser, "How EVA Works Against GATX," *Chief Executive* (January–February 1996), 42–43.

21. For examples, see James Aaron Cooke, "Does Your Logistics Operation Add Value?" *Traffic Management, 34:* 12(December 1995), 49–52; and Victor A. Rice, "Why EVA Works for Variety," *Chief Executive* (January–February 1996), 40–41.

22. David Besanko, David Dranove, and Mark Shanley, *Economics of Strategy*, New York: Wiley, 1996, 543.

23. William Q. Judge and Alex Miller, "Antecedents and Outcomes of Decision Speed in Different Environmental Contexts," *Academy of Management Journal, 34:* 2(June 1991), 449–463; K. E. Eisenhardt, "Making Fast Strategic Decisions in High-Velocity Environments," *Academy of Management Journal, 32* (1989), 543–576.

24. James Bredin, "Dominate or Die," *Industry Week, 243:* 16(September 5, 1994), 27–28.

25. S. E. South, "Competitive Advantage: The Cornerstone of Strategic Thinking," *Journal of Business Strategy, 1* (Spring 1981), 16.

26. Tim W. Ferguson, "The Responsibility Addict," *Forbes* (December 4, 1995), 70–72.

27. Donna E. Vinton, "A New Look at Time, Speed, and the Manager," *Academy of Management Executive, 6:* 4(1992), 7.

28. Robert D. Hof, "Inside Intel," *Business Week* (June 1, 1992), 86–94.

29. Thomas A. Stewart, "Brace for Japan's Hot New Strategy," *Fortune* (September 21, 1992), 63.

30. G. Stalk, Jr., "Time—The Next Source of Competitive Advantage," *Harvard Business Review* (July–August 1988), 41–51.

31. Michael Porter, *Competitive Strategy*, New York: The Free Press, 1980.

32. David A. Garvin, "Leveraging Processes for Strategic Advantage," *Harvard Business Review, 73:* 5(September–October 1995), 76–79.

33. Michael Porter, "From Competitive Advantage to Corporate Strategy," *Harvard Business Review* (May–June 1987), 43–59.

34. Jeffrey Pfeffer, "Competitive Advantage Through People," *California Management Review, 36:* 2(Winter 1994), 9–28; Jeffrey Pfeffer, Toru Hatano, and Timo Santalainen, "Producing Sustainable Competitive Advantage Through the Effective Management of People," *Academy of Management Executive, 9:* 1(February 1995), 55–72.

35. Tom Brown, "Manage with a Conscience," *Industry Week, 244:* 1(January 9, 1995), 20–24.

Appendix to Chapter 1:
An Explanation of Economic Value Added

Recall from your finance and accounting course work that firms raise outside capital in two forms: debt and equity. To oversimplify things, debt capital comes from lenders and equity capital comes from investors. To fulfill its fiscal responsibilities, a firm must meet its obligations to both these stakeholder groups. A firm must legally pay lenders the interest associated with debt; failure to do so can lead to ramifications, such as bank foreclosures, that are clearly spelled out in the loan terms. However, what fiscal responsibility does a firm have to its equity investors?

Legally, a stockholder's investment is risk capital, that is, investors accept the risk of losing their investment if the firm does not succeed and, unlike lenders, they have few options for legal recourse if this happens. In other words, a firm bears no legal obligation to give its investors *any* financial return, although its managers must demonstrate that they actively fulfill its fiduciary responsibilities. Without any legal obligation to provide stockholders with a profitable return on their investments, are managers free to ignore shareholders? Well, if you were a shareholder in a firm, would you be satisfied with its managers' performance if the firm never produced a return on your investment? Obviously, the answer is no, but this raises a more difficult question: How much return can you reasonably expect of you firm and its managers?

When stockholders invest in a firm, they generally do so with the expectation that it will offer them returns at least equal to those available elsewhere from comparable investments, and with the hope that they'll be even better. Recall from your economics classes that when a firm generates a return on its stockholders' investments better than what is generally available from other comparable investments, we say that the firm has created economic value (or added economic value) for its stockholders. In other words, the value of the economic returns created by this investment is greater than returns stockholders could have realistically expected from comparable alternative investments. If the returns are not as great, then the firm and its managers are said to have destroyed economic value. In other words, the investor received less economic value from this investment than what could have been realistically expected from making comparable alternative investments, and the investor is therefore worse off financially.

Note that the preceding paragraph refers to *comparable* alternative investments. In this case, comparable means investments that pose approximately equal risks. Comparable risk is important because rational investors will expect greater returns for accepting greater risks. Consider two investment opportunities. Investment A has a 90 percent chance of giving you a 15 percent return on your investment, while investment B has only a 50 percent chance of giving a 15 percent return. Which investment would you take? Of course you would choose A and its surer returns. But what if B had a 50 percent chance of giving you a 30 percent return? Then you might be willing to invest in B, even though it is riskier than A, because it offers greater returns.

Investors constantly evaluate similar risk-return tradeoffs, and this is reflected in their financial expectations for a firm: the riskier an investment, the greater a return investors expect. Therefore, when measuring how well a firm meets its financial responsibilities to investors, we must always take into consideration the riskiness of the investment, and compare a firm's financial returns to those typically available from similarly risky investment alternatives.

The technical details of how this number is calculated are beyond the scope of this text, but in general terms, the cost of equity capital is the cost of risk-free capital plus any adjustments for the risk inherent in stocks in general and this stock in particular.[1] In one common method for calculating this, we start with the expected risk-free rate (i.e., the rate available from investing in government bonds assumed to be risk free (which is usually around 6 percent), and add a risk premium. The amount of the adjustment is equal to the premium generally associated with stocks as a group (which has historically been about 6 percent) times a measure of this particular stock's riskiness. The individual stock's riskiness is measured by how volatile it is relative to the rest of the market. The statistic measuring this relative volatility is commonly known as beta. A beta of 1 signifies average volatility or risk, and betas above or below 1 signify more or less risk than average. (Betas are published in a number of references cited in the appendix to Chapter 3.) Assume a firm has a somewhat risky stock with a beta of 1.25; a rough approximation of its cost of equity capital would be 13.5 percent [= 6% + (1.25 × 6 percent)].

Note from this formula that a firm with average riskiness (a beta equal to 1) would have a cost of equity of 12 percent, which explains why many managers use this as a rough approximation. For example, Coca-Cola uses 12 percent for its cost of capital in assessing operations around the world, even though the risks in its various markets differ markedly. The company believes that getting managers to understand they are accountable for covering the cost of equity as well as the cost of debt is the key, and details such as the precise cost of equity are considered less critical. As one manager put it, "We are more concerned that all our managers are shooting at the right target than we are that they hit the bull's eye."

So, with regard to our previous question about how much a firm "owes" its investors, the firm is expected to return to investors an amount equal to what they could realize from comparably risky investment opportunities elsewhere. When a firm is profitable enough to meet its interest obligations on its debt from lenders, as well as give its investors a return equivalent to what they could realistically expect elsewhere for comparable risk, it has met its minimal fiscal responsibility.

The total returns required to meet the needs of both lenders and investors vary according to the firm's riskiness—riskier firms must produce higher returns, because stockholders and lenders aren't willing to fund a risky new biotech R&D venture for the same return offered by, say, a safe and highly stable public utility company. The total returns needed also vary according to the relative amount of capital obtained from lenders versus investors. Lenders can tolerate lower returns on their portion of the total capital invested in the firm because their risks are lower—remember that they can pursue legal recourses if the firm doesn't meet the requirements set forth in the terms of the loan. Because investors have fewer legal guarantees, they assume greater risks, and expect greater returns as a result. Thus, the total returns should reflect a weighted average of the lower returns expected by lenders and the higher re-

---

[1]For details, see Michael C. Ehrhardt, *Search for Value: Measuring the Company's Cost of Capital*, Boston: Harvard Business School Press, 1994.

EXHIBIT 1.7
Two Hypothetical Examples of EVA Analysis

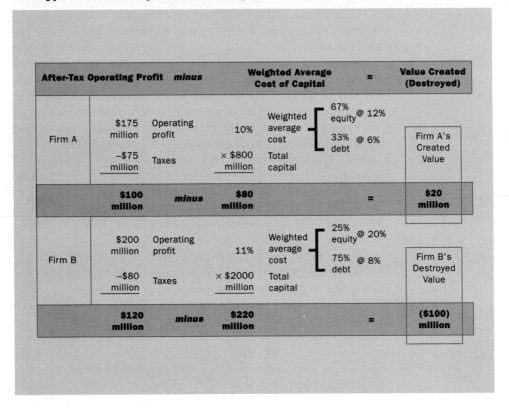

turns expected by investors. Returns required to attract funds from lenders or investors are referred to as *cost of capital*. We can summarize everything said to this point, using somewhat more technical language, as follows: *The financial goal of a for-profit business is to produce returns in excess of its weighted average cost of capital from lenders and investors.*

This statement echoes a central theme found in any basic finance course, and you may already have quite a bit of background on this concept and the details of its use. Our primary interest here is that you understand this crucial point on a conceptual level. But it will help you understand the general concept if you also understand something of the mechanics involved in calculating whether or not a firm is meeting this stated financial responsibility to its stockholders. The simple example provided in Exhibit 1.7 illustrates some of the basic steps involved in determining the economic value added by two hypothetical firms. First, calculate NOPAT (net operating profits after taxes) by subtracting taxes from operating profits. Then, subtract the cost of the firm's capital from this figure. Finally, see if the resulting number is positive. Thus, Firm A is creating economic value and producing wealth for its owners greater than what they could expect from making similarly risky investments elsewhere. On the other hand, Firm B is not offering investors the same levels of returns they can get elsewhere for comparably risky investments, and it has failed to satisfy the goals of an important stakeholder group.

Chapter 2

The Process of Strategic Management

This chapter looks at strategic management from the perspective of how the overall process of developing and implementing plans takes place. Three very different views of this process are considered, and you will be most effective if you view the strategic management process from these three vantage points. The chapter is organized into four parts. The first of these introduces terms distinguishing different types of strategy that will be used in subsequent discussion. The remaining three parts each focus on one of three different views of the strategic management process. The first is the incrementalist view, which suggests that strategic management is largely the process of responding to developments as they unfold. The second is the rational planning perspective. This has been such an influential perspective on how managers attempt to run their businesses that we devote considerable attention to it. Specifically, we look in detail at the concept of the hierarchy of strategic intent and the use of strategic programming to develop rational plans. We end the chapter with an overview of organizational learning, the perspective we emphasize in the rest of this text. Although specific details of organizational learning will be saved for subsequent chapters, here we explain how it draws on and integrates the best elements of both the incrementalist and the rational planning perspectives.

This chapter will help you understand:

- The importance of understanding basic strategic processes
- The differences between intended and realized strategies
- The need for developing a widely understood and accepted hierarchy of strategic intent, incorporating vision, mission, goals, objectives, and plans
- Three complementary perspectives on strategic management: incrementalism, rational planning, and organizational learning
- The elements that constitute the strategic programming approach to strategic management
- The contexts within which strategic programming is most likely to be effective
- The limits to strategic programming and the changes that have led to its decreased use as an approach to strategic management
- The basic elements of organizational learning and how they fit together to provide a complex, but powerful, alternative approach to strategic management

EMERSON ELECTRIC CO.

Emerson Electric Co. is justifiably famous for its nearly 40 years of uninterrupted earnings growth. During all these years, through good times and bad, the corporation's quarterly earnings never failed to increase over the previous quarter's. This unmatched record is the envy of corporations the world over.

What kind of company could manage such performance? The answer may surprise you. Emerson Electric comprises more than fifty operating divisions that make products as staid as torque wrenches and drill presses—hardly the hot growth markets one might expect. So how does Emerson sustain its growth?

A key part of the answer to this question is Emerson Electric's strategic planning process. Fundamental to this process is setting tough targets at all levels of the company and sticking to them. This is accomplished through a commitment to detailed planning and regular follow-up. Each year, top management meets with the leadership of each operating division at its planning conference. Division managers review their plans, while the visiting senior management team challenges it. Each division comes away from this process with an "agreed-to" strategic plan, including specific goals that are consistent with corporate objectives. Then division managers are free to operate with a great deal of autonomy, so long as they meet their targets. Top management monitors key division financials monthly, and meets with each division president and chief financial officer quarterly to review progress against the targets.

You will learn in Chapter 2 that the sort of rigorous planning process Emerson Electric uses is known as strategic programming. Greatly simplified, such a process consists of two parts: (1) establishing plans and (2) monitoring for adherence to those plans. Obviously, this works exceptionally well for Emerson Electric, but what about a software vendor cooperating with a score of independent programmers, or a hospital developing new outpatient services, or a small R&D firm living day to day on government research contracts? Executives at Emerson Electric would be the first to say that while a process based on strategic programming works for them, it may not be the right process for other firms. In this chapter, we consider different strategic management processes, and discover when each is most appropriate.

One of the most fundamental means of approaching strategy is to consider the different processes that strategic management involves.[1] Clearly, to completely understand strategic management, we must have a solid grasp of the processes it entails. In fact, this text is organized into three major parts, each focused on one of the three most fundamental strategic management processes: strategic analysis, strategy formulation, and strategy implementation. This chapter looks at strategic processes from three complementary perspectives. Before we can get into that material, we need to make some distinctions among different forms of strategy because we use these distinctions extensively in our coverage of strategic management processes.

THE DIFFERENT FORMS OF STRATEGY

Exhibit 2.1 depicts five different forms that strategy can take. We will focus on two of these, called *intended strategy* and *realized strategy* by Henry Mintzberg, a leading authority in the field of management.[2] Intended strategies combine an organization's aspirations with its plans for future actions; they are focused on the future and what is meant to be. Realized strategies, on the other hand, refer to the past and depict what actually has come to pass. They reflect how events really unfolded and what an organization ended up doing regardless of its initial intentions.

The relationships and distinctions between intended and realized strategies can be explained using the other forms of strategy identified in our exhibit. *Deliberate strategies* refer to elements of intended strategies that are actually realized; McDonald's consistency in opening its planned number of new restaurants, sometimes as many as one per week, worldwide, over the last 2 decades, is an impressive example of a deliberate strategy. However, intended strategies seldom survive intact: some elements fall by the wayside, while others are added. The plans that never materialize are labeled *unrealized strategy* in Exhibit 2.1. For example, Kmart announced an intended strategy that included rapid growth to reach a goal of $35 billion in annual sales. However, for a variety of reasons including market-share loss to other national chains, increased competition from specialty retailers, and lagging store sales, the plans were never successfully implemented, and Kmart's actual growth rate was only half that needed to reach its goal.[3] Unplanned developments create *emergent strategies*, those that take shape over time without specific initiation. For example, daypacks were originally designed for hiking, but were adopted as replacements for students' book satchels, and backpack manufacturers moved into a new, and much larger, market.

As an illustration of how deliberate and emergent elements combine to produce realized strategies, consider the many changes that occurred in Saturn's strategy from the time initial plans for the new General Motors division were first drawn up until cars began rolling off the line. Exhibit 2.2 details just a few of the ways Saturn's intended strategy changed for the better as unrealized and emergent elements modified

EXHIBIT 2.1

The Realized Strategy Is Usually Both More and Less Than the Strategy That Was Originally Intended

Source: H. Mintzberg and J. A. Waters, "Of Strategies, Deliberate and Emergent," *Strategic Management Journal, 6* (1985), 257–272. Reprinted by permission of John Wiley & Sons Ltd.

EXHIBIT 2.2
Elements of Saturn's Intended and Realized Strategies

Elements of Intended Saturn Strategy	Developments Requiring Strategic Response	Resulting Elements of Realized Saturn Strategy
Economy vehicle (priced around $6,000). Fuel-efficient subcompact offering a product-line extension for General Motors.	Concern for fuel efficiency diminishes after the energy crisis of the seventies. GM loses 11% market share in the U.S. and becomes more concerned about targeting sporty imports.	Sporty compact with $8,000-to-$12,000 price range designed to have the "look and feel of an import."
Heavy automation and emphasis on robots.	Experience in other GM divisions leads to better understanding of the limitations of automation and the importance of "human factors" and workforce involvement.	Balanced mix of advanced and traditional manufacturing technologies; greater emphasis on employee training.
Scale: a $5 billion investment from GM for a plant with annual output of 500,000 cars per year.	More global competitors enter U.S. market, resulting in deteriorating GM corporate performance. GM sees diminished cash flows and develops concerns about sales potential of new Saturn line.	$3 billion investment in a plant with annual output of 240,000 cars.

Source: Author's correspondence with Saturn management.

it. Given the situation in the automobile industry during the 1980s, it was doubtful that Saturn's intended strategy (originally conceived in the late 1970s) would have been appropriate more than a decade later. The realized strategy, however, appeared to be very successful by the early 1990s. Reviews of the car were very positive, consumer demand was strong, and Saturn won numerous industry awards recognizing its excellence.[4]

Saturn's situation is not unique. As we shall see, most successful strategies contain both elements that managers originally intended and unintended elements that emerged over time. In most circumstances, organizational success depends less on blind devotion to implementing intended strategies than skillfully adjusting intentions, plans, and policies as events unfold. This fundamental idea will become clearer as we consider three different views of strategic management in the next sections.

Exhibit 2.3 shows these three perspectives summarized and arrayed along a continuum from the incrementalist to the rational planning perspectives. The middle ground of the continuum, which we call organizational learning, combines elements of both extremes. Although each perspective along the continuum has its advocates, it is fair to say that no one perspective is always more appropriate or otherwise superior to the other three. Each perspective has its uses and limitations, its strengths and

EXHIBIT 2.3
A Continuum of Perspectives on Strategic Management

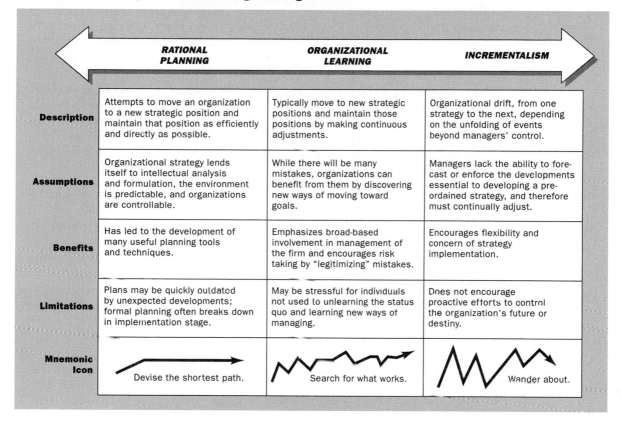

	RATIONAL PLANNING	ORGANIZATIONAL LEARNING	INCREMENTALISM
Description	Attempts to move an organization to a new strategic position and maintain that position as efficiently and directly as possible.	Typically move to new strategic positions and maintain those positions by making continuous adjustments.	Organizational drift, from one strategy to the next, depending on the unfolding of events beyond managers' control.
Assumptions	Organizational strategy lends itself to intellectual analysis and formulation, the environment is predictable, and organizations are controllable.	While there will be many mistakes, organizations can benefit from them by discovering new ways of moving toward goals.	Managers lack the ability to forecast or enforce the developments essential to developing a pre-ordained strategy, and therefore must continually adjust.
Benefits	Has led to the development of many useful planning tools and techniques.	Emphasizes broad-based involvement in management of the firm and encourages risk taking by "legitimizing" mistakes.	Encourages flexibility and concern of strategy implementation.
Limitations	Plans may be quickly outdated by unexpected developments; formal planning often breaks down in implementation stage.	May be stressful for individuals not used to unlearning the status quo and learning new ways of managing.	Does not encourage proactive efforts to control the organization's future or destiny.
Mnemonic Icon	Devise the shortest path.	Search for what works.	Wander about.

weaknesses, and your task is to recognize situations in which each is most appropriate. Although organizational learning is listed second in the exhibit, we discuss it last because it combines elements from the other two approaches and learning about them first will help you understand organizational learning. We begin with incrementalism, move next to rational planning, and then show how elements of the two combine to explain the organizational learning perspective.

THE INCREMENTALIST PERSPECTIVE

The incrementalist view of strategic management assumes that so little of a realized strategy is the result of the intended strategy that managers should not focus their efforts in strategic management on deliberate strategy. Instead, according to this perspective, they should concentrate on how a stream of largely unplanned and uncontrollable events determine the strategic path an organization follows through unrealized and emergent strategies. The arguments for adopting the incrementalist perspective depend heavily on the following three points.

- *The future is unknown and unknowable.* Planning is by definition a future-oriented activity but, unfortunately, our predictions about the future are never entirely accurate. Not only are our forecasts often inaccurate, they are sometimes laughably wrong. Consider that in the 1950s, experts virtually unanimously agreed that the world would never need more than about nine computers at any one time. Today, some models of automobiles have that many computers in a single car! But an inability to foretell the future is not always a laughing matter. For instance, in the 1980s, scores of microcomputer manufacturers went out of business when they mistakenly predicted that the operating system they had adopted would become the industry standard, only to see their system lose out to Microsoft's DOS.

- *External forces are too powerful to be controlled by organizations or their managers.* Although modern-day business organizations may be among the most powerful social institution ever developed, they may still be no match for even greater forces that often work against them. Most students are surprised to learn that the life expectancy of *Fortune* 500 firms, the largest 500 firms in the United States, is consistently less than the life expectancy of a human being. As we discuss later, the environment within which firms operate is filled with powerful forces that help determine an organization's success, despite all its plans and efforts. Government regulations, technological innovations, and changing demographics are just a few of the forces that can, and regularly do, overwhelm an organization, often with very different results from what management intends. For example, the Japanese automobile industry came close to completely dominating the U.S. car market, thanks to a broad set of impressive managerial accomplishments. However, when the yen-dollar exchange rate dramatically reduced the buying power of the U.S. dollar, every Japanese carmaker saw its market inroads blocked by a force it was helpless to overcome. Of course, if the exchange rate should ever reverse itself, this same force will disrupt the plans of U.S. carmakers attempting to sell their products in overseas markets.

- *Managers cannot enforce adherence to their plans.* Even if we could foresee the future and build perfect plans accordingly, you should understand that strict adherence to a plan is difficult to enforce in most organizations.[5] Managers usually lack the power to enforce organizational adherence to plans as they were originally conceived. At one time, executives might have been in a position to manage such adherence to their plans through power and coercion, but that is no longer typical. The joint process of *flattening* organizations (reducing levels in managerial hierarchies) and *empowerment* (decentralizing decision making) that has been so prevalent during the last two decades has dramatically reduced the extent to which decisions made at the top of an organization can be enforced down through the rest of the organization. Furthermore, given the information revolution brought on by computers, middle managers now have access to the data they need to make their own informed judgments and act accordingly.[6] Factory floor workers, meanwhile, are becoming experts at operating today's increasingly complicated and valuable machines, and in many cases they alone know enough to decide what needs doing, and when, and why, and how. This involvement means that individual actions and decisions throughout the organization will inevitably affect any centrally derived formal plans in unforeseeable ways.

Because the future is necessarily uncertain, forces beyond an organization's control often shape plans, and managers are unable to force an entire organization to comply with any particular plan, so scholars have developed the incrementalist perspective on strategic management. This perspective expects managers to constantly readjust strategies as plans are overtaken by developments outside management's ability to predict or control. Incrementalists stress the flexibility to react to unpredictable opportunities and accidents and to "muddle through" without a defined or sustained sense of direction.[7] This perspective also implies that future developments are more or less random, making learning from past experiences difficult.[8] The incrementalist perspective suggests that managerial intellect is no match for the uncertainties that organizations face, and success depends on luck, happenstance, and the ability to adjust to "the breaks." Application 2.1 provides an example of successful use of incremental decision making.

Although the incrementalist depiction of an organization buffeted by forces overwhelming managerial plans is indicative of many organizations, this does not mean that managers are happy about the situation! In other words, it may be a good descriptive model of how things are but few managers are willing to accept it as the model of how things *should* be. Most managers see themselves as participants in a constant battle against the forces that threaten to overwhelm their plans. They do so fully admitting that they are often unsuccessful, but they still refuse to quit. They see value in developing the best possible plans while recognizing that they will not be implemented unchanged and in full. They also recognize the need to skillfully adjust, coping with the unexpected developments—those unrealized elements of strategy that virtually always combine with deliberate strategy to form a firm's emergent strategy. So, while it is important for you to understand and appreciate the incrementalist perspective, it is even more important that you see that organizations expect more of their managers than a resignation to muddle through. In fact, most organizations expect their managers to use some form of rational planning, a perspective of strategic management that in many ways opposes the incrementalist view.

THE RATIONAL PLANNING PERSPECTIVE

Rational planning (also referred to as *formal planning*) is a process or a system for logically approaching the task of identifying the ends an organization pursues and determining the means by which those ends can be reached. Typically, the ends an organization pursues can be "stacked" in a hierarchy ranging from the most broadly defined intentions to the most specifically defined. We call the collection of ends being pursued by an organization its *strategic intent*. According to the rational planning perspective, the means by which these ends are best pursued is *strategic programming*, a process designed to translate strategic intentions into manageable agendas for action.

Application 2.1

Success Through an Incrementalist Approach to Business

The history of Bernie Holzer as an entrepreneur who has managed and founded several businesses provides a wonderful example of the incrementalist approach to strategic management. Bernie's story begins in the middle of World War II when he joined the U.S. Army's famous Mountain Division in hopes of learning to snow ski. He never saw any snow, and his division was assigned to fighting in the hills of Italy where the intensity of the combat led him, like many other soldiers, to go AWOL, absent without leave. He spent several weeks in hiding, during which time his division was overrun and largely captured by German forces, events that Bernie, a Jew, likely would not have survived. Shortly after learning what had happened, Bernie turned himself in and was "busted" to the lowest possible rank as his punishment. This turned out to be the luckiest break of his life.

As the lowest-ranking man in the outfit, Bernie had few privileges, so when the war ended and he was on a troop carrier returning home, Bernie's bunk was confiscated for use as the ship's craps table. With no place to sleep, Bernie stayed up late one night and won nearly $2,000 playing craps. He hired two bodyguards for the rest of the trip home, offering them each 10 percent of his winnings if he made it home safely and with all his money. Once the ship docked, he paid his bodyguards and wired his father the remaining $1,800, which his father immediately invested in AT&T stock on a tip he had overheard.

For the next 4 years, Bernie attended New York University on the GI bill and, upon graduation, he sold the greatly appreciated AT&T stock for enough to buy a small laundromat for sale near his home. He knew nothing about the business, but over the next several years, he was able to expand to a second laundromat and add two dry-cleaning establishments. His small empire was virtually destroyed during the civil riots of the late 1960s, but the properties had been heavily insured. Bernie took the insurance settlement, sold the rest of his assets, and "retired" to Colorado, where he hoped to finally learn to ski.

Upon arriving in Colorado, Bernie was appalled to discover that good bagels were impossible to find. A friend who worked at a local resort restaurant complained of the same problem, so when he stumbled across a local pastry shop for sale, Bernie decided to go into business providing local hotels and restaurants with morning pastries. He or his assistant would get up in the middle of the night, bake the day's pastries, and deliver them on the way to the ski slopes. This business went well until the assistant, after a long and boisterous night of après-ski activities, left the gas ovens on for too long before lighting them, causing an explosion that burned the shop to the ground.

Tired of the snow and cold, Bernie used his insurance to retire once again, this time on a large, comfortable sailboat in Miami. Knowing little about sailing, he sailed in whatever direction seemed easiest until he ended up in the British Virgin Islands just as this area was about to experience a boom in tourism. There he met a local entrepreneur who had an idea for a new business, but no cash to get it started.

The idea was to permanently install mooring buoys that vacationing boat charterers could use instead of having to perform the sometimes tricky maneuver of anchoring for the night. The local contact had already secured an exclusive right from the government to place buoys in the most popular coves and harbors in exchange for the promise to pay $1 each time a mooring was rented. Bernie then met two yacht-delivery captains who were looking for work on the islands to keep them going between delivery jobs. They agreed to learn scuba diving so they could install the mooring buoys underwater. When they were delivering a yacht to the Gulf Coast, where the shrimp business had taken a disastrous downturn, they discovered a sturdy little shrimp boat which they bought for practically nothing and converted to their workboat. In the meantime, Bernie and his partner had convinced local restaurant managers to collect the nightly fee of $15 for buoys placed near their restaurants in exchange for a $4 cut of the revenues.

With all this arranged, Bernie's new business started to resemble a fairy tale even more than his previous lives had. Because his business was so popular with charterers, he was granted a free slip for his live-aboard yacht at the marina of the region's largest yacht charter service. As there was really very little to do in the business (the restaurant owners and delivery skippers did all the ongoing work), Bernie had plenty of time to play tennis and swim at the marina's health club facilities. When he turned 60, he took up the sport of ironman triathlons, so he added biking and running to his daily regime.

In 1995, two hurricanes damaged his boat—but, of course, it was insured. After that he began talking about taking his insurance payment and buying a fleet of ice-

cream trucks. He admitted that he did not know much about the ice-cream business, but he was confident that in the island's tropic heat, the product would be a great business to be in during his (new) upcoming retirement!

In the sections below, we shall take detailed looks at both strategic intent and strategic programming.

The Hierarchy of Strategic Intent

By *strategic intent*, we refer to the purpose(s) of the organization and the ends it pursues.[9] These can be very broad (vision and mission) or more focused (goals and objectives).[10] For example, at the broadest level, your personal intentions may include a vision of a long, happy, fulfilling life, but you may also have a much narrower expectation of making an A in this course. Typically, in order to reach your broader intentions, you must first achieve a series of narrower ones; therefore, it is important that you align your broad and narrow intentions. If you are not careful, you may invest time, energy, and other resources in reaching narrow objectives that do not move you closer to your broader vision.

In the same way, organizations must have a consistent set of narrow intentions that move them toward broader intentions. One of managers' most critical responsibilities is to establish the parameters that shape the values, motives, and actions of others throughout their organization.[11] We will discuss these parameters as a *hierarchy of strategic intent*. As illustrated in Exhibit 2.4, the hierarchy of strategic intent includes five types of elements ranging from (1) a broad *vision* of what the organization should be, to (2) the organization's *mission*, to (3) specific *goals* that are operationalized as (4) various strategic *objectives* to be reached by acting according to specific (5) *plans*. The elements of this hierarchy set forth the ideals and ideas that serve to unify the energy and the forces scattered throughout an organization. They are beginning points for any formal planning process, but they also provide the sense of direction necessary to assure that incremental behavior culminates in overall progress.

Application 2.2 describes part of the hierarchy of strategic intent at Blue Cross/Blue Shield of Texas. In this example, we can see how the various parts (vision, mission, goals, objectives, and plans) support one another and form a logical hierarchy. Study this application, and once you understand the basic nature of the hierarchy of intentions, we can consider each part of such a hierarchy in turn.

Vision

In strategic management, *vision* refers to the category of intentions that are broad, all-inclusive, and forward-thinking. A vision describes aspirations for the future, without

EXHIBIT 2.4
The Strategic Ends Pursued by an Organization Can Be Organized as a Hierarchy of Strategic Intent

Most Integrative

Most Specific

Vision

Mission

Goals

Objectives

Plans

Fewest in Number

Greatest in Number

specifying the means that will be used to achieve those desired ends.[12] When managers refer to a vision, they usually refer to a mental image of some desired future state. One author team calls this *foresight*, a view of how managers hope things will develop.[13] Sometimes, managers also talk about a *shared* vision, meaning that individuals from across the organization have a common mental image and a mutually supported set of aspirations that serve to unite their efforts.

The most effective visions are those that inspire, usually asking employees for the best, the most, or the greatest. It may be the best service, the most rugged product, or the greatest sense of achievement, but it must be inspirational.[14] Steve Jobs's vision of building an "insanely great" computer inspired those working on the invention of the first Macintosh to reach levels of personal achievement most had never believed possible.[15] As one observer puts it, "A vision must have 'mojo,' an appeal to the emotions and aspirations of the troops that goes beyond the usual carrots and sticks."[16]

Mission

Most visions are not written statements—perhaps the points they raise are too ephemeral to look convincing on paper. Of course, this makes them more difficult for organizations, especially larger organizations, to understand and to adopt en masse. Consequently, managers find it useful to move beyond a broad mental vision to develop more specific, and usually written, statements of their organization's mission.

A vision becomes more tangible in the form of a *mission statement*. Such a statement can verbalize the beliefs and the directions in which a visionary manager wants to lead an organization. Exhibit 2.5 presents mission statements from a wide range of firms representing different industries and different organizational sizes.[17]

Excerpts from Blue Cross/Blue Shield of Texas, Inc.'s Strategic Plan

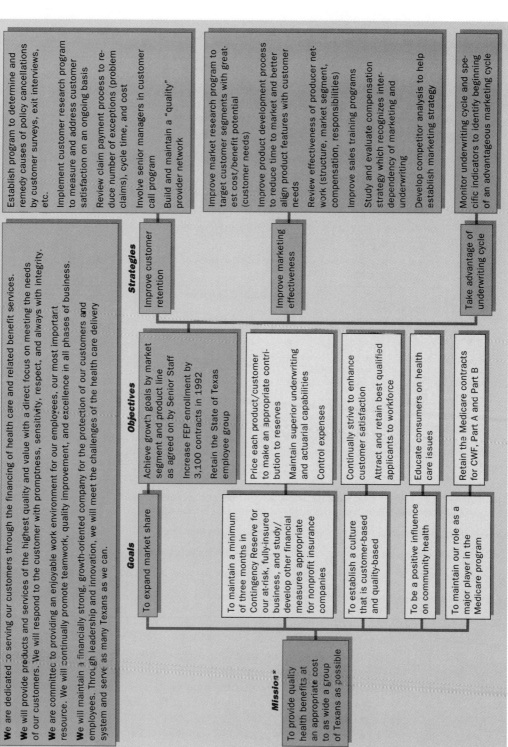

Vision

We are dedicated to serving our customers through the financing of health care and related benefit services.

We will provide products and services of the highest quality and value with a direct focus on meeting the needs of our customers. We will respond to the customer with promptness, sensitivity, respect, and always with integrity.

We are committed to providing an enjoyable work environment for our employees, our most important resource. We will continually promote teamwork, quality improvement, and excellence in all phases of business.

We will maintain a financially strong, growth-oriented company for the protection of our customers and employees. Through leadership and innovation, we will meet the challenges of the health care delivery system and serve as many Texans as we can.

Mission*

To provide quality health benefits at an appropriate cost to as wide a group of Texans as possible

Goals

To expand market share

To maintain a minimum of three months in Contingency Reserve for our at-risk, fully-insured business, and study/develop other financial measures appropriate for nonprofit insurance companies

To establish a culture that is customer-based and quality-based

To be a positive influence on community health

To maintain our role as a major player in the Medicare program

Objectives

Achieve growth goals by market segment and product line as agreed on by Senior Staff

Increase FEP enrollment by 3,100 contracts in 1992

Retain the State of Texas employee group

Price each product/customer to make an appropriate contribution to reserves

Maintain superior underwriting and actuarial capabilities

Control expenses

Continually strive to enhance customer satisfaction

Attract and retain best qualified applicants to workforce

Educate consumers on health care issues

Retain the Medicare contracts for CWF, Part A and Part B

Strategies

Improve customer retention

Improve marketing effectiveness

Take advantage of underwriting cycle

Action Plans

Establish program to determine and remedy causes of policy cancellations by customer surveys, exit interviews, etc.

Implement customer research program to measure and address customer satisfaction on an ongoing basis

Review claim payment process to reduce number of exceptions (problem claims), cycle time, and cost

Involve senior managers in customer call program

Build and maintain a "quality" provider network

Improve market research program to target customer segments with greatest cost/benefit potential (customer needs)

Improve product development process to reduce time to market and better align product features with customer needs

Review effectiveness of producer network (structure, market segment, compensation, responsibilities)

Improve sales training programs

Study and evaluate compensation strategy which recognizes interdependency of marketing and underwriting

Develop competitor analysis to help establish marketing strategy

Monitor underwriting cycle and specific indicators to identify beginning of an advantageous marketing cycle

*Note that this refers to only one element (the last one) of the vision. Other elements of the vision received similar development, but only this one is excerpted here for purposes of illustration. Based on information gathered from company documents available to the public.

EXHIBIT 2.5
Three Examples of Mission Statements

Ford Motor Company

MISSION: Ford Motor Company is a worldwide leader in automotive and automotive-related products and services as well as in newer industries, such as aerospace, communications, and financial services. Our mission is to improve continually our products and services to meet our customers' needs, allowing us to prosper as a business and to provide a reasonable return for our stockholders, the owners of our business.

VALUES: How we accomplish our mission is as important as the mission itself. Fundamental to success for the Company are these basic values:

- People—Our people are the source of our strength. They provide our corporate intelligence and determine our reputation and vitality. Involvement and teamwork are our core human values.

- Products—Our products are the end result of our efforts, and they should be the best in serving customers worldwide. As our products are viewed, so are we viewed.

- Profits—Profits are the ultimate measure of how efficiently we provide customers with the best products for their needs. Profits are required to survive and grow.

ROLM Corporation

ROLM Corporation was founded with four goals:

- To Make a Profit

- To Grow

- To Offer Quality Products and Customer Support

- To Create a Great Place to Work

The four goals are closely interrelated. One cannot exist without the others. In order for ROLM to profit, it must offer quality products and customer support. In order to grow, it must profit. And in order to develop quality products and customer support, ROLM must maintain a work environment conducive to creativity and productivity.

Baxter Travenol Laboratories

At Baxter Travenol, we seek to offer the best products, systems, and services to health-care providers around the world, enabling them to deliver quality care more efficiently. To realize this goal, we will:

- provide quality and value in the goods and services we offer our customers;

- establish and maintain leadership positions in the health-care markets we serve; and

- promote an environment for employees that fosters teamwork, personal growth and respect for the individual.

Achieving these objectives will serve health-care needs worldwide and increase the value of our stockholders' investments.

Although they apply to entire organizations, mission statements are still "personal" in that they are not subject to any well-established rules regarding what they must include. In general, mission statements address issues more explicitly, and can also serve to identify what is unique about the character of the organization,[18] as suggested by Exhibit 2.6.

As this exhibit shows, mission statements commonly address four different types of information in describing the organization's most fundamental intentions. By de-

EXHIBIT 2.6
Key Elements of a Mission Statement

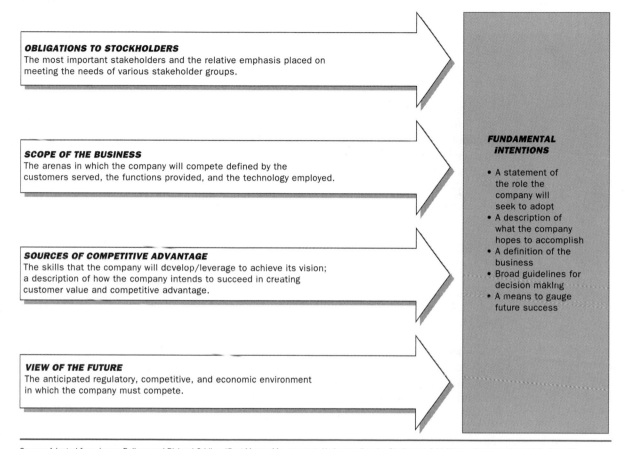

OBLIGATIONS TO STOCKHOLDERS
The most important stakeholders and the relative emphasis placed on meeting the needs of various stakeholder groups.

SCOPE OF THE BUSINESS
The arenas in which the company will compete defined by the customers served, the functions provided, and the technology employed.

SOURCES OF COMPETITIVE ADVANTAGE
The skills that the company will develop/leverage to achieve its vision; a description of how the company intends to succeed in creating customer value and competitive advantage.

VIEW OF THE FUTURE
The anticipated regulatory, competitive, and economic environment in which the company must compete.

FUNDAMENTAL INTENTIONS

- A statement of the role the company will seek to adopt
- A description of what the company hopes to accomplish
- A definition of the business
- Broad guidelines for decision making
- A means to gauge future success

Source: Adapted from James Balloun and Richard Gridley, "Post-Merger Management: Understanding the Challenges," *McKinsey Quarterly* (Fall 1990), 90–102. Reprinted by permission of The McKinsey Quarterly.

scribing perceived obligations to different stockholders, delimiting the scope of the business, identifying the most important forms and sources of competitive advantage(s), and stating assumptions about its future, a firm answers important questions such as:[19]

1. What is our reason for being? What is our basic purpose?[20]

2. What are our obligations to various stakeholder groups?

3. What is the relative emphasis we will place on meeting the needs of different stakeholders?

4. What is unique or distinctive about our organization?

5. What is likely to be different about our business 3 to 5 years in the future?

6. Who are, or who should be, our principal customers, clients, or key market segments?

7. What are our principal goods and services, present and future?

8. What are, or what should be, our principal economic concerns?

9. What are the basic beliefs, values, aspirations, and philosophical priorities of the firm?

By answering these questions, the mission statement helps managers set priorities, guide strategic decision making, and gauge performance. In short, the mission statement's essential role is to help define the business. Defining the business in this manner is such a fundamentally important step in the overall strategic management process that we will return to discuss it in much more detail in Chapter 6.

Goals

As suggested from the examples given earlier in Exhibit 2.5, most mission statements are more specific than anyone's visionary thinking, but they are still hardly concrete directions for action. Therefore, just as mission statements try to make vision more specific, goals are attempts to improve an organization's performance by making mission statements more concrete.[21] The strategic goals identified by most organizations share several features:

■ *They address both financial and nonfinancial issues.* We discussed earlier how an organization's stakeholders can have diverse interests, and given this, it should not be surprising that most organizations list both financial and nonfinancial goals. Explicit discussion of nonfinancial goals often makes it easier for managers to justify efforts aimed at more than just profitability. Exhibit 2.7 gives examples of both types of goals.

■ *They facilitate reasoned trade-offs.* Most businesses pursue a range of goals, as suggested by the exhibit, and these may not always be perfectly consistent with one another. For instance, a firm may have low-cost leadership and good employee relations as simultaneous goals. A recession occurs, and managers are faced with a dilemma. With orders down, maintaining the workforce will incur a loss that may destroy the firm's cost competitiveness, but laying off workers means that employee relations may suffer. Management's task is to make the trade-offs required in such situations, relying on carefully established goals to help with such difficult decisions.

■ *They can be reached, with a stretch.* The best goals are those that require an organization to "stretch" in order to reach them. As Polaroid founder Edwin Land described it, the goals that draw the greatest strengths out of people are those that they feel are "manifestly important and nearly impossible."[22] By constantly setting goals that demand more effort, an organization is more likely to reach its fullest potential. However, this is not meant to suggest that goals should be set arbitrarily high. Unrealistically high goals can actually harm an organization; knowing that

---

EXHIBIT 2.7
Examples of Strategic Goals

Financial Goals

Reynolds Aluminum:
"To be an industry leader in profitability and growth and to achieve an average return on equity of 20 percent."

Boeing:
"Profitability as measured against our ability to achieve and then maintain a 20 percent average annual return on stockholder's equity."

Boeing:
"Growth over the plan period as measured against a goal to achieve: greater than 5 percent average annual real sales growth from 1988 base."

Nonfinancial Goals

Boeing:
"Integrity, in the broadest sense, must pervade our actions in all relationships, including those with our customers, suppliers, and each other. This is a commitment to uncompromising values and conduct. It includes compliance with all laws and regulations."

General Electric:
"We will run only businesses that are number one or number two in their global markets."

General Electric:
"We will be a more contemporary, more accessible, more responsive company, in touch with our customers, firmly in control of our own destiny, driven by more fulfilled people in control of theirs."

Source: Author's correspondence with companies.

goals cannot be attained, the organization ignores them, and so effectively operates without the guidance a goal is meant to offer.[23]

- *They cut across functional areas.* In order to facilitate oversight and administrative efficiency, organizations are broken down into various pieces, usually as departments or functions. However, the goals we are considering cut across these organizational subunits. Thus, they cut across departments and can provide an important integrating force. Without well-understood and accepted organizational goals, individual departments are likely to act independently of one another, severely limiting what the organization as a whole can accomplish. (We will return to the subject of cross-functional coordination in Chapters 4, 5, and 10.)

Objectives

Objectives represent the *operational definitions* of goals, or explanations of abstract concepts that are concrete enough to suggest specific actions. Goals describe in fairly general terms what the organization hopes to accomplish, but objectives detail, in more precise terms, what needs to be accomplished in order to reach the goals. As the

operational definitions of goals, the most helpful objectives have the following characteristics.

- *They can be measured.* Not every objective can be easily measured, but managers
  must still monitor and measure progress. Often, they will use *proxy measures*, metrics that offer approximate indicators of goals that cannot be measured directly.
  For example, in many firms, improved quality is a strategically important goal. Yet
  quality can be a very difficult concept to measure. So, instead, most firms use
  proxies to measure quality objectives such as warranty claims, defect rates, and
  customer satisfaction surveys. In deciding which proxies are best to quantify hard-
  to-measure objectives, managers can use a simple rule of thumb: "Using this
  measurement, will we know when we have reached our objective?"

- *They incorporate a time dimension.* Measurement is usually next to meaningless
  without some time frame. For example, a business that has set the objective of
  moving up from number six to number two in market share in 2 years faces a far
  greater challenge than a similar firm that allows itself 10 years.

- *They reduce conflict.* Clearly stated objectives reduce misunderstandings and rivalry
  among organizational members. Such negative behavior is often a manifestation
  of uncertainty regarding overall firm direction. Objectives form the basis for
  cooperative managerial behavior. Focusing on the overall progress of a firm,
  rather than on the success of organizational subunits, such as individual departments or divisions, facilitates beneficial intraorganizational relationships, such as
  resource and information sharing, and improves overall performance.

Plans

The lowest level in our hierarchy of strategic intent deals with the plans that a manager develops to help accomplish higher-level intentions. These plans typically describe specific tactics, assign responsibilities, identify how resources will be allocated,
schedule activities and efforts, and specify various targets. To use an analogy of computer software, *plans* are the instructional code by which we program our organizations, and *planning* is the equivalent to strategic programming for organizations.[24]
Plans play such an important role in strategic management that you need to study
them in considerable detail. Therefore, the next section is devoted to planning, the
process of strategic programming by which organizations strive to fulfill their visions
and missions and meet their goals and objectives.

Strategic Programming

Under certain circumstances, managers want to ensure that realized strategies are as
similar as possible to deliberate strategies, which, in turn, should be as close as possible to intended strategies. In fact, *strategic programming* can be defined as planning
how the deliberate strategy can best match the realized to the intended strategy. No
one model depicts *the* strategic programming process. Rather, a number of similar
processes typically share several features. Exhibit 2.8 presents a generic model of
strategic programming that incorporates ideas from a variety of sources.[25]

EXHIBIT 2.8
A Generic Model of Strategic Programming

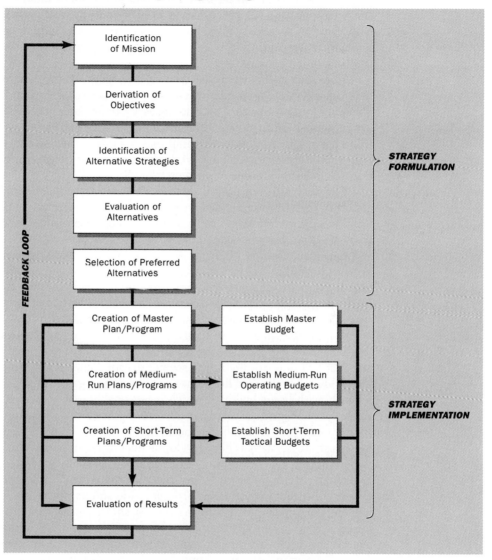

In this exhibit, plan development and implementation takes place in a straightforward linear fashion. Based on a preestablished mission and its corresponding objectives, managers first identify alternative strategies and evaluate them before selecting the preferred option, completing the strategy formulation part of the process. They then implement this strategy through tactics described by a series of increasingly detailed and shorter-range plans, programs, and budgets. In fact, the importance of these three elements gave rise to one of the most common approaches to strategic programming, the so-called planning, programming, and budgeting system, or PPBS.

First used by the U.S. Department of Defense, this approach is still employed in a variety of organizations in both industry and government today.[26] Each level of plans and programs has a corresponding level of budgets by which adherence to the plans is enforced. As the times specified in the plans, programs, and budgets expire, managers evaluate results and use this as input for the next iteration of the process through a feedback loop.

Note that in the rationalist view of management, formulation is a discrete step that logically precedes implementation. This clean separation of formulation and implementation, of planning and doing, is what fundamentally distinguishes strategic programming from incrementalism or organizational learning. Referring again to Mintzberg: "Strategic programming makes sense . . . when the world is expected to hold still or change predictably while the intended strategies unfold, so that formulation can logically precede implementation."[27]

The successful separation of formulation from implementation depends on an ability to foretell the intended strategy that will be effective as the realized strategy. Such *prescience* (knowledge of events before their occurrence) usually requires simple, stable environments in which managers can foretell events with reasonable accuracy and thus plan effective strategies. Only if they are reasonably prescient can managers hope to formulate strategic plans and succeed by carefully adhering to those plans as they implement strategies. Examples of simple, stable businesses in which managers can hope to be reasonably prescient might include restaurant chains, funeral parlors, stone quarries, home construction, and dry cleaners.

Tibbal's Flooring is strikingly successful in using strategic programming. The lumber mill at the heart of the organization is a relatively simple operation that has not changed dramatically in the several decades since it was built. Consumer use of the product has changed little since the business began, and demand has tracked consistently with home building, which is reasonably easy to forecast far enough in advance for management to adjust the firm's purchases and production output. When the CEO of this very profitable business was asked about the need to continually adjust his strategic plans as new developments unfolded, he didn't understand. "No," he said, "nothing gets in the way of our plans—that's why we have them. And once we have them, we're going to follow them or die trying." This managerial mindset is clearly consistent with strategic programming and its two-step sequence of (1) formulate and (2) implement. The firm's success shows clearly that in such a simple, stable business, strategic programming can be quite appropriate as the central process of the overall approach to strategic management. In fact, some businesses that emphasize strategic programming are among the most consistently successful of all.

For example, as described in the opening of this chapter, Emerson Electric has long formulated strategies and used detailed plans, coupled with rigorously enforced budgets to implement them. Although this may sound like an "old-fashioned" approach to management, typically associated with a stodgy, plodding dinosaur-of-a-business, nothing could be further from the truth in Emerson's case. The firm is virtually unmatched for its record earnings growth: at the time of this writing, the firm had not failed to report increased quarterly earnings in nearly 40 years. This period includes some of the most damaging recessions and dramatic economic developments in the history of the U.S. economy—shocks that created major setbacks for most firms. Yet, through it all, Emerson consistently enjoyed earnings growth. Application

Application 2.3

The Planning Process at Emerson Electric

Emerson Electric, the 100+-year-old manufacturer of industrial tools and parts, is justly famous for its strict adherence to strategic programming using a highly regimented approach to formulating and implementing plans. The results are the envy of most of the rest of the corpoate world: The company has an unbroken string of continuously increasing quarterly earnings nearly 40 years long.

The year-long planning process at Emerson culminates in what is known as a planning conference, in which corporate managers and division managers meet to discuss each division's plans and performance. Corporate management sets the stage for these conferences, establishing certain ground rules. The most important rules: first, every division (Emerson has fifty) will prepare a set of four standardized forms to be reviewed in detail during the 1- or 2-day meeting; second, the meetings are confrontational by design. The four standardized forms are:

1. *The Value Measurement Chart.* This table captures information critical to understanding how each business unit creates value for Emerson's stockholders. This includes historical data covering capital investments and returns over the past 5 years, as well as forecasts for the next 5.

2. *The Source of Sales Chart.* This table breaks sales growth down into its different sources: growth in the industry's total market, changes in the division's unit market share, changes in prices, product line extensions, new product lines, and international growth. Differences between forecasted and actual sales are calculated for every source of sales.

3. *The Sales Gap Chart.* In this line chart, sales figures (again broken down into the various sources) are plot-

ted against forecasted growth. Again, coverage is over an 11-year period: 5 years of historical data, this year's data, and a 5-year projection. Performance that does not meet past projections must be explained by the division's management, and a corrective plan for closing the gap must be put in place.

4. *The Profit-and-Loss Chart.* This is a fairly detailed set of income statements covering the 11-year period previously mentioned. Emphasis is placed on recognizing trends and putting plans into place to ward off problems before they get too serious.

Debate over these numbers is intense, given the purposively confrontational atmosphere. As the corporation's chief administrative officer puts it, "The concept is to disagree with the theses being presented irrespective of the thesis."As CEO Charles Knight puts it, "A division president who comes to a planning conference poorly prepared has made a serious mistake."

Between the annual planning conferences, Emerson's corporate managers monitor each division using a monthly President's Operating Report. These reports detail every deviation the division has made from the original plan. Knight explains, "Once we fix our goals, we do not consider it acceptable to miss them."

Sources

Based on information gathered from Charles F. Knight, "Emerson Electric: Consistent Profits, Consistently," *Harvard Business Review* (January–February 1992), 57–70; and Seth Lubove, "It Ain't Broke, But Fix It Anyway," *Forbes, 154* (August 1, 1994), 56–60.

2.3 describes some of the most important features of strategic programming at Emerson. Based on the success of firms such as Emerson, we must conclude that strategic programming is a logical and well-reasoned approach to implementation when used with a thorough understanding of its limitations. Now, let's turn to a discussion of the strengths and limitations of strategic programming.

Strengths of Strategic Programming

Strategic programming's greatest contributions center around its role of facilitating communication about strategic issues and achieving integration across organizational levels and functional specialties.[28] Properly done, rational planning provides the entire organization with a road map that greatly facilitates (but certainly does not replace) personal individual initiative. CEO Carter Fox of Chesapeake Corporation, a $600-million paper-products company, put it this way: "We control the operating units through a system of profit plans and strategic plans. They are rigorously debated and analyzed, but once we have an approved plan, I want people to take the initiative and let me know what is done later."[29] Without coordinating actions from across their organizations through a rational planning process, managers like Fox face a hopeless battle against a set of issues complex enough to challenge their entire organization.

You can see this in Exhibit 2.9, where it is obvious that the steps in the rational planning process require cooperation among managers working at the corporate, business, and operations levels.[30] Consider, for instance, the need to incorporate information on the context within which plans are developed ("strategic context" in the exhibit). The breadth of knowledge required to appreciate the various goals that guide the planning efforts throughout the organization is most likely to be found at the corporate level. However, information about specific competitive environments that particular businesses within the corporation face is most likely to be found within

EXHIBIT 2.9
A Typical Formal Strategic Planning Process

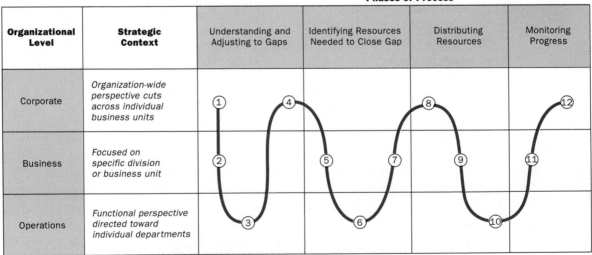

1. Evaluate performance in light of goals and identify gaps.
2. Relate gaps to environmental conditions.
3. Relate gaps to organizational capabilities.
4. Identify future goals, given understanding of gaps.
5. Describe broad action plans aimed at meeting goals.
6. Identify resources required by each function to implement plans.
7. Aggregate needs by function into overall needs of business.
8. Allocate resources across multiple business units.
9. Reallocate resources across multiple functions.
10. Deploy resources within functions.
11. Monitor use of resources within functions.
12. Monitor use of resources across businesses.

the individual business units. Finally, the details of current operational capabilities are most likely to be found within the various functions or departments.

The need to have rational planning serve as a communication and integration device is arguably greater today than ever before. At one time, formal strategic planning was widely viewed as the responsibility of top managers and perhaps a small, centralized planning staff. However, the last decade has witnessed a clear trend toward flattening organizations by removing specialized planning functions and layers of management. Typically, flattened organizations must place more emphasis on decision making lower in the organization, a practice known as empowerment. Ironically, decentralized decision making through flattening and empowerment often makes formal strategic planning even more important: although flattening and empowerment have made strategy enforcement more difficult, they have simultaneously increased reliance on voluntary commitment to the strategy. The formal plan becomes the communications device whereby all the independent organizational members learn of the "big picture" and understand how they can best contribute through individual initiatives.

Peter Drucker, one of the most respected observers of management issues in the last 40 years, likens today's executive and his or her strategic plan to the symphony conductor with a complex musical score to direct.[31] The conductor cannot hope to play each instrument as well as the specialized symphony members can, and so those experts are left alone to perfect their individual contributions. However, the conductor interprets the score and communicates to the orchestra an overall vision for how the piece should sound. Without the conductor and this shared understanding of the score, symphony becomes cacophony. Similarly, without executive leadership and direction provided through some overall strategic plan, decentralization and self-direction result in organizational mayhem.

Limitations to Strategic Programming

Although formal strategic planning can provide the integration and communication that make a valuable contribution to an organization's success, organizations are limited as to how heavily they can rely on strategic programming as the cornerstone of their overall strategic management processes. Strategic programming is applicable only in certain conditions, and these conditions are becoming rare. Additionally, problems with planning and with a command-and-control approach to implementation limit the use of strategic programming. We shall consider each of these four types of limitations in turn.

Required Conditions.[32]   As we have already illustrated by example, strategic programming is most appropriate in organizations facing stable and/or simple conditions—in fact, we see these as necessary conditions for its use. However, beyond these two necessary conditions, there are six other conditions that encourage adherence to intended strategies, as shown in Exhibit 2.10, and we discuss each of the six below.

- *Stability.* Businesses that operate in predictably ongoing ways, free from major unexpected shocks, are said to be stable. For instance, throughout this entire century, Pendleton Woolen Mills has been making the same high-quality shirts and blankets using the same production methods and the same retail distribution system.[33] Such stability allows firms to use strategic programming more viably than would

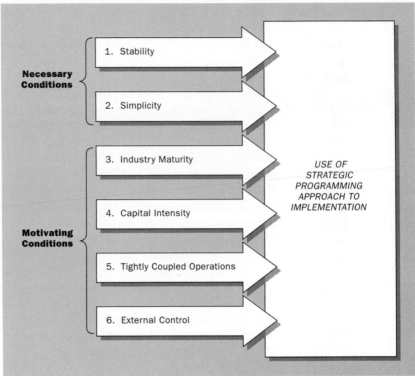

be the case for firms facing dynamic situations. For example, research has deemed
strategic programming ill-suited for dealing with the instability associated with
unexpected events, such as the oil crisis that shook a number of businesses in
1973.[34] Other research suggests that comprehensive planning is more closely
linked to firm performance in stable industries than in unstable industries,[35] and
that dynamic organizations such as start-ups and new business ventures need a
more flexible approach to business management.[36] Finally, interviews with executives reveal a fairly clear consensus that they view planning as being of limited
value where there is substantial uncertainty.[37]

- *Simplicity.* Using programming to implement a deliberate strategy is most appropriate in businesses that are simple enough to know what the right strategy is
before the fact. Or as one research team put it: "Application of the [programming]
model generally depends on being able to see quite clearly which factors we must
take into account in solving the problem, and which we can ignore. . . . [This]
approach is . . . likely to be useful in the planning of simple operations in systems
whose inputs and outputs are reasonably clear."[38] In situations too complex to
allow planners to be prescient about inputs and outputs, adhering strictly to a
mechanistic approach to planning can actually be crippling. As managers in com-

plex environments struggle in vain to adequately capture enough information about inputs and outputs to instill confidence in the intended strategy, the organization bogs down in what has been called the "paralysis of analysis."[39]

- *Industry maturity.* In mature markets, changes are gradual and managers have years of experience to draw on. Thus, they often have great confidence in the intended strategies they design and work aggressively at seeing their implementation as deliberate strategies.

- *Capital intensity.* This is the extent to which the firm has invested in capital equipment. Most such equipment is limited in its use; an assembly line designed for the production of cars cannot be used for anything else—not even for the production of trucks. This inflexibility provides managers an incentive to adhere closely to their intended strategy, because changing their minds would mean that large investments in capital equipment would be rendered obsolete.[40]

- *Tightly coupled operations.* Compare the need for adherence to plans by 100 independent trucking contractors with the need for plan adherence by 100 truck drivers constituting a single, centrally controlled network of trucking services. The independent truckers can adjust their plans "on the fly" as events unfold (more like incrementalism), while the drivers in the tightly linked network must adhere more precisely to prespecified plans (more like strategic programming) in order to avoid mass confusion.

- *Powerful external control.* Organizations under tight control by outside forces typically have a built-in motivation to adhere closely to intended strategies. For example, a business unit that is held accountable to corporate headquarters is more likely to be motivated to stick to an approved plan than a business unit free from this external oversight. The Emerson Electric example you have already seen in this chapter illustrates how a division's deviation from plans is explained and justified at follow-up meetings, providing ample motivation for business-level managers to "make plan." The same goes for firms doing contract work for much larger and more powerful customers—government contractors are a classic example. Unless the contracting agency has signed off on the activity in advance, the budget cannot support it, and seldom is any extra activity added to an established plan. At the same time, nothing planned can be left out, because unspent funds are lost in reduced budgets for the next year. Consequently, management in typical government contractors is focused on careful adherence to the current year's plan.

The six factors identified in Exhibit 2.10 are interrelated and mutually supportive. For example, mature firms tend to be stable and simpler to operate: managers have more experience; equipment associated with many capital-intensive businesses leads to integrated operations with tightly coupled parts; heavy capital investment ties a business to a particular way of doing things, increasing its stability; and so forth. As these various forces reinforce one another and move in concert, we need an overall label that captures the broad picture of the firms that meet these conditions. The label most commonly given to such businesses is *mechanistic organization.* "Mechanistic" is used to connote an organization that is designed to operate reliably in a stable and predictable manner with tightly integrated parts that support one another as do those in a complex machine. We use this label when we are describing firms that meet most or all of the six conditions described above and adhere to a strategic programming approach to implementation as a result of these conditions.

Diminishing Viability of Mechanistic Organizations.   Strategic programming's usefulness in mechanistic organizations would not be a major limitation if mechanistic organizations were the norm. Such firms not only are the exception rather than the rule, but also are becoming even more rare because of several recent trends and developments both outside and inside organizations.[41] Externally, global competition is forcing agile competitors to adjust to fragmenting markets that require greater flexibility in adapting to emerging needs, and mechanistic organizations tend to adapt to such changes slowly. Internally, better-educated employees, coupled with advances in information technology, encourage organizations to get more people involved in planning and decision making so that planning becomes intertwined with doing. Meanwhile, ongoing technological advancements alter competitors' capabilities and customers' expectations, and this requires many firms to evolve continuously. Such trends suggest to managers that the mechanistic organization that began to develop at the turn of this century with the birth of the industrial age is now out of date. Mechanistic organizations can seldom compete in terms of differentiation, cost, and response time with more flexible, flatter organizations. For instance, the narrowly defined goals and divisions of labor common to most mechanistic organizations inhibit the creativity and initiative required to differentiate products in new ways as required by fragmenting markets. The management layers required to enforce adherence to intended strategies often add overhead costs that can leave a firm noncompetitive. Also, standardized procedures and inflexible plans may slow response times and can inhibit a firm's responsiveness in today's competitive environment.

As a result of these external and internal changes and the need to maintain competitiveness, managers seek new models of organization. These new forms of organization are commonly referred to as *organic*, to express the idea that they are lively, dynamic entities that constantly evolve. Organic organizations differ from mechanistic organizations as shown in Exhibit 2.11.

EXHIBIT 2.11
A Comparison of Mechanistic and Organic Organizations

	Traditional Mechanistic Organization	*Emerging Organic Organization*
Employee focus	Internally focused on pleasing supervisor	Externally focused on pleasing customer
Performance standard	Periodically fixed targets	Continuous improvement
Basis of relationships	Vertical, up and down the hierarchy	Horizontal, across functions
Organizational structure	Tall and static	Flat and responsive
Employees' expectations	Expected to comply to direction	Empowered to decide and act
Dominant form of leadership	Command and control	Visionary and enabling

Although it is unlikely that any organization has fully completed the transformation to this organic form, most U.S. organizations are attempting to make such a change. Most international business experts believe that this trend will continue, suggesting that the number of mechanistic organizations depending on strategic programming for strategy implementation will continue decreasing. Application 2.4 describes the type of transformation from mechanistic to organic organization that has become increasingly common.

Problems with Planning.   Planning is the essence of strategic programming. Unfortunately, the very strengths attributed to planning earlier in this chapter (communication, coordination, integration, control) are also its most important weaknesses. Planning works like an organizational gyroscope, constantly exerting righting forces that keep the organization on a constant course, but these same forces must be overcome when a change of course is needed. In other words, strategic programming allows organizations to stick to the straight and narrow path set forth in the intended strategy, and this is good unless the intended strategy was wrong and the path leads in the wrong direction. For example, in managing its doomed venture into facsimile services, Federal Express used the same type of rigorous planning that it uses to operate its package delivery business. In such cases, planning will not only lead the organization astray, but even worse, it may do so with great efficiency! FedEx was able to rapidly open fax services across vast markets, using its elaborate planning process. Regrettably, managers often cannot be certain where their intended strategy will take them until their plans are well underway. Only after investing millions of dollars in this venture did FedEx realize that the economics of faxing favored individually owned machines, rather than centrally located fax centers.

Furthermore, once managers discover they're on the wrong path, planning is particularly ill-suited to changing course. Planning is an inherently conservative process.[42] By this we mean that planning works to conserve the basic orientation of the organization. It moves the organization more expeditiously down a particular path, but seldom leads the organization to seriously question whether it is traveling the *right* path.

Planning may be useful in bringing about incremental changes within an organization, but it does not promote quantum changes, or comprehensive reorientations.[43] Big changes would disrupt all the established thinking (called *paradigms*) on which managers base their plans, and therefore such fundamental changes are ignored—or even avoided—in most planning efforts. In effect, planning and plans place blinders on an organization that limit its field of vision. Of course, this focus is appropriate if (1) it is trained on the right target and (2) the target does not move. However, as we have already discussed, trends increasingly require organizations to hit constantly changing and moving targets, a feat not well suited to planning or strategic programming.

Difficulties with Command and Control.   Even if managers can overcome the problems with planning identified above, new problems arise as managers try to ensure adherence to the resulting plan. Adherence to plans has traditionally depended on successful use of a form of management commonly known as *command and control*, in which managers develop commands reflecting their understanding of plans derived from the intended strategy, and then use organizational control systems to enforce compliance with those commands. In our previous discussion of forces nudging orga-

Application 2.4

General Electric's Salisbury Plant Transforms from a Mechanistic to an Organic Organization

Over the last decade, General Electric has invested heavily in converting many of its business units from fairly mechanistic organizations to more organic ones. It has made this transformation because the corporation is convinced that trends toward greater market instability and complexity will demand that its business units be more responsive. GE's Salisbury plant, a facility that produces electric circuit breakers, is a role model for other business units attempting to make this transformation. CEO Jack Welch regularly sends executive teams to the Salisbury plant for what he calls "a peek into the future."

Before the transformation that took place at the Salisbury circuit breaker plant, it was a classic example of a mechanistic, command-and-control, strategic programming organization. Its circuit breakers were relatively simple, low-technology products sold in a mature domestic market. Senior managers established annual plans complete with detailed objectives and budgets they focused on meeting. Workers were confined to narrowly defined, tightly coupled tasks along a capital-intensive assembly line. The plant employed five layers of management to see that its annual plans were carried out precisely, thereby satisfying the requirements of external managers in GE's corporate headquarters. For years, this had been a simple, stable, and profitable business.

However, by the mid-1980s, the situation had changed. GE faced increasing global competition from strong foreign competitors. The company was becoming dependent on foreign markets, where considerable growth potential remained, for any profits. Volatile economies and government regulations made overseas operations a roller-coaster ride. The Salisbury plant was poorly equipped to cope with this complex, unstable environment, and it became so unprofitable that headquarters threatened to shut it down. This crisis motivated the transformation to a very different-looking organization.

The new plant bears very little resemblance to the old one. The dominant strategic objective has shifted from meeting periodic budget targets to continuous improvement and organizational learning. This has shifted the responsibility for setting targets from the top of the organization, where centralized planning had traditionally

been done, to throughout the organization. The workforce is organized into self-managing teams, each responsible for a different production unit. Each team's elected facilitators lead team members in solving problems and planning changes that the teams believe will improve performance. As their ideas prove out, they work across the organization to spread them. Teams work individually to perform traditional managerial functions like planning, hiring, and capital appropriations requests for their own units. Where teams are linked, cross-functional groups of associates meet weekly to address policy issues as they arise. Without the need for top-down command and control to enforce top-management's plans, the hierarchy has been simplified. It now includes a total of three levels—plant manager, advisers, and associates. Meanwhile computer-based equipment provides the plant with increased flexibility, so production plans can now shift to reflect the constant changes in demand in the new markets the plant is trying to serve. The plant still makes its quarterly reports to corporate headquarters, but everyone seems to place more emphasis on the data the plant tracks internally and reports on a minute-by-minute basis on an electronic scoreboard that hangs above the factory floor. As teams try new ideas, they are able to track the impact they are having on factors affecting the business unit's competitive advantage.

Five years after the transformation process began, results were impressive. Customer complaints about poor quality were down tenfold, costs were down 30 percent, and the average delivery cycle had been reduced from 3 weeks to 3 days. Clearly, for its new environment, the new organic, learning-oriented organization has proven to be far superior to the old mechanistic, strategic programming organization the Salisbury plant used to be.

Sources

Based on information gathered from Steven F. Dichter, "The Organization of the '90s," *McKinsey Quarterly* (Winter 1991), 145–155; John F. Welch, Jr., "Removing Walls," *Executive Excellence, 11* (April 1994), 20; and Joseph D. O'Brian, "GE's 'Work-Outs' Change Role of Management," *Supervisory Management, 39* (January 1994), 6.

nizations toward incremental processes, we have already explained the difficulties managers have in enforcing a plan on today's typical organization.

Now let's summarize the strengths and limitations of strategic programming. The role of strategic programming is valuable when it facilitates communication across the organization about critically important strategic issues, and thereby promotes integration of activities across the firm. However, strategic programming works best when conditions allow managers to cleanly separate strategy formulation from strategy implementation, and, as we have seen, these conditions are only likely to exist in simple, stable businesses. Businesses that are more complex or that operate in more dynamic conditions cannot realistically hope to know what strategy will work in advance of efforts made to implement it. In other words, managers must continually adjust the strategy as they put it in place, and policy formulation overlaps implementation in a process called *organizational learning*.[44] The remainder of this chapter discusses how organizational learning combines elements of incrementalism and rational planning to offer one of the most useful perspectives on the strategic management process.

THE ORGANIZATIONAL LEARNING PERSPECTIVE

This perspective assumes a middle ground between the rational planning and incrementalist perspectives. Both have their strengths and both have their limitations, and organizational learning attempts to capitalize on the advantages and offset the weaknesses of each. Of the three perspectives on strategic management, organizational learning is stressed throughout the remainder of this text, with Chapters 9 to 12 covering in detail what we only introduce here. Exhibit 2.12 makes the point that be-

EXHIBIT 2.12
A Continuum of Approaches to Strategy Implementation

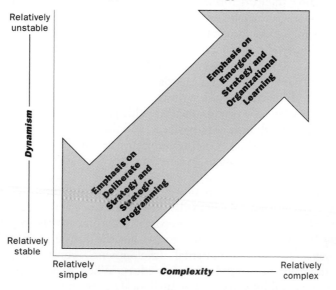

tween the extremes of rational planning's emphasis on deliberate strategy and incrementalism's emphasis on emergent strategies lies an opportunity to mix elements of the two perspectives. And, to quote Mintzberg one final time:

> . . . few if any strategies can be purely deliberate, and few can be purely emergent. One suggests no learning, the other, no control. All real-world strategies need to mix these in some way—to attempt to control without stopping the learning. . . . Thus, emergent strategies are not necessarily bad, and deliberate ones good; effective strategies mix these characteristics.[45]

In Application 2.5, we provide a description of how Honda learned from experience, as it entered the U.S. motorcycle market, instead of just relying on either rational planning or incrementalism.

Organizational learning assumes that, in practice, most detailed rational plans offer only general guidelines for personnel to use in directing their own work. Too much is unknown at any one time to write detailed sets of instructions for individuals, and even what is known today may change tomorrow. In such a situation, strategic management cannot be viewed simplistically as the formal process of coming up with the plan and then seeing that it is implemented. Instead, managers continually rethink and adjust an organization's plans and activities, as described by the incrementalism perspective. However, these continuous adjustments need not be the random wanderings implied by the muddling through of incrementalism. The organizational learning perspective suggests that managers develop plans and then continually adjust them as they gain new insights about how the firm can more successfully reach its goals.

One of the pioneers who developed this middle-ground perspective that mixes elements of rational planning and incrementalism was James Brian Quinn. Quinn's work led him to conclude that the most successful managers are those who willingly concede that they lack the ability to foresee the future and the power to enforce adherence to their plans. Yet, to maintain some sense of mission, these managers are not willing to allow their organizations to drift aimlessly. They manage incrementally, but with a purpose. Quinn labeled this approach to strategic management *logical incrementalism*, to combine the ideas of rational planning with incremental adaptation.[46]

According to this perspective, managers assume that no single point of view dominates an organization's decision making, and that strategically important decisions are constantly being made at all levels of the business and throughout the organization. Managers may have a vision of what they want the organization to be in years to come, but they try to evolve gradually to this position. They do this by attempting to build a strong-but-flexible core business, and then, by continually investing in a number of "side bet" ventures, experimenting to see what else works. They accept these ventures as necessary gambles because managers realize that the future is both unknown and unknowable.

But the unknown and unknowable aspects of the future do not stop managers from trying to understand what will and will not work in moving them toward a vision of what the organization should become, according to the organizational learning perspective.[47] Rather than trying to predict the future, managers seek to become highly sensitive to environmental developments, constantly scanning the world around them for new trends and new ideas. When they observe these new trends, managers respond by carrying out small-scale experiments to see how the organiza-

Honda's Entry into the United States: Success Through Organizational Learning

Honda's entry into the U.S. market provides a good counterexample to Emerson Electric's approach. While Emerson places tremendous emphasis on figuring out in advance what needs to be done and then doing it (strategic programming), the eventual success of Honda's entry was based largely on the organization's ability to try out unproven ideas, build on what worked, and learn from its mistakes (organizational learning). Because the company was entering a complex market it knew nothing about and had neither the money nor the time to do much research or planning, it had little choice but to learn as it went along.

Today, Honda is known as a successful competitor in a number of markets: motorcycles, automobiles, lawn mowers, and a wide variety of products powered by small gasoline engines, such as portable electric generators. However, when it first entered the U.S. market, the firm was unable to offer even a single successful product. The company started in Japan soon after World War II, and for a decade it sold products that ranged from complete failures to marginal successes.

By 1958, the firm finally had a successful product in Japan (a small 50 cc motorbike designed to suit the requirements of Japanese housewives) but exports to the rest of Asia totaled only 1,000 units a year. The poor roads and low disposable income levels across Asia at this time appeared to limit further opportunities there, and Europe's market appeared to be completely dominated by a number of very strong brands. With nowhere else to turn, the firm decided to approach the U.S. motorcycle market with modest ambitions and virtually nonexistent plans. Executives later recounted, "In truth, we had no strategy other than the idea of seeing if we could sell something in the United States. . . . We did not discuss profits or deadlines for breakeven."

In fact, the only structure to the entry timetable was created by Japan's Ministry of Finance, which was clearly skeptical of Honda's chances for success. Toyota had just launched the Toyopet in the United States, and it had failed miserably; what chance did a weaker firm have of succeeding? The ministry stalled but eventually granted funding dependent on a 5-month entry schedule, a schedule intended to convince the firm to give up its idea.

However, Honda scrambled to make the deadline and secure the funding. In doing so, the company depended even less on planning than it had in the past. Mr. Honda, the founder, was especially confident that the larger motorcycles (250 cc and 350 cc) the firm planned to export would be successful, not because of any market research but because he felt the shape of their handlebars looked like the eyebrows of Buddha, which he thought would be a strong selling point.

The firm did not know that motorcycle sales in the United States are seasonal, with a peak season from April to August. Its first shipment of motorcycles arrived in the United States in August of 1959 and mostly sat idle until April of the next year. Soon after the first units were sold, customers started returning with complaints about leaking oil and clutch failures that occurred because U.S. riders rode their motorcycles much farther and faster than Japanese riders rode theirs. The company spent the month of April 1960 airfreighting failed machines back to Japan, where an R&D group worked around the clock, first to diagnose and then to fix the problems with a new head gasket and clutch spring.

The company had always assumed that the largest market for its motorcycles would be "macho males in black leather jackets," and it resisted exporting its line of smaller, 50 cc machines (designed to satisfy the tastes of Japanese housewives) for fear they would damage its image. However, the company did ship several of the small machines to the United States, where Honda employees used them to run errands around Los Angeles. These machines attracted considerable attention, especially from Sears, Roebuck, which proposed to distribute the smaller motorcycles. Honda resisted until its larger machines started breaking down, at which point it had little choice but to start shipping smaller machines.

The smaller motorcycles were well received by sporting goods dealers (rather than motorcycle dealers), who sold them to "normal, everyday Americans." For 4 years, the company had a marketing campaign that tried to appeal to both the "leather jacket" and the "everyday American" market. In 1963, an undergraduate advertising major at UCLA working on a class assignment developed an advertising campaign with the theme "You meet the nicest people on a Honda," which was aimed squarely at the market for the smaller machines. The student passed the idea on to a friend working at Grey Advertising, which bought the rights to the idea and eventually sold it to

Application 2.5 (cont.)

Honda as part of a marketing strategy aimed directly at the large untapped market of "everyday Americans." The Nicest People campaign was a major success, and by 1994, nearly one out of every two motorcycles sold in the United States was a Honda. From a humble base, the company built the corporation we know today.

Sources

Based on information gathered from Richard T. Pascale and E. Tatum Christiansen, *"Honda (B),"* Boston: Harvard Business School (case study), 1989; Richard T. Pascale, "Perspectives on Strategy: The Real Story Behind Honda's Success," *California Management Review, 26* (1984), 51.

tion as a whole might best adapt. Realizing that they cannot hope to spot all important trends and run all the needed organizational experiments, managers encourage similar testing throughout the organization. Thus, according to this perspective, the role of upper management is to build an organization in which all members continuously question the status quo, search out ideas for improving the status quo, conduct experiments to see which of these ideas are most fruitful, and then move to spread what has been learned from these experiments throughout the organization.

The need for organizational learning has become more apparent as a form of competitive rivalry known as *knowledge-based competition* has emerged. This emphasis on knowledge as a competitive weapon is entirely in keeping with the resource-based view (RBV) of firms that we will emphasize in later chapters. The RBV focuses on an organization's internal resources as the key to its success in competition. One of the key resources that an organization can draw upon in establishing a competitive advantage over its rivals is superior knowledge.[48] Consider the importance Boynton and Bart give to knowledge as a critical resource for competition, as shown in the following quotation:

> The very definition of the firm must change in a subtle yet critical way. Instead of the firm being defined by the products and services it produces at any given time, it must now be defined by the specific process know-how or competence it brings to the competitive market. Therefore, the *knowledge* [emphasis in original text] the firm possesses, develops, and enhances, represents the basis for competition.[49]

The organizational learning perspective offers us a very powerful lens for viewing and studying organizations. It combines the best elements of the incrementalist and rational planning perspectives, and also is a very natural complement to the resource-based view of competition and knowledge-based competition we will cover in Chapter 4. Note, however, that although the organizational learning perspective offers these important advantages, this does not make it *the* right approach. Rather than becoming mired in the effort to identify a single best approach, it may be more useful to learn how to use all three perspectives. This text draws heavily from all of them.

In the chapters that follow, you will learn about many planning methods and analytical techniques that have grown out of the rational planning perspective with its theme of applying reason and intellect to overcome the obstacles that stand between an organization and its goals. However, we carefully present the limitations of these tools, and stress that managers need to remain flexible in adapting to developments as they unfold in a very incrementalist fashion. Finally, we stress organizations' need to continually learn about what will and will not work for them through an ongoing process of experimentation that results in continually adjusting the means by which strategic intent is pursued. We will give particular emphasis to organizational learning in our coverage of strategy implementation (Chapters 9 to 12). In these chapters, you will see how leaders can use a variety of organizational levers to create learning organizations. However, before we can get to that material, we need to cover the topics of strategic analysis (Chapters 3 and 4) and strategy formulation (Chapters 5 to 8).

Summary of Managerial Practices to Adopt from This Chapter

- One of the most important responsibilities of management is to lead the organization to develop a hierarchy of strategic intent that incorporates a consistent and mutually supportive set of vision, mission, goals, and objectives.

- As a leader developing a vision, seek out the ideas and ideals that will inspire an organization and motivate its members to work toward greatness.

- In developing a mission statement, remember that organizations serve multiple stakeholder groups and identify how your organization will address the needs of its most important stakeholders.

- Develop goals that support the organization's mission, that address the need for balance among various stakeholder groups, and that "stretch" the organization.

- In identifying objectives, develop measurable targets, but be mindful of the possible unintended consequences of such measurement.

- Remember the difference between an intended strategy and a realized strategy and be careful not to confuse the two in your consideration and discussion of strategy.

- Strategies for simple, stable businesses may be successfully implemented using strategic programming, while strategies for organizations facing complex and/or unpredictable situations will usually require organizational learning, and overwhelming complexity and dynamism may force adoption of an incrementalist approach.

- Remember the key distinguishing feature between strategic programming and organizational learning: In strategic programming, the firm can realistically separate planning and doing, strategy formulation and implementation. In organizational learning, a firm assumes that it cannot realistically tell in advance how the future will unfold or what will work, and it therefore intertwines formulations and implementation, continually adjusting its strategy as it gains new insights through a trial-and-error process of learning by doing.

- Do not assume that either a pure strategic programming approach or a pure organizational learning approach is right for your organization. Most organizations need a blend of the two and, consequently, managers need to understand both.

- You should recognize that although there is nothing inherently wrong with strategic programming, the incidence of "mechanistic" organizations that can successfully depend on this approach is shrinking. Shifts in the nature of business have made it more important for organizations to become more "organic" and to place greater emphasis on organizational learning.

■ Remember the limitations of each of the three major perspectives on strategic management: rational planning, incrementalism, and organizational learning. Develop a willingness to draw from all three perspectives to improve your effectiveness.

Questions for Discussion and Review

1. Describe an example that illustrates the various forms of strategy identified in Henry Mintzberg's model (Exhibit 2.1).

2. What is the incrementalist approach and under what conditions is it most relevant to the practice of strategic management? What are its limitations?

3. What are the major elements of the hierarchy of strategic intent and how do they support one another?

4. Describe strategic programming. Where is this rational planning approach to strategic management most useful and what are its limitations?

5. Explain this statement: "Organizational learning is a middle-ground perspective that attempts to draw upon the strengths and overcome the weaknesses of incrementalism and the rational planning perspective."

Notes

1. Katherine Zoe Andrews, "It's All in the Process," *Harvard Business Review, 73* (September–October 1995), 10–11.
2. See Henry Mintzberg, *Mintzberg on Management*, New York: The Free Press, 1989, esp. chap. 2.
3. Subrata N. Chakravarty, "The Best-Laid Plans . . . ," *Forbes, 153:* 1(January 3, 1994), 44–45.
4. D. Stovicek, "Manufacturing Excellence Awards: The Five Winners," *Automation, 38* (1991), 18–28; J. B. Treece, "Here Comes GM's Saturn," *Business Week* (April 9, 1991), 56–62.
5. P. C. Nutt, "Identifying and Appraising How Managers Install Strategy," *Strategic Management Journal, 8* (1987), 1–14.
6. R. W. Goddard, "The Rise of the New Organization—Doing Business in the 1990s: It Was Never Like This Before," *Management World, 19* (1990), 3–5.
7. C. Lindblom, "The Science of Muddling Through," *Public Administration Review* (1959), 79–88; D. Braybrooke and C. E. Lindblom, *A Strategy of Decision: Policy Evaluation as a Social Process*, New York: The Free Press, 1963.
8. Gerry Johnson, "Rethinking Incrementalism," *Strategic Management Journal, 9* (1988), 75–91.
9. See Gary Hamel and C. K. Prahalad, *Competing for the Future*, Boston: Harvard Business School Press, 1994; find an extension of these concepts in Christopher A. Bartlett and

Sumantra Ghoshal, "Changing the Role of Top Management: Beyond Strategy to Purpose," *Harvard Business Review* (November–December 1994), 79–88.

10. Some theorists have attempted to carefully distinguish among the different types of goals according to the level of specificity or breadth. See, for example, M. D. Richards, *Setting Strategic Goals and Objectives*, 3d ed., St. Paul, MN: West Publishing Co., 1987. Unfortunately, writers in management literature do not agree on whose set of distinctions and definitions is correct, and carefully considering all the options creates a semantic hurdle we will not attempt to clear. To avoid further complicating matters, we will simply describe our terminology without discussing options we could have chosen or justifying our particular selections. We have used *intentions* to refer to desired future states, regardless of the level of specificity. Where the level of specificity is important to note, we use vision, mission, goals, and objectives to refer to increasingly detailed and specific types of goals.

11. For a description of how this works within Levi Strauss & Co., see R. Howard, "Values Make the Company: An Interview with Robert Haas," *Harvard Business Review, 68* (1990), 132–144; and Russell Mitchell and Michael Oneal, "Managing by Values," *Business Week* (August 1, 1994), 46–52.

12. B. B. Tregoe, "Implementing the Vision: The Lessons Learned," *Planning Review, 18* (January–February 1990), 39–44, 48.

13. See Hamel and Prahalad, *Competing for the Future*; and related discussion in Bernard C. Reimann, "Gary Hamel: How to Compete for the Future," *Planning Review, 22*: 5(September–October 1994), 39–43.

14. BankAmerica Corporation provides a good example. See R. N. Beck, "Visions, Values, and Strategies: Changing Attitudes and Culture," *Academy of Management Executive, 1* (1987), 33–41.

15. Frank Rose, *West of Eden: The End of Innocence at Apple Computer,* New York: Viking/Penguin, 1989, 81.

16. W. Keichel, "A Hard Look at Executive Vision," *Fortune, 120* (1989), 207–211.

17. Additional examples, literally hundreds of them, can be found in Patricia Jones and Larry Kahaner, *Say It and Live It: The Fifty Corporate Statements That Hit the Mark*, New York: Doubleday/Currency, 1995; John Graham and Wendy Havlick, *Mission Statements: A Guide to the Corporate and Nonprofit Sectors*, New York: Garland, 1995; and for a detailed look at one visionary's view of the future and his company's place in it, see Richard Brandt, "Bill Gates's Vision," *Business Week* (June 27, 1994), 56–62.

18. J. H. Want, "Corporate Mission: The Intangible Contributor to Performance," *Management Review* (August 1986), 50–54.

19. For additional guidelines in preparing mission statements, see J. A. Pearce II and F. David, "Corporate Mission Statements: The Bottom Line," *Academy of Management Executive, 1* (1987), 109–115; V. McGinnis, "The Mission Statement: A Key Step in Strategic Planning," *Business* (July 1981), 39–43; L. Nash, "Mission Statements: Mirrors and Windows," *Harvard Business Review, 66* (1988), 155–156; and J. H. Want, "Corporate Mission," *Management Review* (August 1988), 46–50.

20. In general, nonprofit organizations appear to have considered these particular issues more thoroughly than for-profit firms. See discussion in Peter Drucker, "What Business Can Learn from Non-Profits," *Harvard Business Review, 67* (1989), 88–93.

21. Anne M. O'Leary-Kelly, Joseph J. Martocchio, and Dwight D. Frink, "A Review of the Influence of Group Goals on Group Performance," *Academy of Management Journal, 37*: 5(October 1994), 1285–1301.

22. Tom Peters, *Thriving on Chaos*, New York: Knopf, 1987, 402.

23. Strat Sherman, "Stretch Goals: The Dark Side of Asking for Miracles," *Fortune, 132:* 10 (November 13, 1995), 231–232.

24. Our discussion of strategic programming draws heavily from Henry Mintzberg, *The Rise and Fall of Strategic Planning*, New York: The Free Press, 1994, 333. For a condensation of key points, refer to Henry Mintzberg, "The Fall and Rise of Strategic Planning," *Harvard Business Review, 72:* 1 (January–February 1994), 107–114.

25. Elements of this model and corresponding discussion can be found in Igor Ansoff and Edward McDonnell, *Implanting Strategic Management*, 2d ed., New York: Prentice-Hall, 1990; George S. Day, *Strategic Market Planning: The Pursuit of Competitive Advantage*, St. Paul, MN: West Publishing Co., 1984; Arnoldo C. Hax and Nicolas S. Majluf, *The Strategy Concept and Process: A Pragmatic Approach*, Englewood Cliffs, NJ: Prentice-Hall, 1991; and George A. Steiner, *Strategic Planning: What Every Manager Must Know*, New York: The Free Press, 1979.

26. Alaric Sample, "Resource Planning and Budgeting for National Forest Management," *Public Administration Review, 52* (July–August 1992), 339–346; L. R. Jones, "Policy Development, Planning, and Resource Allocation in the Department of Defense," *Public Budgeting and Finance, 11* (Fall 1991), 15–27.

27. Mintzberg, *The Rise and Fall of Strategic Planning*, 341.

28. See Ann Langley, "In Search of Rationality: The Purposes Behind the Use of Formal Analysis in Organizations," *Administrative Science Quarterly, 34* (December 1989), 598–631; and Henry Mintzberg, "Rethinking Strategic Planning Part II: New Roles for Planners," *Long Range Planning, 27:* 3 (June 1994), 22–30.

29. T. A. Stewart, "New Ways to Exercise Power," *Fortune, 120* (1989), 52–64.

30. In more complex multinational corporations, the cycles must be expanded to include international-level operations within the overall process, but the fundamental ideas remain the same.

31. P. F. Drucker, "The Coming of the New Organization," *Harvard Business Review, 66* (1988), 45–53.

32. This section draws heavily on Mintzberg, *The Rise and Fall of Strategic Planning*, 342–351.

33. Phyllis Berman, "From Sheep to Shirt," *Forbes* (May 22, 1995), 162–164.

34. See Henry Mintzberg, "Rethinking Strategic Planning Part I: Pitfalls and Fallacies," *Long Range Planning, 27:* 3 (June 1994), 12–21; H. Gomer, L'Utilization des systèmes formels de planification d'entreprise face à la "Crise Petrolière," Thèse doctorat troisième cycle, Institut d'Administration des Entreprises, Université de Grenoble, 1974; E. A. Murray, Jr., "Strategic Choice as a Negotiated Outcome," *Management Science* (May 1978), 960–972.

35. J. W. Fredrickson, "The Comprehensiveness of Strategic Decision Processes: Extension, Observations, Future Directions," *Academy of Management Journal, 27* (1984), 445–466; J. W. Frederickson and T. R. Mitchell, "Strategic Decision Processes: Comprehensiveness and Performance in an Industry Within an Unstable Environment," *Academy of Management Journal, 27* (1984), 399–423.

36. Rita Gunther McGrath and Ian C. MacMillan, "Discovery-Driven Planning," *Harvard Business Review, 73:* 4 (July–August 1995), 44–54; Amar Bhide, "How Entrepreneurs Craft Strategies That Work," *Harvard Business Review* (March–April 1994), 185.

37. J. S. Armstrong, "The Value of Formal Planning for Strategic Decisions: Review of Empirical Research," *Strategic Management Journal, 3* (1982), 197–211.

38. R. Normann and E. Rhenman, *Formulation of Goals and Measurement of Effectiveness in the Public Administration*, Stockholm: SIAR, 1975, 44.

39. William Sandy, "Avoid the Breakdowns Between Planning and Implementation," *Journal of Business Strategy, 12* (September–October 1991), 30–33.

40. S. Kukalis, "Strategic Planning in Large U.S. Corporations—a Survey," *OMEGA, 16* (1988), 393–404; S. Kukalis, "The Relationship Among Firm Characteristics and Design of Strategic Planning Systems in Large Organizations," *Journal of Management, 15* (1989), 565–579.

41. The following material draws extensively from Steven F. Dichter, "The Organization of the '90s," *McKinsey Quarterly* (Winter 1991), 145–155.

42. See discussion in Mintzberg, *Rise and Fall of Strategic Planning*, chap. 4.

43. D. Miller and P. H. Freisen, *Organizations: A Quantum View*, Englewood Cliffs, NJ: Prentice-Hall, 1984.

44. According to Mintzberg, it is not even accurate to talk about strategy formulation in most organizations because so little of their realized strategy is the result of a formulated intended strategy. He prefers to talk about *strategy formation*, a term reflecting the fact that many realized strategies are formed of numerous elements of the emergent strategy, rather than formulated whole as intended strategies. Yet, even Mintzberg acknowledges that most strategies are a blend of intended and emergent elements, indicating the value of strategy formulation as part of the overall strategic management process. See his earlier quotes in this chapter and also his *Rise and Fall of Strategic Planning*, 23–29.

45. Mintzberg, *Rise and Fall of Strategic Planning*, 25.

46. James Brian Quinn, *Strategies for Change: Logical Incrementalism*, Homewood, IL: Irwin, 1980; also James Brian Quinn, *Intelligent Enterprise*, New York: The Free Press, 1992.

47. Major works on organizational learning include Peter M. Senge, *The Fifth Discipline: The Art and Practice of the Learning Organization*, New York: Doubleday/Currency, 1990; Peter M. Senge et al., *The Fifth Discipline Fieldbook*, New York: Doubleday/Currency, 1990; and Mintzberg's treatment of strategy "formation" in *The Rise and Fall of Strategic Planning*.

48. Quinn, *Intelligent Enterprise*; Ikujiro Nonaka, "The Knowledge-Creating Company," in Robert Howard, ed., *The Learning Imperative: Managing People for Continuous Innovation*, Boston: Harvard Business Review, 1993, 41–56.

49. Andrew C. Boynton and Victor Bart, "Stable Organization," *California Management Review, 34* (Fall 1991), 55.

Part Two

STRATEGIC ANALYSIS

In the next two chapters, you will learn how to assess the strengths, weaknesses, opportunities, and threats that face managers and shape strategies. SWOT analysis (for strengths, weaknesses, opportunities, and threats) is one of the most basic analytical tools used to study strategies.

Chapter 3 discusses thorough external analysis of a firm's opportunities and threats—those positive and negative forces at work outside the firm, in its external environment. Opportunities arise with decreasing government regulation, improving demographic trends, or technological advances, but threats may loom from strengthening international competition, decreased public support for business in general, or government subsidies of competing technologies. We emphasize understanding how the external environment impacts a firm's ability to achieve a competitive advantage through shaping the firm's structural position.

In Chapter 4, we describe how to perform a complete internal analysis to assess a firm's strengths and weaknesses—positives and negatives specific to particular firms. Strong patent protection, an experienced workforce, or a brand name that is well known strengthens a firm, while cost structures that aren't competitive, slow and cumbersome organizational practices, or a reputation for poor quality products or services weakens it. To assess strengths and weaknesses, we emphasize understanding how a firm's process execution impacts the competitive advantages it can attain and sustain.

Although we separate external and internal analysis into two chapters, you shouldn't view them as unrelated, but as complementary, necessary components of a complete strategic analysis. Your goal as a manager is to develop strategies that build strengths and overcome weaknesses so your firm can take advantage of its opportunities and avoid its threats. To reach this goal requires you to perform solid internal and external analyses of your firm and its environment and to understand the relationships between the two.

	Positives	Negatives
Internal	STRENGTHS	WEAKNESSES
External	OPPORTUNITIES	THREATS

The Architecture of Strategy

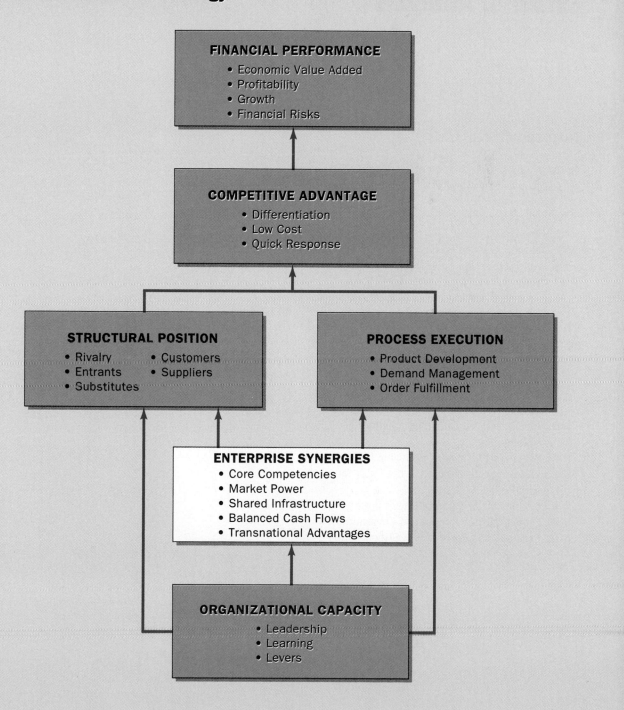

Chapter 3

External Analysis

CHAPTER OUTLINE

I. Two Levels of Environmental Analysis: The General Environment and the Competitive Environment
   A. The General Environment
   B. The Competitive Environment

II. A Detailed Look at Rivalry
   A. Levels of Rivalry: Perfect Competition Versus Pure Monopoly
   B. Factors Affecting the Approach to Rivalry: Avoided Competition Versus Hypercompetition

III. Cooperation in a Competitive Environment

IV. Processes for Analyzing the External Environment
   A. Focusing Your Analysis: Industry Versus Strategic Groups
   B. Environmental Scanning: Gathering Intelligence
   C. Scenario Planning: Organizing Information

V. How Strategy Can Influence the External Environment
   A. Changing the General Environment
   B. Changing the Competitive Environment
   C. Ethical Considerations in Shaping the Environment

We begin our treatment of strategic analysis by looking outside the organization at the environment within which a firm operates and at the structure of its industry. This chapter consists of five parts. We start by introducing various elements of the environment as organized into two levels: the general environment and the competitive environment. We emphasize the competitive environment and analyze the five forces at work there. In the second part of the chapter, we take a detailed look at one competitive force in particular, namely rivalry, and explore what influences different levels of rivalry and the approaches to rivalry taken by competitors. In the third part of the chapter, we briefly consider the irony of how cooperation may be one of the most effective means of addressing the competitive pressures of intense rivalry. The fourth part discusses methods used to analyze the environment and, in the final part of the chapter, we look at how an organization can use strategy to shape its environment.

This chapter will help you understand:

- The important role the external environment plays in strategic analysis
- What elements of both the general and the competitive environments should be considered in a thorough environmental analysis
- When to focus analysis of the competitive environment on a strategic group rather than on the broader industry
- Use of the five forces model to analyze the competitive environment
- The different levels of rivalry and what factors influence the level of rivalry observed in a particular industry
- The benefits of cooperation within a competitive environment
- How to gather intelligence about the external environment and organize it into strategy-shaping scenarios
- How the external environment shapes strategy and how, within limits, strategies can be used to influence the environment

Microsoft®

You may remember, from an economics course, the concept of diminishing returns: the more one sells a product, the more difficult it is to sell more of it as the market grows satiated. However, Microsoft's track record sets this pillar of economic theory on its head—the more Microsoft sells products, such as its Windows operating system, the more the market wants them. Call it the law of "increasing returns": as the installed base of an operating system like Windows grows, more software developers focus on it. As more Windows-compatible software becomes available, more customers buy Windows, and the cycle continues. Bill Gates, Microsoft's CEO, calls this phenomenon "positive feedback" in his book *The Road Ahead*.[1]

Turning such positive feedback into competitive advantage is the core of Microsoft's strategy. Microsoft focuses on selected core technologies (such as operating systems and programming languages) and then encourages others to develop compatible products. Around 85 percent of all PCs are shipped with Windows preinstalled, and Microsoft's aim is to make Windows the sun around which a collection of software products and computing services revolve.

How does Microsoft do this? By staging regular conferences for independent software developers, offering "DevCasts" in which top Microsoft development people are broadcast nationwide by satellite, selling tens of thousands of a software developer's kit that includes 12 CD-ROMs of technical advice and enough software to start your own software company for only a few hundred dollars,

and dispensing reams of technical information to software developers through one of the most active servers on the Internet. Note that in pursuing this strategy, Microsoft, itself a software developer, is cooperating with thousands of other companies that could be considered competitors. The goal of this cooperative strategy is to ensure that Microsoft and its allies win against competing collections of companies and technologies.[2]

The combination of Microsoft's leading position and the law of increasing returns has brought Microsoft phenomenal success with today's technology, but what about tomorrow? Thousands of programmers and engineers are trying every day to devise the next generation of technology in hopes of replacing Microsoft as the market leader by becoming kingpins of their own powerful coalitions of competitors. With its future in constant threat, Microsoft continues to invest heavily in pioneering new technologies. Efforts to move Windows into the corporate world, add Internet features, and develop new products and services offered over the Internet are examples. All are aimed at maintaining Microsoft's leadership position in its highly competitive marketplace.

In this chapter, you will discover how to analyze a competitive marketplace and understand which players in it hold the most power and why. You will also learn how cooperative strategies, such as Microsoft's, are sometimes the key to success in competitive marketplaces. In short, you will discover the relationship between a firm's position in its environment and its success in attaining and sustaining a competitive advantage.

TWO LEVELS OF ENVIRONMENTAL ANALYSIS: THE GENERAL ENVIRONMENT AND THE COMPETITIVE ENVIRONMENT

The external environment plays a critical role in shaping the destinies of entire industries as well as those of individual businesses. The most basic tenet of strategic management is that a manager must adjust strategy to reflect the environment in which a business operates.[3] Research on the subject has repeatedly found strong links between business performance and the alignment between a firm's environment and its strategy. One study analyzed data on 1,638 businesses scattered across eight different environments in two different time periods, and found that the environment-strategy link was consistently an important factor in explaining differences in the businesses' financial performance levels.[4] Similar conclusions have come from research on businesses at different stages of development, such as start-ups,[5] and on businesses in different parts of the world.[6]

In general, the external environment influences strategy in different ways, such as:

- *Providing opportunities and holding threats.* The external environment is the source of many of the opportunities and threats good strategies are meant to capitalize on and also the source of threats they are meant to avoid.

- *Shaping the "rules" of how firms in a given industry compete.* As you will learn, the structure of the industry in which a firm competes can have a profound impact on the nature of the competition that firm faces.

- *Influencing the availability of critical resources.* For example, demographic trends may influence the availability of suitable employees or interested customers.

- *Affecting the likely returns from alternative investments.* Ultimately, a firm does not exist in a vacuum in which it alone can determine its destiny. Rather, organizations exist amidst a blend of opportunities and threats to which a company must respond, and this response helps determine its financial returns.[7]

The conclusion is inescapable: to begin understanding what makes a successful business, one must first consider the environment in which a firm operates and the alignment of that firm's strategy to that environment. However, "the environment" covers a lot of territory—essentially everything outside the organization's control. To be practical, as a manager, you must focus your attention on the parts of the environment that will most affect your business. For this reason, let's consider what parts of the environment are most important for strategic analysis.

First, consider the general environment, which consists of factors external to the industry that may have a significant impact on strategy.[8]

The General Environment

Six broad dimensions appear most relevant: *demographic, sociocultural, political/legal, technological, macroeconomic,* and *global.* Exhibit 3.1 gives examples of factors in each of

EXHIBIT 3.1
Examples of Dimensions in General Environment Assessment

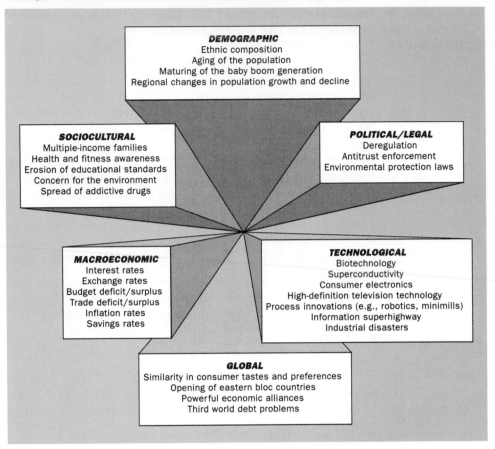

DEMOGRAPHIC
Ethnic composition
Aging of the population
Maturing of the baby boom generation
Regional changes in population growth and decline

SOCIOCULTURAL
Multiple-income families
Health and fitness awareness
Erosion of educational standards
Concern for the environment
Spread of addictive drugs

POLITICAL/LEGAL
Deregulation
Antitrust enforcement
Environmental protection laws

MACROECONOMIC
Interest rates
Exchange rates
Budget deficit/surplus
Trade deficit/surplus
Inflation rates
Savings rates

TECHNOLOGICAL
Biotechnology
Superconductivity
Consumer electronics
High-definition television technology
Process innovations (e.g., robotics, minimills)
Information superhighway
Industrial disasters

GLOBAL
Similarity in consumer tastes and preferences
Opening of eastern bloc countries
Powerful economic alliances
Third world debt problems

the six dimensions.[9] These factors often overlap, and developments in one area may influence those in another. For example, development of high-definition television (technological) by Japanese and European companies (global) forced the U.S. government to reevaluate provisions of the antitrust laws (political/legal) that could prevent U.S. companies from engaging in collective research and development activities. Systematic analysis of the factors comprising the general environment can identify major trends in various industry segments. Exhibit 3.2 shows how environmental trends can influence various industries in different ways.

Perhaps the most important thing to note as you look at this exhibit is that the positive and negative impacts are labeled *potential*.[10] In virtually every industry listed, managers have been able to develop strategies to take advantage of the potential opportunities and avoid the potential threats they have identified. For example, while many universities have seen a drop in enrollment because of the aging U.S. population, others have developed strategies to attract nontraditional students and, consequently, have seen their enrollments increase. (We look at how strategies can be used to shape the external environment in the closing section of this chapter.)

EXHIBIT 3.2
Impact of General Environmental Trends

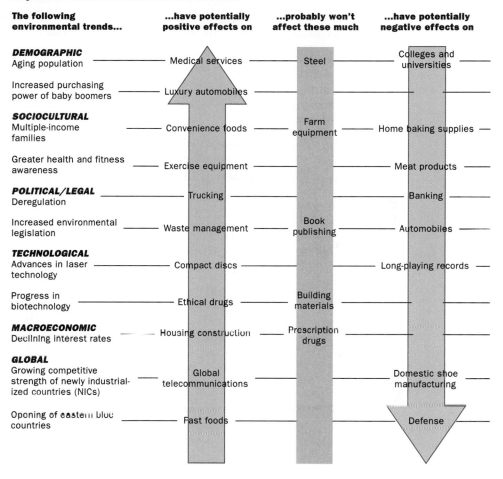

The following environmental trends...	...have potentially positive effects on	...probably won't affect these much	...have potentially negative effects on
DEMOGRAPHIC Aging population	Medical services	Steel	Colleges and universities
Increased purchasing power of baby boomers	Luxury automobiles		
SOCIOCULTURAL Multiple-income families	Convenience foods	Farm equipment	Home baking supplies
Greater health and fitness awareness	Exercise equipment		Meat products
POLITICAL/LEGAL Deregulation	Trucking		Banking
Increased environmental legislation	Waste management	Book publishing	Automobiles
TECHNOLOGICAL Advances in laser technology	Compact discs		Long-playing records
Progress in biotechnology	Ethical drugs	Building materials	
MACROECONOMIC Declining interest rates	Housing construction	Prescription drugs	
GLOBAL Growing competitive strength of newly industrialized countries (NICs)	Global telecommunications		Domestic shoe manufacturing
Opening of eastern bloc countries	Fast foods		Defense

Successful strategic adjustments to environmental changes such as these require that managers be aware of several aspects of the link between the general environment and an organization's strategy:

■ *The general environment can hold either opportunities for, or threats to, entire industries* . . . For example, an aging population offers opportunities for expansion in health care services, whereas rising interest rates have a detrimental effect on the demand for "big ticket" items such as homes and automobiles.

■ *. . . but the impact of an environmental trend often differs significantly for different firms within the same industry . . .* Consider this example from the airlines industry. The restructuring of the U.S. economy in the 1980s led to greatly reduced numbers of managers and sharply curtailed business travel budgets. Consequently, personal travel became a larger part of airline revenues than business travel. But many of the full-service airlines were developed around the concept of business travel, and their cost structure was ill-suited to serving the more cost-conscious personal traveler. On the other hand, some of the newer airlines, built around the concept of providing low-cost/low-service travel between smaller cities, are ideally suited to take advantage of the same environmental change that is crippling many of their older competitors.[11]

- *. . . and the same environmental trend can have different effects on different industries.* Growing awareness about health and fitness helped industries such as exercise equipment and athletic shoes, but fast food restaurants and meat and dairy products suffered.

- *Developments in the general environment can change competitive battle lines.* For example, deregulation (a political/legal change) in the financial services, telecommunications, and airline industries has opened them to new forms of competition.[12]

- *Many developments in the general environment are difficult to predict with any degree of accuracy; others are readily predictable.* Macroeconomic developments, such as interest rates, the rate of inflation, and exchange rates, are extremely difficult to predict. However, some trends in the general environment, such as demographic data on population distribution by age, ethnicity, and income levels, can be forecast accurately.

- *Finally, the dimensions of the general environment with the strongest influence on business may differ from one country to another.* For example, research has shown that economic and political issues are much more significant to firms in Nigeria than to firms in the United States.[13] One of the greatest challenges facing managers of multinational corporations is to adjust their strategies to fit the general environments of diverse countries.

In summary, it is clear that the general environment contains many potentially significant opportunities and threats and that an important part of strategic management is identifying these and developing or adjusting strategies accordingly. But thorough environmental analysis must go beyond consideration of the general environment to include analysis of the competitive environment facing an organization.

The Competitive Environment

The *competitive environment*[14] refers to the situation facing an organization within its specific arena of operation. In considering competition, one most naturally considers a firm's immediate rivals (and that is where we direct much of our focus later in this chapter), but the five forces framework, the most widely known tool for analyzing the competitive environment, was developed to broaden your thinking about how forces in the competitive environment shape strategies and affect performance.[15] It helps you see that there are important competitive forces beyond direct rivals that deserve your attention (see Exhibit 3.3). Together, these five forces determine the nature and extent of competition and shape the strategies of firms in their particular competitive arenas. You should understand how each of these forces affects an industry's environment so that you can identify the most appropriate strategic position within your industry. Exhibit 3.4 lists important questions to ask and issues to consider for a thorough five forces analysis. Now, let's look closer at each of the five forces.

EXHIBIT 3.3
The Five Forces Model of Competition

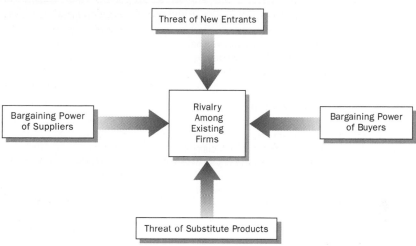

Threat of New Entrants

When a business begins operation in a new market, we say it has *entered* that market; when it ceases to operate in a market, we say it has *exited*. A new entrant in an industry represents a competitive threat to established firms, sometimes called the *incumbents*. The entrant adds new production capacity and the potential to erode the market shares of incumbents. The entrant may also bring substantial resources (such as a large advertising or R&D budget) that were not previously required for success in the industry. To reduce these threats, incumbent firms depend on what we call *barriers to entry* to discourage new entrants. Major entry barriers include:

Economies of Scale.   These exist whenever large-volume firms (more likely the incumbents than the entrants) enjoy significantly lower production costs than smaller-volume operators. This discourages new firms with less volume and higher production costs from entering the market. For instance, it is difficult for a new firm to enter the paper business because efficient production requires production volumes larger than a start-up can reasonably expect to achieve, forcing the new entrant to operate at a cost disadvantage.

Learning or Experience Effects.   As firms produce, they grow more efficient as experience teaches better ways of doing things. This allows their costs per unit to decline along a path we call the *experience curve*, or the learning curve. Because incumbents have more experience than new entrants, their costs will normally be lower. For instance, any firm trying to enter the integrated-circuit business faces a tremendous challenge to learn how to be cost competitive in a market where experienced incumbents are already producing millions of products.

Cost Disadvantages Independent of Scale.   These advantages are unrelated to the size of the operation. They may include proprietary product knowledge, such as patents;

EXHIBIT 3.4
The Five Forces Applied

To Analyze:	Ask These Questions:	Consider These Issues:
Customers	How critical am I to my customer? How critical is my customer to me? How many alternatives does my customer have? Can my customer demand pricing concessions? Would I profit from a cooperative alliance with this customer?	Brand identity Switching costs Product differences Impact on quality/performance Likelihood of backward integration Buyer concentration : supplier concentration
Suppliers	Should I form an alliance with this supplier? What options do I have besides this supplier? What options does this supplier have besides me? Is this particular supplier critical to my success? Is the good or service being supplied critical to my success? Can this supplier force its cost increases on me in the form of higher supply prices?	Supplier concentration Differentiation of supplies Threat of forward integration Substitute supplies available Likelihood of forward integration Importance of volume to supplier Supplies' impact on cost or differentiation Impact of supplies on cost or differentiation Switching costs of suppliers and firms in industry Supply costs relative to total purchases in industry
New entrants	Who would be most likely to want to enter this market? Why? How can I retaliate when a new entrant comes into this market? What would discourage new competitors from entering this market? How can my advantages as an incumbent be made more obvious to would-be entrants? As an incumbent, what advantages would I have that new entrants would need to overcome? How can I signal my intention to retaliate *before* a new competitor actually enters this market?	Switching costs Government policy Economies of scale Expected retaliation Capital requirements Access to distribution Proprietary learning curve
Substitutes	If goods or services like the ones I offer did not exist, how would my customers meet their needs that I'm supplying today? How easy would it be to convince my customers to adopt an entirely different approach to meeting the needs I fill for them? Are there alternatives to my goods and services that are radically cheaper or better? Is anyone trying to develop a totally different approach to serving my customers? Who outside my industry would be most interested in stealing my customers?	Switching costs Buyer propensity to substitute Number of dimensions of customer value Relative price performance of substitutes
Rivalry	Who are my most powerful competitors? How do I compare to these powerful competitors? Is there a way that I can reduce the level of rivalry in this market? What are my competitors' different sources of marketplace power? What factors are likely to heighten or diminish competition in this industry? Do my competitors aggressively combat one another, or is there more of a live and let live attitude?	Exit barriers Brand identity Industry growth Switching costs Product differences Diversity of competitors Concentration and balance of rivals

favorable access to raw materials, such as mineral rights; favorable locations; and government subsidies.

Product Differentiation.   If differences in physical or perceived characteristics make an incumbent's product unique in the eyes of the consumer, new entrants must overcome the resulting brand loyalty.

Capital Requirements.   If the amount of investment required to enter an industry (plant and equipment costs, working capital, etc.) is high, the number of entrants who can afford to "ante up" may be limited. For example, would-be entrants into the cement business find accumulating the required capital for a new operation to be a serious deterrent.

Switching Costs.   Switching costs are the expenses or simply the "hassle" of moving from one supplier to another. Sometimes, costs incurred by a customer in switching from one supplier to another (either psychological costs or financial costs) make it difficult for new entrants to attract customers.

Access to Distribution Channels.   Costs or other restrictions associated with developing a means to distribute a product or service may make it difficult for a new entrant to move its products to or through the market. Firms that enter the soft drink business have found this a major barrier, because most bottlers are already aligned with an incumbent producer.

Anticipated Growth.   Interest in entering a new market diminishes as growth opportunities decline. Incumbents in a rapidly growing market are less likely to respond to a new entrant when the market's growth offers enough opportunities to share. But a new entrant into a slowly growing market can expect a strong competitive response from incumbents, because the entrant's growth will probably come at the expense of incumbents' sales.

Although this is a reasonable general-purpose list of entry barriers, the specific factors that deter new entry vary among industries. In the brewing industry, production differentiation is a major deterrent to new entry, while in heavy manufacturing industries, entry is more difficult because of the substantial capital requirements. U.S. agricultural producers have been frustrated by limited access to distribution channels in Japan and other countries, and in the commercial software industry, switching costs involved in retaining employees sometimes cause continued use of existing packages even when better products from new entrants are available.

Bargaining Power of Suppliers

Suppliers can have an important effect on an industry's profit potential. For example, they may pass through their cost increases as higher prices or cut their costs by reducing the quality of their goods and services. But to make any of these changes "stick," suppliers need bargaining power over their customers. Following are some conditions that make suppliers powerful.

1. *Relative lack of importance of the buyer to the supplier group.* Some customers are more important than others because of the size of their purchases or the prestige

that comes from supplying them. For example, McDonald's is a much more important customer for soft drink producers than a small diner would be. If a customer is not particularly important to the supplier, the supplier is less likely to offer the most favorable terms to win or retain that customer.

2. *Importance of the supplier's product to the buyer.* This is just the converse of the preceding point. McDonald's finds it important to carry the most popular line of soft drinks, therefore increasing Coke's bargaining power.

3. *Greater concentration among suppliers than among buyers.* An industry's concentration, usually measured as its *concentration ratio,* is the proportion of the industry's total output accounted for by the largest firm in the industry. A concentrated industry is one in which a few large firms dominate, giving them greater power over those who do business with them. Conversely, firms in low-concentration industries that supply a highly concentrated customer industry are often in a weaker bargaining position. For instance, there are numerous companies that make sweeteners, but the soft drink industry they supply is dominated by just two companies, Coke and Pepsi. Consequently, Coke and Pepsi can shop around the world for their sweeteners, but the sweetener producers are limited in their options. This shifts bargaining power away from them and toward their customers.

4. *High switching costs for the buyer.* The airlines' use of frequent flyer programs is an obvious attempt to reduce their customers' flexibility by raising their switching costs. Flying on a competitor's flights generates no frequent flyer mileage, and joining multiple frequent flyer plans greatly dilutes the benefits of membership, so a customer is effectively "locked in" to a particular airline.

5. *Credible threat of forward integration by suppliers. Forward integration* would involve a supplier's move into a later stage of the manufacturing process or distribution, that is, into direct competition with its customers. A supplier's ability to threaten such a move keeps pressure on its customers' profit margins because the customers will not want to encourage increased competition from the supplier's forward integration. Many computer manufacturers sell hardware to value-added retailers who develop specialized software applications to run on the hardware, and then sell the complete system to the end consumer. These value-added retailers must be mindful of the threat that IBM could easily integrate forward and sell complete systems directly to the consumer.

Bargaining Power of Customers

Buyers can exert bargaining power over a supplier's industry by forcing its prices down, reducing the amount of goods they purchase from the industry, demanding better quality for the same price, or demanding better terms. For example, national chains, such as Wal-Mart, have become such powerful customers that they can often ignore well-entrenched industry practices. Many manufacturers are willing to give a 2 percent discount if bills are paid within 15 days, a standard industry practice. However, with many of its suppliers depending on Wal-Mart for as much as half their total sales, the giant retailer can often get away with paying its bills after 30 days, and then taking the 2 percent discount on the gross bill (which would include items such as shipping costs) rather than the net bill.[16] It's because of strong-arm tactics such as these that some manufacturers have a policy of avoiding national chains.[17]

Factors that lead to greater customer power include:

1. *Undifferentiated or standard supplies.* For a commodity good or service, a customer can easily shop around for the most favorable terms. How many sources of copy paper are there? The large number of suppliers keeps prices down for such products.

2. *Credible threat of backward integration by buyers. Backward integration* would involve a buyer's moving into an earlier stage of manufacturing or distribution, that is, moving into its supplier's business. Brewing and soft drink firms ensure favorable terms from can suppliers by constantly threatening to integrate backward into can production.

3. *Accurate information about the cost structure of the supplier.* This allows customers to exercise more precision in negotiating prices of supplies. One large consumer products firm insists on having the same cost data as managers in firms that make their products for just this reason. When its suppliers' costs come down, it insists on proportional decreases in price.

4. *Customers' price sensitivity.* A customer is likely to be more price sensitive if (1) the supplies in question represent a significant fraction of the buyer's total cost; (2) the supplier's product is unimportant to the overall quality of the customer's final product, so it is possible to "cut corners"; or (3) the customer already has very low profit margins.

5. *Greater concentration in buyer's industry than in supplier's industry, and relatively larger-volume purchases.* These two factors imply that buyers are larger and more powerful than suppliers. In other words, the buyer is more important to the supplier than the supplier is to the buyer.

Threat of Substitute Products

The availability of substitutes places an upper price limit on an industry's products. When relative prices rise above that of the substitute product, customers tend to switch to the substitute. For example, retail stores don't compete just against each other but against mail order catalogs as well. Consequently, managers must closely monitor substitute products that are showing improvements in performance and/or declines in price.

Two trends in the general environment, deregulation and technological advances, have given rise to a large number of substitutes that have successfully taken market share away from traditional firms. For instance, deregulation of banking has allowed a wide range of financial businesses to provide many services that were once only available from banks. Similarly, technological advances based on CD-ROMS are proving viable substitutes for conventionally printed reference books. CD-ROM versions of reference works are already outselling conventionally published works, and with advantages like these, growth of the electronic substitutes will make digital publishing a $50 billion industry by the year 2000, only 15 years after the medium was first introduced. Meanwhile, traditional stalwarts of conventionally published reference works, who failed to develop their own CD-based substitutes, are threatened with extinction.

Intensity of Rivalry Among Competitors

Direct rivals are competitors that sell basically the same products or services, and the *intensity of rivalry* relates to the fierceness with which these rivals jockey one another for competitive position and superiority. Understanding rivalry is critical to an understanding of strategic management because, as we stress throughout this text, attaining a competitive advantage is a basic requirement for achieving above-average rates of return and creating economic value. And a firm's competitive advantage, that is, its standing relative to its rivals in terms of the customer value it can provide, is obviously influenced by the level of rivalry that exists between that firm and its rivals. In the 1960s, when Anheuser-Busch decided to develop the first nationwide beer, the brewing industry was fragmented, regionalized, and "sleepy." This made it easy for Anheuser-Busch to make rapid strides and position itself as a dominant player. However, the brewing industry is intensely rivalrous today and any firm hoping to establish a competitive advantage can expect a fight every step of the way. Rivalry is such a critical determinant of competitive advantage that we need to look at it in more detail than the other four forces we've just discussed.

A DETAILED LOOK AT RIVALRY

In this section, you will learn about different levels of rivalry and the forces that influence rivalry.

Levels of Rivalry: Perfect Competition Versus Pure Monopoly

Let's begin further exploring rivalry by looking at Exhibit 3.5, which shows a continuum describing different types of competition. To understand this important exhibit, compare its two extremes, perfect competition and pure monopoly. Perfect competition exists when rivals are comparable to one another in terms of quality, cost, and speed, or any other factor that provides a competitive advantage. This is often an ideal situation for customers because there are several firms to choose from, all struggling to provide the best possible customer value. However, in the absence of any significant competitive advantage, all the rivals fail to achieve profits much above the minimal levels required for their continued existence, or what might be called *subsistence-level profits*. So, although the total value provided to customers may be positively impacted by perfect competition, firm profits are not.

This is just the reverse for pure monopolies at the opposite extreme of our continuum. A monopoly exists when a firm does not face direct competition for its cus-

EXHIBIT 3.5
Continuum of Types of Competition

PURE MONOPOLY	AVOIDED COMPETITION	HYPERCOMPETITION	PERFECT COMPETITION
Typically, one form provides good or service that customers value	Typically, a small number of players	Typically, several players aggressively position against each other	Typically many players, all more or less at parity with one another in terms of quality, cost, and/or speed
No, or very limited, direct competition	Rivals work to segment market or otherwise position around each other while avoiding head-to-head competition	Emphasis is placed on either gaining an advantage, negating a competitor's advantage, or both	No one firm dominates the others
Low level of competition allows abnormally high levels of profits	Where rivals' segments overlap, emphasis is placed on tacit collusion to limit price wars or other forms of severe competition	Innovation is used to obsolete old goods and services in search of the latest improved means of providing customer value	With parity on quality and speed, competition often shifts to price and costs
Little competitive pressure to provide higher levels of customer value	Barriers to entry are used to limit threat of new entrants	Nature of competitive advantage is constantly being redefined	Absence of competitive advantage limits profitability
In free-market economies, government regulation is usually developed to limit monopolistic behavior and encourage competition as a means of improving value available to consumers	Differentiation is used to limit threat of substitutes and reduce customers' power	Market leadership continually changes hands or threatens to do so	Customer has many comparable options to choose between, but firms see limited profit potential and seek to avoid this form of competition
	Vertical integration (or threat of it) is used to limit power of suppliers and customers	Abnormally high profits are intermittent as competitive advantages come and go	
	To the extent competition is avoided, above-normal levels of profitability can be sustained		

—— **OUR FOCUS** ——

tomers. In the absence of any competitors, there is no direct rivalry or competitive pressure to keep the monopoly's prices low, or its quality and speed at peak levels.[18] And yet, even without offering its customers the best possible levels of value, the monopolist may well be able to enjoy very high levels of profits. Because there is no alternative source for what is being sold, the monopolist can raise prices (or cut corners on quality and speed) and still not lose customers to rivals. Although this is clearly not very good for customers, it can be very good for a firm's financial performance.

As the two extremes of our continuum, it makes sense that pure monopolies and pure competition are opposite conditions. And, yet, there is one ironic similarity between the two. Firms that are in the extremes of pure monopolies or pure competition generally place much less emphasis on rivalry than the firms that fall somewhere in the middle ground of our continuum. As Exhibit 3.6 illustrates, at the extremes of pure monopoly or perfect competition, emphasis on rivalry is reduced, but for very different reasons. A pure monopolist, such as a public water utility, faces no competition, and therefore has little reason to focus on rivalry. At the other extreme, firms engaged in perfect competition, such as farmers, do not typically engage in fierce rivalry either. Because the profit potential is very limited and because their competitors are so many, farmers tend to adopt a "live and let live" mentality. In fact, it is not unusual to see a farmer help a neighbor, even though technically speaking the neighbor is a competitor.[19]

The vast majority of all firms face a level of rivalry somewhere between the two extremes of a pure monopoly and perfect competition. This is true because of two off-

EXHIBIT 3.6
The Nature of Rivalry Across Four Types of Competition

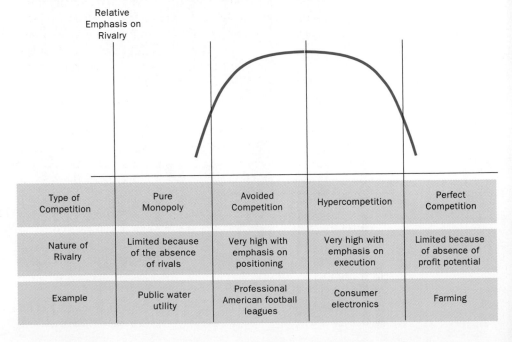

Type of Competition	Pure Monopoly	Avoided Competition	Hypercompetition	Perfect Competition
Nature of Rivalry	Limited because of the absence of rivals	Very high with emphasis on positioning	Very high with emphasis on execution	Limited because of absence of profit potential
Example	Public water utility	Professional American football leagues	Consumer electronics	Farming

setting forces. On the one hand, in the interest of maintaining competition and the higher levels of customer value it produces, governments have created regulations that prohibit monopolies from developing or persisting.[20] On the other hand, a need to produce more than subsistence-level profits drives managers to work hard at avoiding pure competition. Consequently, most firms find themselves pushed into a middle ground by these opposing forces.

Anywhere in this middle ground, firms are usually very concerned with rivalry and how to best address the competitive forces they face. In addressing these competitive forces, firms tend to emphasize one of two approaches to rivalry. One approach is to avoid head-to-head competition as much as possible, and we refer to this as *avoided competition*. The other approach is to aggressively seek to best rivals in head-to-head competition, a type of behavior known as *hypercompetition*.[21]

To understand the differences in the two approaches, look at competition within U.S. football versus consumer electronics. Football's approach to rivalry typifies avoided competition, while consumer electronics addresses rivalry by engaging in hypercompetition. The football industry is strictly controlled by two organizations, the National Football League and the American Football Conference. These organizations determine everything from when and where a football team may move to how players are hired to how products will be licensed. Consequently, although the teams may be fierce sports rivals on the field, economic rivalry between teams is held strictly in check for their mutual benefit. The situation in consumer electronics is very different. There are dozens of competitors active in each product category, and they are constantly hammering away at one another's competitive position. For example, as soon as one computer manufacturer offers an extra feature, its rivals will seek not only to match it, but also to better it. Such rivalry places intense downward pressure on profit margins. For example, Packard Bell is a fierce competitor that has been able to sell more computers than any of its rivals. However, accomplishing this has forced the company to essentially operate without a profit margin.[22] The general trend toward hypercompetition is having a widespread negative impact on business profits, and the average corporate after-tax return on sales ratio has dropped from around 15 percent to around 5 percent over the past 50 years.[23]

Note that while firms in both the avoided-competition and hypercompetition categories emphasize rivalry as key for financial success, their approaches differ widely in how they go about the process of jockeying for position, as shown in Exhibit 3.6 earlier. The football teams and other businesses in the avoided-competition category focus on achieving a favorable competitive position through changing and controlling the structure of their industry, an approach that stresses what we call *structural position* in the Architecture of Strategy framework we use throughout this text (we look more closely at structural position in Chapter 6). On the other hand, firms in hypercompetitive markets such as consumer electronics concentrate on outdoing one another in executing the processes that yield new forms of customer value, an approach to rivalry that emphasizes what is labeled *process execution* in the Architecture of Strategy framework. (We'll focus on process execution as a source of competitive advantage in Chapter 5.)

This does not mean that managers of football teams are unconcerned with how well their business processes are executed or that consumer electronics firms ignore the potential benefits of improved structural position. Most firms try to use structural position to avoid competition and process execution to improve head-to-head competition. So, although it is difficult to find pure examples of avoided competition or hypercompetition, it is nonetheless clear that some markets tend toward one or the other of the two options. The difference between avoided competition and hypercompetition is fundamental and we need to consider the factors that affect these options and consider how each factor encourages rivalry based on structural position or process execution.

Factors Affecting the Approach to Rivalry: Avoided Competition Versus Hypercompetition

Several categories of factors affect which approach to rivalry firms will adopt. These are summarized in Exhibit 3.7 and are discussed in more detail below.

EXHIBIT 3.7
Summary of Factors Affecting the Approach Taken to Rivalry

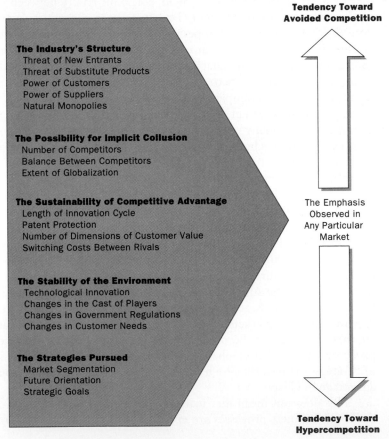

Tendency Toward Avoided Competition

The Emphasis Observed in Any Particular Market

Tendency Toward Hypercompetition

The Industry's Structure
Threat of New Entrants
Threat of Substitute Products
Power of Customers
Power of Suppliers
Natural Monopolies

The Possibility for Implicit Collusion
Number of Competitors
Balance Between Competitors
Extent of Globalization

The Sustainability of Competitive Advantage
Length of Innovation Cycle
Patent Protection
Number of Dimensions of Customer Value
Switching Costs Between Rivals

The Stability of the Environment
Technological Innovation
Changes in the Cast of Players
Changes in Government Regulations
Changes in Customer Needs

The Strategies Pursued
Market Segmentation
Future Orientation
Strategic Goals

The Industry's Structure

Our most important tool for studying industry structure is the five forces analysis, and you are already familiar with this from our previous discussion. But now let's consider how the first four forces affect the force of rivalry.

Threat of New Entrants. If it is easy for new firms to enter the competition against the incumbent rivals, then it is much more difficult for them to successfully avoid the heightened levels of competition associated with hypercompetition. If the incumbents are not continuously providing the market with new forms of value, they open opportunities for new entrants who will. Consequently, the threat of new entrants alone is enough to push incumbents toward hypercompetitive actions.

Threat of Substitute Products. The forces at play through the threat of new entrants also work through substitute products. If there are close substitutes for a given product, then the head-to-head rivals who produce that product have to be aware of what the firms that produce a substitute are doing or threatening to do. If the producers of a substitute threaten to upset the status quo by introducing new rounds of value-improving products, then a manager has little choice but to follow a similarly aggressive strategy.

Power of Customers. As we discussed above, the more closely a firm moves toward perfect competition, the more aggressive it becomes in providing customer value, even at the expense of financial returns. Powerful customers can push their suppliers in this direction, benefiting the customer even if it hurts the supplier's profitability.

Power of Suppliers. This is merely the reverse situation—a supplier is capable of forcing its will on a customer. So, for example, if your key suppliers are all working to limit competition among themselves, this may also limit your ability to engage in hypercompetition. For instance, computer makers could not be effective hypercompetitive rivals if the industries that make key components such as chips and memory storage devices were not also hypercompetitive.

Natural Monopolies. This is not one of the five forces, but a special form of industry structure that limits pressure on firms to engage in hypercompetition. A natural monopoly exists whenever overall customer value is maximized by having a single supplier. A good example is a water utility. Installing the multiple systems required to provide a community's water from multiple suppliers is prohibitively expensive and, consequently, virtually all water utilities operate as pure monopolies in their limited geographic markets. Regulations are typically put in place to keep them from abusing their monopoly status, but they face very limited competition.

The Possibility for Implicit Collusion

Collusion refers to secret agreements between rivals for the purpose of making gains through deceit or fraud. Competitors agreeing to fix prices at high levels to improve profits would be a classic example of collusion. In most developed market economies, government regulations strictly limit any explicit collusion in order to encourage more evenhanded competition. However, even in such regulated economies, there are often opportunities for *implicit collusion*, that is, achieving some of the benefits of col-

Application 3.1

Competing Through Cooperation at Sun Microsystems

The personal computing software industry, once a cottage industry with literally hundreds of small but viable competitors, is now a concentrated industry dominated by a few very large players. Today, Microsoft takes in almost 40 percent of all the revenues generated by this industry, and the giant continues to try to strengthen its grip on the market. Smaller firms are being purchased by the market leaders or forced out of business. The most likely to survive are those firms that are teaming up with one another to take on the giants.

Sun Microsystems, Inc., is one firm that hopes to survive by cooperating with its former competitors as they team up against Microsoft. While Microsoft is dominant in many different product categories, Sun and its new teammates will focus on developing operating systems for entire networks of personal computers, workstations, and low-cost servers, the type of computing environment expected to become the norm in the near future. When Sun began creating the coalition of firms that would challenge Microsoft, the industry giant was selling more operating systems in a week than Sun could sell in a year. However, in the niche that provided operating systems for large networks instead of individual machines or small clusters, most customers felt that Sun's new product, Solaris, was superior to Microsoft's competing product, Windows NT. This seemed to offer Sun a window of opportunity, but how could the firm take advantage of it before Microsoft developed a stronger product?

Sun's answer was to join many of its archrivals in cooperative efforts to take on Microsoft. Solaris's two most important weaknesses were the limited number of applications that would run on it and the need for an easier-to-use object-oriented technology. Solaris could run only

about 8,500 programs, far too few given the 50,000 programs then available for personal computers. To overcome this, Sun agreed to back a joint effort among five competitors (Sun, IBM, Hewlett-Packard, Novell, and Santa Cruz Operations) to develop the Common Open Software Environment, a development that would make different versions of the Unix operating systems look and work the same way. This means that software developed for any one of the five should work on the other four, making software for this operating system much more attractive for program developers. This in turn greatly strengthens the coalition's ability to compete with Microsoft.

In addressing its need for object-oriented technology, Sun turned for help to NeXt Computer, a company that had formerly targeted Sun as its number one rival. Sun agreed to invest $10 million in NeXt in return for the right to use its object-oriented software in the next version of Solaris. This is expected to give Sun a year's lead on Microsoft (as well as on an IBM-Apple venture that is developing similar technology).

While it is still not clear who will survive the ongoing consolidation taking place in the personal computer software business, by teaming up against the industry giant, firms such as Sun appear to be greatly improving their chances of survival. In this case, it seems that perhaps the best way to compete is to cooperate.

Sources
Based on information gathered from G. Paschal Zachary, "Big Bundles: Consolidation Sweeps the Software Industry; Small Firms Imperiled," *Wall Street Journal* (March 23, 1994), A1, A6; Robert D. Hof and Richard Brandt, "Let's Bury the Hatchet—in Microsoft's Back," *Business Week* (December 20, 1993), 40.

Focusing Your Analysis: Industry Versus Strategic Groups

Strategic groups are conceptually defined clusters of competitors that share similar strategies and therefore compete more directly with each other than with other firms in the same industry. They are *conceptual* clusters in the sense that they are grouped together for purposes of improving analysis and understanding competition within their industry—they do not necessarily belong to any formal group, such as an indus-

EXHIBIT 3.8
Dividing the Five Forces Model into Primarily Competitive and Primarily Cooperative Dimensions

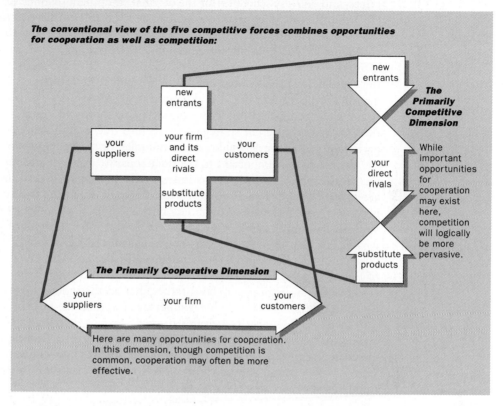

try trade association or a strategic alliance, and they do not necessarily differ in their average profitability.[30]

Research has shown that industries vary greatly in the similarity of their firms in terms of strategies pursued (some industries are very homogeneous while others are very heterogeneous), and we need to analyze the two types of industries differently. For example, there is very little difference in the marketing efforts, research and development expenditures, or capital intensity (measured as the ratio of assets to sales) among the firms operating paperboard mills in the United States. In other words, the paperboard industry is composed of several competitors that look almost identical in terms of the plants they operate, the products they produce, their marketing practices, and so forth.[31] Such an industry is considered *homogeneous*, and it is reasonable for all the competitors in such an industry to be considered part of the same strategic group in a single, industrywide analysis.

However, some industries are *heterogeneous*, comprising multiple strategic groups, and it would be inappropriate and misleading to combine different strategic groups in the same environmental analysis. For instance, consider the bargaining power of the customers served by different strategic groups within the automobile parts industry. Automobile manufacturers are used to dictating terms for product specifications, prices, and delivery schedules for the original equipment manufacturers (OEM) strategic group that supplies parts to assemblers. As a result of this, margins in this industry are notoriously thin, and firms in this strategic group place considerable emphasis on cost control. Now consider the automobile parts manufacturers who supply high-performance replacement parts to individual sports car enthusiasts. In this strategic group, the customer is usually more interested in product performance than cost and, consequently, competitors work at finding means to differentiate the performance capabilities of their products, even if the products cost more as a result. Combining firms in these two very different strategic groups into one overall analysis of the automobile parts–supplier industry could result in muddled or misleading conclusions.

So, when is it important to consider separate strategic groups instead of the industry as a whole, and what constitutes a strategic group? Recall that strategic groups are formed for our benefit to help us better understand the nature of competition in heterogeneous industries. You should only consider separate strategic groups if doing so leads to useful insights that would be missed in an analysis of your industry as a whole. For example, research has shown that strategic groups within the insurance industry not only follow different strategies but also consistently attain different levels of financial performance, so managers in that industry regularly perform analysis focused at the strategic-group level rather than at the industry level.[32] Application 3.2 illustrates differences in the five competitive forces in the pharmaceutical industry.

To determine what constitutes strategic groups, remember that they are merely conceptual clusters to facilitate analysis; we can categorize firms any way we find beneficial or insightful. So, for instance, if it is helpful to know how industry giants differ from smaller firms, one might use size for categorization. Other factors are commonly used to sort strategic groups.

- *Breadth of market.* Is the firm a specialist serving a particular niche within the market (Lamborgini automobiles) or does it serve a broad range of market segments (General Motors)?

- *Product/service quality.* These can often be categorized as standard (Casio watches), premium (Seiko), and luxury (Cartier).

- *Geographic distribution.* It is often important to consider whether a firm is national (such as Wal-Mart) or regional (such as Goody's).

- *Level of vertical integration.* Vertical integration refers to how much of the total processing involved in providing a particular good or service is performed by a single company. A vertically integrated toy company might own its own plastic-injection molding factory, while a toy company that is not vertically integrated purchases its plastic parts from independent suppliers. Given our previous discussion, this distinction is obviously important to bargaining power.

- *Profit/nonprofit.* Some industries (such as hospitals) can be sorted into distinct groups as for-profit and not-for-profit competitors.

This is only a sample of the dimensions that we could use to form strategic groups. Because firms in a strategic group are more or less similar in following a com-

Application 3.2

Strategic Groups in the Pharmaceutical Industry

The pharmaceutical industry is not homogeneous. It comprises three strategic groups, as identified in Exhibit 3.9. Firms that produce patented prescription drugs are notable for research and development programs among the most extensive of any industry. The innovative products they produce are typically patented and available only by prescription, thus the name of this strategic group. On the other hand, over-the-counter drugmakers supply consumers with a broad range of products that do not require prescriptions, including items such as antacid tablets, aspirin, and cough syrups. These products are not generally protected by patents, so their makers attempt to differentiate them through heavy marketing and promotional efforts. A third strategic group in this industry produces generic drugs, which are usually first developed by one of the other two groups and then copied. Without the R&D or

EXHIBIT 3.9
A Map of Strategic Groups in the Pharmaceutical Industry

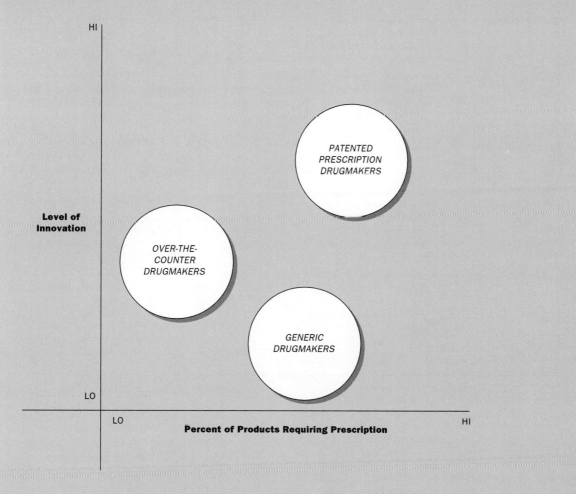

promotional budgets of the patented prescription or over-the-counter drugmakers, generic drugmakers can sell their products on the basis of lower costs.

These groups pursue very different strategies and operate in competitive environments so different as to confound any attempt at industrywide environmental analysis such as use of the five forces framework. This point is illustrated by the very different conclusions

reached about the five competitive forces identified in Exhibit 3.10. Any attempt to do an analysis of the "average" pharmaceutical firm would be meaningless at best and misleading at worst. After all, as indicated by the chart, there really is no average group in the industry—only three very different groups that need to be considered individually.

EXHIBIT 3.10
Illustrative Differences in the Five Forces Across Strategic Groups

Competitive Force	Patented Prescription	Over the Counter	Generic Brands
Bargaining power of buyers	Low—typical for doctor to prescribe medicine and insurance to pay for it.	Moderate—lots of options, but retailers may want leading brands for volume and margin.	High—many undifferentiated options.
Bargaining power of suppliers	Not relevant in many cases—because of vertical integration, key suppliers are in-house.	Low—supplies account for a very small part of product price overall.	Modest—sensitivity to costs keeps greater power in hands of suppliers.
Threat of new entrants	Very low—patent protection and drug approval processes limit new entrants.	Moderate—marketing expenses to launch new brand may be a barrier to entry.	Very high—easy to enter this group with a me-too product.
Threat of substitutes	Low—advanced drugs are often among the most cost-effective medical treatments.	Very high—many substitutes for products like cough syrups, headache remedies, etc.	Moderate—newly patented substitutes may be available that generics cannot yet copy.
Intensity of rivalry	Moderately low—firms compete to be first to market a new pharmaceutical solution, but then patents give them some freedom from head-to-head competition.	High—based on need to differentiate your product from the competition's.	High—based on need to achieve the lowest costs.

---

mon strategy, it is possible to describe a strategic group in just about any way we might describe a strategy. Furthermore, it often makes sense to use different combinations of strategic dimensions to more precisely identify groups. Conceivably, one could combine any number of dimensions; but as a practical matter, we seldom use more than two dimensions at a time. We refer to charts that result from locating the strategic groups within an industry along two (or possibly more) dimensions as *strategic maps*. Application 3.2 uses such a strategic map (Exhibit 3.9) to identify different strategic groups within the pharmaceutical industry.

Environmental Scanning: Gathering Intelligence

Competitive intelligence is information relevant to strategy formulation regarding the environmental context within which a firm competes. Such intelligence has several uses:[33] (1) providing descriptions of the competitive environment that inform strategists and guide strategy formulation, (2) challenging common assumptions about the competitive environments, (3) forecasting future developments in the competitive environment, (4) identifying and compensating for exposed competitive weaknesses, (5) determining when a strategy is no longer viable or sustainable, and (6) indicating when and how strategy should be adjusted to changing competitive environments.

Despite the obvious usefulness of such information, most research in this area suggests that many organizations fail to gather adequate intelligence. You might guess that their intelligence-gathering systems are not sophisticated enough to overcome the complexities of gathering useful intelligence. However, usually, this is not the problem, and some of the simplest intelligence-gathering efforts are also the most effective, as illustrated in Application 3.3.

Researchers have found that organizations regularly overlook some of the most obvious sources of information. Below are several practical sources of useful competitive intelligence.[34]

■ *Information your people already collect.* Experience shows that this is by far the single most important source of competitive intelligence. For example, salespeople in the field are in close proximity to their counterparts from competitive firms, and they will often be the first to hear of new developments underway in rival organizations. Staff members often return with new information from trade shows or industry conferences. Some experts suggest that many large companies already collect 75 to 90 percent of the intelligence they need, but use only a fraction of this useful resource.[35]

■ *Local newspapers.* Some information may not be big enough to warrant national media attention, but could be front-page news at home. Why not subscribe to the newspaper serving the community where your chief competitors have plants?

■ *The government.* Under the Freedom of Information Act, much of the information collected by federal agencies is available to the public. For instance, the EPA requires firms to file information that allows competitors to assess each other's technology and production volumes.

■ *Databases.* There are now hundreds of computerized databases available on everything from mergers and acquisitions to commercial scientific developments. It took less than a minute at a computer terminal in a local library to scan 800 journals and magazines and download abstracts on the 3,176 articles that had been

Application 3.3

A Student's Experience in Collecting Competitive Intelligence

A metal fabrication firm that wanted to grow made inquiries about which rivals might make the most attractive acquisitions. They decided that the ideal candidates for a friendly takeover would be firms located within a 300-mile radius that offered both products and related services in the metal fabrication business. These firms would not be unionized, would have sales between $15 and $50 million, would be growing and profitable, and would have no problems with their local communities. They wanted to find as many such firms as possible, but they did not want anyone else in the industry to know they were shopping for acquisitions. In less than a month, they quietly identified precisely which competitors met all their criteria by using the following procedures to collect competitive intelligence.

They hired an MBA student who was assigned the intelligence-gathering work as part of a summer internship. The intern scanned Dun & Bradstreet databases covering the surrounding states to identify firms in the same industry that were in the right size range and were profitable and growing. This resulted in a list of 137 firms along with their addresses and telephone numbers. A map was used to determine which of them were within 300 miles.

A phone call to each of these was all it took to receive a catalog of their products or services and to ascertain whether or not they were unionized. (In response to questions about why this information was needed, the intern was instructed to politely decline to explain any details and never to pressure anyone for the information. The question never came up.)

Based on a review of this information, the management team identified nine firms that seemed most promising. The intern then spent two weeks traveling to each of the towns in which the competitors were located. There he photographed the facilities, talked to the local newspapers, and had several meals at neighboring diners. Here, conversations with employees covered topics ranging from the working conditions in the plant to the involvement of the company with the local softball league.

Upon returning home, the intern again briefed the management team, which quickly reduced the list to the two firms they considered to be ideal candidates and prepared to approach the firms with an inquiry. Though the intelligence-gathering process had been simple, fast, and cheap, it had also been effective in producing precisely the information on competitors managers needed to formulate a sound acquisition strategy.

written on IBM over the past 3 years. Information on such databases is provided in the appendix to this chapter.

- *Customers and suppliers.* Unless they have signed nondisclosure agreements, these organizations may be willing to provide a wealth of information about what is going on in your market from their standpoint. For example, one of Procter & Gamble's key competitors learned the precise launch date for a new detergent in Europe while visiting the plant that makes packaging equipment for the new product. It took only a few questions about what the machine did, whom it was for, and the delivery date for the competitor to be able to deduce P&G's launch plans with considerable precision.

- *Your competitors.* Many managers are amazed at how forthcoming competitors are with requested information. In fact, the whole concept of competitive benchmarking, discussed in detail in Chapter 5, is based on gathering information from competitors. Approached openly and with some commonsense guidelines (don't ask them anything you don't want to answer about your own firm), many managers are willing to join in an exchange of ideas with their competitors.

Scenario Planning: Organizing Information

The environments surrounding most firms are so complicated that they often threaten to overwhelm strategists. A useful tool for addressing this complexity is a managerial technique known as scenario planning.[36] *Scenarios* are stories about what the future environment might hold and how a firm might respond to this future. Scenarios are useful planning aids because they address two challenges facing those analyzing the environment to improve the strategy formulation process. They (1) direct the attention of those who gather and analyze data, and they (2) help present the assimilated data in a way that is useful for decision making. Typical forecasts give optimistic, pessimistic, and most likely predictions, but scenarios are much richer. They are based on the assumption that it is inappropriate to just identify an outcome and the reasonable highs and lows around it. Instead, scenarios are attempts to identify a set of very diverse alternative futures as a means of preparing managers for unavoidable uncertainties. A scenario for a play does not merely reveal the play's ending, it also explains the developments leading up to the ending. In the same way, a planning scenario does not merely predict how things will turn out, it also attempts to explain what forces will shape the future.[37] Properly constructed scenarios go well beyond mere data to give decision makers a feel for the situations that are likely to unfold.

There are several guidelines for developing useful scenarios:[38] (1) *Avoid focusing exclusively on controllable issues.* Scenario planning is intended to develop alternative views of uncontrollable developments—not simply lay out the plans and outcomes of internally controlled decisions. (2) *Actively seek out contrarian views.* The most helpful scenarios modify current perceptions in fundamental ways. This requires that managers be brutally candid in assessing the situation, which may mean bringing in outsiders with fresh perspectives who will ask questions about things insiders may take for granted. (3) *Do reality checks as scenarios begin to form.* Are the scenarios relevant for the line managers who will determine the firm's future success? Scenarios should address worries that keep line managers up at night. If they do not, they may just be academic exercises with little tangible reward. (4) *Don't get bogged down in two many scenarios or too many details.* A scenario is supposed to help managers understand complexity—not capture all the details. Experts suggest that if you have more than about four scenarios, or if the scenarios become too unwieldy, you should simplify things using Ockham's Razor, the axiom that states, "What can be done with fewer assumptions is done in vain with more." Remember, the purpose of scenarios is to describe different worlds, not to detail all the outcomes possible in the same world.

Although the foregoing discussion makes it clear that the environment can be a powerful influence on firm performance, it would be incorrect to assume that business organizations are inert entities that cannot "push back" against environmental forces. In the following section, we consider how organizations can use strategy to influence their environments.

HOW STRATEGY CAN INFLUENCE THE EXTERNAL ENVIRONMENT

Historically, the external environment was considered beyond the control of the firms that operate within it. This view of the environment explains why so much literature on strategic management has focused on how firms should adapt to their environment. However, organizations are not entirely passive; they regularly attempt to change important elements of both the general and the competitive environments, and we consider changes at both levels below.[39]

Changing the General Environment

Most attempts to influence the general environment fall into two categories, issues management and corporate political activity.

Issues Management

Identifying the events and major trends likely to affect a firm and then developing appropriate responses for shaping these is called *issues management*. A good example of how corporations practice issues management comes from the tobacco industry. Over the past 20 years, the antismoking movement in the United States has resulted in increased regulation, restrictions on product use, increased product-specific taxes, and tarnished images for tobacco companies. Philip Morris, the largest firm in the industry, has been very active in trying to shape a number of elements in the general environment that are related to the antismoking trends. It publishes a magazine (distributed free to smokers) encouraging smokers to be as actively prosmoking as the opposing forces are antismoking. It lobbies government agencies at various levels to limit further smoking regulation, and has given millions of dollars to philanthropic causes in order to improve its public image, like a $30 million television campaign celebrating the Bill of Rights' 200th anniversary. When antismoking forces sought to convince automakers to leave ashtrays off new models, Philip Morris launched an effective ad campaign pointing out that smokers purchase 5 million cars a year. Even though antismoking forces continue to rally, Philip Morris has recently enjoyed record profits from U.S. tobacco sales and has regularly been ranked among the top ten most admired companies in the *Fortune* 500.[40]

Corporate Political Activity

Corporate political activity refers to efforts made by businesses to influence government regulation, in favor of a firm's interests and away from policies that threaten it. It seems to carry a negative stigma; the image is that big business uses questionable means to reach narrowly self-serving ends. Presented in this way, corporate political action certainly sounds nefarious, but it does not have to be. In fact, the political process in a democracy was explicitly designed to allow those being governed (including corporations) to have a role in shaping decisions. Furthermore, when businesses campaign for what they consider to be self-beneficial interests, the public at large is often the cobeneficiary.

Consider the case of the business coalition that set out to "find" more daylight—a part of the environment most observers would certainly view as being fixed. The Daylight Savings Time Coalition was a lobbying effort funded by a group of convenience stores, fast food chains, golf courses, and barbecue-related producers who convinced the U.S. Congress to move the beginning of daylight savings time from the last to the first Sunday in April. Although each of these industries has undoubtedly profited, the change has also proven popular with the public at large. Interestingly, the candy industry was unsuccessful in getting daylight savings time extended from the last Sunday in October until the first Sunday of November. This would have allowed another hour of daylight for children to "trick-or-treat" on Halloween evening, but lawmakers saw the change as too narrowly self-serving for its corporate sponsors and refused to adopt it.

Changing the Competitive Environment

Firms have been successful at reshaping two important elements of their competitive environments: the rate of sales growth and the underlying industry structure.

Sales Growth

This is a critical determinant of the level of rivalry, as we discussed earlier in this chapter. Firms able to alter the underlying demand for their products can have a major impact on how lucrative the environment appears. Changes in demographics that resulted in more women in the workforce outside the home resulted in greatly diminished demand for baking supplies, such as Arm & Hammer baking soda. Many firms supplying domestic goods saw this change in demographics as something that was outside their control and severely limited their potential for growth. Arm & Hammer took a more proactive stance. It developed a campaign that stressed using baking soda for nonbaking purposes, such as an odor absorbent for refrigerators and carpets, an additive to bathwater and swimming pools, and a natural substitute for toothpaste, thereby maintaining a healthy market environment for its product.

Industry Structure

As we saw earlier in our coverage of the five forces model, an industry's structure determines many of the written or unwritten "rules of the game" governing how firms in it compete with one another. Some great firms have been created by astute strategists who understood how these rules can be rewritten. For example MCI, the second-largest long-distance telephone company in the United States, exists because it was able to change the rules. In this case, the rules were, in fact, written: they were the regulations that allowed AT&T to hold a monopoly on the industry. MCI's founder was a leader in efforts to break this monopoly in the early 1980s and open the long-distance industry to competition, an environmental change that allowed MCI to be created.

Ethical Considerations in Shaping the Environment

Business is one of the most powerful social institutions in existence today. With this power comes a responsibility for ethical behavior. This responsibility is perhaps clearest when considering the potential for business to shape its environment. Critics argue that companies such as Philip Morris may wish to bring about changes that are merely self-serving and that may even have extremely negative implications for others. Another example is how firms respond to increasing efforts to reduce pollution through regulation. Managers at such firms find that efforts by individual business or industry coalitions to avoid or lift ecologically sound regulations are inappropriate and that attempts to distort or minimize the scientific evidence on the dangers of pollution are just plain wrong. Our firsthand experience suggests that most firms willingly acknowledge the need for such regulations and work to comply with them.[41] We are encouraged by this and are reminded that there is an important place for the consideration of ethics in any decision to try to influence the business environment. Clearly, not all such attempts at shaping a more favorable environment are unethical, but it is just as clear that some are. Managers have an inescapable responsibility to decide which is which and to behave accordingly.

Summary of Managerial Practices to Adopt from This Chapter

- Make external analysis an important part of your strategy formulation process. Formulate your strategy in the light of a clear understanding of environmental forces most likely to impact your organization.

- In analyzing the general environment, consider each of its six major components: *demographic, sociocultural, political/legal, technological, macroeconomic,* and *global.*

- Where appropriate, in analyzing the competitive environment, focus your analysis on a strategic group rather than an overall industry.

- Regardless of whether you are analyzing the entire industry or a more narrowly defined strategic group, do not fixate on a narrow definition of competition, but consider all five forces in the competitive environment: new entrants, supplier and customer bargaining power, substitute products, and rivalry.

- Be aware of the different levels of rivalry and the factors that lead competitors to particular forms of rivalry and competition. In particular, be familiar with environmental forces associated with the most common forms of rivalry, avoided competition and hypercompetition.

- Instead of viewing your competitive environment in strictly competitive terms, use concepts from evolutionary economics to help identify opportunities to cooperate.

- In gathering the intelligence needed to analyze the environment, do not underestimate the power and usefulness of obvious sources of information.

- The implications of environmental developments will be most clear if information about the environment is organized into scenarios that paint a more meaningful picture of the environment than that obtained from studying the raw intelligence data alone.

- Appreciate the power of the environment and its ability to impact the success of any particular strategy. However, do not underestimate the ability of a well-developed strategy to shape a firm's environment.

Questions for Discussion and Review

1. Describe the most important dimensions of both the general and the competitive environments.

2. Describe the different levels of competitive rivalry and the factors that most affect whether a given set of competitors will more likely engage in avoided competition or hypercompetition.

3. Of the "players" described by five forces analysis (customers, suppliers, producers of substitutes, potential new entrants, you and your direct rivals), which are most likely to engage in cooperative strategies to better compete?

4. Describe (a) the decision to focus on a specific strategic group, (b) environmental scanning, and (c) scenario planning as key to the process of analyzing the external environment.

5. Discuss how strategy can be used to affect both a firm's general and its competitive environments. What ethical considerations should affect a firm's efforts to shape its environment?

Notes

1. James Aley, "The Theory That Made Microsoft," *Fortune, 133* (April 29, 1996), 65–66.
2. Charles Babcock, "Microsoft's Weapon: Keep ISVs Happy," *Computerworld, 29* (January 9, 1995), 8.
3. A thorough discussion of this concept can be found in Thomas C. Powell, "Organizational Alignment as Competitive Advantage," *Strategic Management Journal, 13* (1992), 119–134.
4. N. Venkatraman and John E. Prescott, "Environment-Strategy Coalignment: An Empirical Test of Its Performance Implications," *Strategic Management Journal, 11* (1990), 1–23.
5. For examples, see William Ming-Hone Tsai, Ian C. MacMillan, and Murray B. Low, "Effects of Strategy and Environment on Corporate Venture Success in Industrial Markets," *Journal of Business Venturing, 6* (January 1991), 9–28.
6. J. Justin Tan and Robert J. Litschert, "Environment-Strategy Relationship and Its Performance Implications: An Empirical Study of the Chinese Electronics Industry," *Strategic Management Journal, 15* (1994), 1–20.
7. For example, see Paul Klebnikov, "You Didn't Make the Profit, the Market Did," *Forbes, 154*: 6(September 12, 1994), 184–188.

8. See Lester C. Thurow, "Surviving in a Turbulent Environment," *Planning Review, 23*: 5(September–October 1995), 24–29.

9. For a description of a different but complementary view of the general environment, see Gary Hamel and C. K. Prahalad, "Seeing the Future First," *Fortune, 130*: 5 (September 5, 1994), 64–70.

10. Henry Mintzberg, "That's Not 'Turbulence,' Chicken Little, It's Really Opportunity," *Planning Review, 22*: 6(November–December 1994), 7–13+.

11. Howard Banks, "A Sixties Industry in a Nineties Economy," *Forbes* (May 9, 1994), 107–112.

12. V. K. Narayanan, "How a Broader Environment Can Shape Industry Events," in Liam Fahey, ed., *Strategic Planning Management Reader*, Englewood Cliffs, NJ: Prentice-Hall, 1989, 47–51.

13. Olukemi O. Sawyerr, "Environmental Uncertainty and Environmental Scanning Activities of Nigerian Manufacturing Executives: A Comparative Analysis," *Strategic Management Journal, 14* (1993), 287–299.

14. The competitive environment is sometimes referred to as the *task* or *industry* environment, but the label we are using is in keeping with the emphasis placed on competition and competitive advantage throughout this text.

15. Michael E. Porter has made seminal contributions to the study of competitor and industry analysis. This section draws heavily from his works, particularly *Competitive Strategy: Techniques for Analyzing Industries and Competitors*, New York: The Free Press, 1980; and "How Competitive Forces Shape Strategy," *Harvard Business Review 57*: 2(1979), 137–145. See also Patrick McNamee and Marie McHugh, "Competitive Strategies in the Clothing Industry," *Long Range Planning, 22*: 4(1989), 63–71.

16. Matthew Schifrin, "The Big Squeeze," *Forbes* (March 11, 1996), 45–46.

17. Marcia Berss, "We Will Not Be in a National Chain," *Forbes* (March 27, 1995), 50.

18. To be most accurate, based on our previous discussion of competitive threats coming from substitute producers or potential new entrants, we need to also consider these sources of rivals, rather than just direct rivals. However, our main point here is that in order to behave like a pure monopoly, a firm must not be pressured by competition from *any* fronts, at least in the short run.

19. It is interesting to note that governments usually find it desirable to get involved in using regulations to alter what might otherwise occur at the extremes of pure monopolies and pure competition. For instance, public water utilities answer to regulatory boards that govern price hikes and service levels in the absence of the rivalry that would create similar pressures in other forms of competition. And, in order to ensure a level of profitability acceptable enough so that people will still want to engage in farming, most governments get involved in providing subsidies, limiting output, an so on, essentially moving farming out of the pure-competition category.

20. Ralf Boscheck, "Competitive Advantage: Superior Offer or Unfair Dominance?" *California Management Review, 37*: 1(Fall 1994), 132–151.

21. Richard A. D'Aveni with Robert Gunther, *Hypercompetition: Managing the Dynamics of Strategic Maneuvering*, New York: The Free Press, 1994; Richard A. D'Aveni, "Coping with Hypercompetition: Utilizing the New 7S's Framework," *Academy of Management Executive, 9*: 3(August 1995), 45–60.

22. Damon Darlin, "The Computer Industry's Mystery Man," *Forbes* (April 8, 1996), 42–44.

23. Joe Spiers, "The Myth of Corporate Greed," *Fortune* (April 15, 1996), 67–68.

24. Richard Normann and Rafael Ramirez, "From Value Chain to Value Constellation: Designing Interactive Strategy," *Harvard Business Review* (July–August 1993), 163; Donald J. Bowersox, "The Strategic Benefits of Logistics Alliances," *Harvard Business Review* (July–August 1990), 170; Anne S. Miner, Terry L. Amburgey, and Timothy M. Stearns, "Interorganizational Linkages and Population Dynamics: Buffering and Transformational Shields," *Administrative Science Quarterly, 35* (December 1990), 689–713.

25. Jack Gee, "Partners to Profit," *Industry Week, 244* (April 17, 1995), 13–16; Benjamin Gomes-Casseres, "Group Versus Group: How Alliance Networks Compete," *Harvard Business Review, 72* (July–August 1994), 62–74; Rosabeth Moss Kanter, "Collaborative Advantage: The Art of Alliances," *Harvard Business Review, 72* (July–August 1994), 96–108.

26. James E. Moore, *The Death of Competition*, New York: Harper Business, 1996; James E. Moore, "Predators and Prey: A New Ecology of Competition," *Harvard Business Review* (May–June 1993), 193; Rita Koselka, "Evolutionary Economics: Nice Guys Don't Finish Last," *Forbes* (October 11, 1993), 110–114; Warren Boeker, "Organizational Strategy: An Ecological Perspective," *Academy of Management Journal, 34* (September 1990), 613–635.

27. In some industries, the cost of supplied materials runs 60 to 80 percent of the total manufacturing cost, which makes the supplier-customer dimension critically important. See David Asmus and John Griffin, "Harnessing the Power of Your Suppliers," *McKinsey Quarterly* (Summer 1993), 63–78.

28. Those interested in understanding the managerial processes required to develop and maintain cooperative strategies are referred to Peter Smith Ring and Andrew H. Van de Ven, "Developmental Processes of Cooperative Interorganizational Relationships," *Academy of Management Review 19*: 1(1994), 90–118.

29. For a discussion of how environmental scanning is related to strategy formulation, see Daniel F. Jennings and James R. Lumpkin, "Insights Between Environmental Scanning Activities and Porter's Generic Strategies: An Empirical Analysis," *Journal of Management, 18* (December 1992), 791–803.

30. Robert R. Wiggins and Timothy W. Ruefli, "Necessary Conditions for the Predictive Validity of Strategic Groups," *Academy of Management Journal, 38*: 6(December 1995), 1635–1656.

31. Robert Dooley, Dorn Fowler, and Alex Miller, "The Benefits of Strategic Homogeneity and Strategic Heterogeneity: Theoretical and Empirical Evidence Resolving Past Differences," *Strategic Management Journal* (April 1996), 293–306.

32. Avi Fiegenbaum and Howard Thomas, "Industry and Strategic Group Dynamics: Competitive Strategy in the Insurance Industry, 1970–84," *Journal of Management Studies, 30* (January 1993), 69–105.

33. For a detailed discussion of the following six uses, see Jan P. Herring, "The Role of Intelligence in Formulating Strategy," *Journal of Business Strategy, 13* (September–October 1992), 54–60.

34. Also see Richard S. Teitelbaum, "The New Race for Intelligence," *Fortune* (November 2, 1992), 104–106.

35. Jan P. Herring, "Senior Management Must Champion Business Intelligence Programs," *Journal of Business Strategy, 12* (September–October 1991), 48–52.

36. The company that has made the greatest advances in scenario planning is Royal Dutch/Shell, a global oil company headquartered in the Netherlands. A retrospective on progress made by this company's planning department is given in Paul J. H. Schoemaker

and Cornelius A. J. M. van der Heijden, "Integrating Scenarios into Strategic Planning at Royal Dutch/Shell," *Planning Review* (May–June 1992), 41–46. Other firms' experiences are recounted in Stephen M. Millet, "Battelle's Scenario Analysis of a European High-Tech Market," *Planning Review* (March–April 1992), 20–23; and P. R. Stokke et al., "Scenario Planning for Norwegian Oil and Gas," *Long Range Planning*, 23: 2 (1990), 17–26.

37. Audrey E. Schriefer, "Getting the Most Out of Scenarios: Some Questions and Answers," *Planning Review*, 23: 6(November–December 1995), 37–40; Norman E. Duncan and Pierre Wack, "Scenarios Designed to Improve Decision-Making," *Planning Review*, 22: 4(July–August 1994), 18–25+.

38. These points are drawn from the twenty-five guidelines for scenario planning offered by Daniel G. Simpson, "Key Lessons for Adopting Scenario Planning in Diversified Companies," *Planning Review* (May–June 1992), 10–48.

39. Much of the material in the following two sections was adapted from P. Rajan Varadarajan, Terry Clark, and William M. Pride, "Controlling the Uncontrollable: Managing Your Market Environment," *Sloan Management Review* (Winter 1992), 39.

40. Maria Mallory et al., "Is the Smoking Lamp Going Out for Good?" *Business Week* (April 11, 1994), 30–31.

41. Dorn Fowler, William Judge, and Alex Miller, "What Causes Corporate Environmental Responsiveness," *Corporate and Environmental Strategy*, 3: 3(1996), 43–48.

Appendix to Chapter 3:
Sources of Company and Industry Information*

This appendix provides a brief overview of important sources of information that may be useful while conducting company and industry analyses. Most university libraries and some public libraries carry these reference materials. In addition, there are numerous computer databases available, many of which are available at modest fees to academic users.

We have organized these references into eight categories: Industry Surveys and Rankings, Industry Ratios, Industry Forecasts, National and Industry Statistics, Industry Trade Publications, Magazine/Newspaper Indexes, Databases, and Information on Publicly-Held Corporations.

I. Industry Surveys and Rankings

"Annual Report on American Industry" in FORBES. New York: Forbes, Inc. (first January issue each year)
Covers 1,177 of the largest public companies in 20 major industry groups and 70 subgroups. Compares them in terms of profitability, growth, and marketing performance. Corporations are ranked against their immediate competitors, firms in related industry groups, and against all other companies.
HG5001. F6[1]

---

*This appendix is largely based on materials prepared by Ruthie Brock and Tommie Wingfield, Business Librarians at the University of Texas at Arlington. We gratefully acknowledge their contribution.
[1]Library of Congress and Superintendent of Documents call numbers are provided. Some libraries may use other classifications or variations of these call numbers.

CORPORATE AND INDUSTRY RESEARCH REPORTS (CIRR). Eastchester, NY: JA Micropublishing. 1982–1989. Continued by Bowker Business Research, 1990–1991.
Reports prepared by analysts from investment firms and brokerage houses give analysis, projections, forecasts, market strategies, economic trends, and product developments on over 5,000 companies and 300 industries. Includes comparative data on companies within industries. Full-text reports are in microfiche format. Publication has ceased. See Investext entry below.
HG4001.C531

INTERNATIONAL DIRECTORY OF COMPANY HISTORIES (in five volumes). Chicago: St. James Press.
Narrative histories of 1,250 of the world's largest and most influential companies in 36 industries assembled from magazines, books, annual reports, and material supplied by the companies themselves. Indicates whether the company is public or private.
HD2721. I68 1988

INVESTEXT (CD-ROM). Belmont, CA: Information Access Co. 1990– (monthly)
Similar to CIRR, this source contains full-text reports prepared by analysts from investment firms and brokerage houses which give analysis, projections, forecasts, market strategies, economic trends, and product developments on over 8,000 companies, 2,000 of which are publicly held, and 53 high-tech industries. Includes comparative data on companies within industries. Reports can be printed or downloaded to disk.

MANUFACTURING USA: INDUSTRY ANALYSES, STATISTICS, AND LEADING COMPANIES. First Edition. Detroit: Gale Research.
A comprehensive guide to economic activity in 448 manufacturing industries. Provides unique analysis and synthesis of federal statistics.
IID9721. M364

MOODY'S INVESTORS FACT SHEETS: INDUSTRY REVIEW. New York: Moody's Investors Service. (looseleaf)
Contains key financial information, comparative statistics, operating data, and ratios on over 4,000 companies. Information is arranged into 140 industry groups.
HG4907. M662

STANDARD & POOR'S INDUSTRY SURVEYS. New York: Standard & Poor's Corp. (annual with updates)
Compiling basic data on over 20 leading U.S. industries, the "Basic Analysis" for each industry gives commentary, analysis, projections, and comparisons of leading companies. The "Current Analysis" is a supplement for reporting recent developments in the industry.
HG4902. S82

U.S. Office of Management and Budget, Executive Office of the President. STANDARD INDUSTRIAL CLASSIFICATION MANUAL. Washington, DC: U.S. Government Printing Office, 1987.

The standard industrial classification (SIC) is a numerical system utilized by the U.S. government to facilitate the collection and dissemination of statistics on industries. This manual contains the latest revision of SIC codes and cross reference tables to previous codes.
PrEx 2.6/2: In 27/987

VALUE LINE INVESTMENT SURVEY. New York: A. Bernhard & Co. (loose-leaf with weekly additions)
Analyzes and reports on over 1,700 companies in 90+ industries. Includes a 10-year statistical history of 23 investment factors for each company and an overview for each of the covered industries. Company and industry reports are published quarterly with interim weekly updates.
HG4501. V26

WARD'S BUSINESS DIRECTORY OF U.S. PRIVATE AND PUBLIC COMPANIES. Detroit: Gale Research. (annual)
In addition to the standard alphabetical listing, companies are ranked by sales within four-digit industry (SIC) categories. A special feature section provides totals (sales, employees, number of companies) per industry and revenue per employee of the top 1,000 companies. No minimum sales for inclusion permits some coverage of smaller, private firms.
HG4057. A458

II. Industry Ratios

Dun & Bradstreet Credit Services. INDUSTRY NORMS AND KEY BUSINESS RATIOS. New York: Dun & Bradstreet Credit Services. (annual)
Provides industry norms and key business ratios on 800 lines of business as defined by SIC codes. Ratios for single year only.
HF5681. R25 I52

Robert Morris Associates. ANNUAL STATEMENT STUDIES. Philadelphia: Robert Morris Associates. (annual)
Contains industry norms and financial and operating ratios for about 300 lines of business including manufacturers, wholesalers, retailers, services, and contractors. Includes historical data for 5 years.
HF5681. B2 R6

Troy, Leo. ALMANAC OF BUSINESS AND INDUSTRIAL FINANCIAL RATIOS. Englewood Cliffs, NJ: Prentice-Hall. (annual)
Financial and operating ratios for about 160 industries including banks and financial industries, as well as the usual manufacturing, wholesaling, and retailing industries. Derived from Internal Revenue Service data.
HF5681. R25 A45

III. Industry Forecasts

International Trade Administration, U.S. Department of Commerce. U.S. INDUSTRIAL OUTLOOK. Washington, DC: U.S. Government Printing Office. (annual)

Useful volume for information on recent trends and outlook for 3 to 5 years in over 350 industries. The brief narrative with statistics contains discussions of change in supply and demand for each industry, developments in domestic and overseas markets, price changes, employment trends, and capital investment.
C61.34

PREDICASTS FORECASTS. Cleveland, OH: Predicasts, Inc. (quarterly with annual cumulations)
Gives short- and long-range forecast statistics for basic economic indicators and for individual products by seven-digit SIC number. Accompanying each forecast is a reference to the source from which the statistics were taken.
HC101. P71

IV. National and Industry Statistics

AMERICAN STATISTICS INDEX (ASI). Washington, DC: Congressional Information Service. (monthly with annual cumulations)
Complements Statistical Reference Index by leading to statistical information published in U.S. government publications. Contains an "Index by Category" which identifies sources of statistics reported in specific ways, such as by city or state or by age or sex.
HA195. Z926

Bureau of the Census. U.S. Department of Commerce. ECONOMIC CENSUS PUBLICATIONS (listed below). Washington, DC: U.S. Government Printing Office). (at five-year intervals)
Economic censuses are all taken in the years ending with the numbers 2 and 7. They typically give number of establishments, employment, payrolls, and hours worked. Depending on the census, information is provided on the quantity and value of products shipped and materials consumed, value of retail products sold, value of minerals mined, number of vehicles, vehicle miles, and ton miles transporting freight, etc. In the years between the Census of Manufacturers, the bureau publishes the ANNUAL SURVEY OF MANUFACTURERS, which gives statistics for broad industry groups and selected products. These censuses are:

> Census of Construction Industries
> Census of Manufacturers
> Census of Mineral Industries
> Census of Retail Trade
> Census of Service Industries
> Census of Transportation
> Census of Wholesale Trade

C3.24/4 through C3.257/5

Bureau of the Census, U.S. Department of Commerce. STATISTICAL ABSTRACT OF THE UNITED STATES. Washington, DC: U.S. Government Printing Office. (annual)

Very important statistical reference work because it serves as the primary source for U.S. industrial, social, political, and economic statistics and as a bibliographical guide. Source notes at the foot of each table credit the agency issuing the original data.
C3.134

Bureau of Economic Analysis, U.S. Department of Commerce. SURVEY OF CURRENT BUSINESS. Washington, DC: U.S. Government Printing Office. (monthly) Important source for up-to-date information on the U.S. economy. Includes GNP, personal income, leading economic indicators, U.S. balance of payments, and corporate profits. Beginning April 1990 "Business Cycle Indicators" are also included following the discontinuation of Business Conditions Digest. A historical record of the statistical series (about 1,900) that appear in the SURVEY OF CURRENT BUSINESS is reported in BUSINESS STATISTICS.
C59.11

Internal Revenue Service, U.S. Treasury Department. STATISTICS OF INCOME: CORPORATION INCOME TAX RETURNS. Washington, DC: U.S. Government Printing Office. (annual)
Balance sheet and income statement statistics derived from a sample of corporate income tax returns. Includes tables by industry, with breakdown by asset size, etc.
T22.35/5

STATISTICAL REFERENCE INDEX (SRI). Washington, DC: Congressional Information Service. (monthly with annual cumulations)
Indexes significant statistical information published by industry trade associations, independent research organizations, universities, and state governments. Excellent leads to sources with comparative data. Accompanying microfiche collection includes the full text of many of the publications indexed.
HA214. S73

V. Industry Trade Publications

Trade journals and tabloids are useful sources of information regarding the industries they cover. They frequently publish detailed articles on trends, alert readers to changes in government regulations, announce personnel changes in major companies, cover new products, and can be excellent sources of industry statistics. The following titles are illustrative examples. Many others exist.

> Air Transport World
> American Banker
> Aviation Week and Space Technology
> Best's Review—Life/Health
> Best's Review—Property/Casualty
> Beverage Industry
> Beverage World
> Computerworld
> DM: Discount Merchandiser

DNR: Daily News Record
Data Communications
Editor and Publisher
Electronic Business
Food and Beverage Marketing
Food Processing
Frozen Food Digest
Hotel and Motel Management
Hotels
Infoworld
Nation's Restaurant News
Oil and Gas Journal
PC Week
Packaging
Progressive Grocer
Publisher's Weekly
Restaurant Business
Supermarket Business
Supermarket News
Telephony
Travel Weekly
Vending Times
WWD: Women's Wear Daily

VI. Magazine/Newspaper Indexes

ABI/INFORM. Louisville: UMI/Data Courier (online only, no print version) Frequent updates.
Abstracts of articles covering management, law, taxation, finance, data processing, advertising, human resources, and other areas of vital interest to decision makers in business.

BUSINESS PERIODICALS INDEX (BPI). New York: H. W. Wilson Co. (monthly with quarterly and annual cumulations)
Articles from over 300 key business periodicals covering all aspects of business including management, marketing, economics, finance, accounting, banking, insurance, investments, computers, specific industries, businesses, trades, and topics of current interest. Has a book review section.
HF5001. B8

INFOTRAC (General Periodicals-Academic CD-ROM). Belmont, CA: Information Access Co. 1982– (backfile disk plus monthly updates)
Selected coverage of over 1,000 predominantly business magazines plus 60 days of THE WALL STREET JOURNAL and the business section of THE NEW YORK TIMES.

PAIS INTERNATIONAL IN PRINT. New York: Public Affairs Information Service. (monthly with quarterly and annual cumulations)
Economic and business information, especially related to regulated or recently deregulated industries, and geopolitical, international, or interdisciplinary aspects of business topics. Includes selected books and government publications as well as business periodicals. The title changed in 1991 to include the word "International" to reflect the added emphasis on international coverage and the addition of more foreign language articles.
H83. Z968

PREDICASTS F & S INDEX UNITED STATES. Cleveland, OH: Predicasts, Inc. (weekly with monthly, quarterly, and annual cumulations)
Covers company, product, and industry information from over 750 financial publications, business-oriented newspapers, trade magazines, and special reports. Corporate acquisitions and mergers, new products, market information, technological developments, and social and political factors affecting business are among topics indexed.
HF1040.8. P74

PREDICASTS F & S INDEX EUROPE. Cleveland, OH: Predicasts, Inc. (monthly with quarterly and annual cumulations)
HF1040.9. E8 P72

PREDICASTS F & S INDEX INTERNATIONAL. Cleveland, OH: Predicasts, Inc. (monthly with quarterly and annual cumulations)
HF54. U5 P7

WALL STREET JOURNAL INDEX. Ann Arbor, MI: University Microfilms International. (monthly with quarterly and annual cumulations)
An index to THE WALL STREET JOURNAL in two volumes; the "Corporate" volume is arranged by company and the "General News" is arranged by subject/industry. Includes a separate index for BARRON'S.
HG1. W26

VII. Databases

Academic libraries have access to many of the databases on the Dow Jones News Retrieval System at a special rate. On the "Text" portion, full text articles from the *Wall Street Journal* and many business magazines are available. Full text versions of many cities' newspapers (which often give excellent business coverage) are also available on Datatimes. BRS Information Technologies, ORBIT Search Service, and DIALOG Information Retrieval Service are examples of additional vendors which provide business-related databases, some of which are industry specific.

VIII. Information on Publicly Held Companies

ANNUAL REPORTS AND 10-K REPORTS
Publicly-owned companies must issue annual financial statements to stockholders and file more detailed reports of various kinds with the Securities and Exchange Commis-

sion. Two vendors which make these reports available on microfiche or other formats are:

DISCLOSURE (Corporate reports). Bethesda: Disclosure, Incorporated. Also available as a CD-ROM product and accessible through Dow Jones News Retrieval System, Dialog Information Retrieval Services, and BRS Information Technologies.

Q-FILE (Corporate reports on microfiche: annual reports, 10-K's, 8-K's, Proxy reports). St. Petersburg, FL: Q-Data Corporation.

Moody's Investors Service. MOODY'S MANUALS (listed below). New York: Moody's Investors Service. (annual with updates)
Each of these important manuals covers U.S., Canadian, and other foreign companies listed on U.S. exchanges and includes a brief corporate history, a list of subsidiaries, principal plants and properties; business lines and products; officers and directors; comparative income statements and balance sheet statistics. The blue center sections in each manual provide various industry statistics. Each set also has a looseleaf binder for updates.

    MOODY'S BANK AND FINANCE MANUAL
    HG4961. M65
    MOODY'S INDUSTRIAL MANUAL
    HG4961. M67
    MOODY'S INTERNATIONAL MANUAL
    HG4009. M66
    MOODY'S MUNICIPAL & GOVERNMENT MANUAL
    HG4931. M6
    MOODY'S OTC INDUSTRIAL MANUAL
    HG4915. M68
    MOODY'S OTC UNLISTED MANUAL
    HG4907. M68
    MOODY'S PUBLIC UTILITY MANUAL
    HG4961. M7245
    MOODY'S TRANSPORTATION MANUAL
    HG4971. M74

Standard & Poor's Corp. STANDARD CORPORATION DESCRIPTIONS. New York: Standard & Poor's Corp. (looseleaf)
An excellent financial service, similar to Moody's above, but in looseleaf binders format. Separate volume for DAILY NEWS updates.
HG4501. S7663

Chapter 4

Internal Analysis

CHAPTER OUTLINE

In this chapter, we look inside the firm to assess its internal strengths and weaknesses. The chapter is divided into five parts. In the first, we explain the importance of internal evaluation in an overall strategic analysis. In the second, we explore the resource-based view of the firm, identifying different types of internal resources and describing tests for determining their competitive value. Then we provide frameworks to help identify what to assess for internal analysis. Next, we describe how to use quantitative and qualitative analyses for assessing a firm's strengths and weaknesses in a "balanced-scorecard" approach. In the fifth part, we consider the appropriate comparison standards for internal analysis and explain the value of combining different comparison standards in order to achieve the best possible internal analysis.

This chapter will help you understand:

- The importance of internal analysis in formulating strategies
- The resource-based view of the firm and how it competes
- The three critical types of internal resources: assets, capabilities, and competencies
- The tests that can be used to determine the value of an internal resource for improving a firm's ability to compete
- The use of critical success factors and value chain frameworks to identify key attributes to assess for internal analysis
- The role of core processes in determining a firm's overall ability to compete
- The "balanced-scorecard" approach to multifaceted internal analyses
- The need to combine quantitative and qualitative analysis in assessing a firm's strengths and weaknesses
- The use of industry norms, historical data, and benchmarks as comparison standards

Like all the firms in its industry, Lincoln National Reinsurance Co. sells insurance to insurance companies. To protect itself from the risk inherent in the policies it has sold, an insurance company buys insurance for itself from a company such as Lincoln. To industry experts, reinsurance is viewed largely as a commodity; standard policies offer basic coverage and policies are sold primarily on a price basis in a highly competitive market. However, Lincoln specializes in selling differentiated reinsurance products at premium prices. What competitive advantage allows Lincoln to do what other companies cannot? To understand the answer to this question, you must adopt the "resource-based view" of strategic management found throughout this chapter.

Lincoln recognized two very different types of insurance companies that bought reinsurance. One is the large, sophisticated, experienced insurance company that maintains its own well-staffed technical and research groups. The second type is a very different customer. Changes in the health care industry have encouraged a host of new entrants—such as HMOs and physician groups—into what is effectively the insurance business; and these newcomers often lack the technical expertise to analyze some of the risks they insure. For example, how should a physician group price a group health insurance plan for employees in a cotton mill with an average age of 47, one-third of whom smoke? The larger, more experienced health insurance companies can answer such questions easily, but newcomers are less sure of themselves. Lincoln discovered that such uncertainty meant they could offer something other than a commodity-priced reinsurance policy. Art DeTore, Lincoln's Director of Strategic Planning and Knowledge Management, explains the key to the company's success in seizing this opportunity as "knowing how to link our customers and our competencies." Lincoln accomplishes this in three steps.

Step one: Lincoln places great emphasis on understanding the total set of customer needs for less experienced insurers. These customers need more than just a policy. Instead, they are looking for a partner who can provide the technical and research skills they cannot develop or maintain in house. *Step two:* Lincoln maintains a number of competencies valued by customers in its target market by combining its internal capabilities (such as skills at risk assessment and financial modeling) with its assets (such as cash and sophisticated information technology). *Step three:* Lincoln matches its competencies with customer needs in a process called "mass customization." By maintaining a broad set of technical skills, Lincoln can offer customized solutions for each individual insurer.

Lincoln's story illustrates the practice of "knowledge-based competition." By carefully developing internal resources such as assets and capabilities, Lincoln offers customers a service that makes the company a unique and valuable part of its industry's value chain. Consequently, Lincoln is able to avoid the commodity-based competition that typifies much of the reinsurance industry. In Chapter 4, you will learn how to understand and assess internal resources as a source of advantage in developing successful competitive strategies.

THE IMPORTANCE OF INTERNAL ANALYSIS

Managers perform *internal analysis* to identify strengths to build on and weaknesses to overcome as they formulate strategies for competitive advantage. Research and experience have shown that a firm's overall strengths and weaknesses and its ability to execute may be even more important to its performance than environmental factors.[1] For example, one statistical study compared the relative importance of overall industry variables versus business-specific variables in influencing profitability.[2] The results indicated that a firm's actions and its ability to execute are much more important in determining its financial performance than are conditions in the surrounding industry. One study found that even if the industry itself was quite unattractive and generally unprofitable, firms that produced superior products enjoyed good levels of profitability.[3]

Tecnol Medical Products, a tiny manufacturer of medical face masks, was in the unfavorable business position of facing larger and stronger competitors: Johnson and Johnson and 3M.[4] And to make matters worse, increasing emphasis on cost control in the health care industry was squeezing margins across a broad range of medical supply companies. In this tough environment, Tecnol managed to successfully launch a new line of products by offering a broader range of sizes and lighter-weight masks that made breathing easier. It then improved its market share by offering ever-more sophisticated products while using automated manufacturing techniques to lower its costs and order-completion time. In short, Tecnol developed internal capabilities and process execution that allowed it to overcome environmental threats and its seemingly poor position to achieve a competitive advantage based on differentiated products, low-cost leadership, and shorter response times.

In contrast to the Tecnol example, some competitors holding favorable competitive positions in seemingly attractive environments have suffered when their inability to execute kept them from taking advantage of their situations. One such example is the high-definition television (HDTV) business within the Thomson Consumer Electronics Corporation of France. The French government hoped to make the country one of the leading global competitors in the HDTV industry and, consequently, provided $1 billion in subsidies to Thomson—enough to qualify Thomson's environment and competitive position within its industry as very attractive by any standards. Despite its favorable position, Thomson could not execute the development of new HDTV technology as rapidly as its rivals did. Eventually, other firms developed fully digital HDTV technology far superior to Thomson's, effectively removing Thomson and its government supporters from the HDTV race.

By no means do we intend to downplay the importance of analyzing the external environment and a firm's position within it, but success depends on more than just the external environment.[5] It also depends on a firm's ability to marshal its strengths and overcome its weaknesses: that is, to successfully execute a strategy.[6] This critical point is illustrated in Application 4.1.

Application 4.1

Pathway Bellows Employs Strengths and Offsets Weaknesses

Pathway Bellows, a division of Dover Corporation, designed and manufactured metal industrial expansion joints, devices that allow pipes to expand or contract as they heat and cool in use. Many of the bellows-type expansion joints Pathway produced fit huge pipes (up to 30 feet in diameter) found in very harsh environments, such as chemical processing or steam generation plants. Pathway's competitive strength lay in bellows design and fabrication, but over 20 years, various competitors developed comparable expertise. Competition came to rely more on price cutting, and profit margins eroded. Pathway sought new ways to develop strengths relative to its competitors.

Pathway's analysis uncovered customers' needs for quicker replacement part delivery. When an expansion joint at a chemical or steam plant failed, it very often shut down the operation, and millions of dollars in plant and equipment would sit idle, waiting for a new expansion joint. Pathway reasoned that customers would pay a premium price in return for shorter downtimes. As Pathway's delivery times were no better than its rivals', the management team focused on developing speed as a competitive strength. The plan focused on inventories, cycle-time reduction, and on-site services.

Historically, Pathway held very low inventories and considered their high inventory turnover ratios a measure of success. However, they learned that customers would happily pay huge premiums for simple replacement parts (up to 400%) if it meant a plant could come back on line sooner. Of course, such premiums would more than pay for the inventory-carrying costs of the needed item, so Pathway developed a policy of carrying the industry's largest inventory of the most commonly needed replacement parts.

But many parts (especially larger parts) were custom made and consequently could not be held in inventory easily. Pathway had to completely rethink its design, fabrication, and delivery approaches to speed them up. Previ-

ously, each work order progressed through a series of departments as each completed its work in turn. Delays and bottlenecks often interrupted this sequence, and discoveries made late in the process often required that earlier steps be repeated. Pathway redesigned this work so that a call for new bellows came in to a cross-functional team that stayed with the order until it was filled and, thus, they no longer needed time-consuming "handoffs." With this process change, Pathway was able to establish a competitive advantage in quick response to custom bellows fabrication.

What if the fastest way to get a customer's plant back on line was to repair a bellows, rather than replace it? Pathway had never considered *repairing* bellows because of its historical strength in *selling* them. However, with that strength now matched by rivals, Pathway thought that repairs might be a viable new source of revenues. Consequently, it began training employees to repair in the field. This required a combination of sound practical engineering skills and world-class welding and metal fabrication skills. The company was so successful in developing these organizational capabilities that it developed a totally different approach to replacing/repairing bellows. Its field service crews learned how to build new expansion joints, often even while a plant remained in operation. Pathway offered to have a crew anywhere in the world within 24 hours, and crews developed unique skills such as rebuilding fire-damaged bellows even as internal fires continued to burn. This unique set of production processes led to the creation of a new business unit, which established a strong competitive advantage over rivals and helped Pathway achieve record profit levels.

Pathway's decisions to make the three strategic changes that led to its success were based on a thorough understanding of the firm's historical strengths, the loss of these, and the need to offset the resulting competitive weakness by developing new strengths.

Internal analysis has become so fundamental to good strategic management that a perspective on understanding a firm's overall success as based on its internal resources has emerged. This perspective is called the *resource-based view (RBV)*.

THE RESOURCE-BASED VIEW OF THE FIRM

The Red Cross is a disaster-relief agency that comprises a variety of tangible assets (trucks, mobile hospitals, computers, etc.) and intangible assets (strong morale, a good reputation, brand name awareness, etc.). It also comprises a variety of important capabilities, such as logistical planning, emergency medicine, contingency planning, and fund raising. By combining its assets and its capabilities, the Red Cross has established a competency in fund raising and providing disaster-relief services that makes it a leader in its field. This is a good illustration for understanding several concepts central to the resource-based view.

As depicted in Exhibit 4.1, the resource-based view shows firms as collections of tangible and intangible assets combined with capabilities to use those assets to develop competencies that achieve competitive advantages. This viewpoint fits well with the emergence of *knowledge-based competition*—rivalry in which long-term success depends on what an organization knows and understands. Competitors therefore emphasize capabilities and competencies as the key to their competitive success.[7] Although the language used to describe the resource-based view is somewhat arcane and cumbersome, the underlying concepts are not difficult. Let's look at the most basic building blocks of RBV in more detail.[8]

Three Types of Resources: Assets, Capabilities, and Competencies

RBV has a well-developed set of concepts that help us think about how a firm's internal strengths and weaknesses affect its ability to compete. The sections below provide descriptions and examples of these basic concepts.[9]

Assets

The *factors of production* a firm may draw on in providing is customers with valuable goods and services are called assets. You should note that the resource-based view de-

EXHIBIT 4.1

The Resource-Based View: Relationships Between Assets, Capabilities, and Competencies

$$\begin{pmatrix} \text{Tangible Assets} \\ + \\ \text{Intangible Assets} \end{pmatrix} \times \text{Capabilities} = \text{Competencies} \longrightarrow \text{Competitive Advantages}$$

Assets combined with capabilities produce competencies that can yield competitive advantages.

will first describe each framework and then consider how the three frameworks can be combined.

Critical Success Factors

Many industries have relatively small, but extremely important, sets of factors that are essential for successfully gaining and maintaining competitive advantages. *Critical success factors* (CSFs) describes those areas in which good results help ensure an organization's successful competition and poor results usually lead to declining performance. Application 4.2 shows how strong CSFs impact overall performance in the retail industry, and help explain Wal-Mart's emergence as the world's largest retailer.

Relevant CSFs for individual companies arise from environmental and firm-specific considerations. For instance, a CSF for patented pharmaceutical companies is timely introduction of effective new products. This industry is characterized by intense competition, relatively short product life cycles, and long lead times between basic research, product development, FDA approval, and commercialization. Firms must commit vast resources to R&D to develop new products and to ensure their long-term profitability and cash flow. They must also manage the drug approval process efficiently. Therefore, speed of product development and approval is critical for pharmaceutical firms, but for other firms, CSFs may include manufacturing cost, after-sales service, product image, or other factors that give rise to a competitive advantage.

While specific CSFs vary from business to business, research has identified four major sources of CSFs in general:[13]

- *Industry characteristics.* Critical success factors are often industry-specific. CSFs for supermarket chains include product mix, inventory turnover, sales promotion, and pricing; in the airline industry, fuel efficiency, load factors, and an excellent reservation system are critical. No one set of CSFs applies to all industries, and CSFs change as industries change.

- *Competitive position.* CSFs vary with a firm's position relative to its competition. For example, in a smaller firm within an industry dominated by one or two large competitors, these competitors' actions often produce new and significant problems that become CSFs. At one time, in the personal computer industry, many smaller companies believed that it was critical for them to offer products compatible with IBM's, so IBM's every move took on significance.

- *General environment.* Changes in any of the six dimensions of the general environment (identified in Chapter 3) can affect how CSFs emerge. At the beginning of 1973, virtually no chief executive in the United States would have listed "energy supply availability" as a CSF, but after the oil embargo and the emergence of OPEC, energy supply indeed became critical. Later, as new sources of oil were found and OPEC began to lose its effectiveness as a cartel, energy availability became less critical.

- *Organizational developments.* Internal developments may give rise to new CSFs. Sometimes, short-term issues must be dealt with before the firm can address long-lasting issues. Thus, internal organizational considerations become temporal criti-

Application 4.2

Critical Success Factors for the Discount Department Store Segment

In the late 1980s, Bentonville, Arkansas–based Wal-Mart stores emerged as the nation's largest retailer, surpassing both Sears and Kmart. By 1990, Wal-Mart had sales of $32.6 billion, and grew at an annual rate of 26 percent between 1988 and 1990. During the same period, the sales of its major rivals, Kmart and Sears, were substantially lower, showing annual growth rates of 9.9 and 1.2 percent, respectively. Wal-Mart's astounding growth rate accompanied an equally phenomenal net profit margin of 4.1 percent, nearly twice that of its two rivals. The performance of Wal-Mart's stock made its founder, Sam Walton, one of the richest men in the United States.

As the accompanying table indicates, Wal-Mart compared very favorably with each of its rivals on each of the industry's six critical success factors. Careful attention to every aspect of sales and administrative costs, such as office and retailing facilities as well as shrinkage (defined as the loss in retail dollars due to employee theft, customer theft, and bookkeeping errors), minimized expenses. During the first half of the 1980s, Wal-Mart's sales and administrative expenses as a percentage of sales averaged approximately 16 percent. This compared favorably to Sears and Kmart, which averaged approximately 29 percent and 23 percent, respectively. Also, Wal-Mart's shrinkage rate averaged only 1 percent of sales compared to approximately 2 percent for its rivals. By locating its retail facilities within 1 day's drive from its distribution centers, Wal-Mart replenishes its stores rapidly, allowing higher inventory turns. All of this keeps prices low, thus cultivating a reputation for value in small-town America without sales or markdowns. In contrast,

Sears suffered from its inability to project a consistent image, after it introduced its "everyday low pricing" strategy in 1989. At the time, Leonard Barry, director of the center of retailing studies at Texas A & M University, explained, "Sears is still not competitive in the mind of the consumer, and it doesn't have the prestige of upscale specialty shops. Everday low pricing is not going to get it out of the middle."

Wal-Mart developed and maintained a distinctive organization culture that helped it to achieve dominance in the industry. Employees, referred to as "associates," benefited from an innovative profit-sharing program. The founder, Sam Walton, personally visited each store once a year. Sears, on the other hand, suffered from low employee morale, resulting from frequent layoffs during the late 1980s. Wal-Mart was characterized by having a low turnover in its top management ranks, thus maintaining stability and continuity in its strategies. Wal-Mart was also more successful than its rivals were in converting significant buyer power into lower prices and more reliable supplies.

Sources

Based on information gathered from J. Huey, "Wal-Mart: Will It Take Over the World?," *Fortune* (January 30, 1989), 52–56, 58, 61; F. Schwadel, "The 'Sale' Is Fading as a Retailing Tactic," *Wall Street Journal* (March 1, 1989), B1, B6; P. Baldwin, "Wal-Mart Ranks No. 1 in '90 with $32.6 Billion in Sales," *Dallas Morning News* (February 14, 1991), 1D, 5D; R. Kahn, *Comparison of Expense Rate of Big 3 Retailers,* consultant report (with permission), November 6, 1990.

	Ratings*		
Critical Success Factor	Wal-Mart	Kmart	Sears
1. Low sales and administrative expenses	5	3	1
2. Efficient distribution systems	5	4	4
3. Reputation for value	5	3	2
4. Organization culture	4	2	1
5. Top-management turnover	5	3	4
6. Supplier relationships	4	4	3

*Author's ratings: 5 = very favorable, 1 = very unfavorable.

cal success factors. For example, if several key executives of an investment banking firm quit to form a competing "spinoff firm," rebuilding the executive group would become a first priority for the original organization.

Obviously, there is a great deal of flexibility in identifying what constitutes a CSF. This is both an advantage, because it allows a manager to tailor the general concept to a particular situation, and a disadvantage, because of its lack of specific direction. The value chain is a more directive framework that offers a useful supplement to the study of CSFs.

The Value Chain

This method for assessing strengths and weaknesses divides the business into a number of linked activities that may each produce value for the customer.[14] *Customer value* is a function of factors that usually fall into one of three broad categories: those that differentiate the product, those that lower its costs, or those that allow the organization to respond to customer needs more quickly. The value chain framework helps analyze the contributions of individual activities in a business to the overall level of customer value the firm produces, and ultimately to its financial performance. If each part of the business produces value, the firm should be able to charge more and/or incur lower costs, either of which will lead to a higher profit margin. The value chain framework appears in Exhibit 4.4.

Note that the primary activities are similar to the concept of "line functions," activities directly involved in developing, making, or marketing a particular product or service. Meanwhile, the support activities, similar to the concept of "staff functions," provide support for the firm as a whole. Although categorizing primary and support activities is appropriate for a wide range of firms, you must use judgment as you consider specific activities and particular firms. For example, operating computer systems would normally be seen as part of firm infrastructure; however, similar operations could constitute primary activities in, say, a newspaper, bank, or travel agency. Within

EXHIBIT 4.4
The Value Chain

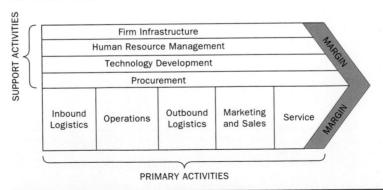

the two broad categories, primary and support, we can identify several more specific categories of activities.

Primary Activities

Primary activities include inbound logistics, operations, outbound logistics, marketing and sales, and service. You may divide these activities further for a thorough internal analysis. Exhibit 4.5 provides a summary of some important factors to consider when evaluating primary activities.

Support Activities

Human resource management, technology development, procurement, and firm infrastructure represent the four major categories of support activities in the value chain model. These provide support for primary activities, and also support each other. For example, a firm must have an effective human resource management strategy to recruit, reward, and retain the research and development (R&D) professionals necessary for technology development activities. These support activities may also be further divided for internal analysis. Exhibit 4.6 summarizes some important factors for you to consider in evaluating support activities.

Strengths and Limitations of the Value Chain Framework

The value chain framework first highlights the importance of customer value. It also provides a useful sense of direction by offering a generic checklist for firm assessment.

EXHIBIT 4.5
The Primary Activities and Factors for Assessment

INBOUND LOGISTICS	OPERATIONS	OUTBOUND LOGISTICS	MARKETING AND SALES	CUSTOMER SERVICE
■ Soundness of material and inventory control systems	■ Productivity of equipment compared to that of key competitors	■ Timeliness and efficiency of delivery of finished goods and services	■ Effectiveness of market research to identify customer segments and needs	■ Means to solicit customer input for product improvements
■ Efficiency of raw material warehousing activities	■ Appropriate automation of production processes	■ Efficiency of finished goods warehousing activities	■ Innovation in sales promotion and advertising	■ Promptness of attention to customer complaints
	■ Effectiveness of production control systems to improve quality and reduce costs		■ Evaluation of alternate distribution channels	■ Appropriateness of warranty and guarantee policies
	■ Efficiency of plant layout and work-flow design		■ Motivation and competence of sales force	■ Quality of customer education and training
			■ Development of an image of quality and a favorable reputation	■ Ability to provide replacement parts and repair services
			■ Extent of brand loyalty among customers	
			■ Extent of market dominance within the market segment or overall market	

PROFIT MARGIN

EXHIBIT 4.6
The Support Activities and Factors for Assessment

- Capability to identify new-product market opportunities and potential environmental threats
- Quality of the strategic planning system to achieve corporate objectives
- Coordination and integration of all value chain activities among organizational subunits
- Ability to obtain relatively low-cost funds for capital expenditures and working capital
- Level of information systems support in making strategic and routine decisions
- Timely and accurate management information on general and competitive environments
- Relationships with public policy makers and interest groups
- Public image and corporate citizenship   **FIRM INFRASTRUCTURE**

- Effectiveness of procedures for recruiting, training, and promoting all levels of employees
- Appropriateness of reward systems for motivating and challenging employees
- A work environment that minimizes absenteeism and keeps turnover at desirable levels
- Relations with trade unions
- Active participation by managers and technical personnel in professional organizations
- Levels of employee motivation and job satisfaction   **HUMAN RESOURCE MANAGEMENT**

- Success of research and development activities in leading to product and process innovations
- Quality of working relationships between R&D personnel and other departments
- Timeliness of technology development activities in meeting critical deadlines
- Quality of laboratories and other facilities
- Qualification and experience of laboratory technicians and scientists
- Ability of work environment to encourage creativity and innovation   **TECHNOLOGY DEVELOPMENT**

- Development of alternate sources for inputs to minimize dependence on a single supplier
- Procurement of raw materials (1) on a timely basis, (2) at lowest possible cost, (3) at acceptable levels of quality
- Procedures for procurement of plant, machinery, and buildings
- Development of criteria for lease-versus-purchase decisions
- Good, long-term relationships with reliable suppliers   **PROCUREMENT**

(PROFIT MARGIN)

Finally, it reminds us that virtually everything an organization does can be managed to improve the firm's overall ability to create value. However, the value chain does not provide a sense of how the various activities interact. As you will see in the next section, this limitation can be overcome by adopting a process/systems view of the business.

Core Processes and Systems

Although the activities within the value chain are individually important, it's their combination that carries the greatest impact on overall value for customers. Groups of activities come together to form what are known as *core processes* and *systems*.

To appreciate the importance of analyzing entire processes or systems rather than individual activities, consider a single activity from the value chain model, say, outbound logistics. Will managing this activity alone provide customers with superior overall value? Not usually. If the activities that make up the value chain are to provide the highest level of customer value, they must be managed as part of a larger business process or system.

Consider this example. The manager of outbound logistics for an institutional furniture manufacturer viewed his job as getting the furniture to the customer as soon and as cheaply as possible. This view seems very reasonable to anyone considering the outbound logistics activity in isolation from other activities or apart from overall customer value. Unfortunately for this manager, many of the organization's customers were buying for newly constructed buildings, and if the furniture arrived too early, the customers had difficulty storing it. The salespeople knew from experience that these customers did not value faster deliveries, but rather, deliveries that arrived precisely on schedule. They also knew customers would happily pay a premium if more precise delivery were available. Not until the manager of outbound logistics saw this activity as a part of the larger process (what we call order fulfillment, below) did he understand how to better manage his part of the business.

Over the last decade, managers have come to accept the need to manage value-creating activities identified in the value chain as part of larger core processes in order to maximize overall value to customers rather than maximizing individual activities within the organization. In fact, as you will discover in Chapter 6, a tremendous worldwide managerial effort is underway to "reengineer" these core processes and systems to provide customers with utmost value. As a future manager, you will operate in a world of business where managers view the overall firm as a collection of value-creating core processes. Therefore, a framework for thinking about businesses in these terms will be useful to you. The framework will probably not be a completely accurate description of any particular business, but like the generic models throughout the text, it will provide a good starting point for your thinking about virtually any business. A framework for viewing a business as a collection of core processes is presented in Exhibit 4.7.

Next, we briefly introduce you to the concept of core business processes. However, because a growing number of firms are adopting the core process perspective, we will return to this topic in greater detail in subsequent chapters. Exhibit 4.7 groups core processes into three categories: primary, support, and control, discussed below.

Primary Processes

At the most basic level, *every* business must develop a product, manage to generate demand for that product, and fulfill orders resulting from that demand. It's difficult to imagine a business that does not include these three processes, regardless of whether it produces a good or a service. In fact, from a customer's perspective, a business exists to carry out these three processes, so we will refer to them as *primary processes*. (These processes also emphasize the primary activities identified earlier as part of the value chain.)

Product Development.   For some businesses, this process involves simply identifying which already existing products to offer. For example, a plumbing supply business must decide which product lines to cover and whether or not to include parts for plumbing gases as well as liquids. But suppose you were opening a day care facility for elderly parents living with their children's dual-career families. You could probably provide services not yet invented, and your firm's product development process could benefit from considerable creativity and innovation. In other words, the product de-

EXHIBIT 4.7
A Generic Model of Core Processes and Systems

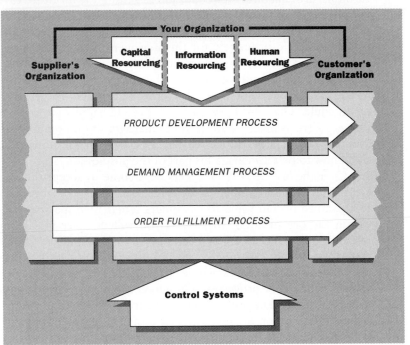

velopment includes both selecting from available products and creating new products through invention and innovation.

Demand Management.   This large process ties together much of the rest of the business.[15] It begins with understanding customers' needs (implying a relationship with the product development process described above) and ends with generating an order for a product or service (linking it to the order fulfillment process, discussed below). Demand management may involve market research, promotion, advertising, sales, packaging, and bookings. Thus, it is obviously related to, but much larger than, the traditional business function of marketing.

Order Fulfillment.   Typically, once demand management has generated an order, a complex set of activities must be coordinated to fill the order as efficiently and effectively as possible. For a manufacturing firm, this process may involve ordering supplies, assembling materials, scheduling production, carrying out production, storing the finished product, shipping the finished product, installing the finished product, and/or servicing already installed products. For a service firm, the process of fulfilling an order will obviously be different, but may not be any simpler. In fact, it may be made more complex by the need to vary services to meet individual needs. Imagine the complex process entailed in delivering such a service as, say, a bank loan; it involves many steps that cut across a variety of functions and/or departments.

Support Systems

In addition to the three primary processes, *every* business must also maintain systems to manage the resources required so that the primary processes can function. These resources include capital, human, and information resources. The *support systems* that manage these resources generally do not serve external customers directly; rather they exist to support the primary processes, as do the support activities identified in the value chain. So, to distinguish between primary processes and support systems, think of primary processes as focused on serving the firm's *external customers* (those who use the final product or service offered by the firm) and think of the support systems as focused on serving *internal customers* (users of the support systems from within the organization). Because the allocation of resources is critical in determining what gets done, the way support systems are managed and resources allocated has a tremendous influence on what strategies the organization can successfully implement. We briefly describe the three support processes here, and then return to them in Chapter 11 to consider in detail their role in strategy implementation.

Capital Resourcing.   This support system entails all the steps involved in obtaining and distributing funds throughout an organization. Funds are primarily obtained as debt (from lenders), as equity (from stockholders), or as retained earnings (from the profits of earlier operations). Funds are usually distributed to reduce liabilities, provide owners with dividends, or pay expenses associated with ongoing operation of the business. Capital-resourcing systems also provide analysis required to determine the most cost-effective means of providing the organization with funds and to allocate available resources effectively.

Human Resourcing.   This system provides the organization with the people and the human capabilities it needs to operate efficiently and productively. It recruits, selects, trains, educates, evaluates, rewards, and promotes individuals. The cliché "people are our most important asset" is quite true here, and the management of this system is often the key to building an organization that is capable of superior competition.

Information Resourcing.   All core processes require information.[16] In fact, we could treat information resourcing as a part of each of the individual processes already identified. However, the information required by one process is often either the same or related to that required by another, so the information-resourcing process is usually coordinated across the entire business.

Control Systems

Finally, every organization has some system of control, either explicit and rigid or implicit and loose. Generally speaking, control systems look at how supporting resources are allocated and used across primary processes. Traditionally, financial budgeting has dominated most organizations' control systems. However, many firms now recognize that this view is too narrow. These firms include a wide variety of behavioral, cultural, and other "soft" elements alongside budgeting as part of a broader-based control system. For instance, as we discussed in Chapter 1, part of EVA's power lies in its ability to provide a new managerial mindset that complements formal managerial systems.

Although it is becoming more common for managers to think of their businesses in terms of core processes and systems, no one has yet developed a standard language for identifying them. For instance, there may be no "demand management" departments, and the business diagram depicted earlier in Exhibit 4.7 certainly should not be considered an organization chart. Instead, this framework offers us a means to conceptualize how activities from across the organization can be managed to provide greater value for customers. As you assess a particular business, rather than focusing on its various activities in isolation from one another, consider how they interact with one another to provide customers with value overall.

Combining the Three Frameworks

As explained earlier, you should develop "fluency" with the critical success factors, value chain, and core process frameworks and be able to mix and match them to suit your particular needs. Each framework has limitations that are best offset by using them in combination. For instance, your understanding of the nature of competition and the expectations of customers in a given industry may allow you to identify the most likely CSFs for a firm in that industry. Using them as a guide, you can begin to hone in on specific activities within the value chain that need special attention. However, to get the most out of these efforts, you must be careful to view and manage them as parts of a broader value-producing core process.

Moving back and forth across these three frameworks will help you identify *what* characteristics to assess, but we still have not addressed the issue of *how* to assess them. We turn to that subject now.

METHODS FOR ASSESSING INTERNAL STRENGTHS AND WEAKNESSES

In this section, we explain how your internal assessment should seek to balance various perspectives, and how it should draw on both quantitative and qualitative analysis.

The Balanced Scorecard

The best internal analysis does not focus on a narrow set of criteria, but instead offers a well-rounded evaluation that views the firm from different complementary perspectives. Although managers can use them individually, these perspectives provide better insights for strategy formulation in combination. Such a broad-based approach has been called the *balanced scorecard* because it does not allow any one perspective to outweigh others in assessing a firm's strengths and weaknesses.[17] To understand the need for the multiple perspectives in the balanced scorecard, refer to Exhibit 4.8 as you consider the following.

Recall from Chapter 1 that we are treating the creation of wealth as the most fundamental goal of strategic management. However, reaching this end requires that we manage through a variety of means. This idea is reflected in the balanced scorecard. The most obvious place to begin assessing a for-profit firm is to consider its financial

EXHIBIT 4.8
The Four Perspectives of the Balanced Scorecard

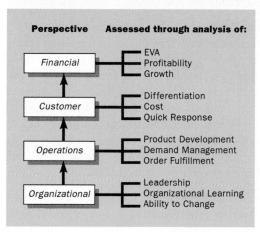

performance. However, most forward-thinking managers and members of the financial community understand that providing superior returns for stockholders usually depends on a firm's sustaining a competitive advantage based on providing superior value for customers.[18] Similarly, providing superior value for customers requires development of operations with necessary capabilities. Finally, developing the required operational capabilities requires an organization of employees with the needed creativity,[19] diversity,[20] skills,[21] and motivations.[22] This implies that performance as assessed in one perspective supports performance in other areas, as depicted by the upward arrows in the exhibit, and that we need to consider all four perspectives in carrying out a complete internal analysis:[23]

1. *The financial perspective.* Does the firm generate financial returns in excess of the total cost of capital, as suggested by the economic value added (EVA) model? We discuss the need for EVA later in this chapter, but, short of a full-blown EVA analysis, what does an assessment of the firm's growth and its profitability suggest about its financial performance? How much financial risk has the firm taken on as a result of its liabilities and debt?

2. *The customer's perspective.* Does the firm provide the customer with superior value in terms of product differentiation, low cost, or quick response? As discussed in Chapter 1, evidence and experience suggest that sustained financial performance ultimately depends on superior performance from the customer's perspective in providing one or more of these forms of customer value.

3. *The operations perspective.* How effectively and efficiently do the core processes that produce customer value perform? Which are the most important sources of customer value? Which need improving to produce greater customer value? How should they be changed?

4. *The organizational perspective.* Can this organization adapt to changes in its environment? Is its workforce committed to shared goals? Does the organization

learn from past mistakes? When it encounters a problem, does it go to work on root causes, or does it only address the superficial symptoms?

These four perspectives are clearly interrelated, as shown in Exhibit 4.8. The structure of the balanced-scorecard framework represents a series of cause-effect relationships in which success measured from one perspective contributes to success as measured from the other perspectives. Although it may be natural to begin with financial analysis, to really grasp a firm's strengths and weaknesses, managers must go further and analyze factors that contribute to the firm's financial performance. This requires moving beyond the financial perspective, and digging deeper into the information available from the other perspectives.

The balanced-scorecard approach to business analysis complements and integrates several of the topics covered so far in this text:

- *Overlaps with text's organizing themes.* If you compare Exhibits 4.8 and 1.6, you will notice substantial overlap between the two. The financial perspective obviously aims at assessing financial performance. Competitive advantage is best assessed from the customer's perspective. Similarly, process execution entails analysis from the operations perspective, and assessing organizational capacity requires adoption of the organizational perspective. In other words, the balanced scorecard is the framework whereby we can assess many of the elements in the organizing themes for the strategic management process advocated in this book.

- *Recognizes stakeholders.* The balanced scorecard is very compatible with a stakeholder perspective. The financial, customer, and organizational perspectives each correspond to critical stakeholder groups: owners, customers, and employees.

- *Reflects a hierarchy of strategic intent.* The balanced scorecard reflects the idea of a hierarchy of intent with elements linked in a series of means-ends relationships. As Exhibit 4.8 illustrates, features assessed in the lower perspectives provide the means for achieving the ends assessed in the higher perspectives.

- *Stresses competitive advantage.* Through the customer perspective, the balanced scorecard explicitly cites competitive advantage as the key to good strategy and the source of superior financial returns.

- *Exhibits versatility.* The balanced scorecard works well in conjunction with various other frameworks, such as critical success factors, the value chain, or core processes. As an example, the balanced scorecard is used in conjunction with the CSF framework in Application 4.3.

As the name suggests, measurement is a central theme for the balanced scorecard. The underlying concept is that properly "keeping score" requires the adoption of numerous perspectives to better understand the firm's varied strengths and weaknesses. As you consider the idea, you will quickly see that it is much easier to keep score on some dimensions than on others. Some lend themselves to assessment using widely accepted quantitative measures. For instance, from within the financial perspective, few would argue that the annual percentage change in earnings is a useful measure for assessing growth. However, we are usually foggier about how to quantitatively measure some of the concepts from within the other perspectives. For instance, how does

Application 4.3

Assessing Strengths and Weaknesses at WMX Technologies

WMX is the world's largest environment services firm, with operations in twenty-one countries and annual revenues in excess of $10 billion. Below, we have identified four critical success factors for a firm such as WMX and provide a brief assessment from the corresponding balanced-scorecard perspective of where the firm stands on each factor.

CSF1.   Raising capital through the stock market. *Assessment from the financial perspective*

Waste treatment is a capital-intensive business; garbage truck fleets, landfills, waste treatment plants, and incinerators are expensive to acquire or build. To feed its hearty appetite for cash, WMX has adopted a unique corporate structure designed to give it the greatest flexibility possible in selling stock to raise more cash. Each of the company's five divisions is a publicly traded corporation, even though WMX owns a controlling interest in each. In this way the corporation controls six corporations' stocks and can issue more of whatever stock is trading at the most attractive prices whenever it needs additional funds: an important strength smaller competitors do not enjoy.

CSF2.   Providing a full line of services that cover customers' entire set of environmental waste problems. *Assessment from the customer perspective*

Most of WMX's customers see waste disposal as a big headache, and they look for simple solutions to a potentially very complex problem. The fewer firms they have to work with to solve their waste problems, the better. For example, Hoechst Celanese recently needed help to redesign its processes in seven specialty chemical plants to make them more "environmentally friendly." WMX was able to put together a total package of technology, engineering, and construction capability that was more comprehensive than anything its competitors could assemble. As a result, WMX was able to win the Hoechst Celanese contract, the largest environment-focused project that had

ever been awarded by the chemical processing industry at that time.

CSF3.   Acquiring suitable landfill sites. *Assessment from the operations perspective*

For the past 20 years, WMX has been following a "land-banking" strategy. The firm bought superior sites for landfills before it needed them, believing that as land became more expensive and regulations became tougher, prices for suitable landfill sites would skyrocket. They have, and now competitors are paying five to ten times what WMX paid, even for geologically inferior sites. In fact, experts predict that regulations will eventually force three of four landfill sites to close, although the demand for landfill space continues to grow. Such events could make the WMX landfill operation the strongest in the industry.

CSF4.   Regulatory compliance. *Assessment from the organizational perspective*

Companies such as WMX exist largely because of environmental regulations, and any failure to comply with them represents a serious weakness. Unfortunately, WMX has had some problems in this area. The corporation was formed in large part by buying up smaller waste management operators. Many of these managers were retained in the company's decentralized organization structure. In several cases, local operators failed to comply with environmental regulations and their actions resulted in WMX's receiving more than its share of citations for pollution and price fixing. In order to address this weakness, the company needs to build stronger organizational control systems to better monitor the actions of individuals throughout its vast empire.

Sources
Based on information gathered from Subrata N. Chakravarty, "Dean Buntrock's Green Machine," *Forbes* (August 2, 1993), 96–100; Richard C. Morais, "A Jagged Line, But the Direction Is Up," *Forbes, 154* (October 24, 1994), 54–58.

one measure commitment to shared goals, a critical dimension under the organizational capabilities perspective? It should be clear from reviewing Exhibit 4.8 that some of the elements identified by the balanced scorecard lend themselves to quantitative measurement while others require a qualitative assessment.

Below, we will consider both quantitative analysis and qualitative analysis. In our experience, students generally find qualitative analysis much more intuitive, so we devote more time to quantitative analysis. This should not be taken as an indication that quantitative analysis is more important—remember, the premise of the balanced-scorecard approach is that managers should adopt a balance of both types of assessment.

Quantitative Analysis

Any strategic analysis depends on thorough appreciation of "the numbers." When managers speak of "running the numbers," they are usually referring to two types of quantitative analysis. One type is based on financial data and the other on nonfinancial data. Financial data analysis is clearly important in assessing a firm from the balanced scorecard's financial perspective. In fact, analysis of financial data is the most basic and universally accepted approach to assessing a firm. However, such analysis has its limits and it is best viewed as only the beginning for a thorough internal analysis. As you will see in the following section, managers have found it useful to go well beyond traditional financial analysis in order to fully quantify their firm's strengths and weaknesses.

Financial Quantitative Analysis

As discussed in Chapter 1, most for-profit businesses consider their owners to be one of the most important stakeholder groups, and they assume that owners of a for-profit business own it for the profit it offers! So, although financial analysis alone can never constitute a complete internal analysis, financial concerns must receive considerable attention in any complete analysis. Exhibit 4.9 shows some of the dimensions that go into a complete financial analysis.

EXHIBIT 4.9
Thoroughly Evaluating a Firm's Financial Position

- Economic value added
- Profitability ratios
- Liquidity ratios
- Leverage ratios
- Activity ratios
- Cost of capital
- Ability to raise additional capital
- Relationships with creditors and stockholders
- Dividend policy
- Match between sources and uses of funds

You may note the emphasis placed on financial ratios. Ratios are simply a way of looking at one number in relation to another number. The traditional mainstay of financial analysis has been the study of financial ratios, called *ratio analysis*. Ratio analysis is so basic to good strategic analysis that we have included an appendix devoted to the subject at the end of this chapter, although most students have covered the topic in previous accounting classes. Four types of financial ratios appear in such analyses:

- *Profitability ratios* provide information regarding a firm's overall economic performance.

- *Liquidity ratios* measure a firm's capacity to meet its short-term financial obligations.

- *Leverage ratios* indicate a firm's financial risk, that is, the relative proportion of its debt to its equity.

- *Activity ratios* reflect a firm's efficient or inefficient use of its resources.

The first three ratios are most useful in assessing the financial performance component of the balanced scorecard. These measures allow you to assess the financial returns (i.e., profitability) of a firm, given the risk associated with its financial liabilities or debt (i.e., liquidity and leverage). The fourth type, activity ratios, is more applicable in assessment from the operations perspective. For instance, inventory turns, an activity ratio that measures the efficient use of inventories, are used for assessing part of the order fulfillment process.

Financial ratios have been widely used since before the turn of the century, and they will undoubtedly remain an important part of business evaluation. However, there are caveats and limitations to using traditional financial accounting. The most important caveat: financial ratios must be viewed within the context of a particular strategy. For example, an escalating debt/equity ratio may be a cause for concern or it may be a reflection of a strategic move to take advantage of an opportunity to quickly expand the business. You will need to consider the strategy a company is pursuing before judging what constitutes a good or bad ratio.

Nonfinancial Quantitative Analysis

One strength of financially based measures is that they reduce everything to a common unit of measure, for example, some currency such as the dollar, the mark, or the pound. But, of course, not every issue of interest to strategists is best measured in financial terms. For instance, financial data are ill-suited to providing strategic insights into important sources of competitive advantage such as product differentiation or quick response. Many factors addressed from the operations perspective are also best quantified using nonfinancial measures, such as development times for new products and advertising recall rates. Finally, it is very difficult to develop financially based measures of most issues assessed from the organizational perspective. To the extent that quantitative data can be used here at all, we are dependent on nonfinancial measures such as absentee rates, employee turnover, and technical literacy rates. Exhibit

EXHIBIT 4.10
Examples of Nonfinancial Quantitative Measures

- ✔ Number of patents
- ✔ Development times for new products
- ✔ Employee turnover
- ✔ Accidents per 100,000 man-hours
- ✔ Customer complaints per week
- ✔ Total cycle time from order to deliveries
- ✔ Market rank
- ✔ Scores on quality assessments
- ✔ Advertising recall rates
- ✔ Absenteeism rates
- ✔ Number of repeat customers
- ✔ Number of regulatory citations
- ✔ Number of new products
- ✔ Customer satisfaction ratings and rankings
- ✔ Capture rate for bidded jobs
- ✔ Number of union grievances
- ✔ Number of retail outlets
- ✔ Number of SKUs (stockkeeping units) inventoried

4.10 provides other examples of nonfinancial quantitative data in what is an illustrative, rather than an exhaustive, list.

Note the variety of scales implied by this list. For example, some items are scaled in units of time (such as product repair turnaround times), others in physical counts (such as number of new distributors added), and others as opinions (such as customer satisfaction ratings). Clearly, "the numbers" entail much more than financial accounting, and managers should develop and track the measures that are most meaningful to the particular strategic issues they face.

Qualitative Analysis

Although quantitative analysis is obviously an important part of strategic analysis, you should not allow it to dominate your assessment of a firm. Many of the most important types of organizational strengths and weaknesses do not lend themselves to quantitative measurement. For example, qualitative information is often the only way to assess such things as employee morale and commitment, the organization's ability to learn from past mistakes, the extent to which different parts of the organization share a common vision and work together as a team, and the use of creativity in overcoming obstacles.

Characteristics such as these are the fundamental underpinnings of an organization's overall strengths and weaknesses. Qualitative information is also an important supplement to quantitative data in understanding basic concepts of what customers value and how they feel about a given product. Finally, assessments of a firm's image and public acceptance depend on qualitative information. In fact, it has been estimated that 80 percent of the information the typical firm needs to make decisions is qualitative, with only 20 percent of the required information residing in "the numbers."[24] Application 4.4 describes how Motorola's decision to invest up to $600 million annually to improve its workforce's capabilities is based largely on qualitative assessment.

Although much of an overall assessment of strengths and weaknesses requires emphasis on qualitative or so-called "soft" data, this "soft" label does not mean such analysis should be any less rigorous or thorough than other forms of organizational assessment. In fact, given the fundamental importance of the "soft" issues, we must be as rigorous and as thorough as possible in analyzing and assessing them.[25] Fortunately, most students find consideration of these factors much more intuitive than

---

Application 4.4

Qualitative Analysis Drives a Major Investment Decision at Motorola

Motorola is widely recognized as one of the best-managed companies in the United States. The firm is dominant in its paging and cellular telephone equipment markets, and its chip business faces demand that regularly threatens to outstrip its production capacity. Much of the firm's success has been attributed to its habit of "doing things by the numbers." The company was the first large corporation to win the Malcolm Baldrige National Quality Award, in large part because of its emphasis on "metrics." In fact, Motorola even named its quality program "Six Sigma" to reflect the measure of defects the company sought to achieve in its operations. (Six Sigma is a statistical term that implies only one defect per million units produced.) It sometimes seems to outsiders that the only things that matter to Motorola managers are the quantitative factors that can be measured and managed "by the numbers."

Recently, the company has decided to spend an estimated $600 million annually by the year 2000 on training and educating its workforce better. This is not only more than Motorola has historically spent; it is far beyond that invested in training by *any* other firm. But perhaps what is most surprising about this decision, for those who know Motorola's "by the numbers" culture, is the fact that the decision to make this gargantuan investment is based almost entirely on "soft" analysis. Granted, a study was done several years ago to try to quantify the value of training and development, but the difficulty of doing so quickly became obvious, and the $600 million decision was not based on the quantitative study. Instead, it was based on the observation and experiences of key managers and reflects a qualitative understanding of how the business works. Gary Langely, manager of human effectiveness for Motorola, explains, "We take it on faith and strong belief that it is improving our bottom line." Gary Tooker, the firm's CEO, explains his support for the investment by arguing, "If knowledge is becoming antiquated at a faster rate, we have no choice but to spend on education. How can that not be a competitive weapon?"

While Motorola's managers may be driven by the numbers, they clearly understand that not everything important to a business is easily quantified, and they are willing to go beyond quantitative analysis when the situation warrants.

Sources
Based on information gathered from Kevin Kelly and Peter Burrows, "Motorola: Training for the Millennium," *Business Week* (March 28, 1994), 158–163; Joseph F. Miraglia, "An Evolutionary Approach to Revolutionary Change," *Human Resource Planning*, 17:2(1994), 1–24.

EXHIBIT 4.11
Important Factors That Lend Themselves to Qualitative Assessment

✔ **CULTURE AND LEADERSHIP**
- The sense of identity and affiliation the firm provides to organizational members
- Consistency of the cultures of subunits with each other and with the overall corporate culture
- Ability of the culture to foster innovation, creativity, and openness to new ideas
- Capacity to adapt and evolve, consistent with the demands of changes in environment and strategy
- Executive, managerial, and employee motivation (based on both monetary and nonmonetary rewards)

✔ **STRENGTH IN THE MARKET**
- The firm's advertising effectiveness
- The product image and perceived quality
- Brand awareness and the strength of the brand name
- Consumer acceptance and trust of innovations from the company

✔ **LEGITIMACY, REPUTATION, AND IMAGE**
- Effectiveness in coping with restrictive regulations (e.g., environmental, antitrust, product liability)
- Relationship with consumer activist groups
- Relationship with the media
- Relationship with policymakers and government officials
- Ability to obtain government grants and funding
- Extent of trade-tariff protection
- Relationship with public interest groups

quantitative analysis. Therefore, we have provided Exhibit 4.11 as a checklist you can use as a starting point to assess a broad range of important qualitative factors.

Any assessment of strengths and weaknesses is meaningless without an appropriate standard for comparison. This fundamental statement applies to both quantitative and qualitative assessments, regardless of whether you are analyzing critical success factors, elements of the value chain, or the core processes, and regardless of what perspective from the balanced scorecard you are using. Therefore, in the following section, we consider the pros and cons of three common comparison standards for internal analysis.

IDENTIFYING APPROPRIATE COMPARISON STANDARDS

Three broad categories of comparison standards prove useful for internal analysis: industry norms, historical performance, and benchmarks. A thorough internal analysis combines all three.

Industry Norms

When managers look for comparison standards, an obvious choice is the norm for their industry. Data on industry norms are widely available and the appendix to this chapter provides several sources of published industry norms. Using such sources to compare your firm against others in its industry serves as a useful "reality check." Suppose your goal is to gain significant market share in a consumer goods company, but you learn that your marketing budget is significantly less than the normal for your industry. Knowing this, you must ask if your campaign is significantly more efficient than your competitors'. If not, is there some other reason you will gain share? If the answer is no, your goal is perhaps unrealistic.

Although they do offer such reality checks, industry norms do not substitute for good judgment and should not be used blindly to establish your firm's behavior, because of the following logical fallacies:

- *Getting stuck in the middle.* Suppose half your competitors excel at cost-related factors and the other half excel at differentiating their premium-priced goods. If you set the average of these competitors as your target, you are likely to be second rate in terms of both cost and differentiation. Customers that value low price will choose one set of your competitors, those who want premium goods will choose the other, and you will be stuck in the middle, excelling at nothing and attracting neither group.[26]

- *Comparing apples to oranges.* Even within the same industry, the strategies pursued and the firms' attributes supporting those strategies vary considerably. In our coverage of external analysis, we stressed focus on the right strategic group in order to complete a meaningful strategic analysis. Because published data are usually industrywide and are seldom organized by strategic groups, you must be careful in using them for comparisons. For example, if your small telecommunications firm supplies a small, highly specialized niche, such as sealed telephone equipment for coal miners and underwater salvage workers, how meaningful are data available on the gigantic general-purpose telephone manufacturing industry?

- *Comparing apples to fruit punch.* Virtually all firms with sales above several million dollars a year are diversified. That is, they have more than one product or service and/or they compete in more than one market. Any data you have on such firms are likely to be simple averages (or possibly weighted averages) of the various businesses they operate. If your firm is not diversified in the same way, how meaningful are these comparisons? A single *Fortune* 500 corporation may consist of dozens, if not hundreds, of different business units. If data on all these businesses are blended, like a fruit punch, meaningful comparisons with such corporations are very difficult.

- *Aiming at mediocrity.* Even if all these other problems can be overcome, you must still question the wisdom of using industry norms as a target. Remember, a norm is an average, and most firms are interested in finding ways to beat industry norms; and they use comparisons to tell them *if* they are doing so, not *how* to do so. To overcome these limitations, managers usually supplement industry norm comparisons with analysis based on their own firm's historical performance.

Historical Performance

One of the best standards of comparison may be your firm's own past performance. A basic tenet of the quality movement is continuous improvement. Whatever you were capable of doing before, try to beat it in the future. Although much can be said for continuous improvement, basing analysis on comparisons to historical performance has obvious limits.

- *More of a bad thing.* Suppose your firm depends on inspection to catch manufacturing errors and the quality inspection function seeks to improve over time by increasing the number of errors caught. This would be a seemingly logical place to make assessments based on historical comparisons, but doing so may lead managers to focus on the wrong type of improvement. Catching more errors is nice, but perhaps an even better improvement would be to reduce the number of errors made in the first place.

- *The illusion of big progress.* Historical trends can be misleading if they entail changes made on a very small base. For example, a sales manager was under pressure to open up new customer accounts, and implemented a program of increased "cold calling" to achieve the targeted growth rate. In the past, salespeople maximized their sales commission by calling on new customers only when they had thoroughly "worked" existing accounts, and the typical salesperson only called on about three new customers per month. As a result of the new program, each salesperson made about one more cold call per month. Annual reviews showed 33 percent more cold calls than before, which sounded impressive. But, actually, the meager four cold calls a month had only minimal impact in helping the organization reach its targeted growth rate.

- *Improving, but not as fast as the competition.* Because customers compare competitors, it is not enough for a company to improve its historical performance. For example, at one point, Xerox Corporation's internal analysis showed productivity growth of 8 percent, and this accomplishment was the source of some pride because it was considerably better than that of the U.S. economy as a whole. However, it was well below the rate of productivity gains being made by the Japanese copier companies that were becoming Xerox's primary competitors. The gap between Xerox and its competition meant that it was not improving rapidly enough to remain competitive, and the company lost its market leadership position to more efficient rivals.

While historical comparisons with past performance are an important form of assessment, the Xerox example illustrates that historical comparisons alone are not enough. *Benchmarking* is a managerial process designed to compensate for the limitations of historical comparisons.

Benchmarks

Through benchmarking, managers seek out the best examples of a particular practice in other companies as part of an effort to improve the corresponding practice in their own firm.[27] Sometimes the search for best practices is limited to competitors, a process called *competitive benchmarking*. Other times, managers may seek out the best practices regardless of what industry they are in, called *functional benchmarking*. Industry-specific standards (such as response times required to repair power outages in the electric utility industry) are best handled through competitive benchmarking, but more generic processes (such as answering 1-800 calls) lend themselves to functional benchmarking because the function is much the same in any industry.

Benchmarking provides the motivation and the means many firms need to seriously rethink how their organizations perform certain tasks. Many resulting advances have been significant enough to receive considerable coverage in the press. As a result, despite its recent development, benchmarking is already widely used. However, the original concept of benchmarking was to study a practice that is the best of its kind. With such rapid adoption, some firms are studying only *good* quality rather than the *best*, and, consequently, some of the power of this process has been lost. Also, benchmarking is often an expensive, time-consuming activity, and unless it results in significant breakthroughs in performance, it may not be worth the investment required.

Combining Different Comparison Standards

Given that industry norms, historical performance, and benchmarking have limitations, it makes sense to use them in combination, allowing the strengths of one standard to offset the weaknesses of another. For example, a firm could study industry norms to assess where it stands on an overall performance dimension, say, its cost of goods sold as a percent of sales. Then it could benchmark the firms that are best at controlling each of its three largest cost categories, say, labor costs, materials costs, and research and development. Based on the results of the benchmarking studies, it could implement major new programs and track improvements in these programs over time using historical comparisons. A thorough internal analysis of a firm's strengths and weaknesses will utilize all three types of comparison standards. Each has its place, and the challenge facing managers is to mix and match to provide the most meaningful internal analysis as a key step in the overall strategic management process.

Summary of Managerial Practices to Adopt from This Chapter

- Understand a firm's internal strengths and weaknesses before attempting to formulate strategies.

- Make sure the strategy you develop reflects this understanding by using insights gained from your assessment of the firm's internal strengths and weaknesses to shape your strategies.

- Recognize that internal resources take three related forms: (1) assets that, when combined with (2) capabilities, result in (3) competencies.

- Use the tests that have been developed as part of the resource-based view of competition to assess the ability of internal resources to yield competitive advantages.

- Identify the critical success factors for your firm and make sure to emphasize them in assessing the firm's strengths and weaknesses and also in formulating strategy.

- Use the value chain framework to help identify the contributions various activities make to the firm's profit margins, and let this information guide your internal assessment.

- Identify the firm's core business processes and carefully assess how well they provide value for both external and internal customers by integrating the contributions of various pieces of the value chain.

- Use a balanced-scorecard approach to evaluating the firm's strengths and weaknesses. You may begin with the financial perspective, but do not stop there. Use the customer, operations, and organizational perspectives to understand the factors that underpin financial performance. Your best chance for influencing financial performance is through factors that only become apparent by adopting these other perspectives.

- Use ratio analysis to assess the financial health of the business in terms of its liquidity, leverage, operating efficiency, and profitability.

- Don't limit your use of quantitative analysis to financial matters. A well-rounded analysis inevitably draws from nonfinancial matters, and these may lend themselves to quantitative analysis, too.

- Incorporate qualitative analysis to cover the important aspects of business that are not easily quantified.

- In making comparisons, mix and match different standards (industry norms, historical data, and benchmarks) to suit your purposes and to overcome the limitations inherent in each.

Questions for Discussion and Review

1. Describe the three major types of resources critical to the resource-based view of the firm.

2. What are the tests that can be used to assess the competitive value of a resource?

3. What are the differences and similarities among the frameworks depicting critical success factors, the value chain, and core processes and systems?

4. What are the four perspectives that comprise the balanced scorecard? Give examples of how each perspective might be assessed using both quantitative and qualitative information.

5. Why is it important to assess a firm's strengths and weaknesses in relative terms? What are the factors a manager should consider to find a comparison standard that is useful in making assessments in relative terms?

Notes

1. Our position is that understanding a firm's competitive advantage (or lack thereof) requires analysis of both. See George S. Day and Robin Wensley, "Assessing Advantage: A

Framework for Diagnosing Competitive Superiority," *Journal of Marketing* (April 1988), 1–20.

2. Richard P. Rumelt, "How Much Does Industry Matter?" *Strategic Management Journal, 12* (March 1991), 167–185.

3. William K. Hall, "Survival Strategies in a Hostile Environment," *Harvard Business Review* (September–October 1980), 75–85.

4. Stephanie Anderson Forest, "Who's Afraid of J&J and 3M?" *Business Week* (December 5, 1994), 66–68.

5. For empirical research on the relationship between the external environment and the use of internal resources for successful competition, see Danny Miller and Jamal Shamsie, "A Contingent Application of the Resource-Based View of the Firm: The Hollywood Film Studios from 1936–1965," *Academy of Management Journal* (Best Papers Proceedings, 1995), 57–61.

6. Matthew J. Kiernan, "The New Strategic Architecture: Learning to Compete in the Twenty-first Century," *Academy of Management Executive,* 7: 1(1993), 7–21.

7. Stan Davis and Jim Botkin, "The Coming of Knowledge-Based Business," *Harvard Business Review, 72:* 5(September–October) 1994), 165–170; Laurence Prusak, "The Knowledge Advantage," *Strategy and Leadership, 24:* 2(March–April 1996), 6–8.

8. Presentations of this theory can be found in J. Barney, "Firm Resources and Sustained Competitive Advantage," *Journal of Management, 17* (1991), 99–20; M. A. Peteraf, "The Cornerstone of Competitive Advantage: A Resource-Based View," *Strategic Management Journal, 14* (1993), 179–191; R. M. Grant, "The Resource-Based Theory of Competitive Advantage: Implications for Strategy Formulation," *California Management Review* (Spring 1991), 119–145; B. Wernerfelt, "A Resource-Based View of the Firm," *Strategic Management Journal, 5* (1984), 171–180; and Kathleen R. Conner, "A Historical Comparison of Resource-Based Theory and Five Schools of Thought Within Industrial Organization Economics: Do We Have a New Theory of the Firm?" *Journal of Management* (March 1991), 121.

9. These sections draw heavily from David J. Collins and Cynthia A. Montgomery, "Competing on Resources: Strategy in the 1990s," *Harvard Business Review, 73:* 4(July–August 1995), 118–128.

10. Ron Ashkenas, "Capability: Strategic Tool for a Competitive Edge," *Journal of Business Strategy, 16* (November–December 1995), 13–15.

11. Philip Selznick, *TVA and the Grass Roots: A Study in the Sociology of Formal Organization,* Berkeley: University of California Press, 1949.

12. James C. Collins and Jerry I. Porras, *Built to Last: Successful Habits of Visionary Companies,* New York: Harper Business, 1994.

13. J. F. Rockart, "Chief Executives Define Their Own Data Needs," *Harvard Business Review,* 57: 2(1979), 81–93.

14. This section draws heavily from Michael E. Porter, *Competitive Advantage: Creating and Sustaining Superior Performance,* New York: The Free Press, 1985, chap. 2. For a useful extension of Porter's original concepts, seen Jeffrey F. Rayport and John J. Sviokla, "Exploiting the Virtual Value Chain," *Harvard Business Review, 73:* 6 (November–December 1995), 75–85.

15. A description of this and other core processes is given in Michael E. McGrath and Richard W. Hoole, "Manufacturing's New Economies of Scale," *Harvard Business Review* (May–June 1992), 94–102.

16. Why information is important in each stage of the value chain is discussed in Michael E. Porter and Victor E. Millar, "How Information Gives You Competitive Advantage," *Harvard Business Review*, *63*: 4(1985), 149–160. Although information processing is not an explicit part of the value chain model, we have chosen to make it explicit in our model of core processes.

17. Robert S. Kaplan and David P. Norton, "The Balanced Scorecard—Measures That Drive Performance," *Harvard Business Review* (January–February 1992), 166; Robert S. Kaplan and David P. Norton, "Putting the Balanced Scorecard to Work," *Harvard Business Review* (September–October 1993), 205; Robert S. Kaplan and David P. Norton, "Using the Balanced Scorecard as a Strategic Management System," *Harvard Business Review*, *74* (January–February 1996), 75–85; and Robert S. Kaplan, "Designing a Balanced Scorecard Matched to Business Strategy," *Planning Review*, *22* (September–October 1994), 15–19.

18. William Copulsky, "Balancing the Needs of Customers and Shareholders," *Journal of Business Strategy* (November–December 1991), 44–47.

19. Gary Hamel and C. K. Prahalad, "Corporate Imagination and Expeditionary Marketing," *Harvard Business Review* (July–August 1991), 184.

20. Taylor H. Cox and Stacy Blake, "Managing Cultural Diversity: Implications for Organizational Competitiveness," *Academy of Management Executive*, *5*: 3(1991), 45.

21. Jeremy A. Klein, Gordon M. Edge, and Tom Kass, "Skill-Based Competition," *Journal of General Management*, *16* (Summer 1991), 1–15.

22. Dave Ulrich and Dale Lake, "Organizational Capability: Creating Competitive Advantage," *Academy of Management Executive*, *5* (February 1991), 77–92.

23. Because each lower scorecard section measures organizational attributes critical to success on the scorecard sections above it, it might be more appropriate to refer to this as a *hierarchical* scorecard. However, we have chosen to keep the original "balanced" scorecard label to avoid confusion and to stress the need to assess both means *and* ends.

24. Gary B. Roush, "A Program for Sharing Corporate Intelligence," *Journal of Business Strategy* (January–February 1991), 4–7.

25. A useful framework for assessing qualitative organizational "vital signs" is provided in P. Lorange and R. T. Nelson, "How to Recognize—and Avoid—Organizational Decline," *Sloan Management Review* (Spring 1987), 41–48.

26. See Michael Porter, *Competitive Strategy*, New York: The Free Press, 1980.

27. A. Steven Walleck and Charles A. Leader, "Benchmarking World-Class Performance," *McKinsey Quarterly*, *1* (1991), 3–23.

Appendix to Chapter 4
Understanding and Analyzing Financial Statements*

Introduction

Evaluating a company involves a multitude of judgmental factors, such as quality of management, the extent of new product development, and marketing acumen. No evaluation can be complete, however, without a thorough financial analysis.

---

*Adapted from D. M. Cordell and D. T. Crary, *Understanding and Analyzing Financial Statements*, published manuscript (with permission).

In what follows we briefly explain some of the basic tools of financial analysis. We begin by describing the major financial statements: the balance sheet, the income statement, and the statement of retained earnings. We show how various items from these statements can be utilized in ratio analysis to further our understanding of the firm's financial situation.

Balance Sheet

Financial analysis of a company begins with a review of its current financial condition. A balance sheet, which is also called a statement of condition or a statement of financial position, provides a snapshot of the firm's financial situation on a particular date.

The balance sheet in Exhibit 4.12 contains three major sections: (1) assets—everything the company owns (even if purchased by credit) or owed to the company; (2) liabilities (debt)—everything the company owes; and (3) stockholders' equity—the difference between the company's assets and its liabilities. The basic accounting identity can be expressed as

$$\text{Assets} = \text{liabilities} + \text{stockholders' equity}$$

This equation must always hold; any change in the total of one side must equal the change in the total of the other side.

As an example, consider a company that wants to purchase a $100 machine (a fixed asset). It may purchase the machine with $100 in cash (another asset), leaving the asset total unchanged. However, it may instead ask the seller to send a bill for the machine. In this case cash does not leave the firm immediately, and the asset total increases by $100. However, the bill from the seller represents a liability, causing the right-hand side of the equation to go up by an equal amount. A more complex example might show the owners of the company infusing $100 cash into the company for purchase of the machine. In this case stockholders' equity is increased concurrently with the cash account; both sides of the equation increase equivalently. Subsequently, the cash account is drawn down for purchase of the machine, changing both the cash and fixed asset accounts but leaving the asset total unchanged.

Income Statement

Traditionally, the income statement has been considered the primary evidence of company performance. As Exhibit 4.13 shows, it presents sales revenue and then subtracts associated expenses and taxes. The income statement is rarely equivalent to a summary of cash flow. An example of why they may differ is that the revenue figures reflect sales for which cash collections have not been received and do not reflect cash collections for previous sales. Another example is that some items, such as depreciation, are deductible expenses on the income statement even though they do not involve a cash flow. Other cash flows, such as repayment of principal on debt and investment in fixed assets, are not reflected on the income statement.

Statement of Retained Earnings

Often attached to the end of the income statement, this simplest of the financial statements is shown in Exhibit 4.14. It examines the change in retained earnings from one year to the next. The statement starts with the retained earnings balance at the begin-

EXHIBIT 4.12
DC Widgets, Inc.: Balance Sheet
(in Thousands of Dollars)

	December 31, 1996	December 31, 1995
Assets		
Current assets		
Cash	$ 187.6	$ 183.6
Marketable securities (note A)	385.5	377.7
Accounts receivable (net of allowance for doubtful accounts of $14.0 in 1991 and $11.25 in 1990)	668.0	575.5
Inventories (note A)	894.6	997.9
Prepayments and deferred charges	21.3	17.3
Total current assets	$2157.0	$2152.0
Property, plant, and equipment		
Land	$1338.0	$1338.0
Buildings and leasehold improvements	2000.0	1750.0
Equipment	5500.0	5312.3
Gross property, plant, and equipment	8838.0	8400.3
Less accumulated depreciation and amortization	−5324.5	−4882.6
Net property, plant, and equipment	$3513.5	$3517.7
Other assets (note B)	142.3	117.3
Total assets	$5812.8	$5787.0
Liabilities and Stockholders' Equity		
Current liabilities		
Accounts payable	$ 536.9	$ 697.5
Wages payable	112.5	197.5
Accrued expenses	30.0	22.5
Accrued income taxes	289.5	287.6
Current maturities of long-term debt	41.7	36.9
Notes payable	7.5	6.0
Total current liabilities	$1018.1	$1248.0
Deferred income taxes	124.1	123.3
Long-term debt		
Mortgage bonds (12% interest, due 1998; net of current maturities; annual sinking fund payment of $25)	$ 409.1	$ 438.9
Debentures (14% interest, due 2004; net of current maturities; annual sinking fund payment of $12)	272.7	292.6
Total long-term debt	$ 681.8	$ 731.5
Total liabilities	$1824.0	$2102.8
Stockholders' equity		
Preferred stock (8% cumulative, $50 par; 10810 share authorized, issued and outstanding)	540.5	540.5

Continued

EXHIBIT 4.12 (cont.)
DC Widgets, Inc.: Balance Sheet
(in Thousands of Dollars)

	December 31, 1996	December 31, 1995
Liabilities and Stockholders' Equity		
Common equity	300.0	300.0
Capital stock ($1 par value, 300,000 shares issued and outstanding; 500,000 shares authorized)		
Paid in capital	508.5	508.5
Retained earnings	2639.8	2335.2
Total common equity	3448.3	3143.7
Total stockholders' equity	3988.8	3684.2
Total liabilities and stockholders' equity	$5812.8	$5787.0

Note A: Significant account policies
  Marketable securities: Recorded at cost, which was the lower of cost or market value in both 1996 and 1995. Market value was $390,000 for 1996 and $410,000 for 1995.
  Inventories: Valued according to the FIFO (first-in, first-out) method.

Note B: Other assets
  Other assets include investment at market value in Western Widget Corporation, an unconsolidated subsidiary. Valued at cost, the Western Widget stock would be worth $115,000.

ning of the year. Because that portion of net income not paid in dividends becomes part of retained earnings, the statement adds net income and then subtracts preferred and common dividends. The resultant figure coincides with the retained earnings line on the balance sheet.

Ratio Analysis

A ratio analysis is an important tool to evaluate the financial condition and performance of the firm. Ratio analysis evaluates a set of financial ratios, looks at trends in those ratios, and compares them to the average values for other companies in the industry. Management uses it to maintain efficient operational control, but it is also invaluable in analyzing a firm for potential debt or equity investment. Four categories of ratios are especially important: liquidity, activity, leverage, and profitability. Below, we define and calculate many representative ratios for DC Widgets, Inc., for 1991.

Liquidity Ratios.   A company's ability to meet its imminent financial obligations is known as liquidity. If the firm is very liquid, it is protected from technical insolvency, which could occur if it were unable to meet an obligation. However, too much liquidity retards profitability unnecessarily. Two widely used liquidity ratios are

$$\text{Current} = \frac{\text{current assets}}{\text{current liabilities}} = \frac{\$2157}{\$1018.1} = 2.12$$

$$\text{Quick ratio} = \frac{\text{current assets} - \text{inventory}}{\text{current liabilities}} = \frac{\$1262.4}{\$1018.1} = 1.24$$

EXHIBIT 4.13
DC Widgets, Inc.: Income Statement
(in Thousands of Dollars)

	December 31, 1996	December 31, 1995
Sales (net of returns and discounts)	$5931.6	$5157.9
Cost of goods sold	−3690.5	−3209.1
Gross profit	$2241.1	$1948.8
Operating expenses		
Selling	$ 155.5	$ 150.1
Administrative	103.7	100.1
Advertising	78.3	62.4
Lease	37.0	37.0
Repairs and maintenance	41.3	25.4
Depreciation	441.9	397.3
Operating profit	$1383.4	$1176.5
Other income	34.7	34.0
Earnings before interest and taxes	1418.1	1210.5
Interest expense		
Note	1.1	0.7
Mortgage bonds	49.1	52.7
Debentures	38.2	41.0
Total interest expense	88.4	94.4
Earnings before taxes	1329.7	1116.1
Provision for income taxes 40%	531.9	446.5
Net income	797.8	669.6
Preferred stock dividends	43.2	43.2
Earnings available to common shareholders	$754.6	$626.4
Average number of shares outstanding	300,000	300,000
Primary earnings per share	$2.52	$2.09
Fully diluted earnings per share	$2.52	$2.09
Dividends per common share	$1.50	$1.40

EXHIBIT 4.14
DC Widgets, Inc.: Statement of Retained Earnings
(in Thousands of Dollars)

	December 31, 1996	December 31, 1995
Retained earnings at beginning of year	$2335.2	$2128.8
Net income	797.8	669.6
Total	$3133.0	$2798.4
Less: Dividends on preferred stock	43.2	43.2
Dividends on common stock	450.0	420.0
Retained earnings at end of year	$2639.8	$2335.2

Although both the current and quick ratios include current liabilities in the denominator, the quick ratio recognizes that inventory is usually less liquid than other current assets. In the case of a long production process or obsolescence, inventory may not provide much liquidity at all because it could not be turned quickly into cash.

Activity Ratios.   In general, activity ratios measure the firm's efficiency in generating sales and making collections.

$$\text{Inventory turnover} = \frac{\text{sales}}{\text{inventory}} = \frac{\$5931.6}{\$894.6} = 6.63$$

$$\text{Average collection period} = \frac{\text{accounts receivable}}{\text{sales per day}} = \frac{\$668}{\$16.25} = 41.1$$

$$\text{Total asset turnover} = \frac{\text{sales}}{\text{total sales}} = \frac{\$5931.6}{\$5812.8} = 1.02$$

$$\text{Fixed asset turnover} = \frac{\text{sales}}{\text{net fixed assets}} = \frac{\$5931.6}{\$5812.8} = 1.02$$

Other things being equal, a high inventory is more efficient because the firm does not have many assets tied up in inventory. However, very low levels of inventory can lead to stock outs and lost profits. Similarly, a short average collection period, although suggesting success in collecting receivables, may also be the result of a credit policy that stifles profitable sales. Total asset turnover and fixed asset turnover measure the company's ability to generate sales for a given level of assets. A higher ratio indicates a more efficient firm, but again one must recognize that an excessively high ratio may suggest that a reduced level of assets may be impeding sales.

Leverage Ratios.   This group concentrates on the amount of financing provided by creditors relative to the amount provided by the owners. Leverage ratios evaluate default risk in that debt payments must be made for the company to remain solvent. Closely related is the concept of financial risk, or variability in earnings per share.

$$\text{Debt ratio} = \frac{\text{total liabilities}}{\text{total assets}} = \frac{\$1824.0}{\$5812.8} = 0.31$$

$$\text{Debt on equity} = \frac{\text{total liabilities}}{\text{total common equity}} = \frac{\$1824.0}{\$3988.8} = 0.46$$

$$\text{Times interest earned} = \frac{\text{EBIT}}{\text{interest expense}} = \frac{\$1418.1}{\$88.4} = 16$$

$$\text{Fixed charge coverage} = \frac{\text{earnings before taxes} + \text{interest expense} + \text{lease obligations}}{\text{interest expense} + \text{lease obligations}}$$

$$= \frac{1329.7 + 88.4 + 37.0}{88.4 + 37.0} = 11.60$$

For each of the first two ratios, a relatively high value suggests that a relatively high proportion of financing is supplied by debt. In the short run, leverage benefits

Part Three

STRATEGY FORMULATION

The key to strategy formulation is to attain and sustain a competitive advantage, and this theme links the four chapters of Part Three. Each chapter shows how this central theme relates to the process of formulating strategies at one of the different conceptual levels illustrated in the exhibit below.

We first look at strategy formulation at the operations level in Chapter 5. This chapter builds on concepts introduced in Chapter 4, where we learned to assess a firm's internal strengths and weaknesses. Now, we explore how managers improve their organization's operating processes in order to produce greater customer value and thereby enhance the firm's competitive advantage in the marketplace.

In Chapter 6, we consider how strategy formulation at the business level impacts competitive advantage. This chapter complements concepts you learned in Chapter 3, where you studied the five forces model and considered structural positioning as a determinant of competitive advantage. In Chapter 6, you will see how a business defines its scope and mission, how it maneuvers to position itself competitively, and how it alters its strategy according to the stages of its market's life cycle—all of which significantly impact the competitive advantage the firm achieves and maintains.

Chapter 7 focuses on strategic management at the corporate level. We explain how the strategic management of diversification dramatically affects competitiveness of businesses within a corporation. Diversification can positively impact business unit competitiveness by yielding synergies that improve individual business units' structural positions or process execution. However, as you will learn, managerial behavior sometimes limits a corporation's effectiveness in building such competitive advantages at the business unit level.

In Chapter 8, we discuss how firms that operate in different countries can best develop competitive advantages across their business units. You will learn that the strongest competitive advantages usually result from integrating a global view of the world as a whole with a more focused perspective that recognizes different needs in individual local markets.

Although we must present these topics in separate chapters to avoid an overload of information, you should remember as we progress through this material that all four chapters are woven together by the common thread of attaining and sustaining a competitive advantage.

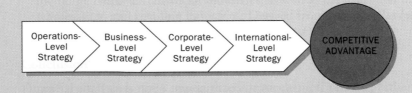

The Architecture of Strategy

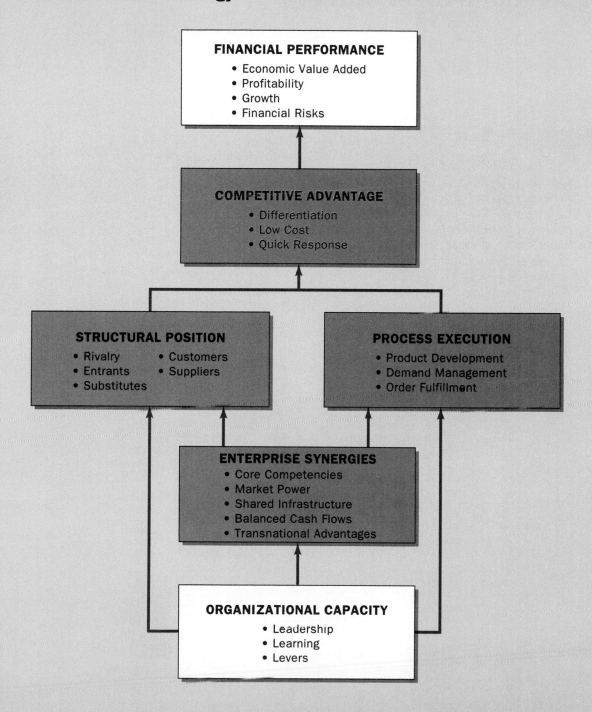

Operations-Level Strategy

CHAPTER OUTLINE

In this chapter we look at how to develop capabilities in process execution that will yield competitive advantages for a firm. This involves applying strategic management concepts to what is known as the operations level, the level at which work inside the organization actually takes place. We focus on how organizations go about improving their process capabilities, including both total quality management and core process reengineering.

The chapter is organized in four parts. The first part explains why it is important to treat operations as a strategic issue. The second describes total quality management (TQM) and core process reengineering (CPR) as complementary approaches to improving process capabilities, while the third part offers guidelines for managing TQM and CPR efforts. The final part of the chapter describes emerging best practices in each of three generic core processes: product development, demand management, and order fulfillment.

This chapter will help you understand:

- The roles process execution and capabilities at the operations level play in creating competitive advantage
- The complementary nature of TQM and CPR as approaches to improving process execution capabilities
- Guidelines for addressing the managerial challenges to using TQM and CPR
- Some of the basic principles employed in process improvement
- How application of the basic principles is leading to the emergence of new "best practices" in three core processes: product development, demand management, and order fulfillment

In 1981, two very significant events occurred in the history of Harley-Davidson, the maker of legendary superheavyweight motorcycles lovingly known to aficionados as "hogs": the company suffered its first loss ever, and its top-management team purchased the company from its corporate owner for $65 million in a leveraged buyout. The new management team, led by CEO Vaughn Beals, had expected the losses—the company had been troubled for several years when they finally bought it, intending a turnaround. Japanese competitors had flooded the U.S. market with low-priced, high-quality products at a time when Harley-Davidson's quality was poor and growing worse. In its last new-model launch before the acquisition, the first 100 units required $100,000 in repairs as they rolled off the assembly line.

After the takeover, Beals and his management team took a benchmarking trip to Japan to study their competitors. There they became convinced that the secret to restoring Harley-Davidson's competitiveness was to improve quality and simultaneously lower costs.[1] To implement this ambitious goal, Harley-Davidson became one of the first American companies to reestablish its market leadership through total quality management. Management went to work on core processes such as supply management, in which they implemented a just-in-time approach to managing inventory; and new-product development, in which they implemented a process that stressed designing products that were easier to manufacture correctly and efficiently. They began an employee involvement program to solicit improvement suggestions from throughout the company and trained the workforce in quality tools such as statistical process control. Meanwhile, Harley-Davidson's marketing experts began to understand what their customers valued in a "hog." They came to see their products as the means by which customers made important personal statements about themselves, transforming themselves into more exciting personalities than their normal day-to-day lives normally offered.

All these efforts paid off: over a 3-year period, Harley-Davidson reduced scrap and rework by two-thirds, and increased inventory turns to 20 (versus a national average of 3.5). Employee productivity increased 40 percent, and delivery of defect-free motorcycles tripled. As such gains began to have an impact on the firm's competitiveness, its position in the market began to improve. Market share in the superheavyweight (850 cc and above) market segment improved from its low of 23 percent in 1983 to today's high of 65 percent. Concurrent with this strengthened competitiveness and market position, financial performance made dramatic improvements. Harley-Davidson began selling stock to the public in 1986, when sales were $300 million and profits were around $4 million. Ten years later, sales continued to grow and reached above $1.5 billion, while profits had risen to $140 million. In other words, net profit margin during this 10-year period had improved sixfold, from 1.5 percent to over 9 percent.

Harley Davidson's dramatic turnaround and continued improvement clearly exhibits how improvements at the operations level can impact a firm's competitiveness and financial performance. In this chapter, we explore how firms implement improvements in operations.

THE STRATEGIC ROLE OF OPERATIONS

Throughout this text we stress that gaining and sustaining competitive advantages are key to superior financial performance. As explained in Chapter 4, one of the two main sources of competitive advantage is a firm's capabilities in process execution.[2] *Process execution* refers to a firm's capacity and its abilities to produce the elements of differentiation, low cost, and quick response that customers value. As one pair of influential writers has put it, "The key to long-term success is being able *to do certain things* better than your competition can. Such superior capabilities provide a competitive advantage that is much more sustainable than one based on something you can build or buy. . . . A company should think of itself as a collection of evolving capabilities, not just as a collection of products and businesses."[3] In other words, a firm's ability to produce the elements of competitive advantage depends on its capabilities,[4] or the internal resources it has to draw from, and this perspective is sometimes referred to as the *resource-based view* of the firm, as discussed in Chapter 4.[5]

At the operations level, these resources are employed to carry out activities that combine to form processes. In his influential article "What is Strategy?", Michael Porter explains the importance of activities at the operations level:

> Ultimately, all differences between companies in cost or price derive from the hundreds of activities required to create, produce, sell, and deliver their products or services, such as calling on customers, assembling final products, and training employees. Cost is generated by performing activities, and cost advantage arises from performing particular activities more efficiently than competitors. Similarly, differentiation arises from both the choice of activities and how they are performed. Activities, then, are the basic units of competitive advantage. Overall advantage or disadvantage results from all a company's activities, not only a few.[6]

Processes are systems of interconnected activities involved in accomplishing an organization's work.[7] For instance, key processes for a bank might include credit management and transactions, while key processes for an airline might be flight operations, route management, and ticketing. These examples refer to fairly large processes, but processes can be even larger; these we call core processes. The framework of core processes we are using in this book appears in Exhibit 5.1.

Exhibit 5.1 identifies three core processes: product development, demand management, and order fulfillment. These can be considered generic core processes because every business develops products, sells products, and fills orders for products, regardless of whether the product is a good or a service. While no single standard identifies all core processes, the three processes shown in this exhibit indicate strong

EXHIBIT 5.1
The Generic Model of Core Processes and Systems Introduced in Chapter 4

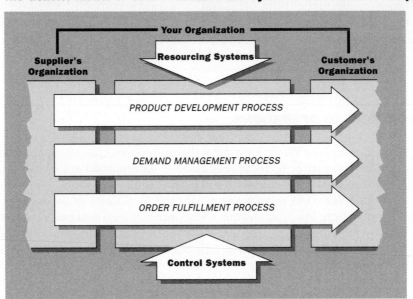

similarities to those identified by other authors. For example, one influential model identifies five "basic" processes—product development, purchasing, production, demand management, and order fulfillment. This model differs from those identified in Exhibit 5.1 only because it separates purchasing and production out of the broader view of the order fulfillment process that is taken here.[8]

While such models divide the organization into separate processes, it is important to understand that fit between the individual processes and fit between the collection of processes and the firm's strategy are more important than any one process in isolation. Exhibit 5.2 depicts three levels of fit. First-order fit refers to simple consistency between a process and the firm's overall strategy. Merck is a leading pharmaceutical company that follows a strategy based on growth through innovation. The company's new-product development process has excellent first-order fit with this overall strategy, as the process has proven capable of generating a long series of successful new products, the engines of Merck's growth.

Second-order fit refers to processes that are mutually reinforcing. The new products developed at Merck are advanced pharmaceuticals, and they require that doctors be educated about their potential and their proper use. Without this critical step, there will be little demand for the new drugs, so the fit between Merck's new-product development process and the educational activities comprised by its demand management process is an important form of second-order fit for this firm.

Third-order fit goes beyond merely aligning processes and refers to a level of organizationwide fit that allows the firm to optimize its core processes. As you will learn in Chapter 11, Merck has developed a system for managing risk and allocating capital that helps it optimize its efforts at producing new products.

EXHIBIT 5.2
Three Levels of Strategy-Operations Fit

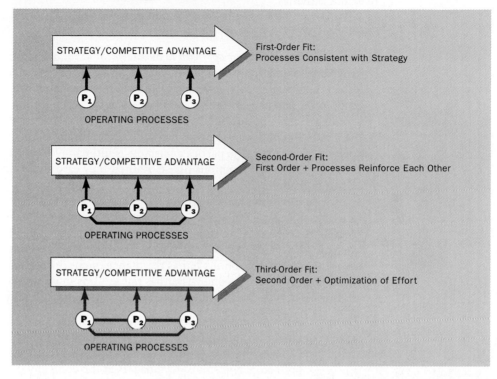

Source: Created from information found in Michael E. Porter, "What Is Strategy?" *Harvard Business Review* (November–December 1996), 61–78.

To understand the importance of seeing how processes fit together as a collective, we can turn again to Michael Porter:

> In all three types of fit, the whole matters more than any individual part. Competitive advantage grows out of the *entire system* of activities. . . .
>
> Strategic fit among many activities is fundamental not only to competitive advantage but also to the sustainability of that advantage. It is harder for a rival to match an array of interlocked activities than it is merely to imitate a particular sales-force approach, match a process technology, or replicate a set of product features. Positions built on systems of activities are far more sustainable than those built on individual activities.[9]

In this chapter we focus on two widely used, complementary approaches to improving a firm's process capabilities in order to achieve fit and sustain competitive advantages.[10] One is commonly known as total quality management (TQM), the other as core process reengineering (CPR).[11] TQM focuses on encouraging a continuous flow of incremental improvements from the bottom of the organization's hierarchy. CPR, on the other hand, is generally more of a top-down approach, aimed at more radical changes in how processes are designed. TQM and CPR are both usually managed as broad-based, multifaceted improvement efforts that entail a variety of initiatives and activities.

TQM and CPR have become popular for improving process execution capabilities for at least five reasons:

- *They encourage a strategic approach to management at the operations level.* Process improvement virtually always cuts across functions or involves multiple departments. When individual departments or functions are managed in isolation, managers tend, in the language of management science, to "reach local maximums while avoiding global optimums." In other words, having managers do what is best for their own functions is no guarantee that the end result will be best for the firm as a whole. Customers, the parties a business is ultimately trying to serve, do not care about the individual functions per se. Rather, they care about the outputs that result from the interplay of all the functions. Consequently, only shortsighted managers focus on individual functions; they must understand how the *interplay* of functions affects customer value. For example, a customer has no use for R&D's creating technological advances manufacturing departments cannot produce. So strategic management at the operations level is best treated not as the management of individual functions but as the management of cross-functional value-producing processes. As one writer has put it, "It is more important for an organization to be cross-functionally excellent than functionally excellent."[12]

- *They get the results managers want.* For example, Globe Metallurgical Inc., the first small company to win the Malcolm Baldrige National Quality Award, carefully studied the financial returns it realized from investing in efforts to improve its processes, both large and small.[13] Managers at the company concluded that the rate of return was 40 to 1. In its first 2 years of work on process improvement, Globe cut its annual operating costs by $11.3 million. After these first big savings, the cost reductions fell to "only" $4 million each year. But the CEO expects the annual cost reductions to continue to grow even higher as his $115-million-in-sales company continues to expand. Further evidence of the success of process improvement efforts: analyses completed by the U.S. General Accounting Office found that among twenty firms that scored high on the Baldrige quality improvement award criteria, employee suggestions were up 17 percent per year, product reliability was improving at a rate of 11 percent per year, order-processing times and inventories were falling at annual rates of 12 and 10 percent respectively, and market share was growing at an annual rate of nearly 14 percent—all strong measures of health.[14]

- *They work equally well for blue-collar and white-collar processes.* Regardless of whether the output is a service or a manufactured good, processes usually share certain elements.[15] Consequently, the tools that are applicable to improving processes on the factory floor typically have analogs for improving processes in the office suite. Managing operations as processes provides a common framework that managers can apply throughout their organizations, and this encourages its widespread use, and thus coordination between functions.

- *They allow organizations to take advantage of several "enabling" developments.* Over the past 10 to 15 years, several developments have taken place that facilitate, or enable, managing operations as cross-functional processes. When work teams were organized around functions, cross-functional work was virtually impossible, but as workforces are organized into cross-functional teams, organizational entities can take a process perspective. At the same time, new managerial techniques are designed for teams instead of individual use. Such cross-functional tools can greatly increase the effectiveness of process improvement efforts.

■ *They fit with an orientation toward interorganizational collaboration.* As organizations practice process management, they grow more adept at looking at the cross-functional issues cutting horizontally across an organization. This ability to work horizontally across *intra*organizational boundaries can be extended to *inter*organizational collaboration with suppliers and customers, a key element of the cooperative strategies discussed in Chapter 3. These two forms of horizontal management are mutually reinforcing, and organizations that use one usually benefit from the other.

While organizations can benefit from improving cross-functional processes as part of an overall strategic effort to gain and hold competitive advantages, many find it difficult. In fact, it is probably fair to say that, when it comes to businesses' gaining significant competitive advantages through TQM and CPR, there have been more failures than successes. Some surveys have shown that up to two-thirds of all U.S. managers believe process improvements in their organizations have failed to produce the expected results, and one study concluded that only 36 percent of the managers surveyed felt that process improvement efforts had any meaningful impact on the competitiveness of their firms.[16] As a consequence of such disappointments, there has been a backlash against TQM and CPR. For instance, when the Baldrige award was first introduced, many managers believed its criteria (which are based on TQM concepts) offered a well-arranged "formula" for running a business.[17] Hundreds of businesses were "phantom" competitors for the award, using the award's criteria to judge their organizations without ever officially entering the competition. However, the Baldrige criteria can no more offer a "one-size-fits-all" formula for business success than any other single managerial framework can, and as it "failed," organizations abandoned it with the same fervor with which they had once embraced it. Applications for the Baldrige award peaked in 1991, just about the same time as "Baldrige bashing" became a popular topic in the business press.[18]

There are two reasons for the problems encountered in achieving real process improvement. First, change is difficult, and many managers struggle with the change from managing individual functions to managing cross-functional processes. (Later in this chapter, we look at steps that managers can take to enhance implementation of process improvement, and you will begin to appreciate the managerial challenges involved.) Second, many managers expect too much from TQM and/or CPR in the first place, ensuring that they will be dissatisfied with them. Clearly, process improvement has its limitations, and managers who overlook these limitations find that the results do not match their expectations.

Despite these stumbling blocks, the basic concepts of process improvement are difficult to dismiss.[19] Though some of the "packaging" associated with TQM and CPR is relatively new, the basic concepts are not. In fact, they have consistently proven their worth over a number of years.[20] As Ray Stata, CEO of Analog Devices, explains, process improvement "essentially involves attention to processes, commitment to customers, involvement of employees, and benchmarking of best practices. It is hard to believe you cannot benefit from that."[21] We agree with Stata and believe the best approach is understanding the essence of process improvement, being aware of both its benefits and its limitations, and working hard at overcoming the difficulties in its implementation.

Because of the backlash against process improvement efforts, many managers have found that the only way to reap the benefits of these approaches is to relabel them with titles such as "Managing for Customer Value" and Motorola's famous "Six Sigma." Regardless of the semantics or program packaging, process improvement is a crucial part of an overall strategic management effort, and its use should not depend on what labels are currently popular. As Tom Vanderpool, a quality expert at Gemini Consulting, puts it, "abandoning the acronyms may be appropriate, abandoning the principles is not."[22]

APPROACHES TO MANAGING AT THE OPERATIONS LEVEL

While TQM and CPR are the most common approaches to process improvement, they share similarities and exhibit distinct differences.

Similarities of TQM and CPR

Because their fundamental objective is to improve process execution capabilities, TQM and CPR have significant similarities in how they are managed:

- *Both aim to improve process capabilities to provide customer value.* The key words here are "process" and "customer value." Alternative approaches to managing at the operations level often focus on improving individual functions as based on internally oriented performance measures.

- *Both consider the needs of internal as well as external customers. External customers* are individuals or other organizations that actually purchase the goods or services your organization sells. *Internal customers* receive the output from one process as the input for their own process within the same organization. TQM and CPR can increase value added for both groups of customers.

- *Both look for opportunities to simultaneously improve multiple dimensions of competitive advantage.* Rather than focusing on quality *or* cost *or* speed, TQM and CPR attempt to improve all of these. While this is not always possible, research and experience indicate that simultaneous improvement is common enough so that this is a reasonable place for managers to start their process improvement efforts.

- *Both are based on a systems view of the organization.* Processes are systems. In simple terms, a *system* is a set of objects and actions involved in transforming inputs into outputs. TQM and CPR are efforts to make the organization's systems as capable as possible in transforming inputs into the outputs desired by customers.

- *Both typically cross intraorganizational boundaries.* Because they are aimed at improving whole processes instead of individual functions or departments, TQM and CPR both require work across the vertical organizational boundaries that usually separate functions and departments from one another.[23] As one manager experienced in both TQM and CPR explained it to us, "Organizations are typically managed at the operations level through a series of vertical stovepipes called departments. Process improvement requires that managers tie together those departments by working through the sewer pipes that cross the organizations horizontally."

- *Both typically cross interorganizational boundaries.* Many processes do not stop with one organization, but continue on into an adjoining organization. Adjoining organizations are usually suppliers or customers, but may also be partners in joint ventures or some other form of strategic alliance. CPR will more likely entail working on process improvements within adjoining organizations, but TQM projects often involve suppliers or customers. We know of one plastic parts supplier who serves two fierce rivals; *both* rivals keep employees at the supplier's plant in order to facilitate TQM improvements in processes that cut across supplier-customer boundaries.

- *Both benefit from benchmarking.* There are often significant differences between typical process performance levels and the levels achieved by the very best competitors. For instance, one study of purchasing processes revealed that while most firms spent 6 weeks processing a purchase order and returned 1.5 percent of the supplies purchased, the best purchasing processes typically require only 10 minutes to process a purchase order and return only .0001 percent of the items purchased.[24] With such tremendous performance differences among firms, there is an obvious opportunity for weaker firms to learn from better-performing firms. As introduced in Chapter 4, *benchmarking* is the study of firms that excel in some process capability to learn new ways of improving processes.[25] CPR allows benchmarking of broad processes, as was the case when Philips Consumer Electronics benchmarked Chrysler's core process for developing new products. TQM benchmarks narrow processes, as when the Internal Revenue Service studied several telephone reservation systems to decrease the number of busy signals received on its 800-number tax-help lines.

- *Both aim at achieving and possibly redefining best-in-class performance.* How much quality is good enough? For many firms, the only answer is for a process to be the best in its class.[26] This may seem like an unlikely goal, and adopting it has certainly driven organizations to adopt some outlandish expectations. For instance, Motorola's Six Sigma program is designed to help the organization reach a target of only two defects per billion. In striving for similar levels of perfection, L. L. Bean has shipped more than 500,000 correctly filled orders in a row. Ambitious targets, perhaps; but in an age of global competition, why should customers settle for second best? We sometimes explain this point to students using a sports metaphor. You may think it ridiculously ambitious to attempt to consistently throw your body over a bar an incredible 8 feet above the ground, as world-class high jumpers routinely do. But as long as plenty of competitors are willing to devote themselves to this goal, any potential Olympic high jumper must do the same. Clearing even 7 feet might sound like an incredible achievement, but it probably would not even warrant an invitation to the Olympic trials in most countries. Global competition among businesses works much the same way, so those who seek to improve process capabilities must often set "best in class" as their goal. Or, as one author put it, "The operational agenda is the proper place for constant change, flexibility, and relentless efforts to achieve best practice."[27]

Differences Between TQM and CPR

As similar as TQM and CPR are, important differences arise between them. These are summarized in Exhibit 5.3 and discussed below.

■ *Differences in general orientation.* TQM and CPR present two ends of a continuum of process improvement efforts, as depicted in Exhibit 5.4. This continuum illustrates differences in terms of two dimensions: the scope of the targeted improvement "site" and the level of improvement sought. TQM efforts tend to focus on more narrowly defined target sites for improvement; that is, the systems they seek to improve are smaller, typically referred to as steps, tasks, or activities. TQM also aims at less ambitious improvement levels than does CPR. At the extreme, TQM

EXHIBIT 5.3
Summary of Differences Between TQM and CPR

TQM		CPR
■ Starts with what is and what works forward to improve	**Approach**	■ Starts with what could be and works backward to rethink
■ Incremental improvements through *kaizen*	**Scope**	■ Radical improvements through reengineering
■ "Scoring" by hitting many "singles"	**"Scoring"**	■ "Scoring" by hitting a few "home runs"
■ Improvements *within* the broader system	**Within/On**	■ Improvements *on* the broader system
■ Bottom up	**Direction**	■ Top down
■ Team members are typically lower-level, "frontline" employees and up to supervisors and lower managers	**Staffing**	■ Team members are typically upper-mid-level managers and up to executive level
■ Empowerment of the many throughout workforce	**Involvement**	■ Leverage of the critical few in management
■ Typically involves 20–100 improvement "sites"	**Numbers**	■ Typically involves 3–5 improvement "sites"
■ Usually cuts across functions and often cuts across whole departments	**Boundaries**	■ Usually cuts across departments and often cuts across whole organization
■ Improvement efforts managed as continuous stream of projects	**Continuity**	■ Redesign is not continuous, so processes can stabilize
■ Customers may often be internal	**Customer**	■ Customers nearly always external

EXHIBIT 5.4
TQM and CPR Emphasize Complementary Elements of Operations Improvement

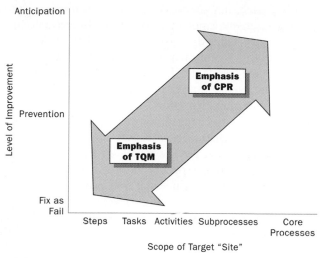

concepts are sometimes applied with a "fix as fail" objective, although TQM is generally meant to avoid this approach to managing operations in favor of more lasting results. Ideally, TQM allows teams to address the root causes of problems and work at problem prevention. At the CPR end of the continuum, the scope of processes addressed is usually broader (subprocesses or core processes) and the objectives for improvement may be more ambitious, often involving improving the ability to anticipate and prevent potential problems.

The conceptual distinctions between CPR and TQM, which appear rather straightforward in Exhibit 5.4, are often fuzzy in practice, and what might be considered TQM in one organization is called CPR (or something similar) in another organization. In fact, even within the same organization, confusion often arises between where TQM stops and where CPR starts, which is why we consider them to be a continuum of shades of gray, rather than black-and-white distinctions.

- *Scope and "scoring."* As suggested in the preceding paragraph, the fundamental difference between TQM and CPR is the scope of its efforts. TQM is intended to result in many incremental improvements, what the Japanese call *kaizen* (continuous improvement) and what Americans often refer to as "hitting singles." CPR, on the other hand, results in radical (as opposed to incremental) changes in processes, sometimes called "hitting home runs," to continue the sports analogy.

- *"Within" versus "on."* Another way of describing the scope of TQM and CPR is to distinguish between working *on* a system (CPR efforts related to redesigning the underlying system of doing things) and working *within* a system (TQM efforts aimed at incremental improvements in a system that otherwise remains unchanged). Obviously, this distinction creates more shades of gray, but it sometimes helps managers understand where to focus their efforts.

■ *Direction and staffing.* A great deal of confusion arises regarding who should be involved in TQM or CPR. While it is fair to say that TQM is more likely to be a bottom-up approach that involves lower-level employees, this should not imply that upper management is not a part of TQM. In fact, perhaps the most common reason TQM efforts fail is the mistaken belief that TQM involves lower-level employees only and that senior management should stand back and, as one CEO told us, "let these people just do it." The proper distinction is the *nature* of senior management's involvement, not its presence or absence. For TQM to succeed, senior management must champion and enable the improvement, overcoming organizational resistance to change, monitoring the TQM effort, and actively and visibly facilitating and encouraging its use. On the other hand, senior management is much more involved in the actual *doing* of CPR—typically, these people alone have the breadth of perspective and the authority required to address the bigger issues involved in reengineering core processes. However, in our experience, even in efforts to reengineer high-level core processes, the actual managers involved in the reengineering work are upper-middle managers working under the endorsement and sponsorship of senior managers. Finally, both TQM and CPR must be organized around desired outcomes stated in terms of improved process capabilities, rather than being organized by functions or departments.[28]

■ *Involvement and numbers.* Another way TQM and CPR differ in terms of staff involvement is that TQM depends on small contributions from many empowered individuals throughout the organization. CPR, on the other hand, depends on leveraging the decisions of a small, but essential, set of upper managers. Of course, this implies that there are usually many TQM projects for every one CPR effort. In our experience, the ratio of TQM to CPR target sites varies anywhere from about 5 to 1 to 50 to 1 in organizations that use both approaches to process improvement.

■ *Boundaries.* We have already emphasized that both TQM and CPR focus on processes that cut across the organization rather than work within single functions or departments. However, TQM usually cuts across functional boundaries, and it often involves several departments. CPR, on the other hand, may cut across several departments and, often, whole organizations.

■ *Degree of continuity.* The concept of *kaizen* at the heart of TQM implies *continuous* improvement. Thus, while individual TQM projects may have more or less clear starting and stopping points, the overall flow of improvement initiatives tends to be unending. This is not the case for CPR initiatives. Constantly reconfiguring the basic architecture of core business processes would be far too disruptive, so an organization must be given an opportunity to stabilize its operations between various generations of process design. This distinction lies at the heart of why the two approaches are complementary, as discussed below.

How TQM and CPR Complement Each Other

Some managers initially see TQM and CPR as incompatible because of the various differences described above. Yet we see these differences as key to the complementary nature of TQM and CPR. If it were not for these differences, the two approaches would be redundant. Despite their differences, the top-down approach of CPR need not conflict with the bottom-up approach of TQM. In fact, as a spokesperson from Andersen Consulting, a leading consultant firm in the area of CPR, put it, "You can't do reengineering without an environment of continuous improvement or TQM." We might just as easily say the converse, because it often doesn't work well to apply TQM to processes that need redesign or replacement through CPR, not just improvement. Our view of the proper relationship between CPR and TQM is depicted in Exhibit 5.5.

In this exhibit, process capabilities improve over time through a series of S-shaped curves.[29] Each S-curve represents another generation of process design, and CPR is what moves an organization from one generation to another. Here we see how CPR involves work *on* the underlying system of doing things that make up a process. We call this type of improvement *dis*continuous, to identify the clear break with the past that distinguishes CPR from TQM. Within each generation of design, employees use TQM to improve process capabilities in an effort to get the most from a particular design. This is working *within* the system, and the smooth S-curves are meant to portray this as being *continuous* improvement. To reach the maximum process execution capability, organizations must employ both types of process improvement. Therefore, we now turn to consideration of the managerial guidelines appropriate for both approaches.

GUIDELINES FOR MANAGING TQM AND CPR

Because of the similarities and differences between TQM and CPR, the two have correspondingly shared and distinct managerial guidelines for their applications. First, we discuss those they have in common.

EXHIBIT 5.5
Kaizen Involves Continuous Improvement; Reengineering Involves Discontinuous Improvement

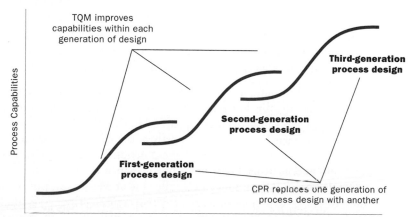

Shared Guidelines for Managing
Process Improvement

Both Should Be Driven by a
Broader Strategy

Assuming that the business strategy focuses on creating and sustaining a competitive advantage based on offering customers superior value (a premise of this book), this strategy should be the starting point for managing either TQM or CPR. TQM and CPR are about improving operations, and only the overall strategy can determine which operations matter most. It has been our experience that without a solid grounding in the broader strategic issues, both TQM and CPR generally slip into addressing less important issues or devolve into efforts to improve internally focused operations through market-blind cost cutting. For instance, the division vice president of washing machines at Whirlpool admitted that process improvement was not linked to a clearly articulated, externally focused strategy, and consequently teams "meandered into discussion of the number of restrooms and the color of their walls."[30] Perhaps the most infamous example of this was General Motors' investment of $50 billion in factory automation, an attempt to reengineer its manufacturing processes aimed at improving internal measures of labor productivity rather than external measures of customer value.[31] At the end of a decade of monumental investing (enough, critics say, for the company to have bought controlling interests in both Toyota and Nissan), GM had little to show in the way of increased competitive advantage, and some have even argued that the huge investments weakened the carmaker's position relative to more externally focused competitors.[32]

To ensure that its process improvement efforts are grounded in a strategic view of providing customers with superior value, Rubbermaid, a firm widely recognized for its successful use of TQM and CPR principles, uses three questions to guide its improvement/reengineering teams:[33]

1. *Who is your customer?* This question forces teams to link their efforts back to customers, encouraging an external focus.

2. *What value are you providing for your customer?* This forces explicit consideration of the specific forms of customer value (within the broader framework of better, cheaper, faster) the process is meant to provide.

3. *What business strategy are you contributing to?* Here managers place process improvement efforts in the context of a broader strategic initiative so that the various efforts throughout the organization are cumulative rather than disconnected.

Richard Heygate, a leading consultant on process improvement at McKinsey & Company, deems this last point one of the most important in determining the overall impact of process improvement efforts. He says the benefits of too many process improvement efforts have "accrued mostly at the individual project level." He goes on to explain, "All too often the sum of these benefits does not add up to anything like the quantum leap in overall corporate performance that managers seek and competition demands." John Hagel, Heygate's colleague at McKinsey, puts it this way: "We did an audit of client experiences with process reengineering. We found lots of examples where there were truly dramatic impacts on processes—60 percent to 80 percent reductions in cost and cycle time—but only very modest effects at the business-unit level, because the changes didn't matter much [from a business strategy standpoint]."[34] To address this problem, Heygate goes so far as to argue that organizations should focus improvement efforts "*only* on those activities that together create distinctive, cross-functional, value-adding processes."[35] And, to repeat, only the firm's strategy can identify which processes these are.

Don't Confuse Means and Ends

Based on the foregoing, we advocate a perspective that sees process improvement "as stepping-stones in an intended direction," with that direction established by the firm's overall strategy.[36] In the complex effort required to manage TQM or CPR, it's easy to forget that they are only means to broader strategic ends, not ends unto themselves. We have been in some organizations where obsession with improvement programs has actually driven employees away from concern for customers and what they value. For instance, we saw one human resource department whose primary concern was reaching the goal of every employee's receiving a targeted number of hours of TQM training—even if doing so meant taking time away from customers! Florida Power and Light's infamous single-minded pursuit of the Deming prize for quality led it to seriously compromise the value it provided customers.[37] A vice president for quality describes another such misguided organization as a "$9 billion company that formed 142 teams as part of its TQM effort and months later found that 100 of the teams were still trying to decide on names for themselves."[38] When an improvement program becomes more important than business results, it's time to seriously rethink the purpose of the program and the values of the organization.

Adjust Application to Fit the Organizational Strengths of the Company

Research shows that process improvement practices may work well in one organization but fail completely in another. Based on a 2-year International Quality Study of 945 managerial practices in 580 businesses around the world, conducted by Ernst & Young, organizational strengths and abilities determine what works. The researchers divided the organizations they studied into three groups they labeled novice, journeyman, and master.

When the researchers compared what worked for each of the three groups, they concluded that no one approach to improvement worked consistently. Instead, firms go through a logical progression in developing their ability to use various process improvement techniques, and those offering the greatest payoffs vary from one developmental stage to another. The head of the research effort explained, "At each level of performance you pull a different set of levers to reap the maximum payoff." For instance, research revealed that if "novice-level" firms attempt to benchmark world-class competitors and implement their findings, they might even hurt themselves, because they are not yet capable of such changes. It is probably better first to benchmark leading competitors and then gradually increase organizational capabilities, aspiring to eventually benchmark world-class practices.

Investments of Time and Money Are Usually Required to Support Improvement Initiatives Adequately

Many companies underfinance and understaff process improvement efforts. Organizations that make unrealistically low investments in TQM or CPR should probably avoid attempting to use these concepts. Nearly two-thirds of the companies involved in reengineering do not have time or money specifically budgeted for its support. We are familiar with one organization that unrealistically planned to invest $400,000 *per year* in a TQM program that was supposed to reverse operating losses of $800,000 *per week*. In another case, reengineering accounted for as little as 5 percent of employees' time, even though the research concluded that a half-time commitment was the realistic minimum required.[39]

One manager told us, "The high-quality people appropriate for improving or redesigning processes cannot be found waiting around in the halls looking for something to do." Her point: those individuals most capable of leading process improvement are the very people the organization thinks it can least afford to give up for new initiatives. Consequently, in staffing such efforts, these valuable people are seldom cut free from their previous responsibilities, and are expected to accomplish process improvement along with everything else. Another manager complained to us that his organization's approach to managing process improvement was what he called "gravy management." He explained, "Rather than push anything off the plates of the busy people involved, our organization ladled process improvement over the top of everything else, hoping it congealed in place before anything important spilled off." Not surprisingly, the organization's improvement efforts never got off the ground.

Many organizations find it difficult to budget money for process improvement. After all, such efforts are generally aimed at saving money, and this obvious argument often stymies advocates of process improvement from beginning initiatives by formally budgeting new funds for the effort. The required money typically comes from reducing other budgetary accounts, and whoever is losing the funds will usually argue that process improvement should "pay for itself." However, process improvement is no different in this regard from most other managerial initiatives: without adequate capital and time allocated for its completion, it will probably never be completed.

Of course, the resources required vary greatly depending on the work being done. Consider the benchmarking examples given earlier. When Philips Consumer Electronics benchmarked Chrysler's product development process, a team spent several months studying the issues involved and traveled as a group to visit Chrysler's facilities for an entire week. However, when the Internal Revenue Service benchmarked telephone reservation systems in order to reduce the frequency of busy signals on its 800-number tax-help lines, a three-person team simply conducted telephone interviews of their counterparts in several other organizations, and the entire project lasted only a few weeks. One general guideline we can offer is that managers should not fall into the trap of believing that process improvement is free.[40] It may pay for itself, and in fact it may offer tremendous returns, but it still requires an investment, and the size of the return is often proportional to the size of the investment.

Managerial Guidelines Unique to TQM or CPR

While the managerial approaches appropriate for TQM and CPR do overlap, there are also subtle but important differences, and organizations that overlook these will likely suffer setbacks. This section presents representative models of the steps commonly involved in TQM and CPR and addresses their unique managerial challenges. These challenges invariably involve implementation issues, but because we explore implementation in detail in Chapters 9 to 12, we shall simply identify implementation challenges here.

Guidelines Unique to TQM

The Steps Involved in TQM Initiatives.   As we have said, TQM is usually managed as a series of projects. In order to facilitate the work of various project teams, organizations usually adopt a particular model or approach for its teams to use, and this approach is used companywide with adaptations made where required by special circumstances. Usually, the approach is broken down into a series of steps the team is to take, and often these steps are presented as a flowchart in keeping with process orientation. Typically, managers keep these frameworks as basic and as simple as possible to facilitate their widespread applicability and use.

The most influential of these models is the "plan, do, check, act" (PDCA) cycle popularized by W. Edwards Deming. Deming was sent to war-ravaged Japan by the U.S. government after World War II to help rebuild that country's economy. He quickly realized that the monumental task would require efforts from hundreds of thousands of individuals, each working on a relatively small part of the whole problem. Yet, to coordinate their activities, these individuals needed a common language of problem solving. Therefore, Deming proposed a simple four-part cycle that could be used by virtually anyone facing virtually any sort of problem.[41] As depicted in Exhibit 5.6, it became known as the PDCA problem-solving cycle.

PDCA systematically addresses a problem by developing a plan for a change, carrying out the plan, checking the effectiveness of its results, and finally doing whatever it takes to close any gaps between the original plan and its results. Because it is so basic, PDCA can be used in virtually any process and at any level within a firm. Companies have customized many variations on this simple idea, and an organization fully committed to *kaizen* will have hundreds, perhaps thousands, of PDCA-like loops in motion at any one time. Where they have been most successful, adaptations of the PDCA loop have become part of employees' language, facilitating communication across functions and between TQM teams. PDCA (or its derivatives) often becomes a set of guidelines for running meetings, a set of standards for evaluating problem-solving efforts, and a means of depersonalizing the process of offering feedback to colleagues. Although the generic structure of the problem-solving process may not be optimal for any particular problem, its ability to unify the thinking of diverse parties generally offsets this limitation.

TQM's Greatest Managerial Challenge.   In our experience, the greatest managerial challenge involved in TQM is making it a way of life rather than an isolated program or project. The power of TQM lies with the masses, hundreds of teams each making

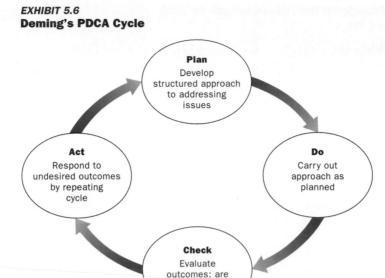

EXHIBIT 5.6
Deming's PDCA Cycle

individual efforts to achieve a greater, shared goal. However, the language used to describe TQM in most of the organizations we have studied suggests that this power has often gone untapped. In these organizations, TQM is seen as the "flavor of the month," a managerial fad that is soon replaced by some other fad. Many believe that the most savvy approach to participating in such programs is to "go through the motions" and "get your ticket punched" by completing some token project. We have seen countless employees who were "playing the game" by selecting a process that can improve dramatically with little effort that offers easily documentable improvements, and that falls more or less under their control. Note that strategic impact is conspicuously absent from this list. Employees may not take TQM seriously because they see it as a short-term project ("This too shall pass") rather than a way of life ("This is the way we get things done around here"). Application 5.1 describes one organization that has been very successful in using TQM and another that has not.[42]

Guidelines Unique to CPR

The Steps Involved in CPR.   While no one model of the steps to CPR is as dominant as the PDCA model of TQM, most approaches share certain basic elements. We present the most common elements for you in Exhibit 5.7, once again trying to be as basic and as simple as possible to increase applicability and promote ease of use.

In this model, a team identifies a strategically important process and then studies it as it currently exists. The team then rethinks the current process, generating possible ideas for change by benchmarking other organizations to identify best practices and/or by considering generic process improvement principles. A sample of such principles is given in Application 5.2.[43]

Application 5.1

Misaree and Nippondenso: Failure and Success with TQM

At Misaree Unlimited (a fictitious name), TQM was greeted with great fanfare, but 2 years later, it was allowed to die a quiet death. Misaree's failure offers a sharp contrast to the success with TQM enjoyed by the Nippondenso plant in Maryville, Tennessee, a manufacturer of alternators, generators, and other automotive electrical parts. This is a world-class operation that has successfully used a wide variety of TQM and *kaizen* concepts to develop nearly perfect production processes.

Misaree made many efforts to apply the basic tenets of quality improvement and *kaizen,* but with virtually no results to show for these efforts. In hindsight, practically everyone involved in the TQM effort admitted that it had been a complete failure. It is instructive to review the reasons for Misaree's failures most commonly cited by its managers and employees as part of a "post mortem":

Lack of strategic focus.   At Misaree, dozens of small teams were told to act independently in identifying a quality problem and attacking it. There was no overall sense of strategic priorities, and there was no opportunity for the various efforts to culminate into anything greater than the sum of its parts. Most teams selected "manageable" problems which allowed them to demonstrate that they were involved, while not taking too much time away from their usual work.

Failure to work across organizational boundaries.   In most cases, the teams defined a "manageable" problem as one that did not require significant amounts of work across organizational boundaries. Team members realized that coordination across departmental boundaries would significantly complicate the quality improvement effort. Several teams rationalized that there were "plenty or problems close to home" and that they did not need to look inside other departments to find quality problems to attack. Others rationalized that they could attack larger processes that crossed organizational boundaries after the organization learned from its experiences with smaller problems. While there was a germ of truth to both of these comments, it was also true that the significant breakthroughs in quality improvement required work across departments and other organizational boundaries.

Attention to "window dressing" over substance.   In well-intentioned efforts to get 100 percent involvement in TQM, managers gave considerable emphasis to having the teams publicize their efforts. They encouraged groups to display statistical process control charts, fishbone cause-and-effect diagrams, and charts of performance improvements. Many teams later admitted that the driving force behind their efforts was to generate the most impressive display possible, while concern for process improvement was almost a side issue.

Lack of involvement from senior management.   Misaree treated TQM as something that lower-level managers, supervisors, and employees did, but not senior managers. Senior managers were "involved" in three ways. First, they were very prominent in the fanfare surrounding the kickoff of Misaree's TQM program. Second, they established a steering committee that met once a quarter in poorly attended meetings to discuss TQM oversight. Third, they selected winning teams from a TQM competition and served as masters of ceremony when quality awards were distributed. As they later admitted, they did not personally serve as role models in applying TQM concepts at higher levels.

This contrasts with Nippondenso, where parts are produced in a high-volume operation with defect rates as low as only a handful per million. A tour of this operation led to the following observations:

Throughout the organization, quality is treated as a strategic issue crucial to success.   Visitors to Nippondenso quickly sense that the entire organization understands that quality is imperative to company success. Senior managers are conversant about the quality improvement initiatives currently underway and can clearly articulate the impact that having the industry's best quality will have on the firm's competitive standing. Line workers can tell you when the last defect occurred, what it was, and what is being done to ensure that it does not occur again. Quality is not seen as someone else's responsibility. Everyone in the organization appears to consider the improvement of quality to near perfection his or her top priority.

While there is tremendous commitment to perfection, there is no effort to hide mistakes.   Walking from one part of the plant to another, visitors regularly mistake the parts or components that are displayed in each work area (often on velvet) as examples of quality parts. Actually, closer inspection will reveal that the items on display are the most recent rejects (often weeks old because so few mistakes are made) complete with documentation about when the problem occurred, why it occurred, and what is being done about it. This is an organization that understands that reaching perfection requires admitting your mistakes and going to work on them.

Quality is an ever-present component of every job.   On the factor floor, each step in the assembly process for the typical part involves both a "checking" and a "doing." The check entails a small quality inspection, typically of an attribute that was determined in the last assembly process just one or two steps up the line. If the product fails this simple inspection (most take only a second or two), no further work is performed on the unit. Instead, the worker performing the check hands the part back upstream where the error was made so that the individual

making it can figure out what went wrong and how to avoid the problem in the future. The nonstop commitment to quality extends all the way to the "executive suite" (actually an open office space just off the factory floor). The company has a strict policy that whenever there is a discovery that a defective part has been shipped, the most senior manager in charge of operations must immediately be informed and must personally head up a detailed investigation of how it happened. This policy is enforced 24 hours a day, 7 days a week.

While Misaree's failures show that good intentions are not enough to ensure success through TQM, Nippondenso's world-class quality is just as convincing in showing that, properly managed, TQM and *kaizen* can provide potent weapons for achieving a competitive advantage through strategic management at the operations level.

EXHIBIT 5.7
A Typical Approach to Managing CPR

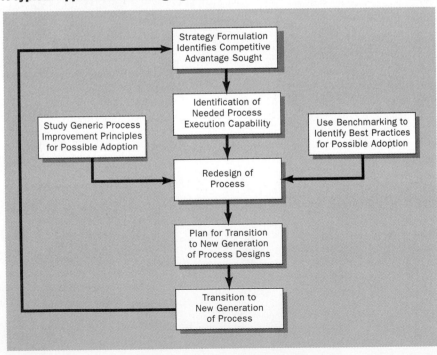

Application 5.2

A Sampler of Principles for CPR

Teams should understand several principles as they begin to improve their processes. In fact, there are far too many to list here, so consider what follows to be a sampler of personal favorites and refer to works referenced throughout this chapter for additional guidelines. The principles listed below have improved process efficiency and effectiveness in a variety of organizations. They can also be applied to both core processes and smaller processes.

■ *Remove non-value-added work.* Perhaps the most basic of all process improvement principles, this suggests that those involved in reengineering should think through all the activities involved in a process and identify those that represent wasted effort in the sense that they produce nothing for which customers are willing to pay. The results of removing non-value-added work are leaner, simpler systems that produce more value for a given level of effort.

■ *Move from serial processing to parallel processing.* Serial processes require that work be done sequentially. Each step takes place only after the preceding step is completed, with a "handoff" separating each two steps in the series. A notoriously inefficient way of doing things, this typically results in processes with very low ratios of value-added to non-valued-added time. It's typically more efficient when steps are completed concurrently, avoiding as many handoffs as possible.

■ *Simplify to reduce the costs of complexity.* Complexity hurts process efficiency and effectiveness by increasing the oversight required, the likelihood of mistakes and rework, and the need for mental effort that could be spent elsewhere. Left unattended, most processes will grow complex just as an unattended boat will grow barnacles. Reengineering allows an opportunity to scrape this growth away and get back to a cleaner, smoother operating process.

■ *Balance flexibility and standardization.* Flexibility refers to the ability to adjust to varying customer needs, tailoring goods or services to maximize the benefits derived by customers. Standardization limits customer options, but it also has the potential to lower costs dramatically. Because customer value is a function of both benefits *and* costs, processes should

be managed to balance the greater benefits offered by flexibility against the cost savings that standardization provides.

■ *Shift from a "push" to a "pull" orientation.* In a push orientation, the organization makes a decision and afterwards attempts to convince customers that the decision was correct. For example, in many manufacturing operations, products are made to inventory, and the firm then works to sell the inventoried goods. In a pull orientation, customers trigger activity, and the challenge becomes one of maintaining the agility to respond to customer needs as they arise. For example, with the just-in-time (JIT) approach, goods are produced not to an inventory but to a customer's order. In customer-driven organizations, customer "pull" tends to be more dominant than organizational "push" across all core processes.

■ *Maximize total customer value.* Managers often take too narrow a view of what impacts customer value. From the customer's perspective, value is a function of *all* the costs and *all* the benefits associated with a good or service. This includes everything from "hassles" involved in the customer's interaction with the product to "psychic income" derived from the customer's association with the product. As more firms improve their products' basic features and prices, the need to find creative approaches to enhancing overall customer value rises.

■ *Move from "arm's-length" relationships to "partnering."* As we have stressed, adopting a process view to operations requires working horizontally across both intra- and interorganizational boundaries. Thus, a different view emerges of the appropriate relationship among the various parties making up the horizontal processes. In most traditional organizations, the various parties involved deal with one another from a distance, in what is commonly referred to as an "arm's-length" relationship. However, the processes most successful at developing new capabilities are usually those in which the various parties involved work closely with one another, as partners.

■ *Build in redundant skills, not redundant people.* The cross-functional teams responsible for the operation of most processes must be able to carry out a wide variety of tasks in a coordinated manner. One approach to ensuring this is to have many people available for each task, to provide redundant backups. The difficulties with this approach are that it is expensive and that it does not foster a cross-functional orienta-tion. Many organizations have found that if they cross-train those who are involved in cross-functional processes, team members can play more than one role (i.e., they have redundant skills). The expenses drop and the team functions better with the various players understanding one another's jobs.

After developing a new process design, a team must undertake a critical step that is too often overlooked: they must develop a plan for moving to the new design without breaking operations by suddenly "turning off" the old process. One of our colleagues describes this problem as analogous to rewiring the electrical systems in a jet-liner while it remains in flight, which sounds just about difficult enough (and scary enough) to be an appropriate analogy. Managing this transition probably presents the most challenging aspect of CPR, as discussed below.

CPR's Greatest Managerial Challenge.   It seems that the greatest challenge in CPR is the transition from the "as-is" process to the newly designed "should-be" process.[44] This transition period is the time span identified in Exhibit 5.8: one experienced reengineer calls it the "crazy time."

Two specific problems arise in this transition period. The first is that organiza-tions cannot usually just shut down while moving from one process to another. This

EXHIBIT 5.8
The "Crazy Time" in CPR

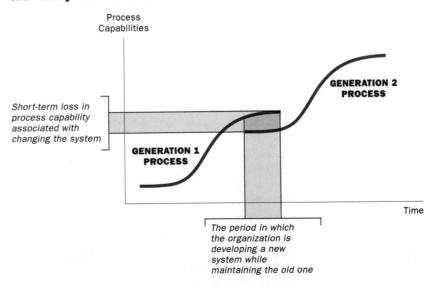

can be seen on the *time* axis of our exhibit. Usually, organizations must continue operating with old processes while bringing new processes on line, and considerable confusion results from the overlap in operating the two processes. To appreciate the challenges involved, imagine that the government had decided that driving on the opposite side of the road would be a worthwhile improvement and that the transition would take place gradually over the next 6 months. Each morning you would try to guess whether your odds for survival in the resulting chaos would be improved by driving on the right- or left-hand side of the road. One thing is for sure: driving in the middle of the road (analogous to adopting a little of the old system and a little of the new system) would be disastrous. As organizations shift from one process to another, they face similar uncertainties.

The second problem with the transition from one process to another can best be seen by looking at the *process capability* axis in Exhibit 5.8. Note that the S-curve for one generation of design usually starts off lower than the upper end of the generation it is meant to replace. Remember, the earlier generation process is probably working better than ever because TQM-like efforts have continuously improved it (a point made earlier in this chapter, in Exhibit 5.5). Consequently, in the beginning, the new way of doing things is probably less efficient and less effective than the old way. This often makes the new generation a very difficult "sell." Resistant managers ask, "Why should we discontinue something that is working better now than ever before?"

Such questioning may seem like undesirable resistance to change. Yet questioning and skepticism is not always a bad thing. American culture, in particular, with its ready acceptance of disposability and its admiration of the "home run," often results in organizations that are too willing to toss out the old and replace it with the "new, improved" model. The costs associated with replacing big organizational processes often run into millions of dollars, and there is little room for blind enthusiasm for change when such amounts are involved.[45]

On the other hand, organizations have often failed to replace older processes when they should have. In debates on the merits of changing from one process to another, asymmetries in the available information often prove fatal to change efforts. An organization more likely knows both the costs and the benefits of the process it has been using than the one it is considering adopting. Furthermore, in considering new processes, managers typically know more about the up-front costs involved than about the future benefits. In fact, many of the benefits of new processes are not only unknown, but also unknowable—simply impossible to foresee or predict. When analysis of a proposed change is based on known costs and unknowable benefits, it is usually difficult to gain widespread support for it. As organizations ponder the trade-offs implied by the overlap in the S-curves shown in Exhibit 5.8, it is not surprising that the transition from one process to another presents the greatest challenge to CPR.

THE BEST PRACTICES IN THREE PRIMARY CORE PROCESSES

Recall from earlier discussion in this chapter that for many firms the appropriate standard for process execution capability is "best in class." As firms across a broad range of industries strive to become the best, certain practices emerge as the best current thinking on managing various processes. In this section, we present three examples of each of these so-called best practices to show you how they apply to product development, demand management, and order fulfillment, the core processes we identified earlier in Exhibit 5.1.[46] Application 5.3 provides examples of how Procter & Gamble has improved in each of the three core processes discussed in this chapter, in an effort to regain its competitive position.

Product Development

Leading organizations around the world are improving the core process of product development (1) to better balance technological capacity and customer satisfaction, (2) to use a concurrent (rather than a serial) approach to development, and (3) to develop goods designed with the product's total life cycle in mind.

Balancing Technological Capacity and Customer Satisfaction

Product development represents one of the most important applications of the principle of moving from a "push" to a "pull" orientation. In adopting a push orientation to product development, firms assume they know what is best for the customer, design what they think the customer needs, and then try to educate the customer about the virtues of the product or service they have developed. In its extreme form, this orientation can lead to internally focused organizations that are virtually out of touch with what customers value. For instance, the U.S. railroad industry once failed to understand that what its customers valued was not just the operation of trains and railyards but expertise and capabilities in logistics.[47] Rail companies did not incorporate other forms of transportation into their networks and lost market share to new transportation firms that offered the greater flexibility of trucking.[48]

At the other extreme, firms can overemphasize customer pull in developing new products if all product developments are only in response to customer-generated "requests." While this treatment of the "customer as king" may sound like the ideal way of ensuring superior customer value, often it is not. Customers may lack the technological expertise to adequately judge whether a technologically advanced alternative would be possible or even desirable. For example, tractor companies might have waited forever before farmers, used to working with horses, requested the modern farm tractor. Most customer-driven innovations are incremental in nature: farmers might have requested a more heat-tolerant breed of workhorse, for example. Such customer-driven innovation often results in a portfolio of marginally different products as a firm tries valiantly to tailor its products to meet the needs of various customers. Yet, for all the resulting variety, such a product line is not usually technologically superior because few, if any, of the products developed by customer pull are based on an understanding of what technology is possible.

Many Japanese consumer products companies have adopted what appears to be a practical approach to balancing technological push with customer pull. As a new technology is developed, they move quickly to get a simple, low-end product based on

Procter & Gamble Manages Core Processes for Customer Value

When market research revealed that families loyal to Procter & Gamble brands were paying $725 more each year than families buying private-label or store brands, senior managers knew that a new strategy was called for. P&G had historically offered retail customers deals that included discounts, but it needed to offer these low prices every day to remain a market leader. However, it was obvious that it could not simply lower prices and hope to maintain decent profits; a new operating strategy was required.

Eleven cross-functional teams examined every part of P&G. For instance, they examined forty-one work processes within the broader core process they called "customer management" (roughly analogous to our "demand management"). The teams operated under four rules: change the work, do more with less, eliminate rework, and reduce costs that do not produce value for the customer. This rethinking led to important changes in P&G's core processes.

New-Product Development

For decades, P&G managed research and development the same way: producing technologically superior goods and depending on marketing to sell them at a premium price that would cover the high R&D costs while still allowing for healthy profit margins. However, most of P&G's opportunities for growth lay outside saturated developed markets, and developing markets cannot pay premium prices for technological marvels. Consequently, P&G reversed its approach to R&D. Now marketing decides first what blend of price and features a particular market most values, providing guidelines for R&D's new-product development. For instance, the company offered Pampers Uni, lower-priced and simpler versions of its sophisticated Pampers diaper line, in developing markets, such as Brazil.

Demand Management

Analysis revealed that P&G had the highest marketing overhead in the industry, undoubtedly because P&G's product line was so complex. Five divisions with three sales layers each sold more than 2,300 stockkeeping units (SKUs) covering 34 product categories and 17 basic pricing brackets. Special deals meant that an average of 55 price changes worked through the system every day.

The quarterly sales promotion plan for health and beauty products (one of five divisions) alone, more than 500 pages long, was sent to every salesperson in the division. To simplify this complex process, P&G reduced the number of pricing brackets from 17 to just 3 and the number of special prices from 55 per day to only 1 per day. It also reduced its number of SKUs by 25 percent.

These changes had a dramatic short-run impact, but another change may have a still greater impact in the long run. Part of the reason P&G's product line was so complex was its practice of introducing a new brand for every significant technological innovation that occurred (e.g., when the company added cold cream to its soap, it created a new brand, and the famous Ivory brand was left unimproved). Customers found the latest technology in newer P&G products but not in the famous brand names they valued. So, as P&G's product line grew more complex, many of the most famous brands saw their market share slowly decline as customers sought out newer brands with enhanced features. For example, P&G's Spic & Span cleaner was not significantly reformulated for 45 years, and its once dominant market share gradually disappeared.

To address this problem, P&G combined its latest technology with its strongest brands, producing such items as Tide with Bleach and Tartar Control Crest. Now, loyal customers find their favorite brands with value-enhancing innovations, and P&G's demand management process is simpler, with fewer brand names to manage.

Order Fulfillment

The U.S. packaged goods industry, of which P&G is a part, is involved in a massive cooperative reengineering effort that will change the way the entire industry operates. This effort is meant to reduce the $30 billion annually the industry must spend on non-value-added activities, such as excess paperwork, handling, and inventories. The end result will be an order fulfillment process based on continuous product replenishment. In this process, when an item is purchased, information from the checkout line automatically triggers the work involved in replenishing the shelf. This largely paperless process reduces mistakes, lowers inventories all along the product pipeline, and improves cash flow.

Under the old process, special deals were constantly

Application 5.3 (cont.)

sending bubbles of artificially created demand through P&G's factories. Though higher capacity was unnecessary most of the time, production facilities were sized to handle even these larger bubbles in a timely fashion. Consequently, capacity utilization was a low 55 percent companywide. As the company moves toward a simpler product line, everyday low pricing, and continuous replenishment, the bubbles are disappearing. Consequently, P&G has been able to reduce its production capacity (closing some thirty plants worldwide) and improve capacity utilization at its remaining plants to 80 percent.

Industry experts believe these changes in core processes have left P&G in a strong competitive position. As one explains, "What we have here is a company that has created a platform to execute a strategy that is dramatically superior to anything its competitors can offer. This new platform is anchored on customer value."

Sources

Based on information gathered from Bill Saporito, "Behind the Tumult at P&G," *Fortune* (March 7, 1994), 74–82; and Zachary Schiller, "A Nervous P&G Picks Up the Cost-Cutting Ax," *Business Week* (April 19, 1993), 28.

that technology onto the market. Usually it is understood that the first generation of the new product is not technologically refined, but once it's in customers' hands, they can begin giving input on potential improvements. Japanese companies then use this customer input to direct further technological improvements, and new generations of the product are quickly on the market as soon as the new technology is refined. Sony uses this approach to first introduce, and then dominate, new-product categories, such as personal entertainment systems, with rapidly evolving and technologically advanced product lines (e.g., its Walkman line).

Using a Concurrent Approach to Development

Organizations enjoy tremendous gains from shifting from a serial approach to product development to a concurrent approach that uses parallel involvement of the various parties involved in developing and launching new products. Development of a new product, be it a good or a service, typically moves through a series of steps as initial concepts are developed and debugged, prototypes are created, and output of the new product ramps up. There are two very different ways of managing progress through these various steps.[49] One approach is to move between the groups involved in each of the steps in a sequential manner, letting each group complete its work before the next begins. The alternative is to adopt a parallel process in which the various groups overlap their work as much as possible. These two approaches are diagrammed in Exhibit 5.9.

The parallel approach manages different steps concurrently; and this approach to product development is sometimes referred to as *concurrent engineering*. Note from the exhibit that even if the time required for each of the individual steps increases, the overlap reduces total time overall. However, this probably understates the net effect of the shift to parallel processing. Experience and research show that, in a shift to a parallel process, each individual cycle time decreases, with a net effect of reduced total product development time. By overlapping their work, the various parties involved in the process can head off problems before they develop. For example, in the sequential

EXHIBIT 5.9
The Impact of Moving from a Sequential to a Parallel Product Development Process

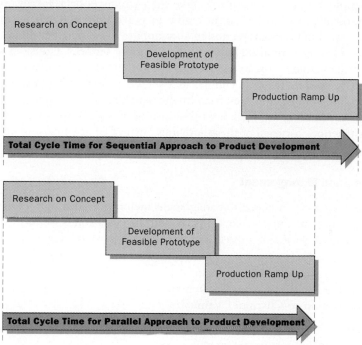

process, R&D "throws new designs over the wall" to manufacturing, the manufacturing engineers immediately see various elements of the product design that will be difficult or perhaps even impossible to produce in large volumes, and the blueprints for the new design iterate back and forth between the two groups as they negotiate a series of engineering change orders. When manufacturing engineers work concurrently with product design engineers, they discover problems sooner, and suitable alternatives develop with fewer false starts and less wasted effort. With such time-savers, product development times often decrease by more than half from shifting from sequential to parallel development.[50]

Designing for a Product's Total Life Cycle

Over their lifetimes, products are built, sold, used, possibly repaired, and finally discarded.[51] If product developers take this into consideration, they can greatly facilitate this cycle and increase the product's value. For instance, Procter & Gamble has always developed products that would provide customers with superior performance. But now P&G has expanded the horizons of product development, using the concept of "cradle-to-grave design." This approach to product development considers everything from sourcing raw material to simplifying manufacturing to providing for environmentally appropriate disposal of postconsumer waste. European government regulations require companies to take their products back for disposal once customers are through with them, so the cradle-to-grave approach may become widespread; it is now used in Germany to design automobiles for easier recycling.

This concept also applies to the design of services. Consider a life insurance policy that is sold by the insurance salesperson, purchased because of the peace of mind it offers, used by the policyholder as a source of borrowing power to help put children through college, and then used by the beneficiaries as a source of inheritance. A well-designed policy will facilitate these various uses with user-friendly forms, reports, and instructions for each of these activities, instead of just focusing on a single user.

Demand Management

Best practices in demand management include (1) shifting focus from customer satisfaction to customer value, (2) balancing the costs and benefits of variety and complexity, and (3) rethinking the importance of customer service in retaining customers.

Shifting Emphasis from Customer
Satisfaction to Customer Value[52]

Many managers equate customer satisfaction with customer value, but doing so masks important opportunities to gain a competitive advantage. Satisfaction measures usually rate how pleased or displeased customers are with a good or service. Collecting information on satisfaction may tell you very little about what customers value. In other words, data on satisfaction with current products may not reveal very much about the perceived importance of benefits derived from potential products. A patient may report that she is very satisfied with the service received during her most recent trip to the dentist, but what she would really value is never having to go to the dentist in the first place. Firms that provide what such customers value are well positioned to leap ahead of competitors that focus merely on customer satisfaction.[53] To better understand the distinction between value and satisfaction, spend some time working through Exhibit 5.10, which deals with what customers value in a car.

Once a firm has worked its way up the hierarchy of customer value depicted in Exhibit 5.10, it can reverse the process by starting at the top and working back down to discover sources of customer value that they might otherwise overlook. For instance, once carmakers began to understand the importance of peace of mind, they added attributes such as roadside service to their car warranties.

Working up and down the value hierarchy requires that demand management develop new approaches to listening to the customer. Customer surveys may be a starting point, but they are more useful for assessing the value being derived from current products than for designing new goods or services. They should never be the full extent of listening to the customer. Organizations interested in more fully understanding what customers value typically use more creative processes for demand management, such as focus groups.

EXHIBIT 5.10
Consumer-Value Hierarchy for Automobiles

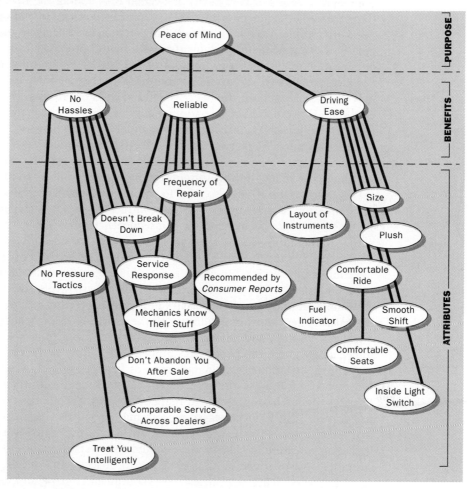

Source: Robert B. Woodruff, David Schumann, and Sarah Fisher Gardial, "Understanding Value and Satisfaction from the Customer's Point of View," *Survey of Business* (Summer–Fall 1993), 33–37. Reprinted by permission of Center of Business and Economic Research, The College of Business Administration, The University of Tennessee, Knoxville.

Balancing the Benefits of Variety with the Costs of Complexity

In well-intentioned attempts to provide customers with sets of product and service attributes they most value, firms often develop vast arrays of different products and services.[54] This would be no problem were it not for the complexity that results. Such complexity stems from the additional inventory, training, forms, oversight, mistakes, suppliers, manufacturing equipment, and waste associated with adding new products to an existing line; every one of these items adds to the cost of operating a business.[55]

If the benefits customers derive from products tailored to their individual needs cannot offset the costs of complexity associated with adding the new good or service to the set already offered, customer value is actually *decreased* by the variety.[56]

For example, a consumer goods firm serving the European market offered combinations of product and packing attributes that grew slowly over the years until the organization maintained an inventory of 362 stockkeeping units (SKUs) for a single product category.[57] When the organization redesigned its demand management process, evaluating both the benefits and the costs of offering such variety, it discovered costs that did not provide additional value. Among the eight brands the firm offered in one product category, fifty-four different ingredients were used in forty-five different formulas. However, tests indicated that consumers were usually able to make distinctions among only twenty-two different product variants, which still says nothing about how many of these variants customers were willing to pay for.

Service organizations also need to balance the benefits of variety against the costs of complexity. A government services contractor was solely dependent on serving a single government agency and was consequently subservient to this customer's every wish. Although this sounds like a good example of the devotion to customer value we espouse, in fact it was not. The government agency had multiple parts that all used the contractor's services, and each part had its own unique set of preferences for carrying on business. The contractor tried to meet these diverse demands by developing an endless set of optional approaches in its various contracts, and a horribly complex bureaucracy developed to administer all the variations. Slowly but surely, the contractor began to bog down under all this administrative weight, and whenever the customer complained, the contractor jumped to respond by developing procedures for expediting the unique combination of steps being criticized. Matters reached a crisis stage when the head of the government agency sent the contractor a chart showing that the volume of contracts had remained constant while the contractor's overhead had tripled. The agency refused to continue paying the high overhead and insisted that the contractor fix the problem. Unfortunately, the contractor never grasped that by failing to carefully balance the benefits and costs of adding new features for the customer, it had driven its cost structure to unacceptable levels. Consequently, the company never changed, overhead costs continued to grow, and, as the agency turned to other contractors, layoffs began. Ironically, the contractor's loss of the agency's contracts was widely blamed on its unwillingness to respond to its customer's needs.

Stressing Customer Retention Through Superior Service

Organizations often pay more attention to gaining new customers than to keeping existing ones, but research into the profitability of old and new customers leads many organizations to seriously rethink their demand management processes in favor of retaining existing customers. Old customers are already a part of your business; they are educated about your product and experienced in using it. The consulting firm Bain & Company discovered that boosting a company's customer retention rate just 2 percent has about the same impact on a firm's profits as decreasing its total cost structure by 10 percent.[58]

Additional research shows that the key to keeping customers is often service.[59] Automobile companies have found that customers who were satisfied with dealer service departments were more than twice as likely to buy the same brand of car again than those who were not satisfied. Similar conclusions result from studying both industrial goods and consumer services. In research on why companies lose industrial customers, 68 percent of all lost accounts were due to company indifference to service, compared to only 14 percent because of dissatisfaction with product attributes and 9 percent because of dissatisfaction with price. In a study of service businesses, nearly 60 percent of the repeat customers cited past satisfaction with the firm as being a primary reason for continued purchase—roughly twice the percentage of those who cited price.

Helping customers resolve problems contributes powerfully to future demand and therefore constitutes a critical element of demand management.[60] Exhibit 5.11 recaps a study of repurchase intentions of customers who had had problems. As you

EXHIBIT 5.11
The Repurchase Intentions of Customers with Problems

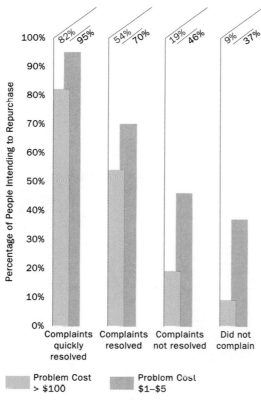

Problem Cost > $100   Problem Cost $1–$5

Source: Daniel P. Finkelman and Anthony R. Goland, "How Not to Satisfy Your Customers," *McKinsey Quarterly* (Winter 1990), 7. Reprinted by permission of The McKinsey Quarterly.

can see, customers whose problems are quickly resolved have a surprisingly high rate of intended repurchase.

GM's Saturn division encountered a similar phenomenon with its first recall. A supplier had provided faulty antifreeze that damaged the cars' aluminum blocks. Saturn quickly replaced the car of every customer affected by the mistake. The move unexpectedly created so much goodwill and brand loyalty with the buying public that Saturn now considers the mistake to have been almost fortuitous. The impact of such customer loyalty can be impressive. One cross-industry study concluded that the return on investment for customer complaint resolution systems runs from 15 to 75 percent for packaged goods companies, 50 to 170 percent in banking, 35 to 400 percent in retailing, and 100 percent or more for consumer durables.[61]

Based on widespread experience, consultants at McKinsey & Company concluded that only about half of total customer satisfaction with a product can be traced back to the product itself. The remaining 50 percent consists of various elements of customer service, including everything from product delivery to billing to training. Anyone trying to improve demand management processes should make every effort to tap the full range of options for delivering value and retaining profitable customers as a result. There are many opportunities for building improved customer service into reengineered demand management processes. Exhibit 5.12 illustrates this point for both consumer goods and industrial goods.

Order Fulfillment

As firms move to improve order fulfillment processes, some of the best practices include (1) moving toward partnerships for strategic sourcing, (2) balancing standardization and customization, and (3) developing a range of "lean" operating practices.

EXHIBIT 5.12
The Relative Importance of Different Sources of Value

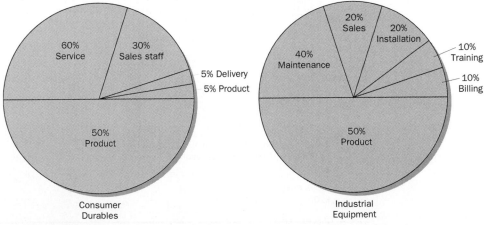

Source: Daniel P. Finkelman and Anthony R. Goland, "How *Not* to Satisfy Your Customers," *McKinsey Quarterly* (Winter 1990), 7. Reprinted by permission of The McKinsey Quarterly.

Moving from Purchasing to Strategic Sourcing

Suppliers play critical roles in many organizations.[62] For instance, purchased goods typically run 80 to 85 percent of revenues for personal computer makers, 70 to 85 percent for consumer electronics makers, and 50 percent for pharmaceutical firms. While the figure is only about 40 percent for the service industry in general, the purchase of supplies still qualifies as one of the most important categories of costs. Given the costs involved, firms have, not surprisingly, found this to be an important area for process improvement.[63]

The standard historical approach to managing purchasing was to maintain arm's-length relationships with suppliers. Suppliers received carefully written specifications to which they responded with bids. Price was usually a deciding factor in evaluating the bids, and the winner was expected to comply strictly with customer specifications. This relationship effectively positioned suppliers and customers as adversaries. More recently, firms have benefited from shifting their focus of competition to rivals (competitors for the same customers), and they have teamed up with their suppliers as allies against common adversaries. Both parties realize their destinies are linked; if one fails, the other suffers too. This perspective allows them to trust each other as allies and to take advantage of each other's expertise in ways that were impossible before. The move away from an arm's-length approach follows an evolutionary process of moving from purchasing to strategic sourcing. Exhibit 5.13 identifies and describes the steps along this evolutionary path, along with the approximate position of various industries and geographic regions. The steps involved in the typical purchasing process appear in Exhibit 5.14.

Traditional purchasing management stresses the latter half of this process, while strategic sourcing stresses the first half. The exhibit indicates that both the range of options and the overall impact of decisions made are sharply curtailed as one moves from the early steps of this process to the later ones. In other words, managers who are rethinking procurement can have a much greater impact on their organization's order fulfillment process by working on issues shown on the left side of Exhibit 5.14.[64]

Motorola has dramatically changed its procurement process by shifting toward a partnering approach. The firm sees its suppliers as important sources of ideas and capabilities that can enhance Motorola's own competitive position. To improve suppliers' capabilities, Motorola sends them through extensive training at "Motorola University," but it does not expect the learning to go all in one direction. In fact, Motorola has come to value its suppliers' expertise so much that it has created a fifteen-member council of suppliers that regularly studies Motorola's own processes and offers ideas on how to improve them. The result: improved production scheduling accuracy and new-product design layout. The firm's vice president of procurement says that strengthened relationships with suppliers enhance the quality, cost, and timeliness of Motorola's products because "every time we make an error it takes people at both ends to correct it."[65]

Balancing the Benefits of Standardized and Customized Production

Traditionally, managers overseeing order fulfillment processes faced a choice between mass production of standardized products and batch production of customized prod-

EXHIBIT 5.13
Stages in Moving from Purchasing to Strategic Sourcing

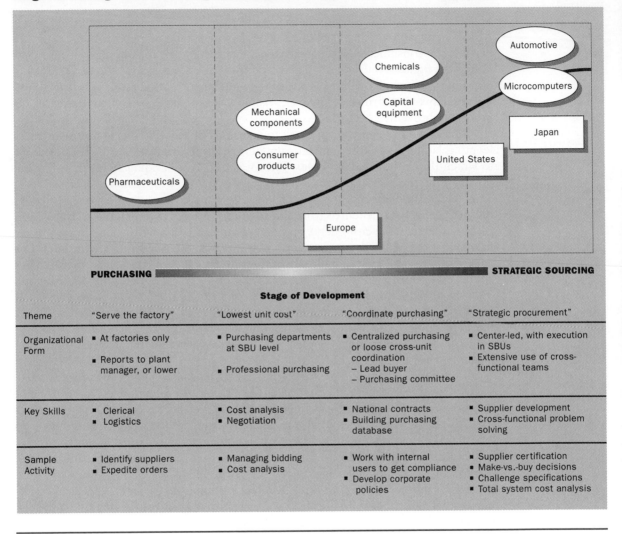

	Stage of Development			
Theme	"Serve the factory"	"Lowest unit cost"	"Coordinate purchasing"	"Strategic procurement"

Organizational Form	▪ At factories only
	 ▪ Reports to plant manager, or lower
		▪ Purchasing departments at SBU level
		 ▪ Professional purchasing
			▪ Centralized purchasing or loose cross-unit coordination
			  – Lead buyer
			  – Purchasing committee
				▪ Center-led, with execution in SBUs
				 ▪ Extensive use of cross-functional teams

Key Skills	▪ Clerical ▪ Logistics	▪ Cost analysis ▪ Negotiation	▪ National contracts ▪ Building purchasing database	▪ Supplier development ▪ Cross-functional problem solving
Sample Activity	▪ Identify suppliers ▪ Expedite orders	▪ Managing bidding ▪ Cost analysis	▪ Work with internal users to get compliance ▪ Develop corporate policies	▪ Supplier certification ▪ Make-vs.-buy decisions ▪ Challenge specifications ▪ Total system cost analysis

Source: Mark Keough, "Buying Your Way to the Top," *McKinsey Quarterly* (Summer 1993), 41–61. Reprinted by permission of The McKinsey Quarterly.

ucts. Businesses that emphasized low cost opted for mass production of standardized goods, which contained costs for several reasons: long, continuous production runs lowered the costly downtime of setting up the equipment to produce another product; focusing on a single product mix allowed the processes to be tailored for utmost efficiency; and all volume was in a narrow product range, allowing the business to move relatively quickly down its learning curve. On the other hand, firms that wished to stress differentiation often took a different approach, offering customized products made in small batches to suit specific customers. Firms could thus carefully match what their

EXHIBIT 5.14
Identifying the Greatest Opportunities for Improving the Procurement Process

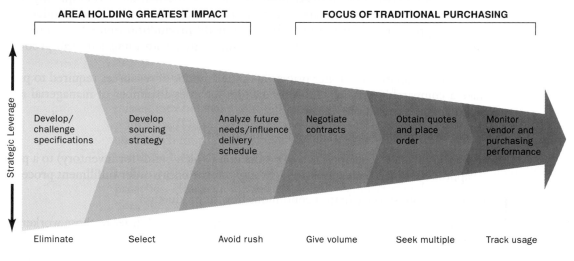

Source: Mark Keough, "Buying Your Way to the Top," *McKinsey Quarterly* (Summer 1993), 41–61. Reprinted by permission of The McKinsey Quarterly.

customers wanted and offset the greater costs involved by charging premium prices. This erstwhile forced choice between these two options contributed to the notion that businesses could successfully pursue *either* low cost *or* differentiation as competitive advantages, but not both. But, as we saw in the previous chapter, this dichotomy has proven false as firms regularly pursue both forms of competitive advantage.

One reason they can do this is an approach to order fulfillment known as mass customization. As the name implies, mass customization attempts to blend the best attributes of mass production and customized production. Doing so is no mean feat, and usually takes a complete redesign of the order fulfillment process with the dual goals of cost-reduction-through-standardization and differentiation-through-customization built in throughout the new process. The transformation has been challenging. To quote one article describing the changes involved, "Toyota—and other firms involved—did not realize that mass customization is not simply an advanced stage of continuous improvement. . . . Successful mass customization calls for more: total transformation of the organization."[66]

Shifting from Mass Production Systems to Lean Production Systems

The last 100 years have seen the development and use of three very different approaches to managing the order fulfillment process.[67] The first of these, craft production, required skilled artisans to fill orders with custom-made products. Craft production has all but disappeared. While consumers can still find tailored suits, custom-designed furniture, and high-performance bicycles that are custom made

13. Bruce Rayner, "Trial-by-Fire Transformation," *Harvard Business Review* (May–June 1992), 116–129; Otis Port and Geoffrey Smith, "Quality," *Business Week* (November 30, 1992), 66–75.

14. U.S. General Accounting Office, "Management Practices—U.S. Companies Improve Performance Through Quality Efforts," Washington, DC: U.S. Government Printing Office, May 1990.

15. Ronald Nicol and Harold Sirkin, "Manufacturing Beyond the Factory Floor: The White Collar Factory," *Target* (Winter 1991), 28–35.

16. Rahul Jacob, "TQM: More Than a Dying Fad?," *Fortune* (October 18, 1993), 65–72; J. M. Juran, "Why Quality Initiatives Fail," *Journal of Business Strategy* (July–August 1993), 35–38.

17. For discussion of this use of the quality award, see David A. Garvin, "How the Baldrige Award Really Works," *Harvard Business Review* (November–December 1991), 80–93.

18. Jim Smith and Mark Oliver, "The Baldrige Boondoggle," *Machine Design* (August 6, 1992), 25–29; John Thackray, "Fads, Fixes, & Fictions," *Management Today* (June 1993), 40–42.

19. Michael Hammer, "Hammer Defends Reengineering," *The Economist* (November 5, 1994), 70.

20. Darrell Rigby, "The Secret History of Process Reengineering," *Planning Review* (March–April 1993), 24–27.

21. Jacob, "TQM," 66.

22. Jacob, "TQM."

23. For research describing the benefits of such horizontal, cross-functional cooperation, see John E. Ettlie and Ernesto M. Reza, "Organizational Integration and Process Innovation," *Academy of Management Journal, 35*:4(1992), 795–827.

24. Port and Smith, "Quality," 72.

25. Jeremy Main, "How to Steal the Best Ideas Around," *Fortune* (October 19, 1992), 102–106; Otis Port and Geoffrey Smith, "Beg, Borrow, and Benchmark," *Business Week* (November 30, 1992), 74–75.

26. Stratford Sherman, "Are You as Good as the Best in the World?," *Fortune* (December 13, 1993), 95–96.

27. Porter, "What Is Strategy?"

28. For amplification of these points, see Michael Hammer, "Reengineering Work: Don't Automate, Obliterate," *Harvard Business Review, 68* (July–August 1990), 104–112.

29. We are indebted to Richard N. Foster for his work on product innovation for this idea, which we have adapted to process innovation; see *Innovation: The Attacker's Advantage*, New York: Summit Books, 1986.

30. Jacob, "TQM," 68.

31. Bristol Voss, "Setting a Course for Radical Change," *Journal of Business Strategy* (November–December 1993), 52–57.

32. For further discussion of how developing capabilities that are not linked to an overall strategy can lead organizations astray, see George Stalk, Jr., and Alan M. Weber, "Japan's Dark Side of Time," *Harvard Business Review* (July–August 1993), 93–102.

33. Jacob, "TQM."

34. Heygate and Hagel are quoted in Thomas A. Stewart, "Reengineering: The Hot New Managing Tool," *Fortune* (August 23, 1993), 41–48.

35. Richard Heygate, "Immoderate Redesign," *McKinsey Quarterly* (Winter 1993), 72–87.

36. This quote and further discussion of this general thesis are found in Hayes and Pisano, "Beyond World-Class."

37. For a look at two misguided quality improvement efforts, see Betsy Wiesendanger, "Deming's Luster Dims at Florida Power & Light," *Journal of Business Strategy* (September–October 1993), 60–61; and Mark Ivey and John Carey, "The Ecstasy and the Agony," *Business Week* (October 21, 1991), 40.

38. Jacob, "TQM," 68.

39. Jill Vitiello in "Reengineering: It's Totally Radical," *Journal of Business Strategy* (November–December 1993), 44–47.

40. This idea has mistakenly spread because of a misunderstanding related to the title of a very influential book. Philip B. Crosby's book *Quality Is Free*, New York: New American Library, 1979, argues that quality efforts will more than pay for themselves, resulting in a net gain rather than a net cost. However, anyone who carefully reads Crosby's work will appreciate that his prescriptions require an investment of time and money.

41. W. E. Deming, "An Interview with W. Edwards Deming: The Roots of Quality Control in Japan," *Pacific Basin Quarterly* (Spring 1985), 3–4.

42. Additional representative models of the steps involved can be found in Alex Miller, *Introducing Process Improvement*, Dayton, OH: National Management Association, 1993; D. Brian Harrison and Maurice D. Pratt, "A Methodology for Reengineering Businesses," *Planning Review* (March–April 1993), 6–11; and Timothy R. Furey, "A Six-Step Guide to Process Reengineering," *Planning Review* (March–April 1993), 20–23.

43. There are a number of books that identify principles that have proven applicable in improving the efficiency and/or effectiveness of a wide range of processes. See, for example, Thomas H. Davenport, *Process Innovation: Reengineering Work Through Information Technology*, Boston: Harvard Business School Press, 1993; Hammer and Champy, *Reengineering the Corporation*; H. James Harrington, *Business Process Improvement*, New York: McGraw-Hill, 1991; Miller, *Introducing Process Improvement*; and Peter M. Senge et al., *The Fifth Discipline Fieldbook*, New York: Doubleday/Currency, 1994.

44. Other managerial challenges inherent in CPR are identified in Robert B. Kaplan and Laura Murdock, "Core Process Redesign," *McKinsey Quarterly* (Spring 1991), 27–43; and John Hagel III, "Keeping CPR on Track," *McKinsey Quarterly* (Winter 1993), 59–72.

45. Jill Vitiello, "Revenge of the Nerds," *Journal of Business Strategy* (November–December 1993), 46–47.

46. In Chapter 11, we will consider how the support processes, which focus more on internal customers, can be reengineered to provide leverage in implementing particular strategic changes in how the organization operates. If you are interested in some of the issues involved in coordinating changes made in support core processes with those described below for primary core processes, you might begin by looking at Sally Solo, "How to Listen to Consumers," *Fortune* (January 11, 1993), 77–78; and Scott A. Snell and James W. Dean, Jr., "Integrated Manufacturing and Human Resource Management: A Human Capital Perspective," *Academy of Management Journal*, 35:3(1992), 467–504.

47. Clearly, the debate over technological push versus customer pull is not new. The arguments on this topic as it applies to the railroad industry were first presented in 1960— see T. Levitt, "Marketing Myopia," *Harvard Business Review* (July–August 1960), 45–56.

While it is not a new idea, it is an idea that each generation of managers appears to rediscover and struggle with.

48. For further discussion regarding the importance of understanding customer value in developing new products, see Fernando Flores, "Innovation by Listening Carefully to Customers," *Long Range Planning, 26*:3(1993), 95–102.

49. Further details on a comparison of these two approaches can be found in chap. 11 of Robert H. Hayes, Steven C. Wheelwright, and Kim B. Clark, *Dynamic Manufacturing*, New York: The Free Press, 1988.

50. For examples and further discussion, see chap. 5 of Joseph D. Blackburn, *Time-Based Competition*, Homewood, IL: Business One Irwin, 1991; and chap. 4 of George Stalk, Jr., and Thomas M. Hout, *Competing Against Time*, New York: The Free Press, 1990.

51. The market life cycle for an entire product category was labeled "the market life cycle" in Chapter 4. We are speaking here of the life of an individual unit rather than an entire product category or market.

52. In most organizations, demand management is assigned the critical task of being the "voice of the customer." This does not mean that this process alone is responsible for representing the interests of the customer—we have stressed throughout this chapter that *every* process is supposed to be managed with the customer's need foremost. However, to avoid the danger that "everybody's responsibility is no one's responsibility," the demand management process is typically singled out for special responsibility in this area, and therefore we are covering the widely applicable concept of customer value under the demand management heading.

53. Gary Hamel and C. K. Prahalad, *Competing for the Future*, Boston: Harvard Business School Press, 1994.

54. Zachary Schiller, "Stalking the New Consumer," *Business Week* (August 28, 1989), 54–62; Mark Alpert, "Hit 'em Where They Used to Be," *Fortune* (October 19, 1992), 112–113.

55. Peter Child et al., "World-Class Operations: The Management of Complexity," *McKinsey Quarterly* (Fall 1991), 52–68.

56. Michael Robert, "Market Fragmentation Versus Market Segmentation," *Journal of Business Strategy* (September–October 1992), 48–53; John Griffin, Scott Beardsley, and Robert Kugel, "Commonality: Marrying Design with a Process," *McKinsey Quarterly* (Spring 1991), 56–69.

57. Peter Cummings, David White, and Stefan Wisniowski, "Strategic Simplicity," *McKinsey Quarterly* (Summer 1991), 80–90.

58. Walecia Konrad, "Small Selling," *Business Week* (August 3, 1992), 46–51.

59. This section draws heavily on research reported in Daniel P. Finkelman and Anthony R. Goland, "How *Not* to Satisfy Your Customers," *McKinsey Quarterly* (Winter 1990), 2–11.

60. Patricia Sellers, "Companies That Serve You Best," *Fortune* (May 31, 1993), 74–88.

61. Finkelman and Goland, "How *Not* to Satisfy Your Customers."

62. Robin Cammish and Mark Keough, "World-Class Operations: A Strategic Role for Purchasing," *McKinsey Quarterly* (Summer 1991), 22–39.

63. James A. Welch and P. Ranganath Nayak, "Strategic Sourcing: A Progressive Approach to the Make-or-Buy Decision," *Academy of Management Executive, 6* (February 1992), 23–31.

64. Mark Keough, "Buying Your Way to the Top," *McKinsey Quarterly* (Summer 1993), 41–61.

65. Myron Magnet, "The New Golden Rule of Business," *Fortune* (February 21, 1994), 60–64.

66. B. Joseph Pine II, Bart Victor, and Andrew C. Boynton, "Making Mass Customization Work," *Harvard Business Review* (September–October 1993), 108–119.

67. This section draws heavily from James P. Womack, Daniel T. Jones, and Daniel Roos, *The Machine That Changed the World*, New York: Rawson Associates, 1990, a report from a 5-year study of the world automobile manufacturing industry conducted by researchers at the Massachusetts Institute of Technology.

68. You may have noticed that there is considerable overlap between these ideas and those discussed throughout the rest of the chapter. In fact, the improvement of core process capabilities across the organization can be viewed as the application of lean concepts organizationwide. For discussion of this idea, see James P. Womack and Daniel T. Jones, "From Lean Production to the Lean Enterprise," *Harvard Business Review* (March–April 1994), 93–103.

Chapter 6

Business-Level Strategy

CHAPTER OUTLINE

THE EL

Firms compete directly with one another at what is called the business level of strategic management, so this chapter will focus on crafting successful competitive strategies. Because competition takes place at the business level, strategic management at this level is crucial to the overall success of the firm. Accordingly, the concept of competitive advantage is the focus of this chapter.

This chapter has four parts that reflect the major considerations in formulating a competitive strategy at the business level. The first part introduces the elements of competition and explains how business-level strategy often entails altering one of these. In the second and third parts of the chapter, we focus in more detail on two of the most important elements of competition: tactics, or maneuvering for competitive advantage; and scope, the breadth of the boundaries used to define a business and its competitive arena. In the fourth part of the chapter, we consider how concepts covered in the first three sections of the chapter play out during a firm's pursuit and maintenance of a competitive advantage over the various stages of the market life cycle.

This chapter will help you understand:

- The five elements of competition: players, added values, rules, tactics, and scope
- The need to build a competitive strategy by first viewing competition through the eyes of the different players involved
- The importance of added value as the ultimate source of competitive advantage and firm performance
- The power inherent in the ability to rewrite the rules of competition
- Four general types of tactics—preemption, attack, deterrence, and response—and more specific examples of each
- The importance and benefits of carefully defining your business
- The three dimensions along which a business can best be defined: functions provided, technologies employed, and customers served
- The advantages and disadvantages of narrowly defining your business by focusing on a particular niche
- The market life cycle and its application to formulating competitive business strategies

EXHIBIT 6.1
The Elements of Competition

Players — the entities that form competitive networks of rivalry. They include your own company, suppliers, customers, potential entrants, substitute producers, competitors, and complementors.

Added Values — the net of plusses and minuses every player brings to the competition. To measure a firm's total added value, first assess the value created by all players, and then see how much this would be diminished by removing the firm in question.

Rules — the structure and system within which competition takes place. Rules may be written (e.g., regulations, antitrust laws, and contracts) or unwritten (e.g., customs, culture, and tacit agreements).

Tactics — the maneuvers undertaken in an attempt to gain, maintain, or regain a competitive advantage. The four general types of tactics are preemption, attack, deterrence, and response.

Scope — this refers to the boundaries of competition. Each player establishes scope through the process of defining its business. A business can be defined along the dimensions of
1. the functions provided,
2. the technologies employed, or
3. the customers served.

petition from perspectives that can guide you to correctly shape your competitive strategy. The exhibit shows competition as a game that is played out on several fields simultaneously. As a manager, you would most naturally view the five forces analysis with your own firm in the center of the field, but, to understand the intricacies of competitive strategy, you also need to understand the game as it is played out on the fields that have your competitors and your complementors at their centers.

To understand the need to view competition through the eyes of the other players involved, consider the case of Holland Sweetener Company. HSC was hoping to cash in on the lucrative profits Monsanto had earned through sales of aspartame, a sweetener that Monsanto sold globally under the brand name Nutrasweet. Monsanto held the patents to aspartame, and this monopoly position had generated profit margins as high as 70 percent, but those patents were just about to expire. HSC hoped to become

EXHIBIT 6.2
The Players and the Fields of Play in Business Competition

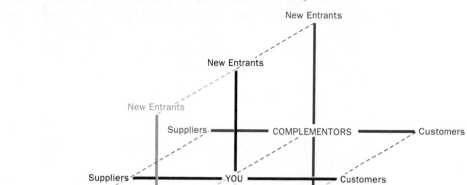

the new European supplier of aspartame to major soft drink producers, such as Coke and Pepsi. HSC's plan was to significantly underprice Monsanto while still making a reasonable profit. Coke and Pepsi would have been delighted to have paid less for aspartame than Monsanto's monopolistic prices but, just as Monsanto's patents were about to expire, they both signed long-term contracts for Nutrasweet, contracts that greatly limited HSC's market potential.

To understand why this move was predictable, HSC should have viewed the competition from both its rivals' and its customers' perspectives. Nutrasweet had a strong brand following, European soft drink consumption was an important growth segment for the firm, and it had both the high prices and the low production costs that would allow it to lower prices relatively painlessly to defend its market. Meanwhile, although they may have wanted to pay less for sweetener, neither Coke nor Pepsi wanted to be the first to drop the "Made with Nutrasweet" labels off their cans, because doing so would have provided the other rival with a potential marketing edge. Consequently, Nutrasweet lowered its prices, Coke and Pepsi signed long-term contracts, and HSC had to look elsewhere for customers. Once we view competition through the eyes of other players, it's easy to see the inevitability of such an outcome.

Added Values

A theme running throughout this text is that, in competitive environments, firm success is directly proportional to the value it creates. This is a fundamental truism because competitive rivalry ensures that a firm cannot take more value away from the marketplace than it brings to the marketplace. If you are my supplier and you try to capture more value than you create, say, by overcharging for inferior goods, I will switch to an alternative supplier. Only if you create value for me will I tolerate your efforts to capture more value for yourself. Therefore, as we have said many times, the essence of strategy is the search for means of establishing a competitive advantage over your rivals by providing superior customer value. Application 6.1 illustrates how a firm can be tremendously successful by adding value for all the players in its competitive marketplace.

To determine how much value you add to your marketplace, look at the total value created by all players involved, and then see how much this total value would be decreased by removing your firm. When you take this broad perspective on value, you may be surprised at all the ways in which your firm creates value. Obviously, a firm hopes to create value by offering goods and services, but this is only one source of value. For example, HSC created value for Coke and Pepsi by providing a competitive threat that forced Monsanto to lower its prices on Nutrasweet, saving the European soft drink industry an estimated total of $200 million annually. While it never sold a product to Coke or Pepsi, HSC still created value, but, unfortunately, the firm was never able to capture the value it had created. With a broader understanding of the means by which it created value for other players, HSC might have tried to capture value from Coke and Pepsi by, say, seeking their help in financing its start-up.

Rules

Every competition is governed by a set of rules, some written and some unwritten. The written rules are obvious—laws, regulations, policies, and contracts; unwritten rules can be just as important, although much less obvious. Unwritten rules include customs, habits, rituals, and tacit agreements that develop over time in particular marketplaces.

Successful competitive strategy often requires firms to change the rules of the game. For example, the U.S. soft drink industry lobbied Congress to pass a law that allowed soft drink concentrate producers, such as Coke and Pepsi, to enforce a bottling network that prohibited bottlers from competing in one another's territories—changing a written rule of competition. Nike changed the unwritten rules of the athletic footwear industry by redefining the basic running shoe. Instead of a relatively heavy, stiff, and uncomfortable all-leather cleated shoe suitable only for runners, Nike offered a light, soft, comfortable nylon shoe that could be worn by anybody as part of a casual wardrobe. Later, Reebok succeeded by rewriting the rules again, this time focusing on females instead of males, as shoe companies had done previously.

When a firm rewrites the rules, it is typically trying to build a competitive advantage by altering its structural position, as discussed in Chapter 3. Nike and Reebok created niches that would serve as beachheads from which they could attack the rest of the market. Both set records for the speed with which they grew to the billion-dollar revenue mark, demonstrating that, when successful, such strategies can produce dramatic results.

To this point, we have been discussing how concepts introduced in Chapter 3 relate to building competitive strategies at the business level. However, in discussing the

Application 6.1

Nintendo's Competitive Strategy: Creating and Capturing Value

Nintendo, the Japanese company that invented and then completely dominated the video game market, provides a nearly perfect example of how to develop a competitive strategy. The company's success arose from maximizing value both created and captured. To understand the power of Nintendo's strategy, we must see it from the eyes of all the other players it affected.

Customers

Nintendo's video games were sold through a highly concentrated market—most units were sold by megaretailers such as Toys "R" Us and Wal-Mart. These are notoriously powerful buyers, known for wrenching the absolute best possible terms from suppliers. However, Nintendo greatly reduced the power these buyers had when it limited its product availability. Although the market could have absorbed 45 million units, Nintendo produced only 33 million units. This scarcity in the face of demand left consumers waiting in lines stretching into the streets. Nintendo units became such a store traffic builder that no retailer could afford to be without it, and the power shifted away from the retailing giants back to Nintendo.

Suppliers

By focusing on older 8-bit chip machines, the most important supply going into a Nintendo unit was essentially a commodity. Several suppliers were all aggressively trying to supply the millions of chips Nintendo needed, and these suppliers were willing to do so at bargain-basement prices.

Substitutes

For children, Nintendo's final consumers, no attractive substitutes for video games existed. The only substitution was the means by which the games would be delivered. This ranged from more expensive dedicated video games to even more expensive computers. Neither were especially strong threats to Nintendo's popularity.

Complementors

In this area, Nintendo's strategy was truly impressive. The most obvious complementors for Nintendo's hardware were game developers, and they threatened to capture much of the value created by the entire marketplace, just as other software developers had done in other segments of the computer industry. However, Nintendo countered this threat through a number of tactics. First, it developed its own in-house game developers so that outsiders knew that they could not push too hard or Nintendo would simply turn to its in-house source. Second, it controlled the number of games that each developer could produce, by limiting licensing to the various programmers, and this prohibited any one developer from becoming too powerful. Third, it required exclusivity from outside developers; in other words, software suppliers had to agree not to program for Nintendo's competitors. This was not a difficult concession to make, because Nintendo already had the largest installed base of games, and every game developer wanted to program for that market. However, this concession created tremendous value for Nintendo.

Competitors

The huge demand for Nintendo systems coupled with its exclusive relationships with game developers meant that very few programmers had an interest in developing games for machines other than Nintendos. This put Nintendo's competitors at a huge disadvantage because they had to develop all their games in-house. Furthermore, Nintendo's advantage increased over time as its larger selection of games increased sales, allowing it to lower its costs, which increased its installed base even more, making game developers even less interested in writing for Nintendo's competitors.

Potential Entrants

The same vicious cycle that hounded Nintendo's competitors effectively precluded entry by new rivals. In fact, the company was only seriously threatened when Sega broke Nintendo's stronghold on software suppliers by developing a 16-bit chip machine. This gave developers a completely new market to write for, and they were suddenly willing to leave the Nintendo fold for the potential this new market offered.

How much value did Nintendo create? To answer this, imagine how much value the video game industry would have captured if Nintendo were suddenly plucked out of the entire network of suppliers, developers, and sellers.

With Nintendo suddenly gone, there would not have been a multibillion-dollar video game industry. And as a result of its brilliant competitive strategy, the firm was able to capture immense value as well. This can be documented by a single particularly startling statistic. Although Nintendo was essentially a one-product company, at the height of its popularity it had a market value well in excess of other well-known Japanese giants such as Sony and Nissan!

last two elements of competition, tactics and scope, we need to introduce several new concepts, so each of these elements of competition warrants its own section and more detailed discussions.

TYPES OF TACTICS

Tactics are maneuvers a business uses in combat with its rivals to address threats and help ensure that a firm's broader strategy is carried out successfully.[4] We can array tactics along either of two dimensions, as shown in Exhibit 6.3.

The most familiar dimension distinguishes between offensive and defensive tactics. *Offensive tactics* are more proactive—instead of waiting for something to happen, the offensive firm moves to take the initiative and to control the competitive situation. *Defensive tactics* protect the status quo or react to events as they unfold. Application 6.2 illustrates offensive and defensive tactics used by global competitors in the luxury segment of the U.S. automobile market.

EXHIBIT 6.3
Four Categories of Tactics

	Anticipatory Tactics	**Tactics of Engagement**
Offensive Tactics	**PREEMPTION** • Pioneering • Intimidation • Capture	**ATTACK** • Frontal Assault • Flanking Maneuver • Siege Warfare • Guerilla Warfare
Defensive Tactics	**DETERRENCE** • Raising Structural Barriers • Increased Expected Retaliation • Lowering Inducements for Attack • Diplomatic Peacekeeping	**RESPONSE** • Counterattack • Fast follower • Retrenchment • Withdrawal

Application 6.2

Attack and Response in the Luxury-Car Market

The early 1980s U.S. luxury-car market was the industry's most profitable segment and its six competitors split the 900,000-unit segment with profits for all. These profits attracted Japanese competitors who attacked the incumbents with high-quality luxury automobiles (regularly top-rated in terms of customer satisfaction) at very competitive prices (typically 30 percent less than comparably equipped competitors' cars). By the end of the decade, fifteen brands of luxury automobiles were available in the United States, and two of these, Lexus and Infiniti, had emerged as the segment leaders. Japanese companies had pulled off one of the most stunningly successful competitive attacks in the history of automaking.

The two leading German luxury-car makers, Mercedes and BMW, especially hard hit by the Japanese attack, saw their U.S. sales drop by nearly 30 percent. Both firms had to respond to this attack but, in doing so, they used very different tactics and got very different results.

Mercedes responded by ceding the low end of the luxury market (the below-$30,000 price range) to the Japanese and focusing on the high end of the segment (the $60,000-and-up price range) where Japanese firms had yet to attack. Mercedes' lowest priced car cost $30,000, but it focused the bulk of its advertising and new-product development on much higher-priced models.

BMW responded by counterattacking. The company focused the bulk of its new-product development and marketing efforts on its 3 Series, its low-end line of automobiles. Within the 3 Series, BMW introduced five successful new models in the $20,000 to $33,000 price range. This helped improve the company's brand image so that "Beemers" became *the* car for young, wealthy, active car buyers—the perfect customer segment for follow-up sales of higher-priced models.

BMW felt compelled to counter the Japanese carmakers' attack by fighting to maintain a strong position in the low end because, managers reasoned, if they failed to put up a successful fight for this segment, the Japanese would use it as a base from which to launch an attack on the higher end of the luxury segment, leaving BMW with no place to run. The counterattack proved very successful. By 1995, sales of Lexus and Infiniti cars were dropping and both companies were developing new lower-priced models, and BMW surpassed Mercedes to become the top-selling German import for the first time.

BMW's success forced Mercedes to rethink its original response and reestablish its commitment to the low end of the luxury segment with its C-class or "Baby Benz" models and plans for a minicar priced at "only" $20,000 for the European market. Because BMW's new models were all built on the same preexisting 3 Series frame, its models remained very cost competitive with the new Mercedes models, and BMW continued its counterattack, introducing the Z3 roadster, made famous by the James Bond movie. Demand for the under-$30,000 car was so great that waiting lists were over a year long.

The second dimension distinguishes between anticipatory tactics and tactics of engagement. *Anticipatory tactics* involve avoidance of head-to-head competition. Anticipatory tactics are the business equivalent of a cold war—maneuvers carried out to gain the upper hand without actually engaging the enemy. *Tactics of engagement* refers to the thrust and parry of actual combat between rivals. By combining these two dimensions, we create a four-celled matrix that organizes a wide variety of commonly observed tactics into more convenient categories labeled preemption, attack, deterrence, and response. Let's consider each of these categories.

Preemption

This category of tactics refers to proactive efforts to keep ahead of competitors by moving first, in order to avoid competition. Common preemptive tactics include pioneering, intimidation, and capture.

Pioneering

In business, pioneer firms break new ground by being first to undertake some endeavor of potentially strategic importance to a broader set of firms. The clearest example of pioneering is opening up a new market, but pioneering can take other forms as well. Firms may be first to form strategic alliances, first to advertise in a new way, first to vertically integrate, first to emphasize outsourcing, first to cut prices, and so forth. In short, *any* leadership in taking action that can be followed or adopted by a broader set of firms can be seen as pioneering. Pioneers hope to gain what are known as *first-mover advantages*, competitive advantages that accrue to market leaders because they are the first to successfully undertake a particular strategic initiative. Considerable research has been done on first-mover advantages, particularly those resulting from entering new markets. (We discuss this research later in the chapter when we look at establishing competitive advantages in the introduction stage of the market life cycle.)

Intimidation

In this case, a firm makes offensive moves to scare off would-be followers. These moves can take several forms. When building up plant capacity in advance of actual increases in demand, a firm is often trying to "bluff" rivals out of adding additional capacity of their own, as we saw in Kellogg's overseas operations in Chapter 4. The other firms will note the industry's expanded level of capacity and rightly conclude that such capacity cannot be supported by the current market. Consequently, they will not increase their own new capacity and, if the market expands, the intimidator will be positioned to gain market share. Other common forms of intimidation include keeping a large "war chest" of cash or other liquid assets on hand that firms could use if a confrontation should flare up, and visibly "staking out turf" by opening new sales offices. A firm can also send clear signals that it intends to survive an impending market shakeout, such as continuing to invest in a business even when its underlying market is shrinking, another intimidating act.

Capture

In this context, capture entails moving offensively to secure assets, rights, or resources in such a way that places would-be rivals at a disadvantage. Patents are the most obvious examples of capture; when a firm has a patented product or process, rivals will have to invent their way around the patents or pay licensing fees to patent holders. Other examples of capture are buying up key real estate to ensure superior locations, leasing scarce mineral rights or otherwise securing access to key raw materials, or securing exclusive or dominant access to major distribution channels.

Attack

Although it is offensive behavior, preemption involves maneuvers that fall just short of the direct confrontation involved in a rival's established position. Let's turn now to consideration of such attacks, and consider the various forms they can take.

Frontal Assault

The most blatant form of offensive behavior, this involves direct attacks on rivals in head-to-head competition. The front in such an attack may be any strategically important aspect of the rival's competitive position: price, image, distribution channels, market share, key customers, and so on. Such assaults are a very expensive form of rivalry and may trigger wars that make the industry less attractive for all firms. Such wars do not end easily. For example, when Pepsi attacked Coke's dominant position with the Pepsi Challenge, it triggered a price war that halved the domestic profit margins of both rivals over 2 decades of fighting.

Flanking Maneuvers

Rather than throwing their firms into frontal assaults, many managers seek to avoid a direct attack by using flanking maneuvers. For example, Hewlett-Packard, a direct rival of IBM in the personal computer market, had little success for all its efforts. However, when the company shifted its emphasis from the computers themselves to developing IBM-compatible printers, that is, to become a complementor (IBM had regularly outsourced this segment of the business), HP was tremendously successful and became a market leader in supplying printers that customers used as part of their IBM-based computer systems.

Siege Warfare

This tactic, sometimes known as encirclement, involves attacking simultaneously on multiple fronts. Attacking firms attempt to totally dominate rivals by reaching a larger number of customers by selling more products, through more channels, and at a broader range of prices. Several national chains of specialty retailers have been successful with this tactic. For example, Circuit City and Office Depot offer a range of products that simply overwhelm mass merchandise retailers' efforts at similar offerings. Further, national chains enjoy a volume level that gives them better margins than smaller, local specialty retailers can enjoy. By successfully attacking their rivals on every conceivable front, these retailing powerhouses have emerged as dominant players in their industries.

Guerilla Warfare

In many ways, this offensive tactic is the opposite of siege warfare. Rather than trying to outlast rivals in all-out confrontations, guerilla tactics call for quick hit-and-run maneuvers.[5] For example, when an upstart rival steals away a major account from its larger competitors, offers a free extended-service contract on all products sold over the next 6 months, and then just happens to come out with a new advertising campaign on the same day the market leader announces its new line of products, the upstart is engaging in guerilla warfare.

Deterrence

Deterrent tactics are meant to influence a rival's calculations about what can be gained from attacking your position. The goal of such tactics is to convince the would-be challenger that the attack would not be a wise option, or to redirect the attack in a way that is less threatening to the defender. In other words, these tactics involve efforts to achieve avoided competition, as discussed in Chapter 3. Most efforts at deterrence involve one or more of the following tactics.

Raising Structural Barriers

Related to the structural issues involved in a five forces analysis. Firms may raise barriers to entry, making it more difficult for rivals to enter the market and increase competition. Such tactics could include lobbying a government for trade barriers limiting foreign competition, tying up distribution channels, raising buyers' switching costs to keep them from "defecting," and plugging holes in established product lines to make it more difficult for a challenger to find a toehold—all aimed at defending an existing market by discouraging new entrants.

Increasing Expected Retaliation to Attacks

Defenders may retaliate against aggressive moves made by rivals in a number of ways that we'll explain below when we discuss the tactic of response. Here we are talking about increasing the challengers' expectations of a response, thereby discouraging the attack in the first place. One means of influencing challengers' expectations is *market signaling*: taking actions that indicate your future intentions in a manner that is highly visible to the rest of your market, such as continued public reference to your willingness to move aggressively against any new entrants. A very common market signal is the advertising tag line. "We will not be undersold," which signals a clear willingness to engage in retaliatory price cutting. Finally, a very aggressive response to one competitor may signal other potential challengers of the retaliation they can expect if they attack.

Lowering Inducements to Attack

The first two deterrent tactics aim to lower the profits a potential challenger can expect from attacking a defender's position. This third tactic differs in that it usually entails a defender's willing acceptance of lower profits to decrease interest in its markets. The profits a defender earns indicate visibly the attractiveness of its position, and high profits attract lots of interest from potential challengers. But lowering profit margins by dropping prices or increasing services may make a challenger see the market as less profitable and less worth attacking. If would-be challengers appear overly optimistic in their market assessments, defenders may publicly discuss market conditions in more realistic, pessimistic terms. Thus, challengers may question their assumptions and become discouraged.

Diplomatic Peacekeeping

These tactics operate behind the scenes and outside the day-to-day fray of market competition. For example, competitors in some markets restrict overly harsh rivalry through an understanding that they will pursue competition on a more civil basis.

These forms of *tacit collusion* amount to unwritten agreements about what actions competitors will or will not take in order to limit head-to-head competition. An example would be a historically established precedent to divide a larger market into regions or segments that rivals are careful not to raid in fear of starting an all-out war. Local businesses that compete with one another in the same metropolitan area, such as hospitals and towing services, often have "an understanding" that divides their markets into territories for this purpose.

Response

Kmart was the largest retailer in the United States, before a relentless attack from Wal-Mart. In one 6-year period, Kmart saw its market position tumble from number one to a distant third, with market share only 30 percent the size of Wal-Mart's. Market research revealed that half of Wal-Mart's customers drove past a Kmart on their way to shop, and that the typical Wal-Mart store produced twice the revenues of the typical Kmart store, though they were of similar size. Clearly, in order to survive, Kmart had to make a meaningful response to Wal-Mart's attack. Firms responding to an attack have several options: counterattack, fast follower, retrenchment, and withdrawal.

Counterattack

Many say that the best defense is a good offense, and an attacked firm can defend itself in a number of offensive ways. For example, it may attempt to leapfrog past the attacker's position by introducing a new generation of products or services. This can be especially demoralizing to a challenger that has just invested heavily to enter a new market, only to discover it needs further investment to remain competitive. A counterattack that uses guerilla warfare tactics disrupts a challenger's test marketing to make it unsuccessful or less meaningful. Another option is litigation, in which a defender seeks legal action based on patent infringements, antitrust considerations, or suits contesting the performance claims of a challenger's products, and so forth.

Fast Follower

This defensive response acts on the dictum "If you can't beat 'em, join 'em." Here, the intention is to copy the actions of a successful challenger as soon as possible. Fast followers are often very successful because they avoid many development costs incurred by pioneers. For example, Forest Laboratories, a pharmaceutical firm that does almost no basic research, chooses instead to simply license technology developed by others. Although it competes in an industry noted for tremendous emphasis on innovation, Forest has succeeded with its follower strategy, enjoying profit margins as high as 25 percent and annual growth rates of over 20 percent.

Retrenchment

This tactic refers to falling back, ceding ground to an attacker, while attempting to maintain the firm's viability. Managers choose retrenchment when they acknowledge that the firm is neither competitive enough to succeed through a counterattack nor nimble enough to be a fast follower. This sounds bleak, but retrenchment is not necessarily the beginning of the end. Many healthy companies have faced life-threatening competitive situations in the past, successfully addressed their shortcomings, and restored themselves. For example, Xerox went through a 2-year period in the early 1980s when managers and analysts thought the firm might face bankruptcy because of crushing attacks from Japanese competitors like Canon and Sharp. Xerox gave up considerable market share under this assault. However, in the decade that followed, the firm managed to fight its way back and regain much of the market share it had lost, by focusing on customer value and reestablishing its competitive advantage.

Withdrawal

Finally, managers sometimes face the possibility that their firms will not be able to successfully defend against attacks and will be forced out of the market. A number of strategies facilitate withdrawal. Although the intricacies of bankruptcy law are well beyond the scope of this book, you should be aware of the potential savings to be had from handling this process well. Most businesses that fold still have value in their assets and, just as in a business that is operating normally, it is management's responsibility to get as much value as possible out of those assets. For example, in the middle of filing for bankruptcy, Revco, the failed drugstore chain, was offered nearly a billion dollars for its assets by a major foreign investment group. We'll return to this topic in Chapter 7, where we discuss corporate divestments.

This discussion should have provided you with a sense of the breadth of options businesses face in developing tactics as part of an overall competitive strategy. Selection of the most appropriate tactics depends on the interplay between the other elements of competition, the last of which is scope.

SCOPE: DEFINING THE BUSINESS

As an element of competition, *scope* refers to the boundaries within which rivalry takes place. Such boundaries are usually not officially prescribed or even uniformly agreed upon by all the players involved. Rather, boundaries vary depending on each player's definition of its own business. For example, if an air conditioner manufacturer defines its business as serving only industrial customers, it automatically sets boundaries for itself that exclude consumer markets and firms that focus on the home air-conditioning market. Properly defining your business is a critical step in the overall process of developing a competitive strategy because:

■ *It clarifies the essential nature of the business and its competition.* Managers can easily lose track of what is and is not essential to a firm and its success, and a clear definition of the business can often highlight issues that might otherwise be overlooked. For instance, MCI was one of several telecommunications startups to enter the long-distance telephone market when AT&T was dismantled. Although MCI managers saw themselves as being in the telephone business, they grew to realize that this perspective did not make them unique, and it did not help explain the tremendous success the firm enjoyed. After all, several new start-ups had entered the business, and they were not all successful. After closer inspection, managers observed that they spent a tremendous amount of time working with government regulators trying to change the telecommunications industry from a regulated monopoly to a less regulated and more competitive market. Much of their success was due to the excellence of this work, and managers came to think of MCI as being not just in the telephone business, but in the government relations business as well. Based on this new understanding, managers gave more consideration in strategic planning to government relations and influenced the firm's structural position.

- *It establishes a focal point for effort and horizons for growth.* By providing a sense of strategic direction, a definition of the business focuses attention toward certain goals and away from others. While overly restrictive definitions run the risk of inducing shortsightedness, without some degree of focus, an organization may not be effective. Such an organization may wander from one opportunity to another and its managers may spend inordinate amounts of time analyzing what could be done, without ever actually *doing* much of anything. A small, entrepreneurial, technology-based business and a leading innovator in finding new applications for carbon fibers exhibited just such behavior. For the first decade of the firm's life, its managers could not resist considering the dozens of potential applications for their new technological discoveries. Their reasoning was that any one of the applications could develop into multimillion-dollar markets, so they could not afford to overlook any of them. Only after the most attractive of these markets became dominated by more focused competitors did the managers finally make crucial strategic decisions regarding which markets to pursue and which to ignore.

- *It facilitates strategic analysis.* Good strategic analysis requires managers to carefully consider the segment or strategic group of the broader industry within which a firm actually competes. A well-developed business definition will clarify this and, in so doing, will help managers perform a more useful analysis of their competitive situation. For example, the Snap-On Tool Company defines its business as providing hand tools for professional mechanics. This definition places it in a strategic group that does not include mass merchandisers, such as Sears, or local retailers, such as the corner hardware store. By focusing on its particular strategic group, Snap-On is better able to tailor its strategy to what its particular market segment requires.

The Dimensions Used to Define Scope

There are two very different ways to define a business. One approach is based on the firm's perspective, which we refer to as the *supply perspective.* The other is from the customers' viewpoint, and we refer to this as the *demand perspective.* As illustrated in Exhibit 6.4 and discussed below, good strategic management requires moving back and forth between both perspectives as the firm's definition emerges along three dimensions.[6]

1. *Functions provided.* This dimension describes *what* a firm does. From the supply perspective, this entails defining what goods and services a firm sells. From the demand perspective, it defines what customer needs a firm fulfills.

EXHIBIT 6.4
Perspective and Dimensions Used to Define the Scope of a Business

	Supply Perspective	Demand Perspective
Functions Provided	The goods and services provided by the business	The customers' needs met by the business
Technology Employed	The means by which goods and services are provided	The functions and processes that intermesh with those of customers to meet their needs
Customers Served	The market segment(s) targeted by the business' marketing strategy	The customers who have needs potentially met by the business's goods and services

2. *Technologies employed.* Adopting a very broad definition of technology, this dimension provides the *how* part of an overall business definition. From the supply perspective, this describes how a firm produces and provides goods and services, and from the demand perspective it describes how a firm's functions and processes fit with its customers' needs downstream.

3. *Customers served.* From the supply perspective, this dimension identifies the target market for a product or service. From the demand perspective, this dimension identifies who has needs that can be met through a particular firm's products and services. The two may or may not overlap. For example, when they were first introduced, many financial planning services were targeted exclusively toward very wealthy individuals. However, a much larger set of customers actually needed these services, and the financial services industry saw explosive growth as it offered new services to this wider market.

As this example suggests, managers often get into trouble when they define their businesses along these dimensions exclusively from the supply or the demand perspective. The U.S. railroad industry provides a classic example:[7] Once by far the most dominant players in the U.S. transportation industry, railroad companies defined their business entirely from the supply perspective, seeing themselves solely as railroad operators. Unfortunately for them, their customers viewed them from the demand perspective, as transportation providers. As changing conditions made alternative forms of transport more viable, railroad operators became less and less important to their customers.

This example reinforces a recurrent theme that you will find throughout these chapters: managers must look at their firms in terms of the value they create for their customers. However, this is not to say that the demand perspective provides the only appropriate definition for a business.[8] Return to the railroads. Part of their business was lost to telecommunications firms that could deliver messages faster and cheaper than mail cars could. Is there any reason to believe that railroad operators could have been effective in competing for this business by attempting to move into telecommunications? Probably not. After all, the skills and competencies required to operate telecommunications systems (i.e., the technology employed as seen from the supply perspective) have little in common with those required to operate railroads. In other words, the insights gained from looking at the business from a demand perspective must be tempered with those gained from using a supply perspective. In fact, the railroads became most effective when they learned how what they did (supply perspective) could fit into the total transportation network their customers needed (demand perspective) by developing coordinated trucking, shipping, and rail operations. There are no examples of railroad companies that successfully transformed themselves into telecommunications businesses.

Now that we have considered the dimensions that define scope, we are ready to regard the relative merits of having a broadly or narrowly defined scope.

Niche Strategies: Reasons to Focus

The extent to which a firm concentrates on a narrowly defined *niche*, or segment, of one of the three dimensions discussed above is referred to as its *focus*. Application 6.3 describes how one firm moved from a narrow to a broad definition of its business along each of the three dimensions.

Several factors impact the extent to which a business should broaden or narrow its focus. The following sections examine these factors.

Differences in Competitive Environments

Sometimes, by focusing on a particular niche, a competitor can avoid head-to-head rivalry with its most fierce competition. For example, by stressing its image as the "Un-Cola," the Seven-Up Company was able to sidestep its larger rivals' "cola wars."

Differences in Value Chains

Sometimes differences in the nature of the activities that make up the value chain involved in providing a good or service preclude a firm from being in that business. Take, for example, custom-published textbooks. Custom publishing assimilates a particular school's or professor's materials and reproduces them with quick turnaround times. Even though the end product doesn't look all that different from mass-produced texts, the activities that make up the value chain in providing custom-published texts are very different. For example, custom publishing typically entails photocopying original materials, while traditional publishing typesets original materials. Consequently, many publishers do not include custom publishing in the scope of their business definition because they would essentially have to develop dual value chains that would then compete with one another.

Differences in the Resource Base Required

Just as broadening the firm's scope may entail development of a new value chain, from the resource-based view of the firm, we can see that it could require firms to develop

Redefining Scope in the Utilities Industry

A municipal utility we'll call Metro Utility Company recently redefined its scope as a key part of developing a new competitive strategy. MetU's mission was narrowly defined, as illustrated in Exhibit 6.5a. MetU served customers within its city's limits; the functions provided were the basic public utilities of electric power, gas, and water. In terms of the technology employed to provide these functions, MetU defined itself as being a "pipes and wires" business, that is, it focused on the *hardware* related to providing basic utilities.

This business definition had served MetU well for nearly 50 years. During this time, state and local regulations granted MetU a monopoly position, and MetU's customers had no other choice for utility service. Then, changes in the competitive environment threatened to disrupt MetU's comfortable situation. Senior managers at MetU predicted that, within 5 to 10 years, customers would have access to other utility providers just as, earlier, telephone customers had been given the right to

choose a long-distance service. MetU's managers knew that to be successful in this new competitive environment, they would need a very different strategy than the one they had used as a monopolist.

As part of developing this new strategy, the management team began to question its definition of the business. The managers realized that to be chosen as a preferred provider of service, they would have to offer customers greater value than competitors could. The search for more value led them to redefine their business along all three previously mentioned dimensions, as shown in Exhibit 6.5b.

Functions Provided

From this perspective, MetU's managers knew that *any* utility could provide basic power, gas, and water services. To differentiate, a competitor should offer new forms of added value, and the management team found two important new sources: (1) services such as advice on energy management and customized billing, and (2) participation

EXHIBIT 6.5a
Narrow Definition of Scope

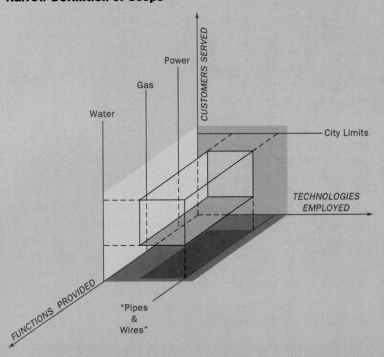

in the region's economic development efforts to offer new and higher-quality jobs. The latter created value not for customers per se, but for the political entities that made important decisions regarding the region's future.

Customers Served

In redefining itself along this dimension, MetU realized several benefits from expanding its horizons to include a broader region. First of all, improved economies of scale allowed it to lower its costs, which had a clear impact on its competitiveness. But the broader definition had other unexpected benefits. For example, by looking at issues on a regionwide basis, the company was better able to provide value through its efforts to be environmentally responsible, because environmental issues, such as water pollution, are regional problems that do not adhere to narrow political boundaries such as city limits.

Technologies Employed

To be effective within the broader definitions of its functions and customers, MetU had to adopt and master a new set of technologies as well. For instance, many of its value-added services went beyond the hardware of "pipes and wires" to involve the company in consulting activities using new technologies such as energy management. An even more radical departure came when the firm realized that it needed to gain expertise in politics to be effective in the economic development of the region.

Merely redefining its scope did not solve any of MetU's problems, but it did prove a critical first step in the overall process of crafting a new competitive strategy for the organization.

EXHIBIT 6.5b
Broader Definition of Scope

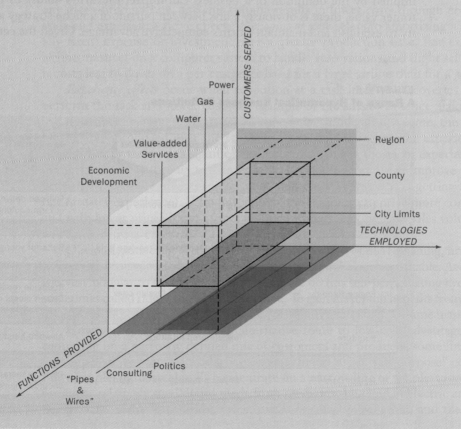

EXHIBIT 6.9
Some Common Characteristics of Market Life Cycle Stages

| Characteristic | Life Cycle Stage | | | |
	Introduction	Growth	Maturity	Decline
Overall market growth	Building rapidly, but on a small base	Faster than GNP	Equal or less than GNP	Decreasing
Product technology	High level of major product innovation, dominant designs not yet established	Dominant design emerges, emphasis placed on product variety	Small incremental innovations, many based on cost savings vs. performance improvements	Little or no change in product
Production technology	Emphasis placed on flexibility, process not fixed until dominant design emerges	As dominant design emerges, production process can become more specialized	Emphasis on efficiency, most likely stage for automation	Little or no change in process
Pricing patterns	Prices are high but volatile	Prices decline rapidly as costs fall and competition rises	Prices decline slowly as productivity allows costs to fall	Prices low, but stable
Promotional efforts	Target innovators and try to build awareness of product	Build brand awareness	Tailor promotion to a variety of market segments	Limit market, largely depend on inertia to maintain viable level of sales
Entry and exit	A few pioneers begin to explore the market	Many firms scramble to enter what appears to be a promising market	As market is saturated, growth slows and shakeout begins	A few survivors remain to serve the market
Nature of competition	Limited, focus is often inward, looking toward product rather than toward competitors	Growth may mask success of competitiors	Competitive rivalry peaks as competitors try to survive the shakeout	As shakeout is completed, survivors seek to de-escalate competition
Capital investment requirements	Substantial, needed to support initial creation of business and/or product	Peak period, needed to fund growth	Reinvestment as needed to maintain viability	Minimal, may in fact "disinvest" by selling off assets
Profitability and cash flow	Unprofitable, substantial negative cash flow	Profitable, but cash flow may still be negative	Profits declining, but larger investment level may mean cash flow is strong	Profits are low, cash flow is small (either negative or positive)

considering the market life cycle. First, the market life cycle is not intended to be used as a short-run forecasting device. Strategists find it more useful to consider the market life cycle as a conceptual framework for understanding what changes *might* occur over time rather than *when* such changes are likely to occur. Second, industry life cy-

Application 6.4

Du Pont's Use of Life Cycles in Strategic Management

E. I. du Pont de Nemours & Company, the giant diversified chemicals company, is a leader in using life cycle models. The company's use of a life cycle model to direct its strategic analysis and its strategic behavior is instructive; it illustrates how managers can adapt the life cycle concept to their particular market's situation.

Managers at Du Pont use what they call the "competitive life cycle" as a framework for their strategic planning process. This model describes the most typical evolutionary path that competitors within the chemical products industry follow. It is an attempt to capture information in the product life cycle, combining with it predictions about how the nature of competition is expected to change. The result is similar to the market life cycle model we have been looking at.

The initial stage of the evolutionary process consists of a market occupied by a single innovative firm, the sole supplier. This firm is the first to offer a new product that almost always has "functional" competition from substitute products but not head-to-head competition from "in-kind" products. At some point, in-kind competitors do enter the market, and this begins the competitive penetration phase of Du Pont's model. Entrants to the market during this phase are forced to offer lower prices to overcome gains made by the first entrant, and there is a widespread struggle among competitors to establish levels of market share that will ensure long-run viability. In Du Pont's experience, as market growth slows, the competitors' relative market shares stabilize, and it labels the

next evolutionary phase share stability. During this time, price and value differences are expected to continually erode, until at some point the product is considered to be an undifferentiated product in the commodity competition phase. Du Pont expects this to be the last phase, except, possibly, for withdrawal.

Although evolution along this path will clearly affect several types of strategic considerations, Du Pont is especially aware of the impact these changes will have on the sort of strategic analysis that is useful in the competitive market's development (see Exhibit 6.10). From the beginning of the sole-supplier stage and continuing throughout the life cycle, the importance of understanding the customer is stressed.

"Value-in-use" analysis, aimed at providing this understanding, acts as a cornerstone of Du Pont's strategic planning. In this analysis, managers perform an economic assessment of a given Du Pont product in several of its most important uses. The goal is to estimate the price at which the product would be equal to the value of a customer's most logical alternative. Because this analysis depends upon the economics facing the customer, Du Pont has found it to be a good means of ensuring that managers clearly understand customers' needs. These needs are expected to change over time, so they repeat value-in-use analysis as the competitive life cycle unfolds.

In trying to maintain or establish viable market portions during the competitive penetration phase, value-in-use analysis is supplemented with "competitor reaction"

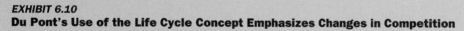

EXHIBIT 6.10
Du Pont's Use of the Life Cycle Concept Emphasizes Changes in Competition

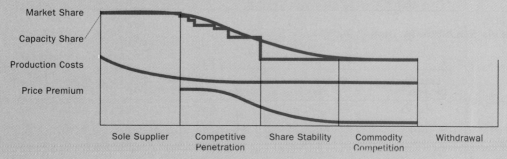

Application 6.4 (cont.)

analysis. Du Pont is interested in maintaining a strong competitive position relative to its competition, to prepare for an eventual industry shakeout. Thus, managers track both Du Pont's behavior and the competition's.

In the final stages of the competitive life cycle, managers use "profitability" analysis as they consider the relative merits of staying in the market or withdrawing. Du Pont has found that the relative stability of the later stages of the life cycle makes it easier to forecast financial performance accurately and to determine the scenarios in which the company will successfully compete.

Source

Based on information gathered from J. B. Frey, Jr., "Pricing and Product Life Cycles," *CHEMTECH* (January 1985), 15–21. Reprinted with permission of The Conference Board.

cles are reversible and repeatable. For example, Tide, a synthetic laundry detergent produced by Procter & Gamble and introduced in 1947, continues to see strong growth today. The product was significantly modified fifty-five times during its first 30 years and demand continues to grow as Procter & Gamble makes improvements, offering a liquid form, packaging innovations, and so on.[14] Tide's continued success suggests that a turnaround phase is an appropriate supplement to the traditional life cycle model, and we shall explore turnarounds after discussion of the first four phases.

Introduction

A market's early stages establish the climate for much of what follows. While firms may enter a market during any stage of its life cycle, studies show that entrepreneurial pioneers who enter the market first gain important advantages.[15] As we discussed earlier in this chapter, such competitive advantages gained by pioneers are called *first-mover advantages*.[16] First movers are notable for their tendency to hold onto competitive advantages and market shares they gain as markets mature.[17] Although market shares tend to become more balanced as markets mature, Exhibit 6.11 documents the finding that market share gained by successful pioneers during the market's introduction stage is often sustained for many years.[18]

EXHIBIT 6.11
Average Market Share by Time in Market

	Consumer Products (%)			Industrial Products (%)		
	Less than 20 Years Old	20 Years Old or More	Average	Less than 20 Years Old	20 Years Old or More	Average
Pioneer	35	27	29	32	28	29
Early follower	17	17	17	22	20	21
Late entrant	11	16	13	15	16	15

Source: Based on information gathered from W. T. Robinson and C. Fornell, "Market Pioneering and Sustainable Market Share Advantages," *PIMSletter on Business Strategy, 39* (1986).

In their early stages, markets begin to establish the "rules of the game" that often translate into important competitive advantages.[19] For instance, as MS-DOS became an industry standard, later entrants into the personal computer market were forced to develop expertise in that operating system or fight the battle of establishing and supporting an alternative one.

Pioneers may gain important competitive advantages in other ways, too. By being the first to offer a particular good or service, pioneers often establish strong brand recognition. Kleenex and Xerox, both pioneers, established such strong name recognition that the entire facial tissue and photocopier markets are often identified by these company names. Such strong recognition may serve as an important switching cost incurred by consumers when moving from one brand to another.[20] Pioneers may also be able to differentiate their products or services by marketing their products before competitors can run countering advertisements.[21] Finally, consumers may consider products and services offered by pioneers as differentiated simply because they are new.[22]

But pioneering does not always yield easily gained or easily sustained competitive advantages.[23] Texas Instruments' expertise in semiconductor design and manufacturing allowed it to gain an impressive market share as a pioneer in the early stages of the digital watch market, while Timex, lacking any competence in the new technology, floundered. However, as the market matured, the basis of competition shifted from electronics design and manufacturing (TI's core competence) to consumer marketing (Timex's core competence). In the end, TI was forced to drop out of the market entirely, taking large writeoffs, while Timex remains a strong competitor. The key to maintaining competitive advantages gained by pioneering a market is to adjust strategy during subsequent market life cycle stages.

Growth

The growth stage of a market's life cycle is often associated with glamour and success.[24] At this stage of the life cycle, demand for the product or service may be growing faster than the industry is able to supply it. Price pressure is minimized, exciting advances are made in new technologies, and sales volume (if not profits) soars. Consequently, we often make invalid assumptions about the benefits of growth. Below, we question three of the most common assumptions and explain how each one can be misleading.

- *Is it easier to gain share in growth markets?* During the growth stage, customers are unlikely to have established strong brand loyalties, making it easier for them to switch suppliers. Because the market as a whole is growing rapidly, competitors may be less likely to retaliate (or, in fact, even notice) when customers are "stolen." This reasoning might be appropriate if the market being considered is for a product or service so radically new that it faces no substitutes from established industries. But, usually, even if new products do not face as much "in-kind" competition (from the same kind of product), they often face "functional" competition (from a different product that is used for a similar purpose). For instance, during much of its growth stage, producers in the digital watch market competed with more established mechanical watch manufacturers who could offer a product that was often more reliable and less expensive. Here, gaining share was not merely a process of convincing shoppers to purchase one digital model over another; it required that consumers choose a digital watch over a mechanical one.

- *Is there less price pressure in growth markets?* Because products in growth markets often enjoy a demand in excess of supply, many growth markets can support premium pricing. During this stage, young firms may be tempted to price their goods unusually high in order to recoup as much of their heavy start-up investment as possible. However, premium pricing at this stage may attract more competitors, so the long-run attractiveness of the market to any particular competitor may decrease. New competitors will reduce the average profits of all competitors in the industry, create a more traumatic eventual market shakeout, and generally make the market more rivalrous. Thus, managers in this situation must balance the need for short-term returns with the need for long-term viability.

- *Is it easier to develop critical areas of expertise in the growth phase?* During the earliest stages of a market's development, technology generally evolves toward a "dominant design"—a fairly standard form of the basic product. For example, the portable computer industry is currently inching its way toward a standard design for laptop batteries, as the number of battery designs in use has dropped from over sixty to around six in the last several years.[25] Participation in this evolutionary process of defining the dominant design is often viewed as essential to achieving and maintaining a competitive position in terms of technological expertise. However, as we have already seen, many fast followers outperform "cutting-edge" firms whose technology they mimic.

Clearly, even though the growth stage may seem more attractive than those that follow, success during this stage still entails aggressive pursuit of a competitive advantage.[26]

Maturity

Markets in the mature stages of their life cycles share four characteristics. First, growth diminishes, which usually means that not all the firms that entered the market in the growth stage can remain viable in the mature stage. Second, by this stage key technology seldom benefits from patent protection, placing competitors on more even footing. Third, cumulative experience (the learning curve) no longer provides an advantage to any one competitor, because experience has already reduced costs to their logical minimums. Finally, few new forms of differentiation are possible, and competitors increasingly compete on the basis of price.

How do firms react to such market characteristics? As markets mature and decline, firms are tempted to compete, not on the basis of product differentiation and premium pricing but, rather, on price competition and commoditylike products. But price competition often proves ruinous to all those involved for at least four reasons:

- *Profits are very sensitive to price.* To understand the impact of price cuts on profits, consider the cost structure of the typical U.S. firm, as reported by the McKinsey & Co. consulting firm, based on analysis of 2,463 firms in the Compustat database.[27] For a typical firm in the researcher's database, a modest 3 percent cut in prices reduced profits by a whopping 37 percent, all other things remaining the same. On the other hand, this research has shown that a 1 percent increase in prices can improve profits in the typical firm by 11 percent. This is a much larger impact than experienced from cutting costs or raising volume, as shown in Exhibit 6.12.

- *Advantages from price cuts are often short lived.* In several industries, a price cut will only remain unmatched until it is discovered. In fact, many consumer retailing businesses, such as food and lumber, advertise a will-not-be-underpriced policy that guarantees the business will match any legitimate price from a competitor.

- *Customers remember low prices and expect them in the future.* Automobile manufacturers have discovered that price rebates are not a one-time thing. Customers who receive a $1,000 rebate on previous purchases may expect a comparable price cut on each subsequent car purchased.

- *Price cuts sensitize customers to shop for low price rather than value and benefits.* If firms emphasize price comparisons, they encourage customers to disregard the potential for adding value to the product through enhanced performance. This narrows competitors' options for differentiating their products, which can develop into a vicious cycle in which price cuts encourage further price cuts, and potential for profitable operations evaporates.

To avoid price wars, many firms adopt a "price war prevention lifestyle," adhering to one or more of the following practices:

- *Avoid strategies that force competitors to respond with lower prices.* For example, keep advertising focused on product benefits instead of prices.

- *Avoid all possible misreads of competition in your market.* For instance, in one industry, a trade journal mistakenly overstated total industry sales by 15 percent and all four of the leading competitors believed they had experienced rapid losses of market share. Consequently, all four dropped prices in an effort to regain market share they had never lost in the first place.

EXHIBIT 6.12
The Predicted Relative Impact of Raising Prices

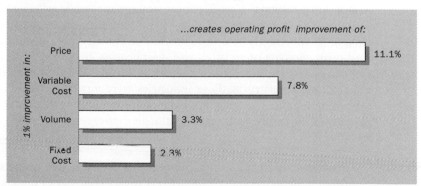

Source: Data from research by Michael V. Marn and Robert L. Rosiello, "Tactical Pricing," *McKinsey Quarterly* (Summer 1992), 75–88.

- *Avoid overreaction to competitors' price cuts.* Price cuts by rivals are often temporary and targeted, for example, to reduce temporarily high inventories. Overreaction can escalate a price war.

- *Use "jawboning" and other forms of market signaling to keep the peace.* Jawboning refers to speaking and writing publicly of the dangers of price competition and your firm's intentions to avoid it. This is one of the most obvious and common forms of market signaling. Others could include publicly observable actions, such as holding prices constant even if the industry's supply prices drop.

- *Reposition your product from a commodity to a differentiated position.* Although not viable for every competitor in every market, this option works for those who are able to establish differentiated niches, and the returns can be impressive. For instance, Perdue Chicken and Orville Redenbacher Popcorn—both branded products with leading positions in their respective markets—hold differentiated positions with what others treat as commodity products, and both enjoy the higher margins that result from the premium prices they are able to charge.

Decline

Most markets eventually face threats from substitute products, satiated demand, or changing customer needs. Consequently, they experience periods of decline, with the majority of competitors facing curtailed operations and/or possible shutdown. Yet there are firms that survive and even thrive against these odds.[28] For example, James B. Beam Distilling Co. saw demand for its straight bourbon products fall sharply as the market moved toward white wines and other pale alcoholic beverages. However, its profits reached all-time record levels when it responded to this change in the market with the introduction of ZZZingers, a line of canned bourbon mixers.

Such an example is not meant to suggest that it is easy for firms to succeed when the overall market trend is on the decline. In fact, rarely can more than one or two competitors survive severe market declines, and strategic management in the decline stage of the market life cycle must accurately assess an individual firm's chances of being among the survivors. Once again, managers must examine what competitive advantage the firm can maintain. Where that advantage cannot support a business, the only rational response is to develop a strategy for "milking" as much as possible from the business before terminating its operations. But, where the firm's competitive advantage is sufficiently strong, appropriate strategy may position the business as a long-term survivor of an otherwise disappearing market. Crown Cork & Seal is famous for using its cost-cutting abilities to survive and be profitable in the bottle cap and steel can industry, as those industries were virtually destroyed by more popular container options. In considering the different levels of sustainable competitive advantages, four distinct alternative strategies emerge: divestment, harvest, niche, and leadership.[29]

1. *Divestment.* Many managers respond to a declining market by selling out. Withdrawal is an appropriate response if it allows recovery of more of the investment than would be available from holding onto the business and implementing one of the three strategies described below.

2. *Harvest.* Unlike divestment, a harvesting strategy is a process of gradually letting a business wither, in a carefully controlled and calculated fashion, as the business continually falls back and retrenches. Typically, managers harvest business so that they produce cash flows that can be diverted to businesses elsewhere in the corporation that have more promising futures, an idea we consider in more detail in Chapter 7, under the discussion of how corporations balance cash flows across business units.

3. *Niche.* As a market declines, pockets of demand often remain capable of supporting one or more businesses. For instance, long after the development of integrated circuits brought on the general demise of the vacuum tube market, a market remained for replacement parts to service equipment with the older technology.

4. *Leadership.* The aim in pursuing this strategic option is to establish a dominant position so that the firm will essentially have the declining market to itself. A firm pursuing a leadership position may use "market signaling" to convey to competitors that other firms' continued participation in the market will be costly. Aggressive pricing, promotion, and product and/or process improvements are all forms of intimidation warning competitors that the signaling firm will not relinquish the market without a fight that will raise the costs (and possibly lower the profits) for everyone involved.

Business Strategies for Turnaround

Each year, thousands of firms face a desperate situation: they must turn their businesses around or face bankruptcy. Turnaround strategies stand on the belief that the market life cycle does not describe an inevitable course of growth followed by decline. We discuss the three phases common to most turnarounds below.

The Evaluation Phase

In hindsight, the need for a turnaround is often painfully obvious. Unfortunately, and perhaps surprisingly, such need is not always clear beforehand, as firms slip toward impending doom. Managers are often surprised to discover that things have gone awry, and that a once healthy business is now in trouble.[30] Two general approaches work well for evaluating a firm's health, in hopes of avoiding such unpleasant surprises. The more obvious approach is to track the firm's financial trends. However, it may be possible to spot warning signals from observing the firm's organizational health. In assessing the organizational health of a business, managers should monitor its "vital signs" for evidence of problems.[31] Organizational trends that typically precede a decline in performance include excess personnel, cumbersome administrative procedures, fear of conflict, and other warning signals, such as losing sight of any clear goals and increasingly ineffective communication.

The Cutting Phase

Once it becomes obvious that a firm must either turn around its performance or risk bankruptcy, the process typically begins with a cutting phase (also known as restructuring) aimed at survival and focused on stopping the hemorrhaging cash flows that often accompany turnaround situations.[32] Sometimes, cuts can be sweeping, taking in large portions of the workforce, entire managerial levels, and even whole operating divisions. Certainly, managers wring cash out of operations through reducing accounts receivable and all forms of inventories, leading or selling underutilized assets, and reducing all discretionary expenses, at least temporarily. Handled improperly, such measures can demoralize managers and other employees, as many firms learned from the repeated rounds of downsizing that took place in the 1980s. Also, turnarounds cannot gut businesses to the extent that no basis for long-term viability remains. Managers must then consider what to build the firm's future on after all the cutting is done.

The Building Phase

After halting the slide toward failure, managers must start and sustain an upturn if the turnaround is to succeed. The building phase most often requires focusing on a segment of a market where the company has some chance for maintaining a competitive advantage. Thus, the process that has been the theme for much of this chapter begins anew: find that overlap of customer needs and company strengths in which the company can compare favorably to its competition and build on that to achieve a sustainable competitive advantage.[33]

Summary of Managerial Practices to Adopt from This Chapter

- Remember that strategy at the business level is crucial to success because it is here that firms compete for customers.

- In crafting competitive strategies at the business level, you should expect to impact one or more of the five "PARTS" of competition: players, added value, rules, tactics, scope.

- One of the most valuable skills in crafting a competitive strategy is the ability to view competition through the eyes of all the other players involved.

- Because of the fundamental law of business competition that says a firm cannot capture more value than it creates, added value should be the centerpiece of any competitive strategy.

- By changing the rules of competition, a firm can alter its structural position with the result of dramatically improving its financial performance.

- In maneuvering for competitive advantage, mix and match your tactics from across four categories: preemption, attack, deterrence, and response. Recognize that there are a variety of options available under each of these categories.

- Define the scope of your business along three dimensions (functions provided, technologies employed, and customers served) and make sure you look at these three dimensions from both supply and demand perspectives.

- Recognize that focus itself does not constitute a competitive advantage. However, the scope of a business has much to do with the competitive advantage(s) it is able to attain. Differentiation is often associated with a narrow scope, while cost leadership is often associated with a broad business definition. But there are many exceptions to these generalities, and your approach to developing a competitive strategy should carefully consider how your particular definition of the business will impact its competitive advantage.

- While not a forecasting device, the market life cycle model helps organize your thinking about the competitive environment. Remember that the most typical pattern is introduction, growth, maturity, decline, and possibly, turnaround. Because the appropriate strategies vary according to the current phase of the market life cycle, adjust your approach to managing accordingly.

- Remember that price warfare, although it may seem appropriate, is usually very damaging to profitability, and some of the most successful mature businesses are those that have found a creative means of avoiding price wars by differentiating themselves.

- When the market is declining, consider alternatives including divestment, harvesting, locating a safe niche, or leadership as the sole survivor in the industry.

- Successful turnarounds typically require a comprehensive evaluation of a firm's problems, precise and purposeful cuts in facilities and personnel, and discovery of the appropriate grounds upon which to build a phoenix business.

Questions for Discussion and Review

1. Describe the five elements in the PARTS model and illustrate how each could affect business-level strategy.

2. Describe the four categories of tactics and provide an example of a tactic in each category.

3. Discuss the three dimensions used to define a business and explain how scope is related to competitive advantage.

4. Describe the four stages of the market life cycle and discuss how the pursuit of competitive advantage changes over the course of the market life cycle.

5. What are the most important phases of the typical turnaround strategy? How do each of these affect competitive advantage?

Notes

1. Kerry McLellan and Allen J. Morrison, *The Diaper War: Kimberly Clark Versus Procter & Gamble*, case study.
2. This material is based on the work of Adam M. Brandenburger and Barry J. Nalebuff, "The Right Game: Use Game Theory to Shape Strategy," *Harvard Business Review*, 73 (July–August 1995), 57–71.

3. Although a detailed look at game theory is beyond the scope of this book, you should be aware that many of the ideas on competitive strategy covered in this chapter have their roots in game theory. For good overviews of this valuable stream of research, see John McMillan, *Games, Strategies, and Managers*, New York: Oxford University Press, 1992; Avinash K. Dixit and Barry J. Nalebuff, *Thinking Strategically*, New York: W. W. Norton, 1991; and Pankaj Ghemawat, *Commitment: The Dynamic of Strategy*, New York: The Free Press, 1991.

4. As this statement suggests, the langauge of tactics is filled with military references. This is because the roots of tactical thinking are from military strategy. For examples, see Sun-tzu, *The Art of War*, trans. by Ralph D. Sawyer, New York: Barnes & Noble, 1994; Michael Howard, "VI: Karl von Clausewitz: Selection B: The Forgotten Dimensions of Strategy," in George Edward Thibault, ed., *The Art and Practice of Military Strategy*, Washington, DC: National Defense University, 1984; and Eliot A. Cohen and John Gooch, *Military Misfortunes*, New York: The Free Press, 1990.

5. Ming-Jer Chen and Donald C. Hambrick, "Speed, Stealth, and Selective Attack," *Academy of Management Journal, 38* (April 1995), 453–482.

6. Derek F. Abell, *Defining the Business: The Starting Point of Strategic Planning*, Englewood Cliffs, NJ: Prentice-Hall, 1979.

7. T. Levitt, "Marketing Myopia," *Harvard Business Review* (September–October 1975), 26.

8. For a good rebuttal to Levitt's emphasis on what we are calling the demand perspective, see the section entitled " 'Marketing Myopia' Myopia," in Henry Mintzberg, *The Rise and Fall of Strategic Planning*, New York: The Free Press, 1994, 279–281.

9. Guidelines for pursuit of niche or focus strategy are provided in Al Ries, "The Discipline of the Narrow Focus," *Journal of Business Strategy, 13* (November–December 1992); and Jaclyn Fierman, "The Fine Art of Niche-Picking," *Fortune* (Autumn–Winter 1993), 80–83.

10. See, for example, Suzanne L. Jennings, "Niches Within a Niche," *Forbes* (April 25, 1994), 122.

11. Michael E. Raynor, "The Pitfalls of Niche Marketing," *Journal of Business Strategy* (March–April 1992), 29.

12. C. R. Anderson and C. P. Zeithaml, "Stage of the Product Life Cycle, Business Strategy, and Business Performance," *Academy of Management Journal, 27* (1984), 5–24.

13. D. C. Hambrick and D. Lei, "Toward an Empirical Prioritization of Contingency Variables for Business Strategy," *Academy of Management Journal, 28* (1985), 763–788; C. W. Hofer, "Toward a Contingency Theory of Business Strategy," *Academy of Management Journal, 18* (1975), 784–810.

14. G. Day, "The Product Life Cycle: Analysis and Applications Issues," *Journal of Marketing, 45: 4* (1981), 60–67.

15. Strategic implications of entry during other stages of the market life cycle are discussed in J. G. Covin and D. P. Slevin, "New Venture Strategic Posture, Structure, and Performance: An Industry Life Cycle Analysis," *Journal of Business Venturing, 5* (1990), 123–135.

16. M. B. Lieberman and D. B. Montgomery, "First Mover Advantages," *Strategic Management Journal, 9* (Summer 1988), 41–58.

17. W. Mitchell, "Dual Clocks: Entry Order Influence on Incumbent and Newcomer Market Share and Survival When Specialized Assets Retain Their Value," *Strategic Management Journal, 12* (February 1991), 85–100.

18. M. Lambkin, "Order of Entry and Performance in New Markets," *Strategic Management Journal* (1988), 127–140; G. L. Urban et al., "Market Share Rewards to Pioneering Brands: An Empirical Analysis and Strategic Implications," *Management Science* (1986), 645–659.

19. Alex Miller, William Gartner, and Robert Wilson, "Entry Order, Market Share, and Competitive Advantage: A Study of Their Relationships in New Corporate Ventures," *Journal of Business Venturing, 4* (1989), 197–209; W. T. Robinson and C. Fornell, "Sources of Market Pioneer Advantage in Consumer Goods Industries," *Journal of Marketing Research, 22* (1985), 305–317.

20. Michael Porter, *Competitive Strategy: Techniques for Analyzing Industries and Competitors,* New York: The Free Press, 1980.

21. R. Schmalensee, "Product Differentiation Advantages of Pioneering Brands," *American Economic Review, 72* (1982), 159–180.

22. J. M. Utterback and J. William, "A Dynamic Model of Process and Product Innovation," *Omega, 3* (1985), 631.

23. Shaker A. Zahra, Sarah Nash, and Deborah J. Bickford, "Transforming Technological Pioneering into Competitive Advantage," *Academy of Management Executive, 9* (February 1995), 17–31.

24. Myron Magnet, "Let's Go for Growth," *Fortune* (March 7, 1994), 60.

25. W. J. Abernathy and J. M. Utterback, "Patterns of Industrial Innovation," *Technology Review, 80* (1978), 41–47.

26. Joseph A. Avila, Nathaniel J. Mass, and Mark P. Turchan, "Is Your Growth Strategy Your Worst Enemy?," *McKinsey Quarterly* (Spring 1995), 48–61.

27. This stream of research is explained in Robert A. Garda, "Tactical Pricing," *McKinsey Quarterly* (Summer 1992), 75–85; Michael V. Marn and Robert L. Rosiello, "Managing Price, Gaining Profit," *Harvard Business Review* (September–October 1992), 18–37; and Robert A. Garda and Michael V. Marn, "Price Wars," *McKinsey Quarterly* (Summer 1993), 87–100.

28. The examples given, as well as several others, are discussed in greater detail in J. Fierman, "How to Make Money in Mature Markets," *Fortune, 112* (1985), 40–47.

29. Discussion of these four types of strategies draws heavily upon Kathryn Harrigan and Michael Porter, "End-Game Strategies for Declining Industries," *Harvard Business Review* (July–August 1983), 111–121.

30. R. A. D'Aveni, "The Aftermath of Organizational Decline: A Longitudinal Study of the Strategic and Managerial Characteristics of Declining Firms," *Academy of Management Journal* (September 1989), 577–605.

31. A more complete discussion of these and other "vital signs" is available in P. Lorange and R. T. Nelson, "How to Recognize—and Avoid—Organizational Decline," *Sloan Management Review* (Spring 1987), 41–48.

32. For guidelines on how to manage the cutting phase, see Eugene F. Finkin, "Using Cost Management Effectively in the Turnaround Process," *Journal of Business Strategy, 13* (November–December 1992), 62–64.

33. For further discussion of the importance of competitive advantage in achieving a turnaround, see C. W. Hofer, "Turnaround Strategies," *Journal of Business Strategy, 1* (1980), 19–31.

Chapter 7

Corporate-Level Strategy

CHAPTER OUTLINE

In this chapter, we focus on strategies for enterprises consisting of more than one business. The General Electric Corporation, for instance, comprises several businesses, including consumer electronics, industrial electronics, heavy locomotives, jet engines, and financial services. Firms that operate more than one business are said to be *diversified*. In this chapter, we consider the role of diversification in the overall strategic management of the firm, why corporations diversify, and how diversification is best managed.

The chapter has five sections. The first explains the role of diversification, the second reviews the most common forms of diversification, and the third describes the means by which firms diversify. The fourth evaluates the various ways in which diversification benefits stockholders, and the final section explores how managerial behavior can limit these benefits.

This chapter will help you understand:

- The importance of corporate-level strategy
- How corporate diversification creates value for stockholders they could not create for themselves
- The forms diversification takes: vertical, horizontal, and global
- The most common means of diversifying: acquisition, strategic alliance, and internal development
- The importance of taking a strategic approach to divestment
- The most common motives for diversification and their relative impact on increasing stockholders' wealth
- How the benefits managers and stockholders receive from diversification may conflict, and how managers' actions may thereby limit stockholders' wealth

When Jack Welch accepted the position of CEO at General Electric, he undertook one of the most massive efforts of corporate restructuring in business history.[1] Over the next decade, GE acquired over 300 businesses for a total of $21 million (including Kidder Peabody and RCA, the owner of NBC) while selling over 200 businesses for a total of $11 billion (including coal mines and manufacturers of TVs and semiconductors).

This is an example of corporate-level strategy on a grand scale. Strategy at the corporate level is focused on diversification into different lines of business. What businesses should the corporation enter or exit? How should it make such moves? How should the corporation strategically manage its businesses? Our answer to all of these questions recalls a now-familiar theme: Build strategies to strengthen the firm's competitive advantages.

Early in his years as General Electric's CEO, Jack Welch adopted a simple, but important, rule that guided many of his decisions on diversification: "If you don't have a competitive advantage, don't compete." Welch insisted that every GE business be (or have a very convincing plan for becoming) number one or number two in its market, vowing to "fix, close, or sell" any business that did not meet this standard. When Welch took over at GE, only Lighting, Motors, and Power Systems were market leaders, but a decade later, every GE business was either a leader in its market or well on its way to becoming one.

Following from this change came some of the most impressive gains in financial performance ever seen in a company as large as General Electric. Productivity grew at rates two-to-five times greater than those of the economy in general. Return on equity grew to 20 percent compared to an average for all large U.S. firms of 12 percent. The corporation's stock rose 500 percent during the time period—two and a half times better than the market average. Market value added (the total value of the company's stock less the value of all investments made in the business) rose to over $60 billion, the second highest of all U.S. firms. In fact, after reviewing a broad range of performance measures, including revenues, profits, market value, and assets, *Forbes* declared General Electric the world's most powerful corporation.

Our focus in this chapter is the central idea at the root of Welch's success—crafting corporate strategies that create competitive advantages throughout a firm's portfolio of businesses.

THE ROLE OF DIVERSIFICATION

Corporate diversification is everywhere. Virtually all of the *Fortune* 1,000 (the largest 1,000 corporations in the United States) are diversified, many of them to a great extent. Some corporations, such as Johnson & Johnson or Textron, for example, consist of dozens—even hundreds—of different businesses. Besides such corporate giants, many smaller firms, some with only a handful of employees, also diversify. For example, one relatively small family business includes car washes, used-car sales, an auto parts store, and a wrecker service—clearly a diversified corporation.

What is the strategic role of diversification? Popular answers to this question have changed dramatically over the last several decades.[2] During the 1960s, diversification fueled tremendous corporate growth as corporations bought up dozens of businesses, regardless of the good or service sold. Managers based this diversification on unrelated businesses on the assumption that good managers could manage *any* business, allowing the formation of huge conglomerates of completely unrelated businesses. In the 1970s, managers began to emphasize diversification based on balancing cash flow between businesses. Corporate managers attempted to diversify so that the resulting portfolio would offer a balance between businesses that produced excess cash flows and those that needed additional cash flows beyond what they could produce themselves. The 1980s brought a broad-based effort to restructure corporations, as managers stripped out unrelated businesses and focused on a narrower range of operations. Restructuring usually also involved downsizing, and the largest corporations shrank in relation to the rest of the economy. In the 1990s, corporations have once again taken an interest in using diversification to grow. But unlike the unrelated diversification that took place in the 1960s, the trend in the 1990s is to diversify into related businesses, or at least into businesses in which the strengths of a particular managerial team fit the needs of the new business being added to the corporation.

So against these continually evolving perspectives, does diversification take any role so fundamental that it never changes? The answer is yes. *The fundamental role of diversification is for corporate managers to create value for stockholders in ways stockholders cannot do better for themselves.*[3] To understand this key statement, you must first realize that when corporate managers diversify a corporation, they essentially invest stockholders' funds in additional businesses. When Coca-Cola bought Columbia Pictures, Coke's stockholders found themselves owning both a soft drink producer and a movie production firm. But stockholders do not need corporate managers to diversify their holdings. Instead, they need only acquire stock in another firm, which they can easily do individually. Were the investors better off having Coke make the investment in Columbia than they would have been if they had invested equivalent funds in Columbia themselves? If Coke did not generate a return from this investment greater than what its stockholders could generate for themselves, Coke's corporate managers did not add value to the stockholders' investments.[4]

Imagine, for example, that 10,000 investors had $400 each to invest in stock. They considered investing half in Samson, Inc., a strong, well-managed company, and half in Underdog, Ltd., a weak, poorly managed company. But an alternative would be for the investors to put all their money into Samson and then have Samson's corporate managers buy Underdog. In the first case, in which the investors buy shares in both companies, the manages from Samson cannot contribute their talents to Underdog's problems because the two firms are still separate entities, even though they do happen to be partially owned by the same people. In the second case, the same people again own parts of both companies, but because the companies have been combined into one corporation, Samson's managers can now go to work on Underdog's problems. In other words, Samson's managers can add value in ways that investors cannot.

How should Samson managers approach their task of adding value by helping Underdog? A corporation's value ultimately depends on how well its various business units perform. Because, as we explained in Chapter 6, superior business-level performance requires a sustained competitive advantage, corporate managers should seek diversification moves that add businesses with competitive advantages or that improve the competitive advantages of their existing businesses.[5] Diversification moves that improve core process execution and/or enhance a business unit's structural position, thereby increasing its competitive advantage, present the most likely ways of investing stockholders' funds better than the stockholders themselves could.[6]

This is the most important role diversification can play, and it is the standard by which we evaluate the benefits of diversification later in this chapter. However, first we need to take a more detailed look at diversification. First, we consider its various forms and then the means by which firms diversify.

We consider three forms of diversification—vertical, horizontal, and global—and three means of achieving that diversification—acquisition, strategic alliance, and internal development. The various forms and means of diversification can be mixed and matched to create a range of options. Exhibit 7.1 gives examples of each of the possible combinations. You may want to mark this exhibit, and use it as a road map as we navigate through a more detailed discussion of each of the forms and means of diversification.

THE FORMS OF DIVERSIFICATION

Diversification typically takes one of three forms, each having its own set of issues, benefits, and limitations.

Vertical Integration

When a corporation performs more than one step of the process involved in converting raw materials into a product delivered and ready for consumption, it is considered to be *vertically diversified*. In Exhibit 7.2, Vertico is a hypothetical vertically diversified corporation consisting of a fishing fleet, which could be managed as one business, and a wholesaling operation, which could be managed separately as a second business.

A vertically diversified corporation integrates its businesses so that one efficiently "feeds" the other. Coordinating upstream operations (those closer to the raw materials) with downstream operations (those closer to the customer) is called *vertical integration*. Vertical integration presents managers with both benefits and limitations.

EXHIBIT 7.1
Combinations of Means and Forms of Diversification

		Forms		
		VERTICAL	**HORIZONTAL**	**GLOBAL**
Means	**ACQUISITIONS**	Time Inc. acquires Warner Communications, creating a vertically integrated entertainment business.	Phillip Morris buys Kraft and General Foods in an effort to diversify out of the cigarette business.	BASF, a German chemical producer, buys Inmont, a U.S. chemicals company, to overcome limited growth opportunities at home.
	STRATEGIC ALLIANCES	Cetus, a leading firm in the biotechnology field, teams up with larger corporations which provide the capital and marketing needed to introduce new Cetus technology.	Dow Chemical and Corning Glass join forces to create a joint venture more profitable than either of its parents.	Fuji Photo Films and Xerox, Inc. form a single import sales operation that later grows to become one of the world's leading producers of photocopiers.
	INTERNAL DEVELOPMENT	Humana develops a full line of health care services, vertically integrating across insurance, hospitals, and follow-up treatment services.	3M consistently gets more than 25% of its revenues from products it has developed within the last 5 years.	Anheuser-Busch attempts to open up new markets by taking Budweiser, its flagship product into Britain.

EXHIBIT 7.2
Vertico and Horizinc, Hypothetical Examples of Vertically and Horizontally Diversified Corporations

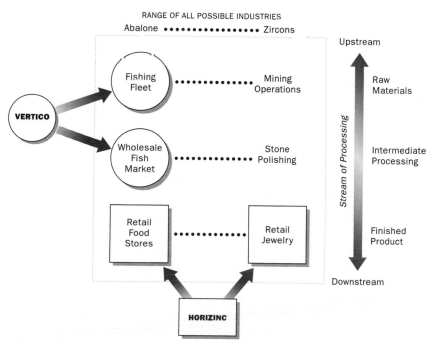

Benefits of Vertical Integration

Vertical integration often eliminates, or at least reduces, the costs of buying and selling (called transaction costs) incurred when separate firms carry out the various steps of converting raw materials to finished goods.[7] When two such steps are integrated, marketing and sales efforts formerly carried out in the upstream business can be eliminated, because the downstream customer is now part of the same corporation.

Corporations also vertically integrate for smoother, better-coordinated operations. For instance, movies have grown increasingly expensive to produce (a big production can easily cost $60 million or more), but vertically integrated studios are less dependent upon the movie itself as their sole means of recouping the investment. If carefully coordinated, a bundle of downstream products building on the foundation provided by the film can dramatically increase the total returns of a movie venture. Such coordination is probably most easily achieved within a single corporate entity, and Walt Disney, for instance, has long excelled at generating profits from products inspired by successful films.

A firm need not be fully vertically integrated to realize important benefits. Many pursue a strategy of *tapered*, or *hybrid*, vertical integration. In these strategies, some elements of the corporation may be fully integrated, while others are not. This allows them to enjoy some of the benefits described above, but involvement with suppliers or customers outside their own corporation also has benefits. For example, working with outsiders keeps insider counterparts "honest" and "on their toes." One steel mill uses a tapered integration strategy extensively. The bolt and screw division depends on insider upstream operations for the bulk of its supplies, but supplements this by purchasing from outside the corporation. If it finds that outsider suppliers offer superior value, it naturally begins to shift more purchases away from its inside suppliers, placing pressure on them to remain competitive. In some cases, when this mill's inside operations cannot remain competitive, it has shut down its own operations and shifted to complete reliance on outside suppliers. Thus there are limits to the benefits of vertical integration.

Limits to Vertical Integration

With vertical integration, unbalanced capacities may limit transaction cost savings. The minimum size a plant can be while still reasonably cost efficient is known as its *minimum efficient scale*. If the minimum efficient scale of one part of a vertically integrated corporation differs radically from that of another, the excess capacity of the larger operation must be disposed of profitably. This usually means that the excess capacity must be sold to other firms. This, unfortunately, incurs the transaction costs vertical integration is designed to avoid. For example, a television tube has a much higher minimum efficient production scale than any other component does. At one time, North American Philips (NAP), producer of Magnavox and Sylvania consumer electronics, sold about half its television picture tubes to firms that produce competing brands. Although NAP could avoid marketing and selling costs through vertical integration only on those tubes it sells in house, it had to produce more than enough tubes for its own consumption to reach minimum efficient scale.

By committing to a corporate strategy of vertical integration, firms may reduce their flexibility and anchor themselves to products or technologies that may become outdated and noncompetitive.[8] Firms that integrate vertically accept responsibility for more than just a wider portion of the production process—they also accept responsibility for remaining innovative in *all* these business segments. For the end product to remain up to date and competitive, the entire chain of vertically integrated subunits must remain innovative. The task of keeping up on so many fronts may be overwhelming, and the corporation may fall behind its more focused competitors.

Vertical integration may make a firm more susceptible to organized labor strikes. For instance, the United Auto Workers is a powerful union that represents the vast majority of General Motors' assembly workers in all of GM's various vertically integrated plants. This gives the union considerable flexibility to decide where to call a strike. For example, when Saturns were in very short supply, the workers at the plant that supplies the Saturn assembly operation with automobile frames went on strike. Because Saturn operates on a just-in-time (JIT) production schedule, it had no reserve inventories of car frames, and within hours the entire Saturn operation was shut down by a strike at a single, relatively small feeder operations upstream. The GM workers at Saturn never went on strike, and the fact that they were out of work because of a parts shortage made them eligible to collect unemployment compensation. In other words, with minimal cost to itself, the UAW was able to shut down the entire Saturn operation, leaving GM responsible for supporting most of the out-of-work union members.

Finally, difficulties may arise in integrating different specializations. The managerial skills and corporate cultures that best serve upstream operations may be incompatible with those required downstream. For example, one vertically integrated high-technology company has various specializations that make up an informal, but well-defined, caste system with the firm. Upstream product design engineers rank much higher than production engineers in this caste system, and both groups generally consider themselves to be superior to downstream service technicians. Because of communication difficulties caused by this attitude, an entire generation of the firm's new products failed. Production engineers were ignored when they complained to design engineers that the new products were needlessly difficult to manufacture. When poorly assembled parts began to break down in the field, service technicians were not given the documentation and supplies required to make the repairs. In fact, they were sometimes forced to go to a local hardware store to buy parts with which to improvise a repair on a machine. Clearly, if a vertically diversified firm is to become truly integrated, it must overcome anything that segregates the various specialists.

When to Integrate Vertically

The level of integration is best adjusted in light of four questions:[9]

1. *Are our existing suppliers or customers meeting the final consumers' needs?* If the firms in the production and distribution chain are doing an adequate job, it is probably unwise to consider taking over their functions by integrating vertically. In this case, managers should concentrate on problem areas. Some extremely successful firms have followed this strategy, keeping only one or two critical business operations in house and outsourcing the rest.[10] A classic example is Nike, which limits its in-house work to athletic shoe design and marketing strategy and outsources

production to manufacturers located primarily in Southeast Asia and distribution to transportation specialists such as Federal Express.

2. *How volatile is the competitive situation?* Highly volatile situations, with changing technologies, evolving customer needs, and unpredictable competitors are poor candidates for vertical integration. Such situations require a flexibility that vertically integrated corporations don't have. Once vertically integrated, a company cannot easily move into and out of the business.

3. *Is it possible to "own" a business without actually buying it?* Many benefits of vertical integration can be obtained by upstream and downstream firms willing to work closely with one another, even though they remain independent businesses.[11] Motorola was one of the first firms to be awarded the Malcolm Baldrige National Quality Award, an award given annually to leaders in total quality management. At one time, Motorola felt so strongly about quality that it decided to require all its hundreds of suppliers to be entered in the Baldrige quality competition and to use the competition as an impetus to upgrade quality. Because Motorola represented a major account for many of its suppliers, they had little option but to comply. In other words, Motorola was able to influence the behavior of its suppliers significantly without actually owning them.

4. *Will vertical integration enhance the business's structural position?* Vertical integration may move you into a line of business that has historically held greater market power and is consequently more profitable.[12] For instance, Bose was once just a manufacturer of high-fidelity audio equipment, but in order to capture the attractive margins available downstream, the firm integrated vertically into direct mail order sales, increasing its total returns. Alternatively, the threat of vertical integration into a business now being operated by powerful suppliers or customers may undermine their power and make them more conciliatory in an effort to keep you out of their business. For instance, the threat that a national brewery might integrate backward into can production is usually enough to reduce the bargaining power of its can suppliers.

Horizontal Diversification

Horizontal diversification entails moving into more than one industry. As Exhibit 7.2 showed, Horizinc, another hypothetical corporation, serves two distinct markets with two very different products. It competes in the seafood industry as a retailer of abalone and in the jewelry business as a retailer of zircons. It is not vertically integrated in either case; although it operates in two industries, it performs only one function (retailing) in the raw-materials-to-finished-goods transformation process of both.

Abalone and zircons represent very different markets, and Horizinc presents an example of unrelated diversification, a strategic decision that has both advantages and disadvantages. In fact, the central issue in managing horizontal diversification is to determine how closely related the new business should be to the old business. The relative financial performance of firms pursuing related versus unrelated diversification is perhaps the single most researched topic in strategic management.[13] Research has produced mixed results, but some consistent evidence suggests that related diversification is somewhat more profitable.[14] Consequently, most corporations seek out opportunities to diversify into businesses that somehow relate to those they already have, although a few *conglomerates* make no such effort and instead pursue a strategy of unrelated diversification.

The Case for Conglomerates

As we mentioned at the beginning of this chapter, building conglomerates of unrelated businesses was widely considered to be an ideal corporate strategy in the 1960s.[15] In the 1960s, firms like Textron, ITT, Gulf & Western, and Teledyne led the way in building vast corporate holdings consisting of every imaginable type of business. For instance, at one time Textron owned Bell Helicopters, Gorham Silver, Homelite Chainsaws, Talon Zippers, and Sheaffer Pens and was also involved in spacecraft propulsion, staplers, chemicals, and air cushion vehicles.[16] Building conglomerates with such diversity rested on the assumption that corporate managers have the expertise to recognize undervalued stocks that many individual investors would miss. Furthermore, the conglomerate builders argued, when it comes to financing acquisitions, corporations have economies of scale that are unavailable to individuals purchasing limited numbers of shares. For example, a corporation may be able to borrow money at a lower rate of interest, or it may be able to lower the per share brokerage commissions on stock purchases by trading very large numbers of shares at once.[17]

The Case Against Conglomerates

Based on a history of the last 30 years of building and managing conglomerates, many managers and researchers today seriously question the wisdom of this corporate strategy.[18] The most important historical arguments against conglomerates are conglomerate discounts and takeover premiums.

Conglomerate Discounts.   A *conglomerate discount* exists when the stock of a conglomerate sells for less than the total of the individual stocks would sell for if each business in the corporation sold its stock separately. Conglomerate discounts are evidence that the market perceives "negative synergy," meaning that the sum of the pieces is worth more than the whole. This perception might arise from a fear that managing a diverse and complex corporation entails excessively high overhead. Or it might reflect a concern that association with a large corporation somehow limits the flexibility of individual business units. In either of these cases, investors appear to be unwilling to pay as much for the corporation as a whole as they would be willing to pay for its dismantled parts. Since their initial popularity in the 1960s, conglomerate stocks have typically sold at such conglomerate discounts.

We measure conglomerate discounts with a *price-earnings ratio (P/E)*, which is simply the price of a share of stock divided by the corporation's annual earnings per share. P/Es indicate investor expectations about the future success of a given corporation; a high P/E means that investors have high expectations for that corporation and will pay relatively more for its stock. In the 1960s, when unrelated diversification was considered to be an ideal corporate strategy, conglomerate stocks traded at a premium relative to the rest of the market. In fact, at the peak of their popularity, conglomerates often sold for over 50 percent more per dollar of earnings than the average corporation did. In other words, the average P/E ratio of conglomerates was about 50 percent greater than the average P/E for other stocks.

This began to change in the 1970s, when conglomerates consistently traded at an average P/E lower than the rest of the market's. When conglomerate stocks trade at average P/Es that are less than the average P/Es of other firms, it indicates that investors value the subsidiary businesses more as individual companies than bundled together. This creates a very volatile situation for corporations and investors alike, one that gave rise to the tremendous volume of divestitures, acquisitions, and takeovers seen in the late 1980s.

The heavy "deal flow" in the late 1980s occurred because investors realized that, with the conglomerate discounts then available, they could acquire a corporation and then sell off its individual parts for more than they had paid for the original corporation as a whole. Without ever having to operate any of the businesses, those involved in such takeovers could make millions. Firms and individuals specializing in this process came to be called *corporate raiders*. To avoid having their corporations dismantled in such "raids," many corporate managers moved to "deconglomerize" first. For instance, in the early and mid-1980s, Gulf & Western sold off businesses producing cement, cigars, video games, apparel, automotive parts, bedding, heavy industrial equipment, wallpaper, horse racing, and sugar. As a more focused corporation with a simpler mix of businesses, Gulf & Western began trading at a P/E very near the average for the market in general, making it an unlikely target for any takeover attempts based on plans to further dismantle the corporation. Reflecting on this metamorphosis, Martin Davis, Gulf & Western's CEO at the time, commented, "Rhyme must follow reason. There must be some kind of fit among diverse operations. A degree of stretching may be acceptable. . . . Stretch too far and the result is greater strain than strength."[19]

After the widespread corporate restructuring that took place in the late 1980s, the "deal flow" declined for a while. Because it has begun to pick up in the mid-1990s, observers note a more widespread effort to pursue related diversification rather than rebuilding unrelated conglomerates.[20]

Takeover Premiums.   The second argument against building huge conglomerates is that if one corporation wishes to buy another, it can expect to pay a *takeover premium*. This is the difference in the normal trading price of the takeover target's stock and the price required to entice stockholders to sell enough shares to give the acquiring firm controlling interest. It is not uncommon to pay a premium of 50 percent or more to acquire controlling interest in a corporation.

For example, before word leaked out that a corporate raider was interested in acquiring United Airlines (UAL) in the late 1980s, stock in the airline sold for about $150 per share. In order to be able to buy a controlling interest in UAL quickly, the raider offered to pay about $240 a share for the stock. The $90 difference represents the takeover premium that managers in the raiding corporation believed they would need to pay in order to obtain a controlling interest in UAL. If, like most individual investors, the raider had decided to buy only a small number of shares in UAL, it would not have had to pay any takeover premium. The smaller number of shares could have been bought at the going market price, but fewer shares would not offer the raider a controlling interest. Therefore, in some ways buying stock in blocks large enough for a takeover is less efficient than individuals' buying stock in smaller amounts.

Takeover premiums and conglomerate discounts combine to create tremendous challenges for corporate managers. If they are not careful, managers may pay a takeover premium for a firm that subsequently becomes worth less because of a conglomerate discount. Because this double-edged danger exists, corporate managers considering diversification should be confident that they can create enough value for stockholders to overcome any takeover premiums and any conglomerate discounts associated with the move.

Global Diversification

The importance of international diversification rose sharply in the past decade. In the 8 years ending in 1993, the annual volume of U.S. acquisitions of foreign business grew by approximately 600 percent.

Chapter 8 discusses international management and global diversification. Here, we simply point out that this form of diversification is another alternative. Returning to Exhibit 7.1 will provide you with some examples of global diversification, but the challenges of international competition are great enough that they merit the separate coverage found in Chapter 8.

THE MEANS OF DIVERSIFICATION

Each of the three forms of diversification discussed in the preceding section can be achieved in different ways. We focus on the three most often employed means of diversification: (1) acquisitions, (2) strategic alliances, and (3) internal development.

Acquisitions

Acquisition refers to the purchase of a company that is already in operation.[21] Acquisition can quickly diversify a corporation and improve the value of stockholders' investment.[22] However, the sharp decline of acquisition activity in the early 1990s occurred, in part, because managers encountered significant problems in managing the acquisition process as limitations to this corporate strategy became evident.[23] The track record of success with mergers and acquisitions is not very encouraging. A study conducted by McKinsey & Company found that only 23 percent of mergers examined over a 10-year period generated returns in excess of the costs incurred by the deal.[24] Yet plenty of acquisitions and mergers have been tremendously successful, resulting in much stronger businesses and greatly increased stockholder value. What managerial practices make the difference between success and failure in acquisitions? We can organize our answer around managerial practices in two stages: preacquisition and

Application 7.1

Chemical Bank and Mannie Hannie: Managerial Efforts Toward a Successful Merger

The third-largest bank in the United States was created when Chemical Bank and Manufacturers Hanover "Mannie Hannie," merged in what industry observers said would "go down in history as one of the greatest mergers ever." Such success was not an accident; managers at both companies worked to ensure it.

To begin with, they made clear what tangible benefits would result from combining the two businesses. Because they were similar, both competing mostly in New York City, the greatest benefit was expected from cutting redundant expenses. As part of the preacquisition analysis, managers drew up a plan to show how the merged banks could cut their combined expenses by $750 million annually in just 3 years. Such a goal might be considered merely posturing for the press; but, in fact, in the first quarter after the merger, the banks reduced their costs by $50 million.

Beyond making sure that the numbers made sense, managers invested heavily in the "people issues" involved in combining the two firms. The CEOs established a great working relationship in which they were able to agree quickly and amicably about who would serve as CEO of the merged organization first and at what point he would be succeeded by his counterpart from the other bank. Similarly, good relationships trickled down across other managerial levels. For instance, the management teams quickly agreed to use Chemical Bank as the name because doing so would save an estimated $50 million in changes for outdoor signs, letterheads, and so on. Thanks to such efforts, within a year of the merger, the two organizations worked smoothly as one, costs were down on increasing revenues, and profits were greater than either bank could have hoped for as a stand-alone operation.

Sources

Based on information gathered from Joshua Mendes, "When Mergers Make Sense," *Fortune* (June 29, 1992), 85; and Anne B. Fisher, "How to Make a Merger Work," *Fortune* (January 24, 1994), 66–70.

postacquisition.[25] Application 7.1 provides an example of a merger that benefited from careful consideration of the pre- and postacquisition issues discussed below, while Application 7.2 provides a counterexample.

Preacquisition Management

Managers can do much to increase their chances of making a successful acquisition even before it takes place, something akin to a "smart shopper" analysis. They must assess two particular elements in detail.

The first of these elements is the deal itself. Managers must answer such questions as:

What is the acquisition going to cost? What are its expected benefits? How will the *acquired* firm benefit?

How will the *acquiring* firm benefit?

How much of the deal can be financed internally, and how much will require outside capital?

Application 7.2

General Motors and EDS: Difficulties in Diversification

For years, information processing had grown more important at General Motors until, by the mid-1980s, the company had more than 100 major computer networks, few of which were capable of communicating with one another. The astronomical cost of such unmanaged growth meant GM might soon be the highest-cost producer of U.S. automobiles. After making two attempts, Roger Smith, GM's CEO, admitted that the company could not get its data processing under control.

Then, in 1984, Smith financed the $2.5 billion acquisition of Electronic Data Systems (EDS), one of the leading companies in the field of computer systems integration, by issuing a special class of stock, GM-E. The GM-E stock sold well, because EDS had a history of 35 percent compound annual profits growth rate. EDS planned to remain a largely independent subsidiary, directed by Ross Perot, who had built EDS on a $1,000 investment. GM would transfer its 7,000-person data processing staff to EDS and would negotiate contracts for EDS to integrate its massive information processing systems. Smith also expressed hope that some of the entrepreneurial EDS style would "rub off" on GM.

A series of unanticipated developments turned the acquisition sour, however, and Perot began a public crusade to "nuke the GM management system." What went wrong? We can learn something of the difficulty of managing diversification by observing several problems with the EDS acquisition:

- *Neither company really understood the needs or capabilities of the other.* Smith thought EDS could facilitate GM's move to automate and computerize its factories but at that time, EDS did not employ a single programmer with expertise in writing code for machine control. Perot believed that Smith had the same managerial style as he. However, GM had 800,000 employees, many of them United Auto Workers union members, and Perot was responsible for only 17,000 fiercely loyal employees in a totally different corporate culture.

- *The structure of the deal inadvertently placed managers from the two organizations in adversarial roles.* When the GM-E stock was created, the contract stipulated that dividends be based on the performance of the EDS subsidiary—not the performance of GM over-

all. Executive compensation at EDS had always depended heavily on stock options to motivate superior managerial performance. Because top EDS managers owned a lot of stock, they had a natural interest in seeing that EDS made the highest possible levels of profit. But their customers inside GM felt EDS would charge higher prices and drive GM's costs up. Angry GM managers saw their operations incurring costs that would improve EDS profits and in turn make EDS managers richer. Four years after the acquisition, many of GM's largest divisions still had not negotiated long-term contracts with EDS for their data processing needs.

- *Managers never adequately specified key relationships before the acquisition.* Discussions before the actual acquisition never broached many issues that eventually became points of conflict. Perot, a self-made multibillionaire, was described by one acquaintance as "a great team player as long as he got to be captain." Yet the contract mentioned in only the most general terms how he was to work for, and report to, Smith. When Smith sent teams of inspectors to oversee operations at EDS, Perot refused to allow them access to "his" company. Meanwhile, Perot insisted that any suggestions for change coming from GM be cleared with him personally before EDS managers undertook them. A managerial gridlock resulted that prevented EDS's integration into GM operations.

- *The cultural difference between the two companies was extreme.* A strong bureaucracy controlled and monitored managerial activity at GM. At EDS, a cultlike following had built up around Perot. Ex-military (a graduate of Annapolis), Perot insisted on conservative dress and patriotic politics; GM people who were transferred to EDS were amazed to learn that beards, long hair, suede shoes, and alcohol at lunch were all strictly forbidden. For decades, GM had adversarial relations with its blue-collar, unionized workforce. In contrast, Perot had made history when he hired a retired Green Beret officer to help him lead a covert operation into Iran to free two EDS workers who were held hostage. EDS recruited people just coming out of the military, and Perot bragged in public that EDS workers were trained to kill a snake when they saw one, as opposed to GM managers, who were instead trained to form a committee to study snakes.

As Perot became publicly vocal in his criticisms, GM decided to remedy the deteriorating situation. Smith offered Perot and his top three executives $750 million for their shares of EDS stock, more than twice the stock's market value, to resign and agree not to set up companies that would compete with EDS. Perot lost his seat on GM's board and agreed to incur a fine of $7.5 million if he continued to criticize Smith or GM publicly. The settle-

ment was so spectacular that it gave rise to a new term for one of the less attractive aspects of the acquisition game: "hush-mail."

Sources

Based on information gathered from J. Schwartz, "Can EDS Prosper Without Its Charismatic Founder?," *Internal Management* (September 1987), 59–62; T. Moore, "Make or Break for General Motors," *Fortune* (February 15, 1988), 32–50; and B. O'Reilly, "EDS After Perot: How Tough Is It?," *Fortune* (October 24, 1988), 72–76.

Will the combined businesses be able not only to repay the cost of making the deal, but also to generate returns for stockholders sufficient to beat any comparable alternative investment?

Beyond such "hard" analysis of the numbers, preacquisition analysis should also include a thorough assessment of a second element—the human, organizational, and cultural aspects of the acquisition. Some managers tend to discount this aspect of the acquisition, arguing that if the numbers look good enough, the "people problems" will resolve themselves. Yet no evidence whatsoever supports this nearsighted conclusion. To the contrary, examples abound in which mergers have failed largely because the individuals in the joining firms simply had tremendous difficulty in getting along with one another. In fact, acquisitions are typified by managerial conflicts that stem from feelings of inferiority in the acquired firm and feelings of superiority in the acquiring firm. Such feelings produce damaging results, such as high managerial turnover.[26]

Although the analysis involved in uncovering potential people problems is likely to be "soft," it is equally important to the hard analysis previously discussed. Consider the hard analysis of the deal and the soft analysis of the people issues to be complementary prerequisites: if either of these turns up discouraging information, the acquisition should probably not occur until the problem is rectified.

While all this takes time, few shortcuts have proven consistently effective. Arthur Andersen, a leading public accounting firm that has successfully pursued a strategy of expansion through acquisition, demonstrates this point well. Andersen courted Asahi Shinwa & Company, a leading accounting firm in Tokyo, for 3 years before actually acquiring the firm. To assess the deal, both parties took long looks at each other's confidential financial statements and other in-house documents. They also emphasized people issues, such as agreeing to maintain Asahi's long-standing compensation package for key partners and ensuring that Asahi would not be crushed under Andersen's greater size. While the preacquisition homework required 3 years, it resulted in one of the strongest accounting and management consulting organizations in Tokyo, something Andersen could never have hoped to accomplish on its own. As Richard

Measelle, the managing partner who oversaw the acquisition, explains, "Sometimes you have to go slow to go fast."[27]

Postacquisition Management

Acquisitions should be chosen for their potential ability to increase the competitiveness of one or the other of the firms involved, thereby creating value for stockholders. However, all the actual value creation to be realized from an acquisition comes after the acquisition takes place. Therefore, firms should invest heavily in managing postacquisition integration. For real value creation, managers must develop a plan to make it happen. At a bare minimum, this plan should reflect the same concern for the hard details associated with the deal and the soft issues concerning people as was appropriate for the preacquisition effort. In other words, it should address the specifics of how the firm will improve competitive advantage as a result of the acquisition, as well as the difficulties that are likely to arise when integrating two organizations that have their own unique cultures.

Regardless of the plan put into place, experience shows that success typically depends as much on the ability of managers to be flexible in adhering to or changing an initial plan as on the quality of the initial plan itself.

Strategic Alliances: Joint Ventures

Diversification by *strategic alliance* refers to arrangements in which corporations join forces to form cooperative partnerships. Typically, neither company owns the other, though often they create a third commercial entity, usually referred to as a *joint venture*, that they co-own.[28] Such arrangements have been growing at nearly 30 percent per year since 1985, according to some experts, and some companies treat alliances as *the* emerging way to carry on business.[29] For instance, IBM is involved in more than 400 joint ventures with firms ranging from Sears to Apple. Strategic alliances make the most sense when each party has strengths that offset the other's weaknesses.[30] A good example is Dow Corning, a successful joint venture that has regularly enjoyed performance levels higher than either of its parents, Dow Chemical and Corning Glass.

Sharing offsetting strengths through such joint ventures has two major benefits. First, neither partner must invest to develop the full range of capabilities required by the new venture. Second, financing should be easier to attract because the new business has two backers instead of just one and the partners can share development risks. Both factors help explain why joint ventures are so common between large corporations and small businesses, especially in the emerging field of biotechnology.[31] Most of the advances in this field are made by small entrepreneurial firms that lack the financial strength to produce goods in this very capital-intensive industry, as well as sales forces to reach the broad range of potential customers. To share these burdens and the substantial risks involved in developing such new products, numerous small biotech firms have teamed up with large corporations. Cetus, a leading biotech firm, has formed a number of such strategic alliances to produce and market some of the first diagnostic instruments based on the new biotechnology. Cetus provides the bulk of the research, while the larger firms typically provide financing, marketing, and manufacturing capabilities.

Perhaps the most serious disadvantage of joint ventures is that achieving close coordination is difficult between two companies that almost certainly have different goals, strategies, procedures, and cultures. Nothing can harm a joint venture's chances of success faster than such incompatibilities. One study revealed that nearly half of all joint ventures that failed experienced conflict between the partners.[32] In order to avoid such conflicts, managers follow these guidelines for the strategic management of joint ventures:[33]

Establish a clear understanding between the partners. At a minimum, potential partners in a joint venture should discuss in some detail (1) the mission of the new business, (2) the market(s) it will serve, (3) the product(s) it will offer, (4) the obligations of each partner, and (5) how the joint venture will be dissolved, if necessary.

Do not depend on a contract to make a joint venture work. Though contracts are necessary, if the partners take an adversarial, legalistic approach to managing the joint venture, it will almost surely fail. Joint ventures succeed often because managers work to make them successful more than because of legally binding agreements. For example, Dow Corning was created with a handshake and was already a promising venture before lawyers eventually finished drawing up the contracts.

Do not try to shortchange your partner. Strategic alliances should be collaborative efforts in which all parties contribute willingly for the good of the partnership. Although each partner must look after its own interests, there is no room for greed in such an arrangement.[34]

Internal Development

Diversification through *internal development* refers to building new businesses more or less from the ground up, a process sometimes referred to as *corporate entrepreneurship*.[35] To create new businesses, corporations have developed four types of programs.[36] In the first, corporations act simply as venture capitalists. *Venture capitalists* provide the funds, sometimes called risk capital, required to start a new business. Exxon Enterprises, Exxon's effort throughout the 1980s to develop new businesses, found this to be its most successful type of corporate entrepreneurship program.[37] Over a 10-year period, the company invested in eighteen new ventures. Six of these became attractive enough so that the corporation eventually bought them. The remaining twelve were never brought into the corporation, but overall they still represented a sound financial investment. Exxon invested $12 million in them, and over a 10-year period they returned $218 million in cash or marketable securities.[38]

A second tactic for fostering corporate entrepreneurship is the *new-venture incubator*. Here the corporation provides funding, low-cost space and equipment, and limited managerial oversight. The ventures supported may start inside the corporate sponsor, or they may be independent start-ups assisted by the corporation. Corporations often use incubator programs to take advantage of excess resources such as extra space, idle equipment, and unused managerial talent.[39] But as they try to coordinate the new venture's use of these resources with those of the established businesses, corporations often encounter difficulties.[40] Kodak encountered difficulties in integrating mainstream businesses with the "new-stream" businesses in its incubator program and eventually closed the program, although it had been modestly successful in creating profitable new lines of business.[41]

A third option, the *idea generation and transfer program*, attempts to birth new business ideas that are then transferred to established operations for further development and ongoing management. Firms have generally had more success with this type of program than with the first two described. Even though corporate resources invested in these idea generation and transfer programs are usually much less than investments in a corporation's venture capital or incubator programs, the results have often been much more significant. For example, Raytheon's New Product Development Center, an idea generation and transfer program, has often produced fifty or more patentable innovations per year.[42] Many of these were important new product enhancements, such as ovens that combined conventional and microwave capabilities and laundries that operated using plastic "credit cards," rather than coins. Such accomplishments can generate important new sources of revenue, but idea generation and transfer programs are usually limited in that they seldom foster innovations leading to the development of entirely new businesses. More typically, as at Raytheon, they lead to new products or product refinements for an existing business.

The last category of corporate entrepreneurship programs is called *intrapreneurship*, because it involves entrepreneurial individuals or small teams working within the corporation to develop their ideas into businesses.[43] Perhaps the corporation best known for pursuing this means of diversification is Minnesota Mining and Manufacturing (3M). This corporation consistently beats its goal of having 25 percent of its revenues generated by products no more than 5 years old. This is accomplished by adherence to a number of practices aimed at spreading an entrepreneurial spirit among its employees.

Unfortunately, not all attempts at fostering corporate entrepreneurship are nearly as successful as 3M's. Internal development is often risky.[44] Of the eighteen new internal ventures Exxon Enterprises tried in the 1980s, as opposed to its venture capital investments mentioned earlier, not one produced a business with significant profits.[45] The risks associated with developing new businesses vary widely, depending on whether or not a market for the product already exists and whether or not the technology is new. Many companies' experiences suggest that almost all new businesses offering familiar product technology to existing markets will be successes, while probably fewer than one in eight new businesses offering new products to an undeveloped market will succeed. Internal development is also very slow. One study found that it takes about 8 years, on average, for new businesses developed internally to break even, and another 4 years for them to reach levels of profitability that match those of typical mature businesses in the United States.[46]

On the other hand, intrapreneurship may offer benefits other than profits per se. Each of the four types of programs discussed above can be as important for its impact on corporate culture as for its impact on diversification or financial performance. Following deregulation of the telephone industry, Bell's Enter-Prize intrapreneurship program was created to transform the firm's culture from one that was heavily dependent on its monopoly position to an entrepreneurial market leader capable of fending for itself in a highly competitive market.[47] During years of operating in a heavily regulated environment, Ohio Bell had developed a culture in which employees were excellent at carrying out orders but unable to direct themselves, and in which there was widespread resistance to any new ideas or management techniques. Under the Enter-Prize program, employees were paid anywhere from $50 to $50,000 for their entrepreneurial ideas on how to make Ohio Bell more competitive. Employees with ideas for potential new businesses were given or loaned resources to test the feasibility of their ideas. While managers estimated that Enter-Prize returned $5 to the corporation for every $1 invested, they insisted that even greater gains came from fostering the more entrepreneurial culture that now pervades and impacts businesses throughout the corporation.

Divestments: The Neglected Side of Diversification

Corporate management must decide not only what businesses the corporation will enter, but also which businesses the corporation will exit. Although the subject receives much less media attention, divesting businesses is an integral part of corporate management. In fact, research shows that corporations will eventually exit many of the markets they enter through diversification long before the markets disappear. In one study, the corporations examined had divested themselves of approximately one-half of all the business units they had ever owned.[48]

Why do businesses divest? While poor performance provides the most obvious reason for selling a business, others also emerge. Corporations may decide to sell off businesses because their assets have more value in some other application. For instance, Greyhound sold a number of its downtown bus terminals because the real estate had much more value as building sites than as bus stations. Sometimes corporations sell businesses to help finance other acquisitions. U.S. Steel (now USX) sold off $3 billion worth of businesses and other assets to finance its purchase of Marathon Oil. A third reason for divestment is to finance ongoing operations. Leveraged buyouts (acquisitions financed mostly by issuing debt) regularly include plans to sell off parts of the new acquisition in order to help generate cash quickly. For instance, when Hanson Trust, one of Britain's largest corporations (built almost entirely through acquisitions), purchased Imperial Group for £2.1 billion, it immediately recouped £1.4 billion by divesting the new acquisition's brewing business.

Because divestments represent an important part of corporate management's responsibilities, they must be managed strategically.[49] Unfortunately, such is not always the norm. Divesting corporations have been described as more interested in minimizing trauma than in maximizing profits. Divestments still symbolize failure to many managers, and the result is that they often jump at a chance to get rid of the "loser" and to distance themselves from the whole affair.

Properly managed, divestments should be considered a part of the overall corporate strategy, not just an isolated quick fix for a troubled business. The business in question should be carefully evaluated, not in terms of its potential in the current setting but in an ideal situation. Then, conduct a systematic search for potential buyers that could offer this ideal setting. Once they are identified, a sales plan should be created to highlight the fit between the particular business and each of the potential buyers. Selling a business involves the same kind of analysis as buying one, with the focus shifting from how the business fits into your corporation to how it fits into someone else's corporation. Because divestment impacts employees and the local community in general, corporate managers should also consider their ethical and social responsibility to manage divestments carefully.[50]

Now that we have considered the forms and means of diversification in some detail, we are ready to evaluate the various benefits that have been attributed to diversification.

EVALUATING THE BENEFITS OF DIVERSIFICATION

Theorists commonly cite six reasons as benefits of diversification. We evaluate these reasons in light of our standard for good corporate management developed in Chapter 1 and in the opening section of this chapter: creating value for stockholders that they cannot create for themselves. We begin with the most powerful reasons for diversifying and then move on to those that are less defensible but still commonly cited as motives for diversification. Exhibit 7.3 arranges the six according to their power to create value.

Capitalizing on Core Competencies

Core competencies are the most significant value-creating skills within a corporation. These skills can often be extended to products or markets beyond those in which they were originally developed.[51] Such extensions represent excellent opportunities for diversification. For example, when it considered diversification targets, Philip Morris believed that the core competence it had developed in marketing cigarettes could apply to other, similar markets. Based on this idea, the company purchased Miller Brewing and then used the Philip Morris marketing skills to move the Miller brand from seventh place to second in its market.

Any core competence that meets the following three requirements provides a viable basis for the corporation to strengthen a new business unit.[52]

EXHIBIT 7.3
Evaluating Reasons to Diversify

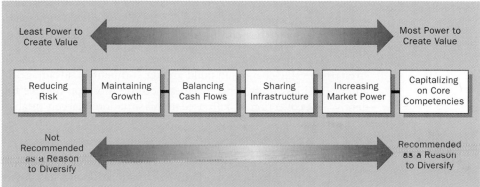

The core competence must translate into a meaningful competitive advantage. In other words, the competence must help the business establish some strength relative to its competitors. Every core process and each of the major activities in the value chain is a viable basis for building on a core competence. For instance, Black & Decker enjoys a core competence in developing products with small electric motors and rechargeable batteries, and has successfully diversified this competence from small power tools for woodworking into higher-margin items such as electric kitchen appliances, miniaturized vacuum cleaners, and rechargeable flashlights.

The new business must have enough similarity to existing businesses to benefit from the corporation's core competencies. This is one reason related diversification is more profitable than unrelated diversification on average. However, this does not necessarily mean that the products themselves must be similar. Rather, at least one element of their value chains must require similar skills in creating competitive advantage in order for the corporation to capitalize on its core competencies. An example is Coca-Cola's move into leisure clothing. At first glance, one might think that soft drinks and sweatshirts have little in common, but in an important strategic sense they are, in fact, closely related; the marketing of both can be based on selling a trademark and an image as much as on selling the product itself. In soft drinks, its core business, Coca-Cola emphasizes marketing as a key component of its value chain by building demand through strong customer awareness. Coke used this same expertise in marketing an image to successfully introduce a line of clothing bearing various Coca-Cola trademarks. In its first full year of business, Coca-Cola Clothes generated $100 million in wholesale revenues—impressive growth in any industry and by far the best in the clothing industry.[53]

The bundle of competencies should be difficult for competition to imitate. As explained in Chapter 4, if the transferred skills are widely available or easily replicated, they are unlikely to provide the basis of a sustainable competitive advantage.[54] An individual core competence need not be unique; rather, it is the *collection* of competencies that should be unique, or at least difficult to replicate. For example, Canon, the Japanese diversified manufacturer, has demonstrated an unmatched ability to enter and dominate markets stretching from photocopiers and cameras to laser printers. Its dominance in these varied markets rests on mastery of crucial technologies for successful engineering and design of all these products. Canon is a world leader in its core competencies of optics, imaging, and microprocessor controls. Other companies are good at one or another of these technologies, but Canon is arguably the best overall. This provides the company with a basis for diversification that competitors cannot easily match.

A corporation that builds on core competencies utilizes skills that combine to strengthen value chains and build greater competitive advantages. This leads to *synergies* among business units, whereby they become more productive together than independently. The collection of skills used in this situation is largely intangible, but, as we discuss in the next section, corporations can also build synergies by sharing tangible resources.

Increasing Market Power

To understand the impact corporate diversification can have on a business unit's market power, compare the structural position of an independent business unit against what it would enjoy as part of a larger corporation. For instance, consider the position of an independent confectioner versus the same business as part of, say, Procter & Gamble on each of the five competitive forces introduced in Chapter 3. Membership in the P&G family can provide the business unit with greater bargaining power vis-à-vis both its suppliers and its customers, as the large corporation carries more clout. With the resources available from the "deep pockets" of a firm like P&G, the individual business unit is also in a much stronger position relative not only to its rivals, but also to threats from substitutes and new entrants. Any competing firm evaluating the strength of our hypothetical candy maker is likely to view it as a much more significant rival if it is part of the P&G corporate behemoth than if it is a single, stand-alone business. Association with the larger corporation may also bring the individual business unit increased visibility and an improved image. If so, this could have a favorable impact on any or all of the five forces affecting the business unit's structural position and ultimately on its competitive advantage.

Corporations may also increase market power by using mergers and acquisitions to consolidate their industries. For instance, Maytag, a leading U.S. manufacturer of domestic appliances, sought to improve its power with suppliers and customers by acquiring a number of business units that both extended and supplemented its core product line. Many of Maytag's acquisitions entailed horizontal diversification in that they moved the firm further into parts of the value chain it had already had a position in; for example, Maytag already manufactured domestic kitchen appliances, but acquisitions gave it a stronger position in manufacturing commercial kitchen appliances. However, a firm can also use diversification to become more vertically integrated and thereby increase its power over suppliers and/or customers by making them a "captive" part of the same corporation. Maytag purchased firms that had once been outside suppliers of component parts such as heating elements for stoves and dishwashers.

Finally, membership in a larger corporate enterprise may provide a business with markets or distribution channels it could not access on its own. A number of attempts to enter the U.S. soft drink market failed because the businesses could not overcome the entry barriers created by that industry's tightly controlled distribution channels. However, the soft drink business unit created inside the Wal-Mart corporation found a ready-made distribution channel provided by the thousands of Wal-Mart retail outlets scattered around the United States. In this way, that soft drink business enjoyed a much more favorable structural position and greater market power as part of the Wal-Mart Corporation than a similar business would have had as a stand-alone entity.

Government agencies that oversee industry competitiveness (such as the U.S. Federal Trade Commission) often place limits on how far a corporation can diversify to gain power, and a move that is believed to place too much power in the hands of a single corporation may be prohibited. For example, government regulators are carefully considering Microsoft's move into on-line services. This diversification move would allow Microsoft to increase its market power by vertically integrating forward; subscribers would be able to download Microsoft software without going through a traditional retailer. Regulators are concerned that this might place too much power in Microsoft's hands, and they are considering stopping the move. However, within such limits, diversification that improves the market power of the various business units constituting the corporation clearly meets our criteria of creating value for stockholders in a way that they cannot replicate themselves.

Sharing Infrastructures

To capitalize on core competencies, firms must share intangible resources, such as skills, know-how, and talent, across business units. Infrastructures, on the other hand, are tangible resources, such as production facilities, marketing programs, purchasing procedures, and delivery routes.[55] These are the basic "nuts and bolts" of any business, and the ability to share these resources can be an important benefit of diversification. Procter & Gamble, for example, uses a common delivery system for various business units. P&G sells a wide range of products that are manufactured in facilities spread over an equally wide geographic area. Yet many of these items share two characteristics: they are destined for the same retail outlets, and they are fairly expensive to ship. Because of this, it is more efficient for P&G's various businesses to share delivery systems. Rather than send an entire truckload of cookies to a single retail outlet, P&G mixes its truckloads to provide the product blend each customer desires. Thus P&G can use one truck with a mix of items to do what otherwise might require a dozen trucks. In addition, because it is inefficient to ship "pure" loads of very light but bulky items (such as potato chips) or very dense goods (such as liquid laundry detergent), P&G saves on fuel bills and road taxes.

Note the two features that allow P&G to benefit from sharing infrastructures. First, the businesses have similar needs—they use the same retail outlets. This is another benefit of related diversification; without similar needs, businesses have no opportunity to share infrastructures. Second, delivery expenses represent a significant part of the value chain for these products, so they help determine the competitiveness of P&G's products. In other words, to be useful, resource sharing must improve competitiveness.

Balancing Financial Resources

Different businesses (even within the same corporation) generate dramatically different levels of cash. Some businesses produce more cash than necessary to continue operating, while others need more than they can produce. Historically, managers in diversified corporations emphasized efficiently balancing cash flows among a corporation's business units. By combining cash producers and cash users in the same corporation, managers can meet the needs of both.

In such a corporation, the sibling businesses become a portfolio of investments, and managers balance cash flow across the family of businesses rather than merely within each individual business. This approach, called *portfolio management*, first became popular in the 1970s, when a number of leading corporations and consulting firms developed several similar frameworks to guide managers in allocating cash among diverse business units.[56] Some of the decisions involved in portfolio management are presented in Application 7.3, which looks at General Electric's efforts to balance the cash flows of its various business ventures.

We shall briefly consider three popular variations of portfolio management and then look at the general benefits and limitations of this approach.[57] The various versions of the portfolio approach are named according to the labels of their grids' axes.

The Growth–Share Matrix

According to the growth–share matrix, developed during the 1970s by the Boston Consulting Group (BCG), two relatively simple factors predict whether an individual

Application 7.3

General Electric Milks a Cash Cow

General Electric pioneered use of portfolio management concepts to direct its diversification efforts. GE's market capitalization (the market value of its stock) is the greatest of any U.S. corporation, and the company still places considerable emphasis on the challenges of managing its huge portfolio of businesses. A recent decision, in which the corporation took $600 million of the cash flows generated by its financial services division and invested the money elsewhere, illustrates the issues involved in portfolio management.

GE Capital Services comprises twenty-four business units that offer a very broad range of financial services, from financing airplanes to selling insurance to investment banking. If the division were a stand-alone corporation, it would be the fifth-largest financial services business in the United States, just behind Merrill Lynch. The division has been tremendously profitable, and GE has historically allowed the division to reinvest the bulk of its profits in itself—in fact, GE even invested an additional $2 billion in the division.

The reason for this huge investment was that Capital Services offered some of the best returns available for GE investments. An analysis done for *Fortune* magazine reported that over a 5-year period Capital Services had an economic value added (EVA) of $1.7 billion compared with an economic value added of *minus* $503 million for the rest of GE (see Exhibit 7.4). In other words, GE poured money into Capital Services because of the superior payback it offered in comparison to all alternatives.

However, in 1993, GE reversed the decision to let Capital Services reinvest its profits, and $600 million was pulled out of the division for use elsewhere. This is a classic example of "milking a cash cow," and it raises all the questions normally associated with such a decision. Given the track record of Capital Services versus the rest

of GE, why did GE think the $600 million could be better invested outside Capital Services? Did this reflect an opinion that Capital Services' future options are limited? Not likely, because the company was still growing at double-digit rates during this time period. Probably GE thought it could use the funds to open up important new international markets, such as China. However, from the standpoint of EVA, GE faces a tremendous challenge in finding a use for the $600 million that will generate a better return for stockholders than that which has historically been produced by the cash cow Capital Services.

Source

Based on information gathered from Stern Stewart and Terence P. Paré, "GE Monkeys with Its Money Machine," *Fortune* (February 21, 1994), 81–87. Copyright © 1994 Time Inc. All rights reserved.

EXHIBIT 7.4
Economic Value Added

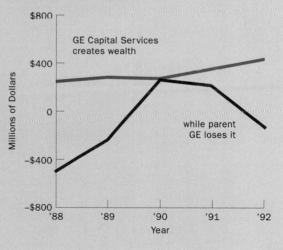

business will be a cash producer or a cash user: (1) the growth rate of the market within which the business competes and (2) its share of that market. Businesses in fast-growing markets usually need more cash to scale up production, open new facilities, advertise, develop new products, and so on. On the other hand, businesses in declining markets may have already lived through their peak periods of product demand and are more likely to have sufficient assets to serve the present dwindling demand. Businesses in this situation generally produce considerable cash but do not have a ready place to invest it. Thus, businesses in growing markets may need more cash than they have, while businesses in mature or declining markets may have more cash than they need. Additionally, businesses with large market shares more likely enjoy economies of scale and greater experience curve benefits. Lower costs mean higher profits, and higher profits mean greater cash flows. In short, the BCG's framework suggests that higher market shares are associated with greater cash flows. Exhibit 7.5 shows the combined effects of market growth and market share, and we can see how each of the four cells of the matrix indicates a different strategy.

Cash cows usually produce far more cash than they can usefully employ in house. Corporations often "milk" such businesses to finance other businesses on which the corporation's future may depend. *Dogs* hold small shares of slow-growing (or even declining) markets and they are unlikely ever to become important sources of cash. In fact, they may be greater users of cash for which there is little likely return. Experts often suggest that such businesses be "harvested" by not investing in them and instead shifting cash flows to more promising businesses. *Problem children* have low market shares of rapidly growing markets. They represent a potential opportunity; if their market shares can be increased, they might become cash cows. However, if they cannot increase market shares before market growth slows, they will, in effect, become dogs. Developing a strategy for problem children means either investing large sums in hope of gaining a viable market share or not investing and possibly missing a growth market. *Stars* are often the hope of the future. They currently hold large market shares in rapidly growing markets, so their cash flows may be minimal or even

EXHIBIT 7.5
The Growth–Share Matrix

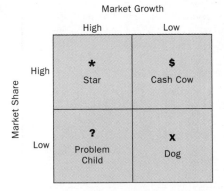

Source: The growth–share matrix was originally developed by the Boston Consulting Group.

negative. Recommended strategy dictates that they be nurtured, maintaining their health and waiting for market growth to slow so that net cash flows will increase. Theoretically, the cash-hungry stars will be transformed into cash-rich cows that can be milked to nurture still another generation of businesses.

The Market Life Cycle–Competitive Strength Matrix

Critics of the growth–share matrix contend that it fails to consider the wide range of factors that affect cash flow beyond market growth and market share. A somewhat more involved picture of the situation facing a business can be depicted by adding a judgmental assessment of the overall competitive strength of the strategic business unit (SBU). A second refinement utilizes the richer concept of the market life cycle as a replacement for market growth. Recall from Chapter 6 that growth rates vary predictably across stages of the market life cycle, but that the life cycle model depicts various strategic issues beyond simply growth. The explicit consideration of the market life cycle found in this portfolio management framework provides a useful bridge between strategy formulation at the business level and at the corporate level. Exhibit 7.6

EXHIBIT 7.6
The Market Life Cycle–Competitive Strength Matrix

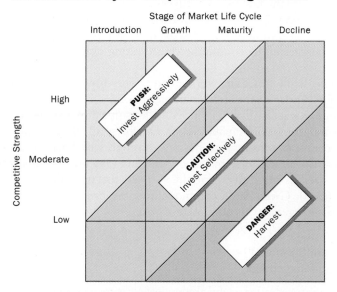

Source: This type of matrix was originally developed by Arthur D. Little, a consulting firm that coupled the matrix to a comprehensive methodology for developing strategic plans.

shows the cash flows and investment requirements at various combinations of competitive strength and market life cycle stages.

While the market life cycle–competitive strength framework obviously provides a richer description than the growth–share matrix, its central message is the same. To see the relationship between these two frameworks, redraw the market life cycle–competitive strength matrix with the growth–share matrix superimposed. This will reveal the similarities of the strategies suggested by the corresponding positions on the two grids. Cash cows will still be in the upper right-hand quadrant, dogs in the lower right-hand quadrant, and so on. The reason for this similarity becomes clear if you remember that market growth is closely linked to the market life cycle and that market share is at once both a cause and an effect of competitive strength.

The Industry Attractiveness–Business Position Matrix

While the market life cycle–competitive strength matrix is more refined than the growth–share matrix, some have found that its coverage of important issues remains limited. An alternative, the broadest portfolio management framework we will consider, is the industry attractiveness–business position matrix. This approach considers matters raised in the other two frameworks and incorporates a range of other considerations, such as those shown in Exhibit 7.7.

Analysts typically combine information about such factors to reach a subjective evaluation of overall industry attractiveness and business position. The strategic implications suggested by combining the resulting evaluation in a matrix are identified in Exhibit 7.8.

Clearly, while this framework entails a very broad set of considerations, it is fundamentally similar to the simpler frameworks described above. All these frameworks share three characteristics: (1) they consider some dimensions of both the external environment and internal capabilities of a business; (2) they simplify information about environmental conditions and business strengths by locating business units graphically on a two-dimensional matrix or grid; and (3) a business unit's position in the matrix is treated as indicative of its likely need for, or ability to provide, financial resources (cash). Given these commonalities, we can evaluate the usefulness of these portfolio management techniques as a group.

Benefits and Limits of Portfolio Management

Portfolio matrices offer useful frameworks for managers to consider potential differences among businesses in the same corporation, and experience shows that they offer several potential benefits:[58] (1) they summarize large amounts of general information about individual business units and overall corporate plans; (2) they focus important differences among businesses and help illustrate the rationale behind corporate plans to invest funds in business A that have been obtained from business B; (3) they provide simple but useful guidelines for checking consistency between a business's requests for resources and opportunities for using these resources effectively; and (4) they suggest reasonable performance levels for business units facing the various

---

EXHIBIT 7.7
Examples of Factors Considered in Constructing an Industry Attractiveness–Business Position Matrix

Industry Attractiveness	*Business Position*

Bargaining power of suppliers/customers
    Relative size of typical players
    Numbers of each
    Importance of purchases from or sales to
    Ability to integrate vertically

Threat of substitute products/new entrants
    Technological maturity/stability
    Diversity of the market
    Barriers to entry
    Flexibility of distribution system

Nature of competitive rivalry
    Number of competitors
    Size of competitors
    Strength of competitors' corporate parents
    Price wars
    Competition on multiple dimensions

Economic factors
    Sales volatility
    Cyclicality of demand
    Market growth
    Capital intensity

Financial norms
    Average profitability
    Typical leverage
    Credit practices

Sociopolitical considerations
    Government regulation
    Community support
    Ethical standards

Level of differentiation
    Advertising effectiveness
    Product quality
    Company image
    Patented products
    Brand awareness

Cost position
    Economies of scale
    Manufacturing costs
    Overhead
    Scrap/waste/rework
    Experience effects
    Labor rates
    Patented processes

Response time
    Manufacturing flexibility
    Time needed to introduce new products
    Delivery times
    Organizational flexibility

Financial strength
    Solvency
    Liquidity
    Break-even point
    Cash flows
    Profitability
    Growth in revenues

Human assets
    Turnover
    Skill level
    Relative wage/salary
    Morale
    Managerial commitment
    Unionization

Public approval
    Goodwill
    Reputation
    Image

---

strategic situations (obviously, the growth and profitability expected of a "star" are quite different from those expected of a "dog").

    While these benefits are important, portfolio management should not be considered the sole, or even the primary, basis for formulating corporate-level plans. It is more appropriately used as a tool that can help initiate a complete corporate strategy.[59] One commonly cited problem is that the simple matrices tend to trivialize

EXHIBIT 7.8
The Industry Attractiveness–Business Position Matrix

Industry Attractiveness

	High	Medium	Low
High	Invest	Selective Growth	Up or Out
Medium	Selective Growth	Up or Out	Harvest
Low	Up or Out	Harvest	Divest

Business Position

Description of Dimensions

Industry Attractiveness: Subjective assessment based on broadest possible range of external opportunities and threats beyond the strict control of management
Business Position: Subjective assessment of how strong a competitive advantage is created by a broad range of the firm's internal strengths and weaknesses

---

Source: This type of matrix was conceived by consultants at McKinsey & Company and managers at General Electric.

thinking. To be fair, this criticism should probably be laid at the feet of those who have misused them; they were never intended to replace careful thought, although in practice they sometimes have done so.

Another problem with portfolio management is that individual businesses can be indistinguishable from one another.[60] No exact principles dictate what constitutes a separate market or an individual product line. For example, should a beverage company treat its coffee and tea operations as two businesses or one? Often yearly planning cycles don't allow enough time for detailed analysis of every SBU in many large diversified firms. Therefore, even the most ardent supporters of portfolio approaches to corporate management "fudge" a little on what constitutes an SBU in their portfolio planning. Firms usually recognize no more than about thirty entities in their portfolios, regardless of how many businesses must be combined to reach this manageable number.[61]

Finally, simple models of portfolio management are generally not very accurate. After 2 decades of use, it is now obvious that models such as the BCG matrix have often led to inappropriate strategic moves because of their inaccuracy. For instance, one study reported that more than half of all businesses that should have been cash users according to the BCG matrix were, in fact, cash providers.[62] On the other hand, roughly one-fourth of all businesses expected to be cash providers were, in fact, cash users. While no similar studies have been carried out for the other portfolio frameworks described here, any framework that reduces a strategic situation to two dimensions will not be highly accurate in its prescriptions.

Thus, portfolio management has become one of the most involved and elaborate approaches to developing corporate strategy. Consequently, our discussion of balancing cash flows has been considerably more extensive than that devoted to the other benefits of diversification. We are now ready to turn to the last two of the six most commonly cited benefits of diversification.

Maintaining Growth

Diversification also provides continued growth. Especially among larger firms, diversification undoubtedly offers one of the most common sources of growth. Using diversification, BASF, the giant German chemical company, was able to maintain a level of growth through the 1980s more typical of rapidly growing start-up businesses, even though it was a mature, multibillion-dollar multinational corporation. In the last half of that decade, BASF grew at an average of 36 percent per year, roughly doubling in size every 2 years, from a base that was already huge.[63]

Is growth always desirable? Considerable argument revolves around the idea that corporations should pursue only moderate levels of growth to generate the best return on stockholder investments. Beyond that, profitability likely declines as the pursuit of high growth levels drives the corporation into more marginal businesses and the cost of operating the increasingly large corporation outstrips the growth in profits that additional businesses might provide. Exhibit 7.9 helps us visualize this relationship.

EXHIBIT 7.9
Typical Trade-off Between Corporate Growth Rate and Corporate Profitability

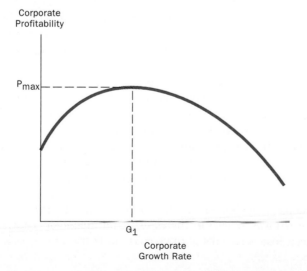

Reducing Risk

Corporate managers sometimes justify diversification on the basis of risk reduction.[64] To understand how diversification relates to risk, first note that different businesses respond differently to particular economic cycles: the demand for luxury cruise vacations typically declines during recessions as consumers look for less expensive recreation, while demand for bus travel typically increases, as this is a relatively inexpensive mode of transportation. We call businesses such as these two *countercyclical*. In order to reduce the risk associated with volatile earnings, a single corporation might decide to diversify its portfolio by holding both a cruise ship line and a bus line. If such countercyclical businesses exist within the same diversified corporation, a bad year for one business can be offset by a better year for the other. In this way, the variability of the overall corporation's earnings would decrease, and stockholder investment is less risky.[65]

However, investors do not need corporate managers to achieve this risk-reducing effect. They can simply invest their individual funds in the different businesses (cruise ship operators and bus operators in this example) to achieve the same risk-reducing effect: a bad year for one of their investments will be offset by the improved performance of their other investment, and the risk associated with their overall portfolio of investments will decrease. In fact, individual investors can usually achieve such risk reduction through diversification at a lower cost than corporate managers can because they do not have to pay the takeover premium a corporation normally has to pay. This being the case, diversification for risk reduction alone hardly meets the goal of having corporate managers create value for an investor in some way that the investor cannot accomplish alone. As we shall see in the next section, forces at play can limit any of the six possible benefits of diversification listed in Exhibit 7.3.

MANAGERIAL BEHAVIOR THAT LIMITS THE BENEFITS OF DIVERSIFICATION

Creating value for stockholders in ways that they cannot do on their own is complicated by the fact that corporate managers do not always benefit from diversification in the same way stockholders do.[66] To appreciate this important point, understand the relationship between corporate managers and the corporation's stockholders. Theoretically, corporate managers are to act as the agents for the stockholders, whose interests they are hired to represent.[67] However, an area of research known as agency theory leads us to ask whether managers always act in stockholders' best interest.[68]

Agency theory suggests that managers will not always place stockholders' interests above their own.[69] In fact, stockholders have been dubbed the "least important constituency" by researchers who have examined how corporate executives manage the diversification process.[70] In managing diversification, corporate managers face a dilemma as they attempt to balance their own interests against those of stockholders.[71] For instance, stockholders often enjoy high profits from the sale of their stock when the firm is taken over. On the other hand, managers of firms that have been taken over often lose their jobs. Critics contend that corporate managers sometimes protect their jobs by using various antitakeover tactics, even though avoiding the takeover often *reduces* the value of stockholders' investments. Such controversial takeover tactics are described in Application 7.4.[72]

In the following sections, we consider how each of the potential benefits of diversification can decrease because of conflicts between the interests of managers and those of stockholders.

Application 7.4

Antitakeover Tactics and the Ethical Issues They Raise

Stockholders can often benefit dramatically from an acquisition; the purchase usually entails a takeover premium that increases the price of the stock they own. But many takeovers involve wholesale dismissal of the management team. Because fighting takeovers is sometimes in management's best interest, the use of antitakeover tactics raises controversial ethical issues. Managers claim that in order to take a long-term perspective toward managing the business, they must feel secure in their jobs. Critics claim that these tactics, sometimes collectively called "shark repellent," insulate managers from market forces which would otherwise require them to do a better job. They argue that the real purpose of shark repellent is self-serving. These critics also point out that the tactics favor certain classes of stockholders (specifically, sharks) above all others. Here is a sample of antitakeover tactics that are controversial because they appear to serve the needs of managers more often than they benefit the firm's owners:

- **Scorched earth:** Selling off key assets in an effort to purposely make the business unattractive to sharks. The assets sold are referred to as the *crown jewels* because they are often those which make the company most attractive in the first place. When sharks threaten, crown jewels may be offered at greatly reduced prices to ensure a quick sale. Obviously, this defense could result in mortally wounding the corporation.

- **White knight:** In order to avoid being acquired in a hostile (unwanted) takeover, managers approach a third firm about acquisition. To induce such a "white knight" to rescue the corporation, the targeted firm's stock is often offered on very favorable terms. When the friendly acquiring firm buys only a portion of the corporation, it is known as a *white squire.*

- **Greenmail:** A financial inducement offered by the threatened firm to stop a shark from acquiring it. The inducement is commonly an offer to buy back (usually at an attractive premium) any of the corporation's stock the shark has already purchased, in exchange for the shark's guarantee that it will not threaten the defending firm. Again, this is special treatment offered only to selected stockholders.

- **Golden parachute:** A high-pay package, often running three times normal annual compensation, that is promised to executives fired as a result of a takeover. Sharks are repelled by the idea of having the management team of the acquired corporation leave *en masse*—especially if they leave with so much cash.

- **Poison pill:** Any of a number of devices aimed at reducing the worth of a company once it has been taken over. For instance, a clause requiring that huge dividend payments be made upon takeover would raise the effective cost of the acquisition, because the shark would have to allow for the cost of meeting the payments. Because there are so many ways to sabotage the future operations of a business, poison pills remain the most popular form of shark repellent.

- **Pac-Man:** A defense based on trying to consume the hunting shark before it attacks. In this situation, offense becomes defense and the hunter becomes the hunted. The risk of using this tactic is that it sometimes sets up a cycle of bid and counterbid in which the prices of both firms escalate. When this happens, the "winner" of the bidding war may be saddled with more debt than it can hope to service.

Capitalizing on Core Competencies

Managers in newly acquired businesses often resent and oppose transferring skills from the core business. Managers good enough at their work to make their business an attractive acquisition may wonder why the new corporate parent presumes to know better. In the case of Philip Morris and the Miller Brewing acquisition, Philip Morris ended up replacing several key Miller executives who resisted the transfer of marketing skills from Philip Morris, even though Philip Morris was undoubtedly one of the best marketers in the world. Philip Morris eventually overcame this obstacle, but other corporations are less fortunate and face continued resistance from their acquisitions.

Increasing Market Power

Any corporate attempt to improve a business unit's market power by enhancing its structural position entails some loss of autonomy or control on the part of the business's managers. To return to our earlier example of a confectioner acquired by Procter & Gamble, to the extent that the candy maker is treated as part of the P&G family, it no longer controls its own destiny. For example, its sales force may no longer be necessary; in order to give the business unit the greatest possible market power, its sales will probably be handled as part of a centralized sales department's responsibilities, with each salesperson handling candy sales along with sales of a variety of other P&G products. This diminished role for managers in the candy business is likely to meet considerable resistance, and they may try to maintain independence from the larger corporation even though doing so will limit the favorable impact on market power the corporate parent offers.

Sharing Infrastructures

Managers may feel threatened when a corporation attempts to have businesses share resources. A corporation may decide to have one set of managers or one set of facilities serve two businesses; in this case, the other managers or facilities will no longer be needed and some managers will lose their jobs. Clearly, managers have good reason to resist such efforts at making the corporation more efficient.

Balancing Financial Resources

While balancing cash flows across businesses sounds logical, consider how managers might respond to having their businesses labeled "dogs." How often are careers advanced by killing off a business efficiently, even if it is done for the good of the corporation? Individual managers often believe that their success depends more on the performance of their particular businesses rather than on the performance of the corporation. In such circumstances, managers find it difficult to sacrifice their businesses for the good of others in the portfolio, even if the corporation as a whole would benefit.

Maintaining Growth

Corporate growth seems to have at least as much to do with improving the welfare of managers as the welfare of stockholders. Managers may be in favor of growth because they expect personal benefits from increasing the size of the corporation. For example, managers in larger corporations typically get paid more than their counterparts in smaller corporations.[73] One study found that, other things being equal, for every 10 percent increase in company size, U.S. CEOs could expect a 2 percent increase in annual pay.[74] This holds true even though larger corporations are not necessarily more profitable.

Larger corporations offer managers more prestige and more perquisites, or "perks." Every year the popular business press celebrates corporate size with listings such as the *Fortune* 500, the 500 largest corporations in the United States. Business professionals consider being a top-ranking executive at a large corporation more prestigious than holding a similar rank in a smaller firm. Corporate jets, executive townhouses, lavish corporate headquarters, and so on, are all expensive perks. Larger corporations are more able to afford such perks, because they represent a smaller percentage of overall corporate assets and expenses.

Managers may also believe that larger corporations offer greater job security. Larger corporations were traditionally more difficult to acquire by takeover, so, by increasing the size of their corporations, managers may think they are reducing the threat of being replaced. With the ever-increasing size of takeover targets, this tactic may no longer work, but for most managers, it remains a major consideration for acquisition.

Both corporations and stockholders can benefit from growth. However, the relationship between corporate size and corporate financial performance is tenuous, and the benefits to growth appear to accrue more directly to managers than to the stockholders they are presumably hired to serve.[75] This suggests that growth alone is not a strong argument for diversifying. It is probably more appropriate to consider growth as a by-product of diversification rather than as a reason for diversifying.

Reducing Risk

As we have seen, individual investors can diversify their stock portfolios using countercyclical stocks to reduce their overall risks, so corporate diversification for the sake of risk reduction does not meet our standards for good strategy. However, some corporate managers may pursue this tactic because it effectively reduces their own risks.[76] When a corporation is involved in a variety of industries, its total earnings are less volatile, which means that the earnings for which corporate managers are responsible are more assured.

Clearly, managers do not benefit from diversification in the same way owners do, and this difference often limits the benefits owners derive from corporate diversification. In fact, if you return to Exhibit 7.3 and compare the things that benefit stockholders and the things that benefit managers, you may reach the conclusion that the two have precisely opposite rankings for the six reasons we have discussed. While stockholders have much to gain from capitalizing on core competencies, improving market power, and sharing infrastructure, managers have much to lose from the same. On the other hand, managers may benefit from maintaining growth and reducing risk, although, as we have seen, there is little opportunity for stockholders to benefit from corporations diversifying for these reasons alone. Balancing cash flows appears to offer mixed results for both parties.

All this suggests that one of the greatest challenges to corporate strategy is overcoming the differences in the motives of owners and managers. One common way of doing this is to tie manager compensation to stock performance. This can be accomplished by granting stock options (options to buy stock at prespecified prices) to managers or by selling stock to all employees on favorable terms. Either option is meant to increase managers' and employees' interest in creating greater value for stockholders, the goal of corporate strategy.

Summary of Managerial Practices to Adopt from This Chapter

- Remember that the key responsibility for managers at the corporate level is to see that stockholders' funds are invested in such a way that they generate more value for the stockholders than stockholders could generate for themselves.

- Corporate managers can continue to invest in their present businesses, or they can invest in different businesses, an option that entails some form of diversification.

- Use the relatively simple three-by-three matrix of "forms by means" to help you sort out options for diversification. The most common forms of diversification are vertical integration, horizontal diversification, and global diversification. Diversification is usually carried out through acquisitions, strategic alliances, or internal development.

- A corporation's level of diversification can also be influenced through divestments as its sells off businesses. Divestments are often poorly managed, but remember that, if they are approached correctly, they too offer opportunities to create value for stockholders in ways that stockholders cannot replicate for themselves.

- As a manager, you should be aware that the benefits you personally receive from diversification are often different from, and sometimes in conflict with, those realized by stockholders. You should consider the needs of both parties carefully in order to reach an appropriately balanced approach to managing at the corporate level.

- Perhaps the best justification for diversification is to be able to capitalize further on core competencies a corporation has already developed, and your organization's core competencies should play an important role in shaping its diversification strategy. Other good reasons for diversifying are opportunities to increase a business's market power, to utilize corporate infrastructures more fully, and to facilitate shifting cash flows from businesses generating excess cash to those needing additional cash.

- Other reasons frequently given for diversification are maintenance of growth and reduction of risk, but it is usually easier to see how managers benefit from these than how stockholders do.

Questions for Discussion and Review

1. Explain the meaning of this statement: "Firms should base decisions on diversification according to the criterion of generating greater returns to stockholders than those stockholders would likely achieve if acting independently."

2. Describe the different forms of diversification and give an example of each.

3. Describe the different means of diversification and give an example of each.

4. Evaluate the most common reasons for diversifying in terms of their impact on competitive advantage and financial performance.

5. Explain how managerial behavior can effectively limit stockholders' benefits from diversification.

Notes

1. Noel M. Tichy and Stratford Sherman, *Control Your Destiny or Someone Else Will,* New York: Doubleday, 1993.

2. Michael Goold and Kathleen Luchs, "Why Diversify? Four Decades of Management Thinking," *Academy of Management Executives,* 7:3 (1993), 7.

3. Michael Lubatkin, "Value-Creating Mergers: Fact or Folklore?," *Academy of Management Executive,* 2 (November 1988), 295–302.

4. You may recall that this is the basic idea behind the notion of economic value added described in Chapter 4; see also Shawn Tully, "The Real Key to Creating Wealth," *Fortune* (September 20, 1993), 38.

5. Alfred Rappaport, "Linking Competitive Strategy and Shareholder Value Analysis," *Journal of Business Strategy* (Spring 1987), 58–67; G. S. Day and L. Fahey, "Putting Strategy into Shareholder Value Analysis," *Harvard Business Review* (March–April 1990), 156–162; Alfred Rappaport, "CFOs and Strategists: Forging a Common Framework," *Harvard Business Review* (May–June 1992), 84–91.

6. Michael Porter, "From Competitive Advantage to Corporate Strategy," *Harvard Business Review,* 65 (May–June 1987), 43–59.

7. O. Williamson, *Markets and Hierarchies: Analysis and Antitrust Implications,* New York: The Free Press, 1975.

8. This point is discussed in some detail in R. H. Hayes and W. J. Abernathy, "Managing Our Way to Economic Decline," *Harvard Business Review* (July–August 1980), 67.

9. These questions are adapted from Kathryn Harrigan's research presented in "Matching Vertical Integration Strategies to Competitive Conditions," *Strategic Management Journal,* 7 (November–December 1986), 535–555; and John Stuckey and David White, "When and When *Not* to Vertically Integrate," *McKinsey Quarterly* (Summer 1993), 3–27. These and additional criteria are discussed in D. B. Ewaldz, "How Integrated Should Your Company Be?," *Journal of Business Strategy* (July–August 1991), 52–55.

10. James Brian Quinn, Thomas L. Doorley, and Penny C. Paquette, "Beyond Products: Services-Based Strategy," *Harvard Business Review* (March–April 1990), 58–68.

11. For a comparison of ownership versus other forms of integration, see Joseph T. Mahoney, "The Choice of Organizational Form: Vertical Financial Ownership Versus Other Methods of Vertical Integration," *Strategic Management Journal,* 13 (1992), 559–584.

12. See discussion of how far to integrate along an industry's "surplus chain" in Alistair M. Hanna and Jerrold T. Lundquist, "Creative Strategies," *McKinsey Quarterly* (Summer 1990), 56–79.

13. J. B. Barney, "Returns to Bidding Firms in Mergers and Acquisitions: Reconsidering the Related Hypotheses," *Strategic Management Journal,* 9 (special issue, 1988), 71–78; V.

Ramanujam and P. Varadarajan, "Research on Corporate Diversification: A Synthesis," *Strategic Management Journal*, *10* (1989), 523–551.

14. Michael Lubatkin, "Merger Strategies and Stockholder Value," *Strategic Management Journal*, *8* (1987), 39–53; S. Chatterjee, "Types of Synergy and Economic Value: The Impact of Acquisitions on Merging and Rival Firms," *Strategic Management Journal*, *7* (1986), 119–140.

15. M. Leontiades, "The Rewards of Diversifying into Unrelated Businesses," *Journal of Business Strategy*, *6* (Spring 1986), 81–87.

16. To learn the fascinating story of how such a corporation was built, read the entertaining *How to Lose $1,000,000,000 and Other Valuable Advice* by Royal Little, Boston: Little, Brown, 1979.

17. For a discussion of the managerial practices that allow firms to better realize the advantages of broad diversification, see Roland Calori and CESMA, "How Successful Companies Manage Diverse Businesses," *Long Range Planning*, *21*:3 (1988), 80–89.

18. For example, research indicates that the best way to protect shareholder value against economic downturns is to diversify only to the extent that "all of one's eggs are in similar baskets"; see M. Lubatkin and S. Chatterjee, "The Strategy-Shareholder Value Relationship: Testing Temporal Stability Across Market Cycles," *Strategic Management Journal*, *12* (May 1991), 251–270.

19. M. S. Davis, "Two plus Two Doesn't Equal Five," *Fortune* (June 25, 1985), 177.

20. William M. Bulkeley, "Conglomerates Make a Comeback—with a '90s Twist," *Wall Street Journal* (March 1, 1994), 1.

21. *Mergers* refers to the act of combining two corporations, but this usually entails one corporation acquiring the other. Therefore, to simplify this material, we do not make a distinction between acquisitions and mergers. For a discussion of the shared strategic goals of mergers and acquisitions, see G. A. Walter and J. B. Barney, "Management Objectives in Mergers and Acquisitions," *Strategic Management Journal* (January 1990), 79–86.

22. For research on how synergies and restructuring are sources of value creation through acquisition, see Sayan Chatterjee, "Sources of Value in Takeovers: Synergy or Restructuring—Implications for Target and Bidder Firms," *Strategic Management Journal*, *13* (1992), 267–286.

23. D. Foust and T. Smart, "The Merger Parade Runs into a Brick Wall," *Business Week* (June 25, 1990), 38.

24. Anne B. Fisher, "How to Make a Merger Work," *Fortune* (January 24, 1994), 66–70.

25. For an in-depth treatment of what managers can do pre- and postacquisition to improve their chances of success, see Philippe C. Haspeslagh and David B. Jemison, *Managing Acquisitions: Creating Value Through Corporate Renewal*, New York: The Free Press, 1991.

26. See Walter R. Nord, "Do Mergers Make Acquired Executives Feel Inferior? You Bet!," *Academy of Management Executive*, *8*:2 (1994), 81–82; and James P. Walsh and John W. Ellwood, "Mergers, Acquisitions, and the Pruning of Managerial Deadwood," *Strategic Management Journal*, *12* (1991), 201–217.

27. Fisher, "How to Make a Merger Work."

28. Kathryn Harrigan, "Joint Ventures and Competitive Strategy," *Strategic Management Journal*, *9* (March–April 1988), 141–158.

29. Stratford Sherman, "Are Strategic Alliances Working?," *Fortune* (September 21, 1992), 77–78.

30. C. E. Schillaci, "Designing Successful Joint Ventures," *Journal of Business Strategy* (Fall 1987), 59–63; David Lei and John W. Slocum, Jr., "Global Strategy, Competence-

Building and Strategic Alliances," *California Management Review* (Fall 1992), 81–97; Joseph L. Badaracco, Jr., "Alliances Speed Knowledge Transfer," *Planning Review* (March–April 1991), 10–16.

31. M. Niederkofler, "The Evolution of Strategic Alliances: Opportunities for Managerial Influence," *Journal of Business Venturing*, 6 (1991), 237–257.

32. P. R. Scanlon, "Collaborative Ventures," *Journal of Business Strategy* (July–August 1990), 81–83.

33. These and other important considerations are discussed in K. R. Harrigan, *Managing for Joint Venture Success*, Lexington, MA: D. C. Heath, 1986.

34. P. Lorange and J. Roos, "Why Some Strategic Alliances Succeed and Others Fail," *Journal of Business Strategy* (January–February 1991), 25–30.

35. For discussion of the determinants of success in corporate entrepreneurship, see S. A. Zahra, "Predictors and Financial Outcomes of Corporate Entrepreneurship: An Exploratory Study," *Journal of Business Venturing*, 6 (1991), 259–285; A. Miller and B. Camp, "Exploring Determinants of Success in Corporate Ventures," *Journal of Business Venturing*, 1 (1985), 87–105; and R. A. Burgelman, "Managing New Venture Division: Research Findings and Implications for Strategic Management," *Strategic Management Journal*, 6 (January–February 1985), 39–54.

36. This typology of new-venture programs was developed in a Harvard Business School research program on corporate entrepreneurship headed by Rosabeth Moss Kanter; see Ian MacMillan, "Introduction of Kanter's Case Series," *Journal of Business Venturing*, 5 (1990), 413.

37. H. Sykes, "Lessons from a New Ventures Program," *Harvard Business Review* (May–June 1986), 69–74.

38. Other corporations have been far less successful in acting as venture capitalists. See R. M. Kanter et al., "Engines of Progress: Designing and Running Entrepreneurial Vehicles in Established Companies," *Journal of Business Venturing*, 5 (1990), 415–430.

39. An often overlooked resource which can be highly valuable to a new corporate venture is the corporation's image. See M. L. Williams, M. Tsai, and D. Day, "Intangible Assets, Entry Strategies, and Venture Success in Industrial Markets," *Journal of Business Venturing*, 6 (1991), 315–333.

40. Alex Miller, Mary Spann, and Linda Lerner, "Competitive Advantages in New Corporate Ventures: The Impact of Resource Sharing and Reporting Level," *Journal of Business Venturing*, 6 (1991), 335–350.

41. R. M. Kanter et al., "Engines of Progress: Designing and Running Entrepreneurial Vehicles in Established Companies; The New Venture Process at Eastman Kodak, 1983–1989," *Journal of Business Venturing*, 6 (1991), 63–82.

42. R. M. Kanter et al., "Engines of Progress: Designing and Running Entrepreneurial Vehicles in Established Companies; Raytheon's New Product Center, 1969–1989," *Journal of Business Venturing*, 6 (1991), 145–163.

43. Gifford Pinchot, *Intrapreneuring*, New York: Harper & Row, 1985.

44. M. Cosgrove, "Roadblocks to New Business Development," *Journal of Business Strategy* (May–June 1991), 53–57.

45. Statistical analysis indicates that 45 percent of the variability in new-venture performance in Exxon Enterprises can be explained by just two factors: market risk and technological risk; Sykes, "Lessons from a New Ventures Program."

46. H. R. Biggadike, "The Risky Business of Diversification," *Harvard Business Review*, 57 (May–June 1979), 103–111.

47. R. M. Kanter and L. Richardson, "Engines of Progress: Designing and Running Entrepreneurial Vehicles in Established Companies; The Enter-Prize Program at Ohio Bell, 1985–1990," *Journal of Business Venturing, 6* (1991), 209–229.

48. Porter, "From Competitive Advantage to Corporate Strategy."

49. See discussion in H. Harowitz and D. Halliday, "The New Alchemy: Divestment for Profit," *Journal of Business Strategy, 5* (Fall 1984), 112–116.

50. E. L. Hennessy, Jr., "The Ethics of Corporate Restructuring," *Directors & Boards, 13* (Fall 1988), 8–12.

51. C. K. Prahalad and G. Hamel, "The Core Competence of the Corporation," *Harvard Business Review* (May–June 1990), 79–91; Amy V. Snyder and H. William Ebeling, Jr., "Targeting a Company's Real Core Competencies," *Journal of Business Strategy, 13* (November–December 1992), 26–32.

52. Prahalad and Hamel, "The Core Competence of the Corporation"; Porter, "From Competitive Advantage to Corporate Strategy."

53. P. Sloan, "Brand Names Seek New Wrinkle with Clothes," *Advertising Age* (April 28, 1986), 28.

54. R. Reed and R. J. DeFillippi, "Causal Ambiguity, Barriers to Imitation, and Sustainable Competitive Advantage," *Academy of Management Review, 15* (1990), 88–102.

55. Porter, "From Competitive Advantage to Corporate Strategy."

56. B. Hedley, "Strategy and the Business Portfolio," *Long Range Planning, 10* (February 1977), 9–15.

57. For a thorough comparison of these various portfolio management techniques, see D. F. Abell and J. S. Hammond, *Strategic Market Planning*, Englewood Cliffs, NJ: Prentice-Hall, 1979.

58. P. Haspeslagh, "Portfolio Planning: Uses and Limits," *Harvard Business Review, 60* (January–February 1983), 58–73.

59. A. C. Hax and N. S. Majluf, *The Strategic Concept and Process*, Englewood Cliffs, NJ: Prentice-Hall, 1991.

60. For an in-depth discussion of the problems of identifying individual businesses within larger diversified corporations, see D. F. Abell, *Defining the Business: The Starting Point of Strategic Planning*, Englewood Cliffs, NJ: Prentice-Hall, 1980.

61. R. A. Proctor, "Strategic Planning: An Overview of Product Portfolio Models," *Marketing Intelligence and Planning, 8*:7 (1990), 4–10.

62. R. D. Buzzell and B. T. Gale, *The PIMS Principles: Linking Strategy to Performance*, New York: The Free Press, 1987.

63. "Capital Cargo—More German Marks for U.S. Chemical Operations," *Chemical Week* (June 25, 1985), 24–27.

64. There are several forms of corporate risk. The risk to which we refer here is technically called business risk. Consideration of other types of risk is not feasible here. Those who need further information on this should see K. D. Miller, "Strategic Risk and Corporate Performance: An Analysis of Alternative Risk Measures," *Academy of Management Journal, 33* (1990), 756–779.

65. Some research suggests that reducing variability in this way improves cash flow and allows corporations to acquire factors of production (e.g., capital equipment) at lower costs, but this is too advanced for coverage here. Those interested are referred to R. Amit and B. Wernerfelt, "Why Do Firms Reduce Business Risk?," *Academy of Management Journal, 33* (1990), 520–533.

66. B. M. Oviatt, "Agency and Transaction Cost Perspectives on the Manager-Shareholder Relationship: Incentives for Congruent Interests," *Academy of Management Review* (April 1988), 214–225; Lubatkin, "Value-Creating Mergers."

67. We are using "agent" here in the legal sense of one authorized to transact business, including executing contracts, for another; S. Davidson, C. Stickney, and R. Weil, *The Language of Business*, New York: Prentice-Hall, 1984.

68. K. M. Eisenhardt, "Agency Theory: An Assessment and Review," *Academy of Management Review*, *14* (1989), 57–74.

69. M. C. Jensen and W. H. Meckling, "Theory of the Firm: Managerial Behavior, Agency Costs, and Ownership Structure," *Journal of Financial Economics*, *3*:4 (1976), 305–360.

70. P. C. Haspeslagh and D. B. Jemison, "Acquisitions: Myths and Reality," *Sloan Management Review*, *28* (Winter 1987), 53–58.

71. R. W. McGee, "Ethical Issues in Acquisitions and Mergers," *Mid-Atlantic Journal of Business* (March 1989), 19–39; P. II. Werhane, "Two Ethical Issues in Mergers and Acquisitions," *Journal of Business Ethics*, 7 (January–February 1988), 41–45.

72. Empirical evidence of how antitakeover measures are used for the benefit of managers rather than owners is presented in James M. Mahoney and Joseph T. Mahoney, "An Empirical Investigation of the Effect of Corporate Charter Antitakeover Amendments on Stockholder Wealth," *Strategic Management Journal*, *14* (1993), 17–31.

73. R. A. Lambert, D. F. Larcker, and K. Weigelt, "How Sensitive Is Executive Compensation to Organizational Size?," *Strategic Management Journal*, *12* (July 1991), 395–402.

74. G. S. Crystal, "Seeking the Sense in CEO Pay," *Fortune*, *119* (June 5, 1989), 88–104.

75. For further discussion of how corporations and managers benefit from growth through diversification, see D. R. Dalton and I. F. Kesner, "Organizational Growth: Big Is Beautiful," *Journal of Business Strategy*, *6* (Summer 1985), 38–48.

76. Walter and Barney, "Management Objectives in Mergers and Acquisitions."

Chapter 8

International-Level Strategy

CHAPTER OUTLINE

The internationalization of competition is inevitable. Future managers in every industry will be either directly involved with or affected by international competition. Tomorrow's winners will be those firms with managers who are comfortable in the international arena. These managers will design strategies that will enable their multinational corporations (MNCs) to establish competitive advantages in specific markets by tapping corporate resources worldwide.

This chapter has four major parts. The first discusses the importance of adopting a global perspective and the advantages and disadvantages of international diversification, while the second reviews options for entering international markets. The third explains how organizations must respond to local markets while tapping global resources if they are to have the strongest possible international strategies. Strategies that do this combine elements of what are known as multidomestic and global perspectives, and the final section details how such combinations result in greater competitive advantages.

This chapter will help you understand:

- The necessity to participate enthusiastically in global competition
- Common strategies for entering international markets and how firms typically progress from one entry strategy to the next
- How dealing with the unique cultures of foreign markets encourages a multidomestic strategy in which individual units freely adjust operations to local needs
- How concern for economic efficiency drives international firms toward a global strategy of tightly integrated operations around the world
- Why the most powerful combinations of competitive advantages are best obtained by mixing elements of both global and multidomestic strategies
- The importance of government support as a fourth source of competitive advantage in the international arena

"Think globally, but act locally." This is a good description of the strategy at Asea Brown Boveri, the $25 billion worldwide giant that produces such products as robots, high-speed trains, turbines, and transformers. The company is headquartered in Europe, has heavy-manufacturing operations around the world, keeps the books in dollars, and conducts business in a variety of languages. CEO Percy Barnevik, the man most responsible for creating this far-flung empire, says that ABB's goal is to make its products more efficiently by uniting a network of manufacturing facilities and technical expertise it has created around the world—a good example of *thinking globally*. But at the same time, ABB strives to meet each country's needs so that its products seem to come from a domestic producer—*acting locally*. Barnevik sums up his opinion of the power of such a strategy by saying, "You want to be able to optimize a business globally—to specialize in the production of components, to drive economies of scale as far as you can. But you also want to have deep local roots everywhere you operate. If you build such an organization, you create a business advantage that's damn difficult to copy."[1]

In this chapter, you will learn how firms such as ABB use their worldwide operations to strengthen their competitive advantages.

THE IMPORTANCE OF A WORLDWIDE
PERSPECTIVE ON STRATEGY

Today's global marketplace calls not only for an international outlook on business in general, but also on formulating competitive strategies in particular.[2] Yet many managers, especially those who deal primarily with lucrative domestic markets, attempt to deny this situation. For instance, with access to what has historically been the strongest economy and the world's single largest market, too many U.S. managers attempt to duck what they view as the unnecessary complexities of international competition. Research reveals that U.S. managers are far less internationally oriented than many of their foreign counterparts. In one survey, only 35 percent of U.S. managers responding thought that work experience abroad was important, compared to 74 percent in the non-U.S. sample. While 67 percent of all American managers saw maintaining an international outlook and perspective as critical to their success, the number is still low compared to managers from other regions. For European managers, the corresponding number was 81 percent; for Latin Americans, 87 percent; and for the Japanese, 100 percent.[3]

This reluctance to pursue international opportunities vigorously can have serious implications for business competitiveness. For example, consider how U.S. carmakers have fared in the global competition for automobile sales. Despite Kuwait's pro-American sentiments after Operation Desert Storm, the Japanese were still able to capture 61 percent of the market for replacement automobiles in this war-torn nation, compared to only a 30 percent market share for U.S. carmakers. "Most U.S. manufacturers only pay lip service to the export market, with the possible exception of Europe," explains Amin Kadri, COO of Alghanum Industries, one of the largest automobile distribution companies in Kuwait.[4] However, analysts question the U.S. economy's supremacy and with home markets maturing or even saturated, the largest new sales markets lie outside the United States.

Still, some firms have tried to avoid the globalization of their industries by concentrating narrowly on their domestic operations and giving limited attention to other developed markets.[5] Unfortunately, this has left them even more vulnerable to the relentless hounding of international competition. For instance, RCA decided to defend itself against the threat of Japanese television manufacturers by concentrating its efforts on the U.S. market. A decade later, RCA was forced to sell its operation to Thomson, a French manufacturer that was willing to compete against the rising Japanese firms.[6]

Discounting worldwide competition represents a serious mistake for several reasons. First, research shows that early entrants into a new internationalized market tend to gain larger market shares and outsurvive later entrants, suggesting that firms not only need to move into international markets—they must do so before other competitors do.[7] Meanwhile, over the past 2 decades, industry after industry has changed from serving simple domestic marketplaces to serving complex world markets.

Second, the trend toward worldwide markets makes it difficult to predict where competitors will spring up. A decade ago, few would have predicted that one of the strongest competitors in the software programming industry, Tata Consultancy Services, would be based in Bombay, India.[8] But since 1950, Indian universities have granted 190,000 science and engineering degrees, third after the United States and the Soviet Union. A workforce with this training will likely excel internationally at programming. Furthermore, because programming requires little capital investment and can be exported electronically, it suits the resources available to Indian firms.

Third, foreign investment is growing as foreign firms buy into U.S. domestic markets. In recent years, foreign investment in U.S. assets has expanded faster than domestic investment in many sectors of the economy.[9] Increasingly, businesses perceived as American are, in fact, foreign owned. For instance, Bruce Springsteen has worked for a Japanese firm ever since Sony purchased CBS Records, and an increasing number of "American" ski resorts and golf courses are owned by Japanese firms. Because of the heavy investments foreign firms have made in U.S. companies, many managers who once thought they worked in a strictly domestic business have become part of the international scene almost overnight.

Fourth, many of the greatest growth opportunities exist overseas in both developed and developing nations. In 1992, the twelve nations in the European Community (EC) began to replace hundreds of national regulations that had previously divided them into separate markets with regulations that would unite them economically.[10] Accomplishing this will make the EC the world's single wealthiest market—larger than the United States, the Soviet Union, or southeast Asia. Meanwhile, large portions of the Soviet bloc began opening borders to international trade in one of the greatest economic revolutions in history.[11] A firm that fails to adapt to such changes by moving toward a worldwide perspective will miss the opportunity to be a major contender in the upcoming century.

While changes in developed nations offer exciting growth opportunities, developing nations no doubt present the greatest growth potential. One MNC, Coca-Cola, has taken advantage of this. In the early 1990s, the firm's soft drinks were consumed at a rate of 274 eight-ounce servings per capita in the United States—perhaps the greatest market penetration in the history of consumer retailing. In other developed nations, consumption is not nearly so high (89 servings per year in Japan and 63 per year in Britain), but competitive substitutes are already well entrenched in these developed markets. The growth potential in the U.S. domestic market and in developed markets around the world is small compared to that in some countries, such as Indonesia, whose 180 million people consumed an average of only 3.2 servings per year, or China, whose 1.2 billion people consumed an average of only .2 servings per year.[12] Recognizing this, Coke is already one of the most fully internationalized firms in the world, with operations in 155 countries, many of which are developing nations. Clearly, developing markets offer tremendous growth potential to firms that until now have considered only developed nations. Exhibit 8.1 presents data that plot market growth potential (workers' earnings) against economic liberalization for a number of different nations.

Examining such data, we can easily see why nations on the northeast rim of this chart, such as Mexico, India, and China, are so attractive to expanding multinational corporations today (see Application 8.1 for an example of how General Electric is responding to this opportunity).

EXHIBIT 8.1

Growing Global Markets Where Rising Affluence Intersects with Economic Freedom

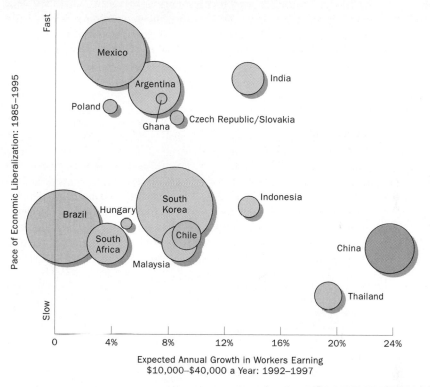

Expected Annual Growth in Workers Earning
$10,000–$40,000 a Year: 1992–1997

Smaller firms can also benefit from global expansion. Industrial giants, such as the firms that make up the *Fortune* 500 (all of which have at least half a billion dollars in annual sales), get much of the media coverage given to world competition. However, their actions should not overshadow the international activity of midsized firms.[13] For instance, roughly 7,500 U.S. firms not in the *Fortune* 500 have sales of more than $100 million. Through the 1980s, the *foreign* sales of these firms grew at an annual rate of 20 percent—five times the growth rate of U.S. firms overall. Many other small businesses with sales of less than $100 million supply foreign markets almost exclusively. Clearly, an organization's size does not limit its potential for worldwide competition.[14]

All these trends have obvious implications for firms that hope to be significant competitors. However, the implications are just as weighty for those who manage such firms. Overseas experience has long been a required rung on the corporate career ladder for companies such as Goodyear and Caterpillar, and is becoming more widespread every day. Most companies depend on foreign nationals to provide the

General Electric Looks to Emerging Nations for Growth

In Chapter 7, Application 7.3 described how General Electric diverted cash flow from Capital Services, its fantastically profitable financial services division, to its foreign operations. They use this cash to develop stronger GE operations around the world, with a clear emphasis on the emerging markets of China, India, and Mexico. These markets contain a total population of nearly 2.5 billion, and GE's sales in them have been growing at around 30 percent per year. This compares favorably to GE's domestic market in the United States, which is only one-tenth the size and in which sales are growing at only about 3 percent per year. With ten times the market size and ten times the growth, GE sees these emerging markets as the key to its future in the next century. In fact, analysts expect that by the end of this century, GE will receive more of its revenues from outside the United States than from inside.

GE brings a powerful combination of skills and resources to its competition for emerging markets. Its product mix is ideally suited to countries with less developed infrastructures of their own. On the one hand, GE can offer high-value items, such as jet aircraft engines, that it manufactures domestically and then exports around the world. On the other, it can set up local manufacture-and-assembly operations for lower-technology appliances. To finance both the domestic and foreign operations, GE Capital Services functions as the firm's own in-house Wall Street investment banker.

GE's far-flung operations are pulled together by a management team that has invested heavily in preparing itself for global competition, developing what GE calls its "global brain." For instance, GE may hire new international managers from outside the corporation on the basis of their proven interest and expertise in a foreign country rather than their technical expertise in GE's product line. When the company requires an insider's expertise, the first step in preparing for the job will often be a 2-month-long crash course in the language and culture of the new country. Meanwhile, to supplement its own managerial talent, GE has entered into international joint ventures in virtually every country in which it operates, giving it access to large pools of local managerial expertise.

Jack Welch, the corporation's CEO, sees this move into global markets, and especially into global developing markets, as being one of the most important decisions he will make at GE. Welch spends several weeks each year traveling to far-flung capitals, personally pushing the plan. He assesses the importance of GE's international initiative this way: "If we are wrong, it's a billion dollars, a couple of billion dollars. If we are right, it's the future of the next century for this company."

Sources

Based on information gathered from Tim Smart, Pete Engardio, and Geri Smith, "GE's Brave New World," *Business Week* (November 8, 1993), 64–70; James R. Norman, "A Very Nimble Elephant," *Forbes, 154* (October 10, 1994), 88–92; Robert Gillespie, "Report Card on Globalization," *Business Quarterly, 59* (Winter 1994), 77–80.

managerial talent required to operate abroad. These managers have a superior grasp of local markets and customs, but many multinational corporations (MNCs) believe that their domestic executives have a better feel for the company's products and its corporate culture. Therefore, overseas offices are typically a blend of nationalities, and executives who aim for the top of an organization are expected to serve on such teams as part of their career paths. Perhaps one of the best indications of how important international experience has become is provided by the Big Three, the largest U.S. carmakers, as they scramble to adjust to the globalization of their industry. Having long been criticized for failing to develop international expertise in their executive ranks, all three are now led by CEOs who have significant overseas experience.

While managers should not make the mistake of discounting the need for a worldwide perspective, they must remember that global diversification has potential advantages and disadvantages.

Advantages of Global Diversification

Expansion into international operations offers several strategic advantages, one of which is lower operational costs.[15] Production costs vary dramatically around the world, making it profitable to establish global operations even when the primary market remains at home. For instance, Nike outsources the production of its athletic shoes to China, where the cost of labor is far below that in the United States, even though most of the Chinese-produced shoes are sold back in the United States.

International expansion can also supplement limited domestic opportunities. Purely domestic firms depend on their home countries for sales and growth. But if a firm grows faster than its home country's economy, it can achieve economies of scale through greater volume by seeking international sales opportunities. In the 1980s, a number of corporations from countries with stronger currencies acquired U.S. businesses at "bargain" rates; for example, BASF AG, a giant West German chemical products company, and a number of other like-minded German chemical corporations bought several billion dollars' worth of U.S. chemical businesses in order to overcome limited growth opportunities at home.[16]

As a third advantage to international operations, many corporations have found that to compete effectively in domestic markets, they must be willing to fight international competitors on their home turf.[17] A global competitor that faces limited competition at home may use its high home-market profits to subsidize its operations in other countries.[18] For example, a U.S. firm may wish to enter the Japanese market in order to drive down the margins its Japanese competitors would otherwise enjoy at home. By doing so, it would hope to limit the ability of Japanese firms to use high profits from their home market to support price competition in the United States. A joint venture between Fuji Photo Film and Xerox provides a classic example of how global diversification can aid a corporation by taking the fight to international competitors.[19]

In the mid-1960s, Xerox established a strategic alliance with Fuji to help overcome difficulties it was having in exporting copiers to the Japanese market. Within 2 decades, what had started out as a simple sales operation had grown into the third-largest producer of its own line of photocopiers—in Japan. Although Fuji Xerox became a freestanding corporation (with sales in the $1.5 billion range), its success in opening the Japanese market and in leading the global fight against other Japanese competitors was vital to Xerox, one of its corporate parents. Xerox managers freely admitted that they had learned much from their Japanese offspring about how to win in international competition for photocopier sales.

Disadvantages of Global Diversification

International operations pose several disadvantages that managers should keep in mind. First, they may face greater and more complex risks than in domestic operations. Corporations that operate in two or more countries must be concerned with currency exchange rates. In the early 1980s, the British carmaker Jaguar went through a radical turnaround process, avoiding bankruptcy and establishing itself as a legitimate competitor in the international luxury-car market. However, the United States was the largest market for Jaguars, and the effects of all the company's advances were wiped out in the last half of the 1980s, when the purchasing power of the U.S. dollar tumbled; the company was eventually taken over by Ford. International operations also face greater social and political risks than domestic operations do. For instance, Iranian businesses with accounts in U.S. banks found their funds confiscated by the U.S. government when Iran took U.S. citizens as hostages. In such cases, politics directly affects the commercial activities of international firms.

A second disadvantage arises because even relatively simple countries have vastly different markets, customers, and ways of competing. Consider the problems encountered by Anheuser-Busch, the leading beer producer in the United States.[20] Because beer is consumed around the world, it might seem a good candidate to take global, especially in a country whose culture is relatively similar to that of the United States. Yet when the company tried to enter the British market, it stumbled, making a number of mistakes in its marketing rollout. Budweiser, its primary product, has a higher alcohol content than most British beers do—a disadvantage because U.K. import duties are based on alcohol content. But the company's marketing campaign could not convince the British that Budweiser was as strong as their own traditional brands, which had noticeably stronger flavor than Budweiser. Ironically, Anheuser-Busch was paying stiffer import duties for Budweiser's higher alcohol content but suffering from the widespread British opinion that all American beers are weak. The marketing expertise that served Anheuser-Busch so well in the United States was initially very ineffective in Britain, and it took years for the company to make the adjustments required. Exhibit 8.2 provides data that illustrate the tremendous differences in

EXHIBIT 8.2
Differences in Market Saturation Across Nations and Regions

	The Americas		Europe				Pacific Rim	
	North America	Latin America	Western Europe	Eastern Europe	Africa	Middle East	South Korea	Singapore
Gross national product ($1,000/capita)	22	2.5	21	2.6	.4	1.8	N.A.	N.A.
Communication (per 1,000 people)								
Radios	2,017	292	817	592	150	318	1,006	643
TVs	798	150	444	308	23	250	210	376
Telephones	788	74	522	108	18	97	296	456
Newspaper circulation	248	87	253	428	11	40	280	280
Transportation								
Passenger cars (per 1,000 people)	575	63	360	65	15	90	27	100
Air travel (passenger miles/ capita)	1,750	225	450	200	90	200	N.A.	N.A.
Energy consumption, all forms (1,000 kilograms of oil equivalent per capita)	8.7	1.1	4.5	2.1	.2	1.3	N.A.	N.A.

consumption patterns around the world. Such data suggest the numerous expansion opportunities that exist overseas, but they also reflect differences in lifestyle and culture that must be addressed to take advantage of those opportunities. Developing a single global strategy that can adequately address such differences is often a difficult, even Herculean, task.

Typical organizational cultures and managerial practices differ dramatically from one nation to another, and what works well in one nation may fail completely in the next.[21] Such differences can affect every aspect of managing, and they require a range of flexibility that most organizations—and most managers—find challenging.[22] Exhibit 8.3 illustrates some of the differences in managerial styles and cultural norms that challenge an MNC operating in the United States, Japan, and Europe. This exhibit describes several stereotypes. Significant differences arise across organizations within each of the countries, but the exhibit indicates the range of styles and cultures found around the world.

EXHIBIT 8.3
A Comparison of Three Management Styles

Categories	American Model	Japanese Model	European Model
Stakeholder Influence	Emphasis on shareholders' profits	Little or no influence by shareholders	Often, greater emphasis placed on stakeholders (e.g., state agencies, unions, large banks, and the church) than on shareholders
Management Orientation	Emphasis on product orientation rather than customer orientation	Emphasis on adaptation to customer needs; perfectionism	People-oriented, with great emphasis on cultural and humanistic values
Individuality	Individualism through personal achievement and professional mobility	Integration of the individual into the firm; emphasis on harmony rather than individual competition	Management of cultural diversity, made necessary by the cultural differences across Europe
Management Style	Functionalism and professionalism	Little distinction between personal life and professional life	Importance of internal (sometimes hard-nosed) negotiations, which can be seen throughout the history of unions in Europe
Temporal Orientation	Ongoing strong competition, which is supposed to bring about customer satisfaction	Long-term growth	Management between extremes and between the long term and short term

Source: Adapted from Norman Blackwell et al., "Shaping a Pan-European Organization," *McKinsey Quarterly* (Spring 1991), 94–111. By permission of The McKinsey Quarterly.

As organizations conclude that the advantages of international operations outweigh the disadvantages, the next question they face is how to enter the international arena.

ENTRY STRATEGIES FOR INTERNATIONAL EXPANSION

The prospect of expanding into international markets can be daunting. Consequently, when firms first enter the international arena, they generally start on a small scale and hope to expand later.[23] They may use a number of different strategies for entering foreign markets. Often called entry strategies, these can be categorized under the headings of exporting (foreign sales), licensing and franchising (contractual arrangements), and joint ventures and wholly owned subsidiaries (foreign investment).[24] Each entails different levels and types of risk and control (see Exhibit 8.4). Typically, firms start with the low-risk/low-control options and then advance to higher levels of risk and control as they gain experience and build confidence.[25] We look at each in turn.

Exporting

Most MNCs got their starts in international business through exporting. In an export operation, firms maintain production facilities at home and transport products abroad. Exporting offers the advantage of not requiring a very substantial presence abroad; usually the firm hires foreign agents to arrange contracts. Foreign investment is minimal because the factory is at home and the products can often be shipped di-

EXHIBIT 8.4
Strategies for Entering Foreign Markets

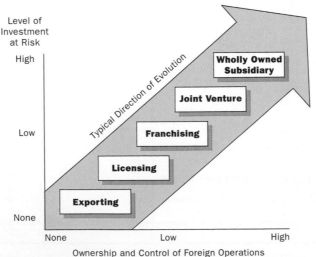

rectly to foreign customers' warehouses. Offsetting these advantages are the high transportation costs associated with exporting and the difficulty of dealing from a distance with problems such as government regulation, cultural differences, and currency exchange.

Licensing and Franchising

Often, firms use contractual arrangements to expand into international markets: licensing and franchising. Both involve contracts between parties in different countries, but franchise contracts cover more aspects of the operation and typically last longer than licensing contracts. A licensor in one country offers limited rights and/or resources to the licensee in a second country. Such rights and/or resources, patents, trademarks, technology, managerial skills, and so on, allow licensees to produce and market a product similar to the one the licensor has already been producing in its home country, without requiring the licensor to actually create a new operation abroad. For example, licensees around the world produce and sell clothing bearing pictures of Mickey Mouse and other Walt Disney characters.

A franchise usually covers a broader "package" of rights and resources, such as production equipment, proven managerial systems, standardized operating procedures, access to advertising and promotional materials, loans and financing, product ingredients, and general management assistance. McDonald's is an obvious example of a corporation with franchise contracts around the world. Franchises often lead to the creation of a new business, in which case the franchise generally stands in perpetuity. On the other hand, licenses are more often granted to businesses that existed before the license was arranged and that will outlive the license contract.

Joint Ventures and Wholly Owned Subsidiaries

The most significant form of foreign involvement entails direct investment in another country. This means that the firm owns assets based in the foreign country, which provides it with greater control than other modes of international expansion. But foreign investment is the riskiest of the global entry strategies.

To avoid facing all this risk alone, many international firms enter into joint ventures in which companies in two different countries join forces to build a third business entity. As with domestic joint ventures, discussed in Chapter 7, both firms contribute capital to create the third business and both share in its returns. The world automobile industry includes numerous international joint ventures. For example, while Mazda fared poorly in its domestic market (Japan), it had a successful international joint venture with Ford that was profitable for both firms.

Alternatively a company may invest in a wholly owned foreign business over which it retains complete control. This arrangement may shorten distribution channels and somewhat simplify logistics. In addition, managers who are actually located on site will be able to perceive changing cultural, economic, and political conditions more quickly. However, a company must make financial and managerial investments to acquire or create businesses in foreign countries, and this investment is subject to a wide range of political and economic risks. This strategy may be most successful for companies that already have experience in other forms of international involvement.

Upon entering the international arena, a firm must decide how to manage its operations.[26] In the remainder of this chapter, we consider the process of formulating strategies for operating businesses in a worldwide context.

MULTIDOMESTIC VERSUS GLOBAL STRATEGIES

A fundamental question facing MNCs concerns the extent to which a corporation with operating units scattered around the world should integrate and/or standardize these operations. The options form a continuum between operations and products that are exactly the same throughout the world and operations and products tailored for each market in which they appear. Companies on either extreme adopt multidomestic or global strategies. Corporations with multiple foreign operations that act independently of one another follow *multidomestic* strategies; each individual operation is treated as an independent business, with the country of each operation essentially becoming its domestic market. On-site managers of such an operation are more or less independent entities, focused solely on their local market and free to develop individually tailored strategies.

At the other extreme, corporations that standardize or tightly integrate operations from country to country follow *global* strategies. These corporations operate all units, regardless of location, under a single unifying strategy. Under such a strategy, on-site managers scattered across various countries all see themselves as serving the same single, homogeneous worldwide market. Firms following a strict global strategy handle adaptations to market needs centrally, because the corporation views the entire world as a single market.

In their purest forms, multidomestic and global strategies differ greatly from each other along two dimension, as illustrated in Exhibit 8.5. First, firms following a pure multidomestic strategy allow managers in each country to adapt their products and services to fit local market preferences, government regulations, technological capabilities, and competitive situations. Consequently, even "sister" business units in the same industries usually offer very different products and services. In contrast, business units in a corporation following a purely global strategy sell very similar products and services. The rationale for this difference can be understood best when you consider a second important difference. In the case of a pure multidomestic strategy, each country's business unit will comprise as much of the value chain as feasible—for example, R&D, marketing, inbound logistics, production, sales, distribution, and service—and its operations will all be tailored to the needs of that country. On the other hand, a firm following a pure global strategy serves its various markets from centralized facilities, limiting replication of the value chain in various countries. For example, R&D, marketing, inbound logistics, and production may be centralized in one location that serves various countries, each of which has its own sales, distribution, and service centers. Global businesses usually locate the centralized portion of their value chains where they have cost advantages or better capabilities.

EXHIBIT 8.5
A Continuum from Global to Multidomestic Strategy

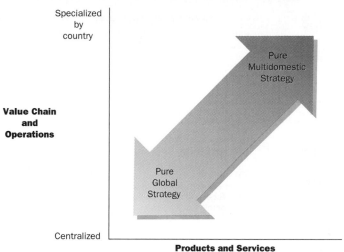

In order for firms to achieve the strongest possible competitive advantages, they must typically combine elements of both global and multidomestic strategy, as illustrated by the Asea Brown Boveri example in the opening part of this chapter.

The proper emphasis on elements of multidomestic and global perspectives depends on the balance of the socioeconomic pressures driving international competitors in two opposing directions. On the one hand, social pressures encourage managers within each country to be responsive to the unique cultural and political circumstances in their narrow slice of the overall world market. On the other hand, economic pressures encourage managers to treat operations in different countries only as part of a greater whole that must be managed for overall efficiency. These social and economic forces are so great that they are commonly referred to as the two "imperatives" facing MNC managers:[27] the social forces encourage firms to operate under a multidomestic strategy, while the economic forces create pressure to use a global strategy.

The following two sections discuss the differences in these two strategies. After these sections, we will explore how responding to conflicting social and economic pressures with a combination of a multidomestic and a global strategy helps achieve the strongest mix of competitive advantages. A summary of some important differences among the multidomestic, global, and hybrid strategic options facing MNCs appears in Exhibit 8.6.

The Social Imperative and Multidomestic Strategies

Three social forces encourage MNCs to adapt the individual parts of their far-flung operations to specific situations. First, cultural differences across countries often ne-

EXHIBIT 8.6
Three Forms of Strategy for International Operations

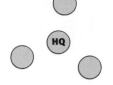

The Multidomestic Strategy

- Units in various countries are independent
- Each unit treats its markets as distinct from all others
- Corporate headquarters is not much more than just another unit

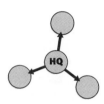

The Global Strategy

- Units in various countries are under centralized control from corporate headquarters
- Headquarters seek out standardized products suitable for a variety of markets
- Production is coordinated centrally to create economies of scale

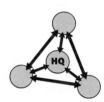

The Hybrid Strategy

- Units coordinate their activities with headquarters and with one another
- Units in various countries may adapt to special circumstances only they face
- Entire organization draws upon relevant corporate resources, wherever they are

cessitate changes in tactics for dealing with stakeholders. Second, governments in countries around the world frequently insist that the actions of MNCs be consonant with their host nations' interests. Third, as industrialization spreads, local competitors scramble to serve narrowing market segments, forcing MNCs to be equally adaptable. When local suppliers can produce tailored products, customers are no longer forced to accept products designed for another market's consumers.

Thus, most businesses adjust the way they do business from one country to the next. Firms must often adapt their products and marketing techniques to suit the host country's particular circumstances. Some adaptations are fairly minor: Hewlett-Packard changes its keyboard layouts to reflect different countries' typing requirements and its business software to match different accounting practices. Other changes are more substantive, as in the case of Avon in Japan.

Avon's door-to-door marketing methods have successfully sold its cosmetics nearly everywhere in the world. However, during its first years in Japan, the company had little success using this approach. After studying the problem, the managers at Avon discovered that Japanese women are often too reserved to make forceful sales pitches to strangers. The company then adjusted its approach to selling in Japan, emphasizing making sales to women who were not strangers and creating an advertising campaign featuring a soft-sell approach with poetic images. After this adjustment, the firm enlisted more than 350,000 saleswomen in Japan and its Japanese sales grew more than 25 percent per year.

The Economic Imperative and Global Strategies

In some industries, the volume necessary to achieve the greatest economies of scale and learning curve effects cannot be reached within a single country. In this case, it makes sense to combine operations in different countries to increase throughput and gain economies of scale. A corporation with global integration can use its network of operating sites to achieve greater overall efficiency than any single site could achieve individually.

For example, Caterpillar, the world's leading producer of heavy earthmoving equipment, utilizes this sort of integration in its worldwide operations. The factories that build Caterpillar products require heavy capital investment, which is best absorbed by high-volume production of a fairly standardized product line. Furthermore, although the company's customers around the world require access to a broad range of earthmoving equipment, specific requirements for each type of machine do not vary much by nation. In other words, one customer may want a particular selection of bulldozers, highlifts, backhoes, and so on, but the equipment required to move dirt is basically the same in any country. Therefore, Caterpillar has its factories within a given country focus on volume production of a relatively narrow range of products, resulting in maximum economies of scale and learning curve effects within each factory. As a result of this focus, no single factory can produce the broad line of equipment that customers need, so each factory cooperates with others in Caterpillar's worldwide system to provide the overall range of products required. When the same parts are manufactured in more than one nation, central design control ensures that these parts are interchangeable and that they will fit on any appropriate Caterpillar, regardless of its country of origin. This is a global strategy, because each country's operation is viewed as a part of a single worldwide plan.

The use of such strategies and the globalization of industries is on the rise because of several trends. The emergence of products with worldwide acceptance, such as Nikon cameras and German engineering services, has facilitated worldwide integration. Development of cheaper, more reliable transportation and worldwide communication networks has also encouraged globalization. Observers of today's international competition refer to a "global village" in which we all live in the same neighborhood and trade in the same shops. Success as a merchant in the global village requires MNCs to understand how to build global strategies.

Combining Global and Multidomestic Outlooks

Because each type of strategy has its advantages, the best approach is usually neither purely multidomestic nor purely global but a combination of both.[28] This becomes most apparent when we see the shortcomings of single-mindedly pursuing an international strategy based on either global integration alone or multidomestic adaptation alone.[29]

Faulty Assumptions Supporting a "Pure" Global Strategy

What assumptions make pursuit of a "pure" global strategy sensible? Theodore Levitt, considered by many to be the father of the concept of global strategies, notes three.[30] Although these assumptions appear perfectly reasonable, critics are quick to point out numerous cases in which one or more of them do not hold.[31]

1. *Customer needs, interests, and tastes are becoming increasingly homogenized.* While in many industries substantial similarities exist between products in different countries (earthmoving equipment, cameras, and soft drinks are just a few examples mentioned in this chapter), substantial differences emerge in many industries.[32] For instance, Findus, the frozen foods division of the Swiss food giant Nestlé, does well marketing fish fingers in the United Kingdom, but in France its successful products are *boeuf bourguignon* and *coq au vin*, and in Italy they are *vitello con funghi* and *braviola*. Even Findus products that ostensibly have international appeal actually differ substantially from country to country. For example, the pizzas Findus sells in Britain include cheese with ham and pineapple toppings on a French bread crust, hardly an internationally accepted recipe for pizza.

2. *Consumers around the world are willing to trade off idiosyncratic preferences in product features for lower price and/or higher quality.* This assumption encourages MNCs to compete with aggressive pricing on low-cost products that meet the common needs of customers around the world. Such a strategy implies a global orientation, with low cost achieved through high volume from standardized production in centralized facilities. Unfortunately, this can lead firms to focus on their least desirable customers. Price-sensitive customers are notorious for lacking brand loyalty, while many premium goods, such as Cartier watches and Godiva chocolates, command a loyal following around the world. Furthermore, any one international competitor's cost position may erode so severely as to make price competition impractical. Host governments may subsidize local competitors, trade tariffs may add costs to exporting, and transportation and distribution costs may favor local suppliers. All this suggests that, in some cases, a focus on price/cost competition will be misguided. In such situations, the link between the economic imperative and global strategies is weakened.

3. *Substantial economies of scale in production and marketing can be achieved by treating the world's markets as homogeneous.*[33] Note the two types of economies of scale mentioned: those related to production and those related to marketing. The economic imperative implies pressure to build large centralized production facilities that supply a wide geographic region covering several countries. However, counterpressures might lead managers of MNCs to adopt more decentralized strategies for their operations, featuring smaller plants that serve local markets. Recent developments in flexible manufacturing have decreased the minimum volume required to reach acceptable levels of production efficiency.[34] In addition, such a localized multiplant strategy can provide a sort of insurance against instability from sources such as fluctuating exchange rates or government regulations.

Finally, in many industries, production costs no longer constitute the major issue in international competition as marketing takes on added importance. Although worldwide marketing campaigns may offer the potential of creating important economies of scale in product development and advertising,[35] experience has yet to yield the widespread gains that some experts have forecasted. Some MNCs have made ambitious attempts to have uniform marketing efforts throughout the world; Gillette's Sensor razor is one example.

Gillette invested $200 million in developing its Sensor razor. Because the razor retails at only $4, the firm wanted to generate the widest possible distribution to create the volume required to amortize the R&D investment.[36] Gillette had developed a successful single advertising campaign to sell its Atra razor throughout Europe, which saved millions in packaging and advertising; with the confidence born of this experience, it launched the new Sensor razor with a single advertising campaign in nineteen markets scattered around the world. The results were excellent, and demand from retailers ran ahead of Gillette's ability to supply the product. Based on this success, the Sensor's global marketing effort may serve as the model Gillette uses in rolling out an entire line of "world" cosmetic products for men.[37]

For every example like Gillette's Sensor, however, a host of other firms have had to tailor their strategies to meet individual market needs. Kellogg's experience in marketing breakfast cereals around the world provides one example. Kellogg has found it must adjust its marketing efforts to the eating habits of each country. In Brazil, where the traditional breakfast is coffee and a roll, emphasis is placed on teaching the consumer to view cereal as a breakfast food to be eaten with milk, rather than a snack food to be eaten alone. But in France, Kellogg's emphasis is placed on convincing the consumer that cold cereals can be nutritious and taste good. Overcoming language differences also requires adjustment in marketing efforts. In Japan, consumers have trouble pronouncing "snap, crackle, and pop," the sounds Kellogg attributes to its Rice Krispies cereal. So in Japan, Rice Krispies go "patchy, pitchy, putchy." And because the name Bran Buds translates roughly into "burned farmer" in Swedish, Kellogg found it beneficial to alter the cereal's name for the Swedish market!

Convergence of Global and Multidomestic Strategies

Reacting to the forces and counterforces driving them to adopt elements of both global and multidomestic strategies, many of the most successful MNCs have converged these strategies. Industries that were once cited as examples of pure multidomestic operations are becoming globalized and vice versa. The consumer electronics industry and the laundry detergent industry provide classic examples of each trend.

Consumer Electronics: From Global Toward Multidomestic.   Until the early 1980s, the consumer electronics industry was marked by its increasing economies of scale in R&D, manufacturing, and marketing, encouraging more global strategies. For example, the minimum efficient production scale for a television set in the late 1970s was around 2.5 million sets per year—forty to fifty times the minimum efficient scale of a plant 20 years earlier. Such tremendous economies of scale assured that only a handful of very-high-volume worldwide suppliers would survive the shakeout that followed the industry's reaching maturity. Matsushita, the Japanese electronics giant that produces the Panasonic and Quasar lines, represents the survivors. Matsushita emphasized worldwide sales of a standardized product line and production in huge centralized plants—a classic global strategy for maximum volume of homogeneous products.

Ironically, Matsushita's success with global strategy pushed some competitors toward a more multidomestic approach. Host governments began to resist what they viewed as a flood of imports upsetting trade balances. Political action, including anti-dumping lawsuits (against exporting goods at unrealistically low prices in order to drive out competition) and limited trade agreements, followed. The cumulative effect of these moves encouraged foreign firms to set up smaller local production facilities scattered around the world. By placing plants inside a number of host nations, an important element of the classic multidomestic strategy, such foreign-owned corporations built up government support in a wide range of countries, not just in their home country.

Meanwhile, niche players attacked global players' formal market, customizing their products to local consumer tastes. So, for instance, the British firm Amstrad introduced a fast-growing line of consumer electronics featuring wood cabinetry and specific types of control panels British consumers wanted. Eventually, the success of firms like Amstrad forced Matsushita to reverse its strategy of offering a limited number of standardized products for sale in markets around the world. In several product categories, the firm has recently more than doubled the number of models available. As a result of its move away from a purely global strategy, Matsushita's sales per individual model have declined sharply, but its overall sales have risen.

Laundry Detergents: From Multidomestic Toward Global. While Matsushita added elements of a multidomestic orientation to its generally global strategy, MNCs that once pursued strictly multidomestic strategies are becoming more global. European laundry detergents have, until recently, been produced primarily by firms pursuing multidomestic operations, a situation created by several factors acting in combination. As recently as 1980, washing machine use varied from less than 30 percent penetration in Britain to more than 85 percent penetration in Germany. Habits and standard practices for washing clothes varied widely, too. In northern Europe, "boil washing" had long been the standard, while in the Mediterranean countries, most washing was done in cold water. Differences in water hardness, fabric mixes, perfume preferences, legislation governing phosphate effluents, and marketing practices (e.g., in Holland, each brand is limited to a certain number of minutes of television advertising per year) also contributed to this multidomestic orientation.

However, this trend has reversed in the past decade or so. Sharply increased sales of washing machines throughout Europe have greatly standardized laundry practices, as has the widespread use of synthetic fibers. In addition, costs rose because of the oil crisis of the mid-1970s; raw materials for producing detergents rose sharply, and a worldwide recession made it impossible to pass increased costs on to consumers. As a result of this dilemma, manufacturers had to actively seek out new means of economizing. The result was a more global perspective. Although they had previously left R&D up to chemical companies that supplied their raw material, some detergent manufacturers found that by standardizing products, they could do the R&D efficiently themselves and thereby achieve a competitive advantage not easily copied by rivals.

Procter & Gamble, for example, benefited from treating laundry detergent R&D as part of an integrated global strategy. One P&G detergent sold with only minor modifications around the world under the label of Tide in the United States, Ariel in Europe, and Cheer in southeast Asia. The product combines major technical advances from the company's research laboratories in Japan, Germany, and the United States. Without global coordination, the technologies resident in the regional laboratories would never have been combined to provide P&G with a product versatile enough to sell in so many different markets.

Hybrid Strategies.   Both of the above examples indicate that MNCs are moving to blend attributes, some reflecting a multidomestic orientation, others with a global perspective. Between the extremes of a purely multidomestic or a purely global strategy lie a number of hybrid strategies sometimes called transnational strategies. In Application 8.2, we see how McDonald's benefits by combining elements of global and multidomestic strategies, and Exhibit 8.7 gives options for various hybrid strategies.

Application 8.2

McDonald's Combines Global and Multidomestic Strategies

McDonald's, the world's most successful fast food restaurant chain, provides a classic example of an MNC that combines elements of both global and multidomestic approaches to international competition. The company, which operates in more than forty countries with over 2,000 outlets outside the United States, realizes more than 40 percent of its growth in sales through international expansion.

One reason for McDonald's success in moving into new countries is its willingness to adapt its operations to the needs of the local partners that it typically uses in its foreign operations. One such partner in Singapore says, "The message that comes out of Chicago [site of the corporation's headquarters] is 'What can we do for you?' rather than 'What did you do and why?'" McDonald's corporate managers regularly depend upon their operators for advice on such matters as menu changes. For instance, beverage selections available on McDonald's menus differ considerably around the world. In Germany, McDonald's sells beer; in Brazil, it serves soft drinks made from the guarana, a berry native only to the Amazon; and in Malaysia it offers milkshakes flavored with durian, a fruit popular locally because of its reported effectiveness as an aphrodisiac.

But the role of local partners and the multidomestic orientation their involvement implies goes far beyond menus. McDonald's is well known in the United States for its cutting-edge work in the area of site selection. However, the company does not automatically presume that this expertise is transferable to every new country it enters. For instance, when McDonald's entered Japan, its local partner steered it away from the suburban locations typical in the United States and toward urban sites that

customers could get to without cars. Den Fujita, president of McDonald's Co. (Japan) Ltd., says, "We don't just sit here and take everything from the United States. We have to make improvements to get better operations."

Ironically, even with this heavy emphasis on local operations, McDonald's provides an excellent example of an MNC with a high level of global integration. For example, on products popular the world over, like its french fries, McDonald's works unceasingly to ensure conformity in all locations. This includes teaching farmers in eighteen selected countries around the world to grow russet potatoes just like those from Idaho.

The company is even more stringent in its requirements for global uniformity in "production" management. Detailed descriptions of standard operating procedures determining product and service consistency fill telephone directory–sized "shop manuals." The firm now operates "Hamburger Universities" in several countries around the world, and because professors are rotated from country to country and every store sends students to a "Hamburger U" somewhere, the corporation can make sure that the "McDonald's experience" is the same for consumers the world over. So while elements of each country's operations are uniquely tailored to what that country needs, this customization takes place within the context of an overall global strategy that emphasizes uniformity.

Sources
Based on information gathered from K. Deveny et al., "Mc-World," *Business Week* (June 25, 1986), 63–68; S. Tully, "Doing Business in One Germany," *Fortune* (July 2, 1990), 80–83; J. Renshaw, "Cultural Savvy—The Essential Factor," *Multinational Business* (Summer 1987), 33–36.

EXHIBIT 8.7
A Continuum of Strategies for MNCs

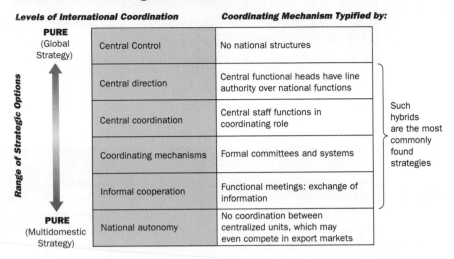

	Levels of International Coordination	Coordinating Mechanism Typified by:
PURE (Global Strategy)	Central Control	No national structures
	Central direction	Central functional heads have line authority over national functions
	Central coordination	Central staff functions in coordinating role
	Coordinating mechanisms	Formal committees and systems
	Informal cooperation	Functional meetings: exchange of information
PURE (Multidomestic Strategy)	National autonomy	No coordination between centralized units, which may even compete in export markets

Range of Strategic Options (vertical axis label)

Such hybrids are the most commonly found strategies (bracket label spanning Central direction through Informal cooperation)

Source: Adapted from Norman Blackwell et al., "Shaping a Pan-European Organization," *McKinsey Quarterly* (Spring 1991), 94–111. By permission of The McKinsey Quarterly.

The organizations associated with these hybrid strategies are some of the most complex because they must try to simultaneously meet the economic and social imperatives previously discussed. In order to successfully implement a hybrid strategy that combines the strength of a global strategy and the flexibility of a multidomestic strategy, an organization must address several paradoxes.[38] For example, firms must be big in order to afford the resources needed to be global powers, but they must narrow their focus to the finer details of tailoring those resources to individual markets. Similarly, an organization must allow its various operating units freedom to develop what local markets demand, but these units must do so within the structure of centralized guidelines and controls.

An approach to sharing power between a central headquarters and decentralized operating units mirrors a form of government organization known as federalism. A federalist system of government is one in which individual states share power with a central national authority. In such a government system, programs may be designed and funded centrally and then administered locally, which is very similar to what we have described as a hybrid strategy.

Federalism, one of the world's oldest political philosophies, is guided by five time-proven principles that also apply to the management of multinational corporations. The principle of *subsidiarity* places power at its lowest possible point in the organization, allowing centralized initiatives to be tailored to fit local conditions. *Interdependence* spreads power around inside the organization, avoiding the risks of an inflexible centralized bureaucracy, on the one hand, and the anarchy of uncoordinated decision making, on the other. *Uniformity* in rules of conduct—establishing common ways of doing everything from collecting financial data to communicating in the same language—is necessary for interdependence to work. *Separation* of responsibility for operations, monitoring, and governing allows managers to focus effectively on different time horizons. *Dual citizenship*, perhaps the most important principle, means everyone in the organization has allegiance to the whole as well as to the individual parts.

These five principles are general enough to be applied regardless of where the organization falls along the continuum depicted in Exhibit 8.7. In other words, managers can adapt the principles of federalism regardless of specific relationships between headquarters and operating units. That is fortunate, because experience shows that no one relationship between headquarters and local operations always works. That relationship needs to vary depending on the importance of the local operation to the future of the firm and the organization's managerial strengths in the specific locale, as shown in Exhibit 8.8.

Regardless of the precise headquarters/local operations relationship sought, federalist principles offer a good starting point in building an organization that combines the required elements of a global and a multidomestic strategy. In the following section, we discuss how such combinations allow MNCs to achieve the strongest possible mix of competitive advantages.

INTERNATIONAL STRATEGY AND COMPETITIVE ADVANTAGE

Businesses that operate across national borders face many of the same competitive challenges that their domestic counterparts do. In particular, as described in Chapter

EXHIBIT 8.8
Options for Interactions Between the Corporate Center and Country Companies

Future Strategic Importance of Country/Region

		Low	High
Current Corporate Skills in Country/Region	**High**	Encourage transfer of skills	Interact as partners
	Low	Manage as "independent" trading post	Promote skills and independence

Source: Ingo Theuerkauf, "Reshaping the Global Organization," *McKinsey Quarterly* (Summer 1991), 102–119. Reprinted by permission of The McKinsey Quarterly.

6, they must strive to achieve sustainable competitive advantages through differentiation, cost, response time, or a combination of these. However, international operations present additional challenges. When firms operate across national borders, political and government issues take on such importance that they provide the basis for a fourth type of competitive advantage—one we shall call "government relations."

Having introduced a fourth source of competitive advantage, we need to consider how blending elements of multidomestic and global strategies can impact each of the four forms of competitive advantage for multinational corporations, as illustrated in Exhibit 8.9 and discussed in more detail below.

Differentiation

Thanks in large part to the power of the Marlboro Man advertising campaign, Marlboro cigarettes have achieved greater worldwide acceptance than virtually any other product in history. This success has derived primarily from brand differentiation through a global marketing campaign. Historically, a single set of advertisements, created in the United States, was used all over the world, wherever cigarette commercials were allowed. This was as pure an approach to global marketing as possible, and it worked well for years. Some have estimated that at times the Marlboro brand alone accounted for 60 percent of Philip Morris's total corporate profits. However, recent evidence shows that even this prime example of pure global marketing is being ad-

---

EXHIBIT 8.9
A Framework with Examples of How MNC Strategy Affects Competitive Advantage

	MNC Strategy	
Sources of Competitive Advantage	*Multidomestic Attributes*	*Global Attributes*
High differentiation	Tailor marketing efforts to fit each individual country.	Market "world" products with standardized advertising copy.
Low cost	Avoid transportation costs and trade tariffs by producing locally.	Use high-volume centralized production facilities to maximize economies of scale.
Quick response	Form joint ventures with local partners to avoid delays in entering new markets.	Combine technology from throughout worldwide operations to innovate faster than individuals can.
Government relations	Build goodwill by working with local government agencies to address problems facing host nations.	Circumvent trade restrictions limiting success of one country's operations by funneling its business through other countries in the global network.

justed for regional differences in what amounts to at least a small step toward a multi-domestic orientation in an effort to maximize market penetration in different countries around the world.[39]

For example, the advertising agency that handled the Marlboro account divided the world into twenty-five primary markets for cigarettes, and its creative people from each region submitted ideas for each year's advertising campaign. In its first year, this approach brought in sixty-nine different suggestions, and the ad agency's top creative directors from around the world selected nine storyboards, which were submitted to Philip Morris for review. Philip Morris approved five of the commercials, from which local managers operating independently in individual countries were free to make their selections. Obviously, this approach is still very much aligned with the notion of worldwide differentiation through global marketing, yet it is increasingly tempered with recognition of the need for flexibility regarding cultural differences.

Other companies have found that global marketing did not work successfully for them and have been much more aggressive than Philip Morris in moving toward multidomestic approaches to achieving differentiation for their products. For instance, when Parker Pen tried to standardize the marketing of its line of ink pens sold in 154 markets around the world, it encountered severe problems. Local managers' authority was sharply reduced, and they resisted the plan. Meanwhile, the new centralized, high-volume plant could not produce adequate numbers of quality pens, and the company began to lose money. The business was eventually sold for only $100 million to a group of managers who had opposed the global strategy from the outset.[40] Once these managers took over, they quickly restored local managers' autonomy, particularly emphasizing decentralized, country-specific advertising. Soon Parker had become the number-one-selling line of pens in many of its markets, and, from a half-million-dollar loss in the year of the takeover, the company rebounded the next year with $23 million in profits.[41] Exhibit 8.10 presents other ways in which multidomestic and global strategies can contribute to the competitive advantage of differentiation.

EXHIBIT 8.10
The Competitive Advantage of DIFFERENTIATION May Be . . .

Facilitated by the Elements of a Multidomestic Strategy, Such as . . .	Facilitated by the Elements of a Global Strategy, Such as . . .
. . . increased freedom of individual business units to adjust promotion and advertising to local tastes	. . . economies of scale in advertising and promotion of images with a worldwide appeal
. . . flexibility in applying local research and development to developing tailored products meeting country-specific needs	. . . the ability to draw upon the resources of a coordinated network of R&D laboratories in developing world products
. . . the ability to adapt after-sales service to the specific cultural norms of a particular market	. . . the creation of a worldwide network offering consistent levels of service, regardless of location

Cost Leadership

As we have noted, the justification for a global strategy is that it will provide greater economies of scale and learning curve effects, thereby providing the competitive advantage of cost leadership. However, firms with low-cost positions have also successfully followed multidomestic strategies, and the key to understanding which is more cost effective in a given situation is understanding what accounts for most of the costs embedded in the industry's value chain. Industries in which proportionally more value is added in upstream activities are more likely to benefit from a global strategy than are those industries in which more value is added downstream.[42] Exhibit 8.11 notes how both approaches can facilitate a cost leadership advantage.

For example, industries such as chemicals, commercial aircraft, computers, and heavy construction equipment all have much of their value added in R&D, product design, and manufacturing activities (all relatively upstream), and each of these industries is dominated by firms with strong global orientations. By centralizing these upstream activities, such firms can lower their costs and gain efficiencies that the multidomestic approach of many smaller efforts scattered across a number of nations cannot provide.

On the other hand, industries such as insurance, prepared foods, and security services all add much of their value in downstream activities such as marketing, sales, and services. These industries tend toward multidomestic strategies because the important activities in their value chains do not lend themselves to mass production at centralized locations. In fact, attempts to centralize such activities would probably induce *dis*economies of scale because coordinating such diversity is so complex. For example, Findus would have difficulty making pizzas in one centralized kitchen to fit all the world's tastes.

Note that the decision to adopt a global or a multidomestic perspective is not nearly as simple as these examples might lead one to think; exceptions abound for every generalization. Remember, the best competitors do not concentrate on just one form of competitive advantage, but struggle to excel on multiple dimensions. Thus, a firm inclined to adopt a global strategy to lower costs might end up pursuing a more multidomestic strategy because of what it offers in the way of differentiation, quick response, or government support.

EXHIBIT 8.11
The Competitive Advantage of COST LEADERSHIP May Be . . .

Facilitated by the Elements of a Multidomestic Strategy, Such as . . .	*Facilitated by the Elements of a Global Strategy, Such as . . .*
. . . decreased shipping and transportation costs inherent in local production	. . . economies of scale gained through centralized production of standardized products
. . . avoidance of trade duties and tariffs by manufacturing within a country that would tax imports	. . . decreased duplication of inventories, which often arises from multiple plants producing similar products

---

Also, note that the decision is not made by MNC managers alone. Quite often, the host country government plays a strong role in determining what the MNC's strategy will be. For example, several Latin American countries do not let foreigners hold a majority of the stock in a local business, while other countries refuse to allow MNCs to operate within their borders without sharing their technology with local manufacturers. In such cases, MNCs either adapt to the situation of the individual nation—a multidomestic response—or choose not to operate in that country at all.

General Electric provides a good example of how other matters may take precedence over concern for cost alone in deciding between a multidomestic and a global strategy. To secure a $450 million contract to build locomotives in China, General Electric had to agree to transfer its locomotive technology to local Chinese manufacturers over the contract's 10-year life. Production of locomotives has tremendous economies of scale and, normally, concern for economic efficiency and cost competitiveness would lead GE to produce the 420 units it required in a centralized factory outside China. However, by taking a less than economically optimal opportunity in locomotives, the company hoped to gain valuable experience in working with the Chinese and improve its competitive advantage in terms of government relations. GE obviously believed the potential gain in government relations was worth the loss of efficiency in locomotive production. Government support may be a useful long-term asset in selling GE's broad range of products in the world's most populous nation.

Quick Response

In the GE example, an MNC entered into a joint venture with a local firm in the host country—a tactic often used to increase the speed with which an MNC enters and penetrates a given national market. Having a local partner can facilitate processes such as obtaining government permits and securing lines of credit from local banks. Local partners also provide valuable information about business practices and essential practical information, such as which local law firm is the best. This means that by adopting a country-by-country approach to international expansion, the MNC is able to respond more quickly to each country's unique situation.

Sometimes, however, a multidomestic approach can actually slow an MNC's response time, resulting in loss of competitive advantage. For instance, Hewlett-Packard traditionally produced versions of its computer software and manuals in local languages for countries outside the United States only after an initial rollout at home. In this approach, it considered each country to be a separate step toward worldwide distribution. But the incremental procedure allowed foreign competitors to learn what was coming to their market long enough before it arrived to adjust their own products accordingly. So Hewlett-Packard adopted a more global approach to the rollout of its new line of highly successful graphics terminals, simultaneously introducing the product and the supporting documentation in fifteen languages.

Otis Elevator also responds more quickly to market opportunities as a result of its global approach to managing innovation. Its latest line of "smart" elevators is the product of R&D at six different research centers in five different countries: France, Germany, Japan, Spain, and the United States. Otis estimates that this global approach cut the development time for the new line of elevators from 4 years to 2 and

---

EXHIBIT 8.12
The Competitive Advantage of QUICK RESPONSE May Be . . .

Facilitated by the Elements of a Multidomestic Strategy, Such as . . .	*Facilitated by the Elements of a Global Strategy, Such as . . .*
. . . joint ventures with local businesses, which provide faster start-ups since local partners "know the ropes"	. . . a centrally coordinated effort, which can bring greater corporate resources to bear on the problems of establishing an operation in a new market
. . . local independence, which allows better responsiveness to local developments	. . . R&D laboratories cooperating with one another on innovations and thus progressing faster than a single independent laboratory could

---

saved the company more than $10 million in design costs. Exhibit 8.12 summarizes some of the ways in which multidomestic and global strategies support the competitive advantage of quick response.

Government Relations as a Source of Competitive Advantage

As discussed in Chapter 3, even strictly domestic firms must be concerned about relationships with the government.[43] When a business operates under the jurisdiction of two or more nations, the problems are compounded, and government relations can become either an invaluable advantage or an overwhelming disadvantage.[44] Government authorities can play many roles, all with potential benefits and costs to international competitors:

- *Regulators* Legalities in business practices often depend on a local government's disposition on a given issue. This disposition can vary greatly between countries and even within one country over time, and the success of an international operation often hinges upon this point. Monsanto, one of the world's largest suppliers of agricultural chemicals, shipped herbicides in bulk to Brazil for many years, where they were then packaged for the South American market. Concerned about its balance of trade, the Brazilian government began to pressure Monsanto to build a factory that would handle the entire production operation, not just packaging. When Monsanto resisted, the government allowed a local company to produce a line of herbicides that Monsanto claims violated its patents. Faced with the resulting local competition, Monsanto was forced to defend itself in the local market by building the plant after all, while fighting for its patent rights in the Brazilian courts. The company's director of international operations admits, "If we had to do it over, we'd have made our investment earlier and avoided all this."

- *Conegotiators* Global competition can create some strange bedfellows, as international firms cultivate a coalition of government support often ranging far outside their home countries. U.S. lawmakers in Washington negotiated against regulators in Europe for the right of Japanese carmakers operating in the United States to export more cars to Europe. Normally, these same U.S. legislators are concerned about regulating the flow of Japanese imports to the United States, but in this case they were allies working as conegotiators in support of the Japanese firms' rights in Europe.

- *Suppliers* In many nations, the state owns important supplier factories or rights to key natural resources. In such situations, the government may supply critical resources such as energy, as many oil and coal reserves are controlled by national governments.

- *Competitors* The public service sector of any nation provides at least some goods and services that can substitute for those that private enterprise provides in other nations. In such cases, these public service organizations constitute a form of competition with actual or potential suppliers from the private sector; for example, privately owned airlines often compete abroad with government-owned airlines.

- *Customers* Depending on the industry, foreign governments may be vital customers whose support is critical for sales volume. Boeing, a leading supplier of commercial aircraft around the world, often sells its planes to, or through, local governments. The power and importance of governments as customers means that Boeing must be open and receptive to unusual business deals that the firm would probably not consider otherwise. In a process known as countertrade,[45] the company has bartered planes for oil, tin, copper, and in one case even feathers! Although the feathers deal fell through, Boeing's director of international sales says, "You can't close the door on anything."[46] Given Boeing's willingness to adapt its practices to local customs, the firm has been able to do well in selling aircraft to wealthy nations in the Middle East. However, Boeing claims that when the U.S. government moved to block the sale of Boeing aircraft to Libya, it angered other Arab nations, which then began to buy aircraft from other countries. Here we see how a firm's home government can influence the firm's success abroad—an international competitor must contend with its own relationship with a host country, as well as cope with relationships between the nations themselves. Application 8.3 illustrates the importance of each of the government roles as they impact a famous international joint venture, Beijing Jeep.

As with the other forms of competitive advantage, a combination of multidomestic and global approaches can also help MNCs obtain government support (see Exhibit 8.13). IBM, which employs a strong global perspective overall, provides many good examples of what an MNC can do within an individual country to achieve local government support by operating in a multidomestic mode. For instance, IBM built support for itself in several Latin American countries by sponsoring nutritional programs for children, and providing advisers for Mexico on agricultural priorities. Meanwhile, halfway around the world, Polaroid, another politically savvy MNC, is helping the Italian government restore Leonardo da Vinci's *Last Supper*. Obviously, such actions are not done strictly as ends in themselves; they help the MNC establish legitimacy with the country's government, creating a comfortable business environment with the support of the local authorities.

Application 8.3

Beijing Jeep: The Many Roles of Government in International Business

When American Motors Corporation entered the Chinese automobile market, it found that government relations were absolutely critical to its success. Everywhere the company turned in this important market, it faced the government acting in a new role. These roles include those discussed in the text:

■ *Regulators* AMC found that a wide range of government offices had authority over its operations, from the head of the Chinese National Automotive Investment Corporation, the national authority governing China's automotive industry, to the local bureaucrats of the Beijing Municipality. AMC managers were regulated on everything—from who they could fire on the job to where they could live off the job.

■ *Conegotiators* Beijing Jeep was a joint venture between American Motors Corporation and the Beijing Automotive Industrial Corporation. As partners, every move each firm made was conegotiated. Negotiations were complex, as each side alternated between negotiating against each other and teaming with each other to negotiate against common adversaries. In the 7 years leading up to the start of production, negotiation was the primary work of managers in both AMC and BAIC.

■ *Suppliers* The Chinese government played a direct role in supplying AMC with everything from employees and a factory to housing and entertainment to electric power and Chinese currency. In fact, while AMC provided a handful of managers and most of the parts re-

quired to actually build a jeep, the Chinese government supplied Beijing Jeep with virtually everything else the joint venture required.

■ *Competitors* Virtually every one of the 160 Chinese firms constituting the Chinese automotive industry was owned and operated by the Chinese government. As would be expected of any competitive rivals, representatives of these various firms actively sought to limit Beijing Jeep's success. They were often very effective, because their position as government insiders gave them a clear advantage over their U.S. rival.

■ *Customers* From the outset, Chinese government officials viewed the primary market for the Jeep to be its military, specifically the People's Liberation Army, rather than its 1-billion-plus population. Ironically, the military's interest was in a four-door soft-top vehicle—a product unlike any AMC sold and one it could not afford to develop. Consequently, AMC's managers faced adversarial customers throughout the early years of Beijing Jeep's life as an international joint venture.

Sources
Based on information gathered from the following: The fascinating story of Beijing Jeep is told by Jim Mann in *Beijing Jeep: The Short, Unhappy Romance of American Business in China,* New York: Simon & Schuster, 1989; Jim Mann, "One Company's China Debacle," *Fortune, 120* (November 6, 1989), 145–152; and Tod O. Clare, "Yin and Yang—And Jeeps in China," *Financier, 10* (October 1986), 24–28.

EXHIBIT 8.13
The Competitive Advantage of GOVERNMENT SUPPORT May Be . . .

Facilitated by the Elements of a Multidomestic Strategy, Such as . . .	*Facilitated by the Elements of a Global Strategy, Such as . . .*
. . . greater goodwill resulting from employing local workforces, rather than simply importing finished goods made elsewhere	. . . greater bargaining power associated with the corporation as a whole, rather than a local operation acting individually
. . . flexibility in adjusting to local laws and customs	. . . flexibility in shifting operations throughout a coordinated network as conditions in specific locales vary

A multidomestic approach is not always the most effective means of dealing with government agencies. In fact, some MNCs deal with government/political pressure by taking advantage of their unified global network of operations. When the German BASF's research on biotechnology came under fire from the "Greens," a collection of environmentally conscious and politically powerful interest groups, the company decided to shift the research being protested in Germany to its facilities in Cambridge, Massachusetts. BASF's experience indicated that the move would offer it a climate in which the community had resolved controversies concerning safety and the environment. Rather than having to fight isolated political movements in any particular country, globally oriented MNCs can shift sensitive work to a location within their worldwide operation that will best fit the values of the local citizens.[47]

Northern Telecom Ltd., the leading Canadian telecommunications firm, made a somewhat similar use of its global operations to overcome trade barriers that were preventing it from penetrating the Japanese market. The Japanese government was under severe pressure from the United States, its largest trade partner, to address the growing imbalance of trade between the two countries. Much of this political pressure was aimed at making it easier for U.S. operations to export products to Japan. Japan responded to this pressure by lifting some key restrictions on U.S. imports, although these restrictions remained in effect against other nations. As a result, it was much easier to export telecommunications devices into Japan from a base in the United States rather than from Canada. Therefore, Northern Telecom operates its Japanese business out of its U.S. subsidiary's headquarters rather than its corporate headquarters in Canada. Again, the global integration of the firm allows it to adjust its operations to fit the political realities it encounters, and government relations come to serve as a competitive advantage rather than as a disadvantage.

Summary of Managerial Practices to Adopt from This Chapter

- Perhaps the most important step toward becoming a more effective manager at the international level is to accept enthusiastically that our world is advancing rapidly and inexorably toward a global marketplace. The most successful firms of the future will be those which embrace this change and build strategies employing corporate resources to strengthen the competitive advantages of their foreign operations.

- A variety of entry strategies are open to most businesses considering international expansion, and managers need to balance the benefits of each option against its risks.

- A useful way of thinking about the strategies pursued by MNCs is to classify them along a continuum between two extremes. One extreme is called multidomestic, because MNCs using it treat their various foreign operations as if they were a collection of independent businesses serving the local domestic markets. At the other extreme of the continuum, MNCs attempt to develop a single global strategy in which all foreign operations are centrally controlled under one unified plan.

- The competitive advantages that are important to a foreign operation overlap with those that are important to domestic businesses. Differentiation, cost leadership, and quick response are powerful weapons, regardless of geography. But in international competition, in which various governments are involved, a fourth form of competitive advantage, government relations, becomes equally important.

- In developing strategies at the international level, managers need to be aware of the social forces working in favor of strategies tailored to individual countries as well as the economic forces that encourage a standardized approach to business worldwide.

- Research and experience suggest that in order to create the strongest combination of competitive advantages, MNCs should blend elements of both global and multidomestic strategies into their worldwide operations. The essence of such a combination is "thinking globally but acting locally."

Questions for Discussion and Review

1. Why must strategists adopt a worldwide view?

2. Discuss the advantages and disadvantages of global diversification.

3. Describe the different entry strategies for international expansion.

4. Explain the most important differences between multidomestic and global strategies.

5. How do hybrid strategies that combine elements of multidomestic and global approaches help firms attain and/or sustain competitive advantages?

Notes

1. J. Kapstein and S. Reed, "The Euro-Gospel According to Percy Barnevik," *Business Week* (July 23, 1990), 64–66.
2. B. S. Chakravarthy and H. V. Perlmutter, "Strategic Planning for a Global Business," *Columbia Journal of World Business* (Spring 1985), 3–10; J. F. Bolt, "Global Competitors: Some Criteria for Success," *Business Horizons* (January–Feburary 1988), 34–41.
3. F. G. Steingraber, "Managing in the 1990s," *Business Horizons* (January–February 1990), 34–41.
4. James B. Treece et al., "New Worlds to Conquer," *Business Week*, (February 28, 1994), 50–52.
5. B. O'Reilly, "America's Place in World Competition," *Fortune, 120* (November 6, 1989), 83–96.
6. R. S. England, "A Lost Opportunity," *Financial World, 158* (May 30, 1989), 18–20.
7. See Briance Mascarenhas, "Research Notes and Communications First-Mover Effects in Multiple Dynamic Markets," *Strategic Management Journal, 13* (1992), 237–243; and Briance Mascarenhas, "Order of Entry and Performance in International Markets," *Strategic Management Journal, 13* (1992), 499–510.
8. R. I. Kirkland, Jr., "Entering a New Age of Boundless Competition," *Fortune, 117* (March 4, 1988), 40–48.
9. S. Hemmerick, "Assets Swell by 20%—But Japanese Outspend U.S. Investors," *Pensions and Investment Age, 17* (October 2, 1989), 33.
10. E. E. Goette, "Europe 1992: Update for Business Planners," *Journal of Business Strategy* (March–April 1990), 10–13.
11. Shawn Tully, "What Eastern Europe Offers," *Fortune* (March 12, 1990), 52–55.
12. I. C. Herbert, "How Coke Markets to the World," *Journal of Business Strategy* (September–October 1988), 4–7.
13. See, for example, M. J. Hardy, "Going Global: One Company's Road to International Management," *Journal of Business Strategy* (November–December 1989), 24–27.
14. N. Gilbert, "How Middle-Sized Corporations Manage Global Operations," *Management Review, 77* (October 1988), 46–50.
15. Michael E. Porter, "The Competitive Advantage of Nations," *Harvard Business Review* (March–April 1990), 73–93.
16. "Capital Cargo—More German Marks for U.S. Chemical Operations," *Chemical Week* (June 25, 1985), 24–27.
17. W. C. Kim and R. A. Mauborgne, "Becoming an Effective Global Competitor," *Journal of Business Strategy* (January–February 1988), 33–37.
18. J. Flanigan, "Multinational, as We Know It, Is Obsolete," *Forbes* (August 26, 1985), 30–32.
19. For details on the important role Fuji Xerox played in helping to improve the competitiveness of Xerox in the United States, see G. Jacobson and J. Hillkirk, *Xerox—American Samurai*, New York: Macmillan, 1986.
20. P. Hemp, "King of Beers in a Bitter Battle in Britain," *Wall Street Journal* (June 9, 1988), 24.
21. Charles Hampden-Turner and Alfons Trompenaars, *The Seven Cultures of Capitalism*, New York: Doubleday/Currency, 1993; Bruno Dufour, "Dealing with Diversity: Management Education in Europe," *Selections, 1* (1994), 7–15.
22. For example, considerable research has been done to document the important differences in effective negotiation tactics across nations; see Stephen E. Weiss, "Analysis of Complex Negotiations in International Business: The RBC Perspective," *Organization*

Science, 4 (May 1993), 269–300; and Nancy J. Adler, Richard Brahm, and John L. Graham, "Strategy Implementation: A Comparison of Face-to-Face Negotiations in the People's Republic of China and the United States," *Strategic Management Journal, 13* (June 1992), 449–466.

23. M. Van Horn, "Market-Entry Approaches for the Pacific Rim," *Journal of Business Strategy* (March–April 1990), 14–19.

24. For another approach to categorizing international strategies, see Allen J. Morrison and Kendall Roth, "A Taxonomy of Business-Level Strategies in Global Industries," *Strategic Management Journal, 13* (1992), 399–418.

25. P. K. Kirkconnell, "Practical Thinking About Going International," *Business Quarterly, 53* (Autumn 1988), 40–45.

26. Clearly, the entry mode cannot be easily separated from the type of operation and form of management that arises postentry; see C. W. L. Hill, P. Hwang, and W. C. Kim, "An Eclectic Theory of the Choice of International Entry Mode," *Strategic Management Journal* (February 1990), 117–128.

27. Y. L. Doz, *Strategic Management in Multinational Companies*, Oxford: Pergamon Press, 1985.

28. This point has been heavily researched and greatly refined by the research team of Christopher Bartlett and Sumantra Ghoshal in *Managing Across Borders: The Transnational Solution*, Boston: Harvard Business School Press, 1989; and Sumantra Ghoshal and Christopher Bartlett, "The Multinational Corporation as an Interorganizational Network," *Academy of Management Review* (1990), 603–625.

29. A. Quelch and E. J. Hoff, "Customizing Global Marketing," *Harvard Business Review* (May–June 1986), 59–68.

30. K. H. Hammonds, "Ted Levitt Is Back in the Trenches," *Business Week* (January 29, 1990), 82–84; Theodore Levitt, "The Globalization of Markets," *Harvard Business Review* (May–June 1983), 92–102.

31. S. P. Douglas and Y. Wind, "The Myth of Globalization," *Columbia Journal of World Business, 22* (Winter 1987), 19–29.

32. S. P. Douglas and C. S. Craig, "Evolution of Global Marketing Strategy: Scale, Scope, and Synergy," *Columbia Journal of World Business, 24* (Fall 1989), 47–59.

33. T. Hout, M. E. Porter, and E. Rudden, "How Global Companies Win Out," *Harvard Business Review* (September–October 1982), 98–108.

34. B. Kogut, "Designing Global Strategies: Profiting from Operational Flexibility," *Sloan Management Review* (Fall 1985), 27–38.

35. R. Friedmann, "Psychological Meaning of Products: A Simplification of the Standardization Versus Adaptation Debate," *Columbia Journal of World Business* (Summer 1986), 97–103.

36. K. H. Hammonds, "How a $4 Razor Ends Up Costing $300 Million," *Business Week* (January 29, 1990), 62–63.

37. J. Levine, "Global Lather," *Forbes* (February 5, 1990), 146, 148.

38. The remainder of this section draws heavily upon Charles Handy, "Balancing Corporate Power: A New Federalist Paper," *Harvard Business Review, 70* (November–December 1992), 59–72.

39. J. S. Hill and J. M. Winski, "Goodbye Global Ads," *Advertising Age, 58* (November 16, 1987), 22.

40. J. M. Winski and L. Wentz, "Parker Pen: What Went Wrong?," *Advertising Age, 1* (January 1, 1986), 60–61, 71.

41. K. Cote, J. S. Hill, and J. M. Winski, "World Brands: Parker Pen Finds Black Ink," *Advertising Age, 58* (July 13, 1987), 49.

42. B. Kogut, "Designing Global Strategies: Comparative and Competitive Value-Added Chains," *Sloan Management Review* (Summer 1985), 15–28.

43. A. J. Prager and J. J. Cala, "Coexisting with Regulators," *Journal of Business Strategy* (January–February 1990), 22–25.

44. P. S. Ring, S. A. Lenway, and M. Govekar, "Management of the Political Imperative in International Business," *Strategic Management Journal* (February 1990), 141–151; P. Choate, "Political Advantage: Japan's Campaign for America," *Harvard Business Review* (September–October 1990), 87–103; S. P. Sethi and K. A. N. Luther, "Political Risk Analysis and Direct Foreign Investment: Some Problems of Definition and Measurement," *California Management Review* (Winter 1986), 57.

45. For guidelines on the important role countertrade plays in international operations, see J. R. Carter and J. Gagne, "The Dos and Don'ts of International Countertrade," *Sloan Management Review* (Spring 1988), 31–37; M. Schaffer, "Countertrade as an Export Strategy," *Journal of Business Strategy* (May–June 1990), 33–38; and Raj Aggarwal, "International Business Through Barter and Countertrade," *Long Range Planning, 22*:3 (1989), 75–81.

46. K. Labich, "America's International Winners," *Fortune* (April 14, 1986), 34–46.

47. W. J. Holstein et al., "The Stateless Corporation," *Business Week* (May 14, 1990), 98–105.

Part Four

STRATEGY IMPLEMENTATION

The four chapters in Part Four deal with the way organizations change to develop capabilities needed to better implement strategy. We cover this material by discussing three complementary topics: learning, leadership, and levers. We believe that organizational learning, first introduced in Chapter 2, is the most viable approach to managing change in the majority of today's businesses. We explain how building a learning organization requires leaders to master the use of a wide variety of change levers.

We begin, in Chapter 9, by describing why organizational change is difficult and how organizations learn to do new things or to do things differently. We conclude this chapter with a discussion of leadership's responsibility to use various levers to help build organizations capable of learning. Each of the three final chapters focuses on a different type of lever for implementing strategic changes.

In Chapter 10, we consider a category of levers for change we call context levers, referring to the general backdrop against which organizational activities take place. Context levers include such things as organization *structure*, informal networks, and corporate *culture.* Chapter 11 describes resourcing and control systems as change levers. Resourcing systems determine how organizations allocate and/or manage critical resources, such as capital, personnel, and information. Through control systems, organizations ensure that resources are allocated and used as intended, and we include both "hard" control systems, such as budgets, and "soft" control systems, such as shared values. You will see how systems management can dramatically affect strategy implementation.

Finally, Chapter 12 returns to the issue of leadership, as we examine how personal actions can be a powerful lever for change. We discover how leaders are found anywhere in the organization, and we focus on the importance of "instrumental" leadership, which manages the many factors that are instrumental in an organization's change effort.

By understanding how these change levers work individually and in concert, you will find yourself in a much better position to lead organizations through the challenging work of strategy implementation and organizational change.

The Architecture of Strategy

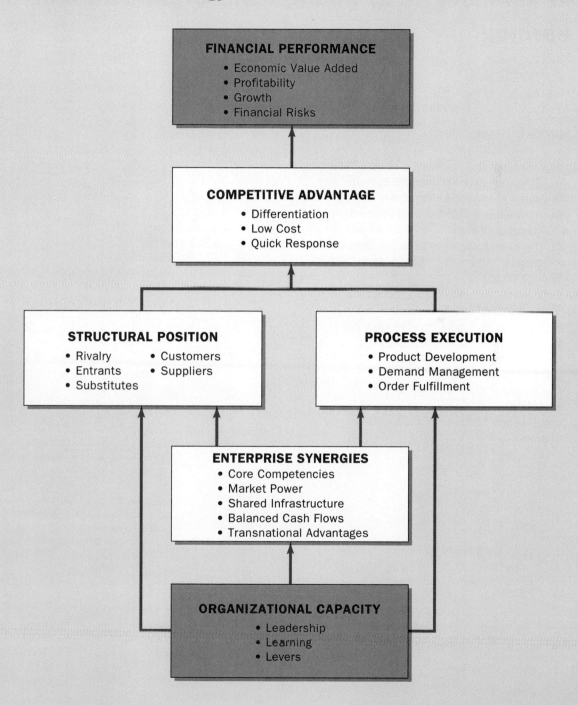

FINANCIAL PERFORMANCE
- Economic Value Added
- Profitability
- Growth
- Financial Risks

COMPETITIVE ADVANTAGE
- Differentiation
- Low Cost
- Quick Response

STRUCTURAL POSITION
- Rivalry
- Entrants
- Substitutes
- Customers
- Suppliers

PROCESS EXECUTION
- Product Development
- Demand Management
- Order Fulfillment

ENTERPRISE SYNERGIES
- Core Competencies
- Market Power
- Shared Infrastructure
- Balanced Cash Flows
- Transnational Advantages

ORGANIZATIONAL CAPACITY
- Leadership
- Learning
- Levers

Chapter 9

The Challenges of Change and Organizational Learning

In this chapter, we consider why organizations and their managers find strategy implementation so difficult, and we focus on organizational learning as the most promising means for addressing the challenges of change. The chapter is organized into five parts. We begin with specific factors that impede strategy implementation and organizational change and then discuss why activity-centered change programs fail. From there, we develop ideas for more successfully managing strategy, first taking a more detailed look at the nature of change and, then, considering what is involved in managing the organizational learning process. In the final section of the chapter, we discuss the need to have leaders play instrumental roles in building learning organizations and we briefly overview organizational levers to use in these efforts. (These levers are studied in more detail in subsequent chapters.)

This chapter will help you understand:

- The factors that make strategy implementation so difficult
- Why strategy implementation based on activity-centered change programs doesn't work
- How adaptive and generative changes require different approaches to strategy implementation
- Single-loop versus double-loop organizational learning
- How the basic elements of organizational learning—discovery and action, fit together to provide a complex, but powerful, approach to strategy implementation
- The critical role leadership plays in building learning organizations
- The need for leaders to support and encourage experimentation, especially experimentation from the middle of the organization, as illustrated by the MOUND model, as the best means of discovering new insights
- The leader's responsibility to act on the results of organizational experiments, backing winners and demonstrating tough love for ideas that don't work

Coworkers James Bulin and John Wolkonowicz sipped their beers in discouraged silence. The two were assigned a fairly menial task, part of the much larger project of designing a new generation of light trucks for Ford Motor Company, and they were frustrated with the job. Ford had long been the leader of the U.S. truck market, one of the most profitable segments of the entire automobile industry. Designers for the new generation of trucks were to build on this foundation without putting the company's market leadership at risk. Bulin and Wolkonowicz were to assemble a pictorial history of truck designs as a resource for the designers and engineers. They were discouraged because they had concluded that truck designs had remained basically unchanged for years. Frustrated by this lack of innovation, they hatched a new plan. Although they did not know it at the time, this was a beginning of a fundamental change in how Ford designs its products.

Without any formal approval or funding, Bulin and Wolkonowicz chose to develop a new approach to thinking about vehicle design. They worked evenings and weekends out of a cramped basement office, maintaining their "official" jobs during the normal workday. They collected myriad examples of how designs for all sorts of products had changed over several decades. They noticed that many product designs changed at similar times, but they couldn't explain this phenomenon. Digging deeper, they collected information about trends in pop music, movies, fashion, wars, and economic

hardship and tried to correlate this information to design trends. They discovered that each generation is profoundly affected by events that occur between their teens and twenties, events that shape everything from their most basic social values to their tastes in consumer goods—including pick-up trucks.

Bulin and Wolkonowicz assembled their data on huge bulletin boards they wheeled around Ford, explaining it to anyone who would listen. Many were initially skeptical, but gradually they influenced first one designer and then another. Eventually, Bulin and Wolkonowicz wheeled their giant bulletin boards in front of the overall design project manager and his boss. These two managers were under considerable pressure to be conservative, so as not to jeopardize the popularity of Ford trucks. However, this new research indicated that if the design team did not develop a very different truck, the new model would be most attractive to a generation of buyers who were no longer in the truck-buying market.

Emboldened with the Bulin and Wolkonowicz data, the project managers pushed Ford's design team to incorporate this new perspective until it finally permeated the project, eventually influencing everything from wheel size to door designs. A year later, the vice president for truck operations saw the developing designs and was so impressed that he increased funding for the new approach and personally backed it.

The new truck was such a market success that it sold at the rate of 800,000 per year, ensuring Ford's market leadership. By now, the Bulin and Wolkonowicz approach to design had been given an official name, value group analysis, and its use had spread to other Ford divisions. The group vice president in charge of overhauling Ford's worldwide vehicle-development process explained that value group analysis had become "one of the building blocks of product development . . . giving Ford a real competitive advantage."

Ford's discovery of a new design process and the changes it wrought throughout the company is an example of organizational learning, the most promising means to bring about organizational change and implement strategies.[1] As you will discover in this chapter, many elements of organizational learning, strategy implementation, and organizational change are counterintuitive. At Ford, where did the learning and change start? How did it grow, and what contribution (or hindrance) came from managers at different organizational levels? Does this example fit your preconceived notions of how large organizations develop new capabilities and improve their competitiveness? Probably not. The impetus for the grand change at Ford was so obscure that when invitations for a celebration with Ford's senior executives were sent to the 400 designers and engineers on the new truck project, Bulin and Wolkonowicz were not even included on the list! Fortunately, the unlikely heroes heard the noise down the hall and investigated just in time to hear themselves singled out for their critically important contribution to fundamentally changing Ford Motor Company and making it a much more effective competitor.

The tale of how Bulin and Wolkonowicz contributed to organizational learning at Ford is a good example of the "middle-out-up-down" change process you will learn about later in this chapter. But we start our discussion of how organizations manage the change process by considering what makes change so difficult.

WHY STRATEGY IMPLEMENTATION IS SO DIFFICULT

Managers intent on implementing strategy must coordinate a broad range of efforts aimed at transforming strategic intentions into action. Resulting actions constitute the firm's realized strategy; and it reflects what an organization has done and ultimately determines how the organization will fare. Strategies that are not implemented, no matter how brilliant they may be, constitute little more than academic exercises. Consequently, the ability to implement strategies is one of the most valuable of all managerial skills.

Unfortunately, strategy implementation skills are not easily mastered. In fact, virtually all managers find implementation the most difficult aspect of their jobs—more difficult than strategic analysis or strategy formulation. One manager explained, "It has been rather easy for us to decide where we wanted to go. The hard part is to get the organization to act on the new priorities."[2] This experience is widespread. U.S. managers now spend an estimated $10 billion annually on strategic analysis and strategy formulation.[3] Managers themselves report that less than half the plans resulting from these efforts are ever implemented.[4] Outside observers put the success rate even lower: less than 10 percent.[5] Several factors impede strategy implementation.[6]

The Organizational Immune System

As strategies change, organizations usually move in new directions: strategy implementation is inextricably connected with organizational change.[7] Yet experience
shows that all organizations suffer from inertia to some degree—they try to maintain
the status quo and resist change.[8] As one researcher put it, "Change theory tells us
that human systems seek homeostasis and equilibrium; i.e., we prefer a predictable,
stable world."[9] Organizations regularly display commitment to the status quo, sometimes even when it yields unsatisfactory results.[10] Because humans naturally resist
change, organizations develop "immune systems" that leaders must overcome if they
hope to implement a new strategy successfully.[11] As examples in the next several chapters will illustrate, these behaviors range from passively rationalizing that change really is not necessary to actively setting out to sabotage change efforts.

Numerous Complex Variables

To translate planned organizational changes (called "intervention activities") into actions that bring desired organizational outcomes requires incorporating numerous

EXHIBIT 9.1
A Theoretical Model of the Dynamics of Planned Organizational Change

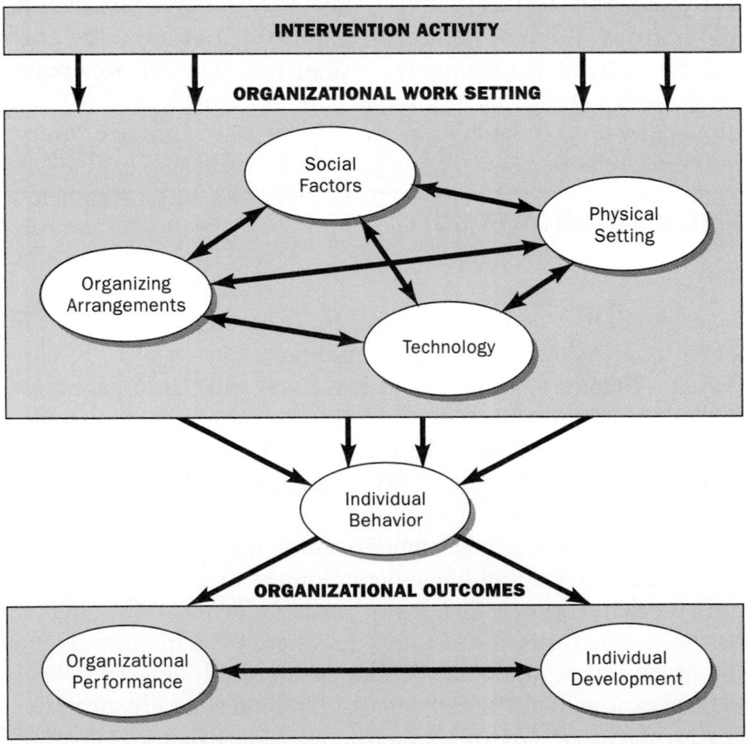

Source: Peter J. Robertson, Darryl R. Roberts, and Jerry I. Porras, "Dynamics of Planned Organizational Change: Assessing Empirical
Support for a Theoretical Model," *Academy of Management Journal, 36* (June 1993), 619–634. Reprinted by permission.

complex variables. Researchers have developed theoretical models of these, and Exhibit 9.1 reproduces one such model. Study how many elements there are in it, remember that all such models necessarily simplify reality, and you will begin to appreciate just how complex strategy implementation is.

The Interconnectedness of Elements Affecting Change

The arrows in Exhibit 9.1 indicate that changing one element of this model has a ripple effect that impacts other parts of the model, which in turn have their own ripple effects, and so on. One manager tried to explain her frustration in dealing with this extensive interconnectedness of factors affecting change in her organization: "I used to think that our organization was like a string: tug on one end of it, and the other end simply moves in the direction you pulled. However, it turned out that the string was really just a thread in a complexly woven fabric: pull on the single thread, and you run the danger of unraveling the whole thing."

The Need to Change "Everything at Once"

Because change factors interrelate, changing only one or two things seldom brings any significant overall organizational change. Managers who hope to change entire organizations by altering only one or two things are searching for a "magic bullet." But research and experience are most convincing on this point: there are no magic bullets.[12] To redirect organizations, managers address many overlapping and related issues, and the resulting impression of needing to change "everything at once" can be overwhelming. Exhibit 9.2 illustrates this point, using the 7-S model developed by consultants at McKinsey & Company who were trying to help managers address the difficulties of strategic change. Use of the 7-S model is illustrated in Application 9.1.

A COMMON PATTERN OF FAILURE: ACTIVITY-CENTERED CHANGE PROGRAMS

Given the difficulties inherent in organizational change and strategy implementation, it is easy to see why efforts at both so often fail. Researchers studying why change efforts are so often unsuccessful note a common failure pattern.[13] Dubbed the "activity-centered" approach to change, it focuses on the *activity* that is to affect the desired change, rather than on the *results* of the change. Managers often promote such activities through programs that become centerpieces of their change efforts. We refer to this approach as *activity-centered change programs*.

Activity-centered change programs are very common and yet consistently unsuccessful. As you read about these programs below, note how each element is individually rational—it makes sense when considered separately. Only when you consider the big picture do you see why activity-centered change programs so seldom work. The most important elements of this approach to change are identified in Exhibit 9.3 and illustrated below with a hypothetical example.

EXHIBIT 9.2
The McKinsey 7-S Framework

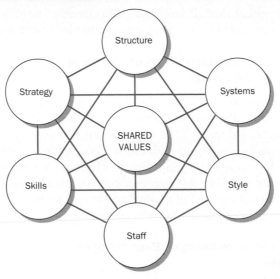

Strategy:	A set of decisions and actions aimed at gaining a sustainable competitive advantage (see Chaps. 1 and 2).
Structure:	The organization chart and associated information that shows who reports to whom and how tasks are both divided up and integrated (see Chap. 10).
Systems:	The flow of activities involved in the daily operation of a business, including its core processes (see Chap. 5) and its support systems (see Chap. 11).
Style:	How managers collectively spend their time and attention and how they use symbolic behavior. How management acts is more important than what management says.
Staff:	How companies develop employees and shape basic values (see human resourcing discussion in Chap. 11).
Shared values:	Commonly held beliefs, mindsets, and assumptions that shape how an organization behaves—its corporate culture (see Chap. 10).
Skills:	An organization's dominant capabilities and competencies (see Chap. 4).

1. *Senior management, dissatisfied with past performance, develops new strategic ideas requiring organizational change.* Dissatisfaction with the past is usually the primary reason for attempting to make a strategic change. For our hypothetical example, assume that, in the face of declining sales, senior managers decide to renew emphasis on customer satisfaction.

2. *They establish a "program" with the intention of producing the desired strategic change.* The intention here is to focus attention on the new idea and generate some excitement about the proposed change. To continue our hypothetical example, a program called "King Customer" is initiated.

Application 9.1

Applying McKinsey's 7-S Model

Consultants at McKinsey & Company developed the 7-S model in the late 1970s to help managers address the difficulties of change. The model shows that organizational immune systems and the many interconnected variables involved make change complex, and that an effective change effort must address many of these issues simultaneously. This is often a daunting managerial challenge. Consider the following case of an Australian company attempting to change the way it managed research and development.

Heightened competition led this firm to devise a new strategy to develop technologically advanced products to reestablish its competitive advantage. Central to this strategy was the firm's R&D laboratory, a facility that had been created to serve the firm's six operating divisions with cutting-edge technology. The firm had fallen far behind its competitors in the technology race, so an obvious problem faced managers before the new strategy, which placed even greater emphasis on technology, could be implemented. However, it was not at all clear where the problem lay or how to fix it. Careful analysis eventually uncovered a whole series of factors that limited the firm's success in commercializing technology. The 7-S framework revealed the following:

Strategy: There was no commonly understood strategy for the lab. For example, the operating division's view of research priorities conflicted with the lab's view.

Structure: The firm's structure clearly separated the lab and the operating divisions, as well as the different departments within the lab itself. The centralized lab and the six operating divisions did not interact; instead, division representatives visited the lab only once a year, on average. Meanwhile, technology commercialization was a strictly sequential process: first invention, then analysis of market potential, then analysis of production issues. The overall process was slow; even worse, many inventions proved nonviable once they reached operating divisions. Also, departments within the lab did not interact, which eliminated the opportunity for cross-fertilization of ideas that had originally motivated managers to create a centralized lab.

Systems: The laboratory was most affected by the system that allocated and controlled the use of capital funds. The lab developed annual budgets for R&D and

top management rubber-stamped them under pressure from the board of directors, who believed "research is good." After funding, there was no system for follow-up on the status of R&D investments or payback from the lab.

Staff: The laboratory was hamstrung by several ineffective and divisive human resource practices. For instance, managers were paid much more than researchers—a practice that encouraged the best researchers to get out of research and into management. Additionally, management pay at the lab was based on department size—encouraging turf battles and animosity among departments.

Skills: Both the laboratory and the operating divisions lacked critical skills for the new strategy's success. The researchers conducted good basic research but had little experience in developing commercially viable technology. The operating division managers knew little about building or marketing technologically advanced products.

Shared Values: The company shared no single organizational culture, and each level or function held different values. The board of directors may have believed "research is good," but the firm's general managers saw the laboratory as a "charity." The lab blamed the company's failures on the operating divisions' inability to utilize the lab's new technology, but the operating divisions thought the failures were due to the lab's inability to develop viable inventions.

Style: The lab managers' leadership style seemed to limit the lab's success. The head of the lab used a dictatorial leadership style, stressing top-down decisions and tight controls. Any celebrations of success were rare and not visible outside the individual lab departments involved.

To address these many problems, management decided to convert from a distant "lab in the woods" operation to a "client service" organization that depended on its service to the operating divisions. Such a transformation required that every one of the items listed above had to be rethought and changed—a mass assault on the old way of doing things. For example, under the "systems" heading, managers established a system that only funded the lab when it "sold" R&D services to operating divisions, and the operating divisions got monthly reports on

Application 9.1 (cont.)

how the lab was fulfilling its R&D contracts with them. Under "structure," the lab reorganized around the product lines represented by each of the divisions, rather than around areas of scientific expertise. As part of addressing "skills," 75 percent of the researchers attended a marketing course to learn about the issues of developing products with customer appeal. When these and many other changes were implemented, the strategy of using technology to reestablish a competitive advantage gradually emerged, and the firm began to win awards for its technologically superior products. The lab's $40 million annual budget began to yield a very attractive return for the business, and it soon became a benchmark operation that other organizations sought to emulate.

Source

This case is discussed in detail in Diane Grady and Tony Fincham, "Making R&D Pay," *McKinsey Quarterly* (Summer 1993), 161–175.

3. *Management of the program is delegated to those in staff positions.* Given senior management's wide-ranging responsibilities, they shift day-to-day oversight for the program to staff personnel who support line managers. Typically, the staff involved have expertise in the area chosen for change. In our example, the director of quality takes responsibility for the King Customer program.

4. *Staff personnel in charge of the program "handle" senior management.* Now, those who initiated the change remain committed to it, but their personal involvement is structured by their "handlers," a term commonly used to describe the staff who organize and orchestrate the activities of campaigning politicians. Similarly, the director of quality prepares several speeches that the CEO delivers during the kickoff for the King Customer program.

5. *The staff in charge of the program focus only on the range of issues under their direct control.* Most staff personnel have no formal authority over most of the organization, and they naturally focus most of their efforts on the limited areas where they have the greatest influence. Thus, changes are made only in staff operations that, hopefully, may indirectly impact line operations. To continue our example, the director of quality creates a new training and development program focused on quality management tools and offered to employees in line positions on a voluntary basis.

6. *Performance is measured by the success of the program rather than the success of the organization.* A widely touted management principle holds that performance evaluation should be limited to matters under the control of the person being evaluated. In our example, everyone in the organization recognizes that many factors influencing customer satisfaction (such as product design, after-sales service, and product pricing) are far outside the quality director's control. Therefore, performance improvement is measured in terms of the *program*'s success rather than in terms of customer satisfaction per se. For instance, success is based on the number of people who graduate from the training and development courses, rather than the improvements in the firm's competitiveness or financial performance.

7. *Even though most of the organization is unchanged, the program is declared a success.* With the narrow performance criteria by which it is judged, the program is "suc-

EXHIBIT 9.3
Activity-Centered Change Programs: A Common Pattern of Failure

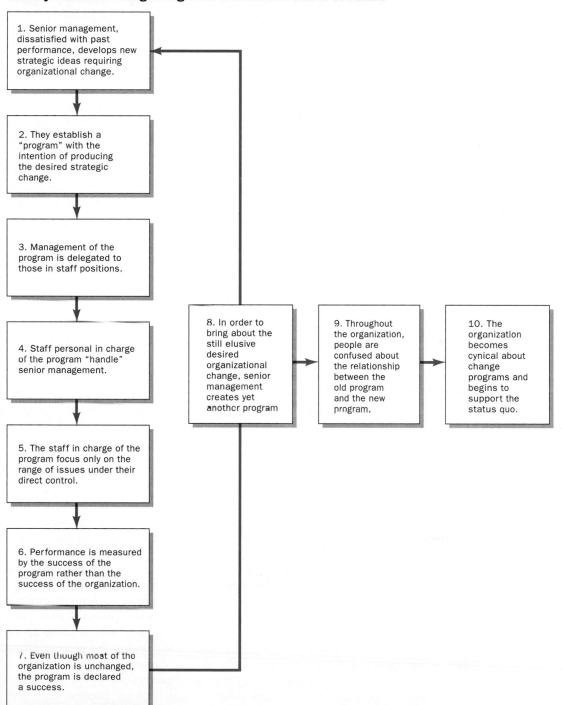

1. Senior management, dissatisfied with past performance, develops new strategic ideas requiring organizational change.

2. They establish a "program" with the intention of producing the desired strategic change.

3. Management of the program is delegated to those in staff positions.

4. Staff personal in charge of the program "handle" senior management.

5. The staff in charge of the program focus only on the range of issues under their direct control.

6. Performance is measured by the success of the program rather than the success of the organization.

7. Even though most of the organization is unchanged, the program is declared a success.

8. In order to bring about the still elusive desired organizational change, senior management creates yet another program

9. Throughout the organization, people are confused about the relationship between the old program and the new program.

10. The organization becomes cynical about change programs and begins to support the status quo.

321

cessful" even if the desired strategic change was never really manifested. Given that the quality director opted to focus on training, a limited activity, it's no surprise that most of the organization was minimally affected by the program. Nonetheless, as performance was assessed in terms of the program's success rather than the overall firm's success, the director of quality has good performance data on the change effort to report back to senior managers.

8. *In order to bring about the still elusive desired organizational change, senior management creates yet another program.* Because the first program was "successful" but still fell short of implementing the desired change, it is easy to conclude that it must be supplemented with another change effort. Although senior managers can see from the quality director's data that the King Customer program was a success in getting many people trained in quality management, many other issues in customer satisfaction remain unaddressed. For instance, cost increases have resulted in rising prices, which customers have complained about. To address this issue, the controller is put in charge of a new program intended to reduce selected costs by 50 percent, called "Have to Halve It."

9. *Throughout the organization, people are confused about the relationship between the old program and the new program.* Because each program typically addresses only a subset of the total issues involved in the desired change, many programs overlap and conflict.[14] When members of the organization learn of the new program, they are unsure of how to balance efforts between the newly acquired quality management tools and the new cost-cutting program. More than one employee is heard to mutter something to the effect that "if they really want to cut costs, they can begin by not pulling us off the line to attend courses like the one I attended last month on quality."

10. *The organization becomes cynical about change programs and begins to support the status quo.* Frustration develops because it is easy to see that even though the King Customer program was declared a victory, the customer is in fact not treated like royalty in most of what the organization does. And because the Have to Halve It program is only the most recent in what is becoming a steady stream of marginally successful programs, each derisively referred to as "the flavor of the month," employees begin to look at each new program as more of a bother than a solution.[15] Consequently, they try to avoid personal involvement in all subsequent programs as much as possible, reminding one another that "this, too, shall pass."

In this scenario, customer satisfaction failed to improve, and the organization in fact became more entrenched in the very status quo that senior managers had originally set out to change. Clearly, this is a failed attempt at strategy implementation and organizational change. But if you review each of the ten steps that led to this undesired outcome, it is also clear that there is some rational logic behind every action taken. In other words, there is no single mistake that derailed the change effort; rather, it was the general approach taken, the activity-centered program approach, that was inappropriate. Although managing through inputs is one of the most commonly observed approaches to implementing strategic change because each step "feels right," it very seldom has the desired impact on results because of the ineffectiveness of the overall process. Before we can move on to a discussion of more promising approaches to strategy implementation, we need to take a closer look at the nature of change.

A MODEL OF CHANGE AND ITS IMPLICATIONS FOR STRATEGY IMPLEMENTATION

Adaptive Versus Generative Changes

Research shows that organizations change and make progress through what has been called the punctuated equilibrium model.[16] As shown in Exhibit 9.4, in a model similar to the one you first saw in Chapter 5, *punctuated equilibrium* entails two levels of organizational change, adaptive and generative. In this view of the change process, progress occurs through an alternating series of long evolutionary periods in which incremental adaptive changes take place, divided by shorter periods of revolutionary upheaval, in which generative changes take place.[17] The adaptive changes are incremental and evolutionary in nature, somewhat analogous to the concept of "working *in* the system" (from Chapter 5) in that they are more likely directed toward changes in day-to-day organizational transactions rather than toward broader organizational transformations. This emphasis on transactions implies that administration is an important part of management's work in changes of this limited scope.[18] On the other hand, generative change more likely entails a quantum breakthrough, a type of change that is not evolutionary but revolutionary; that is, it generates an essentially new way of doing things.[19] We sometimes refer to such changes as "transformational" rather than "transactional," and they require a managerial emphasis on leadership in-

EXHIBIT 9.4

In the Punctuated Equilibrium Model, Progress Depends on Two Types of Change: Adaptive and Generative

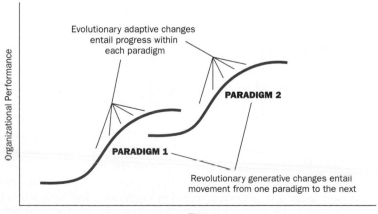

stead of administration. Such changes are roughly analogous to what we called "work-ing *on* the system" in Chapter 5.

The generative changes and revolutionary upheavals shown in Exhibit 9.4 are sometimes called "paradigm shifts." A *paradigm* is an accepted view of the world and how it works, or, as one writer put it, "A paradigm, in its business connotation, is the conventional wisdom about how things have always been done and must continue to be done."[20] As this quotation suggests and research confirms, shifts in paradigms are typified not by smooth transitions but by disruptive breaks.[21] These breaks provide the "punctuation" within the punctuated equilibrium model. Between paradigm shifts we go through relatively stable periods that are closer to equilibrium, during which incremental changes are made within the context of the current paradigm.

Single- and Double-Loop Learning

Coping with these two levels of organizational change entails two corresponding levels of organizational learning. Chris Argyris, a longtime researcher on how organizations learn, calls these single-loop and double-loop learning.[22] The classic example of single-loop learning is the thermostat. Upon discovery of a deviation away from a prescribed temperature, the thermostat triggers the preprogrammed action of heating or cooling. If the thermostat were capable of considering and changing its operation—if it could consider the wisdom of its programming and adjust it accordingly—it would be capable of double-loop learning. In other words, double-loop learning entails questioning and adjusting the underlying policies and objectives that shape the way in which organizations operate. Stephen Covey, an expert on leadership, makes a similar point about levels of learning, using a different metaphor.[23] He says that one level of learning, well suited to management, is like climbing a ladder; but a higher level of learning, one that requires leadership, involves questioning whether or not the ladder is leaning against the right wall.

These examples can help you link single-loop and double-loop learning back to the concepts of adaptive and generative changes introduced in the punctuated equilibrium model. When Argyris's thermostat follows its program without question, all changes are adaptive: when the temperature drops, the thermostat adapts by turning on the heat. However, if the thermostat raises questions about the desired temperature to maintain and adjusts its programming accordingly, the change is generative, because a new program is generated as a result of the change process.

Or consider that an organization attempts to use Covey's ladder in response to a flood. As the water rises, one response would be to climb the ladder to a higher level and wait for a rescue, an adaptive solution for coping with the situation that Covey would equate with management. An alternative is to take the ladder down and use it as a frame for building a raft that can be poled to safety, a generative solution that results in the creation of something entirely different from what was previously available for the organization to draw on. Covey would identify this level of change as one calling for not just management, but leadership. Other experts on the subject have drawn a similar distinction between management and leadership, explaining that management is appropriate for overseeing the transactions involved in single-loop learning, while leadership is required to successfully bring about the transformations entailed in double-loop learning.[24]

In organizational learning, strategy formulation becomes interwoven with strategy implementation, and this interweaving results in a single process formed by blending two ingredients: discovery and action. *Discovery* is the intellectual part of learning—the abstract mental and conceptual process whereby we change our mindsets, thoughts, and opinions about the way things are or should be. *Action* is the behavioral side of learning—what we do differently as a result of new discoveries. Of the two, discovery is closer to strategy formulation, while action is more akin to strategy implementation. As we have stressed, both discovery/formulation and action/implementation are essential to organizational learning. Let us now turn to a more detailed look at discovery and action as the key components of organizational learning.

The Need for Both

Some analysts equate progress with the dramatic disruption that comes with paradigm shifts, but this is not a well-balanced view. To understand why, we can draw an analogy between technological progress and organizational progress. Most people believe that the greatest technological advance in the development of modern lighting was made when Edison invented the electric light bulb. However, Edison's invention is a distant and clearly inferior relative of the light bulbs we have today. True, Edison's creation represents a paradigm shift that resulted in the world's moving from gas to electricity, but afterward there were hundreds of smaller changes that gradually made the light bulb what it is today. In other words, the paradigm shift established a foundation upon which to improve, but the cumulative impact of all these smaller changes has been more significant than the initial improvement from gas to electricity.[25]

The punctuated equilibrium model of organizational progress notes that significant advances take place through *both* evolutionary and revolutionary change and *both* single- and double-loop learning. The double-loop learning entailed in shifting paradigms establishes a new way of seeing the world, a new order of things. But it may take the organization years, even decades, to fully realize the potential gains the new paradigm carries with it through a long period of single-loop learning. So, in order to maximize their progress, organizations must be capable of managing both types of learning and change, or as one research team put it, they need to be "dynamically stable."[26] In other words, an organization needs to be dynamic enough to cope with the double-loop learning and paradigm shifts entailed in the punctuated portion of our model of progress but stable enough to make steady progress through single-loop learning during the periods of relative equilibrium.

Many managers see this as asking too much of them and of their organizations. Business writer Tom Peters reports that many would-be leaders are stymied by what he sees as the ultimate catch-22: "Success is the product of deep grooves. Deep grooves destroy adaptability that is the key to success."[27] Peters's success through "deep grooves" depends on a commitment to holding things relatively stable while endless evolutionary changes are made, an indication of strong faith in the current paradigm. However, faith in the paradigm that deep grooves represent also limits an organization's willingness to break out of the groove and make revolutionary changes. In Peters's view, too many managers want to focus on making progress through evolutionary changes (digging deeper grooves) or revolutionary changes (jumping out of the groove) when what their organizations need is a combination of both types of progress. Another expert on this subject has put it this way:

> The first step in restoring a company's lost vitality is avoiding the false choice between evolution and revolution. . . . Effective renewal requires a combination of step-function changes together with an ongoing process of evolutionary "reconditioning," which enhances learning and helps ready people for the next step-function change.[28]

All of this suggests that organizations need to be proficient at both single-loop and double-loop learning, and with this in mind, we turn now to a description of organizational learning and a discussion of how to manage it.

ORGANIZATIONAL LEARNING

As we have already stated, learning, regardless of whether it is the single-loop or double-loop variety, entails two elements: discovery and action. Application 9.2 shows how Chaparral Steel encourages both elements of learning, and we take a detailed look at both parts below.

Discovery

What should organizations attempt to discover as part of the learning process? For the most part, they do *not* need to discover fundamentally new principles. Ageless principles, such as those underlying the trade-offs depicted in Exhibit 9.5, have organized, managed, and led people for centuries, and rarely do managers discover a completely new management or organization principle.

Consider, for instance, the various quotes presented in Exhibit 9.6. While the concepts being discussed in these quotes are thoroughly modern sounding, each quote is, in fact, decades old. This is not to say that the practice of management has not progressed in the decades since these statements were first made. But fundamental issues have long existed and will long exist, and the search for fundamentally new ideas is not the most useful focus for applied organizational learning. A better focus is a consideration of how managers should address these fundamental issues in a specific organization. In other words, in making the trade-offs given in Exhibit 9.5, what works for your particular situation?

Experimentation: The Key to Discovery

Discovering what works requires that managers understand the causal links between inputs and outputs. In Chapter 4, we described management based on inputs (i.e., managing programs, activities, or efforts without focusing on results) and management based on outputs (i.e., management that stresses performance and results with little consideration given to means), and we discussed the deficiencies of both these approaches. Organizational learning addresses these deficiencies by looking not only at inputs and outputs, but also at the causal links between the two. In other words, understanding what works means understanding how cause X is related to effect Y.

When it comes to searching for cause-effect relationships, perhaps the most suit-

Application 9.2

Chaparral Steel: Habits That Lead to Organizational Learning

Under the leadership of its CEO, Gordon Forward, Chaparral Steel has emerged as one of the most innovative and successful firms in an industry recognized for innovation and success. Asked what explains the firm's success, Forward simply replies, "We are a learning organization." The organization has built its learning ways on four habits, each reflecting different activities, values, and support systems, as shown in the table below.

The first habit is spreading ownership for problem solving organizationwide, a habit based on the assumption that all employees have the potential to contribute to the success of the enterprise, or they would not be there. This attitude may best be summarized in the philosophy of "adultery" as practiced by Forward: "We treat everyone like an adult." Adultery is explained by a foreman as follows: "Whoever comes up with an idea on how to fix something, from the millwright or myself right on up to the top, does it right then." The emphasis is on discovering what works and then standardizing the newly discovered best practice. As the same foreman explains, "If it works, it is the de facto standard. If it improves performance, everyone will imitate it."

The second habit involves actively seeking out and acting on knowledge generated within the firm. For example, Chaparral makes much of the equipment that other steel companies would buy, based on the reasoning that

this gives them insights into how their plants can best work. The company has also made a tremendously high investment in the development of its employees. Its $3^{1}/_{2}$-year program, in which an apprentice progresses to the level of a senior operator, requires successfully completing 7,280 hours of on-the-job training and formal schooling; much of the latter takes place during 4 hours a week of unpaid time. There is impressive data showing that these unusual practices pay off: the two foundries, designed for annual volumes of 250,000 and 500,000 tons, in fact produce more than 600,000 tons and 1 million tons, respectively.

The third habit is an eagerness to tap external expertise. Chapparral builds alliances with firms from around the world with expertise that complements its in-house skills. While many organizations resist outside innovations "not invented here," Chaparral's concern is that innovations are "not reinvented here." Each year, dozens of employees from across the organizational hierarchy travel to visit customers, suppliers, and even competitors who might be able to teach Chaparral some better way of doing things.

The final habit is one of constantly challenging the status quo. As one observer of the company summarized it, "Chaparral employees are skilled experimenters." Forward describes innumerable large and small experiments

Learning Habit	Manifested Activity	Managerial Value	Supporting Systems
Spreading ownership for problem solving organizationwide	Independent discovery of what works	Egalitarianism	Performance-based rewards
Garnering and integrating internal knowledge	Integrating internal knowledge	Knowledge is a "community" resource	Education and development
Creating the virtual corporation to tap external knowledge	Integrating external information	Openness to outside input	Resourcing alliances and networks
Challenging the status quo	Experimentation	Risk is a positive	Hiring practices and career paths

of the "cut-and-try" variety. Often these experiments are not sophisticated, just effective. For instance, Chaparral became the first minimill capable of shaping molten steel in the near-net shape required for large I-beams. The early prototypes for some of the equipment needed for such casting were made from plywood that was continuously soaked with water to keep it from being consumed by the molten steel just long enough for the crews to prove the potential of the design concept.

Perhaps the most important managerial value supporting such experimentation is the firm's tolerance for taking risks and making mistakes. A former mill superin-

tendent championed the installation of a $1.5 million saw for cutting finished beams that, after months of effort, still could not be made effectively. Shortly after the superintendent made the decision to get rid of the saw, he was promoted to vice president of operations.

Sources
Dorothy Leonard-Barton, "The Factory as a Learning Laboratory," *Sloan Management Review, 34* (Fall 1992), 23–38; G. Forward, interviewed by A. M. Kantrow, "Wide-Open Management at Chaparral Steel," *Harvard Business Review* (May–June 1986), 96–102.

able model that emerges is the method of experimentation that allows the most efficient scientific progress, the *scientific method*, shown in Exhibit 9.7. This process begins with a *theory*. While some see little room for theories in something as practical as a business organization's attempting to discover what works, experienced observers find that theories can be both practical and useful to leaders attempting organizational change. For instance, Peter Drucker argued that every business operates on the basis of a theory that reflects assumptions about such things as its environment, its mission, and the competencies it needs to accomplish its mission.[29] Peter Senge, a leading researcher and consultant on learning organizations, refers to such decisions and behavior-shaping assumptions as "mental models."[30] Regardless of the term used, the point is that adjustments to a firm's theory or mental model carry tremendous potential to redirect the organization's thinking and its future prospects. Continuing our description of the scientific method, a *hypothesis* simply speculates about a theorized cause-effect relationship, and presents a testable question about what works, developed as an outgrowth of the theory of the business. Hypotheses are tested by *experimentation*, the *results* of which determine *conclusions*, which then lead to refinements of the *theory*.

The slab-breaking example given in Application 9.3 on Globe Metallurgical provides a simple illustration of each part of the scientific method. In this example, someone hypothesized that a separate slab-breaking step was unnecessary, because dropping the slabs into the truck (an input, or cause) would break them up sufficiently (an output, or effect). The hypothesis was tested by simply trying out the idea, that is, performing an experiment. The result was favorable, and a conclusion was reached that changed the assumptions about how the business could best be operated. While this is a classic example of the use of the scientific method, note that the approach is hardly esoteric. In fact, experimentation and the scientific method are simply the most pragmatic means available for discovering new solutions to practical problems. In fact, studies of especially long-lived organizations have concluded that "the key to survival is the ability to run 'experiments at the margin,' to continually explore new business and organizational opportunities that create potential new sources of growth."[31]

EXHIBIT 9.5
Examples of the Trade-offs Involved in Addressing "Timeless Principles"

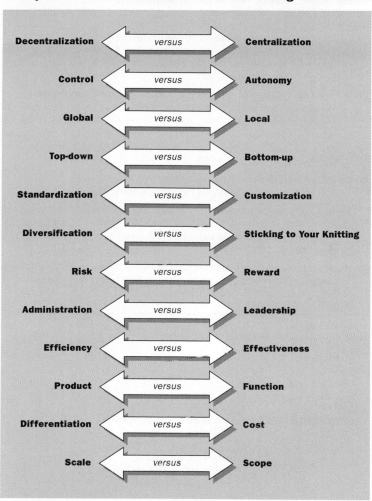

Decentralization	*versus*	Centralization
Control	*versus*	Autonomy
Global	*versus*	Local
Top-down	*versus*	Bottom-up
Standardization	*versus*	Customization
Diversification	*versus*	Sticking to Your Knitting
Risk	*versus*	Reward
Administration	*versus*	Leadership
Efficiency	*versus*	Effectiveness
Product	*versus*	Function
Differentiation	*versus*	Cost
Scale	*versus*	Scope

Developing a Tolerance for Mistakes

Experimentation by definition is a trial-and-error process, and no one is going to be willing to undertake a trial if the risk associated with making an error is too great. Yet without trials and errors, how can organizations hope to make progress on their most challenging problems?[32] Take the issue of total quality management (TQM). One of the most important principles of TQM is the concept of zero defects, perfectly error-free production. One of the ironies of the search for zero defects is that no organization is capable of figuring out how to operate error free without a tremendous amount of trial-and-error experimentation. Thus, the only way to become perfect is to make a lot of mistakes. Therefore, leaders seeking error-free performance need to

EXHIBIT 9.6
Some Quotes About "Modern" Management

On empowering horizontal, cross-functional teams:
> Authority should go with knowledge, no matter if it is up the line or down the line. Emphasize "cross-functioning" and replace vertical authority with horizontal authority.—Mary Parker Follet, *Dynamic Administration,* 1947

On the need for widespread involvement in strategic management issues:
> The more complex an organization becomes, the more sense it makes for top executives to relinquish control. Such delegation will speed and improve decisions because those deciding are close to the problem, reduce friction among executives and increase their desire to do a better job, and allow senior executives more time for planning and thinking.—"The New Management," *Fortune,* 1955

On the importance of customers and quality:
> General Electric is a customer-focused company.—GE CEO, 1956

> To design, process, and sell products competitively in the marketplace, businessmen must take full account of a crucial trend: Customers, both industrial and consumer, have been increasing their quality requirements very sharply in recent years.—"Total Quality Control," *Harvard Business Review,* 1956

On the importance of core competence in establishing a competitive advantage:
> Distinctive competencies are paramount in achieving and maintaining competitive advantage.—Selznick, *Leadership in Administration,* 1957

Source: These and other examples can be found in Robert G. Eccles and Nitin Nohria, *Beyond the Hype: Rediscovering the Essence of Management,* Boston: Harvard Business School Press, 1992.

EXHIBIT 9.7
The Scientific Method as a Model for Discovery

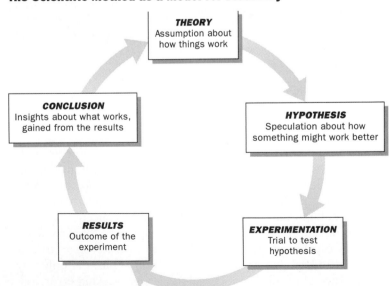

Application 9.3

Globe Metallurgical: A Pragmatic Experimenter

Globe Metallurgical is a small, profitable producer of high-value-added special metals marketed to the chemical and foundry industries worldwide. The company has won quality awards in a number of countries and is considered one of the most innovative in its industry. However, not long ago, Globe was a textbook example of everything that was ailing the rust belt industries of the United States: outmoded equipment, terrible labor relations, undifferentiated products, and uncompetitive cost structures. Arden Sims, the firm's CEO, initially tackled these problems by cutting costs to regain competitiveness. But slashed salaried positions and revamped operations proved ineffective in addressing the competitive situation, and the weakening company was threatened with bankruptcy.

Backed into a corner and fighting for its life, the company began to experiment, and during an 8-year transformation process the firm showed that it was capable of learning dramatically new ways of operating. The changes were not the result of some insightful master plan; rather, faced with a series of crises, Globe set about to find out what might work better than its old ways.

In reflecting on this learning process, Sims said, "I didn't know what would replace the old ways. In some cases, I found the solution myself, in other cases, someone directed me there, and in still other cases, the solution evolved over time through trying one thing, then trying something else." Some of the innovations were the result of serendipity, but, regardless of the source, once a useful insight was discovered, Sims skillfully turned it into a new standard for operating the firm.

One of the most significant periods for learning came while one of the firm's two plants was shut down by a strike. During this period, Sims and a team of thirty-five salaried workers operated the plant by working 12-hour shifts, 7 days a week, for nearly a year. Sims described the period as follows: "The strike was a time of great stress, but also a time of great progress. We experimented with everything. . . . We were operating in a very

fast, continuous-improvement mode. Every day, people would suggest ways to improve the operation of the furnaces or the additive process or the way we transported materials around the plants. I kept a pocket notebook, and if I saw something, I'd jot it down and discuss it with the team over coffee or during a meal. I filled a notebook every day."

The development of a new process for breaking slabs offers a good example of how this learning process took place. Over a meal, workers discussed how to break up metal slabs after they had cooled in trays 8 feet across and 8 inches thick. Traditionally, the slabs had been positioned on top of a grate, where machines broke them into pieces; when the pieces were small enough, they fell through the grate into a transportation bin and were carried away by forklift and dumped into a bulk storage area. However, the two managers who were supervising this process thought that if the slabs were dumped directly into the bed of a dump truck, that alone might break them sufficiently and the pieces could then go directly into the storage bin. With Sims's encouragement, after the meal, the managers rounded up a truck, tried their idea, and discovered that it worked. This eliminated two around-the-clock jobs, or eight positions altogether, an annual saving of more than $300,000 for the reduced labor alone.

Thanks to such changes, a few weeks after the strike began, the plant was actually able to increase its output by 20 percent over prestrike levels, and in the strike's tenth month the plant began to turn a profit.

Sources
Bruce Rayner, "Trial-by-Fire Transformation: An Interview with Globe Metallurgical's Arden C. Sims," *Harvard Business Review* (May–June 1992), 116–129; John S. McClenahen, "Globe's World," *Industry Week, 240* (July 15, 1991), 22–28; "Malcolm Baldrige National Quality Award: Globe Metallurgical Inc.," *Business America, 109* (December 5, 1988), 10–11.

---

be supportive of experimentation and condone mistakes that are made in an effort to improve. Ralph Stayer, the innovative CEO of Johnsonville Foods, sends this same message when he tells his organization, "Anything worth doing is worth doing poorly." In other words, if it is important for us to be able to do something, we ought to be willing to tolerate some mistakes in learning how to do it.

Few students realize that behind most great companies there is a long history of mistakes and failures.[33] Sony's first product, a rice cooker, never worked properly, and its first major innovation, a tape recorder, was a complete flop in the market. (The company managed to survive its early years by stitching wires to cloth to make crude heating pads.) Wal-Mart is the strongest retailer in the world today, but the first store opened by Sam Walton, Wal-Mart's founder, ended nightmarishly, because of several bad business arrangements. Hewlett-Packard had what must have seemed like an unending stream of product failures before finally selling a set of audio oscillators to a struggling young animator named Walt Disney to use on a harebrained movie entitled *Fantasia*. What each of these examples shows is that the key to eventual success is a tolerance for the mistakes inevitably associated with trying anything new.

Leaders can take action to show tolerance for mistakes and thereby encourage experimentation. Bill Gore, the pioneering founder of the privately held W. L. Gore, explained his position on mistakes by using the metaphor of a ship's waterline. He constantly reminded his associates that a ship can tolerate a great many holes above its waterline, while a single one below its waterline will sink it. His message was that an organization should constantly be carrying out small "above-the-waterline" experiments in order to avoid making any big "below-the-waterline" mistakes.

For example, one successful CEO signals his tolerance for making mistakes by telling all new managers that, in their first year, they were to make $50,000 worth of mistakes or they would have to report back to him explaining why they did not. This mandate sounds ridiculous until you consider it from the CEO's position, and he was able to give several reasons why his order made perfect sense. First, the new managers were the least committed to the status quo, and therefore they were the most likely to be willing to try new things if given the freedom to do so. Second, the corporation consisted of some twenty plants, all of which were very similar to one another, so any new discovery made at one plant could be applied at all the others, but any mistake covered up at one plant could also be repeated at all the others. Third, the CEO knew that the new managers were going to make mistakes anyway, so it was much better to sanction them so that they could be openly discussed and addressed, rather than covered up. Finally, the CEO felt that it was important for managers to try things and make mistakes before they were promoted to a level at which mistakes would more likely be measured in hundreds of thousands of dollars than in tens of thousands.

The tolerance for "above-the-waterline" errors and conflicts we have been discussing in this section has implications about where in an organization it is most appropriate to learn through experimentation. Errors made at the top of an organization's hierarchy are more likely to be "below-the-waterline" hits that can sink an organization, which means that senior managers have to be very careful with their experiments. On the other hand, experiments carried out by individuals at the very bottom of the hierarchy are more likely to have a limited impact that falls short of changing the organizationwide mental models involved in organizational learning.[34] This suggests that the middle of the organization is the most fertile ground for organizational learning through experimentation, which leads us to the next section.

Change from the Middle: The MOUND Model of Experimentation and Learning

Organizations often learn most effectively through a process of experimentation described by the MOUND model, for "Middle, Out, Up, 'n' Down."[35] Exhibit 9.8 depicts the process, and the example below illustrates it.

- *The "middle" phase.* In the early 1980s, Northern Telecom Inc. (NTI), the U.S. division of the Canadian-based telecommunications equipment maker, was experiencing dangerously low levels of financial performance.[36] Concern for the firm's chances of survival was widespread, and many different ideas floated around about what the organization should do to save itself. Deep inside the operations group, a small band of first- and second-line managers began to wonder if the major problem with NTI was that it was just too slow. Competitors could develop new products faster than NTI, and they could bring these new products to market faster. In a technology-driven business like telecommunications, being slow was a serious competitive disadvantage. To test their hypothesis about what should be done to improve NTI, this group began to make small experiments: small enough, in fact, so that they did not have to get anyone's permission or any specially allocated funding to do so. Most of these early experiments were directed at learning how to work horizontally and do the parallel development work described in Chapter 5.

EXHIBIT 9.8
The MOUND Model of Change

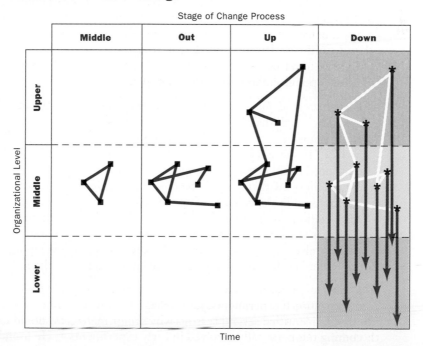

- *The "out" phase.* The group's initial experiments tested new ways of involving Manufacturing in the product development process so that, when designs came out, they were manufacturable and the manufacturing operation was already set up to produce them. The group first tried this new approach (an approach now widely known as concurrent engineering) on a single component part, but as the idea proved to have merit and the group members learned more about how to speed up the process, their confidence grew and they advocated spreading the practice to other units similar to their own.

- *The "up" phase.* Although the experiments had made some impressive improvements, they were still isolated enough so that they had virtually no impact on the firm's financial security. However, over the course of more than a year of experimenting with faster ways of bringing new products to market, the growing band of middle managers involved in the process began attracting increasing attention from senior managers, who were still desperately looking for ways to improve the firm's financial performance. When a new chief financial officer was promoted out of a unit that had enjoyed some success with reducing product development cycle times, he took news of the middle-management experiments to senior management. With the promising results of the low-level experiments to back him up, he was able to convince the other senior managers of the division to seriously consider personally endorsing speed as a competitive weapon for NTI.[37]

- *The "down" phase.* Despite the top-management team's skepticism, results now coming from the middle of the organization were too impressive to ignore. After taking a tour to personally observe the results of the experiments, the president announced that speed was essential to NTI's success as a competitor in the telecommunications industry. Senior management pushed metrics into place to evaluate most parts of the business on their reductions in cycle time, changes were made to the organization to allow it to work faster, and parts of the organization that had never paid much attention to speed now placed great emphasis on it.
    Three points emerge from this example:

- *A supporting role for senior managers.* Our culture enjoys the image of a powerful hero who single-handedly works miracles to save organizations. But the NTI example shows a very different leadership role. Although the publicity associated with NTI's success gave much of the credit to the president for birthing the idea that speed could become a competitive weapon, the president himself insisted during an interview that it would be more appropriate to say that he acted as midwife who assisted in the delivery of an idea conceived and gestated much lower in the organization. In this model of discovery through experimentation, the role of leaders is to nurture an environment in which experimentation can take place. As we have already suggested, one of the keys to this is developing a culture that not only tolerates, but also encourages, making mistakes in the name of learning.

- *Reasons to limit senior-management involvement early in the process.* In his research on organizational experiments, James Brian Quinn, a leading expert on strategic change, identified several reasons why senior managers should carefully avoid becoming too personally involved in early experiments.[38] He found that the most ef-

fective top executives often avoided becoming personally identified with early experiments in order (1) to avoid escalating attention to any one hypothesis until it
had been proven, (2) to allow ownership and commitment for an idea to grow
through the organization, (3) to avoid having their personal credibility damaged
by an idea that did not work out, and (4) to delay top management's commitment
to something until the last moment and thus obtain the best possible match between what the organization did and what changing conditions dictated.[39]

■ *The importance of middle-up influence.* Although middle managers are often labeled
as stumbling blocks to organizational change,[40] this model of change places
tremendous responsibility on them. As Quinn describes the process of discovery
through experimentation, "The guiding executive merely provides broad goals, a
proper climate, and flexible resource support. From there on, the real momentum
comes from below, with the executive making the final choices based on performance shoot-outs." This conclusion is very similar to one reached by Michael
Beer when he summarized his research on how firms make organizationwide
changes. His research team made an in-depth study of six different types of efforts
to make wholesale changes in organizations, and they found only one that had
been truly successful. "With this one," he reports, "the change began way before
the CEO became fully aware of it. It was started in a small plant by some innovative managers. The top learned about it from the lowest level and then spread the
best practices around the company."[41] This is an excellent description of the
MOUND model of learning.

The MOUND model does not in any way diminish the critical role of leadership
in learning. Although senior managers should not be too personally involved in many
of the experiments that lie at the heart of organizational learning, leaders are still critical to supporting the experimentation process and seeing that the organization acts
on the results.

Action

When most people think of learning, they focus on discovery, the act of obtaining
new knowledge. We think discovery alone falls short of the mark. Knowledge without
action offers little value to organizations attempting to improve their performance, in
the same way that strategy formulation without strategy implementation contributes
little practical significance. Senge has argued that one of the most fundamental misunderstandings about organizational learning is the idea that "learning or knowledge
does not need to be related to action."[42]

In their seminal research on what distinguishes excellent companies from all others, Tom Peters and Robert Waterman concluded:

> There is no more important trait among the excellent companies than an action orienta-
> tion . . . a bias for action, for getting on with it. Even though these companies may be ana-
> lytical in their approach to decision making, they are not paralyzed by that fact as so many
> seem to be. In many of these companies, the standard operating procedure is "Do it, fix it,
> try it."[43]

As this quotation suggests, too many companies seem willing to analyze a problem but unwilling to act on the analysis.[44] Most managers will admit that their organizations already know how to do things better than they are in fact done. Most organizations evidence a breakdown between what we know (discovery) and what we do (action).

Three factors contribute to this breakdown. First, it is much easier to talk about what should be done than to actually do it. Actually trying to do something new is what triggers the organizational "immune system" and the resistance to change we introduced earlier. Second, new thoughts can be private, and so no one may know if they are wrong, but changes in organizational action are public, and mistakes are visible to others. Finally, to make a new action "stick," firms often change a wide variety of organizational factors such as rewards, structure, and culture, and these changes may create hurdles that seem too great to clear.

Because of such factors, organizations often gravitate to analysis of the most intractable and difficult-to-solve problems, because the impossibility of solving such problems excuses the organization from doing anything at all. One organization typifies this approach especially well. Corporate headquarters pressured the firm to improve earnings growth, and the top-management team met and identified twelve different areas of opportunity—so far, so good. But then the team refused to narrow down the list or to focus on actually taking advantage of one or two opportunities. Instead, they insisted on detailed studies of all twelve options. These studies lasted nearly a year, and during this time more than one of the managers revealed that they were happy to work on them because they knew nothing would ever be done with them—and they were right! Each of the studies concluded that growth based on the particular opportunity under consideration would depend on something outside the firm's control or something virtually impossible to change (such as changes in federal regulations that might create new demand for the product), and thus it gave the management team a good excuse for not taking any action at all.

Several factors about this company and its experience make this story sad. First, its management team chose to engage in "busywork" rather than meaningful activity. Second, the organization lacked a shared vision of how to attack problems. Third, the organizational culture encouraged managers to identify what could *not* be done about a problem rather than actually do something about it. Finally, the organization was filled with roadblocks that limited progress and provided ready excuses for inaction.

You may conclude that this organization was exceptionally poorly run and that this is atypical, but we have seen many such organizations. And yet there are counterexamples, organizations that eagerly seek out opportunities to discover new insights and then act on them—organizations that prefer action and change to justification of the status quo. These learning organizations share one important feature: they are influenced by leaders who encourage and facilitate both the discovery *and* the action entailed in organizational learning. Leaders can encourage their organizations to act on their discoveries using two complementary means. We describe these as backing winning ideas and exercising "tough love" on ideas that prove less promising.

Backing Winners

In order for experiments to result in organizationwide change, senior managers must back the most promising results. This is the "down" phase of the MOUND model of organizational learning. Research shows that organizations become emboldened to make major changes through reinforcement of smaller changes that are headed in the right direction.[45] Michael Beer again:

> In order for change to spread throughout an organization and become a permanent fixture, it appears that early successes are needed. . . . When individuals, groups, and whole organizations feel more competent than they did before the change, this increased sense of competence reinforces the new behavior and solidifies learning-associated change.[46]

In other words, one of leaders' key roles is to ferret out which experiments offer the most promising results and then to back these winners. But what does a leader actually do in backing a winner? In the following three chapters, we will consider in more detail the "levers" leaders can use to back winning ideas and spread the new discoveries and actions that result from the learning process throughout the organization. We discuss these as context levers, systems levers, and action levers. As you will learn, each type of lever offers leaders an opportunity to facilitate learning and spreading new organizational practices. However, before we move on to these chapters, we want you to understand that the complement to supporting selected new initiatives is deemphasizing others, a part of leadership we call "tough love."

Exercising Tough Love

Although leaders may devote themselves to encouraging experimentation, at some point, they must acknowledge that a given idea is not panning out and it is time for the organization to move on to other possibilities. At this time, senior managers must decide which of the competing ideas win the "shoot-out," and therefore should be spread throughout the organization, while other options are actively discouraged.

Managers often don't like the negative connotations of this outcome. Many believe they should be more patient than demanding, and therefore they are unwilling to step in and take a firm stance that distinguishes between ideas they consider to be supportable and ideas they should not support. Yet a great deal of research, experience, and common sense indicates that leaders should be intolerant of ongoing poor performance if they expect their organizations ever to enjoy superior performance.

We explain this need for leaders to be firm by using the concept of tough love, which was originally developed to explain why loving parents sometimes need to be strict disciplinarians. No one benefits from leaders who are afraid to take a stand or demand results. When the experiments are over and the winner of the shoot-out is obvious, leaders should let it be known in no uncertain terms what the organization will and will not tolerate in the future.

Handled correctly, this toughness can be a great opportunity to reinforce continued experimentation, but it is easy to handle this part of learning poorly and thereby discourage or demoralize the organization. The best way for a leader to practice euthanasia for less promising options while encouraging further experimentation is to openly discuss why an option won't work. Candor signals the leader's serious interest in results and discernment of what should and should not be supported. If a leader can openly discuss a failure and doles out no punishment, this goes a long way toward signaling that mistakes are okay if made for the sake of learning. In turn, employees don't find it necessary to hide mistakes, allowing errors to be caught sooner in the future. And if the leader can encourage those involved in less-promising experiments to learn from their results, no one need consider the experiment a failure. As Thomas Watson, the CEO responsible for IBM's early success, used to tell managers who had tried something that had not worked out, "That's an expensive bit of management training you've just had, but it's cheap if you profit from it."[47]

In encouraging candor, we do not mean to appear overly harsh here, but occasionally leaders must take tough stands. As Mike Walsh, the former CEO of Tenneco we quoted earlier, once put it, "I believe there is a shortage of people who realize that a CEO's job is to lead."[48] Or as William Wiess, the CEO of Ameritech, explained:

> The best way I know to get people to accept the need for change is to not give them a choice. The organization has to know that there's a leader at the top who has made up his mind, that he is surrounded by leaders who have made up their minds, and that they're going to drive forward no matter what.[49]

More than one CEO has helped bring about important organizational transformations by making statements similar to this one: "We have discovered what we think will be a better way of doing things, and we hope you will be part of our future success. But if you think you might stand in the way of our progress, allow me to help you find the best available outplacement service right now." To close this discussion, we return to Arden Sims, the CEO who led Globe Metallurgical's transformation from a moribund traditional organization to a successful learning organization, for his comments on the need for what we have called tough love on the part of leaders:

> I've found that one of the most important components of a successful transformation is to gain the respect of your work force. I don't mean the workers have to like you, although that helps, but they have to understand that you will stand your ground when it comes to forcing through big changes. . . . It's a shame, but I think a lot of senior managers have lost their resolve and their ability to face up to hard work. Change is never easy, and there are no special formulas, no quick fixes. You just have to roll up your sleeves and keep working at it without backing down.[50]

INSTRUMENTAL LEADERSHIP AND THE LEVERS FOR CHANGE

After extensive research on leadership, John Huey concluded that today's corporate leaders "will face two tasks: first, to develop and articulate exactly what the company is trying to accomplish, and second, to create an environment in which employees can figure out what needs to be done and then do it well."[51] Huey's statement echoes the most significant theme of this chapter—the importance of a leader's successfully facilitating and setting the direction for the discovery and action that organizational learning requires.

 This perspective, referred to as the *instrumental view* of leadership, focuses on the most important actions taken by leaders that facilitate change. In building organizations that can both discover and take action, leaders must address a wide variety of issues. As we explained earlier in this chapter, organizational change is a complex phenomenon with many interrelated parts. No "magic bullets" will allow leaders to work wonders by addressing only one or two of these parts. For example, charisma has long been seen as critical to leadership in bringing about organizational change. But we see charisma as just one of the many forces that can work for—or against—change. Leaders need to be more than just charismatic; they need to be "organizational architects," capable of creating entirely new organizations by reshaping all of the many forces affecting change.[52] Paul Allaire, CEO of Xerox, makes this point when he urges leaders not to become too enamored with organizational structure, an element of change discussed in Chapter 10, that managers often treat as a magic bullet. Speaking of successful changes that have taken place at Xerox, Allaire says:

> Changing the structure is only part of it. We are also changing the process by which we manage, the rewards and other mechanisms that shape those processes, and the kind of people we place in the key managerial positions. Finally, we are trying to change our informal culture—the ways we do things, the behaviors that drive the business. In fact, the term "reorganization" doesn't really capture what we are trying to do at Xerox. We are redesigning the "organizational architecture" of the entire company.[53]

Managers at AT&T observed a similar need for broad-based change when they attempted to develop greater entrepreneurship in the company after the telecommunications industry was deregulated. They believed that to bring about desired organizational changes, they had to address the six broad categories of constraining forces identified in Exhibit 9.9.

Researchers studying British Airways' dramatic transformation from a second-rate carrier to world-class reached a similar conclusion: "The change involved a multifaceted effort that used many leverage points to initiate and support the changes."[54] The concept of "leverage points" seems to capture the essence of the work that leaders face if they want to build learning organizations. In thinking of how organizations are moved to implement significant changes, we are reminded of the process used to get a train back onto a track after it derails. The wreckage often prohibits train-mounted cranes from approaching close enough to be useful. Because they cannot rely on this single powerful magic bullet, the cleanup crews use a very different approach: masses of people attack the problem with levers—simple prize poles that, individually, would be totally ineffective, but collectively can slowly untangle the worst wreck and move salvageable equipment back onto the track. We believe the work of putting an organization "on track" requires three types of levers, as depicted in Exhibit 9.10 and discussed in the next three chapters.

In Chapter 10, we will discuss the importance of formal organizational structures and informal organizational processes as context levers that either facilitate or constrain organizational change. In Chapter 11, we will consider how resourcing systems and control systems influence successful change efforts. Finally, Chapter 12 will look at the critical role of a leader's personal actions as a lever for change, focusing on the use of power, communication skills, and the importance of being a role model for advocated changes. As we will see in these upcoming chapters, only through the use of the largest possible set of levers can organizations hope to bring about the changes needed to implement their strategies. Aligning and coordinating the effects of all these levers is the goal of instrumental leadership and the key to successfully implementing strategic change.

EXHIBIT 9.9

Constraining Forces That Affect Strategic Change at AT&T

Systems	Structures	Strategic Direction	Policies and Procedures	People	Culture
Misdirected reward and evaluation systems	Too many hierarchical levels	Absence of innovation goals	Long, complex approval cycles	Fear of failure	Ill-defined values
Oppressive control systems, inflexible budgeting systems	Overly narrow span of control	No formal strategy for entrepreneurship	Extensive documentation requirements	Resistance to change	Lack of consensus over priorities
Arbitrary cost allocation systems	Responsibility without authority	No vision from the top	Overreliance on established rules of thumb	Parochial bias	Lack of fit
Overly rigid, formal planning systems	Top-down management	Lack of commitment from senior executives	Unrealistic performance criteria	"Turf" protection	Values that conflict with entrepreneurial requirements
	Restricted communication channels	No entrepreneurial role models at the top		Complacency	
	Lack of accountability			Short-term orientation	
	Bloated staff functions			Inappropriate skills/talents	

Source: Michael H. Morris and Don J. Trotter, "Institutionalizing Entrepreneurship in a Large Company: A Case Study at AT&T," *Industrial Marketing Management, 19* (May 1990), 135. Copyright 1990 by Elsevier Science Inc. Reprinted by permission of the publisher.

EXHIBIT 9.10
The Levers Available for Affecting Change

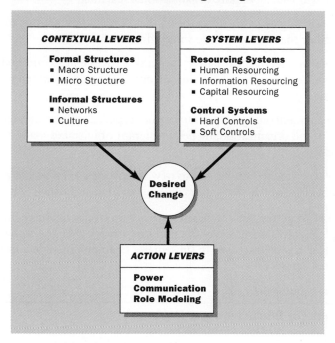

Summary of Managerial Practices to Adopt from This Chapter

- Expect implementation of a strategy to be much more challenging in practice than strategic analysis or strategy formulation.

- Remember that strategy implementation and organizational change will require you to address a large number of interconnected factors simultaneously. A framework such as the McKinsey 7-S model (or the levers model you will study in later chapters) can be useful in helping you identify these factors.

- Do not fall prey to the apparent logic of using an activity-centered change program as your primary means of implementing a strategy. Though each step seems rational by itself, the overall impact of this approach is minimal.

- Remember that organizations engage in two types of learning, single-loop and double-loop, and that both require oversight, although they place different demands on managers and leaders.

- In thinking about the approach to strategy implementation that is appropriate for you, consider (1) the level of change desired and (2) the situation facing the organization. Evolutionary changes or strategies for simple, stable businesses may be successfully implemented by using strategic programming. Revolutionary changes, or strategies for organizations facing complex and/or unpredictable situations, will usually require organizational learning.

■ Treat learning as a two-step process that couples new actions to new discoveries; remember that one is of little value without the other.

■ The best model of the discovery process is the scientific method of theory, hypothesis, test, result, and conclusion, and it is readily adapted to organizational learning.

■ As a leader, encourage experimentation, especially experimentation in the middle levels of the organization, by being tolerant of mistakes made as part of the learning process.

■ Once experimentation has led to new discoveries, a leader has a responsibility to make it clear which alternatives will be pursued and which will not.

■ The key to getting an organization to act on its discoveries is instrumental leadership. It involves using levers to build support for change throughout the organization. Key levers (discussed in subsequent chapters) include context, systems, and personal action.

Questions for Discussion and Review

1. What factors make implementation and strategic change so difficult?

2. What are activity-centered change programs? Why do they seldom produce significant organizational change?

3. What are adaptive and generative changes and how do they relate to single-loop and double-loop learning?

4. What is entailed in the discovery part of organizational learning and what can managers do to facilitate discovery as a key part of organizational learning?

5. What is entailed in the action part of organizational learning and what can managers do to facilitate action as a key part of organizational learning?

Notes

1. Keith Naughton, "How Ford's F-150 Lapped the Competition," *Business Week* (July 29, 1996), 74–76.
2. Steven W. Floyd and Bill Wooldridge, "Managing Strategic Consensus: The Foundation of Effective Implementation," *Academy of Management Executive*, 6:4 (1992), 27.
3. Arnold S. Judson, "Invest in a High-Yield Strategic Plan," *Journal of Business Strategy, 12* (July–August 1991), 34–39.
4. William A. Schiemann, "Why Change Fails," *Across the Board, 29* (April 1992), 53–54.
5. Judson, "Invest in a High-Yield Strategic Plan."

6. For additional discussion of the barriers to change, see Richard Heygate, "Accelerating Front-Line Change," *McKinsey Quarterly* (Winter 1992), 134–147.

7. We consider the two to be so tightly linked that we cannot talk about strategy implementation without talking about organizational change, and we tend to use these terms interchangeably. See Terry L. Amburgey and Tina Dacin, "As the Left Foot Follows the Right? The Dynamics of Strategic and Structural Change," *Academy of Management Journal, 37* (December 1994), 1427–1452, for a discussion of the links between the two.

8. For research on what factors determine the strength with which managers resist change, see Donald C. Hambrick, Marta A. Geletkanycz, and James W. Fredrickson, "Top Executive Commitment to the Status Quo: Some Tests of Its Determinants," *Strategic Management Journal, 14* (1993), 401–418.

9. Edgar H. Schein, "How Can Organizations Learn Faster? The Challenge of Entering the Green Room," *Sloan Management Review, 34* (Winter 1993), 85–92.

10. Joel Brockner, "The Escalation of Commitment to a Failing Course of Action: Toward Theoretical Progress," *Academy of Management Review, 17:1* (1992), 39–61.

11. Preston G. Smith, "Why Change Is Hard," *Across the Board, 30* (January–February 1993), 55–56.

12. See, for example, the low success rate "proven" change programs had in a study of thirteen firms reported in Dexter Dunphy and Doug Stace, "The Strategic Management of Corporate Change," *Human Relations, 46* (August 1993), 905–920.

13. This section is built upon the work of Michael Beer, Russell A. Eisenstat, and Bert Spector in "Why Change Programs Don't Produce Change," *Harvard Business Review, 68* (November–December 1990), 158–166; and Robert H. Schaffer and Harvey A. Thomson in "Successful Change Programs Begin with Results," *Harvard Business Review* (January–February 1992), 80–89.

14. Research has shown that this form of confusion is among the most common reasons for failure among change programs; see R. Krishnan et al., "In Search of Quality Improvement: Problems of Design and Implementation," *Academy of Management Executive, 7:4* (1993), 7.

15. This is most likely to become a problem in organizations that are inclined to pursue the most recent managerial fads or fashions. For a theoretical discussion of why organizations are so inclined, see Eric Abrahamson, "Managerial Fads and Fashions: The Diffusion and Rejection of Innovations," *Academy of Management Review, 16* (July 1991), 586–612.

16. This model of change was originally developed by a naturalist to describe how species arise and evolve; see N. Eldredge and S. Gould, "Punctuated Equilibria: An Alternative to Phyletic Gradualism," in T. J. Schopf, ed., *Models in Paleobiology*, San Francisco: Freeman, Cooper, 1972. It has since been found to be widely applicable to understanding how organizations change; see Connie J. G. Gersick, "Revolutionary Change Theories: A Multilevel Exploration of the Punctuated Equilibrium Paradigm," *Academy of Management Review, 16* (January 1991), 10–36.

17. Stephen J. Mezias and Mary Ann Glynn, "The Three Faces of Corporate Renewal: Institution, Revolution, and Evolution," *Strategic Management Journal, 14* (1993), 77–101; W. Abernathy and J. Utterback, "Patterns of Industrial Innovation," in M. Tushman and W. Moore, eds., *Readings in the Management of Innovation*, Boston: Pitman, 1982, 97–108;

D. Miller and P. Friesen, *Organizations: A Quantum View*, Englewood Cliffs, NJ: Prentice-Hall, 1984.

18. The distinction between managing transactions and leading transformation is explained in John P. Kotter, *A Force for Change: How Leadership Differs from Management*, New York: The Free Press, 1990; and Abraham Zaleznik, "Managers and Leaders: Are They Different?," *Harvard Business Review* (March–April 1992), 126–135.

19. Peter M. Senge, "The Leader's New Work: Building Learning Organizations," *Sloan Management Review, 32* (Fall 1990), 7–23.

20. John Huey, "Nothing Is Impossible," *Fortune* (September 23, 1991), 134–140.

21. T. S. Kuhn, *The Structure of Scientific Revolution*, 2d ed., Chicago: University of Chicago Press, 1970.

22. Chris Argyris, "Double Loop Learning in Organizations," *Harvard Business Review* (September–October 1977), 115–125.

23. Stephen R. Covey, *The Seven Habits of Highly Effective People: Powerful Lessons in Personal Change*, London: Simon & Schuster, 1989.

24. Once again, the distinction between managing transactions and leading transformation is explained in John P. Kotter, *A Force for Change: How Leadership Differs from Management*, New York: The Free Press, 1990; and Abraham Zaleznik, "Managers and Leaders: Are They Different?," *Harvard Busienss Review* (March–April 1992), 126–135.

25. This example is taken from R. E. Gomory, "From the 'Ladder of Science' to the Product Development Cycle," *Harvard Business Review, 67* (November 1989), 99–105.

26. Andrew C. Boynton and Victor Bart, "Stable Organization," *California Management Review, 34* (Fall 1991), 53–66.

27. Tom Peters, "Part Two: Get Innovative or Get Dead," *California Management Review, 33* (Winter 1991), 9–23.

28. Tsun-yan Hsieh, "The Road to Renewal," *McKinsey Quarterly* (Summer 1993), 28–37.

29. See Peter F. Drucker, "The Theory of the Business," *Harvard Business Review* (September–October 1994), 95–104.

30. See Peter M. Senge, *The Fifth Discipline: The Art and Practice of the Learning Organization*, New York: Doubleday/Currency, 1990, chap. 10.

31. From the Shell research group, as quoted in Senge, "The Leader's New Work."

32. For an explanation of the critical importance of making mistakes in the process of double-loop learning, see Shlomo Maital, "The Ramparts of Failure," *Across the Board, 29* (January–February 1992), 51–53.

33. James C. Collins, "Sometimes a Great Notion," *Inc., 15* (July 1993), 90–91.

34. This is not meant to discount the value of innovation at the bottom of the organization. In fact, as we discussed in Chapter 5, we see the culmination of many such innovations as being the key to continuous improvement through *kaizen*. However, in the present discussion of organizational learning, we are more interested in experiments large enough to constitute something more than incremental innovations, and those experiments are more likely to take place at a higher level of the organization.

35. See discussion in I. Nonaka, "Toward Middle-up-down Management: Accelerating Information Creation," *Sloan Management Review* (Spring 1988), 9–18.

36. Roy Merrills, "How Northern Telecom Competes on Time," *Harvard Business Review* (July–August 1989), 108–114.

37. For research on such upward influence, see Jane E. Dutton and Susan J. Ashford, "Selling Issues to Top Management," *Academy of Management Review, 18* (1993), 397–428; R. Mowday, "The Exercise of Upward Influence in Organizations," *Administrative Science Quarterly, 23* (1978), 137–156; and W. K. Schilit, "An Examination of the Influence of Middle-Level Managers in Formulating and Implementing Strategic Decisions," *Journal of Management Studies, 24* (1987), 271–293.

38. James Brian Quinn, *Strategies for Change: Logical Incrementalism*, Homewood, IL: Irwin, 1980.

39. Additional reasons for top managers to avoid making decisions that will shape the learning process too early can be found in H. E. Wrapp, "Good Managers Don't Make Policy Decisions," *Harvard Business Review, 45* (September–October 1967), 91–99.

40. W. D. Guth and Ian C. Macmillan, "Strategy Implementation Versus Middle-Management Self-Interest," *Strategic Management Journal, 7* (July–August 1986), 313–327.

41. Michael Beer, as quoted in Brian Dumaine, "Creating a New Company Culture," *Fortune* (January 15, 1990), 127–131. Details of Beer's research can be found in Beer, Eisenstat, and Spector, "Why Change Programs Don't Produce Change."

42. David E. Meen and Mark Keough, "Creating the Learning Organization," *McKinsey Quarterly* (Winter 1992), 58–77.

43. Thomas J. Peters and Robert H. Waterman, Jr., *In Search of Excellence: Lessons from America's Best-Run Companies*, New York: Harper & Row, 1982, 13.

44. See discussion in Bernard C. Reimann and Vasudevan Ramanujam, "Acting Versus Thinking: A Debate Between Tom Peters and Michael Porter," *Planning Review* (March–April 1992), 36–43.

45. Jay A. Conger, "Leadership: The Art of Empowering Others," *Academy of Management Executive, 3* (1989), 17–24.

46. Michael Beer, *Organizational Change and Development*, Santa Monica, CA: Goodyear, 1980, 64.

47. Toni Mack, "Eager Lions and Reluctant Lions," *Forbes* (February 17, 1992), 98–101.

48. Jacqueline M. Graves, "Leaders of Corporate Change," *Fortune* (December 14, 1992), 104–114.

49. Joyce E. Davis, "A Master Class in Radical Change," *Fortune* (December 13, 1993), 82–90.

50. Bruce Rayner, "Trial-by-Fire Transformation: An Interview with Globe Metallurgical's Arden C. Sims," *Harvard Business Review* (May–June 1992), 116–129.

51. John Huey, "The New Post-Heroic Leadership," *Fortune* (February 21, 1994), 44.

52. David A. Nadler and Michael L. Tushman, "Beyond the Charismatic Leader: Leadership and Organizational Change," *California Management Review, 32* (Winter 1990), 77–97.

53. Robert Howard, "The CEO as Organizational Architect: An Interview with Xerox's Paul Allaire," *Harvard Business Review* (September–October 1992), 106–121.

54. Leonard D. Goodstein and W. Warner Burke, "Creating Successful Organization Change," *Organizational Dynamics, 19* (Spring 1991), 5–17.

Chapter 10

Context Levers

This chapter is the first of three that will describe different levers that can be used to bring about organizational change and implement strategies. In this chapter, we will focus on how different elements of the organizational context, structure, and nature of the internal working environment shape everyday actions, and thus serve as a potentially powerful lever for change. The chapter is organized into five parts, the first of which overviews the different dimensions of organizational context and explains the importance of context in strategy implementation. The remaining four parts take detailed looks at the four most important dimensions of organizational context: macro-organizational (organizationwide) structure, micro-organizational (organizational subunit) structure, informal networks, and organizational culture. In each of these sections, we describe alternatives and explain and illustrate how the most appropriate alternative depends on the type of strategy being pursued.

This chapter will help you understand:

- The importance of organizational context as a subtle but powerful means of influencing the everyday behavior of people throughout an organization
- The need to view context along two dimensions: formal versus informal and organizationwide versus organizational subunit
- Alternative macro-organizational structures and the advantages and disadvantages of each
- Trends toward developing new forms of organization to address some of today's most pressing business issues
- The need to match an organization's macrostructure to its strategy
- Differences between groups and teams
- The different types of microstructures and the type of behavior each encourages
- The different types of informal networks and the roles they play in an organization
- Some of the most common problems of networks and how to address them
- The nature of organizational culture and how managers can shape it

Perhaps you have never heard of Kyocera Corporation, but this company is one of the most respected in Japan, where it and its CEO have won numerous achievement awards and honors, and Kyocera's core business holds a 65 percent share of the multibillion-dollar global market for the ceramic forms that house and protect integrated circuits. Its success can be attributed in large part to the "Amoeba Management System"—with its unique organization structure and culture.

Amoebas are single-cell organisms with indefinite, changeable forms. Kyocera's founder, Dr. Kazou Inamori, long ago adopted the amoeba as the model for structuring his organization. Today, Kyocera organizes its 15,000 employees into hundreds of "amoebas" that each consist of anywhere from seven to seventy individuals. These small units constantly change and reconstitute themselves with little centralized control over how or when they divide or reorganize. Each amoeba operates as a tiny independent business within the much larger corporation, from which they all receive support. Each amoeba carries its own planning, quality control, accounting, and personnel management. Amoebas may be internal suppliers or customers for other amoebas, and there may be several amoebas that perform basically the same function in competition with one another. Depending on its success and the demand for its work, an amoeba will expand, contract, or even redefine its mission.

Organization culture is as important a part of the Amoeba Management System as organization structure. Some describe Kyocera's culture as a mixture of Zen Buddhism and Soviet-style socialism, with a company motto of "Respect the divine, and love people." Members of amoebas are expected to feel intense loyalty to the company, but are still free to question its existing conventions. Days begin with organizationwide exercises and talks about the Kyocera philosophy, and end with joining other employees at local karaoke bars. Employees are encouraged to marry other employees and to be buried at the company's cemetery. However, they are also encouraged to openly question anyone in the corporation, no matter how senior, to take risks, to be entrepreneurial, to "regularly do what no one has ever done before."

Some describe Japanese business culture as being staid, tradition-bound, unquestioning of authority, and not very creative. But the organization structure and corporate culture that results from Kyocera's Amoeba Management System disproves such stereotypes—this is one of the most flexible and innovative companies anywhere. The corporation boasts both strong profits in its core businesses and healthy growth from its many new products developed for a variety of different markets. In this chapter, you will learn how such factors as organization structure and corporate culture help determine which strategies firms can successfully implement.

THE IMPORTANCE AND DIMENSIONS OF CONTEXT

Peter Senge, writing about building learning organizations, illustrates how important organizational context can be by asking managers to identify the person with the greatest impact on the success of a pleasure cruise aboard a large luxury liner.[1] Most identify the ship's captain; others will identify the social activities director; and a few will even identify the head chef. Senge argues that all these are wrong answers—that the person having the greatest impact on the success of the cruise is the designer. After all, the designer determines the context within which all the other individuals will work, and the design of the ship does much to determine the effectiveness of individuals in all roles. In the same way, those who design organizations and determine the context within which others will work have a tremendous influence on their success. Paul Allaire, CEO of Xerox, makes this point when he describes the CEO as an "organizational architect."[2] Senge's ship's designer and Allaire's organizational architect possess tremendous power and influence in their ability to shape the context within which people go about their everyday business. Such subtle but powerful shaping is one of the most effective levers available to managers who seek to bring about strategic change. In discussing the most important forms of context levers, Allaire emphasizes what he calls two elements of organizational architecture. As he explains:

> The first we call "hardware." These are the things managers usually think of as organizational structure, the formal processes by which things get done. . . . "Software" is the most difficult to describe, but probably the most important: the informal networks and practices linking people together, the value system, the culture. Any company that leaves these out of its organizational change effort is making a big mistake.

In this chapter we consider elements of organizational context that mirror Allaire's description of architectural hardware and software, as shown in Exhibit 10.1.

The first element of context we consider is structural in nature and concerns how firms are formally organized. We devote considerable attention to the structure of the organization as a whole, which we refer to as *macro-organizational structure*. But we also consider the structure of the subunits, such as groups and teams, that make up the larger organization—we refer to these as *microstructures*. Structures are powerful levers for implementing strategies because they identify and determine formal authority by specifying the so-called chain of command. Over the last 10 years, businesses have increased emphasis on developing new approaches to authority in organizations by changing the chain of command. For example, throughout this text, we have spoken of the trends toward flatter organizations, empowered workers, and self-directed work teams, all developments that reduce reliance on a top-down chain of command. However, this trend notwithstanding, organizations still depend on formal authority as their primary source of government, and you need to understand the different forms of formal organizational structure and what they imply about who holds authority over whom, and why.

While no one would deny the power of formal structure and the authority it con-

EXHIBIT 10.1
A Framework for Thinking About the Four Elements of Context

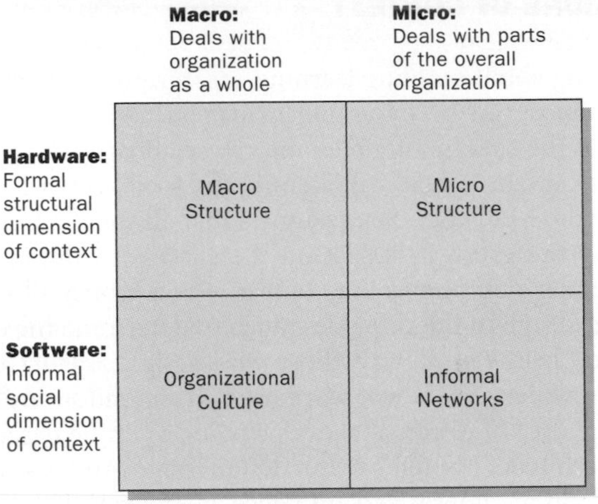

	Macro: Deals with organization as a whole	**Micro:** Deals with parts of the overall organization
Hardware: Formal structural dimension of context	Macro Structure	Micro Structure
Software: Informal social dimension of context	Organizational Culture	Informal Networks

veys, there is also no denying its limits. Organizations are much more than boxes and lines on a chart; they are complex social institutions filled with ever-changing networks and cultures. To understand this side of context, you must study its second element, which we refer to as "informal" to distinguish it from the formal organization. We consider informal networks and organizational culture to be the most important parts of the informal organization.

Where formal organizational structures provide more or less written rules of conduct, networks and culture provide unwritten rules that can be every bit as powerful in shaping behavior and decisions and in affecting the implementation of strategic changes. Consequently, a manager must develop an awareness of how elements of both the formal macro- and microstructures, as well as those of informal networks and culture, affect strategy implementation. Your goal should be to learn how to use all four as levers in helping bring about the strategic changes you desire. We now consider each in turn.

MACRO-ORGANIZATIONAL STRUCTURE

Firms choose various types of macro-organizational (organizationwide) structural forms to further their strategic aims. Each of these structures holds both advantages and disadvantages.[3] Small firms with narrow product-market scopes typically adopt and maintain *simple structures*. When firms grow in overall revenue or engage in vertical integration, a *functional structure* becomes more suitable. As firms expand their product-market scope into unrelated areas, they generally decentralize operations and adopt *divisional structures*. *Matrix* structures address unique sets of organizational contingencies involving the need for both functional-area expertise and coordination across divisional lines. Finally, many firms, especially those with international operations, rely on *combination structures*, in which they blend aforementioned types of organizational structures to match a particular strategic direction. Let's look at each of these first and then consider some of the recently developed trends in organizational structure.

Simple Structure

Simple structure represents one of the oldest organizational forms. Owner-managed companies, predominant during the 1800s, often used simple structures. These organizations are typically limited to a single, or very narrow, product line and a type of structure in which the owner-manager makes all major decisions directly. Owner-managers attempt to monitor all activities, and staffs merely serve as extensions of the top executive's personality.[4] The structure is highly informal with tasks coordinated by direct supervision. Decision-making authority is highly centralized. There is little specialization; few rules and regulations mean that there is a low degree of formalization; and information systems are unsophisticated. Although the chief executive officer or owner-manager participates in all phases of the enterprise, a manager is usually employed to assist in directing day-to-day operations.

Advantages

These simple structures enjoy considerable flexibility. Being small and highly centralized, a firm with a simple structure can move quickly to take advantage of market opportunities. Also, their flat structure allows fast and direct communication, and new-product strategies can be implemented quickly. Because they aren't very complex, these companies seldom experience the same coordination problems that larger firms do, so small firms are often able to outmaneuver larger, formalized, complex organizations.

Disadvantages

A small firm with a simple structure may foster creativity and individualism because of its low level of formalization, but the lack of rules and regulations may also bring problems. Individuals may not clearly understand their responsibilities, which can lead to conflict and confusion. Others may use the lack of regulations to act in their own self-interest, which can lead to an overall decrease in motivation and satisfaction, as well as a possible misuse of organizational resources. Further, a small organization's flat structure provides little opportunity for upward mobility, and without some promise of future advancement, it is difficult to recruit and retain quality personnel. Because of these limitations, as organizations grow, they usually move away from simple structures to those organized around functions.

Functional Structure

As firms begin to grow, they expand their overall scope of operations by further penetrating existing markets, by introducing similar products into additional markets, or by engaging in vertical integration. Functional structures work best in businesses with high production volumes, single or closely related lines of products or services, or some vertical integration. Although growth usually increases an organization's overall complexity, functional structures still provide a high level of centralization, which helps maintain the tight integration and control necessary for linking related product-market activities or the multiple stages of the value chain.

Parkdale Mills, located in North Carolina, provides an effective example of functional organizational structure.[5] Yarn making is a commodity business, and Parkdale, the largest yarn mill in the United States, is generally considered the industry's low-cost producer. The company maintains a narrow product line, a common attribute of functionally organized firms. Tasks are highly standardized, and the company will not change the twist or blend of a yarn for specific customers. Centralized authority rests with a general manager, who operates with a bare-bones staff of ten top executives to oversee the organization's various functions. While the functional structure works well for Parkdale, it is not always so effective. Exhibit 10.2 presents a simplified diagram of a hypothetical functional structure and lists some of the advantages and disadvantages of this form of organization. Let's look at both in more detail.

Advantages

Functional structures offer several advantages that contribute to a firm's effectiveness. Centralized decision making enables the chief executive to integrate operating and

EXHIBIT 10.2
Advantages and Disadvantages of a Functional Structure

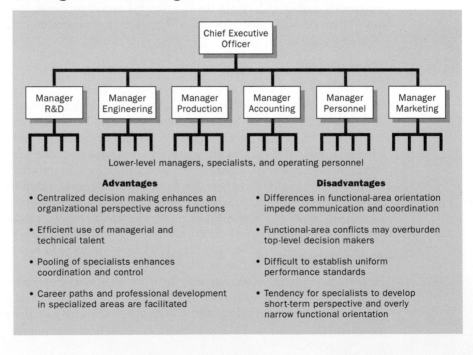

strategic issues. When technical expertise is critical, costly, and scarce, a pool that makes functional experts available maximizes their contributions across the entire organization. This increases the efficient use of managerial talent within functional areas and makes it easier to coordinate efforts of functional-area specialists. Grouping activities by function works particularly well in organizations that operate in relatively similar product and market areas, because cross-product or cross-market coordination is not an issue. A functional structure provides clearly marked career paths for specialists, so it is easier to hire and retain their services. Finally, such people often enjoy working with colleagues who share similar interests.[6]

Disadvantages

Even considering the aforementioned benefits, managers in functionally organized firms must be aware of many potential disadvantages. Coordination and communication may become difficult, because each functional area often forms its own value system, time orientation, and vocabulary. Research and development personnel, for example, may use sophisticated technical jargon and may not react favorably to time pressure when production managers need immediate assistance to solve process design problems. Functional-area conflicts may frequently be referred to senior managers, inundating the senior-management team with time-consuming problems that distract from more important issues.

Control and evaluation are more difficult because there is no one standard performance measure for functional-area managers. Each functional area's contribution to a firm's overall performance merges and overlaps, so managers may feel their performance evaluations and rewards do not reflect their particular contributions. This may be especially true when a major portion of their total compensation is based on the overall profitability of the organization. Because performance evaluation is so difficult, managers may be uncertain about promotion potential, and this may create motivational problems for managers.

Divisional or Strategic Business Unit Structure

A divisional, or strategic business unit (SBU), structure covers a set of relatively autonomous entities governed by a central administration. General Motors was among the earliest firms to adopt a divisional organizational structure. In the 1920s, it formed five major product divisions (Cadillac, Pontiac, Chevrolet, Buick, and Oldsmobile) and several industrial divisions in an effort to make the sprawling GM empire more manageable. Since then, many firms have discovered that, as they diversify into new product-market activities, single functional departments cannot manage the increased complexity of the overall business if functions differ too much from one product market to the next. Operational decision making in such complex businesses places excessive demands on the firm's top management. If top-level managers are to attend to broader, longer-term organizational issues, they must delegate decision making to lower-level managers.

To address the problem, firms organize divisional structures around products and/or markets, often identified as distinct SBUs. Each division or SBU focuses on its own particular issues. Widely diversified corporations may consist of dozens of different divisions, each with its own set of products, services, and/or markets. The percentage of diversified firms in the *Fortune* 500 has increased from only 30 percent in 1950 to approximately 75 percent today. During the same period, the percentage of *Fortune* 500 firms with a divisional structure increased from under 20 percent to approximately 90 percent.[7]

When is a divisional or SBU structure most beneficial? A divisional structure generally improves the efficiency and financial performance of firms that pursue unrelated diversification strategies but decreases efficiency for vertically integrated firms.[8] Vertical integration requires decided interdependence among various stages in the value chain from raw material procurement to distribution to final customers, so centralized control and coordination of activities becomes critical. The decentralization typically associated with a divisional structure would clearly be dysfunctional for such a vertically integrated firm. Exhibit 10.3 depicts a simplified divisional structure and lists some of the advantages and disadvantages of this structure.

Advantages

A divisional or SBU structure avoids many problems typically found in organizations structured by function. In this structure, managers concentrate on their own particular product lines or markets, and they have access to resources and staff functional specialists. Delegating decision making to lower managerial levels moves decisions closer to the products and markets, which facilitates faster decisions from those who are more specialized and knowledgeable in the product area. This allows a high degree of emphasis to be placed on products and markets and improves a firm's ability to adapt during rapid environmental change.

As organizations increase their product-market diversity, they need more general managers—individuals who can comprehend and integrate activities from diverse functional areas. Divisional structures facilitate the training and development of general managers, because these managers are given the authority for formulating and implementing strategy. Many corporations use this type of management development to effectively groom their rising general managers.[9] And because division managers are held accountable for results, internal controls are generally facilitated by a divisional structure.[10]

Finally, as noted above, by delegating operating responsibilities to the semiautonomous divisions, corporate-level executives can spend less time on operating activities and more on identifying strategic or long-term issues for the entire organization.

Disadvantages

Initiating and maintaining a divisional structure increases costs along with the number of personnel and the overhead expense. Administrative functions and the attendant operating and capital expenditures multiply. With the additional hierarchical level, information may be distorted and communication slowed as corporate managers are farther removed from the individual divisions and may even be unaware of significant developments that could impact the corporation.

EXHIBIT 10.3
Advantages and Disadvantages of a Divisional/SBU Structure

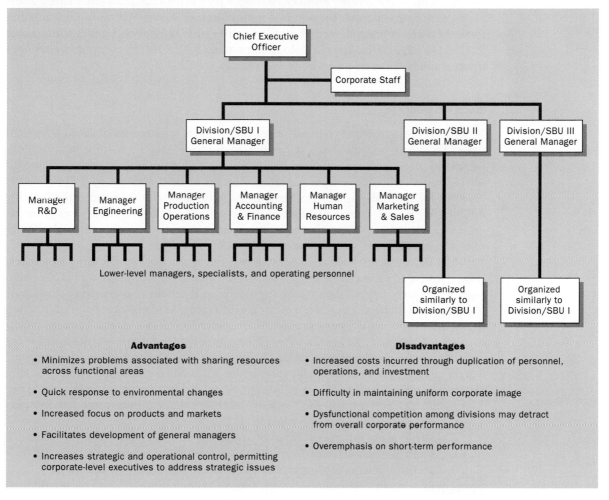

Advantages

- Minimizes problems associated with sharing resources across functional areas

- Quick response to environmental changes

- Increased focus on products and markets

- Facilitates development of general managers

- Increases strategic and operational control, permitting corporate-level executives to address strategic issues

Disadvantages

- Increased costs incurred through duplication of personnel, operations, and investment

- Difficulty in maintaining uniform corporate image

- Dysfunctional competition among divisions may detract from overall corporate performance

- Overemphasis on short-term performance

A common problem with divisional structures is an overemphasis on short-term profitability. The intense pressures placed on divisional or SBU managers to meet short-term return on investment (ROI) targets and to contribute to corporate earnings per share often foster a lack of concern for expenditures with slower paybacks, such as investments in R&D and marketing research. Sometimes, rather than focusing on competing with marketplace rivals, divisions spend more energy on competing with one another for corporate resources, which may eventually lead to an erosion of overall corporate performance. Some writers believe that this short-term focus played a major part in the decline of the international competitiveness of U.S. industry during the past few decades.[11]

Maintaining a consistent corporate image may also be more difficult in divisional organizations. In some instances, using a single company trademark or brand can enhance the perceived value of new or poorly performing products by transferring the identifiability and customer loyalty of stronger products to them. In other cases, a single defective product that is associated with customer dissatisfaction can damage the reputation of a company's entire line. Companies such as General Motors and Procter & Gamble have developed multiple brand names, while 3M, in contrast, has chosen to use a single name on a multitude of products.

Matrix Structure

As we have seen, managers typically must choose between two fundamental structural types: functional and divisional. However, many firms face a situation in which departments need both expertise within functions and coordination across divisional lines. Matrix structures offer a potential solution to this dilemma by increasing the capacity for information handling and decision making within organizations and by establishing formal, lateral channels of communication that complement existing hierarchical channels.[12] Thus, the matrix structure attempts to combine the advantages of both functional and divisional structures.

The matrix is designed to cope with the varied activities required in a complex, project-oriented business. Aerospace firms were among the first to use a matrix structure in the early 1960s, when technology developed rapidly. Aerospace projects progress through many phases, each requiring a different mix of resources. Different types of engineers and support personnel become involved at various stages: innovative conceptual designers are used in the initial phase, persistent and detail-oriented people are necessary in the development phase, and technically skilled customer service personnel are required for the field service phase. Finally, some participants with comprehensive expertise stay with a project from beginning to end.[13] The matrix structure was created to provide management with the flexibility to ensure that a proper combination of organizational resources is always available.

This structure combines two lines of authority: a vertical line from the functional managers and a horizontal line from the project, program, geographic area, or divisional director. Functional departments contribute specialist groupings and functional-area expertise, while project departments provide the direction for scheduling, budgeting, and general administration for particular projects.[14] Top management and support functions (e.g., personnel, security, and purchasing) are generally outside the matrix and are structured with more traditional line and staff designations. Exhibit 10.4 presents a diagram of a matrix organization and lists some of its advantages and disadvantages.

Advantages

The dual-authority structure of the matrix has several potential advantages, such as flexibility, faster response time, close working relationships among departments, and better coordination through enhanced communication, which increases the opportunities for those in lower levels of the hierarchy to work on more significant cross-functional issues. Matrix structures are intended to respond to market changes more quickly. For example, if engineers assigned to a single product group are unable to

EXHIBIT 10.4
Advantages and Disadvantages of a Matrix Structure

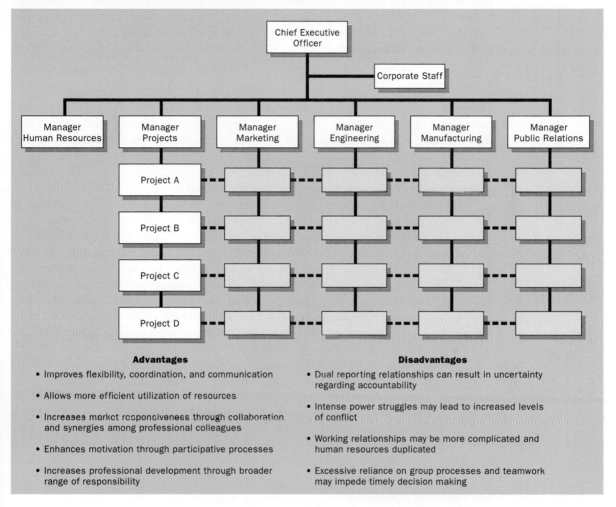

Advantages	Disadvantages
• Improves flexibility, coordination, and communication	• Dual reporting relationships can result in uncertainty regarding accountability
• Allows more efficient utilization of resources	• Intense power struggles may lead to increased levels of conflict
• Increases market responsiveness through collaboration and synergies among professional colleagues	• Working relationships may be more complicated and human resources duplicated
• Enhances motivation through participative processes	• Excessive reliance on group processes and teamwork may impede timely decision making
• Increases professional development through broader range of responsibility	

implement changes to satisfy customer requirements, they can call on engineering groups in other product areas and can collaborate with professional colleagues. At the same time, this structure forms communication and relationships across these boundaries that bring the diverse viewpoints and perspectives of different specialties and departments together into interdisciplinary project teams.

This structure also allows more efficient utilization of resources, and a number of projects or products share individuals or groups of technical specialists, as well as equipment. Remember, one of the major disadvantages of divisional structures is duplication of resources. Matrix organization reduces such redundancy.

Employees who work in a matrix structure seem more motivated. Because they use project teams extensively, such firms tend to have more participatory and democratic cultures than those with functional organization structures. Career development is facilitated, as employees take advantage of opportunities to expand their experience and perspective. When they take account of a wider range of issues than those particular to their own specialties, they demonstrate their capabilities and enhance their promotional prospects.[15]

Disadvantages

During the 1970s, the matrix system spread to health care organizations, construction companies, electronics firms, banks, and other industries.[16] These firms believed that they needed a new approach to adapt to changing markets, more rapid product obsolescence, intensified international competition, heightened social consciousness, and increasing government regulation. However, by the late 1980s, many firms became disenchanted with the matrix structure and abandoned it.

The potential advantages of a matrix structure are difficult to realize fully, and in fact many of its most promising aspects often backfire.[17] If dual-authority structures are not carefully and explicitly documented, informal mechanisms may develop to coordinate critical tasks, leaving employees uncertain about their accountability to various supervisors. Similarly, disagreements among project and functional supervisors over shared resources may lead to power struggles. When project managers and functional managers disagree on project goals and the use of available technology, they may escalate conflict by referring decisions up the chain of command rather than solving problems themselves, which defeats the purpose of freeing upper management from such day-to-day responsibilities.

Another common problem with matrix structures is that they may diminish efficiency if the dual-command structure leads to an excessive number of managers. Dual command does not necessarily require doubling the managerial workforce. Small divisions rarely need a full complement of top managers, full-time project managers, and full-time functional-area managers if projects or functions are similar enough to be directed by a single manager; in practice, complex matrix-based organizations often become "top-heavy."

International Operations: Implications for Organizational Structure

As international operations become important to a firm's overall organization, managers must make corresponding changes in the firm's structure. As organizations expand into foreign markets, they usually follow a pattern of structural change that closely parallels their changes in strategy. Some factors that influence this are (1) the amount of product diversity, (2) the extent to which a firm depends on foreign sales, (3) the type of strategy that drives a firm's international operations,[18] (4) the extent of vertical integration, and (5) the sophistication of a firm's technology.

Recall from Chapter 8 that social and cultural imperatives drive multidomestic strategies and encourage managers within each country or geographic area to be responsive to local conditions. International division and geographic-area structures are consistent with this orientation. In both cases, local managers maintain a high level of autonomy to operate their product divisions within their geographic market's constraints and demands. As a firm's foreign sales increase as a percentage of its total sales, it will likely move from an international division structure to a geographic-area division structure. As a multidomestic firm's product diversity grows, it will likely benefit from a worldwide product division structure. However, when a firm has significant product-market diversity resulting because it has acquired a series of highly unrelated international enterprises, we are likely to see a worldwide holding company structure. Such firms are characterized by very little commonality among products, markets, or technologies and do not require integration.

Global strategies are driven by economic pressures that require managers to view operations in different geographic areas as only one component of a larger operation that must be managed for overall efficiency. Here, division managers view the marketplace as homogeneous and devote relatively little attention to local market, political, and economic factors. Firms with low levels of product diversity may find the worldwide functional structure appropriate, while firms with higher levels of product diversity may opt for a worldwide product division structure or a worldwide matrix structure, depending on their levels of foreign sales.

Emerging Horizontal Organizations

Consider how a customer encounters an airline company: a baggage handler curbside at the terminal entrance, followed by a ticket agent at the counter, then a gate attendant, flight attendants, and, finally, a baggage handler who returns the customer's luggage after the flight. Customers encounter most organizations in a similarly horizontal fashion. But most organizations are structured vertically. If these vertical units are insulated, uncommunicative groups, as they often are, each time the customer is "handed off" from one unit to another, there is a chance that something will be dropped. Recall how many times you have had to supply your college or university with the same information—name, identification number, address, and so on. That happened because the first unit you encountered did not communicate your information to all the other units, even though the vast majority of students will need to have this information on file in precisely the same places you do. In many such cases, vertically oriented organizations are structured for their own convenience rather than for the value that can be created for customers. If we want to emphasize customer value, we must rotate our organizations 90 degrees and begin to see them as customers do, as shown in Exhibit 10.5.

This customer orientation is a motivating factor behind the shift to managing processes rather than functions that is a recurring theme throughout this text. Cross-functional processes follow a perspective much closer to the customer's, and we have already discussed how customer value benefits from this switch. Here we want you to consider what is actually involved in shifting the organization's macrostructure in order to facilitate *process management* rather than management of individual departments. Here is a description of what appears to be the most promising process for bringing about this shift in organization.[19]

EXHIBIT 10.5
The Need to Build Horizontal Organizations

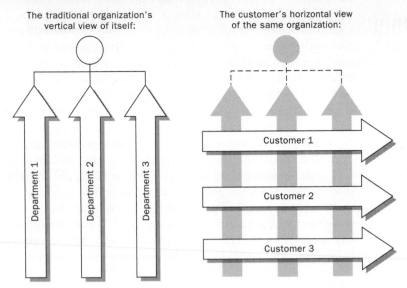

Customers have a view of organizations that is usually 90 degrees off the organization's view of itself.

Application 10.1 describes the efforts and successes of several firms that have attempted to shift from a vertical orientation to a horizontal one. Many of these companies are considered the bellwethers of industry, and most observers feel that their experiments with horizontal organization will establish trends that will be widely adopted in the near future.

1. *Identify the core processes necessary to establishing and maintaining your competitive advantage.* Chapters 4 and 5 presented our model of generic core processes (product development, demand management, and order fulfillment), but each organization should look at its own situation and identify what suits its particular strategy best.

2. *Organize significant "chunks" of the firm around these processes.* Some support groups may not be organized around processes, but the "line" activities involved in directly serving external customers should be organized around the processes customers care about the most.

3. *Assign an owner and a cross-functional team to each core process and to its individual subprocesses.* These teams become the building blocks of the organization. The vertical hierarchy is replaced with a series of means-ends relationships in which various subprocesses support one another and determine the success of the overall core process.

4. *Let customers influence how you measure performance.* The process was established to improve customer value. Therefore, it makes sense for customer satisfaction

Application 10.1

Industry Trendsetters Move Toward a Horizontal Organization

As organizations become more horizontally oriented in order to serve customers better, a number of leading corporations have begun to experiment by "flipping the organization on its side." This entails organizing around processes instead of functions or products, as the following examples indicate:

- Chrysler used a process approach to introduce the successful Neon subcompact in a fraction of the time—and at a fraction of the cost—normally required to develop a new car.

- AT&T units have experimented with making up annual budgets based not on functions or departments but on processes, such as maintaining a worldwide telecommunications network.

- GE's lighting business has been reorganized around 100 processes worldwide that are overseen by a senior leadership team which is itself cross-functional.

- Xerox has replaced parts of its complex matrix organization with one in which people are assigned to "microenterprise units" responsible for the entire process of developing a product or service, bringing it to market, and growing the business to a meaningful size.

- When Merck and Astra formed a joint venture to market new drugs, they chose to forgo creating functional departments and instead structured the entire organization around six "market-driven business processes." The director of strategic planning explained the move by saying, "A functional organization wasn't likely to support our strategic goals of being lean, fast, and focused on the customer."

- Hallmark discovered that the handoffs involved in developing a new card within its strictly functional organization resulted in a process that ran as long as 25

months. The firm has since replaced this organization with one in which cross-functional teams are organized around holidays and other card-giving occasions, dramatically reducing the product development cycle time.

- Eastman Chemical has even experimented by replacing senior managers with horizontally oriented teams. For instance, the position of senior vice president for manufacturing operations has been replaced by a "self-directed work team" comprising all of its plant managers.

What all these examples have in common is that they represent an effort to deemphasize the vertical dimensions of an organization and increase emphasis on the horizontal dimension. While the range of experiments taking place indicates that we have no single agreed-upon way of bringing about such a switch, the diversity of firms involved indicates that there is a broad-based interest in the change. Because many of these firms are considered trendsetters, it is likely that if their experiments continue to prove successful, the emphasis on horizontal organizations will spread to other firms. This will have important implications for new managers coming into industry. As one consultant who has observed this transformation has remarked, "Your career will be dependent on your ability to work across boundaries with others very different from you."

Sources

John A. Byrne, "The Horizontal Corporation" *Business Week* (December 20, 1993), 76–81; George Stalk, Jr., and Jill E. Black, "The Myth of the Horizontal Organization," *Canadian Business Review, 21* (Winter 1994), 26–28; Ronald K. Chung, "The Horizontal Organization," *Business Credit, 96* (May 1994), 21–24.

to be the measure of success. Departmentally specific performance measures designed for a vertically oriented organization usually don't work for a horizontally oriented organization.

5. *Change the appraisal and reward system to one that stresses team results, not individual results.* The big benefit of shifting to cross-functional processes is that it gives members of the organization an opportunity to align themselves with one

another. However, evaluating and rewarding team members as individuals will greatly limit the emphasis placed on team success.

6. *Encourage teams to strip out work that does not add value for the customer, allowing them to highlight value-creating work.* This will clarify the key roles that suppliers and customers play as members of the extended process team. Encourage this sort of upstream and downstream thinking and involvement.

7. *Revamp support systems (such as training, budgeting, and planning) to facilitate the new structure.* If these internally focused staff systems are left just as they were when the organization was vertically oriented, they will encourage the line organization to retain vertical orientation.

Selecting the Most Appropriate Macrostructure

We have covered several alternatives for structuring organizations. By this point, you are probably wondering how to choose among the various options. The answer depends on your chosen strategy and your organization's environment.[20] For instance, if your firm is pursuing a low-cost strategy in a mature, stable business, it is probably best served with a simple functional organization. This structure is also suited to the strategic programming approach to strategic management (see Chapter 2), in which formulation and implementation are clearly distinct. Any changes required are relatively small and easily planned well in advance, so strategic programming is an efficient means of strategy implementation and a good fit with the functional organization.

If your firm operates in a more volatile environment in which customer needs are changing and you hope to compete on a differentiation basis, you will probably be better served by a divisional structure. Such an organization will also be well suited to making more radical shifts in what it offers to customers as their needs and values change. However, it will probably not be terribly efficient in its operations on a day-to-day basis because it will lack the strong functional focus that is usually linked to achieving the highest levels of efficiency. We describe such an organization as more capable of breakthrough learning but less interested in incremental learning.

Organizations with strategies that require both types of learning and that want to combine the strengths of functional and divisional structures should consider a matrix structure. But traditional matrix organizations usually place greater emphasis on one dimension than the other, and managers must match this emphasis to their particular strategic needs.

MICRO-ORGANIZATIONAL STRUCTURE

Although the macro-organizational structures are critical context elements in terms of their impact on strategy implementation, much of the real work of organizations takes place in individual groups, teams, and departments within the broader organization. You should also remember that you will probably be able to influence one of these smaller units much sooner than you can influence the organization as a whole. For both these reasons, you need to understand these smaller organizational units as a second critical element of organizational context.

Traditionally, the basic units within the broader organization were departments, but that is changing as firms become more interested in managing cross-functional processes (as discussed in Chapter 5) than single-function departments. As organizations make this change, the team is emerging as the most important organizational unit. Application 10.2 provides an example of the importance of teams and illustrates many of the concepts that we discuss in this section.

What Makes a Team?

In their influential writing on teams, Jon Katzenbach and Douglas Smith, consultants with McKinsey & Company, define a team as "a small number of people with complementary skills who are committed to a common purpose, performance goal, and approach for which they hold themselves accountable."[21] This is a very broad definition, which could be interpreted to include many different types of suborganizational units. This flexibility is valuable because organizations use teams for many different purposes. However, you should not interpret this definition as covering just any group.

All teams are groups, but not all groups are teams. Committees, councils, and task forces are all groups, but few of them operate as teams. The key difference between a group and a team is the unit's performance. A group's performance is a function of what its individual members do. A team's performance depends on individual efforts as well as contributions that can be made only by two or more people working together to produce a combined product and meet a mutually held goal. In the best working groups, individuals come together to work alongside one another, but the focus is always on individual goals and individual accountability. When the members of a group become more concerned about their mutual goals and accountability than their individual goals and accountability, they meet the criteria set forth in our definition of a team. This shift does not happen quickly, nor is it always an easy process, as suggested by the model of how teams evolve from groups presented in Exhibit 10.6.

During the *forming* stage identified in the exhibit, groups attempt to define their tasks and decide how to accomplish them, while at the same time they sort out how the various group members will relate to one another. During the *storming* phase, members begin to sense what it will take to work together as a team, and they struggle with the group-to-team transition. This usually entails some combination of defensive behavior, competition to establish strength within the group, the creation of factions, "choosing sides," and establishing a "pecking order." This is often the most stressful period of team formation. In *norming*, members accept the fact that they must work as a team, reconcile competing loyalties, and establish ground rules or norms by which team members will cooperate. The emphasis here is on developing a harmonious set of relationships that will allow former group members to be team members. In the *performing* stage, the team has settled its relationships and validated its expectations and can turn to the work for which they are mutually accountable. At this stage, the unit is capable of more work in concert than the sum of their individual efforts would have produced.[22]

Application 10.2

Thermos: Success Through Teams

When Monte Peterson took over as CEO of Thermos, a division of the Japanese manufacturer Nippon Sanso, he faced a significant problem. The $225 million division depended on gas and electric outdoor cooking grills for a significant part of its business, but these products were looking like profitless commodities as market growth went flat and the entire industry began to cut prices. The highly departmentalized functional bureaucracy at Thermos appeared unable to do anything differently to address the problem, and Peterson could feel the division's future slipping away. To remedy the situation, he formed cross-functional teams to develop new products and bring them to market, in what has been called a "textbook lesson for any manager looking to use teamwork to revitalize a corporation."

Peterson wanted a completely new concept in grilling, so he created a team that had very limited connections to the "old" organization. He pulled individuals from every major department and function together and made the new team's success their collective responsibility. Initially, some team members resisted the change in focus and the shared responsibility that team membership required, but Peterson patiently reminded them that this was their best opportunity to have a significant impact not only on their company but on the entire industry, painting what he called a vivid "picture of the difference between winning and losing."

To make it clear that this team was to operate differently from the way things had been done before, it was given the name Lifestyle Team, suggesting that it was more important for the group to focus on its customers' lifestyles than on any one function or even on the design of any one grill. In fact, the team began its work by trying to forget every preconception and assumption about grilling and by going into people's backyards to "discover" how people actually grill.

As the team began to rethink grilling, it drew on Thermos's core competence in vacuum technology, used to keep liquids cold or hot in the firm's famous brand of Thermos bottles, to develop a concept for a totally new type of grill. Using the same vacuum bottle technology, the team was able to build an electric grill that got hot enough to sear foods, producing the cookout taste and the grill lines customers said were critical.

A product this different created problems for virtually every function represented on the team. Consequently, the team rotated leadership as the greatest responsibility for the design-and-rollout process shifted from one department to another. During the early stages, R&D took the lead, then Production, then Marketing. However, all the functional experts on the team remained involved throughout the process. For instance, when a designer proposed that the grill should have tapered legs, the production experts stepped in to show how such legs would greatly increase manufacturing costs, and the marketing experts concluded that customers would not be willing to pay for them. In the old Thermos organization, the production group would not have known about the tapered legs until production had already been scheduled and product drawings arrived.

Once the team members developed a prototype they could all agree on, they were not dismissed from the team and sent back to their former departments. Instead, they were given the responsibility of taking their prototype on the road to test and sell it. Thermos gave 100 units to employees, who were told to use them frequently to uncover flaws, while other units were taken to numerous retail trade shows around the country. Soon after the new units hit the market, it became apparent that the team had produced a winner. The new grill won four design awards, the company's grill revenues climbed 13 percent in the design's first year, and the company forecasted that the new unit would be the first of a series of similarly designed grilling products that would soon boost the division's share of the grill market from 2 percent to 20 percent.

Sources

Brian Dumaine, "Payoff from the New Management," *Fortune* (December 13, 1993), 103–110; Fara Warner, "Message in a Bottle: Thermos Updates Its Image," *Brandweek, 35* (January 31, 1994), 32.

Alternative Team Structures

Just as not all groups are teams, not all groups are organized the same way—and the way groups are organized has a big impact on whether members will work as a group

EXHIBIT 10.6
The Group-to-Team Evolutionary Process

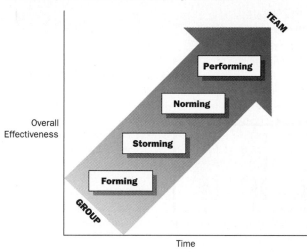

Overall
Effectiveness

Time

Source: Based on work presented in Peter R. Scholtes, *The Team Handbook*, Madison, WI: Joiner Associates, 1988.

or as a team. We can see this clearly in comparing the different ways in which organizations go about integrating activities across different departmental areas.[23] Compare the four options depicted in Exhibit 10.7.

- *Departmental organizations.* In these groups, integration occurs primarily through oversight and coordination provided by general managers. This approach works for many organizations, especially smaller, simpler ones. But when cross-departmental integration is required, the organization can arrive at a bottleneck if general management is unable to address more than a few integration issues at a time—a point we discussed earlier under the disadvantages of functional organization. For this reason, most larger organizations do not depend on this form of integration.

- *Liaison groups.* Firms may create task forces, committees, or councils to which each department sends a representative in a liaison role. This type of organization is appropriate when the purpose of the group is really interdepartmental coordination rather than integration. Universities use this form of organization extensively, and it works reasonably well in keeping various departments informed of developments and in coordinating individual activities, such as allocation of parking spaces, approval of new courses, or creation of handbooks on student conduct. However, such groups are virtually incapable of dealing with more integrative tasks. Because most strategic issues are integrative by nature, this form of organization doesn't work well in dealing with significant strategic issues.

- *Project units.* To settle integrative issues, firms often choose this third option. They establish a project team consisting of a project manager and members in various departments. Sometimes this form of organization is further divided into

EXHIBIT 10.7
Options for Organizing Cross-Functional Integration

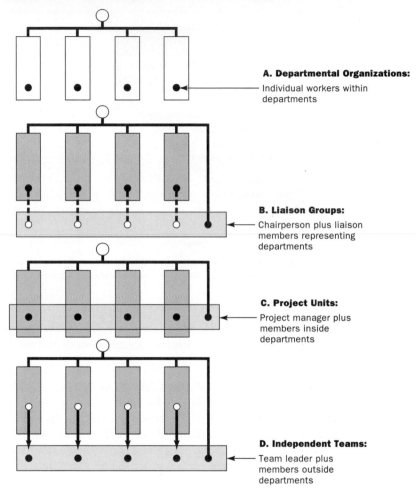

A. Departmental Organizations:
Individual workers within departments

B. Liaison Groups:
Chairperson plus liaison members representing departments

C. Project Units:
Project manager plus members inside departments

D. Independent Teams:
Team leader plus members outside departments

Source: Based on work presented in Robert H. Hayes, Steven C. Wheelwright, and Kim B. Clark, *Dynamic Manufacturing,* New York: The Free Press, 1988; and Takahiro Fujimoto, ''Organizations for Effective Product Development,'' Ph.D. dissertation, Harvard Business School, 1989.

two types, according to the power and influence the project manager holds. If project managers' authority and power over team members are less than those of the team members' department heads, they are what researchers have dubbed "lightweight" project managers. On the other hand, a project manager who has more power than department heads do (especially power to hire, fire, and promote members of the team) is called a "heavyweight" project manager. In matrix structures, where organization is based on project units, this issue may be more formalized, but many organizations often mix these two types of projects indiscriminately. This is not a good idea; a unit's structure should reflect its purpose. If a project unit needs to overcome individual interests and focus on the mutual accountability—that is, if it needs to work as a team—then project managers need more clout. If the project manager is a lightweight compared to department heads, the members of the unit will probably remain loyal to their individual departments and behave as a group of individuals rather than as a team. Many organizations make this mistake, causing their teams to fall short of their goals.

- *Independent teams.* The last option creates a team that operates *outside* the organization's conventional departments. In this arrangement, team members do not report to their department heads but rather to team leaders. This allows considerable latitude in doing whatever the team needs, with minimal concern for department-specific issues. This type of structure is sometimes called a "skunk works," named after the character in the *Li'l Abner* comic strip who everyone else avoided because he worked at the skunk works, an illicit distillery. In a similar fashion, members of an independent team remain part from the rest of the organization. As illustrated by Application 10.2, radically new products most often result from teams' working in such skunk works. In the 1950s, the legendary Kelly Johnson successfully used the skunk-works concept to create product design teams at Lockheed that made incredible advances in aircraft design very quickly and very cost-effectively. Johnson recruited the most talented people from throughout the corporation, isolated them from the rest of the organization, and had them focus exclusively on working together to develop aircraft that the rest of the world could not begin to imagine. In a time when engineers still used slide rules instead of computers, he used this form of microstructure to develop three of the most important, trendsetting jet aircraft designs of that era, including the famous "Blackbird" spy plane, an aircraft so advanced that it can only be piloted by qualified astronauts and is still the most advanced aircraft of its type more than 40 years after its initial development.[24]

Selecting Between Alternative Team Structures

Johnson's success with skunk works should not be taken as an indication that this, or any other option, is inherently superior to all others. The most appropriate option depends on what an organization needs to accomplish. Eric Olson at the University of Colorado conducted research on forty-five product development efforts and concluded that, just as we saw for macrostructures, there are clearly "different horses for different courses" for microstructures.[25] As shown in Exhibit 10.8, coordinating cross-departmental projects depends on the need for group activity versus teamwork and the desire for maintaining status quo versus breaking with tradition.

According to this exhibit, using an independent team to make a simple product modification does not make sense; teams take too long, and the issue might better be handled by a general manager who simply makes a decision and informs the relevant departments. At the other extreme, Olson found that when faced with the task of developing an entirely new product, an independent team clearly represents the best choice. In between these extremes, when firms extend an existing product line or refine a component of a preexisting design, the project unit option would be more appropriate, with a heavyweight project manager in charge of an effort responsible for

EXHIBIT 10.8
EXHIBIT 10.8
Match Options for Microstructure to What the Organization Wants to Accomplish

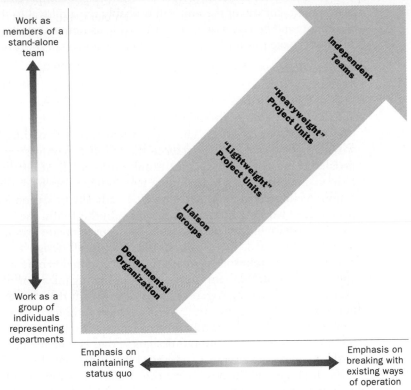

larger, more innovative steps and lightweight managers responsible for smaller product extensions or refinements. If the unit is not innovating but scheduling production across various departments, departmental liaisons can probably coordinate activities. Finally, if the organization requires very little integration across departments, a simple departmental organization might be sufficient. Just as we saw in considering options for macrostructures, when selecting between the various options for microstructures, managers should carefully consider the strategic issue or change to be addressed.

INFORMAL NETWORKS

Informal networks are communication channels outside the formal chain of command. Organizational members rely on these to make contact with one another on a reasonably regular, sustained basis. Regardless of the formal macro- or micro-organizational structures in place, much of what gets done in organizations takes place through informal networks.[26]

Why Are Informal Networks Important?

Informal networks are important for organizational effectiveness for two reasons. First, formal organizations are too often inefficient, and second, formal organizations cannot hope to identify all the roles an organization's members must play.

To begin understanding the first of these reasons, consider the simple organizational chart shown in Exhibit 10.9. Let's assume that the organization depicted in this exhibit needs to plan next year's operations and that the only way the individuals in the three departments coordinate their activities is through the formal communication channels depicted in the chart. Let's also assume that all communications are 90 percent effective (in other words, 90 percent of what is said by one party is understood by the next party). Let's also assume that departments are involved sequentially: Sales announces its plans for promotions in the upcoming year, and, based on that input, Manufacturing establishes a production plan for the year that is then passed on to Purchasing to place orders for required parts. How effective will this organization be? The effect will be the same one you may have observed in the childhood game "Gossip." As each party communicates with the next, the message becomes more garbled, until, in the end, it comes out sounding nothing like the original. With 90 percent communication efficiency (an unrealistically high number, given our experience), by the time the message is communicated through formal channels, only 43 percent of it remains intact (calculated as $.90^8$). Given this overall inefficiency in the flow of information through a formal chain of command, it comes as no surprise that organizations depend so heavily on their informal networks.[27]

The second reason why informal networks are so powerful is that most people in organizations play more roles than can be captured on organizational charts. The macrostructures and microstructures we discussed in the previous two sections assume that people in organizations play one, maybe two, roles and therefore fit neatly into boxes. While organizational charts are a useful starting point for thinking about

EXHIBIT 10.9
A Hypothetical Example of the Inefficiency of Formal Groups

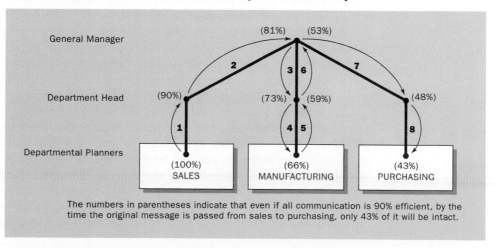

The numbers in parentheses indicate that even if all communication is 90% efficient, by the time the original message is passed from sales to purchasing, only 43% of it will be intact.

how organizations work, we know that they can capture only a small part of how organizations really work, because most people in organizations play many more roles than we can possibly hope to chart on paper. Consider, for instance, a young female production engineer who serves as a member of, say, a reengineering team. On the organizational chart, she is not even listed as a member of this team but as a member of the production engineering department. This is not all that inaccurate; she spends a significant part of her time in the engineering department doing engineering work. But beyond being an engineer, she plays other roles, or "wears many hats," as the saying goes. She wears a second hat when she serves as part of the reengineering team and focuses on what she can do to help the team reach its shared objective. At other times she wears her departmental hat and tries to make sure that her home department is not getting saddled with too much responsibility without the matching resources. At still other times, she wears her professional-woman hat, demonstrating how women can succeed in what has traditionally been a male-dominated field. Most people in large organizations are like this, with many roles beyond the one or two identified for them on an organizational chart. This being the case, we need to move beyond the formal macrostructures and microstructures to study the organization *behind* the charts if we hope to truly understand an organization.

Obviously, informal networks are different from formal macrostructures, but you may not be as clear on how networks differ from the microstructures we have considered as the means of organizing teams and groups. The difference is threefold: First, members of formal groups are usually appointed or recruited, while members of an informal network participate of their own choosing. Second, unlike most teams, which tend to have closed-end objectives, networks are not temporary; they tend to reflect established, ongoing, long-lasting relationships. Third, networks rarely focus on any single problem or issue; rather, they revolve around whatever issue their members find most interesting.

Types of Informal Networks

Researchers have identified three important types of networks.[28] First, *communication networks* connect people to one another so they can address work-related issues. This type of network is widely used to get things done when formal structures are too slow and inefficient, and it is the type most people refer to when they speak of networks in general. But two other types of networks will be important to you as a manager. One is the *advice network*, which connects people who turn to one another to seek counsel, get technical answers, and solve specific problems. Finally, there is the *trust network*, which connects people who are willing to share sensitive information with one another.[29]

As a member of an organization, you will probably be most effective if you participate in all three networks, using them to overcome the limitations of formal organization structures. However, as a leader, your involvement will need to go beyond merely using the networks; you will need to know how to shape them to your organization's advantage. Researchers have identified six different configurations, or shapes, of networks, along with actions managers can take to reinforce or reshape particular network features.[30] Any of the three types of networks identified above can take on any of the six configurations summarized in Exhibit 10.10 and discussed below.

EXHIBIT 10.10
Network Configurations and Appropriate Managerial Actions

Network Type	Configuration (simplified drawing)	Appropriate Managerial Action
1. Healthy		Monitor and maintain health.
2. Imploded	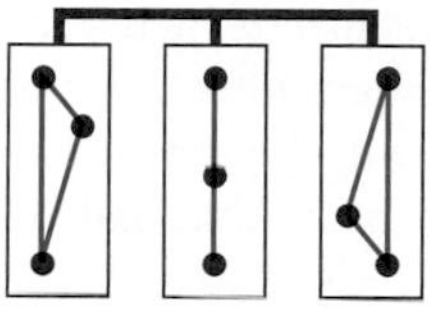	Attack walls dividing departments.
3. Factionalized	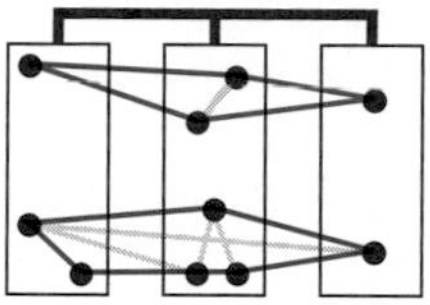	Build bridges between factions.
4. Fragile	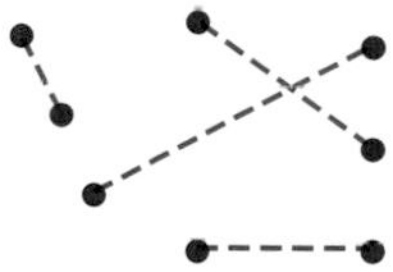	Encourage interaction and team building.
5. Holed	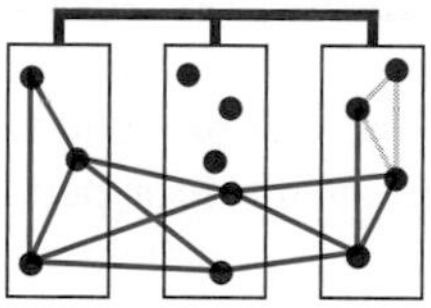	Focus on integrating the missing pieces.
6. Bow Tie	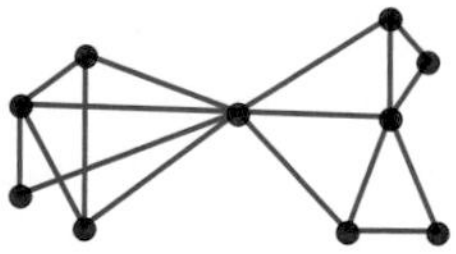	Build connections that don't involve the "knot."

- *Healthy networks* A healthy organizational network is much like air traffic connecting various cities. Important "hub" cities have frequently used direct connections, while smaller cities are connected to the rest of the network like "spokes" off a major city hub, as well as having some direct connections between them. In the same way, a healthy organizational network provides multiple links among a substantial number of individuals who are critical to the organization's success, but not everyone needs to be directly connected to everyone else, as long as they have at least an indirect way of reaching others. (As you might guess, the "hubs" of organizational networks are often individuals who have considerable power and influence in the organization, a point to which we return in Chapter 12.) Managers can maintain the health of such a network by explicitly considering it when making organizational decisions. For instance, when someone who functions as a hub is promoted, how will the network fill the resulting hole? As another example, we know of an organization that had an opportunity to employ a brilliant expert whose talents perfectly matched the firm's most critical deficiency for 3 years before he retired. Despite his fit with the organization's needs, senior managers feared he would still be ineffective, because he was not well connected to the healthy informal network that tied the organization's worldwide operations together. Consequently, they decided to pair the expert with a younger manager who was one of the most popular "hubs" in each of the firm's communication, trust, and advice networks. The pair toured the firm's international operations for 3 years like "twins joined at the hip," to use their own words. As a result, the expert was successful at quickly tapping into the network and the younger manager emerged as the new expert when the older manager was ready to retire.

- *Imploded networks* In this configuration, the informal network closely parallels the formal macro-organizational structure, which, of course, severely limits the benefits of such a network. People tend to talk to others in the same department, and frequently only the most senior people in the department—the department heads—contact other departments. We know of a case where two employees who were from separate departments, but who had been assigned to offices 614 and 514 of the same office building for more than 6 years, met by accident for the first time in a conference center elevator 1,000 miles from home. When separation by one floor is enough to stop any on-the-job contact between departments for 6 years, not much of a network has developed outside departmental lines. Addressing this problem is a bit like trying to get the boys to talk to the girls at their first elementary school dance. One general manager in a research institution addressed this problem by restricting seed money for new research initiatives to interdepartmental projects. In another organization, the general manager agreed to pick up the tab for "power breakfasts" as long as the employees were from different departments.

- *Factionalized networks* These are similar to imploded networks, except that instead of network boundaries being drawn along departmental lines, they are drawn between rival factions. Factional boundary lines often cut across different departments, with the result that cooperation and communication within the divided department suffers. The challenge in addressing this problem is one of peacemaking. Involving a respected, but neutral, third party may be necessary to intervene, open up dialogue, and build bridges between the two factions.

- *Fragile networks* These are simply cases where networks are very weak. Few ties exist; perhaps even these are seldom used. One organization is currently trying to strengthen its fragile networks by insisting that every class in its extensive training program contain no more than a single person from any one department. Other organizations have turned to weekly companywide celebrations or less frequent social events; Outward Bound–type team-building exercises are also popular approaches to strengthening weak networks.

- *"Holed" networks* Sometimes gaps arise in otherwise healthy networks. For instance, one division of a large automobile manufacturer houses all its departments except one in a single location near the division's primary assembly facility. The missing department, Engineering, is located with the rest of the corporation's engineering group in another state. As you might guess, it has never been part of the team in quite the same way as all the other departments. Advances in teleconferencing have gone a long way to address the problems here, but nothing substitutes for regular "live," face-to-face contact, and the hole is still noticeable.

- *"Bow tie" networks* When this type of network is drawn on paper, the reason for its odd name becomes clear. One or two individuals are in the position of the "knot," which lies between a larger subnetwork on either side. This arrangement gives tremendous power to the individual(s) connecting the two networks, which may be good or bad depending on what the organization needs and how the power is used. However, the "knot" may turn into a bottleneck that proves incapable of providing all the needed communication between the two subnetworks, and if a connecting individual ever leaves the organization, the two subnetworks will be isolated from each other. We know of one manager who had long relished her power as the gatekeeper who controlled virtually all contact between two otherwise separate networks. When the organization was small, the situation was of little concern, but as it grew, the need for more extensive communication between the two groups increased, and the single manager severely limited the organization's performance. The problem was eventually solved when senior management found an opportunity to promote the manager to a higher organizational level—to "bump her upstairs"—where she worked with a smaller team of staff specialists who already had good contacts throughout the organization's networks.

As these examples show, managers find power through membership and participation in informal networks that can be personally beneficial. However, the ability to reshape networks offers a different type of power. This power can have an organizationwide impact, and as such it offers an important opportunity to bring about organizational change and implement strategies.

EXHIBIT 10.11
Organizational Culture: Definitions and Perspectives

■ The customary or traditional ways of thinking and doing things, which are shared to a greater or lesser extent by all members of the organization and which new members must learn and at least partially accept in order to be accepted into the service of the firm. (Jacques, 1951)

■ Shared philosophies . . . expectations, attitudes, and norms that knit an organization together. (Kilmann, Saxton, & Serpa, 1985)

■ Artifacts, perspectives, values, and assumptions:
  Artifacts include myths and language that organizational members have in common, technology, dress codes, and frequently repeated rituals and ceremonies.
  Perspectives consist of sets of ideas and actions that people activate when faced with a specific situation.
  Values are guides for overall behavior. These guides include general goals and standards, such as serve the customer, or promote from within.
  Assumptions are the core beliefs which underlie artifacts, perspectives, and values. They form the foundation of culture. (Dyer, 1985, 1986)

■ Basic assumptions and beliefs shared by organization members. (Schein, 1986)

Sources: E. H. Schein, *Organization Culture and Leadership,* San Francisco: Jossey-Bass, 1986; R. H. Kilmann, M. J. Saxton, and R. Serpa, "Five Key Issues in Understanding and Changing Culture," in R. H. Kilmann, M. J. Saxton, and R. Serpa, eds., *Gaining Control of the Corporate Culture,* San Francisco: Jossey-Bass, 1985; E. Jacques, *The Changing Culture of a Factory,* London: Tavistock, 1951; W. G. Dyer, Jr., "The Cycle of Cultural Evolution in Organizations," in R. H. Kilmann, M. J. Saxton, and R. Serpa, eds., *Gaining Control of the Corporate Culture,* San Francisco: Jossey-Bass, 1985; W. G. Dyer, Jr., *Cultural Change in Family Firms: Anticipating and Managing Business and Family Transitions,* San Francisco: Jossey-Bass, 1986.

ORGANIZATIONAL CULTURE

In this final section of our discussion of organizational context, we consider culture by defining it, describing why it is so important, and discussing the effort required to change it in an attempt to use it as a lever for implementing strategy.

What Is Culture, and
Why Is It Important?

Organizational cultures can be viewed as systems of shared values (about what is important) and beliefs (about how things work) that shape a company's behavioral norms (the way "we do" things "around here").[31] Exhibit 10.11 provides other definitions of and perspectives on organizational culture, all of which are consistent with this view.

At the heart of all these definitions is the notion of *shared values.* A value is "an enduring preference for a mode of conduct or an end-state."[32] Managers are frequently unaware that their daily activities are usually governed by culture and shared values. As our definitions of culture and value suggest, we are dealing here with the "givens," or what is taken for granted, about how work is to be done and how one should interact with others. Seen from this perspective, culture reflects many unstated but mutually held beliefs.[33] An organizational culture is powerful because it automatically shapes the way members see their world and behave.[34] Any culture is deeply rooted in beliefs and values that members have internalized, and when beliefs and values are held without challenge for a long period of time, they are even less likely to be questioned. Violations of norms that grow out of cultural values tend to result in pressure to conform, in what amounts to a form of organizational inertia.

The power of culture as a context lever lies in the fact that these inertial forces can be either beneficial or detrimental.[35] Having a stable, widely understood view of "the way we do things around here" can be very beneficial as long as the way we do things works—but what if it stops working? We know of a hospital that demonstrates both the benefits and the detriments of a strong culture. For years, this hospital had benefited from an organizational culture that placed tremendous emphasis on pampering patients. For example, if a patient wanted a different brand of ginger ale than the one the hospital normally carried, someone popped over to get it from a local grocery store. No one worried too much about the costs incurred by such service. While such extras could not be billed to the patient's insurance company, enough other things could be billed to insurance companies, on what amounted to a cost-plus basis, that the hospital could afford such niceties.

But as health care costs soared nationwide, insurance companies began to change their method of payment. Rather than covering a fixed percentage of whatever the patient's bill might be, they began using prespecified standard rates, paying a fixed amount for a specific hospital service regardless of the hospital's actual cost. The capitated rates reflected no-frills service, so that whenever the hospital offered the out-of-the-ordinary pampering that had made it so popular, it now did so at a loss. Though the hospital's management immediately recognized the need for a different approach to operating the hospital, individuals throughout the organization were slow to change, and many continued to offer little extras on an unofficial basis. This may sound like a good example of being dedicated to customer service, but as long as employees insisted on offering the old frills, the hospital could never compete profitably in the new price-sensitive marketplace. Unable to match competitors on the prices it could offer insurance companies for fixed-rate services, the hospital began to lose market share, and soon it was forced to reduce its workforce by a third. The culture that had once provided the key to the organization's success now threatened to destroy it, as management struggled with one of the toughest challenges of leadership: changing an organization's culture.

Changing an Organization's Culture

In their best-selling book *Corporate Cultures*, T. E. Deal and A. A. Kennedy conclude that real and enduring change in an organization's culture "costs a fortune and takes forever."[36] But the results can be worth it, as illustrated in Application 10.3.

Although each situation is unique, here are some general guidelines for bringing about significant changes in an organization's culture:[37]

Application 10.3

Kodak Changes Its Culture and Its Performance

Chuck Trowbridge dramatically reversed the sagging performance of Eastman Kodak's copy products group by imparting a culture dedicated to excellence—he envisioned becoming a world-class manufacturing organization. However, implementing such a culture was not easy. When Trowbridge became the general manager of the newly formed group, sales had recently grown to nearly $1 billion. But costs were high, profits were negligible, and problems popped up nearly everywhere. Changing the culture required developing many forms of written communication as well as enhancing face-to-face communication.

Central to Trowbridge's efforts was the vital role played by Bob Crandall, head of the group's engineering and manufacturing operations. To align people with the new direction, Crandall set up several mechanisms: he organized weekly meetings with twelve managers who reported directly to him; monthly "copy product forums" included different employees from each of his departments; quarterly meetings with all 100 of the supervisors under him, to discuss recent improvements and new projects for achieving higher performance; and quarterly "state of the department" meetings, in which his managers met with all of the employees in their departments. In addition, Crandall held weekly meetings with his managers and his organization's largest supplier, the Kodak Apparatus Division, which supplied one-third of the parts used in the design and manufacture of his products. Trowbridge and Crandall also used many forms of written communication in implementing the new culture. Employees received a newsletter, *Copy Products Journal,* once a month, and a program called "Dialog Letters" allowed employees to anonymously ask top executives questions and be guaranteed a reply. Perhaps the most powerful form of written communication consisted of charts that vividly reported measures of quality, cost, and delivery for each product against different targets. A prominent chart reporting quality levels and costs for the various work groups was displayed in a main hallway near the cafeteria, and 100 smaller versions were displayed throughout the manufacturing area.

Performance improvements associated with the new organizational culture began to appear within 6 months and continued to increase. Such favorable results helped make the efforts more credible and increased employees' commitment to the changes. Viewed over an extended period, the improvements were striking. Defects per unit declined from 30 to 0.3–a hundredfold improvement. Also, over a 3-year period, costs on another product line decreased 24 percent, on-time deliveries increased from 82 percent to 95 percent, and productivity measured in units per manufacturing employee doubled.

Source

Based on information gathered from J. P. Kotter, *A Force for Change,* New York: The Free Press, 1990, 52–55.

- *Understand the current organizational culture so you know where you stand.*

- *Avoid head-on confrontations with the old guard if at all possible.*

- *Change the management leadership.*[38] A gradual shift may be appropriate, or top executives may have to "clean house" and bring in all new managers.

- *While vision statements can be important, don't count on them alone to bring about cultural change.* Words become empty and hypocritical if those using them neglect to change their own behavior. Leaders must "live the new culture."

- *Create new organizational folklore.* The definition of a myth is "a fictional tale that offers insight into a deeper truth." Organizations help themselves understand who they are by the stories they tell one another about themselves.[39]

- *Use symbols to instill new thinking.* Symbols often become the subject of new organizational folklore and myths. For instance, we know of one organization where, even 10 years after the fact, employees still gleefully tell the story of how their CEO tried to flush the company's oversized policy manual down the toilet.

- *Persevere.* Significant changes in organizational culture can take anywhere from 5 to 10 years to complete.

In the remaining two chapters, we will be pointing out other ways in which leaders can affect organizational culture, from changing the way they personally operate to changing the way the firm's support systems operate. But regardless of how change is brought about, altering an organization's culture has a powerful impact on its behavior and the strategy it can hope to implement successfully, which makes organizational culture one of the most important levers for strategic change. When used in concert with the other context levers of macrostructure, microstructure, and informal networks, the result can be an especially strong impetus to change.

Summary of Managerial Practices to Adopt from This Chapter

- Organizational context is easily overlooked as a lever for change because it works in the background. However, it has a powerful effect on organizational actions, and you should consider it one of the strongest levers available to help bring about strategic change and implement strategies.

- In thinking about organizational context, keep two dimensions in mind. One distinguishes between "hardware" and "software" issues, while the other distinguishes between what applies organizationwide versus what applies only to part of the organization. This conceptual framework will help you identify elements of organizational context that apply to macrostructure, microstructure, informal networks, and organizational culture, giving you the widest possible set of influence points.

- There are many alternative forms of organizational structure, all of which have advantages and disadvantages. No one structure is necessarily right for a particular organization. The most appropriate alternative depends on the nature of the strategy the firm is pursuing.

- Regardless of the macrostructure chosen, much of the day-to-day work done by the organization will take place within organizational subunits. The behavior of individuals in these groups or teams is greatly influenced by the subunits' formal structures. Just as the most appropriate macrostructure depends on the organization's purpose, the most appropriate microstructure depends on each subunit's purpose. Consider the purpose, and match the structure to it.

- Informal networks allow organizations to overcome the limitations inherent in any formal organization. Your effectiveness as a manager and leader will depend in part on your use of the organization's informal networks. Not all networks work as well as they could, and steps can be taken to address the most common network ailments. Taking such steps is an important responsibility of leadership.

- Organizational culture has a tremendous "inertial" effect in determining what organizations will and won't do. Consequently, it is perhaps the most powerful type of context lever. However, it is also a very difficult lever to manipulate; changing cultures is a slow, demanding process. There are certainly ways in which you can influence your organization's culture, but you should expect any change to take place over a number of years, and only then with constant effort.

- The way to have the greatest impact on organizational change and strategy implementation is to understand the roles of each of the different elements of organizational context and to use these in concert to shape the day-to-day behavior of people throughout the organization.

Questions for Discussion and Review

1. Give three examples and explain how organizational context influences the behavior of members in an organization.

2. List advantages and disadvantages of different forms of macro-organizational structure and explain how to select the most appropriate of these for a particular organization.

3. Describe what makes a team and how to choose between several alternative team structures.

4. Describe various forms of informal networks and tell what role each plays inside an organization.

5. Explain what organizational culture is and how managers can use it to implement strategic change.

Notes

1. Peter M. Senge, *The Fifth Discipline: The Art and Practice of the Learning Organization*, New York: Doubleday/Currency, 1990.
2. Robert Howard, "The CEO as Organizational Architect: An Interview with Xerox's Paul Allaire," *Harvard Business Review* (September–October 1992), 106–121.
3. The pioneering work regarding the evolution of a firm's strategy and its relationship to structure (i.e., simple, functional, divisional) is known as the Scott Stages Model. It is discussed in J. R. Galbraith and R. K. Kazanjian, *Strategy Implementation: The Role of Structure and Process*, 2d ed., St. Paul, MN: West Publishing Co., 1986.
4. R. E. Miles, "Adaptations to Technology and Competition: A New Industrial Relations System for the 21st Century," *California Management Review*, 31 (1989), 9–27.

5. P. Berman, "The Fast Track Isn't Always the Best Track," *Forbes* (November 2, 1987), 60–64.

6. M. Jelinek, *Organizations by Design: Theory and Practice*, Plano, TX: Business Publications, 1986.

7. The seminal works relating strategy to structure are A. D. Chandler, *Strategy and Structure*, Cambridge, MA: MIT Press, 1962; and R. P. Rumelt, *Strategy, Structure, and Economic Performance*, Boston: Division of Research, Harvard Business School, 1974. This trend was also observed in other industrial countries such as England, Spain, and Germany; see D. Channon, *The Strategy and Structure of British Enterprise*, London: Macmillan, 1973; L. Franco, *The European Multinationals*, Greenwich, CT: Greylock, 1976; and H. Thanheiser, *Strategy and Structure of German Firms*, unpublished doctoral dissertation, Cambridge, MA: Harvard Business School, 1972. Evidence of the increasing popularity of the divisional form of organizational structure and some of the dysfunctions associated with it is provided by C. W. Hill, M. A. Hitt, and R. E. Hoskisson, "Declining U.S. Competitiveness: Reflections on a Crisis," *Academy of Management Executive, 2* (1988), 51–60.

8. R. E. Hoskisson, "Multidivisional Structure and Performance: The Contingency of Diversification Strategy," *Academy of Management Journal, 30* (1987), 625–644.

9. T. A. Stewart, "Westinghouse Gets Respect at Last," *Fortune* (July 3, 1989), 92–94, 96, 98.

10. An interesting perspective on the advantages of a divisional type of organization structure is provided in Oliver Williamson, *Markets and Hierarchies: Analysis and Antitrust Implications*, New York: The Free Press, 1975. Williamson argued that the divisional form of organizational structure (also referred to as a multidivisional, or M-form, structure) helps to overcome the problems relating to both internal and strategic control that are generally faced by diversified firms. Diversified firms that retain a functional organizational structure, he advised, will have not only lower efficiency because of a loss of internal control but also a weaker long-term perspective because of a loss of strategic control. Information overload for the CEO will result because of the need to process too much information. With the formation of relatively autonomous divisions and the delegation of operating responsibilities that are implicit in a divisional form, the role of top corporate executives becomes one of allocating resources as well as evaluating opportunities for and threats to the entire organization.

11. The seminal article on the issue of overemphasis on a short-term orientation by U.S. corporations is R. H. Hayes and W. J. Abernathy, "Managing Our Way to Economic Decline," *Harvard Business Review, 58* (1980), 67–77.

12. W. F. Joyce, "Matrix Organization: A Social Experiment," *Academy of Management Journal, 29* (1986), 536–561.

13. K. L. Kelley, "Are Two Bosses Better than One?," *Machine Design* (January 12, 1984), 73–76.

14. Kelley, "Are Two Bosses Better than One?"

15. E. W. Larson and D. H. Gobeli, "Matrix Management: Contradictions and Insights," *California Management Review, 29* (1987), 126–138.

16. C. E. Kur, "Making Matrix Management Work," *Supervisory Management, 27* (1982), 37–43.

17. This section draws heavily on the work of S. M. Davis and P. R. Lawrence, "Problems of Matrix Organizations," *Harvard Business Review, 56* (1978), 131–142; and Larson and Gobeli, "Matrix Management."

18. J. M. Stopford and L. T. Wells, Jr., *Managing in the Multinational Enterprise*, New York: Basic Books, 1972; J. D. Daniels, R. A. Pitts, and M. J. Tretter, "Strategy and Structure of U.S. Multinationals: An Exploratory Study," *Academy of Management Journal, 27* (1984), 292–307.

19. These steps reflect personal experience as well as the opinions of various authors on the subject; see Frank Ostroff and Douglas Smith, "The Horizontal Organization," *McKinsey Quarterly* (Winter 1992), 148–167; and John A. Byrne, "The Horizontal Corporation," *Business Week* (December 20, 1993), 76–81.

20. Sumantra Ghoshal and Nitin Nohria, "Horses for Courses: Organizational Forms for Multinational Corporations," *Sloan Management Review, 34* (Winter 1993), 23–35.

21. Jon R. Katzenbach and Douglas K. Smith, *The Wisdom of Teams*, Boston: Harvard Business School Press, 1992, 112.

22. This model of team development, as well as a wealth of other valuable information on teams and teamwork, is provided in Peter R. Scholtes, *The Team Handbook*, Madison, WI: Joiner Associates, 1988.

23. Robert H. Hayes, Steven C. Wheelwright, and Kim B. Clark, *Dynamic Manufacturing*, New York: The Free Press, 1988.

24. Clarence L. "Kelly" Johnson with Maggie Smith, *Kelly: More than My Share of It All*, Washington, DC: Smithsonian Institution Press, 1987.

25. Brian Dumaine, "Payoff from the New Management," *Fortune* (December 13, 1993), 103–110.

26. Patricia A. Galagan, "Managing the White Space: The Work of Geary Rummler," *Training and Development, 46* (August 1992), 26–30; Christopher A. Bartlett and Sumantra Ghoshal, "Matrix Management: Not a Structure, a Frame of Mind," *Harvard Business Review* (July–August 1990), 168.

27. Charles C. Snow, Raymond E. Miles, and Henry J. Coleman, Jr., "Managing 21st Century Network Organizations," *Organizational Dynamics, 20* (Winter 1992), 5–20.

28. David Krackhardt and Jeffrey R. Hanson, "Informal Networks: The Company Behind the Chart," *Harvard Business Review* (July–August 1993), 104–111.

29. While these descriptions are of networks of individuals found within a single organization, research has found that there are analogous forms of networks between organizations. See Raymond E. Miles and Charles C. Snow, "Causes of Failure in Network Organizations," *California Management Review, 34* (Summer 1992), 53–72; and Snow, Miles, and Coleman, "Managing 21st Century Network Organizations."

30. Krackhardt and Hanson, "Informal Networks."

31. B. Uttal, "The Corporate Culture Vultures," *Fortune, 66* (October 17, 1983), 68–72.

32. Paul McDonald and Jeffrey Gandz, "Getting Value from Shared Values," *Organizational Dynamics, 20* (Winter 1992), 64–77.

33. V. Sathe, "Implications of Corporate Culture: A Manager's Guide to Action," *Organizational Dynamics, 12* (1983), 4–23.

34. A. Wilkins, "The Culture Audit: A Tool for Understanding Organizations," *Organizational Dynamics, 12* (1983), 24–38.

35. George D. Gordon and Nancy DiTomaso, "Predicting Corporate Performance from Organizational Culture," *Journal of Management Studies, 29* (November 1992), 783–798.

36. T. E. Deal and A. A. Kennedy, *Corporate Cultures*, Reading, MA: Addison-Wesley, 1982. See also J. Richard Harrison and Glenn R. Carroll, "Keeping the Faith: A Model of Cultural Transmission in Formal Organizations," *Administrative Science Quarterly, 36* (December 1991), 552–582.

37. G. C. Gordon, "Five Key Issues in Understanding and Changing Culture," in R. H. Kilmann, M. J. Saxton, and R. Serpa, eds., *Gaining Control of the Corporate Culture*, San Francisco: Jossey-Bass, 1985; B. Nixon, "Strategy and Culture—Bridging the Gap," *Accountancy* (July 1987), 90–92; B. Dumaine, "Creating a New Company Culture," *Fortune* (January 15, 1990), 127–131.

38. McDonald and Gandz, "Getting Value from Shared Values."

39. David M. Boje, "The Storytelling Organization: A Study of Story Performance in an Office-Supply Firm," *Administrative Science Quarterly, 36* (March 1991), 106–126.

Chapter 11
Systems Levers

In this chapter, we consider how an organization's support systems can hinder or facilitate successful implementation of its strategy. Properly managed, these support systems provide a powerful lever for strategy implementation. The chapter is divided into five parts. The first overviews resourcing and control systems and describes their importance in shaping both an organization's actions and the strategy that emerges as a result of those actions. The next three sections look at systems that allocate three basic resources: information, people, and capital. The final section of the chapter explains how organizations control the use of allocated resources and monitor the organization's progress toward its goals, effectively using control systems as levers for strategic implementation.

This chapter will help you understand:

- The importance of organizational support systems and how small changes in the way systems are managed can impact the strategy an organization is able to implement, making them powerful levers
- The difference between resourcing systems and control systems and how they complement each other
- The power of information to serve as an integrating device in fragmented organizations
- How what we measure influences what we do; the need to supplement traditional accounting-based measures with complementary nonfinancial measures
- The critical importance of human resources in determining a firm's organizational capabilities
- The way evaluation and rewards shape people's motives and incentives and thereby affect the actions they take
- The need for organizational controls and how control systems act as levers for change
- The benefits and limits of controls based on inputs, those based on outcomes, and those based on understanding how processes convert inputs to outcomes

MERCK

Imagine that you manage a business that is heavily dependent on research and development for its success, but the average new product costs as much as $400 million and takes nearly 10 years to develop. Now, imagine this new product has a 70 percent chance of failing to return your investment once it reaches the market. Faced with these odds, most managers would probably do as little R&D as possible.

This is precisely the situation facing Judy Lewent, chief financial officer of Merck & Co., Inc., but she is convinced that for Merck, a leader in the drug industry, "the route to success is to put *more* money at risk."[1] As Lewent sees it, without investing the billions required to develop the next generation of drugs, Merck has no future. Consequently, to be successful in pursuing Merck's strategy of technological leadership in the pharmaceutical industry, Lewent and her staff of 500 financial experts must develop systems that allow Merck to manage its risks rather than minimize them.

Lewent believes that, in the typical corporation, the finance function serves the role of "traffic cops," telling others what they can*not* do. She sees her role at Merck in a very different light. Her goal is to turn her staff into experts that serve as valued partners in helping those elsewhere in the organization effectively discover what they *can* do in developing new products for Merck.

For example, when the initial financial analysis indicated that Avid, a new veterinary antiparasitic agent that offered tremendous animal health advantages, could not be profitably manufactured and marketed, Lewent's team went to work to see if somehow it could be made viable. They discovered that packaging costs were eating up projected gross margins, as the project's sponsor had intuitively feared but lacked the hard data to prove. With data in hand, the finance group brought together the project's sponsor, the marketing department, and manufacturing experts to quickly change the packaging and save the project.

Merck's finance department shows how organizational systems impact strategy implementation. As "traffic cops," they would soon strangle the flow of Merck's pipeline of new products. But as service partners, the company's systems for allocating capital and controlling its use play a critical role in implementing Merck's strategy of technological leadership. In this chapter, you will learn how organizational systems can dramatically affect success, and how they can be managed to facilitate strategy implementation and encourage the development of valuable organizational capabilities.

SYSTEMS AS IMPLEMENTATION LEVERS

In this chapter, we define *systems* as established procedures by which organizations allocate resources and monitor their use. We refer to two broad categories of systems: resourcing and control. While we look at control systems as a whole, we further categorize an organization's resourcing systems into three distinct types that reflect three basic resources organizations depend on: information, people, and capital. Both resourcing systems and control systems serve the needs of internal customers—those in the organization's core processes—who, in turn, are externally focused, serving customers outside the organization. You may remember seeing these distinctions made in previous chapters, using a model reproduced here as Exhibit 11.1.

In discussing this exhibit (in Chapter 5), we wrote about the importance of core processes to the success of a firm; these processes do much to determine sustainable competitive advantages. With this in mind, you can begin to understand how vital support systems are. Without the resources (information, people, capital) basic to their operation, core processes cannot offer the value customers need, and they will cease to provide an effective source of competitive advantage. At the same time, without controls, the core processes are likely to move in different directions, squandering the resources they are allocated because they lack coordination.

EXHIBIT 11.1
A Generic Model of Core Processes and Systems

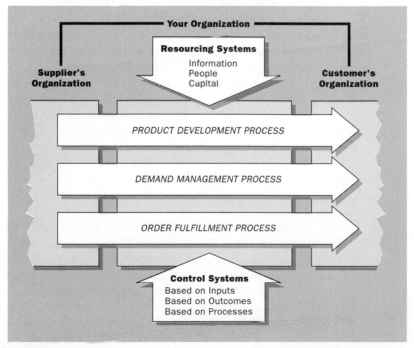

Beyond the fairly obvious idea that support systems must contribute to the success of the firm's core processes, resourcing and control systems affect strategy implementation in more subtle ways. The way in which information is collected and provided, the general approach to developing human resources, the mind-set behind the capital allocation system, and the extent to which the firm emphasizes input- versus outcome-oriented controls are all examples of how these support systems help determine the strategic actions organizations will take, and we discuss them in detail below. It is not enough to understand the need for resourcing and control systems; you must also understand how small differences in the management of these can affect the operation of the core processes and, through that, the success of the entire organization. Application 11.1 provides several examples of how firms were limited or adversely affected by small but important features of their support systems.

An interesting point to note about the examples given in this application is that, in every case, the organization had strong resourcing and control systems in place. It was not the presence of these systems that made the difference but the nature of how they were managed. Consequently, as you read through this chapter, don't expect boldfaced messages about how every organization must carefully manage the way it allocates or controls its resources. That message will be there, but it's more important for you to understand how small changes in the management of resourcing and control systems can have big impacts on the strategy a firm implements. As you consider the impacts the finer points of a support system can have, we suggest you use the standards shown in Exhibit 11.2 to help you decide what constitutes the best alignment between a given strategy and the systems that support it.

As shown in this exhibit, some support system features actually work against the strategy the organization is trying to implement. A classic example is an organization that attempts to compete on differentiated levels of customer service—but focuses its information system on costs, and hires whoever will accept its low wages. Perhaps it refuses to invest in the equipment and materials required to satisfy customers, and its control system is designed to pinpoint any deviation from preapproved actions. Obviously, such a firm will not be very successful in implementing its intended strategy. In fact, this is so obvious that you may conclude that such a ridiculous situation would never actually develop. Unfortunately, it does develop, and far too often. Many organizations' support systems have not changed in decades, regardless of shifts in the firm's strategy. These systems may have made perfect sense at one time, but they do not fit with current strategy. It is not at all unusual to see an organization's intended strategy and its systems totally out of alignment and at odds with each other. For example, organizations too commonly pursue goals (such as growth) that are not supported with rewards (such as bonuses based on cost cutting).

At the second level of Exhibit 11.2, we find firms whose systems are well enough aligned that they do not exert any counterpressure on the firm's strategy, but at the same time they have no positive impact either. For example, many firms state that "people are our most valuable asset" and, consequently, invest in developing a high-quality workforce. Yet their definition of what constitutes quality in a workforce is vague enough that it could apply to any number of organizations and any number of actions.

The highest level of strategy system alignment is one in which, by looking at the attributes of the systems in place, we can "work backwards" and correctly deduce

Application 11.1

Examples of Support Systems Gone Awry

As we study organizations, examples of mismanaged support systems abound, serving as stumbling blocks, tripping up efforts to improve an organization or implement beneficial changes. Here are examples (from disguised organizations) of how each of the support systems discussed in this chapter can negatively affect implementation.

Information Resourcing

The top-management team of a vertically integrated manufacturing firm was convinced that some of its products were consistently being sold at a loss and set out to fix the problem. Unfortunately, the corporation's management information system was not able to provide it with the data required to answer the basic question of what it cost to produce any given product. Each of the businesses at the various states of the vertically integrated production sequence had its own ways of collecting and analyzing data, and these approaches were not compatible with one another. So while there were plenty of data on each step in the manufacturing process, they could not be combined, and so no one had accurate data on the total cost of making any one of the firm's many products.

Human Resourcing

The director of a once successful training and development organization could not figure why demand for the organization's programs had fallen off consistently over a 3-year period. When a group of outsiders was brought in to study the problem, they quickly found it. The organization's staff was paid on the basis of "podium time," the amount of time spent in front of a class delivering a course, while development of new course material was not a compensated activity. In the organization's early years, this had not been a problem, because it was clear that, before instructors could teach, they would have to develop course materials. Later, however, there was little

incentive to develop new materials, because the only pay came from teaching the same old courses. The organization's course catalog had not been changed for almost 4 years, and its programs no longer appealed to customers.

Capital Resourcing

The chief financial officer of a large multinational corporation placed a moratorium on any request for construction of new buildings. The idea was that in order to reduce the level of capital investments the corporation had been experiencing, emphasis should be placed on renovating existing buildings instead of building new ones. To get around the new rule, an enterprising country manager with totally inadequate office space decided to "renovate" his building by razing everything but its elevator shafts and reconstructing a new building around the old elevators. The resulting capital costs were much greater than they would have been if the old building had been sold and a new one built, but of course funds were not available for new buildings.

Control Systems

A large contractor for the federal government was concerned that the costs associated with a part of its operations were much higher than necessary. The team of engineers responsible for the relevant part of the process knew there were at least two other countries in which a very similar process was being carried out at much lower cost. Although the potential cost savings would have amounted to several million dollars over the lifetime of the contract, the contractor chose not to send the engineers on the international benchmarking trip they proposed. The contractor's agreement with the government did not allow it to claim expenses for international travel, and without the ability to pass the cost of the trip on to the government agency that would ultimately benefit from it, management was unwilling to approve the trip.

much of the firm's strategy; that is, these systems are so clearly oriented to supporting a given set of organizational priorities that those priorities become obvious from simply studying the systems. Relatively few organizations fall into this category, but those that do are consistently superb in their ability to remain focused on the strategy they

EXHIBIT 11.2
Three Levels of Strategy System Alignment

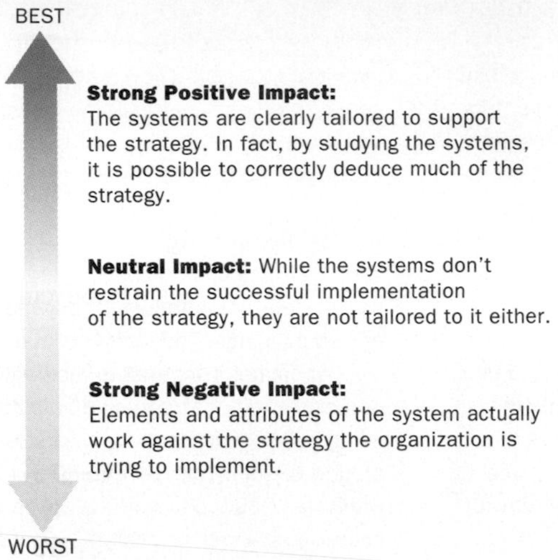

BEST

Strong Positive Impact:
The systems are clearly tailored to support
the strategy. In fact, by studying the systems,
it is possible to correctly deduce much of the
strategy.

Neutral Impact: While the systems don't
restrain the successful implementation
of the strategy, they are not tailored to it either.

Strong Negative Impact:
Elements and attributes of the system actually
work against the strategy the organization is
trying to implement.

WORST

are pursuing and successfully implementing. In fact, in some of these organizations it would be almost impossible for the firm to make a change in strategic direction without first altering its support systems, which is precisely why we see support systems as such strong levers for influencing strategy implementation. Your goal as a manager should be developing an ability to fine-tune resourcing and control systems to further strategic aims. This is not an easy task or one that can be mastered quickly, but you can begin to develop these skills by understanding the basic issues raised in the following sections.

Exhibit 11.2 illustrates a central premise of this chapter: systems must follow strategy. As we move through our discussion of various systems, we will not always point out how they should be linked to strategy. This would be needlessly tedious, because so many of the linkages are fairly obvious. However, toward the end of this chapter, when we come to some of the more difficult topics, we make such linkages more explicit—specifically, how certain features of support systems make them more appropriate for either strategic programming or organizational learning.

INFORMATION-RESOURCING SYSTEMS

As a critical lever for strategy implementation and organizational change, information resourcing plays dual roles. One role is to connect various parts of the organization, facilitating coordination and integration; the second is to provide better measures, thus influencing an organization's behavior. We discuss both roles below.

Information as a Source of Integration

In Chapter 10, we studied various ways of separating organizations into departments and/or units at both macrolevels and microlevels. Complex organizations must make such separations to structure their work. Without a separation of groups and individuals, we would be unable to bring about any meaningful specialization of tasks, and our organizations would become mere collectives of generalists. The cornerstone of the industrial revolution lay in the division of labor and the productivity gains that specialization provided. While specialization and division of labor continue to be fundamental tenets of organizing, they sometimes create stumbling blocks to strategy implementation. In fact, organizations must continually struggle to find ways of integrating their many parts—putting the pieces back together—so that they are more than simply groups of independent specialists.

Thus, what departmentalized, fragmented organizational structures divided and separated during the industrial revolution, information-resourcing systems are now attempting to reconnect and integrate in what has been called the "information revolution." Peter Drucker says that a guiding principle in this information revolution is that "the purpose and function of every organization, business and nonbusiness alike, is the integration of specialized knowledge into a common task."[2] As another observer of the information revolution put it, "The genius of the industrial revolution was separation—the breaking up of work into its component parts. . . . Today's principle is unification. . . . company departments are fusing and enterprises are growing so closely allied with customers and suppliers that boundaries between them seem to dissolve."[3]

In order to achieve such integration, firms must treat information differently from the way they have in the past. In the traditional approach to managing information, most organizations had a group of specialists who handled a management information system (MIS) that was focused on efficient mass production of information. This simply extended the industrial revolution's approach, with its emphasis on specialization, efficiency, and mass production, to a new area of business operation. But applying such industrial revolution–type thinking to the way we collect and treat data often results in an organization's misusing its information resources terribly.

Consider the case of Ameritech, a multibillion-dollar telecommunications services corporation serving a five-state region in the midwestern United States.[4] An analysis of the firm's traditional management information system found that it mimicked a small factory operating at the height of the industrial revolution. Massive machines turned out reams of reports that were pushed out to recipients with minimal attention paid either to their value or to the recipients' needs. One expert spent a week each month producing a twenty-five-page report that not one person had ever used. When the MIS team shifted its self-concept from that of a function responsible for producing data to that of a source of vital integrating information that the entire organization should be able to use freely, the results were startling. When end users became the focus of what came to be seen as an information-resourcing support system, the team reached dramatically different conclusions on how data should be collected and treated. It eliminated 6 million pages of reports—a stack four times the height of the corporation's forty-one-story headquarters in Chicago. This is a good example of how a support system is meant to operate not for its own sake but for the sake of the core processes whose needs it serves.

The Ameritech example also illustrates that if information is to integrate organizations, it must first be considered an accessible resource for its users to draw on rather than as merely the pushed output of a centralized data collection system. Furthermore, as we shall see, to be more effective, information needs to be readily available for those throughout the organization—not just for upper management. To help maintain these distinctions, we shall refer to the information-resourcing system as opposed to the management information system. The integration at the heart of the information-resourcing system takes place at three levels, as we show in Exhibit 11.3 and discuss below.[5]

■ *Team level.* Here, the information-resourcing system facilitates communication between individuals who are already connected through membership in some organizational subunit. A good example is Kmart's "SWAT" team program—at each store, a group of experts from various functions were assigned to tackle new problems across store operations every day. The team members were not merely to fix the problem but to take action to ensure that the problem did not arise again. The process of tackling daily assignments was modeled on *Hill Street Blues,* once a popular television series on police work. The series began every episode with each two-person squad car team receiving its daily assignment. At Kmart, each problem was assigned a "squad car," the "driver" of which was expected to take action on the assigned problem within 4 hours while his or her buddy provided "backup." In *Hill Street Blues,* the patrols stayed in touch with one another through their radios and a central dispatcher. At Kmart, team members used a computerized information network that let them call in "reinforcements" when they needed help on a problem or pass a problem over to a teammate if the "chase" took them outside their "jurisdiction." Without this network, individuals would have been scurrying throughout Kmart, cut off from the rest of the team and seriously compromising the effectiveness of the effort. Dave Carlson, the chief information officer (CIO) at Kmart, described the importance of the network to the SWAT team effort this way: "The availability of the network is the critical enabler. People from different locations—including their homes—and different groupings can function together as a team."

■ *Organizational level.* At this level, the information-resourcing system provides data from across the organization. Firms have traditionally placed more emphasis on developing information systems to facilitate connections here than at the other

EXHIBIT 11.3
Information Resourcing Can Provide Three Levels of Integration

Level of Integration	Type of Information Resourcing	Impact of Information Resourcing	Intended Result
Organizational subunit	Network for work groups	High-performance teams	Business process improvement and redesign
Organization	Integrated organizational systems	Cross-functional integration	Organizational transformation
Interorganization	Data exchange between organizations	Extended concept of enterprise	Improved external relationships

two levels. For example, many multiservice banks have adopted a strategy in which any client is treated as a customer of the entire bank, not just of the individual services with which the client is in contact at any one particular time. So, for instance, a person assisting with a credit card issue can also answer a customer's question about mortgage rates. Of course, this means that everyone must have access to information about every service provided by the bank and the capability of pulling up that information on demand to assist customers as new questions arise. Such a capability is considered a prerequisite for successfully implementing a strategy based on relationship banking, in which a bank establishes such a close relationship with its customers and their various financial issues that they do not consider going outside that bank for any financial services. Thus information resourcing can act as a critical lever in implementing strategies and in helping create a competitive advantage.

- *Interorganizational level.* In the last decade, firms have made major efforts to extend the reach of information-resourcing systems beyond the boundaries of single organizations. Much of this effort used information to tie together various parts of the industry's value chain by connecting suppliers and customers. This is partly why Toys 'R' Us emerged as the world's biggest children's specialty retailer. Using its electronic data interchange (EDI) capabilities, the firm was able to provide continuous updates for its best suppliers on what products were selling. These continuous updates allowed suppliers to schedule further deliveries and adjust merchandise blends without store purchase orders, achieving a level of supplier-customer integration its competitors could not match.

    A more recent trend in the development of information-resourcing systems at the interorganizational level is designing systems that connect rivals with one another in order to facilitate mutually beneficial cooperation. For example, the seventeen largest hotel chains in the United States have joined to create an information-resourcing system provided by a joint venture known as The Hotel Industry Switch Company (THISCO). THISCO's mission is to provide competing hotel chains with the capability of switching reservations so that a traveler at any individual hotel in the system can use that hotel to make arrangements to stay at any of the other hotels. This offers members a service that hotels outside THISCO simply cannot offer, an important competitive advantage (although it must be managed carefully in order to avoid the illegalities of collusion).

    As these examples illustrate, information-resourcing systems can serve as important means of integrating organizations at multiple levels, thus helping to address the problem of fragmentation created by departmentalized organizational structures and specialized individual tasks. Beyond this, information-resourcing systems also have a strong impact on an organization's actions not only through the data they provide but, more specifically, what the systems measure. We now turn to a consideration of how measurement affects organizational action.

Measurements as a Determinant of Organizational Action

The management axiom "What gets measured gets done" indicates the importance of measurement as a lever for bringing about strategic change. Consider, for example, the current change in hospital performance measures and its impact on strategy implementation. For years, insurance and government health programs reimbursed hospitals on a cost-plus basis. When a hospital provided a service, it billed an insurance company or government agency for that service plus an additional profit margin.[6] Under this arrangement, nursing operations were measured by the revenues they generated (the more service, the more revenues; the more revenues, the more profit), and this measurement provided an incentive for hospitals to offer every conceivable service. However, in the early 1990s, to control escalating costs, insurance companies and government agencies began shifting to payment based on a fixed price. This meant hospitals received a prenegotiated payment for a given type of illness, regardless of the costs they actually incurred while treating the illness. Any additional service represented an expense that had to be deducted from the fixed amount of revenue stipulated by the contract. Therefore, hospitals began to measure nursing operations based on their costs. So, to maximize the performance measure, they provided the minimal level of service consistent with acceptable health care quality. This swing in employee attitudes and actions from maximum service to minimum service came by making a relatively straightforward change from measuring performance as revenue to measuring performance as cost.

As this example illustrates, managers need to be very careful about what they measure, because a small difference in what is measured can have a big impact on an organization's actions and strategy implementation. Traditionally, management information systems have relied on accounting measures of financial activity. As we explained in Chapter 4 when we introduced the concept of the balanced scorecard, the financial perspective is an important one—arguably even the most important one in a for-profit business—but it is certainly not the only appropriate set of measurement criteria.[7] Even when measuring financial performance, there is room for using measures that go well beyond traditional financial accounting data. One writer identified the belief that standard accounting statements and forms can provide a clear picture of strategic position as the number one misconception of strategic management.[8] Below, we show you some less conventional financial measures and some nonfinancial measures that can supplement more traditional accounting data in measuring business performance from each of the four perspectives making up the balanced scorecard.

1. Financial Perspective

For years, a standard approach to measuring performance from the financial perspective was based on something called the Du Pont model, so named because it was first developed at Du Pont, the giant diversified chemical corporation. A simplified version of the Du Pont model is presented in Exhibit 11.4.

The idea behind the model was that return on investment (ROI) is the best overall financial measure of performance, and therefore all organization members ought to understand what determines ROI and how their individual pieces of the organization affect it. As you can see, this model is a tree diagram; along the various branches ROI is broken down into its component parts (for example, ROI = ROS × Sales/Investment). Using such a framework, a department head could see how an increase in department expenses and an increase in fixed capital would have a negative impact on ROI if they did not yield more-than-offsetting increases in sales quantities or

EXHIBIT 11.4
The Du Pont Model of Financial Performance

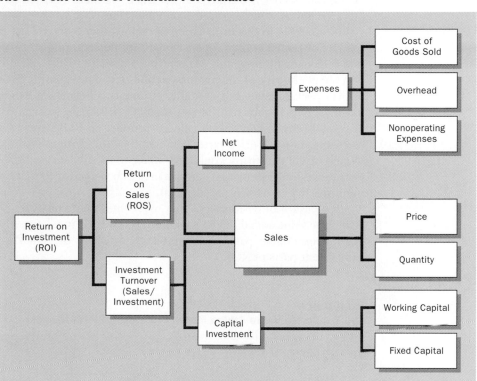

prices. Mathematically, this model is not wrong; but reliance on it has limitations, the three most important of which are discussed in the sections that follow.

Profitability Is Not the Best Measure of the Creation of Wealth.   As we have maintained since Chapter 1, a for-profit business must focus primarily on creating wealth for owners. Given the importance of this goal, it is clear that managers need accurate measures of how much wealth their firms actually create. While measures of profitability such as ROI certainly correlate with the creation of wealth, they are not the best possible measures.

As we explained in Chapter 4, these measures fail to consider the total cost of capital. Specifically, they fail to consider the opportunity costs an investor incurs when investing in a particular business. The *opportunity cost* is the difference between the return received from the investment made and what investors might have received from other possible investments. As a proxy for measuring the return an investor could have received elsewhere, we estimate an average risk-adjusted rate of return and use this as a standard for evaluating the investment actually made. If the actual investment's return is better than the average risk-adjusted rate of return available from other investments, we conclude that the actual investment has created value for the investor. However, if the actual investment does not at least equal the average risk-adjusted rate of return, the investor is worse off for having made this investment. When this occurs, we conclude that the investment resulted in decreased wealth or, more graphically, in destroyed economic value.

Notice that in this explanation of opportunity costs, we use the *risk-adjusted* average rate of return as the proper standard for determining a firm's performance. Traditional accounting measures of performance such as ROI fail to incorporate information about the risk of the investment and may consequently provide a distorted view of firm performance. For example, assume two businesses average a 4 percent ROI, but firm A is highly volatile and regularly has huge swings in its profits and stock prices, while firm B has never failed to produce an ROI of near 4 percent in the last 10 years and its stock price varies consistently with changes in the overall stock market. Which of the two firms would you prefer to own? Because firm B offers less risk, rational investors consider its performance to be superior to that of firm A, even though the firms' average ROIs are identical.

A measure of performance that overcomes many of ROI's inherent limitations is economic value added (EVA).[9] We introduced EVA in Chapter 1, but now let us identify its component parts in Exhibit 11.5, much as the Du Pont model showed the component parts of ROI.

EXHIBIT 11.5
The Economic Value Added Model of Financial Performance

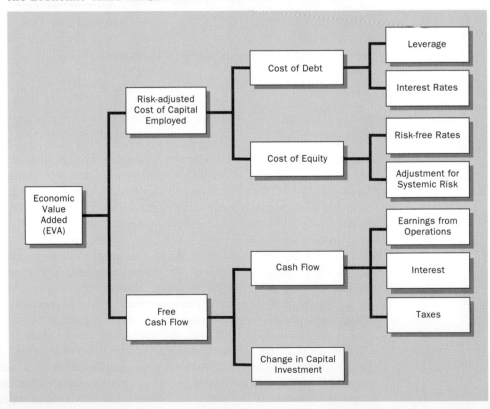

This model shows that EVA is the result of cash flows in excess of the risk-adjusted cost of the capital employed to generate the cash flows. But not all factors determining EVA are reported as part of standard financial accounting procedures. For instance, the weighted cost of capital must be estimated using stock market data that don't show up in financial accounting reports. The necessity of employing non-traditional data and using traditional data in nontraditional ways has limited the use of EVA to a relatively small number of pioneering organizations. However, its use is expanding rapidly, and it is expected to become a standard approach to measuring financial performance over the next decade or so. As a future manager, you should understand the basic concepts underlying EVA, and that is why we have consistently stressed the significance of this measure throughout this text.

Denominator Management.   A second problem with the Du Pont model and similar accounting-based measures is that managers who focus on ROI very quickly realize that the easiest way to improve it is to decrease investment, the denominator in the ratio. Investment is more easily controlled than profit (the numerator), and so-called denominator management often prevails in organizations focused on making short-term improvements in ROI.[10] However, failure to reinvest usually leads to a weakened business. So, albeit inadvertently, through using denominator management to maximize ROI, many managers slowly kill off their businesses for the sake of "improving" performance!

To avoid such detrimental decision making, many firms seek to supplement more traditional accounting measures of performance with additional measures that discourage denominator management. One of the best supplemental measures is EVA, but, as we have already noted, use of this measure is not yet widespread because it is difficult to calculate and interpret. However, as a compromise, some accounting-based measures of financial performance can provide useful supplements to measures of profitability such as ROI. Application 11.2 describes how Allied Signal has made good use of two such measures.

Historical Versus Future Orientation.   A third important drawback to using accounting-based measures of financial performance is that they are historically oriented, while the strategies you will most likely implement must be future oriented. As one writer has explained this dilemma, "Depending on an accounting department to reveal a company's future will leave it hopelessly mired in the past."[11] In their book *Competing for the Future*, Gary Hamel and C. K. Prahalad identify two ways that companies can address this problem.[12]

First, they can guard against "valueless growth," which occurs when sales increase without increasing cash flows. In other words, the company is bigger but is not creating more economic value. A simple way of guarding against valueless growth is to track revenue versus inflation-adjusted profits per employee, which can show if growth is doing anything other than expanding the operation's size. Similarly, comparing trends in revenues, profits, and free cash flow readily shows when growth is actually producing value and when it is not.

Hamel and Prahalad also recommend tracking "investment share" to encourage future-oriented thinking. Many firms track market share (their sales relative to competitors' combined sales), but this measures past accomplishments. A more future-oriented measure is to track investment share (your investments in your business ver-

Application 11.2

Allied Signal: New Measures to Speed an Organizational Transformation

Lawrence A. Bossidy was well known inside Allied Signal Corporation, the $12 billion diversified producer of equipment for the aerospace and automotive industries, as a CEO who was impatient with the traditionally slow pace of organizational change. Bossidy set as his personal goal an unusual measure of cycle-time reduction: he wanted to bring about a complete transformation of the corporation's culture, operations, and performance in 5 years, about half the time that had been required by comparable transformations at firms such as General Electric. Early in the transformation process, Bossidy became convinced of the power of measurement in bringing about change and implementing new strategies.

For example, Allied, like many organizations, initially placed most of the emphasis of its cost-cutting effort on reducing labor costs. However, in its capital-intensive operations, labor amounts to no more than about 25 percent of total costs, so focusing on it limited the success of the cost reduction efforts. Then Bossidy began tracking what he called "total cost productivity." This was calculated as sales, discounted for price increases that cannot be attributed to increases in value (e.g., inflation), divided by all costs (including plant and equipment costs, materials, and labor). This measure encourages managers to look well beyond labor reduction as a source of productivity gains. Explains one manager affected by the new measure, "If I had to get 6 percent productivity growth from labor alone, there'd be nobody left in about 3 years. The real opportunities are in raising the value of what you sell and cutting materials costs."

Another measure that Bossidy adopted has proven useful at a number of other firms: working capital turnover. This is the number of times working capital cycles through the business each year. Because working capital is affected by everything from purchasing supplies to billing for sold goods, it is difficult to generate improvements in one part of the business by hiding something elsewhere. For example, if a manager tries to cut corners in shipping and billing, this will show up later as errors that slow down collections and raise accounts receivable. Another advantage of working capital turnover is that it is easy to measure using conventional accounting data: add accounts receivable and inventory, subtract accounts payable, and divide the difference by sales. The Boston Consulting Group's research has shown that firms with high working capital turnover also score high on productivity and cash generation, making this measure a possible substitute for managers who lack the data to calculate economic value added. For example, Allied Signal calculated that if it could increase the turnover of its working capital to five times a year instead of four, the corporation could generate another $500 million in cash, creating significant value for stockholders.

Sources

Thomas A. Stewart, "Allied Signal's Turnaround Blitz," *Fortune* (November 30, 1992), 72–75; Noel M. Tichy and Ram Charan, "The CEO as Coach: An Interview with Allied Signal's Lawrence A. Bossidy," *Harvard Business Review* (March–April 1995), 68–78.

sus the combined investments of your competition in their businesses). Assuming that investments are made for the sake of future performance, and assuming that all firms' investments have a comparable impact, this measure is one way of estimating your firm's preparedness for future competition.

Beyond measures from the financial perspective, measures from the other three levels of the balanced scorecard—the customer, operations, and organizational perspectives—can shape organizational action. While an exhaustive discussion of all such measures is beyond the scope of this text, below we give two examples of such measures for each of the remaining three perspectives from the balanced scorecard.

2. Customer Perspective

Measuring Customer Satisfaction and Value.   Throughout this text we have emphasized customer value as a key concept of successful strategic management. Successfully implementing strategies often entails measuring customer value in order to know what problem areas exist, to motivate increased emphasis on customers, or to track improvements in customer service and satisfaction.[13] Developing useful measures of customer value is a two-step process. First, talk to customers to see what matters most to them. Second, regularly collect data on how well you meet or exceed customers' expectations in these areas. Meeting customers' expectations is the key to providing customer satisfaction, but exceeding customer expectations is often a better indication that you are providing the greatest possible levels of customer value.

Measuring Industry Leadership by the Customers You Serve.   Hamel and Prahalad suggest that one of the best ways of assessing whether your firm is a leader or a laggard in its industry is to identify your leading customers or clients and then to track how many of those depend on you as a key supplier.[14] This is an application of the old expression "The best dancers always get the best dance partners." When explaining the logic of a particular company's tracking this measure, Hamel and Prahalad asked, "How could the company become the premier service provider in its industry if its clients were anything but premier in their own industries?"

3. Operations Perspective

Time-Based Measures of Operation.   Given that speed and response time can create key competitive advantages, you will not be surprised to see time-based measures identified here as important for use in implementing strategies.[15] Time-based measures can supplement more traditional accounting measures because they measure the physical as opposed to the financial.[16] For example, a time-based measure of a logistics system might track how long it takes to physically move a product from your shipping dock to a customer's shipping dock, while a financial measure would track the expenses incurred in delivering the product. Physically based measures are often simpler to use, easier to interpret, and better for pinpointing areas in which business processes can be improved or redesigned with the greatest impact. For example, it might be very difficult to compute the financial cost of making two delivery runs a day (e.g., should overhead allocations to the shipping department be doubled?), but it is easy to clock how the change impacts delivery times.

Measures of Innovation.   One of the most important determinants of tomorrow's growth and success is today's level of innovation and the development of new products and services. But innovation is very difficult to measure.[17] For example, we can track R&D budgets fairly easily, but spending on R&D may not actually produce viable products that result in growing sales. To address such difficulties, firms pursuing a strategy that emphasizes innovation and/or growth should track different stages of the innovation process. They might measure concept development using expenditures for basic research (as opposed to product development) and the number of new concepts being explored at any given time. Actual product development can be measured using development budgets and measures of the time required to move a product from the concept stage to production. Commercialization of innovation can be tracked by following the percentage of revenues generated by new products in the last 1, 3, or 5 years. By looking at such a blend of measures, managers can obtain a more accurate assessment of the product development process overall.

4. Organizational Perspective

Measures of Organizational Development.   Organizational capacity is so difficult to measure that, typically, we can rely only on proxies to provide some rough approximation of strengths or weaknesses. For example, some managers track union grievances as a measure of employee morale, though they recognize that this is a crude approximation at best. Tom Peters has suggested that firms measure investments in organizational capacity to assess their abilities to compete in the future.[18] Specific measures he has identified include the number of hours or dollars invested annually in skill upgrading and the percentage of all compensation that is based on a pay-for-knowledge program in which pay is linked to employees' mastering new skills.

Early Warning Signals.   Some of the most desirable measures are those that help an organization spot threatening trends before problems actually arise. Banks emphasize such measures because of their interest in identifying potential loan default situations before they actually develop.[19] Given that the organizational perspective is the foundation on which everything else in the balanced scorecard rests, it should not be surprising that many early warning signals such work identifies deal with organizational capacity issues.[20] For example, too many unexpected, irregular events may indicate that managers are operating in a reactive mode; constantly reshaping organizational structures may indicate that the organization senses a problem for which it does not have a clear solution; and unusually high levels of conflict and shortened tempers may indicate that employees are suffering from stress and may have an intuitive sense that something is amiss. While these items do not lend themselves to quantitative measurement, it may be useful to track them in a nonquantitative fashion in order to help identify potential threats.

Note that these examples are meant to be illustrative rather than exhaustive. Managers should use their creativity and judgment in developing measures from all four perspectives of the balanced scorecard to help focus attention and action on the strategies they attempt to implement.

Performance measures from the organizational perspective remind managers how important people are as a critical organizational resource. In the next section, we consider how elements of the system for managing this critical resource can affect an organization's ability to implement a competitive strategy successfully.

HUMAN-RESOURCING SYSTEMS

One lever that managers consistently identify as critical to their ability to implement strategies is how an organization manages its human resources.[21] Changes in the way this system is managed are both facilitated and required by changes occurring in other

parts of many organizations.[22] Here we look at several examples of the most important of these changes before focusing in on perhaps the most powerful implementation lever provided as part of the human-resourcing system—how people are evaluated and rewarded.

New Approaches to Managing
Human Resources

In the past, many businesses, and sometimes entire industries, were well known for
their hard-nosed, adversarial approach to managing their human resources. The function of the personnel department was to hire the required laborers and to negotiate
with unions to hold wages and benefits as low as possible. The attitude at many factories was once typified by statements such as "Check your brain at the door" and "We
hired you for your muscle, not your mind." In short, the workforce was treated as if it
had little to contribute to a business other than physical labor. Today, the workforce is
more often viewed as a crucial source of competitive advantage.[23] Consider the
human resource management described in the following examples:[24]

- Canada's Northern Telecom now considers labor expenses to be a fixed investment rather than a variable expense. The company believes that it has invested so
  much in training its workers and that they have become so skilled that they are far
  too valuable for the company to consider laying them off in response to a decline
  in volume. Labor is now treated as a component of overhead.

- Saturn completely rewrote the automobile industry's typical labor-management
  agreement in establishing itself as a new General Motors division. The agreement
  specifies that labor and management share responsibility for many of the tasks
  they held individually in the past. For instance, both groups have input as to how
  work is to be scheduled. In fact, the list of shared responsibilities of Saturn managers and United Auto Workers union officials is much longer than the list of either group's separate responsibilities.

- Texas Instruments (TI) has implemented a plan calling for 100 percent involvement of its employees as part of a companywide quality improvement effort. Results to date show impressive returns that indicate the contributions employees
  can make if given the right opportunities. At one of the plants leading in this
  movement, more than 60 percent of all hourly workers implemented ten or more
  of their own ideas for better performance. While only half of the more than 7,000
  total ideas had their impact on profitability quantified (employees are not required
  to quantify cost savings in order for their ideas to be implemented), those that
  they did quantify provided more than $7 million of additional profits. Note the
  significance here: TI has more than fifty plants, and the improvements mentioned
  here were for just one plant in just 1 year.

- Realizing the need to develop the potential of both their labor force and their
  managerial teams, corporations are investing millions of dollars in continuing education and management development programs. Motorola's programs have become a "university" with a multimillion-dollar annual budget. Xerox invested
  $125 million in one corporationwide development program aimed at educating all

its employees, management and labor alike, in using an identical set of problem-solving tools.[25]

These examples clearly show that some American managers have come to see their employees as important sources of expertise who support the firms' efforts to gain and sustain a competitive advantage.[26] As a result of this change, these firms and others now have an entirely different approach to managing their human-resourcing system. Many of these changes are identified in Exhibit 11.6, and below we discuss one of them in detail: rewards, arguably the most powerful implementation lever within the human-resourcing system.

The Critical Role of Rewards in Implementing Strategies

The title of one of the best-known articles ever published in an academic management journal succinctly explains the importance of rewards in implementing strategies: "On the Folly of Rewarding A While Hoping for B."[27] While the relationship between rewards and actions is not perfectly straightforward, in general, people value and respond to rewards, and rewards provide a tremendously powerful lever for affecting employee and management behavior. Though we might all agree with this general statement, managers sometimes fail to properly match evaluation and reward systems to the strategic changes they are attempting to make, and the results are usually unsatisfactory.

For example, we once spoke to a manager who enthusiastically described her plans to implement a team-based approach to quality improvement and cost reduc-

---

EXHIBIT 11.6
Traditional and Emerging Ideas of Human Resource Management

Traditional	*Emerging*
Emphasis solely on physical skills	Emphasis on total contribution to the firm
Expectation of predictable, repetitive behavior	Expectation of innovative and creative behavior
Comfort with stability and conformity	Tolerance of ambiguity and change
Avoidance of responsibility and decision making	Accepting responsibility for making decisions
Training covering only specific tasks	Open-ended commitment: broad, continuous development
Emphasis placed on outcomes and results	Emphasis placed on processes and means
High concern for quantity and throughput	High concern for total customer value
Concern for individual efficiency	Concern for overall effectiveness
Functional and subfunctional specialization	Cross-functional integration
Labor force seen as a necessary expense	Labor force seen as critical investment
Workforce is management's adversary	Management and workforce are partners
Evaluation and rewards focused narrowly on work output	Evaluation and rewards defined broadly, depending on strategy

tion. She had been given this high-visibility assignment by the division CEO, and she described plans that included extensive training, numerous teambuilding exercises, countless speeches, contests, posters, videos, newsletters, and so on. We then asked her how evaluation and rewards were being changed to facilitate teamwork. Her response was that the CEO was a big believer in personal accountability and that the divisionwide method for evaluating and rewarding people reflected this emphasis on the individual; from the department heads on down, individuals were evaluated in comparison to one another and rewarded accordingly. Our advice was that she forget about her other efforts until something could be done about the evaluation and reward process. She replied that because the assignment had come from the CEO, she could not delay in taking action. Two years later we had an opportunity to inquire about her success in implementing the team-based approach. Despite 2 years of tremendous effort, her results had been negligible. The biggest problem, as she saw it, was that people were expected to cooperate with one another in teams but were evaluated and rewarded for competing against one another.

This is one of many examples that illustrate how evaluation and rewards motivate people. An appropriate reward system plays a critical role in motivating managers to conform to organizational strategies, achieve performance targets, and reduce gaps between organizational and individual goals. In contrast, an improperly designed reward system can lead to behaviors that detract from an organization's performance or that create lower morale and dissatisfaction. Application 11.3 provides two more examples of different incentive systems and their contrasting effects on an organization's performance.

While effective evaluation and reward systems are crucial throughout an organization, perhaps the greatest leverage comes from the systems used to evaluate and reward executives and managers. Changes here can have a ripple effect down through the ranks, while changes in line employee evaluation and rewards may not have an upward effect. Reflecting the recognized importance of managerial evaluation and reward as an implementation lever, several new approaches to evaluating and rewarding senior management have emerged in recent years.[28]

For example, organizations are increasingly using reward systems in which employees share in the risks and benefits of their firm's performance through *profit-sharing* or *gain-sharing* plans.[29] Profit sharing links individual rewards to a firm's overall financial performance, while gain sharing can link rewards to virtually any type of performance measure. Often, such plans enable organizations to become more competitive.[30] For example, Au Bon Pain, a specialty bakery, initiated profit sharing of up to 50 percent of store profits. Some store managers were able to earn up to $100,000 when the industry norm was abut $25,000. (Meanwhile, entry-level workers were paid up to $25,000 a year, including bonuses.) Shortly after this program was initiated, performance improved dramatically, and annual employee turnover was reduced to around 75 percent versus over 200 percent for the industry as a whole.

Many firms have adopted *deferred stock option plans* to compensate top management for achieving certain performance levels over several (usually 3 to 5) years rather than just 1 year. This change addresses the dysfunctional effects of rewarding solely on the basis of short-term performance. With deferred stock options as rewards, executives can build personal financial bases that increase with time, motivating a longer-term orientation.

Reward Systems: Unsuccessful and Successful

The Evans Products Company, with headquarters in Portland, Oregon, was once a large, successful conglomerate competing in the housing, railcar, forest products, retail home center, and industrial products businesses. Its organizational structure was highly centralized, with clearly delineated profit centers. Its executive compensation plan set bonuses as a direct correlate of earnings so that financial incentives were directed toward meeting ambitious sales goals. Though the company's future had once looked very bright, it eventually went bankrupt.

Why did Evans fail? Not because of a dysfunctional culture or the lack of an explicit reward system. Rather, its reward system was inconsistent with deteriorating competitive and economic conditions. The housing and railcar businesses went into a cyclical downturn typical of these industries, but, driven by the sales-based incentive plan, mangers were unwilling to let sales and profits decline. Instead, they elected to encourage sales growth by providing liberal financing to customers. The company put railcars out on lease and sold houses to customers in order to counteract for the overall corporation's negative cash flow. The company continued to "borrow short and lend long" until it finally ran out of cash and exhausted all its credit lines—and went bankrupt.

A unique reward system devised by Larry Phillips, CEO of Phillips–Van Heusen (a manufacturer of shirts, sweaters, and casual shoes), illustrates some of the important principles of effective reward systems. In 1987, Larry Phillips decided to award his eleven top executives $1 million each if the firm's earnings per share (EPS) increased at a 35 percent compounded annual rate over a

4-year period. This generous incentive was structured so that the first $500,000 could be earned incrementally if EPS goals were met each year and the other $500,000 if the firm achieved the overall goal. As one would probably expect, Phillips–Van Heusen's sales and earnings increased dramatically as a result of the program, and targets were regularly attained or only narrowly missed. These financial results are all the more impressive given the extensive debt the firm took on to repel a corporate raider, as well as the continuing large investments necessary to build new businesses.

Phillips's incentive program was clearly consistent with his overall strategy. The corporation's growth objectives were consistently met. Linking the incentive to overall corporate performance also encouraged cooperation among the business units. Phillips commented that the pay plan "put everybody in his own confessional. Now each of these guys is terribly supportive of every other division of this company. You don't find that very often in corporate America." Because they had incremental annual incentives, the top executive team also had a built-in motivation to focus not only on the 4-year objective but on the annual objectives as well.

Sources

Doran Twer, "Linking Pay to Business Objectives," *Journal of Business Strategy, 15* (July–August 1994), 15–18; C. Knowlton, "11 Men's Million-Dollar Motivator," *Fortune* (April 9, 1990), 65–66, 68; A. Zaleznik, "The Leadership Gap," *Academy of Management Executive* (April 9, 1990), 7–22.

The *weighted strategic factors* approach to executive rewards recognizes differences in strategic positions and types of financial performance that it's reasonable to expect across different business units within a diversified firm. We saw such differences in comparing expected cash flow from stars versus cash cows when studying portfolio management techniques in Chapter 7. In the weighted strategic factors method, corporations identify a variety of different performance measures and match the weights assigned to these to the situations facing each business unit, incorporating them into managers' incentive packages. For example, a firm might identify these four performance standards: return on assets, cash flow, progress against plan on identified strategic projects, and market share. The manager of a high-growth business might be rewarded on these four factors according to a weighting of 20, 0, 45, and 35 percent, respectively, while a mature low-growth business might use weights of 50, 50, 0, and 0 percent.

Finally, *strategic funds deferral* encourages managers to view developmental expenses differently from expenses that are necessary to sustain current operations. Here, otherwise traditional measures of financial performance, such as ROI, are calculated for current operations only, while the long-term investments associated with strategic projects are excluded. This allows separate performance evaluations for long-term and short-term investments, encouraging managers to take more future-oriented perspectives and not overemphasize short-term goals.

These are only a few of the many different approaches taken when using evaluation and reward systems as a lever for implementing strategic change. To be effective, the use of any such system should be closely matched to the situation a firm faces as well as to its particular strategy. To this point, we have considered how managing two of the three critical resources, information and people, is linked to the type of strategy a firm can implement. In the next section, we look at how allocation of the last of the three critical resources, capital, can affect strategic change.

CAPITAL-RESOURCING SYSTEMS

Another important lever for implementing strategy is a firm's system for allocating capital resources. The availability of capital to pay for proposed actions strongly determines managers' efforts; it is one of the most direct ways of influencing what strategic actions will be taken and what realized strategies will emerge. For decades, the traditional means of allocating resources has been capital budgeting. Besides allocating capital resources, the budget process also provides a set of standards for judging a company's performance. This second use of budgets is a subject we will cover later in our discussion of control systems; for now, we concentrate on the part of budgeting that involves how firms allocate funds and consider how this serves as a lever for strategy implementation. Our discussion covers two topics: the theory and practice of conventional capital allocation and a value-based approach to capital resourcing.

The Conventional Capital Allocation
Process: Theory and Practice

You learned about the theory of how capital should be allocated in your finance classes when you studied discounted cash flow (DCF) analysis. As a refresher, we present a greatly simplified version of that theory.[31] DCF analysis revolves around efficient use of funds. Money can be invested in a variety of ways, from building a new factory to investing in government bonds, all of which offer different combinations of expected risks and returns. Comparing these alternatives is further complicated because of the time value of money: alternative A offers you a $1 million payback in 5 years but is not nearly as attractive as alternative B, which offers the $1 million payback a year from now. With alternative B, you have an additional 4 years to put the $1 million to work generating further returns, while alternative A has you waiting 4 years. This is a simple example with obvious preferences, but what if you were like one chief financial officer we know (the CFO usually oversees the capital-resourcing system), who has 200 alternatives to consider, each having paybacks that vary in length from 1 to 10 years, in patterns from regular to highly variable, in riskiness from extremely speculative to extremely safe, and in total investment amounts from hundreds of thousands to hundreds of millions of dollars? Such a confusing set of alternatives typically faces managers who allocate capital in most significant-sized corporations.

To make such varied alternatives more comparable, DCF analysis was developed to reduce the various complex combinations of risks and returns to one or two numbers that could be compared across alternatives. The most commonly used number is the *net present value* (NPV). To calculate it, managers look at the projected outflows and inflows of cash associated with an investment alternative, discount these for the time value of money (i.e., flows in the future are less significant than those occurring sooner), and reduce the whole thing to a single number, the NPV. In theory, managers should be indifferent to taking the amount of money calculated as the NPV right now or undertaking the investment alternative. In other words, NPV analysis is designed to equate the investment's future cash flows to some amount of cash today. Using this technique, the CFO in our previous example could conceivably perform 200 discounted cash flow analyses and simply choose the options offering the greatest NPVs.

Unfortunately, the practice of capital resourcing is not nearly as straightforward and "clean" as the theory of DCF might suggest.[32] For example, the CFO described earlier faced the following problems in actually using DCF to allocate capital. While any alternative that entailed an investment of $1 million or more required a proposal backed up by DCF analysis and a predicted NPV, of the roughly 200 proposals that resulted, the formal review process could hope to give serious consideration to only a few dozen. And even with only these few dozen, the financial managers who administered the capital-resourcing system lacked the technical expertise to evaluate and challenge the assumptions built into most of the alternative analyses. This was a serious issue, because the CFO suspected that most of the analyses had been "cooked"; that is, he believed the managers proposing the investments had worked backward from an NPV they felt would get their projects funded and had adjusted the predictions and assumptions to yield the "right" answer. He knew that another tactic managers regularly use to get their projects funded is claiming that regardless of the financial return, their projects are strategically important for higher-order, difficult-to-quantify reasons, such as worker safety or customer service. But even more troubling was the fact that about 60 percent of all capital was allocated in amounts that fell below the established $1 million hurdle. He believed that many multimillion-dollar projects had been subdivided to avoid the formal DCF-based allocation process. But he was also sure that simply lowering the cutoff would not work—his team couldn't keep up with the proposals it already had.

This situation is not uncommon. Some argue that the root of the problem is overreliance on the mechanics of the analytical tool at the expense of using capital efficiently. In the next section, we consider how the right values play a helpful role in shaping how an organization allocates and uses its capital resources.

A Value-Based Approach to Capital
Resource Allocation

We stress throughout this text that the real power behind many management concepts (especially more complex financial concepts, such as EVA) is not so much the
mechanics involved in the analysis as the concepts behind the mechanics. Such is the
case for DCF. Thomas Copeland and Kenneth Ostrowski, consultants who have
spent years working at improving firms' capital-resourcing systems, explain this point
as follows:

> Using the proper analytic methods does not, and cannot, by itself, ensure real capital effi-
> ciency. . . . It starts, instead, with a managerial understanding of the forces that drive the
> demand for capital and shape the ways in which capital-dependent projects get defined and
> implemented at the front lines of an organization. And it rests on a managerial process that
> aligns the day-to-day behavior and mindset of the employees who plan and execute such
> projects with the organization's overall value-creation objectives.[33]

These authors describe a shift from emphasizing mechanical analysis to emphasizing the use of reason and common sense, influenced by values reflecting the firm's
strategy and by an awareness of how efficient use of capital resources is critical to the
strategy's success. In our earlier example, the CFO and his department focused more
than 80 percent of their efforts on evaluating proposals that accounted for less than 20
percent of the firm's capital allocations. The rest of the capital was allocated to proposals that never received much attention from the finance department or that fell
below the $1 million hurdle. Experts Copeland and Ostrowski would argue that the
team could have had a much greater impact on capital efficiency by focusing more of
its efforts on (1) shaping the organization's values toward caring about capital efficiency and (2) educating people about how to use capital more efficiently.

Consider the following illustration of such a value-based approach to managing
the capital-resourcing system. A moderate-sized regional hospital faced severe cash
flow problems as a result of the sort of decreased payments from insurance companies
and government health programs we described earlier in this chapter. The organization had always made rigorous use of formal DCF analysis, but in the new health care
environment, the CEO and CFO felt that concern for capital efficiency needed to go
further. These executives were particularly concerned about management of all the
funds that were spent outside the formal capital-budgeting process (such as supplies
ordered).

As a result of this concern, they assigned a team to study how staff throughout the
hospital ordered and used supplies and to address problems they discovered in order
to improve the organization's use of its capital. The team found that employees
treated supplies as if they were virtually free. Many of the most commonly used supplies were very inexpensive on a per unit basis, and it was easy for employees to ignore
this cost when looking at the total cost of operating the hospital. For example, disposable gloves were stored everywhere in bulk dispensers, and if two pairs were pulled
out instead of one, employees simply threw away the second pair. The team also
found that for the sake of convenience, medical supplies were typically ordered from
central stores in large quantities, even though many of these were perishable and
often the total amount ordered could not all be used before some was out of date and

had to be destroyed. The research team found that on some highly perishable items, it was common for 20 percent to be discarded later as out of date.

When faced with such widespread waste at the frontline staff level, the investigating team quickly realized that the solution was not tighter specifications built into a centrally administered resource allocation process. Instead, the key to addressing this problem was explaining to workers how such isolated actions cumulatively amounted to millions of wasted dollars. The team gained the commitment of frontline workers by explaining that, because the most obvious way for the hospital to recover its losses was to undertake a reduction in the workforce, by reducing waste, employees would actually be helping to save their own jobs. Application 11.4 provides another example of the impact of values on capital resourcing, describing the changes in values CEO Paul Allaire brought about in order to affect how capital resources were allocated and used at Xerox.

Copeland and Ostrowski observe that if an organization changes its values at the grassroots level, it can usually reduce its capital expenditures by 10 to 25 percent without any reduction in the quality of goods or services offered to customers. They describe one company that reduced its working capital by a half-billion dollars in one year by bringing about widespread capital resource conservation at the grassroots level. As they explain, "This dramatic improvement had nothing to do with budgeting methodology [which remained unchanged] but everything to do with developing a value-based approach to capital management throughout the organization."[34]

Having discussed how allocating the critical resources of information, people, and capital can affect strategy implementation, we are ready to shift to a different, but closely related, topic. In the remainder of this chapter, we consider the control systems that organizations rely on to see that allocated resources are used as intended and that the desired results are achieved.

CONTROL SYSTEMS

So far we have been talking about systems for developing and allocating resources. In this last section, we shift our focus to a consideration of how organizations control the way resources are used and how strategies are thereby implemented. Control systems deal with the fundamental question of whether or not resources (information, people, and capital) are being used to move the organization closer to its goals and what should be done if this is not the case. In this section we discuss the need for organizational control in the midst of the many trends and developments that are intended to free up organizations. Then we compare three alternative approaches to control and look at their relationships within the broader strategy implementation effort.

The Continuing Need for Control

In a world in which businesses are attempting to decentralize decision making to the lowest possible level, encourage entrepreneurship throughout the ranks, flatten organizational hierarchies, and empower individuals to act independently, organizational

Application 11.4

Xerox: Changing the Values That Drive Its Capital-Resourcing System

As part of his effort to make Xerox a more competitive rival, Paul Allaire, the corporation's CEO, attempted to change the way individuals throughout the organization viewed the capital-resourcing system. To understand the change he tried to bring about, consider the way in which R&D resources were allocated. Allaire wanted to alter this system from one that reflected the values of a welfare state doling out funds based on centralized planning to one that would reflect the values of entrepreneurs seeking out venture capital.

Under the old system, an annual ritual that went by the grandiose name of "resource optimization," the top-management team took the R&D budget, which typically ranged from $800 million to $900 million, and allocated it to major priorities. They then used these priorities to decide which projects would get funded and at what levels. This system made sense if it was assumed that the top-management team was the only group that knew the firm's strategy and/or it was assumed that the top-management team knew how best to implement the strategy. Allaire did not think either of these conditions existed at Xerox, and he greatly disliked the values the old system had been built on.

"It was as if the people who actually had to spend the money were living in a welfare state. They told us what they needed—'I need $50 million' . . . then they waited. At some point, somebody would come back to them and say, 'What will happen if you only get $30 million instead of $50 million?' And then they would revise their plans according to the new figure. Finally, someone would come back yet again and say, 'Okay, you get $35 million.' That's how the process worked. It was completely crazy."

What Allaire developed as an alternative was a system that placed greater responsibility for deciding how funds will be allocated lower in the organization. Division heads were told to set their own priorities and to determine what funds they would need to reach their targets. Then they were evaluated on how efficiently they were able to use the capital they were allocated to reach the targets they set. Such a system was based on a very different set of values than the former system had been. It assumed that division-level managers knew what their strategic priorities were and should be and that they were in a better position than senior corporate executives to decide how funds should be allocated in pursuit of those priorities. Allaire's new capital allocation system was much more aligned with the concept of discovery and organizational learning, while the old system had been closer to that of strategic programming.

In describing the way division heads throughout the organization should approach the new capital-resourcing system, Allaire explained, "[T]hey should be coming to corporate management the way an entrepreneur goes to a venture capitalist or banker. . . . We shouldn't be starting out with a fixed R&D budget. How the hell is anybody smart enough to say what the right amount should be?"

Sources

Preston Townley, "Decentralizing for Competitive Advantage," *Across the Board* (January 1994), 24–29; Robert Howard, "The CEO as Organizational Architect: An Interview with Xerox's Paul Allaire," *Harvard Business Review* (September–October 1992); James T. C. Teng, Varun Grover, and Kirk D. Fiedler, "Redesigning Business Processes Using Information Technology," *Long Range Planning, 27* (February 1994), 95–106.

control may seem irrelevant. However, these trends are in fact making control even more critical. Without effective controls in place, greater autonomy can result in an organization's being pulled in so many conflicting directions that it fails to progress toward any goal. Procter & Gamble was a pioneer in employing many of these autonomy-enhancing concepts 10 years before most firms began to experiment with them. For a long time, P&G's leadership interpreted the new ideas as a need for deemphasizing individual accountability, but eventually the firm's position on this point changed. When the firm's annual earnings growth fell from 30 percent to near zero,

Chapter 12

Action Levers

This chapter is premised on the notion that leaders, through their own individual actions, can exert power and influence over what strategies are implemented and how organizations are changed. We expand on this premise by considering a number of different forms of power and influence resulting from actions taken by managers and leaders. We begin with a discussion of formal authority as one of the more obvious forms of power, but we argue that sole reliance on this form of influence is very limiting. We then consider how other forms of power and influence can serve as useful supplements to formal authority and argue for a "full portfolio" in which a variety of different types of actions are taken to provide a leader with the most effective mix of power and influence. Separate sections are devoted to coverage of four of the most influential types of leadership actions: organizational politics, negotiation, communication, and serving as a role model. In each of these sections, we explain the need for the action under consideration and offer basic guidelines for effectively using this type of action as a source of power and influence in the strategy implementation process.

This chapter will help you understand:

- The power of mundane, everyday acts to influence strategy implementation and organizational change
- The continuing need for leaders to exercise power and influence even in organizations that emphasize empowerment and decentralization
- The limits of relying on formal authority as a primary form of power or influence
- The range of options available to leaders interested in supplementing a command-and-control approach to leadership with less heavy-handed action
- The inevitability of organizational politics and an approach to making them a constructive force for change
- The pervasive need for managers and leaders to engage in negotiation, and some basic guidelines for effective negotiating
- The critical need for effective communication and steps toward improving the communication process
- The fundamental need for leaders whose actions can serve as role models for the rest of the organization and some of the most powerful ways in which a leader's actions can do this

CEO David Kearns of Xerox Corporation faced a tremendous challenge: just 2 years before, he became the company's highest-ranking officer. Xerox was the dominant leader in the U.S. photocopier market, with sales growth of a billion dollars a year. Now, however, the product line was aging, growth was flat, Japanese competitors were making major inroads into the U.S. market, and profits were down. This situation was so bad that some analysts speculated that Xerox, inventor of xerography, was now headed toward bankruptcy.

As CEO, Kearns had a clear responsibility—lead 125,000 Xerox employees in saving the company—but the means to accomplish this were anything but clear. Fortunately for Xerox, Kearns's actions constituted a textbook example of sound leadership, as he led the organization to develop and implement its Leadership Through Quality strategy. Eight years later, as Kearns prepared to leave Xerox, the company had won quality awards with its new product line, once again firmly led the global photocopier market, was regaining its lost market share, and enjoyed near-record levels of profitability. What specifically did Kearns do to effect this remarkable turnaround? To insiders, three practices stand out.

Communication Kearns proved effective in communicating the severity of the company's problems as well as his vision of how Xerox would save itself. Although he was a great inspirational speaker, he did not limit communica-

tion to the spoken word. For example, he used symbolism as a communicative device when he insisted Leadership Through Quality would never be referred to as "LTQ"—signaling that the strategy was much more than merely the current acronym.

Use of Power Kearns was never known as an overly tough or demanding boss—rather, his reputation was for being a caring and nurturing "people person." However, one circumstance was always sure to bring out a very different side of his personality as he drew upon the full power of his position as CEO. More than once, doubters questioned the need for the tremendous emphasis on quality, complaining, "All this quality stuff is getting in the way of other things we need to be doing." At this, the normally mild-mannered Kearns took on a steely countenance, as the room grew quiet and he soberly explained, "Quality is not in the way—it is the way, and if you cannot understand this distinction, the company will be happy to provide you with the very best outplacement services available."

A Role Model Kearns's use of communication and power were vital to the Xerox turnaround, but people most remember the role model he provided during the tough times at his company. One retired executive recalls, "David is the only CEO I've ever observed who committed to a demanding course of action and then unflinchingly supported it no matter how tough things got. No matter what we threw at him, he never blinked." Kearns's personal commitment to Leadership Through Quality was so evident that employees began to say: "He doesn't just talk the talk, he walks the talk." This popular phrase spread beyond Xerox and, today, a leader who demonstrates commitment to a strategy by personal actions is said to "walk the talk."

Through personal behavior such as selectively drawing on formal authority, communicating effectively, and maintaining steadfast visible support for his strategy, David Kearns dramatically changed Xerox Corporation, leading the way to great performance improvements.

POWER AND INFLUENCE THROUGH PERSONAL ACTIONS

This chapter shows how a manager's personal actions can be a powerful lever for influencing strategy or bringing about organizational change. It may seem ironic that in a text devoted to establishing an organizationwide, unified approach to strategy, we would end by discussing actions taken on the individual level.[1] But, however paradoxical it may appear, we believe this is an appropriate wrap-up for our treatment of strategy. While we may speak of teams, organizations, and firms in anthropomorphic terms as though they were capable of action, the entities themselves are not. Actions are taken by individuals, and, regardless of our emphasis on the collective, each of us ultimately acts individually.[2]

Before getting into a discussion of how individual actions can be levers for influence, we need to clarify a possible misconception. Contrary to what you may expect, we do *not* focus this chapter on great acts of leadership, power, or influence. By "great acts," we mean those pivotal incidents, often described as watershed events, that single-handedly alter an organization's course. Such events are important and make for good reading, but, for the most part, organizational progress depends on actions that are altogether mundane and commonplace.

This opinion is shared by David Whitman, the CEO responsible for much of Whirlpool's success in transforming itself from an also-ran in the U.S. home appliance market to an aggressive leader in the emerging global market for home appliances. His comments on how this dramatic transformation took place emphasize how powerful many small acts of leadership can be:

> I want to make it clear that the art of management is not confined to orchestrating the creation of a bold vision, a great plan, or even one set of actions that cause an organization to face up to the need for change. It must also encompass relentless follow-through, [and] meticulous attention to detail. . . . These are not glamorous functions, but . . . without them, the organization cannot maintain interest or momentum, and the initiative—no matter how spectacular the fireworks of the start-up—will fizzle out.[3]

Examples of the unglamourous but important actions Whitman stressed are identified in Exhibit 12.1 and illustrated in Application 12.1.[4]

EXHIBIT 12.1
Examples of Everyday Actions That Shape Organizational Outcomes (grouped by chapter section)

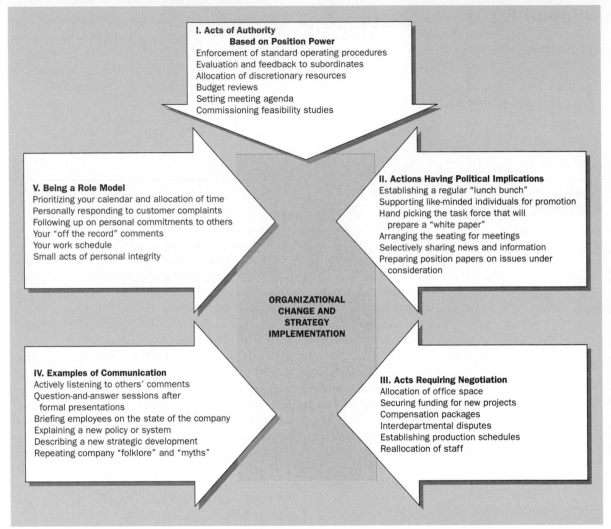

At first, such everyday acts as these may seem boring, but seen in a different light, they become the source of considerable excitement. If organizational progress really depended entirely on watershed events and grand actions, few of us would ever have much impact on our organizations. But organizational progress is actually affected by so many different individuals, and through so many small, everyday events, that we all play a role in shaping our organizations' futures. With this in mind, in this chapter we echo a theme first sounded in our opening chapter, in which we argue that the practice of strategic management is not limited to a particular organizational level.

Application 12.1

Wal-Mart: Influencing Others Through Day-to-Day Actions

Every week, fifty to sixty corporate officers and regional managers board Wal-Mart's fleet of fifteen corporate aircraft to travel from store to store to reinforce the Wal-Mart culture and solve practical business problems. The typical manager in this group will spend 200 days per year doing this, in a job that has a life expectancy of only about 8 years before burnout occurs. Here are a few examples of the mundane things managers do on these trips and the impacts their actions have on the rest of the organization.

■ A regional manager stops by a new store and finds several problems. The store manager begins to make excuses, but the regional manager steps to a computer terminal and starts pulling up comparisons between the store's performance and that of other stores of comparable age in comparable markets. Rather than criticizing the local manager, the regional manager keeps saying, "You have tremendous potential for improvement." The message is clear to the store manager: While there is no way for me to hide poor performance, my regional manager is a resource I can count on to help me figure out how to improve.

■ At every store visited, the regional managers continually ask associates (Wal-Mart's term for employees) what management can be doing to help them out. The message: The late Sam Walton's concept of servant-leadership is alive and well in this organization; managers still value employees and count on them for the continued success of the organization.

■ While making the rounds with several local managers in tow, a regional manager is accosted by an elderly customer who demands to know where the advertised weeding tools are. The regional manager takes down the customer's name, telephone number, and address, promising to take care of the problem. It is discovered that Wal-Mart doesn't carry the product—the advertisement was a cable channel promotion. However, within a week a weed grubber is purchased and shipped to the customer along with a friendly letter. The message: Wal-Mart cares about its customers, and it's everyone's responsibility to take care of them.

■ Back at corporate headquarters for the weekend, all the traveling managers attend a 7:00 A.M. Saturday meeting to go over their week's work and decide what needs doing to keep operations improving. For example, regional managers decide that one reason so many new stores appear to have stock-out problems is that managers appear to be waiting for corporate headquarters to give them directions. The team agrees that a video should be made immediately and shipped to all new store managers to explain that they are responsible for this critical activity. The decision is made to make the video that day and spend the extra $1,200 to express it to all managers overnight so it will be in their hands by the time the team of roving executives begins a new round of visits on Monday. The message: Don't wait. Do it now. Stay after it.

With Wal-Mart managers constantly driving home messages such as these, it is small wonder the firm has become the nation's largest retailer and is still growing.

Sources
Bill Saporito, "A Week Aboard the Wal-Mart Express," *Fortune* (August 24, 1992), 77–84; John Huey, "America's Most Successful Merchant," *Fortune* (September 23, 1991), 46–59; John O. Burdett, "The Magic of Alignment," *Management Decision, 32*(2) (1994), 59–63.

Granted, some things about strategic management more naturally take place at the highest organizational levels, and we identify those, but we also discuss a range of actions that are in no way limited to high-ranking organizational members.

Regardless of where in the organization they occur, in terms of bringing about strategic change and facilitating strategy implementation, the most important individual actions are those that influence others. Through power and influence on others, a leader achieves the leverage critical to an organization's success, as we discuss below.

The Continuing Need for Power and Influence

Power is the potential ability to influence behavior and to change the course of events by overcoming resistance and convincing people to do things they would not otherwise do.[5] Power and influence are subjects often approached with disdain and apprehension. Many people consider it more socially correct to be critical of power than to speak of how to get more of it and use it to your advantage. And yet power is essential to change, progress, and improvement. As Warren Bennis and Burt Nanus, noted authorities on leadership, have explained, "Power is at once the most necessary and the most distrusted element exigent to human progress."[6]

The application of too much power is to be reviled, but the absence of power is to be lamented. Although power has been and continues to be abused, it is hard to imagine that the best response to this problem is to do away with it. We may be uncomfortable with the idea of using power to achieve our own ends, but we must also be dismayed when crises arise because of its absence. Jeffrey Pfeffer, author of *Managing with Power,* contends that "one of the major problems facing organizations today is not that too many people exercise too much power, but rather the opposite: too few people exercise enough power."[7] Bennis and Nanus reach a similar conclusion: "These days, power is conspicuous by its absence.... There is something missing ... POWER, the basic energy to initiate and sustain action translating intentions into reality, the quality without which leaders cannot lead."[8]

As these quotes suggest, power is an essential part of implementation. If an organization wants to see its strategies implemented, it must rely on leaders who understand the sources and uses of power and act accordingly. Power carries so many negative connotations primarily because it is usually defined too narrowly. Power and influence can take many forms, and, to be effective in using them, you need to move beyond overly simplistic negative stereotypes. We can classify the alternate forms power takes by considering its sources and its uses, as shown in Exhibit 12.2.

EXHIBIT 12.2
Sources and Uses of Power and Influence

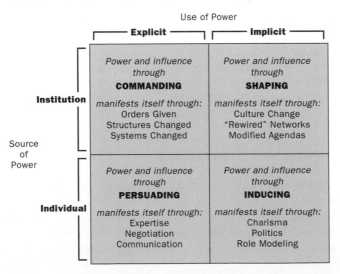

Alternate Forms of Power and Influence

Exhibit 12.2 identifies both institutions and individuals as sources of power. Institutional power, based on formal authority granted by the organization, allows one to govern the actions of others. The amount of institutional power is typically a function of one's position in an organization: the higher one's position, the greater the power granted by the institution. This relationship between hierarchical level and this type of power explains why we often speak of someone's having "power over" something or someone.

But many influential people have power that does not come from their institutional positions. A classic example is the computer "whiz kid" who holds greater power than organizational ranking would suggest because he or she alone really understands how the company's computers work. This form of influence is known as *expert power*. Or there may be someone to whom others regularly defer out of respect and admiration, even though this person is not in a formal position to exercise such influence, an example of *referent power*.

In examples such as these, the source of the power is not the institution but the individual. Power that stems from within an individual is usually formed over time as a result of many actions and through interactions with others.[9] Power that comes from within an individual rather than from an institution is considered "power through," rather than "power over." The types of power derived *through* negotiation, political maneuvering, and communication stem from what an individual does personally rather than what an institution grants.

Again referring to Exhibit 12.2, we see that, regardless of its source, power can be used in a fashion that ranges from explicit (overt or blatant) to implicit (unobtrusive or subtle). When supervisors give workers orders, they use explicit power; those being influenced are aware of it. But not all uses of power are nearly so obvious. When a leader consistently identifies goals in the same order, an implicit message is being sent that the first goal has the highest priority. Over time, this will influence the thoughts and actions of others without the leader's ever having explicitly stated that the first goal should be given priority. By combining the two sources and the two uses of power, we are able to identify four types of power or influence: commanding, shaping, persuading, and inducing.

Commanding

Much of what people find most unattractive about power is found in the northwest corner of Exhibit 12.2, where influence comes in the form of commands. Here, power derived from institutional sources is used explicitly: based on formal authority, a manager gives orders and uses rewards or punishments to enforce them. We call this combination of source and use of power *commanding*. This type of power is readily abused; when abused, it manifests itself in ways that range from petty favoritism to fascism. Naturally, such misuse of power is disliked and discouraged. However, it would be a gross overstatement to say that explicit use of institutionally derived power is always bad. Many circumstances exist in which such power is very appropriate—a classic example is military action. Military operations depend on a command-and-control form of power in which the source of authority is specified by the institution and the use of authority is often necessarily explicit.

But the use of commands is not limited to military applications. As we have seen in previous chapters, the command-and-control approach to implementing a plan of action is neither inherently right nor inherently wrong for business organizations. Its use depends on the situation at hand. In the simple and/or stable situations in which strategic programming is feasible, a command-and-control approach to implementation may be not only reasonable but desirable. In such a situation, institutionally derived power used in an overt manner may effectively keep an organization on track and moving, as we saw in the Emerson Electric example in Chapter 2. However, as we have also discussed, the number of organizations that are able to rely exclusively on strategic programming is shrinking. This suggests that, for most leaders to be effective as possible, they will need forms of influence well beyond formal authority.[10]

For example, the previous two chapters discussed how organizational structure and systems can serve as important levers in bringing about organizational change. Ability to control these levers is directly proportional to institutional power. Those who are higher in an organization can have a much greater impact on the organization's structure (both macro and micro), as well as its resourcing and control systems. Controlling these organizational elements is not as blatant as issuing commands, but it can have an even greater impact. Commands usually apply to a fairly small subset of the organization, but altering the context and systems of an organization may have a much farther-reaching effect. By using institutionally granted authority to control these elements of the organization, managers can exert a tremendous amount of power to help bring about desirable changes. Though less obtrusive than commands, changes in the formal elements of organization structure and systems are still fairly explicit and obvious uses of institutionally derived power.

Research shows that explicit uses of institutionally granted power are often less effective than other, less heavy-handed approaches that are more implicit. For instance, one study found that of seven forms of power surveyed, coercive power (the one closest to our "commanding" category) was the least effective.[11] Such research findings suggest that most managers need to use other forms of power. We advocate that managers develop and employ all the different combinations of sources and uses of power. Moving away from the northwest corner and drawing on other forms of power from throughout this exhibit is what we call using a "full-portfolio" approach to power. By developing a full portfolio, you can become less reliant on commanding and other uses of obtrusive formal authority. You should recognize that we are not decrying the use of power altogether. While we stress the need for *decreased* reliance on commanding, at the same time we stress the *increased* use of other forms of power. For example, we will argue that one of the most effective uses of institutional power is "shaping" instead of commanding.

Shaping

As we have discussed in Chapter 10, an organization's context, its networks and culture, provide the backdrop against which everyday behavior plays out. We are often unaware of precisely how these elements of context affect us, although when we stop and consider, most of us will agree that their impact is immense. This being the case, there is an opportunity for leaders who can shape networks and culture to have a more important, if less obvious, impact on their organizations than they might have by relying on their formal authority.[12] For example, research has shown that, in today's flatter organizations, networks are emerging as particularly important sources of power. One study concluded that one of the most important differences between influential managers and less successful managers was their connection to and use of a network of resource persons—a balanced web of relationships with superiors, subordinates, peers, and other key players.[13] Another concluded that "the ability of managers to get things done depends more on the number of networks in which they're centrally involved than on their height in a hierarchy."[14]

Beyond shaping elements of the organization's networks and cultures, those granted power by the institution can use it to shape agendas, both literally and figuratively. Although this use of power is not often discussed, we find it to be among the strongest uses of formal authority. For example, several CEOs have used their position in an organization's hierarchy to shape the entire organization's agenda. In one case, the CEO, having become convinced that the organization needed to become more involved in international competition, made it a practice of putting any issues dealing with international affairs at the top of the agenda for all his weekly meetings with the VPs. This ensured that adequate time was available to discuss them, but often there was no time left to discuss other items the CEO considered less important. Thus, over several months, the organization made progress on international issues while other concerns were left on the back burner.

This CEO shaped a literal agenda, but many leaders figuratively shape their organizations' agendas by moving certain topics to the forefront of people's minds.[15] Consider the CEO of one hospital who explained that his most important job was to "get the concept of competition on the radar screens of everyone in [the] organization." While hospitals once considered themselves genteel organizations with more important things to worry about than competition, changes in the industry have now brought hospitals into competition not only with one another but with doctors and insurance companies as well. Unless this CEO could get this concept internalized by people throughout his organization, there was little hope the hospital would prosper in the new environment. Therefore, he used his position to frame issues in terms of competition, to ask questions that required those around him in the organization to think about competition, and to establish competition as a frequent topic of conversation and thought throughout the organization.

Without formal authority from the institution, the CEO would not have been nearly as successful as he was in bringing about this change. But while he used formal authority, he used this power in a manner that was less obtrusive than issuing orders. In fact, to those caught up in the day-to-day operation of the hospital, it was not always clear why competition kept coming up as a topic of discussion, and many of them saw their insights into competition and its importance as being something they had discovered on their own as a result of personal initiative. Lao Tsu, the sixth-century B.C. Chinese philosopher, made a similar point:

> The wicked leader is he who the people despise.
> The good leader is he who the people revere.
> The great leader is he who the people say, "We did it ourselves."

This proverb recognizes unobtrusive forms of power as more effective than command-and-control tactics. For instance, we are convinced that if the hospital CEO in our example had simply issued a decree insisting that people change their attitudes to think more competitively, he would have failed miserably. There is much merit in attempting to supplement explicit forms of institutional power with subtle efforts to influence others in less obtrusive ways.

Persuading and Inducing

So far, we have been focusing on the upper half of Exhibit 12.2, which may have given you the mistaken impression that power depends on organizational position and other sources of institutional authority. Although it is an undeniable fact of life that "rank has its privileges," not all forms of power are derived from institutional sources. In fact, researchers learned that personal power (found in the lower half of Exhibit 12.2) is generally more effective than position power (the upper half of the exhibit).[16]

In the lower half of the exhibit, you can see other forms of power that stem from within the individual. These are available to individuals at all levels of the organization, regardless of their rank or formal authority. When used explicitly, individual power manifests itself through acts of expertise, negotiation, and communication. When used in a less overt manner, individual power is seen through acts of charisma, politics, and providing a role model that others aspire to follow.

All these forms of power are found in the lower half of Exhibit 12.2. Of the six, we have already addressed the limits of charisma and the need for expertise in Chapter 9. This leaves politics, negotiations, communication, and role models, and we turn now to these forms of individual power in the following four sections.

ORGANIZATIONAL POLITICS

In this section, we discuss the nature of organizational politics and offer guidelines for using political forces constructively.

The Pervasive Nature of Organizational Politics

More than 30 years ago, esteemed political scientist Norton Long wrote, "People readily admit that governments are organizations. The converse—that organizations are governments—is equally true but rarely considered." Like it or not, organizations have many of the same characteristics as governments do, chief among these being politics. As Jeffrey Pfeffer puts it, "[O]rganizations, particularly large ones, are like governments in that they are fundamentally political entities. To understand them, one needs to understand organizational politics, just as to understand governments, one needs to understand governmental politics."[17] Experienced managers agree with these theorists, but they are not necessarily happy about it, as shown by the data reported in Exhibit 12.3.

EXHIBIT 12.3
Experienced Managers Have Mixed Opinions on Organizational Politics

	Percentage Agreeing
Organizations are political entities:	
The existence of workplace politics is common to most organizations.	93.2
The higher you go in organizations, the more political the climate becomes.	76.2
Politics are important to individual success:	
Successful executives must be good politicians.	89.0
Powerful executives don't act politically.	15.7
You have to be political to get ahead in organizations.	69.8
People are divided regarding the desirability of organizational politics:	
Organizations free of politics are happier than those where there are a lot of politics.	59.1
Politics in organizations are detrimental to efficiency.	55.1
Politics help organizations function effectively.	42.1
Top management should try to get rid of politics within the organization.	48.6

Source: Jeffrey Gandz and Victor Murray, "The Experience of Workplace Politics," *Academy of Management Journal, 23* (1980). Used with permission.

These data show that experienced managers recognize organizations as political entities and that successful or powerful executives must behave politically. However, about half the respondents believe politics are detrimental to organizational efficiency and a happy organizational life and think management should try to rid organizations of their politics. Although we empathize with this desire, it is not realistic. For one thing, even if half the people may want to be rid of politics, half do not. As long as there is such a large number of managers who "believe in" politics, organizations will be political entities. But beyond such simplistic arguments, there are more complex forces at work to sustain politics in organizations. Note that 42 percent of the managers surveyed believe that politics help organizations function effectively—almost as many as those who believe that politics are detrimental. Who is right? Perhaps both. In Application 12.2, a seasoned manager reflects on his experiences with politics and argues that politics are neither inherently good nor inherently bad, but what you make them.

Henry Mintzberg, whose theories of management we have drawn from heavily throughout this text, also agrees that politics are neither inherently good nor bad. He sees a definite place for politics in bringing about needed organizational change. He argues that, most of the time, organizations benefit from avoiding the divisiveness that politics foster. However, he also argues that this is not always the case and that sometimes an organization needs to be shaken up by its politics in order to bring about needed changes. He writes, "Most of the time, the cooperative pulling together . . . is to be preferred, so that the organization can pursue its established strategic perspective. But, occasionally, when fundamental change becomes necessary, the organization has to be able to pull apart through the competitive force of politics."[18]

If you read this quote carefully, you can identify the conditions under which Mintzberg believes politics are most likely detrimental and most likely beneficial.

Application 12.2

An Experienced Manager Shares His Views on Politics

Politics has been called the art of getting things done. Politics run through organizations of all sizes from families to villages to corporations to nations. They are not basically good or bad; they are neutral, to do with as we will. Political goodness or badness flows from the intent and impact of our actions.

Let's not fool ourselves. We won't be very effective if we ignore the politics of the organization, the "art of getting things done." Politics involves knowing who to work with and how to work with them. If you want to change the system, you had better understand how it works. You can try to avoid the politics of your company, but you cannot stay outside of politics. It automatically includes you as a force whether you include yourself or not.

In my new position I tried to apply the abilities that had worked well in my previous job. I worked as a direct contributor on projects rather than as a manager. I tried to measure my success by the project's success. Some of that worked, but something important was missing. My boss eventually took me aside to talk with me about the realities of life in the corporation. He pointed out that it

was a very political organization and that my department's effectiveness depended on my understanding how the company really worked. He told me that there was no excuse for my failing to do this. He was right; I was avoiding politics like the plague! And the more I avoided politics, the less I knew about what was going on in the political realms that were so important to the company's direction. Knowing less about what is happening is not the way to become influential; it does not lead to sound management decisions.

A "good working environment" is not achieved by removing politics, since we could not do this even if we wanted to. Instead, we need to recognize that we are participants in our company's politics. We need to know the kind of political atmosphere we wish to create and do our part to bring it to reality.

Source

Geoffrey M. Bellman, *Getting Things Done When You Are Not in Charge,* San Francisco: Berrett-Koehler, 1992, 75, 76, 77, and 78. Used with permission.

These times correspond to the periods of relative stability and quantum change we first identified using the punctuated equilibrium model in Chapter 9. During "equilibrium," when an organization hopes to adhere to what Mintzberg calls "its established strategic perspective," the absence of politics is beneficial, as it fosters the cooperation and efficiency that facilitate the incremental changes that are dominant during these periods. That is why Mintzberg writes, "[P]olitics often impedes necessary [incremental] change and wastes valuable resources." However, the paradigm shifts that form the "punctuation" part of the model are so difficult to bring about that only powerful political forces may be strong enough to cause a break with past thinking and allow a new order to emerge. In describing the disruptive nature of such paradigm shifts, Mintzberg concludes that "political challenge may also be the only means to promote really fundamental change." Summarizing the alternating need for political tension and apolitical harmony, he concludes, "The organization must, in other words, pull apart before it can pull together again."

This suggests that managers should be very sophisticated in their use of politics, knowing not only how to employ politics to get things done but when to downplay politics and encourage harmony. With the need for such political sophistication in mind, we offer the following advice to those who seek to harness political forces.

Guidelines for Organizational Politics

- *Admit that politics are inevitable.* Politics exist whenever different groups have different ideas that they want to see implemented and the individuals in these groups work to see their shared ideas moved forward. Can you imagine an organization in which this did not happen? In which no one shared ideas about what should happen and/or no one was willing to work to see their ideas advanced? Surely such a lethargic organization could not survive long. Most organizations are filled with politics, and the key to success as a leader in such organizations is not avoiding politics, but carefully controlling how you engage in politics and how they are allowed to affect your organization.

- *Resolve to practice principled politics.* People find politics most abhorrent when they are used for personal gain. Recall from Exhibit 12.3 that 70 percent of the respondents agreed that "you have to be political to get ahead in organizations." Although it is true that political behavior is often directed at furthering one's personal advantage, this is not politics' only role. As we discussed above, politics can be a constructive force for bringing about desirable organizational change. The concept of "principled politics" arises from the notion that the primary role of politics should be strengthening the organization, not the politician.

- *Recognize that, when you want to get something done, it will be considered both politically and objectively.* Because politics are inevitable, plan for them. Recognize that, as you advance your ideas, they will meet with resistance from others who have different ideas they want to advance. Some of the resistance your ideas meet comes from concern about their merits as assessed from an objective standpoint. Other resistance is more political in nature. Either form of resistance can stop your progress, and it is myopic to focus exclusively on one or the other.

- *Be clear up front about what you will and won't do.* The politically heated moment in which your adrenaline is flowing and events are unfolding rapidly is not the place or time to wonder whether you will regret a particular course of action later on. Think things over beforehand, and come to some clear personal guidelines about how you will behave under a broad set of varying scenarios. Use this forethought to keep yourself in check and avoid doing anything under pressure that you would not do normally.

- *Use openness and honesty to undermine unprincipled politics.* The mold of unprincipled politics cannot stand the light of public scrutiny. Let others know what you will and won't do. Openly talk about your motives and why you want to advance the ideas you are pushing. Ask people not to share opinions about others with you unless they are comfortable repeating those statements publicly. When you disagree with others, be willing to share your reasons. Deal with people face-to-face, and avoid behind-the-scenes, "smoke-filled-rooms" politics that can be so corrupting and destructive.

The approach you take to negotiation impacts your effectiveness in practicing principled politics, a subject we discuss in the next section.

THE MANAGER AS NEGOTIATOR

Managers negotiate constantly.[19] You may be familiar with the use of the term "negotiation" to describe talks between organized labor and management—union contract negotiation—but this is actually one of the least commonly occurring subjects of negotiation. Many organizations do not have unionized labor, and most of those that do negotiate new contracts only periodically. However, other forms of negotiation take place continuously in all organizations.[20] Exhibit 12.4 is a short list of the endless topics of negotiation that can be found in the typical organization.

As this exhibit illustrates, getting things done inside an organization virtually always requires negotiation, and it is no coincidence that the most effective leaders are usually good negotiators. Fortunately, negotiating skills are another one of the dimensions of leadership that are easily learned—good negotiators are made, not born. The topic of negotiation has received considerable research, and some of the generally agreed-upon recommendations stemming from that research follow in the next section.

The Value of Principled, Relationship-Focused Negotiation

The stereotype of a negotiator is someone who is "trying to get all of theirs, plus most of mine."[21] Such an attitude is terribly destructive to relationships, as the "loser" of a negotiation approached in this way probably won't feel kindly toward the "winner." Given the importance of relationships to a manager's continued effectiveness, this approach to negotiation is clearly shortsighted.[22] You may win the negotiation battle but in so doing lose the larger war. The potentially ruinous impact of "winning" a negoti-

---

EXHIBIT 12.4
Examples of the Ubiquitous Nature of Negotiation in Managing

A purchasing department negotiates with a vendor for better trade terms.

A plant manager negotiates with a marketing manager over what product changes will actually be implemented.

A director of administration negotiates with a computer installation technician regarding when an installation will actually take place.

Two department heads negotiate the allocation of shared overhead.

An employee negotiates for a pay raise.

A supervisor negotiates with her direct reports to get a rush order expedited.

A CEO negotiates a joint venture agreement with a key customer.

A customer negotiates a settlement to a warranty claim.

A CFO negotiates for more favorable terms on a line of credit.

A contractor negotiates for a deadline extension.

A department head negotiates to save jobs in his section during companywide downsizing.

---

ation causes most effective managers to choose a different approach to negotiation.[23] Their goal is to reach an agreement that is fair to both sides and thereby improve the relationship between two parties. This approach has been labeled "principled" or "relationship-focused" negotiation.[24]

This obviously makes sense in an organization where the manager expects to continue working with the other party after the negotiation ends. But what about negotiations with parties you may never see again, so-called episodic negotiations? Is principled or relationship-focused negotiation a rational choice then?[25] In a surprising number of cases, there are good reasons to approach these as principled, relationship-focused negotiations as well. For example, one company—we'll give it the pseudonym "Craft"—was negotiating to buy the plant and equipment of a former competitor that had decided to get out of the business. Given that the assets were being acquired from a firm that would no longer be around, what possible importance could be assigned to the relationship? Wouldn't it make more sense just to get the price down as low as possible? In response to such questions, the Craft management team considered their options and unanimously agreed that they were interested only in negotiations based on principle and stressing a continued relationship. Their reasoning:

1. *Even if the other business would no longer be around, others in the industry would be, and they would surely learn about how Craft had acquired the failed firm's assets.* Any unfavorable reputation could adversely affect the firm's ability to negotiate with other businesses for their assets as the shakeout continued. And even if they never bought any other assets, Craft managers believed it would be valuable for them to be recognized as a team that did not kick the competition when it was down.

2. *If Craft was successful in making the acquisition, it would be faced with new challenges, and dealing with these challenges would be greatly facilitated if both sides of the negotiation felt good about the way they had been handled.* For example, the process involved in moving the acquired assets to Craft's production site would not be easy, and Craft's managers did not want it to be further complicated by any ill will between their organization and the other firm. In addition, once all the equipment was moved and reinstalled, Craft would need to hire some more managers and operators, and the former employees of the shutdown business would be strong candidates for these new positions.

3. *Finally, Craft's managers did not feel comfortable taking advantage of their favorable position.* They agreed that, if the tables were turned, they would want to be treated decently and fairly, and they were determined to use this as their standard for negotiation.

As explained in Application 12.3, Craft's use of principled, relationship-focused negotiation set aside many of the practices that are sometimes adopted in negotiations and instead adopted practices such as those discussed below.

Effective Negotiating Practices

■ *Understand the implications of no-agreement alternatives.* The most fundamental goal of any negotiation is to achieve through the negotiation what you could not

Application 12.3

A Chemical Processor Uses Principled Negotiation Successfully

Craft Chemicals, a pseudonym for a real firm, used several elements of principled negotiation discussed in this chapter to help implement its growth strategy. The business was a chemical processor in a segment of the industry that had overbuilt capacity. The segment's product—let's call it "philmite"—had tremendous potential for a wide range of uses, but there was no way the market could absorb the capacity chemical firms around the world had scrambled to build. A shakeout was inevitable, and Craft was determined to emerge from the shakeout not just as a survivor but as the industry leader.

A major opportunity arose when a competing company—call it Pickull Chemical—decided to shut its philmite plant down just 3 years after building it. If the Craft team could acquire the assets of that plant cheaply enough, it could afford to move them to its own production site, economically expanding the site's capacity and solidifying the firm's position in the consolidating market. The engineers who managed the Craft philmite operation had never negotiated for such an acquisition, but, by using some very basic negotiating principles, they made the acquisition on very favorable terms. In reflecting on what had worked best for them, the Craft management team singled out two principles.

Stress Creating Value Rather Than Dividing Value

The Pickull negotiating team assumed that talks would begin with offers and counteroffers and that dickering would continue from there. However, the Craft team asked that negotiators postpone all offers until after lunch and spend the morning getting to know each other.

Craft then used this period to help each side identify the other's primary concerns and issues. Based on these insights, the team later tailored the deal so that it created greater value for *both* sides. For example, Pickull's managers were concerned about where they were going to find jobs, and Craft's managers were concerned about how they would be able to oversee dismantling the Pickull plant while continuing to operate and expand their own facilities. The value-creating solution was to have Pickull's managers stay on the job to oversee the dismantling, freeing Craft's managers to concentrate their efforts at home.

Negotiation *with* Each Other Instead of *Against* Each Other

Pickull had arranged the meeting room with the sides facing each other across a long table, a classic confrontational setting. However, Craft's team had anticipated this possibility, and its members were prepared for it. They set up a flip chart at one end of the table, and, as the terms of the deal began to develop, they put them on the flip chart. Throughout the negotiation, they focused on the flip chart and the terms of the deal, rather than on their "adversaries" across the table. They rotated their chairs slightly to have them facing the flip chart rather than squaring off against the Pickull team, and they constantly offered subtle encouragement for Pickull to join them in focusing on problems rather than on each other. Whenever the tone of the negotiation started to heat up, the Craft team found they could diffuse things quickly by directing attention toward the common problem of filling out the pages of the flip chart rather than besting each other.

achieve otherwise. If you cannot reach a better outcome than that available without reaching a negotiated agreement, then why accept such an agreement? In other words, your alternative to a negotiated agreement is the theoretical threshold below which you will not reasonably settle, and we call this limit the no-agreement alternative, or NAA.[26] While you should not enter into any agreement that offers an outcome less preferable than your NAA, in most cases you can accomplish more through working cooperatively with others than you can on your own, and negotiations offer the potential for outcomes that are far superior to your NAA.

- *Do not negotiate on position.* In the stereotypical negotiation, two parties open with offers at opposite extremes and then, through rounds of counteroffers, move toward a position somewhere in the middle. This is called negotiating on position, and it probably causes negotiations to end in failure more than anything else. It encourages a tug-of-war mentality in which the purpose of the negotiation is to overpower the other side and drag it to your preferred position. When you operate under this mentality, each move toward the other side is considered a concession that leaves you worse off, and the negotiation usually becomes an argument over who will get what rather than an opportunity for collaborative problem solving. The classic parable illustrating the folly of negotiating over position is the story of the two cooks who have a fight over a lemon each wants to use in completing prized recipes. They focus on who will get the lemon, never realizing that one recipe calls for only the juice while the other requires only the zest from the peel.

- *Emphasize creating value rather than dividing value.* As illustrated by the parable of the lemon, the common perception of negotiation is that it is a form of arguing about who will get what, and many negotiators concentrate on dividing the potential value between the parties involved. However, relationship-focused negotiators concentrate on creating value for both parties. Said differently, the former is focused on dividing the pie, while the latter is focused on making the pie bigger. There is a common tendency for the focus in negotiations to keep shifting toward the division of value, but this is shortsighted. If negotiators focus on creative approaches to how collaborative efforts can benefit both parties, it is often possible for a pie to grow so large that even taking a smaller piece of the total will result in getting more than would be available otherwise. This is illustrated in Exhibit 12.5.

EXHIBIT 12.5
The Potential Impact of Focusing on Creating Value Rather Than on Dividing Value

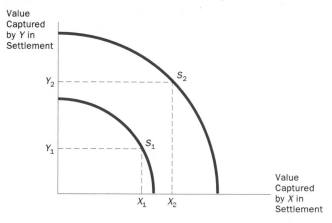

In settlement S_1, X captures a much higher percentage of the total value than Y (i.e., $X_1 > Y$).

In settlement S_2, X captures a smaller percentage of the total value (i.e., $X_2 = Y_2$) while still capturing more value in absolute terms than is captured in S_1 (i.e., $X_2 > X_1$).

■ *Negotiate* on *the problem, not* against *the person.* It is all too common for negotiators to fall into the trap of defining their success as "beating the other person" or "teaching them a lesson." Such a mind-set reflects a presumption that you are to judge the other party's position, and this is not conducive to relationship-based negotiating. A much more productive mind-set is to think of yourself and your counterpart as cojudges who are attempting to reach a common understanding of how a case should be decided. This mind-set shifts the focus from negotiating *against* other people to negotiating *with* them on a problem.[27]

These and other simple guidelines for effective negotiations can be learned and made habitual through practice. To the most effective leaders, such guidelines have become second nature, and these leaders approach the many negotiations that are part of their daily lives as opportunities to influence others in ways that are mutually beneficial and that serve to strengthen working relationships and further enhance their effectiveness. Another set of skills to learn and practice deals with communication, our next topic.

COMMUNICATION

You have probably never thought of communication as a form of power, but consider our definition of power. If power is the ability to influence others to behave in ways they otherwise would not, surely communication is one of power's most important forms. CEO Ray Strata is widely recognized for his success in developing Analog Devices as a learning organization. After years of involvement in this effort, he had this to say about the importance of communication:

> There are many impediments to organizational learning, but the most basic is communication. . . . Only in recent years have I begun to fully understand how profoundly the words that come out of my mouth and my pen affect organizational performance both for better and for worse. When you think about it, the only thing that a manager does that is visible to the organization is listen and speak. . . . We can change each other by what we say and how we listen.[28]

As Strata's statement suggests, there are two parts to communication, what we say and how we listen; given communication's importance as a source of power, you will need skill at both to be an effective leader.[29] Strata also mentions the importance of the written word. While written communication is important, especially when establishing formal statements such as missions and policies, research shows that on a day-to-day basis people are more likely influenced by a spoken rather than a written message.[30] Therefore, in the sections below, we focus on listening and speaking as basic elements of communication.

Listening

In writing about the importance of communication as a leadership skill, observers comment that while listening is the element of communication that is used most, it is clearly the part that is taught and emphasized the least.[31] This is probably because listening appears to be less important to *influencing* others than it is to *being influenced* by others. When we listen, we allow input from someone else, and this appears to shift control over to that person. Consequently, many people equate speaking with power and influence and listening with being influenced. This is a confused and detrimental conception.

Listening is, in fact, the first step toward influencing through communication. Only by understanding what others are thinking and feeling can we hope to influence their actions. Note here that we emphasize listening for understanding, as opposed to listening for the purpose of evaluation. The difference between the two is important. As Carl Rogers, the famous psychologist, wrote to managers reading the *Harvard Business Review*, "I've found that there is one main obstacle to communication: people's tendency to *evaluate*. Fortunately, I've also discovered that if people can learn to *listen* with understanding, they can mitigate their evaluation impulses and greatly improve their communication with others."[32]

Rogers argued that managers focus on evaluation because they assume the purpose of their conversations is to win someone over to their way of thinking by the use of logic. According to Rogers, a manager further assumes that by evaluating what the other person says, he or she can discover flaws in the logic. Naturally, it follows that, by pointing out these flaws, the manager can correct the other person's mistaken views and convince him or her that the manager's views are more valid. But this approach to conversation often brings debate, argument, and hardened feelings instead of useful changes in attitudes and behaviors. In contrast, the concept of listening for understanding is one of seeking to genuinely understand the other point of view, not to find flaws in it but to develop empathy. As Rogers explains, "This means seeing the expressed idea and attitude from the other person's point of view, sensing how it feels to the person, achieving his or her frame of reference about the subject being discussed."

Rogers saw the difference between listening for purposes of evaluation and listening for purposes of understanding as subtle, but critical, to successful communication. While the two often look and feel the same, he described empathic understanding as being focused more on understanding *with* a person rather than understanding *about* a person, the latter of which he linked to evaluation. He thought that distinctions between these two were so subtle that managers often confused them and listened for purposes of evaluation even when they meant to listen for understanding. To help address this confusion, he proposed a simple but effective rule: "Before each person speaks up, he or she must first restate the ideas and feelings of the previous speaker accurately and to that speaker's satisfaction." Using this rule has come to be known as *active listening*, a form of listening in which a listener actively seeks to fully understand the situation facing the speaker.[33]

One of the benefits of active listening is that it clarifies what Chris Argyris, another psychologist who has been very influential on the practice of management, calls the "left-hand column" of conversations. Argyris developed an exercise for improving communication that lists what was actually said on the right-hand side of a page and then annotates this with descriptions of the thoughts behind each comment on the left-hand side of the page. Studying this left-hand column can bring about the empathic understanding that Rogers advocated, in large part because it is effective in uncovering the hidden assumptions we all make throughout our conversations. Exhibit 12.6 provides a simple example.

Our exhibit shows that Pat and Fran continually fail to communicate what they are thinking and feeling. They are both concerned with positioning themselves favorably relative to the other, and neither is making any effort to understand the other person's views or to test his or her own assumptions about what the other needs. Consequently, they both fail to bring about the beneficial results they sought upon entering the conversation. Only by listening actively, in an effort to develop an empathic understanding of each other's situation, can we hope to uncover Argyris's left-hand column. And only by making the left-hand side of our conversations more explicit can we ever hope to achieve positive, constructive communication that will influence the actions of others in our organizations.

Speaking

As we have seen, in conversation, active listening is probably more important than speaking in bringing about the understanding on which communication is based. However, one form of communication in which speaking is critical is that of giving

EXHIBIT 12.6
The Power of the "Left-Hand" Column

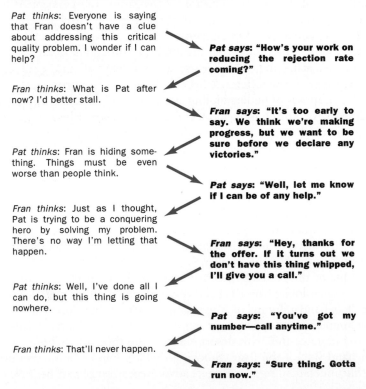

Pat thinks: Everyone is saying that Fran doesn't have a clue about addressing this critical quality problem. I wonder if I can help?

Pat says: "How's your work on reducing the rejection rate coming?"

Fran thinks: What is Pat after now? I'd better stall.

Fran says: "It's too early to say. We think we're making progress, but we want to be sure before we declare any victories."

Pat thinks: Fran is hiding something. Things must be even worse than people think.

Pat says: "Well, let me know if I can be of any help."

Fran thinks: Just as I thought, Pat is trying to be a conquering hero by solving my problem. There's no way I'm letting that happen.

Fran says: "Hey, thanks for the offer. If it turns out we don't have this thing whipped, I'll give you a call."

Pat thinks: Well, I've done all I can do, but this thing is going nowhere.

Pat says: "You've got my number—call anytime."

Fran thinks: That'll never happen.

Fran says: "Sure thing. Gotta run now."

speeches. Question-and-answer time notwithstanding, for the most part public speaking engages the speaker in a monologue rather than a dialogue, and, with less opportunity to listen, emphasis naturally shifts to the speaking side of communication.

In his book *Executive Speeches*, Brent Filson asserts that communication is the most important element of leadership and that, by becoming better speakers, leaders can make both themselves and their companies stronger.[34] Experts have identified several key points you should understand about how to be a more effective leader by improving your speaking abilities.[35]

- *Delivery is just as important as content.* Too many managers devote their efforts to ensuring that the content of their message is correct, without realizing that the style and manner of delivery affect how the content is received.[36] Experienced speechwriters argue that making a favorable impression with the delivery is what defines a successful speech, because the delivery is what the audience will usually remember, rather than the content of the speech itself. Research backs up this opinion. According to one study, an audience typically remembers only 7 percent of what is said but 30 percent of how the speaker sounded and 55 percent of how the speaker looked.[37]

- *Tell a story.* Regardless of the audience's sophistication, they all respond to stories. A good story captures attention in a way that simple prose cannot. Obviously, the story must illustrate a central point and not be merely a distraction. In our experience, the leaders who are the most effective speakers are virtually always great storytellers.

- *Seek to connect with your audience by relating to their situation.* When Joseph Javorski took over as head of the human resource department at Norton, Inc. (a large, diversified manufacturing firm), his first task was to develop and help deliver a new training program for the firm's supervisors that would improve their effectiveness in a flattening organization. Initially, he made little progress—it seemed that all that the supervisors could focus on was the threat to their jobs from Norton's organizational flattening. As head of HRM, a department that was heavily involved in decisions on how to flatten Norton, Javorski was seen as the source of their problems rather than the solution. However, when he explained that he too had once been a frontline supervisor and that he too had been personally threatened by flattening and downsizing, he saw a dramatic change from confrontation to cooperation on the part of the supervisors.[38] Here you can see the importance of relating to audiences personally.

- *Use visuals.* You have heard that a picture is worth a thousand words. Let's assume you are a manager in a company that has been through a period of rising costs that have forced prices up, resulting in diminished sales and dropping market share. Explaining this with tables of numbers and the accompanying prose required to clarify the tables is cumbersome and ineffective. However, as illustrated in Exhibit 12.7, this message is easily conveyed visually. Although no one could be expected to leave your presentation remembering the information on the left-hand side of this exhibit, it is not unreasonable to expect the visual graphs on the right-hand side of the exhibit to "stick" in the minds of an audience.

EXHIBIT 12.7
Charts and Figures Are More Effective Forms of Communication Than Tables of Data Are

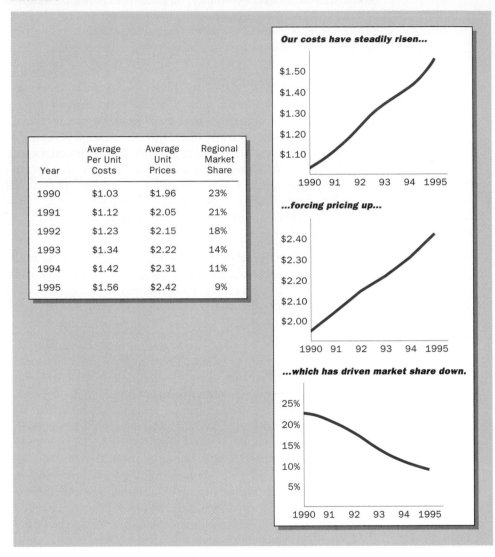

Year	Average Per Unit Costs	Average Unit Prices	Regional Market Share
1990	$1.03	$1.96	23%
1991	$1.12	$2.05	21%
1992	$1.23	$2.15	18%
1993	$1.34	$2.22	14%
1994	$1.42	$2.31	11%
1995	$1.56	$2.42	9%

Our costs have steadily risen...

...forcing pricing up...

...which has driven market share down.

- *Strike the right tone.* Consider what tone will have the desired effect on your audience, and be consistent in delivering it. Humor is usually appropriate but should be used carefully—too much will trivialize your presentation, and humor that fails to amuse is deadly. Credibility is usually enhanced by linking your topic to broader, more universal issues (such as the need for cost controls not for their own sake but because of price pressures brought about by increased global competition), but too much emphasis on the bigger picture can make your presentation come across as theoretical and thus irrelevant. Reading formally prepared text is almost always inappropriate for business presentations; more informal—though still well-organized—comments are usually more effective.

- *Pick your main point, and focus on it.* Contrary to what you might hope, few people in your audience will carry away more than one point. Therefore, you need to consider what that one point will be and focus on its delivery. Strip away all the clutter that might obscure your central theme. Plan on repeating your main point several times in different words. We know of several experienced executives who claim that people in their organizations need to hear a point four or five times before they start to believe and accept it. An old rule for effective speaking is "Tell 'em what you're gonna say, say it, and tell 'em what you said"—in other words, focus on your central point and use repetition to drive it home.

- *Use coaching to improve.* You can greatly improve speaking abilities through practice and coaching, and this need not be an elaborate process. Find people whose speaking skills you admire, note what makes them so effective, emulate them, and ask them to give you feedback on your own speaking. In fact, there is much to be said for "self-coaching." Have your presentation videotaped, and study it to find ways to improve. Repeat the process to continually refine your speaking abilities. Even experienced speakers find it educational to see themselves on tape.

THE LEADER AS ROLE MODEL

We want to end our text by reinforcing something that we first said in Chapter 1 and that we have tried to reinforce throughout our chapters: Strategic management is a set of skills available to any individual at any level throughout an organization who wishes to take a lead in shaping the destiny of the firm. Engaging in the strategic management process requires individual actions, the subject of this entire chapter, and the most important of those demonstrate and reinforce the type of behavior the firm is trying to develop organizationwide. In other words, your actions as a leader should make you a role model that others can follow. This type of role-model behavior is commonly referred to as "walking the talk"—not just giving lip service to the firm's goals and strategies but living an organizational life every day that demonstrates commitment to the strategy through personal actions.

As Robert Haas, the CEO of Levi Strauss & Company whom we have quoted several times, put it, "There is a gap between what the organization says it wants and what it feels like to work there. Those gaps between what you say and what you do erode trust in the enterprise and in the leadership, and they inhibit action. The more you can narrow that gap, the more people's energies can be released toward company purposes."[39] Closing the gap of mistrust that Haas identifies requires more than speeches or published mission statements or poster campaigns. Nothing will establish trust in a leader's personal commitment to an organization like observing that his or her actions continually depict and reinforce the ideals the organization has set forth. Words are important, as we have already discussed, but there is much truth in the axioms "Actions speak louder than words" and "Seeing is believing." Or, as Max De-Pree, CEO of Herman Miller, was fond of saying of leadership, "It's not what you preach but how you behave."

This may appear so obvious to you that it need not be said, let alone stressed. Unfortunately, strong evidence suggests that we cannot stress it enough. Too many leaders still "talk a good game," but fail to personally deliver actions that support their words. As James O'Toole, management professor and leadership expert, puts it, "Ninety-five percent of American managers today say the right thing. Five percent actually do it."[40] There is research to support O'Toole's opinion. A study by Booz Allen & Hamilton, an international management consulting firm, surveyed the management teams at twenty-seven *Fortune* 500 manufacturing and service firms, with the following results:[41]

■ Even though most of the managers reported that their firms' future was more dependent on technological advances that would enhance customer satisfaction than on cost control, most of the CEOs still acted as if cost control was their top priority. For example, although 85 percent of the accounting departments reported directly to the CEO, only 30 percent of the R&D groups did.

■ Despite the nearly universal talk about empowerment, many organizations still fail to practice it. The research showed that a fourth of the time, even managers as high as the corporation's CEO got personally involved in tactical decisions at the individual business-unit level, such as product pricing and changes in packaging. We once spent a morning with a COO of a 20,000-member organization with revenues of $2 billion. This organization was attempting to lower its costs by streamlining its operations, but the COO complained bitterly that his people just refused to show any personal initiative, saying, "They know what needs to be done; now why don't they just do it?" As we left his office, he turned to a large stack of forms that required his approval, including one that already had six approval signatures. This particular approval was for reimbursing $2.00 worth of gasoline that an employee had put into a company car when it had run out of fuel on the road. Who was in a better position to do something about this organization's requiring such approvals by the second-highest executive in the organization, the COO or the employee who bought the gas?

■ Although virtually all the companies surveyed paid lip service to quality, customer satisfaction, and maintaining superior service levels, virtually none of the top executives actually tracked these on a regular basis. Yet every top executive regularly tracked cost, profits, and stock performance.

These are just a few of many common inconsistencies between words and actions, and rectifying such inconsistencies may be the single most important thing an individual leader can do to influence the rest of the organization. If a leader's actions are to consistently match his or her words, it is important that they be based on personal convictions rather than a prescribed script. Playacting is not sustainable; eventually a leader will drop the façade, personality will show through, and employees will be more confused or disillusioned than ever. Only leadership actions that stem from deeply held personal convictions can consistently shape an organization's behavior. As

Tsun-yan Hsieh, a leadership expert at McKinsey & Company, explains, "Successful leaders . . . are not deliberately 'acting' as much as they are doing what they believe in—living it, personifying it."[42]

Two leaders famous for such no-pretense actions were Ray Kroc, the founder of McDonald's, and Sam Walton, the founder of Wal-Mart. The many restaurant managers who got a visit from Ray Kroc knew he was committed to cleanliness when he scoured their parking lots, picking up trash, before coming inside to talk to the manager. Kroc was also well known for spending many of his Saturdays "scrubbing." This entailed his doing everything from scraping gum off the pavement to cleaning out mop buckets and grease traps. Sam Walton made a similarly strong impression on his employees. It was one thing to say that he wanted everyone in the Wal-Mart operation to be cost conscious; it was another thing altogether for him to hold board of directors meetings in a company warehouse and specify that corporate headquarters should have the same decor as the company's regional truck depots did.

As these examples illustrate, there is no limit to the actions leaders can take to demonstrate their personal belief in and commitment to an organization's strategy. However, five categories of action appear especially important to us: emphasis on different roles, time allocation, acts of symbolism, displaying vulnerability, and encouraging leadership in others.

Emphasizing Different Roles

In his book *Getting Things Done When You Are Not in Charge*, Geoffrey Bellman identifies several roles that individuals who are not in positions of formal authority can play in influencing their organizations. These include the roles of administrator, problem solver, planner, strategist, and transformer, among others.[43] Bellman argues that too many people who lack formal authority believe that the roles of planner, strategist, and transformer are beyond their reach, and they therefore settle for the less influential roles of administrators and problem solvers. However, as Bellman explains, with forethought and effort, the roles of planner, strategist, and even transformer are open to virtually anyone in an organization. Given the emphasis we have placed throughout our chapters on the need for strategic management skill to be developed and used throughout organizations, Bellman's position is one we heartily endorse.

The key to ensuring that you play the right roles depends heavily on the personal agenda you set and follow. Does your personal agenda reflect an emphasis on reactively responding to problems, or does it place stress on actively getting out ahead of events and trying to shape the future? Although those higher in the organization may dictate what general issues you are to focus on, within such assignments virtually every individual has considerable latitude on the relative emphasis he or she places on being reactive or active. Perhaps the best way to see this is to study the implementation issues life cycle depicted in Exhibit 12.8, a complicated exhibit that makes several important points.

First, note that the model in the exhibit identifies various stages implementation efforts commonly progress through in a pattern that constitutes a life cycle model. There is a period of gestation before an implementation issue emerges during which the forces that will give rise to it are already at work. After the implementation issue

EXHIBIT 12.8
Different Roles Involved in Stages of the Implementation Issues Life Cycle

Stage of Implementation Issues Life Cycle

| Gestating | Emerging | Forming | Solidifying | Permeating |

Typical
Emphasis of
Effort

Ability to Affect
Organizational
Outcomes

| Transformer | Strategist | Planner | Problem Solver | Administrator |

Roles Played in Each Stage

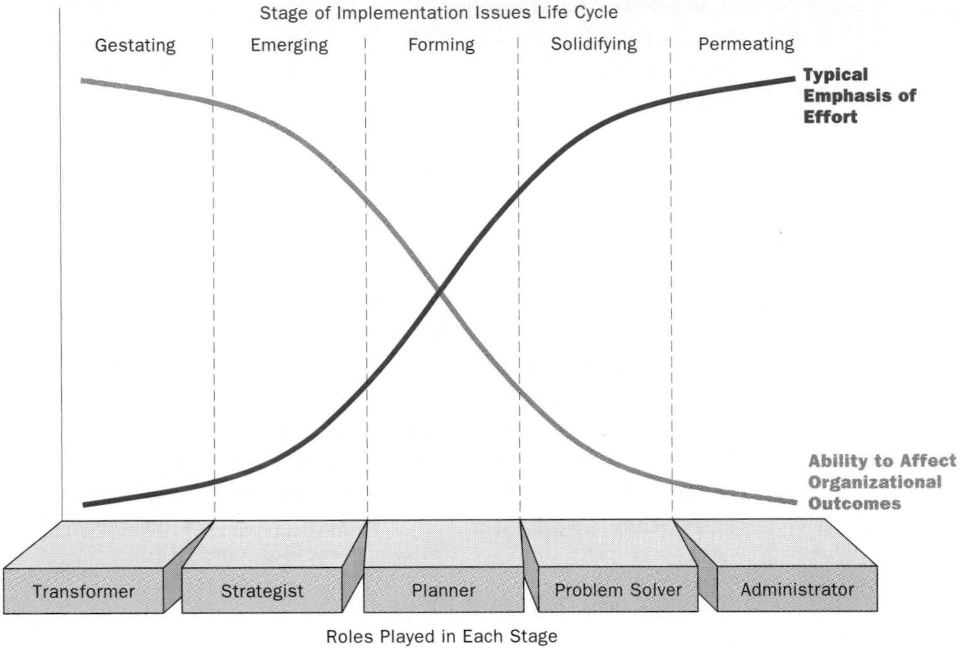

emerges, its various dimensions begin to take shape, and then to become established, in the forming and solidifying stages. In the final stage of the life cycle, permeating, the implementation issue becomes an established part of everyday organizational life. An example will help clarify these different stages.

An international manufacturer of industrial fasteners watched its operating margins shrink to unacceptable levels because of a combination of consolidation in its domestic markets and heightened levels of competition in its foreign markets. Cost control had always been important to the firm, but it became especially critical during a time of low earnings that served as the gestating period (stage 1) for a number of changes that helped the firm implement better cost controls. For example, travel expenses emerged (stage 2) as one of the costs that had been growing the most rapidly. Although increased foreign competition had necessitated more international travel, travel arrangements continued to be left up to each individual to handle as preferred. To address travel costs, a task force was created (stage 3) to form the plans, policies, and recommended practices required to lower travel expenses. These changes were not put into place instantly but solidified (stage 4) over the course of a year, as problems inherent in a more centralized approach to travel arrangements were encountered and then resolved. Eventually, these changes permeated the organization (stage 5) and became the accepted way of controlling travel expenses. In most organizations, implementing a strategy entails countless efforts such as this that collectively shape the way things get done in the organization and help determine how strategies will be implemented.

The second important point to note from this exhibit is the differences in the roles entailed in addressing implementation issues at various stages of the life cycle. These correspond to the roles identified earlier from Bellman's work. Once a new set of policies or practices has developed and permeated the organization, administrators deal with it on a day-to-day basis. In our example, the centralized travel office books flights, collects frequent flyer bonuses, and reimburses travel expenses as it administers the smoothly running program. But before the program could run smoothly, several problems involving various departments' policies and practices had to be resolved, requiring members of the travel policy committee to act as problem solvers. Occasionally, problems still pop up that require someone to play this role, but much less frequently now. It is fair to say that most of the labor-hours this organization devoted to this issue have involved problem solving in the solidifying stage and ongoing administration of the programs in the permeating stage.

Yet some of the most influential decisions were made much earlier. For instance, when the whole matter was still gestating, someone decided that a useful focus would be how much it cost to travel on a per trip basis, as opposed to redefining the issue by focusing on reducing the need to make trips in the first place. For example, someone could have played the transformer role by developing changes that required less travel in the first place, maybe by opening up regional sales offices in more parts of the world and thus limiting the need for flights to and from the company's headquarters city. Once the focus became lowering costs per trip, the task force made a few critical decisions that resulted in a move toward a centralized approach to travel arrangements. Bellman calls those involved in shaping these sorts of decisions strategists (although this is obviously a narrower interpretation of the word than we have been using throughout this text). Once the decision was made to move toward centralized travel arrangements, there were several weeks during which ideas were developed regarding how the centralized office would operate, a form of work that emphasized the planning role.

The final point to note from Exhibit 12.8 is that while more hours are typically devoted to the later stages of the life cycle, the best place to impact the overall process is in its early stages. Once an issue evolves to the point that policies and plans are solidified, all one can do is to react to problems as they occur, and once the smoothly operating procedures are in place, all that is left to do is administer the process, which entails a lot of effort but produces little significant change. On the other hand, when the implementation issues are still gestating and emerging, one or two key decisions can greatly affect the type of problems that will be addressed and thereby have a great impact on everything that follows. Between these two extremes, there is a middle ground in which planners have a moderate degree of flexibility to affect future directions through shaping and framing how an organization will go about addressing the issue. Most people (managers included) spend their lives playing right-hand roles in the reactive mode of responding to issues that have been shaped by others. But the most influential roles, the leadership roles, are on the left-hand side of this exhibit. These are the individuals who actively shape issues in their earliest stages of development.

To be a more effective leader, you should constantly ask yourself what role you play in helping the organization implement its changes. For most people, it is easy to slip into the right-hand roles, but keeping focused on the left-hand roles takes a conscious effort. Administering programs and solving problems are roles that offer a lot of positive reinforcement; it's easy to look back over a day spent on these activities and feel the sense of accomplishment that comes from checking lots of things off a "to do" list. The left-hand roles require "messy" work where objectives are ambiguous, progress is difficult to measure, and solutions are in the distant future. And yet it is here that the greatest ability to shape the future exists; this is the work of leadership. One of the best ways of tracking what roles you play in implementing strategies and strategic changes is to consider how you allocate your time, our next subject.

Allocation of Time

William O'Brien, the CEO of Hanover Insurance, a firm widely recognized as one of the most effective at organizational learning, was interviewed by Peter Senge, who asked what concrete steps a top manager could take to begin moving toward a learning organization. O'Brien's reply: "Look at the signals you send through the organization. . . . One critical signal is how you spend your time."[44] We wholeheartedly agree. Time is one of a leader's most precious resources, and how it's spent is one of the clearest signals of a leader's priorities.

Few outsiders realize just how busy the life of a senior manager is. It is not unusual for senior managers of large corporations to work six 12-to-14 hour days a week before taking a "day off" and working only 4 to 6 hours.[45] The work pace is usually frantic. Research shows that in the typical 12-hour workday, less than 20 percent of the time goes unscheduled, and half of this 20 percent is usually spent in unscheduled meetings. This means that only about 10 percent is available for the manager to be alone, and half of this time will be interrupted after less than 10 minutes. To help keep this amount of work organized, the typical senior manager depends on numerous staff members. For example, the head of one $6 billion conglomerate in the United States employs three executive assistants and four secretaries. Even with such help, the administrative loads can be burdensome. The head of one pharmaceutical firm found he received more than 300 pages of material a day, excluding the numerous magazines, journals, and newspapers he read. Given the overwhelming nature of their jobs, it is not surprising that most senior managers are not able to manage their time in the way they feel it would be most useful, as described in Exhibit 12.9.

As this exhibit shows, the typical senior manager believes he or she should be spending more time on strategy development and organizational leadership but instead feels forced to spend more time on monitoring performance and external stakeholders. Categories such as these are very broad, and, while they are useful for understanding the nature of senior managers' work, they are not specific enough to show the impact of managerial focus on strategy implementation. However, other research shows a clear link between the allocation of managers' time and the strategic direction of their organizations.[46] Our personal experience suggests that one of the best ways of gaining insight into future organizational directions is identifying the specific issues to which the firm's senior leaders allocate their time. Others recognize this connection as well, and, therefore, observing how leaders spend their time is a common means of discerning organizational priorities and shaping individual actions. In fact, aspiring young managers are frequently advised to watch how senior managers allocate time and let their own calendars mirror these priorities. In such cases, what a

EXHIBIT 12.9
Top Executives Often Don't Spend Their Time as They Feel Would Be Most Desirable

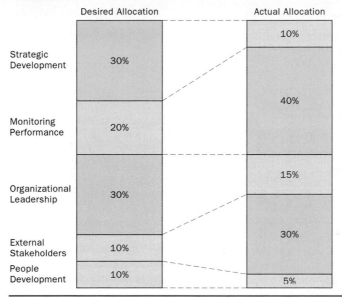

Source: Robert J. McLean et al., "Leveraging CEO Time," *McKinsey Quarterly* (Fall 1991), 106–115. Used with permission.

leader puts on his or her calendar becomes one of the many symbols that others look to in shaping their own behavior.

Acts of Symbolism

When we were discussing organizational culture in Chapter 10, we explained that part of the way in which an organization's culture is established and understood is through the use of symbols and symbolic acts. Among the most important of these symbolic acts are those performed by leaders. This statement applies to leaders in positions of authority, but it also applies to leaders whose influence is based on referent power. By definition, individuals with referent power are considered role models by others, and their actions can become symbols even if they were not originally intended to be symbolic acts. Consequently, acts of individuals throughout an organization's hierarchy can become influential, culture-shaping symbols, and it is important that you carefully consider the potential symbolic implications of your actions, regardless of your position in the managerial hierarchy. We saw this earlier, in the application on Wal-Mart managers, and Application 12.4 gives another example of how the actions of individuals throughout an organization can take on symbolic importance.

Having said that the acts of individuals throughout an organization can become important symbols, we must admit that the acts of senior leaders, especially the CEO and members of top management, are especially powerful sources of symbolism. The most successful executives are aware of this and use this fact to their advantage in im-

---

Application 12.4

Xerox: Individual Acts Become Culture-Shaping Symbols

The development of the 914 copier launched Xerox Corporation and marked the beginning of a decade of record-breaking growth in the 1960s that the firm now calls the "atomic decade." The 914 copier moved Xerox to the billion-dollar sales level (and undreamed-of profits) faster than any company in history. *Fortune* ranked the 914 the most successful product ever marketed in the United States. In the 1980s, Apple Computer, Compaq Computer, and Reebok received much acclaim for reaching the billion-dollar mark still faster, but Xerox set its record at a time when the dollar was worth three times as much. Just 2 years after the 914 was introduced, Xerox made the *Fortune* 500 list, and, just 8 years after that, Xerox was ranked the 60th largest firm in the United States.

Meeting the demands of such rapid growth depended on a workforce that was totally committed to the firm and what it was trying to do. For example, the massive, basic R&D effort required to initially develop the 914 had left the company so poor it could not afford to rent a building with round-the-clock heating. Yet in order to refine the machine to make the promised spring shipping date, engineers had to work 24 hours a day. Consequently, engineers at Xerox's Rochester, New York, plant spent much of the winter of 1959–1960 working without heat. Because the machines themselves gave off some heat, the engineers, bundled in hunting jackets and insulated boots, huddled under blankets draped over their equipment to trap what warmth they could. As a group, they worked 24 hours a day, 7 days a week, under these conditions to get the new product out on time.

This kind of determination did not stop once the machine was developed. As customers discovered the convenience of photocopying, demand quickly grew and far exceeded even the wildest dreams. To meet this demand required still further acts of heroism. In one such instance, low supplies of a part made by a vendor in Chattanooga threatened to shut down production in Rochester. The director of manufacturing and a purchasing agent made an emergency trip to acquire the needed components, but their plane was diverted to Washington, D.C., because of a snowstorm in Tennessee. The railroad from D.C. to Chattanooga would not accept their airline tickets as credit, so the pair tracked down a local Xerox employee to borrow money for tickets. When they finally reached Chattanooga, they had to drive the taxi from the station because the local drivers were unaccustomed to driving on ice. Once they got the parts, they split up and took alternate routes back to Rochester, in hopes of improving the chances of one person's getting through. In the end, the unshaven pair traveled 72 hours nonstop, living on peanut butter sandwiches and sleeping in their seats—but the production line never stopped.

Acts of personal commitment such as these became important symbols in establishing a "can-do" culture that was critical to Xerox's early success, and they live on today as part of the folklore that still shapes Xerox's future—more than 3 decades after they first took place. It is significant that these were not the actions of just the CEO or the company's founder. While those individuals did play a tremendously influential role in shaping Xerox through their personal actions, they were clearly not alone. Individuals *throughout* the organization can display leadership and exert influence through their own personal actions, which can later take on symbolic importance.

---

plementing their strategies. For example, in describing the critical role Motorola's CEO Bob Galvin played in instilling that organization's famous commitment to quality, here's how the firm's director of training portrayed one of Galvin's symbolic acts:

> Since Bob Galvin believed quality training was useless unless top managers gave quality even more attention than they gave quarterly results, he dramatized the point at the operations review meetings. He insisted that quality reports come first, not last, on the agenda, and then he left before the financial results were discussed.[47]

It is possible for a wide range of different types of leadership actions to take on symbolic importance: traveling economy class, working weekends, eating in the company cafeteria, moving your office out into the open, getting rid of management's reserved parking spots, and so on. However, when it comes to building a learning organization, one particular category of actions provides especially important symbols. We are speaking of acts that display the leader's vulnerability.

Displays of Vulnerability

Throughout our treatment of strategy implementation, we have explained that, although most organizations use some blend of both, organizational learning is becoming more important than strategic programming as the overall approach to implementing strategies. We also stressed in Chapter 9 that if organizational learning is to spread throughout an organization, managers and employees must feel that the rest of the organization will be tolerant of the mistakes that are inherent in experimentation. To demonstrate such tolerance, leaders need to accept their own vulnerability and openly admit that they, too, are capable of making mistakes.

Unfortunately, admitting such vulnerability is very difficult for most leaders. A big part of the problem lies in the fact that organizations have traditionally depended so heavily on strategic programming to get things done, and strategic programming encourages leaders to act as if they are invulnerable and mistakeproof. Remember that strategic programming depends on being able to foretell the future with enough certainty so that plans can be formulated and then implemented with little or no alteration. This alone would tend to make leaders assume a posture of invulnerability, but when this is coupled with the command-and-control approach to leadership that is often an inherent part of strategic programming, the pressure on leaders to be infallible is immense. To encourage organizational learning, leaders must overcome the pressures they feel to appear invulnerable. If a leader cannot admit to making mistakes, why would others feel safe in doing so? As one author has put it, "Unless leaders willingly model vulnerability for their people, they cannot create a culture where vulnerability is acceptable."[48]

In his extensive studies of how individuals and organizations learn, Chris Argyris has reached a similar conclusion about the importance of leaders' admitting that they are capable of mistakes and that this vulnerability is not only inevitable, but also entirely acceptable. In fact, given that mistakes are increasingly impossible to avoid in today's ever more complex and unstable business environment, the futility of trying to avoid and/or hide mistakes can actually be more damaging to a leader's credibility than simply admitting vulnerability in the first place. Argyris describes a CEO who made this discovery the hard way:

> Finally, the CEO discovered that many of the tacit evaluations and attributions he had listed turned out to be wrong. Since he had never expressed these assumptions, he had never found out just how wrong they were. What's more, he learned that much of what he thought he was hiding came through to his subordinates anyway—but with the added message that the boss was covering up.[49]

Such covering up is in sharp contrast to the behavior regularly displayed by leaders in the organizations that are most successful in instilling learning. For example, at Chaparral Steel, a minimill that has long stressed organizational learning as the key to its sustained competitiveness, leaders almost appear to boast of past mistakes they have made.[50] Of course, what they are actually proud of is not their mistakes but the learning that resulted from making and correcting them. Leaders' admitting vulnerability to mistakes blurs the distinctions between them and those they lead, and it is important for encouraging others to take on leadership roles themselves.

Encouraging Leadership in Others

We end our last chapter by reemphasizing the message you heard in the opening of our first chapter: Strategic management is not a function limited to one part or level of an organization; it is a set of skills that can and should be used throughout. This being the case, one of the most important acts of leadership is encouraging others to take the initiative of thinking for themselves and acting accordingly. The potential benefits of such "self-leadership" include increased employee commitment, as well as innovation stemming from heightened motivation and unleashed employee capabilities.[51] Given such returns, some leaders are motivated to encourage self-leadership in others based on a "boundless optimism about the potential of ordinary people to accomplish extraordinary things." For example, as CEO of Herman Miller, Max DePree explained why he was convinced that his employees were capable of leading themselves: "Take a thirty-three-year-old man who assembles chairs. He's been doing it several years. He has a wife and two children. He knows what to do when the children have earaches and how to get them through school. He probably serves on a volunteer board, and when he comes to work, we give him a supervisor. . . . He doesn't need one."

This is very different from the attitude seen in many organizations. Henry Ford once complained that his workers tried to think for themselves far too much, saying, "Why can't I just hire their hands and leave their heads out of the picture?" The value to be placed on employees who can think for themselves is a reflection of an organization's general approach to strategy implementation. When firms take a strategic programming approach, it is easy to see employees as cogs in a great machine, sticking to a predetermined plan and routine, relentless and unthinking. More managers than we like to admit have this view of employees and empathize with Ford's desire to use the hands without the head.

Yet, an overwhelming set of forces is driving more and more managers away from such a mind-set and toward one that seeks to fully utilize the capabilities of every member of their organizations. These managers realize that they alone are simply not capable of dealing with the complexities their firms face, and they are looking for help wherever they can find it in the organization. Such optimism about the capabilities of individuals throughout the organization goes hand in hand with the concept of the learning organization. No matter where they are in the organizational hierarchy, individuals are encouraged to seek out the discoveries that will lead to more effective actions. By encouraging such self-leadership, organizations can begin to tap the skills and capabilities of the entire workforce rather than just those of the managerial elite.

Approaching leadership as the task of freeing individuals to direct themselves turns many of our strongest notions of leadership on end. The definition of leadership changes to become one of leading others to lead themselves. The measure of a leader's strength becomes the ability to maximize the contributions of others through recognition of their abilities to guide their own destiny, rather than the leader's ability to bend the will of others to fit his or her own. This may appear to fly in the face of the rest of this chapter. After all, we began this chapter by talking about the importance of a leader's power and influence in determining the actions of others, and now we are ending it with talk of the importance of freeing people to direct their own activities.

The key to resolving this seeming contradiction lies in understanding the unifying power of good strategic management. The goal of self-leadership is not to turn people loose to wander in all directions but to free them to push the organization in an agreed-upon direction. The freedom granted allows them to engage in the strategic management process as full-fledged *participants*, rather than being relegated to receiving output from the process in the form of directions from superiors. Of course, for them to be effective in participating as self-directed organizational members in the firm's strategic management process, there must be an effective strategic management process in place, and members from throughout the organization must understand how it works and how they can contribute to it. The purpose of this text is to prepare you to make such contributions to the future of the organizations you join.

Summary of Managerial Practices to Adopt from This Chapter

■ Remember that even mundane acts of leadership can exert considerable leverage on the strategy implementation process and organizational change.

■ Recognize that while there is a time and a place for exercising power based on formal authority in explicit ways (i.e., commanding), reliance on this form of power alone is often detrimental to a leader's effectiveness.

■ Some forms of influence are so unobtrusive that they are not recognized as forms of power. These "implicit" forms of power are among the most effective ways for an individual leader to affect organizational outcomes.

■ The most effective leaders employ a "full-portfolio" approach to leadership in which they mix and match different sources of power and influence to suit the situation at hand.

■ While politics are an inevitable part of organizational life, they are inherently neither good nor bad, but what you make them. Resolve to practice principled politics, and, by adhering to a few critical guidelines, you can ensure that you will meet this resolution.

■ As a manager, expect to negotiate every day. Recognize that the most effective negotiations are those that strengthen your relationship with the other party. Practice making the guidelines for principled or relationship-focused negotiation an internalized part of your everyday behavior.

■ Effective leadership depends on effective communication, and effective communication begins with effective listening. To influence others, you should first strive to understand them.

■ Remember that, in communicating, delivery is usually just as important as content in influencing others. Practice improving your delivery by using simple guidelines to make yourself a more effective speaker.

■ To help bring about desired organizational changes, your actions should serve as role models for others. By being an effective leader, you can encourage others to be the same, facilitating organizationwide participation in the strategic management process.

Questions for Discussion and Review

1. Discuss the continuing need for power and influence and the alternative forms they take.

2. Debate both sides of the issue of developing personal expertise in organizational politics.

3. Why is negotiation a valuable managerial skill? What are the most important points to remember about being a successful principled negotiator?

4. Develop a personal list of listening and speaking practices you feel a manager should employ to effectively instigate organizational changes.

5. Describe the various ways leaders serve as role models, providing examples (either real or hypothetical) to illustrate.

Notes

1. Abraham Zaleznik, "The Leadership Gap," *Academy of Management Executive, 4* (1990), 7–22.
2. Stanley M. Herman, *A Force of Ones: Reclaiming Individual Power in a Time of Teams, Work Groups, and Other Crowds*, San Francisco: Jossey-Bass, 1994.
3. Regina Fazio Maruca, "The Right Way to Go Global," *Harvard Business Review* (March–April 1994), 134–145.
4. David A. Nadler and Michael L. Tushman, "Beyond the Charismatic Leader: Leadership and Organizational Change," *California Management Review, 32* (Winter 1990), 77–97.
5. Jeffrey Pfeffer, "Understanding Power in Organizations," *California Management Review, 34* (Winter 1992), 29–50.
6. Warren Bennis and Burt Nanus, *Leaders: The Strategies for Taking Charge*, New York: Harper and Row, 1985, 6.
7. Pfeffer, "Understanding Power," 32.
8. Bennis and Nanus, *Leaders*.
9. Robin Fincham, "Perspectives on Power: Processual, Institutional, and 'Internal' Forms of Organizational Power," *Journal of Management Studies, 29* (November 1992), 741–759.
10. Thomas A. Stewart, "New Ways to Exercise Power," *Fortune* (November 6, 1989), 52.
11. Carl E. Pitts, "For Project Managers: An Inquiry into the Delicate Art and Science of Influencing Others," *Project Management Journal, 21* (March 1990), 21–23, 42.
12. David Krackhardt, "Assessing the Political Landscape: Structure, Cognition, and Power in Organizations," *Administrative Science Quarterly, 35* (June 1990), 342–369.
13. Bernard Keys and Thomas Case, "How to Become an Influential Manager," *Academy of Management Executive, 4* (November 1990), 38–51.
14. Rosabeth Moss Kanter, "The New Managerial Work," *Harvard Business Review* (November–December 1989), 85–92.
15. For evidence of the importance of managerial focus, see Richard A. D'Aveni and Ian C. MacMillan, "Crisis and the Content of Managerial Communications," *Administrative Science Quarterly, 35* (December 1990), 634–657.
16. Gary Yukl and Cecilia M. Falbe, "Importance of Different Power Sources in Downward and Lateral Relations," *Journal of Applied Psychology, 76* (June 1991), 416–423.
17. Pfeffer, "Understanding Power."
18. Henry Mintzberg, "The Effective Organization: Forces and Forms," *Sloan Management Review, 32* (Winter 1991), 54–67.
19. David A. Lax and James K. Sebenius, *The Manager as Negotiator*, New York: The Free Press, 1986.
20. Margaret A. Neale and Max H. Bazerman, "Negotiating Rationally: The Power and Impact of the Negotiator's Frame," *Academy of Management Executive, 6* (1992), 42.
21. Len Leritz, *No-Fault Negotiating*, New York: Time Warner, 1987.

22. Leonard Greenhalgh, "Relationships in Negotiations," *Negotiations Journal* (July 1987), 235–243.

23. Leonard Greenhalgh, "The Case Against Winning in Negotiations," *Negotiations Journal* (April 1987), 167–173.

24. Roger Fisher and William Ury, *Getting to Yes: Negotiating Agreement Without Giving In*, New York: Penguin Books, 1981.

25. Margaret A. Neale and Max H. Bazerman, *Cognition and Rationality in Negotiation*, New York: The Free Press, 1991.

26. This concept is also known as BATNA, for "Best Alternative to a Negotiated Agreement," but we find that NAA (as in "*Naa, I don't think so*") is more memorable. See Fisher and Ury, *Getting to Yes*, for a discussion of BATNA.

27. While cultural differences require that prescriptive advice for negotiations must be culture-specific, focusing on the problem rather than the person appears to be effective in a number of cultural settings; see Nancy J. Adler et al., "Strategy Implementation: A Comparison of Face-to-Face Negotiations in the People's Republic of China and the United States," *Strategic Management Journal, 13* (1992), 449–466.

28. Ray Strata, "Organizational Learning in Practice," *McKinsey Quarterly* (Winter 1992), 79–82.

29. For a discussion of the importance of conversation to leadership in building the learning organization, see William N. Isaacs, "Taking Flight: Dialogue, Collective Thinking, and Organizational Learning," *Organizational Dynamics, 22* (Autumn 1993), 24–39.

30. Robert G. Eccles and Nitin Nohria, *Beyond the Hype*, Boston: Harvard Business School Press, 1992.

31. T. Ballard Morton, "Leadership," *Business Horizons, 33* (November–December 1990), 3–7.

32. Carl R. Rogers and F. J. Roethlisberger, "Barriers and Gateways to Communication," *Harvard Business Review, 69* (November–December 1991), 105–111.

33. See John Gabarro, "Retrospective Commentary," *Harvard Business Review, 69* (November–December 1991), 108–109.

34. See a discussion of Filson's work in "If You Want to Lead, First Learn to Speak," *Success, 39* (April 1992), 42–43.

35. The following points were gleaned from a variety of sources, including Floyd Wickman, "Getting Them to 'Buy In' to Your Message," *Supervisory Management, 37* (June 1992), 8; Matt Hughes, "Tricks of the Speechwriter's Trade," *Management Review, 79* (November 1990), 56–58; and Arnold Zenker, "Ten Sure Ways to Score with an Audience," *Training and Development, 46* (April 1992), 19–21.

36. Anne G. Perkins, "Communication: The Perils of Poor Delivery," *Harvard Business Review, 72* (January–Febuary 1994), 9.

37. Gary W. Hankins, "It's Not Only What You Say," *Industry Week, 240* (January 7, 1991), 42.

38. Kerry Rottenberger-Murtha, "Passing On the Motivation," *Sales and Marketing Management, 145* (October 1993), 147–148.

39. Tomas L. Brown, "Walking the Talk," *Industry Week, 241* (January 20, 1992), 33.

40. John Huey, "The New Post-Heroic Leadership," *Fortune* (February 21, 1994), 42–56.

41. Ronald Henkoff, "CEOs Still Don't Walk the Talk," *Fortune* (April 18, 1994), 14–15.

42. Tsun-yan Hsieh, "Leadership Actions," *McKinsey Quarterly* (Fall 1990), 42–58.

43. For the complete list, see chap. 21 of Geoffrey M. Bellman, *Getting Things Done When You Are Not in Charge*, San Francisco: Berrett-Koehler, 1992.

44. Peter M. Senge, "The Leader's New Work: Building Learning Organizations," *Sloan Management Review, 32* (Fall 1990), 7–23.

45. Data reported in this section are based on diary studies reported in Robert J. McLean et al., "Leveraging CEO Time," *McKinsey Quarterly* (Fall 1991), 106–115.

46. Anne M. McCarthy et al., "Changes in the Time Allocation Patterns of Entrepreneurs," *Entrepreneurship: Theory and Practice, 15* (Winter 1990), 7–18.

47. William Wiggenhorn, "Motorola U: When Training Becomes an Education," *Harvard Business Review* (July–August 1990), 233.

48. Emil Bohn and Bill Adams, "I'd Rather Be Dead than Empowered," *Executive Excellence, 10* (March 1993), 16–17.

49. Chris Argyris, "Teaching Smart People How to Learn," *Harvard Business Review* (May–June 1991), 191.

50. Dorothy Leonard-Barton, "The Factory as a Learning Laboratory," *Sloan Management Review, 34* (Fall 1992), 23–38; G. Forward, interviewed by A. M. Kantrox, "Wide-Open Management at Chaparral Steel," *Harvard Business Review* (May–June 1986), 96–102.

51. Much of the material in this section is drawn from Charles C. Manz and Henry P. Sims, Jr., "Superleadership: Beyond the Myth of Heroic Leadership," *Organizational Dynamics, 19* (Spring 1991), 18–35. See also Manz and Sims, "Leading Workers to Lead Themselves: The External Leadership of Self-Managing Work Teams," *Administrative Science Quarterly, 32* (1987), 106–129.

Part Five

CASES IN STRATEGIC MANAGEMENT

The twelve chapters presented in the first four parts of this text present the concepts, tools, perspectives, frameworks, and models essential to understanding strategic management. Part Five offers you the opportunity to apply what you have learned from the chapters in real-world settings documented as case histories. With this emphasis on application, the purpose of these cases is not so much to teach you strategic management as it is to make you a better strategic manager.

We organized these cases in groups focused on specific industries or on specific concepts. Your instructor may assign a selection of cases from a variety of these groups to provide you with a well-rounded development opportunity. Regardless of the categories of cases assigned, you will discover that what you get out of case analysis and discussion is directly proportional to what you put into it. To assist you in being as productive as possible in your preparation of cases, we offer the following guidelines (you'll find these discussed in more detail in the students' preface to this text).

1. Read quickly and highlight selectively.
2. Study case tables and figures.
3. Determine type of issues raised and recommendations required.
4. Identify the most useful analytical and decision-making tools.
5. Reread, analyze using tools, and prepare recommendations.
6. Prepare rough notes capturing key points.
7. Organize your overall set of results.
8. Present your results in a concise, hard-hitting style (written or oral).
9. Actively look for new insights from others' comments.
10. Consider how to apply what you have learned in subsequent analysis.

CASE 1

Jim Thompson Thai Silk Company*

As he looked back on his 20 years as Managing Director of Jim Thompson Thai Silk Company (JT), Bill Booth felt considerable pride. The company had grown to become, by 1994, Thailand's leading retailer of native silk, commanding an enviable two-thirds share of the premium tourist market. It had also expanded far beyond its original base of merely retailing products produced by others, to become the country's only fully integrated producer of native silks.

Recent developments were threatening to undermine this hard-earned success, however. Bangkok's increasing auto congestion, escalating air pollution, and soaring AIDS infection rate were causing foreign tourists—JT's primary customers—to avoid the city as a travel destination. Since JT's shops were all located in Bangkok, its revenue and profitability were falling. Eager to find a way to reverse this decline, Booth had established strategic planning as a major priority for the coming year.

EARLY HISTORY

JT was founded in 1951 by James Thompson, an American who arrived in Thailand at the end of the Second World War as a member of the U.S. Office of Strategic Services, predecessor to the Central Intelligence Agency. A member of a prominent Delaware family and a graduate of Princeton University, Mr. Thompson determined to make a career in Thailand following cessation of hostilities. Becoming interested in the commercial potential of native silk, he opened a shop in Bangkok to retail fabric produced by local weavers. The store's reputation for superb quality and innovative design made it particularly popular among tourists and foreigners stationed in Bangkok—two groups able to afford its prices, which were well above those of most local competitors.

With expansion of tourism and the U.S. troop buildup in Southeast Asia in connection with the Vietnam War, JT grew rapidly. Then, a strange event occurred. During a 1967 Easter holiday in a Malaysian jungle resort, Mr. Thompson mysteriously

*Prepared by Robert A. Pitts, Gettysburg College. This case won the 1995 Curtis E. Tate Outstanding Case Research Award for its selection as the best case presented at the 1994 National Case Research Association Annual Meeting. The author thanks company management for their helpful cooperation in developing this material.

disappeared and, despite a lengthy search lasting many months,[1] was never seen again. JT's Board appointed as acting Managing Director an American who had been Assistant Manager under Mr. Thompson. When this individual died seven years later, Bill Booth was appointed Managing Director.

Booth had arrived in Southeast Asia in the early 1960s as a member of the U.S. military in Vietnam. Struck by the beauty and vitality of nearby Thailand, he settled there at the completion of his military assignment. Booth devoted his early months in the country to intensive study of the Thai language, and eventually became very fluent. Following an unsuccessful attempt to enter the local silk business on his own, he joined JT in 1964. Subsequently, Booth held a variety of positions before being appointed Managing Director in 1974.

EXPANSION

Under Booth's direction, JT expanded into each successive stage of the silk production process. The first step in this process began in 1974, when it established a sewing venture in partnership with a prominent Thai businesswoman. Four years later it acquired a printing plant in partnership with a West German textile printer. In 1979, it entered the weaving business, choosing to establish this activity on a wholly-owned basis rather than through joint venture, and to locate it not in Bangkok, where its sewing and printing plants were situated, but in northeastern Thailand, where many of its contract weavers resided. Finally, in 1988 it entered into sericulture (the breeding of silkworms for production of raw silk fiber) and spinning (twisting together of fibers to produce yarn), establishing these operations on a wholly-owned basis and locating them near its weaving mill in northeastern Thailand. (See Exhibit 1 for map of Thailand; Exhibit 2 for basic facts about the country.)

The company's expansion into production had been motivated in part by a desire to improve product uniformity. Booth noted, for example, that this objective had influenced JT's entry into weaving.

> During the early years, we left weaving entirely in the hands of contract weavers. This arrangement worked fine so long as final sales went primarily to tourists buying through our retail outlet. It became a stumbling block to expansion of our home furnishing business, however. Owners of hotels, office buildings, apartments, and condominia from time to time need to replace wall covering and upholstery fabric, and when they do, they need replacement material that precisely matches the color of original fabric. Our contract weavers were unable to meet this requirement, so we entered weaving ourselves. We can now replicate orders much more precisely.

Another objective motivating the company's move into weaving had been a desire to improve delivery capability. Booth provided the following details.

---

[1]For an excellent account of this search, see William Warren, *Jim Thompson: The Legendary American of Thailand*, Jim Thompson Thai Silk Company, 1993.

EXHIBIT 1
Jim Thompson Thai Silk Company Map of Thailand

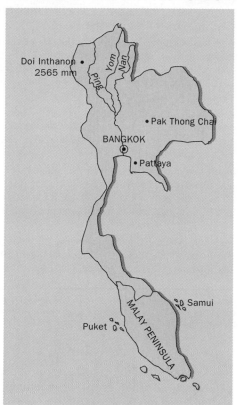

Contract weavers are sometimes unreliable about meeting delivery schedules. This posed little difficulty as long as our business was primarily retail, since our well-stocked store always contained plenty of merchandise for tourists to make their selection. It became a problem as we tried to expand our home furnishing business, however. Delay in receipt of wall covering or upholstery material can postpone occupancy of a new building, and late occupancy imposes a serious cost on a building's owner. By bringing weaving under our direct control we have significantly improved our ability to deliver on time.

A third objective motivating JT's expansion into production had been a desire to establish secure sources of supply. During the 1980s, JT experienced increasing difficulty obtaining raw silk in quantities needed to feed its weaving operation. Shortages were caused in part by a decline in the acreage Thai farmers devoted to mulberry cultivation. Total acreage devoted to this end fell from about 60,000 hectares in the mid-1970s to less than 40,000 hectares in the early 1990s. (One hectare = 10,000 square meters, or 2.417 acres.) This decline was caused by migration of villagers from the depressed silk producing regions in the northeast to Bangkok in search of higher paying jobs, and by conversion on the

---

EXHIBIT 2
Jim Thompson Thai Silk Company

Facts About Thailand

Overview: Size: 198,000 square miles (slightly more than twice the size of Wyoming); 1993 population 59 million; 1993 population growth rate 1.4%; ethnic divisions: Thai 75%, Chinese 14%; religions: Buddhism 95%, Muslim 3.8%; literacy rate 93%; capital city: Bangkok (1993 population 5.9 million); 1992 gross domestic product $103 billion; 1992 per capita gross domestic product $1,800; 1992 annual inflation rate in consumer prices 4.5%.

Government: Until 1932 the country was ruled as an absolute monarchy. Since that date it has experienced a series of relatively bloodless military coups and new constitutions. Though officially a constitutional monarchy, it operates in fact as a benign military dictatorship. It is unique among South Asian nations in never having experienced European rule.

Economy: The economy is relatively free of controls on private enterprise that are common in other developing countries. The dominant sector is private, only 10% of manufacturing output being produced by government-owned entities. The Industries Promotion Act of 1962 provides companies operating in designated industries guarantees against nationalization, and exemptions from import duties, export duties, and many taxes.

Currency: The Thai "baht" is freely convertible into foreign exchange. Its value against the dollar has remained very stable over a long period of time. U.S. $1 = 25.28 baht (April 1993), 25.400 baht (1992), 25.517 baht (1991), 25.585 baht (1990), 25.702 baht (1989), 25.294 baht (1988).

Sources: *Encyclopedia of the Third World*, Volume III, Facts On File (New York, 1992); *The Statesman's Year-Book 1994–1995*, St. Martin's Press (New York, 1994); *The World Fact Book 1994–95*, Central Intelligence Agency, Brassey's (Washington, 1994); *The Europa World Yearbook 1994*, Volume III, Europa Publications Limited (Rochester, Kent, England, 1994).

---

part of many remaining farmers to other crops—particularly to cassava, which was increasing in demand in Europe. Since mulberry leaves constitute a silkworm's chief diet, declining mulberry cultivation led to reduction in output of raw Thai silk.

Developments in China, where JT historically obtained a large share of its silk supply, also contributed to the problem. China produced more than half of the world's raw silk output, and supplied almost 90% of world exports. The Chinese government had long encouraged silk production, but in the 1980s began to allow silk producers to cultivate other crops. Thus freed from government constraint, many farmers switched out of mulberry into more lucrative crops such as fruits and vegetables. As silk output fell, prices on the world market climbed, leading remaining producers to skirt official channels and sell their output at elevated prices through Hong Kong's black market.

A fourth factor motivating JT's expansion into production had been a desire to improve technology. The Thai silk industry was dominated by very small producers employing traditional handicraft methods. As a consequence, the technology employed generally was quite rudimentary. Raw silk, for example, was produced mainly by farm women and children in the poor northeast portion of the country, while most weaving was carried out by individuals working in very small family operations. These players lacked resources to underwrite significant improvement in technology. JT had undertaken production in part to bring its substantial resources to bear on this problem.

TECHNOLOGY TRANSFER

Each successive step into silk production had obliged JT to acquire new technology. Generally, needed expertise was not available in Thailand. Consequently, JT had been obliged to seek it abroad. JT had used several approaches over the years to secure foreign technology. One was to form joint ventures with foreign firms. JT had used this method, for example, to secure initial technology for its printing plant. Its joint venture partner in this activity was a small West German textile printer with a reputation for very high quality. This firm had helped select initial equipment for the printing venture, arrange factory layout, and oversee early start-up; and had assigned one of its senior engineers—Mr. Czerny—to assist the venture on a continuing basis. Making visits to Thailand four times each year, Czerny had counseled JT not only on printing matters, but on a host of other textile-related issues as well, in the process becoming an integral member of JT's management team.

A second method JT had used to obtain foreign technology was to send company personnel abroad for technical training. It had used this device, for example, to obtain technology for its sericulture operation. During early development of this operation, JT employees had made extended visits to China to receive training at the Chinese Sericulture Research Institute. Employees hired to operate the company's spinning machines had also traveled to China for technical training.

Yet another device JT had used to obtain technology from abroad was to bring foreign experts to Thailand to train company employees. Experts from China's Sericulture Research Institute, for example, had made numerous trips to Thailand to train JT employees in mulberry cultivation, silkworm rearing, and cocoon production techniques, and several of its technicians were in Thailand as late as 1994 providing such training.

The network of relationships which Booth maintained with knowledgeable foreigners had also helped the company obtain foreign expertise. One key individual in this network was Henry Thompson, nephew of Jim Thompson and heir to his interest in the company. A resident of the U.S. with extensive business experience and a keen interest in JT's welfare, Henry had provided thoughtful counsel on many occasions during the course of the company's development.

PRODUCTION ACTIVITIES

As a result of this expansion, JT by 1994 was no longer simply a retailer of silk fabric made by others, but was involved in each stage of the complex process through which the delicate filament produced by a silkworm is transformed into such products as fabric, blouses, and pillow cases. Key activities JT performed in bringing about this transformation were sericulture, spinning, weaving, printing, and sewing (see Exhibit 3 for summary).

Sericulture

Silk thread is made from a fine, lustrous fiber produced by a silkworm when it forms a cocoon near the end of its life cycle. A silkworm's sole diet is mulberry leaves. Silk

EXHIBIT 3
Jim Thompson Thai Silk Company

Activity	Output	Vertical Production Flow*		
		Supply†	Employees	Location
Sericulture	Cocoons	66%	150††	PTC§
Spinning	Yarn	22%	250	PTC
Weaving	Fabric	100%	1,500	PTC
Printing	Printed fabric	100%	100	Bangkok
Sewing	Accessories	100%	350	Bangkok

*This exhibit describes JT's silk production activities only. The company also produced small quantities of cotton fabric. However, most of the cotton fabric it sold to retail and home furnishing customers was purchased from outside suppliers.
†Percent of JT's requirements supplied internally.
††JT also utilized approximately 1,500 contract farming families in a broad area surrounding its sericulture facility to raise silkworm eggs to the cocoon stage.
§Pak Thong Chai. Sericulture, degumming, and spinning were carried out in upper Pak Thong Chai Province; weaving was performed in the provincial capital and in a nearby village.

production therefore commences with the growing of mulberry trees. JT cultivated mulberry trees on a 900-acre plantation at the upper end of a farming valley in Pak Thong Chai Province, about 150 miles northeast of Bangkok. The 150 workers employed in this operation picked leaves from mulberry trees, conveyed them to a large rearing house, and fed them to silkworms placed there on trays stacked on long racks. Eggs produced by these silkworms were sold to approximately 1,500 contract farming families down from a peak of 48.5 tons the previous year.

Weaving

Yarn produced by its spinning operation and that procured from outside sources was conveyed to JT's weaving mill located in the town of Pak Thong Chai about 15 miles from the company's sericulture operation. This facility was the largest hand-weaving operation in the country. Yarn entering the mill was first dyed to give it a particular color, then woven into fabric on one of the 537 hand looms installed in the facility. In addition to this mill, JT also operated a satellite weaving mill, containing 277 hand looms, in a nearby village. Looms at both locations had been designed and built by company technicians. Most of the company's 1,500 weavers were women. Because hand weaving was a slow, tedious process, a weaver typically added during an eight-hour shift only two or three meters to the length of the fabric being produced on her loom. Fabric width was generally about one meter.

JT also operated several power looms at its Pak Thong Chai facility, mainly to weave cotton fabric. Total output from these machines amounted to just 38,000 meters of fabric in 1993, compared to 593,000 meters of fabric produced on the company's hand looms.

Printing

A portion of the fabric produced by JT's weaving mills was shipped to its printing joint venture near Bangkok. The latter was equipped with both tables for hand printing and with state-of-the-art machines for high-speed machine printing. In 1993, this facility processed 355,000 meters of hand printed silk fabric, 191,000 meters of hand printed cotton fabric, and 984,000 meters of machine printed cotton and synthetic fabric. Most of this output went for JT's internal use. JT was negotiating to purchase its joint venture partner's 26% interest in this operation in exchange for JT stock, with the understanding that the joint venture partner would continue to provide technical help following transfer of ownership. The latter showed interest in this arrangement, but was seeking an increase in the fee it received for technical assistance from the current level of 2% of printing revenues to 5%. Anticipating favorable conclusion of this negotiation, JT was planning the orderly transfer of printing equipment to a new printing facility it was building adjacent to the company's weaving mill in Pak Thong Chai. The planned move to this facility would enable the company to avoid problems arising from increasingly stringent water pollution regulation in the Bangkok area.

Sewing

A portion of the fabric leaving its weaving and printing mills went to JT's sewing joint venture in Bangkok. The latter's 350 skilled seamstresses produced more than 500,000 different pieces of merchandise in 1993. High-volume items were neckties, purses, and pillow cases. JT was negotiating to buy out its partner in this venture as well.

OTHER ACTIVITIES

In addition to the production operations noted above, JT supported activities in finance, purchasing, design, and sales (see Exhibit 4 for a more complete list).

Finance

JT's original capital had been supplied by Jim Thompson and two other Americans (49%), and 29 Thai weaving families and silk traders (51%). Very few of the shares issued to the latter had subsequently changed hands except by inheritance. The widow of one of the original American shareholders had recently sold her 25% stake to a large Japanese department store chain for a price reputed to be $25 million. This firm, which operated two stores in Thailand—both located in Bangkok—was now JT's largest shareholder.

JT's growth over the years had been financed largely by retained earnings. As a result, the company had issued very few new shares since its inception, and had resorted to no borrowing on a long-term basis. Despite its recent profit decline and its

---

EXHIBIT 4
Jim Thompson Thai Silk Company Management

Managing Director: W. M. Booth

Deputy Managing Director: Pichet Buranastidporn

Division Managers:
  Production: Surindr Supasavasdebhandu
  Purchasing: Supphong Mangkonkarn
  Design Advisor: Gerald W. Pierce
  Accounting: Mrs. Warunee Tanatammatorn

Department Managers:
  Executive Secretaries: Miss Supaporn Tongperm
                          Miss Nithima Smitharak

  Advisor: Chob Pundee
  Design: Tinnart Nisalak
  Design Liaison: Mrs. Sirilak Sirisant
  Merchandise/Warehouse: Mrs. Panya Yothasiri
  Marketing: Mrs. Veronique De Champvallier
  Retail: Mrs. Jeannie Cho Menge
           Mrs. Lorna M. Jarungklin
           Mrs. Aporn Yordmuang

  Computer Processing: Sakda Siriphongwatana
  Internal Audit: Kosol Jirabunjongkij
  Home Furnishing: Mrs. Chidchanok Supavaradom
  Dispatching: Mrs. Kanchana Pundee
  Personnel: Prachuab Chirakarnphong
             Somchai Apisithwanich

Source: 1993 Annual Report.

continued dividend payout, which had averaged 30% of earnings in recent years, JT was accumulating funds in excess of the amount needed to operate its business. In early 1994, this excess was invested mainly in short-term certificates of deposit (see Exhibit 5 for financial summary).

Purchasing

JT purchased large quantities of silk cocoons from suppliers located in Thailand, and significant amounts of silk fiber and silk yarn from both domestic and foreign sources. It also purchased large quantities of cotton fabric from outside sources. To deal with increasing shortages of domestic raw silk, it had established remote buying stations in various parts of Thailand beginning in the early 1980s. In 1993 these stations purchased a total of 90.5 tons of fresh cocoons, and 134 tons of silk yarn.

Design

Creative design was frequently mentioned by JT managers as one of JT's primary strengths, serving to differentiate it from competitors, and enabling it to command premium prices. In 1994 the design department employed more than 30 individuals devoted to developing new fibers, new color formulations, new weave patterns, new

EXHIBIT 5
Jim Thompson Thai Silk Company: Selected Financial Data
(baht in millions, except as otherwise noted)

	1993	1992	1991	1990	1989	1988	1987	1986	1985	1984
Revenues	$ 847	$ 810	$ 914	$ 991	$931	$774	$667	$481	$382	$354
Expenses										
Cost of sales	$ 428	$ 401	$ 462	$ 514	$488	$400	$377	$268	$213	$219
Selling and admin-										
istrative expenses	160	147	151	156	139	119	88	75	58	51
Interest	2	0	0	0	0	0	0	1	1	1
Income tax	77	78	106	111	106	89	70	48	44	33
Total expenses	$ 667	$ 626	$ 719	$ 782	$734	$608	$535	$392	$316	$304
Net profit	$ 181	$ 184	$ 195	$ 209	$197	$167	$132	$ 90	$ 66	$ 50
Current assets										
Cash and short-term										
investment	$ 288	$ 221	$ 232	$ 158	$ 71	$ 82	$172	$158	$131	$ 88
Receivables	53	32	38	55	35	33	26	24	24	20
Inventories	564	531	473	433	476	414	227	152	135	130
Other	21	20	35	53	7	2	8	6	2	2
Total current assets	$ 927	$ 804	$ 778	$ 698	$589	$531	$433	$341	$292	$240
Fixed assets										
Inv. in subs.	$ 28	$ 39	$ 77	$ 77	$ 49	$ 34	$ 33	$ 31	$ 21	$ 26
Property, plant,										
equipment	406	395	279	226	201	127	77	62	47	40
Other	8	4	3	1	1	0	2	3	3	0
Total fixed assets	$ 442	$ 438	$ 359	$ 304	$251	$161	$112	$ 96	$ 71	$ 66
Total assets	$1,369	$1,242	$1,137	$1,002	$840	$693	$545	$438	$362	$306
Current liablities										
Bank debt	$ 2	$ 2	$ 4	$ 5	$ 4	$ 13	$ 8	$ 12	$ 12	$ 14
Accounts payable	26	15	12	19	10	11	12	19	17	15
Accrued expenses	15	19	31	4	6	5	3	4	3	2
Income tax payable	40	33	58	57	55	47	39	28	23	17
Other current liabilities	8	20	5	22	23	19	9	5	4	3
Total current liabilities	$ 91	$ 89	$ 110	$ 107	$ 98	$ 95	$ 71	$ 68	$ 59	$ 51
Shareholders' equity	1,279	1,153	1,027	895	742	598	474	370	303	256
Total liabilities and										
shareholders' equity	$1,369	$1,242	$1,137	$1,002	$840	$693	$545	$438	$362	$306

Source: Annual Reports (errors due to rounding) $1 U.S. = 25.28 baht (April 1993).

print designs, and new garments. A weave designer from Ireland and a print specialist from Taiwan had recently joined the group. Having outgrown its former quarters in the company's headquarters building located in downtown Bangkok, the department had recently moved to a new location on the outskirts of the city.

Sales

JT's sales revenue derived from three major markets—retail (80% of the 1993 total), home furnishing (9%), and export (11%).

Retail sales: JT operated five retail outlets, all located in Bangkok. Its flagship store was located adjacent to its headquarters building in the heart of Bangkok's commercial district. It was designed to resemble a Siamese palace of an earlier era, with several tiers of sloping tile roofs. The building's sumptuous interior was lined from floor to ceiling with teak shelves containing the largest selection of Thai silk fabric in the world; and its many nooks and crannies contained a vast assortment of colorful purses, neckties, and pillow cases. A mezzanine displayed garments representing the latest ready-to-wear women's fashions. Home furnishing fabrics were displayed on the store's second floor; home decorative merchandise—including sisal carpeting, antique furniture, porcelain vases, hand-painted wall panels, and Oriental room screens—on the third. In addition to its main store, JT operated four "satellite" outlets in other parts of the city. Three of the latter were located in the lobbies of luxury hotels, while the fourth was located on the ground floor of Bangkok's recently opened World Trade Center. All four satellite outlets had been established during the past two years.

JT's retail merchandise was typically priced 15% to 20% above levels charged by rivals. Popular items were printed neckties (priced at $35.70 in early 1994), head scarfs ($31.00), printed cushion covers ($18.90), and printed silk napkins ($11.00). Retail prices were scrupulously maintained, the only exception to this policy being huge clearance sales which JT held twice a year in the ballroom of a large Bangkok hotel. Prices at these biennial events were typically set 50% or more below retail list. These sales lasted three Sundays in a row, and were so popular that JT limited attendance to approximately 5,000 "invitation only" customers.

In early 1994 there were dozens of competitors selling high-priced silk and cotton merchandise to foreign tourists in Bangkok. However, the number of such rivals had decreased over the years, and several powerful competitors of an earlier era had all but collapsed. In the meantime, JT had grown to become the undisputed leader of the industry, commanding an estimated two-thirds of the entire premium market.

Home furnishing sales: JT sold drapery, wall covering, and upholstery fabric directly to local hotels, office buildings, condominiums, and housing projects. Its sales effort was focused mainly on interior designers who were chief decision makers in this market. It had recently opened a home furnishing showroom dedicated to such designers on the third floor of its headquarters building. Key purchase considerations in this market were design, price, and delivery. Numerous suppliers, many larger and more highly automated than JT, served the market. Despite this handicap, JT's sales of home furnishing fabric had nevertheless grown in recent years. A sizeable portion of these sales consisted of cotton fabric, the bulk of which JT purchased from contract suppliers and sold under its own brand.

Export sales: JT's export sales were handled by commissioned agents located in more than two dozen countries throughout the globe. Most export sales consisted of home furnishing fabric. Major export markets were the U.S., Japan, United Kingdom, Germany, France, Hong Kong, and Singapore. Sales to Europe had declined somewhat in 1993, but were expected to increase in 1994 as a result of the recent appointment of a new distributor in Germany. Initiatives planned for 1994 included an international advertising program, larger than any ever mounted before; a new showroom scheduled to open in London; and increased effort in several growing Asian markets including Korea, Taiwan, and the Philippines.

REASONS FOR SUCCESS

When asked for reasons for the company's success, JT executives cited the following key factors.

Outside experts: Frequent use of outside experts was widely cited as a key contributor to the company's success. Surindr Supasavasdebhandu, Production Manager, provided two examples:

> Mr. Czerny has helped us enormously over the years—in identifying the most appropriate machinery for our needs—often relatively inexpensive second hand equipment; in installing new equipment; and in adapting machinery to our particular needs. He is very patient and knows how to work with our employees.
>
> At the time we first set up our sericulture operation, two experts from the National Sericulture Institute in China came here to work with us. They provided us a great deal of help getting started. Now, their experts come here for shorter assignments to help us with particular problems as they crop up.

Continual innovation: Surindr explained that JT had not merely duplicated technology brought in from the outside, but had often significantly adapted it to the company's special needs. He offered the following examples.

> When we first began dyeing we brought in experts from several big organizations in Thailand to advise us on boiler design. We didn't stop there, however. I took a course in thermodynamics so that I could understand what happens inside a boiler. We installed a microprocessor to control the process. As we accumulated knowledge over time, we made continual modifications. I could relate similar stories in our reeling and weaving operations. We are forcing ourselves to continually improve, to compete with ourselves for greater efficiency and higher reliability.

Willingness to invest: The company's willingness to invest, even in projects which did not appear to show adequate return on investment, was felt to be another important contributor to the company's success. Pichet Buranastidporn, Deputy Managing Director, offered the following example:

> It was hard to justify our silk plantation on straight ROI criteria. However, this facility has provided us important intangible benefits. It gives us protection in the event raw silk prices suddenly rise. It also enhances our reputation by making us a fully integrated producer.

Leadership: Executive leadership was another factor cited as critical to the company's success. Booth pointed to the exceptional capability of his senior managers, all of whom were Thai.

> The textile industry is considered low-tech by most Thai managers—not a very exciting area to be in. Because of this stigma, it's hard to attract really good managers to a company like ours. Another problem is the reluctance of many Thai managers to question higher ups. Because of this trait, even individuals who are very qualified technically often don't have the independence of mind to become really effective managers. We have been very lucky to avoid these difficulties. Pichet and Surindr, for example, approach their jobs with [a] great deal of independent judgement. This quality has helped them develop into very capable, imaginative managers. Perhaps their strong roots in Chinese culture, which encourages more independence of mind, fosters this quality. It might also come from the fact

that the three of us joined the company at about the same time and have grown up here to-gether, so just naturally consider ourselves as equals.

Pichet and Surindr, in turn, spoke highly of Booth's contribution. Surindr offered the following details:

Bill arrives early, and leaves late—seven days a week—setting a good model for the rest of us to follow. He spends much of his time visiting our different operations, raising questions and providing information everywhere he goes. He doesn't try to make decisions for us, but instead helps us think more clearly about the situations we're facing.

Pichet felt that the decision process which had evolved under Booth's leadership had contributed to the company's success.

We spend a lot of time discussing an issue before a decision is made. Deliberations usually take place in the evening, often over drinks, and are very informal. This kind of setting helps generate a lot of good ideas. It also provides plenty of opportunity for potential obstacles to surface. When obstacles emerge, we go back to the drawing board to study details more carefully. When a decision finally emerges, we have generally thought it through very thoroughly.

While extolling JT's many strengths, several executives felt that the company suffered weakness in the area of marketing. One described the problem as follows:

In the past, demand at our retail store was so strong we didn't have to worry much about marketing. Our big challenge was to produce enough to meet demand. The situation is very different today. With retail sales declining, we must now find new customers, decide which ones we can serve most effectively, devise strategies for reaching new segments, etc. These are essentially marketing tasks. Since we have never had to look too hard for customers, our marketing skills are not yet very well developed.

The condominium market here in Bangkok illustrates the problem. Bangkok has experienced a phenomenal boom in condominium construction over the past decade. These units need to be furnished, their owners have plenty of money to pay for the very best, and Jim Thompson has an outstanding reputation for design and quality. Yet, we have garnered very little of this market.

Another illustration of the problem is our experience at the World Trade Center. When we began opening satellite retail outlets a few years ago, our policy was to confine them to luxury hotels. Consequently, we made no effort to secure space in the World Trade Center which was scheduled to open in 1992. Only after an intense sales campaign by the Center's management were we finally persuaded to open an outlet there. To our great surprise, results at the Center have been spectacular.

BOOTH'S ROLE

Close observation of Booth's interactions with staff and others showed him performing a variety of different roles in managing the company.

Booth frequently brought together key people whose interaction could benefit the company. He performed this role, for example, during a day-long visit to the company's production operations in Pak Thong Chai. Accompanying him on this visit were a young Thai male named Tamrong, who managed the company's printing joint venture, Czerny, and Surindr. A major purpose of the visit was to provide these three an opportunity to plan a proposed move of printing equipment from its current location in Bangkok to Pak Thong Chai. During much of the day the three discussed logistics of moving this equipment and locating it properly in the new facility being prepared by Pak Thong Chai.

Since Czerny spoke no Thai and Surindr and Tamrong spoke no German, discussions among the three took place in English. For the most part this solution presented no difficulty. However, there were occasions when one of the three became confused. At such moments, Booth would interject a brief clarifying comment—in German to Czerny, in Thai to the other two.

Also accompanying Booth on this trip was the representative of a major Brazilian raw silk producer. He had been invited to visit Pak Thong Chai in part to comment on the company's procedures for buying raw silk. He spent the better part of an hour examining raw silk fiber piled on tables in the JT's receiving area. During his inspection, he asked numerous questions about location of suppliers, storage procedures, treatment of incoming material, etc. Since he spoke no Thai and JT's purchasing personnel spoke no English, Booth played the role of interpreter.

Booth's input to conversations most frequently took the form of questions posed to clarify specific points. For example, during a discussion of spinning defects which took place on the floor of the spinning room in Pak Thong Chai, Booth asked whether the source of the problem might be insufficient maintenance frequency. This question in turn led to extensive discussion of the plant's equipment maintenance procedures.

Yet another role which Booth performed on a regular basis was that of gracious host. He took obvious pleasure in treating his Pak Thong Chai visitors to lunch at an outdoor restaurant, and later in the afternoon, during a meeting in the weaving factory's conference room, to cold beverages and appetizers. He also graciously received the steady stream of visitors who arrived at his well-appointed office on the top floor of the company's headquarters building in Bangkok. Visitors included department managers, lower-level employees, suppliers, customers, and directors. Each was cordially received, offered coffee or tea (in the evening, beer), and engaged in pleasant conversation. Not infrequently, several visitors were seated around the table in his office, engaged in lively discussion of topics ranging from developments in European weaving technology to hazards of restoring antique Thai houses.

DIFFICULTIES IN THE RETAIL MARKET

Dollar sales at JT's flagship retail outlet had declined 11% since the peak level reached in 1990, and unit sales had fallen even further. While these declines had been offset somewhat by increases at the company's new satellite outlets, so the company's overall retail sales had dropped in recent years.

JT managers attributed this decline to a variety of adverse environmental developments occurring in Bangkok. Rapid industrialization was destroying many of the charms which once attracted tourists to the city—its easy-going pace, distinctive Oriental architecture, and vast network of canals. Auto congestion was becoming so severe that several hours were sometimes needed to travel just a short distance within the city. This development was of special concern to JT because most customers traveled by taxi to reach its flagship store. Air pollution had reached an alarming level. So had the city's AIDS infection rate, particularly among bar girls who constituted an attraction for some male visitors to the city. Recessions in Japan and Europe, which historically supplied a large proportion of JT's customers, also played a role.

These developments, together with the Iraq war and a brief military coup occurring in Bangkok in 1991, caused the number of tourists visiting Thailand to decline that year for the first time in many years (see Exhibit 6). While tourist activity had recovered somewhat since then, visitors were beginning to skirt Bangkok and travel directly to resorts elsewhere in the country. An article appearing in a recent issue of the *Bangkok Post* provided the following details about this trend.

> One of the major areas of concern is visitor arrivals from Japan which have tapered off. Although Japan's economic woes are said to be partly responsible, the TAT [Tourist Author-

---

EXHIBIT 6
Jim Thompson Thai Silk Company

	I—International Tourist Arrivals in Thailand (in thousands)							
	1986	**1987**	**1988**	**1989**	**1990**	**1991**	**1992**	**1993**
Malaysia	653	765	868	736	752	808	729	830
Japan	259	342	449	556	652	560	570	582
Taiwan	111	195	189	400	503	454	407	525
Singapore	194	240	249	290	336	320	324	364
Germany	119	148	190	222	243	257	276	320
U.S.	196	236	258	267	285	248	274	278
Korea	31	37	65	112	148	180	204	271
Hong Kong	84	132	154	396	383	341	291	265
China	—	—	—	—	61	75	129	262
U.K.	147	184	280	200	238	198	236	250
Australia	95	111	138	219	252	203	208	205
France	100	132	157	187	194	173	194	202
Others	829	961	1,234	1,225	1,252	1,270	1,294	1,407
Total	2,818	3,483	4,231	4,810	5,299	5,087	5,136	5,761

	II—Tourist Expenditures in Thailand (% of total)		
	1986	**1990**	**1993**
Shopping	27.4	39.0	42.8
Accommodations	26.6	23.1	23.0
Food & beverages	16.9	15.1	15.1
Local transit	15.6	13.3	10.7
Entertainment	10.0	7.6	5.1
Other	3.5	1.9	3.3
Total	100.0	100.0	100.0

Source: Tourist Authority of Thailand.

ity of Thailand] is also blaming a spate of adverse publicity over sex, AIDS, and environmental problems in Thailand. The main turn-off appears to be more Bangkok than Thailand. Visitor arrivals in January–September 1993 (by nationality) showed a total of 433,485 Japanese visitors to Thailand (down 1.28% on the same period in 1992) but 374,138 arrivals at Bangkok airport (down 14.21% on Jan.–Sept. 1992).

This indicates that more Japanese are bypassing Bangkok and taking advantage of the increasing number of direct flights to Puket [a popular resort on Thailand's southwest coast]. Japanese tour operators note that the environment-and-safety conscious Japanese are showing strong signs of general disgust with the capital city's traffic problems. Strong marketing by new Puket developments like the Pacific Islands Club and the new Sheraton Grande are also diverting the Japanese from Bangkok.[2]

OPTIONS FOR IMPROVEMENT

In light of these developments, JT managers were seeking ways to reduce the company's dependence on Bangkok's tourist market. During the early weeks of 1994, four options for achieving this objective were under consideration.

1. Develop a mail order catalogue displaying accessories such as neckties, purses, blouses, etc.; target the catalogue to foreigners who had already purchased JT products during visits to Bangkok.

2. Open a retail store in a major foreign city such as New York, Paris, or Tokyo.

3. Open a retail shop at a Thai beach resort such as Puket (an island off the south coast, in the Indian Ocean), Samui (an island in the Gulf of Siam), or Pattaya (a resort on the Gulf of Siam's east coast). All three locations were growing very rapidly. Puket and Samui were still relatively unspoiled. Pattaya, however, was beginning to experience its own brand of environmental degradation. An article appearing in a 1991 issue of *The Economist* provided the following details.

> Twenty-five years ago Pattaya was a sleepy fishing village. Then it was discovered by American soldiers on R&R from Vietnam, and the Thai brand of sun, sea, and sex was invented, beginning a boom in tourism. Today Pattaya is a mess. Uncontrolled building has ruined its shoreline. The sea is coated with a film of raw sewage. Last year so many tourists died in mysterious circumstances that even the shady mafia that controls the town was embarrassed. An alarming proportion of the bar girls, many of whom are in fact transvestites, are HIV positive. Lucky is the hotel with 10% of its rooms occupied.[3]

4. Expand sales to the domestic home furnishing market.

JT managers were particularly enthusiastic about the last of these options, for several reasons. The domestic home furnishing market experienced little adverse effect from the city's traffic congestion. Indeed, the market may have actually benefitted from such congestion, since an increasing number of people were moving from the

---

[2]*Bangkok Post*, December 30, 1993, p. 45.
[3]*The Economist*, July 6, 1991, p. 78.

outskirts of Bangkok to downtown condominiums near their work locations to avoid traffic jams during commuting hours. A heady construction boom was taking place in the city, and new units being built need furnishing. And JT's reputation for creative design and good quality were highly prized by interior decorators who acted as prime decision makers in the market.

The home furnishing market presented JT with a major challenge, however. Most home furnishing sales consisted of relatively low-priced cotton fabric produced by suppliers utilizing high-speed mechanical looms. JT's weaving expertise, by contrast, lay in hand weaving. To compete more effectively in the home furnishing market, JT would need to significantly improve its skill in high-speed mechanical weaving.

In an effort to improve its ability in this area, JT had purchased six high-speed mechanical looms (second hand) during the past several years. JT's personnel had experienced difficulty operating the equipment, however, and trained operators were not available in Thailand. To overcome this obstacle, JT had sent several of its operators to Germany to receive training from the firm which had sold it the equipment—Rohleder GMBH. Rohleder was the world's eighth largest, and Germany's second largest, manufacturer of upholstery fabric used for couches, chairs, etc. When difficulties persisted following the trainees' return to Bangkok, JT had approached Rohleder for further assistance. Ensuing conversations revealed that Rohleder was interested in establishing its own weaving facility in Asia in order to gain access to low-cost Asian labor and to better serve its growing base of Asian customers. Lacking operating experience in the region, it hoped to secure an Asian partner, and enquired whether JT would consider joining it in constructing a jointly owned weaving mill in Thailand.

Investigation revealed that Rohleder's existing weaving mill, located near Frankfurt, was one of the most technically advanced in the world. Its entire output of fabric was sold to wholesalers who in turn sold, often under their own brands, to interior decorators and furniture manufacturers. Wholesalers generally gave Rohleder very high marks for quality and technical sophistication. Though more than 70 years old, Rohleder was still controlled by its founding family.

While Rohleder's skill in mechanical weaving—the very capability JT needed to improve its position in the home furnishing market—made the proposed venture with Rohleder attractive, Booth felt that the other options under consideration also offered promise. He hoped that the planning effort scheduled for the coming weeks would help clarify the pros and cons of all the options open to the company, so that he and his managers could make an optimal decision regarding the company's future direction.

http://parcy.parliament.go.th/files/mainpage.htm

INDUSTRY SPECIFIC: APPAREL

Cabriole*

> This is just plain crazy. The endless pressure with no rewards but huge risks is demoralizing. I find that owning and managing a small business during difficult times is infinitely more complex than people realize.
>
> There were different alternatives that I had considered prior to my decision to close the company. I set a number of different deadlines to check our progress.

Susan White, sole owner of a custom fitness wear/body wear company, was reflecting upon her decision to close Cabriole (the French word *cabriole* means "leap," and refers to a ballet step), the business she had founded and run for 13 years. In some ways it really didn't seem to make sense. Ever since she had announced her decision to close the company, sales had picked up. Loyal customers had been coming in or calling in orders to stock up with merchandise, because they didn't know where they would be able to find a comparable product once Cabriole closed its doors. In fact, sales in November 1991 had been over $45,000, the best in 4 months. (See Exhibits 1 to 3 for financial statements.) It was true that she had been discounting her merchandise 35 to 40 percent, but everyone loved the product and claimed there was no substitute. Could she really turn her back on them when the industry was perceived to be booming? On the other hand, Susan had started the business to sell a good product and do something she enjoyed. She loved to design body wear and then see how it really complemented the body. However, the constant financial pressures and 18-hour days had taken their toll. White commented on starting the business:

> I had two disadvantages when I started Cabriole. I started it as a custom leotard business with no organized business plan, no organizational chart, and no organized financial plan. The second disadvantage that I had was that I brought 150 percent effort to every job. That is so innate in me that it took a while for me to realize that the trait is certainly not universal.
>
> I didn't even realize that I was really starting a company, much less one that at one point would reach a million dollars in sales. For me, that was pretty awesome, to take it

---

*Prepared by Raymond M. Kinnunen and James F. Molloy, Jr., Northeastern University. Management cooperated in the field research for this case, which was written solely for the purpose of stimulating student discussion. All events and individuals are real, but names have been changed at the organization's request. Videotapes of Susan White in a question-and-answer session with an Executive MBA class at Northeastern University may be purchased from the authors at Northeastern University, College of Business, Boston, MA 02115. Copyright © 1994 by the *Case Research Journal* and R. M. Kinnunen and James F. Molloy, Jr.

EXHIBIT 1
Cabriole, Inc.: Balance Sheet as of December 31
(in thousands of dollars)

	1991	1990	1989	1988	1987	1986	1985	1984	1983	1979
Current assets										
Cash	$ 3.0	$ 0.1	$ 0.1	$ 2.5	$ 15.2	$ 29.4	$ 8.5	$ 5.4	$ 1.4	$ 0.6
Accounts receivable	64.2	88.3	70.0	76.7	91.3	119.0	121.4	118.9	103.2	1.9
Merchandise inventory	76.2	255.0	322.0	229.1	142.9	177.5	215.2	152.9	114.5	17.6
Prepaid expenses	10.1	93.8	55.1	31.4	8.3	59.8	21.7	4.3	3.2	1.3
Total current assets	$ 153.5	$ 437.2	$ 447.2	$ 339.7	$ 257.7	$385.7	$366.8	$281.5	$222.3	$21.4
Property and equipment										
Manufacturing equipment	$ 14.7	$ 14.7	$ 14.7	$ 14.3	$ 13.6	$ 13.6	$ 13.6	$ 9.3	$ 8.2	$ 1.2
Other equipment	119.1	104.0	102.0	97.4	83.3	80.4	47.9	24.3	13.9	0.0
Other assets	15.0	36.6	28.6	31.9	33.7	31.8	17.9	35.6	36.5	0.0
	$ 148.8	$ 155.3	$ 145.3	$ 143.6	$ 130.6	$125.8	$ 79.4	$ 69.2	$ 58.6	$ 1.2
Less: Accumulated depreciation	119.8	114.0	112.5	93.6	73.2	53.2	40.0	41.8	26.9	0.0
Total property and equipment	$ 29.0	$ 41.3	$ 32.8	$ 50.0	$ 57.4	$ 72.6	$ 39.4	$ 27.4	$ 31.7	$ 1.2
Total assets	$ 182.5	$ 478.5	$ 480.0	$ 389.7	$ 315.1	$458.3	$406.2	$308.9	$254.0	$22.6
Current liabilities										
Notes payable	$ 383.7	$ 419.0	$ 460.1	$ 365.9	$ 330.7	$209.1	$138.0	$144.4	$111.6	$ 2.1
Capital lease obligations	0.0	3.6	3.0	2.5	3.7	3.2	3.2	0.0	0.0	0.0
Accounts payable	13.3	98.0	109.0	114.9	41.5	153.4	101.3	58.9	55.9	2.9
Accrued expenses	14.2	6.3	19.3	13.7	21.5	16.0	15.9	8.2	17.2	1.2
Total current liabilities	$ 411.2	$ 526.9	$ 591.4	$ 497.0	$ 397.4	$381.7	$258.4	$211.5	$184.7	$ 6.2
Long-term debt										
Notes payable	$ 0.0	$ 22.0	$ 0.0	$ 0.0	$ 28.1	$ 36.8	$ 1.8	$ 13.8	$ 24.7	$ 3.6
Capital lease obligations	0.0	3.7	1.7	1.3	4.0	7.7	10.0	0.0	0.0	0.0
Notes payable—shareholder	292.6	290.0	276.0	153.4	56.1	27.7	124.7	80.9	25.2	11.5
Total long-term debt	$ 292.6	$ 315.7	$ 277.7	$ 154.7	$ 88.2	$ 72.2	$136.5	$ 94.7	$ 49.9	$15.1
Total liabilities	$ 703.8	$ 842.6	$ 869.1	$ 651.7	$ 485.6	$453.9	$394.9	$306.2	$234.6	$21.3
Shareholders' equity										
Capital stock	$ 47.4	$ 1.3	$ 1.3	$ 1.3	$ 1.3	$ 1.3	$ 1.3	$ 1.3	$ 1.3	$ 1.3
Additional paid-in capital	459.2	468.0	236.2	236.2	236.2	236.2	106.2	46.2	46.2	0.0
Deficit	(1,027.9)	(833.4)	(626.6)	(499.5)	(408.0)	(233.1)	(96.2)	(44.8)	(28.1)	0.0
Total shareholders' equity	$ (521.3)	$ (364.1)	$ (389.1)	$ (262.0)	$(170.5)	$ 4.4	$ 11.3	$ 2.7	$ 19.4	$ 1.3
Total liabilities and shareholders' equity	$ 182.5	$ 478.5	$ 480.0	$ 389.7	$ 315.1	$458.3	$406.2	$308.9	$254.0	$22.6

EXHIBIT 2
Cabriole, Inc.: Income Statement
Year Ended December 31
(in thousands of dollars)

	1991	1990	1989	1988	1987	1986	1985	1984	1983	1979
Sales	$ 515.3	$ 829.4	$ 799.2	$756.6	$ 999.4	$ 745.3	$881.6	$698.7	$591.6	$19.1
Costs of goods sold	398.1	523.8	475.2	435.7	633.0	476.9	511.4	403.0	349.4	11.2
Gross profit on wholesale	$ 117.2	$ 305.6	$ 324.0	$320.9	$ 366.4	$ 268.4	$370.2	$295.7	$242.2	$ 7.9
Income from retail operations	5.9	(16.7)	2.8	2.6	3.7	(7.1)	0.0	0.0	0.0	0.0
Gross profit	$ 123.1	$ 288.9	$ 326.8	$323.5	$ 370.1	$ 261.3	$370.2	$295.7	$242.2	$ 7.9
Operating expenses										
Design	$ 1.3	$ 2.9	$ 0.0	$ 0.7	$ 19.1	$ 27.1	$ 0.0	$ 0.0	$ 0.0	$ 0.0
Selling	123.4	222.6	176.7	159.6	246.9	171.7	182.6	167.8	121.9	1.3
Shipping	0.9	0.4	11.9	26.6	26.4	28.0	0.0	0.0	0.0	0.0
Administrative	103.5	178.4	179.2	161.2	179.9	132.4	141.7	96.0	84.7	4.5
Retail	0.0	C.0	0.0	0.0	0.0	0.0	9.4	17.9	11.1	0.0
Total operating expense	$ 229.1	$ 404.3	$ 367.8	$348.1	$ 472.3	$ 359.2	$333.7	$281.7	$217.7	$ 5.8
Operating income (loss)	$(106.0)	$(115.4)	$ (41.0)	$ (24.6)	$(102.2)	$. (97.9)	$ 36.5	$ 14.0	$ 24.5	$ 2.1
Other income										
Miscellaneous	$ 1.6	$ 3.6	$ 0.5	$ 3.5	$ (25.7)	$ 0.1	$ 0.9	$ 1.0	$ 1.0	$ 0.0
Interest	(80.4)	(75.2)	(76.6)	(55.4)	(45.8)	(32.1)	(33.5)	0.0	(19.5)	(0.4)
Loss on bad debts	(2.6)	(1.1)	(5.5)	(7.5)	(6.5)	(7.0)	(7.0)	(26.1)	(4.2)	0.0
Abandonment of assets	0.0	0.1	(2.0)	0.0	0.0	0.0	(4.8)	(5.2)	0.0	0.0
Net rental income (loss)	(6.3)	(19.0)	(2.5)	(7.5)	5.3	0.0	0.0	0.0	0.0	0.0
Relocation expense	0.0	0.0	0.0	0.0	0.0	0.0	(43.3)	0.0	0.0	0.0
Total other income (loss)	$ (87.7)	$ (91.6)	$ (86.1)	$ (66.9)	$ (72.7)	$. (39.0)	$ (87.7)	$ (30.3)	$ (22.7)	$ (0.4)
Net income (loss)	$(193.7)	$(207.0)	$(127.1)	$ (91.5)	$(174.9)	$(136.9)	$ (51.2)	$ (16.3)	$ 1.8	$ 1.7

Notes: In years 1980–1986, the fiscal year ended March 31. The figures for 1979 are for the 7-month period ending October 31. Figures for 1991 include amounts through November 30.

EXHIBIT 3
Cabriole, Inc.: Schedule of Retail Operations
Year Ended December 31
(in thousands of dollars)

	1991	1990	1989	1988	1987
Sales	$36.2	$ 39.8	$31.8	$34.8	$65.1
Cost of goods sold					
Merchandise inventory—beginning	$13.0	$ 12.0	$ 9.6	$17.1	$24.5
Transfers from wholesale stock	18.3	26.5	19.2	13.2	35.7
Total available	$31.3	$ 38.5	$28.8	$30.3	$60.2
Less: Merchandise inventory—end	8.9	13.0	12.1	9.6	17.1
Total cost of goods sold	$22.4	$ 25.5	$16.7	$20.7	$43.1
Gross profit	$13.8	$ 14.3	$15.1	$14.1	$22.0
Operating expenses					
Payroll	$ 0.2	$ 17.5	$ 4.1	$ 4.6	$ 7.6
Commissions	0.0	1.3	0.3	0.6	2.1
Advertising	0.3	0.7	1.1	0.5	0.1
Credit card charges	1.4	1.2	1.3	1.0	1.0
Depreciation	0.0	0.2	0.4	0.4	0.4
Factory overhead applied	5.4	5.6	4.1	3.2	5.8
Medical insurance	0.0	1.2	0.3	0.0	0.0
Payroll taxes	0.0	2.4	0.5	0.6	0.7
Postage	0.5	0.6	0.0	0.0	0.0
Store expenses	0.1	0.3	0.0	0.5	0.6
Total operating expenses	$ 7.9	$ 31.0	$12.1	$11.4	$18.3
Operating income	$ 5.9	$(16.7)	$ 3.0	$ 2.7	$ 3.7

from zero to a million dollars. I just started it because whenever I made anything, it just plain worked well. So I just kept selling it, making it, and selling it.

THE HISTORY OF CABRIOLE

In 1978 Susan White started Cabriole as a custom leotard manufacturer, designing leotards and body wear primarily for theater and dance clientele. Originally, the company catered to a niche within the body wear market—that of professional performers who demanded style, functionality, and quality. Initially, Cabriole's product proved to be superior to anything on the market for two reasons. First, it was designed to move with the body. The fabrics were excellent in quality and retained their shape despite rigorous exercise or washing. Secondly, the designs sculpted the body and were flattering to the wearer. Patterns were made to accommodate a variety of body sizes. The Cabriole designs seemed to have the optimal combination of style and functionality.

Tights retailed in the $26 to $32 range and leotards from $32 to $40, and it was not uncommon for a buyer to spend between $75 and $100. Through referrals and word of mouth, the product quickly gained acceptance, and sales began to accelerate.

In 1980 Susan moved operations from her home to a 2,500-square-foot retail store located in a town just outside of the city of Boston. She had been using a studio in her home and renting the basement of the house next door. The volume of sales seemed to justify the move. Cabriole used the front of the store to merchandise body wear, while the back was used for production. At the time that the enterprise moved to the new location, five employees assisted Sue with the cutting of fabric, sewing, and sales. By 1985, sales exceeded $698,000, and Cabriole employed twenty people. Sales grew to the extent that more space was needed, and Sue decided to look for a larger facility.

In 1985, the "Massachusetts Miracle" was at its height: real estate values in New England were rapidly escalating, high-tech start-ups in electronics and computer science were mushrooming on Route 128 just outside of Boston, college enrollments were at an all-time high, and jobs for graduates were plentiful. Susan found an excellent building with 14,500 square feet of space only a short distance from her rented facility. The building was acquired by Susan and her husband for $840,000, and they spent an additional $110,000 for necessary improvements. The business only needed a third of the space, but Susan was confident that she could find tenants to fill the space and that Cabriole plus the renters would be able to pay the mortgage. With the encouragement of her banker Susan made the investment and in September of 1985, Cabriole moved to its new warehouse. Susan used a small portion of the space to open an outlet store; the majority of the space, approximately 5,000 square feet, was devoted to production.

Susan commented on the purchase of the building:

> As it turned out, leasing the building was a huge responsibility and huge distraction from running Cabriole. At the time I moved over to that building it took another year to lease out the space. I had to manage a whole building, find tenants, do all of the managing of the lease, etc. It was a whole other business which also ate up a lot of capital.

Up to that point in time, Susan was the only member of management. After consultation with her banker and accountant, she decided to hire a few more professionals to help with the workload. In October of 1985 she found an experienced production manager, Jim, through an advertisement in the *Boston Globe*. Susan interviewed Jim with the help of an industry consultant; she received glowing reports from references contacted by telephone, and the banker and accountant agreed that Jim seemed ideal for the new position. The following March, Susan hired a production assistant, Tommi, at Jim's recommendation. They had worked with each other in the past. Concurrent with the move to the new building, operations were being computerized. Tommi took over coordinating the installation of the computer system. From 1985 to 1987, revenues continued to climb, but overall profits and margins declined.

Shortly after he was hired, Jim suggested that to ease the problems associated with growth, the fabric cutting be partially subcontracted to a local firm which he knew. Also, after reviewing Cabriole's records, he noted that the waste on the Nylon/Lycra fabric had been only 3 percent in the past. The industry norm was 8 percent, and Jim suggested that Cabriole was probably now experiencing levels of shrinkage closer to the industry average, which would account for the lower margins. To compensate for this he recommended that Cabriole adjust its price to improve margins.

About the same time Susan noted increasing delays in obtaining accurate and timely reports. For example, Susan was not receiving timely reports of gross profits per month. Investigation showed that the record-keeping system was more than adequate. When asked, Jim and Tommi explained that computer breakdowns and slowness in inputting data were causing the reporting delays. In late 1987, the bookkeeper gave notice, and Susan had to take direct control of the records in order to get the much-needed management information. She was forced now to monitor every bill and especially those of the contractor.

MARKETING AT CABRIOLE

Initially, sales had come in through referrals and networking. As Susan realized how popular her products were becoming, she was confident she had a hit. She knew she had a good product, but needed more stores to carry the product. In 1980, Susan simply started calling department stores, and convinced the better ones to offer her line. Cabriole's relationship with the department store chains was very unbalanced. Small manufacturers were very dependent on the large stores, and often had to acquiesce to outrageous terms to guarantee floor space for the product. The stores typically placed large orders, and frequently returned half for full refund. Fed up with this treatment, Cabriole dropped the department store accounts in 1983.

Sue was eager to pursue other distribution outlets, but faced a major hurdle. The fitness industry was so young that little if any information was available. Until 1987, the industry didn't have a trade show. Fitness was included as part of tennis trade shows, but was relegated to a corner, next to information on racket stringing and tanning beds. Not surprisingly, data on competitors was hard to get. Body wear, as a category of clothing, was classified in the athletic gear category, which included everything from sweatpants and T-shirts to baseball caps. Publicly traded companies such as Danskin might release sales figures in annual reports, but the published figures were usually vague and/or inconsistent.

Despite these barriers, Cabriole established 500 to 800 accounts nationwide by exhibiting in regional and national trade shows. These included elite spas, dance and fitness wear stores, and health clubs. Several collegiate athletic teams, including Princeton, wore Cabriole items. Cabriole also developed a mail-order catalog, and built its mailing list over the years from loyal clients. In Susan's view, once someone tried a Cabriole product, they were hooked. The product lasted much longer and retained its shape better than anything offered by competitors. Although Cabriole had a strong following with individual consumers, retailers were much more fickle. With so many manufacturers to choose from, customers often played one manufacturer against another to get the best prices and terms.

Despite the trend toward body wear as "street" clothes and the increased competition, Cabriole resolved to keep its product marketed to the upscale, fashion-oriented consumer who was concerned with both form and function. Susan was convinced that the quality of the product would sell itself and justify the higher price.

THE FITNESS CRAZE

During the eighties—at the same time that Cabriole was establishing itself—Americans became more and more concerned with appearance and health. One manifestation of this concern was a huge expansion in the number of health clubs. One of the most popular forms of exercise was aerobics. According to a survey conducted by The NPD Group, Inc., for the National Sporting Goods Association, the total United States market for clothing for aerobic exercising was $831 million in 1990 and $1 billion in 1991, and continued growth was forecast for 1992. The attire de rigueur for the sport was leotard and tights. Research played a role too, as new fabrics were developed and tested to determine the optimal covering for the moving body. Fashion—for both men and women—was entering the weight room and athletic field. Since working out was often synonymous with socializing, having a fitness wardrobe was essential. No longer would a T-shirt and baggy sweats do.

As the public worked out, lycra and spandex moved from the gym and onto the street. Tights, leggings, and cycling shorts could even be found on the fashion runways. The customers of body wear became more sensitive to the colors and prints available. The growth in demand was met by a jump in the number of body wear manufacturers. With increased competition, prices were put under greater pressure. Many manufacturers moved their operations off-shore to Taiwan, China, and Mexico, where labor costs were lower. Some manufacturers also sold their clothing under private labels to outlets such as Sears, Kmart, and JCPenney.

White commented on the competition in 1991:

> Just in body wear and fitness alone, I'd say there must be a minimum of fifty competitors in the United States. I am not counting the ones that make special Halloween costumes. When I started in this business there were probably six. The number of small manufacturers who have already ceased operation is large.
>
> Tights or leggings or pants are also now fashion. Because of that a number of people have said to me, "Wow, you must be doing fabulously now that it's fashion." That is not true because now you have all of 7th Avenue manufacturing it very cheaply. The quality on most of it is poor. It doesn't stretch and it is not made for performance function wear like Cabriole's. It just means that now there are more manufacturers doing more "nickel and diming" who can cut a better deal.
>
> I manufacture a high-quality line that is classical in appearance and also performs well. So much of what is being manufactured is by my standards ugly, and it doesn't work for exercise.

PROBLEMS ARISE

In late 1987, Susan became concerned about the business. Sales had been growing, but the company remained unprofitable. Susan recognized that competition had increased, but she thought Cabriole's positioning as an upscale manufacturer of body wear was somewhat sheltered from market swings. She was forced to lay off some of her staff. Then in 1988, Susan began to hear complaints about the quality of Cabriole's products. This she just could not understand. At the urging of the production manager, all fabric cutting had been contracted out. Stitching was still done in-house. Susan had a direct hand in buying the fabric. White commented:

> In the Spring of 1988 I began to hear complaints about our quality. I heard that our sizing was erratic and that our garments did not fit as they had before. I went to Texas to listen to and see some examples of problems. I became aware that our fabric was not stretching as well as it had. At about the same time Jim, my production manager, went into the hospital for a month.
>
> I took over running production and shipping while Jim was in the hospital. I totally reorganized the systems and the tracking records and hired a new person to manage the computer system. I also set up a tracking record on the contractor cuts in relation to receivings and billings. Jim and his assistant had been handling this before. I made it clear that no bills would be paid when the figures did not totally reconcile.

In April of 1988 Tommi left, supposedly to be committed to a hospital for a manic-depressive disorder. Jim returned in June 1988 only to get sick again in September. It was agreed that Jim would take a medical leave of absence without pay. Susan and a new assistant she had hired continued to manage production, using the new system to monitor contractor cuts and deliveries.

At this point Susan became aware of some irregularities involving Jim, his assistant Tommi, and the cutting contractor. Apparently they had been skimping on the fabric used for her patterns (known in the trade as "shrinking the marker"), stealing the fabric, using it to make their own products, and selling the product under another name. Cabriole had been paying not only for fabric that was put into another firm's products, but even worse, the quality of Cabriole's body wear had suffered. Susan elaborated:

> I realized immediately that we had a big problem; I also began to understand what was behind the problem. I called my lawyer, and we started an investigation that lasted 12 nightmarish days. We arrived unannounced at the business where Cabriole was sending fabric to be cut, and everyone went running. We saw piles of tights stitched in our exclusive colors that had another brand name on them.

Thoughts of closing the business were not new to Susan; when the margins had first started to deteriorate, she had contemplated such a move. Now that this white-collar crime against Cabriole had been unearthed, Susan again considered shutting down. Instead, she terminated the director of sales and saw others leave the business.

Susan was never able to find out exactly who was involved, or when the diversions had started. When asked to estimate the loss, she figured that about $250,000 worth of material had been stolen and that about $40,000 would be needed to replace substandard product with acceptable product. In addition, there were costs that were difficult to quantify: poor public relations, damage to reputation because of shoddy product, and the need to redo all patterns, restaff, and acquire new material. She consulted with lawyers about pursuing charges against Jim and Tommi, but was advised against it. She had hard evidence, but not enough time, money (lawyers estimated that it would cost $80,000 to $100,000 to pursue the case in court), or will. There was indirect evidence that Jim had some shady connections. Too much had happened during the move to the new building and the conversion to the new computer system to believe that Jim and Tommi had engineered the crime by themselves.

From 1988 to 1990, Susan also had problems with the excess space at the new warehouse. She had to find tenants, write a lease, and manage the space. One tenant couldn't keep up with payments. Then in the late 1980s, the real estate market started to soften and Susan couldn't find another tenant. The building which had once been worth $1.4 million was now valued at less that $900,000.

Susan continued to have confidence in her product, and felt the business still had a future. Cabriole concentrated more on signing with sporting goods stores, since that was the direction the industry was moving. Cutting of fabric was once again performed in-house. Closer controls were placed on production so that quality could be ensured. Cabriole worked to rebuild its relationship and reputation with accounts. Susan took complete control into her own hands, cut expenses by laying off more employees, and personally watched the finances very closely.

The best months for Cabriole had been September 1990 through March 1991. In the spring of 1991 Susan felt that if profits could continue through July, Cabriole could offset many of the recent losses. Survival required that the company be profitable during this period.

Calie, Susan's daughter, had joined the company in January of 1989 as director of sales. She had graduated from Connecticut College, completed an executive training program at a large regional retailer, and managed several departments in that chain for 3 years. She had been instrumental in keeping Cabriole in business during some very tough times. Sue explained their thinking as the fall of 1991 approached:

> Through the summer of 1991 Calie felt the same way that I did—that sales would grow and we would be able to turn things around. Something happened in late September. I went down to New York to look at new patterns and prints of materials. I observed that a number of my vendors were in real trouble. Then, as I walked the stores, I realized that the merchandise I was looking at was truly ugly. I also noted that vendors were increasing the prices and increasing the yardages you had to buy, and yet the quality of the goods was inferior.
>
> Calie was at a Texas show of sporting goods dealers, an area that had been building for us. It turned out to be a very poor show. The vendor next to her had sold $100,000 worth of goods in 1990, and $50,000 in the March 1991 show, but at this September show she only wrote $7,000 worth of orders. Calie had written $35,000 at the show in March, but only $6,000 in September. When she got home from the September show, even that buyer turned around and canceled half of the order.
>
> Calie was beginning to reach the same conclusion that I had: we weren't doing anything wrong so it was hard to think of what we could do differently. It seemed to us that our line was complete, and we catered to an appropriate number of different types of stores. In addition, we had brought in very good-looking prints. Nothing was lacking.

In September of 1991, the recession was still impacting retailers. Susan had not seen the upturn she hoped for. In October of 1991 she decided to close the company. She commented on that decision:

> Part of why I finally reached the decision to close was that I couldn't see anything more that I could do. There was no one area that I could see that was wrong. That has been the

most difficult part of the last nine months. I am somebody that loves to see some kind of activity in what I do. We had gotten to a point where I could no longer see that, and it just was not feasible to go on any longer given our continued losses.

I found that there were two very important levels to go through in starting a business. One was figuring out if Cabriole was a viable business. Plus Cabriole was something I had started and operated for thirteen years. It was a very important part of me and an important part of what I have done in my life. I found it took a lot to really step back and look at where Cabriole stood and how I had changed in the thirteen years since I had started the company.

White's decision to close Cabriole had not been an easy one to make. Now she had to develop a viable liquidation plan. Her goal was to liquidate Cabriole in a manner which would satisfy customers, creditors, bankers, and employees without placing herself in complete financial disarray. The major question facing her was how to accomplish that task. At the same time she was considering whether or not to undertake another business venture.

http://www.sportlink.com/apparel/

CASE 3

Product Engineering, Inc.*

INTRODUCTION

Product Engineering, Inc., is a small, family-owned manufacturing firm located in a medium-sized midwestern SMSA. The company was established in mid-1970s to produce a simple mechanical device to monitor the air filters used in internal combustion engines. Since its founding, the firm has expanded from the top of a ping pong table in the founder's basement to a new, modern, 7,000 square foot building housing its manufacturing and administrative facilities. The product has grown from a single design to a family of monitors for use in the air and fuel systems in all types of gasoline and diesel engines. While the firm has expanded steadily and prospered since its founding, its senior management team knows that the firm cannot continue on its present path indefinitely. The world is running out of oil and the internal combustion engine is destined for extinction. To survive, Product Engineering has to look to its environment for new opportunities and map a new course for the future.

PRODUCTS AND OPERATIONS

The main product produced by Product Engineering, Inc., is a small plastic analog device which measures the air pressure coming through the air cleaner of an internal combustion engine. Through use, the air cleaner becomes increasingly clogged with dirt, gradually restricting airflow and reducing engine performance. While many owners just replace their air cleaners at regular intervals, this can be wasteful. Replacing the

---

*Prepared by Lynda L. Goulet and Peter G. Goulet of the University of Northern Iowa, Cedar Falls, Iowa, and intended to be used as a basis for class discussion rather than to illustrate either effective or ineffective handling of the situation. The name of the organization has been disguised to preserve the organization's desire for anonymity. Presented to and accepted by the refereed Society for Case Research. All rights reserved to the authors and the SCR. Copyright © 1995 by Lynda L. Goulet and Peter G. Goulet.

cleaner too soon wastes money on new, unneeded air cleaners. Replacing it too late can result in engine damage. With the addition of PEI's Filter Minder™, the driver can simply look at the colorful gauge inside the product's case and see how much filter capacity remains. (Exhibit 1 shows an example model of the product.) The firm feels that a $500,000 investment in the reusable filter minders added to a fleet of trucks can save the fleet owner as much as $7.5 million in maintenance costs over a three year period.

As of 1995, PEI's product line includes a family of filter monitoring products for the air intake and fuel systems of a variety of on-road and off-road engines. These products are sold primarily to OEMs (original equipment manufacturers). Roughly 80% of sales are concentrated with 20 of these OEMs. The product is produced under the PEI's name, as well as being privately labeled for firms such as Ford Motorcraft, Caterpillar, AC Rochester, Purolator and more than 10 others. Fleet users include Greyhound Bus, Ryder Truck Rental, U.P.S., the U.S. Army, the U.S. Postal Service, and many major truck lines. Although the firm is considering the development of new devices for monitoring usage in other types of filters, its product R&D remains focused on engine applications.

PEI's products are all assembled at the company's only plant from parts purchased from a variety of suppliers. The assembly operation is relatively simple and clean, and does not require a large work force. The firm employs its own designers and quality management personnel. Because its customers are generally large fleet owners and

EXHIBIT 1
PEI Filter Minder™: Private Label Version

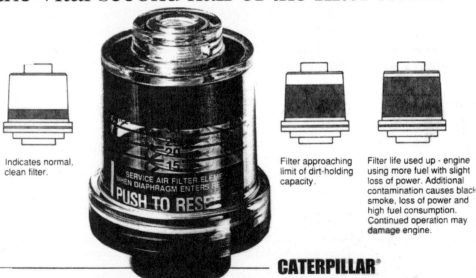

Cat® Air Filter Service Indicator...
the vital second half of the filter team!

Indicates normal, clean filter.

Filter approaching limit of dirt-holding capacity.

Filter life used up - engine using more fuel with slight loss of power. Additional contamination causes black smoke, loss of power and high fuel consumption. Continued operation may damage engine.

CATERPILLAR®

major vehicle manufacturers or suppliers, maintaining very high quality is critical, even for a simple add-on device such as the filter minder. Although PEI is a small firm, it employs a sophisticated computer system which allows it to interface directly with many of its customers. These customers use their computers to send their production schedules and needs directly to PEI, allowing for improved production planning and delivery.

MANAGEMENT AND PLANNING

Although Product Engineering is a small entrepreneurship, it has assembled an experienced management team. PEI's primary owner and CEO is nearing his planned retirement and has been developing his team to provide for a smooth transition in the day-to-day management of the firm. The most recent addition to the staff is a new senior vice president who is responsible for sales management and planning, as well as having other responsibilities. Along with the owner, the firm's board of directors includes the owner's son, who is a scientist and entrepreneur living in Alaska, and his daughter, who is not actively involved in the management of the firm.

PEI has a well-established strategic planning process and utilizes regular meetings of its management and board of directors to update its plan. As management began to develop an agenda for a major planning session in September 1995, the owner's son asked to be allowed to make a presentation of trends expected to affect the energy environment into the 21st century and initiate a discussion of the implications of these trends. Because the firm's products are all related to the internal combustion engine, the future availability of fossil fuels and the implications of their use are critical trends affecting the future demand for the company's products. An annotated summary of the presentation conclusions is presented in Exhibit 2.

Based on this presentation the owner, the firm's managers and directors, and a few invited expert guests were asked to consider the factors that should be assessed as the firm planned its long-run future. They began by discussing the issues raised in the final conclusion shown in Exhibit 2. One guest, a retired automotive engineer and former president of the Society of Automotive Engineers (SAE), urged the group to remember that many of the predictions they had just viewed assumed no new technological innovations. He noted that during this century, innovation had rendered many negative predictions obsolete and produced remarkable unforeseen advancements. Others in the room talked of the need to begin to build formal processes for monitoring environmental change and the need to catalog, store, and communicate this information throughout the company.

Some managers began to consider the firm's products. Should they branch out into new areas and technologies, explore joint ventures, consider integrating their products with other components? What were the major threats to be faced? When should the firm begin to act? Could it grow stakeholder value and still protect its future? What resources would be required to deal with the environment? How could they be obtained?

EXHIBIT 2
Energy Environment Outlook Summary

Summary and Predictions

1. Cheap oil and gas for a few more decades
   - Fool's paradise: not sustainable [fossil fuels predicted to be impractical in 40 years according to Shell Oil CEO]
   - Dependency on Mideast, OPEC [most of the world's oil in these regions]
   - Underpriced—overused [fossil fuel is too cheap and easy to use now]
   - Convulsion [when the oil runs out]? When? How to prevent?

2. U.S. uses 25% of world's energy, with 5% of the population
   - 95% of U.S. energy from fossil fuel
   - Oil imports will be 70% by 2010

3. Hydrocarbon paucity for future generations

4. Efficiency will lead; we must invest [spending money to increase the efficiency of energy uses can be cheaper than developing new sources]

5. Coal cheap and plentiful; [but currently] too dirty to use

6. Oil shale, tar sands [also] costly and dirty

7. Nuclear energy
   - Fission is dirty and dangerous
   - Fusion [perhaps] will be available in 50+ years, but expensive

8. Renewable sources
   - Hydrogen [for combustion], fusion; in the future
   - Electrochemical, not combustion; future uses

9. Public transit will replace private

10. External costs: what, when, how to internalize?

11. PEI position
    - How can the firm maintain and grow stakeholder value?
    - Can PEI remain the filtration monitor leader? What markets and segments?
    - [Should the firm] diversify or metamorphose?

By the end of this planning session, almost all agreed that the future would require the firm to make some changes. They also agreed that much more time would be required to understand the timing and scope of the changes they would have to face and that they did not yet know exactly how to proceed to answer all the questions raised in this initial "futuring" session.

http://www.fenceusa.com/37/

INDUSTRY SPECIFIC: MACHINE MAINTENANCE

CASE 4

Windrock Incorporated, 1996*

"Well, what do you think we should do? Buy or walk?" Ed Flanagan asked. He addressed Steve Follmar and Will Griffith, his friends and coworkers at Windrock, a tiny firm that did R&D on electronic analysis of reciprocating engines. The three of them were huddled in Ed's windowless office among piles of electrical parts and circuit boards scattered on every surface available. Ed's question referred to a decision they had been wrestling with for several days now: whether to buy Windrock, or seek employment elsewhere. Windrock's corporate parent, Computation Systems, Inc. (CSI), had informed them three weeks before that it was closing the books on Windrock and that they had a choice: They could become Windrock's new owners for $250,000 or they could become Windrock's former employees. Their decision was due in two days, and it was far from clear what it should be or what they should do once the decision was made.

THE ENGINE ANALYSIS INDUSTRY

Windrock competed in a highly specialized, but growing, segment of the much larger equipment maintenance industry. U.S. industry was believed to spend some $200 billion annually on equipment maintenance. Estimates found at least 15 percent of all equipment maintenance performed unnecessarily. To understand why, you must understand the three primary approaches to maintaining equipment.

The most common approach, accounting for perhaps 50 percent of all maintenance expenditures, is referred to as "fix-as-fail." As this name implies, maintenance is performed only after a piece of equipment fails; not unlike driving a car until it quits running, and then taking it to a repair shop. While this approach is the simplest, generally speaking, it is also the least cost effective because it entails unscheduled downtime and often requires replacement of parts that could have been repaired.

The second most common approach, probably associated with more than 40 percent of all maintenance expenditures, is preventive maintenance. Under this approach, maintenance is performed on a scheduled basis. This is more cost effective

---

*Prepared by Alex Miller, University of Tennessee.

because it allows work to be scheduled during equipment downtime, and avoids equipment failures. This is analogous to rotating tires and changing oil according to an automobile manufacturer's prescribed schedule.

The third approach to maintenance is predictive maintenance, which involves analysis to determine when a machine is about to encounter problems. This is the most complex and proactive approach, but can be very cost effective. It offers benefits from avoiding unexpected downtimes and high replacement costs associated with equipment failures like preventive maintenance does, but it offers potential cost savings beyond preventive maintenance. Preventive maintenance entails maintenance work on a prescribed schedule, even though not all machines experience wear and tear at precisely the same rates. Consequently, some work is done earlier than necessary and some is done later than might have been preferred. Predictive maintenance sought to avoid these problems by analyzing a particular machine and choosing maintenance work accordingly. For example, with advances in electronics and engine analysis, automobile repairers can perform fairly sophisticated analysis indicating what maintenance an individual automobile needs. While this more sophisticated analysis is typically not cost effective in comparison to preventive maintenance for automobile engines, the opposite is true for more expensive engines and equipment.

Analysis entailed in predictive maintenance involves taking a number of readings on a broad range of parameters covering everything from engine temperature, to chemical analysis of engine oils, to measuring machinery vibrations. Using such data, often in combination, engineers and operators could develop useful guidelines for when and what type of maintenance is needed. While the use of predictive maintenance was less than fix-as-fail or preventive maintenance, it was expected to be the most rapidly growing approach. This growth was expected for two reasons. First, technological advances allowed predictive maintenance to be more accurate and less expensive. Second, advance in operations management (such as the shift from mass production to lean production) was resulting in production processes with much less inventory. Without this inventory, a failure of a link anywhere along the chain of events required in a given operation could rapidly shut the entire process down. A downed production operations could easily cost tens of thousands of dollars an hour, and the threat of such downtime costs effectively increased the value of each machine involved in the process. As stated earlier, predictive maintenance is easier to justify for more expensive machines, so the developments in operations management techniques effectively increased the potential demand for predictive maintenance.

By 1996, Windrock had designed the most sophisticated electronic analyzers available for use in the maintenance and operation of reciprocating machines. "Reciprocating machines" are pumps, compressors, or internal combustion engines that make use of pistons that move back and forth (reciprocate) within a cylinder. Windrock's family of analyzers and sensors were designed to be used in expensive machines costing a million dollars or more. The proper analysis could detect maintenance needs and fine tune engine performance. Such maintenance could save thousands of dollars if it helped operators avoid a part's total failure when it could be repaired rather than replaced. It could also save significant amounts of money by facilitating repairs during planned machine downtimes, rather than unplanned failures. By providing operators with accurate operating data that could be used to fine tune engine settings, Windrock's analyzers could significantly improve engine performance, often gaining 5 percent to 10 percent in engine output without requiring significant investment in new equipment. While Windrock's technical achievements such as these were impressive, they had not come easily, as a review of the company's history will show.

WINDROCK'S HISTORY

Windrock was founded in January 1990 as an R&D subsidiary of CSI, a 12-year-old $20 million publicly traded company that designed, manufactured and sold electronic sensors and diagnostic equipment for preventive maintenance analysis for rotary equipment such as electrical motors. (Such equipment is referred to as "rotary" because its main parts spin around a central shaft.) CSI hoped that Windrock would someday be as successful in the reciprocating analyzer business as the parent company had become in the rotary analyzer business. While the two businesses might appear to be similar, they were actually very different in terms of the technical issues involved, the most common applications for reciprocating versus rotary engines, the industries making up the market, and the competition faced.

CSI expected the Windrock subsidiary to support itself by winning a number of Small Business Innovation Research (SBIR) contracts. SBIR contracts were available through a government program that targeted smaller firms for a portion of the R&D contracts available from a wide variety of federal agencies. Through the fall of 1992, Windrock grew to about 10 employees—mainly graduate-level engineers and scientists—and obtained several grants and contracts to develop products centered around analyzers for reciprocating machines, such as large internal combustion engines. During this time, Windrock's research was focused on developing machine diagnostics and controls, ultrasonic defect sensors, and oil analysis and transducer calibration devices.

From fall 1992 to spring 1994, Windrock focused on developing engine diagnostic monitoring hardware to predict harmful emissions of industrial stationary internal combustion engines. The Gas Research Institute (GRI), an industry research consortium funded by the 200 natural gas pipeline companies in the United States, funded and encouraged this technology, called Parametric Emissions Monitoring (PEM). With GRI's encouragement and support, Windrock began an intensive development effort into modeling engine emissions based on indirect measurement of engine performance. Researchers developed mathematical emissions models that were effective estimates of engine emissions based on such measured parameters as intake pressure, exhaust temperature, intake air temperature, engine speed, engine load, fuel consumption, relative humidity, and so on. This technology proved especially promising because the federal Environmental Protection Agency (EPA) and several state environmental agencies were about to mandate continuous emissions monitoring of stationary engines by operators.

During early 1994, Windrock began to develop the PEM market and products so as to exploit the impending enhanced emissions-monitoring mandates. Market studies showed the PEM market to be extremely attractive, and Windrock, due to research sponsored by GRI, held a leading position in the required technology. However, in the fall of 1994, the United States elected a conservative Congress which soon put a halt to EPA efforts to increase emissions-monitoring policies, and as a result, Windrock's efforts in the PEM field were severely impaired. In fact, during early 1995, it became increasingly evident that the PEM market had all but disappeared. By this time, only Will, Ed, and Steve were working on reciprocating machinery products at Windrock. The team began to focus their efforts on developing hardware and software to be useful and marketable for reciprocating machine condition and performance monitoring.

During July of 1996, CSI management, under pressure to meet quarterly profit and growth projections, decided to liquidate its Windrock subsidiary. In early August, Ed, Will, and Steve were given until the end of the month to decide whether or not they wanted to buy the company for $250,000. There was no offer of employment elsewhere in CSI.

WINDROCK'S PRODUCTS

In the summer of 1996, Windrock offered the following as its product line.

Model 6100

This was a permanently installed on-line reciprocating machine condition monitor. It could receive input from up to 160 sensors and was designed so that a single personal computer (PC) could control and store data for multiple 6100 units. In other words, a technician could remain in one centralized location and simultaneously monitor a number of engines, each with its own 6100 linked via a telephone line or other communication link. The 6100 offered continuous monitoring of static pressure; temperature; oil condition (oxidation and coolant contamination); ignition secondary voltage; machine speed; vibration levels of frequency bands; fuel/air ratio using exhaust oxygen sensor; and vibration and angular velocity versus crankshaft position. The unit could also provide calculations of horsepower per cylinder, compressor valve loss, compressor valve efficiency, rod loading, compressor gas capacity. The price of a 6100 varied tremendously depending on the number of sensors installed. (Sensors were standard off-the-shelf items that Windrock marketed for prices ranging from $500 to $1,500, reflecting the industry standard 100% markup.) A 6100 with a typical number of sensors was expected to cost about $30,000 installed.

Model 6200

This was a transportable on-line reciprocating machinery condition monitor that offered all the features of the 6100 except that it was repackaged for portable use. The electronics were housed in a tackle-box-type enclosure connected to sensors. Data was communicated to a PC for storage and analysis. Because it was designed with portability ("or at least 'lugability' ") in mind, the 6200 was usually sold with only a few sensors. This, and the fact that there were no installation costs for Windrock, allowed the price to stay in the $15,000 to $20,000 range.

Model 6300

This was a truly portable reciprocating machine analyzer that was handheld and battery powered. It featured 4-channel simultaneous data collection, and all data collection and analysis could be done on board the analyzer with no external computer required. Except for the smaller number of channels available for input, the 6300 could perform all the monitoring and analysis performed by the 6100. In fact, the 6300 was essentially the 6100 software coupled with new housing, battery power, and a 486 computer chip, and, while no units had yet been sold, it was to be priced at $30,000, just like the typical 6100. Windrock was very optimistic about the 6300's potential and the sales material describing the product is provided in Exhibit 1.

Model 6400

This was a specialty product designed for extremely rugged applications. Its initial application had been on-line, installed in huge drag-line shovels operating in open pit

EXHIBIT 1
Sales Material for Model 6300

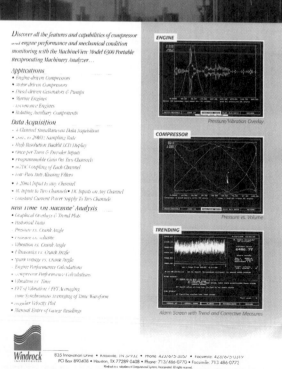

mines. This system was similar to the 6100 on-line monitoring system except that it did not need connection to a PC for data storage. The unit collected data continuously and compared collected data to preset alarm limits. Though only four units had been installed (at $15,000 each), and these were for a single customer, the units had proven to be very reliable, and the customer reported he was very pleased with their service.

Model 6500

As of August 1996, the 6500 was only a concept and some preliminary designs. The future product was intended to be a stand-alone peak pressure and horsepower balancing meter with a target price between $5,000 and $7,000. It was to be a handheld walk-around data collector that would measure the peak pressure and horsepower of each cylinder of a large engine, and allow the engineer or operator to adjust the engine so that all cylinders produced an equal portion of the power, maximizing the efficiency and life expectancy of the engine.

WINDROCK'S MARKET

Windrock saw its market as users of large reciprocating engines and compressors (worth $1 million and up) and a niche market for monitoring drag-line shovels in mines. Its main market comprised seven distinct segments:

Natural Gas Pipelines

Pipeline companies use natural gas–fired reciprocating engines that power reciprocating compressors to deliver natural gas through pipelines to users. (The natural gas pipeline companies also used centrifugal machines to pump gas, and about half of all pumps were centrifugal types for which Windrock's technology was inappropriate.) Pipeline companies require a pumping station about every 200 miles of pipeline. A pumping station usually uses about five to eight machines for gas pumping, with a total station horsepower of about 12,000 to 20,000 HP. Independent market surveys showed about 5,000 domestic reciprocating machines were being used to pump natural gas. Windrock was very optimistic about this market segment for two reasons. First, this was the segment with which Windrock was most familiar thanks to its years of R&D for the Gas Research Institute. Second, Windrock's analyzers could be used for both the engines and the pumps they powered because both were reciprocating designs. Despite these advantages, Windrock had yet to sell an analyzer to this market segment.

Gas and Oil Field Production

Reciprocating engines and compressors are heavily used in the production of oil and natural gas from wells both on land and offshore. Engine-driven compressors are used to pump natural gas from wells for delivery to pipelines. In addition, many reciprocating machines are used to inject natural gas back into oil wells in order to pressurize the oil well to improve the crude yield from the well. This technique is used extensively on offshore production units. Windrock's analyzers could be used on both the engines and the compressors and pumps they are powering. Windrock lacked reliable data on the size of this market segment, but the company believed it was conceivable that every offshore drilling platform or oilpatch could justify investing in the type of analysis Windrock's technology offered.

Petrochemical Production

The oil-refining and chemical industries have many electrical motor-driven reciprocating compressors that are critical components of their operation. Typically, these units are used for hydrogen and other non–natural gas compression duties where the gas is used in the refining process. When one of these units fails, that portion of the refinery is effectively shut down until the machine is repaired or replaced. Based on Steve Follmar's experience with this industry, Windrock estimated that about 2,000 of these critical machines could use the technology of on-line or portable performance monitoring to increase the availability and profitability of the refining and chemical industry.

Marine Propulsion

The marine shipping industry relies heavily on very large reciprocating diesel engines for propulsion and power generation. Windrock felt this was a prime market opportunity for both continuous and portable monitoring by its products. Windrock felt that the leading competitor in this market was relatively weak because its products had a historical record of being unreliable and hard to use. Windrock lacked any basis for estimating the size of this market.

Electricity Generation

Using stationary generators for production of electrical power was becoming increasingly popular domestically for both standby emergency power (backup power supplies for critical applications like hospitals) and co-generation facilities (continuous generation with excess power sold back to local utilities). This segment was largely untapped, and Windrock was pioneering entry into this market thanks to a $70,000 purchase order from Brooklyn Union Gas Co. The analyzer purchased was to be permanently installed at an unmanned co-generation plant at a New York hospital. For this particular application, Windrock built in the "intelligence" required for its analyzer to automatically place telephone calls and page engineers and operators whenever it detected problems in an engine. In the foreign market, diesel engine–driven generators represent a substantial portion of total electric power generation, particularly in third world and island nations. Windrock did not know what the size of this market was, but it was believed to be "huge."

Railroads

Railroads operate large fleets of diesel-powered locomotive engines. Windrock did not know if there was a potential market or not for onboard monitoring systems to be installed aboard locomotives. But, Windrock had had a number of discussions with CSX, a large railroad company, about providing a Test Stand (monitoring and diagnostic system) at each of its overhaul centers to allow for automated data acquisition and analysis capabilities of its diesel engines prior to a major overhaul. It is anticipated that this system would be a slightly modified version of the 6100, and Windrock was excited about potential demand in this market segment.

Mining

Open pit mines rely on self-propelled drag-line shovels for extracting materials. These are large complex machines in a very demanding environment. Windrock had designed and manufactured a custom system for Barrick Goldstrike mines, a well respected company in the mining industry. Barrick Goldstrike reported that the system had already saved them hundreds of thousands of dollars in maintenance costs and downtime by detecting and alarming on a number of developing problems. One instance alone saved an estimated $250,000 because of early detection and correction of a developing gearbox problem.

WINDROCK'S COMPETITION

The market for reciprocating engine analyzers was dominated by two or three firms that accounted for an estimated 90 percent of all sales.

Beta Products

Windrock considered its major competition to be Beta Products, a subsidiary of Liberty Technologies, Inc. Beta produced portable instrumentation, using hardware and technology first assembled around 1985 that had undergone little improvement in recent years. Windrock believed that Beta had a long history of uneconomical production and largely ineffective sales strategies. But, Beta had still been effective in gaining market share since it had faced little competition in recent years due to the slow decline of GET (see below). Beta's portable reciprocating analyzer, the RECIP-TRAP, was priced in the $35,000 to $55,000 range, depending on options selected, and Windrock estimated that between 500 and 600 of the units had been sold, with recent sales running at about 50 units per year. The RECIP-TRAP featured one megabyte of memory that could be downloaded to a PC, but the process typically required 30 minutes to complete. A small (1.5" × 7") graphics screen was also available, but Windrock's engineers considered the screen to be of such low resolution that it was primarily useful for checking to see that the analyzer was receiving a good signal. Windrock believed that Beta held approximately 90 percent of the market for portable reciprocating analyzers.

Gas Equipment Testing (GET)

This company had long produced what was generally considered to be the best instrument for reciprocating machine analysis available. GET's main product was the

PFM 2000 Reciprocating Machine Analyzer, first introduced in 1980. It was a very reliable and accurate analyzer, but the equipment was very large and not portable. It also required 110VAC power and it was rack mounted (i.e., it was designed to be stored permanently on an erect frame). It was common to see the GET analyzer rack mounted in a van that could be parked near the engine to be analyzed and connected via long cables. Though accurate, the equipment was difficult to use, needing at least two people to operate, and it required years of experience to best evaluate its output. The typical engine analysis required between two and three hours, and the original models could not download data to a PC. Instead, the GET analyzer used a standard oscilloscope as its display device, and its only recording device was a camera that could take black and white Polaroid "instant" pictures of the oscilloscope's screen. Records from the typical analysis on these models might entail as many as 150 such photographs. More recent models could store one megabyte of information, but this only included data reading on one pressure plus two calculated variables. GET had done little in recent years to improve the product, and Windrock felt the company only existed at a "subsistence level." The PFM 2000 was priced in the $45,000 to $65,000 range depending on options, and Windrock thought that between 300 and 400 units had been sold.

Bentley-Nevada

This was the third firm Windrock could identify in its market. Although Bentley-Nevada was a much larger company than the other competitors and it provided a wide range of products related to engine operation, Windrock felt Bentley-Nevada's greatest threat to Windrock was its on-line products. Although the capabilities of Bentley's reciprocating analyzers were limited, Windrock felt the size of Bentley warranted its close observation.

WINDROCK'S SALES AND MANUFACTURING PLANS

Windrock currently had contracts with five independent sales representatives in the United States and was negotiating with two additional firms. All these representatives were experienced with predictive maintenance products, and all but two had ongoing relationships with CSI. The CSI sales department had also expressed a strong interest in partnering with Windrock to provide its CSI customer base with reciprocating machinery products to complement CSI's rotary machine analyzers. Windrock believed it to be in its best interest to develop a close working relationship with CSI's Domestic Sales Department to gain access to its large customer base; however, details had not yet been arranged.

CSI also had a worldwide distribution network of independent representative firms which Windrock could potentially access if it decided to pursue international sales. Windrock had already begun discussions with a number of these firms both in Latin America and the Middle East. The company hoped to begin pursuing international sales of the Model 6300 Portable Analyzer as soon as it had adequate field experience to assure that it was free of design defects. International sales of on-line systems would require significant local support and technical expertise, but the company hoped to develop a plan to provide training, installation services, and technical support for international sales.

CSI had offered to manufacture all or any portion of Windrock products for 7 percent over CSI's cost. This was to include purchasing and inventorying components, and testing of final assemblies. CSI had capabilities for a wide variety of manufacturing technologies including surface-mount automated equipment, and a testing department that met many of the industry's most stringent certification standards.

WINDROCK'S MANAGEMENT TEAM

In August of 1996, Windrock employed three individuals: Will Griffith, Steve Follmar, and Ed Flanagan. Griffith received his BS and MS degrees in Mechanical Engineering from the University of Tennessee. After graduate school, he took a position in 1987 with Alcoa, providing technical and engineering support for a large automated materials-handling system. After that work was completed, he started work for Windrock when it was an R&D subsidiary for CSI. His first assignment was research on a flow-calibration procedure for NASA. After that, he joined the small research team that was doing contract research for the Gas Research Institute on improving diagnostics for the large reciprocating engines that were used to pump natural gas through the network of gas pipelines. This was the work that eventually led to the development of Windrock's product line, and from the outset of this work, Will took the lead in developing Windrock's analyzer software. The hardware in Windrock's products was largely available "off the shelf," but the company's software was proprietary, and had resulted from several years of funded research.

Steve Follmar received his BS in business from California State at Fullerton. Upon graduation, he accepted a sales position with Bentley-Nevada, an engineering and construction company, where he worked for 13 years, specializing in sales of instrumentation primarily for large-scale petroleum production. He spent several years as head of the Gulf Coast region, the company's largest sales territory. He left the company to join Tri-Sea, a start-up business that produced triple redundant fault-tolerant digital engine governors for critical applications such as the space shuttle. Tri-Sea fared poorly in competition with older and larger competitors in its markets, and after 11 months, Follmar moved to Beta, an upstart competitor against Bentley-Nevada in the engine diagnostics market. Within four years, Beta grew from $1 million in sales to $7 million in sales, at which time it was sold to Liberty Technologies. At that point, Follmar came to Windrock, where he focused on developing a market for the company's portable analyzers.

Ed Flanagan received his BS and MS degrees in Electrical Engineering from the University of Tennessee. Upon graduation, he went to work in Martin Marietta's aerospace division, where he helped design the electronics for missile guidance systems. After two years, he transferred to Martin Marietta's nuclear division, where he did development work on instrumentation for chemical analysis. He was hired by Windrock as one of its earliest employees to do work on data acquisition under research contracts on engine performance from GRI and the Department of Defense. Ed provided the electronic designs for Windrock's hardware.

THE DECISION AND THE FUTURE

When CSI decided to close down Windrock, it offered Will, Steve, and Ed an opportunity to buy the company for $250,000. CSI provided Windrock with the balance sheet presented in Exhibit 2. Will, Steve, and Ed collaborated to generate the projected balance sheet and income statement presented in Exhibit 3 and Exhibit 4, respectively. CSI's offer required 10 percent of the purchase amount at closing, with the remainder financed by a five-year interest-free loan from CSI that was to be secured by Windrock stock along with the personal guarantees from Will, Steve, and Ed. The deal included very strong "no-compete" language that worked each way to protect

---

EXHIBIT 2
Windrock Balance Sheet, August 5, 1996

Assets

Current assets	
Accounts receivable	$ 92,121
Inventory	190,130
Total current assets	$282,251
Fixed assets	
Computer equipment	$ 11,793
Machinery and equipment	1,288
Furniture and fixtures	2,254
Vehicles	17,176
Less: Accumulated depreciation	(25,925)
Total fixed assets	$ 6,586
Other assets	
Deposits	$ 2,943
Total other assets	$ 2,943
Total assets	$291,780

Liabilities and Stockholders' Equity

Current liabilities	
Accounts payable	$ 13,294
Total current liabilities	$ 13,294
Stockholders' equity	
Common stock	$ 10,000
Additional paid-in-capital	947,429
Retained earnings	(509,572)
Profit year-to-date (aftertax)	(169,372)
Total stockholders' equity	$278,485
Total liabilities/stockholders' equity	$291,779

EXHIBIT 3
Windrock Five-Year Plan Pro Forma Balance Sheet
(in thousands of constant dollars)

	Opening	1996	1997	1998	1999	2000	2001
Current assets							
Opening cash		$ 0	$(128)	$(143)	$ (20)	$260	$ 774
Cash flow		$(128)	$ (15)	$ 122	$280	$515	$ 792
Cash balance		$(128)	$(143)	$ (20)	$260	$774	$1,566
Opening accounts receivable	$ 92						
Write down	$(70.8)						
Adjusted accounts receivable	$ 21.3						
Accounts receivable	$ 21	$ 101	$ 133	$ 197	$271	$368	$ 485
Opening inventory	$ 190						
Write down	$ (20)						
Adjusted opening inventory	$ 170						
Inventory (2 months' COGS)	$ 170	$ 178	$ 203	$ 241	$292	$361	$ 452
Work in progress	$ 0	$ 11	$ 15	$ 22	$ 30	$ 41	$ 54
Fixed assets							
Opening fixed assets							
Computer equipment	$ 12						
Machinery & equipment	$ 1						
Furniture	$ 2						
Vehicles	$ 17						
Less: Accumulated depreciation	$ (26)						
Total opening fixed assets	$ 7						
Total fixed assets	$ 7	$ 17	$ 21	$ 23	$ 24	$25	$ 26
Accounts payable	$ 13	$ 11	$ 15	$ 22	$ 30	$41	$ 54

both Windrock and CSI. Finally, the contract stipulated that CSI would agree to manufacture Windrock products for 7 percent over its costs and that CSI would agree to represent Windrock products through the CSI's distributor network. There was no offer to find jobs for the Windrock employees inside CSI if they decided not to buy the business.

Will, Steve, and Ed were given approximately three weeks to accept or reject the offer. They had never planned to become entrepreneurs, and wondered if they were cut out for it. The two leading firms in the market had only sold about 1,000 machines in over a decade of trying, and Windrock had sold only a handful of products in its entire lifetime. Will, Steve, and Ed acknowledged that the executives at CSI who wanted to be rid of Windrock had much more business experience than the three of them, and they wondered how they could expect to make something of a business that CSI was giving up on. With their experience, all three men felt that they could

EXHIBIT 4
Windrock Five-Year Plan Pro Forma Income Statement
(in thousands of constant dollars)

Sales and Contribution	Assumed Rates	1996	1997	1998	1999	2000	2001
6100 sales		$ 75	$200	$ 300	$ 450	$ 600	$ 900
COGS	14%	11	28	42	63	84	126
Sales commission	15%	11	30	45	67	90	135
Contribution		53	142	213	320	426	639
6200 sales		$ 40	$ 80	$ 160	$ 200	$ 300	$ 400
COGS	18%	7	14	29	36	54	72
Sales commission	15%	6	12	24	30	45	60
Contribution		27	54	107	134	201	268
6300 sales		$165	$495	$ 660	$ 770	$ 825	$ 825
COGS	18%	30	89	119	139	149	149
Sales commission	15%	25	74	99	116	124	124
Contribution		111	332	442	516	553	552
6400 sales		$ 0	$ 90	$ 150	$ 300	$ 600	$ 900
COGS	25%	0	16	27	54	108	162
Sales commission	15%	0	14	23	45	90	135
Contribution		0	60	101	201	402	603
6500 sales		$ 0	$ 21	$ 42	$ 84	$ 126	$ 210
COGS	20%	0	4	8	15	23	38
Sales commission	15%	0	3	6	13	19	32
Contribution		0	14	28	56	84	141
Total sales		$280	$886	$1,312	$1,804	$2,451	$3,235
Total COGS		$ 48	$151	$ 225	$ 307	$ 418	$ 547
Total sales commission		$ 42	$133	$ 197	$ 271	$ 368	$ 486
Total contribution		$191	$602	$ 891	$1,227	$1,666	$2,203
Salary #1 Steve		$ 25	$ 60	$ 60	$ 70	$ 80	$ 100
Salary #2 Will		23	55	60	70	80	100
Salary #3 Ed		25	60	60	70	80	100
Salary #4 other		51	152	156	186	186	186
Benefits		10	26	27	32	34	39
Factory expenses		3	6	6	6	6	6
Shop supplies		3	6	6	6	6	6
Equipment maintenance		1	3	3	3	3	3
Warranty		8	27	39	54	74	97
Rent		3	7	7	7	7	7
Depreciation		2	6	7	8	8	8
Extraordinary start-up expense		13					
Total managed costs		$167	$408	$ 431	$ 512	$ 564	$ 652
Telephone expense		$ 3	$ 7	$ 7	$ 7	$ 7	$ 7
Travel expense		20	48	48	48	48	48
Auto expense		5	12	12	12	12	12
Business promotion		3	6	6	6	6	6
Liability insurance		3	9	13	18	25	32
Professional fees		6	5	5	5	5	5
Job training—expense		2	5	5	5	5	5
Office supplies		1	1	1	1	1	1

(Continued)

EXHIBIT 4 (continued)
**Windrock Five-Year Plan Pro Forma Income Statement
(in thousands of constant dollars)**

Sales and Contribution	Assumed Rates	1996	1997	1998	1999	2000	2001
Building maintenance		1	2	2	2	2	2
Bad debts		6	18	26	36	49	65
Memberships/associations		1	1	1	1	1	1
Advertising		13	30	30	30	30	30
Cartage and delivery		1	1	1	1	1	1
Total expenses		$ 65	$145	$157	$172	$192	$ 215
Income before taxes		$ (38)	$ 49	$301	$542	$909	$1,335
IBT carried forward		$ (38)	$ 11	$301	$542	$909	$1,335
Income tax		$ 0	$ 3	$ 75	$135	$227	$ 334
Income after taxes		$ (38)	$ 46	$226	$406	$682	$1,001

get jobs elsewhere in a reasonably short amount of time, but with families to raise and bills to pay, unemployment was not something to be taken lightly. Of course, the same could be said for going into debt to buy an unproven company. On the other hand, Will, Ed, and Steve had worked hard to develop the product, and had always assumed that there was a market for it that CSI would be able to profitably tap.

As the three friends sat and pondered what their decision should be, they realized that the decision on whether or not to buy the business depended in large part on what they could do with it once it was purchased, and they were not sure what this might be. If they were to buy the business, they had to put their money down and sign the contract in 48 hours, and the hours seemed to slip by more quickly as the deadline approached.

http://www.jdedwards.com/industry/webaec/ppmout.htm
http://www.compsys.com/

INDUSTRY SPECIFIC: PLASTICS

CASE 5

Fraser River Plastics Ltd.*

It was early in 1993. Elinore Wickham-Jones, President of Fraser River Plastics Ltd., was uneasy about the crosscurrents of opinion that were developing regarding the company's future direction. Although the differences of view had perhaps been held for some time, they had surfaced in recent weeks as the merits of several projects—among them a move toward international expansion and an acquisition—were being reviewed. There was, Wickham-Jones felt, more than normal agitation in the atmosphere. Lines were hardening on the questions of how aggressively, and in what direction, the company should proceed.

THE CANADIAN PLASTICS PROCESSING INDUSTRY IN 1993

Although the history of plastics and plastic products goes back over 100 years, in 1993 the industry was still generally regarded in North America as young and growing. In fact, it had only been since the Second World War that plastic had begun to achieve its status as a major primary or substitute manufacturing material.

In 1993, there were over 1,400 firms engaged in plastic processing in Canada, with most of the companies located in Ontario and Quebec. Of these Canadian firms, the majority had sales of less than $2 million. The bulk of company shipments constituted proprietary products. The remainder were either produced on a custom basis or as "captive operations" for a larger manufacturing entity. This breakdown, however, was difficult to confirm precisely, due to the variety of business practices in which any one manufacturing concern engaged.

In terms of the future, world shipments in the plastic processing industry were estimated in 1993 to be moderately "favourable" given the tentative signals of economic recovery. The factors contribution to this projection were an anticipated moderate level of economic growth; a continuing substitution of plastics for traditional materials; and the emergent growth in the manufacturing sector. Costs depended largely on the type of process used. For instance, reinforced plastic products (e.g., boats and storage tanks) were relatively labour-intensive, whereas extrusion products (e.g., pipes, films, etc.) were relatively capital-intensive.

In comparison with other global industries the plastics industry was still considered a labour-intensive area. For example, in plastics the capital investment per production-related employee ranged between Cdn$5,000 and $42,000, while in petrochemicals it was about Cdn$200,000.

It was anticipated that Canadian plastic manufacturing capacity would be sufficient to meet Canadian demands. In addition, Canadian resin prices, which at one time exceeded world prices by 10 percent, were seen as becoming more competitive with U.S. and other international prices, given the recent Canada–U.S. Free Trade Agreement. The prospect, in 1993, of a potential free trade agreement between Canada, the United States, and Mexico was expected to result in significant downward pressure on world prices and consolidation of the North American industry participants through mergers and bankruptcies.

CORPORATE HISTORY

The Early Years: 1984 to 1988

In the fall of 1984, two Vancouver, British Columbia, businessmen, Herbert Rudd and Oliver Farthingham, visited Portland, Oregon, on a tour sponsored by the Vancouver Board of Trade. Of the several plants they visited, one facility, Damian Plastics Inc., particularly caught their attention. This plant used an injection moulding process to manufacture heavy plastic products such as utility crates, garbage cans, and packing cartons. Damian used advanced techniques to minimize the raw material weight in the large products it produced, while retaining, through unique design, the essential rigidity and toughness. Both men, and especially Farthingham, who had experience in plastics, felt there was a ready market for the products in Canada because (1) they would have a competitive edge over comparable but more expensive plastic products and (2) they could be used instead of their metal counterparts. The two men returned home with a tentative licensing agreement for all of Canada which included technical assistance from Damian and access to all mould designs.

The immediate problem facing Rudd and Farthingham was raising the $160,000 equity needed to build a plant and get into operation. By November, they had put together a group of local businesspeople and raised the required funds. Some of the backers, like Elinore Wickham-Jones, were associated with wholesale and industrial supply firms and could assist by providing initial markets for the new plant's output. On December 9, 1984, the company was incorporated under the name of Fraser River Plastics Ltd. Its three major shareholders were Farthingham (20 percent), Wickham-Jones (18 percent), and Rudd (13 percent). Farthingham became Fraser River's first president. Rudd was made secretary-treasurer, and Wickham-Jones became a vice president.

Rudd located a 2-acre site for the company's manufacturing plant in Chilliwack, British Columbia—a small town near Vancouver. Tenders were called on the building's construction in February 1985, and manufacturing equipment was ordered. During this early period, the company was being run by the three officers on a part-time basis, since all had their own full-time businesses as well. On April 1, 1985, Gunther Heinzman, a former plant manager of a Victoria plastics firm, was hired as general manager of Fraser River.

Heinzman recalled:

> Elinore took me out to the site in Chilliwack. It was just a ploughed field! A few days later we did the first public showing of our products at a trade fair in Victoria. All that I had available was two plastic garbage cans, three sizes of the packing cartons, and six pieces of Damian's literature.
>
> One week later, the first carload of products arrived from Portland. Most of it had to be stored in a small warehouse owned by one of our shareholders since there were no storage facilities yet.

In August 1985, production began at Chilliwack while finishing touches were made on the plant. There was a ready and substantial demand for the products. The price, although high, was accepted, and the products were acceptable substitutes for conventional products. It was not long before the company was operating in the black.

Through 1986, the company's operations expanded dramatically. A temporary office annex was erected at the Chilliwack site, and the plant's capacity was increased to accommodate demand. Substantial orders for the company's products also came in from Alberta. To cut transportation costs and get local exposure, Fraser River purchased an empty plant in Calgary, ordered equipment, and hired a general manager to take charge there. The Calgary plant was in full operation by June 1986.

In time, Fraser River's success became known among those familiar with plastics processing. Not surprisingly, in 1987 another group of entrepreneurs set up a facility to produce similar injection moulding products; their plant was in Prince Rupert, British Columbia. Fraser River had no legal remedy, since the products and processes it licensed from Damian were poorly protected by patents. In addition, the initial barriers to entry—such as the special moulds and know-how—started to crumble. Although the new firm marketed its products under its own name, there was little, save some cosmetic design differences, to distinguish the Prince Rupert products from those manufactured by Fraser River. As one company executive put it, "The plant in Prince Rupert was the first time we really experienced direct competition."

Fraser River's response was an offer to purchase the Prince Rupert competitor. This offer was accepted in November 1987, and Fraser River retained the old company's major shareholder as general manager. The purchase was not well received, however, by the Prince Rupert company's minority shareholders. They took their proceeds from the sale and shortly thereafter set up another injection moulding plant, in Nanaimo, British Columbia.

By 1988, Wickham-Jones and Farthingham had become concerned about the limitations of the present three-person board in light of the company's growth and changing external circumstances. There were also signs, particularly in relation to the acquisition of the Prince Rupert company, that some of Fraser River's minority shareholders were disturbed and would like to see a broader representation of views at the board level. As a consequence, three new members were added to Fraser River's board: Owen Palmer, head of a local supermarket chain; Joanna Young, a management consultant who ran the local office of a large national firm; and Michelle O'Reilly, Fraser River's legal counsel.

Up to this point, the organization of the company had been loosely structured. Each of the firm's plants—in Chilliwack, Calgary, and Prince Rupert—had its own managers and field sales force reporting to Gunther Heinzman, the company's general manager. Wickham-Jones, Farthingham, and Rudd were considered the overall management committee. They had the primary responsibility for major decisions such as site selection, price, expansion, and capital investments, but they were also involved on an ad hoc basis in many overlapping operating functions.

The First Transition: 1989 to 1992

At the suggestion of Farthingham, Joanna Young reviewed the company's organization in early 1989 to "assess the marketing strengths and weaknesses of the company and to suggest desirable changes." Her principal recommendation was as follows:

> There is a clear need for greater continuity, consistency and detail in the top supervision of overall operations. The current dispersed nature of responsibilities among the company's executives should be focussed in the hands of a single chief executive with time for close day-to-day contact with the organization. As chief executive officer, this person would be responsible for all company operations and for initiating and implementing policy changes with the concurrence of the board.

Prior to submitting her report, Young reviewed its content with Farthingham and discussed the need for a full-time president. Farthingham agreed with the notion, but noted that his own commitments in other companies prevented him from assuming this expanded role. It was not, in any case, his cup of tea: "I've always considered myself a front-man, an entrepreneur, a hustler." As a consequence, Farthingham suggested that he become chair and Wickham-Jones become president. In taking on the president's role, Wickham-Jones agreed to reduce the time spent on her family business and to run Fraser River on a full-time basis.

At the time of the reorganization, Gunther Heinzman was made manufacturing vice president. Although his title changed, his operating duties with respect to plant operation and supervision remained the same.

Heinzman commented on the reorganization:

> It was an inevitable change. As general manager, I didn't have the time needed to run the sales organization. I didn't like the pressure at the top. Besides, my strength is manufacturing. That's what I know best and that's where I'm most comfortable.

Shortly after the reorganization, Lucas Feck was hired for the position of marketing vice president. Feck recounted his early days:

> I suppose it was the entrepreneurial attitude and capabilities of the people at Fraser River which attracted me to the company. It was like running my own business; there was freedom to run things as I thought they should be.

When I joined, Fraser River had experienced no stiff competition from new entrants yet. The company was begging for more structure and policies in its administration. For instance, at Calgary, the sales manager had no fixed sales price. Hell, there wasn't even a price list, so no one in the marketplace—including our customers—knew what the prices of the products were from one day to the next. There was no fixed collection policy for the company, and there was a high turnover in sales personnel.

During my first eighteen months, I restructured the sales organization. I set up the company's first sales forecast and budgets for each territory and established a reporting system so that salespeople knew how they and their region were doing on a monthly basis. I even instituted an advertising budget—another first!

Throughout 1989, the company continued to grow. Demand was strong and prices were reasonable in spite of the advent of significant competition and an emerging economic recession. The year was also marked by two acquisitions: Beaver Plastics in Vancouver, British Columbia, and Simcoe Plastics of Kamloops, British Columbia.

Beaver Plastics was a company owned by Farthingham which manufactured plastic pipe using an extrusion moulding process. In late 1989, Farthingham expressed concern over having to wear two hats in promoting the products of both Fraser River and Beaver. Even customers were associating the two firms as one. Sales representatives from the two companies often called on the same wholesaler/distributor accounts. In fact, some of Fraser River's fittings were made to fit the plastic pipe produced by Beaver. At the same time, Fraser River was looking for opportunities to expand its product lines. With this in mind, in early 1990 Farthingham offered his company for sale to the board of Fraser River. The sale was negotiated for cash and debt, and by year's end Wickham-Jones reported that the sales, profits, and growth resulting from the acquisition were "very encouraging."

Simcoe Plastics was a family-owned operation which manufactured plastic shower curtains and raincoats using a manufacturing process known as calendering. In October of 1989, Wickham-Jones heard the company was for sale. She believed that the purchase of Simcoe would provide Fraser River with instant product diversification as well as give Fraser River the capability of producing other items, such as plastic wall coverings and backing for upholstery fabrics.

Fraser River completed its purchase of Simcoe by November 1989. The most significant operational change involved experimentation with the production of plastic coated wall coverings. By doing so, the company hoped to take up the apparent slack in Simcoe's manufacturing facilities.

Despite the worsening recession, Fraser River concluded its 1990 fiscal year on a particularly strong note (see Exhibit 1 for 5-year financial statements). The strong profit showing, however, did not completely compensate for a number of developing problems:

1. The plant manager in the Calgary manufacturing facility was fired because of a failure to reduce inefficiencies and waste in the plant.

2. Inefficiency was also a problem at Simcoe, although the waste factor had been reduced substantially since the company's acquisition. Simcoe was experimenting with production of new plastic products. Costs there were mounting rapidly, a matter of increasing concern to Fraser River executives. Some blamed these prob-

EXHIBIT 1
Fraser River Plastics Ltd.: Consolidated Statement of Operations (Audited, December 31, 1992) with Comparative Figures for 1991, 1990, 1989, 1988 (in thousands of dollars)

	1992	1991	1990	1989	1988
		Balance Sheet			
		Assets			
Current assets					
Cash	$ 25	$ 30	$ 5	$ 565	$ 110
Term deposits and marketable securities	—	583	2	—	690
Accounts receivable	2,453	1,155	1,215	423	540
Inventories	3,827	2,625	1,923	2,163	357
Deposits	13	25	140	2	3
Total current assets	$ 6,318	$4,418	$3,285	$3,153	$1,700
Property, plant, and equipment, at cost					
Less: Accumulated depreciation	4,453	2,935	2,743	1,940	1,468
Other assets	17	28	7	15	60
Excess of cost of subsidiaries over the net book value of acquired assets, at cost less amortization	105	145	185	105	130
Total assets	$10,893	$7,526	$6,220	$5,213	$3,358
		Liabilities and Shareholders' Equity			
Current liabilities					
Bank overdraft and loan	$ 2,348	$ 863	$ 515		
Accounts payable and accrued charges	892	1,042	338	$1,063	$ 145
Income and other taxes payable	618	738	962	1,065	260
Royalty payable	—	—	70	90	400
Total current liabilities	$ 3,858	$2,643	$1,885	$2,218	$ 805
Deferred revenue	28	33	33		
Long-term debt	3,150	1,120	1,282	715	875
Total liabilities	$ 7,036	$3,796	$3,200	$2,933	$1,680
Shareholders' equity					
Preferred shares	—	—	—	—	$ 253
Common shares	$ 205	$ 205	$ 205	$ 32	32
Contributed surplus	70	70	70	70	70
Retained earnings	3,582	3,465	2,745	2,198	1,323
Total shareholders' equity	$ 3,857	$3,740	$3,020	$2,300	$1,678
Total liabilities and shareholders' equity	$10,893	$7,536	$6,220	$5,233	$3,358
	Statement of Income and Selected Financial Ratios				
Net sales	$16,445	$15,750	$10,903	$7,835	$5,403
Cost of sales	11,228	10,765	7,178	3,990	3,455
Gross profit	$ 5,217	$ 4,985	$ 3,725	$3,845	$1,948
Selling, general, and administrative expenses	$ 3,605	$ 2,750	$ 1,898	$ 838	$ 655
Royalty expense	332	332	332	625	338
Total	$ 3,937	$ 3,082	$ 2,230	$1,463	$ 993

(Continued)

EXHIBIT 1 (continued)

Operating profit	$ 1,280	$ 1,903	$ 1,495	$2,382	$ 955
Interest and other income	128	135	40	163	80
Total	$ 1,408	$ 2,038	$ 1,535	$2,545	$1,035
Interest, long-term debt	$ 493	$ 138	$ 92	$ 70	$ 77
Amortization of excess cost of subsidiaries over net book value of acquired assets	40	40	35	27	
Total	$ 533	$ 178	$ 127	$ 97	$ 77
Earnings before income taxes	$ 875	$ 1,860	$ 1,408	$2,448	$ 958
Income taxes	480	825	610	1,208	453
Net earnings	$ 395	$ 1,035	$ 798	$1,240	$ 505
Earnings per common share	$ 0.08	$ 0.20	$ 0.15	$ 0.24	$ 0.10
Dividends paid	278	315	251	365	
Dividends per common share	0.05	0.06	0.05	0.07	
Selected financial ratios					
Current assets/current liabilities	1.6	1.7	1.7	1.4	2.1
Total assets/total liabilities	1.5	2.0	1.9	1.8	2.0
Long-term debt/equity	0.8	0.3	0.4	0.3	0.5
Gross profit/net sales	0.32	0.32	0.34	0.49	0.36
Inventory turnover	2.9	4.1	3.7	1.8	9.7
SG&A expense/gross profit	0.69	0.55	0.51	0.22	0.34
EBIT/gross profit	0.17	0.37	0.38	0.64	0.49

lems on overreliance on the management that Fraser River had inherited when it bought Simcoe. For example, the plant manager, who had remained when the firm was acquired by Fraser River, did not have the necessary qualifications to successfully oversee the plant's experimental work. As a consequence, he was fired in May 1990, and Heinzman was instructed to supervise more closely the operation of the plant and its product development activities.

3. Two large competitors had entered Fraser River's traditional markets. One, Moldform Ltd., was a subsidiary of a large conglomerate organization. The other, Plastech Ltd., was a division of a company involved in other plastic processing operations. Both operated in British Columbia and Alberta. Market shares were unknown, but a rough estimate gave Fraser River about 40 percent of the western market and 15 percent each to Moldform and Plastech. The balance of 30 percent was made up by many small companies manufacturing partial lines and capitalizing on low overheads and local contacts to operate.

In 1991, the demand for Fraser River products in British Columbia softened, due mostly to increased competition and local market saturation.

To expand the market, the company built a manufacturing facility in Winnipeg, Manitoba. Sales of Fraser River's products in mid-Western Canada had risen during the past several years, but transportation costs had reduced the firm's competitive position and profit margin. The risk of entering the region against established competition was accepted by company executives. The company also had encouraging internal projections covering the size and future growth of the eastern market. (Exhibit 2 shows financial results by separate facilities, through 1992.)

At a board meeting, Wickham-Jones later informed the other members that because of the decline in market growth and increasing competition, particularly in British Columbia, she and Marketing VP Lucas Feck were investigating numerous potential corporate acquisitions for Fraser River, including a car dealership, a precision tool manufacturing operation, a hotel, and a corrugated steel manufacturing operation. To date, no "deal" has been consummated.

In September 1992, Wickham-Jones hired Clayton Dunwood as Fraser River's vice president for administration. Dunwood assumed complete responsibility for the accounting and financial affairs of the company. Wickham-Jones felt that Dunwood would be of particular help to her in the area of investigation of future corporate acquisitions. However, Lucas Feck continued to be especially disappointed with Fraser River's efforts in this area. He commented on Fraser River's need for new companies:

> Since 1989 I have been pushing other senior managers to find new areas for investment and growth. Fraser River's bread-and-butter products have become commodity items. The industry is easy to enter. We have to have other businesses to support the overheads which have built up in the company. When I look at our markets here in British Columbia, I don't see anywhere to go, . . . and it looks like it's going to be an uphill battle to crack the eastern market. That's why I firmly believe that we should be planning our growth more— with, say, 20 percent coming from new acquisitions.
>
> We haven't had a new company here in some time. It's very frustrating when you consider the number of firms that we've looked at. Of course, you get people like Joanna Young and that lawyer, O'Reilly. Whenever we bring a good acquisition to the board, they're always harping on how there are better deals around. Yet, they can't suggest any themselves.

Through 1992, Wickham-Jones also pursued another venture. Through various publications, she was aware of the need for the type of products produced by Fraser River in other parts of the world, particularly in the lesser developed countries (LDCs) in Asia. This represented an opportunity for Fraser River, with its accumulated expertise in plastic products. Wickham-Jones concentrated her efforts on finding a partner to provide the acumen and international contacts which Fraser River lacked. Preliminary discussions were held with one such partner—a Canadian manufacturer of logging and sawmill equipment with sales offices in a number of foreign countries and a record of joint venture projects with nationals of those countries (mainly to set up logging and sawmill operations). The proposed agreement was for the two companies to form a joint venture limited partnership supplying capital, equipment, and expertise for new ventures in the manufacture of plastic products. Hopefully, Canadian-based resin suppliers could be brought into the deal. Conscious of the reactions multinationals received when they "invaded the LDCs," the joint venture company was to keep a low profile in its international undertakings.

By December, Wickham-Jones reported that she had identified several countries in Asia as possible sites for a first undertaking. The pursuit of the joint venture's arrangements was, for the most part, being conducted by Wickham-Jones alone. She was, many felt, personally committed to the project and was devoting more and more of her time to it. Wickham-Jones commented:

EXHIBIT 2

Fraser River Plastics Ltd.: Unaudited Operating Statements (Unconsolidated)
(in thousands of dollars)

	Chilliwack & Prince Rupert			Calgary			Manitoba & Toronto*			Beaver Plastics		Simcoe Plastics	
	1992	1991	1990	1992	1991	1990	1992	1991	1990	1992	1991	1992	1991
Dollar sales	$6,365	$6,790	$6,115	$6,710	$5,180	$4,365	$ 335	$403	$75	$2,950	$3,660	$1,303	$1,318
Discounts	275	220	310	153	183	175	20	33	5	57	50	28	20
Net sales	$6,090	$6,570	$5,805	$6,557	$4,997	$4,190	$ 315	$370	$70	$2,893	$3,610	$1,275	$1,298
Cost of goods sold	4148	4,420	4,075	4,412	3,332	2,748	312	280	50	2,265	2,765	930	1,073
Gross margin	$1,942	$2,150	$1,730	$2,145	$1,665	$1,442	$ 3	$90	$20	$ 628	$ 845	$ 345	$ 225
Operating costs	1,382	1,093	920	1,190	847	657	153	95	48	733	580	278	313
Royalty†	165	192	192	167	140	137							
Pretax profit (loss)	$ 395	$ 865	$ 618	$ 788	$ 678	$ 648	$ (150)	$ (5)	$(28)	$ (105)	$ 265	$ 67	$ (88)

*Toronto sales operations have been supplied with production from Manitoba and British Columbia plants.

†Each of the plants producing injection moulded products pays a royalty fee internally to Fraser River Plastics Ltd. The parent company in turn pays a royalty fee to its licensor (Damian) based on the total company production of such products, but to a limit of $332,000 as of 1991.

Sure, I'm committed. I really believe we can turn Fraser River into a worldwide organization and provide a useful service to other countries at the same time.

And, yes, this project is taking up a lot of my time. But that's because we don't know anything about operating on an international level. Once I know what's involved, I'll probably hire another vice president and put him in charge of our international operations. In addition, the universities are full of young aggressive people who can be brought on board to help "fill the gaps" created in Fraser River. . . . We should also be able to buy talent either from the market or other organizations. . . .

Exhibit 3 shows Fraser River's corporate structure as of the end of 1992, and Exhibit 4 is an unofficial organization chart for corporate headquarters.

THE SITUATION IN EARLY 1993

In January 1993, Wickham-Jones received drafts of Fraser River's financial statements for the 1992 fiscal year (see Exhibits 1 and 2). Overall, growth in company sales was sluggish, as a result of sharper competition—in particular, from smaller, local plastic manufacturing plants. These plants had contributed to the considerble market erosion experienced by Fraser River, especially in British Columbia. The company's share in Alberta, on the other hand, had remained strong. Profits had slipped a bit due to interest payments.

EXHIBIT 3
Fraser River Plastics Ltd. Corporate Structure

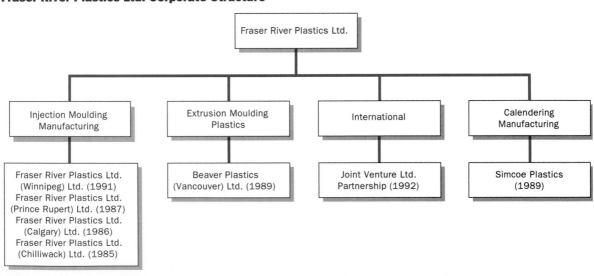

Notes: 1. All companies 100% owned by Fraser River Plastics Ltd. except potential joint venture (50%).
2. It was a general corporate policy to incorporate a separate company for each plant and business to ensure maximum limited liability.

Case writers' summary. No official organization charts existed at the company.

EXHIBIT 4
Fraser River Plastics Ltd. Corporate Headquarters Organization Chart (1992)

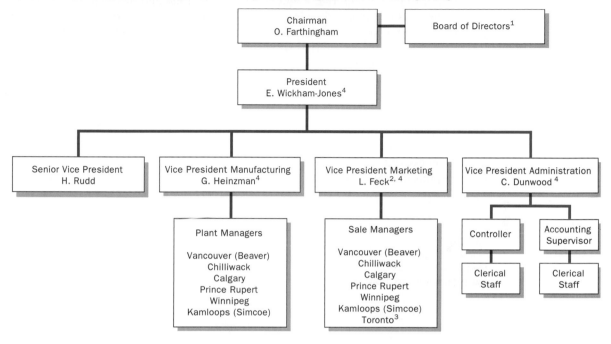

Notes: 1. Board members include O. Farthingham (Chairman), E. Wickham-Jones, H. Rudd, J. Young, M. J. O'Reilly, and Grant Ackerfeldt.
2. Feck was also President of Beaver Plastics Ltd.
3. One sales representative only.
4. Wickham-Jones's and Feck's offices are located in one corner of a wholesale warehouse owned by Wickham-Jones in Vancouver. Heinzman and Fraser River's accounting staff, on the other hand, are situated one hour's drive away at the Chilliwack plant. This arrangement suited Feck because he had been made President of Beaver Plastics—which was also located in Vancouver.

Case writers' summary. No official organization charts existed at the company.

Unfortunately, Simcoe Plastics had not made much progress. To improve the situation, a qualified and experienced plastics engineer had been hired in late 1992 to take over the plant. The board considered making Simcoe more independent, by hiring a general manager, but that action had been deferred for the moment.

Beaver Plastics was also in trouble. The British Columbia market for extruded pipe was saturated and extremely competitive. At present, there were few growth prospects unless the international and eastern projects began to take off. Unfortunately, the eastern market had become a sore spot. Acceptance of Fraser River's products had not been as favourable as initially thought. Despite this, Wickham-Jones forecast that within 2 years the Manitoba plant would be self-supporting.

In the meantime, two specific issues had arisen that required action. The first concerned the proposed international joint venture. Fraser River's potential partner in that venture had reported that preliminary inquiries conducted by its office in Indonesia had revealed substantial interest on the part of both government officials and local businesspeople. A request had been made for Fraser River to send an investigative team to Indonesia. Wickham-Jones felt that if she delayed a response too long, the "partner" might begin to doubt Fraser River's good faith or abilities to proceed.

In addition, Wickham-Jones had heard of another plastics company which was for sale and which, if acquired, might serve to strengthen and broaden Fraser River's product line. The company involved, Plasti-Weave, was located in Kelowna, British Columbia—approximately 80 kilometres away from the Chilliwack facility. Plasti-Weave was a very small operation with sales of less than $1 million in 1992 (see Exhibit 5). It had developed a significant and potentially patentable process for "weaving" plastic strips into strong sheets that could be used as substitutes for jute in carpet backing, furniture manufacture, etc. In 1992, Plasti-Weave realized that a major expansion would be required to exploit the potential of the new product. A new plant and warehouse would have to be built in Kelowna at an approximate cost of $750,000. The owner of Plasti-Weave, Clifford Bell, who was also the inventor of the manufacturing process, did not want to commit himself to this level of debt at the age of 62, or to be responsible for managing the company. Two recent heart attacks had resulted in

---

EXHIBIT 5
Fraser River Plastics Ltd.: Plasti-Weave Financial Statements—Year Ended December 31, 1992
(in thousands of dollars)

	1992	1991
Balance Sheet		
Current assets	$800	$619
Fixed assets (net)	70	57
Other assets	9	7
Total assets	$879	$683
Current liabilities	$183	$114
Deferred taxes	1	—
Long-term shareholder loan	77	64
Capital stock	1	1
Retained earnings	617	504
Total liabilities & equity	$879	$683
Statement of Income		
Sales	$950	$616
Other income—interest	4	2
Cost of goods sold	556	345
Expenses	192	148
Income taxes	77	28
Net income	$129	$ 97
Dividends paid	$ 16	$ 12
Selected financial ratios		
Current assets/current liabilities	4.4	5.4
Total assets/total liabilities	3.4	3.8
Long-term debt/equity	0.12	0.13
Gross profit/net sales	0.41	0.44

his decision to sell, if the price was right. However, one of the conditions of sale was that he be retained as a consultant to the company for at least 10 years.

Wickham-Jones was enthusiastic about acquiring Plasti-Weave, but was unsure what the board's reaction would be in light of the $1 million asking price. She was confident, nevertheless, that the board would approve the deal—if she pushed hard enough for it.

FRASER RIVER'S EXECUTIVES LOOK TO THE FUTURE

As the company considered 1992 results and considered the various paths it might follow in 1993, key executives voiced their own points of view.

Oliver Farthingham—Chairman of the Board

Oliver Farthingham began his own business on graduation from high school. He had interests in an automotive body repair business and a partnership in a Canadian distributorship for narrow-aisle forklift trucks. As chairman of the board, Farthingham's day-to-day involvement with Fraser River was limited, but this did not stop him from what he liked to do best—promote the Fraser River name. In fact, he was regarded as one of the most outspoken people in the company. Farthingham commented on Fraser River and its operations:

> As chairman, I'm a "positive thinker." I'm sure not a worrier. . . . I'm a doer and a real strategist. I also think that I have an ability to persuade people and inspire confidence.
>
> Although my job and title around here have changed, I still have the reputation for being a "high price" zealot. Fraser River's prices have generally been the highest in the industry. Sometimes our shareholders question me on this point. I always tell them that we're not in business to make plastic products—but rather to make profits. People respect me for that.
>
> The world is full of pessimists and timid people. That's not my style. I'm quite innovative and have a knack for foresight. Look at our acquisitions. For instance, there's our plant in Prince Rupert. It made us look strong in our clients' and competitors' eyes. Sure, it's not as strong today due to the competition, but that's because the guy we have running the show there has lost his aggressiveness.
>
> As for the purchase of Simcoe, I don't buy the stories about our failure in developing new products there. The problem is that we've just been fooling around and haven't devoted our full efforts to these experimental projects.
>
> Plastics, unfortunately, is a cyclic industry controlled by the economy, crude oil supplies, and costs. This means, therefore, that we have to look for new products and new companies. We should especially be considering more exciting ventures like sports bars, cappuccino kiosks or even roller blade clubs. They're the rage in the U.S. right now. Market demand is phenomenal—200 percent annually. Competition is low. We can get in on the ground floor. And we can buy the managerial talent we need to run them for us. They are opportunities that won't wait for us.

The pessimists, however, say that we don't have the resources to handle these deals. Well, Fraser River has been in this position in the past and we've survived. Look at how we originally got started. To be an entrepreneur takes guts! I'm a risk taker and I know when the odds are in our favour. We can't afford to burden ourselves with negative thoughts.

I feel I have a personal obligation to all of our shareholders to keep our reputation and profits the most attractive in the industry. After all, we still have the same number of shareholders we started out with. To keep them, we have to show them that their investment is better left in the company and to reward them with bigger dividends. We also have to provide them with some vehicle for eventually cashing out. So, I guess this means we'll have to consider going public. I think it would enhance our image greatly too.

Elinore Wickham-Jones—President

Elinore Wickham-Jones had accomplished two of the major objectives in her life—she was financially well off and she had built a company "from the ground up." Wickham-Jones had used most of her personal savings to invest in the formation of Fraser River. As vice president, she had been known for her analytical brilliance. When she became president, she committed herself to making the company grow into a national plastic manufacturing concern.

From 1985 to 1991, we managed to grow in spite of ourselves and our mistakes. To our credit, though, we moved quickly, we were flexible, and did not get bogged down in bureaucracy or paperwork.

Today, not all of our operations are as strong as we'd like, but there is still potential in them. Take Beaver Plastics, for instance. It was a natural combination with Fraser River. Sure, things are slow right now, but once we establish ourselves out east or in other new territories, we will be all right.

Simcoe Plastics is another case in point—and there, our plant manager was not as good as we thought he was. We've learned a lot from our R&D work at Simcoe—even though it cost us $200,000.

I'd like to see Fraser River grow on an even-keel basis through acquisitions and international expansion. Of course, we're only interested in profitable and growing ventures. But we can't afford to be in it just for the money. We need to maintain our profits so that we can fund other projects as opportunities present themselves.

That's why I'm particularly keen on both our Plasti-Weave acquisition proposal and the joint venture. Right now, we're heavily committed to what are essentially simple plastic products in just one market, Canada. Consequently, we have to reduce the associated risks. We haven't begun to exploit the American market opened to us through the Canada–U.S. Free Trade Agreement, and with a North American Free Trade Agreement soon to be completed, markets in Central and South America are becoming available.

Unfortunately, these new programmes always seem to bring us back to the issue of financing. So, we need more capital and that probably means an equity issue. The question, however, becomes one of when and how.

Herbert Rudd—Senior Vice President

Herbert Rudd completed his schooling up to the tenth grade, but left because his parents needed him to work on the family farm. Like most farmers, Rudd became an expert in home repairs. After he left home, he worked for a small home contractor until he decided to start his own construction business.

As senior vice president, Rudd's primary responsibility had been to represent the company at industry and trade fairs and exhibits both in Canada and abroad. He commented:

> Oliver and I are the real entrepreneurs in this company. So, we make decisions primarily on gut-feel. But I do think I have good business sense and that's what I use to guide me in my judgments.
>
> Looking back, I feel our biggest mistake has been the operation of large plants such as we have in Chilliwack and Calgary. Right now, small competitors have lower overhead and transportation costs and a more competitive price.
>
> The joint venture project is a fantastic concept with unlimited potential for our company. I can't give any firm projections, but something tells me that this is the right road to go on. Look at Mexico. There are more people earning over $50,000 per year than there are living in Canada. I expect a western hemisphere free trade agreement by the year 2000. Some people are worried about staffing international ventures. Heck, there's a lot of talent in this company that's just not being used. After all, a boy doesn't become a man until he has a man's job to do.
>
> Looking at the products we manufacture, though, I can't honestly say if they're better than everybody else's. I know they do the same job. But, looking at them, there's nothing to distinguish them from your ordinary loaf of bread. I also think that we have a problem communicating to our customers. Our salesmen could do a better job finding out what our customers want and what new products we should be producing.
>
> Another major concern of mine is that we're just a limited product company and there's too much risk in it. That's why I'm in favour of diversification. And I really don't care what sort of companies we acquire. We can always hire someone to run them for us.

Lucas Feck—Vice President (Marketing)

Lucas Feck received his bachelor's degree in commerce from a large American university. Upon graduation he joined a multinational chemical company which operated a subsidiary in Canada. Within 4 years, he became its general manager. After the subsidiary was purchased by another multinational conglomerate, Feck became disenchanted and resigned to start his own small business. Despite the new company's success, Feck became bored and sold his interest. He went back to school and earned an M.B.A. After graduating, he contacted several large executive placement firms, looking for a position in a small to medium-sized growth business. This led to his being hired as marketing vice president for Fraser River Plastics.

Feck was by far the most avid promoter of expanding the company by means of acquisitions. Because Feck had been actively involved in a number of acquisition investigations which had failed to result in a concrete purchase, he had come to believe that the company's present structure was standing in the way of its ability to make acquisitions.

> Our neck is really in the noose today because of the competition we're up against, especially in British Columbia. So I'm pretty strong on the idea of acquisitions. They're the key to our future. Personally, I believe we could run or manage any type of company— hotels, food processing, even steel corrugation plants. Others don't.

Take this Plasti-Weave acquisition. It's a natural combination with our business—plastics. But, better still, it represents a real chance for Fraser River to latch onto a proprietary item. It involves a new technology. We can get the jump on the industry and at the same time start moving out of our "commodity product" line.

As for the joint venture idea, I think we have some real problems because we've never considered: (1) who's going to be moving from Fraser River to staff the project, and (2) who we're going to find to fill the gaps created in Fraser River. I've been pushing Elinore on this point, but she keeps saying, "not to worry."

I think our biggest problem around here, however, has to be that senior management is perpetually caught up 110 percent with day-to-day tasks. I don't think that we'll ever find any new growth or good acquisitions as long as we don't free up some of our time. Elinore Wickham-Jones has a problem divorcing herself from finance and administration. She's also been spending a lot of her time these days on the joint venture project. . . . That's her style though.

Oliver Farthingham's style, however, is to "represent" the company. He shouldn't be doing that as chairman of the company. He should be setting goals. After all, isn't the board responsible for the overall direction of the company? So what if "management" wants to do one thing. The board can just overturn it.

I do know this. . . . I only get my kicks from challenges. Day-to-day work is a necessity, of course, but it's not challenging to me. I'm not interested in managing a division. I just want senior management responsibility and exciting work. Otherwise, I get bored.

Gunther Heinzman—Vice President (Production)

Heinzman was in charge of the company's six plants located in Chilliwack, Vancouver (Beaver), Prince Rupert, Calgary, Winnipeg, and Kamloops (Simcoe). Each plant had its own production manager reporting directly to Heinzman.

A native of Germany, Heinzman had emigrated to Canada with his parents. His first job was in a small manufacturing concern, working on the production line. Since then, he had spent most of his life in production.

I learned this business from the ground up. Every free moment I had during the day and at night was spent reading every trade journal I could get my hands on. But, I guess you could say that even today, I'm kept pretty busy just keeping my end under control.

I've never been a frivolous person. I suppose it comes from my German background. That's why I have always run a tight ship. If Elinore ever told me to cut costs, I wouldn't know where to start because I think we're already at maximum efficiency. And I've tried to instill this objective into each one of my plant managers. I've trained every one of them, except the Simcoe manager, and I'm very proud of them. Naturally, I'm a little more liberal today but I like to do things as cheap as possible. Sometimes, Elinore has to say to me: "Don't hold the penny so close to your eye, Gunther, that you can't see the dollar behind it."

When I look at our acquisitions, there are some real lessons to be learned. I don't regret our purchase of the Prince Rupert plant because it has always supported itself. The manager there runs the company as if it was his own. After all, it used to be his own. Simcoe, however, should be a warning to future acquisitions. And, as for this Plasti–Weave deal, I won't say anything about it because I don't know anything about it. And that's because I haven't been involved in the discussions.

I'm not opposed to acquisitions but I'm naturally afraid of things that I don't know too much about. Elinore, of course, is more enthusiastic about acquisitions. Me, I'm a little more nervous about them. We have three different kinds of production processes here already—for injection, extrusion, and calendering—and I'm not sure how much more work I could handle.

As for this joint venture project, Elinore is again playing her cards close to the vest and I don't think it's such a good idea. It's a big responsibility for her to be carrying alone. Besides, I'm a nationalist. Canada has been good to me and to this company. I think we could spend our dollars much wiser here.

http://www2.plasticsresource.com/Docs/apc

CASE 6

Badger Plastics: The Acquisition Process*

Jack Davis grumbled to himself. The leaves on the trees outside his office window in Troy, New York, had assumed brightly splashed hues of orange, red, and yellow in the fading late-afternoon light of that mid-October day in 1990. His mood, however, was more somber. As chief operating office of Newchem Corporation, he had been asked by his boss, Phil Connors, Newchem's president, to look over a potential acquisition, Badger Manufacturing. Badger had two divisions, Cleantech and Plastics. Cleantech, both Davis and Connors agreed, should be a real winner and was the reason this acquisition was being pursued. It manufactured one of the leading products in the newly emerging industry of liner systems for sanitary environmental landfills. The liners, legislated by the government, prevented pollution from waste disposal from leaking into the groundwater. The problem was with the other division, Badger Plastics, which was in the injection molding business. The division had been losing money in recent years, according to the financials Badger had provided Newchem (see Exhibit 1).

Badger Plastics custom-produced molded plastic pieces for use in the medical, aerospace, and defense industries. The injection molding industry was highly fragmented, very competitive, and possessed low barriers to entry. It had over 2,200 companies ranging from divisions of multibillion-dollar corporations to companies with less than $1 million in annual revenue. The largest twenty-four companies, each with annual revenue between $75 and $200 million, accounted for 12 percent of the market in 1990. The typical company in the industry generated about $4 million per year in revenue and employed about 50 people. The top company in the industry produced gross margins of about 22 percent, while the average company produced margins of about 10 percent.

As far as Davis could see, Badger Plastics had no distinct competitive advantage. In fact, relatively little proprietary knowledge or equipment existed in the industry. Most companies who contracted with injection molders dealt with several suppliers and often conducted highly competitive bidding processes among the suppliers. Usu-

---

*Copyright © 1995 by the *Case Research Journal* and Thomas M. Begley, Northeastern University and Nanyang Technological University, Singapore. Management cooperated in the field research for this case, which was written solely for the purpose of stimulating student discussion. All events and individuals are real, but names and the industry have been changed at the organization's request. The author thanks company executives, especially "Jack Davis," three anonymous reviewers for the *Case Research Journal*, and Marianne Penney for their assistance in the development of the manuscript.

EXHIBIT 1
Financial Information on Badger Plastics, 1988–1990
(in thousands of dollars)

	1988*	1989	1990
Sales volume in pounds	5,450	5,050	4,565
Net sales	$12,000	$11,300	$10,500
Net sales per pound	$ 2.20	$ 2.24	$ 2.30
Cost of goods sold per pound	$ 2.10	$ 2.15	$ 2.14
Gross profits	$ 600	$ 450	$ 735
Gross margin	5%	4%	7%
Operating expenses	$ 1,500	$ 1,400	$ 1,365
% of sales	12.5	12.4	13
Earnings before interest and taxes	$ (900)	$ (950)	$ (630)
% of sales	$ (7.5)	$ (8.4)	(6.0)

*Fiscal year runs October 1 through September 30.

ally, the primary selection criterion was the ability to deliver quality parts on time. If several companies satisfied this criterion, price became the determiner. Often a company would choose a primary supplier and designate one or more secondary suppliers. For example, the primary supplier might receive an order for 70 percent of the parts needed while two secondary suppliers received orders for 15 percent each.

BADGER PLASTICS

After three visits to Badger Plastics' single plant, in Racine, Wisconsin, early in the negotiations, Davis had concluded that the division was a dog. Though most members of the middle management team seemed competent, they were befuddled by their inability to put the division in the black. Problems could not be blamed on the plant and equipment because both were in good condition and only about 5 years old—relatively new by industry standards. The plant was operating at full capacity and, in fact, had a modest backlog of orders. The plant's 120 employees, who had been told the division was in danger of being shut down if it could not become profitable, seemed to be working hard. Even so, financial results were little better for the most recent reporting periods than for earlier ones. In addition, the division was run by a bright, aggressive Stanford MBA who was frustrated at its failure to even come close to reaching the $12 million revenue target he had set for 1990 (see Exhibit 1). To top it off, Newchem had no experience in this industry. Davis had never managed an injection molding operation.

As much as he liked the Cleantech division, Davis had decided the acquisition would be a mistake because prospects were so poor for the Plastics business. Since the owners would only sell the two divisions together, Davis now understood why previous suitors had backed off. Citing the negative information he had gathered, Davis had argued several times in the preceding months against the acquisition. In spite of his protests, Newchem had just signed a purchase and sale agreement to purchase Badger, with final terms depending on the results of the *due diligence* process. Worse yet, in a meeting just after the purchase and sale agreement was signed, Phil Connors dropped another bomb that sent Davis searching for the bottle of Maalox he kept in his desk drawer. "When we acquire Badger, Jack, I'm going to put you in charge of the Plastics division. This project is your baby; and from now on treat it as your highest priority. I'll give you a year to turn a profit there. If you can't, we'll try to find someone who can."

Connor's remarks contained elements of challenge and threat. Davis knew he was a candidate to succeed Connors when he retired in 2 years, and Connors seemed to see this assignment as a test of Davis's qualifications. If he turned the division around, his prospects for becoming Newchem's president would be considerably bolstered.

NEWCHEM CORPORATION

Newchem Corp. was a relatively small company in the chemical industry. Originally an internally generated start-up division of a Fortune 500 oil company, Newchem was sold in 1980 when the parent company decided to go in a different strategic direction. Purchased by a group of investors led by Elden Lappas, an entrepreneur whose experience was primarily in automotive parts manufacturing, the company originally sought to grow through internal development. In 1985, seeking to buffer Newchem against the cyclical swings in the chemical business and wanting to achieve a size that would allow the company to go public, Lappas had decided to pursue a strategy of acquisition of companies "downstream" in the process, that is, companies that might use the chemical products Newchem sold in their own manufacturing processes. Between 1985 and 1990, the company made three acquisitions, all manufacturing firms with $4 to $6 million in annual revenues. Newchem sought firms with growth potential, often ones in which an infusion of cash could fuel growth. It assigned one of its own senior managers, usually Jack Davis, to oversee operations and make selective changes in policy and personnel as the situation evolved. Since these acquisitions had consumed substantial cash in its attempts to grow, Newchem did not have large cash reserves in 1990 to invest in newly acquired businesses. Elden Lappas, after conferring with the board of directors, had decided to invest any available funds in Badger's Cleantech division. Badger Plastics would be left to sink or swim on its own. Lappas had told Connors, "If you can't turn that division around, we'll try to sell it. If we can't find a buyer, we'll shut it down." Exhibit 2 reports Newchem's financial performance between 1987 and 1990.

JACK DAVIS

After obtaining a B.S. degree in chemical engineering from Penn State, Jack Davis had started his career as a chemical engineer for a Fortune 500 chemical company.

EXHIBIT 2
Financial Information on Newchem, 1987–1990
(in thousands of dollars)

	1987*	1988	1989	1990
Net sales	$15,000	$20,000	$29,000	$30,000
Gross profit	$ 5,250	$ 7,800	$10,730	$10,500
Gross margin	35%	39%	37%	35%
Earnings before interest and taxes	$ 1,800	$ 3,400	$ 4,900	$ 3,900
Operating margins	12%	17%	17%	13%
Depreciation and amortization	$ 1,100	$ 1,200	$ 1,800	$ 2,400
Interest expense	$ 1,350	$ 1,600	$ 2,300	$ 3,000
Net income	$ 300	$ 1,100	$ 1,600	$ 500

*Fiscal year runs October 1 through September 30.

After 9 years with the company, he was promoted to plant manager of a small plastics extrusion manufacturing plant. A year later, when the division of which the plant was a part was sold to a specialty plastics company, Davis stayed with the plant. Two years later, in 1985, the entire specialty plastics company was acquired by Newchem. Recognizing Davis's managerial potential, Newchem transferred him to its corporate headquarters, putting him in charge of the operational side of its due diligence process for new acquisitions. Davis had performed well in that capacity, and had been promoted to chief operating officer of Newchem in 1988. In that job, he had concentrated on increasing production efficiencies in Newchem's existing businesses and overseeing the due diligence process of potential acquisitions. While Phil Connors and Bart Yablonski, Newchem's chief financial officer, dealt with the financial and legal concerns of these acquisitions, Davis evaluated their administrative structures and operations. Commenting on his role, he observed:

> [Newchem's] CEO and chief financial officer spent their time interacting with opposing counsel and the banks, putting the financing together and negotiating a definitive agreement. I was the guy on-site who was interacting with [Badger Plastics'] managers and conducting the nitty-gritty tire-kicking parts of the due diligence process.

THE CURRENT POSITION OF BADGER PLASTICS

When Davis reviewed a summary of Badger Plastics' financials, he cringed (see Exhibit 1). The earnings before interest and taxes (EBIT) for fiscal 1990, which had ended in September, were projected to show a loss of $630,000, amounting to a negative 6 percent of sales. Even worse, this performance was the best in recent years. His initial efforts to find out why the division was losing money proved less than satisfying. Badger senior managers claimed to be as baffled about the losses as he was. Initially asserting that the most recent year's losses were due to not reaching the $12 million sales target, the executives quickly backed off when Davis asked them how an incremental $1.5 million in revenues would have generated at least a 40 percent profit margin. "Materials constitute 45 percent of your selling price, labor adds another 18 percent, and energy adds 4 percent. You already have three shifts working steadily 5 days a week and cannot show me any plans for productivity improvement. Show me the math that would get you to break even," he challenged them. In addition, he suspected the operations managers of overestimating productive capacity and underestimating costs to show that they were meeting their production goals. If their data were fudged, unaware senior managers would seriously overestimate production capabilities and profit potential.

Though Davis was unsure about the reasons for the losses, he knew a few things about acquisitions because of work on Newchem's last two acquisitions and his prior experience of twice working for a firm that was acquired. First, he was entering a crucial phase in the process. Information obtained during the due diligence phase could be vital in helping address problems as soon as the acquisition was finalized. Second, getting the work force on his side could make or break the acquisition. By now, rumors would be flying around the plant about what was happening. Employees would be highly anxious, fearful for their jobs, and very wary about the trustworthiness and intentions of the acquirer. Davis suspected that overhead costs were a key culprit in the plant's lack of profitability. If that turned out to be true, layoffs might well be in the offing. He knew from previous experience that it was difficult to seek employee trust and increased productivity at the same time other employees were being laid off.

Third, since employees knew the company was losing money, they might be more open to prospects for change than if the company had been profitable. Fourth, in previous acquisitions, Davis had seen several of the best people leave just prior to or after the sale date. Their loss had been a major blow to the successful operation of the acquisition. If at all possible, he needed to find a way to keep Badger's best people. Since the country was in the middle of a recession and manufacturing jobs were on the decline, he knew that the average employee would have difficulty finding employment elsewhere but the best ones would be highly mobile.

DUE DILIGENCE

As Davis contemplated the challenges, he guessed the financing and final negotiations would take another 6 to 8 weeks to complete. Since it was now mid-October, the final sale probably would occur in December. He wondered how to put the intervening weeks to best use. The due diligence clause in the purchase and sale agreement provided some boundaries on how much freedom the current owners might allow Davis in seeking information about Badger Plastics:

> Between the date hereof and the closing date, Newchem shall have, subject to sensitive information to be agreed upon by the parties, reasonable access upon reasonable prior notice, to all facilities, records, and personnel of the business in connection with its due diligence review of the business and the completion of the transaction. Newchem agrees that notice of all due diligence activities at Badger Plastics' facilities shall be given to Peg O'Brien or such other individual as Badger Plastics may designate.

Due diligence stipulations were designed to allow the potential purchaser the right to inspect the financial records, property, equipment, and personnel of the target and to verify its sales by matching goods shipped and invoices sent with monies received. At the same time, it permitted the seller to continue to run the business without undue interference. The definition of "reasonable access" was nebulous, and Davis knew his ability to interact freely with Badger Plastics employees would depend at least partly on the relationships he established with Plastics' managers. It would also depend on how near the closing date of the sale was: the nearer the sale date, the more access he would be allowed. In addition, Davis knew that it did not work to the seller's advantage to attempt to cover up major deficiencies in the company's property, buildings, or equipment because as part of the sales agreement the seller would be required to put a sizable sum in an escrow account to pay for problems discovered after the sale.

Davis wondered what to do next. "I'll probably have to do more than just watch the leaves dancing on the trees outside my window," he muttered to himself as he redirected his attention to the discouraging Badger Plastics spreadsheet on his desk.

http://www.manufacturing.net/magazine/id/archives/1996/ind1201.96/12intro.htm

CASE 7

Ben & Jerry's Homemade Inc.: "Yo! I'm Your CEO!"*

"Ben & Jerry's Grows Up"
—*The Boston Globe*

"Ben, Jerry Losing Their Values?"
—*The Washington Times*

"Ben & Jerry's Melting Social Charter"
—*The Washington Post*

"Life Won't Be Just a Bowl of Cherry Garcia"
—*Business Week*

"Say It Ain't So, Ben & Jerry"
—*Business Week*

The headlines said it all. Ben & Jerry's, the company that had built its success as much on its down-home image and folksy idealism as on its super-rich ice cream, was at a crossroads. Having been started in 1978 in a renovated Vermont gas station by childhood friends Ben Cohen and Jerry Greenfield, the unconventional company soon grew into a $140 million powerhouse that was rivaled only by Häagen-Dazs in the superpremium category of the ice-cream market. With its many donations and policies promoting corporate responsibility, Ben & Jerry's took great pride in its success combining social activism with financial viability. But in mid-1994, the outlook was not so rosy. Sales were flat, profits were down, and the company's stock price had fallen to half what it was at the end of 1992. In its 1993 annual report, Ben & Jerry's admitted that some flavors of its "all natural" ice cream included ingredients that were not, in fact, all natural. And staffers within the company reportedly criticized it for lack of leadership.

On June 13, Ben & Jerry's announced that Ben was stepping down as CEO, and that it would abandon its longtime cap on executive salaries in order to help it find a

---

*Prepared by Katherine A. Auer, Indiana University, and Alan N. Hoffman, Bentley College. Please address all correspondence to: Dr. Alan N. Hoffman, AGC 320, Department of Management, Bentley College, 175 Forest Street, Waltham, MA 02154-4705, (617) 891-2287, AHOFFMAN@BENTLEY.EDU, (617) 237-0627 (fax). Printed by permission of Dr. Alan N. Hoffman, Bentley College.

new one. The message was clear: Ben & Jerry's was no longer the company it once was. For many, the question then was, what would it become?

THE CONTEST

With a marketing flair befitting its tradition of wacky promotional tactics, Ben & Jerry's set out to find its new leader by announcing the "Yo! I'm Your CEO!" contest. Customers were asked to send in a lid from a container of their favorite Ben & Jerry's ice-cream flavor along with a 100-word essay explaining "Why I Would Be a Great CEO for Ben & Jerry's." The winner would get to run the company, the runner-up would get a lifetime supply of ice cream, and the losers would get a rejection letter "suitable for framing."

"We have never had an experienced CEO and we have reached the point in our life when we need one," said Ben, adding that he planned to continue with the company as chairman and concentrate on "fun stuff" like product development.

But the search wasn't all fun and games. Ben & Jerry's also announced that it would abandon its longtime policy that no executive be paid more than seven times the salary of the lowest-paid employee, and hired an executive recruiting firm to help find the right person. Under the old policy, Ben was paid $133,212 in 1993 and no bonuses; the going rate for executives at companies of like size was $300,000 to $500,000.

"I think we are looking for a rare bird," said Ben. "I guess there are about 5 or 10 executives who will be interested and have the skills." The key, he added, is experience in keeping "everyone aligned and moving the same direction" as the company grows—something he admitted he was learning but not good at. "I haven't found the happy medium between autocratic and laissez-faire," he explained.

Some 22,500 aspiring leaders around the world flooded the company with their responses, which were as varied as the flavors in its ice-cream line. Entries came from places as far away as Australia, Thailand, East Africa and Saudi Arabia. An entire fifth-grade class sent in letters, with offers from some of the students to develop new flavors. One woman sent in a near-nude photo of herself, while an advertising executive attached his resume to a Superman costume.

An Indiana schoolteacher scrawled her essay on a painting of a woman reading a book, while Allen Stillman, head of New York restaurant chain Smith & Wollensky, put a full-page ad in *The New York Times*: "I propose a whole new line of flavors," he wrote. "Red Meat Swirl, Potato Gravy Chunk, Starchie Bunker." Stillman also proposed a merger and a new name: Ben Smith & Jerry Wollensky Steaks and Shakes.

Other response tactics included a resume written entirely on a giant sheet cake, another engraved on a brass plaque and mounted on marble, and one written in crayon by a hopeful couple's 2$1/2$-year-old son. A Milwaukee car salesman sent in a mock two-foot-wide lid of a New York Super Fudge Chunk carton, folded in half. When the lid was unfolded, an electronic device made a sound like a telephone ring; the opener then read "Please call me—I'm the one you want to be your CEO."

"Some of them may not be right for the CEO's job, but they sure would be right for marketing jobs," Ben said. "We may not have to advertise for people for the next several years."

THE WINNER

On February 2, 1995, Ben & Jerry's announced that it had at last found the leader it wanted: Robert Holland Jr., a former partner at management consultancy McKinsey & Co. By taking the helm of Ben & Jerry's, the 55-year-old MBA became one of the most visible African-American chief executives among the nation's publicly traded corporations.

Holland was found not through the essay contest, but through New York executive recruiter Russell Reynolds. Some 500 candidates were initially considered by that firm, and Ben & Jerry's board members ultimately reviewed about 15 applicants. The race eventually narrowed down to six competitors (one of whom did come from the essay contest), and from there, it came down to two finalists, both of whom spent considerable time over dinner and ice cream with Ben, Jerry and board members. Rumor had it that Holland's competitor preferred frozen yogurt, while he himself was a passionate ice-cream fan.

Having grown up in Michigan, Holland spent 13 years as an associate and partner at McKinsey, where he worked with consumer and industrial clients including the soft-drink division of Heineken. He left McKinsey in 1981, going on to become an independent consultant and businessman. Among his subsequent roles were chairman of Gilreath Manufacturing Inc., a plastics injection-molding company, and chairman and CEO of Rokher-J Inc., a White Plains, N.Y., consulting and takeover firm. Holland earned his MBA at Baruch College in New York.

But at least as important as his experience in turning troubled companies around were Holland's social values. He was chairman of the board of trustees at Spelman College in Atlanta, a school traditionally attended by black women, as well as the founder of a dropout-prevention program for Detroit high-school students and a board member of the Harlem Junior Tennis program for inner-city youth.

"We were very impressed not only with Bob's operational expertise, but with his social commitment, as expressed in both his business experience and his active involvement with the nonprofit sector," said Ben.

Holland's salary was to be $250,000 plus options on 180,000 shares of stock and a bonus of up to $125,000 if he met certain financial goals. Though significantly higher than what Ben had been earning, that was still at the low end of the pay scale for CEOs at midsized manufacturers, and reportedly less than what Holland had been earning as a management consultant.

Though he didn't submit an essay as part of the contest, Holland did submit something—a poem—upon request after he was chosen. The poem, entitled "Time, Values and Ice Cream" (see Exhibit 1), reflected his background in poor, working-class, south-central Michigan.

Though his appointment at Ben & Jerry's made Holland one of just a few African-American CEOs at public companies, Holland declined to be called a role model for other blacks, calling the term "too presumptuous." Nevertheless, he said, "I'm looking forward to dispelling whatever concerns people have."

In any case, Holland faced a formidable challenge at Ben & Jerry's. The company was expected to post its first quarterly loss ever for the fourth quarter of fiscal 1994, and when Holland's appointment was announced, Chuck Lacy, the company's longtime president, resigned.

EXHIBIT 1
Time, Values and Ice Cream*
By Robert Holland

Born before the baby boom
as war drums raged cross distant waters—way
beyond my family's lore since our 1600s coming to this far off land called
America.

T'was a simple time, as I grew tall.
Shucks! Uncle Sam really wanted you (so the poster said)—pride
in work, parades and proms, company picnics 'tween eve'ns spent with "Suspense,"
"The Shadow," and everybody's "Our Miss Brooks."
Good ole days in the summertime, indeed! . . . in
America.

Yet, some nostalgia stayed 'yond one's grasp,
like Sullivans',
the ice cream place on Main—swivel stools, cozy booths, and sweet,
sweet smells with no sitting place for all of some of us.
Could only dream such humble pleasure. Sometimes, dear 'Merica,
of thee I simply hum.

Much, so much has changed in twenty springs. Sputnik
no longer beeps so loud;
Bay of Pigs, Vietnam and contentions in Chicago . . .
come and gone . . .
All that noise almost drowning out "One small step for man . . ."
and ". . . Willie, time to say goodbye to baseball."
Confusing place, this melodious mix,
called America.

Now I sit by eyeing distant twilight,
Engineer and MBA,
smiling wide on M.L.K.'s day,
CEO of Cherry Garcia and Peace Pops' fountain
having not forgotten the forbidden seats of Sullivans',
with miles to go before we sleep . . .
and time left yet to get there.
Only in America!

---

*Only 100 words before translation from the language of Chunky Mandarin Orange With Natural Wild Brazil Nuts.

While Holland won the executive slot, what some may say was the better prize—a lifetime supply of ice cream—went to three runners-up. Among them was Taylor James Caldwell, the toddler, by then three years old, who had submitted an entry for his parents. In addition, about 100 honorable mentions received limited-edition T-shirts.

THE "GOOD OLD" DAYS

The birth of Ben & Jerry's can be traced to a $5 correspondence course in ice-cream making taken by Ben Cohen and Jerry Greenfield. The duo, who had been friends since growing up together in Merrick, N.Y., then gathered $12,000 ($4,000 of which was borrowed), and in May 1978 opened an ice-cream shop in a renovated Burlington, Vt., gas station. Featuring an antique rock-salt ice-cream freezer and a Volkswagen squareback for its delivery van, the shop soon became popular for its innovative flavors made from fresh Vermont milk and cream.

At the heart of Ben & Jerry's was the very distinct business philosophy shared by its founders. In essence, they believed that companies have a responsibility to do good for society, not just for themselves. This philosophy is best explained by the company's three-part mission statement, formally stated in 1988 and reproduced here in its entirety:

"Ben & Jerry's is dedicated to the creation and demonstration of a new corporate concept of linked prosperity. Our mission consists of three interrelated parts:

Product mission: To make, distribute and sell the finest quality, all-natural ice cream and related products in a wide variety of innovative flavors made from Vermont dairy products.

Social mission: To operate the company in a way that actively recognizes the central role that business plays in the structure of society by initiating innovative ways to improve the quality of life of a broad community—local, national and international.

Economic mission: To operate the company on a sound financial basis of profitable growth, increasing value for our shareholders, and creating career opportunities and financial rewards for our employees.

Underlying the mission of Ben & Jerry's is the determination to seek new and creative ways of addressing all three parts, while holding a deep respect for the individuals, inside and outside the company, and for the communities of which they are a part.

This unconventional philosophy touched everything the company did, from the way it treated its employees to the way it dealt with its suppliers.

The company enjoyed a strong team and family-oriented atmosphere, for example, supported by progressive family-leave, health-insurance and other benefit plans. Reasoning that happy employees would reduce stress and improve the workplace in general, Ben & Jerry kept the culture extremely casual and relaxed, and had even formed a "Joy Committee" to spread joy among its employees. Some of the spontaneous events coordinated by the Joy Committee included an Elvis Presley recognition day, with an Elvis look-alike contest, a Barry Manilow appreciation day, and a car race derby in which employees raced their own toy cars. Pranks abounded at all gatherings, including the annual shareholders' meetings, and most were followed by entertainment such as 1960s musicians Richie Havens, Livingston Taylor, and dozens of other bands. In essence, Ben and Jerry truly seemed to live by their motto, "If it's not fun, why do it?"

Yet in its desire to create a healthy and equitable workplace, Ben & Jerry's did more than just promote fun and games: The longtime cap on executive salaries required that no executive be paid more than seven times the salary of the lowest-paid employee. Typical staff meetings included all employees, not just executives, and issues affecting women, minorities and gays in the workforce were always discussed openly.

In choosing suppliers for the ingredients of its products, Ben & Jerry's tried to be equally responsible. For example, the brownies used in its Chocolate Fudge Brownie ice cream were bought from a bakery in Yonkers, N.Y., that hired undertrained and underskilled workers and used its profits to house the homeless and teach them trades. Ben & Jerry's Rainforest Crunch ice cream featured nuts grown in South American rain forests; the firm paid the harvesters directly, and donated a portion of the proceeds from sales of the ice cream to environmental preservation causes. Wild Maine Blueberry ice cream was made with blueberries grown and harvested by the Passamaquoddy Indians of Maine. Fresh Georgia Peach ice cream was made from Georgia-grown peaches as part of the company's policy of supporting family farms.

Similarly, for the milk and cream that forms the bulk of its products, Ben & Jerry's was committed to buying from Vermont dairy farms, to whom it paid above-market prices. When rBGH, a genetically engineered drug to increase cows' milk production, was approved by the FDA, Ben & Jerry's declared it would buy only from farms not using the drug, citing health concerns and a desire to protect smaller farms. To ensure that its products stayed wholesome and pure, the company paid the premium to suppliers in exchange for their written assurance that they would not use rBGH.

Finally, the company also established the Ben & Jerry's Foundation, which donated 7.5 percent of its pretax profits to nonprofit organizations. These causes included, among others, the American Wildlands in Montana; Burch House in New Hampshire (a safe house); the Burlington Peace and Justice Coalition in Vermont; the Citizens Committee for Children in New York (aid for drug-addicted pregnant women); Natural Guard (an environmental group for school-age children and teens); the Brattleboro Area AIDS Project (providing free services to HIV-positive individuals and their families); and the Massachusetts Coalition for the Homeless.

Such efforts won the hearts of scores of like-minded consumers, many of whom had grown up in the same socially conscious generation as Ben and Jerry. Indeed, because of its values and its unconventional nature, the company had to do very little marketing: Media coverage of its various antics was virtually guaranteed on a regular basis, providing free publicity for the company, its products and its values. Thanks in part to the size of the "baby-boomer" generation of which its leaders were a part, Ben & Jerry's flourished in the 1980s, growing to more than 100 franchises. In 1984 the company went public in Vermont, and by 1986 it had achieved 100 percent growth.

RECENT TROUBLES

While Ben & Jerry's thrived during the 1980s, the 1990s presented a very different picture. One of the primary reasons was that the baby-boom generation—Ben & Jerry's primary target market—was entering middle age and becoming more health conscious. Whereas during the 1980s these consumers enjoyed the socially conscious self-indulgence of Ben & Jerry's ice cream, they had since become averse to high-fat foods such as superpremium ice cream. At the same time, new labeling requirements imposed by the FDA meant that customers could see with painful clarity the amount of fat each scoop of Ben & Jerry's ice creams contained, thus bringing home the reality about their less-than-healthful nature.

One step Ben & Jerry's took to respond was to introduce a reduced-fat, reduced-calorie ice milk, called Ben & Jerry's Lite. That line failed, reportedly due to poor quality, but the subsequent introduction of a low-fat, low-cholesterol frozen-yogurt line met with much better success. In addition, the company was expected to begin rolling out the first flavors in its non-fat yogurt line by the summer of 1995. Nevertheless, the fact remained that ice-cream sales were slowing.

Ben & Jerry's was also facing increased competition from the deep-pocketed Häagen-Dazs, which had expanded its selection of flavors to better rival Ben & Jerry's (including its chunky "Extraas," a low-fat ultrapremium ice cream as well as frozen yogurt) and had brought on a price war by reducing its prices and offering a variety of promotions and discounts. During the weakened economy of the 1990s, competing on price became the name of the game.

Indeed, the superpremium category as a whole was witnessing increased competition from lower-cost, lower-fat premium ice creams. Among those were Edy's, manufactured by Dreyer's, which produced roughly half of Ben & Jerry's output. Not only that, but Dreyer's had recently received a huge cash infusion from Nestlé, giving the firm increased competitive muscle.

Despite the fact that U.S. ice-cream exports had tripled in recent years, and the fact that Häagen-Dazs had already begun exporting (even opening a factory in France), Ben & Jerry's so far had paid little attention to markets outside the United States. Said Chuck Lacy, the company's president, "It's something that we're starting to think about, but we've got a lot of work to do here in the U.S." Sales to restaurants was another option for growth outside of the heated grocery-store market, but again, Lacy said, while "there's huge potential, it's a completely different business. It requires completely different distributors and sales staff, a completely different head."

Software glitches, meanwhile, had repeatedly delayed the opening of Ben & Jerry's new $40 million ice-cream plant in St. Albans, which had been planned to dramatically increase production. But with sales down, it was not even clear that the company would be able to use even half the plant's capacity when it did finally open, making it a roughly break-even proposition.

Management problems were also plaguing the firm, reducing morale and drawing criticism from employees, who said there was a lack of direction. By the end of 1994, the mood had reportedly become so dark that the company asked author Milton Moskowitz to remove it from the most recent edition of "The 100 Best Companies to Work For in America."

Finally, on December 19, 1994, Ben & Jerry's had announced that it expected to report a loss of $700,000 to $900,000 for the fourth quarter of 1994—its first since going public in 1984.

THE INDUSTRY LANDSCAPE

The packaged ice-cream industry included ordinary, premium, and superpremium products. These types were distinguished primarily by their butterfat content and density, as well as the freshness of their ingredients and the way they were blended and treated.

Ordinary ice creams typically contained the minimum of 10 to 12 percent butterfat and the maximum proportion of air; one four-ounce scoop contained 150 calories or less. Premium ice creams contained 12 to 16 percent butterfat and less air than regular types; a four-ounce scoop usually contained 180 calories. Superpremium ice creams, which included Ben & Jerry's, generally contained about 16 to 20 percent fat (excluding add-ins) and less than 20 percent air. The caloric value of a four-ounce scoop was generally about 260 calories. This type of ice cream was characterized by a greater richness than the other types, and was sold in packaged pints priced between $2.29 and $2.89 each.

The total annual sales in U.S. supermarkets for the ice-cream and frozen-yogurt market as a whole were more than $3.6 billion in 1994. The superpremium market (ice cream, frozen yogurt, ice milk and sorbet) accounted for about $415 million. Ninety-three percent of American households consumed ice cream, but demand was seasonal, with summer levels as much as 30 percent higher than those in the winter. Sales for frozen yogurt (superpremium and regular) were $550 million in supermarkets in 1994; Ben & Jerry's was clearly ahead of Häagen-Dazs in the superpremium frozen-yogurt market.

Gross margins in the ice-cream industry as a whole were about 30.6 percent, compared with only 20 percent for the frozen-food department as a whole. Premium and superpremium varieties outperformed other ice-cream types, accounting for 45.8 percent of sales and 45.9 percent of profits of the ice-cream category as a whole, and earning a gross margin of 31.5 percent.

The superpremium ice-cream and frozen-yogurt business was highly competitive. Ben & Jerry's principal competitor was The Häagen-Dazs Company, Inc., which roughly matched Ben & Jerry's 42 percent share of the market; others, including Columbo, Dannon, Healthy Choice, Simple Pleasures, Elan, Frusen Glädje, Yoplait, Honey Hill Farms and Steve's, constituted less than 10 percent of the market.

Häagen-Dazs was owned by The Pillsbury Company, which in turn was owned by Grand Metropolitan PLC, a British food and liquor conglomerate with resources significantly greater than those of Ben & Jerry's. Häagen-Dazs entered the market well before Ben & Jerry's, and also became well-established in certain markets in Europe and the Pacific Rim. And to compete with Ben & Jerry's, it introduced in 1992 its Extraas line of products that included a variety of add-ins like cookies, candies and nuts.

Ben & Jerry's also competed with several well-known brands in the ice-cream novelty segment, including Häagen-Dazs and Dove Bars, which are manufactured by a division of Mars, Inc. Both Häagen-Dazs and Dove Bars achieved significant market share before Ben & Jerry's entered their markets.

MARKET SHARE

The total U.S. sales for superpremium ice cream, frozen yogurt, ice milk and sorbet were more than $415 million in 1994. The market was dominated by Haagen-Dazs and Ben & Jerry's: In 1993, the former held 62 percent of the market while Ben & Jerry's held 36 percent, but by early 1995, both held roughly 42 percent.

Häagen-Dazs had entered the superpremium market back in 1961. Though success was not achieved overnight, the brand remained on the market and became the industry leader. Early success was linked to word-of-mouth advertising, but by 1983

Häagen-Dazs spent $14 million on advertising, while average ice-cream manufacturers spent less than 1 percent of sales on advertising.

When new competitors began entering the market in the early 1980s, namely Ben & Jerry's, Häagen-Dazs attempted to keep them out by threatening distributors. Ben & Jerry's fought back with a lawsuit and a campaign including bumper stickers and T-shirts displaying the statement "What's the Pillsbury Doughboy Afraid Of?" The litigation was settled and the campaign brought to an end within about a year.

Between 1989 and 1993, overall growth in the market had been sluggish, rising by only 14 percent. During that same time period, however, Ben & Jerry's market share rose by 120 percent, while Häagen-Dazs' share decreased by 10 percent. In 1992, Ben & Jerry's increased its U.S. market share by 10 percent; Häagen-Dazs, on the other hand, lost 8 percent. Thus, while Ben & Jerry's entered late into the mature, low-growth ice-cream market, it gained substantial market share, primarily at the expense of Häagen-Dazs.

Ben & Jerry's products were distributed primarily by independent regional ice-cream distributors. With certain exceptions, only one distributor was appointed to each territory. In some areas, subdistributors were used. Ben & Jerry's trucks also distributed some of the ice cream and frozen yogurt sold in Vermont and upstate New York. Ben & Jerry's had a distribution agreement with Dreyer's whereby Dreyer's had exclusivity, in general, for sales to supermarkets and similar accounts of Ben & Jerry's products in most of its markets outside New England, upstate New York, Pennsylvania and Texas. Net sales to Dreyer's accounted for about 54 percent and 52 percent of Ben & Jerry's net sales for 1993 and 1994, respectively.

While Dreyer's marketed its own premium ice cream, as well as frozen dessert products made by other companies, it did not produce or market any other super-premium ice cream or frozen yogurt. Were it to begin doing so, Dreyer's would lose its exclusivity as a Ben & Jerry's distributor.

Because of instances of legal action over distribution agreements, manufacturers and distributors generally opted for verbal rather than written contracts.

In recent years, two independent distributors claimed that Ben & Jerry's and Dreyer's had squeezed them out of the business, and at least three others claimed they had lost access to the brand after building it for years. Furthermore, Amy Miller, founder of Amy's Ice Creams in Austin, Texas, claimed that Ben & Jerry's pressured the best distributor in that area to not carry Amy's pints or risk losing the immensely popular Ben & Jerry's. But Ben and Jerry categorically denied any such involvement, and was backed up by the distributor. There were also a few other instances in which distributors claimed that they had been pressured to not carry brands competing with Ben & Jerry's. Said one retailer, who sued Ben & Jerry's after it cut him off, "corporately, they are absolutely vicious."

Ben & Jerry's admitted that while its relationships with Dreyer's and other distributors have been generally satisfactory, they were not always easy to maintain. But alternatives were few: According to the company, the loss of one or more of the related distribution agreements could have a material adverse effect on the company's business.

When it came to choosing suppliers, Ben & Jerry's insistence on social responsibility earned it much acclaim, but developing such relationships was not always easy. Its search for the perfect coffee bean, for example, took more than five years and led to one of its most complex, yet successful, supplier relationships. The company's goal was to give much of the profits back to the grower, rather than to a middleman broker; accomplishing this required a significant commitment of time and resources to learn each party's needs and expectations.

Because working directly with suppliers required so much energy, Ben & Jerry's planned to establish only one or two relationships each year. R&D, quality assurance, finance and manufacturing all had to be involved in the evaluation and education of each new supplier. Although the work involved was much more than would have been required if it simply made calls to existing suppliers, Ben & Jerry's felt the result made it worthwhile.

FINANCE

Ben & Jerry's sales had been steadily increasing from 1988 through 1992, but then slowed dramatically in 1993. Sales increased by about 30 percent annually from 1990 to 1992, but that dropped to 6 percent in 1993. Furthermore, the company indicated that virtually all of its growth in 1993 came from its frozen-yogurt line, which grew by 35 percent during that year. Sales for fiscal 1993 were $140 million and $149 million for fiscal 1994. (See Exhibits 2 and 3.)

Net income had grown steadily along with sales growth, and exceeded that pace during 1991 and 1992. While sales grew at 26 percent and 36 percent during 1991 and 1992, respectively, net income grew at 42 percent and 81 percent. During 1993, sales grew 6 percent while net income grew at 7 percent. For 1994, however, the company reported a new loss of $1.87 million.

The company's net profit margin was 5.1 percent, compared with the industry average of 3.4 percent. The net loss per share for 1994 was ($0.26); during previous years, earnings per share had risen steadily, from $0.32 in 1988 to a high of $1.07 in 1992, then falling to $1.01 in 1993. Consequently, its stock price had since been driven down nearly 50 percent from its 1993 high of $32 by investors impatient with the company's lack of momentum. On February 1, 1995, the company's stock price was $12.125.

MARKETING

Product

Ben & Jerry's "product" was a carefully orchestrated combination of premium ice-cream products and social consciousness—"Caring Capitalism"—created through bottom-up management and cause-generated marketing and public-relations efforts. The physical products included superpremium ice cream, in both chunky and smooth flavors, low-fat frozen yogurt, and ice-cream novelties. The company operated in the focused niche of superpremium ice-cream products, with the driving competitive factor traditionally being diversity and uniqueness of flavor.

EXHIBIT 2
5-Year Financial Highlights
(in thousands of dollars except per share data)

	Year Ended				
	12/31/94	12/25/93	12/26/92	12/28/91	12/29/90
	Summary of Operations				
Net sales	$148,802	$140,328	$131,969	$96,997	$77,024
Cost of sales	109,760	100,210	94,389	68,500	54,203
Gross profit	39,042	40,118	37,580	28,497	22,821
Selling, general and administrative expenses	36,253	28,270	26,243	21,264	17,639
Asset write-down	6,779				
Other income (expense)—net	229	197	(23)	(729)	(709)
Income (loss) before income taxes	(3,761)	12,045	11,314	6,504	4,473
Income taxes	(1,893)	4,845	4,639	2,765	1,864
Net income (loss)	(1,868)	7,200	6,675	3,739	2,609
Net income (loss) per common share*	(0.26)	1.01	1.07	0.67	0.50
Weighted average common shares outstanding*	7,148	7,138	6,254	5,572	5,225
	Balance Sheet Data				
Working capital	$ 37,456	$ 29,292	$ 18,053	$ 11,035	$ 8,202
Total assets	120,295	106,361	88,207	43,056	34,299
Long-term debt	32,419	18,002	2,641	2,787	8,948
Stockholders' equity†	72,502	74,262	66,760	26,269	16,101

*The per share amounts and average shares outstanding have been adjusted for the effects of all stock splits, including stock splits in the form of stock dividends.
†No cash dividends have been declared or paid by the company on its capital stock since the company's organization. The company intends to reinvest earnings for use in its business and to finance future growth. Accordingly, the board of directors does not anticipate declaring any cash dividends in the foreseeable future.

As such, the primary marketing goal at Ben & Jerry's was to develop and deliver great new products and flavors. It maintained a full-time research & development team dedicated to the development of unconventional, cutting-edge flavors. It is this strength that had placed Ben & Jerry's at the forefront of the superpremium ice-cream market, with six of the Top 10 and 13 of the Top 20 Best Selling Flavors.

In its traditional line, Ben & Jerry's distinguished its flavors and products through "chunkiness," maintaining specifications not only for chunk size, but for number per spoonful and quality of the fruits and nuts they contain. Although such requirements added a great deal more to the cost of the finished product, the enhancement in taste differentiated Ben & Jerry's product from the competition.

The company also distinguished its product by its use of pure, natural and socially conscious milk from Vermont dairy farmers who agreed not to use rBGH. The FDA allowed the voluntary labeling of dairy products made from non-rBGH–treated cows, so Ben & Jerry's aggressively promoted its products' purity on its packaging.

Ben & Jerry's products were sold by the pint in recycled paperboard cups, a practice that was standard in the superpremium market. Ben & Jerry's arrived at that strategy based on the demographics of its target market—25- to 40-year-old consumers in

EXHIBIT 3
Consolidated Balance Sheets

	12/31/94	12/25/93
Assets		
Current assets		
Cash and cash equivalents	$ 20,777,746	$ 14,704,795
Accounts receivable, less allowance for doubtful accounts:		
$504,000 in 1994 and $229,000 in 1993	11,904,844	11,679,222
Inventories	13,462,572	13,452,863
Deferred income taxes	3,146,000	1,689,000
Income taxes receivable	2,097,743	
Prepaid expenses	534,166	847,851
Total current assets	$ 51,923,071	$ 42,373,731
Property, plant and equipment, net	57,980,567	40,261,538
Investments	8,000,000	22,000,000
Other assets	2,391,465	1,725,316
Total assets	$120,295,103	$106,360,585
Liabilities and Stockholders' Equity		
Current liabilities		
Accounts payable and accrued expenses	$ 13,914,972	$ 12,068,424
Income taxes payable		344,519
Current portion of long-term debt and capital lease obligations	552,547	669,151
Total current liabilities	$ 14,467,519	$ 13,082,094
Long-term debt and capital lease obligations	32,418,565	18,002,076
Deferred income taxes	907,000	1,014,000
Total liabilities	$ 47,793,084	$ 32,098,170
Commitments and contingencies		
Stockholders' equity		
$1.20 noncumulative Class A preferred stock—$1.00 par value, redeemable at the company's option at $12.00 per share; 900 shares authorized, issued and outstanding, aggregate preference on voluntary or involuntary liquidation—$9,000	$ 900	$ 900
Class A common stock—$.033 par value; authorized 20,000,000 shares; issued: 6,290,580 shares at December 31, 1994, and 6,266,772 shares at December 25, 1993	208,010	207,224
Class B common stock—$.033 par value; authorized 3,000,000 shares; issued: 932,448 shares at December 31, 1994, and 947,637 shares at December 25, 1993	30,770	31,271
Additional paid-in capital	48,366,185	48,222,445
Retained earnings	25,316,309	27,185,003
Unearned compensation		(19,815)
Treasury stock, at cost: 69,032 Class A and 1,092 Class B shares at December 31, 1994, and 66,353 Class A and 1,092 Class B shares at December 25, 1993	(1,420,155)	(1,364,613)
Total stockholders' equity	$ 72,502,019	$ 74,262,415
Total liabilities and stockholders' equity	$120,295,103	$106,360,585

the upper middle class sector who had no children. People in this segment did not need to purchase larger quantities of ice cream at one time.

Ice-cream pints accounted for only about 13 percent of supermarket ice-cream sales. Nonetheless, Ben & Jerry's strategy had been to obtain an increasingly large piece of a shrinking pie, but that was becoming more difficult as the competitive landscape changed.

It soon became apparent that the company would have to work harder to continue success based on its "new flavor" strategy because competitors began imitating its flavors with rapidly increasing speed. While originally it could count on about six months before imitations arrived, Ben & Jerry's now "owned" a flavor for only about 60 days. As a result, the company revised its marketing goal to establish a standard of product quality that cannot be imitated, to introduce more "euphoric" new flavors and to improve the selection of the company's flavors in grocery stores.

In March 1994, Ben & Jerry's had introduced its line of Smooth, No Chunks flavors in response to market research indicating that a large portion of the super-premium market did not like chunks. The company targeted the segment that was "just too tired to chew" at the end of a busy day and who would rather "experience their ice cream without having to exert too much energy." That move placed Ben & Jerry's in a fortified position in its battle with Häagen-Dazs.

Other product innovations included novelty items such as Brownie Bars, which failed, and Peace Pops, which were marginally successful. Peace Pops were wrapped in a message to redirect 1 percent of the military budget to social programs; they did well only at convenience stores, suggesting to the company that they were primarily impulse buys. Recently, 70 percent of the Pops were sold in convenience stores.

Place

Ben & Jerry's marketed its superpremium ice-cream products to supermarkets, grocery stores, convenience stores and restaurants that had demonstrated corporate consciousness in the way they did business. Roughly 105 Ben & Jerry's franchises or licensed "scoop shops" existed across the United States, in addition to some in Canada and Israel and a 50-50 joint venture in Russia. In addition, in March 1994 the company began shipping a small amount of its products to small specialty stores in the United Kingdom.

The company had also attempted to increase its distribution channels by offering gifts by mail. This concept featured a brochure advertising earthy, tie-dyed gifts, as well as ice cream, coffee and candy, and offered consumers the ability to have the ice cream dry-ice packed and delivered overnight anywhere in the country. So far, the concept has met with limited success, due in part to limited promotion.

Restaurants were another venue the company was exploring in order to maintain growth, but to date, Ben & Jerry's has not placed this opportunity as a primary goal. The same is true for global expansion. The company had been successful abroad, but efforts had been haphazard and cause-generated, and outcomes had been based solely on luck. The company admitted that it did not have an international strategy and that true commitment to global exporting would require that it learn much more about the market—something it has not made a current priority.

Price

Ben & Jerry's ice-cream products were premium-priced at the high end of the ice-cream market. A pint of ice cream retailed for approximately $2.69. Although this pricing strategy worked extremely well within the exploding market of the late 1980s and early 1990s, it had been experiencing some difficulty in recent years, as demand shifted toward lower-priced and/or private-label products in grocery stores. Price elasticity had declined, and whereas before Ben & Jerry's could impose significant price increases (8 percent in 1991, 4 percent in early 1993), price became the pivotal issue.

Pricing pressure also resulted from the apparent consolidation of sales in a few players' hands and the stagnation of the market, with new forms of pricing competition coming into play. Until recently, all superpremium ice-cream and frozen-yogurt makers priced their products roughly equivalently. But Häagen-Dazs, the "sleeping giant" that had allowed Ben & Jerry's to gain market share at its expense during the late 1980s, had recently "woken up" and soon started "throwing dollars and incentives at the marketplace."

Häagen-Dazs was much bigger than Ben & Jerry's and so capable of waging a significant price war without fear of any lasting harm. The result was two-for-one sales and discounts in certain parts of the country. Ben & Jerry's guardedly followed suit with price discounts and store coupons for $1.49 pints, recognizing that the battle had become solely financial.

Promotion

Ben & Jerry's product promotion relied primarily on cause-generated marketing. It was the company's belief that marketing should not be performed simply to sell the product, but to have an effect on society. This marketing theory was called "Edible Activism."

The company's cause-related events included such things as traveling vaudeville shows in buses with solar-powered freezers—the more unconventional and politically correct, the better. The largest part of Ben & Jerry's budget went to major music festivals around the country, including the Newport Folk Festival in Rhode Island. In addition, the company's own plant was the largest tourist attraction in Vermont, hosting 275,000 visitors annually; thus, just by opening its own doors, Ben & Jerry's was promoting its products.

The company's socially conscious practices also earned it regular publicity, thereby saving it millions in public expenditures annually. As Ben once said, "the media can supply the ink and Ben & Jerry's will supply the wackiness."

Responsibility for marketing had not been farmed out to outside design and advertising firms. Rather, the company chose to maintain control for this function in-house. In March 1994, for example, Ben & Jerry's had created its first 30-second commercial to sell its new Smooth, No Chunks flavors; directed by Spike Lee, the ad featured socially minded stars who received nothing but a lifetime supply of ice cream for their efforts. The $6 million campaign to launch the line also included print ads featuring high-profile activists such as Carlos Santana, Bobby Seale and Pete Seeger.

As competitive pressures increased and market growth slowed, Ben & Jerry's was forced to reexamine its exclusive use of socially oriented promotion. Many publicity events were abandoned so that funds could be diverted instead to promotional priorities such as store coupons and price discounts. While apparently rational, such a shift also garnered criticism that the company had been simply using the "world's ills and social needs to sell a product."

Operations

In February 1995, Ben & Jerry's had two manufacturing plants located in Waterbury and Springfield, Vermont; its St. Albans plant, whose opening had been delayed several times, was currently scheduled to come online in the second half of 1995. The company's main factory, in Waterbury, was located just over the hill from company headquarters, and generally operated two shifts a day, six days a week. Production averaged about 4.7 million gallons a year. The Springfield plant was used for the production of ice-cream novelties, bulk ice cream and frozen yogurt, and packaged pints; its production averaged about 1.2 million dozen novelties, 2.3 million gallons of bulk ice cream and frozen yogurt, packaged pints and quarts per year. It, too, operated six days a week. Overall, the company had a maximum manufacturing capacity at its own facilities of about 10.2 million gallons per year of packaged pints.

During 1992 and 1993, Ben & Jerry's had increased its manufacturing capacity to support its phenomenal sales growth. After seeing a surge in sales in the winter of 1991, the company added pint production lines at its Springfield plant and at the St. Albans Cooperative Creamery, in space loaned to the company by the site's family farmer owners.

The new St. Albans plant would have a maximum ice-cream and yogurt production capacity of about 17 million gallons per year when operated six days a week. It was being built with energy-efficient lighting, motors and compressors to reduce the total amount of energy required for production. At the same time, Ben & Jerry's was investing $2 million in the Waterbury plant to improve efficiency there. In the early 1990s the company was fined for dumping too much waste into the Waterbury system; since then, it launched a pilot cleanup project using a solar greenhouse to treat sewage.

The production equipment used at Ben & Jerry's was not the most efficient available; in fact, the only new machine added in recent years had been a wrapping machine, which replaced an antiquated predecessor. The company felt that increased automation might eliminate jobs, which would undermine its philosophy of social responsibility. In discussing the labor-intensive nature of the packaging line, the company has said that it would choose versatility over speed, should the choice be necessary. It admitted that there were several new machines available that were faster than what it currently used: It took the company about two hours to change from one size-packaging capability to another.

Until the new plant was ready, Ben & Jerry's had a manufacturing and warehouse agreement with Edy's Grand Ice Cream, a subsidiary of Dreyer's Grand Ice Cream Inc., to manufacture certain pint ice-cream flavors at its plant in Fort Wayne, Indiana. The agreement was set in accordance with Ben & Jerry's quality-control specifications, and used dairy products shipped from Vermont. About 5 million gallons, or 40 percent of the packaged pints, were manufactured under this agreement in 1994, compared with about 37 percent in 1993. For 1995, the company expected that to be 2 million gallons.

HUMAN RESOURCES

Since its inception, Ben & Jerry's had been run entrepreneurially by Ben and Jerry and "built on the cult of these two counter-cultural personalities." As the company grew to almost 600 employees, the challenge became to maintain the original spirit while managing an increasingly large organization.

The key to Ben & Jerry's human resources success lay in keeping employees at all levels involved in bottom-up decision making. The company attempted to create ownership at all levels and followed the new-age management model of worker empowerment. Because they had the power to make decisions and influence how things were done, employees were energized and committed.

Of course, as the company grew, it became difficult to preserve the feel of a small company in which people matter amid the firm's transformation into an immense corporate entity. Both Ben and Jerry drew considerable praise from those inside as well as outside the company for their efforts to achieve this, and were viewed by many as the company's two biggest assets.

At the same time, however, there were those who criticized the company for "not walking its talk" in terms of employee treatment. Despite the firm's much hailed and publicized politically correct culture, for instance, employees nonetheless held less than half of 1 percent of company stock. And while Ben and Jerry frequently drew attention to the fact that their own salaries were a relatively paltry $130,000 per year, they failed to note that their combined stock was worth in excess of $50 million.

Finally, known for occasionally getting bored with the daily grind and going off on some sabbatical, Ben and Jerry did not enjoy an untarnished reputation on Wall Street. The company's stock consistently underperformed the market and irritated many investors, largely as a result of the firm's insistence on putting its principles—the promotion of charity, peace and environmental preservation—ahead of its public shareholders.

The benefits offered to employees at the company were widely regarded as being on the cutting edge. Tuition reimbursement, flexible spending accounts, opinion surveys, evaluate-your-boss polls, paid health-club fees, 12 unpaid weeks of maternity, paternity and adoption leave, child-care centers, free body and foot massages, sabbatical leave, profit sharing, paid adoption expenses, wellness plans, an insurance plan that covered unmarried heterosexual and homosexual domestic partners, and free ice cream were all among the offerings employees could take advantage of. Ben & Jerry's management also reflected a commitment to minorities and women. Of the five senior positions filled in 1990, four were held by women or minorities.

Minimum wage at Ben & Jerry's was $8 per hour. While top salaries had been capped at roughly $150,000 (the sum earned in 1993 by Charles Lacy, president and COO), that policy was abandoned with the hiring of Holland. Nevertheless, while the average per capita income of Vermont residents was $17,436, the lowest-paid employee at Ben & Jerry's earned salary and benefits worth roughly $22,000.

Not surprisingly, the result of all its attention to employees earned Ben & Jerry's a generally happy workforce; its turnover rate was only 12 percent.

THE CHALLENGE

When Robert Holland took the helm as CEO, Ben & Jerry's future direction was far from clear (see Exhibit 4). While the company had built its success by selling high-fat

---

EXHIBIT 4
CEO's Letter

Dear Shareholders,

As I said at the press conference announcing my appointment as CEO of Ben & Jerry's, it is difficult to say what you are going to do for a company when you are speaking to people who know more about that company than you do.

I came to Ben & Jerry's because I like what I see in this Company. Ben & Jerry's enjoys a tremendous consumer franchise. It has consistently delivered pleasant surprises to its followers in the form of great products and a unique commitment to innovation both in the marketplace and in its vision of the critical role business must play in improving our society. This is a consumer franchise fairly brimming with goodwill between customers and the Company.

I have run businesses of my own and have consulted with many others. What I intend to offer to Ben & Jerry's is the business management and strategic planning skills that it has been my good fortune to learn throughout my career. Despite the difficulties Ben & Jerry's has noted in its most recent results—which are a combination of internal issues and marketplace conditions—I see a host of opportunities in front of this unique Company. As this Annual Report is being prepared, I am brand-new on the job. As such, it is more my task to begin the process of assessing and prioritizing these opportunities than to describe them in detail here.

What impresses me most is what is already here. The people resources of this Company are a tremendous asset; these are skilled, dedicated people whose talents and experience I can complement but not supplant. High on my list of priorities is to analyze the strengths and the deployment of our people and to fill what missing pieces may exist. I stress, though, that much of what we need is already well rooted in the functions and the traditions of this Company.

It is true that I did not write an essay for the "Yo! I'm Your CEO!" contest until I had been selected for the position. There were, as I hear it, some strong entrants from the contest though. The contest itself was a perfect snapshot of what is unique and wonderful about Ben & Jerry's, for two reasons. First, the Company had the imagination to see that it made sense to cast a wide net in its search; that the regular route—a standard executive search—might not be the only place to find what it was looking for. (As the founders note in their letter in this Annual Report, if they had taken the regular route, they would not have gotten to where the Company is today.) Second, the contest created an explosion of creativity and fascination on the part of customers and friends. Precious few companies have the kind of rapport with their customers that can endanger such excitement. I have seen it clearly in the many letters sent to me since my arrival here, without return addresses, that simply say, "Good luck!" or "Welcome to our family."

In the poem I wrote to celebrate the spirit of the contest and the Company, I closed with the words, ". . . with miles to go before we sleep . . . and time left yet to get there. Only in America." I ask you for a bit of that time to make real what I know that Ben & Jerry's can do. I want my actions to speak best, not my words on this page. It is my belief and commitment that next year at this time, you will be close to as glad to have me here as I am today to be here.

With thanks & best wishes,

Bob Holland

ice creams to consumers who were willing to pay more for the unique flavors and for Ben & Jerry's social causes, those days were gone. Health concerns, increased competition, pressure on prices and its own massive size meant that Ben & Jerry's had to change. For Holland, the question was not "if" but "how."

Selected Sources

Allen, Robin Lee. "Demographics Changing, Shaping Industry." *Nation's Restaurant News*, October 28, 1991, p. 42.

Annual Report, Ben & Jerry's Homemade Inc.

"Ben, Jerry Losing Their Values?," *The Washington Times*, June 27, 1994, p. A17.

"Ben & Jerry's: A Firm with a View." *Packaging Digest*, January 1993, p. 50.

"Ben & Jerry's Finally Scoops Up New CEO." *The Chicago Tribune*, February 2, 1995, p. 1.

"Ben & Jerry's Names Cream of the Crop." *The Washington Post*, February 2, 1995, p. D11.

"Ben & Jerry's Projecting Loss for Fourth Quarter." *Ice Cream Reporter*, January 20, 1995, p. 1.

Bittman, Mark. "Ben & Jerry's Caring Capitalism." *Restaurant Business Magazine*, November 20, 1990, p. 132.

Britt, Bill. "Häagen-Dazs Pushes Cold Front Across World." *Marketing (UK)*, October 4, 1990, pp. 30–31.

Bryant, Adam. "Ding-a-Ling Marketing: An Ice Cream Truck Not Just for Kids." *The New York Times*, August 21, 1992, p. 3.

Calta, Marialisa. "Ice Cream Sorcerer." *The New York Times*, March 21, 1993, p. 66.

Carlin, Peter. "Pure Profit: For Small Companies That Stress Social Values as Much as the Bottom Line, Growing Up Hasn't Been an Easy Task." *The Lost Angeles Times*, February 5, 1995, p. 12.

Carton, Barbara. "A Ben & Jerry's Principle Hits a Melting Point: Seeking New CEO, Firm to Scrap Pay Ceiling." *The Boston Globe*, June 14, 1994, p. 1.

Collins, Glenn. "Ben & Jerry's Talent Hunt Ends." *The New York Times*, February 2, 1995, p. D1.

Feder, Barnaby J. "Ben Leaving as Ben & Jerry's Chief." *The New York Times*, June 14, 1994, p. D1.

Forseter, Murray. "Ben & Jerry's Caring Capitalism." *Chain Store Age Executive with Shopping Center Age*, December 1991, p. 12.

Glassman, James K. "Inside Scoop." *The Washington Post*, June 19, 1994, p. H1.

Henriques, Diana B. "Ben & Jerry's—and Dreyer's?" *The New York Times*, June 16, 1991, p. 27.

Hitchner, Earl. "We All Scream for Ice Cream: Ben and Jerry's Homemade Inc." *National Productivity Review*, December 22, 1994, p. 114.

Horwich, Andrea. "Ice Cream Still America's Favorite Dessert?" *Dairy Foods*, August 1990, p. 42.

Hwang, Suein L. "Marketscan: While Many Competitors See Sales Melt, Ben & Jerry's Scoops Out Solid Growth." *The Wall Street Journal*, May 25, 1993, p. 1.

"Ice Cream Firm Names New CEO: Ben & Jerry's Uses Traditional Search." *The Houston Chronicle*, February 2, 1995, p. 2.

"The Ice Cream Market Grows Up." *Frozen and Chilled Foods*, April 1992, p. 25.

Katz, David M. "How Ben & Jerry's Mingles Conscience with Profit Motive." *Property & Casualty/Risk & Benefits Management Edition*, June 3, 1991, p. 9.

Kuhn, Mary Ellen. "Ben & Jerry's Suffers Some Growing Pains: Ben and Jerry's Homemade Inc." *Food Processing*, September 1994, p. 56.

Laabs, Jennifer J. "Ben & Jerry's Caring Capitalism: Ben and Jerry's Homemade Inc." *Personnel Journal Optimas Award*, November 1992, p. 20.

LaFranchi, Howard. "Häagen Dazs Invades Europe, Sans Bowl." *The Christian Science Monitor*, August 19, 1993, p. 7.

Lager, Fred. "Chico," in *Ben & Jerry's: The Inside Scoop*. New York: Crown Publishers, 1994.

Larrabbe, Kathryn. "Ben Cohen Runs a Business with a Mission." *Business Insurance*, April 1990, p. T27.

Linsen, Mary Ann. "Slow Going for Ice Cream." *Progressive Grocer*, March 1991, p. 117.

Lowery, Mark. "Sold on Ice Cream." *Black Enterprise*, April 1995, p. 60.

Mann, Ernest J. "Ice Cream, Part 1." *Dairy Industries International*, July 1991, p. 15.

Manor, Robert. "Ben, Jerry Aren't Above Making a Profit." *Star Tribune*, July 5, 1994, p. 6B.

Maremont, Mark. "Say It Ain't So, Ben & Jerry." *Business Week*, June 13, 1994, p. 6.

Maremont, Mark. "They're All Screaming for Häagen Dazs." *Business Week*, October 14, 1991, p. 121.

Mathews, Jay. "Ben & Jerry's Melting Social Charter: Ice Cream Maker Abandons Progressive Pay Policy to Find New CEO." *The Washington Post*, June 14, 1994, p. D3.

"More than an Ice Cream . . . Ben & Jerry's Is Social Responsibility." *Chain Store Age Executive*, August 1991, p. 81.

Norris, Floyd. "Market Place: Low-Fat Problem at Ben & Jerry's." *The New York Times*, September 9, 1992, p. 6.

O'Donnell, Claudia Dziuk. "The Story Behind the Story: Two Dairy Processors Tell a Tale of Fruits, Flavors and Nuts; Dean Foods Co.; Ben & Jerry's Homemade Inc." *Dairy Foods Magazine*, May 1993, p. 53.

Palmer, Thomas. "News in Advertising." *The Boston Globe*, November 11, 1990, p. A4.

Pandya, Mukul. "The Executive Life: Ice-Cream Dream Job Is Tempting Thousands." *The New York Times*, July 10, 1994, p. 21.

Pereira, Joseph, and Joann S. Lublin. "Ben & Jerry's Appoints Holland President, CEO." *The Wall Street Journal*, February 2, 1995.

Rosenberg, John S. "Growing Pains: After a Remarkable Adolescence, Is Ben & Jerry's Settling into Middle Age? *Vermont Magazine*, November–December 1993, p. 44.

Ryan, Nancy Ross. "Frozen Assets." *Restaurants & Institutions*, March 25, 1992, pp. 118–126.

Saulnier, John M. "Ice Cream Serves Up Sweetest Profits of All in Retail Frozen Food Cabinet." *Quick Frozen Foods International*, January 1992, p. 134.

Seligman, Daniel, and Patty de Llosa. "Ben & Jerry Save the World." *Fortune*, June 3, 1991, p. 247.

Shao, Maria. "Ben & Jerry's Grows Up." *The Boston Globe*, July 3, 1994, p. 65.

Shao, Maria. "The New Emperor of Ice Cream." *The Boston Globe*, February 2, 1995, p. 35.

Shao, Maria. "A Scoopful of Credentials: CEO Holland Brings an Activist's Blend to Ben & Jerry's." *The Boston Globe*, March 1, 1995, p. 1.

Smith, Geoffrey. "Life Won't Be Just a Bowl of Cherry Garcia." *Business Week*, July 18, 1994, p. 42.

Sneyd, Ross. "Ben & Jerry's Set to Appoint New CEO." *The Associated Press*, January 31, 1995.

Stableford, Joan. "Ben & Jerry's Sweetens Its Success by Helping Others." *Fairfield County Business Journal*, March 4, 1991, p. 1.

Wallace, Anne. "Ben Cohen to Step Down as CEO of Ben & Jerry's." *The Associated Press*, June 13, 1994.

Windle, Rickie. "Ben & Jerry's Creams Amy's." *Austin Business Journal*, October 4, 1993, p. 1.

"World Screams for America's Ice Cream." *The Christian Science Monitor*, September 28, 1990, p. 8.

http://www.benjerry.com/

CASE 8

Tootsie Roll, Inc.*

"Tootsie Roll's good fortunes are an accumulation of many small decisions that were probably made right plus bigger key decisions, such as acquisitions, that have been made right, and a lot of luck."

—Mel Gordon, CEO Tootsie Roll, 1993

INTRODUCTION

Tootsie Roll Industries, Inc., a niche candy maker, has often been voted one of *Forbes* magazine's "200 Best Small Companies of America." A top quality producer and distributor of Tootsie Rolls and other candy, Tootsie Roll Industries maintains a 50% market share of the taffy and lollipop segment of the candy industry, and sales have increased each year for the past nineteen years. The world's largest lollipop supplier, the company produces approximately 16 million lollipops and 37 million individual Tootsie Rolls a day.

EARLY HISTORY

In 1896, Leo Hirschfield, a young immigrant from Austria, set up a small shop in Brooklyn, New York, to make candy from a recipe he had brought from Europe. As he rolled the sweet, chewy chocolate candies, his thoughts wandered to his young daughter, Clara "Tootsie" Hirschfield, and he named his new confection the "Tootsie Roll." He wrapped the Tootsie Rolls individually in paper to keep them clean and sanitary, and priced them at a penny each.

Hirschfield's Tootsie Rolls were an immediate success, and demand quickly outpaced supply. Hirschfield realized he would need more capital to promote and expand

*Prepared by Sharon Ungar Lane and Alan N. Hoffman, Bentley College. Please address all correspondence to: Dr. Alan N. Hoffman, AGC 320, Department of Management, Bentley College, 175 Forest Street, Waltham, MA 02154-4705, (617) 891-2287, AHOFFMAN@BENTLEY.EDU, (617) 237-0627 (fax). Printed by permission of Dr. Alan N. Hoffman, Bentley College.

his business. After just one year, he merged his operation with a local candy manufacturer, Stern & Saalberg, which incorporated eight years later, and officially changed its name to the Sweets Company of America in 1917.

From 1922 to 1966, the Sweets Company of America set up manufacturing facilities around the United States to meet growing demand for Tootsie Roll products. Having captured America's sweet tooth with the Tootsie Roll, the company expanded its product line in the 1930s, developing a series of companion products such as the first soft-centered lollipop, the Tootsie Pop, which had a Tootsie Roll center and a hard candy outside.

In 1962, Ellen and Melvin Gordon took over as President/Chief Operating Officer and Chief Executive Officer/Chairman of the Board, respectively. In 1966, the Gordons changed the company name to Tootsie Roll Industries, Inc., and opened a large manufacturing facility in Chicago (which subsequently became the company's world headquarters). In the late 1960s, Tootsie Roll began exploring foreign markets, establishing a subsidiary in Mexico and licensing a firm in the Philippines to produce and distribute Tootsie Rolls. After a positive response in both these countries, the company expanded to Canada in 1971.

Amazingly enough, as the Tootsie Roll celebrates its 100th birthday in 1996, the candy still tastes exactly the same as it did when it was first hand-rolled by Leo Hirschfield. The company's success, as nineteen consecutive years of record sales and fourteen consecutive years of record earnings confirms, is based on strong consumer awareness of the Tootsie Roll brand name, and strategic acquisition of other well positioned and highly recognized brand names to leverage its existing operations. The Gordons own 66% of the voting rights and 47% of the company's stock, and continue to control the company, which remains exclusively a candy company making the very best quality candy for the market it knows best.

THE CANDY INDUSTRY

The United States' largest manufacturing sector, the processed food and beverage industry, is composed of two primary divisions: lower value-added and higher value-added food processors. Higher value-added processors, such as candy manufacturers, make retail-ready, packaged, consumer brand name products which have a minimum of 40% of the industry shipment value added through sophisticated manufacturing. Candy is a $20 billion retail industry worldwide, and accounts for about one-third of the dollar-value of the snack-food market (the largest segment of the higher value-added division). Tootsie Roll Industries occupies a niche market within the Standard Industrial Classification (SIC) code 2064 (candy and other confectionery products) which includes taffies, lollipops and chewing gum. The U.S. confectionery market generates approximately $9.7 billion in annual sales.

Candy is not yet a "mature" industry in the United States. The compound annual growth rate for candy in the past ten years has been close to 6% a year, a very solid gain in an industry that is supposedly mature. In fact, within the chocolate confectionery subcategory, the U.S. ranks eleventh in the world in per capita consumption and fifth in the world in growth since 1980. Based on current demographics, many analysts believe that there will be further growth for confectioneries. A "baby boomlet" is on the way, significantly increasing the teenage population. By the time the population bulge peaks in the year 2010, it will top the baby boom of the 1960s in both size and duration. According to government statistics, the percentage of children between the ages of 5 and 14 will rise during the 1990s, increasing from 14.2% of the population in 1990 to 14.5% in the year 2000. This trend will serve as a strong foundation for increasing consumption of confectionery products through the end of the century. Nevertheless, spending for food and drink as a percentage of all personal consumption is declining in the United States, and most manufacturers recognize that future opportunities lie in using profits from domestic sales to penetrate foreign markets.

Many U.S. producers now use complex processing methods and efficient, automated manufacturing operations which yield comparable quality at lower cost, and are finding a growing international market for their products. Despite recessionary economic conditions and reduced discretionary income, foreign consumers purchase U.S. higher value-added foods and beverages because U.S. products compare favorably with similar products made elsewhere, offering equal or better quality at a lower price. Today, the top five importers of U.S. products are: Japan, Canada, Mexico, South Korea, and the Netherlands. Foreign demand for U.S.-produced higher value-added products (including candy) has increased since 1993, thanks primarily to the rapid growth of the middle class in developing and emerging nations, and growth in the new markets of the former Soviet bloc nations.

However, the candy industry has recently faced several industry curbs. New nutritional labeling requirements were imposed by the Food and Drug Administration in 1990 to regulate serving size, health messages, and the use of descriptive terms such as "light" and "low fat." The Federal Trade Commission also developed stringent sale-date requirements and strict guidelines for documenting environmental claims on packaging. These new regulations were imposed under costly, disruptive, difficult-to-meet deadlines, and posed a particular threat to many foreign food and beverage processors, who are not accustomed to such extensive product analysis and disclosure. For Tootsie Roll, this major packaging revision was costly, and involved detailed laboratory analysis and package modification of every item the company produces.

Candy is still a treat for all ages. People that loved Tootsie Rolls when they were children often buy them for their children and thus the Tootsie Roll perpetuates itself. The baby boom generation grew up with Tootsie Roll products; therefore name recognition is very high among this group. While parental purchases may increase due to brand recognition, the baby boomers are becoming increasingly more concerned with their health and their children's diet. As a result, baby boomers are purchasing less candy for themselves and their children. Thus, as people become more health and weight conscious, their demand for sugar-based products decreases. Additionally, as this consumer group gets older, their concern for dental health becomes greater. Candy has been identified as a major cause of dental decay, and hard, sticky, or chewy snacks, such as Tootsie Rolls, cannot be eaten by people who have had various kinds of dental work. Also, some parents do not buy candy because they are concerned that sugar causes hyperactivity in some children.

Children are Tootsie Roll's primary target market. Children ages 6 to 17 created the greatest demand for confectionery products. Candy was the second most requested snack food among 6 to 12 year olds; only ice cream was higher in demand, according to a study by the Good Housekeeping Institute. This group (ages 6 to 17) spend $60 billion of their own money annually with two-thirds of this spending on candy, snacks and beverages.

TOOTSIE ROLL—1996

Tootsie Rolls are unique, and occupy a niche of the candy market which includes taffies, lollipops and chewing gum. Tootsie Roll Industries' competition is other candy and ready-to-eat snack food manufacturers. Tootsie Roll Industries commands 2%–3% of the overall market as the eighth largest candy manufacturer, following Hershey (27%), M&M Mars (25%), Nestlé (10%), Brach (6%), Huhtamaki (4%), Storck (3%), and RJR Nabisco (3%). (See Exhibit 1.) Although Tootsie Roll has captured only 2%–3% of the total candy market, it continues to be the leader in its own segment, where it maintains a 50% market share. Tootsie Roll's strengths are brand loyalty, established shelf space, state-of-the-art manufacturing facilities and the fact that there are fixed price ceilings for candy products. Also, as the United States becomes a more nutrition oriented society, Tootsie Rolls have another advantage because they contain no cholesterol and have less saturated fat than other leading candy bars.

Tootsie Roll uses many suppliers for sugar, corn syrup, cocoa, and milk, and adapts to fluctuations in commodity prices by changing the formula and size of its products to keep total costs relatively constant. For example, Tootsie Roll can substitute corn syrup for some of the necessary sugar, thus decreasing its dependency upon

EXHIBIT 1
Top Ten Candy Brands—5 Year Average Market Share

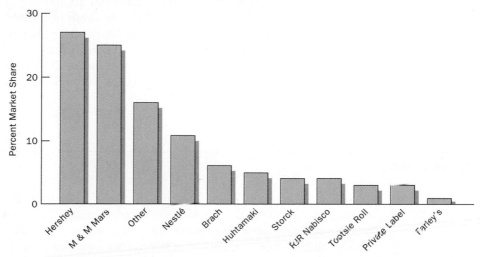

a given commodity or supplier. Tootsie Roll also reduces and controls costs by owning its own refinery. The company can thus buy raw sugar and make, rather than buy, processed sugar, decreasing its dependence on processed sugar suppliers. When natural disasters affect the availability or price of one of its ingredients, for instance, sugar or cocoa, as did floods along the Mississippi River in 1993, the company usually decreases the size of its product to keep the selling price constant.

Tootsie Roll Industries' vertically integrated structure supports its drive for competitiveness, keeping total costs down and maintaining its leading edge in technology. In addition to the sugar refinery, Tootsie Roll owns its own advertising agency, so that commissions flow back into it. The company also makes the sticks for its lollipops, has a print shop for color printing, and owns a machine shop where new machinery is built and existing machinery rebuilt. Tootsie Roll Industries also constantly upgrades its manufacturing equipment to maintain the utmost efficiency.

Tootsie Roll's objectives, which have made it one of America's strongest companies, are, and have always been:

1. Run a trim operation

2. Eliminate waste

3. Minimize cost

4. Improve performance

To be competitive in the candy world market, where margins are limited, one must produce top quality candy highly efficiently. Tootsie Roll has spent millions of dollars on state-of-the-art expansion and automation of its five production facilities (Chicago, Massachusetts, New York, Tennessee and Mexico). Much of its equipment is designed specifically for Tootsie Roll. As Mel Gordon, CEO and Chairman of the Board of Tootsie Roll Industries, explains, "Anybody can buy machinery and in that way become state-of-the-art, but if you develop your own adaptations to the machinery so that it runs faster and runs better for your products, or you develop in-house machinery that does what nobody else in the market can do, then you're ahead of state-of-the-art. We've strived in the last 15 years to be ahead of state-of-the-art." However, the one aspect of its operations the company has not been able to control is the power of its packaging material suppliers. Increased demand has led to dramatic price increases in paper, board, plastics and foil. To insulate itself from price fluctuations, Tootsie Roll has, whenever possible, negotiated fixed price contracts with its packaging suppliers.

ACQUISITIONS

Tootsie Roll Industries often generates more cash than it needs for internal growth, and can therefore consider complementary acquisitions. Following strict criteria, such as a strong brand name, and a preference for non-chocolate (such as hard candies and chewy candies) over chocolate so as not to compete in its own niche, Tootsie Roll has made several key acquisitions of proven brands to expand its product line, increase its shelf space, and spur growth. As President Ellen Gordon explains, "We add new lines only when it benefits our product in quality and efficiency."

Two of Tootsie Roll's earliest acquisitions (1972) were the Mason Division of Candy Corporation of America, which makes such well known products as Mason Mints, Mason Dots, Mason Licorice Crows, and Mason Spice Berries; and the Bonamo Turkish Taffy Company. In 1985, Tootsie Roll acquired Cella's Confections, which makes chocolate covered cherries; and in 1988, it acquired the Charms Company, thereby becoming the world's largest manufacturer of lollipops. Charms' principal product, the Blow Pop, a lollipop with a bubble gum center, makes a nice complement to the highly successful Tootsie Pop. Shortly after the acquisition of the Charms Company, Mel Gordon observed, "We specialize in hard candies such as Tootsie Pops and Blow Pops and all the flat pops that Charms makes. That's a big niche for us, to be the world's largest manufacturer of pops. Also, we're in chewy candy with the Tootsie Roll and the growing Frooties and Flavor Roll lines. We feel that in those two areas we have a certain dominance and we'd like to keep our expertise focused in those areas."

In November 1993, Tootsie Roll purchased the chocolate and caramel division of the Warner-Lambert Company, which makes the popular brands Junior Mints, Charleston Chew, Sugar Daddy, Sugar Babies and Pom Poms. The acquisition of these new lines places Tootsie Roll Industries in more competition with other major chocolate manufacturers such as Hershey and M&M Mars, and provides it with a number of new products which clearly complement its "chewy" candy product line. Over the years, Tootsie Roll has carefully and selectively acquired seventeen popular candy brands, enlarging its niche in the candy and other confectionery segment of the higher value-added products market.

DISTRIBUTION/ADVERTISING

Tootsie Roll Industries uses over 100 public and contract brokers to distribute its products to nearly 15,000 customers. (See Exhibit 2.) To market the newly acquired

EXHIBIT 2
Tootsie Roll Industries—5 Year Sales History

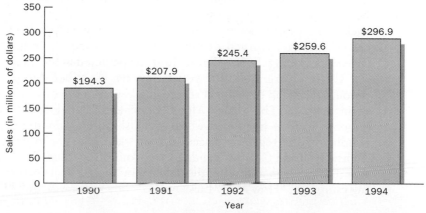

Warner-Lambert brands more effectively, Tootsie Roll created new packaging for them which resembled the packaging of its more established Tootsie Roll products and capitalized on the synergies of Warner-Lambert products with its existing lines.

In addition to using its distribution network to increase sales of Warner-Lambert products, Tootsie Roll is pushing those products generally associated with movie theatres, such as Junior Mints, into mainstream retail outlets: convenience stores, grocery stores, drug chains and warehouse club stores. Convenience stores and supermarkets have traditionally been the dominant candy retailers, but have recently been losing sales to discount stores and drugstore chains. Right now, all four venues share equally in confectionery sales. However, most candy purchases are impulse buys made while waiting in line at a store, and many supermarkets have switched to candy-free aisles, thus reducing these impulse sales. As impulse sales opportunities are diminished, the customer must search for the product. A consumer is unlikely to undertake a search unless desire is heightened through advertising. Parents are the target market that advertisements must reach. However, marketing efforts often tend to focus on children, who are not always the purchasers. These eager consumers purchase through and with the acceptance of their parents.

Tootsie Roll has most recently focused its sales efforts on the more rapidly growing classes of trade such as warehouse clubs. In the candy industry it is difficult to gain shelf space particularly when competing with large companies such as Hershey and M&M Mars. It appears that Tootsie Roll has begun to make progress toward this objective. Tootsie Rolls are beginning to appear in warehouse stores, such as Sam's, BJ's Warehouse and COSTCO, with large packages of traditional Tootsie Rolls and bags of multi-colored Tootsie Roll pops.

Candy regularly shows the strongest gains from promotion and merchandising, clearly evident by the significant increases in candy sales during major holiday periods—Valentine's Day, Easter, Halloween, and Christmas. In fact, candy has shown a stronger response to promotions than any other snack category.

The third quarter has always been the strongest for Tootsie Rolls due to increased Halloween sales. However, Halloween is changing. Grocery retailers report that there is a noticeable shift in consumer behavior because of concern for child safety. In the last several years, Halloween celebrations have moved from the streets, "trick or treating" door to door, to indoor parties sponsored by schools, churches, and, more recently to enclosed shopping malls, thereby reducing purchases for candy that used to be given to trick or treaters. Also, parents have been reluctant to purchase any products that could be easily tampered with, particularly at Halloween. The way Tootsie Roll products are packaged creates a potential concern. Individually wrapped and not sealed products can be tampered with and are thus negatively impacted by an accident such as the 1982 Tylenol poisoning. In fact, Tootsie Roll sales suffered in the wake of that national scare.

While Tootsie Roll's 100-year history has contributed to its wide product recognition, a tradition of national advertising begun in the early 1950s on television programs such as "The Mickey Mouse Club" and "Buffalo Bob" has successfully made "Tootsie Roll" a household word, establishing its domestic market; and schedules continue to be regularly placed in both electronic and print media. Although the Tootsie Roll and Charms brands are well known, as Ellen Gordon puts it, "it's important to keep them in front of the public." In Tootsie Roll's memorable 1970s advertising campaign, "How Many Licks?" a little boy asks a wise owl, "How many licks does it take to get to the Tootsie Roll center of a Tootsie Pop?" Consumers became actively involved as they tried to answer the question for themselves. Although the company has had several successful advertising campaigns since then, it currently spends very little on advertising (approximately 2% of sales, concentrated on television), relying instead on nostalgia and its 100-year-old brand. Internationally, however, aggressive advertising programs support the brands in Mexico as well as in the Pacific Rim markets and certain Eastern European countries.

THE GORDONS

Tootsie Roll Industries, Inc. has been run since 1962 by the husband and wife team of Ellen Gordon, President and Chief Operating Officer, and Melvin Gordon, Chairman of the Board and Chief Executive Officer. The couple owns 47% of the company stock, most of which was inherited by Ellen Gordon, whose family has been Tootsie Roll's largest shareholder since the early 1930s.

Ellen and Melvin Gordon have been working together since the 1960s. They are quick to state that they have an open door policy, but often do not attend annual meetings, saying that they already know what has happened. Together with five other executives, they plan all of the company's marketing, manufacturing and distribution strategies, but the Gordons alone determine Tootsie Roll's corporate vision by controlling strategic planning, decision making, and the setting of corporate goals. Ellen, 64, and Melvin, 75, have no immediate plans to retire, and insist they want to continue working, though, on a number of occasions, they have expressed the desire to have one of their four daughters (none of whom currently works for Tootsie Roll) take over the management of the company. "We hope that our children, or the management that we are building up in the company, will be able to run the company someday," the Gordons claim, but they have no definite strategic plan for passing on the succession.

Tootsie Roll's strong performance and superior balance sheet (see Exhibits 3, 4, and 5) should make it a prime target for a takeover, but the Gordons' determination to maintain control over Tootsie Roll Industries may be one reason why Wall Street has shown little interest in the company. The majority of Tootsie Roll's voting stock, 66%, is controlled by the Gordons and the couple says they have no intention of selling the company. Ellen Gordon explains, "We're busy making Tootsie Roll products and selling them. We're kind of conservative and we don't make projections."

Although Tootsie Roll does not intend to sacrifice long-term growth for short-term gains, its strategy has simply been to focus on making Tootsie Rolls, rather than on preparing forecasts or strategic planning. Over the years, several key acquisitions have enhanced Tootsie Roll's product line, but these acquisitions have generally been made as opportunities have presented themselves within its niche market, and not necessarily as part of a well thought out strategic plan. The Gordons remain arrogant in their view of the market. Ellen Gordon repeated states, "No one else can make a Tootsie Roll."

Recently, Tootsie Roll Industries took advantage of an opportunity related to the location of its headquarters in Chicago. The lease on its 2.2 million square foot facility in Chicago was due to expire and the landlord was not willing to renew it. Tootsie

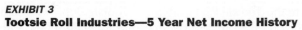

EXHIBIT 3
Tootsie Roll Industries—5 Year Net Income History

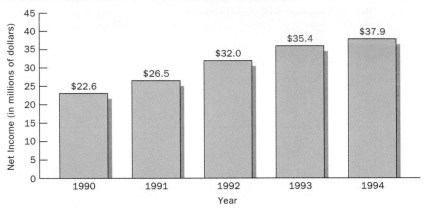

Roll faced the possibility of relocating to a less expensive territory because with a low ticket item like candy, every penny counts, but the company did not wish to relocate. At the same time, the city did not want Tootsie Roll Industries to leave because it feared the resulting rise in unemployment. Thus, Ellen Gordon was able to leverage the firm's 850 jobs into a lucrative package of incentives to stay headquartered in Chicago. The deal signaled a national trend: small companies are more likely to get big tax concessions and other perks as city economies increasingly depend on them. The Gordons' negotiations garnered $1.4 million in state and local tax exemptions over the next fifteen years, a $20 million low-interest rate loan to buy the Tootsie Roll plant, $200,000 in job training funds, and the creation of a state enterprise zone located in the plant for tax breaks on machinery and utilities. In turn, Gordon agreed to add 200 workers over five years and start a loan program for employees to buy homes in Chicago.

Tootsie Roll has remained an independent company for its 100-year history and Ellen Gordon feels that its independence has been a great strength: "As we have grown beyond a small entrepreneurial company we have been able to retain some of our entrepreneurial philosophy and way of doing business." The Gordons are determined to continue as an independent company "for generations to come," but Ellen claims, finally, that the key to their success is ". . . fun. Whenever I tell people I work in a confectionery company there's always a smile. That's very important—the magic of candy."

GLOBAL OPPORTUNITIES

The United States accounts for 90% of Tootsie Roll's sales; the remaining 10% of Tootsie Roll products are sold in foreign markets. Mexico is Tootsie Roll's second largest market, and Canada is third. However, because U.S. consumer spending for food and drink as a percentage of all personal consumption is declining, Tootsie Roll

EXHIBIT 4
Consolidated Statement of Earnings and Retained Earnings, Tootsie Roll Industries, Inc. and Subsidiaries
(in thousands of dollars except per share data)

| | For the year ended December 31 | | |
	1994	1993	1992
Net sales	$296,932	$259,593	$245,424
Cost of goods sold	155,565	133,978	127,123
Gross margin	$141,367	$125,615	$118,301
Operating expenses			
Marketing, selling and advertising	$ 44,974	$ 40,096	$ 38,958
Distribution and warehousing	20,682	17,655	16,959
General and administrative	13,017	12,837	13,186
Amortization of the excess of cost over			
acquired net tangible assets	2,706	1,510	1,265
	$ 81,379	$ 72,098	$ 70,368
Earnings from operations	$ 59,988	$ 53,517	$ 47,933
Other income, net	1,179	4,193	3,989
Earnings before income taxes	$ 61,167	$ 57,710	$ 51,922
Provision for income taxes	23,236	22,268	19,890
Net earnings	$ 37,931	$ 35,442	$ 32,032
Retained earnings at beginning of year	96,647	90,285	83,507
	$134,578	$125,727	$115,539
Deduct			
Cash dividends ($.42, $.35 and $.27 per share)	$ 4,580	$ 3,769	$ 2,947
Stock dividends	22,235	25,311	22,307
	$ 26,815	$ 29,080	$ 25,254
Retained earnings at end of year	$107,763	$ 96,647	$ 90,285
Earnings per common share	$ 3.50	$ 3.27	$ 2.95
Average common and class B common			
shares outstanding	10,848	10,848	10,848

and other candy manufacturers have begun to recognize that future growth opportunities lie in using domestic profits to penetrate foreign markets.

Tootsie Roll needs to increase its sales and distribution internationally to continue to grow as the U.S. market moves toward maturity. As trade barriers decrease, Tootsie Roll's opportunities to expand internationally are growing especially because foreign demand for U.S.-produced higher value-added products, including candy, has increased significantly since 1993. The predicted reduction or elimination of the European Community confection tariffs and variable levies on ingredient composition may also facilitate export growth into Eastern Europe. (See Exhibit 6.)

Tootsie Roll Industries has begun slowly and cautiously working toward worldwide market penetration, targeting export growth to the Far East and Europe, where per

EXHIBIT 5

Consolidated Statement of Financial Position, Tootsie Roll Industries, Inc. and Subsidiaries
(in thousands of dollars)

	December 31	
	1994	1993
Assets		
Current assets		
Cash and cash equivalents	$ 16,509	$ 1,986
Investments held to maturity	45,861	54,217
Accounts receivable, less allowances of $1,466 and $2,075	22,087	20,656
Inventories		
Finished goods and work-in-process	16,704	17,186
Raw materials and supplies	12,464	12,108
Prepaid expenses	3,094	3,667
Deferred income taxes	2,168	2,094
Total current assets	$118,887	$111,914
Property, plant and equipment, at cost		
Land	$ 6,672	$ 4,231
Buildings	26,982	25,347
Machinery and equipment	109,438	107,685
Leasehold improvements	6	10
	$143,098	$137,273
Less: Accumulated depreciation and amortization	57,450	50,574
Total property, plant and equipment	$ 85,648	$ 86,699
Other assets		
Excess of cost over acquired net tangible assets, net of accumulated amortization of $9,966 and $7,260	$ 98,668	$101,375
Other assets	6,880	3,952
Total other assets	$105,548	$105,327
Total assets	$310,083	$303,940
Liabilities and Shareholders' Equity		
Current liabilities		
Notes payable to banks	—	$ 22,601
Accounts payable	$ 6,124	6,259
Dividends payable	1,219	1,026
Accrued liabilities	17,046	17,919
Income taxes payable	1,872	3,057
Total current liabilities	$ 26,261	$ 50,862
Noncurrent liabilities		
Deferred income taxes	$ 7,716	$ 6,364
Postretirement health care and life insurance benefits)	4,993	4,498
Industrial development bonds	7,500	7,500
Term notes payable	20,000	20,000
Other long-term liabilities	3,152	2,373
Total noncurrent liabilities	$ 43,361	$ 40,735

(Continued)

EXHIBIT 5 (continued)

Shareholders' equity		
Common stock, $.69⁴/₉ par value—		
25,000 shares authorized—		
7,306 and 7,069, respectively, issued	$ 5,074	$ 4,909
Class B common stock, $.69⁴/₉ par value—		
10,000 shares authorized—		
3,542 and 3,465, respectively, issued	2,459	2,406
Capital in excess of par value	132,997	111,108
Retained earnings, per accompanying statement	107,763	96,647
Foreign currency translation adjustment account	(7,832)	(2,727)
Total shareholders' equity	$240,461	$212,343
Commitments		
Total liabilities and shareholders' equity	$310,083	$303,940

---

capita confectionery consumption is 40% higher than in the U.S. Tootsie Roll currently holds licenses in several countries and regions including the Philippines, Colombia, Europe, the Far East and Latin America. In addition, the company opened a sales office in Hong Kong in 1992 for sales to China, Korea and Taiwan, and exports products to the Middle East, Eastern Europe and Central and South America. However, this international activity remains a very small percentage of Tootsie Roll's total sales.

Since the Gordons are not getting any younger, the future of Tootsie Roll candy will depend on several key decisions they will make over the next few years. Perhaps the time has come for Mel and Ellen to think ahead while they are still on top.

EXHIBIT 6
Tootsie Role Industries—Percent of Foreign Sales

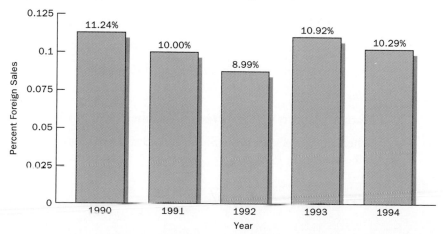

References

Bloomberg. New York, March 1995.

Brown, R. H., & Garten, J. E. *Forecasts for Selected Manufacturing and Service Industries.* U.S. Industrial Outlook 1994, U.S. Department of Commerce, January 1994.

Dow Jones Stock Quote Reporter Service.

Hershey Foods, Inc. 1994 Annual Report.

Industry Norms and Key Business Ratios—One Year. Dun & Bradstreet Information Services, 1993–1994.

Jorgensen, J. *Encyclopedia of Consumer Brands.* Detroit: St. James Press, 1994.

Keith, H. "Green" Package Blues. *Snack Food,* February 1995, pp. 58–61.

Keith, H. Packaging 2000: Virtually Real. *Snack Food,* January 1995, pp. 52–53.

Kimbrell, W. Way to Grow. *Snack Food,* May 1994, pp. 22–25.

Labate, J. Tootsie Roll Industries. *Fortune,* January 10, 1994, p. 109.

Littman, M., & Rogers, P. *Snack Food* Salutes the Top 100 Manufacturers in the Industry. *Snack Food,* December 1994, pp. 32–37.

Market Share Reporter—1995. New York: Gale Research, 1991.

Marketing. *Wall Street Journal,* August 26, 1992, p. B1.

Moody's Industrial Manual. New York: Moody's Investors Services, 1994.

Moskowitz, M., Levering, R., & Katz, M. *Guide to Company Profiles.* New York: Bantam/Doubleday Dell Publishing Group, 1990.

Sparks, D. Tootsie Roll: Don't Bite Yet. *Financial World,* April 26, 1994, p. 16.

Springen, K. Bigger Breaks for Small Business. *Working Woman,* November 1993, pp. 17–18.

Standard NYSE Stock Reports. New York: McGraw-Hill, Vol. 61, No. 241, Sec. 50.

Stauffer, C. Formulating the Fat Out. *Snack Food,* January 1995, pp. 46–48.

Tootsie Roll Industries, Inc. 1994 Annual Report.

Value Line.

Warner-Lambert Co. *Snack Food,* December 1994, p. 40.

When Employees Own Big Stake, It's a Buy Signal for Investors. *Wall Street Journal,* February 13, 1992, p. C1.

http://www.foodweb.com/

CASE 9

Goodyear: The Gault Years*

In June 1991, The Goodyear Tire and Rubber Company announced its board of directors election of Stanley C. Gault, an outside member of the board since 1989, as chairman and chief executive officer to succeed Tom H. Barrett, who retired after 38 years of service with Goodyear. The board of directors, in a statement released after the election meeting, commented:

> Goodyear is exceedingly fortunate that Stan Gault has agreed to lead the company for at least the next three years. In addition to being one of America's most able corporate managers, with an outstanding record of accomplishment at Rubbermaid, he brings to Goodyear the unique advantage of having both the perspective of an outsider as well as a thorough knowledge of the company's businesses gained from his service as Goodyear director.[1]

Acknowledging his election to Goodyear's prestigious top management positions, Gault responded:

> I am very pleased to be joining the team at Goodyear, which is the greatest name in the rubber industry. It has a superior brand franchise, high-quality products, state-of-the-art technology and manufacturing facilities, broad distribution, and very promising new products scheduled to be introduced later this year. Although the rubber business is experiencing industry-wide problems, I am confident that Goodyear shareholders can look forward to a bright future. As a strong believer in hands-on management and open communication between corporate managers and the investment community, I intend to keep our lenders and shareholders fully informed about the company's progress.[2]

BACKGROUND

Goodyear Tire and Rubber Company, in the fall of 1986, under the leadership of then chairman of the board and chief executive officer, Robert Mercer, operated in a mature, concentrated, and highly competitive global market.

---

*Prepared by Bernard A. Deitzer, Alan G. Krigline, and Thomas C. Peterson, College of Business Administration, The University of Akron, Akron, Ohio. Used with permission of the authors.
[1]Goodyear Tire and Rubber Company, Public Relations Release #06155-91, June 1991.
[2]Ibid.

At the same time, Goodyear had incurred $3.7 billion in crippling long-term debt. A legacy of both the 1986 successful takeover defense against Anglo-French financier Sir James Goldsmith, and Celeron, a money-losing California-to-Texas oil pipeline, that was the last vestige of Goodyear's mid-1980s attempt to diversify from rubber into defense and oil.[3]

Until then, Goodyear was the world's largest and most profitable tire and rubber products business, selling original equipment tires to the automotive industry. The company was now positioned behind Michelin/Uniroyal Goodrich in the world tire market.

During this period from 1982–1986, Goodyear's principal business was the development, manufacture, distribution, and sale of tires for most applications.

The company also manufactured and sold a broad array of rubber, plastic, and metal products for the transportation industry and various government, industrial, and consumer markets. Goodyear was a multi-product, diversified conglomerate. Goldsmith, however, changed all that.

PRE-GOLDSMITH GRAND STRATEGY

Goodyear's grand strategy was to maintain its position as the world's number one tire manufacturer while reducing its dependency, roughly 80 percent, on the uncertain demand for original equipment tires and related products supplied to the cyclical new-car industry.

Goodyear planned to generate one-half of its sales volume from tires and rubber products, one-quarter from sales volume of its subsidiary Goodyear Aerospace, and another quarter from its Celeron oil and natural gas operations.

Additionally, Goodyear planned for above-average rubber industry returns to stockholders, while reducing its dependence on the automotive industry.

Meanwhile, in 1985, Chairman Mercer emphatically enunciated Goodyear's approach to go "global." This meant a marketing and distribution approach involving a single strategy for the world, a global strategy, instead of tailoring products and distribution to individual national or regional markets.[4]

Two areas most affected by the Goldsmith takeover attempt were financial and structural. It included buying back 43 percent of its outstanding shares, while long-term debt was increased by $2.6 billion to 72 percent of total capitalization.

In restructuring, Goodyear sold its oil and natural gas reserves for $685 million; sold the assets of two Arizona subsidiaries involved in agricultural products, real estate development, and a resort hotel for $220 million.

It sold Goodyear Aerospace to Loral Defense Systems for $588 million; Motor Wheel Corporation in a leveraged buyout to its management; and also closed plants in Cumberland, Maryland, and Toronto, Canada.

[3]Jung Ah Pak, "Gault on Fixing Goodyear's Flat," *Fortune*, July 15, 1991, p. 104.
[4]Annual Reports, Goodyear Tire and Rubber Company, Akron, Ohio, 1982–1988.

Other casualties were reduced R&D spending, the loss of 6,786 jobs, and placing the ill-fated Celeron All-American hot-oil pipeline up for sale, after its completion, for $1.3 billion.[5]

At this juncture in 1988, Goodyear was reorganized into two major divisions, tire and non-tire products, each operating independently from the other. Formerly separated geographic business units were combined into global units.

Goodyear's management was now flatter with fewer layers of middle management between top and bottom, all with the collateral expectancy of improving performance in overall corporate operations and services.

GOODYEAR'S BUSINESS IN 1995

Goodyear's business, in 1995, was comprised of three major business segments: tires, general products, and oil transportation. The company also has the Kelly-Springfield Tire Company, a wholly-owned subsidiary.

Tires

The tire segment develops, manufactures, distributes, markets, and sells tires and rubber supplies to both automotive, original equipment, and replacement markets. This segment had sales of $10.5 billion in 1994.

General Products

The general products division, which generated $1.7 billion in sales in 1994, is separated into two divisions: engineered products and chemical products.

The engineered products division makes vehicle components; industrial rubber products, such as belts, hose, pipe lining, tank treads, and shoe products, while the chemical products division supplies synthetic rubber and organic chemicals used in rubber and plastic processing to Goodyear itself, as well as other customers.[6]

Oil Transportation

The All-American Pipeline subsidiary segment was profitable for the first time in 1994. Goodyear's Celeron subsidiaries are engaged in the operation of the All-American Pipeline systems, a crude oil pipeline which extends from Gaviota, California, to McCamey, Texas, and related crude oil transportation and trading activities.

---

[5]Adapted from "Goodyear: Beyond Goldsmith," in *A Strategic Management Case*, by Bernard A. Deitzer, Alan G. Krigline, and Thomas C. Peterson, The University of Akron.
[6]Annual Reports, Goodyear Tire and Rubber Company, Akron, Ohio, 1991–1994.

Service and Distribution

Goodyear also provides vehicle repairs and other services at its approximately 1,900 retail tire and service centers and other worldwide distribution centers. The company manufactures its products in 33 plants in the United States and 39 plants in 27 other countries. Goodyear also operates two rubber plantations in Southeast Asia.[7]

KELLY-SPRINGFIELD

The company serves the replacement tire market by manufacturing and marketing radial passenger tires; radial and bias light truck tires; radial and bias medium truck tires; and radial and bias farm tires both front and rear.

Headquartered in Cumberland, Maryland, the subsidiary operates with approximately 7,000 associates and has the capacity to produce 123,000 tires daily.

Kelly-Springfield is generally considered to be the industry's largest producer of private label tires for independent distributors and mass marketers.

Strategically, Kelly brand, associate brand, and private brand tires provide Goodyear with total market coverage at virtually all price points.[8]

THE GOODYEAR CHALLENGE

When asked the reason for undertaking the enormous challenge confronting him at Goodyear, Gault answered:

> Well, frankly, the decision was 98 percent emotional because Goodyear is the last American-owned tire company. All the other brands, with the exception of a much smaller Cooper, are now owned by foreign companies, and they will never return to this country.
>
> Therefore, I decided that I was willing to change my life for three years if there was any way I could lead the charge to rebuild Goodyear. It was mentioned to me more than once that I was a prime candidate for the Maalox moment.[9]

GAULT WHILE AT RUBBERMAID

Gault had retired in May 1991 as chairman and chief executive officer of Rubbermaid, Incorporated, of Wooster, Ohio, which he joined in 1980 after a 31-year career with General Electric.

---

[7]Annual Reports, Goodyear Tire and Rubber Company, Akron, Ohio, 1991–1994.
[8]Goodyear Tire and Rubber Company Corporate Document.
[9]Jacqueline M. Graves, "Leaders of Corporate Change," *Fortune*, December 14, 1992, p. 104.

When Gault became CEO in 1980, Rubbermaid was a slow-growth consumer products business with rising overhead costs, declining productivity, and complacent personnel. Product development lagged, profit margins were depressed, and relations with retail customers were flagging.

Gault wasted no time in restructuring Rubbermaid's operations and installing a new management team. As leader, he set the tone and pace, defined objectives and strategies, and demonstrated what he expected from both management and staff.

Gault strategically cut unprofitable lines of business and searched for complementary acquisitions. He engineered a strong focus on product quality, insisted on higher standards of job performance, revamped an in-place corporate culture, and reorganized Rubbermaid into nine decentralized units.

Under Gault's hands-on administration, Rubbermaid sales rose from $241 million in 1980 to $1.8 billion in 1992. During the same period, net income increased from $21 million to $163 million in 1991 and $184 million in 1992. Total corporate assets in 1980 were $225 million and $1.3 billion in 1992.

In sum, Gault had transformed Rubbermaid from a parochial manufacturer of a limited line of mundane household utensils to a celebrated world-class marketer of over 2,000 consumer-directed products.[10]

GAULT'S INITIAL STRATEGY AT GOODYEAR

Shortly after accepting the greatest task of his already-illustrious career, Gault set out to formulate and then communicate to both Goodyear associates and the business community his personal business philosophy, slated to underscore the company's operations in the 1990s.

"A tremendous change was needed at Goodyear," Gault believed, "a cultural change involving everyone in the organization. When you're in this kind of jam, time is not on your side."[11]

"Furthermore, there is no quick fix or instant formula for success," remarked Gault. "It is a matter of returning to basic business concepts that in today's high technology–driven society often gets forgotten."

"Included necessarily," said Gault, "are the company's operational plans, its overall essential objectives and supporting strategies, its critical resources and competition. All the factors taught in Business Management 101."[12] (See Exhibit 1.)

"What we needed," Gault strongly insisted, "was a road map for our journey and then to explain that map to every one of our 107,000 Goodyear associates throughout the world."[13]

These were Gault's bedrock fundamentals he wanted to firmly establish at the onset. After which he planned to review all company operations; press hard to reduce

[10]Annual Reports, Rubbermaid, Incorporated, Wooster, Ohio, 1992–1993.
[11]Graves, "Leaders of Corporate Change."
[12]Stanley C. Gault, remarks in 4th Annual CEO Report, "Tire Review," December 1991.
[13]Ibid.

EXHIBIT 1
Gault's Basic Business Concepts

- Do we have a mission? What statement or message does my company portray to my potential customers and to my associates? What sets my company apart from my competition?

- What are the key environmental factors in the area in which we operate? Are we protecting the environmental conditions for the area in which we are located?

- What is the nature of our competition? Do we know our competitor's product line and policy strategy, financial strengths and weaknesses?

- What are our long-term objectives? Do we have a business plan? Do we work this plan? Does my supplier interact with my long-term objectives with products, training, business systems, brand and retail advertising?

- Do we have strategies to accomplish our objectives? Has competition changed product lines and pricing strategies? Has our customer base shifted geographically or demographically? How are we going to reach new markets?

- What resources do we now have? What are needed for the future? What are future job requirements and how are we going to get them?

- And last, do we have a contingency plan? What might go wrong? What impact will it have on my business and how can we counteract it?[14]

---

[14]Remarks by Stanley C. Gault in 4th Annual CEO Report, "Tire Review," December 1991.

---

costs, identify corporate assets to sell in order to reduce debt; and most of all, to eventually create a world-class, market-driven, customer-oriented tire manufacturing operation. All the while serving as the implacable strategist and consummate representative of Goodyear, as evidenced by the awards and recognitions in Exhibit 2.

GAULT'S OTHER HONORS

In addition, Gault serves on the boards of directors of Avon Products, International Paper Co., PPG Industries, Rubbermaid, Inc., the Timken Company, and the New York Stock Exchange.

Gault is also chairman of the board of trustees of the College of Wooster, and has served on the board of trustees of the Ohio Foundation of Independent Colleges.

He is a director and honorary vice chairman of the National Association of Manufacturers, having served as the 1986–87 chairman of the board.

He was appointed by President Reagan, and subsequently President Bush, to the Advisory Committee for Trade Policy and Negotiations. He is chairman of the Task Force on Industrial Subsidies. Gault also serves on the executive committee of the board of trustees of the National Invention Center.[15]

---

[15]Goodyear Tire and Rubber Company Corporate Document.

EXHIBIT 2
Stanley C. Gault: Awards and Recognitions

1987   Named American Manager of the Year by the National Management Association.

1987   Received the Ohio Foundation of Independent Colleges Hall of Excellence Award.

1988   Received the Management Excellence Award from the Society for Advanced Management (SAM).

1989   One of six managers highlighted by *Business Week* in the category "The Best of Managers" in the January 9, 1989, "The Best of 1988" issue.

1989   Named one of Industry's best CEOs in a survey by *Industry Week* magazine.

1990   Named the Rubber Industry Executive of the Year by *Rubber and Plastic News.*

1990   Inducted into the National Sales Hall of Fame sponsored by the Sales and Marketing Executives of Greater New York.

1990   Inducted into the Housewares Club of New England Entrepreneurs Hall of Fame.

1991   Presented with the Ohio Governor's Award, state's highest honor, for excellence in business.

1991   Recipient of Plastic Academy's Daniel E. Fox Lifetime Achievement Award.

1992   Honored as the outstanding CEO of the year by *Financial World* magazine.

1992   Recipient of the honorary degree Doctor of Laws, from College of Wooster.

1992   Honored by Sales and Marketing Executives International as Marketing Statesman of the Year.

1994   Elected by *Fortune* magazine to the Fortune Junior Achievement National Business Hall of Fame.

1995   Received the Silver Award for outstanding contributions in the rubber products and components industry in *Financial World* magazine's annual "CEO of the Year" competition.

GAULT'S PRINCIPLES

These are a simple set of business principles that I have honored throughout my career—essential elements that contributed to my prior and personal success. Some say I'm a zealot on these points.

They are low cost, high quality, and customer satisfaction. They are new-product development, aggressive merchandising and new-customer and new-business development. Undeniably, they are the prudent management of assets entrusted to us; good communications and sound human relationships with all associates; and a commitment to a total quality culture which by itself will be the single-most important force for success in the 1990s and beyond.[16]

---

[16]Graves, "Leaders of Corporate Change."

GAULT'S TWELVE OBJECTIVES

After reviewing everything he could, and in as much detail as possible for 45 days, Gault developed 12 objectives to lead Goodyear out of its internal depression and onto the road to success. He termed them "How to Manage Goodyear Successfully in the 90s." (See Exhibit 3.) "Our objectives are extremely ambitious but are doable. We attacked debt reduction through asset sales and an equity offering, while achieving working capital reductions and capital expenditures below depreciation."[17]

GAULT'S TEACHABLE MOMENTS

Gault enjoys a compelling instinct for making the appropriate "teachable moment." His approaches are legendary.

The day the new CEO moved into his spacious Goodyear office, he was handed a fistful of keys to the numerous beautifully paneled cabinets built into the walls. "I don't want these, I like things unlocked," Gault reacted. "But sir," came the reply, "a lot of people come in here at night for cleaning, you understand: union people." "I don't give a damn," said a seemingly irritated Gault. "This company should be run on the basis of trust."[18]

[17]Stanley C. Gault, remarks to Avon Products Financial Conference, New York, September 1994.
[18]Peter Nulty, "The Bounce Is Back at Goodyear," *Fortune*, September 7, 1992, p. 71.

EXHIBIT 3
Gault's Twelve Objectives for the 1990s

1. Achieving significant debt reduction.
2. Increasing the company's financial performance.
3. Holding a quality leadership position.
4. Striving to be a low-cost producer.
5. Providing superior satisfaction in meeting customer expectations.
6. Increasing market share.
7. Introducing new, exciting, customer-oriented products.
8. Strengthening merchandising, advertising, and distribution programs.
9. Enhancing shareholder value.
10. Expanding the company's global presence.
11. Being a socially responsible corporation.
12. Maximizing the company's human resource capability.[19]

---

[19]Stanley C. Gault, remarks to Avon Products Financial Conference, New York, September 1994.

Gault describes his management style as very involved. He wants to know what is going on in every part of the company and is known to read every report that crosses his desk. Yet he is most concerned with what is going on in the marketplace. Gault regularly browses in stores on Saturdays, both Goodyear's and rivals as well—testing the tire market and talking with Goodyear managers and customers.

Gault is not only a blizzard of activity, but his presence seems to permeate Goodyear headquarters. A Goodyear associate for human resources observed that he never heard Gault give a direct order. "But we all know exactly what he expects of us."[20]

At Goodyear, he deliberately discontinued using the word "employee" and instituted the word "associate" companywide because "that was a leveling action." An African-American employee with 35 years of service questioned its application to him as well. Gault assured him that it did apply, absolutely, to him, a mill worker, and Gault as chairman of the board and chief executive officer. In affirmation, Gault later visited the associate's work station. With support of Goodyear's noted grapevine and electronic mail, the incident was around the world in 60 seconds.[21]

GOODYEAR'S PARTNERSHIPS

A strong segment of Gault's business philosophy is the premise that meaningful partnerships are the foundation for success.

"Partnerships," Gault explained, "is what enables us to make continuous improvements. It is the willingness of people to look at something and say, 'If we meet each other half way, we can work cooperatively together, we can improve everything together.' It is those partnerships between people, between companies, with customers and with suppliers, that create greater value for all concerned."[22]

Gault insisted his compensation be tied to the price of Goodyear's stock, an unprecedented arrangement at the firm. "If we can do the job together, as a team, and can show earnings growth, it makes sense for me to benefit in an equal fashion with other shareholders. My ship will rise or fall with the value of the stock and the performance of the company."[23]

GOODYEAR RESTRUCTURED

Goodyear, under Gault, in early 1995 was a leaner and more profitable business. It had slashed costs and improved operating performance, boosted overall quality pro-

[20]Ibid.
[21]Graves, "Leaders of Corporate Change."
[22]Excerpted from Stanley C. Gault's comments at Goodyear's Vendor Awards Program, Akron, Ohio, September 1991.
[23]Ibid.

duction and reduced once-strangling debt in an attempt to best its international adversaries like Bridgestone/Firestone, Inc., Continental A.G., and Michelin S.A.

Structurally, it had replaced a formal hierarchical and engineering-directed focus with more emphasis on innovative product development and broadened sales and marketing services in a globally oriented environment.

Goodyear trimmed its workforce from 108,000 in 1991 to 85,000 in 1995. And, it sold billions in non-core assets. Strategically preparing for the twenty-first century, the firm had expanded its presence in the world's growing tire market.

Underscoring this commitment, Goodyear had restructured the organization into eight SBUs (strategic business units) (Exhibit 4).

The SBUs, organized by product and market, are responsible for sales growth, profitability, and customer satisfaction. Objectives of the SBUs are firmly linked with Goodyear's corporate objectives.

Multifunctional teams comprising R&D, engineering, production distribution, finance, human resources, and other functions cooperate to deliver the quality product or service.[24]

---

[24]Adapted from Stanley C. Gault's remarks at the Industrial Research Institute Annual Meeting, Virginia, May 1993.

EXHIBIT 4
SBU Chart

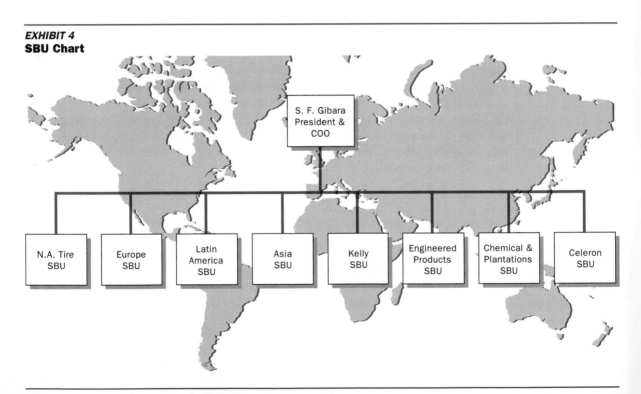

Regional tire operations serve auto, truck, aircraft, farm specialty, and construction markets. The non-tire business units provide rubber and plastic products for automotive and industrial markets and crude oil transportation services (Exhibit 5).

GOODYEAR'S DEBT REDUCTION INITIATIVES

In July 1991, shortly after Gault accepted his greatest managerial challenge, his initial strategy for Goodyear's reconstruction was to center on two major objectives: reducing corporate debt and cutting costs.

Goodyear, according to Gault, would accomplish these by increasing revenues and by the expansion and enhancement of the firm's marketing, sales, merchandising, and advertising effort to gain a larger share of the market. It would, furthermore, seek to improve operations performance.

EXHIBIT 5
Serving Customers Worldwide

Goodyear strategic business units are organized to meet customer requirements and global competition. Regional tire operations serve auto, truck, aircraft, farm, specialty, and construction markets. The non-tire business units provide rubber and plastic products for automotive and industrial markets and crude oil transportation services.

Strategic Business Unit	Products and Markets	Geographic Markets Served
North American Tire	Original equipment, replacement tires for autos, trucks, farm, aircraft, construction	United States, Canada, export
Kelly-Springfield	Replacement tires for autos, trucks, tractors	United States, Canada, export
Goodyear Europe	Original equipment, replacement tires for autos, trucks, farm, construction	Europe, Africa, Middle East, export
Goodyear Latin America	Original equipment, replacement tires for autos, trucks, tractors	Central, South America, export
Goodyear Asia	Original equipment, replacement tires for autos, trucks, farm, aircraft, construction	Southeast, Western Asia, North Pacific Rim, export
Engineered Products	Auto belts, hose, body components, industrial products	Worldwide
Chemicals	Synthetic and natural rubber, chemicals for internal, external customers	Worldwide
Celeron	Crude oil transportation, related services	Operates only pipeline from U.S. West Coast to Texas
Goodyear Racing	Tires for all major motor racing series	Worldwide

Source: Annual Report, Goodyear Tire and Rubber Company, Akron, Ohio, 1994, p. 5.

Oppressively, total debt in 1990 had reached $3.7 billion, and was costing the company $1 million daily in interest. Gault candidly outlined his options. "We have to go through and review every asset that we have and look at disposing of some, particularly those that do not relate directly to the tire business. We are a tire company. Nothing is sacred. We'll look at everything, research and development, capital expenditures, the company's 1,200 retail stores, even the Goodyear Blimp."[25] (See Exhibit 6.)

"One of the things that's different here from my past experience, even at GE, is the debt," recalled Gault. "At GE, we were very thrifty people. And at Rubbermaid, we drove debt down to where it was 5 percent of total capitalization. So, I'm not used to spending more than a million dollars a day for interest, every day of the week, even on Saturdays, Sundays, and holidays. That we cannot live with."[26]

---

[25]Jonathon D. Hicks, *New York Times*, June 9, 1991, p. C4.
[26]Ah Pak, "Gault on Fixing Goodyear's Flat."

EXHIBIT 6
Goodyear's Debt Reduction Initiatives

1991	Sold 12 million shares common stock at $50 per share. Gault, in 4th quarter, made 39 personal presentations in 13 days in 13 cities in Europe and the States.
1991	Scottsboro, Alabama, tire cord textile plant sold in 4th quarter to Akzo N.V. for $95.0 million.
1991	Goodyear's New York apartment sold.
1991	Goodyear's corporate aircraft sold.
1991	Houston blimp base closed and for sale.
1991	Corporate limousines replaced with inexpensive models.
1992	Madison, Kentucky, specialty tire plant sold in 3rd quarter.
1992	Closed Celeron Corporation's subsidiary office in Texas.
1992	Closed European headquarters and relocated its top executives to Akron as part of reshuffling European operations. Laid off 100 associates.
1992	Blown and cast film business assets sold to Huntsman Holdings Corporation for $105.5 million.
1992	Sold the industrial and commercial films business in 2nd quarter for a gain of $9.1 million.
1992	Sold polyester resin business assets in 4th quarter to Shell Oil Company for $308.4 million. Consisted of a plant in West Virginia and a technical center in Akron, Ohio. Approximately 700 production, marketing, and administrative associates were employed.
1993	Sale pending on Reneer Films subsidiary in 1st quarter.
1993	Sold rubber roofing business in 1st quarter.
1993	Air Treads subsidiary sold. Aircraft Wheel and Brake closed its Kingston, Ontario, facility in 2nd quarter for a $3.1 million reduction.
1993	Lowered debt to $1.4 billion from $1.9 billion in 1992 and $3.7 billion in 1990.
1994	Employment continued downward to approximately 89,000 associates from 91,000 in 1993 and 108,000 in 1991.[27]

[27]Source: Adapted from Annual Reports and Corporate Documents, Goodyear Tire and Rubber Company, Akron, Ohio, 1991–1994.

GAULT'S PANACHE

While attacking corporate debt, Gault symbolically removed over 25 light bulbs from wall sconces, lamps, and chandeliers in his suite, leaving him to work in a comfortable, clublike dimness that he calculates, by way of his GE experience, saves Goodyear $230 a year. After that, lights were turned out in halls and offices all over the company.[28]

Gault created quite a stir around Akron when he suggested using low-cost overhead transparencies instead of high-cost slides. That saved $1,500 per meeting and with no loss in the information presented.[29]

"Associates in one department carefully looked at their lighting needs and learned they could save $5,000 a year by turning off unnecessary fixtures," allowed Gault. "If each associate saves just one dollar a day in the way he or she performs their work, we will save more than $25 million a year. I'll get the debt down in every way I can." To reduce operating expenses, Gault is known to bring along stationery and postage stamps to his office for personal use.[30]

GOODYEAR SELLS STOCK TO REDUCE DEBT

In October 1991, Goodyear announced plans to sell 10 million shares of common stock to raise an estimated $400 million to retire a portion of its burdensome debt load of $3.6 billion. Analysts pointed out that Goodyear is reselling 20 percent of the stock it bought back in early 1987 after financier Sir James Goldsmith agreed not to take over the company. Goodyear then paid $50 a share in the buyback of 50 million shares.[31]

GAULT'S PERFORMANCE RECORD

In Gault's first year of leadership, there was a positive savings of nearly $135 million between 1991 earnings and a loss in 1990. Earnings were $96.6 million, which included a $43.2 million gain from a divested asset sale, compared with a loss of $38.3 million in 1990.

Debt was reduced by approximately $1 billion with the sale of non-tire related businesses. Goodyear's Scottsboro, Alabama, textile facility was the first divested.

In a slack economy, 1991 Goodyear sales were $10.9 billion, slightly below its prior-year sales record of $11.3 billion. Earnings per share for 1991 were $1.61 com-

[28]Nulty, "The Bounce Is Back at Goodyear."
[29]Hicks, *New York Times.*
[30]Ibid.
[31]Donald Sabath, "Goodyear to Issue More Stock," *Cleveland Plain Dealer,* October 3, 1991, p. C1.

pared with a loss of 66 cents during 1990. Operating margin was 7.2 percent in 1991, compared to 5.4 percent.

The debt-to-debt-plus-equity dropped significantly to 49.2 percent at year-end from 63.3 percent in 1990.

Improved results reflected the benefits of personnel reductions, cost-reduction programs, productivity improvement, price increases, and lower material costs.[32]

TURNAROUND YEAR

For 1992, Gault again planned to improve operating margins, reduce debt and interest expense, and control capital spending.

Under Gault, the firm led the tire industry in all-time quarterly sales records and exceeded its 6 percent growth objective.

Operating income increased by $327 million, compared with 1991. Debt, concurrently, was reduced by $697 million to below $2 billion, originally a 1994 forecasted objective.

Sales in 1992 reached $11.8 billion, the highest in Goodyear's 94-year history. Consolidated debt dropped to $1.9 billion against $2.6 billion in 1991.

Operating margin was 9.4 percent in 1992, compared with 7.2 percent the previous year. Goodyear's annual stock dividend was increased to $1.00 per share from 40 cents in order to share the company's improved financial performance.

Goodyear's stock appreciably outperformed Standard & Poor's 500 Index during 1992 as its capitalized market value approached $5 billion, compared with $3.8 billion in 1991 and $1.1 billion in 1990.

Consistent with its debt-reduction plans, Goodyear continued to sell operations not directly related to the tire business. Sold were an interest in a chemical facility in Brazil, the industrial and commercial films unit, and the polyester operation. These asset sales, coupled with improved operating performance, enabled the firm to reduce debt by $697 million during 1992 and slash interest payments by $85 million over the period.[33]

GOODYEAR'S 1993 FINANCIAL PERFORMANCE

A resuscitated Goodyear in 1993 outpaced the industry as it recorded a third consecutive year of improved financial performance. The company validated its commitments to greater profitability, debt reduction, industry leadership, growth, customer needs, and greater performance.

Record sales of $11.6 billion were achieved compared with 1992's $11.4 billion, which excluded the sales from divested assets.

Earnings in 1993 surpassed those of all other major global tiremakers. Combined

[32]Annual Report, Goodyear Tire & Rubber Company, Akron, Ohio, 1991, pp. 2–4.
[33]Annual Reports, Goodyear Tire and Rubber Company, Akron, Ohio, 1991–1992.

income before extraordinary charges increased to $488.7 million, or $3.33 per share in 1993, including a 10 cent per share nonrecurring gain on the sale of assets, compared with 1992 income before extraordinary charges of $367.3 million, or $2.57 per share.

Goodyear's common stock in 1993 again outperformed the Standard & Poors 500 Index, while its market value grew almost 40 percent, and nearly seven times since year-end 1992. A two-for-one stock split doubled the number of authorized shares to 300 million.

There was a 20 percent dividend increase, raising the quarterly dividend to 15 cents a share on the split shares.

Continuing its commitment to debt reduction, Goodyear lowered debt to $1.4 billion from $1.9 billion in 1992, and $3.6 billion three years ago.

Major debt rating agencies correspondingly upgraded the firm's long- and short-term debt ratings to investment grade.

Debt reduction in 1993 resulted from improved operating performance, divestment of certain non-core businesses, and the redemption of Euro Convertible Debentures, $117 million of which was converted into common stock.

Debt-to-debt-plus-equity ratio reduction to nearly 38 percent, coupled with lower interest rates, lowered 1993 interest expense by almost one-third, compared to 1992.

The All-American Pipeline subsidiary entered into long-term crude oil transportation agreements with several major offshore California oil producers. These agreements were scheduled to produce significant cash flow beginning in 1996.

As a percent of sales, Goodyear's cost of goods sold declined 3.3 points during the past three years, through higher capacity utilization and lower material costs.

Sales, administrative and general (SAG) expenses as a percent of sales, declined 1 percentage point on growing sales.

Goodyear's employment levels continued downward to 92,000 associates from 108,000 in 1990, while output per man-hour improved.[34]

PERFORMANCE PLAN PLUS OBJECTIVES

During 1994, Gault initiated ambitious plans to strengthen Goodyear's strategic focus on growth consistent with earnings improvement.

The Performance Plan Plus objectives (Exhibit 7) were to encourage greater geographic and business diversification, establish higher expectations for business unit revenue, and provide additional capital and technology to support aggressive growth plans.

Significant earnings improvement in 1994 derived from Goodyear's greater commitment to geographical diversity through global expansion. International operations accounted for a significant increase in revenues, unit sales of tires and rubber products, and segment operating income.

Since the second quarter of 1991, Goodyear achieved 15 consecutive quarter-to-quarter improvements in net income. Income from continuing operations in 1994 reached an all-time high of $567 million, a 16 percent increase over 1993.[35]

[34]Annual Report, Goodyear Tire and Rubber Company, Akron, Ohio, 1993, pp. 2–4.
[35]Remarks by Stanley C. Gault at Annual Meeting of Shareholders, Akron, Ohio, April 1995, pp. 2–4.

EXHIBIT 7
Gault's Performance Plan Plus (PPP)

1. We will increase sales between 4.5 and 5 percent per year . . . twice the projected industry growth rate.

2. Our operating margin at the segment level will reach 12 percent . . . never before accomplished. We were at 10 percent in 1993 . . . but at 6 percent in 1990.

3. Capital expenditures will range between $500 and $700 million annually . . . a significant increase.

4. We will lower our sales, administrative, and general expenses to below 15 percent of sales . . . we were over 18 percent earlier.

5. Our debt-to-debt-plus-equity ratio will decline to 25 to 30 percent . . . down from 63 percent in 1991.

6. Our dividend policy guideline will be to ask our board to pay out 20 to 25 percent of prior year's earnings.[36]

---

[36]Goodyear Tire and Rubber Company Corporate Document.

GOODYEAR'S 1994 ACHIEVEMENTS

At Goodyear's annual stockholder's meeting, Gault recalled that "the year 1994 was truly remarkable as we recorded significant progress in our quest to be the best tire and rubber products company in the world."[37]

"For the fourth consecutive year," he proudly announced, "we achieved improved financial performance and in the process, broke every performance record in the Goodyear history book."[38] (See Exhibits 8 to 11 for a summary of Goodyear financial progress from 1992 to 1994.) The 1994 results:

- Sales of $12.3 billion were the highest in Goodyear history.

- Income of $567 million from continuing operations was an all-time high, surpassing 1993 by 16 percent.

- Every geographic region reported record tire unit sales.

- Tire segment sales for the first time exceeded $10 billion.

- Rating agencies raised Goodyear's rating for commercial paper and senior debt.

- A new four-year financial plan—entitled "Performance Plan Plus"—was launched.

- Interest expense was the lowest since 1986.

- Debt declined to the lowest level in a decade.

---

[37]Ibid.
[38]Ibid.

EXHIBIT 8
Consolidated Balance Sheet
(in millions of dollars)

	December 31	
	1994	**1993**
Assets		
Current assets:		
Cash and cash equivalents	$ 250.9	$ 188.5
Short-term securities	15.4	39.2
Accounts and notes receivable	1,524.7	1,314.2
Inventories	1,425.1	1,349.8
Prepaid expenses	406.6	371.1
Total current assets	$3,622.7	$3,262.8
Other assets:		
Investments in affiliates, at equity	$ 133.4	$ 107.2
Long-term accounts and notes receivable	208.5	173.6
Deferred charges and other miscellaneous assets	775.9	604.6
	$1,117.8	$ 885.4
Properties and plants	4,382.8	4,287.9
Total assets	$9,123.3	$8,436.1
Liabilities and Shareholders' Equity		
Current liabilities:		
Accounts payable—trade	$1,013.9	$ 870.0
Compensation and benefits	745.2	657.1
Other current liabilities	259.8	269.6
United States and foreign taxes	326.2	373.1
Notes payable to banks and overdrafts	213.0	313.1
Long-term debt due within one year	13.9	41.0
Total current liabilities	$2,572.0	$2,523.9
Long-term debt and capital leases	$1,108.7	$1,065.9
Compensation and benefits	2,173.4	2,101.0
Other long-term liabilities	322.1	321.8
Minority equity in subsidiaries	143.9	122.7
Shareholders' equity:		
Preferred stock, no par value:		
Authorized, 50,000,000 shares, unissued	—	—
Common stock, no par value:		
Authorized, 300,000,000 shares		
Outstanding shares, 151,407,285 (150,515,374 in 1993)	$ 151.4	$ 150.5
Capital surplus	918.5	878.0
Retained earnings	2,194.5	1,740.9
	$3,264.4	$2,769.4
Foreign currency translation adjustment	(421.7)	(422.4)
Minimum pension liability adjustment	(39.5)	(46.2)
Total shareholders' equity	$2,803.2	$2,300.8
Total liabilities and shareholders' equity	$9,123.3	$8,436.1

Source: Annual Report, Goodyear Tire and Rubber Company, Akron, Ohio, 1994, p. 25.

EXHIBIT 9
Consolidated Statement of Income
(in millions of dollars, except per share data)

	Year Ended December 31		
	1994	1993	1992
Net sales	$12,288.2	$11,643.4	$11,784.9
Cost of goods sold	9,271.4	8,713.0	8,971.8
Selling, administrative, and general expense	1,958.2	1,922.1	1,997.3
Interest expense	129.4	162.4	232.9
Other (income) and expense	(37.9)	(79.1)	(147.3)
Foreign currency exchange	77.6	113.1	77.1
Minority interest in net income of subsidiaries	23.8	27.0	23.2
Income before income taxes, extraordinary items and cumulative effect of accounting changes	$ 865.7	$ 784.9	$ 629.9
United States and foreign taxes on income	$ 298.7	$ 296.2	$ 262.6
Income before extraordinary items and cumulative effect of accounting changes	$ 567.0	$ 488.7	$ 367.3
Extraordinary item—early extinguishment of debt (net of tax of $6.1 in 1993, $6.4 in 1992)	—	(14.6)	(15.3)
Cumulative effect of change in accounting for postemployment benefits (net of tax of $55.2)	—	(86.3)	
Transition effect of change in accounting for non-pension postretirement benefits (net of tax of $617.0)	—	—	(1,065.7)
Cumulative effect of changes in accounting for income taxes	—	—	55.1
Net income (loss)	$ 567.0	$ 387.8	$ (658.6)
Per share of common stock:*			
Income before extraordinary items and cumulative effect of accounting changes	$ 3.75	$ 3.33	$ 2.57
Extraordinary item—early extinguishment of debt	—	(.10)	(.11)
Cumulative effect of change in accounting for postemployment benefits	—	(.59)	—
Transition effect of change in accounting for non-pension postretirement benefits	—	—	(7.46)
Cumulative effect of change in accounting for income taxes	—	—	.39
Net income (loss)	$ 3.75	$ 2.64	$ (4.61)
Average shares outstanding*	151,203,885	147,086,828	142,808,424

*1992 has been restated to reflect the two-for-one stock split in May 1993.
Source: Annual Report, Goodyear Tire and Rubber Company, Akron, Ohio, 1994, p. 24.

EXHIBIT 10

Consolidated Statement of Shareholders' Equity
(in millions of dollars, except per share data)

	Common Stock		Capital Surplus	Retained Earnings	Foreign Currency Translation Adjustment	Minimum Pension Liability Adjustment	Total Shareholders' Equity
	Shares	Amount					
Balance at December 31, 1991 after deducting 52,328,368 treasury shares:	70,663,515	$ 70.7	$639.1	$2,208.5	$(187.2)	—	$2,731.1
Net loss for 1992				(658.6)			(658.6)
Cash dividends 1992—$.275 per share*				(39.3)			(39.3)
Common stock issued (including 1,580,945 treasury shares):							
Dividend reinvestment and stock purchase plan	45,281		3.1				3.1
Stock compensation plans	1,535,665	1.5	46.3				47.8
Foreign currency translation adjustment					(153.8)		(153.8)
Balance at December 31, 1992 after deducting 50,747,423 treasury shares:	72,244,461	$ 72.2	$688.5	$1,510.6	$(341.0)	—	$1,930.3
Net income for 1993				387.8			387.8
Cash dividends 1993—$.575 per share				(84.9)			(84.9)
Stock dividend 1993	72,689,064	72.6		(72.6)			
Common stock issued (including 5,584,285 treasury shares):							
Dividend reinvestment and stock purchase plan	66,589	.1	3.0				3.1
Stock compensation plans	2,605,544	2.7	74.8				77.5
Conversion of debentures	2,909,716	2.9	111.7				114.6
Foreign currency translation adjustment					(81.4)		(81.4)
Minimum pension liability adjustment						(46.2)	(46.2)
Balance at December 31, 1993 after deducting 45,163,138 treasury shares:	150,515,374	$150.5	$878.0	$1,740.9	$(422.4)	$(46.2)	$2,300.8
Net income for 1994				567.0			567.0
Cash dividends 1994—$.75 per share				(113.4)			(113.4)
Common stock issued (including 891,911 treasury shares):							
Dividend reinvestment and stock purchase plan	96,691	.1	3.5				3.6
Stock compensation plans	795,220	.8	37.0				37.8
Foreign currency translation adjustment					.7		.7
Minimum pens on liability adjustment						6.7	6.7
Balance at December 31, 1994 after deducting 44,271,227 treasury shares	151,407,285	$151.4	$918.5	$2,194.5	$(421.7)	$(39.5)	$2,803.2

*Cash dividends per share for 1992 have been restated to reflect the two-for-one stock split in May 1993.

Source: Annual Report, Goodyear Tire and Rubber Company, Akron, Ohio, 1994, p. 26.

EXHIBIT 11
Consolidated Statement of Cash Flows
(in millions of dollars)

	Year Ended December 31		
	1994	1993	1992
Cash Flows from Operating Activities			
Net Income (loss)	$ 567.0	$ 387.8	$ (658.6)
Adjustments to reconcile net income (loss) to net cash provided by operating activities:			
Depreciation	410.3	392.9	445.8
Deferred tax provision	99.8	(36.3)	(36.0)
Accounts and notes receivable	(192.4)	(10.9)	(219.6)
Inventories	(63.9)	(100.2)	(71.9)
Accounts payable—trade	139.7	(48.1)	124.2
Domestic pension funding	(238.8)	(82.2)	(172.7)
Other assets and liabilities	42.9	117.8	162.1
Accounting changes	—	86.3	1,065.7
Asset sales	—	(24.7)	(164.2)
Workforce reductions and other non-cash charges	—	—	120.3
Early extinguishment of debt	—	20.7	21.7
Total adjustments	$ 197.6	$ 315.3	$1,275.4
Net cash provided by operating activities	$ 764.6	$ 703.1	$ 616.8
Cash Flows from Investing Activities			
Capital expenditures	$(523.0)	$(432.3)	$(366.6)
Asset dispositions	19.0	83.6	425.3
Short-term securities acquired	(287.1)	(157.5)	(121.1)
Short-term securities redeemed	310.6	214.2	95.8
Other transactions	(15.7)	9.8	10.5
Net cash (used in) provided by investing activities	$(496.2)	$(282.2)	$ 43.9
Cash Flows from Financing Activities			
Proceeds from sale of foreign currency exchange agreements	—	4.1	44.5
Short-term debt incurred	$ 385.6	324.8	442.8
Short-term debt paid	(395.7)	(487.6)	(325.6)
Long-term debt incurred	52.9	2.7	124.4
Long-term debt and capital leases paid	(166.4)	(385.8)	(909.3)
Common stock issued	41.4	195.2	50.9
Dividends paid	(113.4)	(84.9)	(39.3)
Net cash used in financing activities	$(195.6)	$(431.5)	$ (611.6)
Effect of exchange rate changes on cash and cash equivalents	(10.4)	(8.4)	(5.0)
Net increase (decrease) in cash and cash equivalents	$ 62.4	$ (19.0)	$ 44.1
Cash and cash equivalents at beginning of the period	188.5	207.5	163.4
Cash and cash equivalents at end of the period	$ 250.9	$ 188.5	$ 207.5

Source: Annual Report, Goodyear Tire and Rubber Company, Akron, Ohio, 1994, p. 27.

- Celeron became the turnaround story of the year.

- Successful negotiation of U.S. labor agreements.

- Celebrated the 300th victory on the Formula One Grand Prix circuit; 300 consecutive victories in Indy Car racing.[39]

At the meeting, an exuberant Gault hailed Goodyear's achievements for 1994, as Goodyear made significant progress in its quest to be the best tire and rubber products company in the world.

GOODYEAR'S MARKETING MISSION

Many American businesses are struggling to survive because of the failure to focus effectively on their marketing and sales objectives.

The science of sales and marketing is an American creation served by the free enterprise system and we cannot allow it to become stagnated by reluctance to adjust to a changing environment of more demanding and more resistant consumers.[40]

Gault envisioned Goodyear's marketing mission to be a three-pronged challenge.

First, to do the complete marketing job by applying proven tenets of good marketing better and sooner than smart aggressive competitors.

Second, to serve as a catalyst for change—to motivate and encourage the entire organization to support its marketing plans by serving the customer in a truly market-driven manner.

Third, to be involved in the external activities that affect marketing's ability to perform, to assume a greater role in influencing economic, social, and political policies affecting those businesses, and to study and understand issues and then to participate in their resolution.[41]

DISTRIBUTION'S NEW KID ON THE BLOCK

In Gault's opinion, "the retail tire marketer is in the midst of great change. The way tires were sold yesterday isn't necessarily the way we'll be selling tomorrow."

"For example," he continued, "there's a totally new kid on the block—the warehouse clubs. Just 10 years ago, this channel of distribution for tires didn't even exist. Today, 6 percent of all replacement tires are sold in those outlets. And, this trend is only starting. Moreover, tires sold through service stations, department stores, and even tire dealerships, are continuing to lose market share."[42]

---

[39]Ibid.
[40]Excerpted from remarks by Stanley C. Gault before the Timken Corporate Forum, Canton, Ohio, April 26, 1993.
[41]Ibid.
[42]Adapted from Stanley C. Gault's presentation to the Harvard Business School Club of Cleveland, Cleveland, Ohio, May 13, 1993.

"The customer," conceded Gault, "wanted convenience in buying; quick service, low prices, a large selection from which to choose, and in the case of Sears, to use a specific credit card."[43]

GOODYEAR'S NEW DISTRIBUTION STRATEGY

As Gault attempted to regain market share, his first steps were to centralize Goodyear's sales organization, narrow its existing structure, and increase local and national advertising. (See Exhibit 12.)

Alone among U.S. tire manufacturers, Goodyear's channels of tire distribution originally were to OE (original equipment) manufacturers or to affiliated dealerships, franchised or company-owned.

However, in spring of 1992, Goodyear, in a strategic marketing move to reclaim a share of the U.S. replacement car tire market, announced it would sell Goodyear brand tire lines through Sears, Roebuck & Co., Kmart, Wal-Mart, and others like Big O. Market share had fallen from about 15 percent to 12 percent since 1987. Goodyear hoped to sell up to 2.5 million additional tires each year through Canadian Tire and Discount Tire, and the new distribution channels.

A major reason for the slide was that Goodyear was not stocking tires where customers would buy them. As Gault saw it, "we're not serving the market with what the customers wanted, but what the manufacturing plant wanted to build."[44]

Increasingly, it appears, consumers were buying tires at multi-brand discount outlets, as well as warehouses (Exhibit 13).

Sensing potential hostility of Goodyear dealers, Chairman Gault addressed the company's 600 franchises and 4,000 independent dealers at their Las Vegas convention.

---

[43]Ibid.
[44]Gault, Harvard Business School Club of Cleveland.

EXHIBIT 12
Goodyear's Advertising Expenditures[45]
(in millions of dollars)

	1992	1993	1994
1. Sales	$11,784.9	$11,643.4	$12,288.2
2. Advertising costs	$266.5	$248.2	$248.2
3. Advertising costs, % sales	2.26	2.13	2.02

[45]Source: Annual Reports, Goodyear Tire and Rubber Company, Akron, Ohio, 1992–1994.

EXHIBIT 13
Market Share and Distribution Channels[46]

	1994	1993	1992	1991	1990	1985
Estimated Share of the Domestic Passenger Tire Retail Market (based on retail sales)						
Tire dealerships*	54.0%	54.0%	54.0%	54.0%	54.0%	55.0%
Chain/department stores	19.0%	19.0%	19.0%	19.0%	18.0%	19.0%
Tire company stores	11.5%	12.0%	12.0%	12.0%	13.0%	10.0%
Warehouse clubs†	8.5%	8.0%	8.0%	7.0%	6.0%	2.0%
Service stations	5.0%	5.0%	5.0%	6.0%	7.0%	9.0%
Auto dealerships	1.0%	1.0%	1.0%	1.0%	1.0%	2.0%
Misc. outlets	1.0%	1.0%	1.0%	1.0%	1.0%	3.0%
Distribution Channels—How Passenger Tires Reach the Domestic Retail Supplier						
Independent dealers	66.0%	66.0%	66.0%	67.0%	67.0%	68.0%
Chain, dept., and discount stores, clubs, misc.	20.0%	20.0%	20.0%	19.0%	18.0%	17.0%
Tire company stores	12.0%	12.0%	12.0%	12.0%	13.0%	12.0%
Oil companies	2.0%	2.0%	2.0%	2.0%	2.0%	3.0%

Of an estimated 169.5 million replacement passenger tires handled directly in 1994 (both retail and wholesale, but counted only once):

- Independent dealers accounted for 111.9 million units;
- Chain and department stores and warehouse clubs handled 33.9 million units;
- Tire manufacturer-owned stores handled 20.3 million units;
- Oil companies supplied their dealers with 3.4 million units.

*Large dealers, defined as independent dealers with 30 or more retail outlets, make up 29% of this total, or 15.5% of the entire replacement passenger tire market.
†Warehouse clubs have increased their U.S. unit total by 80% in the last five years.
[46]Source: *Modern Tire Dealer,* Facts Issue, Twenty-ninth Edition, Bill Communications, Inc., Akron, Ohio, January 1995.

"Goodyear dealers," he guaranteed, "can only lose if we don't generate more funds to support you. Actually, you should be critical of us if we don't take action to expand our business so we can provide the necessary support to our dealer structure."[47]

GAULT'S SUCCESS FORMULA

Goodyear's chief strategist was committed to create shareholders' value by generating consistent earnings growth and delivering high value-added products to the customer.

---

[47]Zachary Schiller, "Goodyear Is Gunning Its Marketing Engine," *Business Week,* McGraw-Hill, March 16, 1992, p. 42.

"It's no secret," Gault declared. "Success comes from the development of market-driven products combined with brand name associated with high quality and offered at true value price."[48]

With a bit of chutzpah, as he did while at Rubbermaid, Gault shops competitive stores and asks people why they bought competitive products or why, in this case, they didn't buy Goodyear tires. "Selling isn't just the role of sales and marketing people. Communicating the benefits of our product is everybody's job in a company."[49]

At a recent plastics industry convention, he asked the audience to please check their tires. If they didn't have Goodyear, then please get a set. He didn't want them driving around on inferior, competitive products.[50]

GOODYEAR'S BLIMPS

For over 25 years Goodyear's blimps, synonymous with Goodyear itself, have been deployed nationwide for the purpose of community relations, providing broadcast quality pictures.

Central to the firm's worldwide promotional efforts, the omnipresent blimps, *Spirit of Akron*, based in Akron, Ohio; the *Eagle*, based in Los Angeles, California; and the *Stars and Stripes*, based in Pompano Beach, Florida, not only advertise Goodyear tires but have emerged as aerial participants in dramatic events that overwhelm their commercial mission.

The blimps have provided more than 2,000 telecasts, including 15 Super Bowls, 15 World Series, the 100th anniversary of the Statue of Liberty, and broadcasts for the *Today Show* and *Good Morning America*.

The blimp was invited to the farewell salute to *Cheers* in California. The popular program was charging $650,000 for 30 seconds on the show. It had 91 million viewers. Goodyear had its most enduring corporate image name recognized for free.

They were witness to the October 1989 earthquakes during the Candlestick Park World Series. And the *Stars and Stripes* was a familiar image in the skies over South Florida in the aftermath of Hurricane Andrew, flashing vital messages in Creole, Spanish, and English.

Surprisingly, Goodyear does not charge for blimp coverage. Instead, it is free in return for any free advertising the sight of the blimp might generate.

While the existence of the blimp was threatened because of the hostile takeover attempt by Goldsmith, it was Stanley Gault who envisioned the importance of the blimp. He changed its colors to blue, silver, and gold, and originated the idea to put "No. 1 In Tires" on its sides.[51]

---

[48]Nulty, "The Bounce Is Back at Goodyear."
[49]Stanley C. Gault's remarks at an Investor Presentation, New York, November 1991.
[50]Nulty, "The Bounce Is Back at Goodyear."
[51]Abe Zaiden, "Executive Strives for Free TV," *Cleveland Plain Dealer*, June 27, 1993, p. 2.

GOODYEAR'S MARKETING PERFORMANCE

Apparently, Gault's marketing strategies were paying off. In 1994, Goodyear held first position in the estimated U.S. replacement passenger tire brand shares (Exhibit 14) and first in the estimated U.S. replacement light truck tire brand shares (Exhibit 15).[52]

Goodyear, in 1994, consistently ranked high in achieving its brand share of the U.S./Canadian OE (original equipment) passenger and light truck vehicle market (Exhibit 16). And Goodyear regularly held first place in the U.S./Canadian OE passenger and light truck tire market share from 1990–1994.[53] (See Exhibit 17.)

Goodyear in 1994 was third among the world leaders in new tire sales (Exhibit 18). Evidently the company suffered a 26.5 percent drop in its stock price from year-end 1993 to year-end 1994 from $45.75 to $33.62, a result of lower sales. Bridgestone, Michelin, and Pirelli, meanwhile, experienced increases in their stock prices while Continental suffered a decrease.[54] Goodyear, however, in 1994 held the first position among the U.S./Canadian leaders in new tire sales.[55] (See Exhibit 19.)

GOODYEAR'S AQUATRED

During the fall of 1991, Goodyear launched the Aquatred, a radically different, all-season, wet traction tire, with a 60,000 mile treadlife guarantee. The Aquatred has a deep center groove and unique tread design which squirts water from the tire. The system helps prevent cars and light trucks from hydroplaning.

While introducing Aquatred, Gault assured, "Customers want safety and reliability. And they will buy features. We're bringing out a tire that truly addresses aquaplaning. Someone might say 'I live in Phoenix, that surely isn't my problem.' Oh yes it is. Three days a year in Phoenix it rains like crazy. You hit the intersection. You're not used to the wet road, and you're taking off. That is a salable characteristic."[56]

The Aquatred qualifies as a "pivotal product" in Goodyear's history as well as the tire industry itself. It is a highly important and integral part of a strategic plan to revitalize Goodyear and inject new life into a mature commodity industry.[57]

According to Goodyear sources, the Aquatred was in development for almost a decade, mostly because of its unusual appearance. It has a large, rounded indentation in the center of the tread that helps channel water from under the tire. John Fiedler, former executive vice president of the North American tire division, critically remarked, "Around here, we called it the baby's butt, and you don't want to put an ugly tire on the market."[58]

---

[52]*Modern Tire Dealer,* Facts Issue, Twenty-ninth Edition, Bill Communications, Inc., Akron, Ohio, January 1995.
[53]Ibid.
[54]Ibid.
[55]Ibid.
[56]Ah Pak, "Gault on Fixing Goodyear's Flat."
[57]Nulty, "The Bounce Is Back at Goodyear."
[58]Ibid.

EXHIBIT 14[59]
**Estimated 1994 U.S. Replacement
Passenger Tire Brand Shares
(based on 169.9 million shipments)**

Brand	Percent
Goodyear	16.0%
Michelin	8.0
Firestone	7.5
General	4.5
BFGoodrich	4.0
Cooper	4.0
Kelly	4.0
Sears	4.0
Bridgestone	3.5
Multi-Mile	3.0
Uniroyal	2.5
Cordovan	2.0
Dayton	2.0
Dunlop	2.0
Pirelli	2.0
Sentry	2.0
Falls Mastercraft	1.5
Herculles	1.5
Patriot	1.5
Summit	1.5
Yokohama	1.5
Delta	1.0
Laramie	1.0
Lee	1.0
Monarch	1.0
Montgomery Ward	1.0
National	1.0
Regul	1.0
Remington	1.0
Sigma	1.0
Spartan	1.0
Star	1.0
Stratton	1.0
Toyo	1.0
Others	9.5

[59]Source: *Modern Tire Dealer,* Facts Issue, Twenty-ninth Edition, Bill
Communications, Inc., Akron, Ohio, January 1995.

EXHIBIT 15[60]
**Estimated 1994 U.S. Replacement Light
Truck Tire Brand Shares***
(based on 25 million shipments)

Brand	Percent
Goodyear	13.0%
BFGoodrich	8.5
Michelin	7.0
Firestone	6.5
Cooper	5.5
Kelly	5.5
General	5.0
Multi-Mile	5.0
Bridgestone	4.0
Armstrong	3.0
Cordovan	3.0
Dunlop	3.0
Uniroyal	3.0
Dayton	2.5
Falls Mastercraft	2.5
Lee	2.5
Sears	2.5
Remington	2.0
Road Tamer	2.0
Toyo	2.0
Summit	1.5
Hankook	1.0
Kumho	1.0
Monarch	1.0
Sigma	1.0
Star	1.0
Yokohama	1.0
Others	5.0

*Because numbers are rounded to the nearest one-half percent,
total may exceed 100%. Brands must have at least 1% of market in
shipment numbers to be listed at 1%.
[60]Source: *Modern Tire Dealer,* Facts Issue, Twenty-ninth Edition, Bill
Communications, Inc., Akron, Ohio, January 1995.

Gault, nonetheless, ended the snail-like product development of the tire and ordered that three other tires in the pipeline be introduced at the same time.

Almost simultaneously, Goodyear issued a new stock offering. Gault, the irrepressible marketer, visited 13 cities in 13 days, holding 39 meetings with potential investors. At the conclusion of his tour, the stock had reached $50, and he had sold 12 million shares instead of the intended 10 million, raising more than $170 million more than planned.

EXHIBIT 16
Estimated 1994 Brand Shares[61]
(U.S./Canada passenger/LT vehicles)*

Chrysler		**Mazda**	
Goodyear	85.0%	Firestone	40.0%
Michelin	15.0%	Bridgestone	27.0%
Ford		Goodyear	20.0%
Firestone	36.5%	Dunlop	10.0%
Goodyear	25.0%	Michelin	3.0%
Michelin	25.0%	**Nissan**	
General	11.5%	Goodyear	26.0%
Uniroyal	2.0%	Firestone	22.0%
General Motors		Michelin	22.0%
Goodyear	33.0%	General	15.0%
Uniroyal	26.0%	Dunlop	9.0%
Michelin	16.0%	Uniroyal	6.0%
General	15.0%	**Nummi**	
BFGoodrich	6.0%	Goodyear	41.0%
Firestone	4.0%	Firestone	30.0%
BMW		Dunlop	15.0%
Michelin	100.0%	Bridgestone	14.0%
CAMI		**Saturn**	
Goodyear	84.0%	Firestone	100.0%
Uniroyal	16.0%	**Subaru**	
Diamond Star		Bridgestone	80.0%
(Chrysler-Mitsubishi)		Goodyear	20.0%
Goodyear	71.0%	**Toyota**	
Bridgestone	29.0%	Dunlop	33.0%
Honda		Goodyear	22.0%
Michelin	44.0%	Firestone	17.0%
Goodyear	30.0%	Bridgestone	14.0%
Dunlop	15.0%	Michelin	11.0%
Bridgestone	11.0%	Yokohama	2.0%
Isuzu		General	1.0%
BFGoodrich	75.0%	**Volvo**	
Uniroyal	15.0%	Goodyear	80.0%
Goodyear	10.0%	Michelin	20.0%

*Excluding imports.
[61]Source: *Modern Tire Dealer,* Facts Issue, Twenty-ninth Edition, Bill Communications, Inc., Akron, Ohio, January 1995.

BEST-MANAGED BRAND

Goodyear owns one of the "best-managed" and most-valuable brand names in the world according to *Financial World* magazine's fourth annual trade name evaluation and ranking (Exhibit 20).

EXHIBIT 17
U.S./Canadian OE Passenger/LT Tire Market Share[62]
(excluding imports)

	1994	1993	1992	1990
Goodyear	40.0%	40.0%	38.0%	36.5%
Michelin	18.0%	18.0%	17.0%	15.7%
Firestone	15.7%	15.4%	15.0%	17.0%
General	9.7%	10.0%	10.3%	12.0%
Uniroyal	9.5%			
		12.0%*	14.0%*	17.0%*
BFGoodrich	2.0%			
Dunlop	2.5%	2.5%	2.5%	1.5%
Bridgestone	2.5%	2.0%	3.0%	.3%
Yokohama	.1%	.1%	.2%	

*The Uniroyal and BFGoodrich brands were calculated as one before 1994.
[62]Source: *Modern Tire Dealer,* Facts Issue, Twenty-ninth Edition, Bill Communications, Inc., Akron, Ohio, January 1995.

EXHIBIT 18
World Leaders in New Tire Sales[63]
(in billions of U.S. dollars)

	1994*	1993
Groupe Michelin	11.5	10.87
Bridgestone Corp.	10.7	10.64
Goodyear Tire & Rubber	10.4	10.0
Continental AG	4.0	3.8
Sumitomo Group	3.4	3.3
Pirelli	3.3	3.0
Yokohama	2.6	2.56
Toyo	1.2	1.3

*MTD estimates.
[63]Source: *Modern Tire Dealer,* Facts Issue, Twenty-ninth Edition, Bill Communications, Inc., Akron, Ohio, January 1995.

By comparing brand value with an estimated industry average, the magazine determined the Goodyear name is the 20th best-managed brand.

Based solely on estimated monetary value, the Goodyear brand ranked 24th, with a value of $4.66 billion among the 282 trade names considered; the Bridgestone brand, 32nd at $3.76 billion; the Michelin brand, 49th at $2.66 billion; the Pirelli brand, 197th at $299 million; and the Continental brand, 225th at $179 million.

OTHER TIRE LINES

The pioneering Aquatred was followed by the Intreped, a lower-priced version for more price-conscious consumers.[64]

---

[64]Goodyear Tire and Rubber Company Corporate Document.

EXHIBIT 19
U.S./Canadian Leaders in New Tire Sales
(in billions of U.S. dollars)[65]

	1994*	1993
Goodyear/Kelly	6.0	5.4
Michelin North America	4.2	4.0
Bridgestone/Firestone	3.1	2.7
Continental General	1.2	1.3
Cooper	1.1	.95
Dunlop	.65	.6
Pirelli Armstrong	.6	.7
Yokohama	.41	.40
Toyo	.265	.26

*MTD estimates.
[65]Source: *Modern Tire Dealer,* Facts Issue, Twenty-ninth Edition, Bill Communications, Inc., Akron, Ohio, January 1995.

EXHIBIT 20
Comparative Value of Tire Brands

Tire Brand	Company	Brand					
		Current Value (in millions)	One-Year Change in Value (%)	1994 Sales (in millions)	1994 Income (in millions)	Operating Margin (%)	Ratio of Brand Value to Brand Sales
Goodyear	Goodyear Tire & Rubber	$4,660	4%	$7,320	$653	9%	0.6
Bridgestone	Bridgestone	3,762	7	6,626	683	10	0.6
Michelin	Michelin	2,656	41	8,080	553	7	0.3
Pirelli	Pirelli	299	65	2,503	100	4	0.1
Continental	Continental	179	30	1,316	59	5	0.1
Category average		—	29	—	—	—	0.4

Source: *Financial World,* August 1, 1995, p. 69.

The next introduction was the Eagle Aquatred for high-performance tires, a market segment where wide, high-adhesion tires are the vogue. But, wider tires are more susceptible to hydroplaning, so a performance tire with dual aqua channels became a big hit.

Most recently, Goodyear introduced the Aquatred II, an updated version of the original Aquatred. The Aquatred II offers a deeper aqua channel and a longer tread-life warranty.

The newest member of Goodyear's aqua-channel family, the Wrangler Aquatred for sport-utility vehicles, was unveiled in a 1995 Super Bowl commercial.[66]

[66]Ibid.

RUN FLAT TIRES

By mid-1993, Goodyear, Bridgestone, and Michelin had all engineered and marketed run flat tire systems. The complete system, including tires, special wheels, and electronic sensor system, then cost about $5,000.

Goodyear's tire, which does not require a special rim, the Eagle GS-C EMT, is an option on all 1994 Chevrolet Corvette models. Bridgestone's Expedia 5-01 A/M Run Flat is sold only as an option to the Callaway Corvette, a customized version of the Chevrolet sports car.[67]

GOODYEAR EMT

Goodyear EMT (extended mobility tire) run flat option was scheduled for the 1995 model year. It is capable of traveling at least 50 miles at 55 mph, with zero air pressure. At reduced speeds, range could be as much as 200 miles.[68]

JUST TIRES

In another strategic move, Goodyear in 1993 inaugurated Just Tires, a tire sales only group of company stores. Just Tires offers no auto repair service, provides tires only and those services directly related to mounting, balancing, and alignment. Goodyear's new logo was "Just Tires . . . Fast Service . . . and Low Prices."[69]

 Goodyear planned to expand its Just Tires chain of retail stores by more than 250 locations nationwide over the next several years.

Goodyear, in May 1994, converted 31 retail stores to the Just Tires format and planned to expand Just Tires primarily through conversion of existing retail stores.

GOODYEAR'S RESEARCH AND DEVELOPMENT

Early on, Gault sensed that if Goodyear was to survive and eventually prosper, it must develop a total commitment to R&D and to quality products and services.

For many years, in Gault's opinion, "Goodyear's management viewed R&D as an upstream link in the value chain. There was a linear model involving research, development, engineering, distribution, and marketing. Products evolved at one end and then filtered down to the customer. The product development effort really came out of R&D and not out of the marketing function."

"All too frequently," he concluded, "we wanted customers to buy what we wanted to make or what we wanted to sell rather than saying: 'Tell us what you want and need and we'll supply it for you.' Now, Goodyear has a new model for business. First mar-

---

[67]Stuart Drown, "The Race to Drive with a Flat," *Akron Beacon Journal*, June 28, 1993, p. D1.
[68]Jim McCraw, "Throw Away the Spare," *Popular Science*, May 1993, p. 88.
[69]Annual Report, Goodyear Tire and Rubber Company, Akron, Ohio, 1994, p. 4.

keting establishes customer needs. Then, the team members comprising R&D, engineering, production, distribution, finance, and human resources work together to deliver the product or service."[70]

Goodyear's policy on R&D expenditures is directly related to its sales (Exhibit 21).

U.S. TIRE INDUSTRY—RESEARCH AND DEVELOPMENT

Despite the rubber industry's recovering sales in 1993, R&D budgets for 1993 remained flat.

Industry analysts surmised that R&D is experiencing a flattening out which is probably reflective of modern scientific equipment—you can do more with a lot fewer people. There's less model building and prototyping.[71]

GOODYEAR'S TQC PROGRAM

Underscoring Goodyear's research and development efforts is its total quality culture. "I am known as a zealot (at Rubbermaid a 'sonofabitch') on quality," confessed Gault. "And, I won't tolerate shoddy merchandise. I expect our products to be the best in the industry. Every department in this entire global company is developing a total commitment to quality in every aspect of its operations."[72]

Presently, 51 percent of Goodyear's tire sales are now from tires on the market for less than five years, which continues to rise from the emphasis that Gault has placed on new-product development.[73]

---

[70]Remarks by Stanley C. Gault at Avon Products Financial Conference, New York, September 1994.

[71]Bryan Kodish, "R&D Expenditures Flat in 1993," *Rubber and Plastic News*, Crain Publications, Akron, Ohio, July 4, 1994.

[72]Adapted from Stanley C. Gault's address to the Industrial Research Institute Annual Meeting in Hot Springs, Virginia, May 1993.

[73]Nulty, "The Bounce Is Back at Goodyear."

EXHIBIT 21
Goodyear's R&D Expenditures[74]
(in millions of dollars)

	1991	*1992*	*1993*	*1994*
1. Sales	$10,906.8	$11,784.9	$11,643.4	$12,288.2
2. R&D expenditures	$330.0	$325.9	$320.0	$340.0
3. R&D, % of sales	3.0	2.8	2.8	2.8

[74]Source: Annual Reports, Goodyear Tire and Rubber Company, Akron, Ohio, 1991–1994.

Goodyear has monthly meetings in Akron open to all associates where teams of fellow associates explain how this commitment to quality has solved seemingly insolvable problems, bettered working conditions, reduced costs, improved product quality, and brought associates together.

Every meeting is videotaped, and tapes are distributed to the company's 88 plants around the world. Gault also chairs bi-monthly meetings at which employees demonstrate improvements they have made and receive awards.[75]

Supporting Goodyear's commitment to its TQC program are its mission statement and guiding principles (Exhibit 22), which provide a foundation for its applications to the company's quality improvement program.[76] (See Exhibit 23.)

GOODYEAR: A GLOBAL PLAYER

In early 1995, an optimistic Gault felt that "Goodyear is less vulnerable to regional swings in product demand than in the past. The firm's continued strategic focus is that of a growth company capable of consistent earnings improvement in worldwide emerging markets."[77] (See Exhibit 24.)

[75]Goodyear Tire and Rubber Company Corporate Document.

[76]Adapted from Stanley C. Gault's address to the Industrial Research Institute Annual Meeting in Hot Springs, Virginia, May 1993.

[77]Glenn Gamboa, "New Goodyear Becomes a Global Player," *Akron Beacon Journal*, April 16, 1995, p. C1.

EXHIBIT 22
Goodyear's Quality Principles[78]

Mission

Our mission is constant improvement in products and service to meet our customers' needs. This is the only means to business success for Goodyear and prosperity for its investors and associates.

Guiding Principles

Customer Satisfaction: Everything we do is directed to the satisfaction of present and future customers. Quality is defined by the current expectations, as well as by future needs and desires, of our customers.

Process Improvement: Results are achieved through the management of processes. All processes—and the resulting products and services—can be improved, forever. The improvements may take the form of revolutionary changes, innovations, or the accumulation of many small steps. The improvements may involve such areas as quality, cost, delivery, or time.

People: We value the commitment, knowledge, and creativity of the men and women of Goodyear. Everyone has the ability to contribute to our mission of constant improvement. Cooperation and respect among individuals and departments are fundamental to success.

Action Based on Facts: Sound business decisions are based on sound data and rigorous analysis. Facts are reviewed in an atmosphere without blame. Understanding and use of data collection and analysis is vital in all areas.

Quality Is the Key to Customer Satisfaction

---

[78]Source: Goodyear Tire and Rubber Company Corporate Document.

EXHIBIT 23
Continuous Quality Improvement Program[79]

Implementing Goodyear's total quality control program is its Continuous Quality Improvement Program (CQI). Seen as "a systematic, organization-wide approach for continually improving all processes that deliver quality products and services."

While pursuing CQI, Goodyear's management and associates are urged to stick to four basic principles:

- Develop a strong customer focus, including the needs of both external end users and internal co-workers, and other departments;

- Continually improve all processes. Identify those processes that are a sequence of repeatable steps that lead to some desired end or output. Improve the processes by use of planning, doing, checking, acting cycle.

- Involve employees. Encourage teams—train them—support them—use their work—celebrate their accomplishments.

- Mobilize both data and team knowledge to improve decision making. Use graphically displayed numbers and word data. Develop team consensus on root cause(s) of a problem and plan for improvement. Provide a safe and efficient outlet for ideas at all levels.

---

[79]Source: Goodyear Tire and Rubber Company Corporate Document.

Today, more than 40 percent of Goodyear's record 1994 revenues and 45 percent of unit sales of tires and rubber products were achieved outside the United States, and more than 50 percent of segment operating income came from international operations. (Exhibits 25 and 26 present industry and geographic segment data.)

The business is strategically poised not only to increase its market leadership in North America, but also to grow faster than the industry around the world. It intends to increase sales by twice the industry rate—about 2.5 percent—in the United States and plans revenue growth in Europe of about 5 percent.[80]

---

[80]Annual Report, Goodyear Tire and Rubber Company, Akron, Ohio, 1993, p. 5.

EXHIBIT 24[81]
Goodyear's Emerging Markets

	China	India	Indonesia	Commonwealth of Independent States
Economic growth (real GDP)	9.5%	4.4%	6.0%	Undergoing economic reform
Population (millions)	1,193	875	195	294
% of world population	22%	16%	3.6%	5.4%
Persons per car	663	356	151	22
Vehicles in use (millions)	6.1	4.7	2.9	28.0
Tire market in 2000 (millions)	66	12	10	61

---

[81]Source: Annual Report, Goodyear Tire and Rubber Company, Akron, Ohio, 1993, p. 5.

EXHIBIT 25
Industry Segments
(in millions of dollars)

	1994	1993	1992
Sales to unaffiliated customers:			
Tires	$ 9,427.6	$ 8,853.3	$ 8,661.4
Related products and services	1,080.6	1,110.2	1,108.7
Total tires	$10,508.2	$ 9,963.5	$ 9,770.1
General products	1,700.9	1,618.0	1,953.9
Oil transportation	79.1	61.9	60.9
Net sales	$12,288.2	$11,643.4	$11,784.9
Income (loss):			
Tires	$ 1,010.6	$ 998.5	$ 763.4
General products	170.9	177.8	362.7
Oil transportation	11.8	(11.6)	(15.8)
Total operating income	$ 1,193.3	$ 1,164.7	$ 1,110.3
Interest expense	(129.4)	(162.4)	(232.9)
Foreign currency exchange	(77.6)	(113.1)	(77.1)
Equity in net income of affiliated companies	25.7	17.6	10.5
Minority interest in net income of subsidiaries	(23.8)	(27.0)	(23.2)
Corporate revenues and expenses	(122.5)	(94.9)	(157.7)
Income before income taxes, extraordinary items and cumulative effect of accounting changes	$ 865.7	$ 784.9	$ 629.9
Assets:			
Tires	$ 5,490.7	$ 5,127.9	$ 5,049.8
General products	636.4	566.9	615.6
Oil transportation	1,398.6	1,413.2	1,487.7
Total identifiable assets	$ 7,525.7	$ 7,108.0	$ 7,153.1
Corporate assets	1,464.2	1,220.9	1,302.9
Investments in affiliated companies, at equity	133.4	107.2	107.7
Assets at December 31	$ 9,123.3	$ 8,436.1	$ 8,563.7
Capital expenditures:			
Tires	$ 425.4	$ 356.5	$ 291.4
General products	90.2	67.7	65.7
Oil transportation	7.4	8.1	9.5
For the year	$ 523.0	$ 432.3	$ 366.6
Depreciation:			
Tires	$ 309.4	$ 305.0	$ 348.4
General products	55.1	47.5	56.2
Oil transportation	45.8	40.4	41.2
For the year	$ 410.3	$ 392.9	$ 445.8

Source: Annual Report, Goodyear Tire and Rubber Company, Akron, Ohio, 1994, p. 40.

EXHIBIT 26
Geographic Segments
(in millions of dollars)

	1994	1993	1992
Sales to unaffiliated customers:			
United States	$ 7,130.5	$ 6,777.4	$ 6,787.3
Europe	2,279.8	2,233.3	2,476.1
Latin America	1,512.5	1,403.5	1,325.1
Asia	711.6	644.9	654.0
Canada	653.8	584.3	542.4
Net sales	$12,288.2	$11,643.4	$11,784.9
Inter-geographic sales:			
United States	$ 373.9	$ 296.9	$ 290.4
Europe	92.5	78.4	66.5
Latin America	159.2	107.7	87.4
Asia	490.7	346.6	325.9
Canada	269.1	233.6	195.3
Total	$ 1,385.4	$ 1,063.2	$ 965.5
Revenue:			
United States	$ 7,504.4	$ 7,074.3	$ 7,077.7
Europe	2,372.3	2,311.7	2,542.6
Latin America	1,671.7	1,511.2	1,412.5
Asia	1,202.3	991.5	979.9
Canada	922.9	817.9	737.7
Adjustments and eliminations	(1,385.4)	(1,063.2)	(965.5)
Total	$12,288.2	$11,643.4	$11,784.9
Operating income:			
United States	$ 591.5	$ 590.5	$ 654.3
Europe	212.0	221.5	216.8
Latin America	278.2	271.1	155.5
Asia	81.3	70.0	82.9
Canada	30.3	12.0	4.0
Adjustments and eliminations	—	(.4)	(3.2)
Total	$ 1,193.3	$ 1,164.7	$ 1,110.3
Assets:			
United States	$ 5,467.3	$ 5,113.4	$ 5,143.0
Europe	1,541.3	1,433.8	1,462.0
Latin America	809.4	799.2	854.6
Asia	645.4	471.6	466.0
Canada	538.9	521.8	541.4
Adjustments and eliminations	(12.4)	(10.9)	(11.0)
Total identifiable assets	$ 8,989.9	$ 8,328.9	$ 8,456.0
Investments in affiliated companies, at equity	133.4	107.2	107.7
Assets at December 31	$ 9,123.3	$ 8,436.1	$ 8,563.7

Source: Annual Report, Goodyear Tire and Rubber Company, Akron, Ohio, 1994, p. 41.

GOODYEAR'S GLOBAL PROGRESS

The company's increasing progress reflects its regional trade agreements in Latin America, which stimulated the growth of export sales and enabled Goodyear plants to regionalize production for high-capacity utilization.

Goodyear Brazil is an export leader, shipping tires to 83 countries from its modern Americana export center.

Goodyear Latin America remains the quality tire leader for the region.

Goodyear's expansion in the Asian growth market advanced as the Chinese government granted approvals for the Goodyear Dalian joint venture to manufacture tires in China. Production began at an existing plant in Dalian, Liaoning Province, the first half of 1995. Other joint tire ventures are being sought in the world's most populous nation.

The joint venture with CEAT Ltd., in India, for a new tire plant is proceeding on schedule. Production was scheduled to begin early in 1996.

The performance of the Asian region has improved since new capacity came on-stream in Thailand. Construction began on expansions in Malaysia and Indonesia.

In Europe, Goodyear is pursuing acquisitions and business development in the new market economies of the former communist countries.[82]

Gault remains convinced that "all these actions translate into growth in financial sources in technical capability, in competitive ability, and growth as a stronger supplier for its customers worldwide."[83]

GOODYEAR'S NEW PRESIDENT

In April 1995, at the annual shareholder's meeting, Gault ended months of speculation when he announced Samir F. Gibara as Goodyear's new president and chief operating officer. Gibara previously had been vice president of Strategic Planning and Business Development, as well as acting chief financial officer.

Egyptian-born Gibara, fluent in several foreign languages, worked in a variety of international management positions to improve the firm's standing as a global competitor.

Gault, who intends to retire at year-end, refused to name a successor to his role as chairman and chief executive officer.

"The board," he pledged, "made an outstanding choice in the selection of Sam Gibara who has all the credentials and experience to lead and successfully manage a global enterprise, such as Goodyear, today and into the future."[84]

http://www.goodyear.com/

---

[82]Annual Report, Goodyear Tire and Rubber Company, Akron, Ohio, 1994, p. 13.
[83]Ibid.
[84]Donald Sabath, "Goodyear Picks a New CEO," *Cleveland Plain Dealer*, April 11, 1995, p. C1.

CASE 10

Titeflex Corporation:
The Turnaround Challenge*

On December 1, 1988, Jon H. Simpson, 41, became president of Titeflex Corporation, a firm that sold $45 million worth of high-performance hoses to the aerospace, industrial, and automotive sectors. Simpson had worked for many years in the R&D Department of the 3M Company and, more recently, as vice president of Operations in CHR Industries, which, like Titeflex, was a part of the Bundy Group of companies. In January 1988, when Bundy brought in the Boston Consulting Group (BCG) to study Titeflex's operations, Jon Simpson was asked to get involved with the project. Within a year, two important events occurred: first, the British engineering conglomerate, Tube Investments (TI), acquired the Bundy Group; second, TI assigned Jon Simpson to manage the Titeflex subsidiary.

The promotion transformed Simpson's life. Suddenly, he found himself in Springfield, Massachusetts, managing a new division under a new set of (British) bosses. Simpson noted that it felt good to have been promoted but admitted that the task before him in Titeflex was daunting. To be sure, the company was profitable and its sales were growing, but competitors were nibbling away at Titeflex's market share, production was slow, deliveries were more often late than on time, and relations between management and Titeflex's union were abysmal.

Sir Christopher Lewinton, the CEO of Tube Investments, had divested nearly 70 percent of the group's assets and bought nearly a billion dollars worth of new companies since becoming TI's head in 1985. He wanted TI's seventy companies to be worldwide leaders in technology and market share in their respective niches. Lewinton believed in giving his companies a great deal of autonomy, but expected their sales

Faculty members in nonprofit institutions are encouraged to reproduce this case for distribution to their students without charge or written permission. All other rights reserved jointly to the author and the North American Case Research Association (NACRA).

*Copyright © 1995 by Ravi Ramamurti and Northeastern University by Ravi Ramamurti of Northeastern University. Robert Millen's contributions to the case are gratefully acknowledged. Management cooperated in the field research for this case, which was written solely to stimulate student discussion. All events and individuals are real. Used by permission. Copies of a videotape to accompany this case may be obtained from the Videocase Resources Center (Attn: Ms. Susan Skalder), Hayden 313, Northeastern University, Boston, MA 02115, (617) 373-3255.

and profits to grow at 15 percent per annum while yielding at least a 15 percent return on sales and a 30 percent return on net assets before interest and taxes.

As CEO, Simpson said he felt sandwiched between irate customers, warring employees, and demanding superiors. How should he deal with his customers? What could he do to improve Titeflex's operations and relations with the union? Would he be able to change the culture within Titeflex? How should he handle his bosses in England? It seemed there was so much to do and so little time. Simpson wondered what his priorities ought to be, where he ought to begin, and how he ought to proceed.

BRIEF HISTORY

Titeflex was founded in 1916 by Westinghouse Corporation. At that time, flexible hoses were made either from metal or natural rubber. Titeflex introduced a hose made from interlocking brass strips tacked with string. These early hoses were used in industrial and automotive applications as well as in World War I aircraft engines. With the advent in the 1930s of synthetic rubber and plastics that could withstand the corrosive effects of fuels and oils, Titeflex shifted its emphasis to shielded metal conduits. During World War II, every B-17 and B-24 was equipped with a Titeflex ignition harness. In the late 1950s, Titeflex began developing metal hose products with inner cores made of Teflon for use in fuel and oil systems in jet engines. In 1971, Titeflex reentered the industrial hose market, and, in 1978, the automotive market. In 1978, Bundy Corporation added Titeflex to its Performance Plastics Group.

MARKETING AND SALES

According to customers that Simpson met in his first few days in the company, Titeflex had a reputation for producing "pricey" products of excellent quality. A total of 100,000 different hoses varying in size, shape, fittings, and type of protective sleeving were offered by Titeflex. Customers for these hoses were concentrated in three market segments: aerospace (50 percent of sales), industrial (30 percent of sales), and automotive (20 percent of sales).

Aerospace

Titeflex's Marketing Department estimated that with 35 percent of the market in the early 1980s, Titeflex ranked second in market share in the aerospace segment. Its customers included all aircraft engine and airframe manufacturers worldwide. Titeflex and two other firms accounted for 90 percent of all sales, with the remainder shared by several smaller competitors. Few competitors existed in this segment because of the long time required to demonstrate effectiveness in usage and the need to be certified as a qualified supplier. While the number of pieces sold was small (ten units per day), the parts were highly customized for each client and involved large margins. Some complex hoses went through all forty-four manufacturing departments, traveling $2^{1}/_{2}$ miles from start to finish. In recent years, Titeflex's market share had declined to approximately 25 percent; in 1988, sales to this segment were expected to be 10 percent below the 1987 level. Indeed, two of Titeflex's largest customers told Simpson that they were seriously considering dropping Titeflex as a supplier.

While products for the aerospace segment were highly engineered, the rate of technological change was small until a new series of aircraft was announced. Then the technological change was substantial. Continued success in the market depended both on delivery and price for existing products and on technological advances for future products.

Demand in this market had boomed in the 1980s, thanks to the defense buildup in the United States and the growth of the commercial airline industry. However, the outlook for the future was somewhat bleak due to the thaw in East-West relations and the shakeout occurring in the airline industry.

Industrial

Industrial applications of hoses ranged from oil field equipment to refrigeration equipment. Half of all sales were to equipment OEMs, and the other half to distributors. Many firms participated in this segment, including a number that competed primarily on price. Titeflex held only 1 to 2 percent of the overall market for industrial hoses but as much as 20 percent of the market for the high-pressure/high-temperature segment, where price was less important than quality and reliability.

A key feature in the replacement portion of this market was rapid response to customer requests. In contrast, in the OEM segment meeting delivery schedules, rather than immediate response, was crucial. Product customization was not as critical as in the aerospace market, and unit demand was roughly twice as large. Titeflex's Marketing Department estimated that demand would grow in line with the general economy.

Automotive

As automobiles and their engines become smaller, engine temperatures and vibration effects increased dramatically. Titeflex had a technological advantage when entering this market because these problems had been solved 10 years earlier in aerospace applications. Demand was somewhat seasonal, according to the automotive companies' production schedules, as well as cyclical, according to overall economic performance nationwide.

Price competition was intense. Margins were low in contrast to those in the other two markets, but there was little variety in products. A customer might expect 2,000 hoses to be shipped per day. Late deliveries could shut down an engine assembly or components plant, and customers would not accept early delivery. Technological change was continuous, although changes were small when compared to those encountered in aerospace. Of the three markets served by Titeflex, the automotive segment was expected to grow the fastest.

Sales and Marketing Organization

Titeflex had separate sales and marketing departments for the aerospace segment and the industrial and automotive segments, both based in Springfield. (Exhibit 1 shows Titeflex's organizational structure in 1988.) Salespersons were paid a base salary plus commission. The Sales Department was the principal contact point with customers, and other forms of contact between customers and Titeflex employees were strongly discouraged. For instance, when customers visited the company to follow up on orders, they were whisked away to a small room in the Sales Department and not permitted to wander around the offices or on the shop floor.

Competitors

Titeflex's strongest competitor in high-performance hoses was Aeroquip Corporation, based in Jackson, Michigan, which was also the leading supplier to the aerospace segment. The other major competitor, Stratoflex, was based in Dallas, Texas. Stratoflex had become increasingly aggressive after it was acquired by Parker Hannifin, which invested heavily in the firm's modernization. Both companies were reducing their costs and improving customer service at a brisk pace. As of 1988, no foreign competitor of any significance had emerged.

ORGANIZATION AND OPERATIONS AT SPRINGFIELD

In 1988, Titeflex employed about 750 people. Nearly 600 worked in its largest facility, in Springfield, and the rest were employed in plants and offices located in Canada and France. About half the employees at Springfield were shop-floor workers, while the rest worked in front office jobs: operations planning, engineering, quality control, sales, finance/MIS, R&D, and human resource management (see Exhibit 1). Bundy had invested significant sums to expand and modernize the Springfield plant and strengthen the MIS system. However, Bundy had not tampered with Titeflex's organization or management methods.

The Sales Department took 3 to 5 weeks for order entry and processing, while Operations took about 7 to 10 weeks to manufacture a standard made-to-stock product, for a total of 10 to 15 weeks from order receipt to shipment—provided all went according to plan. In the Operations function, there were five to six levels in the hierarchy from the head of the department to the shop-floor employee. A purchase order for a bearing to fix a machine might require seven or eight signatures. Departmental loyalties were strong, and interdepartmental coordination was achieved primarily through formal meetings. Said one busy executive: "We have morning meetings, afternoon meetings, quality review meetings, engineering review meetings, purchasing meetings, make-buy meetings, and meetings to schedule meetings!"

The production process for an average hose began with the Plant Engineering Department, which developed the drawings required for manufacture—unless the customer supplied drawings with the order. The basic hose was manufactured in the Hose Fabrication Department, while parts and fittings were manufactured in the Ma-

EXHIBIT 1
Titeflex Organizational Structure and Staffing, December 1988

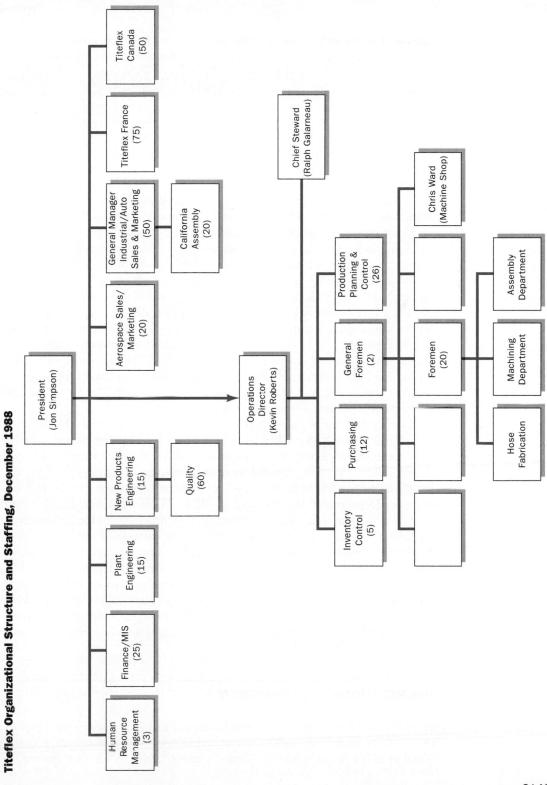

chining Department. Each of these departments had a handful of very expensive pieces of equipment that were common to the manufacture of all parts. In the Assembly Department, hoses and fittings made by Hose Fabrication and Machining were assembled with outside parts to make finished products for the aerospace, industrial, and automotive markets.

In all departments, workers and equipment were organized by type of activity rather than type of hose or type of customer. For instance, the same machine or worker might be used in the fabrication of a $10,000 hose for a jet engine and a $50 exhaust-recovery hose for a car. Most machine operators—direct workers—were paid on a piecework basis. Material handlers moved work from one location to the next; the company had designed special carts to minimize damage during such transportation. Indirect workers of this sort accounted for about 20 percent of the shop-floor work force.

Shipments were frequently held up for want of outside parts or internal production bottlenecks, leading in some cases to delays of several weeks and infuriated customers. To alleviate this problem, Titeflex built up inventories of parts and work-in-process at all stages; by 1988, inventories had risen to 4 months of sales. A computerized Materials Requirement Planning (MRP) system introduced in the mid-1980s at a cost of nearly $1 million generated very detailed reports on schedules, inventories, and manufacturing costs (by order, by department, etc.). In addition, Production Planning and Control (PPC) held periodic meetings to review the status of various jobs. When all else failed, the "sales action" group in the PPC Department shepherded high-priority orders through the production maze to placate angry customers. Despite this, in 1988 only a fourth of all industrial orders and a tenth of all aerospace orders were delivered on time.

Titeflex had the reputation of shipping high-quality products. A large Quality Department, which reported to the Engineering Department rather than the Operations manager, inspected parts and subassemblies at every stage of the production process, sending anything that fell short of specifications for rework. Typically, 25 percent of the output had to be reworked. A competent fifteen-person New Products Engineering Department was engaged in R&D. This department had recently been downsized and was quite heavily focused on new products for the automotive industry.

Several of the most senior executives were included in an incentive plan that awarded bonuses at the end of the year based on the company's overall performance. The accounting system yielded cost data on individual departments and generated profit numbers for the company as a whole. Titeflex had no scheme for employee stock ownership, although a few senior executives were believed to own Bundy stock. John Makis, who headed Titeflex from 1980 to 1988, had been with the company for more than 30 years and was described by a colleague as "conservative and cautious."

MANAGEMENT-UNION RELATIONS AT SPRINGFIELD

Ralph Galarneau (an imposing 6 feet 1 inch tall and 265 pounds) was chief steward of Titeflex's Springfield union. Galarneau had joined Titeflex at age 19, following in the footsteps of his father, who was himself a union leader in Titeflex. Although workers voted (over his objections) in 1976 to join the Teamsters Union rather than remain an independent union, Galarneau remained an influential member of the union, eventually becoming its head. Like Galarneau, who was 42, the average Titeflex worker was about 40 years old, had been with the organization 20 years, and had at least a few relatives working in the company.

Historically, union contracts had been negotiated annually, usually through a contentious process that involved a 1- or 2-week strike. In addition, workers went on wildcat strikes from time to time. The contract stipulated work rules in detail, including who could perform which tasks: for instance, only welders could weld, and only material handlers could move materials. In 1987, management and the union signed a 3-year contract for the first time, one that would expire in April 1990. Although Ralph Galarneau represented workers at contract negotiations, the local Teamsters Union business agent formally signed the contract.

Kevin Roberts, head of Operations, represented management in contract negotiations. One subordinate described him as "brilliant," while another noted that Roberts had a large following among the supervisory staff within Operations. According to one employee, "Kevin and Ralph play cat and mouse day in and day out." Roberts expected his foremen to take disciplinary action against troublemakers on a regular basis; in turn, Galarneau filed grievances with Kevin Roberts at the rate of at least one per day, and often pursued individual cases for as long as possible. Workers were subject to "progressive discipline"; that is, they could be fired only after a long series of prior warnings and hearings. Typically, only one or two workers were fired every year. However, when demand slackened, layoffs were permitted on a reverse seniority basis. Reflecting on the work environment, Chris Ward, a supervisor, said: "It's unfortunate, but true, that in this company to get work out of your guys and to keep your bosses happy you've got to be an s.o.b.!"

Once signed, the contract became the primary basis for union-management relations. As one employee put it, "Both management and union walk around with copies of the contract in their back pockets." There was minimal interaction between front office people, such as engineers and salespersons, and shop-floor workers. Although in the 1960s and 1970s management and workers had celebrated special times like Christmas together, in recent years each had organized its own holiday parties.

JON SIMPSON

Jon Simpson earned degrees in polymer chemistry from Duke University and the University of Arizona before joining the 3M Company in 1969 as a bench chemist. Eleven years later, he had become supervisor of an R&D lab employing seventy scientists. In 1980, he left 3M to become vice president of R&D at CHR Industries, a Bundy company within the Performance Plastics Group based in New Haven, Connecticut. CHR made high-performance pressure-sensitive tapes and silicone rubber products for the aerospace and electronics industries. Like Titeflex, CHR worked with Teflon technology and served some of the same end users. CHR workers were members of the United Rubber Workers Union. In 1982, Simpson became vice pres-

EXHIBIT 2
Titeflex Corporation: The Turnaround Challenge
Trends in Performance Indicators,
1988 vs. 1987 (1987 = 100)*

Indicator	1987	1988[†]
1. Sales		
Aerospace	100	89.5
Industrial	100	113.1
Automotive	100	146.3
Total	100	107.4
2. Quality		
Returns	100	102.3
Rework	100	105.4
3. Inventory	100	116.5
4. Overhead/sales ratio	100	110.0
5. Pretax return on net assets[‡]		
before interest (EBIT/NA)	100	94.6
6. Return on Sales	100	87.3

*As Titeflex did not report divisional financial results, the actual amounts are not shown in this table; only changes in each item in 1988 relative to 1987 (base year) are shown. Thus, the table gives some idea of the trends in performance at the time Simpson took over as head of Titeflex (December 1988).
[†]Estimates as of December 1988.
[‡]Net assets equal gross fixed assets less accumulated depreciation.

ident of Operations at CHR, with continued responsibility for R&D. Describing that stint, Jon Simpson said:

> At 3M, I was used to managing professionals doing R&D. It was always very gentlemanly. At CHR, they ate me alive when I tried managing in that style. So, I turned into a Genghis Khan. At the end of the day, my blood pressure was high, theirs was high, and we all went home with knots in our stomach. But I fought and I won every goddamn battle with the unions. And I won it bloody and I won it dirty, but I won every battle. I wouldn't even let 'em win the small ones!

In 1988, when Bundy brought in the Boston Consulting Group (BCG) to study Titeflex's operations, Jon Simpson was asked to take time away from CHR to help with the project. Over a period of 9 months, he spent 2 days a week in Springfield serving as an internal consultant to the BCG team, whose mission was to flow-chart organizational processes in every area to identify how efficiency and speed of response could be improved. In August 1988, Bundy transferred Simpson to Titeflex with the intention of making him head of Titeflex's industrial and automotive businesses, leaving the aerospace/marine business under the charge of another general manager. This plan went astray when Tube Investments (TI) bought Bundy and announced its decision to divest all four subsidiaries in Bundy's Performance Plastics Group, including CHR Industries and Titeflex. After further study, however, TI pulled Titeflex out of the divestment package because its technology was seen as having value for Bundy's automotive business as well as for TI's flourishing aerospace business. Christopher Lewinton then made Jon Simpson president of all of Titeflex.

THE TASK AHEAD

In 1988, Titeflex earned a 5 percent margin on $45 million in sales and a return on net assets (gross fixed assets less accumulated depreciation) before interest and taxes of 20 percent. (See Exhibit 2 for the trend in several performance indicators in the 2 years prior to Simpson's arrival at Titeflex.) In recent years, sales had grown at 6 to 7 percent per year, with growth in the automotive segment offsetting sluggish growth in the industrial sector and negative growth in the aerospace market. Meanwhile, Titeflex's costs were rising faster than sales. Customers were also beginning to expect their suppliers to provide more and better service for less money.

Simpson estimated that Titeflex had a 15 to 20 percent cost disadvantage relative to its major competitors on account of its location in Massachusetts, where taxes and wages were higher than other parts of the country. However, moving to a different location could be an expensive proposition; among other things, a new facility would have to be recertified before it could supply the aerospace industry. In addition, Simpson believed the work force in western Massachusetts was highly skilled and had a strong work ethic.

Simpson wondered what course of action he ought to take in the coming weeks and months.

http://www.socplas.org/

CASE 11

ValuJet and the U.S. Airline Industry in 1996*

On May 11, 1996, at 2:17 P.M., ValuJet Flight 592 took off from the Miami International Airport bound for Atlanta, Georgia. Eight minutes after takeoff, the aircraft wheeled around to return to Miami, reporting smoke in the cockpit. Seconds later the DC-9, carrying 105 passengers and 5 crew members, crashed into the Florida Everglades and disappeared in the mud, water, and swamp grass. There were no survivors.

THE WIDESPREAD EFFECTS OF THE CRASH

At the time of the crash, ValuJet shone as a symbol of success in a challenged industry. It was one of the very few fast-growing profitable airlines, and one of the few start-up ventures in the industry to have flourished. Its success in the no-frills, low-fare market cast it as the new model for aspiring ventures. The Clinton administration, and most particularly Department of Transportation Secretary Federico Pena, held it up as proof that the administration's "open skies" policy of continued worldwide deregulation was sound and workable.

The media coverage of the crash publicized serious shortcomings on the part of both ValuJet and the Federal Aviation Administration (FAA). Despite immediate statements by ValuJet President Lewis Jordan, FAA Administrator David Hinson, and Secretary Pena, that ValuJet was a safe airline, the investigations prompted by the accident revealed that ValuJet had the worst safety record of any major airline. Since beginning operations in October 1993, ValuJet had incurred a total of 284 FAA citations for service difficulties. The company's record of 3.06 accidents per 100,000 departures compared unfavorably with the 0.43 average for 14 other low-fare airlines. At the time of the crash in May, and because of this history of safety problems, ValuJet was in the midst of a 120-day FAA surveillance that had begun in February.

As the investigation continued, the revelation of more serious shortcomings on the part of both ValuJet and the FAA tarnished the airline, humiliated the agency, em-

---

*This case was prepared by John B. Gallagher, The University of Tennessee, Knoxville, under the direction of Alex Miller. Copyright © 1996 by John B. Gallagher and Alex Miller. Reprinted by permission of authors.

barrassed the Clinton administration, and led to congressional hearings. Fallout from the accident included additional restrictions placed on all airlines and significant loss of business to other low-fare airlines. It also precipitated a criminal investigation by federal officials from the FBI and the Transportation Department.

The discovery that the airline had not been in full compliance with safety regulations for as much as a year prior to the accident had major ramifications for both ValuJet and the FAA. On June 17, the carrier handed its air carrier certificate over the FAA and ceased operation. One day later, Anthony Broderick resigned his position as the associate administrator for regulation and certification for the FAA. This was the first FAA resignation ever linked to a particular accident.

Some experts openly speculated that this crash would result in major changes to the industry, similar to previous crashes that had permanent effects. The 1931 accident that killed Knute Rockne resulted in a ban on wooden structural parts. The 1935 accident that killed Senator Bronson Cutting led to the creation of the Civil Aeronautics Board (CAB) in 1940, and the crash of a DC-10 in Chicago in 1979 effectively grounded that aircraft model. The ValuJet Flight 592 crash raised immediate questions about the entire industry. Issues such as safety, particularly low-fare airline safety, airline management practices such as outsourcing, and the functioning of the FAA received close scrutiny and renewed criticism. One reporter characterized ValuJet as a casualty of deregulation, implying that industry dynamics and competitive forces had created circumstances which made accidents inevitable.

DEREGULATION RESHAPED THE INDUSTRY

Prior to the Airline Deregulation Act of 1978, the Civil Aeronautics Board (CAB) controlled routes, established fares, and licensed new entrants. Deregulation gradually phased out all CAB regulations and eliminated restrictions on entry, routes, and fares. The intent was to permit market forces to shape capital investment, pricing, and service decisions. Capital decisions include investment in airplanes, and in facilities for maintenance, storage, baggage handling, and passenger terminals. Airplanes, however, are mobile assets. Airlines can shift planes into and out of service and even transfer them by sale or lease to another airline with relative ease. Competition dictates shifting assets to maximize return. Pricing decisions include fares and fare structures that can respond to demand. Service decisions involve flight schedules and rates, also responsive to demand. All of these decisions could improve if airlines were free to make them in a competitive environment.

Deregulation provided that environment. The resulting dramatic changes encompassed route structuring, technological innovation, federal government oversight, and industry consolidation. At the same time, the industry witnessed significant growth accompanied by relentless pressure to reduce costs and improve efficiency.

Changes in Route Structures

One of the most significant developments in the industry since deregulation has been hub-and-spoke route networks. In the United States, particularly with vast geographical areas to cover, point-to-point service connecting two cities is expensive and highly variable in demand. As a result, major airlines developed hub-and-spoke systems. Hub cities were popular or strategically important destinations connected to smaller spoke or feeder destinations. Major airlines provided service from hub to hub and relied on smaller commuter or regional airlines to fly the spoke routes. This system allowed for more efficient collection and transfer of passengers.

For example, Atlanta is a hub city for Delta Airlines. A flight from Greensboro, NC, may carry 30 passengers, 10 of whom are traveling to Orlando, 14 to New Orleans, 4 to New York, and 2 to Boston. Similarly, a flight from Kansas City to Atlanta may carry 50 passengers, 20 of whom are traveling to Orlando, 16 to New York, 11 to New Orleans, and 3 to Atlanta. Flying spoke routes from Greensboro to Atlanta and from Kansas City to Atlanta, all 80 passengers will deplane in Atlanta. Thirty will board a plane for Orlando, 24 a plane to New York, with 4 continuing to Boston, and 22 will board a plane to New Orleans. Although this network requires frequent plane changes for passengers, and may increase their total travel time, it allows an airline to utilize capacity more efficiently than operating separate flights from Greensboro and from Kansas City to all those destinations.

Technology Innovations

The need for efficiency led the major airlines to develop their own proprietary customer reservation systems or CRS's. These extensive computer systems listed the airlines' scheduled flights and allowed airline agents and travel agents to sell tickets and route passengers easily through the hub-and-spoke system. They allowed passengers to select airlines on the basis of schedules, fares, and connections. The availability of flights and the interconnections between hub-and-spoke flights appeared seamless to customers, through an arrangement known as code sharing. This was an agreement between two or more airlines to list their respective flight schedules on the same CRS, and schedule connecting flights accordingly. The CRS also provided updated information about the availability of seats on any given flight and the planned type of aircraft.

Federal Government Oversight

The Airline Deregulation Act required that the Civil Aeronautics Board be dismantled in 1984. This left the Federal Aviation Administration as the primary federal agency responsible for oversight of the aviation industry, with a broad double mission: to promote air travel, and to regulate it. Traditionally, the FAA interpreted the mission of promoting air travel to mean facilitating the entry of new airlines, and the mission of regulating travel to mean enforcing safety and controlling air traffic.

Critics of the FAA charged that the agency had not adapted to the changed environment shaped by airline deregulation. They complained that administrators were too close to the industry, and too slow to adopt new technology. There had been considerable media coverage regarding FAA failure to take swift action in areas where airlines were moving aggressively to contain costs, such as outsourcing critical maintenance to subcontractors. In congressional hearings following the ValuJet crash, the

FAA conceded it was unprepared to handle oversight responsibility for this growing practice.

Consolidation of the Industry

Deregulation intensified the level of competition in the industry and brought significant consolidation of carriers through bankruptcies, acquisitions, and mergers, often with a high degree of government or court involvement in the process. An increase in market concentration resulted (see Exhibit 1). At the same time, it encouraged almost continual attempts to start new airlines, most of which have failed.

Despite the high failure rate, start-up efforts continue. Since 1993, thirty-nine new carriers were certified by the FAA, eight in the first months of 1996 alone. Exhibit 2 lists several of those ventures, including the size of their fleets, and financial

EXHIBIT 1
Concentration Among Major U.S. Carriers

1985 Rank	Company	% Market Share	1995 Rank	Company	% Market Share
1	American	13.3	1	United	21.0
2	United	12.5	2	American	19.3
3	Eastern	10.0	3	Delta	16.0
4	TWA	9.6	4	Northwest	11.7
5	Delta	9.0	5	Continental	7.5
6	Pam Am	8.1	6	USAir	7.2
7	NWA	6.7	7	TWA	4.7
8	Continental	4.9	8	Southwest	4.4
9	People Express	3.3	9	America West	2.5
10	Republic	3.2	10	America Trans Air	1.2
	Others	19.4		Others	4.5

Source: Standard & Poors Industry Survey, February 1996.

EXHIBIT 2
Recent Airline Start-up Ventures—1995 Data

Airline	Date Started	Fleet Size	Revenue (in thousands of dollars)	Income (in thousands of dollars)
Air South	August 1994	7	$ 2 6,600,000	$ (4,700,000)
Frontier Airlines	July 1994	7	14,250,000	(986,301)
Kiwi International	September 1992	15	170,000,000	(770,000)
Nations Air	March 1995	3	12,500,000	(8,400,000)
Reno Air	July 1992	24	11,800,000	(1,500,000)
ValuJet	October 1993	51	367,800,000	67,800,000
Vanguard Airlines	December 1994	7	14,500,000	(6,100,000)
Western Pacific	April 1995	12	55,000,000	(10,500,000)

Source: *USA Today,* February 12, 1996.

data. Company founders and investors tried to exploit special niches, or to fill gaps in point-to-point service left by the majors when they restructured routes and forged regional alliances. Often the relative ease of starting an airline attracted entrants. The fledgling companies usually ran short of cash when larger competitors matched their service and fares, and declared bankruptcy.

Successes are few and notable. Observers most often credit Southwest Airlines as a model for starting an airline company. Started in 1973, Southwest created a favorable cost structure by utilizing only one style of aircraft, the 737, and offering only minimal services. It pioneered the no-frills approach and began providing point-to-point short-haul service between cities with a lot of traffic. The formula proved successful and made Southwest one of the largest airlines in the United States.

Generally, the competition brought about by deregulation had improved service, saved consumers money, and made U.S. carriers more competitive in the international arena. However, some regional and metropolitan areas have seen fares increase while services deteriorate. Managers and labor unions note intensified friction in their relationships. Quality of the flying experience declines as passengers encounter delays and crowded flights. Finally, airlines face drastically changed rules of competition.

THE NATURE OF DEREGULATED COMPETITION

Bankruptcy, consolidation, and rare start-up success in the deregulated environment clearly demonstrate that profits are elusive. During the first four years of the 1990s, the industry had collectively managed to lose 13 billion dollars (see Exhibit 3), mostly due to price wars and fare reductions. The industry had too much capacity and could not fill enough seats to cover its costs. In contrast, the first four months of 1996 were perhaps the brightest since 1979. (Exhibit 4 presents several years of composite revenue data.) In late April 1996, the reported first quarter results of major airlines in the United States showed impressive profits, the result of cost-reduction efforts, moder-

EXHIBIT 3
Composite Industry Data: Airline Earnings and Book Value 1987–1994

Year	Earnings	Book Value
1987	8.27	151.42
1988	33.76	177.98
1989	18.5	198.51
1990	−21.35	167.47
1991	−31.08	131.26
1992	−48.48	27.83
1993	−26.73	24.23
1994	−15.77	93.82

Source: Standard & Poors Industry Survey, February 1996.

EXHIBIT 4
Composite Industry Data: Airline Revenue 1987–1994

Year	Revenue
1987	541.54
1988	847.20
1989	994.26
1990	1,106.22
1991	990.74
1992	1,051.99
1993	1,126.62
1994	796.16

Source: Standard & Poors Industry Survey, February 1996.

ate growth in demand, and no added capacity. This performance came on the heels of 1995, the industry's best year ever, when operating profits were more than five billion dollars, and net earnings in excess of two billion.

Domestic airlines reporting record profits in the first quarter of 1996 included Continental, AMR Corp. (the parent of American Airlines), Northwest, and America West. Southwest and ValuJet reported improvements over last year's earnings, and airlines reporting bottom-line losses but still significantly improved operating profits were UAL Corp. (the parent of United Airlines) and Delta Airlines, although Delta reported non-recurring charges that resulted in a net loss. Finally, USAir, TWA, and the Alaska Air Group reported red ink, but still improved figures.

Industry analysts and executives shared optimism that the overcapacity that fueled price wars and fare cutting during the 1980s and early 1990s had been eclipsed by the growth in demand. Historically, airlines had always added capacity and ordered planes at the first hint of profits, but apparently not this time. Although orders for new aircraft had risen dramatically during 1995 (see Exhibit 5), most experts expected airlines to use new planes to upgrade fleets and remove older planes from service, not put more available seats on the market. For example, ValuJet, the launch customer for McDonnell-Douglas's MD-95, had decided even before the crash to scale back its planned delivery of new planes.

EXHIBIT 5
Civil Transport Aircraft Backlog (as of December 31, 1995)

	1991	1992	1993	1994	1995
Transports:					
No. of aircraft on order	2,781	2,329	2,023	1,741	1,869
Value (in millions of dollars)	108,833	96,724	77,735	67,709	N.A.

Customer Demand for Air Travel

Generally, demand for air travel is cyclical, and follows overall economic trends. Since 1978, the number of domestic passengers in the United States increased 62%, and the total number of passengers increased 79%. These passengers include two distinct groups of customers, business travelers and leisure travelers. Often, passengers are in both segments, traveling for business one time and vacation the next, or combining the two in one trip.

Business travel tends to increase in times of economic expansion, and to reflect the level of business activity taking place between cities, regions, or countries. Leisure travel also reflects general economic conditions. Vacationers use air travel more in times of relative prosperity and vacation closer to home in recessionary times. They may choose to not fly at all. In early 1996, growth in leisure travel had outstripped that of business travel and accounted for nearly 60% of all U.S. traffic.

Business travel is more sensitive to changing services and technology. Business travelers value services such as scheduled flight frequency and timely connecting flights, but also value reasonable fares. Leisure passengers view flights as a way of getting to the place on the ground where they really want to spend their money. They value low fares and make travel decisions sometimes exclusively on price.

Specifically, then, the price of fares has a direct effect on demand for air travel, as does the relative ease and cost of air travel compared to the ease and cost of alternate modes of travel. High fares reduce demand for travel; low fares stimulate demand. In the past several years, some airlines, particularly ValuJet, have demonstrated that, with low enough fares, travelers who have never flown before will abandon automobiles and get on an airplane.

Yield Management

Profitability is not assured simply by expanding the customer base and stimulating demand. The keys to airline profitability lie in cost containment and revenue maximization. Costs are rigidly fixed, but revenues are highly volatile. Furthermore, most of an airline's costs are incurred before any revenue is earned. This set of relationships encourages airlines to view costs and revenues very differently. They look to develop a cost structure that will maintain expenses at or near a particular level over a fairly extended time. Within this time period, they then look to maximize revenue on any given flight. Since there is a certain fixed cost required to get a plane in the air, any revenue is preferable to an empty seat. Achieving this balance between costs and revenue is complex and involves issues of capacity, scheduling, route selection, fare structure, and levels of service. This situation may trigger price wars if a particular airline needs to fill seats.

Capacity is a function of the types of aircraft flown and the frequency with which they fly. Aircraft types differ by size, seating configuration, fuel efficiency, and runway needs. Different types of aircraft therefore suit certain routes and service patterns better than others. Routes can be either short- or long-haul, depending on the distance covered, but most routes also experience peak demand periods when there are more passengers per flight. Thus, suitable aircraft available at the right time can contain costs and enhance revenue.

Airlines use load factors as the measure of capacity utilization. The load factor is the percentage of seats filled by paying passengers compared to the total number of seats available on the flight. If there are 64 paying passengers on a 100-seat airplane, the load factor for that flight is 64.0. Load factors for individual flights are aggregated over time for all flights and provide an ongoing measure of capacity utilization.

Yield is a measure of fare prices. Yield measures the total dollars of revenue generated by the seats that are full, and is expressed on a per-seat, per-mile basis. It measures the average fare per mile per passenger, and is aggregated over all flights to provide an ongoing measure. High yields, indicating high average fares, can sometimes offset low load factors, or nearly empty planes. Low yields, indicating low average fares, may not always offset high load factors even when the plane is full. While yield measures the average fare paid by a passenger per seat, and the success of the airline at garnering high fares, the load factor determines how full the plane actually was. Increasing load factors by substantively discounting fares can drive the revenue generated from any given flight below the fixed costs required to get airborne. This relationship often leads airlines to calculate break-even load factors or break-even yields for use in price decisions.

Because yield is a measure of average fares based on occupied seats, the industry also measures revenue per available seat mile (RPM), which is the total passenger revenue distributed over all scheduled seat capacity. Total costs are also calculated on a per available seat mile (ASM) basis, and represent the airline's total cost distributed over all scheduled seat capacity. All airlines measure operating costs in costs per ASM, and in early 1996, costs ranged from as low as 6.5 cents per ASM for ValuJet, to over 12.0 cents per ASM for USAir. (Exhibit 6 provides industry cost comparisons.) Operating margin is the comparison between these two measures.

Cost Containment

Major cost factors include salaries for all pilots, flight attendants, and ground attendants, maintenance costs, reservation system costs, fuel costs, advertising expenses,

---

EXHIBIT 6
Comparison of Costs, 1994 (cents/ASM): Selected U.S. Airlines and Industry Average

Expense	Delta	USAir	Southwest	ValuJet	Industry
Salaries	2.78	3.57	1.89	1.23	2.65
Benefits	1.09	1.42	0.81	0.54	1.02
Total labor	3.87	4.98	2.70	1.77	3.66
Fuel	1.05	1.06	0.98	1.47	1.05
Depreciation	1.41	1.75	1.03	0.19	1.43
Commissions	0.93	0.95	0.53	0.26	0.82
Advertising	0.20	0.26	0.34	0.72	0.24
Maintenance	0.39	0.64	0.63	0.72	0.45
Other	1.71	2.12	1.08	1.90	1.67
Total expense	9.56	11.76	7.28	7.03	9.33

Source: Kidder, Peabody & Company, 12/7/94.

airport terminal expenses, and landing fees. Wages remain the single largest cost component and most airlines relentlessly pursue reductions in labor, either through personnel reductions or contract negotiations, and more recently, through employee stock payments. The industry has been heavily unionized and the relentless pressure to reduce labor cost has fostered permanent acrimony between the airlines and organized labor.

Fuel costs are next largest after wages. The rising 1990–91 petroleum costs attributable to the Iraqi invasion of Kuwait and the resulting Persian Gulf war significantly contributed to the industry's poor performance during that time. A third major cost factor involves the method of financing aircraft. Differences between the treatment of lease fees compared to interest expense on debt can distort operating margins.

Other significant costs arise in ticketing and reservations. In February 1995, the carriers capped the commissions paid to travel agents with savings estimated to exceed $500 million in the first year. Where feasible, information technology has revamped the entire process of selling seats and issuing tickets. Direct dial, Internet access, and captive software permit direct purchase of seats by consumers, and electronic reservations permit ticketless travel.

The most significant and controversial approach to containing costs involves the practice of outsourcing. Outsourcing is the farming out of work, such as maintenance, to other companies who specialize in performing those services and are willing to provide them at prices below an airline's in-house costs. Outsourcing typically entails bidding out work to suppliers that are geographically diverse, and thus hard to monitor. Usually, these services are contracted for at a relatively fixed cost and for a specific period of time. An airline knows what its costs will be for certain expenses and does not have to invest in the facilities, employees, or training to accomplish these items as part of its own operations. The contractor, or supplier, can also achieve cost efficiencies and expertise by specializing only in certain services. Beyond maintenance, outsourcing is also used for training pilots and flight crews, drafting operations and flight manuals, and filing records and documents required by FAA regulation.

The start-up of Presidential Air provides an example of the use of outsourcing to create a "virtual airline." Presidential began in February 1996, providing service from Southern California, through Houston, to Atlanta. Launched by a real estate entrepreneur with no airline experience and a prior conviction for fraud, Presidential parlayed over $4 million in loans and credits from aircraft leasing and jet fuel companies into a balance sheet strong enough to win government approval. It hired consultants to handle the federal certification process, Continental to train its flight attendants and retrain its pilots, and America West to provide ground attendants. Presidential performed no activities in-house.

Revenue Enhancement

Yield management refers to the complex array of practices that airlines use in seeking that profitable balance between higher fares and possible empty seats. The most prevalent technique employs advance ticket purchases. Business travelers booking at the last minute with little flexibility and few alternatives will pay higher fares. Passengers who can book flights early find that airline will secure that commitment with lower fares.

Additional techniques used to manage yield include quietly discounting fares as the departure data draws closer, and establishing different structures for round-trip tickets, long duration stays, and Saturday night stay-overs. Airlines can also expand or contract the number of seats assigned to coach, economy, or first-class seating as a way of improving yield. As a result, passengers on the same flight rarely pay the same fare.

The availability of fare and scheduling information due to the widespread use of CRS's has armed consumers with competitive information and diminished passenger loyalty to particular airlines. Airlines have responded with features, such as frequent flyer programs, that attract repeat passengers with the promise of free tickets, package deals with car rental and hotel chains, and senior citizen discounts.

Industry analysts and executives believe future tactics to generate profits will require an increasing focus on smaller market segments, or customer groups. A narrower focus affords the best opportunity to create workable cost structures. It minimizes the number of aircraft types a company has to own or lease, fixes maintenance costs and crew costs, and more narrowly defines competition. This means market segmentation will become an increasingly important factor in continuing profitability.

MARKET SEGMENTATION

The U.S. Department of Transportation classifies airlines according to the size of their revenue bases (Exhibit 7). "Majors" are airlines with more than $1 billion in annual revenues. "Nationals" are airlines with revenues between $100 million and $1 billion and "regionals" are airlines with revenues less than $100 million. Industry insiders, analysts, and government publications and reports use these classifications widely. Most airlines use these designations to describe themselves as well. However, these classifications have nothing to do with geographic markets served. Further, they do nothing to describe the customer base or market segment that a given airline is attempting to serve. For example, several airlines with annual revenues large enough to be classified as nationals, such as America Trans Air, operate primarily charter flights. Others, such as Tower Air and Continental Micronesia, conduct primarily international operations. Still others, such as ValuJet, have increased revenues rapidly by serving particular market segments with specific routes.

Most experts, however, including airline executives, clearly see an industry in the United States that is segmented along markets served, rather than revenues generated. Examples include the short-haul segment of routes up to 150 miles, which cannot be served economically by jets, or the high-frequency, low-cost, point-to-point service routes favored by Southwest. Existing segments based on markets rather than revenues include national airlines, global airlines, regional or community companies, and niche competitors.

National, global, and regional airlines all offer "full service." Full service airlines provide complete passenger service including baggage checking and handling, baggage forwarding, even to competing airlines, and sophisticated computer reservation systems and capabilities. They provide different seating classes, from economy to first class, assign seats based on passenger preferences, serve meals and liquor, and show

EXHIBIT 10
Global Airlines, 1994: Includes Total Domestic and International Operations for All Airlines (in millions of dollars)

Airline	Revenues	Expenses	Net Income	Load Factors*
Air France(93)	5,472.2	6,110.0	(1,378.5)	N.A.
American	14,876.9	13,965.3	228.0	65.5
British Airways	8,693.5	7,948.2	430.0	N.A.
Continental	4,645.4	4,731.7	(613.3)	63.6
Delta	12,197.7	12,412.8	(273.7)	64.5
Japan Airlines	8,183.3	8,456.4	(236.5)	N.A.
Lufthansa(93)	7,795.4	7,802.4	(67.2)	68.7
Northwest	8,875.1	7,998.6	295.5	70.2
Qantas	4,090.3	3,820.1	83.6	72.8
Singapore Airlines	3,051.5	2,724.5	455.1	N.A.
TWA	3,160.4	3,377.8	(411.7)	64.5
United	13,389.7	12,876.7	51.0	69.5

*Load factors are as of July 1, 1995.
Sources: *Air Transport World*, 10/95; *Aviation Week & Space Technology*, 1/8/96.

ship carriers for certain nations view the global arena as a lucrative growth area, and are competing for favorable government treatment, landing rights, and passengers. Many global airlines are forming partnerships or alliances that provide worldwide service using code-sharing arrangements.

Regionals

Regional airlines in the United States are experiencing the fastest growth of any segment. These are smaller carriers that generally fly the spoke routes through alliances with larger national airline partners. Regional airlines offer the nationals a way to cut costs while maintaining brand loyalty. Three long-standing examples of these partnerships are Delta's link with Comair, American's with Midway, and Continental's with Frontier.

The 125 regional carriers that were operating in 1994, serving a total of 806 airports throughout the country, flew 13.3% more RPM's than in 1993. (Exhibit 11 provides data on several regional companies.) Much of the growth occurred when the nationals abandoned unprofitable routes, expecting their regional partners to meet the residual demand.

Flights by regional airlines typically average 210 miles, compared to flights by national airlines, which average 679 miles. Regionals therefore use smaller aircraft suited for shorter distances and fewer passengers. These aircraft subject passengers to cramped seats and to bumpy flights due to flying in lower and more turbulent altitudes. As these airlines grow, they are investing in new-generation turboprops and 50-seat jets that provide significant improvements. Turboprops can provide efficiency and comfort on flights up to 600 miles in length, while jets can profitably replace majors on long unprofitable routes.

EXHIBIT 11
Operating Statistics: Regional Airlines, 1994

Airline	RPM's (in millions)	ASM's (in millions)
Atlantic Coast	372.7	789.9
Atlantic Southeast	777.4	1,690.6
Comair	1,074.8	2,135.9
Great Lakes	222.7	506.8
Horizon	813.3	1,331.8
Mesa	1,099.7	2,172.9
Mesaba	315.3	698.2
Skywest	499.2	1,021.7
Trans States	335.6	683.3

Source: *Aviation Week & Space Technology*, 1/8/96.

The newer aircraft provide operating benefits as well. With the added comfort and extended range, they allow regionals to link more cities with point-to-point service. In some cases, regionals can even bypass some hub cities. These aircraft types can be used on existing routes to more precisely match peak and off-peak demand, reducing operating costs even further. (Exhibit 12 provides data on several regional airlines.)

Niche Players

Airlines that selectively identify niches and attempt to devise a way to serve them continually enter the market. Southwest, despite its size, began by selecting a niche market, eschewing hub-and-spoke arrangements in favor of short-haul, high-frequency, point-to-point service with low fares and no frills. Kiwi International was looking to

---

EXHIBIT 12
Regional Airlines, 1994
(in millions of dollars)

Airline	Revenues	Expenses	Net Income	Load Factors*
Atlantic Coast	158.9	182.2	(23.3)	46.4
Atlantic Southeast	312.1	227.8	84.3	44.6
Comair	360.7	313.7	47.0	50.1
Great Lakes	68.8	63.6	5.2	43.3
Horizon	256.9	244.0	12.9	57.5
Mesa	396.1	347.8	48.3	49.9
Mesaba	137.7	125.9	10.8	46.1
Skywest	225.4	205.1	20.3	46.4
Trans States	144.2	123.7	20.5	46.1

*Load factors are as of July 1, 1995.
Sources: *Aviation Week & Space Technology*, 1/8/96; *Air Transport World*, 10/95.

extend low-fare, no-frill flying to the international arena. Presidential Air was originally conceived to provide vacation trips strictly to resort properties. (Exhibit 13 reports data on the most prominent niche airlines.)

The distinction of niche players is the attempt to differentiate product. This may limit flights to a select set of routes, with only certain types of planes, unusual combinations of service, or no service, and flights at odd hours or according to very atypical schedules.

Niche airlines usually lack formal operating or marketing agreements with other airlines, although some may have code-sharing arrangements. The no-frills approach is favored by many niche airlines because containing costs is critical. This often involves advance notice, advance payment, and fees for ticket changes and cancellations. ValuJet had successfully distinguished itself as a niche player.

THE DIFFERENTIATION OF VALUJET

From the beginning, ValuJet was different. Founded by three individuals with more than a century of combined airline experience, its strategy was carefully conceived. In 1992, Robert L. Priddy, Timothy P. Flynn, and Maurice J. Gallagher, Jr., pooled $1.0 million each to purchase 1.5 million shares in a new company they called Charter Way. The founders recruited Lewis Jordan from his position as President and Chief Operating Officer of Continental Airlines, to be the President of the new company, and Steve Nevin from his position as the head of the McDonnell-Douglas Finance Corporation to be the Chief Financial Officer. Priddy began his career with Southern Airways in 1966, then moved on to be one of three founders of Atlantic Southeast Airlines. Following that, he held executive positions at Air Midwest, and then Florida Gulf Airlines. Like Priddy, Jordan also had started his career with Southern Airways,

EXHIBIT 13
Niche Airlines, 1994
(in millions of dollars)

Airline	Revenues	Expenses	Net Income	Load Factors*
Air South	6.7	15.9	(9.1)	47.3
Frontier	24.5	32.7	(8.1)	44.2
Kiwi International	117.2	135.1	(17.9)	71.4
Midway	31.5	52.9	(21.4)	47.4
Reno Air	195.5	209.4	(13.9)	59.1
Southwest	2,591.9	2,275.2	316.7	64.2
ValuJet	133.9	99.4	34.5	66.6
Vanguard	0.8	8.9	(3.1)	46.0

*Load factors are as of July 1, 1995.
Sources: *Aviation Week & Space Technology*, 1/8/96; Standard & Poors Industry Survey, 2/1/96.

but moved to Continental in 1962. Nevin's role at McDonnell-Douglas, leasing aircraft to companies worldwide, gave him invaluable knowledge of the whereabouts of good used aircraft.

In October of 1993, before the first plane ever took off, the company had raised another $13.0 million through a private placement of an additional 3.25 million shares at $4.00 each. It used the capital to purchase two used DC-9's from Delta Airlines for $2.0 million apiece. After considering painting the planes a stark white with a solitary black stripe and calling itself "Generic Air," the company adopted a blue and yellow color scheme, unveiled a cartoon plane character known as "Critter," renamed itself ValuJet, and started flying on October 26, 1993.

The company decided to base its operation out of Atlanta, Georgia, one of the busiest airports in the country, and the principal hub for Delta Airlines. Initial service consisted of eight flights total each day from Atlanta to three cities in Florida: Jacksonville, Orlando, and Tampa. The founders reasoned that of the 20 million people a year driving to Florida, a significant number would choose to fly rather than drive if the price was right.

Throughout 1994, the company expanded its fleet by an average of 1.5 aircraft per month. ValuJet went public in June of 1994, selling 3.2 million shares at $12.50 a share. By the fourth quarter, the company was flying 103 flights per day. A second focus city, Washington, DC, was added, and flights were servicing 10 cities from there. Total fleet size consisted of 27 DC-9's with service to 23 cities in 14 states and 2 countries. By the end of 1995, the company had added Boston and Orlando as focus cities, raised the fleet to 45 DC-9's and one MD-80, and was flying to 31 cities in 19 states with as many as 320 departures each day. Exhibit 14 provides the most recent operating data from the first quarter of 1996.

Strategy

From its inception, ValuJet followed a very deliberate strategy. It flew a single aircraft type. It offered single-class service, served no meals, assigned no seats, and offered a simple (and low) fare structure including no round-trip discounts or extended stay requirements. One-way fares ranged from $39 to $119.

It avoided flying too many daily flights between points and, as a result, did not siphon off traffic from larger competitors. It created a collegial atmosphere for both employees and passengers, promoted casual attire, provided children's games in waiting lounges, and board games in flight.

EXHIBIT 14
ValuJet: First Quarter 1996, Selected Operating Statistics

Passenger Revenue (in millions of dollars)	ASM's (in millions)	Cost/ASM (in cents)	RPM's (in millions)	Yield (in cents)
105.6	1,322	7.00	767	13.77

Source: Kidder, Peabody & Company, 12/7/96.

ValuJet's major innovation was its use of technology, and nowhere was this more apparent than in its electronic ticketing. The company determined early on to issue no paper tickets, held its breath to gauge initial passenger reaction, and was rewarded when passengers loved it. The technology saved millions in personnel, accounting, ticket printing, distribution, tracking, and storage costs.

In addition to paperless tickets, ValuJet had no frequent flyer programs, and participated in no code-sharing or customer reservation systems. As a result, less than 25% of its tickets were sold through travel agents, further reducing costs. It developed and maintained a paperless electronic reservation system and completely computerized accounting procedures.

The other critical components to its low-cost structure were aircraft ownership costs and outsourcing. This strategy led ValuJet to initially purchase used aircraft. The DC-9's it purchased to begin operations cost approximately $2 million each. Additional aircraft purchased as it grew were also used DC-9's. Using the same aircraft for all flights simplified pilot and crew training and spare parts requirements. The older used aircraft that ValuJet flew incurred higher fuel costs due to inefficiency, but this was offset by reduced acquisition costs. The company incurred higher maintenance costs as well, due to frequency of repairs and cost of parts, but this was offset by outsourcing all maintenance to subcontractors.

Financial Performance

ValuJet was profitable in its second month of operations, and was paying bonuses to permanent employees within a year of the start-up. Profits continued month after month, and the airline consistently enjoyed operating margins greater than 25%, almost unheard of in the business. (The Appendixes at the end of the case contain complete financial statements.) As one analyst put it, "ValuJet's management know the business, they know their markets, they are motivated to do well by their stock. They like what they do, they keep in simple, and they do it well." (Financial data from the first quarter of 1996 are in Exhibit 15.)

Cash reserves grew to nearly $128.0 million at the end of 1995. At the same time, book value of the firm was in excess of $150.0 million, and nearly $200.0 million in May of 1996. The company's stock was trading at $21.00 per share.

In general, analysts and industry experts continued to be optimistic about ValuJet's future (see Exhibit 16). The major obstacles that anyone could see on the horizon for the company included the spectre of rising fuel costs that would affect ValuJet more

---

EXHIBIT 15
ValuJet: First Quarter 1996, Selected Operating and Financial Statistics

Revenues (in millions of dollars)	Expenses (in millions of dollars)	Net Income (in millions of dollars)	Load Factors (%)	Break-even Load Factor (%)
110.0	92.5	10.7	58.0	47.8

Source: Kidder, Peabody & Company, 12/7/96.

EXHIBIT 16
ValuJet: Investment Analyst Highlights

Share price (12/95)	$21
Book value/share (12/95)	$2.97
ROE (1996E average)	46.7%
Shares outstanding (in millions)	54.6
Market capital (in millions)	$1,146.6
LT liability % of capital	33.3%
Est. 5-year EPS growth	15%
Institutional ownership	18.6%

Source: Kidder, Peabody & Company, 12/7/96.

---

adversely than other airlines because of the used aircraft, and the decreased availability of good used aircraft itself. ValuJet was growing faster than the supply of good used planes, and faced the prospect of considerable increase in its ownership costs. Of course, another obstacle would be a serious crash involving significant loss of life.

AFTERMATH OF THE CRASH

The smoke in the cockpit reported minutes before Flight 592 crashed was determined by investigators to be the result of an intense fire on board the plane. On June 17, ValuJet's flight operations were halted. After 15 weeks of intense scrutiny and correction of numerous deficiencies, the source of the fire *still had not* been identified, but wide speculation ties it to oxygen canisters in the hold. The oxygen canisters had been mis-marked by SabreTech, a contractor to whom ValuJet had outsourced work.

On August 29, 1996, the FAA granted ValuJet tentative approval to resume operations. The tentative approval was to operate only nine planes between Atlanta and four other cities. The DOT granted final approval to the airline on September 26. The following day, a federal court removed the final legal obstacle by denying an appeal from the flight attendants' union. The flight attendants alleged that the airline was still unsafe and that planes should be kept out of the air.

On Monday, September 30, the first flight since June 17 took off from Hartsfield International headed for Dulles Airport outside Washington, DC. The one-way fare was $19 dollars.

http://www.valuejet.com/

APPENDIX—VALUJET FINANCIAL STATEMENTS
Statement of Cash Flows (in thousands of dollars)

	For Year Ending 12/31/95
Cash flow provided by operating activity:	
Net income (loss)	$ 67,762
Depreciation and amortization	15,147
Net incr. (decr.) assets/liabilities	21,421
Other adjustments, net	9,456
Net cash provided (used) by operations	$ 113,788
Cash flow provided by investing activity:	
(Incr.) Decr. in PP&E	$(139,128)
Net cash provided (used) by investing	$(139,128)
Cash flow provided by financing activity:	
Issue (purchase) of equity	$ 435
Incr. (decr.) in borrowing	67,773
Net cash provided (used) by financing	$ 68,209
Net change in cash or equivalents	$ 42,869
Cash at year beginning	85,077
Cash at year ending	$ 127,947

Source: ValuJet 1995 Annual Report.

CASE 12

Southwest Airlines*

> The work force is dedicated to the company.
> They're Moonies basically. That's the way they operate.[1]

> —Edward J. Starkman, Airline Analyst, Paine Webber

Ann Rhoades, VP—People for Southwest Airlines, was packing her briefcase at the end of a 17-hour day. Tomorrow was an off-site meeting with the top nine executives of Southwest Airlines. The agenda for the meeting was to review Southwest's competitive position in light of recent actions by United and Continental, both of whom had entered Southwest's low fare market. That day's *New York Times* (September 16, 1994) had an article which characterized the situation as a major showdown in the airline industry:

> "This is a battle royal that has implications for the industry," said Kevin C. Murphy, an airline stock analyst at Morgan Stanley. The battle will, after all, be as much a test of strategy as a contest between two airlines. United and other big carriers like USAir and Continental have decided that they can lower their costs by creating a so-called airline-within-an-airline that offers low fares, few frills, and frequent service. The new operations are unabashedly modeled after Southwest, the pioneer of this strategy and keeper of the healthiest balance sheet in the industry.[2]

The reasons for this competition were easy to understand. Over 45 percent of United's revenues came from passengers who flew through its California hubs. As a market, the California corridor was the most heavily traveled in the U.S., with 80 percent more traffic than the Boston–New York–Washington corridor. Yet, United's share in this market had fallen from 38 percent in 1991 to 30 percent in 1993. During the same period, Southwest's had increased from 26 percent to 45 percent. Other airlines, like Continental, had also been hurt by Southwest's competition. Southwest's success spawned a number of imitators, including new airlines like Kiwi and Reno Air as well as major airlines like United and Continental. Concerned with this new competition, the market had driven down Southwest's stock price and analysts were raising questions about how sustainable Southwest's advantage really was.

---

*This case was prepared by Professors Charles O'Reilly and Jeffrey Pfeffer as a basis for class discussion rather than to illustrate effective or ineffective handling of an administrative situation. Support for this case was provided by the Human Resources Initiative of the Graduate School of Business.
[1]Peter Elsworth (1991). "Southwest Air's New Push West." *New York Times*, June 16, 1991.
[2]Adam Bryant (1994). "United's Bid to Rule Western Skies." New York Times, September 16, 1994.

Rhoades, a former marketing executive with an MBA from the University of New Mexico and a background in banking, had joined Southwest in 1989 to help transform the so-called People Department (Human Resources in most organizations). Southwest had always believed that an important part of its competitive advantage rested with its people and how they were managed. Ann's job was to help leverage this advantage. At tomorrow's meeting she would be asked to review Southwest's current position in light of the new competition. She had prepared a brief overview of what she saw as the major threats and opportunities of the competition and an assessment of Southwest's strengths and weaknesses in light of these changes. However, she wanted to reflect one last time on these issues to be sure she was not missing anything. Her major concerns were whether Southwest was getting the most in competitive advantage from its own people, and whether the competition could imitate its successful human resource practices.

BACKGROUND

History

On June 18, 1971, Southwest Airlines, headquartered at Love Field in Dallas, began flying with three Boeing 737 aircraft, serving the Texas cities of Dallas, Houston, and San Antonio. Southwest's competition was Texas International and Braniff, and, to a lesser extent, Continental. Continental used every political and regulatory means to ensure that Southwest would not get off the ground, including keeping Southwest out of the recently built Dallas–Fort Worth airport and waging a four-year legal battle that left Southwest almost bankrupt at the time of its first flight. One outcome of the legal battle was the so-called Wright Amendment, named after James Wright, then Speaker of the U.S. House of Representatives. The Wright Amendment prohibited any air carrier from offering direct service into Love Field from any place beyond Texas and the four contiguous states of Oklahoma, Louisiana, Arkansas, and New Mexico. This law meant that passengers flying into Southwest's central location at Love Field from destinations beyond these four states would have to purchase separate tickets for each leg of the trip and could not check baggage through to their final destination. Furthermore, neither airlines nor travel agents were permitted to advertise connections through Love Field. Ostensibly, this law was intended to encourage traffic through the new Dallas–Fort Worth hub. In fact, it was aimed at stopping Southwest.

Herb Kelleher, CEO and one of the airline's founders and then Southwest's corporate counsel, said, "You know, anger can be a great motivator. For me, this became a cause. I was a crusader freeing Jerusalem from the Saracens."[3] More recently, he was quoted as saying, "I have told people that I would retaliate if I became very angry, but now I think I would revise that. Let's just say that if I become peckish, I will attack."[4]

---

[3]Edward Welles (1992). "Captain Marvel." *Inc.*, January 1992.
[4]Kenneth Labich (1994). "Is Herb Kelleher America's Best CEO?" *Fortune*, May 2, 1994.

This aggressive, underdog spirit still pervades the company, especially among longer serving employees. Many see the goal of keeping this spirit alive as one of the firm's great challenges. Delise Zachry, an instructor from the People Training Department, noted, "In 1971, 198 people got together and did something that was impossible. Now we need to update the culture to today's problems."

In the early days, Southwest gained attention by putting its flight attendants in hot pants and using its location at Love Field to launch an advertising campaign with "Make Love, Not War," a theme that is still used today when Southwest refers to itself as the "Love" (LUV) airline. This designator is Southwest's stock ticker symbol. All aircraft have a small heart emblazoned on their sides and hearts are used prominently on corporate communications and advertising. From its inception, Southwest has encouraged its employees to identify with others at the company, deliver great customer service and have fun. It has also pursued a low fare strategy.

In the mid-80s USAir and American, attempting to increase their share of the valuable California market, purchased Air California and Pacific Southwest Airlines (PSA), two successful regional carriers. However, American soon withdrew from some cities and routes when they could not be served profitably. USAir made a number of marketing and service mistakes and also cut back service in the region. Southwest seized the opportunity to expand in California. From basically a zero market share in California in 1989, Southwest moved to the leading airline in passenger boardings in 1993 and now serves 10 cities in the state with more than a 70 percent average market share for city-pairs served.

The Current Situation

From the beginning, Southwest has maintained the same strategy and operating style that it maintains to the present. It concentrates on flying to airports that are underutilized and close-in to a metropolitan area—e.g., Love Field in Dallas, Hobby in Houston, San Jose and Oakland in the Bay Area, Midway in Chicago—although it does fly to major airports like LAX and SFO. The company also began flying fuel-efficient 737s, and now has over 200 of them, the only type of aircraft it flies. Southwest service involves frequent on-time departures as well as low cost fares. It emphasizes point-to-point routes, with no central hub and an average flight time of 65 minutes. According to its 1993 annual report, 80 percent of its customers fly non-stop to their final destination. By avoiding a hub and spoke system, it is able to avoid the delays often associated with connecting flights. This makes short-haul trips more attractive to travelers who might otherwise consider driving. It also pays off in shorter turnaround times (70% of the flights had a 15-minute ground time in 1991) and higher equipment utilization. For example, Southwest aircraft spent an average of 11 hours in the air daily compared to an industry average of 8, and they averaged 10.5 flights per gate versus 4.5 for the industry.

Following this strategy, Southwest has always seen itself as competing not so much with other airlines as with surface transportation. For instance, in 1993 the average passenger fare was roughly $60 for a trip of 500 miles. In 1984 the comparable numbers were $49 and 436 miles. For example, in August of 1994 the round-trip fare from Oakland to San Diego, a distance of over 1,000 miles, was $135. Southwest uses these low fares and frequent flights to increase passenger volume two to three times.

For example, somewhere around 8,000 people used to fly between Louisville and Chicago weekly; after Southwest entered the market, that number climbed to 26,000. It dramatically lowered the fares and increased the frequency of flights. For instance, in August of 1994 it flew 39 times round-trip daily between Dallas and Houston, 25 times between Phoenix and Los Angeles, and 20 times between Sacramento and Los Angeles. When American moved out of the San Jose hub because it was losing money, Southwest moved in and was profitable from the first day of service. In 1992, it was the leading carrier in passenger boardings in 27 of the 34 airports served. It dominated most of the major markets with almost 70 percent of the intra-Texas and over 50 percent of the intra-California markets in 1994.

Consistent with the strategy of low costs, low fares, and frequent flights, Southwest also keeps its fares simple. Unlike other airlines that rely heavily on computers and artificial intelligence programs to maximize flight revenue, Southwest typically offers only two fares on a route, a regular coach fare (there is no first or business class) and an off-peak fare. It also tries to price all fares the same within a state (for instance, currently $69 to fly anywhere within California). Southwest has never sold interline connections to other carriers and has been unwilling to pay to be part of other airlines' reservations systems. As a result, only 55 percent of Southwest's seats were booked by travel agents compared to 90 percent of tickets for major airlines. In 1994, United announced that its Apollo System would no longer carry Southwest's schedules or issue its tickets. This makes issuing tickets more difficult for travel agents, who often have to call the airline rather than working through a computer as they do with other airlines—a clear incentive to travel agents not to book Southwest flights.

To further simplify its operations, Southwest has never offered meal service on its flights. Meals can add $40 per passenger to the cost of a flight. Instead, passengers on Southwest are served beverages, peanuts (referred to as "frills"), and on longer flights, crackers or other light snacks such as cookies. There is no assigned seating. Upon arrival at a Southwest gate, each passenger holding a reservation is given a reusable plastic boarding pass with numbers from 1 to 137, the maximum load of the 737 aircraft. Passengers are loaded in groups of 30 and the boarding passes are collected for use on the next flight. Standby passengers are boarded if seats are available, in the order in which they sign up at the departure gate.

Although it is not connected to other airlines' reservation systems or affiliated with other frequent flyer programs, Southwest does have its own frequent flyer club ("The Company Club"), also a model of simplicity. It is based on the number of trips flown, not the mileage. Members keep a card that is stamped every time a plane is boarded. After they accumulate 16 segments, a free ticket is awarded and a Company Club card is issued. The card is then read into the computer system for each trip. This approach economizes on operating costs since it requires no effort to keep track of mileage. Based on some negative advertising by United about Southwest's frequent flyer program, Herb Kelleher recently sent a letter to all Company Club members detailing how awards from Southwest took less mileage to obtain and were more widely available than at other airlines. Kelleher argues that the program ". . . is the greatest value because it gives you free travel faster, for much less money, without giving up great service." For instance, after 50 round-trips within a 12-month period, a companion flies free with a Company Club member, even if the club member is traveling on an award ticket.

Overall, Southwest Airlines has been profitable in every one of the last 21 years, a record achieved by no other major U.S. airline. It was consistently profitable even during the 1991–1992 period, during which some 40 percent of the total capacity of the U.S. airline industry was seeking bankruptcy protection or ceased operation completely. Exhibit 1 presents selected financial and operating data for the last 10 years. According to *Money* magazine, for the 20-year period 1972–1992, Southwest's stock earned the highest returns of any publicly traded U.S. stock—a compounded return of over 21,000 percent. Only Wal-Mart comes close to being as good an investment over this period.

Competitive Advantage

Although the reasons for Southwest's success were many, one highly visible advantage could be seen in its cost structure. Kelleher recognized that short-haul flying was inherently more costly than longer flights (the plane is taking off and landing more often and has to be handled at every gate). He understood that the lowest-cost provider could leverage that cost advantage most where costs are highest. Exhibit 2 shows the costs per available seat mile for two comparable quarters in 1993 and 1994. Southwest's costs averaged roughly 7.1 cents while the larger airlines had costs up to 10 cents or more per mile, 20–30 percent higher. This achievement is even more striking when noting that Southwest's costs in 1984 were 5.86 cents. So, over a decade its costs had increased by only about 20 percent.

Part of this cost advantage derives from the remarkable productivity Southwest gets from its work force. For example, it routinely has an aircraft turnaround of 15 minutes from the time it arrives at the gate until it leaves (see Exhibit 3 for the anatomy of a 15-minute turnaround). United and Continental average 35 minutes. Southwest's gates are typically handled by a single agent and with a ground crew of six or fewer, rather than the three agents and twelve ground crew common at other airlines.

These low costs also come from other sources. Southwest pilots, for example, spend more time in the air than pilots at other airlines. While pilots at United, American, and Delta earn up to $200,000 a year for flying an average of 50 hours a month, Southwest's pilots average $100,000 a year flying 70 hours a month. Flight attendants and pilots help clean the aircraft or check passengers in at the gate. Harold Sirkin, an airline specialist with BCG, said, "Southwest works because people pull together to do what they need to get a plane turned around. This is a part of the Southwest culture. And if it means the pilots need to load bags, they'll do it."[5]

Southwest's employees also routinely volunteer to help customers in need. Once a customer arrived at the airport for a vacation trip with his dog in tow, only to learn that he couldn't bring the dog with him. Rather than have him cancel the trip, the gate agent took care of the dog for two weeks so the fellow could enjoy his holiday. Another employee accompanied an elderly passenger to the next stop to ensure that she was able to change planes. Stories of this sort abound.

These efforts pay off in employee productivity. In 1993, for example, Southwest had an average of 81 employees per aircraft while United and American had 157 and

---

[5]E. Scott Reckard (1994). "Shuttle Dogfight Good News for Air Travelers." *San Francisco Chronicle*, October 2, 1994.

EXHIBIT 1
Ten-Year Financial Summary
(Selected Consolidated Financial Data is in thousands of dollars, except per share amounts)

	1993	1992	1991	1990
	Selected Consolidated Financial Data			
Total operating revenues	$2,296,673	$1,802,979	$1,379,286	$1,237,276
Operating income	$291,973	$193,804	$72,611	$87,261
Net income	$154,284	$97,385	$33,148	$50,605
Net income per common and common equivalent share	$1.05	$.68	$.25	$.39
Cash dividends per common share	$.03867	$.03533	$.03333	$.03223
Total assets	$2,576,037	$2,368,856	$1,854,331	$1,480,813
Long-term debt	$639,136	$735,754	$617,434	$327,553
Stockholders' equity	$1,054,019	$879,536	$635,793	$607,294
	Consolidated Financial Ratios			
Return on average total assets	6.2%	4.6%	2.0%	3.5%
Return on average stockholders' equity	16.0%	12.9%	5.3%	8.4%
Debt as a percentage of invested capital	37.7%	45.5%	49.3%	35.0%
	Consolidated Operating Statistics			
Revenue passengers carried	36,955,221	27,839,284	22,669,942	19,830,941
Load factor	68.4%	64.5%	61.1%	60.7%
Average length of passenger haul	509	495	498	502
Trips flown	546,297	438,184	382,752	338,108
Average passenger fare	$59.97	$58.33	$55.93	$57.71
Passenger revenue yield per RPM	11.77¢	11.78¢	11.22¢	11.49¢
Operating revenue yield per ASM	8.35¢	7.89¢	7.10¢	7.23¢
Operating expenses per ASM	7.25¢	7.03¢	6.76¢	6.73¢
Fuel cost per gallon (average)	59.15¢	60.82¢	65.69¢	77.89¢
Number of employees at year end	15,175	11,397	9,778	8,620
Size of fleet at year end	178	141	124	106

EXHIBIT 2
Airline Costs per Available Seat Mile

	3rd Quarter 1993	3rd Quarter 1994
Southwest	7.13	7.03
Continental	7.64	7.56
United	8.11	8.32
American	8.06	8.08
TWA	9.23	8.66
Delta	8.66	8.95
Northwest	9.36	9.79
USAir	10.94	10.74

Sources: Company reports and *The Economist*, November 5, 1994.

1989	1988	1987	1986	1985	1984
		Selected Consolidated Financial Data			
$1,057,729	$860,434	$778,328	$768,790	$679,672	$535,948
$102,040	$85,890	$30,447	$88,963	$78,524	$68,497
$74,505	$57,952	$20,155	$50,035	$47,278	$49,724
$.54	$.41	$.14	$.34	$.34	$.38
$.03110	$.02943	$.02890	$.02890	$.02890	$.02890
$1,423,298	$1,308,389	$1,042,640	$1,061,419	$1,002,403	$646,244
$354,150	$369,541	$251,130	$339,069	$381,308	$153,314
$591,794	$567,375	$514,278	$511,850	$466,004	$361,768
		Consolidated Financial Ratios			
5.5%	5.1%	1.9%	4.8%	5.6%	8.1%
12.9%	10.8%	4.0%	10.3%	11.4%	14.7%
37.4%	39.4%	32.8%	39.8%	45.0%	29.8%
		Consolidated Operating Statistics			
17,958,263	14,876,582	13,503,242	13,637,515	12,651,239	10,697,544
62.7%	57.7%	58.4%	58.8%	60.4%	58.5%
517	516	577	542	472	436
304,673	274,859	270,559	262,082	230,227	200,124
$54.21	$55.68	$55.66	$54.43	$51.91	$48.53
10.49¢	10.79¢	9.65¢	10.05¢	11.00¢	11.12¢
6.86¢	6.47¢	5.84¢	6.11¢	6.88¢	6.71¢
6.20¢	5.82¢	5.61¢	5.41¢	6.08¢	5.86¢
59.46¢	51.37¢	54.31¢	51.42¢	78.17¢	82.44¢
7,760	6,467	5,765	5,819	5,271	3,934
94	85	75	79	70	54

152, respectively. The industry average was in excess of 130. Southwest served an average of 2,443 passengers per employee while United and American served 795 and 840, about the industry average. This means that Southwest needs a smaller load factor to break even than the other carriers (usually around 55 percent). Second, the point-to-point strategy and the use of less congested airports improves the efficiency of flight operations and helps ensure high levels of aircraft utilization. Finally, by using a single type of aircraft, Southwest was able to save on maintenance and training costs.

But Southwest is not just a low fare/low cost carrier. It also emphasizes customer service. In fact, the word "Customer" is always capitalized in all Southwest corporate communications, whether it is the Annual Report or an internal newsletter. Colleen Barrett, executive vice president—Customers and highest ranking woman executive in the airline industry, insists on this. She is also adamant about treating employees as internal customers and tries to make sure that Southwest is a comfortable and fun

---

EXHIBIT 3
Anatomy of a 15-Minute Turnaround

7:55	Ground crew chat around gate position
8:03.30	Ground crew alerted and move to positions
8:04	Plane begins to pull into gate; crew move toward plane
8:04.30	Plane stops; jetway telescopes out; baggage door opens
8:06.30	Baggage unloaded; refueling and other servicing underway
8:07	Passengers off plane
8:08	Boarding call; baggage reloading, refueling complete
8:10	Boarding complete; most of ground crew leave
8:15	Jetway retracts
8:15.30	Pushback from gate
8:18	Pushback tractor disengages; plane leaves for runway

Sources: Subrata Chakravaty, "Hit 'em Hardest with the Mostest," *Forbes*, September 16, 1991.

place to work. "If you're comfortable, you're smiling more and you give better service," Barrett says. "It doesn't take a rocket scientist to figure that out."[6] The results are undeniable. In the airline industry service is measured by on-time performance, having the fewest lost bags, and having the fewest number of customer complaints. If an airline is the best in all three categories in a single month, it wins the so-called "Triple Crown." Southwest has won the monthly Triple Crown 24 times. In 1992, the Department of Transportation began giving an annual Triple Crown. Southwest won the award in 1992, 1993, and 1994.

Leadership at Southwest

While a number of industry experts attributed Southwest's accomplishments to its unwavering adherence to its low cost niche strategy, others disagreed and argued that its real competitive advantage lay in its leadership. A recent *Fortune* article, for instance, was entitled "Is Herb Kelleher America's Best CEO?"[7] The piece cites a U.S. Department of Transportation report as noting that Southwest was the "principal driving force for changes occurring in the airline industry," and credits Kelleher with much of this. The author quotes Michael Derchin, a veteran airline analyst who has been monitoring Southwest almost from its beginning, as saying, "I think Herb is brilliant, charming, cunning, and tough. He is the sort of manager who will stay out with a mechanic in some bar until four o'clock in the morning to find out what is going on. And then he will fix whatever is wrong." In his view, the difference between Southwest and other carriers is ". . . in the effort Herb gets out of the people who work for him." The *Fortune* writer, Ken Labich, concluded his article by noting that "the greatest obstacle to long-term prosperity at Southwest may be Kelleher's mortality."

Although Southwest is headquartered in Dallas, Herb Kelleher isn't a native Texan. He is not a pilot either. He's a lawyer who grew up on the East Coast, majored

---

[6]Jeff Pelline (1993). "Southwest Air's Driving Force." *San Francisco Chronicle*, June 10, 1993.
[7]Kenneth Labich (1994). Ibid.

in philosophy and literature, graduated from NYU Law School, clerked for a New Jersey Supreme Court justice, and practiced law in Newark, New Jersey. After visiting his wife's parents in San Antonio, he announced that he wanted to move to Texas. By the mid-1960s he was happily practicing law in San Antonio. One day in 1966 a client named Rollin King described his experience in California on PSA, a short-haul commuter airline, and suggested that Texas could benefit from a similar operation. The two sketched out some plans, borrowed money, and started Southwest.

From the beginning, Herb has adopted a visible, hands-on, slightly over-the-top style—always ready to promote a party and have fun. He appeared one Halloween at a Southwest maintenance hangar dressed in drag with a feathered boa imitating Corporal Klinger from the television program *M*A*S*H*. He's also appeared in print advertisements and at company parties dressed as Elvis Presley. (Ann Rhoades suggested that this was fine, but they try not to encourage him to dress like Ethel Merman.) He's renowned for his love of Wild Turkey bourbon. When Herb met the president of the company that produces it, he told him that he may be just a man to most people, ". . . but to me he is a god."[8] While recovering from minor surgery, he received over 3,000 cards and gifts from employees, including an intravenous drip setup—but with Wild Turkey rather than saline solution. He also smokes five packs of cigarettes a day. He says, "I've always felt that there's no reason that work has to be suffused with seriousness, that professionalism can't be worn lightly. Fun is a stimulant to people. They enjoy their work more and work more productively." He believes that "you don't have to surrender your individuality to work for Southwest Airlines." This is seen in the phrase sometimes heard at Southwest, "Work is important . . . don't spoil it with seriousness."[9]

And Kelleher does have fun. He constantly interacts with customers and Southwest employees. He routinely visits maintenance facilities in the early morning hours. Tom Burnett, the Teamster leader who represents Southwest mechanics and cleaners, says, "Let me put it this way. How many CEOs do you know who come into a cleaners' break room at 3 A.M. on a Sunday passing out doughnuts or putting on a pair of overalls to clean a plane?"[10] Once while rushing to catch a flight at Love Field, he stopped his car in the loading zone and began talking with a Southwest employee. After an animated few minutes, he realized he was late and rushed off to make his plane. When he arrived in Houston, a Southwest employee asked him if he knew where his car was. He'd left it idling at curbside. Kelleher has also appeared in television ads for American Express—not because he's such a big user, but because he has lost more cards during a year than any other AMEX customer. Colleen Barrett, an EVP of the company, is always sticking money in his pockets since he routinely forgets his wallet. Reflecting on Herb's propensity to engage people in conversation, she says, "I could add four hours to Herb's day if I could get him to walk and talk at the same time." One friend says, "There is an unwritten rule that, if you don't want to stay up all night drinking and talking, then you stay the hell away from Herb."[11]

---

[8]Kenneth Labich (1994). Ibid.

[9]Evan Ramstad (1991). "Cattle Call Carrier Lassos Riders, Profits." *San Francisco Chronicle*, April 7, 1991.

[10]Bridget O'Brian (1992). "Southwest Airlines Is a Rare Carrier. It Still Makes Money." *Wall Street Journal*, October 26, 1992.

[11]Kenneth Labich (1994). Ibid.

This philosophy pervades the entire company. Serious attention is paid to parties and celebrations. Every year, for instance, each station (city) is given a budget for parties for the employees and their families. Most stations supplement this by doing their own fund raising. Up until several years ago, all Southwest employees used to fly to Dallas for the annual company party. Now that the company has grown too large for that, it holds a rolling party in several cities with Herb and the senior managers moving from one location to another. Celebrations and contests occur continually, including chili cookoffs and Christmas parties. The Love Field corporate headquarters in Dallas is filled with pictures of Southwest employees at parties, awards, trips, celebrations, and banners. In fact, there is no corporate art in the headquarters. All paintings and sculptures, and there are many, are those donated by employees.

Colleen Barrett also reflects the relaxed management style. Officially, she is responsible for communication, marketing, public relations, people (human resources), governmental affairs, and scheduling (see Exhibit 4 for an organizational chart). She is also heading the merger efforts with Southwest's recent acquisition of Morris Air. Unofficially, she has been described as a combination of den mother, management guru, and customer ombudsman. She is a stickler for detail and provides the organizational counterweight to Kelleher's sometimes chaotic style. "She's the backbone of the airline," said one employee. Colleen claims that "the company is only as good as its people," and constantly reinforces that theme. "We'll never jump on an employee for leaning too far toward the customer, but we come down on them hard for not using common sense."

For instance, about four years ago she became concerned with the size and geographic dispersion of the company and set up a culture committee consisting of 65 people from all levels and regions of the company. This committee meets with Colleen four times a year for a full day to preserve and enhance the Southwest spirit. After determining that some distant locations were operating functionally but without

EXHIBIT 4
Southwest Airlines Organizational Chart

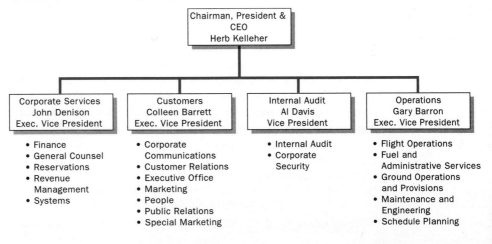

the teamwork that Southwest values, members decided to try to reduce this tendency. One outcome was a systematic effort for groups of employees to express their appreciation to others for their contributions. So, for instance, the pilots held a barbecue for the mechanics on the flight line at 3:00 A.M. Other groups, including pilots, decided to thank the reservations agents by coming in and spending a shift with them. Even the officers and directors of the company have a program, called "Day in the Field," that requires them to spend one day per quarter working in a front-line job. Colleen is adamant that this means really work, not stand around and drink coffee.

THE PEOPLE DEPARTMENT

About five years ago the human resources function at Southwest was renamed "The People Department." This reflected a concern that the old human resources group was, in the words of John Turnipseed, manager of People Services, "a police department." To counteract this, Ann Rhoades first threw away the 300-page corporate handbook and brought in new people with marketing backgrounds. Currently, to join the department an employee must first have line experience. She sees the role of the People Department as saying "yes" rather than "no" and wants employees to "Do what it takes to make the Customer happy." Employees are the customers of her group. Although it deals with approximately 18,000 employees, the People Department has a staff of about 100. All members of the department sign the department's mission statement, which is prominently displayed in a very large poster on the wall of the headquarters' office. It reads:

> Recognizing that our people are the competitive advantage, we deliver the resources and services to prepare our people to be winners, to support the growth and profitability of the company, while preserving the values and special culture of Southwest Airlines.

Ann takes this charge seriously and believes in what she calls the two Cs: compassion and common sense. She worries about maintaining the culture and tells people to break the rules if they need to. While in many companies human resources is considered a backwater, the People Department at Southwest is "like the keeper of the flame," says Treasurer John Owen.[12] Ann notes that "most HR people have no courage. They never take a chance. No guts. No capability of making a decision. They're so afraid of being fired. . . . We need to have confidence in people doing the right thing." To do this, she believes, it is imperative that you get the right people into HR to begin with. This also underlies the Southwest policy of hiring and firing for attitude. Her department is also continually feeding back information to employees such as on-time performance, turnaround times, number of customers boarded, or the cost of a day's health care for the airline in terms of the number of bags of peanuts served on the flights. The intent is to keep people focused and make them aware of how their actions affect costs.

---

[12]Wendy Zellner (1995). "Go-Go Goliaths." *Business Week*, February 13, 1995.

Recruiting

To ensure that it gets the right people, Southwest is extraordinarily selective in its recruiting. In 1993, it had 98,000 job applicants. Of these, roughly 16,000 were interviewed, and 2,700 hired—including one aspiring employee who submitted her resume on the icing of a large sheet cake, demonstrating the creative spirit that Southwest looks for. To ensure fit, there is an emphasis on peer recruiting. For example, pilots hire other pilots, often coming in on their day off to do background checks. As Ann noted, "They can get far more information in a phone call to the chief pilot of another airline than anyone else." They even turned down a top pilot who worked for another major airline and did stunt work for movie studios. Even though he was a great pilot, he made the mistake of being rude to a Southwest receptionist. Teamwork is critical. As Ann noted, "If they say 'I' too much in the interview, they don't get hired." She described how one group of eight applicant pilots were being kidded about how seriously they were dressed (dark suits and black shoes and socks). They were encouraged to loosen up. Six of them accepted the invitation to wear the standard Southwest Bermuda shorts and interviewed for the rest of the day in suit coats, ties, Bermuda shorts, and dress shoes and socks. They were the six hired.

To further screen for the Southwest spirit, customers are sometimes involved in the interviewing for new flight attendants. The process consists of an application, a phone screening interview, a group interview, three additional interviews (two with line employees), and a consensus assessment and a vote. During the interview process, the applicant will come into contact with other Southwest employees. These people are also invited to give their assessments of whether the person would fit in at the company. The entire process focuses on a positive attitude and teamwork. For example, applicants are given crayons to draw a picture that tells the story of their lives. The firm looks for people who are willing to draw outside the lines. Even its advertisements emphasize the Southwest spirit. One ad for people with computer skills showed a picture of a techno-nerd, with tape holding his glasses together, and emphasized that "we're not looking for your average computer geek." Others convey a sense for the type of employee Southwest wants to attract.

As befits a company where selection is important, Southwest has spent a lot of time identifying the key components comprising effective performance and behavior. For instance, the People Department identified its top 35 pilots and systematically interviewed them to identify common characteristics. One key trait identified was the ability to work as a part of the team. This is now used as a part of the pilot selection process. The company believes that most skills can be learned and doesn't screen heavily on these except for certain specialist jobs, like pilots and mechanics. Attitudes are what count. Kelleher says, "We draft great attitudes. If you don't have a good attitude, we don't want you, no matter how skilled you are. We can change skill levels through training. We can't change attitude."[13] For example, John Turnipseed described an EEO complaint for not hiring a person for a position who had 15 years of experience while selecting a person who had no experience. Southwest successfully made the case that the culture was critical and had to be considered in selection.

---

[13]Subrata Chakravaty (1991). "Hit 'em Hardest with the Mostest." *Forbes*, September 16, 1991.

An important awareness on the part of the People Department is that the company rejects more than 95,000 applicants each year. These are all potential customers. Therefore, the recruiting process is designed to not make applicants feel inferior or rejected. Ann claims that some people have told her they had a better experience being rejected by Southwest than they did being hired by other companies. Rita Bailey, a corporate employment manager, always tries to call any internal or managerial applicants that are turned down. She uses this as a chance to counsel them, trying to be honest but not damaging their self-esteem. She invites them to call again if they want to talk more. She is concerned not only with how well people will do at the jobs they are applying for, but also with how they'll do in the next job. She says, "It's important to do it this way or you're setting people up to fail when they get promoted."

The company hires very few people with MBAs, and even those that do get hired are selected for their fit, not for their credentials. In fact, it prefers people without extensive industry experience. For example, 40 percent of its pilots come directly from the military, 20–30 percent from small commuter airlines, and the rest from the major airlines. To encourage employees to help in the recruitment effort, Southwest offers a free space-available pass (which permits a person to travel free when the plane isn't full) to any employee who recommends someone who is hired to fill a position that is difficult to fill, such as in finance or information systems. Southwest doesn't have a nepotism policy (except for officers) and has 481 couples who work for the company. When these people describe the firm as "family," a common reference throughout the airline, they really mean it.

Training

Given the emphasis on selecting for attitudes and fit and the importance of culture, it follows that training is an important part of Southwest. In 1993 alone, 6,500 employees went through Southwest's University for People. Headed by Liz Simmons and with a staff of eight, the training group offers a variety of courses ranging from the "New Hire Celebration" (it's not called orientation) designed to get new employees enthused and excited, to senior management courses. Delise Zachry believes that "our level of external service is only as good as our internal service." She worries that the success of the company may induce a sense of complacency and noted that all the positive press accounts don't help.

New flight attendants go through four weeks of classes, typically with less than 5 percent attrition. Much of this training is oriented toward customer service—"the care and feeding of customers." Customer expectations about service are quite high, and these are communicated to both new and experienced employees. All new hires are exposed to the history, principles, values, mission, and culture of the company. They are also told how the company views leadership and management. In all training, there is an emphasis on teamwork and team building, all in good humor. For instance, new hires often do a celebratory skit at the conclusion of their training. One new pilot class donned dark sunglasses and white canes and stumbled into Kelleher's office.

For managers, there is a three and a half day course on leadership, pricing, revenue management, and on how the business works. A member of senior management always attends a two-hour session and talks openly with the participants. Training is

Southwest's policies stood out—labor peace, trust, non-adversarial relations, open sharing of information, and high productivity.

More recently, several other airlines were undergoing employee buyouts. By 1994, TWA was largely employee-owned. Northwest narrowly avoided bankruptcy when its unions agreed to an eleventh hour swap of wage concessions for an ownership stake. United has followed suit. USAir was offering stock and board seats in return for employee wage concessions. Continental Airlines had also emerged from Chapter 11 with what the press claimed was a more employee-oriented management. Executives at Delta said they would announce their plans for a new low fare strategy in the coming months. The pilots at American suggested a similar strategy to management.

But it wasn't these general trends that concerned Ann as much as two direct threats. Both United and Continental had begun low cost airlines-within-an-airline to challenge Southwest directly. They were not only directly imitating the Southwest strategy; they were also using their policies and procedures. An old adage at Southwest was not to provoke its major competitors. Obviously, it had done more than provoke them; it had challenged them directly.

Continental Lite

Under the guidance of CEO Bob Ferguson, Continental Airlines emerged from its second bankruptcy, in April 1993. In May, Ferguson announced his plan to split the company into two operations: one that would concentrate on short-haul, low fare flights (named Continental Lite or CALite), and the other featuring first class service at business class prices. He believes that because of its low cost structure, lower even than Southwest, Continental would be able to compete successfully. While imitating many of Southwest's practices, including the use of humor by flight attendants, Ferguson believes that he can attract the business traveler. By concentrating primarily on the East Coast market, he can take advantage of greater density, shorter flights, and avoid competing directly with Southwest, at least in the short term.

Continental Lite was rolled out in October 1993, with 173 daily departures from 14 cities. By summer, it had expanded to 28 percent of Continental's capacity, with plans to ultimately grow to 40 percent. Fares were cut dramatically. For example, the Newark-Greensboro went from $273 to $99 and the Greensboro-Greenville from $226 to $59. The early results, however, are mixed. CALite currently is flying with about 59 percent of its seats filled. Customer reaction is not always positive. Some frequent flyers were miffed that there was no priority boarding or meal service. Flight attendants are concerned about the increased workloads (like Southwest, they clean cabins between flight segments) and lack of breaks between flights. Ground crews are trying hard, but turnarounds are still taking over 30 minutes rather than the hoped-for 20. Even the pilots were upset until the company began providing meals for them during their busy schedules. (In one instance, a flight was delayed while the pilots ate in the airport terminal.) In March of 1994, Continental had the worst marks of any domestic airline in terms of customer complaints, on-time performance, and mishandled baggage.

Financial results are also not yet up to expectations. Continental lost $38.5 million on revenues of $39 billion from April 1993, when it emerged from bankruptcy protection, through the end of 1993. Management expects to break even in the second half of 1994 and doesn't see these results as a disaster. Chief Financial Officer Daniel Garton says that only 20 percent of CALite's routes are losing money and notes that because USAir and Delta responded aggressively to Continental's fare cuts, profits have been weaker than expected.[19] Some airline industry observers believe that Continental's costs may still be too high.

This is also complicated because CALite still relies more heavily on one-stop and connecting passengers than does Southwest. The clear trend in the industry has also been for fewer business travelers. In 1982, over 50 percent of travelers paid full economy fare or higher (e.g., business class). Currently, that figure is less than 40 percent. Gordon Bethune, Continental's COO, says, "Up to a two-hour flight, it's already a commodity business. A $10 difference will grab anybody's passenger these days."[20] Flights of up to two hours represent over 60 percent of domestic traffic.

Ferguson, whose style has been described as "harsh and uncommunicative," is undeterred. A 1972 graduate of Lehigh University with a degree in finance, he began his career at Bankers Trust making loans to the airline industry. He left Bankers to move to one of his clients, Braniff International, and subsequently left Braniff to join Frank Lorenzo at Texas Air. While there, he helped Lorenzo buy People Express, a successful low fare carrier in the early 1980s that failed in 1986 after overexpanding. A harsh taskmaster, Ferguson has been known to drive executives away. Since he took over in 1991, at least a dozen top managers have left. One commented on his management style by noting that "it's very pointed, even nasty. If he doesn't like an idea, he seems to go out of his way to ridicule it."[21] Another said, "He can't resist reverting to Lorenzo-style management." Ferguson admits to not suffering fools easily and says, "I will not tolerate not doing a good job. I will tell you in front of yourself, 20 people, 100 people." A person familiar with his style claims that "Ferguson has to become more people-oriented and depend more on the recommendations of his management team."[22] He denies that he has people-skill problems and has plans to give as much as 4 percent of the stock to employees. He has also hired Donald Valentine as marketing chief for CALite; Valentine was previously head of Marketing for Southwest. Ferguson concedes that CALite has had some start-up pains and hasn't operated very efficiently so far but sees this as just the usual problems of changing the organization.

United's Shuttle

On July 28, 1994, United announced what had been the year's worst-kept secret: On October 1st it would begin its own airline-within-an-airline on the West Coast. The goal of this operation, named "The Shuttle," was to cut costs by 30 percent on these routes and regain the market share that Southwest had captured. To do this, United aimed at reducing its costs per available seat mile to 7.4 cents. The Shuttle was sched-

---

[19]Wendy Zellner (1994). "Why Continental's CEO Fell to Earth." *Business Week*, November 7, 1994.
[20]Howard Banks (1994). "A Sixties Industry in a Nineties Economy." *Forbes*, May 9, 1994.
[21]Wendy Zellner (1994). "This Is Captain Ferguson, Please Hang on to Your Hats." *Business Week*, May 23, 1994.
[22]Wendy Zellner (1994). Ibid.

uled to begin with 184 daily flights on 13 routes, expanding to almost 300 flights by year end. United announced that it would match the going price on all routes on which it went head-to-head with Southwest. Its service would include advance seat assignments, a first-class cabin, and United's frequent flyer mileage program. "People want to fly us because they can consolidate their frequent flier miles and get better service," said United's senior vice president for planning.[23]

Herb Kelleher referred to United's announcement as a "declaration of war" and intimated that Southwest might begin flying other United routes to drain revenue. He also talked about raising fares on longer routes to generate revenue to lower the bar without hurting its own profits. On August 30, Kelleher sent a memo, entitled "Commencement of Hostilities," to all Southwest employees detailing Southwest's response to United's challenge. This memo concludes:

> Southwest's essential difference is not machines and "things." Our essential difference is minds, hearts, spirits, and souls. Winston Churchill stated: "Success is never final." Indeed, "success" must be earned over and over again or it disappears. I am betting on your minds, your hearts, your souls, and your spirits to continue our success. Let's win this one and make aviation history—again!

The president of America West, a Phoenix-based low fare airline that had been bloodied by Southwest, said, "Taking on Southwest head-to-head is unwise for anyone."[24]

On July 12, United had completed negotiations for an employee buyout. In return for 55 percent of the company, employees, excluding the 17,000 flight attendants who voted not to participate in or agree to work rule changes, promised $4.9 billion in wage cuts and productivity gains. As a part of this agreement, Steve Wolf, the former CEO, was required to step down and was replaced by a Chrysler executive, Gerald Greenwald, with no previous airline industry experience, but who was reputed to be a good people person. Wolf claimed that he left United in good financial shape with great success on its overseas routes and a fleet that averaged only nine years old. Wolf estimated that the $1 billion in losses in 1992 would have been a $700 million profit if United hadn't been competing with Southwest. "We just need to come up with a strategy that will offset their competitive advantage," he said.[25]

Unfortunately, not everyone is sure that The Shuttle can succeed. The culture at United is almost the opposite of that at Southwest. One pilot claimed, "We live by the letter of the law, in every way." Another noted that "mechanics and pilots have always had a rift between them. . . . That's a conflict as old as aviation history." Another worried, "As for management, I don't know if they can change their culture. There's a lot of dinosaurs over there at headquarters. There are a lot of power struggles over there, and they worry more about those than they do running the airline." One cynic claimed that "most of the expansion we've done over the past few years a blind man could have accomplished. I wouldn't really credit Steve Wolf with any of that." These sentiments were not restricted solely to the pilots. Based on interviews around the air-

[23]Wendy Zellner (1994). "Dogfight over California." *Business Week*, August 15, 1994.
[24]Wendy Zellner (1994). Ibid.
[25]Kenneth Labich (1994). "Will United Fly?" *Fortune*, August 22, 1994.

line, Ken Labich, at *Fortune*, reported mixed opinions about the future among United employees.[26]

> You've also got to hope that the way we do things will change. [United] is the kind of place where management usually thinks they are way up there, and the rest of us are way down here. They want to make sure the shareholders get what they want, but they don't care much about the employees. All that's got to change.
>
> —Mechanic

> I'm afraid a lot of people are still looking at the situation as us versus them—management versus labor, union versus non-union. . . . there are clearly union people out there who are saying, "Wait till we take over." I don't know how we will ever get out of that.
>
> —Planner

> We've always been treated like angry children who don't deserve what they get. Upper management has been adversarial and confrontational with us for over 10 years now; I don't think Mr. Wolf liked the flight attendants at all. We are managed differently from the other groups. We're disciplined if we're sick more than 3 days per month or if we arrive late for a flight. . . . We're the only group that has to hop on a scale every month. Pilots certainly aren't held to those standards. When it comes to the boys in the cockpit, things are different. The pilots stay in downtown hotels, and we're stuck out at the airport. When we have to deadhead, they fly in first class and we're in the back of the plane. That says it all. . . . The irony, of course, is that the bosses . . . ought to think a lot harder about how we feel if they want to keep their customers happy. We're the people who spend all the time with the passengers. To the public, we are United.
>
> —Flight Attendant and Union Representative

> People think a reservation job is easy, but it's actually very difficult. Customers aren't nice on the phones any longer, like they were when I came here 15 years ago. . . . they're rude to us. Then we get so busy, with so many calls on hold, that we can't spend time with people and provide the good service.
>
> —Reservation Agent

> I'd say there has been an intense lack of trust toward management among the people I work with. We feel that they haven't been dealing straight with us for a long time. They wanted to satisfy shareholders and if people lost their jobs—well, that's business these days. . . . There's been turmoil since 1985, when people on Wall Street started looking at us like we were some cash cow they could milk.
>
> —Ramp Agent

Although the head of the new airline had not yet been announced, the betting was on Alan "Sky" Magary. Magary, a veteran with 24 years in the industry, was an innovator, credited with ideas such as foot rests and smoke-free flights. A former Northwest executive described how when Magary was there, he came up with the idea of using patterned fabrics for the seats to disguise coffee stains. Magary had spoken publicly about the potential for The Shuttle and United's plans to reduce costs to 7.4 cents a seat mile. There was some skepticism about this goal among industry analysts, one of whom commented "only a deranged MBA could have thought this up."[27]

---

[26]Kenneth Labich (1994). Ibid.
[27]Susan Chandler (1994). " 'Sky' Magary Picks a Dogfight." *Business Week*, September 19, 1994.

The Off-Site Meeting

As Ann pondered the situation, she wondered if this competitive threat could seriously damage Southwest, and what actions, if any, Southwest's senior management should take. Could United and Continental really imitate the Southwest approach? Of course, the threat was made more complicated because of the size and growth of Southwest. With 14,000 employees, it was no longer the small firm it had been. She worried that this could affect the family feeling. She also worried about the overconfidence their success could breed. Herb had been quoted in a recent interview as saying, "We have to be the world's first company to refute the old law that companies die from excessive prosperity."[28] How could they avoid these attitudes? There was also the tricky problem of succession. Herb had been at the head of the company since 1963. How would the organization deal with this problem if it became necessary? It was clear to her that the success of the company really did rest with the human resources, and her job was to ensure that these were managed effectively. But what should management be doing to deal with these problems? Well, she had seven hours before tomorrow's 7 A.M. meeting to reflect on her options.

http://www.iflyswa.com

---

[28]Howard Banks (1994). Ibid.

CASE 13

Dell Computer Corporation*

Customer satisfaction and customer service are two of the most repeated catch phrases in major corporations, especially from producers rather than the consumers. Michael Dell does not want service and satisfaction to simply be repeated by his corporate employees and support staffs; he requires them to practice what he preaches. In fact, the corporate culture—as clearly stated by Michael Dell (*Personal Selling Power*, March, 1993)—". . . is very simple. Responsive, customer focus, high intensity level."

Dell's commitment to this concept of customer satisfaction and service—known at Dell as Direct Relationship Marketing—can be shown through the policies of the corporation. First, there is an unconditional thirty-day money-back guarantee for all of Dell's computer systems and a "no questions asked" return policy.

Second, Dell's toll-free technical support organization is available from 7:00 A.M. to 7:00 P.M., coast to coast (including Mexico). These technicians solve 95 percent of customer problems in less than six minutes. Additionally, a TechFax system is available twenty-four hours a day, seven days a week. Customers can request technical information through a fax catalogue, and problem-solving instructions are returned by fax. A third-party network of on-site service representatives can be dispatched when problems are not solved over the phone. If necessary, unresolved problems are expedited to the design engineers to ensure complete customer satisfaction. Dell users can also access an on-line technical support group via CompuServe. Finally, Michael Dell openly invites customers to write or call him with comments about the quality of Dell's products and the level of support received from service and support personnel.

This emphasis on quality and service has won accolades from customers and industry analysts. Dell has consistently been recognized as the best in customer support and satisfaction, ahead of all other computer manufacturers. J. D. Power and Associates, known for its automobile rankings, again in 1994 rated Dell number one in customer satisfaction in its third annual end-user survey for the computer industry.

The most publicized story of a company start-up in the computer industry is that of Steven Jobs and Stephen Wozniak designing and marketing Apple computers. These young entrepreneurs took a concept from a garage manufacturing base and developed Apple into a multimillion-dollar organization. The story of Michael Dell and the development of the Dell Computer Corporation rivals that of Jobs and Wozniak.

---

*Prepared by Bill J. Middlebrook, Michael J. Keeffe, and John K. Ross III, Southwest Texas State University.

In 1983, Dell, then a freshman pre-med student at the University of Texas, decided to earn additional money by selling disk-drive kits and random access memory (RAM) chips at computer user meetings in Austin, Texas. Within a few months, he had sufficient funds to acquire excess personal computers (PCs) at reasonable prices from IBM dealers having difficulties meeting their sales quotas. He modified these machines and began selling them through contacts in the local area and was reported to be grossing approximately $80,000 per month by April 1984. In May 1984, Dell formed the Dell Computer Corporation to sell PCs Limited brand computers and conducted operations out of his dormitory room. After dropping out of school (against his parents' wishes), he began attending computer trade fairs, where he sold these IBM PC-compatible computers, one of the first custom "clones" on the market.

The results of Dell's endeavors were immediate. During the first year of business, sales were approximately $6 million and grew to $257 million within the next four years. In 1988, the brand name was changed to Dell and sales continued to grow such that by 1990 the organization had sold $546 million in PC-compatible and peripheral equipment and $2.1 billion in fiscal 1993 (Dell's fiscal year ends in January). The most recent figures are shown in Exhibits 1 and 2.

In 1987, Dell established its first international subsidiary in the United Kingdom to enter the growing European computer market. European countries had a lower PC saturation rate than the United States, and there were no large PC manufacturers in

---

EXHIBIT 1
Percentage of Consolidated Sales

	Year Ended		
	Jan. 30 1994	Jan. 31 1993	Feb. 2 1992
	Net Sales		
North America (U.S. and Canada)	68.1%	68.9%	69.6%
Europe	27.2	27.5	27.2
Other international	4.7	3.6	3.2
Consolidated net sales	100.0	100.0	100.0
Cost of sales	84.9	77.7	68.3
Gross profit	15.1	22.3	31.7
	Operating Expenses		
Selling, general, and administration	14.7	13.3	20.5
Research, development and engineering	1.7	2.1	3.7
Total operating expenses	16.4	15.4	24.2
Operating income (loss)	(1.3)	6.9	7.5
Net financing and other income (expense)	—	0.2	0.7
Income (loss) before income taxes	(1.3)	7.1	8.2
Provision for taxes (benefit)	(0.1)	2.1	2.5
Net income (loss)	(1.2)	5.0	5.7
Preferred stock dividends	(0.1)	—	—
Net income (loss) app. to com. stockholders	(1.3%)	5.0%	5.7%

Source: Dell form 10-K fiscal year ended January 30, 1994.

EXHIBIT 2
Five-Year Summary

Date	Sales (in thousands of dollars)	Net Income (in thousands of dollars)	EPS
1993	$2,873,165	$(39,576)	(1.06)
1992	2,013,924	101,642	2.59
1991	889,939	50,911	1.40
1990	546,235	27,232	0.91
1989	388,558	5,114	0.18

Source: Dell form 10-K fiscal year ended January 30, 1994.

Europe. From 1988 to 1991 the organization developed wholly owned subsidiaries in Canada, France, Italy, Sweden, Germany, Finland, and the Netherlands and is in the process of launching other subsidiaries in Europe. An Irish manufacturing facility opened in 1991 to provide systems for the European market. In addition, a support center located in Amsterdam provides technical support throughout Europe. Dell reported that fourth-quarter 1991 international sales were up 109 percent over the same quarter in 1990. By February of 1993, European sales totaled $240 million and constituted 30 percent of total sales (see Exhibit 1). Currently, 40 percent of sales are derived from international subsidiaries after only five years of operations.

In January 1993, Dell made a bold move by entering the Japanese market. Dell Computer of Japan employs a staff of forty workers to provide a full range of sales, service, and technical assistance. Telephone sales are supplemented with an outside sales force and through two major retailers in Tokyo. As the first to attempt telemarketing in Japan, Dell was met with skepticism by some industry observers. Initial reports indicate that the Japanese are very enthusiastic about the marketing approach and are responding in greater numbers than originally forecasted. In fact, the forty people in the Tokyo office are being tested for their ability to handle requests. Although successful, Dell is expected to have less than 1 percent of the Japanese market in 1993.

Dell Computer Corporation is headquartered in Austin, Texas, with approximately 4,200 employees worldwide. Dell had the foresight to surround himself with people having expertise in computer engineering and marketing, and he serves as both chief executive officer (CEO) and chairman of the board of directors (see Exhibit 4 for corporate officers and members of the board of directors). The company still operates on the principles espoused by Dell during its inception: customer service and a personal relationship with Dell system users.

PERSONAL COMPUTER INDUSTRY OVERVIEW

The short history of the PC industry is one of booms and slumps. The stellar performance of the industry during the early to mid-1980s was followed by a consolidation of existing companies and a slowdown in sales during the 1986–1987 period. Industry sales increased through 1990, and projections show that corporate capital-equipment spending should grow at a 7 to 8 percent annual rate into the early 1990s. Some analysts contend that the growth rate of the PC industry is uncertain as the growth rate of the economy slows. For example, Volpe & Covington, a San Francisco–based PC investment consulting firm, believes that a 15 percent long-term growth in revenues for high-end PCs and a 12 percent compound growth rate for the industry is a reasonable assumption. Other analysts contend that PC sales will grow at only 5 to 7 percent in the 1990s, less than half as fast as sales grew in the late 1980s. In 1992, computer and peripheral sales totaled over $142 billion. This amount grew to $155 billion in 1993 and was projected to exceed $167 billion in 1994.

PC Industry Strategies

Two macroindustry strategies for competing in the PC industry can be combined with two macrosegments of the PC market to assess competitors and competitive approaches. First, PC manufacturers can approach the market as either innovators or imitators. IBM is the accepted innovation leader as both computer manufacturers and customers watch IBM's product development and base production and purchase decisions on current IBM products. Other computer manufacturers approach the market as innovators by developing hardware and software to satisfy specific market segments.

Most firms approach the market building clone PCs. These firms (sometimes called value-added remarketers) use the base MS-DOS technology of innovators and attempt to improve on the system configuration and/or differentiate their product on some basis such as marketing channel used, service and support, product reliability, and/or price. Essentially, value-added remarketers buy components and software from various vendors to configure systems sold under their own brand labels. The success of the imitative approaches is evidenced by the performance of companies such as Compaq, Prime Computer, Inc., CompuAdd, and Dell. Many clone firms believe that to be successful in the PC industry, they must be concerned with market pressures to reduce price; thus, they constantly monitor costs and search for ways to reduce those costs.

PC Markets

Macrosegments in the PC industry are usually defined as business, home, government, or education users. Business users want high performance, reliability, and value in a system for their computing needs. State-of-the-art technology, the ability to network and communicate with other systems, customer service and support, and cost are primary purchase determinants for the business user. One of the fastest-growing segments in the business market is the portables market, which is expected to grow at an annualized rate of 20 percent for the next few years.

Home market demand was initially created by innovators, early adopters, and the early majority groups of the adoption or diffusion of innovation cycle. Most home users are price conscious, planning to spend less than $1,200 for a system, and they value ease of operation and service as well as support from the manufacturer. This market should not be as lucrative as it was in the early to mid-1980s, but replacement sales (sales to previous PC owners) and sales to those still intending to buy a home PC should make this market moderately attractive.

Government and education users comprise the remaining macrosegments of the PC market. Both of these segments represent large, important segments yet typically yield lower margins than either the business or home markets. Typical purchase decisions are based on a bidding system, with the contract going to the lowest qualified bidder. The education market was considered important for its proposed ability to generate long-term brand loyalty among early users (students). Apple was one of the earliest entrants into this market. It is questionable, however, if the long-term benefits of brand loyalty by early users are actually realized.

This segment, like the business segment, is interested in integrated systems designed to perform to buyers' specific needs. Increased competition for this market has led to increased downward pressures on prices.

Competitors

Major competitors of Dell include most traditional PC manufacturers such as IBM, Compaq, Zenith, and Tandy. These firms rely on selling through a professional sales force or through retail outlets. Competitors of Dell using a direct marketing and/or retailing approach (primarily value-added remarketers) include CompuAdd, which offers a full line of machines; Northgate, which offers machines similar to Dell at savings of up to $2,000 over Dell equipment; and Everex, which offers machines similar to Dell but claims that they are faster than Dell PCs. CompuAdd is located in Austin, Texas; Northgate in Plymouth, Minnesota; and Everex in Freemont, California. None of these firms have the service and satisfaction reputation of Dell.

Changes in the industry will be driven by several factors as the market matures. First, the Gartner Group, a market research firm, estimates that the number of customers replacing their outdated systems is expected to outnumber first-time purchasers by 1995.

Second, an investment report on the PC distribution industry shows that PC saturation rates are relatively low. Only about 33 percent of white-collar workers use PCs on the job, and only 17 percent of all domestic households have a PC. This becomes more important when one considers that the largest growth opportunities are in small- to medium-sized accounts (businesses with fewer than 500 employees) that employ more than 70 percent of white-collar workers.

Third, the ratio of price to performance for equivalent functions continues to improve approximately 20 to 25 percent per year, which makes the purchase of state-of-the-art machines more attractive to many segments. And fourth, competition should intensify. Value-added remarketers more than doubled during the 1988–1989 period, with the number of firms increasing from 350 to more than 1,000. Coupled with increased demand by business users, improved software and networking capabilities, and increased competition through differentiation and focus-oriented marketing strategies, industry analysts forecast additional changes in both market approaches used by major competitors and further segmentation of the market. The 1990s should be a period of change for the industry, rivaling changes that occurred during the 1980s.

DELL COMPUTER OPERATIONS

Dell's success can be attributed to its commitment to customer service and satisfaction and the marketing of state-of-the-art systems to business users through direct marketing strategies.

Product Line

Dell offers an extensive and competitive product line ranging from inexpensive "first time user" computers to those with the latest technological developments. This strategy has resulted in a continuing evaluation and modification of Dell's product line, with new products constantly being offered and other products being discontinued. Currently Dell is working with Microsoft to deliver factory-installed Windows NT in high-end workstations and networks as the software becomes available. Dell also plans to sell IBM's competing OS/2 operating system preinstalled. The ever-changing demands of computer technology and the market have made product forecasting and planning difficult and risky. For example, during the last quarter of fiscal 1989, Dell overestimated demand and had considerable surplus inventories of finished goods. It attacked this problem and reduced inventories by $36 million in fiscal 1990. Inventory levels for the third and fourth quarters of 1991, respectively, were between 8.6 and 10.3 weeks of sales, below industry averages. In 1993, Dell reported a loss of $75.7 million on sales of $700.6 million. This was after taking $71 million in unusual charges relating to the restructure of European operations. Also included in this loss were the value of inventories and the costs related to notebook computer projects. Michael Dell is predicting a revenue growth of about 70 percent in FY 1994, according to the March 10, 1993, *Wall Street Journal*.

Manufacturing

Dell's computers for the domestic market are manufactured in facilities in Austin, Texas. The purchase of a 126,000-square-foot manufacturing facility in 1989 doubled Dell's manufacturing capability. The 135,000-square-foot facility in Limerick, Ireland, is expected to satisfy the growing international demand for Dell systems.

The manufacturing strategy utilized at Dell is one of building each computer system to the buyer's specifications. Buyers can add options to customize their systems for their own needs. The order is then assembled and shipped with peripherals and upgrades requested by the customer. Manufacturing at Dell actually consists of the assembly and testing of vendor-procured parts, assemblies, and subassemblies. In addition, Dell utilizes a total quality approach where enthusiastic workers compete in product-quality competitions for bonuses and recognition.

Marketing

One factor leading to Dell's success is the organization's marketing style. Dell approaches the market from a service and customer satisfaction standpoint combined with lower prices than comparable brands. Sales leads are generated through several sources, the primary one being advertising in PC and business publications. An outside sales force located in major markets addresses the needs of large corporate customers.

Dell's sales force is channeled according to the market it serves: small/medium business and home users, corporate buyers, and government/education/medical. Each of these sales channels is supported by its own marketing, customer service, and technical support organization. This organizational structure ensures high accountability for the satisfaction of each customer, as well as feedback from daily direct contact with the customer. PC makers dealing through the retail channel do not have this advantage and are not able to respond as quickly to market and service demands as the direct channel. Additional face-to-face exposure occurs at industry shows.

Dell's entire product line is sold by telephone sales representatives who answer more than 8,000 incoming calls on a busy day. In addition to answering customer-initiated calls, the Austin-based sales force responds to sales leads and supports the efforts of its team members in the field.

Sales orders are downloaded to the manufacturing facility several times each day, and all systems are custom-configured according to the customer's specifications. Trucks load at Dell's manufacturing facility throughout the day, and overnight services are utilized for expedited orders. Lead times on most systems vary from three to seven days.

Internationally, Dell is similar in marketing approach and culture to its domestic operation. Dell's wholly owned subsidiaries give it access to over 70 percent of the available worldwide market for PCs.

Dell sells to major buyers through a small (twenty-five person) sales force located in major metropolitan areas throughout the United States and services those accounts with management teams consisting of sales, customer service, and technical support representatives. Dell believes that the small- to medium-sized business represents the greatest growth potential for PC-based systems.

Dell has also arranged to sell its systems through integrators like Electronic Data Systems (EDS) and Andersen Consulting, which sell to multiple workstation customers and thereby increase its sale potential. This move from traditional channels was prompted by the fact that the mail-order market is only 16 percent of a $35 to $40 billion market, less than one-fifth the size of sales of computer stores. Dell currently has 25 percent of the mail-order market.

RETAIL

In 1990, Dell contracted with CompUSA, Inc., a Dallas-based chain of twenty superstores, to sell Dell products through 1993. CompUSA is a computer version of Toys 'R' Us, with approximately 21,000 square feet of retail space per store, a service center with a fast service pickup for corporate clients, and over 5,000 items at discount prices. CEO Nathan Morton, a former senior executive with Home Depot and Target Stores, expected sales to top $1 billion in 1991 after only two years of operations.

CompUSA is adding new stores in major metropolitan areas and sells Dell systems for the same prices as Dell's direct sales.

Dell added Staples Office Supply Superstores to its mass merchandising channel in mid-1991 as well. Staples markets to a less sophisticated computer user than does CompUSA. Although Dell systems are sold through this superstore channel, Dell maintains its same level of customer support to these buyers. Users who purchase Dell systems through CompUSA and Staples are entered into Dell's customer data base as if they had ordered directly through Dell.

Dell's mass merchandising move may provide a serendipitous opportunity for the company even though computer retailing is seen by some industry analysts as poised for a shakeout. Dataquest, Inc., believes that traditional retailers will see their share of PC sales shrink through 1994. Analysts state that marketers will have to move toward the ends of the retail spectrum by either concentrating on high-volume, low-price selling or specializing in market niches or other customized services that mass marketers neglect, in order to be successful. Smaller operations that emphasize service along with price are already showing the greatest gains. Superstores may be one retail format that not only survives the shakeout but prospers. In 1993, Dell began selling its Precision line of computers through Sam's Clubs, a division of Wal-Mart Stores Incorporated. This move is in addition to the agreement with Price Clubs, another mass merchandising chain.

In July 1994, Dell announced that it would abandon efforts to sell its computers through discount stores. Only 2 percent of Dell's sales revenue came from the retail outlets.

Research and Development

During the last few years, Dell's revenue growth has allowed the organization to devote considerable resources to building a first-class technological capability. Research and development spending in fiscal 1989 increased 29 percent over the previous year, doubled in fiscal 1990, and was estimated to be more than $18 million in 1991. Dell's efforts are enhanced since Intel added Dell to its preferred purchaser list in 1989.

During fiscal 1990, the first products to utilize the Dell proprietary integrated circuit chip were shipped to customers. Dell is no longer restricted to standard vendor technologies when customizing its machines for specific usages. In 1990, Dell filed forty-five patent applications to protect Dell-developed technologies and designs.

Finance

Financial summaries of Dell are presented in Exhibits 2 and 3. The organization does not pay dividends to investors, instead relying on appreciation of stock price. It has experienced good sales and profit growth, especially after instituting tighter inventory controls following the overstock of 1989. The 1989 inventory problem caused the stock price to drop 42 percent, from a high of $12 to $7 per share. Dell is currently searching for ways to reduce costs without sacrificing customer service and technological performance of its systems.

EXHIBIT 3

Dell Computer Corporation Condensed Consolidated Balance Sheet (in thousands of dollars)

	Jan. 30 1994	Jan. 31 1993	Feb. 2 1992
Assets			
Current assets:			
Cash and cash equivalents	$ 3,355	$ 14,948	$ 55,460
Accounts receivable, net	410,774	374,013	164,960
Inventories	220,265	303,220	126,554
Other current assets	80,323	80,239	65,814
Total current assets*	$1,048,384	$852,787	$512,180
Property and equipment, net	86,892	70,464	44,661
Other assets	5,204	3,756	2,722
Total assets	$1,140,480	$927,005	$559,563
Liabilities and Stockholders' Equity			
Current liabilities:			
Notes payable	—	—	—
Accounts payable	$ 282,708	$295,133	$ 97,389
Other current liabilities	255,279	198,706	132,145
Total current liabilities	$ 537,987	$493,839	$229,534
Long-term debt	$ 100,000	$ 48,373	$ 41,450
Other liabilities	$ 31,385	$ 15,593	$ 14,399
Common stock	$ 379	$ 369	$ 358
Additional paid in capital	$ 320,041	$177,978	$165,745
Retained earnings	$ 170,790	$208,544	$106,902
Obligations under capital leases	—	—	—
Deferred income taxes	—	—	—
Redeemable convertible preferred stock	—	—	—
Stockholders' equity	$ 471,108	$369,200	$274,180
Cumulative translation adjustment	$ (23,345)	$ (17,691)	$ 1,175
Total liabilities and net worth	$1,140,480	$927,005	$559,563

*Total current assets also includes short-term investments of $337,667 for 1994, $80,367 for 1993, and $164,960 for 1992.
Source: Dell form 10-K fiscal year ended January 30, 1994.

ISSUES AND CONCERNS

The most pressing concern of investors regarding Dell operations is Michael Dell. Dell has been very successful in building his organization with an entrepreneurial style of management. On a scale of one to ten, Dell rates himself ten as a competitor, innovator, goal setter, entrepreneur and exporter. He rates himself lowest in the areas of production and finance. Although Dell was cited as Entrepreneur of the Year by *Inc.* magazine, his critics wonder if he is capable of making the transition of moving the corporation from a Stage 1 entrepreneurial mode to a stage 2 professionally

show, the company grew rapidly, becoming a leading supplier of Ethermodems, a series of broadband Ethernet facility networking products that form the backbone of LANs. Ethermodems are used on large industrial sites and campuses requiring data transmission over long distances.

In October 1986, Bob Badavas was named CEO, Vice President of Finance, and Treasurer. Bob's goal was to go public; he believed that, "if Chipcom is going to be a public company candidate, then we should act like a public company." He implemented a series of budget controls and finance strategies, and met with investment banking firms and financial analysts to see what it would take to go public. Company reps also attended investment conferences to psyche out the criteria potential investors use to make investment decisions, and shop around its strategy for going public.

Chipcom's ability to capitalize on market trends was the key to the company's initial success. In 1988, anticipating the industry's move toward fiber-optic networks, Chipcom created ORnet, a new line of fiber-based products, which created a fault-tolerant network to send signals over longer distances. The Institute of Electrical and Electronic Engineers has adopted Chipcom's fiber-optic cable technology, which is now the draft standard for Ethernet fiber backbone connectivity.

In a top management change in June 1988, John Held, a division manager at GenRad Inc., was appointed President and CEO. Held, a graduate of Yale University with a degree in mechanical engineering, had spent $4^1/_2$ years as a lieutenant on a Polaris nuclear submarine during the 1960s, which served as a model for his management technique at Chipcom. "The military is very much the opposite of what people think. It's very collaborative. You learn to be extraordinarily dependent on your people," according to Held. Held admits to living life on the edge. He is an "extreme skier" and has even been dropped by helicopter 10,000 feet up in the Canadian Rockies. "It's scary but it's fun." This same feeling applies to his business. "You are making moves and decisions that are potentially perilous but exhilarating. It's like a bobsled run." His style jibed with that of Badavas, who remained as CFO and Treasurer.

POSITIONING FOR GROWTH

For Chipcom, 1990 was a year of technological breakthroughs. In April, the company announced a joint technology agreement with Cisco Systems. Successfully recognizing a shift in the market, Chipcom launched its unique Online System Concentrator line, which distributes computer applications across entire organizations. These "smart" switching hubs, a significant advancement in intelligent hub technology, enable users to create large-scale networks that are flexible, manageable, and reliable. Chipcom also introduced a "fault tolerance" design which eliminated downtime for critical network applications to meet complex user needs, and was the first vendor to build products capable of supporting multiple networks in a single concentrator. In 1990, *New England Business* magazine ranked Chipcom number one on its list of the 100 fastest growing private and public companies in the region; and *Inc.* magazine ranked Chipcom number 12 on its list of the fastest growing companies in America.

In 1991, Chipcom became the first provider of port-switching Ethernet capabilities, which allow users to assign any port on certain Ethernet modules to any network within a hub without having to move cables manually. The company was now competing with high-profile, public companies such as Cabletron Systems and SynOptics, pressuring management to become more aggressive in its search for investment banking relationships.

For Bob Badavas, the most challenging aspect of going public was "selling" Chipcom to the public: "Why were we different? Was it a significant difference? How would we stay ahead? These are important questions for prospective investors." Wall Street was beginning to notice Chipcom and the enormous growth potential in the markets it competed in. During 1990, Chipcom became a recognized competitor in the smart hub business, and its profitability increased dramatically. Held credited his employees. "There is a true spirit of cooperation, creative thinking, and problem solving at all levels of the company."

Chipcom selected three investment firms: Adams, Harkness & Hill; Montgomery Securities; and Wessells, Arnold & Henderson to sponsor the initial public offering (IPO) because these firms were well positioned to communicate the Chipcom story. The IPO was announced on February 16, 1991, and Chipcom became a public company on May 3, 1991.

THE COMPETITIVE LANDSCAPE

Competition in the network industry is intense. Analysts believe that as competition increases, price competition will increase as well. In 1992 the average price of a managed port network system was about $120 million. Two years later, the price had dropped to $80 million. The three major requirements for networking systems are reliability, flexibility, and manageability. Early on, companies focused on a particular segment of the market: hubs, routers, or switches. The current "one-stop shopping" trend, however, has firms marketing a full spectrum of networking products, which had led to a number of mergers and buyouts in the industry.

In the summer of 1994, two industry giants, Wellfleet Communications and SynOptics Corporation, merged to form Bay Networks. Chipcom moved to offset this threat by merging with Artel Communications. The merger complemented Chipcom's existing product line by adding the Ethernet-based "Galactica" Switching Hub and "Starbridge" Turbo Hub to the "ONline" System product family and the new "ONcore" Switching System. Chipcom further enhanced its market position in response to the formation of Bay Networks by forming a marketing partnership with IBM, and signing a worldwide sales and marketing agreement with Cisco Systems.

The major competitors in the network industry are:

Bay Networks: The corporation formed in October 1994 when Wellfleet Communications, a major router producer, merged with SynOptics, a leading hub manufacturer, filling critical gaps in each company's product lines to become a full service provider. With 110 offices worldwide, over 1,200 resellers, and 700 direct sales and service personnel, the combined revenues for the new entity were over one billion dollars.

Cisco Systems: With close to half of all the 1994 router sales, Cisco is the leading integrator of router technology in the network industry. Cisco has also formed partnerships with leading hub vendors such as Cabletron, Hewlett-Packard, and Chipcom. Cisco's sales in 1994 were $1.243 billion with close to $315 million in net income, almost double 1993's $649 million in sales and $171 million in net income. The company's five-year growth rate is projected as 105.4%.

3-Com: A network industry pioneer, 3-Com was founded in 1979. Since 1992, 3-Com has acquired BICC Data, Star-Tek, Synernetics Inc., and Centrum Corporation, thus establishing a complete line of networking products. In 1994, sales were close to $827 million but acquisition expenses made net income a negative $29 million.

Cabletron Systems: Cabletron operates at the high end of the hub market. Its new product, MMAC-Plus Chassis Hub, incorporates bridging, routing, and the hub system in one unit. The product is designed for the small office market, but is also a precursor of the direction the industry is headed. The New Hampshire–based company had sales of close to $600 million, with a net income of about $120 million.

INDUSTRY STANDARDS

Standards for the computer industry are written by national and international standards groups, such as ANSI, or by a dominant vendor in the market, such as IBM. For instance, the industry adopted the IBM PC bus ISA (Industry Standard Architecture) as the standard for all PC vendors.

There are a number of large players in the networking industry, but no one company dominates the industry as IBM does the PC market. Therefore, the industry has not yet adopted an industry standard for ATM (Asynchronous Transfer Mode) or fast Ethernet technologies. Companies such as Cisco Systems have already started using a particular technology, hoping to establish the standard. Chipcom is also working on an ATM product. Each competitor wants to design a product that will support whatever industry standard is adopted, to give it a marketing edge over its competitors. An industry standard that differs from Chipcom's product design would threaten the marketability of Chipcom's product, slowing the company's momentum and cutting into its market share while it either fights the standard or redesigns its products. Chipcom has attempted to minimize this threat by aligning itself with industry leaders such as IBM and Cisco, but such alliances cannot guarantee it won't be left in the dust.

ANTI-TRUST LEGISLATION

Because Chipcom's relationships with competitors such as Cisco and IBM can be viewed as collusion by the government, Chipcom has to be concerned with the threat of anti-trust regulation, which would cost them fines and loss of business. The government currently allows some cooperation and consortiums so that U.S. companies can meet the threat of large Japanese companies that are heavily supported by their government, but this climate could easily change with an election of a new President or a shift in Congress.

CHIPCOM'S RISE

In 1991, Chipcom's U.S.-based operations were profitable, but its European subsidiary was losing money. President John Held and Chief Financial Officer Robert Badavas formulated a unique plan to make Chipcom's Income Statement as appealing as possible prior to its IPO, and authorized the sale of Chipcom Europe to a group of Boston venture capitalists for $3.3 million. Chipcom was granted a management contract and an outright call to buy the company back from the investors within two years for a specified amount of Chipcom stock, and went public at $12 a share. Following the IPO, Chipcom negotiated an early buyback of Chipcom Europe at a discount, which allowed Chipcom to maximize its return on the stock sale.[1]

This creative plan seemed to give the company the boost it needed. Growth began in 1991 and was especially strong in 1993 and 1994, with revenues of $150 million and $250 million, respectively. In 1994 resellers rated Chipcom number one among networking hardware vendors in *VAR Business Magazine*'s "Annual Report Card" issue in all four major categories: products, pricing, support, and partnership.

Chipcom's astute international strategy has strongly positioned it in the international market. The company opened new sales offices in Italy, Brazil, Japan, and China in 1994, in addition to its offices in Australia, France, Germany, Israel, Malaysia, and the United Kingdom. International sales grew from $40.1 million or 43.5% of revenue in 1992 to $123.4 million or 46.1% of revenue in 1994. In the first half of 1995, over 50% of Chipcom's sales were derived from international markets. In 1994, Chipcom became the first U.S. networking company to penetrate the People's Republic of China. The Beijing Commodity Exchange uses a Chipcom network to process daily transactions equivalent to over 2 billion U.S. dollars. The company believes its presence in international markets, combined with its aggressive strategies, will provide a solid base for future growth.

PRODUCT LINE

Chipcom, a customer-focused company, designs, manufactures, markets, and supports fault-tolerant intelligent switching systems, including hub, internet, and network management products for remote site, campus, and enterprise network computing environments. Merging with Artel Communications expanded its product line by introducing the Ethernet-based "Galactica" Switching Hub and "Starbridge" Turbo Hub to its "ONline" System product line and the new "ONcore" Switching System. Chipcom's worldwide development and marketing partnership with IBM led to the

---

[1]Richard Phalon, "Prettying the Prospectus," *Forbes*, March 29, 1993, p. 75.

development of an Asynchronous Transfer Mode (ATM) technology strategy.[2] Its agreement with Cisco Systems was enhanced in early 1995 by a program for delivering next-generation networking solutions based on a shared commitment to multivendor standards, Asynchronous Transfer Mode interoperability, and integration of key Cisco technologies into Chipcom's product families.

DISTRIBUTION

Chipcom's channel development strategy focuses on building relationships with a select, worldwide network of resellers which includes value-added resellers, large systems integrators with a global presence, companies with a national reach, vertical market-focused systems integrators, regional resellers, and distributors. Chipcom aggressively sought distribution agreements with companies such as Datacraft, Ericsson, Unisys, Bell Atlantic, Bosch Telecom of Germany, Tai Ji Computer Corp. of China, Comlink, Avon Datacom, and HBO & Co. In 1995, Chipcom expanded its third-party distribution channels to include Hewlett-Packard, British Telecom, Andersen Consulting, and ITS. And, as these channels continued to grow, its VAR sales increased significantly.

FINANCE

In the past few years, Chipcom has experienced tremendous growth in revenue and income. In 1994 alone, revenues increased by 67%, and income by 28%. Chipcom's first quarter 1995 revenues were up 66%, and its net income was up 300% from first quarter 1994. In 1994 Chipcom had sales of $267.8 million, with a net income of $18.6 million, a 50% increase over 1993's sales of $160.5 million, with a net income of $12.3 million.

Chipcom's financial objective is to finance future growth with profits from operations, relying very little on borrowed funds. Presently Chipcom has only $1.84 million in total debt compared to almost $10.7 million in cash and cash equivalents. Its relatively low debt allows the company to save money on interest and maintain tight control because it has not had to venture outside to raise capital. Chipcom has also reduced its overhead expenses as a percentage of revenue. In 1993, the company reduced overhead from 33% to 31% of revenues and further reduced overhead to 27% of revenue in 1994, while continuing to expand its product offerings and making two acquisitions.[3]

Chipcom has continued to increase its earnings per share (EPS), ending 1994 with an EPS of $1.07, a 37% increase over 1993's $.78 per share. Although this is not

---

[2]Business Wire, 7-13-93 (Lexius).
[3]Ibid.

the explosive increase experienced in its charter years, it is still healthy growth. First quarter EPS for 1995 came in at 45 cents, up 300% from the previous year.

MARKETING

Chipcom is the third largest supplier of intelligent hub systems. To effectively market its products, the company has built relationships with a variety of resellers, aggressively pursuing new alliances and joint ventures, as well as expanding already established relationships. Its strength derives from offering a full line of network management products for remote site, campus, and enterprise network computing environments. In addition, the market is very large, domestically as well as internationally, with extensive growth potential. Chipcom has been wise enough to recognize this and has set up sales offices in more than 40 countries worldwide to market and sell its systems and provide prompt professional service of its products for its customers.

Chipcom has worked hard to establish strong partnerships with IBM and other large companies. Because it uses its partners' distribution channels, Chipcom can spend more time and money on its own products, enhancing its already strong reputation for high-quality products.

OPERATIONS

Chipcom's operations objective is to provide a wide range of systems solutions and worldwide support through "best-in-class" service. Chipcom systems are highly reliable, with a design that allows key components to be "hot swapped" for minimal downtime. The company provides flexibility and investment protection by designing next-generation hubs 100% compatible with earlier products. An installed network system can be monitored, controlled, and changed from remote locations.

In a constantly changing industry, research and development is particularly important. The industry average for R&D is about 9% of revenues; however, Chipcom spent 12% in 1994. Designing systems is Chipcom's forté. By focusing on design, management believes, Chipcom can develop new and better products to meet the needs of its current and future customers.

INDUSTRY SHAKEOUT

The computer networking industry is dominated by Bay Networks, Cisco Systems, 3-Com, and Cabletron Systems, each with annual sales of close to a billion dollars. The current industry trend is consolidation through mergers and acquisitions, resulting in bigger and more powerful competitors. As the industry consolidates and its competitors expand their product lines, Chipcom is increasingly at a resource disadvantage, and its reliance on the high-end market may ultimately curtail its growth potential.

According to the CFO of Cabletron Systems, "Chipcom has got a lot of ground to catch up. It is getting harder and harder to become a major player."[4]

1994–1995 MARKET POSITIONING

The importance of providing customers with a complete network system forced Chipcom to offer a greater variety of products. Networked systems users require enterprise networks that integrate hardware-and-software-based technologies to connect and distribute applications across an entire organization. The basis for building this type of system is an intelligent switching hub. Users of this technology require:[5]

Reliability: Enterprise networks must be highly reliable and continuously available in order to minimize the interruption of computer applications. This requires a long mean time between failure, support fault-tolerant and redundant configurations, and the ability for maintenance to be performed while the network is operating.

Flexibility: Enterprise networks must provide flexibility and simple configurations that can grow and change with an organization. This requires that the physical portion of the network be developed for many years of use.

Manageability: Enterprise network managers must have the means to monitor, control, and change the network remotely across all areas of the organization, including numerous detached locations.

Built-in migration: The rapid evolution of network technologies requires that the platforms for the next generation of technologies be compatible with existing products, allowing the user to migrate to new technologies in an efficient and cost-effective manner.

To meet these requirements while becoming a full service provider, Chipcom developed several strategies. By acquiring Artel in 1994, Chipcom became a full service provider. To expand its low-end modular hub products, Chipcom acquired DSI, developers, manufacturers, and distributors of stackable Ethernet hubs, which were then integrated into Chipcom's Onsemble StackSystem.

Chipcom also focused on internal growth and product development. From 1994 to mid-1995, the engineering department grew from 50 to 300 employees. Senior engineers who had been involved in hands-on research, design, and development of products shifted their focus to developing an organizational culture that promoted a tight-knit "family" environment. Consequently, management of new products weakened, and the engineering department became fragmented, increasing development time, and slowing the advent of new products on the market, thus hurting sales to users looking for a full service provider for their networking needs.

The shift of focus by senior engineers had a negative impact on the development of Lightspeed, a high-speed switching technology compatible with DEC's Alpha Chip. Lightspeed's extremely fast transfer time was supposed to set Chipcom apart from its

[4]Lexius Search, *Boston Globe*, February 12, 1995.
[5]Chipcom Proxy Statement/Prospectus, September 11, 1995.

competition. The company had hired five former senior engineers from DEC to design the technology. However, the group's focus shifted, and organizational support waned; yet outside the immediate group no one was aware of the serious problems and delays with Lightspeed. The company still anticipated taking the networking market by storm.

In the meantime, Chipcom moved to diversify its product line. In the spring of 1994 the company embarked on a strategy to enter the telecommunications industry using its existing customer base and distribution channels to move directly into this market. But Chipcom both lacked a comprehensive portfolio of full service products for this market and underestimated the cost of entry into the telecommunications market.

Internal turmoil at Chipcom mirrored the rapid change and uncertainty of the industry as a whole. A number of small networking companies, each vying to become the number one full service provider, began merging to form larger companies. By 1995, three industry leaders had emerged: Cisco Systems, 3-Com, and Bay Networks. The number four company, Cabletron Systems, was half the size of number three, Bay Networks; and Chipcom, the number five company, was half the size of Cabletron Systems. It became apparent that the industry giants were aggressively moving to take over the industry.

THE DIGITAL DEAL

Two of Chipcom's founding executives had previously been at Digital Equipment Corporation (DEC). They brought with them keen engineering and manufacturing ability and a strong relationship with the DEC engineering group. As a result, DEC became a reseller of Chipcom's products in 1987. During 1992 and 1993 Chipcom supplied DEC with intelligent hub systems, realizing $31.2 million and $31.3 million in sales, which accounted for 19.5% and 34.0% of Chipcom's ongoing revenues for 1992 and 1993. In addition to DEC's providing a large revenue stream, Chipcom used the DEC relationship to grow internationally.

In 1994 the relationship with DEC began to change. DEC relinquished many of its outside provider agreements, turning to inside development and manufacturing, and began designing its own hub systems. Chipcom sales to DEC dropped to 10% of revenues in 1994, down from 34% in 1993. At the same time, Chipcom's market share was being eroded as other competitors cut into the hub market.

THE IBM ALLIANCE

In September 1992, Chipcom and IBM agreed to a 5-year alliance to market network related products worldwide, which either party could terminate after April 1, 1994. Each party agreed to provide the other with the internal use and resale of specific hardware and software products. IBM had manufacturing rights to the hub system and licensing rights to some parts of the system. Chipcom manufactured and sold module boards and other components for the hub system to IBM. In forming this alliance, Chipcom beat out industry giant Cisco Systems and was cited in 1993 by *Fortune* magazine as one of the fastest growing companies in America.

In 1993, sales to IBM reached $34.0 million or 21.2% of Chipcom's revenues. In

1994, that figure skyrocketed to $102.4 million or 38.2% of Chipcom's total revenues. For Chipcom, its relationship with IBM was highly significant; but for IBM, a $60 billion company, it was a minor relationship which failed to hold its attention. IBM did not see that the industry was changing rapidly, and it was not keeping pace.

Demand in the computer networking industry slowed. The remaining 62% of Chipcom's customers in the channel gradually cut their orders, operating as value-added retailers with no stock in inventory. IBM, however, lost control of the channel and continued to receive products from Chipcom, creating an inventory imbalance of hub parts and systems. In 1995 Chipcom inputs to IBM far outpaced IBM's output. By spring, Chipcom had pushed $30 million of revenue through the system, leaving IBM with six months of inventory. Chipcom's first quarter 1995 sales to IBM were $30.6 million. Once IBM realized what was happening, it reduced its commitment and IBM sales declined to $16.6 million in the second quarter. And, predictions for future revenues from this alliance were even less than the actual second quarter level.

A TIME OF TRANSITION

In January 1995, after the two previous finance directors had been fired and the position had remained vacant for nine months, Bill Walsh began his new position as Finance Director at Chipcom. Having left the stagnant and depressing environment of Digital Equipment Corporation, he was ready for the fast pace and rising status of one of *Fortune* magazine's top 100 fastest growing companies. As Finance Director he would be involved in top level strategy sessions which would determine the future direction of the organization. It was with great anticipation on his first day that he entered a company-wide meeting to kick off the new year. At that meeting he witnessed a strong culture of team spirit and togetherness, but it was almost as if the company employees were involved in a cult movement, with lots of cheering and screaming to express team spirit. He began to wonder about what he had gotten himself into.

INTERNAL CHAOS

In the months that followed he began to unravel an organization that had been run directly by top level managers, with few management fundamentals and systems in place. Employees were accustomed to going directly to heads of divisions and departments for direction. But as company growth made direct contact with each employee virtually impossible, an infrastructure should have been developed to handle the day-to-day operations and issues that arose. Walsh saw very early on that there was no infrastructure, and that the company was straining from the stress of rapid growth.

Three areas of the organization were in particular disarray: operations, engineering, and finance. In operations and manufacturing, workers had been accustomed to going directly to top management with problems, but now that the organization was too big for top management to be involved in day-to-day operations, there were no systems in place to ensure that work was either not interrupted, or put quickly back on track when problems arose. Manufacturing bogged down, leading to product defects and inefficiency. The time from the beginning of manufacture to shipment of products was too long, and customers became unhappy with slow delivery and missed deadlines. Internally, slow manufacture added to product costs, adversely affecting company finances.

Similarly in engineering, no programs were in place to ensure swift and efficient development of new technologies, the key to survival in the rapid growth networking market. Support from top management for new-product development fluctuated. Senior engineers were easily convinced to move from project to project, which led to the failure of Chipcom's Lightspeed project discussed above. By 1995 it was 12 months behind schedule, costing the company millions of dollars and diminishing investors' faith in the company's potential to compete at the top of the market.

Company finances were also in disarray. (See Exhibits 1 and 2.) The entire staff was accustomed to working directly with the CFO, Bob Badavas, on both day-to-day

---

EXHIBIT 1
Chipcom Announces Q-2, First Half 1995 Results: Condensed Consolidated Balance Sheet (unaudited)
(in thousands of dollars)

	July 1, 1995	December 31, 1994
Assets		
Current assets:		
Cash and cash equivalents	$ 14,833	$ 10,698
Short-term investments	28,390	41,322
Accounts receivable, net	48,563	45,319
Inventories	70,204	58,701
Prepaid expenses and other current assets	4,524	4,830
Deferred income taxes	11,195	11,351
Total current assets	$177,709	$172,221
Fixed assets, net	42,174	34,495
Other assets, including goodwill	16,247	15,137
Total assets	$236,130	$221,853
Liabilities and Stockholders' Equity		
Current liabilities:		
Current portion of long-term debt	$ 996	$ 800
Accounts payable	21,528	25,627
Accrued expenses	24,414	22,955
Income taxes payable	6,232	3,559
Total current liabilities	$ 53,170	$ 52,941
Deferred income taxes	4,919	4,849
Long-term debt	29	284
Other liabilities	5,349	4,843
Stockholders' equity	172,663	158,936
Total liabilities and stockholders' equity	$236,130	$221,853

EXHIBIT 2

Chipcom Announces Q-2, First Half 1995 Results: Condensed Consolidated Statement of Income (unaudited)

(in thousands of dollars, except per share data)

	Three Months Ended		Six Months Ended	
	July 1, 1995	*June 25, 1994*	*July 1, 1995*	*June 25, 1994*
Revenue	$71,511	$61,306	$157,721	$113,188
Costs and expenses:				
Cost of goods sold	$36,042	$28,203	$ 76,820	$ 51,031
Selling, general, and administrative	23,589	15,859	46,730	30,896
Research and development	10,421	7,740	20,642	13,966
Merger related expenses	—	—	—	5,125
Total costs and expenses	$70,052	$51,802	$144,192	$101,018
Income from operations	$ 1,459	$ 9,504	$ 13,529	$ 12,170
Other income (expense), net	404	229	874	536
Income before provision for income taxes	$ 1,863	$ 9,733	$ 14,403	$ 12,706
Provision for income taxes	671	3,601	5,185	4,701
Net income	$ 1,192	$ 6,132	$ 9,218	$ 8,005
Net income per share	$ .07	$ .36	$ .52	$ .47
Weighted average shares outstanding	17,534	17,097	17,725	17,145

business and higher-level concerns. There was no internal financial organization that could run smoothly without his presence, nor any planning procedures and controls over the forecasting process. There were no fundamental management tools such as an information system that linked production and inventory channel management. An operating committee was supposed to review the company's financial situation quarterly, but didn't, and the company did not really have a clear picture of where it stood financially. The finance department employed 50 to 60 people, but had become fragmented during its nine-month period without any leadership. Much of the information being generated was either useless or not utilized properly.

THE STOCK COLLAPSE

Three months after Walsh's arrival things began to get worse. Chipcom's stock plummeted 35%, from $40 to $26 per share during the second quarter of 1995, amidst rumors of the weakening of the alliance with IBM. In addition, a month prior to the severe stock drop, Chipcom's executive team disposed of a large amount of stock, leading other stockholders to suspect insider trading. The Board of Directors began to meet monthly, and demanded full disclosure of the company's operations and investments. Before long, the Securities and Exchange Commission was knocking at Mr. Walsh's door to investigate suspected dumping of Chipcom stock by insiders two weeks before the announcement of the cutback in orders by IBM. The SEC was also trying to determine when the executive team knew of the earnings shortfall for the second quarter, and at what point they should have known about it and disclosed it to the shareholders.

The loss of the DEC account the previous year together with the loss in revenues from IBM was devastating to the organization's financial health. In addition, the larger networking companies were gaining ground through rapid development of new technologies, new acquisitions, and diversification into related business areas. Despite this turmoil, Chipcom was again named one of the top 100 fastest growing companies by *Fortune* magazine for the third year running. The company was at a crossroads. . . .

http://www.chipcom.com/

CASE 15

Intel's Internet Entanglement*

INTRODUCTION

On 26 November 1994, Andy Grove, Chief Executive Officer of Intel, was preparing for his weekly Saturday morning bike ride with his wife. Grove often used this time to mull over what he calls the "concern du jour"—the latest company problem on his desk. Today he was reflecting on the rapidly changing world of computer technology and electronic communications. While his company was one of the powerhouses of the personal computer world, it was becoming increasingly difficult for him to stay in touch with every aspect of the business. Events of the past few weeks had brought that point sharply into focus.

Intel has always been very interested in using any means possible to gauge customer response to its marketplace offerings. The release of the Pentium microprocessor had been very successful, and customer response had been quite positive. Recently, however, disturbing messages had started appearing on the Internet concerning perceived quality problems with the Pentium. It had first come to his attention with Dr. Nicely's message in the "comp.sys.intel" news group on Usenet. Now, as he followed his wife up one of the lion-colored hills above Silicon Valley, he had to determine the best way to respond to the growing problem.[1]

Nicely@2small.2notice.edu

On 30 October 1994, Dr. Thomas R. Nicely, a professor of mathematics at Lynchburg College in Lynchburg, Virginia, sent a message across one of the Internet's Usenet newsgroups about a bug in Intel's Pentium floating point unit (FPU) or nu-

---

*Prepared by Lee T. Perry, Professor of Strategy and Organization Behavior, Monte R. Swain, Price Waterhouse Research Fellow, and Nicholas V. Kovalenko, Graduate Student, Marriott School of Management, 519 Tanner Building, Brigham Young University, Provo, UT 84602, (801) 378-3174, Fax: (801) 378-5933. This case was prepared as a basis for class discussion rather than to illustrate either effective or ineffective handling of a managerial situation.

[1]Source of all personal data on Andrew S. Grove: "Why Andy Grove Can't Stop," *Fortune* (10 July 1995).

meric coprocessor. Professor Nicely originally encountered erroneous results in June 1994, but it took him until 19 October 1994 to eliminate all other likely sources of the error (i.e., software logic, compiler, chipset). He contacted Intel Technical Support regarding the bug on October 24th. Intel's contact person reported back that the bug had been observed on a Pentium 66-MHz system, but he offered no further information or explanation.

Professor Nicely's message described the error with great precision. He wrote:

> . . . the Pentium FPU is returning erroneous values for certain division operations. For example, $1/824633702441.0$ is calculated incorrectly (all digits beyond the eighth significant digit are in error). This can be verified in compiled code, an ordinary spreadsheet such as Quattro Pro or Excel, or even the Windows calculator (use the scientific mode), by computing $(824633702441.0)*(1/824633702441.0)$, which should equal 1 exactly (within some extremely small rounding error; in general, coprocessor results should contain 19 significant decimal digits). However, the Pentiums tested return 0.999999996274709702 for this calculation. [10/30/94]

Professor Nicely tested for the bug on five different Pentium-based systems: a Dell P90, a Gateway P90, a Micron P60, an Insight P60, and a Packard-Bell P60. He did not observe the bug on 486-based or earlier systems. He also observed that when the FPU was locked out, the error disappeared, but this would slow down computations by roughly a factor of ten. While the principal purpose of Professor Nicely's message was to warn other Pentium users, he was also interested in further testing on other Pentium-based machines, 486-DX4s, and the AMD, Cyrix, and NexGen Pentium microprocessor clones.

Only about a thousand visitors posted messages in the "comp.sys.intel" news group during November 1994, the period during which interest peaked about Dr. Nicely's public revelation. Fewer visitors still posted messages reflecting their concerns about and/or support for the Pentium. That was not a lot of people discussing the Pentium chip within the Internet—an international computerized communications system with a total population of several million. How much should Intel, one of America's most powerful companies, worry about a very small group of computer users exchanging views and comments within a system so chaotic that it has been said that "the Internet could be called anarchy . . . if it were better organized"?

BACKGROUND ON INTEL AND ANDY GROVE

Gordon Moore and Robert Noyce founded Intel in 1968. Their goal with the new company was to design, manufacture, and market a new technology—called "semiconductor computer memory"—to replace the magnetic core memory, dominant in computers at that time. Dr. Andrew S. Grove joined Intel soon after its incorporation and eventually became the third head of what Noyce called Intel's "three-headed monster." Andy Grove, a native Hungarian, lived through both the Nazi and Joseph Stalin eras in Eastern Europe and arrived in New York City on a refugee ship in 1957 at the age of 21. Grove is literally a self-made success, putting himself through college in chemical engineering while working as a busboy during the summers. A star student, Andy Grove went on to complete a Ph.D. at UC Berkeley and joined a California start-up company called Fairchild Semiconductor. When his two bosses, Gordon Moore and Robert Noyce, left Fairchild four years later to start Intel, Grove was the first to join the new company. He was initially given charge of operations and spent the next 20 years developing a reputation as a notoriously hands-on manager of Intel's product-development and manufacturing operations. In 1987, Andy Grove was named President and CEO. Ironically, Grove was initially adamant in his disdain for PC computers. Eventually, Grove was forced to deal with his PC as the company began using electronic mail company-wide in 1989. Since then, Grove's attitude has changed mightily to the point where he now believes that the PC is most useful as a communications medium.

In 1971, Intel introduced the world's first microprocessor. Intel microprocessor technology has driven the development of the personal computer industry ever since it was first introduced in the IBM PC in 1978. That first microprocessor, the 8088, used an 8-bit microprocessor running at 4.77 MHz. Five chip generations later (8086, 80286, 80386, 80486), the Pentium (80586) uses a 32-bit microprocessor to run at clock speeds up to 166 MHz. By 1995, Intel had design teams working on the "P6," "P7," and "P8" processors—potential successors to the Pentium.

By the end of 1994, nearly 75% of the world's personal computers used the Intel architecture and annual revenues were rapidly approaching $10 billion. In March 1994, *Business Week* named Intel one of the top ten American companies in terms of profit, one of the top 15 market value winners, and 16th out of the magazine's top 1,000 companies overall. The commercial release of the Pentium chip at the end of 1993, like each of its predecessors, was eagerly anticipated by the huge population of Intel users across all the personal computer markets (e.g., science, education, commercial, government, home, etc.). Pentium sales expanded quickly, eclipsing sales of the Intel 80486 chip. However, in October 1994, Intel's reputation for engineering excellence and product quality collided with messages in the "comp.sys.intel" news group.

BACKGROUND ON THE INTERNET

Since there is no one central authority that "owns" or "runs" the Internet, trying to come up with a precise definition of what is and what is not the Internet is an almost hopeless endeavor. Generally speaking, the Internet is a grand network of computer networks. A central computer neither runs the Internet nor controls its traffic. Rather, the Internet consists of an ever increasing number of Local and Wide Area Networks that have been interconnected through shared data lines and other communications technologies.

The origins of today's Internet are found in the U.S. Department of Defense. During the height of the Cold War, there was great concern over maintaining data flows and communications over a wide area in the event of nuclear attack on the United States. Scientists at the Advanced Research Projects Agency (ARPA) developed a technology called Packet Switching, which allowed data to travel over widely dispersed paths and arrive at a common destination. Accordingly, even if most of the lines were destroyed, data would still be able to travel from one location to another without interruption.

In the 1970s, as military systems moved away from the rudimentary ARPA network into other, more secure means of communications, academic institutions began joining the ARPAnet. Engineering centers such as MIT and Stanford pioneered the use of ARPAnet to distribute and share research and development information. While most of this research was originally funded by and in support of ARPA, use of ARPAnet to promulgate other research and academic communications continued to expand. Soon many universities engaged in computer science research quickly came on-line to share data and communicate electronically with each other. Business and commercial interests gradually began to become aware of this growing network of networks, now being called Internet, and started connecting their internal computer networks to the "backbone" of the old ARPAnet. Today, several companies exist to provide connection to the Internet for individual computers, and the use of dedicated data lines for Internet connection is constantly expanding.

On today's Internet, the most widely used feature is electronic mail, which allows people to communicate with each other literally from anywhere in the world, almost instantaneously. Other popular features include: FTP (File Transfer Protocol), which allows users to transfer computer files from one location to another; Telnet, which allows remote control of a distant computer as if at a local terminal; Gopher, a research tool for finding information on participating computer networks; Chat, a real-time CB-like gathering of various users communicating via typed messages; and News, or Usenet, which facilitates sharing of ideas and information on an almost unlimited number of topics through time-delayed articles posted to individual news groups (see below). It is in Usenet that the "comp.sys.intcl" news group exists.

The prototype for Usenet is the familiar cork bulletin board, on which various individuals post ideas and information about which others comment. Currently there are over 10,000 individual news groups in existence, with more coming on-line every day. These tend to be very topic specific, such as "comp.sys.intel," and run the gamut from highly technical to extremely irreverent. For any topic of interest imaginable, there is probably a news group in existence. Often, as many as 100,000 to 150,000 visitors attend a specific news group such as "comp.sys.intel" each month. Chip Salzenberg offers the following approximate description of Usenet:

> Usenet is a world-wide distributed discussion system. It consists of a set of "news groups" with names that are classified hierarchically by subject. "Articles" or "messages" are "posted" to these news groups by people on computers with the appropriate software—these articles are then broadcast to other interconnected computer systems via a wide variety of networks. Some news groups are "moderated"; in these news groups, the articles are first sent to a moderator for approval before appearing in the news group. Usenet is available on a wide variety of computer systems and networks, but the bulk of modern Usenet traffic is transported over either the Internet or UUCP [UNIX to UNIX Copy Program].[2]

---

[2]This quote is an extract of the article "What Is Usenet, Part 1." Originally written by Chip Salzenberg and edited until 1993 by Gene Spafford (early Usenet administrators at Purdue University), this is one of many "Frequently Asked Questions" lists periodically circulated across Usenet. Although there is no definitive source of information that constitutes the accepted final word, this article, now currently maintained and posted periodically by Mark Moraes, is usually regarded as authoritative. It should be noted that there are also rebuttal articles that present different points of view on what constitutes Usenet.

There is an extensive body of opinion within Usenet as to the care and feeding of news groups, and what constitutes proper behavior, or "netiquette," within these discussions. The above referenced article is but a start. However, though they may be largely unwritten, these rules are quite real, as those who violate them quickly discover.

Nicely@2small.2notice.edu Redux

A second Internet message was sent by Professor Nicely, on 25 November 1994, to respond to an inquiry about a nondisclosure agreement (NDA) he signed with Intel. Professor Nicely's original interpretation of the NDA was that it constituted a voluntary "gag order." This led him to refer all inquiries regarding the Pentium FPU to Intel's representatives between 10 November, the day the agreement was signed, and 22 November. Several complaints were registered with Intel during this period, so on 22 November, Intel representatives informed Professor Nicely that he could freely discuss the discovery and nature of the Pentium FPU bug, since it was work that preceded the signing of the NDA. Intel explained that the primary purpose of the NDA was to ensure confidentiality of information exchanged around consulting work Professor Nicely might perform for Intel in the future.

Professor Nicely also offered his opinion about Intel's response to the FPU bug and advised Pentium users about how to communicate their concerns to Intel. He wrote:

> I cannot speak for Intel regarding its policies on CPU replacement for Pentium systems having the bug; that is a management decision which obviously must take into account the constraints of supply, inventory, logistics, expense, and public relations. To date, I believe Intel has handled the affair in essentially the manner that could usually be expected of most businesses operating in a highly competitive, low-margin, capital-intensive environment. Any Pentium owner who feels the need for a replacement CPU should contact Intel Customer Service and Tech Support at 800-628-8686, or Intel representative John Thompson at 408-765-1279.
>
> . . . Intel has been most cooperative in alleviating difficulties caused for my own research (computational number theory; distribution of twin primes and other constellations, and the sums of their reciprocals) by the presence of the bug. They have shipped replacement chips for the CPUs in the machines I am using, and I have verified that the new chips are free of the bug (zero errors in > 1e15 simulated random divisions). [11/25/94]

Obviously concerned about all the commotion he was causing, Professor Nicely attempted to diffuse concern over the bug. He reminded users about the complex designs of today's microprocessors, which led him to conclude that the discovery of the Pentium FPU bug should not be any great surprise. He reviewed several past, well-publicized bugs involving Intel's 8088, 80386, and 80486 microprocessors, and even Motorola's 68K DRAM memory chip.

The New York Times

The first press reports about the Pentium FPU bug appeared the day before Professor Nicely's second Internet message (24 November 1994). An article by John Markoff, appearing in *The New York Times*, is representative of these initial reports:

SAN FRANCISCO—[A]n error in division has been found in the Pentium, the current top microprocessor from Intel Corp., the world's largest chip maker. . . .

Intel declined to say how many Pentium chips it made or sold, but Dataquest, a market research company in San Jose, Calif., estimated that in 1994 Intel would sell about six million Pentiums, roughly 10 percent of the number of personal computers sold worldwide.

Intel said Wednesday that it did not believe the chip needed to be recalled, asserting that the typical user would have but one chance in more than nine billion of encountering an inaccurate result as a consequence of the error, and thus there was no noticeable consequence to users of business or home computers. Indeed, the company said it was continuing to send computer makers Pentium chips built before the problem was detected. . . .

Intel said the problem came to its attention in June and was corrected then, at the design stage. That change took some time to make its way through the chip production process, and Intel has only recently begun providing its largest customers with the revised chips, the company said.

Intel acknowledged that the flaw could affect certain scientific and engineering applications in rare cases. Stephen L. Smith, the company's engineering manager for the Pentium, said discussions were under way with scientists and engineers.

"Those are exactly the people who should call us," he said. "We're willing to work with them and understand what applications they are using that might be affected."

For Intel, which has spent millions of dollars on an advertising campaign using the slogan "Intel Inside," the news of the defect might create something of a public relations problem. . . .

The Pentium error occurs in a portion of the chip known as the floating point unit, which is used for extremely precise computations. In rare cases, the error shows up in the result of a division operation.

Intel said the error occurred because of an omission in the translation of a formula into computer hardware. It was corrected by adding several dozen transistors to the chip.

The error was made public earlier this month after Thomas Nicely, a mathematics professor at Lynchburg College in Lynchburg, Va., sent a private electronic-mail message to several colleagues, asking them to check their machines for the error. . . .

After the Pentium flaw was made public, Intel began telling users that it had discovered and corrected the flaw in June, and last week it quietly began offering replacement chips to users concerned about the error. . . .

The Weekend Decision

As president of Intel, Andy Grove had a great deal of enthusiasm for the company's latest microprocessor chip. He was confident that the Pentium would establish a new standard in operating performance for PC users, as well as new records in chip sales for Intel. However, this latest row over the Pentium FPU bug was developing a life of its own. The Intel development and production process had certainly resulted in bugs in previous '86 chip architectures; however, those problems had been easily resolved without much public contention. In terms of both customer inconvenience and production redesign, Grove felt that the Pentium bug was comparatively minor relative to previous bugs. Yet, it seemed clear that the possibility of a major public relations disaster was growing.

Without question, Grove felt that any public criticism of the Pentium chip was without basis. The summer of 1994 had been spent using some of Intel's best mathematicians and scientists to analyze completely the nature of the Pentium bug. Several months of testing seemed to indicate that the FPU miscalculation occurred only in extremely rare circumstances. The Intel lab report stated that, other than users of extremely heavy mathematical computations, most PC users would never be affected by the bug. Hence, there was little reason to doubt Intel's position that the Pentium was a great product.

It seemed clear to Andy Grove that the announcement by Professor Nicely (certainly a unique PC user involved in the study of complex mathematics) had simply created a stir among a select group of PC users on the Internet. On 26 November, Grove's mind worked furiously as he pumped his bike up Joaquin Road. It was obvious that this Pentium bug issue should be and could be fully resolved. Intel, deservedly, was the industry leader and had a terrific public reputation. As he turned off Joaquin Road, Grove set out for himself three tasks: (1) determine the product support plan for current Pentium users, (2) outline a public communication plan that resolves the growing overreaction to the bug, and (3) beat his personal record for biking the upcoming Honor Camp Road by 2 minutes!

http://www.intel.com/

STRATEGIC ANALYSIS

CASE 16

The Hue-Man Experience Bookstore*

I began telling everyone who came in the store that this was the largest African-American bookstore in the country. I really didn't know if that was true, but it was the largest one I had ever seen in my travels and everyplace I go I'm always looking for bookstores. Maybe eventually I'll uncover one that's larger and I'll have to acknowledge it, but until then I won't say anything different. So I began to create that image in people's minds, nationally as well as locally.

—Clara Villarosa

What began in 1984 as an attempt to set up an independent business targeted to affluent African-Americans was by 1992 a 3,000-square-foot retailing establishment and North Denver community landmark. The Hue-Man Experience Bookstore specialized in books, cards, jewelry, and artwork by and for people of color (hence the "Hue" in "Human"). While most patrons lived within 5 miles of the bookstore, the Hue-Man Experience Bookstore had gained a national reputation, attracting frequent out-of-town visitors. By 1994, Clara Villarosa was looking at expansion. The availability of the building next door kindled her dream of creating an Afrocentric retail and cultural center.

HISTORY

The Hue-Man Experience Bookstore grew out of the dream of a woman who had already made it in corporate America. Clara Villarosa started out professionally as a psychiatric social worker, working in an outpatient (nonresidential) clinic in Chicago, after receiving a master's degree in social work in 1954. Like many women of her generation, she dropped out of the workforce when her children were born. In 1968, when her daughters were 5 and 9 years old, Clara and her husband moved the family to Denver. Clara soon took a position in the department of behavioral sciences at Denver's Children's Hospital. By the time she left the hospital in 1980, she had become the director of the department of behavioral sciences and assistant hospital administrator. After entering a doctoral program in social work and law, she started a consulting business.

> I wanted to help African-Americans move up the corporate ladder and I thought I could sell that idea to large corporations. As a social worker I had some skills, but I didn't know how to knock on doors, to get a business off the ground. When I ran out of money I took a temporary job at United Bank. I started out in employee relations and moved quickly up the corporate ladder, becoming the vice president of Human Resources within two years. Again I found myself in the position of being the highest African-American on the payroll. But, as often happened in those times, I hit the glass ceiling. People were extremely resentful and angry about African-Americans and affirmative action and I received a significant backlash. So I left the bank. But left the bank with some money. I think they *wanted* me to quit.

Her consulting business had taught her that she wanted to sell something tangible, and at the same time, something that would relate in a positive way to the African-American community.

> And I came up with books, because I've always been a reader. My father was a reader and I grew up immersed in books. We [the African-American community] had had a bookstore in Denver, but there wasn't one now, so my dream was to create the largest African-American bookstore in Denver.

This time, Clara researched her market and wrote a business plan, outlining the financial and marketing requirements of her ethnic bookstore concept. With the help of two friends and her severance from the bank, she got together $35,000 and secured a lease on a two-story row house in a rundown residential/commercial area north of downtown Denver in a predominantly African-American area. The Hue-Man Experience Bookstore opened in 1984. In 1986, realizing that business and friendship don't always mix well, Clara arranged to buy out her partners' shares over a 2-year period by selling shares of the business to interested friends and customers. In 1993, the Hue-Man Experience Bookstore was governed by a nine-member board of directors, elected annually by Clara, who owned 58 percent, and thirty-one shareholders. Financial data for the Hue-Man Experience Bookstore for 1990–1993 are given in Exhibits 1 and 2.

THE BOOKSELLING INDUSTRY

In 1992, book sales in the United States exceeded $16.1 billion, according to the Association of American Publishers. The American Book Trade Directory estimated that there were about 27,000 retailers of books in the United States, 15,700 of which were privately owned independent bookstores. The largest book retailers were general bookstore chains, which had sales of $2.9 billion in 1992 from a total of 2,768

EXHIBIT 1
The Hue-Man Experience Bookstore: Income Statements for 1990–1993 (period ending 12/31)

	1990	1991	1992	1993
Revenue:				
Books	$181,134	$216,922	$272,542	$269,751
Cards	26,024	26,517	25,811	23,106
Prints	13,503	15,579	13,994	9,616
Jewelry	3,903	2,152	1,759	1,438
Miscellaneous	17,274	16,967	14,712	7,154
Catalog	13,098	18,268	21,338	6,828
Tapes and magazines	3,924	2,724	4,342	5,310
Reimbursed postage	1,428	3,070	3,345	2,433
Total revenue	$260,289	$302,198	$357,841	$325,635
Cost of sales:				
Books	$121,719	$143,793	$196,666	$152,104
Cards	14,613	12,769	17,603	14,583
Prints	6,146	11,100	8,487	3,453
Jewelry	956	612	1,435	325
Miscellaneous	8,942	6,396	2,665	5,946
Tapes and magazines	3,568	2,437	8,319	4,044
Catalog	3,336	5,661	779	120
Freight and postage	1,733	2,770	6,663	740
Framing supplies	1,815	590	1,379	538
Inventory (increase)/decrease	(1,094)	5,617	(4,047)	8,034
Total cost of sales	$161,732	$191,743	$239,947	$189,885
Gross margin	$ 98,557	$110,455	$117,894	$135,750
Administrative expenses:				
Officer salary	$ 26,000	$ 26,814	$ 29,599	$ 24,973
Salaries	20,874	27,193	27,647	26,706
Employee benefits	—	160	169	3,454*
Advertising	3,848	4,406	4,740	3,309
Promotional	2,677	1,364	758	13
Accounting and legal	4,008	4,101	3,389	4,256
Vehicle expense	2,822	3,010	3,433	4,517
Bank and credit card service charges	3,791	2,208	6,407	1,175
Janitorial/cleaning expenses	276	164	240	—
Consulting/contract labor	2,568	2,510	328	676
Contributions	864	900	229	293
Dues and subscriptions	907	1,242	933	1,977
License and fees	—	10	26	95
Depreciation	3,015	4,453	4,027	3,997
Entertainment	971	257	1,409	3,299
Travel/conferences	4,011	1,530	1,576	2,082
Rent	9,078	7,677	7,350	12,495
Repairs and maintenance	869	662	2,008	2,609
Security	322	520	458	556
Telephone†	5,147	7,689	9,995	7,577
Utilities	2,445	2,722	2,636	3,055
Insurance	—	1,462	1,104	173
Office supplies and equipment	4,082	3,345	4,259	4,667

(continued)

EXHIBIT 1 (continued)
The Hue-Man Experience Bookstore: Income Statements for 1990–1993
(period ending 12/31)

	1990	1991	1992	1993
Printing	—	—	598	2,194
Store supplies	1,686	3,681	2,722	3,264
Taxes—personal property	148	284	486	—
Taxes—payroll	4,156	4,826	4,970	4,409
Freight and postage	4,242	357	1,254	5,280
Miscellaneous	1,284	319	1,254	436
Total expenses	$111,561	$113,583	$122,655	$127,755
Other income (expense):				
Interest earned	$ 348	$ 283	$ 168	$ 105
Other income	5,000	325	779	7
Interest expense	(566)	(297)	(2,145)	(155)
Bookstore net income (loss)	(8,222)	(2,817)	(5,960)	7,952
Rental income:	—	2,066	16,950	19,536
Administrative expenses:				
Depreciation—building	—	440	2,643	4,423
Repairs and maintenance	—	900	1,682	4,737
Utilities	—	125	1,046	235
Miscellaneous	—	—	—	575
Insurance—property	—	—	2,964	1,226
Taxes—real property	—	134	820	1,948
Interest income—building	—	—	35	131
Interest expenses—building	—	(1,140)	(2,252)	(6,001)
Total building income (expense)	—	$ (639)	$ 5,674	$ 390
Total other income (expense)	$ 4,781	$ (328)	$ 4,475	$ 347
Net income/(loss)	$ (8,222)	$ (3,456)	$ (286)	$ 8,342

*In 1993, Clara added health-care coverage for the employees. Due to the prohibitive costs, this was discontinued by the end of the year, in favor of increased wages.
†Includes Yellow Pages advertising and 1-800 phone lines.

outlets. Exhibit 3 contains sales information for the largest bookstore chains in 1991 and 1992.

Major chain expansion began in the late 1970s to mid-1980s. Mall outlets carrying 1,000 to 20,000 titles proliferated toward the end of the 1980s. As mall growth slowed, the focus changed to superstores, huge discounters which averaged 200,000 titles, five to ten times the number offered by specialty or mall stores. Barnes & Noble opened its first superstore in September 1990, in a Minneapolis suburb. The 15,000-square-foot store was patterned after such well-known independent booksellers as Oxford Books in Atlanta, Powell's Books in Portland, the Tattered Cover in Denver, and Waterstone's in Boston.

The hallmark of the chain superstores was discounting, selling mainly fiction, celebrity biographies, and other books that appeal to the general public. Increasing competition was coming from mail-order catalogs, warehouse clubs, discount retailers, and nonbook specialty stores (such as the Nature Company, Sutton Place

EXHIBIT 2
The Hue-Man Experience Bookstore: Balance Sheets for 1990–1993
(period ending 12/31)

	1990	1991	1992	1993
Assets				
Current assets:				
Cash and cash equivalents	$ 6,401	$ 14,675	$ 11,891	$ 13,787
Accounts receivable—trade	—	—	681	1,998
Prepaid employee benefits	—	—	1,134	—
Inventory—merchandise	61,153	55,536	59,583	65,579
Total current assets	$67,554	$ 70,211	$ 73,289	$ 81,364
Property and equipment:				
Building	—	$ 79,260	$ 79,260	$ 79,260
Construction in progress	—	—	8,900	8,900
Leasehold improvements	$ 6,701	$ 6,701	$ 6,701	$ 6,701
Furniture and fixtures	3,323	3,323	3,323	3,323
Machines and equipment	16,888	21,888	23,943	25,917
Less accumulated depreciation	(13,994)	(18,887)	(25,557)	(33,977)
Other assets:				
Organizational expense	5,056	5,056	5,056	5,056
Less accumulated amortization	(5,056)	(5,056)	(5,056)	(5,056)
Total fixed assets	$13,919	$ 92,286	$ 96,571	$ 90,125
Total assets	$80,473	$162,497	$169,860	$171,489
Liabilities and Stockholders' Equity				
Current liabilities:				
Accounts payable	$11,847	$ 12,060	$ 19,686	$ 14,219
Security deposits	—	870	870	370
Payroll taxes payable	3,429	2,960	2,606	107
Sales tax payable	2,618	3,357	4,596	3,886
Property taxes payable	—	806	792	2,413
Deferred revenue	100	100	2,209	100
Interest payable—SBA loan	—	1,140	1,140	498
Officer loans	4,400	4,400	4,400	4,400
Accrued interest—shareholder	—	—	2,097	2,383
Total current liabilities	22,395	25,694	38,396	28,377
Noncurrent portion—SBA loan	—	72,000	66,948	70,255
Total liabilities	$22,394	$ 97,694	$105,344	$ 98,631
Stockholders' equity:				
Common stock	$46,102	$ 56,282	$ 56,282	$ 56,282
Paid in capital	47,902	47,902	47,902	47,902
Retained earnings	(23,201)	(35,925)	(39,381)	(39,669)
Dividends	(4,502)	—	—	—
Net profit (loss)	(8,222)	(3,456)	(287)	8,342
Total equity	$58,079	$ 64,803	$ 64,515	$ 72,858
Total liabilities and equity	$80,473	$162,497	$169,860	$171,489

EXHIBIT 3
U.S. Bookstore Chain Sales
(Sales of 11 Largest Trade Bookstore Chains, 1992 and 1991)

Chain	Ownership	'92 Sales* (in millions (of dollars)	'91 Sales (in millions of dollars)	% Change	No. Stores at Year End
Waldenbooks	Kmart	$1,146.0	$1,139.0	.06	1,260
Barnes & Noble	Public (in 1993)	1,086.7	920.9	18.0	916
Crown Books	Dart Group	240.7	232.5	3.5	247
Borders Books	Kmart	116.0	82.5	40.6	22†
Books-A-Million	Public	95.1	72.8	30.6	107
Encore Books	Rite-Aid Corp.	65.2	52.3	24.7	103
Lauriat's†	Chadwick-Miller	49.0	46.0	7.0	56
Tower Books†	MTS Inc.	33.0	29.0	13.8	15
Kroch's & Brentano's§	Waldenbooks	30.0§	33.0	−9.0	20
Rizzoli Bookstores§	Private	24.0	21.0	14.3	11
Taylor's Inc.§	Private	20.0	17.5	14.3	11
Totals		$2,905.7	$2,646.5	9.8	2,768

*Figures are for calendar 1992 or most current fiscal year.
†Store totals do not include nine Basset Books transferred to Borders at year end.
†Estimated sales.
§Sales estimate is a projection for year ending June 30, 1993.
Source: *Publishers Weekly,* June 14, 1993.

Gourmet, and Toys 'R' Us). In addition, university bookstores had expanded their stock to include popular books and sidelines such as cards and clothing, and, more recently, books targeted to young adults, known as "generation X" or "13th Gen" books. Both chain and independent bookstores had been increasing their use of book catalogs and newsletters, which promoted bestsellers or discount specials and also served as promotional tools to get more people in the stores.

Profit margins among the large chains were estimated at less than 1 percent, which made volume critical to this business. Exhibit 4 shows estimates of financial performance for 1991 or 1992 based on *Publishers Weekly* data compiled from Barnes & Noble, Books-A-Million, and Crown Books (for chain-store estimates) and American Booksellers Association ABACUS survey results, based on reports from 199 independent bookstore operations.

Fiscal 1993 reports from the large chains showed revenue increases of 19 percent. Profit margins and operating income were similar to 1992 levels, resulting in operating margins for each of the 2 years at 3 percent, nearly twice the independents' 1.62 percent.

Barnes & Noble attributed a 144 percent increase in sales in 1992 to its new superstores. In 1993, 30 percent of Barnes & Noble sales were from its 135 superstores, 77 of which were added in 1993. Another 75 stores were planned for 1994 and for 1995. Encore Books, which operated only one superstore in 1993, planned to open four more by mid-1994. Waldenbook's superstore operations were under the name of Borders, a previously independent 19-store chain purchased by Kmart in the fall of 1992. Borders (which also included Walden's Basset Book Shops) had 30 superstores in 1992 and planned to open 20 more by the end of 1993. Crown planned to increase

EXHIBIT 4
Comparison of Independent and Chain Bookstore Profitability
(Estimates of Bookstore Expenses as % of Total Sales*)

	Chains Composite Dollars (in millions of dollars)	Chains (%)	Sample Independents Composite Dollars	Independents (%)
Net sales:	$1197.8	100	$170.5	100
Receipts from books†	1078.1	90	136.4	80
Receipts from sidelines†	119.7	10	34.1	20
Cost of goods sold	816.3	68.2	106.4	62.4
Gross profit	381.5	31.8	64.1	37.6
Operating, selling, and administrative expense:	317.8	26.5	61.4	36.0
Occupancy costs	—	—	12.3	7.2
Advertising	—	—	4.9	2.9
Depreciation and amortization	27.6	2.3		
Operating profit	36.1	3.0	2.8	1.6
Interest expense	29.9	2.5	.34	0.2
Income before tax	6.2	0.5	2.42	1.4
Income tax	5.5	0.4	.68	0.4†
Net income	0.7	0.1	1.7	1.0

*Calendar year 1991 or fiscal year ending 1992. (Most independents operate on a calandar year; chains report earnings on a fiscal basis.)
†Estimate from anecdotal reports.
Source: *Publishers Weekly,* October 18, 1993.

its 22 superstores to 40 by the end of 1993. Books-A-Million, with 10 superstores in 1992, expected to open 5 more in 1993. Tower Books had 15 stores by the end of 1992; Lauriat's was positioning its new Royal Discount Bookstores as superstores.

Many independent bookstore owners were concerned that the industry was going the way of hardware stores and neighborhood pharmacies. According to John Mutter of *Publishers Weekly*, there was fear that superstores were creating "a concentration of power that threatens the diversity of what gets published and what is available for the public to read."[1] The American Booksellers Association was cooperating with the Federal Trade Commission in investigating business practices and pricing policies which appeared to threaten the small independent book retailers.

While chains offered cheap prices, few could offer the personal service of independents who knew their customers. This was particularly true in the growing breed of specialty bookstores. Some specialty booksellers focused on a particular subject, such as Armchair Sailor in New York, which specialized in nautical books; Victor Kamlin, Inc., in Rockville, Maryland, which specialized in Russian literature; Books of Wonder in New York, which specialized in children's books; Sports Central: The Ultimate Sports Bookstore in Palo Alto; or Books for Cooks in Baltimore. Others, like Salt of the Earth Bookstore in Albuquerque, Midnight Special in Santa Monica, California, and Odyssey Bookshop in South Hadley, Massachusetts, prided them-

[1]Mutter, J. "Heated Competition Gets Hotter," *Publishers Weekly*, January 4, 1993, p. 43.

selves on community involvement by promoting multicultural authors. Some stores focused on one particular market group, such as Charis Bookstore in Atlanta, which positioned itself as a feminist bookstore; OutBooks in Fort Lauderdale and A Different Light in San Francisco, which targeted lesbians and gays; and Shrine of the Black Madonna in Detroit and Hue-Man Experience Bookstore in Denver, which catered to an African-American clientele.

Bookselling and publishing by and for African-Americans had surged since 1988. An increasing interest in African-American culture, aided by school curriculum reforms, fueled a growth in bookstores catering to African-Americans. According to Wade Hudson, who ran Just Us Books in New Jersey, "African-Americans are hungry for knowledge and understanding about their experience, so they are looking for books that provide it."[2] Until recently, these books had been published by small independent publishing operations or by the authors themselves, and sold out of car trunks at book conventions. More recently, the major publishers and national distributors had entered this market, providing easier access to booksellers through mainstream distribution channels.

"Bookstores used to assume there was no market because blacks didn't come in asking for titles like these, but that's because they assumed the stores wouldn't stock them," Mr. Hudson commented. Kassahun Checole, president of the Red Sea Press, the largest distributor of African-American titles, had spent his career in the publishing business. Early in 1992, he told *Publishers Weekly*, "The Red Sea Press now distributes titles from about sixty publishers, approximately half of them African-Americans."[3]

Bookseller and publisher Haki Madhubiti, who had founded the African-American Publishers and Booksellers Association (AAPBA) in 1989, believed that "a good 30 to 35 percent of the people who buy our books aren't black."[4] The AAPBA held trade meetings and special sessions at the American Booksellers Association convention. This group became the first specialty segment within the ABA. As of 1992, there were several such segments, including a travel group and a mystery group, which held roundtable discussions at national and regional meetings and put together newsletters targeting specialty bookstore owners.

THE DENVER MARKET

According to the 1990 census, Colorado had almost 3.3 million residents; nearly 2 million lived in the greater metropolitan Denver area, of whom 460,000 lived within the city limits. While only 4 percent of Colorado's population was black, the city of Denver was nearly 13 percent black; 60 percent of these lived north of downtown.

According to Scarborough Research Corporation, Denver ranked 10 percent above the national average in the popularity of reading in 1993, ranking twenty-second out of 209 surveyed metropolitan areas. Forty-three percent of metropolitan Denver

[2]Goddard, C. "Aiming for the Mainstream," *Publishers Weekly*, January 20, 1992, p. 29.
[3]"Aiming for the Mainstream," p. 30.
[4]"Aiming for the Mainstream," p. 30.

households were considered "avid readers." Both Denver and Boulder, 35 miles away, boasted independent superstores which had been in existence for over 20 years.

The Tattered Cover, a Denver landmark, was located in a former department store in Cherry Creek North, an established shopping area with nearly a million square feet of retail and service businesses. The Tattered Cover had 40,000 square feet of selling space on four floors, and boasted over 220,000 titles. Across the street was the prestigious Cherry Creek Shopping Center. The Cherry Creek center, which had opened in August, 1990, was a 1-million-square-foot mall comprised of luxury and specialty stores (including Doubleday Book Shop and Travelday's Book Shop, both owned by B. Dalton, and Brentano's, owned by Waldenbooks). Recent competitors, located in suburban areas, included five Barnes & Noble superstores, each with approximately 10,000 square feet of selling space. A sixth Barnes & Noble superstore was planned in a renovated theater building about 2 miles east of the Tattered Cover.

There was a wide variation in retail lease rates in Denver, depending upon the location. Rents in Cherry Creek North averaged between $17 and $28 per square foot (calculated on a yearly basis). Rates for the Cherry Creek Shopping Center, immediately south of Cherry Creek North, were about twice that rate.

The Denver area had over one hundred independent retailers of new and used books. Specialty bookstores included Murder by the Book, which specialized in mystery fiction; Astoria Books and Prints, which specialized in rare books and artwork; Hermitage Antiquarian Bookshop, which specialized in collectibles and first editions; Isis Metaphysical Bookstore, which specialized in books on metaphysics, crystals and jewelry, and new-age music; Category Six Books, specializing in gay and lesbian literature; Cultural Legacy, which specialized in books in Spanish; and numerous children's bookstores and religious specialty stores.

The Hue-Man Experience Bookstore was located on Park Avenue West, a well-traveled thoroughfare about a mile north of downtown, bordering the area known as Five Points, named for the five tramway lines that once intersected there. Five Points was one of Denver's largest residential areas, encompassing over 1,000 acres. Five Points had once been known as a cultural center for African-Americans, with more African-American–owned businesses than any other place in the United States except for Harlem. This began to change in 1959 with the passage of Colorado's Fair Housing Act. During the 1960s and 1970s, many of the more affluent African-Americans moved to other, more integrated, neighborhoods. In 1993, the Five Points area was populated with small service and retail establishments and rundown houses. According to 1990 census data, the average household income in Colorado was $36,015 (the U.S. average was $29,199). Half of the residents in the vicinity of Five Points had an annual household income under $35,000; nearly 30 percent of the households reported an annual income under $15,000.

Walking in the vicinity of Five Points was not considered advisable, especially after dark. In 1993, this area had the third highest crime rate in Denver, with 315.2 crimes reported per 1,000 population. In 1992, Five Points had ranked second. The highest crime area (consistently since 1989) was North Capital Hill, which bordered Five Points to the south, with 413.2 crimes reported per 1,000 population in 1993. These numbers included car theft and petty robbery as well as gang violence and homicides, and Five Points was generally viewed as an undesirable part of town.

HUE-MAN'S OPERATIONS AND LAYOUT

The Hue-Man Experience Bookstore began operations in a two-story row house, one of four attached residential apartments. Within 2 years, Clara had expanded her store into the adjacent row house, convincing the landlord to do renovations to connect the two. She thought that with 4,200 titles occupying 3,000 square feet, the Hue-Man Experience was, very likely, the largest African-American bookstore in the United States.

Two cash registers, or point of sale computer terminals, were located just inside the door. Afrocentric greeting cards and note cards were located in a separate room adjacent to the checkout area. Afrocentric art created a backdrop for the checkout area, which was surrounded by a glass case displaying ethnic jewelry. An employee was always on hand to greet people and offer assistance. Each room was arranged around a particular theme or subject. Popular titles and classics were on the main floor, in what was once a living room. Upstairs, there were rooms devoted to sports, religion, music, and children's books.

Specialty cards, calendars, and jewelry comprised approximately 20 percent of sales. Fine art prints and ethnic artwork by local artists were displayed on the walls throughout the store and in two browsing racks. Calendars featuring African-American history and African-American art were also prominently displayed. During the holiday season, two rooms upstairs were full of distinctive boxed Christmas and Kwanzaa cards. People who bought books as gifts could also purchase gift wrapping and gift bags with African designs. As with most specialty stores, these sidelines were an integral part of the store's identity, geared specifically to the African-American market. Cards and jewelry typically have a bigger markup than books, and bring added traffic into the store.

Industry insiders recognized that books are often an impulse purchase, bought on a whim for personal reasons or to be given as a gift. Both small mall boutiques and large chain stores understood the importance of lighting and displays for enticing people to walk in the door to browse. Location and name recognition were also important, especially for independent booksellers.

Because of the fixed maximum price of most items, inventory control was critical to profitability. Computerized inventory control systems attached to point of sale (POS) terminals were considered essential for the success of large stores. These computer programs ranged in price from around $400 (for software which runs on most PCs) to over $5,000 (for systems that included POS terminals, cash registers, and scanners). Some of the more expensive computer systems available could be connected to on-line electronic ordering systems with wholesalers or major distributors to expedite reorders and returns. Others could tie into banking networks for credit card authorization and check scanning. Hue-Man Experience used a program called Booklog, a menu-driven system which was easy to use, even for "noncomputer" people. Booklog kept track of purchases and sales, and these records could be used to track fast- and slow-moving items. Booklog also kept a customer file, which was used for identifying frequent buyers and sending out announcements or newsletters.

Employees were critical to the success of independent booksellers, whose customers relied on service. Many booksellers had difficulty finding qualified employees, people who read and who were knowledgeable about books, who were personable, and who were willing to work hard. Wages in most bookstores ranged from $4.50 to $5.50 per hour, far less than most full-time employment. Despite this, and even given Denver's strong economy, booksellers such as the Tattered Cover and Hue-Man Experience had had no trouble finding competent, well-educated employees who liked their work.

There were four full-time employees at the Hue-Man Experience Bookstore. Turnover was low, with employees typically staying over a year, a rarity in minimum-wage positions. The employees at the Hue-Man Experience Bookstore conveyed a sense of belonging, not only to the bookstore, but also to the cultural community. One employee at Hue-Man Experience Bookstore, a college graduate who majored in African-American Studies, had stayed at the store for over a year because she enjoyed learning more about her culture and interacting with African-Americans in her community.

MARKETING

Clara commented:

I started out with a marketing plan, but there were many flaws because it was based on Anglo book purchasing behavior. We were unable to anticipate the difficulty in getting African-American people to buy books. I had to go back and reevaluate my marketing strategies. We thought people would come because the idea was unique. It was an upscale store with ambiance, patterned similar to Tattered Cover, which really has a national presence. And we thought that people would come—particularly middle-class people with disposable incomes and a higher education level, because that was the population that I was close to. But it took a lot more marketing to get people in. The variable we didn't count on is that the store sells not just books, but culture. The customers we attract have to be culturally connected.

Clara originally put out fliers and took out ads to publicize her store, but quickly realized that she wasn't reaching her market. And she soon understood that the people who came into the store were not the well-to-do clientele that she had envisioned.

We found out that our market was the working class. So we had to direct our advertising to these people. Unfortunately, they don't belong to a lot of groups. They belong to churches, but marketing from churches is very difficult because pastors do not want you to come into their congregation to sell something—other than what they sell. So we've tried to determine what our people buy and why they buy what they buy. We've studied the psycho-demographics of our population and tried to create a presence in the community. And we have tried to create a national presence. People make purchases based on prestige, so the bookstore had to develop prestige.

Clara Villarosa began telling everyone who came in the store that Hue-Man Experience was the largest African-American bookstore in the country. She became an influential figure in the African-American community. She did book reviews on the radio. She was active in community and civic affairs. She was appointed to the governor's council for business development and served on the board of directors of the Small Business Development Center and the Metro Denver Visitors and Conventions Bureau. She was a "friend of the library," she worked with the Denver Center for Performing Arts (DCPA), the Cleo Parker Robinson Dance Company, and Eulipions Cultural Center. As Clara put it, she was willing to be involved in

> . . . anything that's culturally related, because I enjoy ethnic events. I like the theater and the ballet and all of that, so I get involved. DCPA currently performs one black play a year, and maybe someday they'll do two. I host the director and cast for a reception here in the store and I invite my customers in so that they can touch and feel the cast and it advertises the show and helps sell tickets. Cleo Parker Robinson—her dance troupe is an African-American dance troupe, and I work with her and find out what she's doing. Eulipions is an African-American theater company. I was a founding member of their Board of Directors and served for 8 years. If an author—an African-American author—is coming to town to make a speech or presentation, I ask if they want their book sold at the event where they are appearing, and if they would like to come to the store for a signing. And of course they do and of course they will! I'm not stupid! But I really have to hustle and seek out opportunities. And so I've been nominated for a zillion awards and won most of them. I'm a small business, I'm retail, I'm a minority-owned business.

In the 10 years since the store had opened, Clara felt she had become much better at marketing. By the end of 1993, the only paid advertising was in the form of courtesy ads, ads placed in local programs or newsletters. These ads generated goodwill, but Clara did not believe that they generated new business. Word of mouth was the main source of advertising, but it was a sophisticated type of word of mouth, cultivated through sophisticated public relations. Clara had been featured in *Ms. Magazine, Executive Female,* and *Publishers Weekly.* She was on the board of directors of the American Booksellers Association and was a member of the Mountains and Plains Booksellers Association. In 1990, she was instrumental in putting together a feature exhibit entitled "Black and Read: Books by African-American Authors and Illustrators" at the ABA convention, which met in Denver that year.

> African-Americans come to Denver for many conventions, but how do I locate them? By serving on the board [of the Denver Metropolitan Visitors and Conventions Bureau]. I am instrumental in putting together a fact sheet of things to do and places to go in Denver for African-American visitors. For example, there's a convention of African-American educators in Denver this week, and I'm hosting a group of them here on Friday. I'm also learning about other industries, like the hotel industry. Everything becomes part of my marketing strategy.

In 1989, at the suggestion of many out-of-town customers, Clara put together a sixty-four-page mail-order catalog. "They said, 'Send me the booklist.' They like to read it but they don't order. It's a different motivation to pick up the phone and order a book. But the catalog appears to create a feeling of connectedness, and brings them back to the store." Clara financed the newsprint catalog largely through co-op advertising, whereby publishers paid for most of the printing cost of ads for their books.

By 1992, Clara's catalog had been streamlined down to sixteen pages. The catalog was professionally produced, in a format similar to those found in upscale bookstores such as the Tattered Cover. In 1993, she began negotiating with Ingram's, a major book distributor, to jointly produce a catalog that would be distributed to other bookstores. The new catalog would be a glossy version of her newsprint catalog that other bookstore owners could use for their customers.

My name would appear as a by-line and Ingram's would do the layout and pick up the printing costs. Individual bookstores would put their name and address on it for their own customers, which would help them publicize current titles. I know it's a lot of work to design this, but I've already done the work for my own catalog. This way Hue-Man Experience will get national publicity.

Clara also published a quarterly newsletter, highlighting author signings and community events. This newsletter was typically one page, printed on both sides, which could be mailed easily when folded and stapled. Regular customers were on the mailing list; customers who spent at least $10 were added to this list. Clara had found out the hard way that sending out unsolicited newsletters was not an efficient way to bring in new customers. As she put it, regular customers were "the ones most likely to come back and most likely to come to store-sponsored events. They pay for the newsletter."

> PR is critical in this business—community connections. It's interesting, because that's what we built this store on—a community presence. Local people say that we have something of value and this creates pride and ownership. And we perpetuate that image by showing them that we care about them as individual customers and that we care about their community. We find that our customers expect to be treated well, everyone is greeted, everyone is treated warmly, nurtured. We have to recognize our history, based on segregation, discrimination.
>
> You still hear of salespeople demanding IDs and avoiding eye contact with African-American customers. It happens everyplace. Not as often as before, but people are still uncomfortable around African-Americans. Even in Denver, which is a city that's pretty well mixed, an integrated city. There's no central African-American community because Denver was developed as an integrated city and people have dispersed to all areas of the city. People have moved to the suburbs, outlying areas, Aurora, Littleton. These people aren't inclined to drive the distance to the store very often. We have to create a destination place for them. There's no other traffic around here.

PLANS FOR THE FUTURE

In November 1992, Clara Villarosa bought the four houses that comprised the building which contained the bookstore, with financing backed by the U.S. Small Business Administration. She was able to buy the building for $79,000. With her track record as a successful retailer, she was able to secure a $72,000 24-year loan on the building, which appraised for $120,000. Her store occupied two units; the other two were rented to an art gallery and an ethnic apparel retailer.

Clara viewed her business as more than a bookstore. To her, it was a cultural center. She observed, "People who come here are culturally connected." She feared that, in 1993, Denver's African-American population was too dispersed to support a cultural center. She also recognized that there was strength in numbers: a larger concentration of attractive African-American businesses could serve as a catalyst for cultural connections.

> I'd like to create an Afrocentric Marketplace and position it as a minimall. So I bought this building 2 years ago. The other rented spaces in this building are complementary product

lines. One sells African clothing and cloth and accessories and the other is an art gallery. I'd eventually like to work with them to make it a coffee shop also. The rent is fixed, it's stable, so they aren't going to deal with escalating rent costs. I offer limited services; I maintain the property, but we work cooperatively. I know the bookstore is the anchor. They each have their own customer base, but we feed off of each other. We want to create a synergy that will create more traffic for everyone. I'm working on joint PR [with the clothing store and the art gallery].

Around the corner from the Hue-Man Experience Bookstore was another row-house building, which faced the side street. The first floor of this building housed an artists' co-op, a store that sold blues tapes, a custom hat shop, and a caterer. Rents were about $4 per square foot (per year), or $400 per month for each tenant. Three of the leases were month-to-month contracts. The second floor was boarded up and un-inhabitable due to fire damage several years before.

In September 1993, this building went up for sale. By December 1993, the asking price had been reduced from $150,000 to $95,000. The roof had recently been re-paired, but needed replacement. The building would need extensive renovation, esti-mated as high as $200,000, for the upstairs to be used for retail space. One prospec-tive buyer estimated that a new floor could be put in for about $50,000, after which the upstairs could be used as storage.

The Mayor's Office of Economic Redevelopment had targeted the Five Points area for low-interest redevelopment loans. Clara believed that there was potential for a lot of retail activity in this area, but that it would be slow in coming. A light rail transit system, connecting Five Points to downtown, was scheduled to open in Octo-ber 1994.

> I had hoped that the catering operation [around the corner] would also serve food, but she just wants to cater, and my suspicion is that they're not stable tenants. The top floor of the building needs to be renovated for retail or office space. I think the purchase is still an option.

Clara Villarosa was confident that she could get financing for expansion without diluting her ownership in the business. Business loan rates were going for as low as 10 percent. But, even if she could obtain the building at less than the current asking price, she was not sure that this would be a prudent investment. At this point in her life, Clara was particularly concerned about the income potential of any expansion ef-fort. At the same time, she didn't want to give up her dream of creating an Afrocentric Marketplace with national recognition.

http://www.hue-man.com/

STRATEGIC ANALYSIS

CASE 17

Akron Zoological Park, 1994*

As the United States approached the twenty-first century, zoos were perceived as custodians of the cultural wildlife heritage and educators of the skills of conservation. A single zoo could maintain a collection of about 1,500 species of rare and endangered birds and animals. However, a collection of this size represented less than one-half of 1 percent of the species that were expected to become extinct during the next 10 years. Zoos were expected to inform and educate the public.

Zoos were a strong attraction for people of the United States. Each year more people visited zoos than entered the U.S. National Parks. Collectively, more people attended North American zoological facilities and programs than the combined number of persons who attended professional football, basketball, baseball, and hockey games. Zoos have remained a strong attraction for the people of the United States.

During 1991, member institutions of the American Association of Zoological Parks and Aquariums (AAZPA) collectively had 105,903,570 visitors; over $798 million in operating budgets; $441,842,396 in combined capital improvements; 4,241,869 support organization members; over 25,633 acres in parklands; and more than 493,620 specimens from among various species of mammals, birds, reptiles, amphibians, fish, and invertebrates.

Zoological parks, aquariums, and botanical gardens came in all sizes. For example, the largest institution had 4,300,000 visitors and an annual operating budget of $50 million. The smallest institution had 3,000 visitors. Another had a $96,325 budget. Approximately 37 percent of AAZPA member institutions had annual operating budgets of less than $1 million. However, 22 percent had budgets in excess of $6 million. The association, at its 1989 annual meeting, awarded membership to the Akron Zoological Park, in Akron, Ohio. This recognition established that the zoo was one of the best 160 institutions in the Western Hemisphere.

During the late 1970s in Akron, a depressed local economy caused by changes in consumer preferences for radial automobile tires, the internationalization of the rubber industry, the economic ravages of rapidly increasing general price levels, and changes in government priorities almost resulted in the permanent closing of the

*This case was prepared by F. Bruce Simmons, III, of The University of Akron in Ohio, College of Business Administration, as a basis for class discussion rather than to illustrate either effective or ineffective handling of an administrative situation. The cooperation and assistance of the Akron Zoological Park and the people who have commented on various drafts of this case are acknowledged and appreciated. Copyright © 1995 by F. Bruce Simmons, III. All rights reserved to the author.

Akron Children's Zoo. Sagging attendance and a low level of family memberships did not help matters. Faced with the uncertain prospect of continuing its zoo operations, the City of Akron sought to reduce, or eliminate, its financial commitment. As a response, the Akron Zoological Park was organized as an eleemosynary operation under Section 501(c)3 of the Internal Revenue Code. The Board of Trustees then contracted with the city to operate the zoo.

During the 1980s a number of changes significantly affected the major employers in the Akron area. For example, Firestone was purchased by Bridgestone; General Tire changed its name and sold off its broadcasting affiliates and its tire operations; Michelin acquired the combined Uniroyal-Goodrich company; and Goodyear had to sell several of its divisions to fend off an attempted takeover. In the 1980s and 1990s many area corporations delayered, destaffed, and moved to operating under the just-in-time manufacturing philosophy.

HISTORY

Residents of Akron, like people in many other cities, created their zoo by donating animals to their city. Earlier this century, two brown bears were given to the city of Akron. The city fathers constructed an appropriate facility in a neighborhood park. Subsequently, other individuals established a Museum of Natural History near the Perkins Park bears. In 1953, both facilities were combined to create the Akron Children's Zoo. By the late 1970s the city's ability and willingness to satisfactorily husband its animals was questioned. The future of the zoo as a community resource and its continuing operation were in grave danger. In response to this turmoil, the trustees of the Akron Zoological Park contracted with the city to manage and operate the zoo.

While contemplating the future direction of the zoo, and mindful of the severe financial constraints, the zoo's trustees decided to restrict their animal husbandry to North, South, and Central American birds, animals, and reptiles. The older exhibits which displayed the animals in caged exhibits (i.e., Mother Goose style) were eliminated. They were replaced by more natural, native animal environments. These animal exhibits contained the zoo's collection of 183 specimens which represent 66 different species of birds, reptiles, and animals.

During the latter part of the 1980s, the zoo expanded its operations. Although it continued to follow the Western Hemisphere exhibits policy, the zoo opened an animal clinic, renovated its "petting zoo" barnyard, and constructed a gift shop, an alpaca exhibit, a concessions area, a reptile building, and a North American River Otter exhibit. New maintenance facilities and educational display areas were built. Also, the zoo has completed phase one of its educational signs installation.

PURPOSE

The mission of the Akron Zoological Park was to manage its resources for the recreation and education of the people of Akron and surrounding communities and to promote the conservation of wildlife. To be successful, the Akron Zoological Park had to maintain its image as a quality place where its visitors desired to spend time. Zoo personnel sought to keep animal exhibits clean and neat so that they were easy for all to see and enjoy. Throughout the park, flowers and plants were abundant. As resources became available for construction and continuing operations, the zoo added new exhibits and new activities. As a result, attendance increased from 63,034 people in 1986 to a record 133,762 in 1988. As a unique institution, the Akron Zoological Park presented a balanced program of education, recreation, conservation, and scientific activities.

OPERATING SEASON

Because of Akron's northern climate, the zoo was open only from mid-April until mid-October. During the winter months the zoo reopened for 1 week at Halloween and then again for the month of December. During December the zoo was decked out with more than 150,000 Christmas lights. The zoo had a shorter operating season than did many of the other local attractions.

In addition, zoo activities were very dependent on the weather. For example, during 1990 the Akron area experienced the wettest weather in its recorded history. The area received more than 57 inches of rain and snow. Other areas, such as New Orleans, Louisiana; San Juan, Puerto Rico; Miami, Florida; and Mobile, Alabama, were among the lush locales that typically experienced such wet weather. The 1990 precipitation far exceeded even the spring 1989 record. In addition, December 1989 broke local records for the coldest temperatures, the lowest windchill factors, and the most snow. Because of the extreme cold and snow, zoo officials canceled several evenings of the Holiday Lights. Attendance at this event in 1988 was over 48,000. In December 1989 attendance was less than 21,000. Exhibit 1 shows annual attendance at the zoo.

EXHIBIT 1
Akron Zoological Park: Annual Attendance

| Year | Total | Admission Fee | | |
		Adult	Child	Group
1994	134,605	$4.00	$3.00	$2.00
1993	108,659	4.00	3.00	1.50
1992	117,874	4.00	2.50	1.50
1991	125,363	3.00	2.00	1.00
1990	126,853	3.00	2.00	1.50
1989	108,363	2.50	1.50	1.00
1988	133,762	2.50	1.50	1.00
1987	95,504	2.00	1.00	0.50
1986	63,034	1.50	0.75	0.50
1985	63,853	1.50	0.75	0.50
1984	61,417	1.50	0.75	0.50
1983	53,353	1.50	0.75	0.50

Source: Akron Zoological Park, 1995.

Variations in weather also affected crop yields and thus prices of fresh animal foods. A drought in 1988 and too much rain in 1989 and again in 1990 impacted the cost of feeding and sheltering the zoo's animals. In less extreme climatic circumstances the zoo might have been able to achieve target attendance goals. The zoo sought to attract an annual attendance equal to 40 percent of its community. The attendance goal, however, may have been too ambitious. The surrounding community had experienced a declining population level from 524,472 people in 1980 to 514,990 people in 1990. In addition, the target audience for any zoological park tended to be young children and their parents. Yet the Akron community contained a high percentage (approximately two-fifths) of senior citizens. In spite of the demographics, the zoo's annual attendance had doubled since 1983. Observers suggested that the attendance increase occurred because the zoo had become better known as an innovative community resource.

MEMBERSHIP

Membership in the Akron Zoological Park was available to all. Zoo members enjoyed unlimited, no-charge admission to the zoo grounds during the operating season plus reciprocal admission at over 130 zoological parks, aquariums, and botanical gardens. In addition, members received a quarterly newsletter and invitations to members-only events. There were different types of memberships including family, grandparent, donor, patron, zookeeper, safari leader, and director's club. Each type of membership reflected different levels of financial support for zoo activities. Over the decade of the 1980s the number of memberships had increased significantly (see Exhibit 2).

EXHIBIT 2
Akron Zoological Park: Annual Memberships

Year	Total
1994	2,695
1993	2,695
1992	2,021
1991	1,825
1990	1,365
1989	1,100
1988	1,158
1987	1,200
1986	1,036
1985	1,295
1984	986
1983	492
1982	437
1981	312
Cumulative	19,122
Mean	1,366

Source: Akron Zoological Park, 1995.

As the variety and number of zoo activities increased during the decade, membership and attendance more than doubled.

Zoo management felt that providing good customer service for the zoo's clientele paid dividends. Customer service included the provision of exciting events at the zoo. As indicated in Exhibit 3, the zoo promoted several special events during 1992. These events attracted community media recognition. In turn, the community attention resulted in increased annual memberships.

EDZOOCATORS

"Edzoocators" was the name given to the unpaid volunteer group begun in the 1970s. Edzoocators were trained to provide on-site and off-grounds educational programs using the zoo's birds, reptiles, and other animals. The Edzoocators provided guided tours of the zoo grounds, gave presentations at local schools, provided a speakers' bureau, and appeared on radio and television programs. In return they received free admission to the zoo grounds. These volunteers had no responsibility for the direct operations of the zoo. In 1983 the zoo created the position of Education Curator. One aspect of this position was to coordinate the Edzoocators' activities.

EXHIBIT 3
Akron Zoological Park: Special Events in 1992

Activity	*Month*
Snow Bowl	January
Spring Fling	April
Earth Day observance	April
Super Saturday and Keep Akron Beautiful	May
Beastly Black and White Blast	May
Akron Zoo Day at the Cleveland Stadium	May
Sunday Sundae: Zoobilation	June
Recycle with Ohio Zoos	June
Nature Train	June
Zoo Camp	June
Reptile Day	July
Nocturnal Golf Classic	August
Spots and Stripes Celebration	August
Members' Night	September
Boo at the Zoo	October
Annual Birdseed Sale	October
Downtown Yule Display	November
Holiday Lights Celebration	December
Zoorific Birthday Parties	May–September

Source. Akron Zoological Park, 1992

EXHIBIT 14
Akron Zoological Park: Statement of Support, Revenue, Expenses and Changes in Fund Balances for the Years Ended December 31, 1994, 1993, 1992, 1991, 1990, 1989, 1988

	1994	1993	1992	1991	1990	1989	1988
Support and revenue:							
City of Akron grant	$ 250,000	$242,000	$230,000	$200,000	$180,000	$180,000	$175,000
City services in kind	111,685	84,014	145,237	124,915	58,597	55,367	51,160
Donations	129,212	83,805	107,007	111,640	152,289	155,143	227,102
Admissions	224,239	181,815	207,803	198,505	167,307	109,523	113,840
Concessions	106,540	81,553	94,638	87,441	76,788	55,177	54,419
Memberships	95,410	91,229	53,733	48,736	38,800	27,247	24,666
Interest	15,757	12,767	12,798	31,124	32,112	22,291	15,634
Total revenue	$ 932,843	$777,183	$851,216	$802,361	$705,893	$604,748	$661,821
Expenses:							
Program:							
Animal care	$ 174,649	$142,428	$161,362	$131,057	$133,819	$127,410	$113,037
Buildings and grounds	344,138	295,074	318,393	289,746	233,121	189,763	169,870
Cost of concessions	33,357	22,249	23,200	25,124	13,489	14,267	14,434
Education	72,428	52,444	49,022	39,117	26,510	28,509	22,699
Strategic planning	0	0	0	0	0	3,838	0
Visitor services	101,787	72,451	82,130	74,133	0	0	0
	$ 726,359	$584,646	$634,107	$559,177	$406,939	$363,787	$320,040
Supporting:							
Administration	$ 112,439	$141,767	$201,099	$168,477	$228,391	$206,217	$175,426
Promotion	118,092	99,890	85,570	57,816	8,277	15,795	23,903
Legal and accounting	5,100	5,850	4,048	4,200	3,540	3,522	3,401
	$ 235,631	$247,507	$290,717	$230,493	$240,208	$225,534	$202,730
Total expenses	$ 961,990	$832,153	$924,824	$789,670	$647,147	$589,321	$522,770
Capital additions:							
Contributions utilized	$ 584,542	$ 78,400					
Excess (deficiency) of support and revenue over expenses	$ 555,395	$ 23,430	($ 73,608)	$ 12,691	$ 58,746	$ 15,427	$139,051
Operating fund balance: beginning of year	725,562	702,132	775,740	763,049	704,303	688,876	549,825
Operating fund balance: end of year	$1,280,957	$725,562	$702,132	$775,740	$763,049	$704,303	$688,876

Source: Akron Zoological Park.

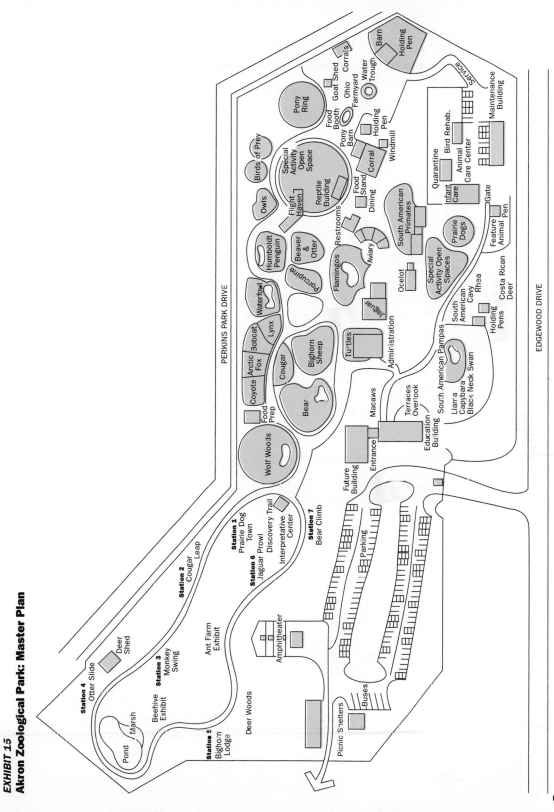

EXHIBIT 15
Akron Zoological Park: Master Plan

C251

EXHIBIT 16
Akron Zoological Park: Visitors Survey, December 1989

Primary Competitors

Other Attractions Visited in 1989	Percent
Cleveland Zoo	51.8
Sea World	45.2
Stan Hywet Hall and Gardens	41.2
Hale Farm and Village	32.2
Geauga Lake Park Amusements	31.2

Reasons Not to Attend

Multiple Reasons Given	Percent
Lack of time	27.2
Not personally able	16.7
Do not like zoos	16.3
No interest	13.6
Kids are grown	12.2
Unable to supply an answer	12.0
Transportation problems	6.1
Unsafe urban neighborhood	2.4
New to area	1.7

Preferred New Projects

New Projects	Response Ranking
Build exhibits for children	First (tie)
Add a railroad	First (tie)
Bring back the bears	Second
Add small cats	Third
Add more monkeys	Fourth

Source: The University of Akron Survey Reseach Center Project Report.

---

also make changes. For example, the terrain hindered access to the grounds for the handicapped and disabled. Also, to improve zoo access, the zoo needed to improve washroom facilities.

Other issues also impacted on the zoo. For example, on special-events days, the crowds numbered 3,000 or more. At such times, parking was inadequate. The zoo did have some space within its fenced perimeter where it could expand parking. Further, by expanding out into the grounds of Perkins Park, the zoo could double its size.

During 1989 the zoo contracted with the University of Akron to conduct a study of zoo customers. The study was based on telephone interviews and consisted of a large sample of 757 usable responses. The survey results are summarized in Exhibit 16.

FUTURE CONSIDERATIONS

Zoos, aquariums, and botanical gardens were evolving away from their origins in the museum community. They had become caretakers of life in an age of extinction. They focused on life and its diverse forms. The employees and board members were concerned about the Akron zoo's future viability, prosperity, and perspective. The various issues provided multiple strategic and operational dilemmas.

Although the zoo made it through these turbulent and difficult times, its President and CEO remained mindful that past achievements did not guarantee future survival. Under the guidance of this CEO, the zoo expanded its operations and facilities, increased its annual attendance, and received AAZPA accreditation. In order to keep the zoo open and financially solvent, the CEO believed she needed to develop more animal exhibits, restroom facilities, parking spaces, and community outreach programs. At the same time, she balanced the costs of this approach with the flows of operating revenues. This approach presented a dilemma. To expand and to construct new exhibits would increase admissions, but it would require increases in both capital and operating funds. Further, extra exhibits could mean that customers would remain longer in the zoo and would likely purchase more concessions and souvenirs. Continued pursuit of its educational and recreational objectives could become a financial burden. Failure to follow its expansion strategy would risk organizational decline and acceptance of the uncertainty of funding. Zoo executive management would not accept secondary community status. What recommendations would you make?

http://www.neo.lrun.com/Akron_Zoological_Park/

STRATEGIC ANALYSIS

CASE 18

Handguns at Wal-Mart*

In the week of December 13, 1993, Wal-Mart President and CEO, David Glass, learned that the store was being sued for negligence in a handgun sale. Wal-Mart was accused of selling a .38-caliber handgun to a mentally-ill man who later brutally murdered his parents. With this new development in a troublesome product category, internal debate over the company's handgun sales policy heated up. Then, on Friday, December 17, when a couple was gunned down in a Wal-Mart parking lot, the debate came to a head.

Events of the preceding six months suggested to management that Wal-Mart should reconsider its policy of selling handguns. Wal-Mart sold handguns in 700 of its 2,022 stores; sales were estimated at $29 million in 1992. Yet it had become increasingly evident that Wal-Mart's handgun sales could expose the company to a substantial legal liability. Wal-Mart's public image also was harmed by incidents connecting the retailer to handgun violence. Polls showed that public opinion was turning abruptly against handguns and that shoppers increasingly did not like shopping for everyday goods in a store that sold handguns. Finally, the so-called Brady Law would soon take effect, imposing a five-day waiting period for handgun purchases and increasing the paperwork for handgun retailers. In the light of these developments, Wal-Mart's management, which had a history of refusing to sell morally questionable products, had to decide what to do with its pistol and revolver product lines.

WAL-MART STORES, INC.

In 1993, Wal-Mart Stores, Inc., based in Bentonville, Arkansas, was the country's largest and fastest-growing retailer. As of January 1993, the company operated 1,880 Wal-Mart discount stores, 256 Sam's wholesale clubs, 64 Bud's warehouse outlets, 4 Hypermart USA hypermarkets, and two distribution subsidiaries, McLane Company,

---

*Todd E. Himstead and Andrew Libuser of Georgetown University Business School prepared this case from public sources under the supervision of Professor N. Craig Smith as the basis for class discussion rather than to illustrate either effective or ineffective handling of an administrative situation. Copyright Todd E. Himstead, Andrew Libuser, and N. Craig Smith, 1995.

Inc., and Western Merchandisers, Inc. By December 1993, the number of discount stores had grown to 2,022. The company operated Wal-Mart stores in 45 states and Puerto Rico, with the highest concentration in the mid-western and southeastern United States. Its revenues in 1992 were $55.5 billion, net income was $2.0 billion, and its 3.6 percent profit margin well exceeded the 2.7 percent retailing industry average. On January 31, 1993, the company had approximately 434,000 full- and part-time employees. Founder Sam Walton had died in 1992, leaving his family with 40 percent ownership in the company. Walton had been well-known for his personal involvement in each store's operations and for having a strong interest in his employees.

Wal-Mart stores typically had thirty-six departments, including apparel, curtains, fabrics and notions, shoes, housewares, hardware, electronics, home furnishings, small appliances, automotive accessories, garden equipment and supplies, toys and sporting goods, cameras and supplies, health and beauty aids, pharmaceuticals, and jewelry. In 1992, the toys and sportings goods department, which included firearms, represented 10 percent of sales.

One of Wal-Mart's key strengths was its purchasing power. Virtually all purchasing and merchandising decisions for stores were controlled from the home office through centralized buying and planning practices. Wal-Mart's success also was attributed to its use of information systems and its strengths in distribution. During the 1993 fiscal year, approximately 77 percent of inventory was sent to stores from Wal-Mart's twenty-two distribution centers while the remainder was shipped directly from suppliers. The company bought in huge volumes and yet could still reach its rural locations with reliable deliveries.

Wal-Mart received much press attention for its propensity to boycott morally sensitive products, a practice typically attributed to listening to customers' wants, which it considered another key strength. For example, the company refused to distribute the following products: the November 1993 issue of *Cosmopolitan* magazine, which bore on its cover the headline "A Matter of Pride: Being a Gay Woman in the 90s"; rock group Nirvana's *In Utero* album, which contained a song called "Rape Me"; and Madonna's *Sex* book, which included photographs of nude men and women, bestiality, and sadomasochism.

FIREARM RETAILING

Firearm retailing was the epitome of a fragmented industry. In 1993, there were approximately 284,000 licensed firearm dealers in the U.S., of which only 20,000 constituted actual stores. Of the stores, more than half were pawnbrokers. Dealers without stores sold guns out of homes and at gun shows and flea markets. To qualify for a dealer's license, an applicant had to pay $10 annually and could not be a convicted felon.

Definitive firearm statistics were not compiled. U.S. federal law prohibited the government from collecting information on firearm sales. Industry analysts estimated that retail firearm sales in 1992 totaled about $1.5 billion, which comprised $488 million for rifles, $433 million for shotguns, and $579 million for handguns. This latter figure reflected the sale of approximately 6 million handguns. Markups from manufacturer to retail could run from 75 to 125 percent; with markups from manufacturer to distributor around 40 to 45 percent, from distributor to retailer around 10 to 15 percent, and from retailer to consumer around 15 to 25 percent.

It was estimated that there were around 200 million firearms owned by consumers in 1992, including 60 million handguns. Sales in the general firearm category were projected to continue growing at a 15 percent annual rate—though there had been a 51 percent increase in handgun sales in 1992 over 1991, an increase attributed largely to concern about pending legislation intended to restrict gun sales.

In 1992, big discount retail chains, the largest of which were Wal-Mart and Kmart, accounted for between 15 to 20 percent of firearm sales. Many retailers, including Target Stores, Sears, Roebuck, J. C. Penney, Montgomery Ward, and Ames Department Stores, had ceased carrying firearms since 1980, citing low profitability, regulatory complexity, excessive paperwork and concern about growing firearm violence. A spokesperson for Sport-Mart commented: "We believe in constitutional rights, but we don't want to be part of the problem. . . . We don't want it [a firearm] to be an impulse item." Kmart stopped selling handguns in its flagship stores, but continued selling rifles and shotguns; it continued to sell handguns through its wholly-owned specialty store subsidiary, Sports Authority. It was estimated that Wal-Mart's market share in 1992 was approximately 5 percent (by value) of the handgun market (the largest share of any retailer) and 7 percent (by value) of the rifle and shotgun market.

Gun regulation varied from state to state, but, in general, dealers were required to have customers complete two forms: one for state police and one for the Federal Bureau of Alcohol, Tobacco and Firearms (BATF). Federal law 18 U.S.C. 921-928 required handgun buyers to file a form (ATF F 4473) providing personal information (name, address, sex, height, weight, race, date and place of birth) and asserting that they were not prohibited from buying firearms. Buyers had to certify that they were not prohibited from purchasing or possessing a firearm by answering "no" to each of the following questions:

- Are you under indictment in any court for a crime punishable by imprisonment for a term exceeding one year?

- Have you been convicted in any court of a crime punishable by imprisonment for a term exceeding one year?

- Are you a fugitive from justice?

- Are you an unlawful user of, or addicted to, marijuana, or a depressant, stimulant, or narcotic drug?

- Have you ever been adjudicated mentally defective or have you ever been committed to a mental institution?

- Have you been discharged from the Armed Forces under dishonorable conditions?

- Are you an alien illegally in the United States?

- Are you a person who, having been a citizen of the United States, has renounced his citizenship?

The buyer was warned that false oral or written statements or exhibiting false or misrepresented identification with respect to the transaction was a felony offense. The seller was required to establish the identity, place of residence, and age of the buyer; typically by inspection of a driver's license. The seller also recorded the type, model, caliber or gauge, serial number and manufacturer of the firearm sold, as well as the seller's federal firearm license number. Multiple purchases (two or more pistols and/or revolvers at one time or during five consecutive business days) required completion of an additional form (ATF F 3310.4).

The paperwork was complex and the BATF believed it especially burdened large, discount stores where sales clerks tended to move between departments. Sears, Roebuck and Company had stopped selling handguns in its stores and catalog in 1963 and other firearms in the early 1980s. A Sears spokesperson commented: "It got too complicated. . . . It became a burden because the regulations vary between states and the federal government."

Firearms were specifically excluded from the Consumer Product Safety Act. However, gun dealers could be held liable for careless sales even when the above legal requirements were observed, as well as for more obviously negligent or reckless sales. Legal liability had become an increasingly important issue for retailers. In 1980, an Arkansas court had established that a retailer has a duty to avoid selling a gun if it has reason to know that the purchaser is likely to harm himself/herself or others. In 1985, a Maryland court ruled that manufacturers and marketers (including retailers) of so-called "Saturday night specials" may be held strictly liable to innocent persons who suffered injuries from criminal use of the guns. The plaintiff had sought strict liability for all handguns, contending that making and selling handguns is an "abnormally dangerous activity" and handguns are "abnormally dangerous products." In restricting its ruling to Saturday night specials, the Maryland Court of Appeals held that the manufacturer or marketer of such a gun "knows or ought to know that the chief use of the product is for criminal activity." The National Rifle Association disputed this assertion, citing self-defense uses.

In 1989, a $1.5 million jury verdict was awarded against Kmart in the Michigan Supreme Court. The case stemmed from the sale of shotgun shells to a "visibly intoxicated person." While no statute specifically prohibited the sale, it violated the common law duty of the dealer to avoid such negligent acts. In a Virginia court in 1992, for the first time, damages were awarded against a gun shop for a "straw sale." The real buyer was a 15-year-old high school student who eventually used the 9mm semi-automatic pistol to kill a teacher during a rampage at the school. Testimony was provided by the straw purchaser himself, who told jurors his 15-year-old cousin accompanied him to the store and selected the weapon in full view of the clerk. According to Larry Weindruck, a spokesperson for the National Sporting Goods Association, "there's an awful lot of liability" associated with retailing handguns.

ARGUMENTS FOR AND AGAINST RETAILER SALES OF HANDGUNS[1]

It was well-established that companies marketing potentially dangerous products, like handguns, should bear some responsibility for consumer safety. Legislation had been

[1]This section is based largely on Charles P. Cozic and Carol Wekesser (ed.), *Gun Control* (San Diego, Greenhaven Press, Inc.: 1992) and "Guns in America," *The Economist*, March 26, 1994, pp. 23–28.

introduced accordingly. However, critics of government regulation argued that the individual consumer was responsible for his or her own safety. They supported protecting and strengthening individual rights in the face of a "paternalistic" society, wherein individual decisions were in danger of being controlled by the government's views of the individual's best interests.

While over 20,000 gun laws had been enacted in the United States to combat gun violence, the frequency of gun-related violence continued to grow. Given the apparent failure of existing gun control laws, opponents concluded that controls could not work, while proponents suggested better enforcement of existing laws or trying different kinds of controls. Several national organizations participated in the gun control debate. The most prominent gun control opponent group was the National Rifle Association (NRA) and its 3.3 million members. Gun control advocacy groups included Handgun Control, Inc., and the Coalition to Stop Gun Violence.

The outcome of the debate on legislation governing gun control would ultimately influence the retailer's burden of compliance with regulations on gun sale. Moreover, the main arguments used by groups for and against gun control also coincided with major arguments for and against retailer sales of handguns. More specifically, the effects of guns on crime and the role of guns in self-defense were important considerations for any responsible retailer in deciding whether to sell handguns. In addition, beliefs about the constitutionality of gun control would at least influence the reaction of some stakeholder groups to a retailer's changes in its handgun sales policy, if not the firm's management.

Handguns and Crime

In the light of growing handgun violence, many Americans were concerned about the ready availability of handguns. In 1991, there were over 22,500 homicides and 30,900 suicides in the United States. Firearms accounted for 15,000 of the homicides and 18,000 of the suicides. Of these, approximately 12,000 homicides and 15,000 suicides involved handguns (there were less than 100 handgun-related murders in Britain, Canada, or Japan). Recent polls showed that 80 to 90 percent of Americans wanted handguns registered and owners licensed. As the result of public concern, Congress and state legislators were considering a new flurry of bills that would limit the sale and use of firearms, especially handguns and assault rifles.

Americans owned a greater number of firearms than citizens of any other Western democracy, and they also used their guns against one another for murder at least 100 times more often than in Japan, Britain, or Australia. More Americans had died from domestic gun use than from all American wars dating back to and including the Revolutionary War of 1776. Although handguns made up only about one-third of firearms in the United States, they accounted for roughly 80 percent of firearm homicides.

Many victims of gun violence viewed guns as threatening, dangerous objects that must be strictly controlled or even banned. Sarah Brady, wife of shot Reagan assistant Jim Brady and chair of Handgun Control, Inc., said to the organization's members: "your continued support and commitment are essential to the success of our fight to save lives by restricting access to guns." People who used guns for protection or sport, however, viewed firearms as useful objects that every American had a right to own. Indeed, as

U.S. President Bill Clinton commented, "I can still remember the first day when I was a little boy out in the country, putting a can on top of a fence post and shooting a .22 [gun] at it." Besides, the manufacture and distribution of firearms by American companies produced economic benefits in the form of commerce and employment.

Gun control supporters often cited studies that indicated firearms were frequently used impulsively, against oneself or others, causing unintentional or intentional injuries and deaths. A study relating Canadian and U.S. homicide rates to their respective gun control policies concluded that the more strict Canadian gun controls resulted in lower murder and accidental death rates. Because of various socio-economic factors, black Americans were eight times more likely to be murdered and one and one half times more likely to suffer aggravated assault than white Americans. In 1992, homicide was the leading cause of death among blacks, aged 15–24; it ranked third among whites of the same age group. It was argued that a decrease in the number of guns in America would reduce the number of crimes committed against blacks.

Others argued that guns did not commit murder and violence; the humans who wielded them irresponsibly did. In fact, gun ownership had little to do with crime. Studies showed that at least 98 percent of gun-owning American adults never became involved in unlawful homicides. Only by removing the causes of crime—poverty and injustice—would violent crime decrease. Studies conducted in New Orleans, Detroit, and Kennesaw, Georgia, showed that serious crime rates plummeted when more people owned guns and were trained in their use. Some argued that reduced availability of guns could even increase crime. Criminals would still obtain guns illegally, while law-abiding citizens would relinquish their weapons and consequently be vulnerable to crime. At Dave's Firearms in Richmond, Virginia, a spokesperson said: "You'll never stop those guns. They come in with the [illegal] drugs."

Gun control opponents also argued that no confiscation effort, however broad or stringent, would disarm hardened criminals, political terrorists, or killers. Many believed the demand for guns could not be legislated away. Also, they suggested that arguments blaming accidents on the misuse of firearms missed the point. Accidents actually called for more safety training and more stringent owner liability for negligence; they were not arguments for restricting gun sales.

Guns and Self-Defense

The relationship between guns and self-defense was also an important consideration in a retailer's decision whether to sell guns. Gun control advocates cited research that showed the home handgun was far more likely to kill or injure family members and friends than anyone who broke into the home and was especially harmful to young adults and children. Guns were used in suicides, homicides, or accidental deaths far more often than for self-defense. The risk handguns posed to society in the form of accidental shootings and crimes outweighed their effectiveness in the area of self-defense. Moreover, without proper training, gun owners, when threatened, often found themselves unable to use the firearm, for either physical or psychological reasons. Often they were disarmed and the weapon used against them. Gun control proponents argued that guns were an illusory means of home protection.

On the other hand, it was also argued that handguns were frequently used in self-defense to prevent or deter crime. The NRA, in particular, claimed over two million protective uses of firearms annually. It was suggested that handguns were used more by law-abiding citizens to repel crime than by criminals to perpetrate crime. Retailer decisions to end gun sales could leave law-abiding people unarmed, but not the criminals. It was argued that because the police could not be everywhere, people needed guns to protect themselves and that many more criminals were killed or wounded each year by armed citizens protecting themselves than by the police. Reduced availability of guns might especially endanger blacks and other minorities; because many minority Americans lived in dangerous, crime-ridden communities, guns were believed to be necessary forms of self-defense.

Gun Control and the Constitution

Of central importance to the gun control debate was the constitutionality of gun control. The Second Amendment, in the Bill of Rights of the United States Constitution, reads, in full: "A well regulated Militia being necessary to the security of a free State, the right of the people to keep and bear Arms, shall not be infringed." It was reasonable to assume that the Second Amendment would be familiar to most Wal-Mart customers who approved of its sale of handguns and to many, if not most, of those opposed.

Gun control advocates interpreted the Second Amendment to allow states to keep militia for their protection against the threat of tyrannical federal governments. As such, individuals did not thereby have the right to keep and bear arms. Hence, the federal government could regulate, to the point of prohibition if necessary, private ownership of guns, since that has nothing to do with preserving state militia. Moreover, changes to American society had altered the role of guns in society. In contrast to the time of the Second Amendment, daily life no longer required guns for hunting or protection in an ordered society. Professional police forces protected individuals. Conditions were such that public ownership of guns threatened, not protected, public safety.

The constitutionality of gun control had been addressed by several court cases in the previous 200 years. These cases all supported the constitutionality of controls on gun sale, purchase, and use. Gun control advocates noted that if the amendment was interpreted to include all citizens and all "arms," convicted murderers and lunatics would be able to access such "arms" as nuclear weapons.

On the other hand, gun control opponents interpreted the Second Amendment to preserve the individual's right to keep and bear arms so that people could protect their absolute individual rights as well as carry out their obligations to assist in the common defense. Not only was the right of the people to keep and bear arms observed prior to the Constitution; the Framers of the Constitution intended to ensure the continued existence of an "unorganized" armed citizenry prepared to assist in the common defense against a foreign invader or a domestic tyrant. In addition, should a tyrannical power overtake the nation, Americans would be able to defend themselves. Because this danger always existed, many opposed gun control.

In sum, it was not clear if handguns constituted a net benefit or harm to society. Gun control advocates and their opponents presented provocative arguments and studies intended to shift government policies to favor their vision of proper handgun marketing. Wal-Mart had found itself embroiled in this debate. It had to decide how arguments about the effects of guns on crime and their possible role in self-defense

Further, with the high cost of each machine and the fast rate of model introductions, Xerox developed a strategy of leasing rather than selling machines to customers. Various options were available, but typically the customers paid a monthly charge on the number of copies made. The charge covered not only machine costs but also those of the paper and toner that Xerox supplied and the service visits. This lease strategy, together with the carefully cultivated service image, served as key safeguards from competition, as it tied the customers into Xerox and significantly raised their switching costs.

Unlike some other American corporations, Xerox had an international orientation right from the beginning. Even before it had a successful commercial copier, Xerox built up an international presence through joint ventures which allowed the company to minimize its capital investment abroad. In 1956, it ventured with the Rank Organization Ltd. in the U.K. to form Rank Xerox. In 1962, Rank Xerox became a 50 percent partner with Fuji Photo to form Fuji Xerox, which sold copiers in Japan. Through these joint ventures, Xerox built up sales and service capabilities in these key markets similar to those it had in the United States. There were some 5,000 salespeople in Europe, 3,000 in Japan and over 7,000 and 3,000 service reps, respectively. Xerox also built limited design capabilities in both joint ventures for local market customization, which developed into significant research establishments in their own rights in later years.

Simultaneously, Xerox maintained high levels of investment in both technology and manufacturing to support its growing market. It continued to spend over $100 million a year in R&D, exceeding the total revenues from the copier business that any of its competitors were earning in the early 1970s, and also invested heavily in large-size plants not only in the U.S., but also in the U.K. and Japan.

Competition in the 1970s

Xerox's PPC patents began to expire in the 1970s, heralding a storm of new entrants. In 1970, IBM offered the first PPC copier not sold by Xerox, which resulted in Xerox suing IBM for patent infringement and violation of trade secrets. Canon marketed a PPC copier the same year through the development of an independent PPC technology which it licensed selectively to others. By 1973, competition had expanded to include players from the office equipment industry (IBM, SCM, Litton, Pitney Bowes), the electronics industry (Toshiba, Sharp), the reprographics industry (Ricoh, Mita, Copyer, 3M, A. B. Dick, Addressograph/Multigraph), the photographic equipment industry (Canon, Kodak, Minolta, Konishiroku), and the suppliers of copy paper (Nashua, Dennison, Saxon).

By the 1980s many of these new entrants, including IBM, had lost large amounts of money and exited the business. A few of the newcomers managed to achieve a high level of success, however, and copiers became a major business for them. Specifically, copiers were generating 40 percent of Canon's revenues by 1990.

Canon

Canon was founded in 1933 with the ambition to produce a sophisticated 35mm camera to rival that of Germany's world-class Leica model. In only two years' time, it had emerged as Japan's leading producer of high-class cameras. During the war, Canon utilized its optics expertise to produce an X-ray machine which was adopted by the Japanese military. After the war, Canon was able to successfully market its high-end camera, and by the mid-1950s it was the largest camera manufacturer in Japan. Building off its optics technology, Canon then expanded its product line to include a mid-range camera, an 8mm video camera, television lenses, and micrographic equipment. It also began developing markets for its products outside of Japan, mainly in the U.S. and Canada.

Diversification was always very important to Canon in order to further its growth, and a new products R&D section was established in 1962 to explore the fields of copy machines, auto-focusing cameras, strobe-integrated cameras, home VCRs, and electronic calculators. A separate, special operating unit was also established to introduce new non-camera products resulting from the diversification effort.

The first product to be targeted was the electronic calculator. This product was challenging because it required Canon engineers to develop new expertise in micro-electronics in order to incorporate thousands of transistors and diodes in a compact, desk model machine. Tekeshi Mitarai, president of Canon at that time, was against developing the product because it was seen to be too difficult and risky. Nevertheless, a dedicated group of engineers believed in the challenge and developed the calculator in secrecy. Over a year later, top management gave its support to the project. In 1964, the result of the development effort was introduced as the Canola 130, the world's first ten-key numeric pad calculator. With this product line, Canon dominated the Japanese electronic calculator market in the 1960s.

Not every diversification effort was a success, however. In 1956, Canon began development of the synchroreader, a device for writing and reading with a sheet of paper coated with magnetic material. When introduced in 1959, the product received high praise for its technology. But, because the design was not patented, another firm introduced a similar product at half the price. There was no market for the high-priced and incredibly heavy Canon product. Ultimately, the firm was forced to disassemble the finished inventories and sell off the usable parts in the "once-used" components market.

Move into Copiers

Canon began research into copier technology in 1959 and, in 1962, it formed a research group dedicated to developing a plain paper copier (PPC) technology. The only known PPC process was protected by hundreds of Xerox patents, but Canon felt that only this technology promised sufficient quality, speed, economy, and ease of maintenance to successfully capture a large portion of the market. Therefore, corporate management challenged the researchers to develop a new PPC process which would not violate the Xerox patents.

In the meantime, the company entered the copier business by licensing the "inferior" CPC technology in 1965 from RCA. Canon decided not to put the name of the company on this product and marketed it under the brand name Confax 1000 in Japan only. Three years later, Canon licensed a liquid toner technology from an Australian company and combined this with the RCA technology to introduce the CanAll Series. To sell the copier in Japan, Canon formed a separate company, International

Image Industry. The copier was sold as an OEM to Scott Paper in the U.S., who sold it under its own brand name.

Canon's research aiming at developing a PPC technical alternative to xerography paid off with the announcement of the "new process" (NP) in 1968. This successful research effort not only produced an alternative process but also taught Canon the importance of patent law: how not to violate patents and how to protect new technology. The NP process was soon protected by close to 500 patents.

The first machine with the NP technology, the NP1100, was introduced in Japan in 1970. It was the first copier sold by Canon to carry the Canon brand name. It produced 10 copies per minute and utilized dry toner. As was the standard in the Japanese market, the copier line was sold outright to customers from the beginning. After two years of experience in the domestic market, Canon entered the overseas market, except North America, with this machine.

The second generation of the NP system was introduced in Japan in 1972 as the NPL7. It was a marked improvement because it eliminated a complex fusing technology, simplified developing and cleaning, and made toner supply easier through a new system developed to use liquid toner. Compared with the Xerox equivalent, it was more economical, more compact, more reliable and still had the same or better quality of copies.

With the NP system, Canon began a sideline which was to become quite profitable: licensing. The first-generation NP system was licensed to 3M, and Canon also provided it with machines on an OEM basis. The second generation was again licensed to 3M as well as to Saxon, Ricoh, and Copyer. Canon accumulated an estimated $32 million in license fees between 1975 and 1982.

Canon continued its product introductions with a stream of state-of-the-art technological innovations throughout the seventies. In 1973 it added color to the NP system; in 1975, it added laser beam printing technology. Its first entry into high-volume copiers took place in 1978 with a model which was targeted at the Xerox 9200. The NP200 was introduced in 1979 and went on to win a gold medal at the Leipzig Fair for being the most economical and productive copier available. By 1982, copiers had surpassed cameras as the company's largest revenue generator (see Exhibits 1 and 2 for Canon's financials and sales by product line).

The Personal Copier

In the late 1970s, top management began searching for a new market for the PPC copier. Canon had recently experienced a huge success with the introduction of the AE-1 camera in 1976 and wanted a similar success in copiers. The AE-1 was a very compact single-lens reflex camera, the first camera that used a microprocessor to control electronically functions of exposure, film rewind, and strobe. The product had been developed through a focused, cross-functional project team effort which had resulted in a substantial reduction in the number of components, as well as in automated assembly and the use of unitized parts. Because of these improvements, the AE-1 enjoyed a 20 percent cost advantage over competitive models in the same class.

After studying the distribution of offices in Japan by size (see Exhibit 3), Canon decided to focus on a latent segment that Xerox had ignored. This was the segment comprised of small offices (segment E) that could benefit from the functionality of-

EXHIBIT 1
Canon, Inc.—Ten-Year Financial Summary
(in millions of yen, except per share amounts)

	1990	1989	1988	1987	1986	1985	1984	1983	1982	1981
Net sales:										
Domestic	¥ 508,747	¥ 413,854	¥ 348,462	¥ 290,382	¥ 274,174	¥ 272,966	¥ 240,656	¥ 198,577	¥ 168,178	¥ 144,898
Overseas	1,219,201	937,063	757,548	686,329	615,043	682,814	589,732	458,748	412,322	326,364
Total	¥1,727,948	¥1,350,917	¥1,106,010	¥ 976,711	¥ 889,217	¥ 955,780	¥ 830,388	¥ 657,325	¥ 580,500	¥ 471,262
Percentage to previous year	127.9%	122.1	113.2	109.8	93.0	115.1	126.3	113.2	123.2	112.5
Net income:	¥ 61,408	¥ 38,293	¥ 37,100	¥ 13,244	¥ 10,728	¥ 37,056	¥ 35,029	¥ 28,420	¥ 22,358	¥ 16,216
Percentage to sales	3.6%	2.8	3.4	1.4	1.2	3.9	4.2	4.3	3.9	3.4
Advertising expense	¥ 72,234	¥ 54,394	¥ 41,509	¥ 38,280	¥ 37,362	¥ 50,080	¥ 51,318	¥ 41,902	¥ 37,532	¥ 23,555
Research and development	86,008	75,566	65,522	57,085	55,330	49,461	38,256	28,526	23,554	14,491
Depreciation	78,351	64,861	57,627	57,153	55,391	47,440	39,995	30,744	27,865	22,732
Capital expenditure	137,298	107,290	83,069	63,497	81,273	91,763	75,894	53,411	46,208	54,532
Long-term debt	¥ 262,886	¥ 277,556	¥ 206,083	¥ 222,784	¥ 166,722	¥ 134,366	¥ 99,490	¥ 60,636	¥ 53,210	¥ 39,301
Stockholders' equity	¥ 617,566	¥ 550,841	¥ 416,465	¥ 371,198	¥ 336,456	¥ 333,148	¥ 304,310	¥ 264,629	¥ 235,026	¥ 168,735
Total assets	¥1,827,945	¥1,636,380	¥1,299,843	¥1,133,881	¥1,009,504	¥1,001,044	¥ 916,651	¥ 731,642	¥ 606,101	¥ 505,169
Per share data:										
Net income:										
Common and common equivalent share	¥78.29	¥50.16	¥51.27	¥19.65	¥16.67	¥53.38	¥53.63	¥46.31	¥41.17	¥34.04
Assuming full dilution	78.12	49.31	51.26	19.64	16.67	53.25	53.37	45.02	38.89	33.35
Cash dividends declared	12.50	11.93	11.36	9.09	11.36	11.36	9.88	9.43	8.23	7.84
Stock price:										
High	¥1,940	¥2,040	¥1,536	¥1,282	¥1,109	¥1,364	¥1,336	¥1,294	¥ 934	¥1,248
Low	1,220	1,236	823	620	791	800	830	755	417	513
Average number of common and common equivalent shares in thousands	788,765	780,546	747,059	747,053	746,108	727,257	675,153	645,473	564,349	515,593
Number of employees	54,381	44,401	40,740	37,521	35,498	34,129	30,302	27,266	25,607	24,300
Average exchange rate ($1 =)	¥143	¥129	¥127	¥143	¥167	¥235	¥239	¥238	¥248	¥222

Source: Canon 1990 Annual Report.

EXHIBIT 2
Canon—Sales by Product
(in millions of yen)

Year	Cameras	Copiers	Other Business Machines	Optical and Other Products	Total
1981	201,635	175,389	52,798	40,222	¥470,044
1982	224,619	242,161	67,815	45,905	580,500
1983	219,443	291,805	97,412	48,665	657,325
1984	226,645	349,986	180,661	73,096	830,388
1985	197,284	410,840	271,190	76,466	955,780
1986	159,106	368,558	290,630	70,923	889,217
1987	177,729	393,581	342,895	62,506	976,711
1988	159,151	436,924	434,634	75,301	1,106,010
1989	177,597	533,115	547,170	93,035	1,350,917
1990	250,494	686,077	676,095	115,282	¥1,727,948

Source: Canon Annual Report, 1981–1990.

EXHIBIT 3
Office Size Distribution, Japan 1979

Copier Market Segment	Number of Office Workers	Number of Offices	Working Population
A	300+	200,000	9,300,000
B	100–299	30,000	4,800,000
C	30–99	170,000	8,300,000
D	5–29	1,820,000	15,400,000
E	1–4	4,110,000	8,700,000

Source: Breakthrough: The Development of the Canon Personal Copier, Teruo Yamanouchi, *Long Range Planning,* Vol. 22, October 1989, p. 4.

fered by photocopiers but did not require the high-speed machines available in the market. Canon management believed that a low-volume "value for money" machine could generate a large demand in this segment. From this analysis emerged the business concept of a "personal side desk" machine which could not only create a new market in small offices, but potentially also induce decentralization of the copy function in large offices. Over time, the machine might even create demand for a personal copier for home use. This would be a copier that up to now no one had thought possible. Canon felt that, to be successful in this market, the product had to cost half the price of a conventional copier (target price $1,000), be maintenance free, and provide ten times more reliability.

Top management took its "dream" to the engineers, who, after careful consideration, took on the challenge. The machine would build off their previous expertise in microelectronics but would go much further in terms of material, functional component, design, and production engineering technologies. The team's slogan was "Let's make the AE-1 of copiers!" expressing the necessity of know-how transfer between the camera and copier divisions as well as the desire for a similar type of success. The effort was led by the director of the Reprographic Production Development Center. This cross-functional team of 200 was the second largest ever assembled at Canon (the largest had been that of the AE-1 camera).

During the development effort, a major issue arose concerning the paper size that the new copier would accept. Canon Sales (the sales organization for Japan) wanted the machine to use a larger-than-letter-size paper which accounted for 60 percent of the Japanese market. This size was not necessary for sales outside of Japan and would add 20–30 percent to the machine's cost as well as make the copier more difficult to service. After much debate worldwide, the decision was made to forgo the ability to utilize the larger paper size in the interest of better serving the global market.

Three years later the concept was a reality. The new PC (personal copier) employed a new-cartridge based technology which allowed the user to replace the photoreceptive drum, charging device, toner assembly, and cleaner with a cartridge every 2,000 copies, thus eliminating the need to maintain the copier regularly. This enabled Canon engineers to meet the cost and reliability targets. The revolutionary product was the smallest, lightest copier ever sold, and created a large market which had previously not existed. Large offices adjusted their copying strategies to include decentralized copying, and many small offices and even homes could now afford a personal copier. Again, Canon's patent knowledge was utilized to protect this research, and the cartridge technology was not licensed to other manufacturers. Canon has maintained its leadership in personal copiers into the 1990s.

BUILDING CAPABILITIES

Canon is admired for its technical innovations, marketing expertise, and low-cost quality manufacturing. These are the result of a long-term strategy to become a premier company. Canon has frequently acquired outside expertise so that it could better focus internal investments on skills of strategic importance. This approach of extensive outsourcing and focused internal development has required consistent direction from top management and the patience to allow the company to become well grounded in one skill area before tasking the organization with the next objective.

Technology

Canon's many innovative products, which enabled the company to grow quickly in the seventies and eighties, are in large part the result of a carefully orchestrated use of technology and the capacity for managing rapid technological change. Attesting to its prolific output of original research is the fact that Canon has been among the leaders in number of patents issued worldwide throughout the eighties.

These successes have been achieved in an organization that has firmly pursued a strategy of decentralized R&D. Most of Canon's R&D personnel are employed by the product divisions where 80–90 percent of the company's patentable inventions originate. Each product division has its own development center which is tasked with short- to medium-term product design and improvement of production systems. Most product development is performed by cross-functional teams. The work of the development groups is coordinated by an R&D headquarters group.

The Corporate Technical Planning and Operation center is responsible for long-term strategic R&D planning. Canon also has a main research center which supports state-of-the-art research in optics, electronics, new materials, and information technology. There are three other corporate research centers which apply this state-of-the-art research to product development.

Canon acknowledges that it has neither the resources nor the time to develop all necessary technologies and has therefore often traded or bought specific technologies from a variety of external partners. Furthermore, it has used joint ventures and technology transfers as a strategic tool for mitigating foreign trade tensions in Europe and the United States. For example, Canon had two purposes in mind when it made an equity participation in CPF Deutsch, an office equipment marketing firm in Germany. Primarily, it believed that this move would help develop the German market for its copiers; but it did not go unnoticed among top management that CPF owned Tetras, a copier maker who at that time was pressing dumping charges against Japanese copier makers. Canon also used Burroughs as an OEM for office automation equipment in order to acquire Burroughs software and know-how and participated in joint development agreements with Eastman Kodak and Texas Instruments. Exhibit 4 provides a list of the company's major joint ventures.

Canon also recognizes that its continued market success depends on its ability to exploit new research into marketable products quickly. It has worked hard to reduce the new product introduction cycle through a cross-functional program called TS 1/2 whose purpose is to cut development time by 50 percent on a continuous basis. The main thrust of this program is the classification of development projects by total time required and the critical human resources needed so that these two parameters can be optimized for each product, depending on its importance for Canon's corporate strategy. This allows product teams to be formed around several classifications of product development priorities, of which "best sellers" will receive the most emphasis. These are the products aimed at new markets or segments with large potential demands. Other classifications include products necessary to catch up with competitive offerings, product refinements intended to enhance customer satisfaction, and long-run marathon products which will take considerable time to develop. In all development classifications, Canon emphasizes three factors to reduce time to market: the fostering of engineering ability, efficient technical support systems, and careful reviews of product development at all stages.

Canon is also working to divert its traditional product focus into more of a market focus. To this end, Canon R&D personnel participate in international product strategy meetings, carry out consumer research, join in marketing activities, and attend meetings in the field at both domestic and foreign sales subsidiaries.

Marketing

Canon's effective marketing is the result of step-by-step, calculated introduction strategies. Normally, the product is first introduced and perfected in the home market

EXHIBIT 4
Canon's Major International Joint Ventures

Category	Partner	Description
Office equipment	Eastman Kodak (U.S.)	Distributes Kodak medical equipment in Japan; exports copiers to Kodak
	CPF Germany	Equity participation in CPF, which markets Canon copiers
	Olivetti (Italy)	Joint venture for manufacture of copier
	Lotte (Korea)	
Computers	Hewlett-Packard (U.S.)	Receives OEM minicomputer from HP; supplies laser printer to HP
	Apple Computer (U.S.)	Distributes Apple computers in Japan; supplies laser printer to Apple
	Next, Inc. (U.S.)	Equity participation; Canon has marketing rights for Asia
Semiconductors	National Semiconductor (U.S.)	Joint development of MPU and software for Canon office equipment
	Intel (U.S.)	Joint development of LSI for Canon copier, manufactured by Intel
Telecommunications	Siemens (Germany)	Development of ISDN interface for Canon facsimile; Siemens supplies Canon with digital PBX
	DHL (U.S.)	Equity participation; Canon supplies terminals to DHL
Camera	Kinsei Seimitsu (Korea)	Canon licenses technology on 35mm camera
Other	ECD (U.S.)	Equity participation because Canon values its research on amorphous materials

Source: Canon Asia, Nomura Management School.

before being sold internationally. Canon has learned how to capture learning from the Japanese market quickly so that the time span between introduction in Japan and abroad is as short as a few months. Furthermore, the company will not simultaneously launch a new product through a new distribution channel—its strategy is to minimize risk by introducing a new product through known channels first. New channels will only be created, if necessary, after the product has proven to be successful.

The launch of the NP copier exemplifies this strategy. Canon initially sold these copiers in Japan by direct sales through its Business Machines Sales organization, which had been set up in 1968 to sell the calculator product line. This sales organization was merged with the camera sales organization in 1971 to form Canon Sales. By 1972, after three years of experience in producing the NP product line, the company entered into a new distribution channel, that of dealers, to supplement direct selling.

The NP copier line was not marketed in the U.S. until 1974, after production and distribution were running smoothly in Japan. The U.S. distribution system was similar to that used in Japan, with seven sales subsidiaries for direct selling and a network of independent dealers.

By the late 1970s, Canon had built up a strong dealer network in the U.S. which supported both sales and service of the copiers. The dealer channel was responsible for rapid growth in copier sales, and, by the early 1980s, Canon copiers were sold almost exclusively through this channel. Canon enthusiastically supported the dealers with attractive sales incentive programs, management training, and social outings. Dealers were certified to sell copiers only after completing a course in service training. The company felt that a close relationship with its dealers was a vital asset that allowed it to understand and react to customers' needs and problems in a timely manner. At the same time, Canon also maintained a direct selling mechanism through wholly owned sales subsidiaries in Japan, the U.S., and Europe in order to target large customers and government accounts.

The introduction of its low-end personal copier in 1983 was similarly planned to minimize risk. Initially, Canon's NP dealers in Japan were not interested in the product due to its low maintenance needs and inability to utilize large paper sizes. Thus, PCs were distributed through the firm's office supply stores that were already selling its personal calculators. After seeing the success of the PC, the NP dealers began to carry the copier.

In the U.S., the PC was initially sold through existing dealers and direct sales channels due to limited availability of the product. Later, it was sold through competitors' dealers and office supply stores, and, eventually, the distribution channels were extended to include mass merchandisers. Canon already had considerable experience in mass merchandising from its camera business.

Advertising has always been an integral part of Canon's marketing strategy. President Kaku believes that Canon must have a corporate brand name which is outstanding to succeed in its diversification effort. "Customers must prefer products because they bear the name Canon," he says. As described by the company's finance director, "If a brand name is unknown, and there is no advertising, you have to sell it cheap. It's not our policy to buy share with a low price. We establish our brand with advertising at a reasonably high price."

Therefore, when the NP-200 was introduced in 1980, 10 percent of the selling price was spent on advertising; for the launch of the personal copier, advertising expenditure was estimated to be 20 percent of the selling price. Canon has also sponsored various sporting events including World Cup football, the Williams motor racing team, and the ice dancers Torvill and Dean. The company expects its current expansion into the home automation market to be greatly enhanced by the brand image it has built in office equipment (see Exhibit 1 for Canon's advertising expenditures through 1990).

Manufacturing

Canon's goal in manufacturing is to produce the best quality at the lowest cost with the best delivery. To drive down costs, a key philosophy of the production system is to organize the manufacture of each product so that the minimum amount of time, energy, and resources is required. Canon therefore places strong emphasis on tight inventory management through a stable production planning process, careful material planning, close supplier relationships, and adherence to the *kanban* system of inventory movement. Additionally, a formal waste elimination program saved Canon 177 billion yen between 1976 and 1985. Overall, Canon accomplished a 30 percent increase in productivity per year from 1976 to 1982 and over 10 percent thereafter through automation and innovative process improvements.

The workforce is held in high regard at Canon. A philosophy of "stop and fix it" empowers any worker to stop the production line if he or she is not able to perform a task properly or observes a quality problem. Workers are responsible for their own machine maintenance, governed by rules which stress prevention. Targets for quality and production and other critical data are presented to the workers with on-line feedback. Most workers also participate in voluntary "small group activity" for problem solving. The result of these systems is a workforce that feels individually responsible for the success of the products it manufactures.

Canon sponsors a highly regarded suggestion program for its workers in order to directly involve those most familiar with the work processes in improving the business. The program was originally initiated in 1952 with only limited success, but in the early 1980s, participation soared, with more than seventy suggestions per employee per year. All suggestions are reviewed by a hierarchy of committees, with monetary prizes awarded monthly and yearly depending on the importance of the suggestion. The quality and effectiveness of the process are demonstrated by a 90 percent implementation rate of the suggestions offered and corporate savings of $202 million in 1985 (against a total expenditure of $2 million in running the program, over 90 percent of it in prize money).

Canon chooses to backward integrate only on parts with unique technologies. For other components, the company prefers to develop long-term relationships with its suppliers and it retains two sources for most parts. In 1990, over 80 percent of Canon's copiers were assembled from purchased parts, with only the drums and toner being manufactured in-house. The company also maintains its own in-house capability for doing pilot production of all parts so as to understand better the technology and the vendors' costs.

Another key to Canon's high quality and low cost is the attention given to parts commonality between models. Between some adjacent copier models, the commonality is as high as 60 percent.

Copier manufacture was primarily located in Toride, Japan, in the early years but then spread to Germany; California and Virginia in the U.S.; and France, Italy, and Korea. In order to mitigate trade and investment friction, Canon is working to increase the local content of parts as it expands globally. In Europe it exceeds the EC standard by 5 percent. It is also adding R&D capability to some of its overseas operations. Mr. Kaku emphasizes the importance of friendly trading partners:

> Frictions cannot be erased by merely transferring our manufacturing facilities overseas. The earnings after tax must be reinvested in the country; we must transfer our technology to the country. This is the only way our overseas expansion will be welcomed.

LEVERAGING EXPERTISE

Canon places critical importance on continued growth through diversification into new product fields. Mr. Kaku observed,

Whenever Canon introduced a new product, profits surged forward. Whenever innovation lagged, on the other hand, so did the earnings. . . . In order to survive in the coming era of extreme competition, Canon must possess at least a dozen proprietary state-of-the-art technologies that will enable it to develop unique products.

While an avid supporter of diversification, Mr. Kaku was cautious.

In order to ensure the enduring survival of Canon, we have to continue diversifying in order to adapt to environmental changes. However, we must be wise in choosing ways toward diversification. In other words, we must minimize the risks. Entering a new business which requires either a technology unrelated to Canon's current expertise or a different marketing channel than Canon currently uses incurs a 50 percent risk. If Canon attempts to enter a new business which requires both a new technology and a new marketing channel which are unfamiliar to Canon, the risk entailed in such ventures would be 100 percent. There are two prerequisites that have to be satisfied before launching such new ventures. First, our operation must be debt-free; second, we will have to secure the personnel capable of competently undertaking such ventures. I feel we shall have to wait until the twenty-first century before we are ready.

Combining Capabilities

Through its R&D strategy, Canon has worked to build up specialized expertise in several areas and then link them to offer innovative, state-of-the-art products. Through the fifties and sixties, Canon focused on products related to its main business and expertise, cameras. This prompted the introduction of the 8mm movie camera and the Canon range of midmarket cameras. There was minimal risk because the optics technology was the same and the marketing outlet, camera shops, remained the same.

Entrance into the calculator market pushed Canon into developing expertise in the field of microelectronics, which it later innovatively combined with its optics capability to introduce one of its most successful products, the personal copier. From copiers, Canon utilized the replaceable cartridge system to introduce a successful desktop laser printer.

In the early seventies, Canon entered the business of marketing microchip semiconductor production equipment. In 1980, the company entered into the development and manufacture of unique proprietary ICs in order to strengthen further its expertise in electronics technology. This development effort was expanded in the late eighties to focus on opto-electronic ICs. According to Mr. Kaku:

We are now seriously committed to R&D in ICs because our vision for the future foresees the arrival of the opto-electronic era. When the time arrives for the opto-electronic IC to replace the current ultra-LSI, we intend to go into making large-scale computers. Presently we cannot compete with the IBMs and NECs using the ultra-LSIs. When the era of the opto-electronic IC arrives, the technology of designing the computer will be radically transformed; that will be our chance for making entry into the field of the large-scale computer.

Creative Destruction

In 1975 Canon produced the first laser printer. Over the next fifteen years, laser printers evolved as a highly successful product line under the Canon brand name. The company also provides the "engine" as an OEM to Hewlett-Packard and other laser printer manufacturers, which, when added to its own branded sales, supports a total of 84 percent of worldwide demand.

The biggest threat to the laser printer industry is substitution by the newly developed bubble jet printer. With a new technology which squirts out thin streams of ink under heat, a high-quality silent printer can be produced at half the price of the laser printer. The technology was invented accidentally in the Canon research labs. It keys on a print head which has up to 400 fine nozzles per inch, each with its own heater to warm the ink until it shoots out tiny ink droplets. This invention utilizes Canon's competencies in fine chemicals for producing the ink and its expertise in semiconductors, materials, and electronics for manufacturing the print heads. Canon is moving full steam forward to develop the bubble jet technology, even though it might destroy a business that the company dominates. The new product is even more closely tied to the company's core capabilities, and management believes that successful development of this business will help broaden further its expertise in semiconductors.

Challenge of the 1990s

Canon sees the office automation business as its key growth opportunity for the nineties. It already has a well-established brand name in home and office automation products through its offerings of copiers, facsimiles, electronic typewriters, laser printers, word processing equipment, and personal computers. The next challenge for the company is to link these discrete products into a multifunctional system which will perform the tasks of a copier, facsimile, printer, and scanner and interface with a computer so that all the functions can be performed from one keyboard. In 1988, with this target, Canon introduced a personal computer which incorporated a PC, a fax, a telephone, and a word processor. Canon has also introduced a color laser copier which hooks up to a computer to serve as a color printer. A series of additional integrated OA offerings are scheduled for introduction in 1992, and the company expects these products to serve as its growth engine in the first half of the 1990s.

MANAGING THE PROCESS

Undergirding this impressive history of continuously building new corporate capabilities and of exploiting those capabilities to create a fountain of innovative new products lies a rather unique management process. Canon has institutionalized corporate entrepreneurship through its highly autonomous and market focused business unit structure. A set of powerful functional committees provide the bridge between the entrepreneurial business units and the company's core capabilities in technology, manufacturing, and marketing. Finally, an extraordinarily high level of corporate ambition drives this innovative engine, which is fueled by the creativity of its people and by top management's continuous striving for ever higher levels of performance.

Driving Entrepreneurship: The Business Units

Mr. Kaku had promoted the concept of the entrepreneurial business unit from his earliest days with Canon, but it was not until the company had suffered significant losses in 1975 that his voice was heard. His plan was implemented shortly before he became president of the company.

Mr. Kaku believed that Canon's diversification strategy could only succeed if the business units were empowered to act on their own, free of central controls. Therefore, two independent operating units were formed in 1978, one for cameras and one for office equipment, to be managed as business units. Optical Instruments, the third business unit, had always been separate. Since that time, an additional three business units have been spun off. The original three business units were then given clear profitability targets, as well as highly ambitious growth objectives, and were allowed the freedom to devise their own ways to achieve these goals. One immediate result of this decentralization was the recognition that Canon's past practice of mixing production of different products in the same manufacturing facility would no longer work. Manufacturing was reorganized so that no plant produced more than one type of product.

Mr. Kaku describes the head of each unit as a surrogate of the CEO empowered to make quick decisions. This allows him, as president of Canon, to devote himself exclusively to his main task of creating and implementing the long-term corporate strategy. In explaining the benefits of the system, he said:

> Previously, the president was in exclusive charge of all decision making; his subordinates had to form a queue to await their turn in presenting their problems to him. This kind of system hinders the development of the young managers' potential for decision making.
>
> Furthermore, take the case of the desktop calculator. Whereas I can devote only about two hours each day to problems concerning the calculator, the CEO of Casio Calculator could devote 24 hours to the calculator. . . . In the fiercely competitive market, we lost out because our then CEO was slow in coping with the problem.

In contrast to the Western philosophy of stand-alone SBUs encompassing all functions including engineering, sales, marketing, and production, Canon has chosen to separate its product divisions from its sales and marketing arm. This separation allows for a clear focus on the challenges that Canon faces in selling products on a global scale. Through a five-year plan initiated in 1977, Seiichi Takigawa, the president of Canon Sales (the sales organization for Japan), stressed the need to "make sales a science." After proving the profitability of this approach, Canon Sales took on the responsibility for worldwide marketing, sales, and service. In 1981, Canon Sales was listed on the Tokyo stock exchange, reaffirming its independence.

Canon also allows its overseas subsidiaries free rein, though it holds the majority of stock. The philosophy is to create the maximum operational leeway for each subsidiary to act on its own initiative. Kaku describes the philosophy through an analogy:

> Canon's system of managing subsidiaries is similar to the policy of the Tokugawa government, which established secure hegemony over the warlords, who were granted autonomy in their territory. I am "shogun" [head of the Tokugawa regime] and the subsidiaries' presidents are the "daimyo" [warlords]. The difference between Canon and the Tokugawa government is that the latter was a zero-sum society; its policy was repressive. On the other

hand, Canon's objective is to enhance the prosperity of all subsidiaries through efficient mutual collaboration.

Canon has also promoted the growth of intrapreneurial ventures within the company by spinning these ventures off as wholly owned subsidiaries. The first venture to be spun off was Canon Components, which produces electronic components and devices, in 1984.

Building Integration: Functional Committees

As Canon continues to grow and diversify, it becomes increasingly difficult but also ever more important to link its product divisions in order to realize the benefits possible only in a large multiproduct corporation. The basis of Canon's integration is a three-dimensional management approach in which the first dimension is the independent business unit, the second a network of functional committees, and the third the regional companies focused on geographic markets (see Exhibit 5).

Kaku feels there are four basic requirements for the success of a diversified business: (1) a level of competence in research and development; (2) quality, low-cost manufacturing technology; (3) superior marketing strength; and (4) an outstanding corporate identity, culture, and brand name. Therefore, he has established separate functional committees to address the first three requirements of development, production, and marketing, while the fourth task has been kept as a direct responsibility of corporate management. The three functional committees, in turn, have been made responsible for company-wide administration of three key management systems:

- The Canon Development System (CDS), whose objectives are to foster the research and creation of new products and technologies by studying and continuously improving the development process;

- The Canon Production System (CPS), whose goal is to achieve optimum quality by minimizing waste in all areas of manufacturing;

- The Canon Marketing System (CMS), later renamed the Canon International Marketing System (CIMS), which is tasked to expand and strengthen Canon's independent domestic and overseas sales networks by building a high-quality service and sales force.

Separate offices have been created at headquarters for each of these critical committees, and over time their role has broadened to encompass general improvement of the processes used to support their functions. The chairpersons of the committees are members of Canon's management committee, which gives them the ability to ensure consistency and communicate process improvements throughout the multiproduct, multinational corporation.

Using information technology to integrate its worldwide operations, Canon began development of the Global Information System for Harmonious Growth Administration (GINGA) in 1987. The system will consist of a high-speed digital communications network to interconnect all parts of Canon into a global database and allow for the timely flow of information among managers in any location of the com-

EXHIBIT 5

Canon Organizational Chart and Operation System

CANON ORGANIZATION CHART

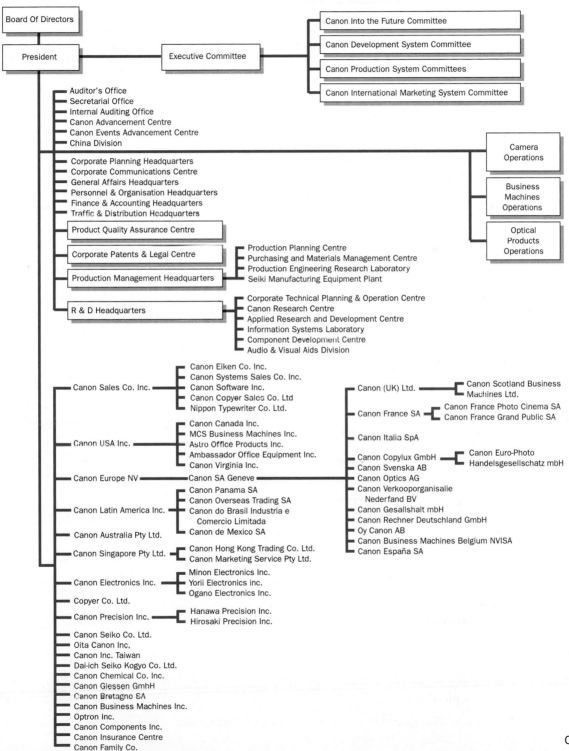

C279

EXHIBIT 5
Canon Organizational Chart and Operation System *(Continued)*

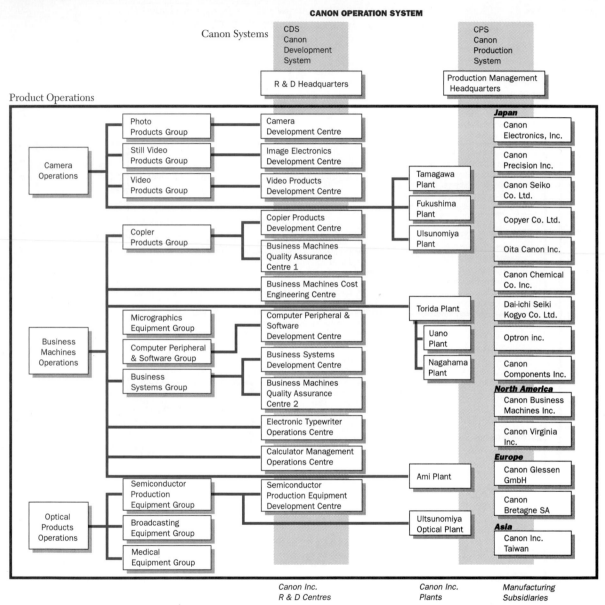

CANON OPERATION SYSTEM

Canon Systems

CDS Canon Development System

CPS Canon Production System

R & D Headquarters

Production Management Headquarters

Product Operations

Camera Operations
- Photo Products Group
- Still Video Products Group
- Video Products Group

Camera Development Centre
Image Electronics Development Centre
Video Products Development Centre

Copier Products Group
- Copier Products Development Centre
- Business Machines Quality Assurance Centre 1
- Business Machines Cost Engineering Centre

Business Machines Operations
- Micrographics Equipment Group
- Computer Peripheral & Software Group
- Business Systems Group

Computer Peripheral & Software Development Centre
Business Systems Development Centre
Business Machines Quality Assurance Centre 2
Electronic Typewriter Operations Centre
Calculator Management Operations Centre

Optical Products Operations
- Semiconductor Production Equipment Group
- Broadcasting Equipment Group
- Medical Equipment Group

Semiconductor Production Equipment Development Centre

Tamagawa Plant
Fukushima Plant
Ulsunomiya Plant
Torida Plant
Uano Plant
Nagahama Plant
Ami Plant
Ultsunomiya Optical Plant

Japan
- Canon Electronics, Inc.
- Canon Precision Inc.
- Canon Seiko Co. Ltd.
- Copyer Co. Ltd.
- Oita Canon Inc.
- Canon Chemical Co. Inc.
- Dai-ichi Seiki Kogyo Co. Ltd.
- Optron inc.
- Canon Components Inc.

North America
- Canon Business Machines Inc.
- Canon Virginia Inc.

Europe
- Canon Glessen GmbH
- Canon Bretagne SA

Asia
- Canon Inc. Taiwan

Canon Inc. R & D Centres   *Canon Inc. Plants*   *Manufacturing Subsidiaries*

pany's worldwide organization. GINGA is planned to include separate but integrated systems for computer integrated manufacturing, global marketing and distribution, R&D and product design, financial reporting, and personnel database tracking, as well as some advances in intelligent office automation. As described by Mr. Kaku, the main objective of this system is to supplement Canon's efficient vertical communications structure with a lateral one that will facilitate direct information exchange among managers across businesses, countries, and functions on all operational matters concerning the company. The system is being developed at a total cost of 20 billion yen and it is targeted for completion in 1992.

Managing Renewal: Challenges and Change

Mr. Kaku was very forthright about some of the management weaknesses of Canon prior to 1975:

> In short, our skill in management—the software of our enterprise—was weak. Management policy must be guided by a soundly created software on management; if the software is weak, the firm will lack clearly defined ideals and objectives. In the beginning we had a clearly defined objective, to overtake West Germany's Leica. Since then our management policy has been changing like the colors of a chameleon.
>
> In the past our management would order employees to reach the peak of Mount Fuji, and then before the vanguard of climbers had barely started climbing, they would be ordered to climb Mount Tsukuba far to the north. Then the order would again be suddenly changed to climb Mount Yatsugatake to the west. After experiencing these kinds of shifts in policy, the smarter employees would opt to take things easy by taking naps on the bank of the River Tamagawa. As a result, vitality would be sapped from our workforce—a situation that should have been forestalled by all means.

Mr. Kaku's first action as president of Canon was to start the firm on the path to global leadership through establishing the first "premier company plan," a six-year plan designed to make Canon a top company in Japan. The plan outlined a policy for diversification and required consistently recurring profits exceeding 10 percent on sales.

> The aim of any Japanese corporation is ensuring its perpetual survival. Unlike the venture businesses and U.S. corporations, our greatest objective is not to maximize short-term profits. Our vital objective is to continually earn profits on a stable basis for ensuring survival. To implement this goal, we must diversify.

By the time the original six-year plan expired in 1981, Canon had become a highly respected company in Japan. The plan was then renewed through 1986 and then again into the 1990s. The challenge was to become a premier global company, defined as having recurring profits exceeding 15 percent of sales. R&D spending was gradually increased from 6 percent of sales in 1980 to 9 percent in 1985 as a prerequisite for global excellence. As described by Mr. Kaku:

> By implementing our first plan for becoming a premier company, we have succeeded in attaining the allegorical top of Mount Fuji. Our next objective is Everest. With a firm determination, we could have climbed Fuji wearing sandals. However, sandals are highly inappropriate for climbing Everest; it may cause our death.

According to Mr. Kaku, such ambitions also require a company to build up the ability to absorb temporary reversals without panic; ambition without stability makes the corporate ship lose its way. To illustrate, he described the situation at Canon during the time the yen depreciated from 236 to the dollar in 1985 to 168 to the dollar in 1986. With 74 percent of Canon's Japanese production going to export markets, this sudden change caused earnings to fall to 4.6 billion yen, one-tenth of the previous year. Some board members at Canon sought drastic action such as a major restructuring of the company and cutting the R&D budget. Mr. Kaku had successfully argued the opposite:

> What I did was calm them down. If a person gets lost in climbing a high mountain, he must avoid excessive use of his energy; otherwise his predicament will deepen. . . . Our ongoing strategy for becoming the premier company remains the best, even under this crisis; there is no need to panic. Even if we have to forgo dividends for two or three times, we shall surely overcome this crisis.

While celebrating the company's past successes, Mr. Kaku also constantly reminds his colleagues that no organizational form or process holds the eternal truth. The need to change with a changing world is inevitable. For example, despite being the creator of the product division-marketing company split, he was considering rejoining these two in the nineties:

> In the future, our major efforts in marketing must be concentrated on clearly defining and differentiating the markets of the respective products and creating appropriate marketing systems for them. In order to make this feasible, we may have to recombine our sales subsidiaries with the parent company and restructure their functions to fully meet the market's needs.

While constantly aware of the need to change, Kaku also recognizes the difficulties managers face in changing the very approaches and strategies that have led to past successes:

> In order for a company to survive forever, the company must have the courage to be able to deny at one point what it has been doing in the past; the biological concept of "ecdysis"—casting off the skin to emerge in new form. But it is difficult for human beings to deny and destruct what they have been building up. But if they cannot do that, it is certain that the firm cannot survive forever. Speaking about myself, it is difficult to deny what I've done in the past. So when such time comes that I have to deny the past, I inevitably would have to step down.

http://www.canon.com/

STRATEGY FORMULATION

Motorola Inc.*

Motorola is one of the world's leading diversified electronics manufacturers, providing wireless communications, semiconductor technology, and advanced electronics equipment and services for worldwide markets. Motorola has been an outstanding success in industries where many U.S. competitors have exited, and during a time when corporate America has been restructuring and retrenching in the face of recession. Motorola's revenues have grown from under $5 billion in 1983 to $16 billion in 1993, with an annual rate of 18% in the last 2 years, fueled by the proliferation of wireless communications in overseas markets. According to former CEO George Fisher, "I see no reason why we can't maintain that pace throughout the 1990s."[1] This tremendous growth has not come at the expense of profits or heavy borrowing: profit margins and ROE have remained stable, with debt accounting for only 24% of capital, which is less than working capital. Motorola employs approximately 107,000 people worldwide and ranks among the top forty U.S. industrial companies in terms of total sales.

What makes Motorola's success even more impressive is the competitors that Motorola has gone up against. In its two main markets, semiconductors and communications, Motorola competes with the elite of Japanese industry in businesses the Japanese government has targeted for nationally supported development. Yet Motorola is the worldwide leader in cellular phones, pagers, two-way radios, and advanced dispatch systems for commercial fleets. In telecommunications, Motorola has alternated between the number one and number two spots, while competing with AT&T and Ericsson. In microprocessing units (MPUs), Motorola is second only to Intel. Motorola does not just compete in these markets, it competes for the leadership position, with innovative products and the most advanced technology. In the words of one observer, "Its excellence lies in good part in a deeply bred ability to continually move out along the curve of innovation, to invent new, related applications of technology as fast as older ones become everyday, commodity type products."[2]

---

*Prepared by Dean Aluzio, University of Connecticut, and Michael Lubatkin, University of Connecticut and Groupe ESC Lyon. Copyright Dean Aluzio and Michael Lubatkin. Reprinted by permission of Michael Lubatkin.

[1]DeYoung, H. Garret, "Motorola's Strength Comes from Growth by Renewal," *Electronic Business,* July 9, 1990, p. 30.

[2]Slutsker, Gary, "The Company That Likes to Obsolete Itself," *Forbes,* September 13, 1993, p. 140.

HISTORY

Paul V. Galvin established the Galvin Manufacturing Corporation in Chicago in 1928. The company first produced a "battery eliminator," which allowed customers to operate radios directly from household current instead of the batteries supplied with early models. Although this venture eventually failed, Galvin was more successful in the 1930s, when another venture successfully commercialized car radios under the brand name "Motorola," a word which suggested sound in motion by combining "motor" with "Victrola." During this period, the company also established home radio and police radio departments, instituted pioneering personnel programs, and began national advertising. In the 1940s, the company started to do work for the government and opened a research laboratory in Phoenix, Arizona, to explore solid-state electronics. The name of the company was changed to Motorola Inc. in 1947.

By the time of Paul Galvin's death in 1959, Motorola was a leader in military, space, and commercial communications, had built its first semiconductor production facility, and was a growing force in consumer electronics. Under the leadership of Paul's son, Robert W. Galvin, Motorola expanded into international markets in the 1960s, setting up sales and manufacturing operations around the world. In the 1970s, the company faced increasing Japanese competition, especially in consumer electronics. The company shifted its focus away from consumer electronics, selling off businesses such as color television. Faced with this stiff competition from overseas, Motorola's management staked the company's future on its ability to renew itself. The company instituted the Participative Management Program, which linked the needs and interests of employees more closely with the needs and interests of the company. In 1979, management began the journey toward total quality in all of Motorola's operations and products. This commitment to quality earned Motorola the coveted Malcolm Baldrige Quality Award in 1988, the first year the award was given.

George Fisher, appointed CEO in 1988, has continued to concentrate Motorola's energies on high-technology markets in commercial, industrial, and government fields, resulting in today's global customer base and strong position across a portfolio of related electronic product lines. Under Fisher's guidance, Motorola has experienced record sales growth in the last 5 years and has moved to the forefront of U.S. industry. Fisher left Motorola in October 1993 to accept the CEO position at Eastman Kodak, leaving the company well positioned to exploit some of the future's most promising markets.

BUSINESS LINES

Motorola serves customers in four interdependent "arenas" of electronics—components, communications, computing, and control. Businesses within and across these arenas are managed as highly decentralized sectors, groups, or divisions, depending on size. There are currently three sectors (Semiconductor Products, Land Mobile Products, and General Systems) and four groups (Paging and Wireless Data, Government and Systems Technology, Information Systems, and Automotive and Industrial Electronics). There is also a New Enterprises unit, which serves as an incubator for new businesses. If a diversified corporation as large as Motorola can be said to have a single strategy, for Motorola the strategy has been to maintain, develop, and exploit expertise and technology to be the world's best manufacturer of products within its traditional arenas, while continually developing new products and technologies that expand, extend, and bridge these arenas.

The *Semiconductor Products Sector* designs and produces a broad line of discrete semiconductors and integrated circuits to serve the advanced systems needs of the computer, consumer, automotive, industrial, federal government/military, and telecommunications markets. The segment accounted for 32% of Motorola's 1992 sales, and in the third quarter of 1993, segment sales rose 31% to $1.51 billion, the 19th consecutive quarter of growth.[3] Motorola is the largest semiconductor manufacturer in North America and ranks fourth in the world, behind Hitachi, NEC, and Toshiba. While observers have pronounced doubts about Motorola's ability to keep pace in semiconductors while investing heavily in its other businesses, management has given its assurances that semiconductors will not be sacrificed. The company's portfolio of more than 50,000 components is the broadest product line in the industry, and Motorola is particularly strong in 8-bit microcontrollers, digital signal processing, logic devices, discrete semiconductors, RISC microprocessors, and 16- and 32-bit microprocessors (see Appendix A for a list of sector and group products). Its MPUs have become the standard in products such as Apple Computers, Sega Game systems, and most new cars rolling out of Detroit. And in a joint venture with IBM and Apple, Motorola is developing the PowerPC family of MPUs, which could threaten Intel's dominant market position. IBM has started volume production of the PowerPC 601, and the smaller, low-power portable computer design Power PC 603, which Motorola will manufacture, is being readied for introduction.[4] The company's MOS-11 fabrication plant in Austin, Texas, is the world's first commercial semiconductor facility to manufacture 8-inch wafers, which allows a higher yield of chips per wafer.

The Semiconductor Products Sector, like other Motorola businesses, has been expanding overseas, particularly in Asia, which is the region with both the highest consumption of semiconductors and the fastest growth in consumption. Ten to fifteen percent of Motorola's semiconductor sales come from Japan, and the Asia-Pacific region led Motorola's 25% growth in orders in the third quarter of 1993.[5] In 1992, 52% of Motorola's sales were outside the U.S. region. Asia accounted for 22%, including Japan, which accounted for 7% of total sales. Overall, the corporation's Asian sales are growing 2 to 3 times faster than sales in the United States and Europe. According to Motorola's director of international operations, Rick Younts, Asia could be Motorola's largest source of revenue within a decade. Motorola's success in penetrating Asian markets is a result of a long-term commitment to the region. The company has been manufacturing for more than 20 years in Korea, Taiwan, and Malaysia. According to

---

[3]Motorola, 1993 Third-Quarter Report.
[4]Ibid.
[5]Ibid.

Younts, Motorola was already moving into the emerging Asian markets just as the rest of the world was realizing their potential importance. This included doing business in China before it started to open up to Western business and competing with the Japanese in Japan and in their sphere of economic influence in Asia. Competing with the Japanese initiated the quality revolution and organizational renewal that transformed the company in the late 1970s and early 1980s. In the words of Younts, "The Japanese were the benchmark for quality." Competing with the Japanese in their domestic market meant that Motorola had to have comparable quality and service: in the opinion of Younts, "The Japanese customer is the most demanding in the world—he does not accept poor service or poor quality."

In businesses such as semiconductors, where volume is the key to success, Motorola had to compete with the Japanese everywhere in the world. Motorola's international strategy has been "to understand culture and market, to be an insider in the markets in which they operate, and to ultimately contribute to the betterment of the welfare and society of these markets." Becoming an insider has meant the distribution of activities throughout the world. The company has been opening design and manufacturing centers around the world to stay close to customers and competitors. Hong Kong has been chosen for development as a regional business center and semiconductor manufacturing site that might one day replicate Silicon Valley's mutually profitable alliance between industry and academia. In Japan, Motorola Nihon has succeeded in getting Motorola components designed into Japanese products. One example is how Motorola worked with Canon to develop the microprocessor controls for a new type of autofocus on Canon's 35-millimeter cameras. Motorola has also teamed up with Toshiba, a leading producer of memory chips. Motorola did not participate in the development of the 256K generation of memory chips and as a result has suffered from a weakness in memory chips ever since. The joint venture, Tohoku Semiconductor Corporation, recently announced plans to build a $727 million plant in Sendai to produce 16K memory chips. The venture currently makes about 9 million components monthly, including DRAMS, MPUs, and microcontrollers, and has been used by the two companies to develop chips for high-density television (HDTV) applications and for Toyota car engines.[6]

The *Land Mobile Products Sector* designs, manufactures, and distributes two-way radios and other forms of electronic communication systems for customers including agriculture, commercial, construction, education, state, government, health care, mining, petroleum, utilities, and transportation companies. The company's involvement in these products stems back to World War II, when Motorola made walkie-talkies for the U.S. Army. Motorola is the leading supplier in the largest segment of this industry, two-way private mobile radios such as those used by taxicabs, police and fire departments, and trucking companies.

The *General Systems Sector* designs and manufactures computer-based cellular telephones and systems, personal communication systems, computers, microcomputer boards, and information processing and handling equipment. Motorola is the world's largest producer of mobile and portable cellular phones and has received more

[6]"Motorola, Toshiba Joint Venture Plans to Build Chip Plant," *The Wall Street Journal*, June 24, 1993, p. B7.

cellular system awards than any other company. More than half of the cellular revenues come from outside the United States, and Motorola has even succeeded in selling cellular equipment to Japan's NTT.

Cellular technology is one of Motorola's greatest successes. Motorola spent 15 years and $150 million developing cellular technology before there was any significant demand.[7] This investment has paid off, for in the last 2 years cellular phones have outsold cord phones, and the customer base of 12 million continues to grow. Yet Motorola management is convinced that it has barely scratched the surface of this market. Chris Galvin, Motorola assistant COO and son of retired CEO Bob Galvin, believes that "at some point during this decade, 20% of all POTS [plain old telephone services] will be portable. That's a tremendous market."[8] The company claims to be the only producer that offers cellular and portable phones as well as related infrastructure, test equipment, and reseller services. Since the average cellular subscriber requires about $1,500 in support equipment and services above the price of the phone, this market represents an incredible growth opportunity.

Motorola's entrance into cellular technology is a representative example of how the company spins off new technologies and businesses. In the early days of cellular technology, Edward Staiano saw that the emerging technology was being treated like a stepchild by the communications group, which back then was mainly involved in two-way radio systems. So Motorola gave Staiano free rein to develop the technology independently. Says Staiano, "So I moved out of the building with a few people, got a building down the road, and we ran basically like a start-up. Motorola is one of the few big companies where you have a pretty good chance of starting up your own business and running it."[9] Staiano is now the president and general manager of the General Systems Sector, and Motorola is now the dominant player in cellular technology.

Motorola not only pioneered cellular technology but it maintains leadership by continuously developing new products and markets ahead of the competition. One notable example is the MicroTac cellular phone Motorola introduced in 1989 as the world's smallest portable cellular phone. The phone was an instant success, and it took 18 months for competitors like NEC, Fujitsu, Mitsubishi, and LM Ericsson to counterattack with competitive products. According to Motorola President Gary Tooker, the phone clearly illustrates how Motorola anticipates customer needs and introduces products that seem ahead of their time. "When we formed the MicroTac team, no one was demanding this product," says Tooker.[10]

Motorola not only anticipates customer needs with innovative products like MicroTac but also creates demand by developing new markets. The General Systems Sector has been investing in cellular network services to create cellular infrastructures in countries that have not yet developed them. Cellular networks may become the primary systems in these countries because of the huge investments needed to connect a country through traditional wired phone lines. Motorola first got involved in network services in Hong Kong 6 years ago. According to Staiano, cellular networks

---

[7]Morone, Joseph G., "Technology and Competitive Advantage—The Role of General Management," *Research • Technology Management*, March–April 1993, p. 17.
[8]DeYoung, H. Garret, "Motorola's Strength," p. 32.
[9]Slutsker, Gary, "The Company That Likes to Obsolete Itself," p. 141.
[10]DeYoung, H. Garret, "Motorola's Strength," p. 33.

did not exist in the colony, so he decided to jump-start them by taking a 30% equity position in a start-up. Motorola originally decided not to compete with equipment customers and thus did not invest in cellular networks in the United States. Realizing what those missed opportunities cost, Staiano now has bids to build cellular systems in six countries (with Motorola equipment), and the network ventures are among Motorola's most profitable and fastest-growing businesses.[11] Motorola also controls radio frequencies previously used for dispatch systems and has the technology to convert these analog systems into high-traffic digital networks that could compete with cellular networks. But according to some Motorola executives, these ventures are just vehicles to promote equipment sales, and the long-term strategy is to exit these businesses once the market is developed.

Motorola's involvement in the European and Japanese markets is especially important for cellular products, for it is expected that Japan and Europe will move more quickly to advanced digital systems than the United States has. Motorola has won several contracts from NTT, the Japanese communications authority, and for the pan-European digital cellular network, or GSM. Motorola is already providing validation systems in several countries and has been chosen to supply operational systems in Sweden, Spain, and the United Kingdom.

The *Paging and Wireless Data Group* designs, manufactures, and distributes products for paging and wireless data systems worldwide. Motorola is the world leader in pagers and paging systems. Pagers receive one-way messages that range from a simple beep to words and numbers that can be stored and displayed on a screen. The devices were used traditionally to contact personnel in the field and prompt a phone call, but customers are now finding more innovative uses for Motorola's pagers. Restaurants are using pagers to let waiters know when orders are finished being prepared. In China, where there is very limited telephone infrastructure, pagers are being used to send coded messages to field personnel, instructing them on their next task.

Motorola's paging operations were previously combined with the land mobile products operations to form the Communications Sector, which accounted for 29% of 1992 sales. The sector was split in 1993, and paging and wireless data operations became its own group. The primary reason for the new organizational structure was to encourage the development of wireless data technology, which was being hindered by the dominant focus of the Communications Sector on land mobile products.

There are currently only about 200,000 users of wireless data systems, including the 50,000 UPS drivers who transmit package tracking data from Motorola equipment in their trucks. Revenues from wireless data services are still small, expected to be $192 million in 1993 and $303 million in 1994, according to Ira Brodsky of Datacomm Research in Wilmette, Illinois.[12] But Robert Growney, executive vice president and general manager of the Paging and Wireless Data Group, expects that the worldwide market will reach 26 million users by the year 2000.[13] At the forefront of this market is the development of personal digital assistants (PDAs), small palmtop com-

---

[11]Slutsker, Gary, "The Company That Likes to Obsolete Itself," p. 143.

[12]Collier, Andrew, and Cray, Dan, "Wireless Data Market Still Up in the Air?" *Electronic News*, July 27, 1992, p. 19.

[13]Slutsker, Gary, "The Company That Likes to Obsolete Itself," p. 142.

puters which could revolutionize the way individuals organize and communicate information while on the go. Motorola has licensed two PDA formats: Apple Computer's Newton Operating System and General Magic's operating system. It has also established a joint venture with Samsung of Korea to manufacture portable palmtop computers. Motorola is also competing with a GE-Ericsson joint venture and AT&T to supply the wireless modems that will make PDAs and the new generation of laptop computers feasible. The Hewlett-Packard 95LX palmtop was one of the first PDAs to be introduced, and Motorola furnished it with DataStream, a nationwide broadcasting service supported by a miniature data transceiver.[14]

Like the General Systems Sector, the Paging and Wireless Data Group has expanded into network development in order to create a demand for equipment. The group has set up paging operations in countries like Brazil, where they do not yet exist, and has been establishing wireless messaging networks in the United States, such as Ardis, a joint venture with IBM, and Embarc, a receive-only E-mail network.

The *Government and Systems Technology Group* specializes in research, development, and production of electronic systems and equipment for the U.S. Department of Defense and other government agencies, commercial users, and international customers. Motorola has excelled in meeting the demands of complex military and aerospace markets, and its equipment has been on board virtually all U.S. space missions. The first words transmitted from the moon to the earth came through a Motorola transponder. The 1988 photos of Neptune taken by *Voyager II* were also sent back to earth by Motorola equipment.

This group is currently involved in the Iridium project, an ambitious attempt to make portable communication possible from any location in the world. The foundation of this global network will be 77 satellites in circular orbits around the earth. While the service will probably be considered too expensive for those accustomed to developed wire and cellular phone service, for travelers in uninhabited locations or underdeveloped countries, the system will provide instant communication to anywhere in the world via portable phone. Motorola has spun off Iridium as an independent entity, selling equity in the project to international consortia, companies, and governments. But Motorola is expected to retain a 15% share and will supply the equipment necessary to make the system work. The $3.37 billion network is scheduled to begin operations in 1998.[15]

The *Information Systems Group* combines the capabilities of the Codex Corporation with those of Universal Data Systems to provide the elements for distributed data and voice networks for the communication of data through telephone lines, from basic modems to network management systems. Codex is helping to drive the analog-to-digital transformation within the industry by providing products that meet the need for analog services today while providing an easy path to meeting future requirements for digital services. Motorola is also developing a wide range of products for the Integrated Services Digital Network (ISDN), including high-speed terminal adapters and products developed in conjunction with Northern Telecom.

---

[14]Weber, Samuel, "Anatomy of Coopetition," *Electronics*, August 1991, p. 37.
[15]"Japanese Consortium to Take a 15% Stake in Motorola Project," *The Wall Street Journal*, April 2, 1993, p. B3.

The *Automotive and Industrial Electronics Group* serves the motor vehicle and industrial equipment industries through the development and production of a variety of electronic components, modules, and integrated electronic systems. High-technology automotive applications include power-train and chassis electronics, power controls, and sensors. Building on a dominant position in certain types of automotive sensors, the company hopes to develop new automotive applications and then leverage the learning and production volume advantages to enter more lucrative markets in medical applications. Some of the newer product developments include engine management controls, antilock braking system controls, truck instrumentation, agricultural monitoring systems, and automotive theft alarms. Motorola is also positioned to develop electronics for the car of the future, such as voice-activated in-dash navigation systems and multiplex systems.

The *New Enterprises* unit manages Motorola's entry into emerging, high-growth and high-technology areas. This outlet for entrepreneurial activity allows Motorola to exploit the initiative of its people in areas not directly related to existing operations. Two current ventures are Dascan and Emtek Health Care Systems. Dascan designs and produces supervisory control and data acquisition (SCADA) systems and cell controller systems for utility markets. Emtek provides clinical information management systems for hospital intensive care units. Successful start-up operations are usually sold off, often to their management, or they are folded back into existing Motorola operations if the corporation sees a strategic fit.

MANAGEMENT PRACTICES

The heart of Motorola is the three-man Office of the Chief Executive, previously made up of CEO George Fisher, President and COO Gary Tooker, and Senior Executive Vice President and Assistant COO Chris Galvin. George Fisher left unexpectedly in November 1993 to assume the position of CEO at Kodak, and a successor has not yet been confirmed. The three members of the Office of the Chief Executive share responsibility for operations, geographic areas, and focused concerns/initiatives. As of October 1993, George Fisher had responsibility for human resources, law, strategy, technology, and external relations. He also had regional responsibility for Japan. The focused corporate activities he oversaw included U.S. government relations, trade, corporate goals, women and minority development, trade policy committee, total quality management (TQM), and product development. Gary Tooker has responsibility for Semiconductor Products, Land Mobile Products, and the Government and Systems Technology Group, and also has finance, quality, and corporate manufacturing reporting to him. His geographic responsibilities encompass the rest of Asia and the Americas. His focused activities include the Iridium project, cycle time, technology transfer, management incentive programs, product improvement, employee empowerment, and the environment. Chris Galvin is responsible for General Systems, Paging and Wireless Data, Automotive and Industrial Electronics, Information Systems, and New Enterprises. He takes geographic responsibility for Europe, the Middle East, and Africa and directs acquisitions, consumer products, personal communications, and the premier employee program.

Despite the importance of the Office of the Chief Executive, Motorola is a highly decentralized company that keeps operating and strategic authority at the business level. Motorola uses financial controls to coordinate businesses, and finance departments report directly to corporate staff, with dotted-line relations to the operating divisions. Finance, research, strategic planning, and quality are all small groups at the corporate level. Corporate staff take responsibility for having expertise in functions whose development cannot be justified on an individual business level. Businesses draw on this expertise and ask corporate staff to be able to get up to speed quickly on new capabilities, such as competitor intelligence. But Motorola is not top heavy; it maintains a good balance between corporate support staff and businesses. In the words of one executive, "It keeps staff small, running tight, and in demand. They can't be running around with time on their hands looking for things to do. If they are, then they are either overstaffed or not staffed with the right people." According to a line manager, "There is not a lot of hands-on, day-to-day involvement by corporate staff. We look to the corporate staff for guidance, advice, and counseling on the future."

Corporate staff in the legal, environmental, quality, human relations, and strategy departments develop and disseminate new ideas and set policy guidelines consistent with Motorola's mission, values, and history. Within these guidelines, Motorola businesses have the autonomy to develop their own strategies. But it is the corporation's mission which unifies and guides business strategy. Corporate headquarters has articulated the corporation's mission:

> In each of our chosen areas of the electronics industry, we will grow rapidly by providing our world-wide customers what they want, when they want it, with Six-Sigma quality and best-in-class cycle time, as we strive to achieve our fundamental corporate objective of Total Customer Satisfaction, and to achieve our stated goals of increased global market share, best-in-class people, products, marketing, manufacturing, technology and service; and superior financial results.[16]

PARTICIPATIVE MANAGEMENT PROGRAM

The cornerstone of Motorola's informal, first-name-only culture is the company's Participative Management Program (PMP).[17] Building on the highly participative style of founder Paul Galvin, Motorola management created a system in the 1970s and 1980s in which employees have a greater stake in Motorola's future than Japanese workers have in Japan's best-run corporations.

The key building blocks of the PMP are work teams of 50 to 250 workers. Each employee shares in a common bonus pool with his or her team members. The idea is that the people in the pool will be responsible for their own performance—as measured by the production costs and materials used that are controllable by the team, by quality, by production levels, by inventory stock and finished goods, by housekeeping

---

[16]Motorola company brochure.
[17]Description of the Participative Management Program adapted, in part, from James O'Toole, *Vanguard Management* (New York: Doubleday and Company, 1985).

standards, and by safety records. Whenever an idea proposed by a team leads to a cost reduction or to production that exceeds target, all team members share in the gains through bonuses that can amount to 41% of base salary (the average varies between 8% and 12%).

An example of how the PMP program has increased worker productivity is the case of an assembly worker in a Fort Worth, Texas, plant. She discovered that one of every ten screws she used to assemble a radio would break. Instead of just throwing the screws away or reporting the problem to a supervisor, the employee called the vendor. After that initial conversation, her work team got together with the vendor and they collectively solved the problem. It turned out that if the screws had proper heat treatment, they wouldn't break. Another example of the trimming of waste is in the use of gold in the production of semiconductors. Before the PMP, something like 40% of the gold used was wasted. After 2 months of analysis, Motorola employees identified some 50 spots in the process where gold was being lost. Ultimately, they reduced waste to zero.

To make this system work at a large corporation, Motorola has established a communications network of hierarchical committees. Each team has one of its members on a steering committee at the next higher level in the company (which, in turn, has a member on another committee at the subsequent higher level). The steering committees perform several critical functions:

1. *Coordination.* A steering committee will act on ideas that come from a working group that require cooperation with one or more other working groups.

2. *Lateral communication.* A steering committee will disseminate the ideas or practices of one working group to other groups, thus facilitating organizational learning.

3. *Downward communication.* A steering committee will ensure that each work group has all the managerial information it requires to do its job.

4. *Upward communication.* Since each steering committee is linked to the next-level steering committee (which, in turn, reports to top management), shop floor issues reach Motorola executives after going through only four levels in the hierarchical chain.

5. *Control.* A steering committee negotiates output standards and measures performance with the work teams that report to it. This is a continuing process in which trust is built by clearly establishing the performance criteria by which work teams will be measured in advance of the evaluation process.

6. *Evaluation.* Based on the negotiated measures of performance, a steering committee evaluates the record of the work teams that report to it and allocates rewards based on a prenegotiated formula.

While it was originally intended for production workers, like the quality and cycle time initiatives, Motorola has applied this idea across the entire organization. Professional, clerical, marketing, research, and other staff people are also organized into teams and partake in a PMP bonus program based on performance measures appropriate to their tasks. The PMP system is buttressed by Motorola's "I Recommend" plan. Every work area in the company has a bulletin board on which employees can post questions or recommendations. The questions and recommendations can be either signed or anonymous. Either way, the supervisor responsible for the area is required to post a reply within 72 hours. In those cases where it is impossible to obtain an answer that quickly, the supervisor must post the name of the person who is working on obtaining the information, along with the date by which a final answer will be posted.

The PMP has made participation the cornerstone of Motorola's culture. The reason the company has institutionalized a level of participation formerly found only in smaller companies or Japanese companies is, according to former chief operating officer William Weisz, because "of our set of assumptions about human behavior." Significantly, in Motorola's employee handbook on PMP, the discussion begins with an elucidation of the company's assumptions about workers and work. (See Appendix B for James O'Toole's summary of Motorola's assumptions.)

QUALITY

Another distinction that sets Motorola apart from other U.S. firms is the commitment to quality and the importance of the corporate quality department. Motorola has adopted quality as the cornerstone of everything the company does. Its goal has been to achieve Six-Sigma quality—3.4 defects per million. Motorola has actually achieved this condition in certain processes and products and now aims for a doubling of quality improvement every 2 years, according to Paul Noakes, director of External Quality Programs. Although quality is the responsibility of line businesses, corporate staff play an important part in coordinating its development and maintenance across the organization. Their role within the company is to teach quality and champion its cause, make sure material and techniques are up to date, and measure customer satisfaction and serve as the customer's advocate. Corporate quality staff are important participants in the semiannual review meetings. Motorola has also taken on responsibility for converting others to the quality gospel. External programs champion TQM and the need for quality while showing other companies how Motorola does it.

Motorola's quality revolution started in 1979 at a meeting of corporate executives when one of the attendees put it bluntly: "The real problem around here is that quality stinks." This started the dialogue on quality that would eventually force Motorola executives to face up to the fact that some of its products and operations did not make the grade. According to Motorola President Gary Tooker, top executives faced a choice: Go back to the fundamentals or continue to lose customers to Japanese competitors with better quality.[18] Going back to the fundamentals meant assuming final responsibility for quality at corporate headquarters. "No one wants to do a lousy job," according to Richard Buetow, vice president and director of quality. "If a company has a quality problem, 95 percent of the fault is with management." So top management began to manage quality into Motorola's operations, aided by a participative management style that made quality everybody's responsibility. To help workers do their jobs better, Motorola now spends about $100 million a year on employee training and insists that every worker take a 1-week company course in a job-related subject. The

[18]DeYoung, H. Garret, "Motorola's Strength," p. 32.

focus on quality has not only resulted in better products, more satisfied customers, and increasing market share; it has also eliminated the need for inspection and testing—a saving that Buetow estimates at 3% to 4% of the cost of sales.[19] (See Appendix C for company financial information, 1988–1992.)

CYCLE TIME

Winning the ongoing corporate battle of constantly improving quality, Motorola's quality department has turned to new ways of helping businesses reach their goal of total customer satisfaction. One important new initiative is the cycle time reduction program. The program was originally a response to customer dissatisfaction with Motorola's long lead times for product design and manufacturing. Through environmental scanning, contact with line businesses, and constant attention to customer satisfaction, corporate staff recognized the need to improve in this area. After the idea had been approved by the CEO's office, the corporate quality department took responsibility for an organizationwide program to reduce cycle time, first in manufacturing and product design, then eventually in all areas of the company's operations. It was not first executed as a pilot program but instead was implemented across the whole organization simultaneously. In a 2-day meeting, corporate staff introduced the problem and initiated discussion on how to reduce cycle times among the 180 to 200 corporate officers responsible for running line businesses. Eventually, corporate quality staff and line business personnel developed a methodology for attacking the problem: first the process is mapped; then it is examined to determine what steps are critical and which are not. Non-value-adding steps are eliminated, the process is simplified, and effort is directed only toward critical value-adding activities.

INTRAORGANIZATIONAL RELATIONSHIPS

Although corporate headquarters staff may seek to actively solve problems, they are not usually perceived as meddling in line affairs. Corporate staff expect problems to be solved at the business level, with expertise and information supplied as necessary. Active involvement often takes forms such as the cycle time initiative or recommendations from the acquisitions office to make strategic investments in other companies. The corporation's ability to look at the company and the environment from a broader perspective than line managers sometimes makes involvement necessary and beneficial. An example is when a major Bell company had ordered some equipment from the cellular division for a major showcase in Baltimore. Due to the fact that the equipment was not in production yet and was still being assembled by engineers, the cellular division was not going to be able to supply it by the deadline. The Bell company

---

[19]Ibid.

thought that the division was holding back on it in order to give priority to equipment Motorola was using to set up its own showcase. Bell complained to Executive Committee Chairman and retired CEO Bob Galvin that the deck was being stacked against it. Galvin intervened by commandeering fifteen engineers from each of the other operating divisions and temporarily putting them on the project so that the deadline could be honored.

The relationships between Motorola's independent businesses are like any vendor-customer relationships. While equipment divisions will buy from the components division when it is the best value, they do not hesitate to go outside the company for vendors. But according to one General Systems Sector executive, divisions are highly motivated to win internal orders. While having in-house customers is a valuable source of feedback, Motorola tries to be close to all of its customers, with semiannual customer surveys and an emphasis on constant horizontal contact. Equipment divisions have their own liaisons with Semiconductor Products, but outside customers have the same access. There is some cooperative development, such as the Integrated Circuit Applications Research Lab (ICAR), which tried to develop future applications of integrated circuits through cooperation with internal users. But the real coordination of independent businesses comes from shared R&D resources and the Management Technology Review process.

RESEARCH AND DEVELOPMENT

As a corporation, Motorola spent $1.3 billion on research and development activities in 1992. Research is a mix of centralized and decentralized facilities. Operating units buy R&D time from various research organizations throughout the organization to work on projects they are interested in. Relationships among businesses, projects, and R&D personnel may become semipermanent. Divisions also have specific research and development activities on a decentralized basis. The corporation sponsors general research in the critical capabilities such as radio and systems, as well as developing new technologies, such as voice coding, that may one day be critical for multiple businesses. Corporate involvement in R&D means not only ensuring a steady stream of developments but also imposing discipline: "We're like kids in a candy shop," Fisher acknowledges. "There are so many opportunities, but we know we can't pursue everything."[20]

MANAGEMENT TECHNOLOGY REVIEW

The Management Technology Review is a distinctive Motorola management practice that integrates the multiple streams of technology at the company. Semiannually, corporate staff review each business in both a business management review and a tech-

---

[20]Ibid., p. 35.

nology management review. Although the issues are obviously intertwined, the two reviews are conducted separately so that conflicting issues do not obscure the review process. In the technology review process, Motorola charts out the expected evolution of products and technology in a technological road map, a forecast of future technological advancement with interim technological milestones, product destinations, and clearly delineated routes to these destinations. This is a very interactive process, and technical people at every level participate. All employees with technical knowledge are involved in generating the initial forecasts and in implementing the plan that will be based on these forecasts. The reviews are always attended by senior staff, such as a member of the CEO's office and the directors of quality, strategy, and R&D, as well as senior people from other businesses. The participation of members of other Motorola businesses is important, for they may know where the required technology is within Motorola, possible outside sources, other possible applications for it, and opportunities to invest or license. During the review, these executives examine the road maps in light of the strength of competitors, experience curves, sales history, and Motorola's own distinctive competencies and interests. From this raw data is created a long-term product plan, a map that indicates when and where to allocate corporate research resources, when to begin product development, when to introduce new products, and when to take existing products out of production.[21]

The review process explicates what each division expects in terms of technological breakthroughs. Since technical advancement of any division is partly dependent on the technical developments of other divisions and outside suppliers, this review/mapping process is a key coordinative mechanism between the different operating divisions. An example of how one division will anticipate technical breakthroughs in another might be when one of the communications equipment divisions calls for the development of a new kind of chip from the Semiconductor division to make a new product feasible. By specifying future technological needs, the corporation can then make sure someone in the targeted division is given responsibility for meeting these needs. To demand a breakthrough from other divisions, managers have to make coherent arguments of why the breakthrough is important and why it is possible. According to one General Systems Sector executive, technologists usually know where to expect the next breakthroughs, and this process stimulates those breakthroughs by creating applications that already demand them.

The Management Technology Review is also an important opportunity for corporate management to realign businesses strategically. Products developed in one division may be transferred to another division or spun off on their own for a number of reasons, usually because a business cannot fund the development of a certain type of technology that will play only a limited role in its current business domain. When the corporation finds a promising technology in danger of being cut, it might decide to accept responsibility for nurturing and developing that technology, giving it time to grow without the profit requirements that constrain the line businesses. Corporate headquarters staff learn about these opportunities through the network of reporting lines, the review process, and informal contact. Businesses are supposed to let it all

---

[21]O'Toole, James, *Vanguard Management*, p. 177.

hang out during the review, and this is encouraged by the Motorola culture of frank, forthright discussion and debate to resolve issues. Another hallmark of Motorola culture that aids in communication is informality, probably stemming from the fact that engineers tend to be informal people. If the CEO has a question, he is likely to talk directly to the engineer directly involved, not to the engineer's boss. "I know technologists throughout the company," Fisher says. "We all understand how the company works, so that nobody's toes get stepped on when I call an engineer to find out how something really works or what his opinion is."[22]

SPIN-OFFS

Creating new products and technologies is the modus operandi of Motorola, according to one executive, and can be compared to the new-business development process at 3M. As a result, employees are very conscious of the opportunities. There are big payoffs for success, and it is seen as a primary way to climb the corporate ladder. The corporation exploits this reservoir of entrepreneurial talent and initiative by giving financial support to initiatives outside a particular business's mission or by transferring responsibility for them to more suitable locations. Many managers have become senior VPs by growing a new business. Cellular and semiconductors are the spectacular examples.

Spin-offs come about for a number of reasons. Often the autonomous initiatives of operating-level engineers will result in products unrelated to the domain of the business where it was developed. When a breakthrough is made, it becomes a candidate for special organizational arrangements to facilitate further development. Pressure from customers who are not satisfied with service for specific products within a division is also a key motivating factor. And if outside consultants, analysts, or the press is pointing out a new technology as being a critical area in the future, Motorola might move to establish a strategic foothold in the area by establishing a spin-off. The process is usually straightforward, as divisions that do not want to use scarce resources to pursue something not directly related to current product lines either seek corporate help or let the technology be separated from the division.

Managers who fail to successfully develop a spin-off are not forced to leave the company. While there is no guarantee that you will get your old position back, this is part of the risk/reward balance of the venture. A high percentage of success and the thrill of being on the cutting edge ensure that there are still plenty of entrepreneurial engineers willing to take this route.

http://www.mot.com/

---

[22]Slutsker, Gary, "The Company That Likes to Obsolete Itself," p. 143.

Appendixes to Case 20

APPENDIX A
Motorola's Products by Sector and Group

Semiconductor Products Sector Products

Bipolar, BiCMOS, and MOS digital ICs
Bipolar, BiCMOS, CMOS, and combined technology semicustom circuits
Custom and semicustom semiconductors
Customer-defined arrays
Data conversion circuits
Digital signal processing
Fiber-optic active components
Field effect transistors (FETs)
Industrial control circuits
Interface circuits

Microcomputers and peripherals
Microcontroller ICs
Microprocessors and peripherals
Microwave transistors
MOS and bipolar memories
Motor control circuits
Open architecture CAD systems
Operational amplifiers
Optoelectronics components
Power supply circuits

Pressure and temperature sensors
Rectifiers
RF modules
RF power and small-signal transistors
SMARTMOS products
Telecommunications circuits
Thyristors and triggers
TMOS and bipolar pager products
Voltage regulator circuits
Zener and tuning diodes

Land Mobile Products Sector Products

Automatic vehicle location systems
Communications control centers
Communications system installation and maintenance
Emergency medical communications systems
FM two-way radio products:
    Base station and repeated products
    Mobile products
    Portable products

FM two-way radio systems:
    Advanced conventional systems
Digital voice protection systems:
    Communication systems
    Trunked radio systems
HF single-sideband communication systems
Integrated security and access control systems
Signaling and remote control systems

Paging and Wireless Data Group Products

Pagers and components
CT2 (telepoint systems)
Radio paging systems

Mobile data systems:
    Data radio networks
    Portable and mobile data terminals
    RF modems

General Systems Sector Products

Cellular mobile, portable, transportable, and personal subscriber products
Cellular radiotelephone systems
Electronic mobile exchange (EMX) series
HD, LD, and HDII series cellular base stations
Microcomputer (VME) board-level products

Multiuser super microcomputer systems and servers
Software for workgroup and network computing communications
Wireless in-building network products

APPENDIX A (continued)
Motorola's Products by Sector and Group

Automotive and Industrial Electronics Group Products

Agricultural vehicle controls	Multiplex systems
Antilock braking systems controls	Power modules
Automotive and industrial sensors	Solid state relays
Automotive body computers	Steering controls
Gasoline and diesel engine controls	Suspension controls
Ignition modules	Transmission controls
Instrumentation	Vehicle navigation systems
Keyless entry systems	Vehicle theft alarm modules
Motor controls	Voltage regulators

Government and Systems Technology Group Products

Fixed and satellite communications systems	Video-processing systems and products
Space communication systems	Intelligent display terminals and systems
Electronic fuze systems	Electronic positioning and tracking systems
Missile guidance systems	Satellite survey and positioning systems
Missile and aircraft instrumentation	Surveillance radar systems
Secure telecommunications	Tracking and command transponder systems
Drone and target command and control systems	Tactical communications transceivers

Information Systems Group Products

Codex Corporation Products

Network management:
  Integrated network management that
  supports emerging international standards
  and complements key de facto industry
  standards

Digital transmission:
  DSU/CSUs, digital platforms, ISDN terminal
  adapters

Analog transmission:
  V.32 and other dial modems, leased line
  modems

Data and data/voice networking:
  T1 and subrate multiplexers, x.25 switches
  and PADs, statistical multiplexers

LAN Internetworking:
  LAN/WAN bridges

UDS Products

Modems

Multiplexers

High-speed digital communication products

ISDN terminal adapters

Micro-to-mainframe plug-in boards

Network management services

Custom data communication products

New Enterprises Organizations

Emtek Health Care Systems   Dascan

APPENDIX B
Summary of Motorola's Assumptions About Workers

1. Employee behavior is a consequence of how workers are treated.

2. Employees are intelligent, curious, and responsible.

3. Employees need a rational work world in which they know what is expected of them, and why.

4. Employees need to know how their jobs relate to the jobs of others and to company goals.

5. There is only one class of employee, not a creative management group and a group of others who carry out orders.

6. There is no one best way to manage.

7. No one knows how to do his or her job better than the person on the job.

8. Employees want to have pride in their work.

9. Employees want to be involved in decisions that affect their own work.

10. The responsibility of every manager is to draw out the ideas and abilities of workers in a shared effort of addressing business problems and opportunities.

APPENDIX C
Motorola Inc. Financial Information
(in millions of dollars)

	1992	*1991*	*1990*	*1989*	*1988*
Net sales	$13,303	$11,341	$10,885	$9,620	$8,250
Manufacturing and other costs of sales	$ 8,508	$ 7,245	$ 6,882	$5,905	$5,040
Selling, general, and administrative expenses	2,838	2,468	2,414	2,289	1,957
Depreciation expense	1,000	886	790	650	543
Interest expense, net	157	129	133	130	98
Total costs and expenses	$12,503	$10,728	$10,219	$8,974	$7,638
Earnings before income taxes and cumulative effect of change in accounting principle	$ 800	$ 613	$ 666	$ 646	$ 612
Income taxes on provided earnings	224	159	167	148	167
Net earnings before cumulative effect of change in accounting principle	$ 576	$ 454	$ 499	$ 498	$ 445
Net earnings	$ 453	$ 454	$ 499	$ 498	$ 445
Net earnings before cumulative effect of change in accounting principle as a percentage of sales	4.3%	4.0%	4.6%	5.2%	5.4%
Net earnings as a percentage of sales	3.4%	4.0%	4.6%	5.2%	5.4%

STRATEGY FORMULATION

Perdue Farms Inc., 1995*

BACKGROUND/COMPANY HISTORY

> I have a theory that you can tell the difference between those who have inherited a fortune and those who have made a fortune. Those who have made their own fortune forget not where they came from and are less likely to lose touch with the common man. (Bill Sterling, "Just Browsin'" column in *Eastern Shore News*, March 2, 1988)

In 1917, Arthur W. Perdue, a Railway Express agent and descendant of a French Huguenot family named Perdeaux, bought 50 leghorn chickens for a total of $5 and began selling table eggs near the small town of Salisbury, Maryland. A region immortalized in James Michener's *Chesapeake*, it is alternately known as "the Eastern Shore" or the "Delmarva Peninsula" and includes part of DELaware, MARyland and VirginiA.

Initially, the business amounted to little more than a farm wife's chore for "pin money," raising a few "biddies" in a cardboard box behind the wood stove in the kitchen until they were old enough to fend for themselves in the barnyard. But, in 1920, when Railway Express asked "Mr. Arthur" to move to a station away from the Eastern Shore, at age 36 he quit his job as Salisbury's Railway Express agent and entered the egg business full-time. His only child, Franklin Parsons Perdue, was born that same year.

"Mr. Arthur" soon expanded his egg market and began shipments to New York. Practicing small economies such as mixing his own chicken feed and using leather from his old shoes to make hinges for his chicken coops, he stayed out of debt and

*Prepared by George C. Rubenson and Frank M. Shipper, both of Franklin P. Perdue School of Business, Salisbury State University, Salisbury, Maryland 21801, Tel. (410) 543-6333, Fax (410) 548-2908, E-mail: fmshipper@ssu.edu; and Jean M. Hanebury, College of Business Administration, Texas A&M University (Corpus Christi), Corpus Christi, Texas 78412, Tel. (512) 994-6015, Fax (512) 994-2725.

Acknowledgments: The authors are indebted to Frank Perdue, Jim Perdue, and the numerous associates at Perdue Farms, Inc., who generously shared their time and information about the company. In addition, the authors would like to thank the anonymous librarians who routinely review area newspapers and file articles about the poultry industry—the most important industry on the Delmarva Peninsula. Without their assistance, this case would not be possible.

prospered. He tried to add a new chicken coop every year. By the time young Frank was 10, he had 50 chickens or so of his own to look after, earning money from their eggs. He worked along with his parents, not always enthusiastically, to feed the chickens, clean the coops, dig the cesspools, and gather and grade eggs. A shy introverted country boy, he went for 5 years to a one-room school, eventually graduated from Wicomico High School, and attended the State Teachers College in Salisbury for 2 years before returning to the farm in 1939 to work full-time with his father.

By 1940, it was obvious to father and son that the future lay in selling chickens, not eggs. But the Perdues made the shift to selling broilers only after careful attention to every detail—a standard Perdue procedure in the years to come. In 1944, "Mr. Arthur" made his son, Frank, a full partner in what was then A. W. Perdue and Son, Inc., a firm already known for quality products and fair dealing in a toughly competitive business. In 1950, Frank took over leadership of Perdue Farms, a company with 40 employees. By 1952, revenues were $6,000,000 from the sale of 2,600,000 broilers.

By 1967, annual sales had increased to about $35,000,000, but it was becoming increasingly clear that additional profits lay in processing chickens. Frank recalled in an interview for *Business Week* (September 15, 1972) ". . . processors were paying us 10 cents a live pound for what cost us 14 cents to produce. Suddenly, processors were making as much as 7 cents a pound."

A cautious, conservative planner, Arthur Perdue had not been eager for expansion and Frank Perdue himself was reluctant to enter poultry processing. But economic forces dictated the move and, in 1968, Perdue Farms became a vertically integrated operation, hatching eggs, delivering the chicks to contract growers, buying grain, supplying the feed and litter, and, finally, processing the broilers and shipping them to market.

The company bought its first plant in 1968, a Swift and Company operation in Salisbury, renovated it, and equipped it with machines capable of processing 14,000 broilers per hour. Computers were soon employed to devise feeding formulas for each stage of growth so birds reached their growth potential sooner. Geneticists were hired to breed larger-breasted chickens and veterinarians were put on staff to keep the flocks healthy, while nutritionists handled the feed formulations to achieve the best feed conversion.

From the beginning, Frank Perdue refused to permit his broilers to be frozen for shipping, a process that resulted in unappetizing black bones and loss of flavor and moistness when cooked. Instead, Perdue chickens were (and some still are) shipped to market packed in ice, justifying the company's advertisements at that time that it sold only "fresh, young broilers." However, this policy also limited the company's market to those locations that could be serviced overnight from the Eastern Shore of Maryland. Thus, Perdue chose for its primary markets the densely populated towns and cities of the East Coast, particularly New York City, which consumes more Perdue chicken than all other brands combined.

During the 1970s, the firm entered the Baltimore, Philadelphia, Boston, and Providence markets. Facilities were expanded rapidly to include a new broiler processing plant and protein conversion plant in Accomac, Virginia; a processing plant in Lewiston, North Carolina; a hatchery in Murfreesboro, North Carolina; and several Swift and Company facilities including a processing plant in Georgetown, Delaware; a feedmill in Bridgeville, Delaware; and a feedmill in Elkin, North Carolina.

In 1977, "Mr. Arthur" died at the age of 91, leaving behind a company with annual sales of nearly $200,000,000, an average annual growth rate of 17 percent compared to an industry average of 1 percent a year, the potential for processing 78,000 broilers per hour, and annual production of nearly 350,000,000 pounds of poultry per year. Frank Perdue, who says without a hint of self-deprecation that "I am a B-minus student. I know how smart I am. I know a B-minus is not as good as an A," said of his father simply, "I learned everything from him."

Stew Leonard, owner of a huge supermarket in Norwalk, Connecticut, and one of Perdue's top customers, describes Frank Perdue as "What you see is what you get. If you ask him a question you will get an answer." Perdue disapproves of the presence of a union between himself and his associates and adds, "The absence of unions makes for a better relationship with our associates. If we treat our associates right, I don't think we will have a union." On conglomerates, he states, "Diversification is the most dangerous word in the English language." His business philosophy is, "I'm interested in being the best rather than the biggest. Expansion is OK if it has a positive effect on product quality. I'll do nothing that detracts from product quality."

Frank Perdue is known for having a temper. He is as hard on himself, however, as he is on others, readily admitting his shortcomings and even his mistakes. For example, in the 1970s, he apparently briefly discussed using the influence of some unsavory characters to help alleviate union pressure. When an investigative reporter in the late 1980s asked him about this instance, he admitted that it was a mistake, saying ". . . it was probably the dumbest thing I ever did."

In 1981, Frank Perdue was in Massachusetts for his induction into the Babson College Academy of Distinguished Entrepreneurs, an award established in 1978 to recognize the spirit of free enterprise and business leadership. Babson College President Ralph Z. Sorenson inducted Perdue into the academy, which, at that time, numbered 18 men and women from four continents. Perdue had the following to say to the college students:

> There are no, nor will there ever be, easy steps for the entrepreneur. Nothing, absolutely nothing, replaces the willingness to work earnestly, intelligently towards a goal. You have to be willing to pay the price. You have to have an insatiable appetite for detail, have to be willing to accept constructive criticism, to ask questions, to be fiscally responsible, to surround yourself with good people and most of all, to listen. (Frank Perdue, speech at Babson College, April 28, 1981)

The early 1980s proved to be a period of further growth as Perdue diversified and broadened its market. New marketing areas included Washington, D.C.; Richmond, Virginia; and Norfolk, Virginia. Additional facilities were opened in Cofield, Kenly, Halifax, Robbins, and Robersonville, North Carolina. The firm broadened its line to include value added products such as "Oven Stuffer" roasters and "Perdue Done It!"—a new brand of fresh, prepared chicken products featuring cooked chicken breast nuggets, cutlets, and tenders. James A. (Jim) Perdue, Frank's only son, joined the company as a management trainee in 1983.

But the latter 1980s also tested the mettle of the firm. Following a period of considerable expansion and concentric diversification, a consulting firm was brought in to recommend ways to cope with the new complexity. Believing that the span of control was too broad, the consulting firm recommended that strategic business units, responsible for their own operations, be formed. In other words, the firm should decentralize.

Soon after, the chicken market leveled off and eventually began to decline. At one point the firm was losing as much as one million dollars a week and, in 1988, Perdue Farms experienced its first year in the red. Unfortunately, the decentralization had created duplication of duties and enormous administrative costs. MIS costs, for example, had tripled. The firm's rapid plunge into turkeys and other food processing, where it had little experience, contributed to the losses. Waste and inefficiency had permeated the company. Characteristically, Frank Perdue took the firm back to basics, concentrating on efficiency of operations, improving communications throughout the company, and paying close attention to detail.

On June 2, 1989, Frank celebrated 50 years with Perdue Farms Inc. At a morning reception in downtown Salisbury, the governor of Maryland proclaimed it "Frank Perdue Day." The governors of Delaware and Virginia did the same.

The 1990s have been dominated by market expansion to North Carolina; Atlanta, Georgia; Pittsburgh, Pennsylvania; Cleveland, Ohio; Chicago, Illinois; and Florida. New product lines have included fresh ground chicken, fresh ground turkey, sweet Italian turkey sausage, turkey breakfast sausage, fun-shaped chicken breast nuggets in star and drumstick shapes, and BBQ and oven roasted chicken parts in the "Perdue Done It!" line. A new "Fit 'n Easy" label was introduced as part of a nutrition campaign using skinless, boneless chicken and turkey products. By 1994, revenues had increased to about $1.5 billion, Frank Perdue was Chairman of the Executive Committee, and Jim Perdue was Chairman of the Board.

In January 1995, Perdue Farms became the third largest producer in the broiler industry when it bought Showell Farms, Inc., of Showell, Maryland, the twelfth largest producer in the United States with about 8,000 employees and revenues of approximately $550,000.

Sitting in the small unpretentious office that had been his dad's for 40 years, Jim looked out the window at the house where he had grown up, the broiler houses Frank built in the 1940s, his grandfather's homestead across the road where Frank was born, and a modern hatchery. "Dad would come home for dinner, then come back here and work into the early hours of the morning. There's a fold-out cot behind that credenza. He got by on three or four hours of sleep a night."

Jim, Frank, and Mr. Arthur Perdue . . . Three Generations of Perdue Farms Leadership

MISSION STATEMENT AND STATEMENT OF VALUES

From the beginning, "Mr. Arthur's" motto had been to ". . . create a quality product, be aware of your customers, deal fairly with people, and work hard, work hard, work hard. . . ." In a speech in September 1991 to the firm's lenders, accountants, and Perdue associates, Frank reiterated these values, saying:

> If you were to ask me what was the biggest factor in whatever success we have enjoyed, I would answer that it was not technology, or economic resources, or organizational structure. It . . . has been our conscious decision that, in order to be successful, we must have a sound set of beliefs on which we premise all our policies and actions. . . . Central to these beliefs is our emphasis on quality. . . . Quality is no accident. It is the one absolutely necessary ingredient of all the most successful companies in the world.

The centrality of quality to the firm is featured in its Mission Statement and its Statement of Values. To ensure that all associates know what the company's mission, quality policy, values, and annual goals are, managers receive a fold-up, wallet-size card with them imprinted on it (see Exhibit 1).

SOCIAL RESPONSIBILITY

To realize its corporate statement of values, Perdue Farms works hard to be a good corporate citizen. Two areas in which this is especially clear are its code of ethics and its efforts to minimize the environmenal damage it causes.

Code of Ethics

Perdue Farms has taken the somewhat unusual step of setting forth explicitly the ethical standards it expects all associates to follow. Specifically, the Code of Ethics calls upon associates to conduct every aspect of business in the full spirit of honest and lawful behavior. Further, all salaried associates and certain hourly associates are required to sign a statement acknowledging that they understand the code and are prepared to comply with it. Associates are expected to report to their supervisor dishonest or illegal activities as well as possible violations of the code. If the supervisor does not provide a satisfactory response, the employee is expected to contact either the Vice President for Human Resources or the Vice President of the division. The code notes that any Perdue manager who initiates or encourages reprisal against any person who reports a violation commits a serious violation of the code.

Minimizing Environmental Damage

Historically, chicken processing has been the focus of special interest groups whose interests range from animal rights to repetitive-motion disorders to environmental causes. Perdue Farms has accepted the challenge of striving to maintain an environmentally friendly workplace as a goal which requires the commitment of all of its associates, from Frank Perdue down. Frank Perdue states it best: "We know that we

EXHIBIT 1
Perdue, Fiscal Year 1994

Mission Statement

Our mission is to provide the highest quality poultry and poultry-related products to retail and food service customers.

We want to be the recognized industry leader in quality and service, providing more than expected for our customers, associates, and owners.

We will accomplish this by maintaining a tradition of pride in our products, growth through innovation, integrity in the management of our business, and commitment to Team Management and the Quality Improvement Process.

Quality Policy

We shall produce products and provide services at all times which meet or exceed the expectations of our customers.

We shall not be content to be of equal quality to our competitors.

Our commitment is to be increasingly superior.

Contribution to quality is a responsibility shared by everyone in the Perdue organization.

Statement of Values

Our success as a company, and as individuals working at Perdue, depends upon:

- Meeting customer needs with the best quality, innovative food and food-related products and services.

- Associates being team members in the business and having opportunities to influence, make contributions, and reach their full potential.

- Working together as business partners by implementing the principles of the QIP so that mutual respect, trust, and a commitment to being the best are shared among associates, customers, producers, and suppliers.

- Achieving the long-term goals of the company and providing economic stability and a rewarding future for all associates through well-planned, market-driven growth.

- Being the best in our industry in profitability as a low-cost producer, realizing that our customers won't pay for our inefficiencies.

- Staying ahead of the competition by investing our profits to provide a safe work environment; to pay competitive wages; to maintain up-to-date facilities, equipment, and processes; and to create challenging opportunities for associates.

- Serving the communities in which we do business with resources, time, and the creative energies of our associates.

FY 1994 Company Goals

1. *People* Provide a safe, secure, and productive work environment.

- Reduce OSHA recordable incidents by 12%.

- Reduce per capita workers' compensation by 28%.

- Implement an associates satisfaction survey process.

- Provide an annual performance evaluation for all associates.

2. *Products* Provide the highest quality products and services at competitive costs.

- Develop an improved measurement of consumer satisfaction.

- Improve the "Customer Service Satisfaction Index."

- Improve our quality spread over competition.

- Consistently achieve a plant weighted ranking score for product quality of 212 points.

- Increase sales from new products.

3. *Profitability* Lead the industry in profitability.

- Achieve a 10% ROAE.

- Broiler Agrimetrics Index to be equal to the Southeast Best Eight Average.

- Turkey Agrimetrics Index to be equal to the Best Eight National Average.

- Increase market share by growing at a rate which exceeds the industry.

must be good neighbors environmentally. We have an obligation not to pollute, to police ourselves, and to be better than EPA requires us to be."

For example, over the years, the industry had explored many alternative ways of disposing of dead birds. Perdue research provided the solution—small composters on each farm. Using this approach, dead birds are reduced to an end product that resembles soil in a matter of a few days. This has become a major environmental activity. Another environmental challenge is the disposal of hatchery wastes. Historically, manure and unhatched eggs that make up these wastes were shipped to a landfill. Perdue produces about 10 tons of this waste per day! However, Perdue has reduced the waste by 50 percent by selling the liquid fraction to a pet food processor who cooks it for protein. The other 50 percent is recycled through a rendering process. In 1990, Perdue spent $4.2 million to construct a state-of-the-art wastewater treatment facility at its Accomac, Virginia, plant. This facility uses forced hot air heated to 120 degrees to cause the microbes to digest all traces of ammonia, even during the cold winter months. In April 1993, the company took a major step with the creation of the Environmental Steering Committee. Its mission is ". . . to provide all Perdue Farms work sites with vision, direction, and leadership so that they can be good corporate citizens from an environmental perspective today and in the future." The committee oversees how the company is doing in such environmentally sensitive areas as wastewater, storm water, hazardous waste, solid waste, recycling, biosolids, and human health and safety.

Jim Perdue sums it up as follows: ". . . we must not only comply with environmental laws as they exist today, but look to the future to make sure we don't have any surprises. We must make sure our policy statement is real, and that there's something behind it, and that we do what we say we're going to do."

MARKETING

In the early days, chicken was sold to groceries as a commodity, i.e., producers sold it in bulk and butchers cut and wrapped it. The consumer had no idea what company grew the chicken. Frank Perdue was convinced that higher profits could be made if Perdue's products were premium quality so they could be sold at a premium price. But the only way the premium quality concept would work was if consumers asked for it by name—and that meant the product must be differentiated and "branded" to identify what the premium qualities are. Hence, the emphasis over the years on superior quality, a higher meat-to-bone ratio, and a yellow skin (the result of mixing marigold petals in the feed), which is an indicator of bird health.

In 1968, Perdue spent $40,000 on radio advertising. In 1969, the company spent $80,000 on radio, and in 1970 spent $160,000, split 50-50 between radio and television. The advertising agency had recommended against television advertising, but the combination worked. TV ads increased sales and Frank Perdue decided the old agency he was dealing with did not match one of the basic Perdue tenets: "The people you deal with should be as good at what they do as you are at what you do."

That decision set off a storm of activity on Frank's part. In order to select a new ad agency, Frank studied intensively and personally learned more about advertising than any poultry man before him. He began a 10-week immersion on the theory and practice of advertising. He read books and papers on advertising. He talked to sales managers of every newspaper, radio and television station in the New York City area, consulted experts, and interviewed 48 ad agencies. On April 2, 1971, Perdue Farms selected Scali, McCabe, Sloves as its new advertising agency. As the agency tried to figure out how to successfully "brand" a chicken—something that had never been done—ad executives realized that Frank Perdue was their greatest ally. "He looked a little like a chicken himself, and he sounded a little like one, and he squawked a lot!" Ed McCabe, partner and chief copywriter of the firm, decided that Frank Perdue should be the firm's spokesperson. Initially Frank resisted. But, in the end, he accepted the role and the campaign based on "It takes a tough man to make a tender chicken" was born. Frank set Perdue Farms apart by educating consumers about chicken quality. The process catapulted Perdue Farms into the ranks of the top poultry producers in the country.

The firm's very first television commercial showed Frank on a picnic in the Salisbury City Park saying:

A chicken is what it eats. . . . And my chickens eat better than people do. . . . I store my own grain and mix my own feed. . . . And give my Perdue chickens nothing but pure well water to drink. . . . That's why my chickens always have that healthy golden yellow color. . . . If you want to eat as good as my chickens, you'll just have to eat my chickens. . . . Mmmm, that's really good!

Perdue's First Television Commercial Featuring Frank Perdue

SCALI, McCABE, SLOVES INC.   TITLE: "MY CHICKENS EAT BETTER THAN PEOPLE"

CLIENT: PERDUE FOODS INC.   LENGTH: 30 SECONDS

PRODUCT: PERDUE CHICKENS   COMMERCIAL NO.: TV-PD-30-2C

1. FRANK PERDUE: A chicken is what it eats. And my chickens eat better than . . .

2. people do. I store my own grain and mix my own feed.

3. And give my Perdue chickens nothing but pure well water to drink.

4. That's why my chickens always have that healthy golden-yellow color.

5. If you want to eat as good as my chickens, you'll just have to eat my chickens.

6. That's really good.

IT TAKES A TOUGH MAN TO MAKE A TENDER CHICKEN. PERDUE

Additional ads, touting superior quality and more breast meat, read as follows:

Government standards would allow me to call this a grade A chicken . . . but my standards wouldn't. This chicken is skinny. . . . It has scrapes and hairs. . . . The fact is, my graders reject 30% of the chickens government inspectors accept as grade A. . . . That's why it pays to insist on a chicken with my name on it. . . . If you're not completely satisfied, write me and I'll give you your money back. . . . Who do you write in Washington? . . . What do they know about chickens?

Never go into a store and just ask for a pound of chicken breasts. . . . Because you could be cheating yourself out of some meat. . . . Here's an ordinary one-pound chicken breast, and here's a one-pound breast of mine. . . . They weigh the same. But as you can see, mine has more meat, and theirs have more bone. I breed the broadest breasted, meatiest chicken you can buy. . . . So don't buy a chicken breast by the pound. . . . Buy them by the name . . . and get an extra bite in every breast.

The ads paid off. In 1968, Perdue Farms held about 3 percent of the New York market. By 1972, one out of every six chickens eaten in New York was a Perdue chicken. Fifty-one percent of New Yorkers recognized the label. Scali, McCabe, Sloves credited Frank Perdue's "believability" for the success of the program. "This was advertising in which Perdue had a personality that lent credibility to the product." Today, 50 percent of the chickens consumed in New York are Perdue.

Frank had his own view. As he told a Rotary audience in Charlotte, North Carolina, in March 1989, ". . . the product met the promise of the advertising and was far superior to the competition. Two great sayings tell it all: 'nothing will destroy a poor product as quickly as good advertising' and 'a gifted product is mightier than a gifted pen!' "

Today, the Perdue marketing function is unusually sophisticated. Its responsibilities include deciding (1) how many chickens and turkeys to grow; (2) what the advertising and promotion pieces should look like, where they should run, and how much the company can afford; and (3) which new products the company will pursue. The marketing plan is derived from the company's 5-year business plan and includes goals concerning volume, return on sales, market share, and profitability. The internal Marketing Department is helped by various service agencies including:

- Lowe & Partners/SMS—advertising campaigns, media buys

- R. C. Auletta & Co.—public relations, company image

- Gertsman & Mcyers—packaging design

- Group Williams—consumer promotional programs

- Various research companies for focus groups, telephone surveys, and in-home use tests

OPERATIONS

Two words sum up the Perdue approach to operations—quality and efficiency—with emphasis on the first over the latter. Perdue more than most companies represents the Total Quality Management (TQM) slogan, "Quality, a journey without end." Some of the key events are listed in Exhibit 2. The pursuit of quality began with Arthur Perdue in 1924 when he purchased breeding roosters from Texas for the princely sum of $25 each. For comparison, typical wages in 1925 were $1.00 for a 10-hour workday. Frank Perdue's own pursuit of quality is legendary. One story about his pursuit of quality was told in 1968 by Ellis Wainwright, the State of Maryland grading inspector, during start-up operations at Perdue's first processing plant. Frank had told Ellis that the standards that he wanted were higher than the government Grade A standard. The first 2 days had been pretty much disastrous. On the third day, as Wainwright recalls,

EXHIBIT 2
Milestones in the Quality Improvement Process at Perdue Farms

1924   Arthur Perdue buys leghorn roosters for $25.

1958   Adopts the company logo of a chick under a magnifying glass.

1984   Frank Perdue attends Philip Crosby's Quality College.

1985   Perdue recognized for its pursuit of quality in *A Passion for Excellence*.
        200 Perdue managers attend Quality College.
        Adopted the Quality Improvement Process (QIP).

1986   Established Corrective Action Teams (CATs).

1987   Established Quality Training for all associates.
        Implemented Error Cause Removal Process (ECR).

1988   Steering Committee formed.

1989   First Annual Quality Conference held.
        Implemented Team Management.

1990   Second Annual Quality Conference held.
        Codified Values and Corporate Mission.

1991   Third Annual Quality Conference held.
        Customer satisfaction defined.

1992   Fourth Annual Quality Conference held.
        "How to" implement customer satisfaction explained for team leaders and QITs.

We graded all morning, and I found only five boxes that passed what I took to be Frank's standards. The rest had the yellow skin color knocked off by the picking machines. I was afraid Frank was going to raise cain that I had accepted so few. Then Frank came through and rejected half of those.

To ensure that Perdue continues to lead the industry in quality, it buys about 2,000 pounds of competitors' products a week. Inspection associates grade these products and the information is shared with the highest levels of management. In addition, the company's Quality Policy is displayed at all locations and taught to all associates in quality training (Exhibit 1).

Perdue insists that nothing artificial be fed or injected into its birds. The company will not take any shortcuts in pursuit of the perfect chicken. A chemical- and steroid-free diet is fed to the chickens. Young chickens are vaccinated against disease. Selective breeding is used to improve the quality of the chickens sold. Chickens are bred to yield more breast meat because that is what the consumer wants.

Efficiency is improved through management of details. As a vertically integrated producer of chickens, Perdue manages every detail including breeding and hatching its own eggs, selecting growers, building Perdue-engineered chicken houses, formulating and manufacturing its own feed, overseeing the care and feeding, operating its own processing plants, distributing via its own trucking fleet, and marketing. Improvements are measured in fractional cents per pound. Nothing goes to waste. The feet that used to be thrown away are now processed and sold in Asia as a barroom delicacy.

Frank's knowledge of details is also legendary. He not only impresses people in the poultry industry, but those in others as well. At the end of one day the managers and engineers of a new Grumman plant in Salisbury, Maryland, were reviewing their progress. Through the door unannounced came Frank Perdue. The Grumman managers proceeded to give Frank a tour of the plant. One machine was an ink-jet printer that labeled parts as they passed. Frank said he believed he had some of those in his plants. He paused for a minute and then he asked them if it clogged often. They responded yes. Frank exclaimed excitedly, "I am sure that I got some of those!" To ensure that this attention to detail pays off, eight measurable items—hatchability, turnover, feed conversion, livability, yield, birds per worker-hour, utilization, and grade—are tracked.

Frank Perdue credits much of his success to listening to others. He agrees with Tom Peters that "nobody knows a person's 20 square feet better than the person who works there." To facilitate the transmission of ideas through the organization, it is undergoing a cultural transformation beginning with Frank (Exhibit 3). He describes the transition from the old to the new culture and himself as follows:

> . . . we also learned that *loud and noisy* were worth a lot more than mugs and pens. What I mean by this is, we used to spend a lot of time calling companies to get trinkets as gifts. Gradually, we learned that money and trinkets weren't what really motivated people. We learned that when a man or woman on the line is going all out to do a good job, that he or she doesn't care that much about a trinket of some sort; what they really want is for the manager to get up from behind his desk, walk over to them and, in front of their peers, give them a hearty and sincere "thank you."
>
> When we give recognition now, we do it when there's an audience and lots of peers can see. This is, I can tell you, a lot more motivating than the "kick in the butt," that was part of the old culture—*and I was the most guilty!*

Changing the behavioral pattern from writing up people who have done something wrong to recognizing people for doing their job well has not been without some setbacks. For example, the company started what it calls the "Good Egg Awards," which is good for a free lunch. Managers in the Salisbury plant were all trained and asked to distribute the awards by "catching" someone doing a good job. When the program manager checked with the cafeteria the following week to see how many had been claimed, the answer was none. A meeting of the managers was called to see how many had been handed out. The answer was none. When the managers were asked

EXHIBIT 3
Perdue Farms Inc. Cultural Transformation

Old Culture	New Culture
1. Top-down management	1. Team management
2. Poor communications	2. Focused message from senior management
3. Short-term planning	3. Long-range planning
4. Commitment to Quality	4. Expanded commitment to Quality
5. Profitability focus	5. Focus on People, Product, and Profitability
6. Limited associate recognition	6. Recognition is a way of life
7. Limited associate training	7. Commitment to training
8. Short-term cost reduction	8. Long-term productivity improvements
9. Annual goals as end target	9. Continuous Improvement
10. Satisfied customers	10. Delighted customers

what they had done with their award certificates, the majority replied they were in their shirt pockets. A goal was set for all managers to hand out five a week.

The following week, the program manager still found that very few were being turned in for a free lunch. When employees were asked what they had done with their awards, they replied that they had framed them and hung them up on walls at home or put them in trophy cases. The program was changed again. Now the "Good Egg Award" consists of both a certificate and a ticket for a free lunch.

Perdue also has a beneficial suggestion program that it calls "Error Cause Removal." It averages better than one submission per year per three employees. Although that is much less than the 22 per employee per year in Japan, it is significantly better than the national average in the United States of one per year per five employees. As Frank has said, "We're 'one up' . . . because with the help of the Quality Improvement Process and the help of our associates, we have *thousands* of 'better minds' helping us."

MANAGEMENT INFORMATION SYSTEMS (MIS)

In 1989, Perdue Farms employed 118 IS people who spent 146 hours per week on IS maintenance—"fix it"—jobs. Today, the entire department has been reduced to 50 associates who spend only 52 hours per week in "fix it," and 94 percent of their time building new systems or reengineering old ones. Even better, a 6-year backlog of projects has been eliminated and the average "build-it" cost for a project has dropped from $1,950 to $568—an overall 300 percent increase in efficiency.

According to Don Taylor, Director of MIS, this is the payoff from a significant management reorientation. A key philosophy is that a "fix-it" mentality is counterproductive. The goal is to determine the root cause of the problem and reengineer the program to eliminate future problems.

Developer-user partnerships—including a monthly payback system—were developed with five functional groups: sales and marketing, finance and human resources, logistics, quality assurance, and fresh-poultry and plant systems. Each has an assigned number of IS hours per month and defines its own priorities, permitting it to function as a customer.

In addition, a set of critical success factors (CSFs) were developed. These include: (1) automation is never the first step in a project; it occurs only after superfluous business processes are eliminated and necessary ones simplified; (2) senior management sponsorship—the Vice President for the business unit—must back major projects in an area; (3) limited size, duration, and scope; IS has found that small projects have more success and a cumulative bigger payoff than big ones. All major projects are broken into 3 to 6 month segments with separate deliverables and benefits; (4) precise definition of requirements—the team must determine up front exactly what the project will accomplish; and (5) commitment of both the IS staff and the customer to work as a team.

Perdue considers IS key to the operation of its business. For example, IS developed a customer ordering system for the centralized sales office (CSO). This system automated key business processes that link Perdue with its customers. The CSO includes 13 applications including order entry, product transfers, sales allocations, production scheduling, and credit management.

When taking an order, the Perdue salesperson negotiates the specifics of the sale directly with the buyer in the grocery chain. Next, the salesperson sends the request to a dispatcher who determines where the various products are located and designates a specific truck to make the required pickups and delivery, all within the designated 1-hour delivery window that has been granted by the grocery chain. Each truck is even equipped with a small satellite dish that is connected to the LAN so that a trucker on the New Jersey Turnpike headed for New York can call for a replacement tractor if the rig breaks down.

Obviously, a computer malfunction is a possible disaster. Four hours of downtime is equivalent to $6.2 million in lost sales. Thus, Perdue has separate systems and processes in place to avoid such problems. In addition to maximizing on-time delivery, this system gives the salespeople more time to discuss wants and needs with customers, handle customer relations, and observe key marketing issues such as Perdue shelf space and location.

On the other hand, Perdue does not believe that automation solves all problems. For example, it was decided that electronic monitoring in the poultry houses is counterproductive and not cost effective. While it would be possible to develop systems to monitor and control almost every facet of the chicken house environment, Perdue is concerned that doing so would weaken the invaluable link between the farmer and the livestock, i.e., Perdue believes that poultry producers need to be personally involved with conditions in the chicken house in order to maximize quality and spot problems or health challenges as soon as possible.

RESEARCH AND DEVELOPMENT

Perdue is an acknowledged industry leader in the use of technology to provide quality products and service to its customers. A list of some of its technological accomplishments is given in Exhibit 4. As with everything else he does, Frank Perdue tries to

EXHIBIT 4
Perdue Farms Inc. Technological Accomplishments

- Breed chickens with 20% more breast meat
- First to use digital scales to guarantee weights to customers
- First to package fully cooked chicken products on microwavable trays
- First to have a box lab to define quality of boxes from different suppliers
- First to test both its chickens and competitors' chickens on 52 quality factors every week
- Improved on-time deliveries 20% between 1987 and 1993

leave nothing to chance. Perdue employs 25 people full-time in the industry's largest research and development effort, including 5 with graduate degrees. It has specialists in avian science, microbiology, genetics, nutrition, and veterinary science. Because of its research and development capabilities, Perdue is often involved in U.S.D.A. field tests with pharmaceutical suppliers. Knowledge and experience gained from these tests can lead to a competitive advantage. For example, Perdue has the most extensive and expensive vaccination program among its breeders in the industry. As a result, Perdue growers have more disease resistant chickens and one of the lowest mortality rates in the industry.

Perdue is not complacent. According to Dr. Mac Terzich, doctor of veterinary medicine and laboratory manager, Perdue really pushes for creativity and innovation. Currently, the lab is working with and studying some European producers who use a completely different process.

HUMAN RESOURCE MANAGEMENT

When entering the Human Resource Department at Perdue Farms, a visitor first notices a prominently displayed set of human resource corporate strategic goals (see Exhibit 5). Besides these human resource corporate strategic goals, Perdue sets annual company goals that deal with "people." FY 1995's strategic "people" goals center on providing a safe, secure, and productive work environment. The specific goals are included on the wallet-size, fold-up card mentioned earlier (Exhibit 1).

EXHIBIT 5
Human Resource Corporate Strategic Goals

Provide leadership to the corporation in all aspects of human resources including safety, recruitment and retention of associates, training and development, employee relations, compensation, benefits, communication, security, medical, housekeeping, and food services.

Provide leadership and assistance to management at all levels in communicating and implementing company policy to ensure consistency and compliance with federal, state, and local regulations.

Provide leadership and assistance to management in maintaining a socially responsible community image in all our Perdue communities by maintaining positive community relations and encouraging Perdue associates to be active in their community.

Provide leadership and assistance to management in creating an environment wherein all associates can contribute to the overall success of the company.

Be innovative and cost efficient in developing, implementing, and providing to all associates systems which will reward performance, encourage individual growth, and recognize contribution to the corporation.

Strategic Human Resource planning is still developing at Perdue Farms. According to Tom Moyers, Vice President for Human Resource Management, "Every department in the company has a mission statement or policy which has been developed within the past 18 months. . . . Department heads are free to update their goals as they see fit. . . . Initial strategic human resource plans are developed by teams of three or four associates. . . . These teams meet once or twice a year company-wide to review where we stand in terms of meeting our objectives."

To keep associates informed about company plans, Perdue Farms holds "state of the business meetings" for all interested associates twice a year. For example, during May 1994, five separate meetings were held near various plants in Delmarva, the Carolinas, Virginia, and Indiana. Typically, a local auditorium is rented, overhead slides are prepared, and the company's progress toward its goals and its financial status is shared with its associates. Discussion revolves around what is wrong and what is right about the company. New product lines are introduced to those attending and opportunities for improvement are discussed.

Upon joining Perdue Farms, each new associate attends an extensive orientation that begins with a thorough review of the "Perdue Associate Handbook." The handbook details Perdue's philosophy on quality, employee relations, drugs and alcohol, and its code of ethics. The orientation also includes a thorough discussion of the Perdue benefit plans. Fully paid benefits for all associates include (1) paid vacation; (2) eight official paid holidays; (3) health, accident, disability, and life insurance; (4) savings and pension plans; (5) funeral leave; and (6) jury duty leave. The company also offers a scholarship program for children of Perdue associates.

Special arrangements can be made with the individual's immediate supervisor for a leave of absence of up to 12 months in case of extended non-job-related illness or injury, birth or adoption of a child, care of a spouse or other close relative, or other personal situations. Regarding the Family and Medical Leave Act of 1993, although opposed by many companies because its requirements are far more than their current policies, the act will have little impact on Perdue Farms since existing leave of absence policies are already broader than the new Federal law.

Perdue Farms is a non-union employer. The firm has had a long-standing open door policy and managers are expected to be easily accessible to other associates, whatever the person's concern. The open door has been supplemented by a formal peer review process. While associates are expected to discuss problems with their supervisors first, they are urged to use peer review if they are still dissatisfied.

Wages and salaries, which are reviewed at least once a year, are determined by patterns in the poultry industry and the particular geographic location of the plant. Changes in the general economy and the state of the business are also considered.

Informal comparisons of turnover statistics with others in the poultry industry suggest that Perdue's turnover numbers are among the lowest in the industry. Perdue also shares workers' compensation claims data with its competitors, and incidence rates (for accidents) are also among the lowest in the industry. Supervisors initially train and coach all new associates about the proper way to do their jobs. Once they are trained, the philosophy is that all associates are professionals and, as such, should make suggestions about how to make their jobs even more efficient and effective. After a 60-day introductory period, the associate has seniority based on the starting date of employment. Seniority is the determining factor in promotions where qualifications (skill, proficiency, dependability, work record) are equal. Also, should the workforce need to be reduced, this date is used as the determining factor in layoffs.

A form of Management by Objectives (MBO) is used for annual performance appraisal and planning review. The format includes a four-step process:

1. Establish accountability, goals, standards of performance and their relative weights for the review period.

2. Conduct coaching sessions throughout the review period and document these discussions.

3. Evaluate performance at the end of the review period and conduct appraisal interview.

4. Undertake next review period planning.

The foundation of human resources development includes extensive training and management development plus intensive succession planning and career pathing. The essence of the company's approach to human resource management is captured in Frank Perdue's statement:

> We have gotten where we are because we have believed in hiring our own people and training them in our own way. We believe in promotion from within, going outside only when we feel it is absolutely necessary—for expertise and sometimes because our company was simply growing faster than our people development program. The number one item in our success has been the quality of our people.

FINANCE

Perdue Farms Inc. is a privately held firm and considers financial information to be proprietary. Hence, available data are limited. Stock is primarily held by the family and a limited amount by Perdue management. *Forbes* (December 5, 1994) estimates Perdue Farms revenues for 1994 at about $1.5 billion, net profits at $50 million, and the number of associates at 13,800. The January 1995 purchase of Showell Farms, Inc., should boost revenues to more than $2 billion and the number of associates to about 20,000.

The firm's compound sales growth rate has been slowly decreasing during the past 20 years, mirroring the industry, which has been experiencing market saturation and overproduction. However, Perdue has compensated by wringing more efficiency from its associates, e.g., 20 years ago, a 1 percent increase in associates resulted in a 1.3 percent increase in revenue. Today, a 1 percent increase in associates results in a 2.5 percent increase in revenues (see Exhibit 6).

Perdue Farms has three operating divisions: Retail Chicken (62% of sales—growth rate 5%), Foodservice Chicken and Turkey (20% of sales—growth rate 12%), and Grain and Oilseed (18% of sales—growth rate 10%). Thus, the bulk of sales comes from the sector—Retail Chicken—with the slowest growth rate. Part of the

EXHIBIT 6
Annual Compound Growth Rate: Revenues and Associates

	Revenue Growth	Associate Growth
Past 20 years	13%	10%
Past 15 years	11%	8%
Past 10 years	9%	5%
Past 5 years	5%	2%

reason for the slow sales growth in retail chicken may stem from Perdue Farm's policy of selling only fresh—never frozen—chicken.

This has limited its traditional markets to cities that can be serviced overnight by truck from production facility locations, i.e., New York, Boston, Philadelphia, Baltimore, and Washington—which are pretty well saturated (developing markets include Chicago, Cleveland, Atlanta, Pittsburgh, and Miami). On the other hand, food service and grain and oilseed customers are nationwide and include export customers in eastern Europe, China, Japan, and South America.

Perdue Farms has been profitable every year since its founding with the exception of 1988. Company officials believe the loss in 1988 was caused by a decentralization effort begun during the early eighties. At that time, there was a concerted effort to push decisions down through the corporate ranks to provide more autonomy. When the new strategy resulted in higher costs, Frank Perdue responded quickly by returning to the basics, reconsolidating and downsizing. Now the goal is to constantly streamline in order to provide cost-effective business solutions.

Perdue Farms uses a conservative approach to financial management, using retained earnings and cash flow to finance asset replacement projects and normal growth. When it is planning expansion projects or acquisitions, long-term debt is used. The target debt limit is 55 percent of equity. Such debt is normally provided by domestic and international bank and insurance companies. The debt strategy is to match asset lives with liability maturities, and have a mix of fixed rate and variable rate debt. Growth plans require about two dollars in projected incremental sales growth for each one dollar in invested capital.

THE U.S. POULTRY INDUSTRY

U.S. annual per capita consumption of poultry has risen dramatically during the past 40 years from 26.3 pounds to almost 80 pounds in 1990. Consumption continued to grow through 1994, according to a broiler industry survey of the largest integrated broiler companies. Output of ready-to-cook product increased 5.8 percent in 1991,

5.3 percent in 1992, 6.0 percent in 1993, and 7.9 percent in 1994 to 508 million pounds per week.

Recent growth is largely the result of consumers moving away from red meat due to health concerns and the industry's continued development of increased-value products such as pre-cooked or roasted chicken and chicken parts. Unfortunately, this growth has not been very profitable due to chronic overcapacity throughout the industry which has pushed down wholesale prices. The industry has experienced cyclical troughs before and experts expect future improvement in both sales and profits. Still, razor thin margins demand absolute efficiency.

Fifty-three integrated broiler companies account for approximately 99 percent of ready-to-cook production in the United States. While slow consolidation of the industry appears to be taking place, it is still necessary to include about 20 companies to get to 80 percent of production. Concentration has been fastest among the top four producers. For example, since 1986 market share of the top four has grown from 35 percent to 42 percent (see Exhibit 7).

Although the Delmarva Peninsula (home to Perdue Farms Inc.) has long been considered the birthplace of the commercial broiler industry, recent production gains have been most rapid in the Southeast. Arkansas, Georgia, and Alabama are now the largest poultry producing states—a result of abundant space and inexpensive labor. The Southeast accounts for approximately 50 percent of the $20 billion U.S. chicken industry, employing 125,000 across the region. Still, Delmarva chicken producers provide about 10 percent of all broilers grown in the United States. This is due largely to the region's proximity to Washington, Baltimore, Philadelphia, New York, and Boston. Each weekday, more than 200 tractor trailers loaded with fresh dressed poultry leave Delmarva headed for these metropolitan markets.

Seven integrated companies operate 10 feed mills, 15 hatcheries, and 13 processing plants on the Delmarva Peninsula, employing approximately 22,000 people, and producing approximately 10 million broilers each week (see Exhibit 8).

THE FUTURE

Considering Americans' average annual consumption of chicken (almost 80 pounds per person in 1990), many in the industry wonder how much growth is left. For example,

---

EXHIBIT 7
Nation's Top Four Broiler Companies, 1995*

	Million Head	*Million Pounds*
1. Tyson Foods, Inc.	26.70	88.25
2. Gold Kist, Inc.	13.40	44.01
3. Perdue Farms Inc.	10.97†	42.64†
4. ConAgra, Inc.	10.50	37.91

*Based on average weekly slaughter; Broiler Industry Survey, 1995.
†Includes figures for Showell Farms, Inc., which Perdue acquired in January 1995.

EXHIBIT 8
Integrated Broiler Producers Operating on Delmarva Peninsula*

	National Rank
Tyson Foods, Inc.	1
Perdue Farms Inc. (includes Showell Farms, Inc., which Perdue acquired in January, 1995)	3
ConAgra, Inc.	4
Hudson Foods, Inc.	7
Townsend, Inc. (headquarters in Millsboro, DE)	10
Allen Family Foods, Inc. (headquarters in Seaford, DE)	14
Mountaire Farms of Delmarva, Inc. (headquarters in Selbyville, DE)	26

*Delmarva Poultry Industry, Inc.; May 1995 fact sheet.

after wholesale prices climbed from 14 cents per pound in 1960 to about 37 cents per pound in 1989, the recession and a general glut in the market caused prices to fall back (see Exhibit 9). Although prices have rebounded somewhat in 1993 and 1994, in real terms the price of chicken remains at an all-time low. A pound of chicken is down from 30 minutes of an average worker's 1940 wage to only 4.5 minutes of a 1990 wage.

While much of this reduction can be justified by improved production efficiencies, prices are clearly depressed due to what some consider overcapacity in the industry. For example, in 1992, ConAgra, Inc., temporarily stopped sending chicks to 30 Delmarva growers to prevent an oversupply of chickens and several chicken companies have started to experiment with producing other kinds of meat—from pork to striped bass—to soften the impact (Kim Clark, *The Sun*, July 4, 1993).

EXHIBIT 9
Wholesale Price/Pound of Live Broilers as Received by Farmers

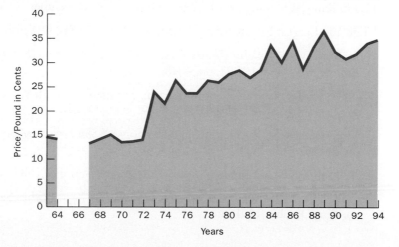

The trend is away from whole chickens to skinless, boneless parts. Perdue has responded with its line of "Fit 'n Easy" products with detailed nutrition labeling. It is also developing exports of dark meat to Puerto Rico and chicken feet to China. Fresh young turkey and turkey parts have become an important product and the "Perdue Done It!" line has been expanded to include fully cooked roasted broilers, Cornish hens, and parts. Recently the company has expanded its lines to include ground chicken and turkey sausage.

Frank Perdue reflected recently that ". . . we have a very high share of the available supermarket business in the Middle Atlantic and Northeastern United States, and if we were to follow that course which we know best—selling to the consumer through the retailer—we'd have to consider the Upper Midwest—Pittsburgh, Chicago, Detroit, with 25 to 30 million people."

PUBLIC SOURCES OF INFORMATION

Barmash, Isadore. "Handing Off to the Next Generation." *The New York Times*, July 26, 1992, p. 1/Business.

Bates, Eric, and Bob Hall. "Ruling the Roost." *Southern Exposure*, Summer 1989, p. 11.

Clark, Kim. "Tender Times: Is Sky Falling on the Chicken Boom?" *The Sun*, July 4, 1993, p. 4F/Business.

"Facts About the Delmarva Broiler Industry—1973." Industry Bulletin, February 25, 1974.

"Facts About the Delmarva Poultry Industry." Delmarva Poultry Industry, Inc., May 1995.

Fahy, Joe. "All Pain, No Gain." *Southern Exposure*, Summer 1989, pp. 35–39.

Flynn, Ramsey. "Strange Bird." *The Washingtonian*, December 1989, p. 165.

"The 400 Largest Private Companies in the U.S." *Forbes*, December 5, 1994.

Gale, Bradley T. "Quality Comes First When Hatching Power Brands." *Planning Review*, July/August 1992, pp. 4–48.

"Golden Jubilee! Company Honors Frank Perdue for His 50 Years of Service." *Perdue Courier* (Special Edition), July 1989.

Goldoftas, Barbara. "Inside the Slaughterhouse." *Southern Exposure*, Summer 1989, pp. 25–29.

Hall, Bob. "Chicken Empires." *Southern Exposure*, Summer 1989, pp. 12–19.

"In the Money: Downhome Retailer Is Nation's Richest, Forbes Says." *The Washington Post*, October 14, 1986.

MacPherson, Myra. "Chicken Big." *The Washington Post, Potomac Magazine*, May 11, 1975, p. 15.

"Nation's Broiler Industry." *Broiler Industry*, January 1995.

Perdue, Frank. Speech at Babson College, April 28, 1981.

Perdue, Frank. Speech to firm's lenders, accountants, and Perdue associates, September 1991.

"Perdue Chicken Spreads Its Wings." *Business Week*, September 16, 1972, p. 113.

Perdue Farms Incorporated—Historical Highlights. Perdue Farms Inc. publication, September 1992.

"The Perdue Story. And the Five Reasons Why Our Consumers Tell It Best." Perdue Farms Inc. publication, October 1991.

Poultry Industry file—miscellaneous newspaper clippings from 1950 to 1994. The Maryland Room, Blackwell Library, Salisbury State University.

Santosus, Megan. "Perdue's New Pecking Orders." *CIO*, March 1993, pp. 60–68.

Scarupa, Henry. "When Is a Chicken Not a Football?" *The (Baltimore) Sun Magazine*, March 4, 1973, pp. 5–12.

"Silent Millionaires in America." *Economist*, vol. 270, no. 7072, March 17, 1979.

Sterling, Bill. "Just Browsin'." *Eastern Shore News*, March 2, 1988.

Thornton, Gary. "Data from BROILER INDUSTRY," Elanco Poultry Team, partner with the Poultry Industry, December 1993.

Yeoman, Barry. "Don't Count Your Chickens." *Southern Exposure*, Summer 1989, pp. 21–24.

http://www.perdue.com/

STRATEGY FORMULATION

Rykä Inc., 1994*

> Rykä has a great story to tell. We are the only athletic footwear company that is exclusively for women, by women, and now supporting women.
>
> —*Sheri Poe*

It was the day after Christmas 1990 when Sheri Poe, president and chief executive officer of Rykä Inc. (617-762-9900), knew she was on the verge of the marketing break she'd been waiting for. Poe had sent several free pairs of Rykä athletic shoes to Oprah Winfrey. Now Poe was going to be featured as a successful female entrepreneur on Winfrey's popular talk show, with a television viewing audience numbering in the tens of millions—almost entirely women. Rykä's new line of Ultra-Lite aerobic shoes had just begun to penetrate the retail market. Poe could not have planned for a better advertising spot than Winfrey tossing pairs of Rykä shoes into the studio audience exclaiming, "Can you believe how light these are?"

After the "Oprah" broadcast, the Ultra-Lite line became an overnight success. Lady Foot Locker immediately put the Ultra-Lite shoe line in 200 stores, up from the 50 that had been carrying Rykä's regular line of athletic shoes. Retailers were swamped by consumer requests for Rykä products, and the sharp upturn in consumer demand quickly exhausted their inventories. It took Poe over three months to catch up with the orders. Many industry analysts believe that the shot in the arm provided by the Ultra-Lite sales literally saved the company.

Based in Norwood, Massachusetts, Rykä Inc. designs, develops, and markets athletic footwear for women, including aerobic, aerobic/step, cross-training, walk-run, and walking shoes. The company's products are sold all over the world in sporting goods, athletic footwear specialty, and department stores. As a new entrant in the highly competitive athletic footwear industry, the fledgling Rykä Corporation had no choice but to rely on low-budget "guerrilla marketing" tactics such as the "Oprah" show appearance. Since that time, however, Rykä has turned to more traditional marketing techniques such as radio and glossy magazine advertising. Rykä print ads appear regularly in *City Sports*, *Shape*, *American Fitness*, *Elle*, and *Idea Today*— magazines that particularly target women aged 21–35, who care not just about how they look, but are serious about physical fitness.

---

*Prepared by Valerie Porciello, Alan Hoffman, and Barbara Gottfried, Bentley College.

Rykä today is a company in financial trouble. Net profits have been negative for the last several years. Perhaps a new mission is needed. Rykä's current mission statement is given below:

Rykä shoes are made for top performance. You'll find that Rykä shoes will help you look good and feel great, no matter how demanding your fitness program.

Rykä shoes are designed, engineered, and manufactured by women for women, because a woman's needs in a comfortable, attractive, high-performance athletic shoe are different from a man's.

As you lace up for your first workout in your new Rykä shoes, you'll feel the difference. With every pair of Rykä shoes goes the positive energy of women who believe in other women.

Step forward with confidence, and be your best.

COMPANY BACKGROUND

Rykä was organized in 1987, when it commenced operations. The company was cofounded by Martin P. Birrittella and his wife, Sheri Poe. Prior to founding Rykä, Birrittella had worked at Matrix International Industries as a vice president of sales and marketing from 1980 to 1986. At Matrix, he was responsible for developing and marketing footwear and health and fitness products, and has two patents pending for shoe designs that have been assigned to Matrix. From 1982 to 1985, Sheri Poe was national sales manager for Matrix. She then moved to TMC Group, a $15-million giftware maker based in New Hampshire, where she was national accounts manager from May 1986 to June 1987.

Sheri Poe is one of only two women CEOs in the state of Massachusetts. Poe admits being an exercise fanatic who really knew nothing about making athletic shoes when she cofounded Rykä. In 1986, Poe had injured her back in an aerobics class and was convinced that the injury had been caused by her shoes, which had never fit properly. After an exhaustive search for footwear that would not stress her body, Poe realized that many other women were probably having the same trouble as she was finding a shoe that really fit and decided to start her own women's athletic footwear company. She believed that rather than adapting men's athletic shoes for women, Rykä should design athletic shoes especially suited for women's feet and bodies. Rykä introduced its first two styles of athletic shoes in 1987 and began shipping the shoes a year later.

Poe had considerable difficulty obtaining venture capital to start a women's athletic shoe company. Potential investors questioned her ability to compete with industry leaders such as Nike and Reebok, given that she had no money and no retail experience—then turned down her requests for loans. Ironically, some of those same venture capitalists now call Poe to ask how they can get in on her $8 million business.

Since she couldn't get anything out of the venture capitalists, Poe leveraged her own house, then turned to family and friends to help finance the company. She also continued to search for more open-minded commercial investors and eventually discovered a Denver investment banker who was willing to do an initial public offering. Poe got a $250,000 bridge loan before the initial public offering—which happened to be about the time the stock market crashed in October 1987. Nevertheless, Rykä went public on April 15, 1988, and despite the unstable market, 4 million shares in the company were sold at one dollar each in less than a week. The Denver firm completed a second offering before failing. Poe then turned to Paulson Capital Corporation in Oregon for a third offering in 1990.

SHERI POE

Sheri Poe believes that by having a woman president, Rykä inspires other women to buy the company's products. As she points out, "we're the only company that can tell women that the person running the company is a woman who works out every day." Even Nike doesn't have a woman making all of its product decisions. Poe's image and profile is the most critical component in Rykä's marketing strategy. Rather than using professional models, Rykä's print advertisements feature Poe working out; and in the company's recent venture into television advertising spots, Poe is the company spokesperson. The caption on a recent ad for Rykä's Series 900 aerobic shoes reads, "Our president knows that if you huff and puff, jump up and down, and throw your weight around you eventually get what you want," cleverly referring to Poe's own determination to succeed, and including her audience as coconspirators who know how hard it is for a woman to make it in the business world because they have "been there" themselves.

As part of Rykä's unique marketing strategy, Poe appears on regional television and radio shows throughout the country and has been interviewed by numerous magazines and newspapers. Feature articles on Poe and Rykä have appeared in *Entrepreneurial Woman*, *Executive Female*, and *Working Woman*. Poe has successfully worked the woman angle: she particularly appeals to today's working women because although she has become something of a celebrity, she considers herself a down-to-earth woman who also happens to be a successful executive, and a (divorced, and now remarried) mother. A *Boston Business Journal* article describes her as a CEO whose title "does not cramp [her] style . . . she eschews power suits for miniskirts and jeans, drives herself to work, and lets calls from her kids interrupt her meetings."

THE ATHLETIC FOOTWEAR INDUSTRY

The $11 billion athletic footwear industry is highly competitive. Three major firms control the market: Nike, Reebok, and L.A. Gear. Second string competitors include Adidas, Avia, Asics, and Converse. All of these companies have greater financial strength and more resources than Rykä. While Rykä's sales were $12.1 million in 1992, Nike's were $3.4 billion, Reebok's $3.0 billion, and L.A. Gear's $430 million.

Annual growth in the athletic footwear market has shrunk to approximately 4 percent and it is considered a mature market. Despite the subdued growth characteristics of the overall industry, however, a number of its submarkets are expanding via high specialization, technological innovation, and image and fashion appeal.

Product Specialization

The athletic footwear industry is divided into various submarkets by specialization. Product use categories include: basketball, tennis, running, aerobic, cross-training, walking, etc. Rykä competes only in the latter three markets: aerobic, walking, and cross-training shoes.

Aerobic Segment

The aerobic segment of the athletic shoe industry accounts for approximately $500 million in annual sales. Reebok pioneered the segment and continues to be the industry leader. The market is made up primarily of women and has grown rapidly in recent years. Rykä's number one market is aerobics; 80 percent of Rykä's sales are from the Ultra-Lite and step aerobic lines.

Walking Segment

The second major market Rykä competes in is the walking segment. This high-growth market is now the fourth largest product category in the athletic shoe industry. More than 70 million people walk for exercise and spend $2 billion annually on footwear. Reebok leads this market and is concentrating its marketing efforts on young women. Nevertheless, while the male and younger female walking markets have experienced some growth, the walking segment is primarily focused on women 45–55 years old. Ten percent of Rykä's sales are derived from its Series 500 walking shoe and the company expects the walking shoe segment to be its greatest growth category.

Cross-Training Segment

Rykä also competes in the cross-training segment of the athletic shoe market. Cross-training shoes are popular because they can be used for a variety of activities. Nike created this segment and maintains the lead in market share. Overall sales for the segment are currently at $1.2 billion, and growth is strong. Rykä earns 10 percent of its revenues from its cross-training shoes.

Technological Innovation

Reebok and Nike are fast moving toward the goal of identifying themselves as the most technologically advanced producers of performance shoes. Rykä understands that it must keep up with research and development to survive. Rykä has introduced its nitrogen footwear system, Nitrogen/ES—the "ES" stands for Energy Spheres. The system was developed over a two-year period by a design team with over 35 patents in shoe design and state-of-the-art composite plastics. The idea is that the ES ambient air compression spheres contain nitrogen microballoons that provide significantly more energy return than the systems of any of Rykä's major competitors. Consumer response to the Nitrogen/ES shoe was overwhelming, so Rykä has discontinued sales of a number of models that did not include this special feature.

Two patents were filed for the Nitrogen/ES System. One has been granted; the other is pending. Although patents are intended to provide legal protection, the cost of defending patents can be quite high. With the vast resources available to Rykä's competition, it would be easy for Reebok or Nike to adopt Rykä's technology at little or no risk of an infringement suit. Rykä's limited financial resources would disable the company from enforcing its rights in an infringement action.

Fashion

Rykä has focused on performance rather than fashion because Poe believes that fashion-athletic footwear is susceptible to trends and the economy, but performance shoes will not be affected because women always need to protect their bodies. Nevertheless, a large segment of athletic footwear consumers purchase products based on looks rather than function. In fact, the fashion market is a mainstay of Rykä's major competitors, especially Reebok, the originators of the fashion aerobic shoe market; 80 to 90 percent of fashion aerobic shoe buyers do not participate in the sport.

Although Rykä shoes are as technologically advanced as Reebok, Nike, or L.A. Gear's, they are often overlooked by fashion-conscious consumers unfamiliar with the Rykä name. Despite the fact that Rykä's sales have grown even during these recessionary times, retailers haven't always carried Rykä shoes because they prefer to stock only those brands which are easily recognizable. The lack of a nationally recognized name is a serious concern for any company; thus for Rykä, as for its competitors, expensive, leading edge advertising campaigns have played an essential part in its marketing initiatives.

A ROCKY START

Given the saturation of the athletic footwear market, athletic shoe companies need more than a good product to stay alive; they need powerful marketing and advertising. Rykä concentrates much of its energies on marketing. As a new manufacturer in an already crowded industry, Poe understands the possibility of being marketed right out of business by big competitors with deep pockets like Nike and Reebok. Rykä's approach is to offer similar products, but focus on the most cost-effective ways to reach a target market, thus carving out a niche that the industry giants have overlooked.

To protect a niche, it is critical to stay one step ahead of the competition. Unfortunately for Rykä, Poe had to learn this lesson the hard way. When the company was first founded, it tried unsuccessfully to challenge the brand name manufacturers in all product categories, including running, tennis, aerobics, walking, and cross-training shoes. However, given its limited capital and the huge advertising budgets of Reebok,

Nike, and L.A. Gear, Rykä could not compete in all of these different markets at once. Instead, Rykä cut back and chose to focus on aerobic shoes, and, secondarily, on its walking shoe line. Thus, in addition to limiting product line breadth, Rykä has designed its marketing approach to attract a specific set of customers rather than a broad audience. Poe does not believe that Rykä has to be a giant to succeed. Rather, she contends that Rykä needs to maximize its ability to perform in a particular niche within a large industry.

A NEW DIRECTION

In the already-crowded athletic footwear industry, the various competitors are continually jockeying for a better market position and competitive edge. Currently, women are, and will probably continue to be, the fasting growing segment of the athletic footwear market. Women's athletic footwear accounts for 55 percent of Reebok's sales, 60 percent of Avia's, 45 percent of L.A. Gear's, and 17 percent of Nike's $2.2 billion in domestic sales. In recent years, Reebok and Nike have fought for the number one spot in the women's market, and Reebok initially prevailed; but in each of the past two years, Nike has posted a 30 percent growth in the market. This unparalleled growth in the women's athletic footwear market is the most important trend in the sporting goods industry today, and it is on this niche that Rykä is staking its future.

An important part of the Rykä mission stems from the fact that its shoes are specifically made for women. While the big name shoe companies were merely making smaller sizes of men's shoes made on men's lasts, Rykä developed a fitness shoe built specifically for women, with a patented design for better shock absorption and durability. Rykä had a first mover advantage in this segment and had a sustained competitive advantage in that none of the other companies in the athletic shoe industry can boast having a business strategy focused on women. All other contenders have other lines or are concentrated in other niches. Ultimately, however, it is the Ultra-Lite midsole, Rykä's most significant and successful product advancement, that keeps Rykä up with its competition in its market. The Rykä Ultra-Lite aerobics shoe weighs 7.7 ounces, or roughly 30 percent of the weight of a regular aerobic shoe. Within two months of its introduction in December 1990, the company had sold all of its Ultra-Lites at a unit price of $70 a pair (retail). It took three months before additional shoe orders could be filled. Some investment firms were concerned that Rykä might not be able to capitalize on the success of its new line, given its difficulty keeping retailers supplied with sufficient quantities. Eventually, Rykä did lose some ground to Nike and Reebok—both of which quickly jumped into the lightweight aerobic shoe market. Despite the competition, however, Rykä's Ultra-Lite lines are a success, accounting for close to 90 percent of its total sales today.

After establishing a solid foundation in the aerobics category, Rykä again turned its attention to product differentiation. Its current product line includes the Series 900 Aerobic/Step shoes, the Series 700 Aerobic shoes, the Series 800/Cross-Training shoes, and the Series 500 Walking shoes. To make sure its shoes were not perceived as "too specialized," Rykä designed the Aerobic Step 50/50 and a lightweight version of it, the Step-Lite 50/50, each of which can be worn for both high-impact and step aer-obics. Rykä also designed a dual purpose walk/run shoe, the 570, for women who complement their walking routine with running, but don't want to own shoes for every activity. Rykä is now considering entering the medical footwear market because an increasing number of podiatrists and chiropractors are recommending Rykä walk-ing shoes to their patients.

THE RYKÄ ROSE FOUNDATION

The Rykä ROSE (Regaining One's Self Esteem) Foundation is a not-for-profit orga-nization created by Sheri Poe to help women who have been the victims of violent crimes. The foundation was launched in 1992, and Poe herself personally pledged $250,000. Poe founded the ROSE Foundation because she was raped at age 19. The trauma resulting from the rape led to further suffering from bulimia. She sees herself as a survivor who needed to do something to help fellow victims, "For me, having a company that just made a product was not enough. I wanted to do something more."

Rykä has made a commitment to donate 7 percent of its pretax profits to the foundation and to sponsor special fund-raising events to help strengthen community prevention and treatment programs for women who are the victims of violent crimes. Rykä includes information on the foundation in brochures that are packaged with each box of shoes in the hope that its social conscience may favorably influence some consumers. But for Poe, it is more than a marketing ploy. She considers Rykä's finan-cial commitment to the ROSE Foundation a natural extension of the company's com-mitment to women.

The foundation has created alliances with health clubs, nonprofit organizations, and corporations, in an effort to reach women directly with educational materials and programs. In addition, the ROSE Foundation funds a $25,000 grants program to en-courage organizations to develop creative solutions to the widespread problem of vio-lence against women. One of the foundation's beneficiaries, the National Victim Cen-ter, received an award of $10,000 to set up a toll-free (800) telephone number for victims and their families through which they can obtain immediate information, re-ferrals, and other types of assistance.

Poe hopes that the foundation will act as a catalyst for coalition-building to help stop violence against women. But she also envisions the foundation as a means of in-volving retailers in marketing socially responsible programs directly to women. Lady Foot Locker has taken advantage of this opportunity and became the first retailer to join forces with the ROSE Foundation. In October 1993, Lady Foot Locker con-ducted a two-week promotional campaign in its 550 United States stores in conjunc-tion with the ROSE Foundation. The retailer distributed free educational brochures and held a special sweepstakes contest to raise awareness about the issue of violence against women. Customer response was overwhelmingly positive, and Lady Foot Locker is considering a future partnership with the ROSE Foundation. Foot Locker, Champs, and Athletic X-press have also expressed interest in the foundation.

MVP Sports, a New England retailer, has also participated in Rykä's activities to help stop violence against women. The company, which operates eight stores in the

New England area, sponsored a two-week information-based campaign featuring Sheri Poe that included radio, TV, and newspaper advertisements. In addition, Doug Barron, president of MVP Sports, was so impressed with the concept and progressive thinking of the Rykä ROSE Foundation that he decided his company would donate $2 to the foundation for each pair of Rykä athletic shoes sold during the 1992 holiday season. Poe sees MVP Sports' support as an important first step toward actively involving retailers in Rykä's efforts to help prevent violence against women and is reaching out to other retailers who, she hopes, will follow suit.

Poe considers Rykä and its foundation unique. As she sees it, the company has a great story to tell. It is the only athletic footwear company that is exclusively for women, by women, and now supporting women—"the first athletic shoe with a 'soul.'" And Poe is banking on her hunch that the foundation will appeal to Rykä customers who appreciate the idea that their buying power is helping women less fortunate than they are.

Nevertheless, Poe's choice to make Rykä a socially responsible company right from the beginning, rather than waiting until the company is fully established, has had consequences for its financial status. Some industry analysts have suggested that Rykä would be better off funneling any extra cash back into the company until it is completely solvent, and its product lines and their name recognition are automatic. But others argue that the reputation Rykä has garnered as an ethical company, as concerned about social issues as about the "bottom line," effectively appeals to kind-hearted women consumers. For them, the ROSE Foundation is worth in "good press" whatever it has cost the company in terms of actual investment dollars, because the company has effectively carved out a niche that speaks on many different levels to women's ethical and consumer concerns.

MARKETING

Rykä's promotional strategy is aimed at creating both brand awareness and sales at the retail level. By garnering the support of professional sports organizations early on, Rykä acquired instant name recognition in a variety of key audiences. Rykä entered into a six-figure, eight-year licensing agreement with the U.S. Ski Team which permitted Rykä to market its products as the official training shoes of the Team. In addition, the American Aerobics Association International boosted Rykä's brand name recognition when it replaced Avia with Rykä as the association's preferred aerobics shoes. *Shape* magazine labeled Rykä number one in its aerobic shoe category.

Rykä has also begun sponsoring both aerobics teams and aerobics competitions. In 1992, twenty-five countries competed in the World Aerobic championships in Las Vegas, Nevada. The Canadian Team was sponsored by Rykä Athletic Footwear. Rykä was the premier sponsor and the official shoe of the Canadian National Aerobic championship held in Vancouver, BC. To ensure the success of the event and build awareness for the sport of competitive aerobics, Rykä successfully promoted the nationals through retailers, athletic clubs, and individuals. Given that virtually every previous aerobics competition worldwide had been sponsored by Reebok, Canada's selection of Rykä as its official sponsor marked a significant milestone for Rykä, as well as marking Rykä's international recognition as a core brand in the women's athletic market.

The Rykä Training Body

Early on, Sheri Poe determined that the most effective way to reach Rykä's female aerobic niche would be through marketing to aerobics instructors and targeted Rykä's advertising accordingly. In fact, Rykä spends almost as much as industry leaders on print advertisements in aerobics instructors' magazines and very little on print advertising elsewhere. On the other hand, unlike its big competitors, Rykä does not use celebrity endorsements to sell its products, because the company markets on the theory that women will care more about what feels good on their feet than about what any particular celebrity has to say.

Beyond advertising in aerobics magazines, Rykä has successfully used direct mail marketing techniques to target aerobics instructors. The Rykä Training Body is comprised of more than 40,000 women employed as fitness instructors and personal trainers throughout the country. They receive product information four to six times per year, as well as discounts on shoes. Rykä also has a group of its instructors tied to specific local retailers. The instructors direct their students to those retailers, who then offer discounts to the students. Finally, Rykä-affiliated instructors offer demonstrations to educate consumers about what to look for in an aerobics shoe.

In addition to increasing sales, the relationship between Rykä and the aerobics profession has led to significant product design innovations. Aerobic instructors' suggestions, based on their own experience, as well as on feedback from students in their classes, has led to improvements such as more effective cushioning and better arch support in the shoes. Poe considers these teachers as the link to Rykä's customers. In fact, as a direct result of instructor feedback, Rykä was the first manufacturer to respond to the new step-aerobics trend by developing and marketing lightweight shoes specifically designed to support up and down step motions.

Salespeople

Rykä's marketing efforts are also aimed at the people who sell Rykä products. In Rykä's early days, Poe and her advertising manager, Laurie Ruddy, personally visited retail stores to meet salespeople and "sell" them on Rykä products. Now, the vice president of sales and marketing maintains contact with retailers using incentive programs, giveaways, and small monetary bonuses to keep salespeople excited. The company also provides premiums, such as fanny packs or water bottles for customers.

Advertising Budget

Given the highly competitive nature of the athletic footwear industry, effective advertising is crucial in distinguishing among brands and creating brand preference. Back in 1989, Rykä was particularly capital-intensive, given that it was trying to penetrate the athletic shoe market. Its $3.5 million loss that year is largely attributable to advertising spending of approximately $2.5 million, but that amount was nothing compared to Nike, Reebok, and L.A. Gear, who, combined, spent more than $100 million on advertising during the same period. At that time, Rykä advertised only in trade publications, so recognition among consumers was lagging.

More recently, Rykä ads have appeared in *Shape, City Sports, American Fitness, Elle,* and *Idea Today* magazines. Rykä's brand recognition has grown dramatically, even though Rykä's advertising and marketing budget is only about 9 percent of sales. Poe attributes Rykä's marketing success to its direct marketing techniques, especially its targeting of certified aerobic instructors to wear Rykä shoes.

In October 1992, after three successive quarters of record sales and little profitability, Poe announced that Rykä was going to expand its direct marketing to consumers, even if it required increased spending to penetrate the marketplace beyond aerobics instructors. But Rykä is still in another league compared to industry giants when it comes to budgets. Rykä's total advertising budget is approximately $1.5 million, while Nike spent about $20 million recently on a 1991 pan-European campaign to launch a single product, and Reebok is currently spending $28 million on its "I Believe . . ." ad campaign, which specifically targets women.

OPERATIONS

As is common in the athletic footwear industry, Rykä shoes are made by independent manufacturers in Europe and the Far East, including South Korea and Taiwan, according to Rykä product specifications. Rykä's first three years were rough, in large part because of the poor quality of the products provided by its manufacturer in Taiwan. Now, however, the shoes are made in South Korea with strict quality-control measures in effect. The company relies on a Far Eastern buying agent, under Rykä's direction, for the selection of suppliers, inspection of goods prior to shipment, and shipment of finished goods.

Rykä's management believes that this sourcing of footwear products minimizes company investment in fixed assets as well as reducing cost and risk. Given the extent of the underutilized factory manufacturing capacity in countries outside of South Korea and Taiwan, Rykä's management believes that alternative sources of product manufacturing are readily available, should the company have need of them. Because of the volatility of international and economic relations in today's global marketplace, and in order to protect itself from complete dependence on one supplier, Rykä has resolved to keep itself free of any long-term contract with manufacturers beyond the terms of purchase orders issued. Orders are placed on a volume basis through its agent and Rykä receives finished products within 120 days of an order. If necessary, Rykä may pay a premium to reduce the time required to deliver finished goods from the factory to meet customer demand.

The principal raw materials in Rykä shoes are leather, rubber, ethylvinyl acetate, polyurethane, cambrelle, and pigskin, all of which are readily available both in the United States and abroad. Nevertheless, even though Rykä could locate new sources of raw materials within a relatively short period of time if it needed to for its overseas

EXHIBIT 1
Rykä Inc. and Subsidiary: Consolidated Balance Sheets—Assets

	December 31,	
	1993	1992
Assets		
Current assets		
Cash and cash equivalents	$ 83,753	$1,029,161
Accounts receivable, net of allowance for doubtful accounts of $665,605 in 1993 and $446,034 in 1992	2,789,728	2,958,629
Inventory	3,280,648	3,260,617
Prepaid advertising	0	723,460
Prepaid expenses and other current assets	160,916	240,511
Total current assets	$6,315,045	$8,212,378
Security deposits and other assets	28,253	21,485
Equipment, furniture, and fixtures, net	87,514	85,366
Total assets	$6,430,812	$8,319,229

Source: Rykä Inc. *Annual Report,* 1993.

EXHIBIT 2
Rykä Inc. and Subsidiary: Consolidated Balance Sheets—Liabilities and Stockholders' Equity

	December 31,	
	1993	1992
Liabilities and stockholders' equity		
Current liabilities		
Accounts payable (including $1,028,150 in 1993 payable to factories)	$ 1,324,603	$ 497,179
Payable to lender	2,627,493	3,100,000
Payable to factor	500,000	0
Accrued expenses	525,724	145,000
Notes payable to stockholder	125,000	375,000
Current portion of capital lease obligations	10,405	17,795
Total current liabilities	$ 5,113,225	$ 4,134,974
Obligations under capital leases, less current portion	7,473	17,878
Commitments and contingencies		
Stockholders' equity		
Preferred Stock, $0.01 par value, 1,000,000 shares authorized; none issued or outstanding		
Common Stock, $0.01 par value, 30,000,000 shares authorized; 23,721,356 and 23,101,948 shares issued and outstanding at December 31, 1993 and 1992, respectively	237,213	231,019
Additional paid-in capital	14,780,493	14,214,459
Accumulated deficit	(13,707,592)	(10,279,101)
Total stockholders' equity	$ 1,310,114	$ 4,166,377
Total liabilities and stockholders' equity	$ 6,430,812	$ 8,319,229

Source: Rykä Inc. *Annual Report,* 1993.

EXHIBIT 3
Rykä Inc. and Subsidiary: Consolidated Statements of Operations

	Year Ended December 31,		
	1993	1992	1991
Net sales	$14,350,282	$12,193,643	$ 7,977,925
Cost of goods sold	11,199,119	8,867,375	5,231,346
Gross profit	$ 3,151,163	$ 3,326,268	$ 2,746,579
Operating expenses:			
General and administrative	1,645,553	1,042,211	1,098,925
Provision for losses on doubtful accounts	631,835	197,034	189,000
Sales and marketing	2,085,077	1,526,299	1,098,080
Advertising costs	1,162,825	196,319	298,689
Research and development	361,780	148,958	155,576
Total operating expenses	$ 5,887,070	$ 3,110,821	$ 2,840,270
Operating income (loss)	$ (2,735,907)	$ 215,447	$ (93,691)
Other (income) expense:			
Interest expense	$ 699,231	$ 516,455	$ 418,469
Interest income	(6,647)	(4,195)	(12,648)
Total other expense	$ 692,584	$ 512,260	$ 405,821
Net loss	$ (3,428,491)	$ (296,813)	$ (499,512)
Net loss per share	$ (0.15)	$ (0.01)	$ (0.03)
Weighted average shares outstanding	23,573,316	19,847,283	18,110,923

Source: Rykä Inc. *Annual Report,* 1993.

manufacturers, its business could be devastated by any interruption in operations, whereas Reebok and Nike have large stockpiles of inventory and would be less affected by any difficulties with suppliers.

Distribution

Rykä products are sold in sporting goods stores, athletic footwear stores, selected high-end department stores, and sport-specialty retailers including Foot Locker, Lady Foot Locker, Athlete's Foot Store, Foot Action, US Athletics, Oshman's, and Nordstroms. Rykä's major distribution relationship is with the 476 Lady Foot Locker stores in the United States and 250 Lady Foot Locker stores in Canada. Today, 400 Lady Foot Locker stores display permanent Rykä signage, identifying Rykä as a brand especially promoted by Lady Foot Locker. Both Sheri Poe and Amy Schecter, vice president of retail marketing for Lady Foot Locker, agree that Rykä shoes have seen solid sales in Lady Foot Locker stores, and the Lady Foot Locker's display of permanent Rykä signage expresses the confidence Lady Foot Locker has in Rykä's future success

FOOTACTION USA, a division of the Melville Corporation and the second largest specialty footwear retailer in the country, recently began selling Rykä athletic shoes on a trial basis in 40 stores. The trial was so successful, FOOTACTION agreed

EXHIBIT 4
Rykä Inc. and Subsidiary: Consolidated Statements of Stockholders' Equity

	Common Stock		Additional Paid-in Capital	Accumulated Deficit	Total
	Shares	Amount			
Balance at January 1, 1990	13,242,500	$132,425	$ 7,109,898	$ (5,394,264)	$1,848,059
Issuance of shares for cash in July 1990, in connection with public offering	4,700,000	47,000	4,653,000		4,700,000
Registration costs related to public offering			(1,182,834)		(1,182,834)
Exercise of stock options	62,642	626	21,925		22,551
Net loss				(4,088,512)	(4,088,512)
Balance at December 31, 1991	18,005,142	$180,051	$10,601,989	$ (9,482,776)	$1,299,264
Issuance of shares for services	30,000	300	9,600		9,900
Exercise of stock options	101,000	1,010	24,240		25,250
Net loss				(499,512)	(499,512)
Balance at December 31, 1991	18,136,142	$181,361	$10,635,829	$ (9,982,288)	$ 834,902
Issuance of shares for cash in September 1992, in connection with warrant call	4,021,046	40,210	3,980,836		4,021,046
Redemption of unexercised warrants in September 1992			(169,739)		(169,739)
Registration costs related to warrant call			(644,046)		(644,046)
Exercise of stock options	944,760	9,448	411,579		421,027
Net loss				(296,813)	(296,813)
Balance at December 31, 1992	23,101,948	$231,019	$14,214,459	$(10,279,101)	$4,166,377

Source: Rykä Inc. *Annual Report,* 1992.

to purchase five styles of Rykä shoes for its stores, and today 150 FOOTACTION stores carry Rykä products nationally.

Rykä has received orders from three large retail sporting goods chains, adding well over 200 store outlets to its distribution network. The twelfth largest sporting goods retailer in the country, MC Sporting Goods, based in Grand Rapids, Michigan, now carries five styles of Rykä athletic shoes in each of its 73 stores. In addition, Rykä has received orders from the Tampa, Florida-based Sports and Recreation, which will sell four styles of Rykä athletic shoes in all of its 23 sporting goods stores. Charlie Burks, head footwear buyer for Sports and Recreation, based his decision to stock Rykä shoes on his sense that the chain's customers are looking for new, exciting styles of athletic shoes at affordable prices, and that Rykä delivers on performance, fashion, and value. Rykä shoes are also carried in more than 135 Athletic Express stores.

In the competitive athletic footwear industry, distributors and retailers have considerable clout. Lady Foot Locker and Foot Locker retailers accounted for 13 percent

EXHIBIT 5
Rykä Inc. and Subsidiary: Consolidated Statements of Cash Flows

| | Year Ended December 31, | | |
	1993	1992	1991
Cash flows from operating activities:			
Net loss	$(3,428,491)	$ (296,813)	$ (499,512)
Adjustments to reconcile net loss to cash used for operating activities:			
Depreciation and amortization	51,142	62,711	52,034
Provision for losses on doubtful accounts	631,835	197,034	189,000
Advertising credits	614,217		
Issuance of common stock for services	31,050		9,900
Changes in operating assets and liabilities:			
Accounts receivable	(462,934)	(1,395,354)	(1,152,403)
Inventory	(20,031)	(1,016,458)	(1,293,102)
Prepaid advertising	109,243	(604,099)	
Prepaid expenses and other current assets	79,595	(163,115)	39,043
Accounts payable and accrued expenses	1,208,148	(52,684)	(31,437)
Net cash used for operating activities	$(1,186,226)	$(3,268,778)	$(2,080,477)
Cash flows from investing activities:			
Purchase of equipment, furniture and fixtures, net of capital leases	$ (53,290)	$ (33,398)	$ (6,227)
(Increase) decrease in security deposits and other assets	(6,768)	(5,398)	91,310
Net cash provided by (used for) investing activities	$ (60,058)	$ (38,796)	$ 85,083
Cash flows from financing activities:			
Payable to lender, net	$ (472,507)	$ 200,000	$ 2,300,000
Advances from factor, net	500,000		
Proceeds from notes payble to stockholder	125,000	375,000	
Repayment of notes payable to stockholder	(375,000)		
Repayments of capital lease obligations (32,591)	(17,795)	(32,583)	
Proceeds from exercise of stock options and warrants (net of redemptions)	541,178	4,272,334	25,250
Payment for registration costs		(644,046)	
Net cash provided by financing activities	$ 300,876	$ 4,170,705	$ 2,292,659
Net increase (decrease) in cash and cash equivalents (308,735):	$ (945,408)	$ 863,131	
Cash and cash equivalents, beginning of year	1,029,161	166,030	474,765
Cash and cash equivalents, end of year	$ 83,753	$ 1,029,161	$ 166,030
Supplemental disclosures of cash flow information:			
Cash paid during the year for interest	$ 370,945	$ 548,455	$ 318,469
Cash paid during the year for income taxes	—	—	—
Supplemental disclosure of noncash activity:			
Footwear sold in exchange for prepaid advertising	—	$ 494,856	—
Equipment, furniture and fixtures capitalized under capital leases	—	—	$ 14,698

Source: Rykä Inc. *Annual Report*, 1993.

EXHIBIT 6
Rykä Inc. Percentage of Net Sales by Category for the Years Ended December 31, 1993, 1992, and 1991

Category	1993	1992	1991
Aerobic	65%	80%	80%
Cross-Training	19	5	10
Walking and Walk/Run; Hikers	16	15	10

Source: Rykä Inc. *Annual Report*, 1993.

of Rykä's net sales several years ago, but today, no single customer or group under common control accounts for more than 10 percent of its total revenue.

Human Resources

When Rykä was in its early stages, Poe set out to gain credibility through human resources. The company offered industry-standard salaries, stock options, and the opportunity for significant input into the day-to-day operations of the company. In addition, Poe attracted four top executives from Reebok for positions in sales, advertising, and public relations. This high-powered team performed so effectively that sales doubled between Rykä's first and second years. But total executive compensation was too much for the young company. Poe realized that a change in strategy was necessary, and three of the four Reebok veterans have since left.

Rykä now employs 22 people at its Norwood headquarters, as well as 35 sales representatives across the country. Rykä's small size gives it a certain flexibility, enabling the company to concentrate on continual streamlining and improvement so that new ideas and adjustments can be implemented and in the stores within 120 days.

Rykä recently appointed Roy S. Kelvin as vice president and chief financial officer to reinforce its commitment to the financial community. Poe sees Kelvin, a former New York investment banker, as instrumental to helping the company grow, but there is also a sense in which Poe's appointment of Kelvin is her acknowledgment of the fact that she's competing for funds in an "old-boy's" network, so it is extremely valuable to have an "old boy" to help build up her list of contacts. Kelvin's main priorities are helping to secure domestic financing, reduce operating expenses, and improve profit margins.

FINANCIALS

Rykä originally financed its operations principally through public stock offerings, warrant exercises, and other private sales of its common stock, netting an aggregate of approximately $7.2 million. In July 1990 Rykä completed its public stock offering, which raised net proceeds of $3.5 million, allowing the company to market its prod-

EXHIBIT 7
Rykä Inc., 1993 Representatives

Territory #1 (WA, OR, MT, ID, AK)
  *Peggy Finnigan 714-252-0240
  same (fax)

Territory #2 (Northern California)
  *Pat Miller 707-746-5784
  707-746-5785 (fax)
  P.O. Box 215 and/or 342 East 2nd St.
  Benicia, CA 94510

Territory #3 (TX, LA, MS, AR, OK)
  *Richard Hart 717-792-5774
  717-792-5196 (fax)

Territory #4 (Southern California)
(AZ, NV, CO, WY, UT, NM)
  *Peggy Finnigan 714-252-0240
  same (fax)
  86 Almador
  Irvine, CA 92714

Jeanne Northrop 303-296-0980
303-431-1865
451 E 58th Avenue #3367
Denver, CO 80216

Mindy Jaffe (HI) 808-922-4222
same (fax)
Cellular 808-285-2855
234 Ohua Avenue #118
Honolulu, HI 96815

Territory #5 (FL, Puerto Rico)
  *Pat Best (West Coast)
  813-864-4624
  Sunshine Sports
  3000 34th Street South
  St. Petersburg, FL 33715

  *Al Maduro (East Coast, Puerto Rico)
  305-382-3877
  305-387-9446 (fax)
  Sunshine Sports
  11785 S.W. 134th Ct.
  Miami, FL 33186

Representatives:
Dave Jenkins 407-779-1737
133 North East 1st Street
Satellite Beach, FL 32927

Territory #6 (OH, MI, IN, KY)
  *Dave Phillips 513-459-0121
  same (fax)
  3478 Cutter Lane
  Maineville, OH 45039

Frank Karr 502-425-6502
502-429-6668 (fax)
9013 Cardiff Road
Louisville, KY 40242

Chris Karr 317-257-2260
317-257-4066 (fax)
6242 N Rural Street
Indianapolis, IN 46220

Territory #7 (ME, NH, VT, MA, RI, CT)
  *Bob Morgan 617-383-6346
  617-383-1955 (fax)
  698 Jerusalem Road
  Cohasset, MA 02025

Tom O'Brien 617-471-2472
617-471-2855
189 Everett Street No. 5
Quincy, MA 02169

Territory #8 (NJ, NY, PA, MD, DE, VA)
  *Richard Hart 717-792-5774
  717-792-5196 (fax)
  111 Weldon Drive
  York, PA 17404

(MD, VA)
Keith Jones 301-663-8605
same (fax)
5967 Grove Hill Road
Frederick, MD 21702

Hank Mason 315-652-7416
315-652-1570 (fax)
115 Glenwood Drive
Liverpool, NY 13090

Mike Elison 215-874-4418
same (fax)
422 Camelot Drive
Brookhaven, PA 19015

Territory #9 NYC, NJ
  *Thad Budzinski 609-588-9698

609-588-0019 (fax)
38 Willow Court
Mercerville, NJ 08619

Territory #10 (KS, MO, IA, NE, ND, SD,
WI, MN, IL)
  *Gene Wayenberg 314-997-4696
  314-997-6963 (fax)
  Great Athletic Wear
  1702 Robin Knoll Lane
  St. Louis, MO 63146

Representatives:
((Northern) IL, (Southern) WI)
Rich Neuffer 815-337-0131
9804 Autum Lane
Woodstock, IL 60098

(MN, SD, ND, WI)
Dennis Fitzpatrick 612-641-1417
612-646-5876 (fax)
2095 Shelby Avenue
St. Paul, MN 55104

(KS, MO)
Denny Hobson 913-648-0111
916-648-0669 (fax)
Hobson & Associates
7208 West 80th
Suite 206
Overland Park, KS 66204

Territory #11 (NC, SC)
  *Mark Diehl 704-365-9482
  704-366-1139 (fax)
  5012 Crooked Oak Lane
  Charlotte, NC 28226

Territory #14 (GA, TN, AL)
  *Lissy Cowdery 404-257-0775
  same (fax)
  470 River Valley Road
  Atlanta, GA 30328

Canadian Distributor
  Myke & Christine Penfold
  416-738-5291
  416-738-4818 (fax)
  333 Confederation Parkway
  Concord, Ontario, Canada L4K 4S1

*Head representative.
Source: Rykä Inc. *Annual Report,* 1993.

ucts aggressively. Rykä has sold shares to private investors who control 65 percent of the shares.

Rykä's product costs are higher than those of the industry leaders for several reasons. First, because Rykä is significantly smaller than the industry leaders, it cannot take advantage of volume production discounts. Second, the company has opted to pay somewhat higher prices for its products than would be charged by alternate suppliers in order to achieve and maintain higher quality. Finally, higher production costs have resulted from Rykä's inventory financing arrangement with its Korean Trading company, which includes financing costs, commissions, and fees as part of cost of sales.

Rykä has taken on some formidable competition in the form of Nike and Reebok. For Rykä to prosper, Sheri Poe must successfully carve out a niche in the women's athletic shoe market before the firm runs out of money. Time is becoming increasingly scarce. As indicated on Rykä's financial statements (Exhibits 1 through 6), the company lost nearly $500,000 in 1991 and $300,000 in 1992. Sales are increasing, but profits are nonexistent. Exhibit 7 provides a list of representatives as of 1993. Prepare a strategic plan that will enable CEO Poe to guide Rykä to prosperity in the mid-to-late 1990s.

http://www.ryka.com/

STRATEGY FORMULATION

From Rags Come Riches: Coping in a Commodity Industry*

A PROBLEM AT GROSSMAN INDUSTRIES, INC.

When his phone rang, Chuck Shearer picked it up to discover it was Brad Grossman, President and CEO of Grossman Industries, Inc., of Columbus, Ohio. "Chuck, if you're free, I would like you to come over to my office. I want to explore strategies which would allow us to regain our traditional levels of profitability."

Chuck, the General Manager, was quite familiar with the problem of slipping profit margins. There were a number of reasons for it and many of them were beyond the control of the company. As Chuck slipped on a jacket for the walk over to Brad's office, he began to think about how circumstances were driving the situation.

A HISTORY OF THE INDUSTRY

The textile recycling industry can be traced back about 400 years on the European continent. In the U.S., scrap metal dealers and rag merchants started springing up during the mid-19th century in the country's major industrial centers. Material shortages caused by the Civil War made these industries quite profitable. These companies later became transfer agents for all sorts of secondary materials: rags for felt bills, hemp, jute, and, of course, cotton.

In the early 20th century, rags had become a standard commodity. They were purchased from established vendors and transported to warehouses for sorting into various categories of worth. The rags were cut, compressed into bales, and sold to industry.

By the end of the 20th century, growing environmental concerns placed the "rag merchant" into a new role. In America, only 16% of textiles are recycled, the huge balance ending in landfills across the country. Now, more than ever, textile recycling companies can provide an environmentally correct solution which can also be profitable.

---

*Copyright 1996 by Richard C. Scamehorn, Executive-in-Residence, College of Business, Ohio University, 304 Copeland Hall, Athens, Ohio 45701, Tel: 614-593-2025 (O), 614-687-1842 (H), Fax: 614-593-1388 (O), scamehorn@ouvaxa.cats.ohiou.edu.

THE BACKGROUND OF GROSSMAN INDUSTRIES

Benjamin Grossman started the company in 1925, during the period between W.W.I and the depression. He had three sons: Herb, Marvin, and Arnie. Herb continued to operate the family business and having reached aged 70, retired so that the third-generation Grossman, Bradley, is now the company President.

From humble beginnings, the company now occupies a 10-acre site in south Columbus, Ohio, and has created jobs for more than 200 full-time employees.

"Good morning, Chuck." Brad Grossman was getting a cup of coffee just as Chuck walked in the outer office. "Want a cup?" "Thanks," Chuck said as he emptied a packet of Equal and stirred. "From the way you described this meeting, it sounds like we'll need a whole pot before we finish."

"What do you think is our greatest strength at Grossman?" Brad asked. Chuck sprang back with a knee-jerk reaction, "Product quality, no doubt about it."

QUALITY AS A STRATEGIC ISSUE AT GROSSMAN

"For us, quality is what you ask for, is what you get. We've built our reputation on the quality of the material we have. Our bales of garments are distinguished by the clip which fastens the steel bands of the bundles. We have our own clip, which carries our logo of the world with the word Grossman on it. We've had customers refuse to accept even our own product if it doesn't have our own clip on it. Remember that time when we ran out of our logo clip, and had to use plain steel clips, and a customer refused a shipment and told us, 'Wait, who knows where that came from? We want to see the Grossman name on it!' " "For sure," Chuck reiterated, "quality is our hallmark."

Grossman's customers would pay for quality. Everything had to be functionally working: buttons in place, zippers that worked. Some companies used the old bait-and-hook technique; ship the first few trial orders with very high quality product and then ship junk on the first large production order.

According to Check, "If a customer buys a #2 quality, it's easy to put in some number #3 quality material. Dishonest suppliers can always say, 'Oh, I thought it was #2,' or 'Oh, it looked like a quality #2 garment to me.' When you have an order for 2,000 pounds of quality #2, but you only have 1,800 available, it's easy to 'grow' 200 more pounds by just throwing in 200 pounds of quality #3. You really mix it all up with the other so the customer may never even notice the difference.

"In addition, quality may differ from customer to customer. What may be a quality #2 for a customer in Gahanna might be a #3 quality to a customer in South America. So, there's a lot of room to fudge on quality. You have to know your market and above all, you have to know your customer: what he will accept and what he won't accept."

SOURCES OF SUPPLY

Being located in the Midwest doesn't get Grossman Industries any better clothes. Organizations in Columbus such as the Salvation Army, Goodwill, or Volunteers of

America may be selling to someone in Texas. They send a truck to Columbus, load it, and haul it back to Texas.

Grossman buys primarily from the Midwest, rather than the other large markets in New York, California, or Texas. There is sufficient population in Ohio and its surrounding states to supply their needs and only about 10 to 20% is purchased from the Columbus market.

Buying and sourcing is mostly a matter of supply and demand. A rag merchant from Texas may be telling the Salvation Army in downtown Columbus, "I'll give you 12 cents a pound for your unsorted rags." If Grossman's other sources will sell what they require for 10 cents a pound, then they don't buy in the Columbus market.

The supply of rags "trickles down" from the charities. Discarded wearing apparel is donated to the charities, all of whom maintain thrift shops where a pair of khaki trousers might be priced at $5.00; after a month marked down to $3.00, and if not sold, marked down again to $1.50. If, after another month, it isn't sold, they sell it to a rag merchant for 10 to 12 cents per pound. About 75% of the purchased rags are salable (after grading) "as is." About 20% can be cut into pieces to make "wiping cloths" and sold to industry. The remaining 5% is not useable as a textile and is scrap to Grossman and sold at a scrap price.

THE PROCESS

Rags are received in bulk from hundreds of sources in the Midwest in the form of "loose bales." They are broken apart and loaded onto an elevator belt which moves them to a horizontal conveyor belt on the second-floor level. Here, nearly a dozen workers perform the primary sort: men's vs. women's; shirts separated from skirts from coats from socks from blazers, etc. At this point, quality is not being sorted, only the type of garment and whether for male or female and adult or child.

This sorting is accomplished by large, gravity chutes feeding into very large, wheel-mounted bins on the ground floor. These bins provide the basis for the secondary sort: that of quality. This secondary sort requires more judgment since it is here that Grossman's reputation is maintained. Secondary sorters must use their judgment and experience to segregate quality #1 from #2 and be both consistent and accurate.

After the secondary sort, Grossman has bins with men's white shirts, men's khaki trousers, men's ties, men's cotton shirts, men's wool shirts, etc. (and the same for the various categories of women's, boys', and girls' apparel). In total, there are nearly 100 classifications which are then baled under high compression into 1,000 pound bales for direct shipment either to customers or to finished goods storerooms awaiting a demand by customers.

The work is both fatiguing and boring. Workers must stand, either at the conveyor (for the primary) or at a bin (for the secondary) during sorting and process a high volume of rags. It is necessary to throw the rags into various chutes or bins, which requires expending energy to make this toss. As a result, the work is tiring but not very challenging. The factory is hot in the summer and cold in the winter. The sorting is no small, mean task. Annually, Grossman sorts more than 13,000,000 pounds.

Notwithstanding the hard work, some sorters have been working at Grossman for more than thirty years, and many have worked for more than ten. But there is a downside to the employment picture as well. The turnover of new hires is high. Some workers will work for only two weeks, do a poor job so as to be fired so they will again be eligible to collect unemployment. Others will work for only 2 to 3 days and then file a job injury claim under the worker's compensation law. Both of these require human resource management follow-up action to protect Grossman's position, for if either of these unwarranted claims goes unchallenged, the workers collect money not due to them, at Grossman's expense.

Although the secondary sort requires some judgment and is usually performed by the most dependable employees with the most seniority, it is neither a skilled nor even a semi-skilled occupation. Grossman attempts to pay the U.S. Federal minimum wage of less than $5.00 per hour. However, the economy in Columbus, Ohio, has been so robust for the past five years that unemployment rates have consistently been less than 2.5%. As a result, laborers willing to work for the minimum wage cannot be found. Grossman is forced to pay between $5.00 and $6.00 per hour, depending upon longevity and job performance. In addition, it must offer a "fringe-benefit" package including expensive medical benefits.

Workers in one small section of the company's operation are organized by the Textile Worker's Union, A.F.L./C.I.O., but even the union's international leadership understands the reality that in such a commodity market, low wages are necessary to keep the company viable. As a result, the union makes no effort for milestone wage settlements at Grossman Industries.

THE PRODUCT

Grossman's value added is the grading and sorting of bulk purchases of "rags." Top quality garments, called "vintage," are respected brand labels in excellent condition which might include Saks Fifth Avenue, Brooks Brothers, Pendelton, and others of similar high quality. Those which show no wear and are functional (zippers zip and are not torn) can be sold at premium prices.

As an example, most Levi denim trousers have a small "Levi" red tag sticking out from the edge of the rear hip pocket. Almost all of them are spelled with a lowercase "e." However, a few, rare Levi's were made with an uppercase "E" and have become collector's items. They sell (in the U.S.) for up to $500, but in Japan, where Levis are treasured, the "E" Levis sell for up to $5,000. When a sorter finds one of these, there's true cause to celebrate. Bomber jackets, although not fetching $500 or $5,000, are also vintage garments.

The next level is called premium, consisting of garments which are fully functional, fashionable, and although not famous-maker labels, are in good demand in recycle or consignment goods stores: wool and flannel shirts (men's and women's) along with dresses, ordinary Levi pants and jackets. These command a lesser price than vintage, but a premium over quality #1.

Quality #1 garments are ordinary in nature, not of a particular label, but are 100% functional and have the broadest base of customer demand. Grossman sells nearly all of these to countries on the African continent. Quality #2 and #3 are of lesser grade, semi-functional and just a notch above being cut up for wiping rags. Those below quality #3 are, in fact, cut apart and sold as wiping rags to industry.

Quality levels of vintage down through #3 represent about 75% of the garments received at Grossman. Those cut and sold as wiping rags amount to about 20%. The remaining 5% is either polyester or wool. Polyester is sold to the "shoddy-makers." Shoddy is that grey black mat you find under the carpet of your car. It's an insulation mat used for padding or insulation in a car. Polyester is the only material Grossman sells at a loss. Rather than throwing it away, as an environmentally responsible organization, Grossman sells it at a loss so that it will be productively recycled into further use.

Wool is truly recycled. Grossman ships all of it to Italy, which is one of the few countries in the world that has the manufacturing capability to actually break down the garment made out of wool, and turn it back into a wool fiber, and then re-weave it into a wool garment. In garments labeled "Virgin Wool," it's right off the animal, but if the label just says "100% wool," that wool has been around for a while. Grossman sells wool at cost, but it fits its environmental policy.

Some items present a problem; coats are one of them. With 75% of the product being exported to the African continent, Grossman doesn't want coats. Efforts to sell them in countries like Russia have met with little success. Corruption in Russia is rampant and starting a new, small business virtually necessitates playing ball with organized crime.

The entire industry is looking for an outlet for warm clothing. China is the big potential market which everyone in the industry is trying to break into, but with little success. Much of the year the Chinese wear warm clothing, but getting started is a problem, since small orders just can't be profitable with the very small profit margin. Getting started in China means a small, profitless business for an unknown period.

MARKETS AND CHANNELS

About 75% of Grossman's rags are exported, making it the 5th or 6th largest exporter in the state of Ohio. About 20% is cut up and made into wiping cloths. The remaining 5% is either polyester or wool, and doesn't represent a profitable volume.

The demand for the basic product of bulk, serviceable garments is steady in the United States but continues to grow in Africa.

Some items become hot and command a high premium selling price. Ten years ago it was Izod polo shirts (with the little alligator logo). Everybody wanted them and sellers could demand quite a price for them. Chuck Shearer told all the graders, "Look for the alligators."

Today, western cowboy-style shirts are hot. Denim jackets are too. Bomber jackets are especially hot and command a big selling price. Grossman pays only 10 to 12 cents a pound for these hot items, but can sell them for $3 to $5 each. Unfortunately, they represent only a very small percentage of Grossman's intake.

These hot items are subject to mercurial swings in demand. Japanese teenagers loved the *Beverly Hills 90210* TV show and part of that show was the flannel shirts the actors wore. That made flannel shirts a big demand item in Japan. Chuck Shearer could sell all of those he could get, but he just couldn't find enough. The market would take all grades, all quantities. One year flannel shirts were selling for 50 cents a pound and the next year, because of *Beverly Hills 90210*, they were selling for $5.00 per pound. But just one year later, the market died out and the selling price was back to 50 cents a pound.

The industry doesn't offer terms for credit sales. Selling prices have a very broad range over the various quality levels, but average less than a dollar per pound, FAS, East Coast port of shipment. Seventy-five pecent of Grossman's export sales are by letter of credit and the balance by cash prior to shipment.

COMPETITION

There are about 200 textile recycling companies, or rag merchants, in the United States. The majority are small competitors, with annual sales well below $5,000,000. Only a handful are at annual sales levels in excess of $25,000,000 per year. None is unique, except that the very small ones tend to frequently leave the industry after they realize they will be unable to achieve a market share percentage yielding sufficient volume to realize a reasonable profit. The capability to achieve critical volume of sales is a competitive key to this industry.

There are a number of the larger competitive firms based along the East Coast, particularly from New York to Florida, and a few in Southern California. Being located on the coast, with nearby port facilities, gives these competitors a distinct cost advantage with the huge market on the African continent. Grossman must absorb the freight cost to the Eastern ports, a cost those competitors don't experience.

However, a new form of competition is starting to develop from Grossman's own customers, particularly those in Africa. Buyers are saying, "Why do we need to pay Grossman a profit to collect and grade rags when we can do it ourselves?" It's a classic case of backward vertical integration and because it's easy to do, many are tempted to enter the industry.

The problem with this strategy, of course, is analogous to a new market entry into Africa. Most of these African buyers don't know the channels of supply, and even the few that do, discover they must break apart the buyer-seller relationships which have existed for years. While it appears lucrative for them to integrate backwards, it's pretty tough for them to be successful at the process. Nevertheless, there is some erosion of Grossman's suppliers, tending to cause escalation of the prices paid for rags.

BARRIERS TO ENTRY

The barriers to enter this industry are very low. Large capital investments are unnecessary. Even working capital requirements are low, since most rags are sold soon after grading. Further, it is a simple business. Buy rags, sort them, and sell them. There's nothing complicated about what is done and years of study taken up in technical training aren't required either. Basically, it can be started out of a garage.

There are two factors which cause many industry entrants to fail. The first is a lack of critical sales volume.

The small entrepreneurs may actually start working out of their garages. What they typically fail to realize is that the margins are so small that a respectable profit can only be generated with large volumes. Many also fail to realize that it's a "cash-up-front" business. Start-ups which sell to customers in Africa on credit find it exceedingly difficult to obtain payment. One merchant, being owed a considerable sum, actually went to Africa to demand payment. That was a couple of years ago and he's not been seen or heard of since.

The second factor is the lack of a good reputation. Customers who fly to the U.S. from Africa are highly prone to do business with established firms who have developed a good industry-wide reputation and have developed a satisfactory business relationship with the specific customer. They avoid giving new suppliers "a chance" because they don't want to get stung and they don't have the time or money to experiment.

WHAT THEY ALREADY TRIED

"You know, Brad, it's too bad that maquiladoro concept you tried back in 1991 and 1992 didn't work out," Chuck lamented. "If that had worked, we probably wouldn't be facing the profit issue today."

"Yeh," Brad responded, "but it just wasn't the right stuff for a small company of our size." Brad continued to review the history of their maquiladoro experience just across the Mexican border from Laredo, Texas. "We could move our unsorted rags from the U.S. into a bonded area in Mexico without paying duty or any exhausting paperwork. The Mexican laborers then performed the work at pay levels of less than $1.00 per hour. The graded rags (including any scrap or waste resulting from the sorting) was then returned to the U.S., again duty-free."

This concept, developed with joint cooperation between the Mexican and American governments, provided needed jobs for Mexican workers and, at the same time, low cost production for American companies. The concept is especially attractive for companies who have repetitive, low skilled, routine work requirements where little training or education is required.

Brad continued. "This concept required us to absorb the freight costs from Columbus to Mexico and return; however, with labor costs of about one-fifth of the Columbus labor market, the theoretical savings potential was pretty good.

"Unfortunately, we didn't realize that the corruption of the Mexican officials would consume all the labor savings. Paying off the Mexican labor union leaders to get the union workforce cost a bundle. Then we had to continue to pay them off whenever we had to replace a worker who quit . . . and there were plenty of those.

"And that wasn't the worst of it. Paying off the Mexican customs agents at the border cost even more. The agents always claimed that our shipments returning to the U.S. were not properly documented. They always demanded that our driver unload an entire 40,000 pound truckload for inspection. But, for several hundred dollars, all of this could be avoided. Most of the labor savings were taken by the union officials but the customs officials wanted even more.

"This might work for big companies like Motorola or General Electric, who could find ways to comply or override these corrupt agents' demands. But a small company like us had to pay up. And it wasn't just the money. It really rankled me to pay bribes to do business. We tried for a year, but I finally gave up on the maquiladoro, and that whole experiment cost us a bundle." You could see that Brad was still smarting from a good idea that went sour.

"Well, that's all water over the dam at this point. Let's put our heads together and see what alternative strategic programs we can develop at this point." After several hours of discussion, they had sketched out four possible plans of action.

ALTERNATIVE STRATEGIC ACTIONS IDENTIFIED BY BRAD AND CHUCK

Collect Directly from the Original Owner— Alternative 1

Backward vertical integration by Grossman Industries could be a new strategy. Chuck Shearer could make presentations to Kiwanas, Rotary, and other service clubs as well as much larger organizations like Buckeye Boys Ranch with a pitch. He could offer them a way to generate income for their community service projects without hard work.

It goes like this: Grossman would establish a "drop box" with the service club's name and logo but Grossman would perform all the work of collection: supply the box, place the club's name on the box so that the local community can identify with it and also advertise within the community, "If you're going to donate clothing, give it to the Buckeye Boys Ranch at one of their convenient drop boxes." Grossman would then pick up all the material and pay the service organization a pre-agreed rate per pound.

Although it's recognized that implementation of this plan would take place over the long term, say five years, it is also recognized that perhaps 50% of Grossman's supply could be acquired via this channel.

This alternative is not without cost. The money saved by not paying a profit to the traditional suppliers will be eaten up by the cost of providing the drop boxes and making periodical pickups in addition to the commission paid to the local service organizations.

However, there is a significant hidden advantage. These garments will not be picked over, with most of the vintage and #1 quality garments being sold by the Salvation Army or Volunteers of America now being available to Grossman. Thus, the cream of the merchandise now becomes available at about the same overall cost as the current channels of supply that provide almost none of this quality grade. As a result, Grossman could sell the vintage and #1 quality garments to the thrift and consignment shops in the U.S. and thereby develop a new and highly profitable market segment.

Furthermore, there will be much more quality #1 and #2 rags, which will provide solid reinforcement of Grossman's image as a supplier of quality rags.

Relocate Near a Seaport—
Alternative 2

Relocation of the sorting operations to a small community near an East Coast port city offered possibilities in several areas. First, Grossman would no longer need to eat the freight costs from Columbus to an Eastern port of debarkation for its export shipments to Africa. In addition, the labor market in the Southeastern U.S. is quite different from that of Columbus, Ohio.

As witnessed by automotive, rubber, and other industries who have moved away from Midwest production sites, the work ethic in the Southeast U.S. was quite different: less confrontational with management, lower in cost (although not nearly as low as Mexican labor), and higher in productivity and job attendance.

Relocate Near Mexico and a Seaport—
Alternative 3

Shut down the Columbus operation and relocate the entire company near the Mexican border along the Texas Gulf Coast. This alternative would provide the advantage of low cost Mexican border labor and either Galveston or Corpus Christi as a port of debarkation for exports to Africa.

These locations would not provide sufficient sources of supply as does the Midwest, so some inbound freight costs would be incurred from suppliers, but the penalty Grossman now experiences for freight from Columbus to the East Coast would be eliminated.

Relocate en Route to a Seaport—
Alternative 4

A middle position between Columbus and an East Coast port city also offered advantages. Established sources of supply in the Midwest could be maintained by continuing to utilize Columbus as the central collection point. However, unsorted rags could then be transported part way to the East Coast port city by establishing a new sorting facility in, for example, a small West Virginia community where unemployment is at the highest level in the United States Wages are very competitive as is the work ethic. Educational levels are not high, but that is not a requirement of Grossman's sorting operations.

The sorting could be completed in West Virginia, where inexpensive warehouses could be utilized for finished goods storage prior to export shipment.

DECISION TIME

Brad Grossman looked out his office window and it was dark. "How long have we been at this?" he asked. Chuck looked at his watch. "About five hours and I'm getting hungry!"

Brad wanted to summarize. "Let's jot down all the viable alternatives we reviewed during the past five hours. We can each think them over but we need to come to a decision in the cold light of dawn. We'll meet again tomorrow at 7:30 in my office and determine which one of these would be the best for us. In addition, Chuck, if you think of any other good ones, we can compare those with these four. In any event, I want your recommendation as to which course of action is the best. You'll have to convince me why we should take that action. See you in the morning."

"Goodnight, Brad," Chuck murmured as he walked out of Brad's office looking at the carpeting and wondering what criteria he should use to select the best alternative.

The two had discussed four alternatives, and as soon as he got back to his office, Chuck wrote them all down so he wouldn't forget any. More than one was attractive, but he knew he had to select which one he thought was best and justify his decision. In order to do that, he would also need to briefly explain how the alternative would be implemented.

Chuck wasn't expecting a good night's sleep as his car edged up the ramp to I-270 for the drive home.

http://www.recycle.net/

STRATEGY FORMULATION

Reader's Digest Association*

George V. Grune, Chairman and Chief Executive Officer, reflected upon his years as head of Reader's Digest Association (RDA). He was a member of a triumvirate which had assumed power of the organization upon the death of cofounder Lila Wallace in 1984 at the age of 94. The other cofounder, DeWitt Wallace, had died at 91 in 1981. In the final years of their lives, RDA had run on "automatic pilot," lacking a clear sense of direction. Since their deaths, dramatic changes had taken place at RDA, including a new emphasis on costs and profits, something the Wallaces had not been overly concerned about.

Since 1984, the company had been run as a modern, profit-oriented company, complete with strategic planning. The results had been impressive. Revenues improved from $1.3 billion in 1984 to $2.6 billion in 1992, for a 100 percent increase. Net income went from $21 million in 1984 to $243 million in 1992, for over a thousand percent increase. The change had not been without its price. Under the Wallaces, the company had been a secretive and patriarchal company which took a paternalistic approach to its employees. For example, at Thanksgiving and Christmas, employees were given hams, turkeys, or cash. Under Grune, costs were lowered by cutting staff and overhead. Morale plummeted, and a number of key employees resigned.

Grune believed he had things under control. However, there were some trouble areas. Most of the increases in net income had come from obvious fat cutting, and questions were raised whether real growth could be fostered. Furthermore, a diversification move into specialty magazines had resulted in losses. RDA spent $20 million in an effort to improve its huge database of 100 million households for direct mail marketing, and this resulted in huge cost overruns and delays. *Value Line* reported that despite RDA's increased profits, the analysts were not enthusiastic about RDA's stock.

HISTORY†

RDA was founded in February 1922 by DeWitt and Lila Wallace to publish *Reader's Digest* magazine. DeWitt, a college dropout, was an avid magazine reader who placed the facts he wanted to remember on 3- by 5-inch slips of paper. Before going to bed at

---

*By Dan Kopp and Lois Shufeldt, Southwest Missouri State University. This case was prepared as a basis for class discussion rather than to illustrate effective or ineffective management practices. It was presented at the North American Case Research Association's annual meeting in November 1993. Copyright © 1994 by the *Business Case Journal* and Dan Kopp and Lois Shufeldt.

†This section is a condensed and paraphrased version of the article "Unforgettable DeWitt Wallace," by Charles Ferguson, *Reader's Digest*, February 1987: 1–20.

night, he would review what he had read during the day, and from time to time he would go through his files to refresh his memory. From this practice was born the idea for a magazine that presented information in abbreviated form. DeWitt put together 31 articles, one for each day of the month, which were condensed to two pages or less. The editorial mix of articles consisted of self-improvement, simple answers to complicated problems, super-patriotism mixed with anti-communism, and loads of corn. No advertisements were included in the magazine. Initially 5,000 copies were mailed to charter subscribers who had been sent a direct mail advertisement announcing the new magazine and offering a money-back guarantee if they were not satisfied. The original price was $3 per year. No one requested a refund, and there were no cancellations.

In September 1922, the Wallaces moved to Pleasantville, New York, and continued to mail promotion announcements seeking subscribers. By the end of the magazine's first year, circulation had increased to 7,000. After 4 years, the circulation had improved to 20,000; over the next 3 years, circulation skyrocketed to 216,000. The Wallaces expanded their physical facilities in various Pleasantville office buildings as circulation inched upward.

The Wallaces never divulged the financials on their operations, but *Fortune* magazine reported in 1936 that the magazine had netted the Wallaces $418,000 and had a circulation of 1,800,000. Still, there were no revenues from advertisements. DeWitt Wallace was the primary editor of the magazine, while Lila had little interest in the magazine, even though her name was listed ahead of DeWitt's as editor. Her interests were in artwork, decoration, and homemaking.

At one point, RDA was operating in 14 locations around Pleasantville, and Lila thought it was time to have a central location. She secured architects and supervised the building of the new corporate headquarters. Lila designed the landscaping and interior decoration.

In 1938, a British edition of *Reader's Digest* was printed, followed by other foreign editions. RDA diversified into condensed books in 1950 and started publishing general books, records, and cassettes. The year 1955 marked the inclusion of advertisements to hold down the prices of subscriptions. In 1962, RDA pioneered sweepstakes mailings. By 1980, the Wallaces' wealth was estimated to be $500 million.

The Wallaces were very generous with their wealth. Some of the profits were disseminated to employees. For example, in 1941, $71,040 was distributed to 348 employees earning $250 a month or less. The generosity toward employees continued as long as DeWitt lived. Since the Wallaces were childless, they donated freely to various organizations. Macalester College, for example, received over $50 million, and the New York Public Library was given $1.8 million for refurbishing and restoring the periodicals rooms. New York's Metropolitan Museum of Art received well over $50 million.

DeWitt and Lila retired in 1973 when both were 73; however, DeWitt continued to come to his office and do some work for RDA for the rest of his life.

THE INDUSTRY

According to *U.S. Industrial Outlook 1993*, the first half of 1992 had seen better-than-expected gains in advertising pages after experiencing two consecutive years of sharp page declines. During the same period, circulation for consumer magazines remained flat, due to weakness in single-copy newsstand sales. Total magazine industry sales for 1992 were expected to increase slightly more than 1 percent. Total industry sales were estimated at $21.3 billion.

Uncertainty concerning the economy made publishers cautious. Publishers were hesitant to incur more debt to launch new magazines, acquire other magazines, or upgrade the editorial content of their magazines. Due to stiff competition for limited advertising dollars, many publishers offered advertisers ad rate discounts and special deals to attract more advertising to their magazines. Concentrated efforts were made to refrain from substantially increasing subscription and newsstand prices. Publishers turned their efforts toward other revenue sources.

In 1990 newsstand magazines accounted for 20 percent of total circulation, and subscription sales for 80 percent. Newsstand consumer magazines represented 31 percent of total revenues, and subscription sales accounted for 69 percent. During the recession, newsstand sales suffered more than subscription sales. This was due to more cautious consumer buying habits, higher magazine prices, lack of display space in stores due to the growing number of magazines, and a decline in the number of outlets for publication.

The number of U.S. periodicals in 1991 was 11,239. Of these, 2,276 were consumer and farm magazines, an increase of 750 from the 1981 total. The next year, 1992, saw increases in magazine closings due to a weak advertisement environment, postal increases of magazines, lackluster circulation, and increased competition from other media.

Some publishers registered their environmental concern by using recycled paper stock for their magazines. This practice was not, however, widespread due to problems with the quality, prices, and availability of recycled stock. The industry was facing possible Congressional legislation imposing mandatory use of recycled paper. Although there was opposition among publishers to mandatory use requirements, one source reported that the number of publishers voluntarily using recycled paper had increased from 24 percent in 1991 to 35 percent in 1992.

Due to the saturated condition of the U.S. market, publishers were turning their attention to overseas markets to increase revenues. In 1991 U.S. exports increased 6 percent over the 1991 levels, to $747 million. Major export markets for U.S. magazines in 1991 included Canada (78 percent), the United Kingdom (6 percent), Mexico (4 percent), and the Netherlands (3 percent). The most common forms of global expansion for U.S. magazine publishers included subsidiaries, joint venture operations, and licensing.

During the late 1980s and early 1990s, U.S. publishers had launched a number of foreign editions of popular U.S. magazines, especially in Europe. Due to the recession in Europe, however, the conditions for launching publishing ventures had become unfavorable. Recently, a number of U.S. magazine companies had introduced publications in eastern Europe. However, this region offered little publishing potential for most U.S. publishers due to the lack of currency, few sources of advertising, and poor mail distribution.

During the last 5 years, European publishers, especially German and French firms, had invested heavily in foreign editions of their publications, both in the United States and Europe. United States imports of periodicals increased an estimated 19 percent to $144 million over 1991 imports. Canada captured 60 percent of the market, followed by the United Kingdom, Japan, and Mexico—representing 11, 6, and 4 percent, respectively.

Predictions for the more favorable economic climate in 1993 were for an increase of at least 2 percent in U.S. magazine industry receipts. Also forecast were fewer magazines ceasing publication, a leveling off of total magazine circulation, and an increase in the number of new magazines in special niches. Printing and magazine costs were not expected to increase more than 5 percent, unless demand for recycled paper increased more than anticipated. Postal rates were not expected to increase.

The 5-year outlook predicted that industry receipts could grow at a yearly rate of 1 to 2 percent if the economy grew as predicted. The following trends were predicted.

■ Publishers will be more concerned about the balance between advertising and circulation revenues. There will be less dependence on advertising revenues, with more aggressive advertising strategies competing for limited advertising dollars.

■ Publishers will be more likely to offer a targeted editorial product. Firms which clearly identify their readers, reader interest, and the advertisers who want to reach those readers will have a competitive advantage. The most growth will be experienced by those publications targeting narrowly defined interest areas of readers; for example, more attention will be devoted to reaching minority audiences.

■ To attract readers, more magazines will consider improving their editorial quality.

■ Higher prices are anticipated for subscriptions, which will reduce the dependence of publishers on advertising revenues.

■ With the increase in the number of competitors for advertising dollars, more attention will be focused on providing advertisers with information on audiences they wish to reach.

THE COMPETITION

Reader's Digest magazine competed with other magazines for subscribers, and with magazines, as well as all other media, including radio and television, for advertising. RDA strongly believed that its uniqueness, well-established reputation, and longstanding and extensive international operations gave it a significant competitive advantage.

RDA was also in competition with many other direct mail marketers. In this area also the company strongly believed that its name, image, and reputation, along with its customer list, gave RDA a significant advantage over its competition. Its books and home entertainment products were in competition with other direct mail marketers, as well as retailers. RDA's specialty magazines were in competition with other similar magazines for readers and advertising.

Since RDA was such a diverse firm and competed in select niches, it was difficult to identify direct competitors. Two firms that were in direct competition with RDA were Time Warner, Inc., and Meredith Corporation.

Time Warner, Inc.

Time Warner was the world's largest media and entertainment company. It had operations in magazines (30 magazines, including *Time, People, Sports Illustrated, Fortune,* and *Life*); filmed entertainment (Warner Brothers, Lorimar TV, and Warner Home Video); recorded music and music publishing (Warner Brothers Records, Atlantic Records Group, and Warner/Chappell Music); cable television (American Television and Communications Corporation); programming (HBO, Cinemax, and the Comedy Channel); and books (Time-Life, Book-of-the-Month Club, and Warner Books and Oxmoor House).

Time Warner had 44,000 employees and $13.1 billion in revenues in 1992. According to *Value Line*, the company was positioned for global growth. Time Warner's movie and music businesses were the industry leaders in the United States and overseas. Future growth was expected in the United States, Europe, and Asia as those economies recovered from the recession. Publishing, which amounted to 23 percent of 1992 revenues and 13 percent of operating profits, was seen as less essential to Time Warner.

Meredith Corporation

Meredith was a diversified media company with operations in magazines (15 subscription-based magazines including *Ladies Home Journal, Better Homes and Gardens*, and *Country Home* and 47 special interest publications in the areas of home improvement, decorating, gardening, and family life); book publishing (175 home and family services books); television broadcasting (5 television stations); and real estate marketing and franchising. In fiscal 1993, total sales were $769 million; there were 2,335 employees. Publishing represented 80 percent of revenues and 61 percent of profits.

According to *Moody's Handbook*, earnings were expected to improve through cost reduction and streamling strategies. Furthermore, an agreement with Wal-Mart to establish Better Homes and Gardens Centers in 1994 in more than 2,000 stores, which would carry a variety of gardening-related publications, was seen as of potential benefit to operating profits.

ORGANIZATION

The 1992 10-K form described RDA as

> a global publisher and direct mail marketer of magazines, books, recorded music collections, home videos, and other products.

The company was organized into four business divisions: (1) *Reader's Digest* magazine, (2) books and home entertainment products, (3) special interest magazines and (4) other operations. Exhibit 1 provides revenue and operating profits for each division.

Reader's Digest Magazine

The world's most widely read magazine, *Reader's Digest* was published in 17 languages and 41 editions. The latest foreign language editions included Russian and Hungarian. Worldwide, it was estimated that there were more than 100 million readers. Total circulation was over 28 million, more than *Time, Newsweek, U.S. News & World Report*, and *TV Guide* combined. Approximately 95 percent of the U.S. circulation of *Reader's*

EXHIBIT 1
Revenues and Operating Profit by Business Segment
(dollar figures in millions)

Business Segment	1992	1991	1990	1989	1988
	Revenues				
Reader's Digest magazine	$ 685.0	$ 655.5	$ 623.9	$ 589.4	$ 570.0
Books and home entertainment products	1,744.8	1,500.1	1,220.3	1,086.1	1,017.0
Special interest magazines	75.5	73.7	57.5	47.3	22.6
Other operations	112.9	119.5	111.0	111.6	105.5
Intersegment	(4.2)	(3.7)	(3.0)	(2.4)	(3.1)
Total revenues	$2,614.0	$2,345.1	$2,009.7	$1,832.0	$1,712.0
	Operating Profit				
Reader's Digest magazine	$ 96.8	$ 89.4	$ 75.4	$ 61.6	$ 65.9
Books and home entertainment products	303.0	270.6	228.9	192.3	196.0
Special interest magazines	(19.5)	(29.4)	(25.7)	(17.1)	(14.2)
Other operations	22.2	20.6	21.1	16.5	13.5
Eliminations	—	—	(0.05)	0.05	(0.1)
Corporate expense	(72.3)	(59.2)	(59.6)	(46.6)	(47.8)
Total operating profit	$ 330.2	$ 292.0	$ 240.1	$ 206.7	$ 213.3

Source: RDA *Annual Reports*.

Digest consisted of subscriptions, with the other 5 percent coming from single copy sales at newsstands and in supermarkets. Subscription prices in 1993 were $20.93 per year and $2.15 per single copy. The renewal rate was 70 percent, up from 64 percent in 1985, which indicated that readers were exceptionally loyal.

The magazine was unique, in that 30 percent of its revenues came from advertising, which was 20 percent less than the industry norm. This made the magazine far more recession-resistant than other mass circulation magazines. The magazine provided the company with just 28 percent of total sales and 31 percent of profits.

When asked about the success of *Reader's Digest*, Kenneth Tomlinson, editor-in-chief, replied:

> This magazine is for the people, not for liberal East Coast editors. We keep in touch with what the masses really want to know about. We emphasize RD's special bond with the common man. (Teitelbaum, 1991, 91)

The magazine had a sunken treasure—a mailing list that included 50 million households, which was more than half the households in the United States. Once a household subscribed to the magazine, the details of its spending were accumulated in the RDA database center, which was located some 30 feet beneath RDA's headquarters. Each household was tracked for its purchases and preferences in response to the continual mailings it received. This information was valuable in targeting market segments or testing new products. RDA's mailing list was the best in the business. RDA also had an international list which included a comparable number of households.

The mailing list was used to sell bigger ticket items—books, specialty magazines, videos, and recorded music. Once a household subscribed to *Reader's Digest*, the household was sent a sweepstakes or other mailing that offered another *Reader's Digest* product. Once a household ordered a particular item such as travel books, it could expect to receive similar mailings on products related to its purchase. Offers could be other travel books, travel magazines, or travel videos. One competitor remarked, "They mind their customer base better than anyone in the business." In 1989, *Reader's Digest* sent out more than 600 million pieces of mail. It was estimated that half of the households on the U.S. list had purchased one or more products or received services from RDA within the past 2 years.

According to Patrick Kenney, circulation manager, "*Reader's Digest*'s sweepstakes are seen as an extremely successful way to introduce potential subscribers to the magazine." Although many companies offered sweepstakes at the time, *Reader's Digest*'s sweepstakes were viewed very favorably by its customers.

RDA spent an estimated $20 million on updating the database. According to *Business Week*, the updating experienced significant cost overruns and delays.

Reader's Digest was a global magazine. Exhibit 2 provides 1988–1992 revenues and operating profits by geographic area. Exhibit 3 lists the countries in which *Reader's Digest* competed. The European, Latin American, and Asian/Pacific editions had the largest paid circulation of any magazine in their respective regions. *Reader's Digest* also had the largest paid circulation of any magazine in numerous other countries, including United Kingdom, Germany, France, and Mexico, to name just a few.

EXHIBIT 2
Revenues and Operating Profit by Geographic Area
(dollar figures in millions)

Area	1992	1991	1990	1989	1988
	Revenues				
United States	$1,146.7	$1,038.8	$ 930.4	$ 860.2	$ 819.2
Europe	1,114.0	996.7	793.4	726.6	691.6
Other	362.0	318.1	293.9	253.6	206.8
Inter-area	(8.7)	(8.5)	(8.0)	(8.4)	(5.6)
Total revenues	$2,614.0	$2,345.1	$2,009.7	$1,832.0	$1,712.0
	Operating Profit				
United States	$ 197.3	$ 177.5	$ 151.0	$ 121.4	$ 132.2
Europe	146.5	119.2	100.4	97.4	107.8
Other	58.7	54.5	48.3	34.5	21.1
Corporate expense	(72.3)	(59.2)	(59.6)	(46.6)	(47.8)
Total operating profit	$ 330.2	$ 292.0	$ 240.1	$ 206.7	$ 213.3

Source: RDA *Annual Reports*.

EXHIBIT 3
Global Circulation of *Reader's Digest*

Edition	Circulation Rate Base
Europe	
Belgium–Flemish	80,000
Belgium–French	88,000
Denmark	110,000
Finland	345,000
France	1,077,000
Germany and Austria	1,250,000
Hungary	50,000
Italy	650,000
The Netherlands	390,000
Norway	163,000
Portugal	256,000
Russia	100,000
Spain	74,000
Sweden	149,000
Switzerland–French	85,000
Switzerland–German	256,000
United Kingdom	1,500,000
Asia/Pacific	
Asia–Chinese	300,000
Asia–English	242,000
Australia	476,000
India–English	350,000
India–Hindi	55,000
Korea	120,000
New Zealand	170,000
North America	
Canada–English	1,264,000
Canada–French	319,000
United States–English	16,250,000
United States–Spanish	131,000
Latin America	
Argentina	137,000
Brazil	75,000
Central America	35,000
Chile	38,000
Colombia	55,000
Ecuador	11,000
Mexico	700,000
Peru	33,000
Puerto Rico/Dominican Republic	67,000
Uruguay/Paraguay/Bolivia	36,000
Venezuela	33,000
Other	
Middle East	58,000
South Africa	370,000
Total	27,948,000

Source: 1992 Form 10-K.

In the U.S. market, *Reader's Digest* sold approximately 5 million new subscriptions each year in order to maintain its circulation rate base. New subscriptions were secured primarily by direct mail. New subscriptions were sold at a discount price from both single-copy and regular subscription prices. The largest percentage of subscriptions were sold between July and December of each year, with many of these subscriptions purchased by current subscribers as Christmas gifts.

Reader's Digest offered advertisers different regional editions, major market editions, and test market editions in the United States and the larger international markets. On the average, the U.S. editions contained 160 editorial pages, the highest among any major magazine. About half the articles in *Reader's Digest* were original articles written by staff writers with the balance selected from existing sources. Approximately 500 publications were read each month by editorial staff members to identify possible articles.

Books and Home Entertainment Products

Through direct mail, RDA published and marketed *Reader's Digest* condensed books, series books, general interest books, recorded music collections, and home video products.

Condensed Books

Condensed Books were condensed versions of mostly popular fiction and some nonfiction. The reduced-length versions appealed to consumers who had limited reading time or limited access to retail book stores. Since 1950, Condensed Books had been published in twelve languages and marketed in 21 countries.

International editions of Condensed Books were translated and edited as appropriate for the location in which they were published. Locally published works were also sometimes issued as RDA Condensed Books.

Six volumes of Condensed Books were published each year in the United States. Each volume contained a variety of works. Not all selections were by well-known authors. RDA's research indicated that readers considered enjoyment of the selection to be more important than the fame of the author. Thus, the selected works reflected the traditional values of RDA.

The company automatically shipped regular Condensed Book customers volumes every 2 to 3 months until requested not to do so. Direct mail, with extensive use of sweepstakes entries and premium merchandise offers, was used to solicit new customers.

Series Books

Series books had been marketed since the early 1980s, and there was a strategy for expanding the series book product line. The same marketing strategy was used for the series books as for the Condensed Books. The first volume was shipped free of charge, and subsequent books were automatically shipped until a cancellation notice was received. Some of the series books were part of an open-ended, continuing series, while others consisted of a limited number of volumes.

Series books were published in 7 languages and marketed in 16 countries. More than 11 million series books were sold annually. The internationally marketed series books had global consumer appeal and required only limited adaptation for use in different countries.

General Interest Books

General interest books were first published in 1961. These books included reference books, cookbooks, how-to and do-it-yourself books, songbooks, and special interest books such as history, travel, religion, health, nature, and the home. Hundreds of these books have been published. The criterion of global appeal was used in picking general interest books for publication, so that limited adaptation was required.

The most popular books were *Book of the Road, Do-It-Yourself, You and the Law, Great World Atlas*, and the *Illustrated Guide to Gardening*. More than 5 million copies each had been published of those five books.

More than 23 million general interest books were sold annually. They were published in 11 languages and marketed in 25 countries. Most sales resulted from direct mail announcements, but the books were also distributed to retail outlets, which accounted for a small portion of the sales.

RDA utilized prepublication testing of these books. The customer database provided statistical data which were used to develop a market forecast for the proposed books before substantial expenses were incurred for the creation of the book.

Music

RDA published record music packages, which were sold by direct mail; cassettes and compact discs were sometimes available. Generally, the packages were collections of previously recorded material by a variety of artists. A wide variety of music—from classical to country to easy listening and religious music—was offered. The music packages were multiunit sets, which included three to five cassettes or the equivalent compact discs.

Almost 7 million music sets were sold annually. One four-cassette set sold 1.5 million copies. There were more than 15,000 selections in the music set library.

The same marketing strategy was used for the music sets as for the general interest books. Extensive preproduction research was conducted. The music sets were marketed in 19 countries, with different music products offered in each market.

Video

Home video products were first offered in 1986. A similar product strategy was used for the home video products as with the general interest books. RDA was in the process of expanding its video operations, both domestically and globally. More than 2.5 million home video products were sold annually, and the products were marketed in 14 countries outside the United States.

Special Interest Magazines

RDA first diversified into special interest magazines in 1986. The selection criteria for acquisitions were consistency with the image and editorial philosophy of RDA, and market expertise. Exhibits 4 and 5 provide details regarding RDA's special interest magazines. Each magazine had undergone strategic changes since acquisition, which included upgraded editorial quality, changes in personnel, revised marketing strategies, and a new management infrastructure. RDA utilized its customer data list to promote its magazines.

The special interest magazines had not been profitable (refer to Exhibit 1). However, RDA viewed this division as having long-term growth potential and continued to support it with that in mind. One magazine, *Family Budgets*, a French magazine started by RDA in 1990, had been discontinued. There were no current plans for additional acquisitions, but RDA was open to such acquisitions if appropriate magazines became available.

Other Operations

Other operations included the sales of language courses, consisting of written materials and cassettes, and globes. The revenues for these products were not material to RDA's business.

QSP, Inc., was a wholly owned subsidiary which assisted schools and youth groups in their fund-raising activities. It was one of the largest organizations of its kind in the United States. QSP assisted its clients in planning and running fund-rais-

---

EXHIBIT 4
RDA Special Interest Magazines

Magazine	Year Acquired	Focus	How Sold/Price
Travel Magazine	1986	Practical travel magazine aimed at middle-income travelers	Subscription Travel Club Members/$11.97
Family Handyman	1987	Provides instructions and guidance for "do-it-yourself" home improvement projects	Subscription/$17.93 Newsstand/$2.25 per
New Choices for Retirement Living	1988	Aimed at active mature readers and provides information on entertainment, travel, health, and leisure time activities	Subscription/$19.97
American Health	1990	Provides helpful information on Medicare, nutrition, psychology, and fitness	Subscription/$17.97 Newsstand/$1.95 per
Moneywise (United Kingdom)	1990	Helps families manage their finances	n.a.

Source: Form 10-K, pp. 13–14.

EXHIBIT 5
Selected Information on Special Interest Magazines

	Circulation Rate Base	Number of Advertising Pages Carried	Gross Advertising Revenues
Travel Holiday			
1992	550,000	458	$8,887,500
1991	550,000	450	8,098,900
1990	550,000	413	6,980,400
1989	750,000	392	6,069,600
1988	750,000	393	6,340,000
Family Handyman			
1992	1,000,000	439	$10,779,600
1991	1,000,000	441	11,230,800
1990	1,300,000	378	8,995,200
1989	1,275,000	502	9,834,800
1988	1,200,000	520	10,808,700
New Choices for Retirement Living			
1992	575,000	324	$7,065,800
1991	575,000	323	6,757,300
1990	575,000	381	7,408,400
1989	575,000	451	7,604,200
1988	500,000	387	5,924,100
American Health			
1992	800,000	424	$9,213,300
1991	800,000	295	5,904,700
1990	800,000	603	11,541,500
1989	1,000,000	705	13,033,700
1988	900,000	699	12,101,500

Source: Form 10-K, pp. 13–14.

ing campaigns. Participants sold magazine subscriptions, music products, books, food and gifts. QSP generated its revenue from a portion of the proceeds of each sale. Magazine subscriptions were offered at substantial discount. Several hundred publishers, including RDA, provided the discounts. A large music publisher offered discounted music products.

FINANCES

Exhibits 6 and 7 provide financial data for RDA for the years 1989–1992. The company was privately held until 1989, when it went public. In the *1992 First Quarter Report*, Chief Financial Officer Anthony W. Ruggeiro listed RDA's financial accomplishments:

EXHIBIT 6
Reader's Digest Association, Inc.: Consolidated Statements of Income
(dollars in thousands, except per share data)

	1992	1991	1990	1989
Revenues	$2,613,958	$2,345,068	$2,009,704	$1,832,013
Cost of sales, fulfillment and distribution expense	1,046,906	940,587	786,554	697,654
Promotion, selling and administrative expense	1,236,838	1,112,479	983,017	927,644
	$2,283,744	$2,053,066	$1,769,571	$1,625,298
Operating profit	$ 330,214	$ 292,002	$ 240,133	$ 206,715
Other income (expense)				
Interest and dividend income	$ 52,894	$ 48,724	$ 46,058	$ 38,747
Gain on sale of assets				1,240
Net gain (loss) on marketable securities and short-term investments				(8,550)
Interest expense	(2,933)	(4,078)	(3,554)	(2,843)
Other, net	936	3,415	1,822	(484)
	$ 50,897	$ 48,061	$ 44,326	$ 28,110
Income before provision for income taxes	381,111	340,063	284,459	234,825
Provision for income taxes	146,728	130,923	108,439	83,277
Net income	$ 234,383	$ 209,140	$ 176,020	$ 151,548
Earnings per common share	$ 1.95	$ 1.74	$ 1.48	$ 1.28
Average common shares outstanding	119,800	119,413	118,343	117,796

Source: RDA *Annual Reports.*

- Earnings per share increased from $0.16 in 1984 to $1.95 in 1992.

- U.S. revenues grew from $700 million in 1984 to $1.1 billion in 1992, while international revenues doubled. International revenues are now more than half RDA's total.

- World revenues for *Reader's Digest* maintained a steady 6 percent growth, with operating profits doubling since 1987.

- Revenues for books and home entertainment, RDA's largest segment, have both doubled since 1987.

- Special interest magazines have reported losses to date; however, the loss was reduced by $10 million in 1992. Our focus is to achieve profitability in this area before seriously considering any new acquisitions.

- Cash grew from $131 million in 1984 to $804 million in 1992.

- The balance sheet is very strong; RDA enjoys significant operating growth while generating substantial cash.

EXHIBIT 7
Reader's Digest Association, Inc.: Consolidated Balance Sheets
(dollars in thousands)

	1992	1991	1990	1989
	Assets			
Current assets				
Cash and cash equivalents	$ 292,703	$ 191,634	$ 205,157	$ 331,238
Short-term investments, at cost which approximates market	39,694	169,003	113,709	105,593
Receivables, less allowances for returns and bad debts of $173,630 in 1992, $126,852 in 1991, $101,899 in 1990, and $95,993 in 1989	408,588	334,111	275,261	215,812
Inventories	153,234	135,589	118,213	88,009
Prepaid expenses and other current assets	107,804	83,126	46,899	48,832
Deferred federal and foreign income taxes	—	—	15,952	9,744
Total current assets	$1,002,023	$ 913,463	$ 775,191	$ 799,228
Marketable securities, at cost (market value $559,072 in 1992, $336,828 in 1991, $282,447 in 1990, and $89,948 in 1989)	471,635	289,096	269,526	68,239
Investments in affiliated and other companies, primarily at cost	—	—	25,516	20,010
Other long-term investments	58,363	38,095		
Property, plant and equipment, net	253,666	223,695	231,296	191,070
Deferred federal and foreign income taxes	—	—	15,502	21,252
Intangible assets, net	79,839	90,032	86,651	50,759
Other noncurrent assets	66,783	50,869	30,652	23,138
Total assets	$1,932,309	$1,605,250	$1,434,334	$1,173,696
	Liabilities and Stockholders' Equity			
Current liabilities				
Notes payable	$ 6,386	$ 7,948	$ 5,072	$ 8,078
Accounts payable	171,740	135,449	122,504	108,094
Accrued expenses	229,271	192,085	161,543	149,095
Federal and foreign income taxes	89,991	58,346	58,531	43,956
Advances from affiliated companies	—	—	13,516	12,665
Other current liabilities	17,433	13,066	—	—
Total current liabilities	$ 514,821	$ 406,894	$ 361,166	$ 321,888
Long-term notes payable	11,083	13,975	11,785	11,148
Unearned revenue	383,310	347,033	338,549	296,103
Other noncurrent liabilities	88,217	77,726	88,751	95,317
Total liabilities	$ 997,431	$ 845,628	$ 800,251	$ 724,456
Stockholders' equity				
Capital stock	28,520	29,170	30,240	30,224
Paid-in capital	56,360	36,511	34,095	—
Retained earnings	847,138	709,866	570,041	440,799
Foreign currency translation adjustment	17,970	(15,725)	1,584	(21,583)
Less: Treasury stock, at cost	(15,110)	(200)	(200)	(200)
Unamortized restricted stock	—	—	(1,677)	
Total stockholders' equity	$ 934,878	$ 759,622	$ 634,083	$ 449,240
Total liabilities and stockholders' equity	$1,932,309	$1,605,250	$1,434,334	$1,173,696

Source: RDA *Annual Reports.*

- In the latest Fortune 500 listing we ranked:
  First in publishing and printing industry for ROE
  First for our sales growth
  Third for our profit growth
  Third for our return on assets

CORPORATE STRATEGIC PLANNING

RDA began utilizing the concepts of strategic management when Grune took the helm in 1984. Since that time strategic plans had been updated, and a more sophisticated and mature level of planning had taken place. The strategic plan included a mission component and a strategies component.

Mission

RDA's *1992 Annual Report* summarized its mission in a section entitled "Words We Live By":

> *Focus on Serving the Customer* Providing superior quality service that meets the individual needs of our customer. Developing and delivering products that make a difference in people's lives worldwide.
>
> *Recognition and Concern for Employees* Respecting the individual. Advocating fair treatment for all. Rewarding exceptional performance. Showing commitment to personal and professional growth. Encouraging teamwork.
>
> *Maintain High Ethical Standards* Becoming involved as good corporate citizens wherever we work and live around the world. Treating customers and suppliers with integrity, fairness and respect. Avoiding even the appearance of conflict of interest. Respecting and preserving our environment. Providing leadership in industry, trade and regulatory associations.
>
> *Innovative, Results-Oriented Company* Dedicating ourselves to maximizing the value of the company for share owners.

Strategies (Corporate Strategic Plan)

The corporate strategic plan of RDA incorporated strategies which focused on the basic product lines and operating strengths. Emphasis was placed upon growth and capturing the benefits of globalization. Specific strategies included the following (*1992 Annual Report*, 2–3):

1. Ensure the flagship role of RD magazine as a major profit center and the "front door" to the company to build our customer base. The magazine will always be fundamental to the worldwide reputation and basis for global growth since it is the first contact customers have with the company.

2. Grow current product lines by increasing customer base in countries where RDA does business. Use special interest magazines to bring new customers who are potential buyers of many other products.

3. Develop new products to sell to existing customers. Video products have increased over 2.5 million in 15 countries.

4. Expand current product lines into new countries. General interest books, series books, music, Condensed Books, and *Reader's Digest* magazine have been introduced into such countries as Scandinavia, Finland, South Africa, the eastern part of Germany, and Russia.

5. Maximize global business growth through globalization initiatives. Global management task forces are implementing a global information system and programs for editorial excellence, product quality, effective promotions, customer service.

6. Achieve growth objectives within existing businesses and core skills. Focus is on what RDA does best. Acquisitions will be made only when they fit tightly with core business.

FUTURE OF RDA

Grune reviewed the latest strategic plan as he contemplated the future of RDA and its trouble spots. As he put it:

> These plans are our road map for our future. Based on our recent history, I am confident it will guide us to even greater success.
>
> We are raising the standards for our industry, moving the so-called "barrier of entry" even higher. We will widen our lead over the competition. And we will make newcomers to the industry think twice before they challenge us. We have the systems, the products and the people to strengthen our position as a global publisher and a world leader in direct mail marketing. And we have some unique qualities—competitive advantages that separate us from virtually all of our rivals. (*First Quarter Report 1992*, 5–6.)

REFERENCES

Annual Reports 1990, 1991, 1992. Reader's Digest Association.

Cheever, Benjamin. "Bad Days in Pleasantville." *Nation*, 7 May 1990: 628–632.

Ferguson, Charles. "Unforgettable DeWitt Wallace." *Reader's Digest*, February 1987: 1–20.

First Quarter Report 1992. Reader's Digest Association.

Form 10-K. Reader's Digest Association, 1992.

Kenney, Patrick. "29 Million Readers Can't Be Wrong." *Target Marketing*, October 1989: 18, 24.

"Meredith Corporation." *Moody's Handbook*, 1994.

"Meredith Corporation." *Standard & Poor's*, 11 January 1994: 1478.

"Printing and Publishing." *U.S. Industrial Outlook 1993*.

"Pulp Profits." *Economist*, 20 October 1990: 84–86.

"Reader's Digest." *Value Line*, 4 September 1992: 1804.

Rothman, Andrea. "The Man Who Rewrote Reader's Digest." *Business Week*, 4 June 1990: 148–149.

Teitelbaum, Richard. "Are Times Tough? Here's an Answer." *Fortune*, 2 December 1991: 91.

"Time Warner." *Value Line*. Reader's Digest Association, 4 March 1994: 1770.

http://www.digest.com.pl/

STRATEGY FORMULATION

Birra Moretti*

> We want to keep momentum. Until we overtook Poretti we were pressing to be number three and had something to shoot at. It's a little harder now that we are third. Dreher is a long way away, and we need a share of about 18 percent of Italian production to get the breweries to true efficient scale. So we have to almost double sales again.
>
> Richard Beveridge, February 1993

Key managers of Birra Moretti SpA met in Bologna, Italy, in February 1993 to develop their proposed fiscal year 1994 (ending March 31) comprehensive business plan. In June 1989, Toronto's John Labatt Limited had acquired Birra Moretti along with another Italian brewer, Prinz Brau Brewing Company. Prinz was merged into Moretti in the months after the acquisitions. The new Moretti's unit sales grew from a rate of about 800,000 hectoliters per year (hl/yr)† in late 1989 to 1.2 million in FY1992, and the sales projection for FY1993 was 1.4 million.

To continue its growth strategy in FY1994, Moretti needed an estimated US$15 million from Labatt. Such funding was hardly assured, as Labatt itself was retrenching and restructuring in Canada and the United States. Further, despite a similar infusion during FY1993, Moretti's rate of growth in unit sales had slowed to 5 percent, down from 21 percent the previous year. And earnings before interest and taxes (EBIT) remained negative, as had been true since the 1989 acquisitions.

ITALY AND THE BEER INDUSTRY

Foreign firms obtained control of most Italian brewers during the 1980s. The investments seemed promising at first, as Italians, like other southern Europeans, began to cut their consumption of wine and drink more beer. But beer sales in Italy stopped increasing in 1985, and by 1988, every major Italian brewer was losing money. Further,

---

*Prepared by Arthur Sharplin of the Institute for International Business Studies, Pordenone, Italy, and Waltham Associates, Inc., Austin, Texas. The author thanks Richard Beveridge, Yasmin Ferrari, Adam Humphries, William G. Bourne, Sidney M. Oland, and John Morgan, as well as John Seeger and the anonymous reviewers of the *Case Research Journal*, for their assistance. Management assisted in the research for the case but exercised no editorial prerogative. The case was written solely for the purpose of stimulating student discussion.
†A hectoliter is 100 liters, or 26.4 U.S. gallons.

political uncertainty along with worsening economic and demographic conditions suggested that recovery would not occur soon.

Political and Economic Circumstances

Professor Franco Cazzola, of the University of Florence, described the worsening condition of the Italian government in early 1993, concluding, "An entire political system, faced with a crisis of legitimacy, is now falling to pieces."[1] The head of Italy's ruling Socialist Party and the justice minister had just resigned under charges of corruption. Over 150 members of parliament had been named in criminal inquiries, and 850 lesser Italian officials and business persons had been arrested for various abuses.

Italy's unemployment rate moved up from 9.9 percent in 1991 to 11 percent in 1992. The lire was devalued 7 percent by the Italian government in 1992, and fell even further as a result of financial market pressure. Exhibit 1 gives selected economic statistics for Italy during the years from 1988 to 1992. As the exhibit shows, Italy's population grew by only 600,000 during those years. More relevant to the brewing industry was what had happened to the 15–34 year age bracket, which Italian beer industry association Assobirra called "the formative beer drinking population." This segment peaked at 18 million in 1990, and was projected to fall to 16 million in 2000 and 12 million in 2010.

The Competitors

Exhibit 2 shows all eight Italian brewers' reported production and percentage of the total in the early 1990s. Peroni and Dreher had six plants each, Moretti three, Poretti two, and the others one each. Foreign ownership of the top five in 1989 was as follows:

Dreher   Heineken, Dutch brewer (100%)

Interbrew   Stella Artois, Belgian brewer (100%)

Peroni   BSN Danone, French food group (% unknown)

Moretti   John Labatt Limited, Canadian brewer (100%)

Poretti   Carlsberg, Danish brewer (50%)

EXHIBIT 1
Selected Economic Statistics for Italy

	1988	1989	1990	1991	1992
GDP @ mkt (L'000 bn)	1,092	1,194	1,307	1,427	1,507
Real GDP growth, %	4.1	3.0	2.2	1.4	0.9
Consumer price inflation, %	5.1	6.3	6.5	6.3	5.3
Population, millions	57.4	57.5	57.7	57.8	58.0
12/31 exchange rate (L/US$)	1,388	1,249	1,271	1,240	1,601
12/31 exchange rate (L/C$)	1,163	1,067	1,096	1,041	1,274

Sources: The Economist Intelligence Unit and The Royal Bank of Canada.

EXHIBIT 2
Brewers and Reported Production in Italy for 1990–1992: Years Ended 30 September (in thousands of hectoliters; percentages are % of total)

	1990		1991		1992	
Peroni	4,117	38.3%	3,928	36.6%	3,936	36.0%
Dreher	3,243	30.2%	3,040	28.3%	3,266	29.8%
Moretti	790	7.4%	969	9.0%	1,116	10.2%
Poretti	983	9.2%	1,081	10.1%	1,095	10.0%
Interbrew	749	7.0%	817	7.6%	736	6.7%
Forst	676	6.3%	695	6.5%	647	5.9%
Castelberg*	134	1.2%	157	1.5%	109	1.0%
Menabrea	43	0.4%	43	0.4%	45	0.4%
Total†	10,735	100.0%	10,733	100.0%	10,951	100.0%

*Shut down in summer 1992.
†Totals may not check, due to rounding.
Source: Assobirra.

Several brewers "rationalized" production in 1988–1992, closing and modernizing breweries. But industry profits—and those of each major competitor—remained negative each year.

Imports and Exports of Beer

Richard Beveridge, planning and development director for Moretti, said importers were a big threat, adding, "They can sell in Italy without covering fixed costs." Exhibit 3 shows imports by country of origin for 1990–1992. Imports represented 19.8 percent of consumption in 1992, up from 11.7 percent in 1981. Imports were subject to a 25 percent "value landed" tax, compared to a 19 percent tax on production costs for domestic beer. Only 2 percent of Italian beer production was exported in 1992, but this was up from 1 percent in 1981.[2]

Changing Drinking Patterns

Like other Europeans, Italians shifted to nonalcoholic beverages in the 1980s and early 1990s. From 1981 to 1992, the "share of the throat" (percent of total beverage consumption) for alcoholic drinks in Italy fell from 39 to 25 percent, while the soft drinks share rose from 26 to 46 percent. Italy's per capita beer consumption jumped 30 percent from 1980 to 1985, then flattened, easing down to 22.6 liters in 1991. Of that, 19.5 liters was "normal beer" (not less than 3 percent alcohol by volume), 2.1 liters "special beer" (not less than 3.5 percent), 0.7 liters "double malt/red beer" (not less than 4 percent), and 0.3 liters nonalcohol/low alcohol beer (less than 1 percent).[3] Beer's share of the Italian throat was 6 percent in 1992, back to its 1981 level.[4] Canadean Limited, which studied the industry, concluded:

EXHIBIT 3
**Imports to Italy by Country of Origin 1990–1992: Years Ended 30 September
(in thousands of hectoliters; percentages are % of total)**

	1990		1991		1992	
Germany	927	39.3%	969	39.8%	996	36.9%
Denmark	338	14.3%	372	15.3%	438	16.2%
Belgium/Luxembourg	212	9.0%	264	10.9%	322	11.9%
Holland	302	12.8%	225	9.2%	219	8.1%
France	241	10.2%	170	7.0%	177	6.6%
Austria	133	5.6%	137	5.6%	147	5.4%
Great Britain	73	3.1%	90	3.7%	108	4.0%
Mexico	6	0.3%	43	1.8%	100	3.7%
Czechoslovakia	34	1.4%	34	1.4%	43	1.6%
Former Yugoslavia	27	1.1%	36	1.5%	40	1.5%
Switzerland	27	1.1%	30	1.2%	26	1.0%
Ireland	16	0.7%	21	0.9%	26	1.0%
China	9	0.4%	10	0.4%	16	0.6%
United States	4	0.2%	6	0.3%	15	0.6%
Spain	9	0.4%	7	0.3%	14	0.5%
Other countries	7	0.3%	22	0.9%	17	0.6%
Total*	2,361	100.0%	2,434	100.0%	2,703	100.0%
As % of consumption		18.0%		18.5%		19.8%

*Totals may not check, due to rounding.
Source: Assobirra.

The alleged replacement of wine by beer is a concept in which hardly anyone believes anymore (Italians who do not drink wine during meals have turned massively to bottled water), and beer is hardly perceived as an in-between meals and/or after dinner drink or late night drink.[5]

Beer consumption in Italy, as elsewhere, varied through the year. Exhibit 4 shows Italy's monthly beer production plus imports for 1990–1992.

Marketing Beer in Italy

Historically, the Italian beer industry association Assobirra had run a cooperative advertising program (funded at L10 billion in 1990) for the general category of beer;

EXHIBIT 4
**Italy's Monthly Beer Production and Imports, 1990–1992
(in thousands of hectoliters)**

	Jan.	Feb.	Mar.	Apr.	May	June	July	Aug.	Sept.	Oct.	Nov.	Dec.
1990	901	976	1,238	1,097	1,520	1,521	1,615	1,256	1,096	807	901	556
1991	1,021	1,058	1,134	1,234	1,400	1,337	1,583	1,127	1,011	872	754	619
1992	889	1,163	1,329	1,220	1,404	1,682	1,710	987	998	N./A.	N./A.	N./A.

Source: Assobirra.

that is, ads featured multiple brands. In the 1980s, brewers began to develop their own advertising programs. In 1991, television accounted for 84 percent of Italy's media advertising expenditures for beer, and the trade press and magazines accounted for another 8 percent. Posters and radio advertising had small, declining shares.

Retail prices for bottles, cans, and draught beer in May 1992 averaged L1,600 to L2,000 per liter for normal beers, and L2,300 to L2,500 for premium ones. Each major Italian brewer produced normal and premium beers, and each had several special brands which appealed to small market segments. Exhibit 5 shows the estimated distribution of the retail price of bottled beer and the trend of each component in 1992.

Packaging of beer in Italy in the early 1990s was relatively old-fashioned by North American, or even northern European, standards. Exhibit 6 shows types of packaging for beer sold in Italy in 1991 and 1992. Refillable bottles were declining in use.

Of the European Community (EC) standard size bottles—25, 50, and 75 centiliters (cl)*—25- and 50-cl ones had been introduced by Dreher and Moretti but not by other Italian brewers; practically all the cans were the 33-cl size. Few kegs were sold for other than draught installations. Twist-off caps had not been introduced by domestic producers, nor had flip-in tabs for cans.[6] Glass bottles were bought from an Italian cartel, which attempted to control bottle design and supply as well as price.

Exhibit 7 illustrates the distribution channel for beer sold in Italy in 1991–1992. Brewers sold beer to five thousand or so concessionaires, generally with exclusive territories. Concessionaires distributed the beer to tens of thousands of mostly small retailers. Deposits were charged on crates and returnable bottles at each level, and brewers installed and serviced draught equipment, further tying channel members together. But the relationships were not totally exclusive. Certain concessionaires also sold to other wholesalers, who delivered mixed loads of beer and other products to the tiniest outlets. Some beer was sold directly to consumers from route trucks. And

---

*A centiliter is 0.338 fluid ounce.

EXHIBIT 5
Estimated Distribution of the Retail Price of Bottled Beer, 1992

Acquisition of prime materials and packing	7% (stable)
Overall cost of bottles	10% (increasing)
Production costs[†]	24% (increasing)
Promotion costs	5% (increasing)
Selling and administrative costs	7% (stable)
Manufacturer's margin	2% (stable)
Distributor's margins	45% (increasing)

†Includes 19% value added tax on production costs (VAT), raised from 9% July 1990.
Source: Databank.

EXHIBIT 6
Types of Packaging for Beer Sold in Italy, 1991–1992

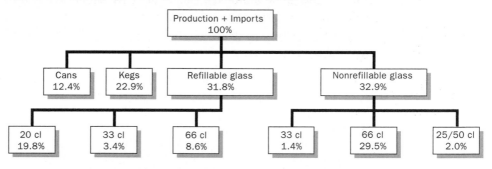

Source: *Il Mondo Della Birra,* December 1992, 30.

an increasing percentage of beer was being purchased by Grande Distribuzione (GD) and Distribuzione Organizzata (DO), centralized buying offices for chain stores and buying groups made up of large supermarkets.[7]

William Bourne, general manager of Moretti, said the concessionaire system was "consolidating" in the early nineties; Beveridge said it was "disintegrating." "Now," added Beveridge, "a concessionaire may sell several competing beers, so is less loyal than in the past. Several have merged with others or acquired them. When a conces-

EXHIBIT 7
Distribution Channel for Beer Sold in Italy, 1991–1992

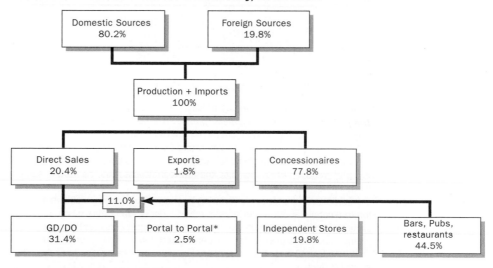

*Sales directly to consumers from route trucks.

Source: *Il Mondo Della Birra,* December 1992, 30.

sionaire grows large enough, above 500,000 hectoliters per year, they can even import economically. Some brewers, including us, have begun to buy up concessionaires."

BIRRA MORETTI AND PRINZ AND 1989

Exhibit 8 describes how beer is made. When acquired by Labatt, Moretti had an ancient 450,000 hl/yr brewery in Udine, in the Friuli region of extreme northeastern Italy (see Exhibit 9). Moretti's 9-year-old packaging plant was in San Giorgio, about 50 km (31 miles) southwest of Udine. The company, which was losing money, was still owned by Luigi Moretti, a fifth-generation member of the founding family. Birra Moretti had agreed to stay out of the south for 10 years in connection with an asset sale in mid-1980. However, the company had a strong distribution system in northeastern Italy and the largest market share in that area of any brewer. The Moretti brewery was operating near capacity in 1989 and frequently dusted central Udine with a sticky white substance which floated up from the brewing kettles. Nearby was a Moretti restaurant and bar, where a unique, nonpasteurized brew was served to the local set. There was also a museum containing memorabilia from the firm's 130-year history. Labatt brewing chief Sidney Oland said Moretti's essential attraction was its "good brand" and solid distribution system in the small area of Italy it served.

Prinz operated a modern 700,000 hl/yr brewery and packaging plant near its headquarters in Crespellano, north-central Italy, and an older 75,000 hl/yr brewery in Baragiano, far to the south. The firm was virtually bankrupt and in disarray. Both breweries were operating far below capacity in 1989, and Prinz's distribution system was collapsing. As Labatt was negotiating to buy Prinz, it discovered Prinz had been inflating sales figures by failing to account for returns, billing some products for later

---

EXHIBIT 8
How Beer Is Made

A modern brewery at first glance appears to be a simple process plant, consisting mainly of stainless steel tanks, hoppers, dryers, filters, pumps, and so forth, connected by pipes and valves. Temperatures, pressures, and product chemistry are tightly controlled throughout, and the system is closed from the atmosphere. An on-site laboratory uses spectrographic analysis and chemical methods to test raw materials and to check the product at various points. Brewery products are also tasted regularly. Staff requirements, including the few technicians required to take samples, record data, or adjust machinery, are low.

Primary raw materials for brewing beer are water, barley malt (which provides starch for conversion to alcohol), about a fourth as much of other cereal grains (such as rice or corn), a much smaller amount of hops (which impart bitterness and aroma), and yeast (to promote fermentation). The cereals and hops are cooked in large steam-jacketed kettles to produce wort, an amber sugar solution. This takes from 2.5 to 3.5 hours, allowing seven to nine batches per day. The residue is usually sold as animal feed.

The wort is fermented in large tanks for about 4 days and the resulting beer aged for about 16 days. Product characteristics—color, taste, alcohol content—are varied by adjusting the variety and amount of malt, grain, and hops used and by modifying the fermentation and aging regimens.

EXHIBIT 9
Map of Italy

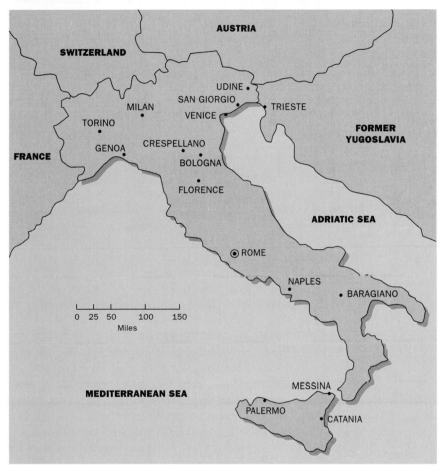

delivery, and even delivering presold beer to alternative customers for cash. By May 1989, prepaid customers were threatening to sue, and unpaid suppliers were refusing to ship. But Oland instructed his negotiating team to go ahead with the acquisition, saying it offered "a chance to buy capacity very cheaply."

BIRRA MORETTI'S NEW CORPORATE PARENT

John Labatt Limited was Canada's leading brewer in the decades before 1980. While Canada's per capita beer consumption fell 7 percent during the 1980s, Labatt gained domestic market share, to 42.3 percent in 1989. Labatt's brewing revenues rose steadily and EBIT increased each period from FY1985 to FY1989, both absolutely and as a percentage of sales. For FY1989, Labatt Brewing Company reported EBIT of C$158 million on sales of C$1.8 billion.

In 1989 Labatt's arch-competitor Molson Companies Limited merged its brewing operation with Carling O'Keefe Breweries of Canada, Ltd., a unit of worldwide brewer Elders IXL Ltd. This gave Molson a 53 percent market share. Still, Oland said, "We had won the battle in Canada. We were making lots of money in brewing and had to decide what to do with it." The Molson merger? "Our weaker competitor combined with our weakest one," said Oland.

During the 1980s Labatt acquired the U.S. brewer of Rolling Rock beer and other U.S. and Canadian firms in food and nonalcoholic beverages, broadcasting, and entertainment. Labatt's total sales more than doubled in the 5 years before 1989. Labatt Food Company, which also included the broadcasting and entertainment activities, earned C$106 million EBIT on sales of C$3.6 billion in FY1989 (ended March 31). About a third of Labatt's C$5.4 billion FY1989 total revenue came from U.S. sales and about 1 percent from beer exported to Europe, practically all to the U.K.

When Labatt Breweries of Europe (LBOE) was formed in 1987, Oland sent John Morgan to London to head it. Morgan chose a young Englishman, Adam Humphries, as his vice president of Finance and brought in a Canadian as vice president of Marketing. Humphries said overseas expansion was undertaken because of GATT (General Agreement on Tariffs and Trade) complaints at home and failing diversification. Indeed, the United States was preparing a charge against Canadian brewers under GATT. U.S. brewers were reportedly more efficient than the Canadians because the latter had to make beer in every province where it was sold, requiring smaller than optimal scale plants. Further, the Food Company's EBIT was only 5.24 percent of sales, compared to Brewing's 8.13 percent.

Whatever the reasons, Morgan and his team pressed ahead in Europe. After converting the U.K. operation to "toll brewing" (hiring domestic brewers to brew beer), and joint-venture marketing, they attempted several large acquisitions, first in the U.K. and then on the Continent. None worked out. One former LBOE official said "pussyfooting" by recalcitrant Labatt directors nixed the bigger deals. Humphries acknowledged, "At corporate there were those who saw European expansion as risky and who needed to be convinced." But Morgan disputed the pussyfooting charge, saying, "Brascan's cash needs were the reason." Brascan, part of the troubled Bronfman financial empire, owned 42.3 percent of Labatt's voting stock. In mid-1988, Morgan started the successful effort to buy Moretti and Prinz. In September that year, he hired Beveridge, then a recent graduate of the London Business School, to do financial analysis.

Before the Italian deals were closed, Labatt sold several of its businesses, ostensibly due to their lack of "strategic relevance." According to Morgan, another reason for the divestments was pressure from Brascan to "maximize cash coming up [Labatt's] corporate chain." Morgan added that Labatt was being "actively marketed" during 1988, although Oland disputed that. "Actually," Oland said, "our plan was to separate the company into brewing and entertainment divisions, both publicly traded. Labatt would own 51 percent of Brewing and 50 percent of Entertainment."

In July 1989, a month after the Moretti and Prinz acquisitions, the Labatt board gave Oland a chance to realize his vision, promoting him to president and CEO of Labatt. Oland soon announced four objectives:

1. Pursue major international growth initiatives primarily by building on the company's strength in Brewing.

2. Rationalize the Food businesses to achieve improved results in fiscal 1991 and to maximize resources for better returns longer term.

3. Divest smaller, nonstrategic operations.

4. Expand the company's Broadcast and Entertainment businesses.

Before Oland's promotion, he and George Taylor, head of Labatt Food Company, had full operating responsibility for their separate divisions. But under Oland, management of the two groups was combined within the "Office of the CEO." A stated purpose of the centralization was to provide "strong senior management leadership in support of the company's strategic thrust toward major international expansion." Taylor was made executive vice president of Labatt.

MANAGEMENT CHANGES AT MORETTI

William Bourne, formerly Labatt's director of international development, had moved to Udine in May 1989 to become *direttore generale* (general manager) of the new Birra Moretti. Although Luigi Moretti kept the title *presidente* for a time, he took no active part in management after Bourne arrived. Morgan fired Humphries, for reasons neither chose to disclose, and moved back to LBOE's London headquarters. (In 1991, Morgan was promoted to president of Labatt Breweries of Canada, replaced at LBOE by Bruce E. Peer, from Canada.) Beveridge stayed behind as Birra Moretti's director of planning and development, a new position. Several of the former Birra Moretti SpA Italian managers kept their jobs, as did most Italian supervisors and workers. In general the Prinz management structure—to the extent it remained in existence—was dismantled, though many operating workers and salespersons were retained.

The new Birra Moretti's Commercial Department (Sales and Marketing) was placed under the direction of former Prinz Commercial Director Marzio Zanardi and moved to Milan in 1989. A young Italian, Michele Pecoraro, was hired as marketing director. Pecoraro's parents lived in Rome, but he had attended college in Canada and worked in marketing for Procter and Gamble there.

Beveridge said, "We had a foothold on the Continent. Now, we had to make it count." Exhibit 10 outlines the ownership and organization of Labatt in July 1989.

THE NEW MORETTI STRATEGIC PLAN

Beveridge sketched out the new Moretti 1989 strategic plan as illustrated in Exhibit 11. He explained, "We believed that from the two organizations we could create a solid national brewer with adequate capacity to service the demand we knew Labatt marketers could generate. And there could have been a good bit of synergy with other acquisitions in Europe we expected to make."

Beveridge continued, "Prinz was the immediate concern. We had to stabilize it as we merged it into Moretti and converted it to a production operation. Prinz was a dis-

EXHIBIT 10
Ownership and Organization of John Labatt Limited, July 1989

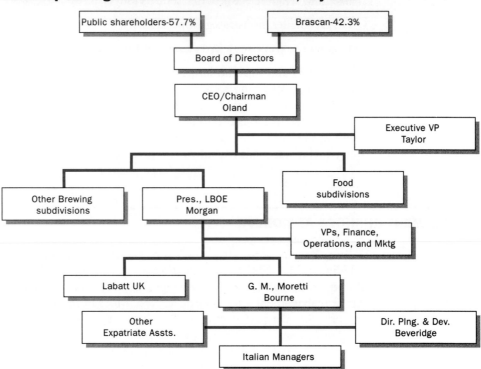

aster." Another former member of the acquisition team added, "The integration phase was totally underestimated. Prinze was just a shell, with a complete breakdown in management and financial systems."

Not until January 1990 did Bourne and his team focus on the operations at Udine and San Giorgio. Beveridge said, "Moretti had operated the same way for ten years, so we thought another few months would not hurt. Actually, it did hurt. Because nothing important had changed at Udine from June through December, everyone had fallen back into the old ways."

Exhibit 12 shows the Moretti organization as it existed from 1990 to 1993. Bourne reported mainly to Peer, whose staff included directors of operations, marketing, and finance. These directors were in frequent contact with their counterparts at Moretti and at Labatt Brewing UK.

PLANT ADDITIONS AND RENOVATIONS

In 1990 and 1992, Moretti built a new US$15 million brewery next to its packaging plant in San Giorgio. The old brewery in Udine was closed and dismantled, parts of it being used in the new facility. Beveridge said:

EXHIBIT 11
Elements of Moretti's Strategic Plan, 1989

Objectives

1. Marketing initiatives—led by marketing group in Milan.
2. Increase sales levels—"push" and "pull" strategies.
3. Increase plant utilization, mainly at Crespellano.
4. Add capacity, mainly at Crespellano.
5. Lower costs—production and distribution efficiencies.

Merger Rationale

Moretti	Prinz
Low-tech plants	High-tech plant
Utilized capacity	Spare capacity
Northeast plant	Central and southern plants
Strong regional distribution	Weak national distribution
Strong brand image	Weak brand image
Premium brands	Price/commodity brands
Operations-oriented	Operations-oriented

Disadvantages

Instability of Prinz operation
Lack of national credibility
Moretti could not sell in Southern Italy before mid-1990
Overabundance of brands and packages
Communication problems (mainly language differences)
Lack of financial systems for combined operation
Lack of management information systems
Lack of a national sales organization

The movement of the brewery to San Giorgio was only a marginal capacity increase—we replaced a 450,000-hectoliter brewery with a 660,000 one. The major reason for Moretti's cash flow problems, and the reason we could buy them, was that the split site was costing them more than US$3 million per year in transport of bulk beer and overhead duplication. At present [February 1993] the overall capacity of Moretti/Prinz is only slightly more than when we started. Eventually, the Crespellano plant will be a minimal-mix, high-productivity brewery, with fully utilized capacity, and the San Giorgio facility will be a "job shop" making shorter runs of premium products. The real benefits in capacity and costs will come as we increase the size of Crespellano.

The Crespellano brewery was renovated in 1990 and 1991, with little change in capacity. But Beveridge said output there could be expanded by 600,000 hl/yr for about US$5 million. Starting in 1990, the brewery at Baragiano was operated only for peak production. A Labatt official said, "We had put some value on the southern brewery but nothing there fit; in fact, in the long term we are still wondering what to do with it." Beveridge explained, "It would probably cost us more to close Baragiano than to keep it running. To replace its 70,000 hectoliters of utilized capacity and to dismiss the thirty employees there might cost US$4 million."

EXHIBIT 12
Birra Moretti Organization Chart, 1993

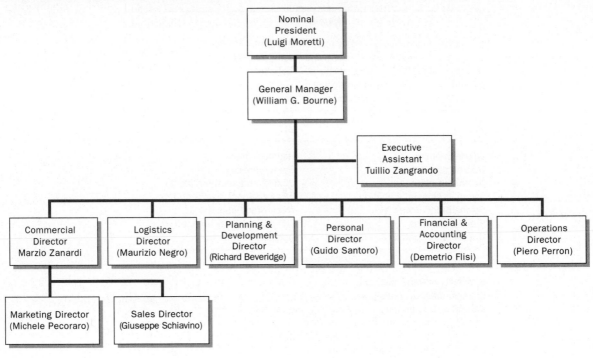

There were other reasons the Baragiano brewery was neither closed nor expanded. It had been built partly with earthquake recovery funds, so as much as US$10 million might have to be repaid to the government if the plant were closed. Also, efforts to enlarge the brewery were reportedly suspended in 1990 after Moretti refused to hire a local official's relative in exchange for a license. Oland had planned to tour the plant before the acquisition, but local officials refused to allow it. "Kidnapping," Oland said. "They were afraid I would be kidnapped."

STAFFING AT MORETTI

During the peak season, from April through August, Moretti breweries operated 24 hours a day, at other times usually 16. Each brewery was shut down for a month each year for maintenance, for 2 weeks at Christmas, and whenever necessary to limit accumulating inventories.

Moretti had 420 employees in 1993, about the same as Prinz and Moretti together in 1989. About 50 were based in Udine, 120 in San Giorgio, 30 in Baragiano, 100 in Milan, and 120 in Crespellano. Yasmin Ferrari, assistant to Guido Santoro, the personnel director at Moretti, described the hiring process:

After a manager calls or writes us about an opening, we check the resumes on hand. If one or more of the applicants fit the job, we refer their resumes to the manager. We try to be there for the first interview, which the manager sets up. A second interview is held before hiring, usually by the manager alone. The Personnel Department only screens; we do not hire. If we don't find a candidate among existing applicants, we call a recruitment agency. Advertising in the paper takes too long, maybe two months by the time a person is hired. For sales jobs, the best recruiting technique is just to put the word out within the company, to take advantage of "networking." Every tenth new hire must come from the waiting list at the local labor office.

Bourne said there was no formal training program, but that there was "considerable ad hoc training, normally initiated by the function or department head."

CULTURAL CHALLENGES

Ferrari said the expatriates were bound together because "it is hard to develop relationships in the Friuli [the region surrounding Udine]. It's tough on the non-Italians." Ferrari's parents were Italian, but she had been born in Australia and had lived in at least six other countries before her recent move to Italy. She said the expatriates were all on a first-name basis. Beveridge added, "There has, historically, been a special relationship among Bill, Michele, John Farris [financial controller, reporting to Flisi], and myself as far as dealing with the wishes of Canada, whereas Marzio [Zanardi—commercial director] has been the person who really understood the dynamics of selling beer in Italy." Beveridge said, "Our goals were not only to streamline the operation and get it working, but also to go from internally oriented, production led, and top down management to externally oriented, marketing led, and bottom up."

Among senior managers, only Zanardi, Pecoraro, Perron (operations director), and Zangrando (executive assistant to Bourne) were bilingual, according to Beveridge, although Bourne classified Maurizio Negro, the logistics director, as "moderately bilingual." Beveridge added, "Schiavino and Flisi are about the same in English as I am in Italian, not fluent but able to get by. Bourne and Santoro are fairly weak in their second language." Most workers and supervisors at Moretti spoke only Italian.

Beveridge described the main problem he felt the expatriate managers faced:

It is this "power distance" thing, which is so imbedded in the Italian culture, as it is in all of southern Europe. Subordinates accept that bosses have power because they are bosses and not just because they are competent—although they may be. And employees do a job a particular way because the boss wants it that way, not because employees believe it is the best way. Bypassing your boss is insubordination. In the traditional Italian company there is no informal "you" [*tu*] at work, only the formal you [*lei*]. Titles, status, and job descriptions become all-important.

To change that, we could change hearts, minds, or people. But in Italy you can't fire anyone except senior managers. So we have to effect massive culture change. And ultimately it has to be the Labatt culture, which involves extremely low power distance. We have to move people in and out without taking six months to learn a new way to think.

Ferrari explained the difficulty of firing anyone:

> You can discharge people, but you have to pay them. For a manager above a certain level it might be a year's salary—whatever the person will accept. Workers have great protection. If you get into financial trouble you can put people on temporary layoff for up to two years, but you have to pay them almost full pay. And people don't want to "leave their chairs," as they say in Italy, even with pay.

Most employees also resisted transfer, many because their spouses worked for the government or agencies controlled by the government, such as banks, schools, and hospitals. Ferrari said:

> To get one of those jobs, one must take a *concorso*, or examination. It takes perhaps a year to prepare for the *concorso*. You tend to pass if you know a member of parliament or other powerful official. Then you go on the waiting list, and may wait a year or two. Of course, all this gets circumvented for those who know the *right* officials. But when you finally get a job, it's for life, and you don't want to leave it. If you try to transfer to, say, Milan, you have to take another *concorso*. Even if you know the right people in Udine, that doesn't mean you do in Milan.

In the first half of 1990, Bourne and his team conducted meetings at each facility to explain how the new company would work. Beveridge said change came, although grudgingly, explaining:

> Workers and supervisors just rolled their eyes, as if they knew nothing would really change. But things did change, and we folded Prinz into Moretti and moved toward a more externally oriented, bottom-up culture. Essentially, the marketing department in Milan is going to run this company, although it might not look like that on paper. And power distance is already [February 1993] going down. Employees of the new Moretti respect the manages, I believe, but they know competence is what counts and they are beginning to communicate up, down, and across the organization.

Beveridge felt that without continued pressure for reform, the Moretti culture would revert. He added:

> I believe that what's happened at Dreher [the Italian brewer which was bought by the Dutch brewer Heineken in the 1980s]. Heineken walked all over that culture and then backed off. Dreher is still aggressive, but they are having trouble responding to what we are doing, or even understanding it. If Heineken people were still running things there, it would be a different story.

Ferrari saw the change as more long-lasting and attributed it mainly to replacing people and flattening the organization structure. She explained, "The majority of the staff employees are new hires, although fewer production workers have been replaced. Only two of the senior managers are here who were here in 1989." Several of the managers had retired and others had accepted severance deals.

Ferrari also felt that employing younger people, some in newly created jobs, had made change easier to implement. She said:

> Michele [Pecoraro] is thirty-one. Only one brand manager is over thirty. Most salesmen are in their twenties and most are recent hires. Even the production staff is quite young, most in their mid-thirties and younger. They know Birra Moretti aims to be a meritocracy, which means they don't get advanced based on who they know, but based on how much they contribute.

Another factor, according to Ferrari, was trying to get everyone to become part of the "family" at Moretti:

> For example, the people here used to hate the annual Christmas party [for employees only]. Mr. Moretti would invite a bunch of city council members and put on a big, formal show. There would be long speeches and it would all be very boring. We had a Christmas party for everybody, spouses included, in the company in 1991—got a popular band, no city council people. The speech was limited to five minutes. Many did not come, saying it would be the same boring thing. But the ones who did come had a blast. Last Christmas, 1992, almost everybody came. One of the neat ideas was to have a singing contest between the two breweries. The San Giorgio brewery was shy and never found a contestant, so Crespellano won. San Giorgio was shamed. Next year, I hear, San Giorgio is determined to win. This kind of thing has done more to change attitudes in the company than any training we could do.

But Ferrari saw less progress in her own department, saying,

> We've got a way to go on that. Santoro is from the old school, where the power distance has to be there. He speaks very little English and does not read it well. I am Santoro's assistant, but I talk with Bill Bourne often. Santoro doesn't like that, and my four Italian colleagues don't do it. They also tend to use formal titles and surnames, not first names. I am trying to introduce internal communications but finding pressure not to do it. They also tend to use formal titles and surnames, not first names. I am trying to introduce internal communications but finding pressure not to do it. For example, I want to post bulletin board notes when we hire a new person—giving a little personal information. Santoro keeps saying no; but he is coming toward it. I can see the fight he is going through.

MARKETING AT MORETTI

Bourne said, "Moretti has concentrated on establishing market position for its brands rather than competing on price simply to gain volume. . . . Aggressive marketing will remain the company's primary tool for maintaining its trend of market-share growth in the face of competitive pricing pressure." Beveridge said Moretti was also trying to reinforce the "push-type" side of its marketing program by purchasing several concessionaires.

Product Realignment

In 1990, Moretti discontinued several brands and began to focus on just three: Prinz Brau and two former Moretti brands, Birra Moretti and Sans Souci. All these were normal beers and all were distributed in bottles and cans. Prinz Brau and Sans Souci were also sold as draught. Moretti continued to make, but not intensely promote, a reddish "double malt" brew called La Rossa and a dark "pure malt," Baffo D'Oro. Baffo D'Oro was targeted at restaurants, bars, hotels, and catering companies, mainly in southern Italy. Two of the former Prinz brands, Wolfsbrau and Castello, were made to special order only.

Prinz Brau was a "price brand" sold mainly to chain stores and buying groups. It was often marketed through "3 x 2" (three for the price of two) promotions using point-of-sale placards. Birra Moretti was a medium-light brew. Advertised as "The Beer for Any Occasion," it was targeted at middle-aged drinkers who preferred a premium beer. Ads, as well as labels on the squat, brown Moretti bottles, showed a mustachioed man in felt hat and dark suit—the "Moretti Man"—holding a mug of beer and blowing the froth aside. Label copy featured the words *Dal 1859* (roughly, "from 1859"), along with mention of brewing by "five generations of Morettis."

Sans Souci, called Moretti's "Rock 'n Roll" beer, targeted younger drinkers. "Males eighteen to twenty-five are just 7 percent of the population in the world but drink 40 percent of the beer," said Beveridge, "and males eighteen to thirty-five consume 70 percent of the beer." Bottles for Sans Souci were amber medium-necks. A sailing ship was shown on labels and some ads showed the face of a young woman looking out over a glass of beer. Beveridge explained,

> The positioning of Moretti and Sans Souci grew out of research into attitudes in Italy. Later, we recognized they were directly comparable to Coke's "The Real Thing" appeal for Moretti and Pepsi's "New Generation" theme for Sans Souci—and we could work by analogy to see what customers might, or might not, accept as elements of positioning. We used a sort of product story for Moretti—the man on the label and the 130-year brewing tradition—but only to emphasize the "Real Thing" idea.

By 1993, selected ads were featuring the "Moretti family" of beers, which then included Labatt Canadian Lager, imported and marketed as a "super-premium" beer. In 1992, about 20,000 hectoliters of Moretti was exported to the United States and a little to Canada. Beveridge saw little chance of exports to the rest of Europe because, he said, "Beer flows south in Europe, not north."

Promotion

Moretti's 1991 advertising expenditures were L19 billion, most for television. Per hectoliter sold, this was more than three times Peroni's spending and over twice that of Dreher. From 1989 to 1992, Peroni dropped 5 percent in market share and Dreher lost 2 percent, while Moretti picked up 3.2 percent.[8]

Beveridge said, "Until we came, everyone was advertising the beer category, and some still are." A marketing research firm employed by Moretti said its new ads were "significantly better remembered" than those of any competitor. "It's all very encouraging," said Beveridge. In addition to its regular ad campaign for Birra Moretti, Moretti used Zucchero, Italy's leading pop singer, to promote Sans Souci, sponsoring over 200 Zucchero concerts in FY1993 alone. The Sans Souci brand also sponsored some concerts by lesser-known artists. Beveridge said competitors soon copied any successful strategy. He noted that Moretti intended to keep up the advertising pressure and was looking at various changes in bottle shapes and sizes, label designs, can and carton designs, and promotional appeals.

Sales and Distribution

Beginning in mid-1900, Moretti intensified its coverage of central Italy and expanded into the south. Under Giuseppe Schiavino, Moretti's national sales director, were four regional sales managers, each of whom supervised several area managers. District sales representatives reported to the area managers. In general, sales representatives solicited orders from concessionaires, handled customer complaints, and prospected for new concessionaires. Moretti contracted with a transport company to deliver beer from its breweries to two "super depots," one outside San Giorgio and the other near Crespellano. Several regional transport companies hauled the beer to Moretti's five regional warehouses and to customer sites.

FINANCE AND MIS

By 1993, Labatt had invested an estimated US$150 million in Moretti. The estimates are broken down in Exhibit 13. Exhibit 14 presents skeleton financial data reported to the Italian government for fiscal years 1990 and 1991.[9] Beveridge said he could not confirm the data in Exhibit 14, adding,

> The report to the Italian government is made according to Italian accounting principles, with Italian tax law as the prime concern. I have never wanted to see the reports after trying to disentangle them during the acquisitions—you have to make so many adjustments to

EXHIBIT 13
Labatt's Estimated Investment in Moretti, March 1993

Transaction Amount	US$
Purchase of Prinz Brau	25 million
Purchase of Birra Moretti	75 million
Construction of San Giorgio brewery	15 million
Additional advances	35 million
Total	150 million

EXHIBIT 14
Moretti Skeleton Financial Data
(in billions of lire)

	1990	1991
Net sales	40.6	68.0
Labor cost	8.5	14.5
Depreciation	4.1	6.5
Other operating costs	41.5	62.8
Operating income	−13.6	−15.8

Source: Databank, Milan.

get them to make sense in GAAP terms. As long as we aren't paying tax, the document has no relevance to strategic decisions. And with capital allowances, goodwill, and prior year losses it will be a long time before we are liable to tax.

For FY1993, unit sales at Birra Moretti increased 5 percent, compared to 21 percent in FY1992, and the company had a loss before interest and taxes of C$3 million on net sales of C$130 million.

At the time of the acquisitions, Moretti had an obsolete Texas Instruments computer and Prinz had an even older IBM machine. Beveridge recruited Marcello Cordioli as manager of Information Systems in June 1992. They purchased a Hewlett-Packard HP9000, connecting it with PC clones through a Novell network. Beveridge said, "When this is fully working, it will be a true 'distributed' computing environment—when we started from almost nothing, it was as easy to go to state-of-the-art as go anywhere else."

Cordioli added, "We already [early 1993] have Crespellano, Milan, San Giorgio, and Udine on the Novell network. I hope we have all four regional offices connected by midyear." He said he would like to see inventory computerized, "from raw materials to the super depots and the regional warehouses." Salespersons telephoned or faxed sales orders to Udine, where they were entered. "The Italian telephone system is not too good and I would not trust a remote workstation for order entry," said Cordioli. "Also, one person can enter all the orders at Udine, rather than having one at each field office."

RESTRUCTURING AT LABATT

Oland fired Morgan in July 1991. "I had good reasons," said Oland, "but you don't tell a person that if he doesn't ask. And John never asked. Anyway, it had nothing to do with Italy—he got a promotion for that." Three months later, Oland was moved down to vice chairman of Labatt and group chairman of Brewing, neither an operating position. He was replaced by George Taylor, former head of Labatt Food Company. Though no reason for Oland's demotion was made public, Oland later explained, "Brascan said I was an 'operator' and they wanted a finance person."

Labatt paid C$3 per share (C$260 million total) as a special dividend in October 1992, about C$110 million of it to Brascan. By February 1993, the remaining "nonstrategic businesses" had been sold and Labatt restructured itself into Brewing and Broadcast segments. The latter included 90 percent interest in the Toronto Blue Jays. Net sales from the remaining businesses were projected to be just over C$2 billion for FY1993, versus C$5.4 billion for all businesses in 1989. Brewing was providing about 75 percent of Labatt sales and 80 percent of earnings in FY1993. A net loss was expected for FY1993, owing to large losses in discontinued operations and about C$45 million in restructuring charges. The rule that Canadian brewers had to brew beer in the province where it was sold was dropped. This allowed Labatt to further "rationalize" its production, an effort which had already begun, with the closing of two Canadian breweries and the announced shutdown of another.

According to Oland, the plan in 1993 was still for Labatt to be a holding company, owning 51 percent of Brewing and 50 percent of Broadcast, with the balance of the stock publicly traded.

DEVELOPING AND NEGOTIATING A NEW COMPREHENSIVE BUSINESS PLAN

On 4 February 1993, before Labatt's FY1993 results were known outside the company, Bourne convened a meeting of sixteen key managers in Bologna to discuss Moretti's FY1994 comprehensive business plan. The plan would include objectives by department, staffing budgets, capital expenditure plans, market analysis, brand plans, and financial projections. Beveridge explained the challenge he said Moretti faced:

> The goal is to constantly improve. The current priority is cultural change—decentralize and reinforce the reduction of power distance, be more cost-aware, and push a marketing attitude through the company. We have approached this in a stepwise way.
>
> Initially the priority was to get basic structure in place, then to build sales: when we had spare capacity coming out of our ears, there was little value in using it more efficiently. Then there was a period of radical change, particularly at San Giorgio, and it was just too difficult. Now we are basically stable but capacity is tight and it costs money to build so we have to examine the profitability of each sale more carefully—it has to cover not only the variable costs but also the capital.
>
> The initial management group can't be everywhere at once so we have to make all the employees understand the basic tradeoffs so they can be involved. Also we want to keep momentum. Until we overtook Poretti we were pressing to be number three and had something to shoot at. It's a little harder now that we are third. Dreher is a long way away, and we need a share of about 18 percent of Italian production to get the breweries to true efficient scale. So we have to almost double sales again.

After Bourne called the meeting to order, Flisi, Zanardi, and the other directors spoke briefly. Flisi presented year-to-date financial results, for the company and for each department, and Zanardi discussed marketing initiatives being undertaken by Peroni and Dreher.

Bourne then handed out sheets containing the proposed departmental objectives for FY1994. Beveridge explained,

> All the individual managers had submitted their first drafts and Bill and I had rewritten them. We developed objectives, strategies, and tactics. We added objectives like "cost consciousness" to the Marketing list and "aiding Marketing in development of products" to the Purchasing list. Bill gave each manager until Monday to make further suggestions and changes.

The meeting concluded with a review of the renovation plans for the new headquarters in Milan. Beveridge said Bourne and his "direct reports" would move there in April, adding, "We think it will promote communication to have all the decision makers in the same office. Udine will become a back office. Unfortunately, Flisi, Negro, and myself will end up spending three days a week on the road visiting our departments."

Bourne and Beveridge met with LBOE President Bruce Peer and his staff in London the following week. At that meeting, Peer raised the possibility of merger with Poretti, which was a subsidiary of Denmark's Carlsberg. Labatt brewed and marketed Carlsberg beer in Canada, so had good relations with that company. He said Poretti was interested, but Carlsberg would demand to control the surviving entity.

Beveridge saw little likelihood that Moretti could be sold for a reasonable price, unless it was to Poretti. He remarked:

> Neither Peroni nor Dreher could expect to gain market share over and above the sum of the shares of the two companies by buying us. So they would have to make cost savings to generate a bid premium. And neither company has done everything they could to cut costs as they lost share in the last few years.

Beveridge suggested trying to buy Interbrew from Stella Artois. "We could add capacity and a second bottling line at Crespellano," he said. "Then, we could dispose of Interbrew's brewery and, by about 1997 or '98, the one in Baragiano."

Bourne expressed pride that Moretti "rewrote the way the beer business operated in Italy" and made the company "a strong viable entity and positioned it for future growth." He admitted Moretti would continue to lose money through FY1994 and might need as much as US$15 million in new funding if it was to continue expanding sales. But Bourne pointed out that the rate of loss was decreasing.

The chances for continued funding seemed to improve in February 1993, when Brascan announced it had agreed to sell its Labatt stock. This eliminated the need for Labatt to throw off cash for the Bronfmans. On the other hand, Labatt was incurring huge restructuring losses as it rationalized production in Canada and disposed of its U.S. dairy operations. It was clear by then that Labatt would report a net loss for FY1993, versus a C$101 million net profit the year before.

Beveridge said, "If Labatt were to refuse further funding, we'd cut marketing and capital. It's the only way to improve cash flow in the short term and would not only get us into positive cash flow but would, since sales growth would slow and maybe even stop, make rationalizing production easier. I would expect, though, that we would be losing share to some degree." As to closing facilities, Beveridge remarked, "The choice is, 'Horrible end or horrors without end?' I suppose in that case we would have to choose a horrible end for some facilities. Fortunately we have, until now, been able to persuade top management that we can't do the job without cash."

As their discussion continued, four alternatives emerged:

- Constantly improve: place priority on cultural change, make sure sales cover both variable and capital costs, keep momentum in sales growth.

- Cut marketing and capital. Rationalize production. Close some facilities.

- Attempt to buy Interbrew from Stella Artois. Add capacity and a second bottling line at Crespellano. Dispose of Interbrew's brewery and, by 1997 or 1998, the one in Baragiano.

- Merge with Poretti. Be prepared to give up control of the surviving entity.

Clearly, the availability of capital from Labatt was key to Moretti's 1994 plan. How could the Italian organization best present its case?

Notes

1. Franco Cazzola, "Clean Hands Dip into the Tangentopoli," *The European*, 25–28 February 1993, 9.
2. Canadean Ltd., *The Beer Service Basic Report Italy* (Basingstoke, Hants, UK: Canadean Ltd., 1992), section 3.
3. Databank SpA, *Competitors Birra: Management Highlights* (Milan: Databank SpA, 1992), 7.
4. Canadean Ltd., section 1.
5. Ibid., sections 2–3.
6. Ibid., section 9, and "Dossier," *Il Mondo Della Birra*, December 1992, 30.
7. Canadean Ltd., section 8.
8. Canadean Ltd., sections 6–7.
9. Databank SpA, Findas: Birra Moretti SpA (Milan: Databank SpA, 1992), 4.

http://www.breworld.com/

CASE 26

Kentucky Fried Chicken and the Global Fast-Food Industry*

During the 1960s and 1970s, Kentucky Fried Chicken Corporation (KFC) pursued an aggressive strategy of restaurant expansion, quickly establishing itself as one of the largest fast-food restaurant chains in the U.S. (see Exhibit 1). KFC was also one of the first U.S. fast-food restaurant chains to expand overseas. By 1990, restaurants located outside of the U.S. were generating over 50 percent of KFC's total profits. By the end of 1994, KFC was operating in 68 foreign countries and was one of the three largest fast-food restaurant chains operating outside of the U.S.

Japan, Australia, and the United Kingdom accounted for the greatest share of KFC's international expansion during the 1970s and 1980s. However, as KFC entered the 1990s, a number of other international markets offered significant opportunities for growth. China, with a population of over one billion, and Europe, with a population roughly equal to the U.S., offered such opportunities. Latin America also offered a unique opportunity because of the size of its markets, its common language and culture, and its geographical proximity to the U.S.

By 1995, KFC was operating successful subsidiaries in Mexico and Puerto Rico. A third subsidiary was established in Venezuela in 1993. The majority of KFC's restaurants in Mexico and Puerto Rico were company-owned. However, KFC had established 29 new franchises in Mexico by the end of 1995, following enactment of Mexico's new franchise law in 1990. KFC anticipated that much of its future growth in Mexico would be through franchises rather than company-owned restaurants. KFC was only one of many U.S. fast-food, retail, and hotel chains to begin franchising in Mexico following the new franchise law. In addition to Mexico, KFC was operating franchises in 20 other countries throughout the Caribbean, and Central and South America by 1995.

COMPANY HISTORY

Fast-food franchising was still in its infancy in 1954 when Harland Sanders began his travels across the U.S. to speak with prospective franchisees about his "Colonel

---

*Prepared by Jeffrey A. Krug, The University of Memphis, Fogelman College of Business and Economics, Department of Management, Memphis, Tennessee 38152, Tel. (901) 678-2972, Fax (901) 678-4990.

EXHIBIT 1
Leading U.S. Fast-Food Chains

Chain	Parent	U.S. Sales (in millions of dollars)		Percent CHG	1995 Units (e)
		1995 (e)	1994		
McDonald's	McDonald's Corporation	15,800	14,951	5.7	10,175
Burger King	Grand Metropolitan PLC	7,830	7,250	8.1	6,400
Pizza Hut	PepsiCo, Inc.	5,400	5,000	8.0	8,725
Taco Bell	PepsiCo, Inc.	4,853	4,200	15.5	6,565
Wendy's	Wendy's International Inc.	4,152	3,821	8.6	4,263
KFC	PepsiCo, Inc.	3,720	3,500	6.3	5,200
Hardee's	Imasco Ltd.	3,520	3,511	0.3	3,405
Subway	Doctor's Associates Inc.	2,905	2,518	15.4	10,351
Little Caesars	Little Caesar Enterprises	2,050	2,000	2.5	4,720
Domino's Pizza	Domino's Pizza Inc.	1,973	1,911	3.3	4,245
Red Lobster	Darden Restaurants Inc.	1,850	1,798	2.9	700
Denny's	Flagstar Cos. Inc.	1,810	1,672	8.3	1,578
Arby's	TriArc Corp.	1,730	1,770	−2.3	2,678
Dunkin' Donuts	Allied Domecq PLC	1,426	1,332	7.0	3,074
Shoney's	Shoney's Inc.	1,277	1,317	−3.0	907
Olive Garden	Darden Restaurants Inc.	1,250	1,146	9.1	479
Dairy Queen	International Dairy Queen	1,185	1,160	2.2	4,935
Jack in the Box	Foodmaker Inc.	1,082	1,036	4.4	1,240
Applebee's	Applebee's International	1,012	881	15.0	551
Big Boy	Elias Bros. Restaurants	1,010	1,050	−3.8	858
Long John Silver's	Long John Silver's Restaurants	986	931	5.9	1,564
Cracker Barrel	Cracker Barrel	970	787	23.3	257
Chili's	Brinker International Inc.	950	885	7.35	446
Sonic Drive-In	Sonic Corp.	880	756	16.45	1,500
T G I. Friday's	Carlson Hospitality Worldwide	870	774	12.4	310
Outback Steakhouse	Outback Steakhouse Inc.	822	549	40.8	279
Ponderosa	Metromedia Co.	741	751	−1.3	680
IHOP Restaurants	IHOP Corp.	729	631	15.5	684
Boston Market	Boston Chicken Inc.	725	384	88.9	825
Popeye's	America's Favorite Chicken	689	610	13.0	932
Total		74,196	68,872	7.7	88,526

(e) 1995 sales estimated.
Source: *Nation's Restaurant News.*

Sanders Recipe Kentucky Fried Chicken." By 1960, "Colonel" Sanders had granted KFC franchises to over 200 take-home retail outlets and restaurants across the United States. He had also succeeded in establishing a number of franchises in Canada. By 1963, the number of KFC franchises had risen to over 300 and revenues had reached $500,000.

By 1964, at the age of 74, the Colonel had tired of running the day-to-day operations of his business and was eager to concentrate on public relations issues. Therefore, he sought out potential buyers, eventually deciding to sell the business to two Louisville businessmen—Jack Massey and John Young Brown Jr.—for $2 million. Massey was named chairman of the board and Brown, who would later become Governor of Kentucky, was named president. The Colonel stayed on as a public relations man and goodwill ambassador for the company.

During the next five years, Massey and Brown concentrated on growing KFC's franchise system across the United States. In 1966, they took KFC public and the company was listed on the New York Stock Exchange. By the late 1960s, a strong foothold had been established in the United States, and Massey and Brown turned their attention to international markets. In 1969, a joint venture was signed with Mitsuoishi Shoji Kaisha, Ltd., in Japan, and the rights to operate 14 existing KFC franchises in England were acquired. Subsidiaries were also established in Hong Kong, South Africa, Australia, New Zealand, and Mexico. By 1971, KFC had 2,450 franchises and 600 company-owned restaurants worldwide, and was operating in 48 countries.

Heublein, Inc.

In 1971, KFC entered negotiations with Heublein, Inc., to discuss a possible merger. The decision to seek a merger candidate was partially driven by Brown's desire to pursue other interests, including a political career (Brown was elected Governor of Kentucky in 1977). On April 10, Heublein announced that an agreement had been reached. Shareholders approved the merger on May 27, and KFC was merged into a subsidiary of Heublein.

Heublein was in the business of producing vodka, mixed cocktails, dry gin, cordials, beer, and other alcoholic beverages. It was also the exclusive distributor of a variety of imported alcoholic beverages. Heublein had little experience in the restaurant business. Conflicts quickly erupted between Colonel Sanders, who continued to act in a public relations capacity, and Heublein management. In particular, Colonel Sanders became increasingly distraught over quality control issues and restaurant cleanliness. By 1977, new restaurant openings had slowed to about 20 per year (in 1993, KFC opened a new restaurant on average every two days). Restaurants were not being remodeled and service quality was declining.

In 1977, Heublein sent in a new management team to redirect KFC's strategy. Richard P. Mayer, who later became chairman and chief executive officer, was part of this team (Mayer remained with KFC until 1989, when he left to become president of General Foods USA). A "back-to-the-basics" strategy was immediately implemented. New unit construction was discontinued until existing restaurants could be upgraded and operating problems eliminated. Restaurants were refurbished, an emphasis was placed on cleanliness and service, marginal products were eliminated, and product consistency was reestablished. By 1982, KFC had succeeded in establishing a successful strategic focus and was again aggressively building new units.

R. J. Reynolds Industries, Inc.

On October 12, 1982, R. J. Reynolds Industries, Inc. (RJR), announced that it would merge Heublein into a wholly owned subsidiary. The merger with Heublein represented part of RJR's overall corporate strategy of diversifying into unrelated businesses. RJR's objective was to reduce its dependence on the tobacco industry, which had driven RJR sales since its founding in North Carolina in 1875. Sales of cigarettes and tobacco products, while profitable, were declining because of reduced consumption in the U.S., due mainly to the increased awareness among Americans regarding the negative health consequences of smoking.

RJR's diversification strategy included the acquisition of a variety of companies in the energy, transportation, and food and restaurant industries. RJR had no more experience in the restaurant business than did Heublein when Heublein purchased KFC in 1971. However, RJR decided to take a hands-off approach to managing KFC. Whereas Heublein had installed its own top management at KFC headquarters, RJR left KFC management largely intact, believing that existing KFC managers were better qualified to operate KFC's businesses than were its own managers. By doing so, RJR avoided many of the operating problems that Heublein had experienced during its management of KFC. This strategy paid off for RJR, as KFC continued to expand aggressively and profitably under RJR's ownership.

In 1985, RJR acquired Nabisco Corporation for $4.9 billion. Nabisco sold a variety of well-known cookies, crackers, cereals, confectionaries, snacks and other grocery products. In October 1986, Kentucky Fried Chicken was sold to PepsiCo, Inc.

PEPSICO, INC.

Corporate Strategy

PepsiCo, Inc. (PepsiCo), was first incorporated in Delaware in 1919 as Loft, Inc. In 1938, Loft acquired the Pepsi-Cola Co., a manufacturer of soft drinks and soft drink concentrates. Pepsi-Cola's traditional business was the sale of its soft drink concentrates to licensed independent and company-owned bottlers, which manufactured, sold, and distributed Pepsi-Cola soft drinks. Today, Pepsi-Cola's best known trademarks are Pepsi-Cola, Diet Pepsi, Mountain Dew, and Slice. Shortly after its acquisition of Pepsi-Cola, Loft changed its name to Pepsi-Cola Co. On June 30, 1965, Pepsi-Cola Co. acquired Frito-Lay Inc. for three million shares, thereby creating one of the largest consumer companies in the United States. At that time, the present name of PepsiCo, Inc., was adopted. Frito-Lay manufactures and sells a variety of snack foods. Its best known trademarks are Frito's brand Corn Chips, Lay's and Ruffles brand Potato Chips, Doritos and Tostitos Tortilla Chips, and Chee-tos brand Cheese Flavored Snacks. Eight of the top ten snack chips in the U.S. market during 1995 were Frito-Lay brands. In 1994, 63 percent of PepsiCo's net sales were generated by its soft drink and snack food businesses (see Exhibit 2).

Beginning in the late 1960s, PepsiCo began an aggressive acquisition program. Initially, PepsiCo pursued an acquisition strategy similar to that pursued by RJR during the 1980s, buying a number of companies in areas unrelated to its major businesses. For example, North American Van Lines was acquired in June 1968. Wilson Sporting Goods was merged into the company in 1972 and Lee Way Motor Freight was acquired in 1976. However, success in operating these businesses failed to live up to expectations, mainly because the management skills required to operate these businesses lay outside of PepsiCo's area of expertise.

In 1984, then-chairman and chief executive officer Don Kendall decided to re-

EXHIBIT 2
**PepsiCo, Inc.: 1994 Operating Results
(in millions of dollars)**

	Beverages	*Snack Foods*	*Restaurants*	*Total*
Net sales	$9,687.5	$8,264.4	$10,520.5	$28,472.4
Operating profit	1,217.0	1,376.9	730.3	3,324,2
Percent net sales	12.6%	16.7%	6.9%	11.7%
Assets*	$9,566.0	$5,043.9	$7,202.9	$24,792.0
Capital spending†	677.1	532.1	1,072.0	2,288.4

*Assets include corporate assets of $2,979.2 million.
†Capital spending includes corporate allocation of $7.2 million.
Source: PepsiCo, Inc., *Annual Report,* 1994.

structure PepsiCo's operations. Most importantly, PepsiCo would divest those businesses which did not support PepsiCo's consumer product orientation. PepsiCo sold Lee Way Motor Freight in 1984. In 1985, Wilson Sporting Goods and North American Van Lines were sold. Additionally, PepsiCo's foreign bottling operations were sold to local businesspeople who better understood the cultural and business conditions operating in their respective countries. Lastly, Kendall reorganized PepsiCo along three lines: soft drinks, snack foods, and restaurants (see Exhibit 3). All future investment would be directed at strengthening PepsiCo's performance in these three related areas.

When Wayne Calloway became chairman of the board and chief executive officer

EXHIBIT 3
**PepsiCo, Inc.: Principal Divisions
(Executive Offices: Purchase, New York)**

Beverage Segment	Snack Food Segment	Restaurants
Pepsi-Cola North America, Somers, New York	Frito-Lay, Inc., Plano, Texas	PepsiCo Worldwide Restaurants, Dallas, Texas
PepsiCo Foods and Beverages International, Somers, New York		PepsiCo Restaurants International, Dallas Texas
		Kentucky Fried Chicken Corporation, Louisville, Kentucky
		Pizza Hut Inc., Dallas, Texas
		Taco Bell Corp., Irvine, California
		PepsiCo Food Systems, Dallas, Texas

Source: PepsiCo, Inc., *Annual Report,* 1994.

of PepsiCo in 1986, he expanded PepsiCo's soft drink segment to include non-soft drink beverages such as tea, sports drinks, juices, and bottled water. These included, among others, ready-to-drink Lipton Tea; All Sport, which has become the nation's second best-selling sports drink; and Aquafina Bottled Water. In addition, several new organizations were created to maximize synergies across PepsiCo's related businesses. These included PepsiCo Foods and Beverages International, designed to coordinate efforts between PepsiCo's beverage and snack food segments and PepsiCo Worldwide Restaurants, created to maximize synergies across PepsiCo's restaurant companies (see Exhibit 3).

Restaurant Business and Acquisition of Kentucky Fried Chicken

PepsiCo first entered the restaurant business in 1977 when it acquired Pizza Hut's 3,200 unit restaurant system. Taco Bell was merged into a division of PepsiCo in 1978. The restaurant business complemented PepsiCo's consumer product orientation. The marketing of fast food followed much of the same patterns as the marketing of soft drinks and snack foods. Therefore, PepsiCo's management skills could easily be transferred among its three business segments. This was compatible with PepsiCo's practice of frequently moving managers among its business units as a way of developing future top executives. PepsiCo's restaurant chains also provided an additional outlet for the sale of Pepsi soft drink products. In addition, Pepsi soft drinks and fast-food products could be marketed together in the same television and radio segments, thereby providing higher returns for each advertising dollar.

To complete its diversification into the restaurant segment, PepsiCo acquired Kentucky Fried Chicken Corporation from RJR-Nabisco in 1986 for $841 million. The acquisition of KFC gave PepsiCo the leading market share in three of the four largest and fastest-growing segments within the U.S. quick-service industry. At the end of 1994, Pizza Hut held a 28 percent share of the $18.5 billion U.S. pizza segment, Taco Bell held 75 percent of the $5.7 billion Mexican food segment, and KFC held 49 percent of the $7.7 billion U.S. chicken segment. (See Exhibits 2 and 4 for business segment financial data and restaurant count.)

PepsiCo's success during the late 1980s and early 1990s can be seen by its upward trend in *Fortune* magazine's annual survey of "America's Most Admired Corporations." By 1991, PepsiCo was labeled the fifth most admired corporation overall (of 306 corporations included in the survey). However, PepsiCo's ranking fell to 14th place in 1993, 26th place in 1994, and 72nd place in 1995. PepsiCo's fall in the rankings is partially the result of changes made in *Fortune*'s survey methodology in 1994. In particular, it increased the number of industry groups from 32 to 42 (e.g., by adding computer services and entertainment) and divided some industry groups into their components (e.g., by dividing the transportation group into airlines, trucking, and railroads). Home Depot, Microsoft, and Walt Disney, which were added to the survey in 1994, were all ranked in the top ten most admired corporations in America that year.

However, part of PepsiCo's decline in the *Fortune* rankings is the result of a decline in operating profits among its restaurant chains, which declined $48 million in

EXHIBIT 4
PepsiCo, Inc.: Number of Units Worldwide

Year	KFC	Pizza Hut†	Taco Bell*	Total
1989	7,948	7,502	3,125	18,575
1990	8,187	8,220	3,349	19,756
1991	8,480	8,837	3,670	20,987
1992	8,729	9,454	4,153	22,336
1993	9,033	10,433	4,921	24,387
1994	9,407	11,546	5,846	26,799
Five-Year Compounded Annual Growth Rate				
	3.4%	9.0%	13.3%	7.6%

*Taco Bell data include 178 Hot 'n Now and 53 Chevy's restaurants.
†Pizza Hut data include 25 East Side Mario's restaurants and 197 D'Angelo Sandwich Shops.
Source: PepsiCo, Inc., *Annual Report*, 1994.

1994. Much of the decline was the result of increased administrative and support costs, international development costs, and higher store operating costs. In fact, a nearly two-year decline in earnings led PepsiCo to move the international operations of KFC, Pizza Hut, and Taco Bell to the newly formed PepsiCo Restaurants International (PRI) group in Dallas, Texas, in 1994.

PepsiCo	Ranking
1995	72
1994	26
1993	14
1992	9
1991	5
1990	6
1989	7
1988	14
1987	24
1986	25

FAST-FOOD INDUSTRY

U.S. Quick-Service Market

According to the National Restaurant Association (NRA), 1995 food-service sales will hit $289.7 billion for the approximately 500,000 restaurants and other food outlets making up the U.S. restaurant industry. The NRA estimates that sales in the fast-food segment of the food industry will grow 7.2 percent to approximately $93 billion in the

United States in 1995, up from $87 million in 1994. This would mark the second consecutive year that fast-food sales exceeded sales in the full-service segment, which are expected to grow to $87.8 billion in 1995. The growth in fast-food sales reflects the long, gradual change in the restaurant industry from an industry once dominated by independently operated sit-down restaurants to an industry fast becoming dominated by fast-foot restaurant chains. The U.S. restaurant industry as a whole is projected to grow by 4.7 percent in 1995.

Sales data for the top 30 fast-food restaurant chains are shown in Exhibit 1. Most striking is the dominance of McDonald's. Sales for 1995 are estimated at $15.8 billion, which would represent 17.3 percent of industry sales, or 21.3 percent of sales of the top 30 fast-food chains. McDonald's strong per restaurant sales are more striking given that McDonald's accounts for under 12 percent of the units of the top 30 fast-food chains. U.S. sales for the PepsiCo system, which includes KFC, Pizza Hut, and Taco Bell, are estimated to reach $14.0 billion in 1995, which would represent 15.0 percent of the fast-food industry and 18.8 percent of the top 30 fast-food chains. The PepsiCo system will grow to an estimated 20,490 restaurants in 1995. McDonald's holds the number one spot in the hamburger segment, while PepsiCo holds the leading market share in the chicken (KFC), Mexican (Taco Bell), and pizza (Pizza Hut) segments.

Major Business Segments

Six major business segments make up the fast-foot market within the food service industry. Exhibit 5 shows sales for the top 64 fast-food chains in the six major segments for the years 1993 through 1995, as compiled by *Nation's Restaurant News*. Sandwich chains make up the largest segment, with estimated sales of $41 billion in 1995. Of the 18 restaurant chains making up the sandwich segment, McDonald's holds a 34 percent market share. Sandwich chains, faced by slowed sales growth, have turned to new menu offerings, lower pricing, improved customer service, co-branding with other fast-food chains, and have established units in non-traditional locations to beef up sales.

Hardee's and McDonald's have successfully introduced fried chicken in many of their restaurants. Burger King has introduced fried clams and shrimp to its dinner menu in some locations and Jack in the Box has introduced chicken and teriyaki with rice in several of its California units, in order to appeal to its Asian-American audience. In order to broaden its customer base, McDonald's has installed 400 restaurants in Wal-Mart stores across the country. In addition, it has cut its building costs for its conventional stand-alone units from $1.6 million to $1.1 million in order to counter reduced profit margins resulting from lower pricing. Co-branding is also a potential source of expansion for many fast-food chains. PepsiCo plans to add Taco Bell signs and menus to approximately 800 existing KFC restaurants over the next few years. This would increase Taco Bell's 4,500 unit U.S. system by almost 18 percent.

The second largest fast-foot segment is pizza, long dominated by Pizza Hut. Pizza Hut expects sales to top $5.4 billion in 1995, which would represent a 53 percent market share among the eight competitors making up the pizza segment. Two years ago, Little Caesars overtook Domino's as the second largest pizza chain, despite

EXHIBIT 5

**U.S. Sales of the Top Fast-Food Chains by Business Segment Sales
(in billions of dollars)**

Business Segment	Number of Chains	1993	1994	1995(e)
Sandwich chains:	18	$41.0	$44.0	$47.2
(McDonald's, Burger King, Taco Bell, Wendy's, Hardee's, Subway, Arby's, Dairy Queen, Jack in the Box, Sonic Drive-In, Carl's Jr., Roy Rogers, Whataburger, Checker's Drive-In, Rally's, Blimpie Subs & Salads, White Castle, Krystal)				
Pizza chains:	8	10.2	10.5	11.2
(Pizza Hut, Little Caesars, Domino's, Papa John's, Sbarro The Italian Eatery, Round Table Pizza, Chuck E. Cheese's, Godfather's Pizza)				
Family restaurants:	11	7.6	8.0	8.6
(Denny's, Shoney's, Big Boy, Cracker Barrel, IHOP, Perkins, Friendly's, Bob Evan's, Waffle House, Coco's, Marie Callender's)				
Dinner houses:	15	7.6	8.7	9.8
(Red Lobster, Olive Garden, Applebee's, Chili's, T.G.I. Friday's, Outback Steakhouse, Ruby Tuesday, Bennigan's, Chi-Chi's, Ground Round, Lone Star, Fuddruckers, Hooters, Red Robin Burger & Spirits, Stuart Anderson's Black Angus)				
Chicken chains:	6	5.0	5.6	6.4
(KFC, Boston Market, Popeye's, Chick-fil-A, Church's, Kenny Rogers Roasters)				
Steak restaurants:	6	3.0	3.0	3.2
(Ponderosa, Golden Corral, Sizzler, Ryan's Western Sizzlin', Quincy's)				
Top fast-food chains	64	$74.4	$79.8	$86.4

(e) 1995 sales figures estimated.
Source: *Nation's Restaurant News.*

the fact that Domino's operated more outlets. Little Caesars is the only pizza chain to remain predominately a take-out chain. Home delivery, which has been successfully introduced by Domino's and Pizza Hut, was a driving force for success among the market leaders during the 1970s and 1980s (Little Caesars has also recently begun home delivery). However, the success of home delivery has driven competitors to look for new methods of increasing their customer bases. Increased competition within the pizza segment and pressures to appeal to a wider customer base have led pizza chains to diversify into non-pizza menu items, to develop non-traditional units (e.g., airport kiosks), and to offer special promotions. Among the many new product offerings, Domino's has introduced chicken wings; Little Caesars, Italian cheese bread; and Pizza Hut, stuffed crust pizza.

The highest growth segment in 1995 was the chicken segment. Sales are estimated to increase by 14.3 percent in 1995 over 1994. Dinner houses, which have outgrown the other five segments over the last few years are expected to increase sales by 12.6 percent in 1995. Both the chicken and dinner house segments are growing at almost twice the rate of the sandwich, pizza, and steak restaurant segments. Red Lobster remains the largest dinner house and is expected to surpass $1.8 billion in sales for its fiscal year ending May 1995. This would make Red Lobster the eleventh largest chain among the top 100. Olive Garden is expected to hit the $1.3 billion sales mark for 1995. Olive Garden is currently running a strong second place within the dinner house segment behind Red Lobster.

The dinner house segment should continue to outpace most of the other fast-food segments for a variety of reasons. Major chains still have low penetration in this segment, though Darden Restaurants Inc. (Red Lobster and Olive Garden) and PepsiCo, Inc. (Fresh-Mex), are poised to dominate a large portion of this segment. A maturing population is already increasing demand for full-service, sit-down restaurants. Eight of the fifteen dinner houses in this segment posted growth rates in sales of over 12 percent in 1995. Lone Star Steakhouse & Saloon, Outback Steakhouse, Fuddruckers, Applebee's Neighborhood Grill & Bar, T.G.I. Friday's, Red Robin Burger & Spirits Emporium, Ruby Tuesday, and Hooters grew at rates of 65, 50, 32, 23, 19, 15, 15, and 12 percent in 1995, respectively.

KFC continues to dominate the chicken segment, with projected 1995 sales of $3.7 billion. Its nearest competitor, Boston Market (formerly Boston Chicken), is a distant second with projected sales of $725.0 million. Popeye's Famous Fried Chicken and Chick-fil-A follow with projected sales of $689.2 and $507.2 million, respectively. KFC holds a market share of 58 percent in the chicken segment, while Boston Market and Popeye's hold shares of 11.3 and 10.8 percent, respectively. Other competitors within the chicken market include Church's, Kenny Rogers Roasters, Bojangle's, El Pollo Loco, Grandy's, and Pudgie's.

Despite KFC's continued dominance within the chicken segment, it has lost market share over the last two years to both Boston Market and Kenny Rogers Roasters, new restaurant chains which have emphasized roasted chicken over the traditional fried chicken offered by other chicken chains. Boston Market has been particularly successful in creating an image of an upscale deli offering healthy, "home-style" takeout products. Early in 1995, it changed its name from Boston Chicken to Boston Market. It thereafter quickly broadened its menu beyond rotisserie chicken to include ham, turkey, and meat loaf. KFC has quickly followed by introducing its $14.99 Mega-Meal, which is designed to compete with Boston Market as a home-replacement alternative. It is also aggressively pushing home delivery to support its home-replacement strategy. KFC has also introduced its "Colonel's Kitchen" in Dallas and is testing a full menu of home-meal replacement items.

Industry Consolidation

Although the restaurant industry has outpaced the overall economy in recent years, there are indications that the U.S. market is slowly becoming saturated. According to the U.S. Bureau of Labor, sales of U.S. eating and drinking establishments increased by 2.7 percent in 1992. Following a period of rapid expansion and intense restaurant building in the U.S. during the 1970s and 1980s, the fast-food industry has apparently begun to consolidate. In January 1990, Grand Metropolitan, a British company, purchased Pillsbury Co. for $5.7 billion. Included in the purchase was Pillsbury's Burger King chain. Grand Met has already begun to strengthen the franchise by upgrading existing restaurants and has eliminated several levels of management in order to cut costs. This should give Burger King a long-needed boost in improving its position against McDonald's, its largest competitor in the U.S. market. In 1988, Grand Met purchased Wienerwald, a West German chicken chain, and the Spaghetti Factory, a Swiss chain. In addition, General Mills spun off its Red Lobster, Olive Garden, and China Coast franchises in early 1995 in order to concentrate on its core businesses.

Perhaps most important to KFC was Hardee's acquisition of 600 Roy Rogers restaurants from Marriott Corporation in early 1990. Hardee's immediately began to convert these restaurants to Hardee's units and quickly introduced "Roy Rogers" fried chicken to its menu. By the end of 1993, Hardee's had introduced fried chicken into most of its 3,313 domestic restaurants. While Hardee's is unlikely to destroy the customer loyalty that KFC has long enjoyed, it has cut into KFC's sales as its widened menu selection appeals to a variety of family eating preferences.

The effect of these and other recent mergers and acquisitions on the industry has been powerful. The top ten restaurant chains now control over 55 percent of all fast-food sales in the U.S. The consolidation of a number of these firms within larger, financially more powerful firms should give these restaurant chains the financial and managerial resources they need to outgrow their smaller competitors.

Demographic Trends

Intense marketing by the leading fast-food chains will likely continue to stimulate demand for fast food in the U.S. through the year 2000. However, a number of demographic and societal changes are likely to affect the future demand for fast food in different directions. One such change is the rise in single-person households, which has steadily increased from 17 percent of all U.S. households in 1970 to approximately 25 percent today. In addition, disposable household income should continue to increase, mainly because more women are working than ever before. According to Standard & Poor's *Industry Surveys*, Americans will spend 55 percent of their food dollars at restaurants in 1995, up from 34 percent in 1970. In addition to the effect of a greater number of dual-income families and less time for home food preparation, growth of fast-food sales has been stimulated by an increase in the overall number of fast-food chains, easier access to fast-food chains in non-traditional locations such as department stores and airports, and the greater availability of home delivery and take-out service.

In addition to these demographic trends, a number of societal changes may also affect future demand for fast food. For example, microwaves have now been introduced into approximately 70 percent of all U.S. homes. This has already resulted in a significant shift in the types of products sold in supermarkets and convenience restaurants, which have introduced a variety of products that can be quickly and easily prepared in microwaves. In addition, the aging of America's Baby Boomers may change the frequency with which people patronize more upscale restaurants. Therefore, these various demographic and societal trends are likely to affect the future demand for fast food in different ways.

International Quick-Service Market

Because of the aggressive pace of new restaurant construction in the U.S. during the 1970s and 1980s, future growth resulting from new restaurant construction in the U.S. may be limited. In any case, the cost of finding prime locations is rising, increasing the pressure on restaurant chains to increase per restaurant sales in order to cover higher initial investment costs. One alternative to continued investment in the U.S. market is expansion into international markets, which offers large customer bases and comparatively little competition. However, few U.S. restaurant chains have yet defined aggressive strategies for penetrating international markets.

Three restaurant chains which have established aggressive international strategies are McDonald's, Pizza Hut, and KFC. McDonald's currently operates the most units within the U.S. market. McDonald's also operates the largest number of fast-food chains outside of the U.S. (4,710), recently overtaking KFC, which long dominated the fast-food industry outside of the U.S. KFC ended 1993 with 3,872 restaurants outside of the U.S., 838 fewer than McDonald's. However, KFC remains the most internationalized of all fast-food chains, operating 43 percent of its total units outside of the U.S. In comparison, McDonald's operates 34 percent of its units outside of the U.S. Pizza Hut presently operates in the most countries (80); however, over 88 percent of its units are still located in the U.S.

Exhibit 6 shows *Hotels'* 1994 list of the world's 30 largest fast-food restaurant chains. Several important observations may be made from these data. First, 17 of the 30 largest restaurant chains (ranked by number of units) are headquartered in the U.S. This may be partially explained by the fact that U.S. firms account for over 25 percent of the world's foreign direct investment. As a result, U.S. firms have historically been more likely to invest assets abroad. However, while both KFC and McDonald's operate over 3,800 units abroad, no other restaurant chain, U.S. or foreign, has more than 1,500 units outside of the U.S. In fact, most chains have fewer than 500 foreign units and operate in less than 22 countries.

There are a number of possible explanations for the relative scarcity of fast-food restaurant chains outside of the U.S. First, the U.S. represents the largest consumer market in the world, accounting for over one-fifth of the world's gross domestic product (GDP). Therefore, the U.S. has traditionally been the strategic focus of the largest restaurant chains. In addition, Americans have been more quick to accept the fast-food concept. Many other cultures have strong culinary traditions which have not been easy to break down. The Europeans, for example, have long histories of frequenting more mid-scale restaurants, where they may spend several hours in a formal setting enjoying native dishes and beverages. While KFC is again building restaurants in Germany, it previously failed to penetrate the German market because Germans were not accustomed to take-out food or to ordering food over the counter. McDonald's has had greater success penetrating the German market because it has made a

EXHIBIT 6
The World's 30 Largest Fast-Food Chains
(year-end 1993, ranked by number of countries)

	Franchise	Location	Units	Countries
1	Pizza Hut	Dallas, Texas	9,500	80
2	McDonald's	Oakbrook, Illinois	13,993	70
3	KFC	Louisville, Kentucky	9,000	68
4	Burger King	Miami, Florida	7,121	50
5	Baskin Robbins	Glendale, California	3,557	49
6	Wendy's	Dublin, Ohio	4,168	38
7	Domino's Pizza	Ann Arbor, Michigan	5,238	36
8	TCBY	Little Rock, Arkansas	7,474	22
9	Dairy Queen	Minneapolis, Minnesota	5,471	21
10	Dunkin' Donuts	Randolph, Massachusetts	3,691	21
11	Taco Bell	Irvine, California	4,800	20
12	Arby's	Fort Lauderdale, Florida	2,670	18
13	Subway Sandwiches	Milford, Connecticut	8,477	15
14	Sizzler International	Los Angeles, California	681	14
15	Hardee's	Rocky Mount, North Carolina	4,060	12
16	Little Caesar's	Detroit, Michigan	4,600	12
17	Popeye's Chicken	Atlanta, Georgia	813	12
18	Denny's	Spartanburg, South Carolina	1,515	10
19	A&W Restaurants	Livonia, Michigan	707	9
20	T.G.I. Friday's	Minneapolis, Minnesota	273	8
21	Orange Julius	Minneapolis, Minnesota	480	7
22	Church's Fried Chicken	Atlanta, Georgia	1,079	6
23	Long John Silver's	Lexington, Kentucky	1,464	5
24	Carl's Jr.	Anaheim, California	649	4
25	Loterria	Tokyo, Japan	795	4
26	Mos Burger	Tokyo, Japan	1,263	4
27	Skylark	Tokyo, Japan	1,000	4
28	Jack in the Box	San Diego, California	1,172	3
29	Quick Restaurants	Berchem, Belgium	876	3
30	Taco Time	Eugene, Oregon	300	3

Source: *Hotels,* May 1994.

number of changes in its menu and operating procedures in order to better appeal to German culture. For example, German beer is served in all of McDonald's German restaurants. KFC has had more success in Asia, where chicken is a traditional dish.

Aside from cultural factors, international business carries risks not present in the U.S. market. Long distances between headquarters and foreign franchises often make it difficult to control the quality of individual franchises. Large distances can also cause servicing and support problems. Transportation and other resource costs may also be higher than in the domestic market. In addition, time, cultural, and language differences can increase communication and operational problems. Therefore, it is reasonable to expect U.S. restaurant chains to expand domestically as long as they can achieve corporate profit and growth objectives. However, as the U.S. market becomes more saturated, and companies gain additional expertise in international business, we should expect more companies to turn to profitable international markets as a means of expanding restaurant bases and increasing sales, profits, and market share.

KENTUCKY FRIED CHICKEN CORPORATION

Management

One of PepsiCo's greatest challenges when it acquired Kentucky Fried Chicken in 1986 was how to mold two distinct corporate cultures. When R. J. Reynolds acquired KFC in 1982, it realized that it knew very little about the fast-food business. Therefore, it relied on existing KFC management to manage the company. As a result, there was little need for mixing the cultures of the two companies. However, one of PepsiCo's major concerns when considering the purchase of KFC was whether it had the management skills required to successfully operate KFC using PepsiCo managers. PepsiCo had already acquired considerable experience managing fast-food businesses through its Pizza Hut and Taco Bell operations. Therefore, it was anxious to pursue strategic changes within KFC which would improve performance. However, replacing KFC with PepsiCo managers could easily cause conflicts between managers in both companies, who were accustomed to different operating procedures and working conditions.

PepsiCo's corporate culture has long been based heavily on a "fast-track" New York approach to management. It hires the country's top business and engineering graduates and promotes them based on performance. As a result, top performers expect to move up through the ranks quickly and to be paid well for their efforts. However, this competitive environment often results in intense rivalries among young managers. If one fails to perform, there is always another top performer waiting in the wings. As a result, employee loyalty is sometimes lost and turnover tends to be higher than in other companies.

The corporate culture at Kentucky Fried Chicken in 1986 contrasted sharply with that at PepsiCo. KFC's culture was built largely on Colonel Sander's laid-back approach to management. As well, employees enjoyed relatively good employment stability and security. Over the years, a strong loyalty had been created among KFC employees and franchisees, mainly because of the efforts of Colonel Sanders to provide for his employees' benefits, pension, and other non-income needs. In addition, the Southern environment of Louisville resulted in a friendly, relaxed atmosphere at KFC's corporate offices. This corporate culture was left essentially unchanged during the Heublein and RJR years.

When PepsiCo acquired KFC, it began to restructure the KFC organization, replacing most of KFC's top managers with its own. By the summer of 1990, all of KFC's top positions were occupied by PepsiCo executives. In July 1989, KFC's president and chief executive officer, Richard P. Mayer, left KFC to become president of General Foods USA. Mayer had been at KFC since 1977, when KFC was still owned by Heublein. PepsiCo replaced Mayer with John Cranor III, the former president of Pepsi-Cola East, a Pepsi-Cola unit. In 1990, PepsiCo named Kyle Craig, a former Pillsbury executive, as president of KFC's U.S. operations.

Most of PepsiCo's initial management changes in 1987 focused on KFC's corporate offices and U.S. operations. In 1988, attention was turned to KFC's international division. During 1988, PepsiCo replaced KFC International's top managers with its own. First, it lured Don Pierce away from Burger King and made Pierce president of KFC International. However, Pierce left KFC in early 1990 to become president of Pentagram Corporation, a restaurant operation in Hawaii. Pierce commented that he wished to change jobs partly to decrease the amount of time he spent traveling. PepsiCo replaced Pierce with Allan Huston, who was formerly senior vice president of operations at Pizza Hut. However, by the end of 1995, most of KFC's new top management team had either left the company or moved on to other positions within the PepsiCo organization. John Cranor III resigned in 1994, Kyle Craig resigned in 1994 to join Boston Market, Allan Huston (president of KFC International) became president and chief executive of Pizza Hut, and Robert Briggs (vice president of international finance for KFC International) left to become the president of Arby's International.

An example of the type of conflict faced by PepsiCo in attempting to implement changes within KFC occurred in August 1989. A month after becoming president and chief executive officer, John Cranor addressed KFC's franchisees in Louisville, in order to explain the details of a new franchise contract. This was the first contract change in thirteen years. The new contract gave PepsiCo management greater power to take over weak franchises, to relocate restaurants, and to make changes in existing restaurants. In addition, existing restaurants would no longer be protected from competition from new KFC restaurants. The contract also gave management the right to raise royalty fees on existing restaurants as contracts came up for renewal. After Cranor finished his address, there was an uproar among the attending franchisees, who jumped to their feet to protest the changes. The franchisees had long been accustomed to relatively little interference from management in their day-to-day operations. This type of interference, of course, was a strong part of PepsiCo's philosophy of demanding change.

As a result of sluggish performance in its restaurant businesses and a desire to consolidate restaurant operations in order to maximize synergies, PepsiCo created two new divisions to oversee its restaurant businesses in late 1994: PepsiCo Worldwide Restaurants and PepsiCo Restaurants International. Both are based in Dallas, Texas. David Novak was named president of KFC (see Exhibit 7). Roger Enrico, vice-chairman of PepsiCo and former CEO of Frito-Lay, was named chairman and CEO of PepsiCo Worldwide Restaurants. Laurence Zwain, formerly president of KFC International, was named president and chief operating officer of PepsiCo Restaurants International. Then in October 1995, James H. O'Neal, who had been president of PepsiCo Foods International-Europe, was named to the new position of chairman and CEO of PepsiCo Restaurants International. Zwain retained his title and would report to O'Neal. O'Neal would report directly to Enrico.

EXHIBIT 7
KFC Organizational Chart

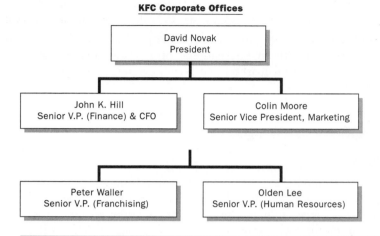

Source: PepsiCo, Inc., *Annual Report*, 1994.

Operating Results

KFC's recent operating results are shown in Exhibit 8. In 1994, worldwide sales, which represent sales of both company-owned and franchised restaurants, reached $7.1 billion. Since 1987, worldwide sales have grown at a compounded annual growth rate of 8.2 percent. KFC's domestic market share remained at about one-half of the $7.7 billion U.S. market in 1994. KFC corporate sales, which include company-owned restaurants and royalties from franchised units, reached $2.6 billion, up 14 percent from 1993 sales of $2.3 billion. New restaurants and higher volume contributed $193 million and $120 million to corporate sales, respectively.

EXHIBIT 8
KFC Operating Results

	Worldwide Sales (in billions of dollars)	KFC Corp.* Sales (in billions of dollars)	KFC Corp.* Profit (in millions of dollars)	Percent of Sales
1987	$4.1	$1.1	$ 90.0	8.3
1988	5.0	1.2	114.9	9.5
1989	5.4	1.3	99.4	7.5
1990	5.8	1.5	126.9	8.3
1991	6.2	1.8	80.5	4.4
1992	6.7	2.2	168.8	7.8
1993	7.1	2.3	152.8	6.6
1994	7.1	2.6	165.2	6.2
7-year growth rate	8.2%	13.6%	9.1%	

*KFC corporate figures include company restaurants and franchise royalties and fees.
Source: PepsiCo, Inc., annual reports for 1988–1994.

KFC's worldwide profits increased by 8 percent to $165 million in 1994. KFC's operating profits from international operations represented about 40 percent of worldwide profits in both 1993 and 1994. Profits rose as the result of additional units, higher volume, and increased franchise royalties, which were partially offset by a sales mix shift to lower-margin products, lower pricing, and higher administrative and support costs. Growth in international profits was highest in Australia (now KFC's largest international market) and New Zealand. Profits were lowest in Mexico and Canada.

Business Level Strategies

Marketing

As KFC entered 1996, it grappled with a number of important issues. During the 1980s, consumers began to demand healthier foods and KFC was faced with a limited menu consisting mainly of fried foods. In order to reduce KFC's image as a fried chicken chain, it changed its logo from Kentucky Fried Chicken to KFC in 1991. In addition, it responded to consumer demands for greater variety by introducing a variety of new products. Consumers have also become more mobile, demanding fast food in a variety of non-traditional locations such as grocery stores, restaurants, airports, and outdoor events. This has forced fast-food restaurant chains in general to investigate non-traditional distribution channels and restaurant designs. In addition, families continue to seek greater value in the food they buy, further increasing the pressure on fast-food chains to reduce operating costs and prices.

Many of KFC's problems during the late 1980s surrounded its limited menu and its inability to quickly bring new products to market. The popularity of its Original Recipe fried chicken allowed KFC to expand through the 1980s without significant competition from other chicken competitors. As a result, new product introductions were never an important part of KFC's overall strategy. However, the introduction of chicken sandwiches and fried chicken by hamburger chains has changed the make-up of KFC's competitors. Most importantly, McDonald's introduced its McChicken sandwich in the U.S. market in 1989 while KFC was still testing its new sandwich. By beating KFC to the market, McDonald's was able to develop a strong consumer awareness for its sandwich. This significantly increased KFC's cost of developing consumer awareness for its chicken sandwich, which was introduced several months later.

The increased popularity of healthier foods and consumers' increasing demand for better variety has led to a number of changes in KFC's menu offerings. In 1992, KFC introduced Oriental Wings, Popcorn Chicken, and Honey BBQ Chicken as alternatives to its Original Recipe fried chicken. It also introduced a dessert menu, which included a variety of pies and cookies. In 1993, KFC rolled out its Rotisserie Chicken and began to promote its lunch and dinner buffet. The buffet, which includes 30 items, had been introduced into almost 1,600 KFC restaurants in 27 states by the end of 1993.

One of KFC's most aggressive strategies was the introduction of its "Neighborhood Program." By mid-1993, almost 500 company-owned restaurants in New York,

Chicago, Philadelphia, Washington, D.C., St. Louis, Los Angeles, Houston, and Dallas had been outfitted with special menu offerings to appeal exclusively to the Black community. Menus were beefed up with side dishes such as greens, macaroni and cheese, peach cobbler, sweet-potato pie, and red beans and rice. In addition, restaurant employees have been outfitted with African-inspired uniforms. The introduction of the Neighborhood Program has increased sales by 5 to 30 percent in restaurants appealing directly to the Black community. KFC is currently testing Hispanic-oriented restaurants in the Miami area, which offer such side dishes as fried plantains, flan, and tres leches.

As the growth in sales of traditional, free-standing fast-food restaurants has slowed during the last decade, consumers have demanded fast food in a greater variety of non-traditional locations. As a result, distribution has taken on increasing importance. KFC is relying on non-traditional units to spur much of its future growth. Distribution channels which offer significant growth opportunities are shopping malls and other high-traffic areas which have not traditionally been exploited by fast-food chains. Increasingly, shopping malls are developing food areas where several fast-food restaurant chains compete against each other. Universities and hospitals also offer opportunities for KFC and other chains to improve distribution. KFC is currently testing a variety of non-traditional outlets, including drive-thru and carry-out units; snack shops in cafeterias; kiosks in airports, stadiums, amusement parks, and office buildings; mobile units that can be transported to outdoor concerts and fairs; and scaled-down outlets for supermarkets. In order to help its KFC, Taco Bell, and Pizza Hut units more quickly expand into these non-traditional distribution channels, PepsiCo acquired a partial share of Carts of Colorado, Inc., a manufacturer of mobile merchandise carts, in 1992. Additionally, KFC and Taco Bell plan to add the Taco Bell menu to existing KFC restaurants in 1996 and 1997. This "dual branding" strategy would help PepsiCo improve economies of scale within its restaurant operations and enable KFC restaurants to improve its customer base by widening its menu offerings.

Operating Efficiencies

While marketing strategies traditionally improve a firm's profit picture indirectly through increased sales, improved operating efficiencies can directly affect operating profit. As pressure continues to build on fast-food chains to limit price increases in the U.S. market, restaurant chains continue to search for ways of reducing overhead and other operating costs in order to improve profit margins. In 1989, KFC reorganized its U.S. operations in order to eliminate overhead costs and to increase efficiency. Included in this reorganization was a revision of KFC's crew training programs and operating standards. A renewed emphasis has been placed on improving customer service, cleaner restaurants, faster and friendlier service, and continued high-quality products. In 1992, KFC reorganized its middle management ranks, eliminating 250 of the 1,500 management positions at KFC's corporate headquarters. More responsibility was assigned to restaurant franchisees and marketing managers and pay was more closely aligned with customer service and restaurant performance.

Restaurant Expansion and International Operations

While marketing and operating strategies can improve sales and profitability in existing outlets, an important part of success in the quick-service industry is investment growth. Much of the success of the top ten competitors within the industry during the late 1980s and early 1990s can be found in aggressive building strategies. In particular, a restaurant chain is often able to discourage competition by being the first to build in a low population area which can only support a single fast-food chain. Additionally, it is equally important to beat a competitor into more largely populated areas, where location is of prime importance. Internationally, KFC was operating 4,258 restaurants in 68 countries at the end of 1994. KFC is now the third largest quick-service, and largest chicken, restaurant system in the world. In the future, KFC's international operations will be called on to provide an increasing percentage of KFC's overall sales and profit growth as the U.S. market continues to saturate.

MEXICO AND LATIN AMERICA

KFC was one of the first restaurant chains to recognize the importance of international markets. In Latin America, KFC was operating 205 company-owned restaurants in Mexico, Puerto Rico, Venezuela, and Trinidad and Tobago as of November 1995. In addition, KFC had 173 franchisees in 21 countries throughout Latin America, bringing the total number of KFC restaurants in operation in Latin America to 378 (see Exhibit 9).

Through 1990, KFC concentrated its company operations in Mexico and Puerto Rico and focused its franchised operations in the Caribbean and Central America. However, by 1994, KFC had altered its Latin American strategy in a number of ways. First, it began franchising in Mexico, mainly as a result of Mexico's new franchise law,

EXHIBIT 9
KFC (Latin America) Restaurant Count
(as of November 30, 1995)

	Company Restaurants	Franchise Restaurants	Total Restaurants	Countries
Mexico	129	29	158	1
Puerto Rico	64	0	64	1
Venezuela	4	0	4	1
Virgin Islands	8	0	8	1
Trinidad and Tobago	0	26	26	1
Franchises	0	118	118	19
Total	205	173	378	24

Source: PepsiCo, Inc.

which was enacted in 1990. Second, it expanded its company-owned restaurants into the Virgin Islands and Trinidad and Tobago. Third, it reestablished a subsidiary in Venezuela in 1993. KFC had closed its Venezuelan operations in 1989 because of the high fixed costs associated with running the small subsidiary. Last, it decided to expand its franchise operations beyond Central America. In 1990, a franchise was opened in Chile and, in 1993, a new franchise was opened in Brazil.

Franchising

Through 1989, KFC relied exclusively on the operation of company-owned restaurants in Mexico. While franchising was popular in the United States, it was virtually unknown in Mexico until 1990, mainly because of the absence of a law protecting patents, information, and technology transferred to the Mexican franchise. In addition, royalties were limited. As a result, most fast-food chains opted to invest in Mexico, using company-owned restaurants rather than through franchising.

In January 1990, Mexico enacted a new law which provided for the protection of technology transferred into Mexico. Under the new legislation, the franchisor and franchisee are free to set their own terms. Royalties are also allowed under the new law. Royalties are currently taxed at a 15 percent rate on technology assistance and know-how and 35 percent for other royalty categories. The advent of the new franchise law has resulted in an explosion of franchises in fast-food, services, hotels, and retail outlets. In 1992, franchises had an estimated $750 million in sales in over 1,200 outlets throughout Mexico.

At the end of 1989, KFC was operating company-owned restaurants in three regions: Mexico City, Guadalajara, and Monterrey. By limiting operations to company-owned restaurants in these three regions, KFC was better able to coordinate operations and minimize costs of distribution to individual restaurants. However, the new franchise legislation gave KFC and other fast-food chains the opportunity to more easily expand their restaurant bases to other regions of Mexico, where responsibility for management could be handled by individual franchisees.

Economic Environment and the Mexican Market

Many factors make Mexico a potentially profitable location for U.S. direct investment and trade. Mexico's population of over 91 million people is approximately one-third as large as the U.S. This represents a large market for U.S. goods. Because of its geographical proximity to the U.S., transportation costs from the U.S. are minimal. This increases the competitiveness of U.S. goods in comparison with European and Asian goods, which must be transported at substantial cost across the Atlantic or Pacific Ocean. The U.S. is, in fact, Mexico's largest trading partner. Over 65 percent of Mexico's imports come from the U.S., while 69 percent of Mexico's exports are to the U.S. market (see Exhibit 10). In addition, low wage rates make Mexico an attractive location for production. By producing in Mexico, U.S. firms may reduce labor costs and increase the cost competitiveness of their goods in world markets.

Despite the importance of the U.S. market to Mexico, Mexico still represents a

EXHIBIT 10
Mexico's Major Trading Partners

	1988		1990		1992	
	Percent Total Exports	Percent Total Imports	Percent Total Exports	Percent Total Imports	Percent Total Exports	Percent Total Imports
U.S.	72.9	74.9	69.3	68.0	68.7	65.2
Japan	4.9	6.4	5.8	4.5	3.2	6.3
West Germany	1.3	3.5	1.4*	4.2*	N/A	5.1
France	1.8	2.0	3.5	2.3	2.0	2.7
Other	19.1	13.2	20.0	21.0	26.1	20.7
Percent total	100.0	100.0	100.0	100.0	100.0	100.0
Value (in millions of dollars)	20,658	18,903	26,773	29,799	46,196	62,129

*Data include East Germany.
Source: *Business International*, 1994.

small percentage of overall U.S. trade and investment. Since the early 1900s, the portion of U.S. exports to Latin America has declined. Instead, U.S. exports to Canada and Asia, where economic growth has outpaced growth in Mexico, have increased more quickly. Canada is the largest importer of U.S. goods. Japan is the largest exporter of goods to the U.S., with Canada close behind. While the value of Mexico's exports to the U.S. has increased during the last two decades, mainly because of the rise in the price of oil, Mexico still represents a small percentage of overall U.S. trade. U.S. investment in Mexico has also been small, mainly because of government restrictions on foreign investment. Instead, most U.S. foreign investment has been in Europe, Canada, and Asia.

The lack of U.S. investment in and trade with Mexico during the 20th century is mainly the result of Mexico's long history of restricting trade and foreign direct investment in Mexico. In particular, the Institutional Revolutionary Party (PRI), which came to power in Mexico during the 1930s, has traditionally pursued protectionist economic policies in order to shield its people and economy from foreign firms and goods. Industries have been predominately government-owned or -controlled and production has been pursued for the domestic market only. High tariffs and other trade barriers have restricted imports into Mexico and foreign ownership of assets in Mexico has been largely prohibited or heavily restricted.

In addition, a dictatorial and entrenched government bureaucracy, corrupt labor unions, and a long tradition of anti-Americanism among many government officials and intellectuals have reduced the motivation of U.S. firms for investing in Mexico. As well, the 1982 nationalization of Mexico's banks led to higher real interest rates and lower investor confidence. Since then, the Mexican government has battled high inflation, high interest rates, labor unrest, and lost consumer purchasing power (see Exhibit 11). Total foreign debt, which stood at $125.9 billion at the end of 1993, remains a problem.

EXHIBIT 11
Economic Data for Mexico

	1989	1990	1991	1992	1993
Population (millions)	84.5	86.2	87.8	89.5	91.2
GDP (billions of new pesos)	507.6	686.4	865.2	1,019.2	1,127.6
Real GDP growth rate (percent)	3.3	4.4	3.6	2.8	0.6
Exchange rate (new pesos/dollars)	2.641	2.945	3.071	3.115	3.106
Inflation (percent)	20.0	26.6	22.7	15.5	8.6
Current account (in billions of dollars)	(5.8)	(7.5)	(14.9)	(24.8)	(23.4)
Reserves (excl. gold in billions of dollars)	6.3	9.9	17.7	18.9	25.1

Source: *International Financial Statistics,* International Monetary Fund, 1995.

Investor confidence in Mexico has, however, improved since December 1988, when Carlos Salinas de Gortari was elected president of Mexico. Following his election, Salinas embarked on an ambitious restructuring of the Mexican economy. In particular, Salinas initiated policies to strengthen the free market components of the economy. Top marginal tax rates were lowered to 36 percent in 1990, down from 60 percent in 1986, and new legislation has eliminated many restrictions on foreign investment. Foreign firms are now allowed to buy up to 100 percent of the equity in many Mexican firms. Previously, foreign ownership of Mexican firms was limited to 49 percent. Many government-owned companies have been sold to private investors in order to eliminate government bureaucracy and improve efficiency.

Privatization

The privatization of government-owned companies has come to symbolize the restructuring of Mexico's economy. On May 14, 1990, legislation was passed to privatize all government-run banks. By the end of 1992, over 800 of some 1,200 government-owned companies had been sold, including Mexicana and AeroMexico, the two largest airline companies in Mexico, and Mexico's 18 major banks. At least 40 more companies were scheduled to be privatized in 1993. However, more than 350 companies remain under government ownership. These represent a significant portion of the assets owned by the state at the start of 1988. Therefore, the sale of government-owned companies, in terms of asset value, has been moderate. A large percentage of the remaining government-owned assets are controlled by government-run companies in certain strategic industries such as steel, electricity, and petroleum. These industries have long been protected by government ownership. As a result, additional privatization of government-owned enterprises until 1993 was limited. However, in 1993, President Salinas opened up the electricity sector to independent power producers and Petroleos Mexicanos (Pemex), the state-run petrochemical monopoly, initiated a program to sell off many of its non-strategic assets to private and foreign buyers. This was motivated mainly by a desire by Pemex to concentrate on its basic petrochemical businesses.

North American Free Trade Agreement (NAFTA)

Prior to 1989, Mexico levied high tariffs on most imported goods. In addition, many other goods were subjected to quotas, licensing requirements, and other non-tariff trade barriers. In 1986, Mexico joined the General Agreement on Tariffs and Trade (GATT), a world trade organization designed to eliminate barriers to trade among member nations equally. As a result of its membership in GATT, Mexico dropped tariff rates on a variety of imported goods. In addition, import license requirements were dropped for all but 300 imported items. During President Salinas' administration, tariffs were reduced from an average of 100 percent on most items to an average of 11 percent.

On January 1, 1994, the North American Free Trade Agreement (NAFTA) went into effect. The passage of NAFTA, which included Canada, the U.S., and Mexico, created a trading bloc which has a larger population and gross domestic product than the European Union. Over the next several years, all tariffs on goods traded among the three countries will be phased out. Given that Canada is the U.S.'s largest trading partner and Mexico the U.S.'s third largest trading partner, the absence of tariffs and reduced restrictions on investment should result in increased trade and investment among the three countries. In particular, Mexico should benefit from the lower cost of imported goods and increased employment from higher investment from Canada and the U.S. Canada and the U.S. should benefit from lower labor and transportation costs from investing in Mexico.

Foreign Exchange and the Mexican Peso Crisis of 1995

Between December 20, 1982, and November 11, 1991, a two-tiered exchange rate system was in force in Mexico. The system consisted of a controlled rate and a free market rate. A controlled rate was used for imports, foreign debt payments, and conversion of export proceeds. An estimated 70 percent of all foreign transactions were covered by the controlled rate. A free market rate was used for other transactions. On January 1, 1989, President Salinas instituted a policy of allowing the peso to depreciate against the dollar by one peso per day. The result was a grossly overvalued peso. This lowered the price of imports and led to an increase in imports of over 23 percent in 1989. At the same time, Mexican exports became less competitive on world markets.

Effective November 11, 1991, the controlled rate was abolished and replaced with an official free rate. In order to limit the range of fluctuations in the value of the peso, the government fixed the rate at which it would buy or sell pesos. A floor (the maximum price at which pesos may be purchased) was initially established at Ps 3,056.20 and remained fixed. A ceiling (the maximum price at which the peso may be sold) was initially established at Ps 3,056.40 and allowed to move upward by Ps 0.20 per day. This was later revised to Ps 0.40 per day. On January 1, 1993, a new currency was issued—called the new peso—with three fewer zeros. The new currency was designed to simplify transactions and to reduce the cost of printing currency.

When Ernesto Zedillo became Mexico's president in December 1994, one of his objectives was to continue the stability in prices, wages, and exchange rates achieved by ex-president Carlos Salinas de Gortari during his five-year tenure as president. However, Salinas had achieved stability largely on the basis of price, wage, and foreign exchange controls. While giving the appearance of stability, an over-valued peso continued to encourage imports which exacerbated Mexico's balance of trade deficits. Mexico's government continued to use foreign reserves to finance its balance of trade deficits. According to the Banco de Mexico, foreign currency reserves fell from $24 billion in January 1994 to $5.5 billion in January 1995. Anticipating a devaluation of the peso, investors began to move capital into U.S. dollar investments. In order to relieve some of the pressure placed on the peso, President Zedillo announced on December 19, 1994, that the peso would be allowed to depreciate by an additional 15 percent per year against the dollar compared to the maximum allowable depreciation of 4 percent per year established during the Salinas administration. Within two days, continued pressure on the peso forced the Zedillo administration to allow the peso to float against the dollar. By mid-January 1995, the peso had lost 35 percent of its value against the dollar and the Mexican stock market plunged 20 percent. By November 1995, the peso had depreciated from 3.1 pesos per dollar to 7.3 pesos per dollar.

The continued devaluation of the peso resulted in higher import prices, higher inflation, destabilization within the stock market and higher interest rates, as Mexico struggled to arrange continued payment of its dollar-based debts. In order to thwart a possible default by Mexico on its dollar-based loans, the U.S. government, International Monetary Fund, and World Bank pledged $12.5, $11.4, and $1.0 billion (a total of $24.9 billion) in emergency loans to Mexico. In addition, President Zedillo announced an emergency economic package called the "pacto," which included reduced government spending, increased sales of government-run businesses, and a freeze on wage increases.

Labor Problems

One of KFC's primary concerns is the stability of Mexico's labor markets. Labor is relatively plentiful and cheap in Mexico, though much of the workforce is still relatively unskilled. While KFC benefits from lower labor costs, labor unrest, low job retention, absenteeism, and punctuality continue to be significant problems. A good part of the problem with absenteeism and punctuality is cultural. However, problems with worker retention and labor unrest are mainly the result of workers' frustration over the loss of their purchasing power due to inflation and past government controls on wage increases. *Business Latin America* estimated that purchasing power fell by 35 percent in Mexico between January 1988 and June 1990. Though absenteeism is on the decline due to job security fears, it is still high, at approximately 8 to 14 percent of the labor force. Turnover also continues to be a problem. Turnover of production line personnel is currently running at 5 to 12 percent per month. Therefore, employee screening and internal training continue to be important issues for foreign firms investing in Mexico.

Higher inflation and the government's freeze on wage increases has led to a dramatic decline in disposable income since 1994. Further, a slowdown in business activity, brought about by higher interest rates and lower government spending, has led many businesses to lay off workers. By the end of 1995, an estimated one million jobs had been lost as a result of the economic crisis sparked by the peso devaluation. As a result, industry groups within Mexico have called for new labor laws giving them more freedom to hire and fire employees and increased flexibility to hire part-time rather than full-time workers.

RISKS AND OPPORTUNITIES

The peso crisis of 1995 and resulting recession in Mexico left KFC managers with a great deal of uncertainty regarding Mexico's economic and political future. KFC had benefited greatly from the economic stability brought about by ex-president Salinas' policies during his 1988–1994 tenure. Inflation was brought down, the peso was relatively stable, labor unrest was relatively calm, and Mexico's new franchise law had enabled KFC to expand into rural areas, using franchises rather than company-owned restaurants. By the end of 1995, KFC had built 29 franchises in Mexico. KFC planned to continue to expand its franchise base and to rely less heavily on company-owned restaurants as a cornerstone of its strategy to maintain its market share against other fast-food restaurants, such as McDonald's and Arby's, which were pursuing high growth strategies in Mexico.

The foreign exchange crisis of 1995 had severe implications for U.S. firms operating in Mexico. In particular, the devaluation of the peso resulted in higher inflation and capital flight out of Mexico. The Bank of Mexico estimated that $7.1 billion fled the country during the first three months of 1995. In order to bring inflation under control, the Mexican government instituted an austerity program in early 1995 which included reduced government spending and a freeze on wage increases. Capital flight reduced the supply of capital and resulted in higher interest rates. Additionally, the government's austerity program resulted in reduced demand for products and services, higher unemployment, and lower disposable income. Imports from the U.S. dropped dramatically in 1995. About one-third of this decline included the importation of capital goods, such as technology materials and updated machinery, which are critical to Mexico's industrialization program.

Another problem area has been Mexico's failure to reduce restrictions on U.S. and Canadian investment in Mexico in a timely fashion. While the reduction of trade barriers has resulted in greater U.S. exports to Mexico, U.S. firms have experienced problems getting the required approvals for new ventures in Mexico from the Mexican government. For example, under the NAFTA agreement, the United Parcel Service (UPS) was supposed to receive government approval to use large trucks for deliveries in Mexico. As of the end of 1995, UPS had still not received approval. As a result, UPS has been forced to use smaller trucks, which puts it at a competitive disadvantage vis-à-vis Mexican companies, or to subcontract delivery work to Mexican companies that are allowed to use bigger, more cost-efficient trucks. Other U.S. companies, such as Bell Atlantic and TRW, have faced similar problems. TRW, which signed a joint venture agreement with a Mexican partner, had to wait fifteen months longer than anticipated before the Mexican government released rules on how it could receive credit data from banks. TRW claims that the Mexican government slowed the approval process in order to placate several large Mexican banks.

A final area of concern for KFC has been the increased political turmoil in Mexico during the last several years. For example, on January 1, 1994, the day NAFTA went into effect, rebels (descendants of the Mayans) rebelled in the southern Mexican province of Chiapas on the Guatemalan border. After four days of fighting, Mexican troops had driven the rebels out of several towns earlier seized by the rebels. Around 150—mostly rebels—were killed. The uprising symbolized many of the fears of the poor in Mexico. While ex-president Salinas' economic programs had increased economic growth and wealth in Mexico, many of Mexico's poorest felt that they have not benefited. Many of Mexico's farmers, faced with lower tariffs on imported agricultural goods from the United States, felt that they might be driven out of business by the NAFTA agreement. Therefore, social unrest among Mexico's Indians, farmers, and the poor could potentially unravel much of the economic success achieved in Mexico during the last five years.

Further, ex-president Salinas' hand-picked successor for president, Luis Donaldo Colosio, was assassinated on March 23, 1994, while campaigning in Tijuana. The assassin—Mario Aburto Martinez, a 23-year-old mechanic and migrant worker—was affiliated with a dissident group upset with the PRI's economic reforms. The possible existence of a dissident group has raised fears of further political violence in the future. The PRI quickly named Ernesto Zedillo, a 42-year-old economist with little political experience or name recognition, as their new presidential candidate. Zedillo was elected president and replaced Salinas in December 1994. However, political unrest is not limited to Mexican officials and companies. In October 1994, between 30 and 40 masked men attacked a McDonald's restaurant in the tourist section of Mexico City to show their opposition to California's Proposition 187, which would have curtailed benefits to illegal aliens (primarily from Mexico). The men threw cash registers to the floor, cracked them open, smashed windows, overturned tables, and spray-painted slogans on the walls such as "No to Fascism" and "Yankee Go Home."

Despite these worries, the passage of NAFTA, the size of the Mexican market, and its proximity to the United States have resulted in a number of opportunities for KFC and other U.S. businesses. During the first five months of 1995, exports from Mexico to the United States jumped 33.5 percent from the previous year as lower tariffs lowered the price of Mexican goods to the American consumer. In fact, during this period, Mexico ran up its highest trade surplus with the U.S. in Mexico's history.

The peso devaluation has also made it less expensive for U.S. and Canadian businesses to buy assets in Mexico. This has enabled businesses to more easily fund expansion in Mexico through new capital at a lower cost. As well, for companies already operating in Mexico, raw materials can be imported from outside of Mexico by converting dollars into pesos at a more favorable rate.

For many U.S. companies, the protection of technology and patents is a major concern. In June 1991, a new patent law was passed which replaced the old 1976 law. Patents will now last for twenty years rather than fourteen. Chemicals, pharmaceuticals, and animal feed will benefit from product patent protection for the first time, opening up the Mexican market to U.S. firms in these fields. Trademarks are now valid for an initial ten years and are renewable for ten years, up from the previous five-year terms. Patents on industrial designs are now valid for fifteen years, up from seven years. Additionally, a new copyright law was passed in August 1991. The new law will protect sound recordings and computer software for the first time.

KFC's approach to investment in Mexico is to approach it conservatively, until greater economic and political stability is achieved. While resources could be directed at other investment areas with less risk such as Japan, Australia, China, and Europe, the Mexican market is viewed as KFC's most important growth market outside of the U.S. and second largest international market behind Australia. Also, significant opportunities existed for KFC to expand its franchise base throughout the Caribbean and South America. However, PepsiCo's commitments to these other markets are unlikely to be severely affected by its investment decisions in Mexico, as PepsiCo's large internal cash flows could satisfy the investment needs of KFC's other international subsidiaries regardless of its investments in Mexico. The danger in taking a conservative approach in Mexico was the potential loss of market share in a large market where KFC enjoys enormous popularity.

http://www.kentuckyfriedchicken.com

STRATEGY FORMULATION

CASE 27

Whirlpool's Quest for Global Leadership*

In the Chairman's Letter of Whirlpool Corporation's 1995 Annual Report, David R. Whitwam, Chairman of the Board and Chief Executive Officer, stated his disappointment with the company's recent performance:

> On a relative basis, 1995 was a good year for Whirlpool Corporation and we continued to strengthen our position as the global leader in the major home appliance industry. That said, we should have done better. On an operating basis, and compared to our own very high performance expectations, the year was disappointing—for me, our global team and you, our shareholders.[1]

He attributed this disappointing performance partly to manufacturing inefficiencies and start-up costs of a new refrigerator in the U.S., partly to restructuring difficulties in Europe, as well as raw material cost increases combined with minimal growth or even declining demand in North America and Europe. This statement was quite a change in tone compared to his pronouncement a year earlier, when at the same place he had boldly stated that the company had achieved both primary objectives—to produce "strong, short-term results" and to "building competitive advantage by continuing our expanding worldwide enterprise at all levels, and to leverage its best practices and Whirlpool's cumulative size."[2] (For key performance data see Exhibit 1.)

THE U.S. APPLIANCE INDUSTRY

Home appliances were generally classified as laundry (washers and dryers), refrigeration (refrigerators and freezers), cooking (ranges and ovens), and other appliances (dishwashers, disposals, and trash compactors). Many appliance manufacturers also made floor care goods such as floor polishers and vacuum cleaners.

---

*Prepared by Arieh A. Ullmann, School of Management, State University of New York at Binghamton, Binghamton, NY 13902-6015, Tel. (607) 777-6858, Fax (607) 777-4422, ARIEH@BINGVMB.BITNET. Copyright © 1995 by Arieh A. Ullmann, Associate Professor, Binghamton University. Prepared as the basis for class discussion rather than to illustrate either effective or ineffective handling of an administrative situation.
[1]Whirlpool Corporation, 1995 Annual Report, p. 4.
[2]Whirlpool Corporation, 1994 Annual Report, p. 2.

EXHIBIT 1
Whirlpool Corporation: Key Performance Measures

Year	Earnings per Share*	Return on Equity†	Total Return to Shareholders†	P/E Ratio
1990	$1.04	5.1%	2.8%	22.6
1991	$2.45	11.6%	6.7%	15.9
1992	$2.90	13.1%	17.0%	15.4
1993	$3.19	14.2%	25.8%	20.8
1994	$2.10	9.4%	12.0%	23.9
1995	$2.80	11.6%	20.8%	19.0

*Earnings from continuing operations before accounting change.
†Earnings from continuing operations before accounting change divided by average
 stockholders' equity.
†Five-year annualized.

Manufacturing operations consisted mainly of preparation of a metal frame to which the appropriate components were attached in automated assembly lines and by manual assembly. Manufacturing costs comprised about 65 to 75 percent of total operating cost with labor representing less than 10 percent of total cost. Optimal sized assembly plants had an annual capacity of about 500,000 units for most appliances except microwave ovens. Unlike other industries such as textiles, variable costs played an important role in the cost structure; changes in raw material and component costs were also significant. Component production was fairly scale sensitive. Doubling compressor output for refrigerators, for instance, reduced unit costs by 10 to 15 percent. There were also some scale economies in assembly but the introduction of robotics tended to reduce those while improving quality and performance consistency and enhancing flexibility.

Distribution of major appliances occurred either through contract sales to home builders and to other appliance manufacturers predominantly directly or indirectly through local builder suppliers. Traditionally, these customers were very cost conscious and thus preferred less expensive appliance brands. Retail sales represented the second distribution channel with national chain stores and mass merchandisers like Sears, department, furniture, discount, and appliance stores acting as intermediaries. The consolidation of the appliance distributors during the past ten years led to the current situation where about 45 percent of the total appliance volume was being sold through ten powerful mega-retailers, with Sears leading with a market share of about 29 percent. A third, less visible channel was the commercial market such as laundromats, hospitals, hotels, and other institutions.

Industry Structure

Since World War II, when over 250 firms manufactured appliances, several merger waves consolidated the industry while sales grew and prices held. The most recent consolidation occurred in 1986 when within less than one year Electrolux purchased White Consolidated, Whirlpool acquired KitchenAid, and Magic Chef was bought up by Maytag. Maytag's acquisition of Jenn-Air and Magic Chef increased its overall revenues by giving it brand name appliances at various price points. Likewise, Whirlpool's acquisition of KitchenAid and Roper, respectively, broadened Whirlpool's presence at the high end and low end of the market. By the end of 1995, the number of domestic manufacturers varied by type of product between four for dishwashers and fifteen for home refrigeration and room air conditioning equipment.

In the 1980s, the market continued to grow primarily thanks to booming sales of microwave ovens, which tripled from 1980 to 1989, while washers and dryers increased in sales 34 and 52 percent, respectively. Appliance manufacturers realized that they must offer a complete line of appliances even if they did not manufacture all of them themselves, which was one reason for the merger activity and practice of interfirm sourcing. For example, Whirlpool made trash compactors for Frigidaire (Electrolux/White Consolidated); General Electric manufactured microwave ovens for Caloric (Raytheon), Jenn-Air, and Magic Chef (Maytag).

By 1992, five major competitors controlled 98 percent of the core appliance market, each of which offered a broad range of product categories and brands targeted to different customer segments. With 33.8 percent domestic market share Whirlpool was ahead of GE (28.2 percent), a reversal of the leadership position compared to two years earlier. Whirlpool was especially strong in washing machines (1995: 53 percent share), whereas GE was ahead in refrigerators, dishwashers, and electric ranges. In terms of overall market share, Electrolux followed (16 percent), then Maytag (14 percent), and Raytheon (6 percent), respectively.

Throughout the 1980s and into the 1990s competition in the U.S. was fierce. Industry demand depended on the state of the economy, disposable income levels, interest rates, housing starts, and the consumers' ability to defer purchases. Saturation levels remained high and steady; over 70 percent of households had washers and over 65 percent dryers (Exhibit 2). Refrigerator demand stagnated while sales of electric ranges slowed as the microwave oven bloomed. Microwave sales, which had jumped from 3.5 million units in 1980 to over 10 million by 1989, started leveling out, while sales of ranges dropped off drastically due to market maturation.

Factors of Competition

In this environment all rivals worked hard at keeping costs down. Had the appliance manufacturers been making automobiles, the price of a Chevrolet Caprice would have risen from $7,209 in 1980 to $9,500 in 1990 and not $17,370. Over four years, Electrolux spent over $500 million to upgrade old plants and build new ones for its acquisition, White Consolidated Industries. General Electric automated its Louisville, Kentucky, plant, which, over ten years, halved the workforce and raised output by 30 percent.

Toward the end of the 1980s, it became even more important to lower costs, monitor margins, and achieve economies of scale. The Big Four were renovating and enlarging existing facilities. Maytag built new facilities in the south to take advantage of lower cost, non-union labor. Others built twin plants on the Mexican border to profit from cheap labor. A third trend was toward focus factories where each plant produced only one product category covering all price points.

EXHIBIT 2
Global Home Appliance Industry: Saturation Levels by Region, Demand, and Market Growth, 1994–2004

	North America	Europe*	Latin America	Asia
Home appliances				
Refrigerators	100%	100%	70%	30%
Cooking equipment	100	96	90	—
Clothes washers	74	82	40	20
Clothes dryers	70	18	—	—
Dishwashers	51	30	—	—
Microwave ovens	80	40	5	8
Room air conditioners	41	—	10	8
Compactors	5	—	—	—
Freezers	40	40	—	—
Population (in millions)	380	1,100	380	2,900
Annual demand (in million units)	46	75	17	56
Estimated annual growth rate	3%	3%	6–8%	8–9%

*Includes Eastern Europe, Africa, and the Middle East.

Source: Whirlpool Corporation, 1994 Annual Report.

Also, all competitors started to push into the high-end segment of the market, which was more stable and profitable. Once the domain of Maytag, it became increasingly crowded with the appearance of GE's Monogram line, Whirlpool's acquisition of KichenAid, and White's Euroflair models. Quality became an important feature in the competitive game. Maytag used it effectively in its famous ad of the lonely repairman. Defect rates dropped from 20 per 100 appliances made in 1980 to 10 twelve years later. Relationships with suppliers changed as companies used fewer of them than in years past. Contracts were set up over longer terms to improve quality and keep costs low with just-in-time deliveries.

A recent development was the demand by the powerful distributors for faster delivery. Distributors sought to curtail inventory costs, their biggest expense. As a consequence, manufacturers started to improve delivery systems. For instance, General Electric created its Premier Plus Program, which guaranteed three-day delivery. Sales departments were reorganized so that one sales representative would cover all of a manufacturer's brands of a given product category. Customer information services via 800-telephone lines were also strengthened.

Innovation

Two developments, government regulation and advances in computer software, combined with intense competition accelerated product innovation. New energy standards to be enforced under the 1987 National Appliance Energy Conservation Act limited energy consumption of new appliances with the objective to reduce energy usage in appliances by 25 percent every five years. At the same time, the possible ban on ozone-depleting chlorofluorocarbons (CFCs) in refrigerators by 1995 was forcing the industry to redesign its refrigerators. Pressure was also exerted to change washer and dishwasher designs to reduce water consumption and noise levels. In 1989, the Super Efficient Refrigerator Program Inc. (SERP) offered a $30 million award for a refrigerator prototype free of CFCs which was at least 25 percent more energy-efficient than the 1993 federal standards. The winner had to manufacture and sell over 250,000 refrigerators between January 1994 and July 1997.

As the industry globalized (see below), more stringent government regulations outside of the U.S. became an issue. For example, there was a concern that the more stringent environmental standards prevailing in the European Community would become law in the U.S. as well. While Whirlpool supported the more stringent standards, the other competitors, notably GE, opposed them.

Regarding advances in computer technology, new programs using fuzzy logic or neural networks which mimicked the human brain's ability of detecting patterns were being introduced in many industries including white goods. In Asia, elevators, washers, and refrigerators using fuzzy logic to recognize usage patterns were already widespread. In late 1992, AEG Hausgeräte AG, then a subsidiary of Daimler Benz's AEG unit, introduced a washer using fuzzy logic to automatically control water consumption depending on the size of the load and to sense how much dirt remained in clothes.

There were also other innovations. The late 1980s saw new technologies in cooking surfaces: ceramic-glass units, solid elements, and modular grill configurations. Other new customer-oriented features included the self-cleaning oven, automatic ice cube makers, self-defrosting refrigerators, pilotless gas ranges and appliances that could be preset. Also, manufacturers worked hard to reduce the noise level of dishwashers and washing machines. Consumers became more concerned with the way appliances looked. Sleek European styling became fashionable with smooth lines, rounded corners, and a built-in look with electronic controls. Another trend was the white-on-white look which suggested superior cleanability and made the kitchen look larger.

Outlook

For the future, demand conditions in the United States continued to look unattractive, with growth rates estimated around 3 percent based on a 1994 demand of 46 million units (Exhibit 2). At the prevailing saturation levels, demand was mostly restricted to replacement purchases (79 percent) with the remainder going to new housing and new household formation. The industry was so competitive that no single manufacturer could keep an innovation to itself for more than a year without a patent. One of the competitors summarized the situation in the North American appliance industry as follows:

> In the 1980s, four manufacturers accounted for almost all major home appliance sales in the United States, a market where approximately 40 million appliances are sold annually. Each was a tough, seasoned competitor fighting for greater sales in a market predicted to grow little in the decade ahead.[3]

---

[3] Whirlpool Corporation, 1995 Profile.

THE GLOBALIZATION OF THE APPLIANCE INDUSTRY

Foreign Competition

The white goods industry was as American as baseball and apple pie. In 1992, 98 percent of the dishwashers, washing machines, dryers, refrigerators, freezers, and ranges sold in America were made in America. Exports represented around 5 percent of shipments. The manufacturing plants of the industry leaders were located in places such as Newton, Iowa (Maytag), Benton Harbor, Michigan (Whirlpool), and Columbus, Ohio (White Consolidated Industries). Each of the "Big Four" was nearer to a corn stalk than to a parking meter. Combined, these companies practically owned the market for each major appliance with one exception—microwave ovens. These represented the lion's share of imports, which made up about 17 percent of total appliance sales.

The acquisition of White Consolidated Industries by AB Electrolux of Sweden in 1986 marked a major change in the industry. Until then, foreign competition in the United States was largely restricted to imports of microwave ovens, a segment which was controlled by Far Eastern competitors from Korea (Goldstar, Samsung) and Japan (Sharp, Matsushita). Aware of the fate of other industries, many expected that it was only a matter of time before these companies would expand from their beachhead in microwave ovens and compact appliances into other segments.

Europe

Of prime attractiveness to the U.S. manufacturers was Europe. Since 1985, Western Europe was rapidly moving toward a unified market of some 320 million consumers which was not nearly as saturated as Canada and the U.S. (Exhibit 2). Appliance demand was expected to grow at 5 percent annually. Political changes in Eastern Europe integrated these countries into the world trade system and thus added to Europe's long-term attractiveness.

During the 1970s and 1980s the European white goods industry had experienced a consolidation similar to that in the U.S. According to Whirlpool, in 1995 the number of manufacturers in Western Europe was 35, most of whom produced a limited range of products for a specific geographic region.[4] However, since the late 1980s six companies—Electrolux Zanussi, Philips Bauknecht, Bosch-Siemens, Merloni-Indesit, Thompson, and AEG—controlled 70 percent of the market (excluding microwave ovens and room air conditioners). Until the mid-1980s, most companies were either producing and selling in only one national market or exporting to a limited extent to many European markets from one country. Observed Whirlpool's CEO Whitwam: "What strikes me most is how similar the U.S. and European industries are."[5] Re-

---

[4]Whirlpool Corporation, 1994 Form 10-K.
[5]Stewart.

search by Whirlpool also indicated that washers were basically alike in working components around the globe.[6]

The European market was very segmented and consumer preferences differed greatly from country to country with regard to almost every type of appliance: The French preferred to cook their foods at high temperatures, splattering grease on oven walls. Thus, oven ranges manufactured for France should have self-cleaning ability. However, this feature was not a requirement in Germany, where lower cooking temperatures were the norm. Unlike Americans, who preferred to stuff as many clothes into the washer as possible, Europeans overwhelmingly preferred smaller built-in models. Northern Europeans liked large refrigerators because they preferred to shop only once a week; consumers in the south of Europe preferred small ones, because they visited the open-air markets daily. Northerners liked their freezers at the bottom of the refrigerators, southerners on top. In France, 80 percent of washing machines were top-loaders, while elsewhere in Western Europe, 90 percent were front-loaders. Also, European washers frequently contained heating elements, and the typical European homemaker preferred to wash towels at 95 degrees Celsius. Gas ranges were common throughout Europe, except for Germany, where 90 percent of all ranges sold were electric.

Given this situation, some observers were skeptical about the possibility of establishing pan-European models which would yield a sustainable competitive advantage through manufacturing, procurement, and marketing efficiencies. They claimed that the European market was actually made up of many smaller individual markets corresponding to the respective countries. Furthermore, they reasoned, many of these national markets featured strong competitors.

Distribution of white goods in Europe was different from North America. The larger channel, known as the Retail Trade, comprised independent retailers many of which were organized through buying groups or as multiple-store chains. The second channel, the Kitchen Trade, was primarily comprised of kitchen specialists that sold consumers entire kitchen packages. The Kitchen Trade was mainly focused on built-in units and not involved in laundry appliances.

AB Electrolux was a force practically in all of Europe with an overall 25 percent market share. Over 20 years the $14 billion multinational from Sweden had undertaken more than 200 acquisitions in 40 countries which spanned five businesses: household appliances, forestry and garden products, industrial products, metal and mining, and commercial services. Its expertise in managing acquisitions and integrating the newly acquired units into the organization was unequaled. For example, in 1983, Electrolux took over a money-losing Italian white goods manufacturer with 30,000 employees, 50 factories, and a dozen foreign sales companies. Within four years the Swedes turned a company which in 1983 lost Lit. 120 billion into an efficient organization netting Lit. 60 billion. The acquisitions of Zanussi of Italy, Tricity in Britain, and three Spanish companies in anticipation of the changes in Western Europe marked the beginning of a new era in this mature industry as Electrolux sought

---

[6]Kindel.

to establish a pan-European approach to the appliance market, followed by exploring cross-Atlantic opportunities. However, in 1993 Electrolux's pan-European strategy ran into trouble. The recession, combined with Europe's market fragmentation, reduced profits far below the targeted 5 percent margin.

In Germany Bauknecht (Philips), Bosch-Siemens and AEG-Telefunken were dominant; in Britain GEC's Hotpoint, and in France Thompson-Brandt were forces to be reckoned with. Merloni from Italy pursued a different approach by flooding Europe with machines produced in Italy with lower cost labor. In 1987, Merloni gobbled up Indesit, an Italian producer in financial trouble, in order to enlarge its manufacturing base and take advantage of Indesit's marketing position in many European countries. In the late 1980s no brand had more than 5 percent of the overall market, even though the top ten producers generated 80 percent of the volume.

1989 marked the year the Americans landed in Europe. General Electric formed an appliance joint venture with Britain's General Electric Corporation (GEC), which had a strong presence in the low price segment of the European market, especially in the UK, and thus complemented GE's high-end European products. In the same year, Maytag acquired the Hoover Division through the purchase of Chicago Pacific. Hoover, best known for its vacuum cleaners, in the UK also produced washers, dryers, and dishwashers which, however, encountered acceptance problems on other European markets. Hoover was also present in Australia and, through a trading company, serviced other parts of the world. 1989 was also the year in which Whirlpool and N.V. Philips of the Netherlands formed a joint venture which included all of Philips' European appliance division. Thus, within a short time the Americans closed the gap relative to the geographical scope of Electrolux. In spite of concerns about different consumer preferences in Europe, the largest U.S. appliance manufacturers established themselves before the 1992 EU Program became a reality. European Community rules required 60 percent local content to avoid tariffs which, combined with the fear of a "Fortress Europe" protected by Community-wide tariffs after 1992, excluded exports as a viable strategy.

Within a very short time further agreements followed which greatly reduced the number of independent competitors in Europe. AEG started cooperating with Electrolux in washer and dishwasher production and development and, in 1994, became part of Electrolux; Bosch-Siemens formed an alliance with Maytag; the European Economic Interest Group combined several manufacturers, with France's Thompson-Brandt as the leader. In spite of this trend toward consolidation in the early 1990s Whirlpool estimated the number of European manufacturers of home appliances to be around 100.[7]

Asia

Asia, the world's second largest home appliance market, was likely to experience rapid economic growth in the near future primarily thanks to the booming economies of the Pacific Rim countries. Home appliance shipments were expected to grow at least 8–9

---

[7]Whirlpool Corporation, 1992 Form 10-K.

percent per annum through the 1990s (Exhibit 2). The biggest promise of course was in the huge markets of the world's most populous states—China and India. However, income levels in these two markets were only approaching levels at which people could afford appliances. The Asian market was dominated by some 50 widely diversified Asian manufacturers, primarily from Japan, Korea, and Taiwan, with no clear leader emerging yet. Matsushita, the market leader, held less than 10 percent outside Japan.

Consumer preferences in Asia were quite different from those in North America and Europe and varied widely from country to country. For example, typical Asian refrigerators ranged from 6 cu. ft. to 10 cu. ft. due to the lack of space. Since owning a refrigerator represented a status symbol, refrigerators were often placed in the living room. Such a prominent display created a demand for stylish colors and finishes. In India for example, refrigerators in bright red or blue were popular. In terms of technology, both direct-cool and forced air models were common in Asia, whereas in Europe direct-cool prevailed, and in North America the forced air version. Clothes washers had to be portable, because living quarters tended to be small and because usually there was no basement to permanently keep washers hooked up to a water supply and drain. Often, they were stored in an outside hallway and moved into the bathroom and kitchen for use. Also, they had to be delivered to large apartment blocks with no elevators and thus had to be carried up many flights of stairs. Therefore, washers tended to be designed as lightweight products on wheels equipped with handles for each relocation. Technological designs varied, even though vertical axis machines dominated. The clothes themselves also represented a challenge since these ranged from the yards of fabric used in Indian saris to simple cotton dress and western style clothing. Clothes dryers were virtually unknown. Washing habits were different, too. For instance, Japanese usually washed with cold water. But in order to get their clothes clean, Japanese machines have soak cycles which can range from 30 minutes to several hours. Two-burner, tabletop cooking units replaced the ranges used in North America and Europe, reflecting the differences in cooking styles. In addition, kitchens were much smaller and baking was virtually unknown as were dishwashers. In air conditioning, split-system units were the dominant version in Asia. In regions where air conditioners were used a better part of the year, consumers didn't want to block out limited window space. Split-system units were installed high on the wall, often out of reach, making remote controls an important feature.

Latin America

Another market promising attractive growth in appliances was Latin America once these countries would emerge from decades of political instability, economic mismanagement, and hyperinflation (Exhibit 2). Indeed, much of this was happening in the 1990s accompanied by efforts to lower tariffs, which would stimulate trade. In 1994, the white goods industry in Latin America comprised about 65 competitors. Whirlpool expected appliance shipments to expand at a faster pace than in North America and Europe.[8]

---

[8]Whirlpool Corporation, 1992 Annual Report.

EXHIBIT 3
North American Appliance Group in Early 1996

Principal Products	*Major Brand Names*	*Principal Locations*	
Automatic dryers	Acros*	Corporate, regional,	Sales offices:
Automatic washers	Admiral (Canada)	research & engineering center:	U.S.:
Built-in ovens	Chambers	Benton Harbor, Michigan	Atlanta
Dehumidifiers	Crolls*		Boston
Dishwashers	Coolerator		Charlotte
Freezers	Estate	Subsidiaries:	Chicago
Ice makers	Inglis	Inglis Ltd.	Dallas
Microwave ovens	KitchenAid	Mississauga, Ontario	Dayton
Ranges	Roper	Whirlpool Financial Corp.	Denver
Refrigerators	Speed Queen (Canada)	Benton Harbor, Michigan	Kansas City
Room air conditioners	Supermatic*		Knoxville
Trash compactors	Whirlpool	Affiliates:	Little Rock
		Vitromatic S.A. de C.V.	Los Angeles
		Monterrey, Mexico	Miami
			Minneapolis
		Manufacturing facilities:	New York City
		Benton Harbor, Michigan	Orlando
		Celaya, Mexico	Philadelphia
		Clyde, Ohio	Pittsburgh
		Evansville, Indiana	San Francisco
		Findlay, Ohio	Santurce (Puerto Rico)
		Forth Smith, Arkansas	Seattle
		Greenville, Ohio	
		Lavergne, Tennessee	Canada:
		Marion, Ohio	Laval, Quebec
		Mexico City, Mexico	Mississauga, Ontario
		Monterrey, Mexico	Vancouver, British Columbia
		Montmagny, Quebec	
		Oxford, Mississippi	Mexico:
		Puebla, Mexico	Guadalajara, Jalisco
		Reynosa, Mexico	Mexico City, Distrito Federal
		Tulsa, Oklahoma	Monterrey, Nuevo León

*Affiliate owned.

WHIRLPOOL CORPORATION

Company Background

In early 1996, Whirlpool Corporation, headquartered in Benton Harbor, Michigan, was one of the world's leading manufacturers and marketers of major home appliances. The company's plants were located in 12 countries and it distributed its products in over 140 countries under 28 brand names (Exhibits 3 to 7). Whereas fifteen years earlier, Whirlpool executives had perceived the world primarily as consisting of the U.S. and Canadian markets with some marginal sales in Latin America and limited export opportunities, the company had transformed itself and now the world encompassed three major regions: North America with 46 million units sold annually

EXHIBIT 4
Whirlpool Europe B.V. in 1996

Principal Products	Major Brand Names	Principal Locations	
Automatic dryers	Bauknecht	European operations center:	Sales offices:
Automatic washers	Ignis	Comerio, Italy	Athens, Greece
Dishwashers	Laden		Barcelona, Spain
Freezers	Whirlpool	Subsidiaries:	Brussels, Belgium
Microwave ovens		Whirlpool Europe B.V.,	Budapest, Hungary
Ranges		Eindhoven, Netherlands	Comerio, Italy
Refrigerators		Whirlpool Tatramat a.s.,	Dublin, Ireland
		Poprad, Slovakia	Eindhoven, Netherlands
			Espoo, Finland
		Manufacturing facilities:	Herlev, Denmark
		Amiens, France	Lenzburg, Switzerland
		Calw, Germany	Lisbon, Portugal
		Cassinetta, Italy	London, UK
		Naples, Italy	Moscow, Russia
		Neunkirchen, Germany	Oslo, Norway
		Norrköping, Sweden	Paris, France
		Poprad, Slovakia	Poprad, Slovakia
		Schorndorf, Germany	Prague, Czech Republic
		Siena, Italy	Stockholm, Sweden
		Trento, Italy	Stuttgart, Germany
			Vienna, Austria
			Warsaw, Poland

EXHIBIT 5
Latin American Appliance Group in 1996

Principal Products	Major Brand Names	Principal Locations
Automatic washers	Brastemp*	Regional headquarters:
Dishwashers	Consol*	São Paulo, Brazil
Dryers	Eslabon de Lujo	
Freezers	Semer*	Subsidiaries:
Microwave ovens	Whirlpool	Latin American Sales and Service
Ranges		Company, Miami
Refrigerators		South American Sales Company, Grand
Room air conditioners		Cayman
		Whirlpool Argentina S.A., Buenos Aires,
		Argentina

*Affiliate owned.

EXHIBIT 6
Asian Appliance Group in 1996

Principal Products	*Major Brand Names*	*Principal Locations*	

Automatic washers
Microwave ovens
Refrigerators
Room air conditioners
	Bauknecht
	Ignis
	KitchenAid
	Raybo
	Roper
	Whirlpool
	
	Under license:
	  Kelvinator (India)
	  Narcissus
	  SMC
	  Snowflake
	  TVS
		Regional headquarters &
		  technology center:
		  Singapore
		
		Regional offices:
		  Hong Kong
		  New Delhi, India
		  Singapore
		
		Subsidiaries:
		  Beijing Whirlpool Snowflake
		    Electric Appliance Co.,
		    Ltd., Beijing
		  Kelvinator of India,
		    New Delhi, India
		  Whirlpool Narcissus
		    (Shanghai) Co. Ltd.,
		    Shanghai, China
		  Whirlpool Washing Machines,
		    Ltd., Madras, India
		
		Affiliates:
		  Great Teco Whirlpool Ltd.,
		    Taipei, Taiwan
		  Beijing Embraco Snowflake
		    Compressor Co. Ltd.,
		    Beijing, China
			Manufacturing facilities:
			  Beijing, China
			  Faridabad, India
			  Pondicherry, India
			  Shanghai, China
			  Shenzhen, China
			  Shunde, China
			
			Sales offices:
			  Auckland, New Zealand
			  Bangkok, Thailand
			  Guanzhow, China
			  Ho Chi Minh City, Vietnam
			  Hong Kong
			  New Delhi, India
			  Noble Park, Australia
			  Petaling Jaya, Malaysia
			  Seoul, South Korea
			  Shanghai, China
			  Singapore
			  Tokyo, Japan	

EXHIBIT 7
Changes in Whirlpool's Global Presence, 1988–1995

	1988	*1995*
Revenues	$4.41 billion	$8.35 billion
Market position	Leader in North America; affiliates in Brazil, Canada, India, and Mexico	No. 1 in North America No. 1 in Latin America No. 3 in Europe Largest western appliance company in Asia
Manufacturing locations (incl. affiliates)	4	12
Brands (incl. affiliates)	14	28
Market presence		>140
Employees	29,110	45,435

(1994), consisting of Canada, Mexico, the U.S.; Europe with 50 million units (Western, Central, and Eastern Europe, Africa, the Middle East); Asia, representing a total demand of 56 million units; and Latin America, comprised of the Caribbean and Central and South America with 17 million units.

Located two hours by car from Chicago, Whirlpool was founded in St. Joseph, Michigan, in 1911. At the time, it was producing motor driven wringer washers under the name Upton Machine, with the hopes of selling them in quantities to large distributors. In 1916, the first order from Sears, Roebuck and Co. marked the beginning of an enduring relationship with Sears as the oldest and largest customer, representing 20 percent of Whirlpool's 1995 sales. In 1948, the Whirlpool brand automatic washer was introduced. This established the dual distribution system—one product line for Sears, the other for Nineteen Hundred. The Nineteen Hundred Corporation was renamed Whirlpool in 1950 with the addition of automatic dryers to the company's product line. In 1955, Whirlpool merged with Seeger Refrigerator Co. of St. Paul, Minnesota, and the Estate range and air conditioning divisions of R.C.A. In 1957, Whirlpool entered the foreign market through the purchase of equity interest in Multibras S.A. of São Paulo, Brazil, later renamed Brastemp S.A. In 1967, Whirlpool was the first competitor in the industry to take advantage of AT&T's new 800-line service and created the Cool-Line Telephone Service, which provided customers a toll-free number to call for answers to questions and help with service.

In the mid-1980s, the limited growth potential of its established markets motivated Whirlpool to undertake a major examination of the industry. Top management decided "to remain focused on major home appliances but to expand into markets not already served by Whirlpool."[9] In 1986, the KitchenAid division of Hobart Corporation was purchased from Dart & Kraft, which marked Whirlpool's entry into the upscale segment of the appliance market as well as into small appliances. In the same year, Whirlpool sold its central heating and cooling business to Inter-City Gas Corp. of Canada. In 1985 Whirlpool purchased the assets of Mastercraft Industries Corp., a Denver based manufacturer of kitchen cabinets. A year later a second cabinet maker, St. Charles Manufacturing Co., was acquired through the newly formed Whirlpool Kitchens, Inc. However, in March 1989, Whirlpool Kitchens was sold due to lack of fit.

North American Appliance Group

The North American Appliance Group (NAAG) was formed in 1989 out of the operations in the U.S., Canada, and Mexico (Exhibit 3). After several plant closings and a reshuffling of product lines between plants, a streamlined organization with a unified strategy was formed, originally around four brands. In 1992 Whirlpool reorganized its North American operations behind a strategy to create a "dominant consumer franchise" (DCF). For Whirlpool, a DCF existed "when consumers insist on our brands for reasons other than price, when they view our products as clearly superior to other appliances, when they demonstrate strong loyalty in their future purchase decisions."[10] Such a strategy required, above all, a better understanding of consumer needs; merely improving product quality and keeping costs low was deemed as neces-

---

[9]Whirlpool Corporation, 1994 Profile.
[10]Whirlpool Corporation, 1994 Annual Report, p. 9.

sary but not sufficient. The objective was to become more customer focused which entailed a functional organization which functions dealing with four core processes: product management, brand management, trade partner management, and logistics. Unlike the traditional functional organization, the new approach employed cross-functional teams within each function with Product Business Teams at the center.

To support its DCF strategy, Whirlpool announced a multitude of new products aimed at six discrete appliance consumer segments labeled: (1) the Traditionalist, (2) the Housework Rebel, (3) the Achiever, (4) the Self-Assured, (5) the Proven Conservative, (6) the Homebound Survivor.[11] KitchenAid brand appliances were marketed to upscale consumers who look for style and substance, typically found among Achievers; Whirlpool was positioned as the brand that helps consumers to manage their homes better, for instance, Housework Rebels. Roper brand appliances were value-priced and offered basic styling and features and were a good match for the Self-Assured. The Estate brand line was limited to a few high-volume models and distributed through warehouse club outlets. The Kenmore Appliance Group was dedicated to serve Whirlpool's single largest customer—Sears, Roebuck and Co.

In June 1993, Whirlpool was named the winner in the $30 million Super Efficient Refrigerator Program, a success which CEO Whitwam attributed to the multidisciplinary team which had been assembled from all over the world. The SERP models eliminated CFCs completely by using a different refrigerant. Also, a different, environmentally safe blowing agent was used which is needed to expand foam insulation between the walls of the refrigerator liner and cabinet. Energy efficiency gains were achieved through better insulation, a high-efficiency compressor and an improved condenser fan motor in conjunction with a microchip-controlled adaptive defrost control which incorporated fuzzy logic. Whirlpool had entered the SERP contest because it was consistent with the company's strategy to exceed customer expectations. Jeff Fettig, Vice President, Group Marketing and Sales for NAAG, commented: "The SERP program allowed us to accelerate the development process and bring these products to the market sooner. Future products will be designed with these consumer expectations [regarding environmental friendliness] in mind, giving people even more reason to ask for a Whirlpool-built product next time they are in the market for a major home appliance."[12]

After an energy-efficient refrigerator with a CFC-free sealed system which was launched in March 1994, the company announced that it would introduce a new clothes washer in 1996 that would use a third of the water and energy of a conventional washer. The company hoped that consumers would be willing "to pay a premium price for the new washer."[13] In its 1993 Annual Report Whirlpool announced that since 1988 NAAG had increased its regional market share by nearly a third, also thanks to Inglis, Ltd., the Canadian subsidiary, and Vitromatic S.A., the Mexican affiliate.

In late 1994 Whirlpool initiated a major restructuring initiative closing plants and reducing headcount in an effort to reduce costs. In 1995, Montgomery Ward, the second largest home appliance retailer in the U.S., became a Whirlpool customer.

---

[11]"Fleet of Foot."

[12]Whirlpool Corporation, World Washer news release.

[13]Whirlpool Corporation, 1994 Annual Report, p. 10.

Whirlpool's Globalization

In 1995, Whirlpool's efforts to establish a global presence were more than ten years old. Already in its 1984 Annual Report Whirlpool announced that it had concluded a two-year study and adopted a plan for the next five years. Among the steps mentioned were developing new international strategies and adding sound new businesses which would complement existing strengths. The strategy was based on the assumption that, in spite of the differences in consumer habits and preferences, it was possible to gain competitive advantage by leveraging a global presence in the various regional markets. In the 1987 Annual Report CEO Whitwam elaborated on the company's rationale for globalization:

> The U.S. appliance market has limited growth opportunities, a high concentration of domestic competitors and increasing foreign competition. Further, the U.S. represents only about 25% of the worldwide potential for major appliance sales.
>
> Most importantly, our vision can no longer be limited to our domestic borders because national borders no longer define market boundaries. The marketplace for products and services is more global than ever before and growing more so every day.
>
> Consumers in major industrialized countries are living increasingly similar lifestyles and have increasingly similar expectations of what consumer products must do for them. As purchasing patterns become more alike, we think that companies that operate on a broad global scale can leverage their strengths better than those which only serve an individual national market. Very likely, appliance manufacturing will always have to be done regionally. Yet the ability to leverage many of the strengths of a company on an international basis is possible only if that company operates globally."[14]

Whirlpool Trading Corporation was formed to consolidate existing international activities and explore new ventures. In January 1985, the company increased its equity interest in Inglis, which dated back to 1969, from 48 percent to more than 50 percent. In the following year, Aspera S.r.l. in Torino, Italy, a large compressor maker, was purchased from Fiat.

Already in the late 1950s Whirlpool had undertaken the first expansion beyond the U.S. borders when it entered Brazil, followed by Canada in 1969 (Exhibit 8). In 1976 Whirlpool strengthened its position in Brazil. However, globalization truly took shape in the 1980s when Whirlpool added Mexico, India, and Europe through a series of joint ventures. The moves in South America and Asia were motivated by the expectation that climbing disposable incomes in these continents would result in a growing demand for appliances that would "at least partially mirror the American consumer boom of the 1950s and 1960s."[15]

Among Whirlpool's top management David R. Whitwam was known as a champion of Whirlpool's globalization. Whitwam had succeeded Jack Sparks, who had retired in 1987 after 47 year of service, including five as CEO. Sparks had given Whirlpool the focus it had lacked. It was not an easy task to follow in the footsteps of such a distinguished leader.

Born in Madison (Wisconsin), Whitwam graduated from the University of Wisconsin with a B.S. in economics with honors. After eight years in the United States Army and the Wisconsin National Guard he joined Whirlpool as a marketing manage-

---

[14]Whirlpool Corporation, 1987 Annual Report, p. 5.
[15]Whirlpool Corporation, 1989 Annual Report, p. 9.

EXHIBIT 8
Milestones of Whirlpool's Globalization

1957   Whirlpool invests in Brazilian appliance market through purchase of equity interest in Multibras S.A., renamed Brastemp S.A. in 1972.

1969   Entry into the Canadian appliance market through a 52% equity interest in Inglis, Limited. Sole ownership established in 1990.

1976   Increased investment in Brazil through purchase of equity interests in Consul S.A., an appliance manufacturer, and Embraco S.A., a maker of compressors.

1986   Purchase of majority interest in Aspera S.r.l. of Fiat S.p.A., a manufacturer of compressors, located in Turin and Riva, Italy.

1987   Entry into the Indian appliance market through TVS Whirlpool Limited, a 33% each joint venture company formed with Sundaram-Clayton Limited of Madras.

        Ownership in Inglis, Limited, increased to 72%.

1988   Vitromatic, S.A. de C.V. is formed with Vitro, S.A., of Monterrey, Nuevo León, to manufacture and market major home appliances for Mexican and export markets. Whirlpool has a 49% interest.

        Whirlpool operates a maquiladora, Componentes de Reynosa, in Reynosa, Tamaulipas, to manufacture components for final assembly in the U.S.

1989   Whirlpool and N.V. Philips of the Netherlands consummate an agreement under which Whirlpool acquires a 53% interest in a joint venture company made up of Philips former major domestic appliance division. The new company, Whirlpool International B.V. (WIBV), will manufacture and market appliances in Western Europe. The joint venture brand names are Bauknecht, Philips, Ignis, and Laden.

        North American Appliance Group formed from streamlined U.S., Canadian, and Mexican operations.

        Affiliates in Brazil, India, and Mexico complete construction of facilities and start producing the "World Washer."

1990   A program is launched to market appliances in Europe under the dual brands Philips and Whirlpool.

        Formation of a joint venture company with Matsushita Electric Industrial Co. of Japan to produce vacuum cleaners for the North American market.

        Creation of Whirlpool Overseas Corporation as a wholly owned subsidiary to conduct industrial and marketing activities outside North America and Western Europe.

        Inglis, Limited, becomes a wholly owned subsidiary.

1991   Whirlpool acquires remaining interest in WIBV from Philips Electronics N.V.

        Creation of two new global business units: Whirlpool Compressor Operations and Whirlpool Microwave Cooking Business.

1992   Creation of Whirlpool Tatramat in the Slovak Republic. Whirlpool Tatramat a.s. will manufacturer clothes washers for Slovakia and neighboring countries and import other WIBV major appliances for sale.

        Begins gradual phase-out of dual-branded advertising to sole Whirlpool brand by removing the Philips name in Europe.

        Whirlpool assumes control of SAGAD S.A. of Argentina from Philips.

        Reorganization of Whirlpool Europe. The name is changed from WIBV to WEBV.

        Creation of a global small appliance business unit.

1993   Reorganization of NAAG.

        WOC is replaced by two separate regional organizations in Latin America and Asia, respectively.

        Start of the implementation of a new Asian strategy with Tokyo as headquarters and regional offices in Singapore, Hong Kong, and Tokyo.

EXHIBIT 8 (Continued)
Milestones of Whirlpool's Globalization

Sales subsidiaries are opened in Greece, Poland, and the Czech Republic.

Inglis Ltd. becomes Canada's leading home appliance manufacturer.

To streamline European operations WEBV sells its Spanish refrigerator plant to IAR/Sital of Italy.

1994   In May Whirlpool announces joint venture with Teco Electric & Machinery Co., Ltd., of Taiwan to market and distribute home appliances in Taiwan.

Whirlpool becomes a stand-alone brand in Europe.

Brazilian affiliates Consul and Brastemp merge to form Multibras.

Acquisition of controlling interest in Kelvinator of India, Ltd., and assumes controlling interest in TVS Whirlpool Ltd.

Whirlpool's Asian headquarters moved to Singapore; number of regions increased from three to four.

Whirlpool exits vacuum cleaner business by selling its minority interest in the joint venture with Matsushita.

Acquisition of majority ownership in SMC Microwave Products Co., Ltd., and Beijing Whirlpool Snowflake Electric Appliance Company, Ltd.

Creation of the Microwave Oven Business unit as a global business unit.

1995   Formation of South American sales company.

New joint venture formed to produce washers called The Whirlpool Narcissus (Shanghai) Co., Ltd.

Acquisition of majority interest in Raybo Air Conditioner Manufacturing Company.

Approval obtained for a joint venture with Shenzhen Petrochemical Holdings Co. to produce air conditioners.

Creation of the Global Air Treatment Unit as a global business unit.

---

ment trainee in July 1968. One year later he was named territory sales manager at the South California sales division and from there job descriptions did not change, only the locations. Whitwam spent time in New York and then in Southern California.

Whitwam moved to corporate headquarters in 1977 when he was named Merchandising Manager for Range Products. From that post came a promotion to Director of Builder Marketing, and then Vice President, Whirlpool Sales, in 1983. In 1985, he was elected to the company's Board of Directors. On December 1, 1987, he assumed his current position as President, CEO, and Chairman of the Board of Whirlpool Corporation. Since then, he has transformed a domestically oriented $4 billion company into a $8 billion global force. Whirlpool's Corporate Vision, which was displayed in many of its publications and throughout its facilities, clearly communicated this orientation:

> Whirlpool, in its chosen lines of business, will grow with new opportunities and be the leader in an ever-changing global market. We will be driven by our commitment to continuous quality improvement and to exceeding all of our customers' expectations. We will gain competitive advantage through this, and by building on our existing strengths and developing new competencies. We will be market driven, efficient and profitable. Our success will make Whirlpool a company that worldwide customers, employees and other stakeholders can depend on.

Whirlpool Europe B.V.

Amongst those most strongly convinced of the promise of the European market was David Whitwam: "The only people who say you can't have a pan-European brand are the people who don't have one themselves."[16] On August 18, 1988, Whirlpool announced a joint venture with N.V. Philips, the second largest appliance manufacturer in Europe behind Electrolux with a broad presence in many markets throughout Europe and also in Latin America. The deal was for a 53 percent interest in Philips' worldwide Major Domestic Appliance Division for $361 million in cash; the new company was called Whirlpool International B.V. In July 1991, Whirlpool exercised its option to purchase from Philips the remaining interest in WIBV and changed the name to Whirlpool Europe B.V. (WEBV) (Exhibit 4). By 1994 with 13 percent market share, WEBV occupied the third position in Europe behind Electrolux (25 percent) and Bosch-Siemens (15 percent). (For financial data see Exhibits 11 and 12.)

Soon after the formation of WIBV, Philips' decentralized organization was phased out and WIBV was split into customer-focused business units. Brands were positioned to fit the niches and conditions in Europe, an approach employed earlier in the U.S. Bauknecht—Philips' most profitable brand—was aimed at the high end of the market, the dual-branded Philips/Whirlpool at the middle, and Ignis was designed for the lower end. Later, in 1995, Whirlpool terminated its successful brand-transfer effort that had cost $110 million and dropped the Philips brand name. The Bauknecht and Philips/Whirlpool Appliance Groups received centralized sales and marketing functions which supported all of Whirlpool's European brands. National sales subsidiaries were consolidated into three sales regions in order to take account of the growing European cross-border trade. The marketing function included separate, brand-oriented components to strengthen brand identity while at the same time ensuring coordination internally. Manufacturing and technology activities were reorganized around product groups and development centers with Germany focusing on laundry and dishwashing products and Italy on refrigeration and cooking. Key support functions (Consumer Services, Information Technology, Logistics, Planning) were maintained as separate, centrally managed entities. Distribution was reconfigured toward a pan-European approach and 10 out of 28 finished goods warehouses were closed. Explained WEBV president Hank Bowman: "The idea is to put systems support in place so we can deliver products more accurately and in a more timely manner."[17] WEBV also assumed responsibility for the Middle East and Africa, which accounted for $100 million in sales, mainly in the form of kits in an attempt to boost local content and thus preempt the emergence of domestic-content rules. In late 1994 yet another reorganization was started to streamline operations on a pan-European basis in conjunction with similar efforts in North America, hoping to achieve annual cost savings of about $150 million per year starting in 1997.

In 1992, WIBV started a four-year effort to redesign its products in order to increase manufacturing efficiency and improve product quality and customer satisfaction. The goal was to renew the entire product line by 1996. Whirlpool had identified

---

[16]Stewart.
[17]Tierney.

what it called a "value gap" in Europe. When benchmarking the European industry's performance against best-in-class North American and Asian players, managers found that European producers delivered significantly lower levels of customer satisfaction. Also, Europeans paid more for their appliances than did their U.S. counterparts. Explained Ivan Menezes, Vice President, Group Marketing, WEBV: "When Whirlpool first came to Europe, the typical appliance cost 50 percent to 100 percent more in terms of daily income. In the U.S., for example, a typical consumer could, in 1991, earn the necessary dollars for a dishwasher in 3.8 days, whereas in Europe, it would have taken 7.5 days. Today that gap has closed by 15 percent to 20 percent for all appliances."[18]

A global outlook was forged in the management team. Managers were rotated between Europe and the U.S. to foster global thinking. The first time this move paid off was in 1991 when the VIP Crisp microwave oven, developed by a new "advanced global technology unit" in Norrköping, Sweden, was introduced and quickly became Europe's best-selling model. The VIP Crisp had a heated base plate which allows Italians to bake crisp pizza crusts and the British to fry eggs. Subsequently, the company started to import the VIP Crisp to the United States.

WEBV also made a series of moves to establish itself in the emerging markets of Central and Eastern Europe, which in 1991 represented about 11 percent of the world appliance market and promised attractive growth opportunities over the long term. Bauknecht was first in setting up a distribution system in East Germany after the opening of the border. In early 1992, WEBV developed distribution networks in the entire region and established a wholly owned sales subsidiary in Hungary. In May 1992, Whirlpool took a 43.8 percent minority investment in Whirlpool/Tatramat a.s., a joint venture in the Slovak Republic, which manufactured and sold automatic washers and marketed products assembled at other WEBV locations. In 1994, WEBV took a controlling interest in this joint venture. A year earlier, sales subsidiaries were opened in Poland and the Czech Republic, adding to WEBV's position in Eastern Europe, and Greece in South Eastern Europe, followed by Russia in 1995. Expansions into Romania and Bulgaria were planned for 1996.

Latin American Appliance Group

Whirlpool's foray overseas started in Latin America when in 1958 the company purchased equity interest in Multibras S.A. of Brazil, a manufacturer of major appliances. Whirlpool's strategy in Latin America called for taking full advantage of this large emerging market by optimally positioning its brands across the entire spectrum based on in-depth consumer research in an attempt to cultivate "Customers for Life."

In the crucial Brazilian market, which accounted for about half of all appliances sold in Latin America in 1994, Whirlpool held equity positions in three Brazilian companies: (1) Multibras, which in 1994 merged three sister appliance makers into one organization and with annual sales of $800 million held the market leader position in Brazil; (2) Embraco, one of the world's largest manufacturers of compressors, exporting to 50 countries on four continents; (3) Brasmotor S.A., a holding company

---

[18]Jancsurak, "Marketing: Phase 2."

with a majority interest in Multibras and a minority interest in Embraco. Whirlpool claimed that based on its own research, it has the second highest brand recognition after Coca-Cola.

In January 1992, Whirlpool strengthened its position in South America by taking over control of SAGAD, Philips' white goods operation in Argentina. Outside of Brazil and Argentina the South American Sales Company, a subsidiary of LAAG, was responsible for sales throughout the region.

Originally, Whirlpool's Latin American operations were part of the Whirlpool Overseas Corporation (WOC) which was formed in Spring 1990 as a wholly owned subsidiary to conduct marketing and industrial activities outside North America and Europe. It included U.S. Export Sales, the Overseas Business Group acquired from Philips in the WIBV transaction, and three wholly owned sales companies in Hong Kong, Thailand, and Australia. Industrial activities encompassed technology sale and transfer, kit and component sales, joint venture manufacturing, and project management for affiliates.

Key responsibilities of WOC also included feeding new technologies from Whirlpool's bases in North America and Europe to its other units, ensuring optimal brand positioning in each country and analyzing specific appliance design for their suitability to various markets. Conditions could vary greatly from country to country. For instance, the company sold so-called giant ovens in Africa and the Middle East. These ovens were 39" and 42" wide compared to the standard 30" in the United States and were large enough to roast a sheep or goat.

In 1993, after exhaustive and detailed analysis of world markets the company decided that its global business interests would be better served by establishing two stand-alone business units, one for Latin America called LAAG, the other, the Whirlpool Asian Appliance Group for Whirlpool's Asian operations (Exhibits 5 and 6).

Whirlpool Asian Appliance Group

When Whirlpool began to pursue perceived business opportunities in Asia, it was not new to the market. It had exported home appliances to the region for over 30 years from the U.S. Thanks to the acquisition of Philips' appliance business, it gained broadened access to Asian markets. However, Whirlpool realized that a viable position in Asia implied more than selling imports from NAAG and WEBV, having kits assembled by licensees, or having appliances built to specification by local manufacturers.

Whirlpool's Asian strategy rested on the "Five Ps"—partnerships, products, processes, people, and a pan-Asian approach. The strategy was broken down into three phases: start-up, building, and market leadership. Based on extensive market research, Whirlpool decided to base its foray into Asia on four specific appliance products—the so-called "T-4": refrigerators, clothes washers, microwave ovens, and air conditioners. For a household with no appliances, a refrigerator was usually the first appliance purchased when income goes up. A clothes washer came next. Air conditioners were important because of the heat and humidity prevailing in much of the region. Microwave ovens had become a truly global appliance with essentially standardized features and design. Whirlpool focused its efforts on China and India, the most populous countries. Market entry was supposed to occur through joint ventures, to be followed later by "greenfield" plants. Based on commonalities identified in the region, Whirlpool planned to use a pan-Asian platform, with modifications made for specific areas given regional preferences. In contrast to other regions, only one brand name—Whirlpool—would be used since the market was not considered mature enough to allow for a multi-brand approach.

In 1987, Whirlpool created a joint venture in India with Sundaram-Clayton, Ltd., called TVS Whirlpool, Ltd., which started to operate a plant producing semi-automatic clothes washers, the so-called "World Washer" (see below), and twin-tub washers for the Indian market.

Whirlpool's Asian expansion gained momentum in 1993 with the creation of the Whirlpool Asian Appliance Group (WAAG) (Exhibit 6) supported by a $10 million investment. A regional headquarters was established in Tokyo and later moved to Singapore, which also became the home of a pan-Asian marketing, product development, and technology center. The Asian market was further subdivided first into three, then four operating regions: Greater China, based in Hong Kong (Peoples Republic, Hong Kong); South Asia, based in Delhi (India, Pakistan, and surrounding markets); North Asia, based in Tokyo (Japan, Korea, Philippines, Taiwan), and Southeast Asia, based in Singapore (Australia, New Zealand).

In 1994, Whirlpool's investment in Asia jumped to over $200 million. Whirlpool announced a joint venture with Teco Electric & Machinery Co., Ltd., to market and distribute home appliances in Taiwan as an insider. In February 1995, Whirlpool acquired a controlling interest in Kelvinator of India, Ltd., one of the largest manufacturers and marketers of refrigerators in that country. Also, Whirlpool obtained a controlling interest and day-to-day management of its existing Indian-based venture, TVS Whirlpool, Ltd. In its 1995 Annual Report to Shareholders the company announced that in the forthcoming year it would create an efficient, customer responsive "Whirlpool of India" organization.

Also, China became the center of a series of joint ventures (for details see Exhibit 8) combined with plant expansions and upgrades which marked an important milestone in that they completed Whirlpool's T-4 strategy in China.

Essential for the long-term strategy was the creation of a technology center in Singapore, where a new generation of products would be designed for the Asian market and which could tap into Whirlpool's expertise gained around the globe. Just like in Latin America, the Worldwide Excellence System (see below) was adapted to the regional circumstances and provided a strong integrating mechanism.

To accelerate the process, Whirlpool assembled global product teams, offered foreign assignments for key personnel within the global organization, and started hiring aggressively within the region.

ORCHESTRATING THE STRATEGY GLOBALLY

Even though Whirlpool by the end of 1995 was a global force, its U.S. exports were less than 10 percent of gross revenues. As Whirlpool expanded its geographic reach (Exhibit 7), it became more and more critical to lay the groundwork so that the company could utilize effectively its experience worldwide in product technology and manufacturing processes and transfer it quickly to wherever it was needed and thereby leverage its global presence to gain sustainable competitive advantage. For this purpose, a number of projects and organizational functions and arrangements were put in place.

Global Business Units

Two product groups were managed and organized on a global platform. The Microwave Oven Business Unit managed microwave oven production and development activities on a global basis with manufacturing and product development facilities in Norrköping, Sweden, and a second, low-cost source in development in China. Whirlpool claimed that once the Shunde facility started operating, it would be one of the world's top five microwave oven manufacturers.

In late 1995 Whirlpool created the Global Air Treatment Unit, which relied on the Lavergne Division in Tennessee, and Shenzhen Whirlpool Raybo Air-Conditioner Industrial Co. Ltd., which had become part of the company a few months before. An aggressive growth strategy had been formulated that anticipated quadrupling volume growth in the first half of 1996 relative to the same period a year earlier.

In addition, Whirlpool Financial Corporation, established in 1957, served manufacturers, retailers, and consumers in the U.S., Canada, and Europe. With assets exceeding $1.9 billion in 1995, it provided inventory and consumer financing to support product sales from the point of manufacture through the market channel to the consumer.

The World Washer

The World Washer represented an effort to create a lightweight compact washer with few parts that could be produced in developing countries where manufacturing technology was not as advanced and which could be sold at a price that put it within reach of many more households than the designs marketed in the industrialized world. The goal of the world washer effort was to develop a complete product, process, and facility design package versatile enough to satisfy conditions and market requirements in various countries, but with low initial investment requirements. At the same time, the World Washer established a beachhead especially against the Far Eastern rivals. Not everybody in the industry shared Whirlpool's vision of global products. Commented Lawrence A. Johnson, a corporate officer of General Electrics' Appliance Division: "We're not in an industry where global products work well. . . . There is also no such thing as a global brand, and it's unlikely that there will be. It's hard to change decades of brand commitment."[19]

As the name indicated, a common design was envisaged for India, Brazil, and Mexico, where the washer was to be produced and marketed. Originally it was planned to replicate the project design in each of the three countries. It eventually

---

[19]Remich, "Speed Saves the Day," p. 29.

proved necessary to devleop three slightly different variations. Costs also varied widely, further affecting both product and process decisions. "In India, for example, material costs may run as much as 200 to 800 percent higher than elsewhere, while labor and overhead costs are comparatively minimal," added Lawrence J. Kremer, Senior Vice President, Global Technology and Operations.[20]

The plants also varied subtly from each other, although the goals were identical—minimizing facility investment and avoiding big finish systems and welding stations requiring extensive machinery for material cleanup and environmental safety. In Brazil, the plant was constructed of precast concrete; it was designed as a creative convection cooling system to address the high humidity. In India, the new facility was built in Pondicherry, just 12 degrees north of the equator. Although the plant looked similar to that in Brazil—except for the overhead fans—the method of construction was different. Concrete was hand mixed on location, then carried in wicker baskets to forms constructed right next to the building site. The Indian construction crew cast the concrete, allowed it to cure, and then, using five or six men, raised each three-ton slab into place using chain, block, and tackle.

Worldwide Excellence System

Established in 1991, the Worldwide Excellence System (WES) was the company's blueprint for how it approached quality, customers, and continuous improvement worldwide. WES combined elements of other well-known quality systems: ISO 9000, the Deming approach used in Asia, and the Baldridge system used in the U.S. Like the Baldridge system, WES used a point system to measure success in implementing the program. WES had seven categories (Exhibit 9). The Leadership and Whirlpool People categories described the involvement of people at all levels in moving the corporation to excellence. Fact-based management, Strategic Planning, and Quality of Process & Products outlined the major internal processes for achieving excellence. Measurement and Results explained the methods used to determine what customers expected, and to assess how well they were being satisfied. The continuous monitoring of Customer Satisfaction was used for unending improvement of activities and processes.

Technology Organization

Several of Whirlpool's functions were organized in a fashion to take advantage of the company's technical know-how scattered around the globe. The goal was to develop advanced, innovative products and move them to market quickly and competitively. As mentioned earlier, an early success in this area occurred in late 1991 when the VIP Crisp microwave oven, developed in Norrköping, Sweden, was introduced and quickly became Europe's best-selling model.

A Global Procurement organization bought all material and components to support the company's appliance production facilities. From procurement centers in the

---

[20]Whirlpool Corporation, World Washer news release.

EXHIBIT 9
Worldwide Excellence System

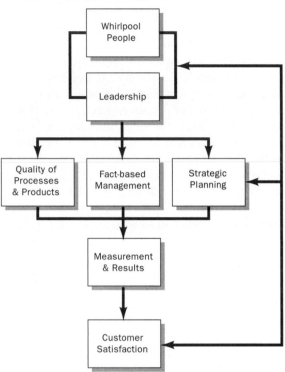

U.S., Italy, and Singapore, it bought finished products, commodities sourced on a regional or global basis, and standardized parts and components. Most other parts and material were sourced from suppliers located near the production facilities where they were used. In developing countries, this often implied educating and assisting local suppliers in attaining Whirlpool standards.

Corporate Technology Development developed product and process technology capabilities and provided technical services to Whirlpool businesses. While centrally managed from the corporation's technology center in Benton Harbor, technology development activities were geographically dispersed in Europe, Asia, and North America.

Advanced Product Concepts looked beyond current product needs for appliances Whirlpool was making. It was responsible for developing new product concepts that were identified through market research.

Advanced Manufacturing Concepts was responsible for bringing new manufacturing processes into the corporation and identifying and developing simulation tools and best practices to be used on a global basis.

Strategic Assessment and Support identified and evaluated non-traditional new product opportunities in cooperation with other units of Whirlpool. Also, it established corporate policy regarding product safety, computer-aided design, and manu-

EXHIBIT 10

Eleven-Year Consolidated Financial Review
(in millions of dollars, except per share data)

Year Ended December 31

	1995	1994	1993	1992	1991	1990	1989	1988	1987	1986	1985	1984
Consolidated operations:												
Net sales	$8,163	$7,949	$7,368	$7,097	$6,550	$6,424	$6,138	$4,306	$4,104	$3,928	$3,465	$3,128
Financial services	184	155	165	204	207	181	136	107	94	76	67	63
Total revenues	$8,347	$8,104	$7,533	$7,301	$6,757	$6,605	$6,274	$4,413	$4,198	$4,004	$3,532	$3,191
Operating profit	$396	$397	$482	$479	$393	$349	$411	$261	$296	$326	$295	$288
Earnings from continuing operations before income taxes and other items	242	292	375	372	304	220	308	233	280	329	321	326
Earnings from continuing operations before accounting change	209	158	231	205	170	72	187	161	187	202	182	190
Net earnings	209	158	51	205	170	72	187	94	192	200	182	190
Net capital expenditures	480	418	309	288	287	265	208	166	223	217	178	135
Depreciation	282	246	241	275	233	247	222	143	133	120	89	72
Depreciation	100	90	85	77	76	76	76	76	79	76	73	73
Consolidated financial position:												
Current assets	$3,541	$3,078	$2,708	$2,740	$2,920	$2,900	$2,889	$1,827	$1,690	$1,654	$1,410	$1,302
Current liabilities	3,829	2,988	2,763	2,887	2,931	2,651	2,251	1,374	1,246	1,006	781	671
Working capital	(288)	90	(55)	(147)	(11)	249	638	453	444	648	629	632
Property, plant, and equipment—net	1,779	1,440	1,319	1,325	1,400	1,349	1,288	820	779	677	514	398
Total assets	7,800	6,655	6,047	6,118	6,445	5,614	5,354	3,410	3,137	2,856	2,207	1,901
Long-term debt	983	885	840	1,215	1,528	874	982	474	367	298	125	91
Total debt—appliance business	1,535	965	850	1,198	1,330	1,026	1,125	441	383	194	64	53
Stockholders' equity	1,877	1,723	1,648	1,600	1,515	1,424	1,421	1,321	1,304	1,350	1,207	1,096
Per share data:												
Earnings from continuing operations before accounting change	$2.80	$2.10	$3.19	$2.90	$2.45	$1.04	$2.70	$2.33	$2.61	$2.72	$2.49	$2.59
Net earnings	$2.80	$2.10	$0.67	$2.90	$2.45	$1.04	$2.70	$1.36	$2.68	$2.70	$2.49	$2.59
Dividends	$1.36	$1.22	$1.19	$1.10	$1.10	$1.10	$1.10	$1.10	$1.10	$1.03	$1.00	$1.00
Book value	$25.08	$22.83	$22.80	$22.67	$21.78	$20.51	$20.49	$19.06	$18.83	$18.21	$16.46	$14.97
Closing stock price—NYSE	$53\frac{1}{4}$	$50\frac{1}{4}$	$66\frac{1}{2}$	$44\frac{5}{8}$	$38\frac{7}{8}$	$23\frac{1}{2}$	33	$24\frac{3}{4}$	$24\frac{3}{8}$	$33\frac{7}{8}$	$24\frac{11}{16}$	$23\frac{1}{4}$

facturing; addressed environmental and regulatory issues and intellectual property rights.

THE RACE FOR GLOBAL DOMINANCE

Whirlpool was by no means alone in its effort to establish a global position of strength. Everybody in the industry was pursuing similar strategies.

Electrolux, the leader in Europe, continued to expand aggressively using its strong pan-European as well as local brands. Plans included establishing market share leadership in Central and Eastern Europe by the year 2000. A $100 million investment in China included a joint venture to manufacture water purifiers, another for compressors, and a vacuum-cleaner plant. Vacuum-cleaner manufacturing capacity was also increased in South Africa. In India Electrolux established itself through acquisitions of majority holdings in production facilities for refrigerators and washing machines. In Thailand, Indonesia, Malaysia, and Singapore the Swedish giant rapidly developed a strong position through a network of retailers. In Latin America finally, the company recently had acquired a minority interest in Brazil's second-largest white goods manufacturer, Refripar.

Besides trying to strengthen its position in North America through its alliance

---

EXHIBIT 11
Business Unit Revenues and Operating Profit
(in millions of dollars)

	1995	*1994*	*1993*
Revenues:			
North America	$5,093	$5,048	$4,559
Europe	2,502	2,373	2,225
Latin America	271	329	303
Asia	376	205	151
Other	(5)	(6)	130
Total appliance business	$8,163	$7,949	$7,368
Operating profit			
North America	$ 445	$ 522	$ 474
Europe	92	163	139
Latin America	26	49	43
Asia	(50)	(22)	(5)
Restructuring*	—	(248)	(23)
Business dispositions†	—	60	(8)
Other	(147)	(154)	(116)
Total appliance business	$ 366	$ 370	$ 504

*Consolidation and reorganization of European and North American operations in 1993 and 1994 and closure of two North American manufacturing facilities in 1994.
†In 1994, the minority interest in Matsushita Floor Care Company was sold as were the European compressor operations to its Brazilian affiliate Embraco, and its refrigerator plant in Barcelona.

with Maytag where it hoped to sell its distinctively European designs beyond the export of 40,000 dishwashers, Bosch-Siemens Hausgeräte GmbH (BSHG) also vied for a larger share in other regions. In China, BSHG had acquired a majority in Wuxi Little Swan Co., a leading manufacturer of laundry appliances. In Brazil, BSHG had purchased Continental 2001, a large appliance producer with sales of $294 million. In Eastern Europe, it had recently completed the construction of a washing machine factory in Lodz, Poland.

EXHIBIT 12
Business Segment Information
(in millions of dollars)

	North America	Europe	Other and Eliminations
Net sales:			
1995	$5,093	$2,502	$ 586
1994	5,048	2,451	450
1993	4,547	2,410	411
1992	4,471	2,645	185
1991	4,224	2,479	54
1990	4,157	2,405	43
Operating profit:			
1995	$ 314	$ 90	$ (38)
1994	311	43	16
1993	341	129	34
1992	359	101	19
1991	314	82	(3)
1990	269	86	(6)
Identifiable assets:			
1995	$2,031	$2,104	$2,033
1994	2,046	1,824	1,410
1993	1,742	1,758	1,154
1992	3,511	1,917	690
1991	3,672	2,284	489
1990	3,216	1,905	493
Depreciation expense:			
1995	$ 140	$ 105	$ 8
1994	141	98	4
1993	137	101	1
1992	142	132	1
1991	129	104	
1990	140	107	
Net capital expenditures:			
1995	$ 262	$ 186	$ 29
1994	269	135	12
1993	188	116	3
1992	174	111	3
1991	183	104	
1990	158	106	1

General Electric Appliances, a $6 billion giant in 1994, was also working hard to establish itself as a global player: "We're focusing our efforts on the world's fastest growing markets, including India, China, Southeast Asia, and South America. . . . We're also strengthening our alliances in Mexico and India, and we developed a number of new products specifically for global markets," explained J. Richard Stonesifer, GEA's President and CEO.[21]

Epilogue

For the fiscal year of 1995 Whirlpool reported per share earnings of $2.80, up from a year earlier but still below the 1993 high. (For a summary of financial results, see Exhibits 1, 10 to 12.) A combination of events and trends had contributed to these results. First, in North America product shipments had declined by 1.4 percent and operating profits had dropped by 16 percent. In Europe, rising raw material costs, fierce competition, and a shift by consumers to cheaper brands and models reduced Whirlpool's shipments by 2 percent while the industry grew by 1 percent. Volume in Latin America was up thanks to robust growth in Brazil in contrast to Argentina, where industry shipments plummeted by as much as 50 percent fueled by the Mexican collapse. Whirlpool Asia reported an operating loss due to the continuing expansion while shipments increased by 193 percent and revenues by 83 percent, respectively. David Whitwam said that the company was ahead of schedule in its restructuring effort in Europe and North America and that he anticipated significant improvements in operating efficiency for next year. Evidently, Whirlpool felt pretty good about its position in the industry as indicated by the quote in his 1995 Letter to Shareholders in spite of the lackluster short-term results (see p. C415).

BIBLIOGRAPHY

Appliance Manufacturer (February 1990), pp. 36–37.

Babyak, R. J. "Demystifying the Asian Consumer," *Applicance Manufacturer,* Vol. 47, No. 2 (Special Section) (February 1995), pp. 25–27.

Babyak, R. J. "Multifaceted Strategy," *Appliance Manufacturer,* Vol. 47, No. 2 (Special Section) (February 1995), pp. 28–29.

Babyak, R. J. "Strategic Imperative," *Appliance Manufacturer,* Vol. 47, No. 2 (Special Section) (February 1995), pp. 19–24.

Botskor, I., M. Chaouli, and B. Müller. "Boom mit Grauwerten," *Wirtschaftswoche,* No. 22 (May 28, 1993), pp. 64–75.

---

[21]Remich, "A Kentucky Thoroughbred," p. 4.

Bower, J. L., and N. Dossabhoy. "Note on the Major Home Appliance Industry in 1984" (Condensed), Case #385-211, Harvard Business School, mimeo.

Bray, H. "Plugging into the World," *Detroit Free Press* (May 17, 1993), pp. 10–11F.

Bylinsky, G. "Computers That Learn by Doing," *Fortune* (September 6, 1993), pp. 96–102.

DuPont, T. "The Appliance Giant Has a New President and a Global Vision," *The Weekly Home Furnishings Newspaper* (July 2, 1987), p. 1.

DuPont, T. "Whirlpool's New Brand Name," *The Weekly Home Furnishings Newspaper* (April 11, 1988).

Echikson, W. "The Trick to Selling in Europe," *Fortune* (September 20, 1993), p. 82.

Fisher, J. D. "Home Appliance Industry," *Value Line* (December 22, 1989), p. 132.

"Fleet of Foot," *Appliance Manufacturer,* Vol. 46, No. 5 (May 1994), pp. 35–38. *Appliance*, June 1991.

Ghoshal, S., and P. Haspeslagh. "The Acquisition and Integration of Zanussi by Electrolux: A Case Study," *European Management Journal*, Vol. 8, No. 4 (December 1990), pp. 414–433.

Hunger, D. J. "The Major Home Appliance Industry in 1990: From U.S. to Global," 1990, mimeo.

Jackson, T. "European Competition Hurts Whirlpool," *Financial Times* (October 14/15, p. 6).

Jancsurak, J. "Holistic Strategy Pays Off," *Appliance Manufacturer,* Vol. 47, No. 2 (Special Section) (February 1995), pp. 3–6.

Jancsurak, J. "Marketing: Phase 2," *Appliance Manufacturer,* Vol. 47, No. 2 (Special Section) (February 1995), pp. 8–10.

Jancsurak, J. "Wanted: Customers for Life," *Appliance Manufacturer,* Vol. 47, No. 2 (Special Section) (February 1995), pp. 36–37.

Jancsurak, J. "Big Plans for Europe's Big Three," *Appliance Manufacturer,* Vol. 47, No. 4 (April 1995), pp. 26–30.

Kindel, S. "World Washer: Why Whirlpool Leads in Appliance: Not Some Japanese Outfit," *Financial World*, Vol. 159, No. 6 (March 20, 1990), pp. 42–46.

Maruca, R. F. "The Right Way to Go Global," An Interview with Whirlpool CEO David Whitwam," *Harvard Business Review* (March–April 1994), pp. 135–145.

Naj, A. K. "Air Conditioners Learn to Sense If You're Cool," *Wall Street Journal* (August 31, 1993), p. B1.

"A Portrait of the U.S. Appliance Industry 1992," *Appliance* (September 1992).

Remich, N. C., Jr. "A Kentucky Thoroughbred That Is Running Strong," *Appliance Manufacturer*, Vol. 47, No. 7 (Special Section) (July 1995), pp. 3–6.

Remich, N. C., Jr. "Speed Saves the Day," *Appliance Manufacturer*, Vol. 47, No. 7 (Special Section) (July 1995), pp. 25–29.

Schiller, Z. "GE Has a Lean, Mean Washing Machine," *Business Week* (November 20, 1995), pp. 97–98.

Standard & Poor's Corp. "Poised for a Moderate Recovery," *Industry Surveys*, Vol. 2 (November 1992), pp. T96–101.

Standard & Poor's Corp. "Waiting for the Next Replacement Cycle," *Industry Surveys*, Vol. 2 (November 1991), pp. T102–105.

Stewart, T. A. "A Heartland Industry Takes On the World," *Fortune* (March 2, 1990), pp. 110–112.

Tierney, R. "Whirlpool Magic," *World Trade* (May 1993).

Treece, J. B. "The Great Refrigerator Race," *Business Week* (July 15, 1993), pp. 78–81.

Weiner, S. "Growing Pains," *Forbes* (October 29, 1990), pp. 40–41.

Whirlpool Corporation. Annual Reports 1987–1995.

Whirlpool Corporation. Form 10-K 1992, 1994, 1995.

Whirlpool Corporation. 1992 Proxy Statement.

Whirlpool Corporation. Profile 1994, 1995.

Whirlpool Corporation. "Whirlpool Corporation Named Winner in $30 Million Super-Efficient Refrigerator Competition," undated.

Whirlpool Corporation. "Whirlpool 'World Washer' Being Marketed in Three Emerging Countries," news release, undated.

Zeller, W. "A Tough Market Has Whirlpool in a Spin," *Business Week* (May 2, 1988), pp. 121–122.

http://www.whirlpool.com/

STRATEGY FORMULATION

Becton Dickinson: Worldwide Blood Collection Team*

In the spring of 1993, Bill Kozy, president of Becton Dickinson VACUTAINER Systems (BDVS) division, discussed the challenges he foresaw for the Worldwide Blood Collection Team (WBCT) he led. Over his four and a half years chairing this team of managers drawn from BDVS operations around the globe, Kozy had seen great growth in the business. (See Exhibit 1.) He was particularly proud of the role the WBCT played in BDVS's two major new product introductions—the HEMOGARD safety closure and the plastic PLUS TUBE line—because they represented the first products developed and launched through the transnational management approach he was trying to develop.

But Kozy knew that he still faced difficult organizational issues as worldwide blood collection evolved from an international business treating overseas operations as appendages, to a genuinely transnational business managing its worldwide portfolio of resources and capabilities as strategic assets. Three major issues concerned him. First, there was the structure of the worldwide blood collection business. As Becton Dickinson's business grew outside the United States and the U.S. market matured, Kozy wondered if the configuration of roles and resources was appropriate. WBCT members were increasingly involved in discussions and negotiations over complex issues of where R&D resources and capabilities should be developed.

Kozy's second issue concerned the need to align human resource systems with the new worldwide strategies, the changing structures such as the WBCT, and the evolving processes for key decisions such as development of worldwide products. He had experienced the difficulties inherent in chairing a team of unevenly matched and skilled managers. And as larger numbers of managers became involved in decisions and actions beyond their traditional areas of responsibility, he wondered how they should be measured and evaluated in terms of their contributions to BD's worldwide businesses.

Finally, Kozy was aware that some of his colleagues still wondered whether the WBCT was the right mechanism for managing BDVS's worldwide business in accor-

---

*Research Associate Kathleen Scharf prepared this case under the supervision of Professor Christopher A. Bartlett as the basis for class discussion rather than to illustrate either effective or ineffective handling of an administrative situation.

EXHIBIT 1

Becton Dickinson & Company: Income Statement
(in thousands of dollars)

Division and Strategy Center	1985 Actual $	1986 Actual $	1987 Actual $	1988 Actual $	1989 Actual $	1990 Actual $	1991 Actual $	1992 Actual $
Worldwide blood collection (including specimen collection):								
Net trade sales	$144,371	$172,770	$198,790	$236,736	$264,533	$293,940	$329,837	$363,376
Gross profit	62,815	77,902	90,443	109,201	118,353	133,234	147,000	163,714
Total expenses	37,188	40,156	46,897	55,114	59,518	65,436	75,970	82,614
OIBT*	23,046	34,950	41,441	48,680	52,562	60,110	60,344	72,732
RONA (pretax—average)	23.94%	30.60%	32.20%	31.00%	25.90%	23.00%	18.00%	23.00%
U.S. blood collection:								
Net trade sales	$ 92,921	$102,823	$110,269	$123,018	$140,886	$149,910	$162,217	$170,670
Gross profit	44,400	48,327	50,723	56,711	62,595	66,860	71,375	74,753
Total expenses	22,780	22,218	22,975	25,013	27,269	38,693	32,759	34,712
OIBT*	19,421	23,978	25,955	29,730	32,990	35,539	33,559	36,529
RONA (pretax—average)	41.70%	41.10%	42.10%	41.70%	35.90%	29.60%	21.20%	25.30%
Europe blood collection:								
Net trade sales	$ 30,204	$ 44,862	$ 56,669	$ 71,879	$ 75,275	$ 93,106	$111,751	$130,174
Gross profit	8,683	17,865	25,501	32,921	33,874	42,829	51,182	60,140
Total expenses	9,661	12,518	15,283	18,869	19,800	23,177	27,448	30,504
OIBT*	(1,055)	5,309	10,218	11,400	11,226	16,144	19,435	25,769
RONA (pretax—average)	(2.8%)	12.20%	20.00%	18.40%	13.00%	14.70%	14.30%	20.30%
Japan blood collection:								
Net trade sales	$ 2,213	$ 3,421	$ 5,719	$ 7,438	$ 8,654	$ 9,074	$ 11,452	$ 14,735
Gross profit	1,237	2,382	3,380	4,626	5,338	4,339	4,972	7,100
Total expenses	1,084	1,532	3,883	5,130	4,978	4,877	6,149	6,692
OIBT*	154	850	(501)	(732)	95	(817)	(1,555)	(92.4)
RONA (pretax—average)	8.50%	45.00%	(16.7%)	(13.7%)	1.50%	(10.7%)	(17.3%)	(0.8%)

Note: Although data have been disguised, key relationships have been retained.

*Operating Income Before Taxes for 1985–1987 includes little or no GCE for international units.

dance with transnational concepts. While he believed this body had played a vital role particularly as it clarified its responsibilities in recent years, perhaps it was time to reevaluate its future role.

HISTORY AND CONTEXT OF BD'S INTERNATIONAL BUSINESS

Founded in 1897 as a manufacturer of clinical thermometers, Becton Dickinson and Company (BD) was a supplier of medical products and diagnostic systems to hospitals, physicians' offices, clinical and research laboratories, and pharmacies. BD had 10 core businesses organized into two product sectors: medical and diagnostic. Major medical sector products included hypodermic needles and syringes, medical gloves, diabetic products, and intravenous catheters. Diagnostic products included blood collection devices, prepared plated media, automated systems to detect and identify bacteria, rapid manual tests for doctors' offices, blood cell analysis systems, and immunocytometry products for cellular analysis.

Although about half of BD's 1992 sales of $2 billion were generated outside the United States, the company's international business had been developed relatively recently. In 1960, BD began to build a European organization whose central role was to expand the market for the very successful line of products the company had developed for the U.S. market. The European operation was built as a portfolio of country subsidiaries whose general managers reported to an area president, who, in turn, was part of the corporate-level international group. Country managers were responsible for sales, marketing, distribution, administration, and compliance with local regulations, whereas U.S. division presidents managed R&D, manufacturing, and other operational issues. (See Exhibit 2.)

During the 1970s, BD transferred the locus of power from the functionally dominated regional office to the national subsidiaries, giving the country managers clear mandate to maximize sales in their countries. Evaluation and compensation still gave country managers little incentive to risk short-term local results in the service of longer-term corporate goals for international market development. Their main complaint was that their performance was often limited because U.S. division managers often filled international orders only when the U.S. demands were covered, and routinely refused to consider new product requests from abroad.

European SBUs

In 1980, BD's senior executives saw the need to respond to several important developments. As the U.S. market matured, growing opportunities in Europe became increasingly attractive. At the same time, several international medical technology companies were focusing their attentions on Europe, posing a threat to BD's position not only in those markets but in the United States as well. As a result, pressure was increasing to reorganize sales and marketing activities in support of international

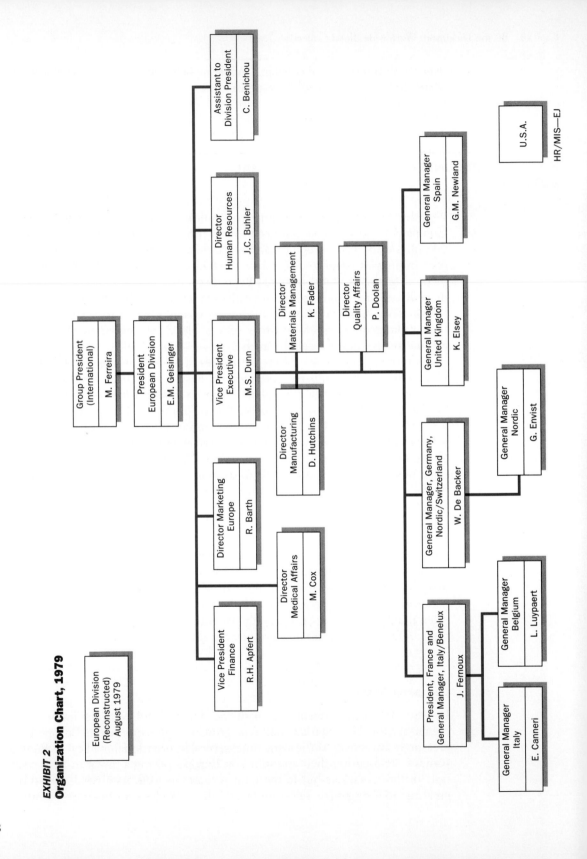

EXHIBIT 2
Organization Chart, 1979

European Division (Reconstructed) August 1979

Group President (International) — M. Ferreira

President European Division — E.M. Geisinger

Vice President Executive — M.S. Dunn

Assistant to Division President — C. Benichou

Director Human Resources — J.C. Buhler

Director Materials Management — K. Fader

Director Quality Affairs — P. Doolan

Director Manufacturing — D. Hutchins

Director Marketing Europe — R. Barth

Director Medical Affairs — M. Cox

Vice President Finance — R.H. Apfert

General Manager Spain — G.M. Newland

General Manager United Kingdom — K. Elsey

General Manager, Germany, Nordic/Switzerland — W. De Backer

General Manager Nordic — G. Envist

President, France and General Manager, Italy/Benelux — J. Fernoux

General Manager Belgium — L. Luypaert

General Manager Italy — E. Canneri

U.S.A.

HR/MIS—EJ

growth, to rationalize international product flows, and to achieve more uniform cost and quality standards worldwide.

Expanding on the Strategic Business Unit (SBU) concept that had been overlaid on the U.S. product divisions to provide them with more strategic focus and discipline, top management decided to create corresponding European SBUs. The head of each European SBU was given the title of president, and treated similarly to a division president in the United States. This status level was higher than that accorded to country managers in Europe. Country level sales and marketing personnel for these products now reported directly to the European SBU presidents rather than to their country manager. The country organizations retained responsibility for accounting, finance, human resource, and other administrative functions; BD's European headquarters coordinated these functions on a Europe-wide basis. The country presidents were still compensated based on their country P&L results, whereas SBU managers were rewarded for their SBU's results Europe-wide.

Although senior managers worked to prepare European managers for a new structure, a manager involved recalled making complex presentations to "a largely unresponsive audience." European managers had just adjusted to a shift from a regionally dominated functional organization to a stronger country system; now they were being asked to buy into a regionally driven structure once again. The changes were traumatic. Under the new hybrid structure, many country presidents felt their roles had greatly diminished. Although they were still BD's legal representatives and managed relationships with local regulatory agencies, unions, medical advisory panels, and the like, their role in broader strategy development, planning, and decision-making processes was unclear. In this environment, border disputes among SBU managers, country managers, and regional and corporate departments erupted frequently.

Differences over many issues such as marketing plans, sourcing, or managing manufacturing assets, arose periodically between U.S. and non-U.S. managers. But it was the conflict over new product development issues that often became the most emotional flashpoint for issues of autonomy, competence, and cultural bias. Because the U.S. divisions still controlled R&D, Europeans accused the U.S. divisions of a strong bias for products with U.S. markets. The U.S. division presidents, on the other hand, found most European product requests poorly documented and reflective of incomplete understandings of the real resource costs of the product development cycle.

Toward Transnational Management

Despite the continued spectacular growth of its European sales and market share, BD Europe posted operating losses for FY 1983–1984. The company was in an investment mode with respect to its European businesses, and the Plymouth plant, which had been built in 1981 as a regional plant for Europe, was not expected to turn a profit until the late 1980s. But senior managers feared that cost and quality goals would be difficult to achieve with the conflict that existed among pivotal players and organizational units, and it seemed unlikely that BD's European situation would permit it to contend successfully with a growing field of competitors.

By 1985, some senior managers were ready to reassess how the company managed its worldwide operations. As a result, BD engaged a consulting company to study the problem. The consultant produced two alternative models ("The Worldwide Product Division" and "Europe as Equal Partner") each described in great detail as to the structural change required. Senior management decided it was not ready for another restructuring, with all the implied turf battles and inwardly focused energy. Instead, it sought a solution that would respond to the external forces for more cross-border coordination, but that would not compromise the country organizations' entrepreneurship and motivation, undermine their excellent relationships with their local markets, or interfere with their need to negotiate with national regulatory, medical, and labor groups.

It was in this context that some senior managers met with Harvard Professor Christopher Bartlett, then undertaking a research project with his colleague Sumantra Ghoshal on worldwide organization.[1] In several sessions with the top team, Bartlett emphasized three core findings from the study:

- The strategic need for companies to build global efficiency, national responsiveness, and a worldwide innovation and learning capacity;

- The need of this multilayered strategic capability for a multidimensional organization, not one structured around traditional dichotomous choices between product and geography, centralization and decentralization; and

- The building of such organizations by changing management culture and values and developing organizational processes and relationships, and not just by changing formal structural design.

International Sector President Clateo Castellini, an Italian national, and Group President Ralph Biggadike, a British national, strongly advocated Bartlett's transnational approach because they saw it as providing a balance between the country structure and the SBU structure debated within BD. After many months of discussion, BD senior managers agreed to make the transnational approach the subject of the 1986 senior management conference. Then in a series of three-day management conferences in 1986 and 1987, Bartlett exposed over 150 of BD's managers to transnational concepts. After analyzing the changes occurring in their businesses, the managers quickly realized the need to build multiple sources of competitive advantage and that doing so would require strong management capability in both the local and global dimensions.

Using frameworks similar to those illustrated in Exhibit 3, the managers spent most of the conference discussing and negotiating what needed to be managed in a more globally integrated manner, what needed to be handled in a more nationally responsive way, and what few issues needed to be handled jointly. As the exhibit suggests, they quickly discovered that there was no single formula and that they had to decide business by business, function by function, and even decision by decision.

Although most issues could be clearly allocated to country or business management, a few vital issues needed to be managed in a shared fashion. To provide a forum

---

[1]Reported in Christopher A. Bartlett and Sumantra Ghoshal, *Managing Across Borders: The Transnational Solution* (Boston: HBS Press, 1989).

EXHIBIT 3
Task Responsibility Framework: VACUTAINER Systems

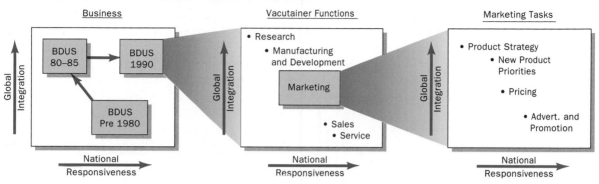

This reflects the preliminary discussions and analysis done at the early transnational management seminars, where managers began to negotiate, business by business, function by function, and task by task, which responsibilities needed to be managed primarily by SBUs in a global manner (the northwest quadrant), which needed to be managed primarily by subsidiaries in a local manner (the southwest quadrant), and which *few key issues* needed to be handled in off-line forums where global and local managers could engage in the more intensive discussions and negotiations that transnational management required (the northeast quadrant). This analysis illustrates the outcomes on discussions about allocation of responsibility for marketing tasks in the Vacutainer Systems business. Similar discussions and analysis were undertaken to determine responsibility for key tasks in all major functions on a business by business basis.

for these decisions, as well as a means to develop relationships between key managers, in late 1986 Worldwide Teams were established for each of the key worldwide businesses. Because each of the businesses had defined its organizational tasks differently, no attempt was made to impose a uniform set of responsibilities on the team. Instead, senior management challenged each team to define its own role in helping manage the worldwide business. Some quickly became active in initiating worldwide projects and coordinating joint decision-making processes; others met less frequently and slipped into the role of communication forums.

THE CHANGES AT VACUTAINER SYSTEMS

One of the businesses affected by all the changes was the BD VACUTAINER Systems (BDVS) Division. BDVS included the U.S. business, which housed all R&D, and the European operations. Manufacturing plants in the United States and Europe reported to the BDVS president through the divisional director of Manufacturing. In Asia and Latin America, however, the VACUTAINER business still reported to the country presidents. (See Exhibit 4.)

BDVS as a Worldwide Business

The first formal "worldwide" meeting of BDVS managers occurred in Annecy, France, in 1982. The meeting was quite formal, with the U.S. group explaining to the Europeans procedures for new product development, product support, and other di-

EXHIBIT 4
Organization Chart, 1986

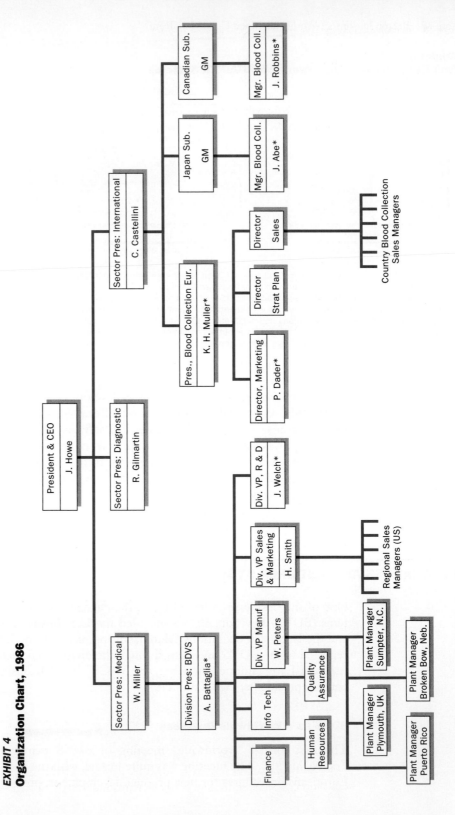

*Member, Initial Worldwide Blood Collection Team

visional functions. In response, the Europeans explained the nature of their market with its diverse pattern of medical practice.

Encouraged by their influence as a united group, the Europeans continued to meet on a somewhat informal and *ad hoc* basis throughout the early 1980s. Then European BDVS President Karlheinz Müller described the spirit of the group:

> After that [Annecy meeting] we had fairly regular meetings and product training for our sales force. It was a relationship we benefited mutually from, initiated really by the people, and tolerated by management.

Through this process of opening communication channels, the non-U.S. managers became conscious that they might be able to have an input into BD's worldwide strategy. This encouraged managers in Europe and Japan to propose new product ideas to the worldwide SBU group in the mid-1980s. The initial response, however, was greatly disappointing for both non-U.S. groups, and by 1985 there was growing cynicism that the worldwide meetings were little more than a means of imposing U.S. strategy on overseas operations.

The stories of the development of two products—HEMOGARD and the PLUS TUBE—will illustrate the challenges BD faced in developing an integrated worldwide management approach.

HEMOGARD™: The European Proposal

In 1980, BD's European sales force began a push to convert European customers from conventional syringes to the VACUTAINER™ blood collection system that had been a major success in the U.S. market. In Europe, however, there was some resistance because of perceived blood exposure safety problems for laboratory personnel removing the VACUTAINER™ rubber stopper, which had to be popped off in order to remove blood for testing. Because this action broke the vacuum in the tube, there was some danger blood would "aerosol"—spray out of the tube onto the worker's skin—or that the tube would actually break, posing a danger of cuts and infection with blood-transmitted diseases such as hepatitis.

The issue became a major topic of discussion in early 1983 at a VACUTAINER™ Europe sales meeting in St. Paul de Vence, France. Several sales and marketing managers reported that some of BD's competitors were developing closures that reduced the danger of worker contamination. Furthermore, they confirmed that BD's ability to convert was being slowed down most in the high-potential markets of the United Kingdom, Germany, and Italy, where safety concerns were the greatest. Following their diagnosis, the group developed drawings and preliminary specifications for the screw-on plastic closure device they envisioned and sent them off to Joseph Welch, head of BDVS's R&D department.

The proposal met with little response due to a number of factors. There were no formal organizational means to translate regional interests into potential R&D priorities. Even new product and product extension ideas generated in the United States were not placed on a clearly prioritized list for R&D attention. Since the proposed screw-on cap represented an expensive product development commitment, U.S. marketing people saw little reason to develop it, believing it would be a niche product with limited demand, even in Europe. Furthermore, BDVS has several large-scale projects on the board, and the Americans saw little need to take a major risk without strong support within R&D and with thinly documented paybacks.

As Müller later acknowledged:

> Since we had 100 million [annual unit sales of tubes] versus 500 million for the United States, it was hard to interest R&D. And our marketing group was not very effective then in submitting the Project Initiation Review properly. Without formal processes, it all had to be done through an informal relationship with Joe Welch.

Nonetheless, within Europe there was a growing sense of frustration as time passed and the screw-on closure was not forthcoming from U.S. R&D. The promise of truly worldwide management seemed hollow.

In June of 1984, after considerable pressure from Müller and his team, Welch agreed to a compromise. He directed his R&D department to develop a mold for an interim product, a press-on plastic cap called the Safety Cap that could be added to existing VACUTAINER products for use in hematology labs. The design was a good deal simpler than the European proposal, and the mold itself was produced in a weekend in BD's machine shop.

In October of 1984, four months after the first Safety Cap molds were produced, Alfred Battaglia became BDVS president and committed himself to "lighting a fire" under the division's product development process. He saw his new division's R&D function as one with many projects but no clear sense of their relative importance and business potential. Instead of relying on personal contacts and the "squeaky wheel" approach that had been the division's *de facto* research priority system, Battaglia encouraged his staff to pursue a clearer and more informed approach to allocating BDVS's resources. To help in this regard, he developed and began to use an R&D priority matrix on which proposed projects were ranked based on a combination of development cost and potential return.

Early in 1985, BDVS began to ship small quantities of Safety Caps for field trials in Europe. The company's accounts were protected more against the incursions of competing safety products, and field data could be fed back to the U.S. R&D engineers still working on the project. Unfortunately, the trials were not very successful, as an engineer involved with the project recalled:

> The Safety Caps didn't exactly take off. They didn't fit in everybody's holders. They didn't fit with competitive needles. We didn't have a very good needle at the time, so a lot of places were using our tube with someone else's needle. . . . It was a son of a gun to push on; it took about 30 pounds of force to put it on . . . [and] it was very smooth and straight-sided, so it was hard to grip with a wet glove.

As BDVS engineers went back to work on the project, Battaglia urged the R&D group to look at the project as one with worldwide significance. Not only did it respond to a growing concern for health care workers' safety, but it also offered a differentiating benefit that could allow BDVS to standardize on a smaller global blood collection tube size, thereby reducing costs.

From the European perspective, however, all they saw was a further delay. Therefore, when key U.S. and European figures met in 1985 at BD's plant in Plymouth, England, Müller expressed his frustration to Battaglia. By this stage, the European team had buttressed its initial proposal with market studies and physicians' endorsements and lined up significant support for the product through direct contacts at the U.S. corporate level. (Müller later characterized his own approach as "table banging.") Battaglia was sympathetic and agreed to commit to the project.

Following this meeting, Welch assigned more R&D resources to the project and moved more aggressively to secure agreement to specifications. New European trials provided input into design decisions, and by March 1986, marketing groups in the United States, Canada, Europe, and Japan had signed off on the specifications for the Safety Cap. Now the challenge was to implement the launch of a product called HEMOGARD™.

PLUS TUBE: The Japanese Proposal

When members of the Blood Collection SBU met in Tokyo in 1985, Japanese managers talked with leading team members about what they saw as a key to VACUTAINER market share in Japan: unbreakable specimen collection tubes. Breakability was much more than an issue of safety to Japanese users. Because of a strong cultural aversion to blood loss, recollecting specimens because of tube breakage was a major problem, and resistance to breakability was seen as a core measure of overall product quality. Although European management viewed the plastic tube as a less urgent, longer-term need, the Japanese group saw it as an urgent priority to defend BD's fragile market share against competitive Japanese products already selling well.

Many BDVS observers realized that demand for relatively light, unbreakable collection tubes would grow as environmental and safety concerns increased worldwide. In both Austria and Japan, local firms had already introduced plastic tubes, and although their market share was small and localized, they looked to be potential threats to BD's penetration of these markets.

Again, the sense of local Japanese managers was that their requests had fallen on deaf ears. Japanese managers felt they had struggled against uncertain supplies and inattention to quality concerns for several years; between 1982 and 1984 BD actually lost part of its small market share in Japan. From their perspective, the HEMOGARD™ project had finally captured attention, and by 1985, was "winning" development resources while their project (dubbed the PLUS TUBE) "lost" because of the originating market's small size. U.S. R&D managers rejected this view and pointed out that the costs and technical challenges entailed in the two projects differed greatly. Whereas HEMOGARD could be developed with existing technologies, the projected plastic tube would require substantial retooling and the location or development of high-performing polymer materials that would not only meet medical standards but also guarantee shelf life, transparency, and other performance characteristics glass tube users had come to expect.

THE WORLDWIDE BLOOD COLLECTION TEAM

The frustration and confusion managers were experiencing on the HEMOGARD and PLUS TUBE projects were symptomatic of the interpersonal tension that existed as BD struggled with how best to manage international expansion. The transnational organizational structure designated to help BD deal with these issues was the Worldwide Blood Collection Team (WBCT) in 1986. (See Exhibit 5.) It was hoped that the new organizational structure, and the changed management approach it required, would help resolve some of the problems.

Early Years: Defining the WBCT's Role

Although the WBCT decided to focus on strategic issues, ability to fulfill that objective was limited by two factors. First, worldwide plans were part of the U.S. division's strategic/operational/financial planning process (SOF), developed by the U.S. staff with limited worldwide consultation. And second, few non-U.S. managers had been trained in BD's strategic planning system, which senior BD managers viewed as central to the firm's management system.

As a consequence, during the first two years of the WBCT's official existence, the team was seen largely as an information-sharing group. Basically, the organization continued to operate as it had under the old SBU model: the U.S. division determined strategy, directed R&D, and controlled manufacturing resources, while overseas operations focused on sales and marketing. Non-U.S. WBCT members, designated by their country or regional managers, tended to be junior to the U.S. team members and less able to commit their own organizations to the WBCT agenda. Some regions' delegates appeared irregularly at team meetings, changed frequently, and did not always command English well enough to participate fully in discussions. As a result, for both HEMOGARD and the PLUS TUBE, continued progress was determined by the originating region's ability to convince the BDVS president and R&D director of the projects' potential.

EXHIBIT 5
Worldwide Blood Collection Team, 1986

- Alfred Battaglia, President, BDVS US
- Hank Smith, Vice President, Sales/Marketing BDVS
- Joe Welch, Vice President/R&D BDVS
- Bill Peters, Vice President/Manufacturing BDVS
- Karlheinz Müller, President, Blood Collection Products Europe
- Pierre Dader, Director of Marketing, Blood Collection Products Europe
- Jun Abe, Manager, Blood Collection and Diabetic Products Japan
- Canadian representative (rotating)

Periodic attender:
- Representative, Latin America

The creation of the WBCT, however, soon had an impact on the development of the HEMOGARD project. In 1986, it was becoming clear to U.S. epidemiologists and to the general public that the AIDS virus outbreaks were early warnings of a pandemic, and the worldwide humanitarian and business potentials of a safety tube closure became more obvious. A BDVS R&D engineer explained:

> The driver was Europe originally, and even in 1984 and 1985 . . . Europeans tended to have a longer view of some trends. They knew about AIDS, and that it was important, and would get worse. In the United States, we were a year or two behind on that curve; awareness peaked around 1986. . . . It was only after the scare hit the United States that we really started cranking [HEMOGARD] up.

With this more widespread support for HEMOGARD, the WBCT provided a useful forum in which to discuss and drive the project. At the team's urging, BDVS R&D director Joe Welch pursued the project aggressively. The WBCT also decided to use the Plymouth, England, plant as the major source for the product.

The PLUS TUBE found a more difficult time claiming the WBCT's attention. First, the team's role was unclear in its early days, and nobody seemed sure of what function to play. Second, the project overlapped with the HEMOGARD launch, and the BDVS R&D and manufacturing staffs were heavily involved with both.

Japanese managers were convinced that the HEMOGARD closure on a glass tube had no future in Japan. They were also greatly alarmed by news that Terumo, BD's major competitor in Japan, was working steadily toward a plastic tube. While the persistent Japanese concerns convinced the U.S. managers to raise the priority of getting a viable product into Japan, even without the breakthrough in plastic technology they had been seeking, there was continuing debate within the WBCT about the worldwide application of plastic tube strategy. In contrast to HEMOGARD, which everyone believed eventually would be a crucial product worldwide, PLUS TUBE was seen by many as a unique Japanese product. Most of the Europeans, for instance, were unconvinced that rapid plastic tube development was necessary to their short-term regional strategy, although some, like Eckhard Lachenauer, believed it would be a key competitive product by 1995. A U.S. participant recalled the flavor of the discussion in 1987 and 1988:

> There seemed to be two camps about whether plastic was necessary. There was a lot of discussion of profits and ROA. We also had to decide how fast we would push the plastic tube, if we did decide to develop it. That was very important because in some instances the coexistence of glass and plastic was an important business strategy for us.

The division and the corporation agreed in 1987 to a staged development scheme, which aimed at supplying the Japanese market as quickly as possible, and moved on toward ultimate goals of shelf life, appearance, cost, and other factors with the help of BD's Research Center in North Carolina.

The debate of PLUS TUBE in the WBCT meetings did serve to increase overall awareness of the project and, as a result, led to some progress in locating suppliers. BD managers in Europe and in Japan ferreted out promising suppliers, licensers, and business partners able to supply technology and materials. For example, Müller introduced Welch to representatives of Greiner, the Austrian company manufacturing plastic blood collection tubes, and Jun Abe of BD's Japanese company put him in touch with Sekisui, a Japanese company interested in a marketing partnership for its plastic technology. In 1987, BD agreed to purchase Greiner's molds and Sekisui's plastic technology.

The Maturing WBCT: Launching World Products

In October of 1988, when Battaglia was promoted to group president, Bill Kozy became BDVS president. By this time the WBCT composition and role had evolved considerably, and Kozy saw the team as a major means to achieve the ambitious growth in international business he and BD expected.

However, from his first meeting with the WBCT, Kozy was aware that it was still struggling with the notion of "transnational management." It was difficult for managers to grasp and embody a change process that was focused not on a structural prescription but on changing processes and relationships and on broadening management mentalities ("creating a matrix in managers' minds," as the transnational model proposed). Kozy described the division's early operating committee discussions:

> In terms of worldwide roles and responsibilities, no one had a clue. A bunch of basically command and control people suddenly became "team members" or "team leaders." Everyone wanted to know what his role was, what he was responsible for. People were still in the political mode of "If you're not going to develop my products, I'm going to tell."

To spark discussion on the team's role, Kozy asked his entire senior staff to read Bartlett and Ghoshal's book *Managing Across Borders* so that the group could discuss it chapter by chapter during its regular meetings. The new division president saw the reading and discussions as a valuable exercise, although some of his staff greeted references to it with wry laughter.

Kozy himself recounted an epiphany of sorts that occurred on a plane during a conversation with his Japanese seatmate. The two men discussed the challenges of international business management, and the Japanese manager said Kozy was lucky to work for a company with the patience to adopt an approach like transnational management, which would clearly require at least 10 years to implement. The extent to which transnational management really was built on changing managers' mentalities and relationships rather than just restructuring reporting relationships suddenly struck Kozy with full force, and the amount of time required to achieve genuine transnational management became clear. He realized that it probably *was* a ten-year process, and that his own division had been struggling with it for only three or four years.

Kozy's commitment to clarify the WBCT's responsibilities and increase its role as a key forum for transnational management exchange was greatly facilitated by the ongoing operations relating to the two new products under development.

HEMOGARD Launch

As the HEMOGARD launch neared, the WBCT was increasingly involved in marketing decisions, some of which did not meet with field sales approval. For technical reasons and to reduce manufacturing costs, BDVS wanted to minimize the number of individual HEMOGARD catalogue numbers. But every time they reduced the size of the product line, the European marketing group would have to lower its forecasts, triggering long debate within the group. Eckhard Lachenauer described the WBCT discussions of the number of VACUTAINER products to be offered with HEMOGARD closures and debates over sales projections as "a constant battle."

Finally, the HEMOGARD line was launched in July 1989. European Director of Operations John Hanson described the launch as the most successful in which he had ever participated, representing to him a truly cross-functional and trans-Atlantic team effort. He recalled the plan's execution:

> By the end of 1988 the real final stage was to involve the plants to bring the product to market. That was the part that was highly successful. It was the first real transnational effort that brought the product to a very aggressive launch date of June 1989. And we slipped by only one month, to July 1989. That I always quote as being truly successful in a worldwide team sense—the plants, R&D, the Supply Chain group, sales and marketing. We had very detailed plans, and they actually happened—that's the amazing part.

Hanson attributed the success of the HEMOGARD launch effort to two central characteristics. First, team roles were made an integral part of members' regular jobs rather than side assignments:

> All of the team assignments and the additional responsibilities these jobs implied were formalized within the framework of their job description. People did the job as they were meant to; this meant that rather than being asked to take on a team assignment on the side.

Second, Hanson believed the launch process was effective because project participants agreed to bypass any existing management information systems that were slow and bureaucratic. For example, new materials management models were developed on local personal computers because existing systems seemed unlikely to support the manufacturing schedules BD contemplated. Furthermore, minutes of the meetings of far-flung teams and committees were faxed to Kozy and Welch within hours. In turn, these managers and their staff responded rapidly to queries, requests, and issues. Hanson recalled:

> The whole key was focus and communication and holding people responsible for what they're actually supposed to do. There's no project now with that weekly communication and weekly meetings. The coordination is not as clear and crisp.

PLUS TUBE Launch

The launch of the PLUS TUBE went less smoothly, but the WBCT's role was also critical in bringing this product to market. The main problem stemmed from BDVS R&D's agreeing to a launch date schedule before completely understanding how challenging a shift from glass to plastic would be. The molds purchased from Greiner produced tubes that did not fit the HEMOGARD closure and had to be modified. In making adjustments, the group quickly learned that plastic was a very different material from glass. But having the WBCT forum at least allowed the problems to be identified quickly and for corrective action to be agreed on and assigned.

Although BDVS originally planned to release the first PLUS TUBEs in late 1988 or 1989, by that date they had not even begun the first Japanese field trials. Eventually trials were conducted and the first products were shipped in 1991. The division and the WBCT were learning that agreement to a marketing strategy did not produce manufacturing capability, as one manager pointed out:

> It took us a year to figure out how to make it work; the schedules were very aggressive. We have learned from this. For the PLUS TUBE we put schedules on products before we figured out how to do it. We're now using a planning method that won't let you commit to a date until you've proved a technology.

Structural Change in the WBCT

At the same time the WBCT was handling the implementation of the two new product launches, it was also engaged in a variety of other issues that required the input and involvement of managers worldwide. Meanwhile, the size and diversity of team membership had grown substantially. By 1990, a few of the most active and influential team members felt that the WBCT was too large and too diversely skilled to make all of the decisions the team's projects required. As Lachenauer explained, "Bill (Kozy) and I realized one day that we could not make all the decisions in the big team. It was taking too much time on tactics and not enough on strategy." The decision was made to form three smaller subteams that could move more efficiently to deal with the strategic, operating, and marketing issues that were becoming increasingly important. (See Exhibits 6, 7, and 8.)

EXHIBIT 6
Worldwide Blood Collection Team Role, 1992

- Develop the worldwide strategy and the strategic goals for the Blood Collection Strategy Center.
- Support development of the regional strategies congruent with the worldwide strategy.
- Recommend the worldwide resource allocation to achieve the maximized effectiveness and efficiency in implementation of the worldwide strategy.
- Review the worldwide business performance to monitor the progress to worldwide strategic goals and to recommend the corrective strategies, if necessary.
- Develop and update the worldwide competitive strategies by integrating the competitive information from the worldwide regions.
- Support developing the regional competitive strategies by releasing the collected competitive information to the worldwide regions.
- Evaluate and prioritize the new product concepts in the worldwide R&D agenda to maintain the optimum resource allocation in PACE.
- Support non-PACE regional product development requirements based upon specifically local customer needs by the worldwide technical support function in the BDVS organization.
- Coordinate worldwide product strategies and rollouts.
- Make recommendations on "global" vs. "local" business activities.
- Coordinate transfer of key skills/capabilities from "Centers of Excellence" to regions.
- Maintain good communications with regional senior managements to help them to develop and implement the well-integrated regional operations strategy with the Blood Collection Strategy Center strategy.
- Identify and locate medical/QA/RA support to the worldwide regions.
- Identify and allocate technical/selling skill training support to the worldwide regions.

Source: *Worldwide Blood Collection Operating Manual*

In 1991 the three members of the Worldwide Strategy Team—Kozy, Lachenauer, and Abe—embarked on a worldwide profiling tour, using BD's long-established strategic profiling process to examine regional strategic potentials and advise regional managers on their role in the worldwide business unit's international strategy. The trio met in Tokyo with managers in BD's Japanese and Asia Pacific blood collection businesses, in Mexico City with their Brazilian and Mexican counterparts, with Canadian managers, and with managers in Europe and the United States. They visited customers in Brazil and Japan. The visits exposed the Strategy Team to the realities of the business outside its major markets, and Kozy returned newly impressed by the potential of markets such as Latin America.

The trip also sensitized the team to the different needs of local markets (e.g., Japanese needs for smaller tubes and some labeling changes). In fact, the Strategy Team members were engaged enough in the problems presented by the Brazilian business that they arranged to visit Brazil. As these visits and exchanges continued, managers recognized that a new level of understanding and cooperation was emerging in subsequent WBCT meetings. Abe commented:

EXHIBIT 7
Transnational Organizational Concept, September 1992

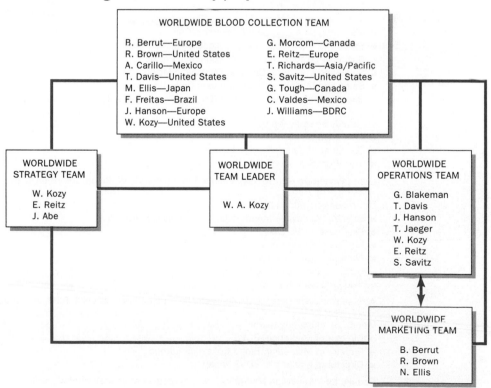

Source: *Worldwide Blood Collection Operating Manual.*

Before when we talked about "worldwide strategy" we really didn't know—we talked only about surface things. That really changed; there were much better suggestions, and much better advice. Now we could see how to use U.S. and even European resources to help.

The other major structural changes related to the management of R&D and technology support. As the HEMOGARD and PLUS TUBE experiences had shown, overseas managers had often experienced difficulty in getting support from the U.S.-based R&D group. The situation was even more difficult for those trying to get technology assistance for older products no longer marketed in the United States, because most R&D staff were tied up in current projects.

EXHIBIT 8
Worldwide Blood Collection Team, 1992

- President, BDVS US
- President, Blood Collection Europe
- Vice President/R&D BDVS
- Director of Marketing, BDVS
- Director, Worldwide Manufacturing and Logistics
- Vice President, Worldwide Business Development
- Corporate Medical Director
- Marketing Director, Blood Collection Europe
- Vice President/General Manager, Diagnostic Canada
- Marketing Manager, Blood Collection Canada
- Sales and Marketing Director, Blood Collection Japan
- Business Director, Blood Collection Asia Pacific
- Sales and Marketing Director, Diagnostic Mexico
- Sales and Marketing Director, Blood Collection Brazil
- Director, Manufacturing Europe (Director Plymouth plant)

Worldwide strategy team:
- President, BDVS
- President, Blood Collection Europe
- Vice President, Worldwide Business Development

Leads Worldwide Strategy development in the Worldwide Blood Collection Team.

Worldwide operations team:
- Director, Worldwide Manufacturing and Logistics (Chair)
- President, BDVS US
- President, Blood Collection Europe
- Plant Manager, Sumter, North Carolina
- Director, Manufacturing Europe
- Vice President/R&D BDVS

Acts as Worldwide Operations Management Team for Manufacturing, R&D, and Supply Chain Management.

Worldwide marketing team:
- Director of Marketing, BDVS
- Director of Marketing, Blood Collection Europe
- Director of Marketing, BDVS Japan

Speaks for "Worldwide Marketing" on key product strategies or new product decisions.

Source: *Worldwide Blood Collection Operating Manual.*

The situation gradually began to improve in the late 1980s, particularly after the arrival of Steven Sous, a BDVS quality assurance (QA) specialist. As a sideline to his domestic responsibilities, Sous took on the role of QA liaison to Japan and from that base gradually expanded his international role. Because of the personal contacts he made during those meetings and in trips to BD locations outside the United States, Sous was increasingly identified as the best person to contact for technical support—especially in the problematic area of support for products deemphasized or discontinued in the United States. As issues in which he was involved came up, he began to attend the WBCT meetings in an unofficial capacity, eventually attending regularly.

When Joseph Welch left BDVS in January of 1990 to become president of BD Labware, and Steven Savitz took his place as VP of R&D, Savitz defined his role as "doing worldwide R&D for the division." His non-U.S. colleagues viewed him as "genuinely transnational." Savitz strengthened the international role Steven Sous had taken, in 1991 giving him the new title of manager, Research and Development Worldwide Technical Support. Sous and his group were responsible for working with the non-U.S. businesses to support and extend products, including responsibility for relatively small projects such as label changes, producing VACUTAINER tubes for high-altitude applications, and packaging variations necessitated by government regulations or differences in device-dispensing practices. Most of these "do it now" projects did not require large financial investment and did not need to wend their way through the division's major project approval and resource allocation process. To deal with demand, Sous hoped to expand his staff by four permanent positions in FY 1992.

During the same period, Kozy and Savitz responded to Lachenauer's long-term lobbying for a Europe-based R&D manager by appointing Chris Dufresne, Manager R&D VACUTAINER Systems Europe in BD's European headquarters. He reported to Lachenauer with a dotted line to Savitz, and was responsible for helping to manage the interface between European management and the U.S. R&D organization, particularly for expediting European new product and product extension ideas. Dufresne's position was a compromise between the European desire to be fully integrated vertically and the U.S. division's desire to maintain control over worldwide R&D efforts.

Dufresne lost no time in becoming a champion for European products. During the May 1992 meetings, he presented an ordered list of potential products for European applications. Many present agreed that his reputation and U.S. experience increased the likelihood that European ideas would be accorded serious consideration by the WBCT and by Kozy and Savitz.

During the May 1992 Toronto meeting, members of the WBCT discussed two important new developments in their technology management. First, BDVS was working with a consultant to refine the project approval and project management processes. Second, they discussed the need for greater non-U.S. participation in the R&D function. Although budget constraints prevented him from further expansion of the R&D organizations in regions outside the United States and Europe, Kozy was sympathetic to the requests. After much discussion, he and WBCT members from Mexico and Japan developed the idea of creating a position within the U.S. R&D organization to be funded jointly by Mexico and Japan.

All WBCT members saw clear evolution toward genuine transnational management in the team's operation. Roles and structures were clarified in practice and in the

"Worldwide Blood Collection Manual" (on which Exhibits 6, 7, and 8 are based). But historic difficulties in achieving a real balance between the power of the U.S. division staff and the rest of the company's interests persisted. During the 1992 Toronto meetings, Lachenauer and Kozy and his staff clearly dominated many discussions from which their non-U.S. colleagues sometimes seemed disengaged. A rapid assessment of the development costs and sales potential of a list of proposed new products and product extensions yielded a priority list intended to guide the U.S. R&D function in its work over the company year, but some team members wondered privately whether they had either the time or the expertise to assess every project fairly. They cited examples of products such as the European-sponsored SEDITAINER tube, whose further development still languished in the face of the American medical directors' disapproval and American marketers' indifference.

THE WBCT IN 1993: ACHIEVEMENTS AND CHALLENGES

After the WBCT met in Geneva in May of 1993, many participants sensed that the group was continuing to evolve toward a genuinely transnational position. Where they once struggled to achieve consensus around uniform global strategies and goals, they were now comfortable with regional variations consistent with overall worldwide strategies and business goals. For example, because European members preferred a marketing strategy that emphasized choice between glass and plastic, the group discussed selling the PLUS TUBE under another name in Europe to avoid implying invidious comparisons to the glass tubes they planned to sell alongside plastic for a few years. U.S. participant Tom Jaeger saw this and other local market-specific discussions as good indications of the WBCT's evolution toward a genuine transnational mentality:

> Even in the most recent meeting before this, we felt there had to be a worldwide consensus on business strategy; now a consensus has arisen that we can have different strategies . . . we need to have everyone understand, and decide on a regional basis exactly what to do. I believe in that—that everyone is the keeper of their own markets.

Furthermore, the WBCT's ability to respond rapidly to worldwide needs had developed considerably. When members representing Japan pushed for rapid expansion of catalogue numbers to include smaller tubes and a wider range of coatings and additives, many were elated by a six-month concept-to-release process for a new additive tube for Japan undertaken in 1992, remarking that without the R&D proposal review and priority-setting capacities of the evolving WBCT, such speed would have been inconceivable.

The group also broadened international participation in R&D decision-making. The European director of Operations and a senior European marketing manager joined the worldwide Project Approval Committee, thereby bringing the group to U.S./European parity. Furthermore, WBCT members had already agreed to place sponsored engineers from Europe, Japan, and Latin America on the U.S. R&D staff.

Members saw considerable change in WBCT team members' ability to communicate and negotiate shared and divergent strategies and operational parameters. A frequent WBCT participant with both R&D and manufacturing experience at BD observed that each member's understanding of the whole range of the business had deepened, and that members had learned how to argue for the projects they supported:

> Because of the Worldwide Team meetings, each of the different regions now looks at their marketplace a little bit differently because at meetings they have to explain to people from other parts of the world what's really going on. They have to get outside their tunnel vision, put a perspective on the whole thing. Someone can't just say, "This is the way it is," so he prepares his data to explain why his perspective might be different from theirs.

However, as he reviewed the WBCT's achievements, Kozy could not help wondering what additional changes would be required to keep the group operating effectively. Questions that particularly concerned him were:

- Does the business have the right configuration of assets and resources? In particular, what are the implications of our recent changes in the R&D function for the future of that key task? Should we try to keep our resources concentrated in the United States and expand the "sponsored liaison" positions, or should we yield to the European lobby for a more fully integrated European development capability? How can we balance the large-scale businesses in the United States and Europe, against the smaller businesses in the rest of the world?

- What changes do we need to make in our human resource policies and practices to move us further towards transnational management? What changes can we make to our human resource management system so we can send people on over-

---

EXHIBIT 9
Senior Management Bonus Plan Changes, 1993

Corporate Officers	Sector Presidents	Division Heads
Old formula:		
50% company (65% EPS vs. budget, 35% strategic)	25% company (65% EPS vs. budget, 35% strategic)	25% company (65% EPS vs. budget, 35% strategic)
25% strategic (function/company)	50% sector (65% OIBT vs. budget, 35% strategic)	50% unit (65% OIBT vs. budget, 35% strategic)
25% individual performance	25% individual performance	25% individual performance
New formula:		
75% company EPS* budget	25% company EPS* vs. budget	25% sector (65% OIBT vs. budget, 35% strategic)
	50% sector OIBT	50% unit OIBT
25% strategic (function/company)	25% strategic (worldwide sector)	25% strategic (worldwide teams)

*As reported for executive officers; FX neutral for other corporate officers.

seas assignment with some assurance that their careers won't be compromised? The new compensation system has been favorably received [see Exhibit 9], and should help us get over the conflict between the WBCT and the regions caused by regional managers' being rewarded for maximizing the local budget, but what else can be done to increase WBCT effectiveness?

- Finally, how should the WBCT's role evolve as we move into the future? Is there need for more structure and more clearly defined roles as some advocated, or should it continue to be managed on a more flexible process-driven manner? What impact will changing membership have on its operation, and can such personal dependencies be managed? Do a few strong managers dominate team meetings, and do we need to find ways to foster broader participation?

http://www.bdpcd.com

STRATEGY IMPLEMENTATION

CASE 29

SOR, Inc.: Issues of Implementation of TQM*

INTRODUCTION

Colbert Turney, Quality Assurance Manager, and Keith Gann, General Manager, had just received some troubling news. Mike Smith, team leader of the Foreign Order Process Team, had resigned from the team. Memos to the team members from the leader had revealed that the group was not functioning effectively. Had these same members not participated in extensive team training in Total Quality Management in 1989 and 1990? Colbert and the management staff felt that they had supported Total Quality and the team concept. The team members had been chosen from various departments at SOR, all of which were somehow involved in the problems in the processing of export sales (see Appendixes 2 and 3). What had gone wrong?

THE BACKGROUND OF SOR, INC.

Shortly after World War II, two machinists, Roy R. Dunlap and Clinton Nelson, met at Nelson's home to plot how they could put together their own business. What soon arose was MechniArts Associates—a tiny machine shop whose first product was a "dial attachment" for feed store platform scales. The product, Tel-A-Dial, was successful, but the new partnership had no means of marketing it. They eventually sold the idea to the Pennsylvania Scale Company.

The partnership found another opportunity in manufacturing a food tray table for TWA. The demand for the product spread to most of the domestic airlines and gave the business a foundation for future growth.

After more than 10 years in business, a former University of Kansas physics professor, Ben Brown, invited Nelson and Dunlap to join with him in developing a pressure switch. Brown had designed the switch but needed a machine shop to manufac-

---

*This case was prepared by Thomas L. Lyon, Ph.D., and graduate students Robert Bennett, Mark Gearin, Thomas Gibbons, Andrea Korff, Ann Marshall, and Steve Streeter, all of the School of Management, Rockhurst College, and is intended to be used as a basis for class discussion rather than to illustrate either effective or ineffective handling of the situation. Presented to and accepted by the refereed Society for Case Research. All rights reserved to the authors and SCR. Copyright © 1995 by Thomas L. Lyon, Ph.D.

ture it. If the product was successful, MechniArts would receive the manufacturing rights and Brown, a royalty.

The arrangement led to the creation of the Static "O" Ring Switch. The company's name was changed to reflect its single-minded attention to the new product: SOR, Inc. These switches are used to sense pressure in tanks and pipes and to turn pumps, heaters, and warning lights on and off. They are used mainly by two industries: petrochemical and nuclear and other power production. The 1990 sales of SOR had reached 16 million dollars. The company enjoyed sales growth and financial success throughout the 1989–1991 period.

Over the years, SOR has subscribed to three business principles which its management believes are the main reasons for the success of the company:

1. "Uncompromising insistence on product quality"

2. "Excellent delivery"

3. "Outstanding customer service"

SOR CHOOSES TO ADOPT TOTAL QUALITY

In early 1989, Colbert Turney faced a very important career decision. He was the drafting and design supervisor at SOR, but was considering a job change within the company that held not only uncertainty, but also a measure of risk. The position was Quality Assurance Manager (QA), and its present manager was about to retire. The position was not easy. The retiring QA Manager reported simultaneously to several department managers. The demands were heavy because customers in the nuclear industry pushed suppliers, such as SOR, to reach ever higher levels of quality.

Yet, SOR and whoever would become the QA Manager were about to face an even more difficult challenge. Motorola, a somewhat insignificant customer in terms of sales, called upon SOR to prepare itself to apply for the Malcolm Baldrige National Quality Award by 1995, if it wished to remain a Motorola supplier (which is still the goal). SOR could easily have afforded to let Motorola's business go and dispense with the monumental task of steering into Total Quality. However, looking ahead, SOR's management assessed the Motorola challenge as just the leading edge of the quality movement. Customer expectations of better quality were increasingly commonplace. It was probably just a matter of time before SOR would be asked to do something similar by other customers. SOR was about to get really serious on quality.

Colbert applied for the job and was accepted. As the new Quality Assurance Manager, Colbert quickly encouraged all of SOR's managers to attend a quality seminar at a local community college. The seminar, Transformation of American Industry (TAI)/Total Quality Management, excited many of the managers about quality concepts. Soon afterwards, Keith Gann, Senior V.P. and General Manager, and Jim Johnson, President and CEO, participated in a quality seminar presented by Motorola. The educational process continued until eventually all of SOR's employees entered the TAI seminar. The focus was on "cross-functional" teams. Employees received 48 hours of classroom training and spent an additional 20 hours on a seven-person team project. The teaching goal of the teams involved several hopeful outcomes:

1. Inculcate the principles of Total Quality Management

2. Instruct team members how to work together to solve problems and help each other

3. Elicit idea generation from the employees

4. Foster feelings of empowerment in the employees to make real changes in the organization

As the teams finished the courses, they returned to SOR to put their new training to work. SOR would rely on these teams as a critical ingredient in pursuing Total Quality. In the ensuing 3-year period, SOR's 188 employees would participate altogether on 62 teams and work on 2,000 ideas. (See Appendix 1, SOR's Quality Position, October 1990.)

SOR had an informal steering committee at the beginning of the TAI process. By the time the Foreign Order Process Team was formed, the steering committee no longer met. Each department Vice President or Director formed teams as needed for special projects/problems in the department. And employees could still form a team if they saw a problem/opportunity and management agreed to support the project.

FOREIGN ORDER PROCESSING AND THE "PROBLEMS" THAT LEAD TO THE FORMATION OF THE FOREIGN ORDER PROCESSING TEAM

SOR sold its products to customers in several countries throughout the world. The International Sales Department entered the foreign orders into the computer, and production built the product. Finished product shipments were sent to specific countries on set days of the week. For example, Canadian orders were shipped on Tuesday, and Japanese orders, on Thursday. The reason given for this consolidation of shipments was that it saved freight costs for the customer. On any shipping day, accounting had to receive paperwork for finished product from the plant by 10:30 A.M. Accounting then processed the invoices and sent them to Carla Fields in the International Sales Department. Carla needed them by 1:30 P.M. so she could complete the necessary export documents and pass them along to shipping. The Shipping Department required all of the papers and invoices by 3:00 P.M. to ship that afternoon.

One of the first activities of the team was to describe the process by using the flow charting tool that they had learned in the TAI/Total Quality Management seminar (see Appendix 3). Senior management had proposed this particular process for improvement because it believed the process was very cumbersome, resulted in too high an error rate, and was an important interface with the customer and, therefore, impacted customer satisfaction.

PERSPECTIVES ON THE "PROBLEMS" FROM TEAM MEMBERS WHO WERE INVOLVED IN THE FOREIGN ORDER PROCESSING

Carla Fields, Traffic Coordinator Many errors were made, mostly from problems with the flow of paperwork. Some orders were shipped without all of the paperwork, and some paperwork did not match the parts shipped. This caused orders to be delayed by customs at the border. She could not type the international documents without the invoices. She was receiving invoices as late as 2:30 P.M., which gave her only half an hour to get the documentation ready for orders due to go out that day.

Dave Fisher, VP—Finance It was not uncommon for the plant to bring orders to the accounting office for shipment that day after 10:30 A.M. This, in fact, became a common occurrence. As a result, paperwork to Carla was late, which delayed foreign orders scheduled to leave that same day. Each department in the process blamed the others for the problems.

Steve Engel, Inside Sales Representative: Canada It was taking 5 days to ship an export order, and he was receiving many complaints from his customers. He believed that the consolidation of orders for shipping finished products to specific countries on set days of the week was the reason. Even though cost savings to the customers on freight charges was the incentive, no one had surveyed the customers to ask if the shipping delay was worth the savings.

Melvin Hobbs, Manager of Final Assembly and Shipping If he did not receive the paperwork early enough in the day, his shipping department did not have enough time to ship the order. He felt that the delay in receiving the paperwork originated in accounting. This delay kept Carla from having enough time to process her part of the paperwork, and therefore, she was late in getting the paperwork to shipping.

THE TAI TEAM FORMED TO ADDRESS THE "PROBLEMS" AND IMPROVE FOREIGN ORDER PROCESSING

The Viewpoints of the Members on Their Team's Performance (See Appendix 2 on Team Progression and Memos)

Mike Smith, Drafting and Design Supervisor and Team Leader A fellow employee in production solicited his participation on the team. Although Mike had no knowledge or direct experience in foreign orders, he agreed to join and eventually became the team leader. He understood that the team's purpose was to streamline and improve the foreign order process. He had no direct stake in the activities of that process, but felt committed to help the team achieve its mission. He began experiencing frustration when some members displayed disinterest and participated only sporadically in the activities. Some came late or not at all to the team meetings. Lack of commitment at a personal level was one possible explanation. Training should not have been the problem. Before this group had formed, Mike and the others attended and completed the TAI–TQM course at the County Community College. The program had given them all the tools: Pareto charts, baselines, and data collection systems. Mike thought the group was composed of the appropriate people and was neither under- nor overstaffed. When asked whether management effectively explained and supported Total Quality, he recalled that a few members of his team still remained unconvinced about the usefulness of the concepts. In fact, some seemed threatened by the team. He viewed SOR's management as highly employee-oriented and sincere about achieving Total Quality. Still, decisions occasionally came down, which, in the opinion of some employees in the plant, appeared inconsistent with accomplishing that goal. Unable to reverse the squabbling and apathy that infected the team, Mike resigned from the group.

Pat Jones, Inside Sales Representative: Asia Pat had new hope for the implementation of a solution when he was drafted onto the team with Mike Smith as facilitator. He felt that the team members showed commitment to the process during the first few meetings, but the commitment vanished and turned into disillusionment. Members began showing up late, and much of the meeting time was consumed by complaining and finger-pointing. The friction in the group seemed to stem from the members who were directly involved in the ordering process; no one wanted to evaluate his/her own responsibilities. The team asked Pat to share in the collection of data. He disagreed and was reluctant to provide the data. Consequently, a serious disagreement between Pat and Mike arose. Pat differed from other team members, in that he believed the real problem lay at the end of the process. The conflict over this issue finally led to Mike asking Pat to resign. The complaining and dissension did not stop. Team members had lost all interest in the process. Soon afterwards, Mike advocated dissolving the team entirely. Pat came to the conclusion that Mike was at a disadvantage because, although he was the facilitator, he was also the only member who had no stake in the ordering process. Mike tried to lead by TAI principles, but felt that because of the members' particular backgrounds, the group needed tighter controls to follow the principles and procedures of team problem resolution.

Steve Engel, Inside Sales Representative: Canada In describing the team and its progress, Steve thought that in spite of the team members being very close to the process, it did not appear that solving the problem was very high on their priority list. When meeting, they discussed and argued without focusing on the problem at hand. When Mike Smith joined the team, Steve thought he added a bit of "neutralness" and hoped it would help them reach a solution. Even Mike's entrance did not help, as members still did not respond.

Larry DeGarmo, Manager of International Sales Larry felt he came into this team at a
disadvantage, since he was not aware of earlier group discussions that had taken
place prior to his entrance. He thought the root of the problem continued to
elude the group.

Melvin Hobbs, Manager of Final Assembly, Temperature Line, and Shipping Melvin
thought the team had all the tools and knew how to use them, but it still had trouble defining the problem. In his view, this occurred because the team members actually involved in the foreign order process were too protective of their territory.
The protectiveness fed on itself, slowed, and finally stopped the progress of the
team. When Mike became involved, Melvin believed it was a good idea. He felt
that people outside the process could break down the noncooperation of those involved in the process. However, Mike had no effect, and those members outside
the process soon became disinterested.

Dave Fisher, VP—Finance According to Dave, each team member was very territorial,
not wanting to admit to any weakness in his or her area nor give on any point. All
this led to more bickering and trading blame. With its leader out of the group and
the team still sputtering, management felt it had to intervene in order to make the
team function effectively and fix the foreign order processing problem.

When Mike Smith resigned, Melvin Hobbs thought a member of senior management should participate in the team. He believed that this team needed someone with
authority who could get the team moving and solve the problem. It was at this time
that Keith Gann joined the team.

Keith originally wanted to better handle the order process without adding staff.
Keith ultimately decided to create a position accountable for handling all the foreign
order paperwork by restructuring some responsibilities—an idea he had previously
rejected.

Although most of the team members agreed that the solution worked, and customers were purportedly more satisfied with the delivery service, many of the team
members were also skeptical of the outcome because of the forced solution.

APPENDIX 1

SOR's Quality Position, October 1990

It is SOR's policy to market only products of a quality that shall merit and earn customer satisfaction by performing reliably and effectively in accordance with customer
needs.

SOR is actively engaged in a companywide quality/productivity improvement
process. Over 90 percent of our employees have been trained through a 6-day (48-
hour) training course. The program is called Transformation of American Industry
(TAI).

Transformation of American Industry (TAI) focuses on implementing the business philosophy of Dr. W. Edwards Deming and the statistical techniques devised by Dr. Walter Shewhart. Training includes 48 hours in a classroom setting combined with hands-on experience. Each class consists of six or seven employees representing a cross-section of the company. TAI introduces a team approach to attaining quality goals. The program guides the teams through a step-by-step process of change, thus improving quality, productivity, and competitive position. The program is compatible with and advocates the utilization of "just-in-time" and "value analysis" concepts. Upon conclusion of the sessions, team members make a presentation to management, reviewing the tangible results of the training.

Team members learn how to . . .

- Work smarter.

- Do it right the first time.

- Reap the benefits of change.

- Identify and improve processes.

- Remove barriers that inhibit process improvement.

- Implement Dr. Deming's principles of management.

- Apply Statistical Process Control (SPC) techniques.

- Apply the power of the team concept using the TAI process.

- Improve quality while increasing productivity and profitability.

- Create an atmosphere whereby everyone works more effectively.

- Eliminate mass inspection by building quality into the product or service.

- Understand that process improvement needs to be constant and forever.

- Understand that business starts with customer requirements and satisfaction.

Eighteen teams have completed the TAI training and all have submitted project booklets. Some of the teams have continued intact as a team. Other teams have completed their projects and have formed new teams.

One team has studied ways to collect SPC data from our lathes and milling machines through an automated collection system. They attended seminars on various automated systems, interviewed sales representatives, called other manufacturing firms and tried different brands of systems. The team then made a proposal to management. Management approved the collection unit and all of the calipers, micrometers, and depth gauges needed.

The accompanying list of TAI projects shows the broad scope of ideas and projects to improve SOR. The 564 hours of formal quality productivity training is only a start. With a list of 1,736 ideas, we will be busy and see great stories in the next few months.

SOR has purchased a Coordinate Measuring Machine. The CMM measures parts through the use of an electronic probe that senses surfaces and compares their location by means of a computer program. With the CMM, parts are measured faster and more accurately than with manual calipers, micrometers, or gauges. The computer also stores the measurements and does a complete statistical printout of the parts features.

SOR relies on outside suppliers for many of its parts such as nameplates, wires, paint, castings, flanges, and some machined components. The supplier rating system is constantly being monitored to assure that we have the best suppliers and parts coming into SOR. Each week a team of SOR people consisting of the General Manager and a representative from Purchasing and Quality Assurance visits a supplier. During the visit a tour of their facility is made. Usually the team is asked to speak to the supplier's whole workforce. Quality goals are explained to the supplier's workers and the importance of their parts to SOR is emphasized. On every visit, SOR has found that there are ways to help the supplier deliver a better product. Often the supplier or its workers will ask about a dimension or feature on our parts which gives them difficulty. On some occasions the feature can be redesigned to simplify the manufacturing process.

Since 1983, SOR has supplied switches to the nuclear industry that are 1E qualified. Any supplier of 1E qualified products to the nuclear industry is subject to audits of their quality system by the nuclear users. SOR's nuclear QA program has been audited by nuclear utilities over 100 times. Two audits were by the Nuclear Regulatory Commission. As the nuclear industry has become more stringent on QA requirements, SOR has maintained its name on the utilities approved lists. The commercial QA nuclear program implements the same techniques and quality principles as the nuclear program and has successfully passed all commercial audits. A copy of SOR QA manuals will be made available upon request to any responsible party.

Colbert Turney, QA Manager

APPENDIX 2

The Foreign Order Process Team started in the fall of 1989 and was disbanded in the fall of 1991.

Team I-A Fall 1989	Team I-B
Steve Engel—Inside Sales Representative: Canada	Steve Engel
Teresa Berry—Sales Secretary	Pat Jones
Pat Jones—Inside Sales Representative: Asia	Lana Ellis
Lana Ellis—Accounting and Insurance Clerk	Linda Woods
Linda Woods—Shipping Coordinator	Melvin Hobbs
Melvin Hobbs—Manager, Final Assembly and Shipping	Carla Fields—Traffic Coordinator

Team I-C	Team I-D Fall 1991
Steve Engel	Steve Engel
Pat Jones	Linda Woods
Lana Ellis	Melvin Hobbs
Linda Woods	Carla Fields
Melvin Hobbs	Dave Fisher—Vice President, Finance
Carla Fields	Larry DeGarmo—Manager, International Sales
John Reese—Shipping Coordinator	Keith Gann—General Manager
Mike Smith—Drafting and Design Supervisor	

Team membership changed over time. Only Hobbs, Woods, and Ellis were on the team the entire time period. Company policy was that individuals might be asked to be on a team, but participation was voluntary. Teams 1-A through 1-D represent the membership composition over the time period from 1989 through 1991.

INTER - OFFICE CORRESPONDENCE
SOR   P. O. Box 591   11705 Blackbob Road

Olathe, Kansas 66061

TO: Linda Wood, Steve Engel,   FROM: Mike Smith
      Melvin Hobbs, Lana Ellis,
      Pat Jones, Carla Fields   DATE: April 4, 1991

SUBJECT: TAI-FOREIGN ORDER PROCESSING MEETING MINUTES FROM 4/2/91

The team had decided at the last meeting to collect data so that a baseline for improvement could be established. Unfortunately, not everyone collected data. Those of you who did, the Team thanks you for your efforts. We re-discussed the importance of collecting data in helping to make future decisions. As a team, we should help each other out as we go through the process of improvement.

As outlined in our meeting minutes of 3/13/91, all members of the team need to make an effort to continue data collection or at least start collecting.

We will meet again on 4/9/91, from 12:30 to 1:30, in the Mfg. conference room to review the data collection progress.

Mike Smith

MS/lg
04049101

cc: Joel Bradley
    Larry DeGarmo
    Colbert Turney

INTER - OFFICE CORRESPONDENCE

SOR   P. O. Box 591   11705 Blackbob Road

Olathe, Kansas 66061

TO: Linda Wood, Steve Engel,   FROM: Mike Smith
      Melvin Hobbs, Lana Ellis,
      Pat Jones, Carla Fields   DATE: April 16, 1991

SUBJECT: TAI-FOREIGN ORDER PROCESSING

Due to the lack of commitment from team members and minimal progress since our
first meeting February 2, 1991, I recommend that the team be dis-banded due to
the following reasons:

   1)   Not showing up at scheduled meetings on time or not at all.

   2)   Lack of completing volunteered assignments, (i.e., flow charting,
         data collecting).

   3)   Lack of group participation.

Mike Smith

MS/lg
04169106

cc: Keith Gann
    Colbert Turney

APPENDIX 3

The foreign order process flow chart depicts five distinctive sub-processes within
SOR. They are labeled A through E on the flow chart.

A represents the sales process, and Jones, Engel, and DeGarmo all played a role in
the team from this area of SOR.

B represents the manufacturing process, and Hobbs was the team leader from manufacturing at SOR.

C represents shipping, and Woods and Reese were team members from the process
area of SOR.

D represents the accounting and invoicing process, and Ellis and Fisher were team
members from this area of SOR.

E represents the traffic process at SOR, and Fields was the team representative from
this area.

FOREIGN ORDER PROCESSING

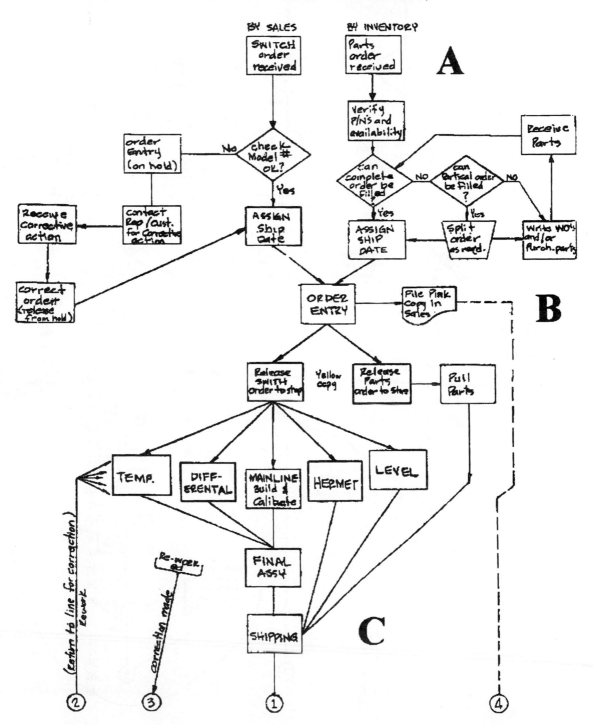

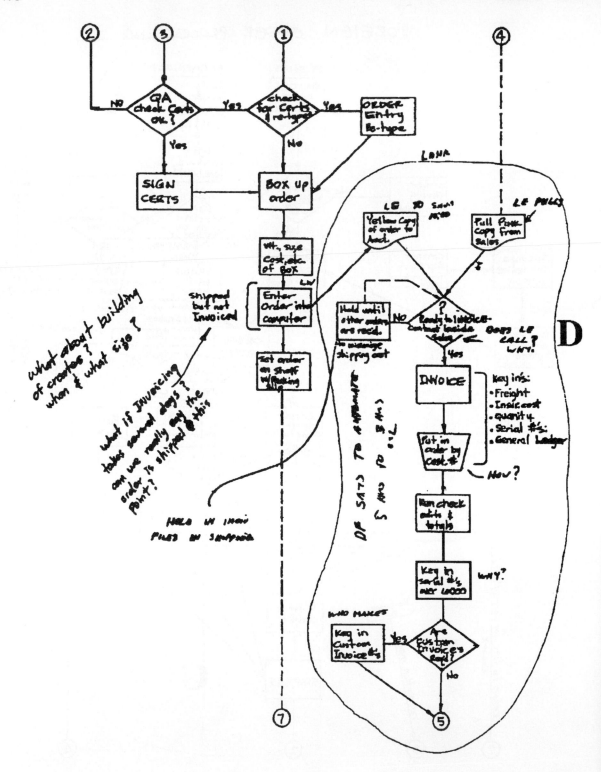

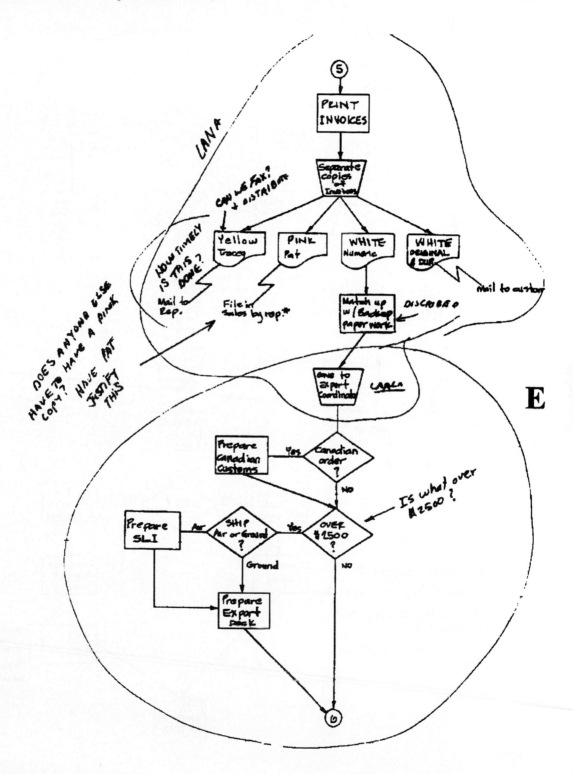

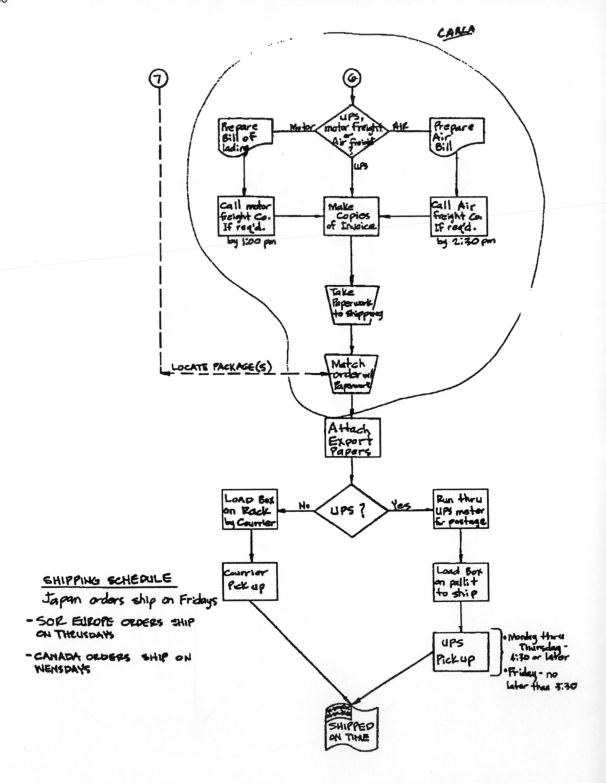

CARLA

SHIPPING SCHEDULE
Japan orders ship on Fridays

- SOR EUROPE ORDERS SHIP
  ON THRUSDAYS

- CANADA ORDERS SHIP ON
  WENSDAYS

SOR

May 23, 1991

Documentation Requirements for Projects & Foreign Orders

1)Direct Foreign Orders

Purchase orders from foreign customers with payment terms of Cash Against Documents or Cash In Advance - The P.O. will indicate which freight forwarder is to be used, documents required to allow the goods into the country and for payment purposes. We have to coordinate with production/shipping to find out when the goods will be ready and call (most of the time it is long distance and this will have to be considered if a traffic coordinator will handle these orders) the freight forwarded to find out where the goods are to be sent. The packing list must contain the total cartons, total gross and net weights and carton dimensions. If it is an air freight order, generally we can give the weights and dimensions to the freight forwarder on the phone and they will give us the address. Prior to invoicing, the weights and dimensions have to be entered on the order (the person will have to be trained in order entry procedures and have a terminal). The goods are invoiced and all paperwork from accounting must be returned to the person handling the order as:

1) 4 copies of the invoice and packing list must go to the freight forwarder, 2) SLI must be completed so the goods can leave the USA, 3) duplicate invoice is to be put with the backup paperwork on the job for future reference in case there are problems with the units or replacements are needed, 4) a letter has to be included with the documents advising the freight forwarder whether the goods are to go freight collect or prepaid, if a special airline is to be used, whether or not legalized documents are needed, whether or not SOR will do the banking, and to return the original AWB to SOR (a typewriter will be required for this job), 5) once the AWB is returned, the original invoice, packing list, AWB and other documents as required on the order must be mailed to the customer for payment. At this point, the Numeric copy of the invoice and related documents are to be stapled and returned to the sales area for filing.

P. O. Box 15964 • 14685 W. 105 St. • Lenexa, Kansas 66215 USA • (913) 888-2630 • FAX (913) 888-0767

SOR INC. Static "O" Ring CONTROL DEVICES INTERNATIONAL TELEX NUMBER 499-2783 SOR UI

SOR

If you want to relieve sales of Letters of Credit and Cash Against Document procedures, this should be handled by Accounting as these are accounting functions (getting payment from the customer). Review of P.O.'s and doing L/C's requires a person who can handle detail work. The work area must be free of distractions and have quiet surroundings as concentration to detail is critical. A traffic coordinator in the shop doing accounting functions would be a mistake.

Larry DeGarmo

P. O. Box 15964 • 14685 W. 105 St. • Lenexa, Kansas 66215 USA • (913) 888-2630 • FAX (913) 888-0767

SOR INC. Static "O" Ring CONTROL DEVICES INTERNATIONAL TELEX NUMBER 499-2783 SOR UI

http://www.sor.com/

STRATEGY IMPLEMENTATION

Kyocera Corporation, 1996*

Kyocera is a world leader in applied ceramics technology, a major force in the Japanese telecommunications industry, and a global competitor in a wide range of products including electronic and optical components, instruments, and equipment. Exhibit 1 presents a 10-year financial summary of the company. The company's accomplishments are widely recognized both in its home country of Japan as well as abroad:

> From its inception in 1959, a small electronics maker in Kyoto grew to become a legend in Japanese business. Kyocera was seen as more than simply a solid company in its field; it was widely regarded as one of the best all-around companies in Japan, a model for executives to look up to.—*Tokyo Business*

> What company do the Japanese admire most for entrepreneurship and technological progress? Sony? Honda? Toyota? Guess again. In four surveys over the past five years—most recently in a sampling of 15,000 Japanese executives published by the principal national business newspaper—top honors have gone to an outfit called Kyocera Corp. . . . Kyocera's success provides vivid lessons in how to make things well, how to manage people, how to innovate, and how to diversify.—*Fortune*

KYOCERA—A COMPANY OF PARADOXES

The company's success has been attributed to a unique and often paradoxical blend of culture, leadership, organization structure, and corporate strategy. Although Kyocera competes in numerous high-visibility markets, the company made its reputation in markets unfamiliar to most people. Kyocera introduced some of the first laptop computers (sold by Radio Shack under the Tandy brand), manufactured VCR equipment for Hitatchi, and produced the Yashica line of cameras. However, its excellence in producing ceramic products for markets obscure to the general public earned Kyocera respect the world over.

The ceramics in which Kyocera specializes transform the ancient craft into an exciting technology with a seemingly endless array of applications. Kyocera's high-tech ceramics bear little resemblance to traditional ceramic tiles or teapots. Most of its products are complex, highly purified synthetic materials with exotic names such as zirconia and silicon nitride. Ceramic products range from metal cutters, synthetic

---

*Written by Alex Miller, University of Tennessee at Knoxville.

EXHIBIT 1
Kyocera Corporation: Financial Summary
(in millions of dollars)

	1996	1995	1994	1993	1992	1991	1990	1989	1988	1987
				Income Statement						
Revenues	$7,000*	$5,741	$4,177	$3,755	$3,412	$3,280	$2,668	$2,566	$2,403	$1,892
Operating income	N.A.	1,091	694	610	521	564	513	526	444	339
Depreciation	N.A.	327	269	268	203	169	133	114	112	107
Interest expenses	N.A.	24.5	13.0	28.6	26.2	26.7	30.4	12.3	10.7	3.9
Pretax income	N.A.	935	668	428	436	464	454	464	403	259
Effective tax rate	N.A.	47%	46%	51%	53%	51%	53%	52%	55%	54%
Net income	550*	498	359	208	204	229	214	225	181	120
				Balance Sheet						
Cash	N.A.	$2,578	$2,291	$1,525	$1,583	$1,644	$1,436	$1,857	$1,623	$1,333
Current assets	N.A.	5,174	4,143	3,201	3,093	3,106	2,683	2,925	2,723	2,178
Total assets	N.A.	8,924	6,839	5,403	5,017	4,793	4,126	3,951	3,606	2,922
Current liabilities	N.A.	1,450	988	794	1,058	867	729	583	568	410
Long-term debt	N.A.	525	461	85.0	78.0	361	413	558	346	414
Common equity	N.A.	6,659	5,270	4,447	3,824	3,506	2,908	2,760	2,643	2,054
Total capital	N.A.	7,187	5,734	4,534	3,903	3,868	3,325	3,321	2,992	2,471
				Other Financial						
Capital expenditures	N.A.	$ 438	$ 224	$ 273	$ 290	$ 247	$ 204	$ 148	$ 133	$ 93.0
Cash flow	N.A.	$ 825	$ 628	$ 476	$ 407	$ 398	$ 347	$ 339	$ 293	$ 227
Average annual P/E ratio	N.A.	25.0	30.9	48.1	29.5	36.3	40.5	33.7	29.4	34.6
Relative P/E ratio	N.A.	1.68	2.03	2.84	1.79	2.32	3.01	2.55	2.44	2.31
High stock price	$155.0	$184.0	$154.3	$122.9	$ 74.5	$103.0	$126.0	$ 92.9	$ 91.2	$ 94.0
Low sock price	$126.5	$123.0	$104.0	$ 64.5	$ 51.0	$ 60.0	$ 74.0	$ 66.9	$ 68.0	$ 45.7
Stock beta	.70	N.A.	N.A.	N.A.	N.A.	N.A.	N.A.	N.A.	N.A.	N.A.
Translation rate (¥/$)	105	107	89	103	116	133	141	158	132	125

*Estimates.
Sources: Value Line; Standard & Poor's Stock Reports.

jewels, scissors and knives that need no sharpening, heating elements, artificial joints and teeth, engine parts, temperature sensors, and printing heads for fax machines.

The company's greatest success has come in producing ceramic packages for integrated circuits (ICs). Kyocera holds 65 percent of the global market for IC ceramic packages. These packages hold delicate semiconductor chips and protect them from all matter of harm. The ceramics involved are produced by purifying and homogenizing ceramic powder, forming it to the desired shape, firing it using exacting procedures, and then further processing it as needed for specific applications, including glass coatings, metal plating, and attaching metal parts.

Making ceramic packages requires highly technical work, but many firms possess the technical skills required to make the parts in small quantities. Historically, Kyocera's expertise lay in producing them by the millions at very low cost and very high quality, a self-perpetuating form of expertise. As one industry observer explained: "In a business such as ceramic packaging, big is beautiful. The more products you make, the more experience you get. Feeding this knowledge back in the production line enables you to improve quality and reduce costs."

Although prototypically Japanese in many of the ways it manages people (such as stressing lifetime employment), Kyocera is very atypical of Japanese firms in other regards (such as assigning jobs strictly on merit without regard to seniority). Many of its manufacturing practices—such as simultaneous *kaizen* improvement of quality, cost, and delivery—follow a decidedly Japanese approach which contrasts noticeably with Kyocera's emphasis on innovation and growth through original research which is considered atypical of Japanese firms. The stereotypical Japanese strategy begins with a low-end product sold at home, and improves the product over time, establishing a strong domestic presence in Japan, before moving into global distribution. Kyocera has regularly followed part of this strategy: it often moves into a new market with a low-end product. But it typically develops a strong base for the product *outside* Japan before focusing on domestic sales in the company's home market. For instance, in laser printers, Kyocera became a prominent competitor in Europe while capturing only 2 percent of the Japanese market.

Many of the Kyocera paradoxes can be traced back to the company's history and its enigmatic founder Kazuo Inamori, his philosophies on life and business, and the unusual company culture these forces combine to create.

COMPANY HISTORY

Kazuo Inamori was born in 1932, the son of a printer whose family business was closed by World War II. The family struggled economically, and young Inamori had to negotiate with his father to be allowed to continue his education. He attended little-known Kagoshima University in the backwaters of Kyushu, and graduated in 1955. After graduation, he could only find a job working as a chemical engineer at the tiny Shofu Kogyo Company, where he worked on new ceramic products for 4 years. When Shofu's union went on strike, Inamori convinced his subordinates to keep working for the sake of their customers. After arguments with Shofu's research director about the director's treatment of subordinates and lack of vision about ceramics' future, Inamori left the company and founded Kyoto Ceramics (since shortened to Kyocera) with seven friends and an investment of ¥8,000 (the equivalent of approximately $10,000 in 1959).

The early years at Kyoto Ceramics were not easy. For several years, the company only had 24 employees, who worked 16-hour days (including Saturdays) before retiring in the company dormitory. They visited with their families only on an occasional Sunday. Still, the struggling company found the Japanese market offered little enthusiasm for its products.

Initially, Kyocera used a very unsophisticated approach to management. Some of the tiny company's first successes were largely due to management's ignorance of conventional business practices. For example, unaware that established industries in Japan were spending 20 percent of their revenues on sales, general, and administrative expenses, Kyocera held these to 12 percent by relying on its own salaried sales force instead of paying distributors, a "mistake" that added eight percentage points to the company's pretax profit margin.

The company's early products were as unsophisticated as its management practices. The firm first sold simple thread guides to the textile industry, where its porcelain could hold up well to the wear of thread and fabrics. Inamori's goal of becoming a major industrial supplier of ceramic parts was stymied by resistance encountered in the Japanese market. As he later explained, Inamori came to believe that "in Japan, corporate history and appearances are critical factors in determining business relationships. Japanese society is very conservative and this favors established giants. But one can do business in the United States as long as one has creativity, innovative products, and integrity." Consequently, in 1963, Inamori traveled to the United States, hoping to find customers who could provide him with greater legitimacy back in his home country. He targeted the emerging U.S. semiconductor industry as a key market for ceramic applications.

In the United States, Kyocera developed a reputation for happily accepting the technical challenges competitors refused. The company defined itself more in terms of customer service than in terms of products, considering itself a "producer of high-technology solutions." The firm's service soon became legendary among Silicone Valley chipmakers where Kyocera considered no "garage inventor" too small to be served. The company provided design and technical assistance to all customers and potential customers at no extra charge, and its nothing-is-too-much-trouble attitude eventually won the hearts of engineers at many U.S. chipmakers, such as Intel and Motorola.

Many outside the industry attribute Kyocera's success in IC ceramic packages to the development of leading technology. However, industry insiders explain it differently. Bob Johnstone, a business reporter for *Far Eastern Economic Review*, concluded from his in-depth historical analysis of the company that Kyocera's success had little to do with its technology and everything to do with how it related to customers. Johnstone wrote: "Kyocera has contributed no major innovations to ceramic microchip packaging. . . . When Kyocera set up shop in California's Silicone Valley in 1969, U.S. firms such as RCA had already established most of the basic skills needed to make IC packages. And, even today, rivals such as IBM and NGK Spark Plug can run rings around Kyocera when it comes to materials science." Johnstone concluded that the key to understanding Kyocera's success lay in its unbeatable customer service.

Asa Jonishi, Kyocera's first U.S. salesperson, readily admitted the company's success "was not really technology, it was service." Jonishi explained that when U.S. chipmakers had a problem, Kyocera made heroic efforts to respond overnight while competitors regularly took weeks to find a solution. When customers needed samples of a new product, Kyocera worked around the clock to be the first to supply them. When customers had problems with quality, Jonishi himself rushed to the factory to weed out defective parts. A former Kyocera international executive who became a consultant to the semiconductor industry confirmed Jonishi's point: "Direct personal service is their secret. Kyocera has 12 direct sales offices in North America, with 50 salespeople in the field at once, each supported by customer-service people and administrative assistants. No rival ceramic package supplier comes close to matching Kyocera's strength on the ground."

An example of such service occurred in the late 1960s, when Kyocera lavished special attention on Fairchild Semiconductor Corporation, the seminal firm in its industry. Kyocera salespeople visited every day, developing relationships with everyone from shipping clerks to the president. In 1971, Fairchild decided to abandon its struggling ceramic packaging business. It outsourced production of those parts to Kyocera, and sold its ceramic packaging plant to Kyocera for this purpose. With Fairchild out of the business, Kyocera became the only company left in this niche market. But this monopoly position did not ensure its success. The new factory went through seven plant managers trying to solve the problems of making a viable ceramic package for Fairchild's semiconductors. Kyocera's devotion to the Fairchild business paid off unexpectedly. As Fairchild itself struggled, numerous employees left the firm to strike out on their own. These so-called "Fairchildren" included the founders of Intel, National Semiconductor, and Advanced Micro Devices, all of whom left Fairchild as devoted Kyocera fans.

CHAIRMAN KAZUO INAMORI

Kazuo Inamori, Kyocera's Chairman, prided himself on being fiercely un-Japanese on one point: his maverick nature. Throughout his career, he has constantly defied the Japanese establishment, regularly blasting his native country for being too concerned with maintaining the status quo. Highly creative himself, Inamori devoted tremendous time and energy encouraging young engineers to "do things no one has ever done before." As he explained it, much of his emphasis on the need for mavericks to resist the traditional Japanese system stemmed from his personal history at the time he founded Kyocera:

> Japan's traditional environment is that of the rice-farming village. Each village had a presiding patriarch whose job, from season to season, was to maintain a peaceful environment. If there is an individual who does extraordinary things, he is left out because he harms the harmony of the village. This goes against the spirit of independence, of entrepreneurship.

But I was the one who acted against the village patriarch. I was the outlaw who was about to be expelled.

Instead of being "expelled," the "outlaw" eventually became one of Japan's most highly respected corporate leaders. He was named Japan's most effective manager twice by *Nikkei Business*, a leading Japanese business magazine, and the press called him "the quintessential Japanese manager" of "the perfect company." But he was also called the "myth-breaker from Japan" and his company was regularly criticized on a number of fronts. Like his company, Inamori is an enigma comprising many paradoxes:

■ Though he has been identified as a follower of Max Weber, a founding father of socialist thinking, he has also been called "the most capitalistic guy in Japan."

■ While he has been accused of "making money like a thief," he is also a philanthropist who has given away millions. (Inamori gave $100 million to establish the Inamori Foundation to administer the $320,000 Kyoto Prizes for innovators in fields overlooked by the Nobel awards.)

■ Although outsiders see him as Kyocera's "monarch and god," and its "absolute autocrat," he insists that employees inside the organization must feel free to question anyone, including himself.

■ When he could not find a job upon graduation, he thought, "Perhaps I should become a Robin Hood type outlaw, . . . a gangster boss in southern Japan," but more recently, he has threatened to quit work at Kyocera to become a monk.

■ He insists that "I am not influential, so I can't have a strong voice. I am not powerful enough to change opinions." But he has also boasted that his managers disseminate his strategic philosophy "the way Christ's disciples spread his teachings."

■ Inamori self-effacingly calls himself "a country boy," claiming that he is too unsophisticated to use anything as complex as a corporate strategy and seemingly bragging about how little he knew about business when he founded Kyocera. Yet, he also talks about God-given talents for which he sees no bounds, and in a company brochure he proclaimed that "after 30 years of continuous refinement, Kyocera technology is today expanding toward microcosmic and macrocosmic levels that defy limitations."

None of these seeming contradictions are more paradoxical than Inamori's perspective on business. Dubbed Inamorism, his philosophy can be viewed as a combination of Zen Buddhism and Soviet-style socialism that results in a tremendously successful capitalist enterprise.

INAMORISM

The business philosophy of Kyocera's founder, Inamori, provides a central set of ideas by which the company is managed. Inamorism has been described in detail in 40 booklets that are widely circulated throughout the company. Here are several ideas comprised by Inamorism:

- The corporate motto is "Keiten Aiijin," which translates to English as "Respect the divine and love people." The importance of these two ideas has been explained by Kyocera managers: "We are a technology company. The further and deeper we venture into the boundaries of scientific facts, the more we are overwhelmed by the works of the divine." And "Business is but people working together for a common goal. It is through our relationship with other people that things are achieved. Improvement and happiness are only possible on the common basis of mutual love and respect."

- "Act like a vagabond." This statement was meant to convey the importance of independence and self-reliance. Such attributes were deemed essential to creativity, free thinking, and the focused pursuit of one's dreams. Inamori insisted that all employees should be free to tell anyone else in the organization—including Inamori himself—precisely what they thought as long as they were motivated by the good of the company and not by ego.

- "Only the individual who is willing to challenge the accepted beliefs and to put in the effort to break down such barriers can open the door to the future."

- "The essential nature of human beings is to pursue virtue. If you can feel that you have devoted yourself to your work, have been useful to society, and have been happy yourself, then you have a successful life."

- "Work is life. It is obvious that man does not work just to earn money. He seeks mental satisfaction; in other words, he tries to find meaningful joy in his work. What you have to do is change your arduous work into something that is worth living for."

- "One should always seek righteousness and not the easy way out. Unsuccessful people do not have tenacity: if something goes wrong, they give up easily. Never give up. As far as I know, there is no project that we have started on which we have given up. Because we continue until we are successful, we never fail."

- "Decisions should reflect a clear and pure mind that can see the truth. An egotistical mind can only see complications." Inamori taught that if you have a sincere and honest attitude, then suddenly, you can develop a sixth sense, a flash of insight he called "whispered revelations from God."

- Depth over breadth. "You can only become well-versed in the universe if you pursue one thing in depth. That is because inside of every fact or matter or thing lies the truth that governs them all."

- "A person who can manage a great business is a person who can give profit to his customers. Satisfying customers' needs while trying to maximize profit—this is business."

- "When a company is no longer on the offensive, that company is already beginning to go downhill."

- "Development is the continued repetition of destruction and construction."

KYOCERA'S CULTURE

Inside Japan, Kyocera maintains a culture that descends from the tiny organization Inamori founded more than 40 years ago, tempered by Inamori's philosophies and leadership. Its largest plant is located in Kagoshima, Inamori's birthplace on the southern island of Kyushu. Fresh out of high school, the youngsters who work at the manufacturing facility come from nearby farms and face few employment opportunities besides Kyocera. Young employees still live in dormitories, and the workforce joins in formations each morning for 10 minutes of teaching and mediation on Inamorism followed by physical exercises. At these morning rituals, foremen snap the plant manager military-style salutes and report the number of workers present. To instill a team spirit and encourage competitiveness, employee battalions face each other in intramural sports during off-hours. Employees are encouraged to marry other employees, and those spouses outside the workforce are often offered cottage industry jobs involving labor-intensive hand inspection of critical component parts. Upon their death, all employees have the right to be interred at the company cemetery on a monastery hillside near Kyoto. (Inamori has said that he wants to develop three-dimensional holographic images of deceased leaders so future employees can see images of past heroes when they visit the cemetery for posthumous advice in the form of recorded messages.)

Another holdover from Kyocera's early days is a managerial cultural norm of working long hours. In a speech to other business leaders, one senior executive from Kyocera described the managerial work norm as follows: "Most of the people who started with the company were working 15–16 hours every day including Saturday. . . . Working hours were gradually reduced, and now the professionals at Kyoto work only about 12 hours a day and only occasionally work on Saturdays." Social commentators have harshly criticized Kyocera for demanding what some consider to be excessively long hours, but Kyocera executives have responded by saying, "You may ask if they are workaholics, but how many of you know people who have achieved success without working hard?"

Insisting that success depends on devotion to a higher calling than self-interest, Inamori has built a distinctly Japanese reward system for Kyocera employees. In his book of philosophy, he explains, "we don't think in terms of individual rewards. We don't buy individuals' loyalty with monetary incentives or titles. Rather, we believe that individual workers endowed with superior capabilities should contribute their capabilities for the good of the entire group." Consequently, outstanding employees or leaders get no extra pay, though they may score points toward a promotion.

Inamori, and others on the Kyocera management team, have sought out various ways to break down barriers between organizational levels and to build employee loyalty. In Japan, Kyocera's executives wear the same modest celery-green uniform as the lowest employee in the hierarchy, and Inamori regularly joins workers and managers at Kyoto's footloose *karaoke* bars where he sings with a powerful baritone voice. The company has inspired levels of employee loyalty unusual even in Japan. During the oil crisis in the 1970s, the employees' union even went so far as to suggest a wage freeze in order to preserve the company's competitiveness. In return for such cooperation, the company seldom lays off an employee. It keeps the workforce lean in good times, depending on employees to use overtime to meet the demand. When demand drops, excess workers have been given brooms and paint brushes and told to go to work on the plant.

A key to sustaining Kyocera's culture is the corporation's "amoeba" management system, which Inamori and Kyocera have developed over the company's last 40 years. This management system is an obvious attempt to re-enact the earlier days of Kyocera's history over and over again within hundreds of micro-organizations scattered throughout the larger corporation.

THE AMOEBA MANAGEMENT SYSTEM

In the world of biology, an amoeba is a single-cell organism with no fixed shape that ceaselessly wanders about in search of what it needs to support itself. At Kyocera, amoebas are independent self-responsible units of 3–80 employees, that compete, contract, and cooperate among themselves and with outside sources to make a profit. Depending upon their success, amoebas can grow or contract, divide or multiply. The 13,000 Kyocera employees are grouped into around 800 amoebas, but the mix of amoebas changes daily with 40 or so amoebas being disbanded and a similar number of new ones created each month.

The objectives for some amoebas are established before the teams are formed, but other teams are formed first and expected to identify their own objectives. Kyocera's management doctrine states that "the company will only move forward if all amoebas pull in the same direction." While amoebas operate with a great deal of autonomy, responsibility for setting the overall direction falls to division managers. They achieve this by limiting amoeba responsibility to a prespecified range of products or services. Changes in these can be initiated by amoeba members, but they can only be implemented with the approval of division management.

Most amoebas focus narrowly on manufacturing or sales, and Kyocera treats all such amoebas as profit centers. As such, they are expected to produce products of the highest quality, achieve timely deliveries, negotiate the best selling prices, minimize production costs, and develop new products and/or services. The company treats some centralized functions for which no intuitive price can be established (e.g., quality control) as cost centers, called *hans*, rather than as amoebas, and allocates costs from these departments to the amoebas on the basis of the estimated benefit each amoeba receives.

If an amoeba cannot sell all its products or services in-house, it is encouraged to go outside the company for sales, and this keeps amoeba leaders aware of market prices and competitive developments. On the other hand, Kyocera places considerable emphasis on *not* going outside the company to buy a product or service offered by an amoeba in-house. If a supplier amoeba cannot outperform external suppliers, it is under constant pressure from both its internal customer amoeba and from higher management to improve its competitiveness. If using internal sources adversely affected amoebas, they go to outside suppliers—as long as the decision is clearly being made for the long-term good of the corporation. Such decisions are seldom made.

Amoeba heads typically serve in dual roles as team member and team leader. They are usually selected to be amoeba heads by the individual to whom they report, typically a division manager. Selection is based on qualifications (measured as technical and leadership abilities plus motivation to make the amoeba the best possible), not seniority. Day-to-day operations in the manufacturing and sales amoebas are not directly managed by central headquarters, although they depend on headquarters for support and advice. Amoeba heads and the managers to whom they report share supportive relationships. Division managers are most often former amoeba heads from within the same division. This practice ensures that managers have an intimate understanding of the issues amoeba heads face, so they can offer timely and useful advice. However, if the amoeba head disagrees with this advice, he or she has the option of consulting a level higher in the organization for discussion and resolution of the problem.

While the position of amoeba head carries considerable responsibility, such as responsibility for performance monitoring and reporting, it offers few perquisites. Heads receive the same workspace and employee benefits as other team members. Occasionally, due to poor amoeba performance, a head is replaced. The manager who had originally recruited and promoted the amoeba head makes this decision, but usually with consensus from all members of the amoeba team. Replaced heads transfer to other amoebas, and managers take great care to see that the individuals fit into the new groups in order to be assured of success.

The amoeba team proposes plans in discussion with upper management and bases performance goals on past performance tempered with consideration of future opportunities. They use two planning horizons to establish performance goals: a year and a month. The annual master plan reflects the amoeba's overall strategy, and monthly plans help ensure that the amoeba realizes its strategy. The master plan depicts an aggressive set of goals; monthly plans contain more realistic estimates of what an amoeba could accomplish short term. Performance against the monthly plan is publicized daily, and performance against the annual plan is reviewed monthly and posted publicly. Master plans can be revised mid-year to reflect changing conditions, but monthly plans are not altered once master plans with which they are linked are set into motion.

Kyocera evaluates performance against plans using both quantitative data and judgment. Quantitative measures vary depending on the nature of the work, but might include net production, manufacturing yields, manufacturing lead times, processing times, or added value. One measure used by almost all amoebas is value added per labor hour. Value Added is calculated as Amoeba Shipments − [(Internal Purchases + External Purchases) + (Internal Expenses + External Expenses)]. Internal expenses include salaries, interest payments, factory payments, selling expenses, etc. External expenses include raw material expenses, outsourced services, utility costs, etc. Value Added Per Labor Hour is used to show the contribution to creating value the average amoeba member makes with each hour of labor. Evaluation using such measures focuses first on performance against plan, and then on performance improvement over time, comparing the most recent 6 months to the preceding 6 months.

Amoeba members are expected to be experts at whatever they do, no matter how mundane the task. Inamori insisted that every position carries with it the responsibility to seek out creative solutions for improving *every* task for the betterment of the whole. All employees rotate through a variety of tasks, becoming experts in each, and constantly seeking to improve performance of the task at hand for the good of the company and society as a whole.

MANAGEMENT BY MEETINGS

The independence of the amoebas contrasts sharply with an elaborate web of meetings through which Kyocera's various initiatives are tightly integrated and monitored. Four organizational levels hold regular meetings: corporate, division, sales and manufacturing, and individual amoeba.

Inamori chairs the monthly corporate-level meetings, which typically begin at 9:00 A.M. and sometimes last until midnight. From 120–140 managers attend, and 40 or so address the larger group. Division managers speak first, followed by leaders from their manufacturing and sales groups. During these meetings, anyone is free to ask questions, although most questions come from Inamori. Known for his ability to analyze complex financial statements in only moments, he often asks pointed questions, and his reactions to poor performance range from long, heated discussions to incidents of throwing objects such as shoes and ashtrays. Poor performance is not determined by bottom-line figures alone, but instead takes into consideration the challenges facing a division. For instance, the solar energy group went for more than 20 years without having consistent profits, but it was not criticized as long as it was able to report continued progress and improvement.

Division-level meetings follow a format similar to the corporate-level meetings, but division heads play Inamori's role at these meetings. Accordingly, sales and manufacturing groups hold their monthly meetings, and individual amoebas meet regularly—sometimes once a day—to discuss management issues. Large numbers of people attend lower-level meetings, then a subset of the larger group attends the next-higher-level meetings and presents "macroscopic" overviews backed up with "microscopic" details available upon request. Bi-annual week-long meetings at which Inamori presides complement the monthly meetings, and involve 150–200 managers from overseas operations.

DIVERSIFICATION

In its early years, Kyocera focused exclusively on ceramics, but during the 1970s and 1980s, the corporation diversified into a variety of different businesses. Exhibit 2 provides a breakdown of recent corporate sales and profits by division.

Many of the new businesses were acquired when they were on the verge of collapsing. For instance, Kyocera moved into the calculator business, the citizens' band (CB) radio business, and the camera business, by buying companies which were all on the brink of bankruptcy. The company entered other new businesses as start-ups,

EXHIBIT 2
Kyocera Corporation: Sales* (and Operating Margins†) by Business Line

	1994	*1995*	*1996†*	*1997†*
Ceramics and components	$4,069	$3,961	$4,475	$5,050
	(17.1%)	(21.8%)	(20.0%)	(20.0%)
Electronic equipment	$1,060	$1,671	$2,525	$3,300
	(15.6%)	(25.8%)	(22%)	(20%)
Cameras and optical	$473	$416	$450	$450
	(8.4%)	(9.9%)	(10%)	(10%)
Company total	$5,802	$6,048	$7,450	$8,800
	(16.1%)	(22.1%)	(20%)	(19%)

*In millions of dollars.
†Before interest and income.
†Forecast.
Source: Value Line.

such as DDI Corp., the cellular network and long-distance service Inamori helped to create in 1985 when it became apparent that Japan would deregulate its telecommunications industry. In still another approach to diversification, Kyocera bought international companies that needed access to capital to fund growth. In 1989, Kyocera spent $250 million to buy Elco Corporation, a maker of electrical connectors, and $560 million for AVX Corp., the largest U.S. maker of multilayer ceramic capacitors, providing expansion capital for both businesses.

Kyocera's diversification strategy regularly found alternative uses for new assets if the initial plan for their use failed. For example, the company tried unsuccessfully to enter the consumer electronics, the photocopier, and the cash register businesses. While none of these attempts survived, the effort and investment put into developing each of them flowed into other businesses in which Kyocera was more successful. The consumer electronics business provided the experience necessary for making cordless and cellular telephones, and Kyocera's successful laser printer business traced its roots back to the failed photocopier business. And, although the company no longer produces cash registers, it does produce sophisticated point-of-sales retail systems. Kyocera's diversification may appear to have produced what one critic called "a lot of carnage," but as another observer put it, "Nothing is wasted."

Inamori dismissed critics of the corporation's diversification efforts as "not clever." As he explained in the early 1990s: "After we acquired a nearly bankrupt telecommunications company, they all said, 'Kyocera has gotten into an unprofitable march.' But that was the start of our vertical integration into telecom, which we completed after establishing DDI. Telecom will be a third of Kyocera's sales and it will be very profitable. I would say we have started to see the synergy effect."

This synergy effect was attributed to Kyocera's vertical integration. In justifying his diversification strategy to the financial community, Inamori repeatedly railed against the Japanese practice of building *keiretsu*—industrial cartels that interlocked dozens of Japanese companies and operated with and through the powerful Japanese Ministry of Trade and Industry to manipulate and control much of the Japanese economy. Inamori drew a sharp distinction between Kyocera's portfolio of vertically integrated businesses and other forms of Japanese corporate structure. He explained, "We don't belong to any groups. We protest at these tendencies and expect changes in the future." However, Kyocera built a collection of businesses linked through what Inamori described as "vertical diversification," that produced many of the same advantages as a keiretsu. President Kensuke Itoh explained: "We are unique in terms of the success of our diversification efforts. We are vertically diversified. We make materials, use those materials to make parts and devices, and then use those parts and devices to make useable finished products."

The Ecosys printer provides an example of Itoh's point. Ecosys was a light-emitting diode (LED) printer with a per-page operating cost about 65 percent lower than comparable laser printers. Kyocera originally entered the laser market with a conventional product, only to find it could not compete with Canon, the market leader. However, when another division in the corporation developed a proprietary amorphous silicon drum and a ceramic-based toner, the office equipment division was able to produce a very cost-competitive copier because the copier's drum—a key component in the printer cartridge—so rarely needed replacing. The Ecosys printers did very well in Europe, eventually capturing about 9 percent of that market.

But, critics say, for every Ecosys success story there are several counter examples of vertical integration that never panned out. Material companies around the world have spent hundreds of millions of dollars in trying to develop a ceramic engine block, as well as individual parts such as cylinder heads and cams, for internal combustion engines. Most have long since concluded that the application does not represent a feasible use of ceramics, while Kyocera continues to invest in the technology's development. Finally, Yuzuru Hayashi, Kyocera's director of corporate technology, explains: "You might think we are stupid, but there is nothing at this stage which indicates that ceramic engines will pay off." Asked why the company continued to invest in ceramic engine R&D, Hayashi shrugs, "For us it was an article of faith."

Inamori argues that the company's considerable financial success provides it with the breathing room needed to justify long-term R&D projects, such as ceramic engines. One Kyocera observer explained that Inamori sees such projects as "a proper balance between the dream of doing something difficult and the practical considerations of making a profit."

GLOBAL MANAGEMENT

Kyocera diversified not only in terms of the products it sold but in terms of the international markets it served as well. Managers at Kyocera spoke of three "profitability pillars" in the corporation: telecommunications in Japan, plus semiconductors and office equipment in the global market. Kyocera's approach to global operations often differs markedly from that of other Japanese firms. For instance, Inamori has placed two Americans on his board, which is very unusual for a Japanese firm.

But one of the most unusual aspects of Kyocera's approach to global operations is its CEO's strong stance in favor of free trade and heightened international competition. While most Japanese business leaders support efforts to protect their domestic operations using a complex set of international trade regulations that serve to limit entry of foreign competitors, Inamori has repeatedly lashed out against protectionist international trade policies in Japan: "The government's paternalism in 'maintaining order' has become a pretext for protecting existing interests, and the interest of the public is low on the list of priorities."

Kyocera's efforts on behalf of international trade and global competition are not limited to Japan. When asked about the U.S. Department of Commerce's concern that American semiconductor makers might be too dependent on Japanese suppliers for their IC housings, another Kyocera executive explained to the U.S. press that "it would be desirable if the U.S. government pushed some U.S. companies into making ceramic packages. The more competition, the better the products will be. After all, ceramic packaging started in the U.S."

Most of Kyocera's competition in the ceramic packaging business was located in Asia. NGK (which specializes in ceramics for spark plugs) and Sumitomo Ceramics, both Japanese firms, offered IC ceramic packaging comparable to Kyocera's. Samsung Electronics, a Korean company, also offered ceramic packages, though only on the low end of the market. In the United States, Kyocera's strongest competitor was Coors Porcelain Co., a division of the Coors Brewing Co. Coors triggered the U.S. Department of Commerce's interest in the ceramic packaging industry when it claimed that Kyocera domination of the industry constituted a threat to national security and economic competitiveness. Interestingly, Kyocera's defense came primarily from its U.S. customers, firms such as Motorola and Intel, that were well-connected in Washington, D.C. These firms lobbied on behalf of Kyocera, explaining that the U.S. semiconductor industry—of critical importance to the nation's economy—was absolutely dependent on the tiny parts Kyocera supplied.

ISSUES FOR THE FUTURE

In its core business area of ceramic housings for semiconductors, Kyocera faces its most important threat from plastics. In the early part of the 1990s, Kyocera's IC packaging business did not grow as rapidly as the semiconductor industry it supplied. (The early 1990s saw roughly 5 percent growth for ceramic housing versus double digit growth for semiconductors.) This was because plastic proved to be an effective low-cost alternative (with costs 30–50 percent less than ceramics) for housing many of the semiconductors used in the personal computer industry. However, by the mid-1990s, chip producers engaged in a fierce battle to produce faster chips. These faster chips produced greater amounts of heat than plastic housings could withstand. For example, Intel's Pentium chip produced 16 watts of heat, and the plastics available at that time could handle no more than 5 watts. (Kyocera played major roles in developing the ceramic packages for Intel Corporation's 80486 and Pentium chips as well as performing the same roles for Motorola Inc.'s PowerPC chip.) But most analysts expected plastics to be improved, so the real question for the long term was one of cost effectiveness and reliability. Some felt that ceramics had an advantage over plastics on these concerns. As one ceramics salesperson explained: "Someday plastics may replace ceramics, but the real question is can you guarantee reliability. When customers are paying $900 for chips like the first-generation Pentium, who cares if the packages cost $10?"

Another issue for the company concerns whether Kyocera's culture can be sustained as the company expands. There are signs of changes even within Japan, but as the company expands well beyond the initial base it established in Kyoto, maintaining its culture is becoming a special challenge. A Japanese business writer concluded that even domestically, Kyocera found its demanding hours to be "an obstacle in attracting the high-quality recruits the company needs to remain competitive." But the countries outside of Japan within which the company now operates include a wide range of cultures, not all of which are compatible with Kyocera's culture developed in a rural southern Japanese environment. For example, the amoeba management system that Kyocera relies on exclusively in Japan is not so evident in operations elsewhere. The company applies a "diluted' version of its management philosophy and practices in its San Diego, California, facilities, where 1,200 employees make ceramic packages. Instead of daily exercises, for instance, the San Diego plant employees follow an abbreviated version twice a week. And, although the San Diego workers like the job security and egalitarian manner in which they are treated, managers report that "their eyes glaze over when we talk philosophy." One vice president at the San Diego operation explained that the company was clearly not for everybody: "Two of my three kids probably couldn't work here. They're too independent."

One writer describes another issue concerning Kyocera as "Breaking the 'Inamori Dependency.' " Managers and directors at Kyocera agree that "a post-Inamori system does not yet exist" in the organization, and one observer put it this way:

> Kyocera's history is also the history of "Inamori Magic." Inamori announced proposals and then convinced his company that they were the right moves. As his vision proved on-target time and time again, employees came to believe in their leader's infallibility. Many inside and outside the company agree that Kyocera's rapid growth would not have been possible without Inamori's charisma.

The issues leave many long-time Kyocera watchers wondering about the corporation's future, and calling for a new vision for the company. In an article entitled, "Whither the Perfect Company—Can the 'Kyocera Myth' Be Revived?" *Tokyo Business* wrote:

> Inamori's [inevitable] withdrawal will probably further speed up Kyocera's evolution from an unusual, outstanding firm to simply an ordinary company. However, this shift is not necessarily a symptom for decline and can also be seen as a step toward a new growth period. Those responsible for the "post-Inamori" era need the courage to carve out a new vision for the future.

BIBLIOGRAPHY

Tatsuya Anzai, "Whither the Perfect Company—Can the 'Kyocera Myth' Be Revived?" *Tokyo Business Today 62* (February 1994), 48–50.

Robin Cooper, "Kyocera Corporation: The Amoeba Management System," case study published by Harvard Business School (1994).

Thomas Easton, "A Smart Japanese Buy," *Forbes 156* (November 20, 1995), 80–83.

Jonathan Friedland, "Companies: Samurai Sorcerer," *Far Eastern Economic Review 156* (June 3, 1993), 60–62.

Hideki Ishida, "Amoeba Management at Kyocera Corporation," *Human Systems Management 13*:3 (1994), 183–195.

Bob Johnstone, "The Customer Is King," *Far Eastern Economic Review 156* (June 3, 1993), 62–64.

Arthur Jonishi, "Kyocera Leader Outlines Success of Early Venture Business," *Business Japan* (October 1986), 39–41.

Kathleen Morris, "Born Again," *Financial World 163* (June 7, 1994), 62–67.

Christopher Parkes, "Rebel Without a Strategy," *Business* (January 1991), 64–67.

Nancy Rothbard and John P. Kotter, "Kyocera Corporation," case study published by Harvard Business School (1991).

Gene Rylinsky, "The Hottest High-Tech Company in Japan," *Fortune 121* (January 1, 1990), 82–88.

Shirley Skeel, "Not So Small, but Still Beautifully Put Together," *Management Today* (December 1990), 26.

Lewis H. Young, "Market Leader Kyocera Invites Competition," *Electronic Business Buyer* (December 1993), 86–90.

Milan Zeleny, "Amoeba: The New Generation of Self-Managing Human Systems," *Human Systems Management 9*:2 (1990), 57–59.

http://www.Kyocera.com/

STRATEGY IMPLEMENTATION

CASE 31

General Electric: Managerial Practices under Jack Welch*

Jack Welch became CEO and chairman of General Electric Company (GE) in April 1981. The organization he found himself heading was quite different from the GE of today both financially and managerially. Selected financial information from this period is shown in Exhibit 1, and a description of managerial changes from this period follows.

JACK WELCH AND GE: BEFORE APRIL 1981

John F. Welch, Jr., joined GE Plastics in 1960 after earning his Ph.D. in chemical engineering from the University of Illinois. When he received only the standard raise after his first year of employment, he quit work at GE because he believed he deserved more. Although he was talked into returning by his boss's boss, he was never again given simply the same raise as everyone else. In 1968, at only 33 years of age, Jack Welch became the company's youngest general manager ever. Welch's marketing acuity was in large part responsible for the success he achieved at Plastics, as GE overtook Du Pont, the market leader, in plastic sales for the automotive industry. Earnings at Plastics increased at a compound rate of 34 percent under Welch, and at 37 he was asked to head up the components and materials group, which added GE Medical Systems to his responsibilities.

Welch was not even included in the original list of candidates expected to succeed Reginald Jones as CEO, so his selection was a surprise to many. Welch was widely viewed as a maverick and a renegade. In contrast, Jones had developed GE's reputation for stability, sound management, and predictable earnings increases. However, Jones later explained that he was looking for someone to take GE to the next level—someone who could effect change.

Welch became a serious contender for the position in 1977, when Jones reorganized the company into six sectors and appointed one of six potential CEOs to each

---

*Prepared by Michelle Wright, University of Tennessee, under the direction of Alex Miller. Reprinted by permission.

EXHIBIT 1
General Electric Company and Consolidated Affiliates: Selected Financial Data
(in millions of dollars, except per share data)

	1994	1993	1992	1991	1990
Revenues	$ 60,109	$ 55,701	$ 53,051	$ 51,283	$ 49,696
Earnings from continuing operations	5,915	4,184	4,137	3,943	3,920
Earnings (loss) from discontinued operations	(1,189)	993	588	492	383
Earnings before accounting changes	4,726	5,177	4,725	2,245	4,303
Net earnings	4,726	4,315	4,725	2,636	4,303
Dividend declared	2,546	2,229	1,985	1,808	1,696
Earned on average shareowner's equity	18.1%	17.5%	20.9%	12.2%	20.2%
Per share*					
Earnings from continuing operations	$ 3.46	$ 2.45	$ 2.41	$ 2.27	$ 2.21
Earnings (loss) from discontinued operations	(0.69)	0.58	0.34	0.28	0.21
Earnings before accounting changes	2.77	3.03	2.75	2.55	2.42
Net earnings	2.77	2.52	2.75	1.51	2.42
Dividend declared	1.49	1.305	1.16	1.04	0.96
Stock price range	$54\frac{7}{8}$–45	$53\frac{1}{2}$–$40\frac{3}{8}$	$43\frac{3}{4}$–$36\frac{3}{8}$	39–$26\frac{1}{2}$	$37\frac{3}{4}$–25
Total assets	$194,484	$251,506	$192,876	$166,508	$152,000
Long-term borrowings	36,979	28,194	25,298	22,602	20,886
Shares outstanding—average (in thousands)	1,708,738	1,707,977	1,714,396	1,737,863	1,775,104
Shareowner accounts—average	458,000	464,000	481,000	495,000	506,000
Employees at year end:					
United States	156,000	157,000	168,000	173,000	183,000
Other countries	60,000	59,000	58,000	62,000	62,000
Discontinued operations (primarily U.S.)	5,000	6,000	42,000	49,000	53,000
Total employees	221,000	222,000	268,000	284,000	298,000

*Per share data reflect 2-for-1 splits in April 1983, April 1987, and April 1994.

Sources: General Electric Company, 1985 *Annual Report,* 1990 *Annual Report,* and 1994 *Annual Report.*

one. Welch was put in charge of Consumer Products and Services. The field was narrowed to three in 1979 as John F. Burlingame, Edward E. Hood, Jr., and Welch were all named vice chairmen. Burlingame's age and Hood's reserve showed Welch to be the best fit for the future of GE. In December of 1980, Welch was unanimously voted in by the Board of Directors as CEO-elect. The news made many GE employees nervous. John T. Cornell, a Paine Webber analyst, was quoted as saying, "The word inside the company is that he's chomping at the bit to go crazy once he takes over."[1]

The corporation Welch was asked to head was very complex. In 1981, there were nine organizational layers between the CEO and the shop floor. The numerous layers of middle management gave employees comfort. Everyone knew that there was plenty of room for upward movement, and GE's renowned ability to develop managers meant that there would be little outside hiring for the sought-after positions.

---

[1]William D. Marbach and Susan Dentzer, "General Electric's New Hi-Tech Boss," *Newsweek,* April 6, 1981, 76.

EXHIBIT 1 (continued)
General Electric Company and Consolidated Affiliates: Selected Financial Data
(in millions of dollars, except per share data)

1989	1988	1987	1986	1985	1984	1983	1982	1981
$ 54,574	$ 50,089	$48,158	$42,013	$28,285	$27,947	$26,797	$26,500	$27,240
—	—	—	—	—	—	—	—	—
—	—	—	—	—	—	—	—	—
3,939	3,386	2,119	2,492	—	—	—	—	—
3,939	3,386	2,915	2,492	2,336	2,280	2,024	1,817	1,652
1,537	1,314	1,209	1,081	1,020	930	852	760	715
20.0%	19.4%	18.5%	17.3%	17.6%	19.1%	18.9%	18.8%	19.1%
—	—	—	—	—	—	—	—	—
—	—	—	—	—	—	—	—	—
4.36	3.75	3.20	2.73	5.13	5.03	4.45	4.00	3.63
1.70	1.46	1.325	1.185	2.23	2.05	1.875	1.675	1.575
64³/₄–43¹/₂	47⁷/₈–38³/₈	66³/₈–38³/₄	44³/₈–33¹/₄	73³/₈–55⁵/₈	59³/₈–48¹/₄	58⁷/₈–45³/₈	50–27¹/₂	35–25³/₈
$128,344	$110,865	$95,414	$84,818	$26,432	$24,730	$23,288	$21,615	$20,942
16,110	15,082	12,517	10,001	753	753	915	1,015	1,059
904,223	901,780	911,639	912,594	455,381	453,680	454,768	454,078	455,056
526,000	529,000	491,000	492,000	506,000	520,000	501,000	502,000	514,000
243,000	255,000	277,000	302,000	—	—	—	—	—
49,000	43,000	45,000	71,000	—	—	—	—	—
—	—	—	—	—	—	—	—	—
292,000	298,000	322,000	373,000	304,000	330,000	340,000	367,000	404,000

The company was divided into 150 business units, each dedicated to a single product or product line. These units were equipped with support staff from all functional areas and grouped into businesses which were in turn grouped into sectors. GE's extremely diverse business portfolio encompassed everything from appliances to aerospace to information services. GE was a financially strong company; however, its growth rate was approximately equal to that of the gross national product.

> The trouble with such diversity is that it is impossible to be outstanding in so many fields. In a few, yes, but not in all. Even before he became chairman and CEO . . . Jack Welch . . . identified this as one of GE's major problems. . . . In short, the laggards, businesses like large transformer and TV set manufacturing, tie up capital and management talent without earning a commensurate return. Individually they do okay, but overall they have a negative effect.[2]

Welch took on the task of "taking GE to the next level" by articulating a new vision, focusing the organization on specific values, and developing new management

---

[2]Howard Banks, "General Electric—Going with the Winners," *Forbes*, March 26, 1984, 97–98, 102.

processes. Exhibit 2 summarizes many of the ideas developed and implemented under Welch, each of which is further developed below.

THE VISION: CHANGING THE GE PORTFOLIO

In the early 1980s, four main goals were responsible for driving GE's major business portfolio decisions. To remain a part of GE, individual business units were required to:

- Be No. 1 or No. 2 in the market they served

- Maintain substantially above average real return on investments

- Possess a competitive advantage

- Leverage existing strengths at GE such as technology, capital intensity, and management expertise

Even before Welch began preaching "No. 1 or No. 2," he changed the organizational chart. In the summer of 1981, Welch added two new sectors: Technical Systems and Services and Materials. Technical Systems was composed of the electronics-intensive operations of Aerospace, Industrial Electronics, Medical Systems, Advanced Microelectronics, and Mobile Communications. The Services and Materials sector focused on high-growth business units—GE Credit Corporation, Information Services, Engineering Materials, Plastics, Batteries, and Electromaterials. This rearranging was the genesis of Welch's strategic vision for GE.

In 1982, Welch made a sketch on the back of an envelope to answer critics who expressed the sentiment that GE was simply a conglomerate (Exhibit 3). He grouped the company's portfolio of businesses into three circles: core manufacturing units, technology-driven businesses, and services. Each of the units in the circles was made up of many previously stand-alone operations. Only businesses that were number one or two in their respective markets were allowed in the circles, and every business outside the circles would be fixed, sold, or closed.

EXHIBIT 2
Vision, Values, and Processes

Vision	Values	Processes
No. 1 or No. 2	Self-Confidence	Work-Out
+	↓	(internally and externally)
"Boundaryless company"	Simplicity	
(internally and externally)	↓	
	Speed	

Source: Russ Merck and Mike Grabarek, "Customer Focused Process Improvement Techniques," Presentation for GE Technical Leadership Development Course, August 16–21, 1992.

EXHIBIT 3
GE's Portfolio of Businesses as Classified by Welch

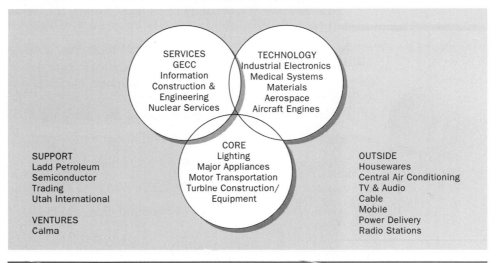

SERVICES
GECC
Information
Construction &
Engineering
Nuclear Services

TECHNOLOGY
Industrial Electronics
Medical Systems
Materials
Aerospace
Aircraft Engines

CORE
Lighting
Major Appliances
Motor Transportation
Turbine Construction/
Equipment

SUPPORT
Ladd Petroleum
Semiconductor
Trading
Utah International

VENTURES
Calma

OUTSIDE
Housewares
Central Air Conditioning
TV & Audio
Cable
Mobile
Power Delivery
Radio Stations

Source: Noel M. Tichy and Stratford Sherman, *Control Your Destiny or Someone Else Will* (New York: HarperBusiness, 1994), p. 107.

Welch's first 4 years were marked by divesture of business units which did not make the grade and reduction of the workforce. During this time, he liquidated one-fifth of GE's $21 billion asset base and cut the workforce by more than 18 percent. By 1986, he had reduced the workforce by more than 100,000. Miscellaneous corporate staff was also pared down from 2,100 to 900, and the second and third layers of management—sectors and groups—were eliminated. The cuts earned Welch the nickname "Neutron Jack" because where he "hit," the workers were gone while the buildings were left standing.

Welch argued these cuts were necessary to ensure the health of the company as a whole. In 1984, he pointed out that "overstaffing and incompetence are not only bad for a company but put every job in jeopardy."[3] Furthermore, Welch referred to the company's actions as a "renewal process" and one in which displaced workers were provided a "soft landing." In 1990, he explained, "We had to be hard-headed about the company's long-run competitiveness, but we could afford to be soft-hearted in dealing with the people we let go."[4] Evidence of the care taken to address personnel issues comes in the fact that during these 4 years of heavy layoffs, plant closings, and asset sales, there were no strikes. GE was careful to announce layoffs and closings well in advance and made extensive efforts to help people find new jobs.

Even so, pruning the workforce and changing GE's portfolio took an emotional toll not only on displaced workers but also on those workers who remained. In 1986, an executive in one of GE's mature businesses said,

---

[3]Ibid.
[4]Stephen W. Quickel, "Welch on Welch," *Financial World*, April 3, 1990, 64–65, 68.

Morale stinks. People are looking for jobs or waiting for a nice severance package. They talk openly about it. He is skeptical of Welch's ability to do more than cut costs. "I don't see the greatness that everybody says is here," he says. "I could understand if out of this devastation came something we could look to as the wave of the future. But I see a void.[5]

In Welch's first 2 years alone he sold 71 businesses while acquiring, starting, or forming joint ventures for 118 businesses. Many of these decisions were made in an effort to move the company away from traditional electrical products and into more high-technology and service-oriented areas.

Businesses divested which fell outside of the circles in Exhibit 3 include:

- Central Air Conditioning, sold in 1982

- Utah International, sold in 1984 for $2.4 billion

- Housewares, sold to Black & Decker in 1984 for $300 million

- Consumer electronics, traded to Thomson of France in 1987 for medical diagnostic business

- Semiconductor business, sold to Harris Corporation in 1988

- Ladd Petroleum, sold in 1990 to Amax Oil and Gas Inc. for $515 million

By 1984, GE's image had shifted in the eyes of investors from a toaster oven and lightbulb company to a major player in high-growth areas such as plastics, medical diagnostic systems, and financial services. Alan Benasuli of Drexel Burnham Lambert was quoted as saying, "GE is no longer a highly cyclical GNP-type company. It is now a highly diversified technology and services company."[6] For further evidence of this transformation, revenue from "core" manufacturing operations had dropped from half of GE's earnings in 1980 to about a third.

While performance and market share goals shaped GE's portfolio in the 1980s, the vision of a boundaryless company shaped the way business would be done in the 1990s. In the 1990 *Annual Report*'s Letter to the Share Owners, Welch and his vice chairmen defined this "vision for the 1990s." According to their description, in a boundaryless company, suppliers are partners and customer needs are the focus of all employees. Internally, functional silos are torn down as cross-functional teams work together to solve problems. Welch believed that boundarylessness would have been unachievable without cutting the workforce. According to him,

> It's terrible to take out people. It's the worst part of the job. But we had to get rid of anything that was getting in the way of being informal, of being fast, of being boundaryless. You can't say to a big bloated bureaucracy, "Let's be boundaryless," because they've already got defined slots. Unless you clear the forest, you don't see anything.[7]

---

[5]Peter Petre, "What Welch Has Wrought at GE," *Fortune*, July 7, 1986, 43, 45.
[6]Philip Mattera, "A New P/E for the New GE," *Fortune*, January 9, 1984, 114.
[7]Charles R. Day, Jr., and Polly LaBarre, "GE: Just Your Average Everyday $60 Billion Family Grocery Store," *Industry Week*, May 2, 1994, 14, 16.

Welch said that any organizational boundary was a "toll gate"—an impediment to speed, the "indispensable ingredient of success in this decade." Welch further argued that "boundary-busting" would lead to greater profitability and higher market share through improved responsiveness to customers.

VALUES: CHANGING THE GE CULTURE

Welch found it abundantly easier to change GE's business portfolio than to change its culture. Nevertheless, he stuck to the task. Welch believed that "changing culture starts with an attitude." So he began shaping GE's attitude through key words and ideas. The 1981 *Annual Report*'s Letter to the Share Owners included three basic ideas for "attitudinal positioning": reality, excellence, and ownership:

1. Reality means understanding both the marketplace and corporate social responsibilities.
2. Excellence spurs the company to build upon its reputation for quality through the best efforts of employees.
3. Ownership drives decisions down to the operating levels within the company while requiring employees to take full responsibility for these decisions.

The process of moving from key words to an explicit statement of company values was a "brutal process," according to Welch. It took the Executive Management Staff 3 years to complete the first draft of the document, which was based on consultations with Welch and his vice chairmen, Larry Bossidy and Edward Hood, as well as feedback from 5,000 employees during management training sessions. This first "discussion" draft was finished in 1985. After much debate a revised version of the statement of values was completed in 1987. The following GE values were listed in the 1991 *Annual Report*'s Letter to Share Owners:

- Create a clear, simple, reality-based customer-focused vision and are able to communicate it straightforwardly to all constituencies.

- Understand accountability and commitment and are decisive . . . set and meet aggressive targets . . . always with unyielding integrity.

- Have a passion for excellence . . . hate bureaucracy and all the nonsense that comes with it.

- Have the self-confidence to empower others and behave in a boundaryless fashion . . . believe in and are committed to Work-Out as a means of empowerment . . . are open to ideas from anywhere.

- Have, or have the capacity to develop, global brains and global sensitivity, and are comfortable building diverse global teams.

- Stimulate and relish change . . . are not frightened or paralyzed by it. See change as opportunity, not just a threat.

- Have enormous energy and the ability to energize and invigorate others. Understand speed as competitive advantage and see the total organizational benefits that can be derived from a focus on speed.

In 1989, GE values were first used to evaluate the performance of top managers. Business leaders were required to rank their officers on a scale of 1 to 5 for each business and individual characteristic in the value statement. At that time, the business characteristics included: lean, agile, creative, ownership, and reward. Individual characteristics were: reality, leadership, candor/openness, simplicity, integrity, and individual dignity.

A short time later the value criterion was utilized for all yearly employee performance appraisals. Entry-level professionals in GE's many development programs such as the Edison Engineering Program, Manufacturing Management Program, and Financial Management Program were rated every 6 months, following each work assignment, on their display of GE values.

In 1991, Vice Chairman Larry Bossidy acknowledged that even with GE's progress to date,

> I'd be less than candid if I told you we had all the answers on how to go about changing the corporate culture. We still have autocrats—highly successful '70s and '80s style people—and we're not sure what to do with them. . . . We've learned to have patience as well. There are no quick fixes, no instant culture changes. What we have set out to do will take years—maybe a decade.[8]

MANAGERIAL PROCESSES

GE was founded in 1878 by the inventor of the lightbulb, Thomas Edison. Throughout the company's existence it has been as well known and admired for its management acuity as for its products. GE was the first corporation to systematically apply a number of management concepts that are now well established "standards," including strategic planning, decentralization, and market research. Such topics formed the core curriculum at GE's Management Development Institute in Croton-on-Hudson, New York. Dubbed by *Fortune* "The Harvard of Corporate America," "Crotonville" was established in the 1950s and charged with the mission "to enhance GE's competitiveness in a global environment by providing . . . a broad array of experiences which serve as an instrument of cultural change."

The open, honest exchanges which frequently took place in the "Pit" at Crotonville were a very powerful experience for the 20,000 or so professionals fortunate enough to attend management training there. However, it was not enough to penetrate and transform the approximately 300,000 employees throughout GE as of 1988. To truly realize changes in the mind-set and culture of such a monstrous organization as GE would require a mechanism which would directly involve employees from all levels. Work-Out was developed to fulfill this need.

---

[8]Lawrence W. Bossidy, "Why Do We Waste Time Doing This?" *Across the Board*, May 1991, p. 20.

EXHIBIT 4
Management's View of Work-Out

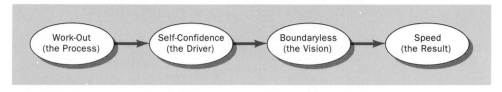

Source: General Electric Company, 1990 *Annual Report,* p. 3.

Work-Out

The four main goals of Work-Out were to:

1. Build trust

2. Empower employees

3. Eliminate unnecessary work

4. Create a new paradigm

Work-Out was designed to begin the process of totally "redefining the relationship between boss and subordinate." The main objective of Work-Out was to instill GE values of speed, simplicity, and self-confidence in every single employee regardless of rank or function (Exhibit 4). In Welch's words,

> Work-Out is absolutely fundamental to our becoming the kind of company we must become. That's why I'm so passionate about it. . . . Work-Out is the next generation of what we're trying to do. We had to put in a process to focus on and change how work gets done in this company. We have to apply the same relentless passion to Work-Out that we did in selling the vision of number one and number two globally.[9]

Exhibit 5 shows the basic steps involved in the Work-Out process. The format for Work-Out in its original form was very similar to a New England town meeting. Management would choose a group of 40 to 100 employees from across functions and ranks. The group would go to an off-site conference center or hotel for approximately 3 days. The first day typically began with the business leader setting a tentative agenda for the 3 days. After this was accomplished, the leader would leave. An outside facilitator would then help the employees organize themselves into five or six groups, each of which would work on a portion of the agenda. For the remainder of the first day and the entire second day the teams would discuss problems, argue over solutions, and prepare their presentations for the following day. On the third day, the business leader would return. With the leader at the front of the room, each team would present its recommendations. The leader could make only one of three responses: yes, no, or need more information.

---

[9]Noel Tichy and Ram Charan, "Speed, Simplicity, Self-Confidence: An Interview with Jack Welch," *Harvard Business Review,* September–October 1989, 116, 118–120.

EXHIBIT 5
The Seven Steps of Work-Out

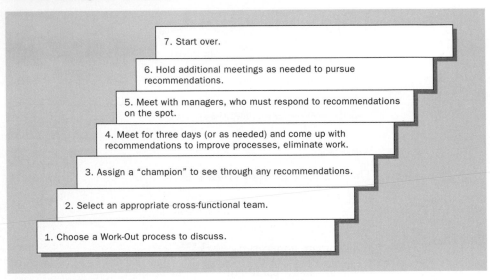

7. Start over.

6. Hold additional meetings as needed to pursue recommendations.

5. Meet with managers, who must respond to recommendations on the spot.

4. Meet for three days (or as needed) and come up with recommendations to improve processes, eliminate work.

3. Assign a "champion" to see through any recommendations.

2. Select an appropriate cross-functional team.

1. Choose a Work-Out process to discuss.

Source: Adapted from Judy Quinn, "What a Work-Out!" *Sales & Marketing Management,* November 1994 (suppl.), p. 61.

If more information was requested, the leader was required to establish a team and the group had to agree on a deadline for providing the needed information. If the leader approved of a recommendation, the previously determined "champion" of the measure had the responsibility to ensure that it was carried out. An approved recommendation received the necessary resources in time, capital, and management support required for implementation. Meetings of team members and other necessary personnel would be held as needed. Recommendations which were not approved could be resurrected in future Work-Out sessions, because the process of continuous improvement was never complete.

The first Work-Outs occurred in March 1989. They began slowly with Plastics, then NBC, then Lighting. Although no one kept count of the exact number of Work-Out sessions or attendees, Welch estimated that between 20,000 and 25,000 employees attended Work-Out sessions in 1990. The attendee estimate for 1991 was up to 40,000. While the essence of Work-Out has not changed over the years, it has become broader and less structured. Work-Out sessions have occurred on site and have started including customers and suppliers as well as employees.

Work-Out Success Stories

Managers' buy-in gives Work-Out its unique success. "That's what's missing from most quality and employment programs," says Robert Tomasko, consultant with Washington, D.C.–based management consulting firm Arthur D. Little Inc. . . . "Usually a group writes up recommendations, files a report and that's it. It just disappears into space. That can't happen at GE."[10]

There are numerous success stories from GE businesses that took the "Work-Out challenge":

■ At Aircraft Engine's plant in Lynn, Massachusetts, Work-Out proposals saved more than $200,000 in plant services. The majority of the cost savings were attributed to the insight of frontline employees. Their input resulted in the cycle time for combustion liners for jet engines dropping from 30 weeks to 10 days.

■ GE Plastics' plant in Burkville, Alabama, was trying to increase the percentage of product that emerges from processing as salable pellets without having to be melted and run through extruders ("first-pass yield"). The product was Lexan, which is used in applications ranging from automobile bumpers to milk bottles. Line workers determined that new procedures were necessary to accomplish this task. These workers wrote the new procedures manual themselves in 3 months. As a result of their efforts, waste was reduced by 37 percent with an investment of only $10,000.

■ At GE Appliances (GEA), Work-Outs directed the development of a build-to-order manufacturing scheme called Quick Response—a faster, more flexible just-in-time production cycle. Application of process mapping guided measures which reduced inventory by $200 million and cycle time by more than 75 percent.

■ A locomotive paint shop in Erie, Pennsylvania, found that many of its problems stemmed from the inconsistency of the paint. At that time, GE was using two different suppliers. The Work-Out team convinced its boss to use only one supplier. The team went further to meet with the supplier's chemist and together write standards for paint color and consistency. Team members' efforts reduced painting time by more than an entire shift.

■ GE Monogram Retailer Credit Services manages charge cards for Montgomery Ward. Teaming together, they cut the time needed to open a new customer account from 30 minutes to 90 seconds by tying GE's mainframes directly into Montgomery Ward's cash registers.

Best Practices: Learning from Others

Work-Out and its complementary program, Best Practices, were developed almost simultaneously. While GE employees generally looked for innovation internally, Welch realized that they were missing the opportunity to learn from other companies' breakthroughs. Lessons learned from other companies could serve to spark new ideas in Work-Out teams.

Welch put Michael Frazier of GE's Business Development Staff in charge of

---

[10]Judy Quinn, "What a Work-Out!" *Sales & Marketing Management*, November 1994 (suppl.), 61–62.

compiling a list of companies with higher productivity than GE. Frazier and his team began their task in the summer of 1988. The initial list of candidates, numbering 200, was derived from both the business press and GE executives. After a preliminary screening, the list contained twenty-four companies. Nine companies agreed to participate, including AMP (an electronic components maker), Ford, Chapperell Steel, Wal-Mart, Sanyo, Toshiba, Xerox, Hewlett-Packard, and one other unnamed Japanese company.

The ten members of Frazier's team spent the next year in on-site data gathering at these companies. The primary assignment was not to record details but to determine each company's secret of success. Upon completion of the process, the team found some striking similarities among the companies. Six common characteristics of these companies were:

1. Instead of managing people, they managed processes.

2. They relied on practices such as benchmarking and process mapping to improve their operations.

3. They emphasized *kaizen*, or continuous improvement.

4. These companies were all customer focused and used customer satisfaction as their primary performance measurement.

5. Their products were designed with attention to manufacturing constraints.

6. They approached their relationship with suppliers as partners.

In addition to these broad ideas, team members came back with case studies. One such case relays the story of a Japanese company in the washing machine market. It realized that in order to respond to market demands, it would have to switch from producing only a few different models to producing a wide selection. The company created a flexible production system and in 5 years doubled the number of new washers introduced. The business doubled its manufacturing capacity and sales per employee while also improving quality. The capital outlay for the project was only $2 million to $3 million each year over the 5 years.

Best Practices was a rude awakening for GE. While there had already been many Work-Out successes, they were mainly "low-hanging fruit." Stepping up to the next level would require a shift in focus. To facilitate the dissemination of Best Practices, Crotonville developed two courses. The first course was given to employees of GE's ten manufacturing businesses. The second course was targeted to the service businesses, based on research at companies such as American Express. The three central themes of the classes were:

- GE has much to learn from other companies.

- There is tremendous value in continuous improvement.

- Processes need owners.

The final theme forged a link between Best Practices and Work-Out. Like Work-Out, Best Practices was an ongoing exercise. Some of the recent additions were

EXHIBIT 6
GE Corporate Structure, 1994

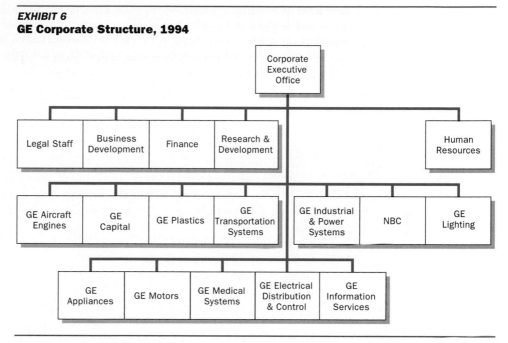

Source: Noel M. Tichy and Stratford Sherman, *Control Your Destiny or Someone Else Will* (New York: HarperBusiness, 1994), p. 346.

American Standard's "Demand Flow Technology" and Caterpillar's part standardization disciplines. Using the "Demand Flow Technology" technique, American Standard had doubled and tripled its inventory turnover rates. GE applied this system in Power Systems, Plastics, and Medical Systems, achieving double-digit improvement in working capital turnover. Using Caterpillar's part standardization approach resulted in a reduction in product introduction cycle times by more than half in Appliances and Power Systems.

Stretch: The Latest Step

GE's most recent operating principle is called *stretch*. In the 1994 *Annual Report*'s Letter to the Share Owners, Jack Welch and Vice Chairman Paolo Fresco say, "Stretch, in its simplest form, says, 'Nothing is impossible,' and the setting of stretch targets inspires people and captures their imaginations."

Dubbed as the most "New Age" of Welch's concepts by the *Journal of Business Strategy*, stretch used dreams to set business targets. Stretch pushed for seemingly unobtainable goals instead of calculating down to the hundreds place a proposed increase in inventory turns or operating margin. Welch gave an illustration to explain stretch:

> The CEO of Yokogawa, our Japanese partner in the Medical Systems business, has a wonderful phrase. He talks about "bullet-train thinking." He says if you want to increase the speed of the bullet train 10 mph, you add a little more horsepower. . . . But if you want to

take it from 150 mph to 300 mph—double the speed of the bullet train—you've got to think about whether or not you widen the track, change the suspension system. You've got to think out of the box. It's not the same train with a little tweak. *It's a whole new thought.* So all the talks are about big things! Double the speed of the bullet train—don't go 10 miles an hour faster. That's what stretch is.[11]

WHAT THE FUTURE HOLDS

While there remain pockets of resistance, outside observers concur that Work-Out has largely changed the culture at GE. Along with Best Practices, it has been an invaluable tool for improved process and total company performance. Observers also agreed that the elimination of layers within the organization facilitated the pace of change by allowing for "boundaryless" behavior. GE's simplified structure is illustrated in Exhibit 6.

Looking to the future in the 1994 Letter to the Share Owners, Welch and Fresco wrote, "Using 100% of the minds and passion of 100% of our people in implementing the best ideas from everywhere in the world is a formula, we believe, for endless excitement, endless growth and endless renewal." However, it was unclear what GE's next steps should be in order to ensure that this ambitious goal will be reached.

BIBLIOGRAPHY

Banks, Howard, "General Electric—Going with the Winners," *Forbes*, March 26, 1984, pp. 97–98, 102.

Beatty, Richard W., and David O. Ulrich, "Re-energizing the Mature Organization," *Organizational Dynamics*, Summer 1991, p. 22.

Bossidy, Lawrence W., "Why Do We Waste Time Doing This?" *Across the Board*, May 1991, p. 20.

Cosco, Joseph P., "General Electric Works It All Out," *Journal of Business Strategy*, May–June 1994, pp. 48–50.

Day, Charles R., Jr., and Polly LaBarre, "GE: Just Your Average Everyday $60 Billion Family Grocery Store," *Industry Week*, May 2, 1994, pp. 14, 16.

D'O'Brian, Joseph, "GE's 'Work-Outs' Change the Role of Management," *Supervisory Management*, January 1994, p. 6.

"The $5-Billion Man: Pushing the New Strategy at GE," *Fortune*, April 18, 1983, p. 6.

General Electric Company, *Annual Report*, 1981, 1985, 1988, 1990, 1991, 1994.

---

[11]Day and LaBarre, "GE."

Gravin, David A., "Building a Learning Organization," *Harvard Business Review,* July–August 1993, p. 86.

Harris, Marilyn A., and Christopher Power, " 'He Hated Losing—Even in Touch Football,' " *Business Week,* June 30, 1986, p. 65.

Harris, Marilyn, Zachary Schiller, Russell Mitchell, and Christopher Power, "Can Jack Welch Reinvent GE?" *Business Week,* June 30, 1986, p. 64.

Mann, Robert W., "A Building-Blocks Approach to Strategic Change," *Training & Development Journal,* August 1990, p. 23.

Marbach, William D., and Susan Dentzer, "General Electric's New Hi-Tech Boss," *Newsweek,* April 6, 1981, p. 76.

Mattera, Philip, "A New P/E for the New GE," *Fortune,* January 9, 1984, p. 114.

Merck, Russ, and Mike Grabarek, "Customer Focused Process Improvement Techniques," Presentation for GE Technical Leadership Development Course, August 16–21, 1992.

Morrison, Ann M., "Trying to Bring GE to Life," *Fortune,* January 25, 1982, pp. 51, 53.

"Out for a 'Helluva Good Time,' " *Fortune,* January 12, 1981, p. 15.

Petre, Peter, "What Welch Has Wrought at GE," *Fortune,* July 7, 1986, pp. 43, 45.

Quickel, Stephen W., "Welch on Welch," *Financial World,* April 3, 1990, pp. 64–65, 68.

Quinn, Judy, "What a Work-Out!" *Sales & Marketing Management,* November 1994 (suppl.), pp. 61–62.

Stewart, Thomas A., "GE Keeps Those Ideas Coming," *Fortune,* August 12, 1991, pp. 42–45.

Tichy, Noel, and Ram Charan, "Speed, Simplicity, Self-Confidence: An Interview with Jack Welch," *Harvard Business Review,* September–October 1989, pp. 116, 118–120.

Tichy, Noel M., and Stratford Sherman, *Control Your Destiny or Someone Else Will* (New York: HarperBusiness, 1994), pp. 16, 59, 62, 65, 70, 95, 102–103, 107–109, 172, 252, 346.

Tichy, Noel, and Stratford Sherman, "Walking the Talk at GE," *Training & Development,* June 1993, pp. 29, 32.

Welch, John, "Competitiveness from Within—Beyond Incrementalism," transcript of speech, 1984.

http://www.ge.com

STRATEGY IMPLEMENTATION

W. L. Gore & Associates, Inc., 1996*

> To make money and have fun.
> —W. L. Gore

THE FIRST DAY ON THE JOB

Bursting with resolve, Jack Dougherty, a newly minted M.B.A. from the College of William and Mary, reported to his first day at W. L. Gore & Associates on July 26, 1976. He presented himself to Bill Gore, shook hands firmly, looked him in the eye, and said he was ready for anything.

Jack was not ready, however, for what happened next. Gore replied, "That's fine, Jack, fine. Why don't you look around and find something you'd like to do?" Three frustrating weeks later he found that something: trading in his dark blue suit for jeans, he loaded fabric into the mouth of a machine that laminated the company's patented GORE-TEX®[1] membrane to fabric. By 1982, Jack had become responsible for all advertising and marketing in the fabrics group. This story is part of the folklore of W. L. Gore & Associates.

Today the process is more structured. Regardless of the job for which they are hired, new Associates[2] take a journey through the business before settling into their own positions. A new sales Associate in the fabrics division may spend 6 weeks rotating through different areas before beginning to concentrate on sales and marketing. Among other things the newcomer learns is how GORE-TEX fabric is made, what it can and cannot do, how Gore handles customer complaints, and how it makes its investment decisions.

---

*Frank Shipper, Department of Management and Marketing, Franklin P. Perdue School of Business, Salisbury State University, Salisbury, Maryland, 21801, (410) 543-6333, FAX (410) 548-2908, >fmshipper@ssu.edu<; and Charles C. Manz, Department of Management, College of Business, Arizona State University, Tempe, Arizona 85287, (602) 965-3431.

[1]GORE-TEX is a registered trademark of W. L. Gore & Associates.

[2]In this case the word "Associate" is used and capitalized because in W. L. Gore & Associates' literature the word is always used instead of "employees" and is capitalized. In fact, case writers were told that Gore "never had 'employees'—always 'Associates.'"

Anita McBride related her early experience at W. L. Gore & Associates this way: Before I came to Gore, I had worked for a structured organization. I came here, and for the first month it was fairly structured because I was going through training and this is what we do and this is how Gore is and all of that. I went to Flagstaff for that training. After a month I came down to Phoenix and my sponsor said, "Well, here's your office; it's a wonderful office" and "Here's your desk," and walked away. And I thought, "Now what do I do?" You know, I was waiting for a memo or something, or a job description. Finally after another month I was so frustrated, I felt, "What have I gotten myself into?" And so I went to my sponsor and I said, "What the heck do you want from me? I need something from you." And he said, "If you don't know what you're supposed to do, examine your commitment, and opportunities."

BACKGROUND

W. L. Gore & Associates evolved from the late Wilbert L. Gore's experiences personally, organizationally, and technically. He was born in Meridian, Idaho, near Boise in 1912. By age 6, according to his own account, he was an avid hiker in the Wasatch Mountain Range in Utah. In those mountains, at a church camp, he met Genevieve, his future wife. In 1935, they got married—in their eyes, a partnership. He would make breakfast and Vieve, as everyone called her, would make lunch. The partnership lasted a lifetime.

He received both a bachelor of science in chemical engineering in 1933 and a master of science in physical chemistry in 1935 from the University of Utah. He began his professional career at American Smelting and Refining in 1936. He moved to Remington Arms Company in 1941 and then to E. I. DuPont de Nemours in 1945. He held positions as research supervisor and head of operations research. While at DuPont, he worked on a team to develop applications for polytetrafluoroethylene, referred to as PTFE in the scientific community and known as "Teflon" by DuPont's consumers. (Consumers know it under other names from other companies.) On this team Wilbert Gore, called Bill by everyone, felt a sense of excited commitment, personal fulfillment, and self-direction. He followed the development of computers and transistors and felt that PTFE had the ideal insulating characteristics for use with such equipment.

He tried many ways to make a PTFE coated ribbon cable without success. A breakthrough came in his home basement laboratory while he was explaining the problem to his 19-year-old son Bob. The young Gore saw some PTFE sealant tape made by 3M and asked his father, "Why don't you try this tape?" Bill then explained that everyone knew that you cannot bond PTFE to itself. Bob went on to bed.

Bill Gore remained in his basement lab and proceeded to try what everyone knew would not work. At about 4:00 A.M. he woke up his son, waving a small piece of cable around and saying excitedly, "It works, it works." The following night father and son returned to the basement lab to make ribbon cable coated with PTFE. Because the breakthrough idea came from Bob, the patent for the cable was issued in Bob's name.

For the next 4 months Bill Gore tried to persuade DuPont to make a new product—PTFE coated ribbon cable. By this time in his career Bill Gore knew some of the decision makers at DuPont. After talking to a number of them, he came to realize that DuPont wanted to remain a supplier of raw materials and not a fabricator.

Bill and his wife, Vieve, began discussing the possibility of starting their own insulated wire and cable business. On January 1, 1958, their wedding anniversary, they founded W. L. Gore & Associates. The basement of their home served as their first facility. After finishing dinner that night, Vieve turned to her husband of 23 years and said, "Well, let's clear up the dishes, go downstairs, and get to work."

Bill Gore was 45 years old with five children to support when he left DuPont. He put aside a career of 17 years, and a good, secure salary. To finance the first 2 years of the business, he and Vieve mortgaged their house and took $4,000 from savings. All their friends told them not to do it.

The first few years were rough. In lieu of salary, some of their employees accepted room and board in the Gore home. At one point 11 Associates were living and working under one roof. One afternoon, while sifting PTFE powder, Vieve received a call from the City of Denver's water department. The caller indicated that he was interested in the ribbon cable, but wanted to ask some technical questions. Bill was out running some errands. The caller asked for the product manager. Vieve explained that he was out at the moment. Next he asked for the sales manager and finally, the president. Vieve explained that they were also out. The caller became outraged and hollered, "What kind of company is this anyway?" With a little diplomacy the Gores were able eventually to secure an order for $100,000. This order put the company on a profitable footing and it began to take off.

W. L. Gore & Associates continued to grow and develop new products, primarily derived from PTFE. Its best known product would become GORE-TEX fabric. In 1986, Bill Gore died while backpacking in the Wind River Mountains of Wyoming. He was then chairman of the board. His son Bob continued to occupy the position of president. Vieve remained as the only other officer, secretary-treasurer.

THE OPERATING COMPANY

W. L. Gore & Associates has never had titles, hierarchy, or any of the conventional structures associated with enterprises of its size. The titles of president and secretary-treasurer continue to be used only because they are required by the laws of incorporation. In addition, Gore has never had a corporatewide mission or code of ethics statement; nor has Gore ever required or prohibited business units from developing such statements for themselves. Thus, the Associates of some business units who have felt a need for such statements have developed them on their own. When questioned about this issue, one Associate stated, "The company belief is that (1) its four basic operating principles cover ethical practices required of people in business; (2) it will not tolerate illegal practices." Gore's management style has been referred to as unmanagement. The organization has been guided by Bill's experiences on teams at DuPont and has evolved as needed.

For example, in 1965 W. L. Gore & Associates was a thriving company with a fa-

EXHIBIT 1
International Locations of W. L. Gore & Associates

cility on Paper Mill Road in Newark, Delaware. One Monday morning in the summer, Bill Gore was taking his usual walk through the plant. All of a sudden he realized that he did not know everyone in the plant. The team had become too big. As a result, he established the practice of limiting plant size to approximately 200 Associates. Thus was born the expansion policy of "Get big by staying small." The purpose of maintaining small plants was to accentuate a close-knit atmosphere and encourage communication among Associates in a facility.

In 1995, W. L. Gore & Associates consisted of over 44 plants worldwide with approximately 6,000 Associates. In some cases, the plants are grouped together on the same site (as in Flagstaff, Arizona, with ten plants). Overseas Gore's facilities are located in Scotland, Germany, France, and Italy, and the company has two joint ventures in Japan (see Exhibit 1). Gore manufactures electronic, medical, industrial, and fabric products. In addition, it has numerous sales offices worldwide including Eastern Europe and Russia.

Gore electronic products have been found in unconventional places where conventional products will not do—in space shuttles, for example, where Gore wire and cable assemblies withstand the heat of ignition and the cold of space. In addition, they have been found in fast computers, transmitting signals at up to 93 percent of the speed of light. Gore cables have even gone underground, in oil drilling operations, and underseas, on submarines that require superior microwave signal equipment and no-fail cables that can survive high pressure. The Gore electronic products division has a history of anticipating future customer needs with innovative products. Gore electronic products have been well received in industry for their ability to last under adverse conditions. For example, Gore has become, according to Sally Gore, a leader in Human Resources and Communications, ". . . one of the largest manufacturers of ultrasound cable in the world, the reason being that Gore's electronic cables' signal transmission is very, very accurate and it's very thin and extremely flexible and has a very, very long flex life. That makes it ideal for things like ultrasound and many medical electronic applications."

In the medical arena, GORE-TEX–expanded PTFE has been considered an ideal replacement for human tissue in many situations. In patients suffering from cardiovascular disease the diseased portion of arteries has been replaced by tubes of expanded PTFE—strong, biocompatible structures capable of carrying blood at arterial pressures. Gore has a strong position in this product segment. Other Gore medical products have included patches that can literally mend broken hearts by sealing holes, and sutures that allow for tissue attachment and offer the surgeon silk-like handling coupled with extreme strength. In 1985, W. L. Gore & Associates won Britain's Prince Philip Award for Polymers in the Service of Mankind. The award recognized especially the life-saving achievements of the Gore medical products team.

Two recently developed products by this division are a new patch material that is intended to incorporate more tissue into the graft more quickly and GORE™ RideOn[3] Cable System for bicycles. According to Amy LeGere of the medical division, "All the top pro riders in the world are using it. It was introduced just about a year ago and it has become an industry standard." This product had a positive cash flow very soon after its introduction. Some Associates who were also outdoor sports enthusiasts developed the product and realized that Gore could make a great bicycle cable that would have 70 percent less friction and need no lubrication. The Associates maintain that the profitable development, production, and marketing of such specialized niche products are possible because of the lack of bureaucracy and associated overhead, Associate commitment, and the use of product champions.

The output of the industrial products division has included sealants, filter bags, cartridges, clothes, and coatings. The specialized and critical applications of these products, along with Gore's reputation for quality, have had a strong influence on industrial purchasers. This division has introduced Gore's first consumer product— GLIDE®[4]—a dental floss. "That was a product that people knew about for a while and they went the route of trying to persuade industry leaders to promote the product, but they didn't really pursue it very well. So out of basically default almost, Gore decided, Okay, they're not doing it right. Let's go in ourselves. We had a champion, John Spencer, who took that and pushed it forward through the dentist's offices and it just skyrocketed. There were many more people on the team but it was basically getting that one champion who focused on that product and got it out. They told him it 'Couldn't be done,' 'It's never going to work,' and I guess that's all he needed. It was done and it worked," say Ray Wnenchak of the industrial products division. Amy LeGere added, "The champion worked very closely with the medical people to un-

---

[3]GORE RideOn is a registered trademark of W. L. Gore & Associates.
[4]GLIDE is a registered trademark of W. L. Gore & Associates.

derstand the medical market like claims and labeling so that when the product came out on the market it would be consistent with our medical products. And that's where, when we cross divisions, we know whom to work with and with whom we combine forces so that the end result takes the strengths of all of our different teams." Bob Winterling of the fabrics division explained, "The product champion is probably the most important resource we have at Gore for the introduction of new products. You look at that bicycle cable. That could have come out of many different divisions of Gore, but it really happened because one or two individuals said, 'Look, this can work. I believe in it; I'm passionate about it; and I want it to happen.' And the same thing with GLIDE floss. I think John Spencer in this case—although there was a team that supported John, let's never forget that—John sought the experts out throughout the organization. But without John making it happen on his own, GLIDE floss would never have come to fruition. He started with a little chain of drugstores here, Happy Harry's I think, and we put a few cases in and we just tracked the sales and that's how it all started. Who would have ever believed that you could take what we would have considered a commodity product like that, sell it direct for $3–$5 apiece? That is so un-Gorelike it's incredible. So it comes down to people and it comes down to the product champion to make things happen."

The Gore fabrics division has supplied laminates to manufacturers of foul weather gear, ski wear, running suits, footwear, gloves, and hunting and fishing garments. Firefighters and U.S. Navy pilots have worn GORE-TEX fabric gear, as have some Olympic athletes. The U.S. Army adopted a total garment system built around a GORE-TEX fabric component.

GORE-TEX membrane has 9 billion pores randomly dotting each square inch and is featherlight. Each pore is 700 times larger than a water vapor molecule, yet thousands of times smaller than a water droplet. Wind and water cannot penetrate the pores, but perspiration can escape. As a result, fabrics bonded with GORE-TEX membrane are waterproof, windproof, and breathable. The laminated fabrics bring protection from the elements to a variety of products—from survival gear to high-fashion rainwear. Other manufacturers, including 3M, have brought out products to compete with GORE-TEX fabrics. The toughest competition came from firms that violated the patents on GORE-TEX. Gore successfully challenged them in court. In 1993, the basic patent on the process of manufacturing ran out. Nevertheless, as Sally Gore explained, ". . . what happens is you get an initial process patent and then as you begin to create things with this process you get additional patents. For instance, we have patents protecting our vascular graft, different patents for protecting GORE-TEX patches, and still other patents protecting GORE-TEX industrial sealants and filtration material. One of our patent attorneys did a talk recently, a year or so ago, when the patent expired and a lot of people who were saying, Oh, golly, are we going to be in trouble! We would be in trouble if we didn't have any patents. Our attorney had this picture with a great big umbrella, sort of a parachute, with Gore under it. Next he showed us lots of little umbrellas scattered all over the sky. So you protect certain niche markets and niche areas, but indeed competition increases as your initial patents expire." Gore, however, has continued to have a commanding position in the active wear market.

To meet a variety of customer needs, Gore introduced a new family of fabrics in

EXHIBIT 2
Gore's Family of Fabrics

Brand Name	*Activity/Conditions*	*Breathability*	*Water Protection*	*Wind Protection*
GORE-TEX®	Rain*snow*cold*windy	Very breathable	Waterproof	Windproof
IMMERSION™ TECHNOLOGY	For fishing and paddle sports	Very breathable	Waterproof	Windproof
OCEAN TECHNOLOGY	For offshore and coastal sailing	Very breathable	Waterproof	Windproof
WINDSTOPPER®	Cool/cold*windy	Very breathable	No water resistance	Windproof
GORE DRYLOFT™	Cold*windy*light precipitation	Extremely breathable	Water resistant	Windproof
ACTIVENT™	Cool/cold*windy*light precipitation	Extremely breathable	Water resistant	Windproof

the 1990s (Exhibit 2). The introduction posed new challenges. According to Bob Winterling, ". . . we did such a great job with the brand GORE-TEX that we actually have hurt ourselves in many ways. By that I mean it has been very difficult for us to come up with other new brands, because many people didn't even know Gore. We are the GORE-TEX company. One thing we decided to change about Gore four or five years ago was instead of being the GORE-TEX company we wanted to become the Gore company and that underneath the Gore company we had an umbrella of products that fall out of being the great Gore company. So it was a shift in how we positioned GORE-TEX. Today GORE-TEX is stronger than ever as it's turned out, but now we've ventured into such things as WindStopper®[5] fabric that is very big in the golf market. It could be a sweater or a fleece piece or even a knit shirt with the Wind-Stopper behind it or closer to your skin and what it does is it stops the wind. It's not waterproof; it's water resistant. What we've tried to do is position the Gore name and beneath that all of the great products of the company."

Bill Gore knew that products alone did not a company make. He wanted to avoid smothering the company in thick layers of formal "management." He felt that hierarchy stifled individual creativity. As the company grew, he knew that he had to find a way to assist new people and to follow their progress. This was particularly important when it came to compensation. W. L. Gore & Associates developed its "sponsor" program to meet these needs.

When people apply to Gore, they are initially screened by personnel specialists. Those who meet the basic criteria are given interviews with other Associates. Before anyone is hired, an Associate must agree to be his or her sponsor. The sponsor is to take a personal interest in the new Associate's contributions, problems, and goals, acting as both a coach and an advocate. The sponsor tracks the new Associate's progress,

---

[5]WindStopper is a registered trademark of W. L. Gore & Associates.

helping and encouraging, dealing with weaknesses, and concentrating on strengths. Sponsoring is not a short-term commitment. All Associates have sponsors and many have more than one. When individuals are hired initially, they are likely to have a sponsor in their immediate work area. If they move to another area, they may have a sponsor in that work area. As Associates' commitments change or grow, they may acquire additional sponsors.

Because the hiring process looks beyond conventional views of what makes a good Associate, some anomalies have occurred. Bill Gore proudly told the story of "a very young man" of 84 who walked in, applied, and spent 5 very good years with the company. The individual had 30 years of experience in the industry before joining Gore. His other Associates had no problems accepting him, but the personnel computer did. It insisted that his age was 48. The individual success stories at Gore have come from diverse backgrounds.

An internal memo by Bill Gore described three roles of sponsors: helping a new Associate get started on a job, seeing that an Associate's accomplishments are recognized, and ensuring that an Associate is fairly paid. A single person can perform any one or all three kinds of sponsorship.

In addition to the sponsor program, Bill Gore articulated four guiding principles:

1. Try to be fair.

2. Encourage, help, and allow other Associates to grow in knowledge, skill, and scope of activity and responsibility.

3. Make your own commitments, and keep them.

4. Consult with other Associates before taking actions that may be "below the waterline."

The four principles have been referred to as Fairness, Freedom, Commitment, and Waterline. The waterline terminology is drawn from an analogy to ships. If someone pokes a hole in a boat above the waterline, the boat will be in relatively little real danger. If someone, however, pokes a hole below the waterline, the boat is in immediate danger of sinking.

The operating principles were put to a test in 1978. By this time word about the qualities of GORE-TEX fabric was being spread throughout the recreational and outdoor markets. Production and shipment had begun in volume. At first a few complaints were heard. Next some of the clothing started coming back. Finally, much of the clothing was being returned. The trouble was that the GORE-TEX fabric was leaking. Waterproofing was one of the major properties responsible for GORE-TEX fabric's success. The company's reputation and credibility were on the line.

Peter W. Gilson, who led Gore's fabrics division, recalled: "It was an incredible crisis for us at that point. We were really starting to attract attention; we were taking off—and then this." In the next few months, Gilson and a number of his Associates made a number of those below-the-waterline decisions.

First, the researchers determined that oils in human sweat were responsible for clogging the pores in the GORE-TEX fabric and altering the surface tension of the membrane. Thus, water could pass through. They also discovered that a good washing could restore the waterproof property. At first this solution, known as the "Ivory Snow solution," was accepted.

A single letter from "Butch," a mountain guide in the Sierras, changed the company's position. Butch described what happened while he was leading a group: "My parka leaked and my life was in danger." As Gilson noted, "That scared the hell out of us. Clearly our solution was no solution at all to someone on a mountaintop." All the products were recalled. Gilson remembered: "We bought back, at our own expense, a fortune in pipeline material—anything that was in the stores, at the manufacturers, or anywhere else in the pipeline."

In the meantime, Bob Gore and other Associates set out to develop a permanent fix. One month later, a second generation GORE-TEX fabric had been developed. Gilson, furthermore, told dealers that if a customer ever returned a leaky parka, they should replace it and bill the company. The replacement program alone cost Gore roughly $4 million.

The popularity of GORE-TEX outerwear took off. Many manufacturers now make numerous pieces of apparel such as parkas, gloves, boots, jogging outfits, and wind shirts from GORE-TEX laminate. Sometimes when customers are dissatisfied with a garment, they return them directly to Gore. Gore has always stood behind any product made of GORE-TEX fabric. Analysis of the returned garments found that the problem was often not the GORE-TEX fabric. The manufacturer ". . . had created a design flaw so that the water could get in here or get in over the zipper and we found that when there was something negative about it, everyone knew it was GORE-TEX. So we had to make good on products that we were not manufacturing. We now license the manufacturers of all our GORE-TEX fabric products. They pay a fee to obtain a license to manufacture GORE-TEX products. In return we oversee the manufacture and we let them manufacture only designs that we are sure are guaranteed to keep you dry, that really will work. Then it works for them and for us—it's a win-win for them as well as for us," according to Sally Gore.

ORGANIZATIONAL STRUCTURE

W. L. Gore & Associates has been described not only as unmanaged, but also as unstructured. Bill Gore referred to the structure as a lattice organization (see Exhibit 3). The characteristics of this structure are:

1. Direct lines of communication—person to person—with no intermediary

2. No fixed or assigned authority

3. Sponsors, not bosses

4. Natural leadership defined by followership

5. Objectives set by those who must "make them happen"

6. Tasks and functions organized through commitments

EXHIBIT 3
The Lattice Structure

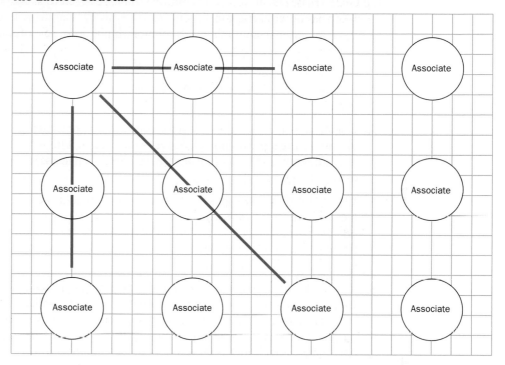

The structure within the lattice is complex and evolves from interpersonal inter-actions, self-commitment to group-known responsibilities, natural leadership, and group-imposed discipline.

Bill Gore once explained the structure this way: "Every successful organization has an underground lattice. It's where the news spreads like lightning, where people can go around the organization to get things done." An analogy might be drawn to a structure of constant cross-area teams—the equivalent of quality circles going on all the time. When a puzzled interviewer told Bill that he was having trouble under-standing how planning and accountability worked, Bill replied with a grin: "So am I. You ask me how it works? Every which way."

Outsiders have been struck by the degree of informality and humor in the Gore organization. Meetings tend to be only as long as necessary. As Trish Hearn, an Asso-ciate in Newark, Delaware, said, "No one feels a need to pontificate." Words such as "responsibilities" and "commitments" are commonly heard, whereas words such as "employees," "subordinates," and "managers" are taboo in the Gore culture. This is an organization that has always taken what it does very seriously, without its members taking themselves too seriously.

For a company of its size, Gore has always had a very short organizational pyra-mid. As of 1995 the pyramid consists of Bob Gore, the late Bill Gore's son, as president and Vieve, Bill Gore's widow, as secretary-treasurer. All the other members of the Gore organization were, and continue to be, referred to as Associates.

Gore has never had any managers, but it has always had many leaders. Bill Gore described in an internal memo the kinds of leadership and the role of leadership as follows:

1. The Associate who is recognized by a team as having a special knowledge, or experience (for example, this could be a chemist, computer expert, machine operator, salesman, engineer, lawyer). This kind of leader gives the team *guidance in a special area.*

2. The Associate the team looks to for coordination of individual activities in order to achieve the agreed upon objectives of the team. The role of this leader is to persuade team members to *make the commitments* necessary for success (commitment seeker).

3. The Associate who proposes necessary objectives and activities and seeks agreement and team *consensus on objectives.* This leader is perceived by the team members as having a good grasp of how the objectives of the team fit in with the broad objective of the enterprise. This kind of leader is often also the "commitment seeking" leader in 2 above.

4. The leader who evaluates relative contribution of team members (in consultation with other sponsors), and reports these contribution evaluations to a compensation committee. This leader may also participate in the compensation committee on relative contribution and pay and *reports changes in compensation* to individual Associates. This leader is then also a compensation sponsor.

5. The leader who coordinates the research, manufacturing, and marketing of one product type within a business, interacting with team leaders and individual Associates who have commitments regarding the product type. These leaders are usually called *product specialists.* They are respected for their knowledge and dedication to their products.

6. *Plant leaders* who help coordinate activities of people within a plant.

7. *Business leaders* who help coordinate activities of people in a business.

8. *Functional leaders* who help coordinate activities of people in a "functional" area.

9. *Corporate leaders* who help coordinate activities of people in different businesses and functions and who try to promote communication and cooperation among all Associates.

10. *Entrepreneuring Associates* who *organize new teams* for new businesses, new products, new processes, new devices, new marketing efforts, new or better methods of all kinds. These leaders invite other Associates to "sign up" for their project.

It is clear that leadership is widespread in our lattice organization and that it is continually changing and evolving. The situation that leaders are frequently *also* sponsors should not confuse these different activities and responsibilities.

Leaders are not authoritarians, managers of people, or supervisors who tell us what to do or forbid us doing things; nor are they "parents" to whom we transfer our own self-responsibility. However, they do often advise us of the consequences of actions we have done or propose to do. Our actions result in contributions, or lack of contribution, to the success of our enterprise. Our pay depends on the magnitude of our contributions. This is the basic discipline of our lattice organization.

Many other aspects of the Gore culture have been arranged along egalitarian lines: parking lots with no reserved parking spaces except for customers and disabled workers or visitors; dining areas—only one in each plant—set up as focal points for Associate interaction. As Dave McCarter of Phoenix explained: "The design is no accident. The lunchroom in Flagstaff has a fireplace in the middle. We want people to like to be here." The location of a plant is also no accident. Sites have been selected on the basis of transportation access, a nearby university, beautiful surroundings, and climate appeal. Land cost has never been a primary consideration. McCarter justified the selection by stating: "Expanding is not costly in the long run. The loss of money is what you make happen by stymieing people into a box."

Bob Gore is a champion of Gore culture. As Sally Gore related, "We have managed surprisingly to maintain our sense of freedom and our entrepreneurial spirit. I think what we've found is that we had to develop new ways to communicate with Associates because you can't communicate with 6,000 people the way that you can communicate with 500 people. It just can't be done. So we have developed a newsletter that we didn't have before. One of the most important communication mediums that we developed, and this was Bob Gore's idea, is a digital voice exchange which we call our Gorecom. Basically everyone has a mailbox and a password. Lots of companies have gone to E-mail and we use E-mail, but Bob feels very strongly that we're very much an oral culture and there's a big difference between cultures that are predominantly oral and predominantly written. Oral cultures encourage direct communication, which is, of course, something that we encourage."

Not all people function well under such a system, especially initially. For those accustomed to a more structured work environment, there can be adjustment problems. As Bill Gore said: "All our lives most of us have been told what to do, and some people don't know how to respond when asked to do something—and have the very real option of saying no—on their job. It's the new Associate's responsibility to find out what he or she can do for the good of the operation." The vast majority of the new Associates, after some initial floundering, have adapted quickly.

Others, especially those who require more structured working conditions, have found that Gore's flexible workplace is not for them. According to Bill, for those few, "It's an unhappy situation, both for the Associate and the sponsor. If there is no contribution, there is no paycheck."

As Anita McBride, an Associate in Phoenix, noted: "It's not for everybody. People ask me do we have turnover, and yes we do have turnover. What you're seeing looks like utopia, but it also looks extreme. If you finally figure the system, it can be real exciting. If you can't handle it, you gotta go. Probably by your own choice, because you're going to be so frustrated."

In rare cases an Associate "is trying to be unfair," in Bill's own words. In one case the problem was chronic absenteeism and in another, an individual was caught stealing. "When that happens, all hell breaks loose," said Bill Gore. "We can get damned authoritarian when we have to."

Over the years, Gore & Associates has faced a number of unionization drives. The company has neither tried to dissuade Associates from attending an organizational meeting nor retaliated when flyers were passed out. As of 1995, none of the plants has been organized. Bill believed that no need existed for third-party representation under the lattice structure. He asked the question, "Why would Associates join a union when they own the company? It seems rather absurd."

Overall, the Associates appear to have responded positively to the Gore system of unmanagement and unstructure. Bill estimated the year before he died that "the profit per Associate is double" that of DuPont.

The lattice structure has not been without its critics. As Bill Gore stated, "I'm told from time to time that a lattice organization can't meet a crisis well because it takes too long to reach a consensus when there are no bosses. But this isn't true. Actually, a lattice by its very nature works particularly well in a crisis. A lot of useless effort is avoided because there is no rigid management hierarchy to conquer before you can attack a problem."

The lattice has been put to the test on a number of occasions. For example, in 1975, Dr. Charles Campbell of the University of Pittsburgh reported that a GORE-TEX arterial graft had developed an aneurysm. If the bubble-like protrusion continued to expand, it would explode. Obviously, this life-threatening situation had to be resolved quickly and permanently.

Within only a few days of Dr. Campbell's first report, he flew to Newark to present his findings to Bill and Bob Gore and a few other Associates. The meeting lasted 2 hours. Dan Hubis, a former policeman who had joined Gore to develop new production methods, had an idea before the meeting was over. He returned to his work area to try some different production techniques. After only 3 hours and 12 tries, he had developed a permanent solution. In other words, in 3 hours a potentially damaging problem to both patients and the company was resolved. Furthermore, Hubis's redesigned graft went on to win widespread acceptance in the medical community.

Some outsiders have had problems with the idea of no titles. Sarah Clifton, an Associate at the Flagstaff facility, was being pressed by some outsiders as to what her title was. She made one up and had it printed on some business cards: SUPREME COMMANDER (see Exhibit 4). When Bill Gore learned what she did, he loved it and recounted the story to others.

Eric Reynolds, founder of Marmot Mountain Works Ltd. of Grand Junction, Colorado, and a major Gore customer, raised another issue: "I think the lattice has its problems with the day-to-day nitty-gritty of getting things done on time and out the door. I don't think Bill realizes how the lattice system affects customers. I mean after you've established a relationship with someone about product quality, you can call up one day and suddenly find that someone new to you is handling your problem. It's frustrating to find a lack of continuity." He went on to say: "But I have to admit that I've personally seen at Gore remarkable examples of people coming out of nowhere and excelling."

When Bill Gore was asked if the lattice structure could be used by other companies, he answered: "No. For example, established companies would find it very diffi-

EXHIBIT 4
Sarah Clifton's Business Card

W. L. GORE & ASSOCIATES, Inc.

S A R A H   C L I F T O N
SUPREME COMMANDER

1505 NORTH FOURTH STREET
FLAGSTAFF, ARIZONA 86001
PHONE: 602-774-0611
TWX: 910-972-0969

cult to use the lattice. Too many hierarchies would be destroyed. When you remove titles and positions and allow people to follow who they want, it may very well be someone other than the person who has been in charge. The lattice works for us, but it's always evolving. You have to expect problems." He maintained that the lattice system worked best when it was put in place in start-up companies by dynamic entrepreneurs.

RESEARCH AND DEVELOPMENT

Like everything else at Gore, research and development has always been unstructured. Even without a formal R & D department, the company has been issued many patents, although most inventions have been held as proprietary or trade secrets. Any Associate could ask for a piece of raw PTFE (known as a silly worm) with which to experiment. Bill Gore believed that all people had it within themselves to be creative.

One of the best examples of Gore inventiveness occurred in 1969. At the time, the wire and cable division was facing increased competition. Bill Gore began to look for a way to straighten out the PTFE molecules. As he said, "I figured out that if we ever unfold those molecules, get them to stretch out straight, we'd have a tremendous new kind of material." He thought that if PTFE could be stretched, air could be introduced into its molecular structure. The result would be greater volume per pound of raw material with no effect on performance. Thus, fabricating costs would be reduced and profit margins would be increased. Going about this search in a scientific manner, Bob Gore heated rods of PTFE to various temperatures and then slowly stretched them. Regardless of the temperature or how carefully he stretched them, the rods broke.

Working alone late one night after countless failures, Bob in frustration stretched one of the rods violently. To his surprise, it did not break. He tried it again and again with the same results. The next morning Bob demonstrated his breakthrough to his father, but not without some drama. As Bill Gore recalled: "Bob wanted to surprise me so he took a rod and stretched it slowly. Naturally, it broke. Then he pretended to get mad. He grabbed another rod and said, 'Oh, the hell with this,' and gave it a pull. It didn't break—he'd done it." The new arrangement of molecules not only changed the wire and cable division, but led to the development of GORE-TEX fabric.

Bill and Vieve did the initial field-testing of GORE-TEX fabric the summer of 1970. Vieve made a hand-sewn tent out of patches of GORE-TEX fabric. They took it on their annual camping trip to the Wind River Mountains in Wyoming. The very first night in the wilderness, they encountered a hailstorm. The hail tore holes in the top of the tent, and the bottom filled up like a bathtub from the rain. Undaunted, Bill Gore stated: "At least we knew from all the water that the tent was waterproof. We just needed to make it stronger, so it could withstand hail."

The largest medical division began on the ski slopes of Colorado. Bill was skiing with a friend, Dr. Ben Eiseman of Denver General Hospital. As Bill Gore told the story: "We were just to start a run when I absentmindedly pulled a small tubular section of GORE-TEX out of my pocket and looked at it. 'What is that stuff?' Ben asked. So I told him about its properties. 'Feels great,' he said. 'What do you use it for?' 'Got no idea,' I said. 'Well, give it to me,' he said, 'and I'll try it in a vascular graft on a pig.' Two weeks later, he called me up. Ben was pretty excited. 'Bill,' he said, 'I put it in a pig and it works. What do I do now?' I told him to get together with Pete Cooper in our Flagstaff plant, and let them figure it out." Not long after, hundreds of thousands of people throughout the world began walking around with GORE-TEX vascular grafts.

Gore Associates have always been encouraged to think, experiment, and follow a potentially profitable idea to its conclusion. At a plant in Newark, Delaware, Fred L. Eldreth, an Associate with a third-grade education, designed a machine that could wrap thousands of feet of wire a day. The design was completed over a weekend. Many other Associates have contributed their ideas through both product and process breakthroughs.

Even without an R & D department, innovations and creativity continued to work very well at Gore & Associates. The year before he died, Bill Gore claimed that "the creativity, the number of patent applications and innovative products is triple" that of DuPont.

ASSOCIATE DEVELOPMENT

Ron Hill, an Associate in Newark, noted that Gore "will work with Associates who want to advance themselves." Associates have been offered many in-house training opportunities, not only in technical and engineering areas but also in leadership development. In addition, the company has established cooperative education programs with universities and other outside providers, picking up most of the costs for the Gore Associates. The emphasis in Associate development, as in many parts of Gore, has always been that the Associate must take the initiative.

PRODUCTS

Gore's electronic products division has produced wire and cable for various demanding applications in aerospace, defense, computers, and telecommunications. The wire and cable products have earned a reputation for unequaled reliability. Most of the wire and cable has been used where conventional cables cannot operate. For example, Gore wire and cable assemblies were used in the space shuttle *Columbia* because they could stand the heat of ignition and the cold of space. Gore wire was used in the moon vehicle shuttle that scooped up samples of moon rocks, and Gore's microwave coaxial assemblies opened new horizons in microwave technology. Back on earth, Gore's electrical wire products helped make the world's fastest computers possible because electrical signals could travel through them at up to 93 percent of the speed of light. Because of the physical properties of the GORE-TEX material used in their construction, the electronic products have been used extensively in defense systems, electronic switching for telephone systems, scientific and industrial instrumentation, microwave communications, and industrial robotics. Reliability has always been a watchword for Gore products.

In medical products, reliability is literally a matter of life and death. GORE-TEX–expanded PTFE proved to be an ideal material for combating cardiovascular disease. When human arteries have been seriously damaged or plugged with deposits that interrupt the flow of blood, the diseased portions can often be replaced with GORE-TEX artificial arteries. Because the patient's own tissues grow into the graft's open porous spaces, the artificial portions are not rejected by the body. GORE-TEX vascular grafts, produced in many sizes to restore circulation to all areas of the body, have saved limbs from amputation, and saved lives. Some of the tiniest grafts have relieved pulmonary problems in newborns. GORE-TEX–expanded PTFE has been used to help people with kidney disease. Associates have also developed a variety of surgical reinforcing membranes, known as GORE-TEX cardiovascular patches, which can literally mend broken hearts by patching holes and repairing aneurysms.

Through the waterproof fabrics division, Gore technology has traveled to the roof of the world on the backs of renowned mountaineers and adventurers facing extremely harsh environments. Because the PTFE membrane blocks wind and water but allows sweat to escape, GORE-TEX fabric has proved ideal for those who work or play hard in foul weather. Backpackers have discovered that a single lightweight GORE-TEX fabric shell will replace a poplin jacket and a rain suit, and dramatically outperform both. Skiers, sailors, runners, bicyclists, hunters, fishermen, and other outdoor enthusiasts have also become big customers of garments made of GORE-TEX fabric. GORE-TEX sportswear, as well as women's fashion footwear and handwear, have proved to be functional as well as attractive. Boots and gloves, for both work and recreation, became waterproof thanks to GORE-TEX liners. GORE-TEX garments have even become standard items issued to military personnel. Wet suits, parkas, pants, headgear, gloves, and boots have kept the troops warm and dry in foul weather missions. Other demanding jobs have also received the protection of GORE-TEX fabric, with its unique combination of chemical and physical properties.

The GORE-TEX fibers, like the fabrics, have ended up in some pretty tough places, including the outer protective layer of a NASA spacesuit. In many ways, GORE-TEX fibers have proved to be the ultimate synthetic. They have been impervious to sunlight, chemicals, heat, and cold. They are strong and uniquely resistant to abrasion.

Industrial filtration products, such as GORE-TEX filter bags, have reduced air pollution and recovered valuable solids from gases and liquids more completely than alternatives—and they have done so economically. In the future they may make coal-burning plants completely smoke free, contributing to a cleaner environment.

Gore's industrial products division has developed a unique joint sealant—a flexible cord of porous PTFE—that can be applied as a gasket to the most complex shapes, sealing them to prevent leakage of corrosive chemicals, even at extreme temperature and pressure. Steam valves packed with GORE-TEX have been sold with a lifetime guarantee, provided the valve is used properly.

COMPENSATION

Traditionally, compensation at W. L. Gore & Associates has taken three forms: salary, profit sharing, and an Associates' Stock Ownership Program (ASOP).[6] Entry level salary has been in the middle for comparable jobs. According to Sally Gore: "We do not feel we need to be the highest paid. We never try to steal people away from other companies with salary. We want them to come here because of the opportunities for growth and the unique work environment." In the past, Associates' salaries have been reviewed at least once a year and more commonly twice a year. The reviews are conducted by a compensation team at each facility, with sponsors for the Associates acting as their advocates during the review process. Prior to meeting with the compensation committee, the sponsor checks with customers or Associates familiar with the person's work to find out what contribution the Associate has made. In addition, the evaluation team considers the Associate's leadership ability and willingness to help others develop to their fullest.

Profit sharing follows a formula based on economic value added (EVA). Sally Gore had the following to say about the adoption of a formula, "It's become more formalized and in a way, I think that's unfortunate because it used to be a complete surprise to receive a profit share. The thinking of the people like Bob Gore and other leaders was that maybe we weren't using it in the right way and we could encourage people by helping them know more about it and how we made profit share decisions. The fun of it before was people didn't know when it was coming and all of a sudden you could do something creative about passing out checks. It was great fun and people would have a wonderful time with it. The disadvantage was that Associates then did not focus much on, 'What am I doing to create another profit share?' By using EVA as a method of evaluation for our profit share, we know at the end of every month

---

[6]Similar, legally, to an ESOP (Employee Stock Ownership Plan). Again, Gore simply has never allowed the word "employee" in any of its documentation.

how much EVA was created that month. When we've created a certain amount of EVA, we then get another profit share. So everybody knows and everyone says, 'We'll do it in January,' so it is done. Now Associates feel more part of the happening to make it work. What have you done? Go make some more sales calls, please! There are lots of things we can do to improve our EVA and everybody has a responsibility to do that." Every month EVA is calculated and every Associate is informed. John Mosko of electronic products commented, ". . . (EVA) lets us know where we are on the path to getting one (a profit share). It's very critical—every Associate knows."

Annually, Gore also buys company stock equivalent to a fixed percent of the Associates' annual income, placing it in the ASOP retirement fund. Thus, an Associate can become a stockholder after being at Gore for a year. Gore's ASOP ensures that Associates participate in the growth of the company by acquiring ownership in it. Bill Gore wanted Associates to feel that they themselves are owners. One Associate stated, "This is much more important than profit sharing."

Commitment has long been considered a two-way street. W. L. Gore & Associates has tried to avoid layoffs. Instead of cutting pay, which in the Gore culture would be disastrous to morale, the Company has used a system of temporary transfers within a plant or cluster of plants and voluntary layoffs.

MARKETING STRATEGY

Gore's marketing strategy has focused on three assumptions: that it can offer the best-valued products to a marketplace, that people in that marketplace appreciate what it manufactures, and that Gore can become a leader in that area of expertise. The operating procedures used to implement the strategy have followed the same principles as other functions at Gore.

1. Marketing a product requires a leader, or *product champion.* According to Dave McCarter: "You marry your technology with the interests of your champions, since you've got to have champions for all these things no matter what. And that's the key element within our company. Without a product champion you can't do much anyway, so it is individually driven. If you get people interested in a particular market or a particular product for the marketplace, then there is no stopping them."

2. *A product champion is responsible for marketing the product through commitments with sales representatives.* Again, according to Dave McCarter: "We have no quota system. Our marketing and our sales people make their own commitments as to what their forecasts have been. There is no person sitting around telling them that is not high enough, you have to increase it by 10 percent, or whatever somebody feels is necessary. You are expected to meet your commitment, which is your forecast, but nobody is going to tell you to change it. . . . There is no order of command, no chain involved. These are groups of independent people who come together to make unified commitments to do something and sometimes when they can't make those agreements . . . you may pass up a marketplace. . . . But that's

OK, because there's much more advantage when the team decides to do something."

3. *Sales Associates are on salary, not commission.* They participate in the profit sharing and ASOP plans in which all other Associates participate.

As in other areas of Gore, individual success stories have come from diverse backgrounds. Dave McCarter related one of these successes:

> I interviewed Sam one day. I didn't even know why I was interviewing him actually. Sam was retired from AT&T. After 25 years, he took the golden parachute and went down to Sun Lakes to play golf. He played golf a few months and got tired of that. He was selling life insurance.
>
> I sat reading the application; his technical background interested me. . . . He had managed an engineering department with 600 people. He'd managed manufacturing plants for AT&T and had a great wealth of experience at AT&T. He said, "I'm retired. I like to play golf but I just can't do it every day so I want to do something else. Do you have something around here I can do?" I was thinking to myself, "This is one of these guys I would like to hire but I don't know what I would do with him." The thing that triggered me was the fact that he sold insurance and here is a guy with a high degree of technical background selling insurance. He had marketing experience, international marketing experience. So, the bell went off in my head that we were trying to introduce a new product into the marketplace that was a hydrocarbon leak protection cable. You can bury it in the ground and in a matter of seconds it could detect a hydrocarbon like gasoline. I had a couple of other guys working on the product who hadn't been very successful with marketing it. We were having a hard time finding a customer. Well, I thought that kind of product would be like selling insurance. If you think about it, why should you protect your tanks? It's an insurance policy that things are not leaking into the environment. That has implications, big time monetary. So, actually, I said, "Why don't you come back Monday? I have just the thing for you." He did. We hired him; he went to work, a very energetic guy. Certainly a champion of the product, he picked right up on it, ran with it single-handed. . . . Now it's a growing business. It certainly is a valuable one too for the environment.

In the implementation of its marketing strategy, Gore has relied on cooperative and word-of-mouth advertising. Cooperative advertising has been especially used to promote GORE-TEX fabric products. Those products are sold through a number of clothing manufacturers and distributors, including Apparel Technologies, Lands' End, Austin Reed, Timberland, Woolrich, North Face, Grandoe, and Michelle Jaffe. Gore has stressed cooperative advertising because the Associates believe positive experiences with any one product will carry over to purchases of other and more GORE-TEX fabric products. Apparently, this strategy has paid off. When the Grandoe Corporation introduced GORE-TEX gloves, its president, Richard Zuckerwar, noted: "Sports activists have had the benefit of GORE-TEX gloves to protect their hands from the elements. . . . With this handsome collection of gloves . . . you can have warm, dry hands without sacrificing style."

The power of informal marketing techniques extends beyond consumer products. According to Dave McCarter: "In the technical end of the business, company reputation probably is most important. You have to have a good reputation with your company." He went on to say that without a good reputation, a company's products would not be considered seriously by many industrial customers. In other words, the sale is often made before the representative calls. Using its marketing strategies, Gore has been very successful in securing a market leadership position in a number of areas, ranging from waterproof outdoor clothing to vascular grafts.

ENVIRONMENTAL FORCES

Each of Gore's divisions has faced some environmental forces. The fabric division was hit hard when the fad for jogging suits collapsed in the mid-1980s. The fabric division took another hit from the recession of 1989. People simply reduced their purchases of high-end athletic apparel. By 1995, the fabric division was the fastest growing division of Gore again. The electronic division was hit hard when the mainframe computer business declined in the early 1990s. By 1995, that division was seeing a resurgence for its products partially because that division had developed some electronic products for the medical industry. As can be seen, not all the forces have been negative. The aging population of America has increased the need for health care. As a result, Gore has invested in the development of additional medical products and the medical division is growing.

FINANCIAL INFORMATION

As a closely held private corporation, W. L. Gore has kept its financial information as closely guarded as proprietary information on products and processes. It has been estimated that Associates who work at Gore own 90 percent of the stock. According to Shanti Mehta, an Associate, Gore's returns on assets and sales have consistently ranked it among the top 10 percent of the Fortune 500 companies. According to another source, W. L. Gore & Associates has been doing just fine by any financial measure. For 35 straight years (from 1961 to 1995) the company has enjoyed profitability and positive return on equity. The compounded growth rate for revenues at W. L. Gore & Associates from 1969 to 1989 was more than 18 percent discounted for inflation.[7] In 1969, total sales were about $6 million, by 1989, the figure was $600 million. As should be expected with the increase in size, the percentage increase in sales has slowed over the last 5 years (Exhibit 5). Gore financed this growth without long-term debt unless it made sense. For example, "We used to have some industrial revenue bonds where, in essence, to build facilities the government allows banks to lend you money tax free. Up to a couple of years ago we were borrowing money through industrial revenue bonds. Other than that, we are totally debt free. Our money is gener-

---

[7]In comparison, only 11 of the 200 largest companies in the Fortune 500 had positive ROE each year from 1970 to 1988 and only 2 other companies missed a year. The revenue growth rate for these 13 companies was 5.4 percent, compared with 2.5 percent for the entire Fortune 500.

EXHIBIT 5
Growth of Gore's Sales vs. Gross Domestic Product

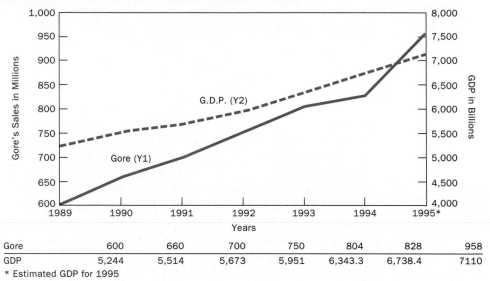

	1989	1990	1991	1992	1993	1994	1995*
Gore	600	660	700	750	804	828	958
GDP	5,244	5,514	5,673	5,951	6,343.3	6,738.4	7110

* Estimated GDP for 1995

ated out of the operations of the business, and frankly we're looking for new things to invest in. I know that's a challenge for all of us today," said Bob Winterling. *Forbes* magazine estimates Gore's operating profits for 1993, 1994, and 1995 to be $120, $140, and $192 million, respectively (Exhibit 6).

When asked about cost control, Sally Gore had the following to say:

> You have to pay attention to cost or you're not an effective steward of anyone's money, your own or anyone else's. It's kind of interesting, we started manufacturing medical products in 1974 with the vascular graft and it built from there. The Gore vascular graft is the Cadillac or BMW or the Rolls-Royce of the business. There is absolutely no contest, and our medical products division became very successful. People thought this was Mecca. Nothing had ever been manufactured that was so wonderful. Our business expanded enormously, rapidly out there (Flagstaff, Arizona) and we had a lot of young, young leadership. They spent some time thinking they could do no wrong and that everything they touched was going to turn to gold. They have had some hard knocks along the way and discovered it wasn't as easy as they initially thought it was. And that's probably good learning for everyone somewhere along the way. That's not how business works. There's a lot of truth in that old saying that you learn more from your failures than you do your successes. One failure goes a long way toward making you say, Oh, wow!

Acknowledgments

Many sources were helpful in providing background material for this case. The most important sources of all were the W. L. Gore Associates, who generously shared their time and viewpoints about the company. They provided many resources, including internal documents, and added much to this case through sharing their personal expe-

EXHIBIT 6
Operating and Net Profits of W. L. Gore & Associates

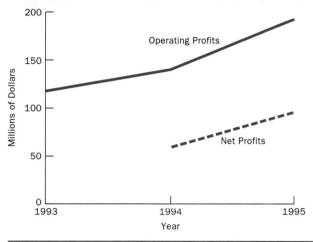

Source: Data from *Forbes Magazine's Annual Report on the 500 Largest Private Companies in the U.S.*

riences as well as ensuring that the case accurately reflected the Gore company and culture.

Bibliography

Aburdene, Patricia, and John Nasbitt. *Re-inventing the Corporation.* New York: Warner Books, 1985.

Angrist, S. W. "Classless Capitalists," *Forbes,* May 9, 1983, pp. 123–124.

Franlesca, L. "Dry and Cool," *Forbes,* August 27, 1984, p. 126.

"The Future Workplace," *Management Review,* July 1986, pp. 22–23.

Hoerr, J. "A Company Where Everybody Is the Boss," *Business Week,* April 15, 1985, p. 98.

Levering, Robert. *The 100 Best Companies to Work for in America.* New York: Signet, 1985. See the chapter on W. L. Gore & Associates, Inc.

McKendrick, Joseph. "The Employees as Entrepreneur," *Management World,* January 1985, pp. 12–13.

Milne, M. J. "The Gorey Details," *Management Review,* March 1985, pp. 16–17.

Posner, B. G. "The First Day on the Job," *Inc.,* June 1986, pp. 73–75.

Price, Kathy. "Firm Thrives Without Boss," *AZ Republic,* February 2, 1986.

Rhodes, Lucien. "The Un-Manager," *Inc.,* August 1982, p. 34.

Simmons, J. "People Managing Themselves: Un-Management at W. L. Gore Inc.," *The Journal for Quality and Participation*, December 1987, pp. 14–19.

Trachtenberg, J. A. "Give Them Stormy Weather," *Forbes*, March 24, 1986, Vol. 137, No. 6, pp. 172–174.

Ward, Alex. "An All-Weather Idea," *The New York Times Magazine*, November 10, 1985, Sec. 6.

Weber, Joseph. "No Bosses. And Even 'Leaders' Can't Give Orders," *Business Week*, December 10, 1990, pp. 196–197.

"Wilbert L. Gore," *Industry Week*, October 17, 1983, pp. 48–49.

EXCERPTS FROM INTERVIEWS WITH ASSOCIATES

The first excerpt is from an Associate that was formerly with IBM and has been with Gore for 2 years:

Q: What is the difference between being with IBM and Gore?

A: I spent 24 years working for IBM and there's a big difference. I can go ten times faster here at Gore because of the simplicity of the lattice organization. Let me give you an example. If I wanted to purchase chemicals at IBM (I am an industrial chemist), the first thing I would need to do is get accounting approval, then I would need at least two levels of managers' approval, then a secretary to log in my purchase and the purchase order would go to Purchasing where it would be assigned a buyer. Some time could be saved if you were willing to "walk" the paperwork through the approval process, but even after computerizing the process, it typically would take one month from the time you initiated the purchase requisition till the time the material actually arrived. Here they have one simple form. Usually, I get the chemicals the next day and a copy of the purchase order will arrive a day or two after that. It happens so fast. I wasn't used to that.

Q: Do you find that a lot more pleasant?

A: Yeah, you're unshackled here. There's a lot less bureaucracy that allows you to be a lot more productive. Take lab Safety, for example. In my lab at IBM, we were cited for not having my eyewash taped properly. The first time, we were cited for not having a big enough area taped off. So we taped off a bigger area. The next time the same eyewash was cited again, because the area we taped off was 3 inches too short in one direction. We retaped it and the following week, it got cited again for having the wrong color tape. Keep in mind that the violation was viewed as serious as a pail of gasoline next to a lit Bunsen burner. Another time I had the dubious honor of being selected the functional safety representative in charge of getting the function's labs ready for a Corporate Safety Audit. [The function was a third level in the pyramidal organization—(1) department, (2) project, and (3) function.] At the same time I was working on developing a new surface mount package. As it turned out, I had no time to work on development, and the function spent a lot of time and money getting ready for the Corporate Auditors, who in the end never showed. I'm not belittling the importance of safety, but you really don't need all that bureaucracy to be safe.

The second interview is with an Associate who is a recent engineering graduate:

Q: How did you find the transition coming here?

A: Although I never would have expected it to be, I found my transition coming to Gore to be rather challenging. What attracted me to the company was the opportunity to "be my own boss" and determine my own commitments. I am very goal oriented, and enjoy taking a project and running with it—all things that you are able to do, and encouraged to do within the Gore culture. Thus, I thought, a perfect fit!

However, as a new Associate, I really struggled with where to focus my efforts—I was ready to make my own commitments, but to what?! I felt a strong need to be sure that I was working on something that had value, something that truly needed to be done. While I didn't expect to have the "hottest" project, I did want to make sure that I was helping the company to "make money" in some way.

At the time, though, I was working for a plant that was pretty typical of what Gore was like when it was originally founded—after my first project (which was designed to be a "quick win"—a project with meaning, but one that had a definite end point), I was told "Go find something to work on." While I could have found something, I wanted to find something with at least a small degree of priority! Thus, the whole process of finding a project was very frustrating for me—I didn't feel that I had the perspective to make such a choice, and ended up in many conversations with my sponsor about what would be valuable. . . .

In the end, of course, I did find that project—and it did actually turn out to be a good investment for Gore. The process to get there, though, was definitely trying for someone as inexperienced as I was—so much ground would have been gained by suggesting a few projects to me and then letting me choose from that smaller pool.

What's really neat about the whole thing, though, is that my experience has truly made a difference. Due in part to my frustrations, my plant now provides college grads with more guidance on their first several projects. (This guidance obviously becomes less and less critical as each Associate grows within Gore.) Associates still are choosing their own commitments, but they're doing so with additional perspective, and the knowledge that they are making a contribution to Gore—which is an important thing within our culture. As I said, though, it was definitely rewarding to see that the company was so responsive, and to feel that I had helped to shape someone else's transition!

http://www.gorefabrics.com/

STRATEGY IMPLEMENTATION

The Lincoln Electric Company, 1996*

THE LINCOLN ELECTRIC COMPANY, 1996

It was February 29, 1996. The Lincoln Electric Company, a leading producer of arc welding products, had just celebrated its centennial year by reporting record 1995 sales of over $1 billion, record profits of $61.5 million, and record employee bonuses of $66 million. This performance followed 2 years of losses—the only losses in the company's long history—stemming from a seemingly disastrous foray into Europe, Asia, and Latin America. (Exhibits 1 and 2 tabulate operating results and ratios for recent years.)

Headquartered in the Cleveland suburb of Euclid, Ohio, the company was widely known for its Incentive Management System. According to the *New York Times*, thousands of managers visited Lincoln's headquarters each year for free seminars on the system, which guaranteed lifetime employment, paid its production people only for each piece produced, and paid profit-sharing bonuses which had reportedly averaged 90 percent of annual wages or salary for the 60-year period from 1934–1994.[1] James Lincoln, the main architect of the Incentive Management System, had been dead 30 years by 1995, but he remained a dominant influence on the company's policies and culture.

Record sales and profits, however, were not of themselves cause for complacence. Lincoln Electric had gone public during 1995 in order to reduce the substantial debts it had run up during its 2 losing years; now the company was subject to public scrutiny and such publications as the *New York Times* and *Business Week* questioned whether the famous Incentive Management System was consistent with the firm's obligations to its public stockholders. Dividends for 1995 amounted to $9.1 million, while bonuses had totalled $66 million. Even at $66 million, however, bonuses equalled only 56 percent of employees' annual pay. Some workers complained loudly that the average $21,000 payment in December was far short of what it should have been.

Lincoln's hometown newspaper, the Cleveland *Plain Dealer*, saw the worker complaints as a sign of increasing strain between management and workers. Characteriz-

*Arthur Sharplin, The University of Texas at Austin, Austin, Texas 78731, 512-343-1804, Fax 343-1785; and John A. Seeger, Bentley College G-308, Waltham, MA 02154-4705, 617-891-2532, Fax 891-2896, e-mail jseeger@bentley.edu. The authors thank Richard S. Sabo of Lincoln Electric for help in the field research for this case, which is written solely for the purpose of stimulating student discussion. Management exerted no editorial control over content or presentation of the case. All events and individuals are real.

EXHIBIT 1
Five-Year Operating Results
(in thousands of dollars, except per share data)

	Year Ended December 31				
	1995	*1994*	*1993*	*1992*	*1991*
Net sales	$1,032,398	$906,604	$845,999	$853,007	$833,892
Income (loss) before cumulative effect of accounting change	61,475	48,008	(40,536)	(45,800)	14,365
Cumulative effect of accounting change			2,468		
Net income (loss)	$ 61,475	$ 48,008	$ (38,068)	$ (45,800)	$ 14,365
Per share:					
Income (loss) before cumulative effect of accounting change	$ 2.63	$ 2.19	$ (1.87)	$ (2.12)	$ .67
Cumulative effect of accounting change			.12		
Net income (loss)	$ 2.63	$ 2.19	$ (1.75)	$ (2.12)	$ .67
Cash dividends declared	$ .42	$ .38	$ .36	$ .36	$ .30
Total assets	$ 617,760	$556,857	$559,543	$603,347	$640,261
Long-term debt	$ 93,582	$194,831	$216,915	$221,470	$155,547

ing Lincoln's work pace as "... brutal, a pressure cooker in which employees are constantly graded and peer pressure borders on the fanatical," reporter Thomas Gerdel said Lincoln "faces growing discontent in its workforce."[2] *Business Week* said, "... Lincoln increasingly resembles a typical public company. With institutional shareholders and new, independent board members in place, worker bonuses are getting more of a gimlet eye." Chairman and CEO Donald F. Hastings had set up a committee and hired Price Waterhouse to study the bonus program and the company's productivity.

"If Lincoln can adapt to new times without sacrificing employee good will," said *Business Week*, "another model pay plan may yet emerge."[3]

A HISTORICAL SKETCH

In 1895, having lost control of his first company, John C. Lincoln took out his second patent and began to manufacture an improved electric motor. He opened his new business with $200 he had earned redesigning a motor for young Herbert Henry Dow (who later founded the Dow Chemical Company). In 1909, John Lincoln made his first welding machine (Exhibit 3 describes the welding process). That year, he also brought in James, his younger brother, as a salesman. John preferred being an engi-

EXHIBIT 2
Financial Ratios, 1992–1994

	Fiscal Year Ending December 31			
	1995	*1994*	*1993*	*1992*
Quick ratio	0.89	0.95	0.74	0.89
Current ratio	2.12	2.17	1.85	2.16
Sales/cash	102.35	86.97	41.51	41.35
SG&A/sales	0.28	0.29	0.33	0.35
Receivables: turnover	7.33	7.19	7.66	7.66
Receivables: days sales	49.11	50.04	47.02	46.98
Inventories: turnover	5.65	5.84	5.89	4.98
Inventories: days sales	63.77	61.66	61.14	72.27
Net sales/working capital	5.48	5.35	5.65	4.94
Net sales/net plant & equipment	5.02	4.92	4.99	4.09
Net sales/current assets	2.89	2.89	2.60	2.66
Net sales/total assets	1.67	1.63	1.51	1.41
Net sales/employees	172,066	159,249	140,159	134,714
Total liability/total assets	0.46	0.64	0.73	0.64
Total liability/invested capital	0.67	0.92	1.13	0.92
Total liability/common equity	0.87	1.90	3.01	2.13
Times interest earned	9.07	6.09	−1.66	−0.84
Current debt/equity	0.00	0.01	0.07	0.07
Long-term debt/equity	0.28	1.00	1.51	1.11
Total debt/equity	0.29	1.02	1.58	1.19
Total assets/equity	1.87	2.87	3.90	3.04
Pretax income/net sales	0.10	0.09	−0.06	−0.04
Pretax income/total assets	0.16	0.14	−0.08	−0.06
Pretax income/invested capital	0.24	0.21	−0.13	−0.08
Pretax income/common equity	0.31	0.43	−0.35	−0.19
Net income/net sales	0.06	0.05	−0.04	−0.05
Net income/total assets	0.10	0.09	−0.07	−0.08
Net income/invested capital	0.15	0.12	−0.11	−0.11
Net income/common equity	0.19	0.26	−0.28	−0.25
R&D/net sales	N.A.	N.A.	N.A.	N.A.
R&D/net income	N.A.	N.A.	N.A.	N.A.
R&D/employees	N.A.	N.A.	N.A.	N.A.

Sources: Disclosure, Inc.; Dow-Jones On-Line News Service.

neer and inventor to being a manager, and in 1914 he appointed James Vice President and General Manager. (A condensed history of the firm is shown in Exhibit 4.)

James Lincoln soon asked the employees to form an "Advisory Board." At one of its first meetings, the Advisory Board recommended reducing working hours from 55 per week, then standard, to 50. This was done. In 1934, the famous Lincoln bonus plan was implemented. The first bonus averaged 25 percent of base wages. By 1940, Lincoln employees had twice the average pay and twice the productivity of other Cleveland workers in similar jobs. They also enjoyed the following benefits:

EXHIBIT 3
What Is Arc Welding?

Arc welding was the standard joining method in shipbuilding for decades and remained so in 1995. It was the predominant way of connecting steel in the construction industry. Most industrial plants had their own welding shops for maintenance and construction. Makers of automobiles, tractors, and other items employed arc welding. Welding hobbyists made metal items such as patio furniture and barbecue pits. The popularity of welded sculpture was growing.

Arc welding employs electrical power, typically provided by a "welding machine" composed of a transformer or solid-state inverter connected to a building's electrical system or to an engine-driven generator. The electrical output may vary from 50 to 1,000 amps at 30–60 volts (for comparison, a hair dryer may use 10 amps at 120 volts) and may be alternating or direct current (AC or DC) of varying wave patterns and frequencies. The electrical current travels through a welding electrode and creates an arc to the item being welded. This melts the actual surface of the material being welded, as well as the tip of the electrode, resulting in deposit of the molten metal from the electrode onto the surface. When the molten metal re-freezes, the pieces being joined are fused into one continuous piece of steel.

Welding electrodes—called "consumables" because they are used up in the welding process—are of two main types, short pieces of coated wire (called "stick" electrodes or "welding rods") for manual welding and coils of solid or tubular wire for automatic and semiautomatic processes. The area of the arc must be shielded from the atmosphere to prevent oxidation of the hot metal. This shielding is provided by a stream of inert gas which surrounds the arc (in "MIG," or metallic-inert gas welding) or by solid material called "flux" which melts and covers the liquefied metal surface. Flux often contains substances which combine with the molten metal or catalyze chemical reactions. The flux may be affixed as a coating on welding rods, enclosed inside tubular welding wire, or funneled onto the weld area from a bin (in "submerged arc" welding). Arc welding produces sparks, heat, intense light, and noxious fumes, so operators usually wear face, body, and eye protection and, if ventilation is inadequate, breathing devices.

Other types of welding include oxy-fuel welding, which uses a flame to melt metals together; tungsten-inert gas (TIG) welding, which employs a tungsten electrode to create an arc to melt a welding rod; induction welding, which uses electrical coils to induce currents in the metal being welded, thereby heating it; resistance welding, which heats the weld joint by passing current directly through it; and plasma-arc welding, which is similar to arc welding but involves higher temperatures and a more tightly constrained arc. Related processes include cutting metals with oxy-fuel torches, laser beams, and plasma-arc systems.

An employee stock purchase plan providing stock at book value.

Company paid life insurance.

An employees' association for athletic and social programs and sick benefits.

Piece rates adjusted for inflation.

A suggestion system with cash awards.

A pension plan.

A policy of promotion from within.

A practice, though not then a guarantee, of lifetime employment.

Base pay rates determined by formal job evaluation.

A merit rating system which affected pay.

Paid vacations.

During World War II the company suspended production of electric motors as demand for welding products escalated. Employee bonuses averaged $2,250 in 1942 (about $20,000 in 1995 dollars). Lincoln's original bonus plan was not universally accepted: the Internal Revenue Service questioned the tax deductibility of employee bonuses, arguing they were not "ordinary and necessary" costs of doing business, and the Navy's Price Review Board challenged Lincoln's high profits. But James Lincoln overcame the objections, loudly refusing to retract the firm's obligations to its workers. Also during World War II, Lincoln built factories in Australia, South Africa, and England.

In 1951, Lincoln completed a new main plant in Euclid, Ohio; the factory remained essentially unchanged in 1995. In 1955, Lincoln again began making electric motors, but they represented only a small percentage of the company's revenue through 1995.

EXHIBIT 4
Condensed History of Lincoln Electric Company

1895	Company founded by John C. Lincoln.
1909	James Lincoln joins as salesman. (General Manager, 1914.)
1934	Bonus plan implemented, at 25 percent of base earnings.
1940	Employees earning double the area's average wage.
1942–1945	Factories built in South Africa (later closed), England (later sold to employees), and Australia. Motor production discontinued.
1951	Main factory built in Euclid, Ohio.
1955	Motor production resumed.
1958	Historic guaranteed employment policy formalized.
1965	James Lincoln's death. William Irrgang President.
1970	Annual revenues reach $100 million for the first time.
1972	Irrgang named Chairman/CEO. Ted Willis becomes President.
1977	New electrode factory built in Mentor, Ohio.
1982–1983	Recession slashes revenues. Employees on 30-hour weeks. ESAB begins global expansion.
1986	Willis named Chairman/CEO. Don Hastings becomes President. International operations include five plants in four countries.
1992	Foreign operations include 21 plants in 15 countries. Long-term debt at $220 million. Hastings named Chairman/CEO. Fred Mackenbach named President.
1992–1993	Global recession. First losses in Lincoln's history. International retrenchment begins.
1995	International operations include 16 plants in 11 countries. Public stock issue provides funds for debt reduction. New motor factory built.

Executive Succession

William Irrgang, an engineer and long-time Lincoln protégé, was President when James Lincoln died in 1965. By 1970, Lincoln's annual revenues had grown to $100 million and bonuses were averaging about $8,000 per employee each year (about $30,000 in 1995 dollars). Irrgang was elevated to Chairman in 1972 and Ted Willis, also an engineer and protégé of James Lincoln, became President. In 1977, Lincoln completed a new electrode plant a few miles from Euclid, in Mentor, Ohio, doubling its capacity for making welding wire and rods.

Lincoln's net sales were $450 million in 1981 and employee bonuses averaged $20,760 (abut $34,000 in 1995 dollars) that year. But sales fell by 40 percent in the next 2 years owing, Lincoln management said, to "the combined effects of inflation, sharply higher energy costs, and a national recession." By 1983, the firm's net income and bonuses had collapsed to less than half their 1981 levels. The following table lists the company's bonus amounts from 1981–1995:

The Lincoln Electric Company Bonus History

Year	Total Dollars (millions)	Number Employees	Percent of Wages	Average Gross Bonus	W-2 Average Earnings for Factory Worker
1981	59.0	2684	99.0	22,009	
1982	41.0	2634	80.1	15,643	
1983	26.6	2561	55.4	10,380	
1984	37.0	2469	68.0	15,044	
1985	41.8	2405	73.2	17,391	
1986	37.7	2349	64.8	16,056	
1987	44.0	2349	70.5	18,791	
1988	54.3	2554	77.6	21,264	
1989	54.5	2633	72.0	20,735	47,371
1990	56.2	2701	71.2	20,821	47,809
1991	48.3	2694	65.0	17,935	39,651
1992	48.0	2688	61.9	17,898	40,867
1993	55.0	2676	63.9	20,585	48,738
1994	59.0	2995	60.2	19,659	55,757
1995	64.4	3396	55.9	*21,168	57,758

*Employee with more than 1 year of service.
Source: Lincoln Electric Company document.

But there was no layoff. Many factory workers volunteered to do field sales work and customer assistance. Others were reassigned within the plants, some repairing the roof of the Euclid factory, painting, and cleaning up. The work week, previously averaging about 45 hours, was shortened to 30 for most nonsalaried workers. Several new products, which had been kept in reserve for just this kind of eventuality, were brought to market. Sales, profits, and bonuses began a slow recovery.

Bill Irrgang died in 1986. Ted Willis took over as Chairman and Don Hastings became President, taking primary responsibility for domestic operations.

THE LINCOLN PHILOSOPHY

Throughout the tenures of these CEOs, the business philosophies first articulated by James Lincoln remained in effect, forming the foundation of the company's culture and providing the context within which the Incentive Management System worked. Lincoln's own father had been a Congregationalist minister, and the biblical Sermon on the Mount, with Jesus' praise of meekness, mercifulness, purity of heart, and peacemaking, governed his attitudes toward business. James never evangelized his employees, but he counseled truthfulness in speech, returning evil with good, love of enemies, secret almsgiving, and quiet trust and confidence.[4]

Relationships with Customers

In a 1947 speech, James Lincoln said, "Care should be taken . . . not to rivet attention on profit. Between 'How much do I get?' and 'How do I make this better, cheaper, more useful?' the difference is fundamental and decisive." He later wrote, "When any company has achieved success so that it is attractive as an investment, all money usually needed for expansion is supplied by the customer in retained earnings. It is obvious that the customer's interests, not the stockholder's, should come first." He added,

> The Christian ethic should control our acts. If it did control our acts, the savings in cost of distribution would be tremendous. Advertising would be a contact of the expert consultant with the customer, in order to give the customer the best product available when all of the customer's needs are considered. Competition then would be in improving the quality of products and increasing efficiency in producing and distributing them; not in deception, as is now too customary. Pricing would reflect efficiency of production; it would not be a selling dodge that the customer may well be sorry he accepted. It would be proper for all concerned and rewarding for the ability used in producing the product.

Lincoln's pricing policy, often stated, was "Price on the basis of cost and keep downward pressure on cost." C. Jackson Graham, founder of The American Productivity Institute, said prices of Lincoln products, on average, grew at only one-fifth the rate of inflation in the decades after 1930. Some prices actually went down. For example, Lincoln welding electrodes which sold for $0.16 per pound in 1929 were $0.05 in 1942. And Lincoln's popular SA-200 welder decreased in price from 1958 to 1965. Until the 1990s, Lincoln was the dominant U.S. producer of arc welding products and was able to keep market prices low, especially for consumables. That changed after Miller Welding Co. grew to match Lincoln in U.S. sales of machines and ESAB became the world's largest supplier of consumables and materials. In 1984, Don Hastings said,

> Right now we are paying the price of not having enough capacity in Mentor [Ohio] to supply our customer demand. We are spending money now. But if we had spent it last year, we would not be having the shortages that we're having right now. We're also allowing our competition to raise prices because there's nothing we can do about it without more capacity.

Lincoln quality was legendary. In the refinery and pipeline industries, where price was seldom the main consideration in purchasing, Lincoln welders and electrodes were almost universally specified for decades. Warranty costs at Lincoln typically averaged under $1/4$ percent of sales. A Lincoln distributor in Monroe, Louisiana, said he had sold hundreds of Lincoln welders and had never had a warranty claim.

Lincoln sold its products directly to major customers and indirectly through distributors, most of which were welding supply stores. Lincoln also licensed hundreds of service centers and trained their personnel to do maintenance and warranty work on Lincoln machines. The company maintained a system of regional sales offices, which serviced both direct customers and distributors. In keeping with James Lincoln's principle that salespersons should be "expert consultants," sales jobs at Lincoln were only open to graduate engineers until about 1992, when Hastings changed the policy; he began to recruit majors in liberal arts, business, and other disciplines into the sales force.

Hastings instituted Lincoln's Guaranteed Cost Reduction (GCR) program in 1993. Under GCR, Lincoln sent teams of engineers, technical representatives, and distributors to customer facilities with a goal to "find ways to improve fabrication procedures and product quality as well as methods to increase productivity." Hastings promised, "The Lincoln Electric Company will guarantee in writing that your company's annual arc welding fabrication costs will be reduced by a specified amount. If you don't save that amount, a check will be written for the difference." Lincoln cited these "successes" in its literature promoting GCR:

> A fabricator of steel buildings found GCR savings of $25,000/year and, as a result of the program, developed an improved welding cost analysis system. A manufacturer of heavy grading equipment verified savings in excess of $50,000/year and productivity gains from 50% to 90%. An automotive manufacturer produced productivity increases, in specific welding operations, exceeding 20%. Resultant savings totaled over $1,000,000 a year.

Relationships with Employees

The company professed to still adhere to the basic precepts James Lincoln set down early in his development of the incentive system:

> The greatest fear of the worker, which is the same as the greatest fear of the industrialist in operating a company, is the lack of income. . . . The industrial manager is very conscious of his company's need of uninterrupted income. He is completely oblivious, evidently, of the fact that the worker has the same need.
>
> He is just as eager as any manager is to be part of a team that is properly organized and working for the advancement of our economy. . . . He has no desire to make profits for those who do not hold up their end in production, as is true of absentee stockholders and inactive people in the company.
>
> If money is to be used as an incentive, the program must provide that what is paid to the worker is what he has earned. The earnings of each must be in accordance with accomplishment.
>
> Status is of great importance in all human relationships. The greatest incentive that money has, usually, is that it is a symbol of success. . . . The resulting status is the real incentive. . . . Money alone can be an incentive to the miser only.
>
> There must be complete honesty and understanding between the hourly worker and management if high efficiency is to be obtained.

"I don't work for Lincoln Electric; I work for myself," said Lester Hillier in the 1994 *New York Times* article. "I'm an entrepreneur," added Hillier, a welder at Lincoln for 17 years. Other workers, asked in April of 1995 about why people worked so hard and what motivated them, responded:

Joe Sirko, Machine Operator Since 1941

People want their bonus. And a decent job. No layoffs. I wanted a job where I could spend all the money I make all year and then I get the bonus. I still do that. I go out and live it up. I go to the races. I go everywhere.

When I came here—under James Lincoln—the jobs were given to family. Almost everybody in here was family. My brother got me in. Somebody else's brother got them in or their dad got them in. It was all family. And J. F. backed that a hundred percent. Family, right on down. If you had someone in your family, they were in. Now, they have three different interviewers down there. They all interview.

They hired a lot of people once, to reduce the overtime, remember, and they had all them people when it slowed down. They were sweeping and cleaning—and they didn't know what to do with them. When James Lincoln was alive, he always got up when he gave the bonus and told them—they would be complaining about overtime—he told them that they would either work, because he didn't want to over-hire all them extra people. He believed in all the overtime.

Kathleen Hoenigman, Wiring Harness Assembler Hired in 1977

I worked in factories before and the factories I worked at either went out of business or moved to another state. I will have to say that my money is more here, but I did always make good money. This is much more, because of the bonus. I invest. I also bought a house. Right now, I give my mother money.

I feel that people here that are making all this money, they work so hard for it that they don't want to spend it stupidly and what they do is invest, for the future. And they also, you know, take care of their family.

I like the challenge. I also like the money and the fact that the money is tied to my own output. You have to be motivated yourself. You want the company to succeed, so you want to do better. By having guaranteed employment, the company has to be strong. To me, guaranteed employment means if there's a slowdown you always have a job. Like they'll always take care of you. Back in 1982, when sales slumped, they put me on the roof carrying buckets of tar.

Scott Skrjanc, Welder Hired in 1978

Guaranteed employment is in the back of my mind. I know I'm guaranteed a job. But I also know I have to work to get paid. We don't come in and punch a card and sit down and do nothing.

Linda Clemente, Customer Service Representative Hired in 1986

Well, I guess the biggest thing is guaranteed employment. And I think most people want to be the best that they can be. For other people, maybe the motivation is the money, because they are putting kids through college and things like that. I mean, it's definitely a benefit and something everybody works for.

Relationships with Unions

There had never been a serious effort to organize Lincoln employees. While James Lincoln criticized the labor movement for "selfishly attempting to better its position at the expense of the people it must serve," he still had kind words for union members. He excused union excesses as "the natural reactions of human beings to the abuses to which management has subjected them." He added, "Labor and management are properly not warring camps; they are parts of one organization in which they must and should cooperate fully and happily."

Several of the plants Lincoln acquired during 1986–1992 had unions and the company stated its intention to cooperate with them. No major Lincoln operation had a union in 1995, although 25 of the Ohio employees did attend a union presentation by the United Auto Workers in December, after the announcement of the 1995 bonus rate. "The attendance, out of a total of 3,400 workers, was disappointing even to organizers," said the Cleveland *Plain Dealer*. Lincoln spokesman Bud Fletcher said, "The secret to avoiding those types of situations is that management has to work twice as hard to provide all the elements that membership in an organization like a union would have. We've got to listen, we've got to sit down, we've got to take our time."

Relationships with Stockholders

Through 1992, Lincoln shareholders received dividends averaging less than 5 percent of share price per year and total annual returns averaged under 10 percent. The few public trades of Lincoln shares before 1995 were at only a small premium over book value, which was the official redemption price for employee-owned stock.

"The last group to be considered is the stockholders who own stock because they think it will be more profitable than investing money in any other way," said James Lincoln. Concerning division of the largess produced by Incentive Management, he wrote, "The absentee stockholder also will get his share, even if undeserved, out of the greatly increased profit that the efficiency produces."

Under Hastings, Lincoln gave public shareholders more respect. Dividends, while limited under certain credit agreements, were increased in 1994 in preparation for the public issue, and again in 1995. And the presence of new outside directors on the Lincoln board (see Exhibit 5) seemed to protect public shareholder interests.

THE LINCOLN INCENTIVE MANAGEMENT SYSTEM

Lincoln's Incentive Management System was defined by the firm's philosophy and by the rules, regulations, practices, and programs that had evolved over the 60 years since its origination:

EXHIBIT 5
Officers and Directors of Lincoln Electric Company

Directors

Donald F. Hastings, 67 *1980
Chairman of the Board and
Chief Executive Officer

Frederick W. Mackenbach, 65,
*1992
Retired President and Chief
Operating Officer

Harry Carlson, 61, *1973
Retired Vice Chairman

David H. Gunning, 53, *1987
Chairman, President and Chief
Executive Officer of Capitol
American Financial Corp.

Edward E. Hood, Jr., 65, *1993
Former Vice Chairman of the
Board and Executive Officer of
The General Electric Co.

Paul E. Lego, 65, *1993
President of Intelligent Enterprises

Hugh L. Libby, 70, *1985
Retired Chairman of the Board
and Chief Executive Officer of
Libby Corp.

David C. Lincoln, 70, *1958
Retired Chairman of the Board
and Chief Executive Officer of
Lincoln Laser Co. and President
of Arizona Oxides LLC

Emma S. Lincoln, 73, *1989
Retired
Formerly an Attorney in private
practice

G. Russell Lincoln, 49, *1989
Chairman of the Board and Chief
Executive Officer of Algan, Inc.

Kathryn Jo Lincoln, 41, *1995
Vice President of The Lincoln
Foundation, Inc., and Vice
Chair/Secretary of The Lincoln
Institute of Land Policy

Anthony A. Massaro, 52, *1996
President and Chief Operating
Officer

Henry L. Meyer III, 46, *1994
Chairman of the Board of Society
National Bank and Senior Execu-
tive Vice President and Chief
Operating Officer of KeyCorp.

Lawrence O. Selhorst, 63,
*1992
Chairman of the Board and Chief
Executive Officer of American
Spring Wire Corporation

Craig R. Smith, 70, *1992
Former Chairman and Chief Exec-
utive Officer of Ameritrust
Corporation

Frank L. Steingass, 56, *1971
Chairman of the Board and
President of Buehler/Steingass,
Inc.

Officers

Donald F. Hastings, 67, †1953
Chairman and Chief Executive
Officer

Anthony A. Massaro, 52 †1993
President and Chief Operating
Officer

David J. Fullen, 64, †1955
Executive Vice President
Engineering and Marketing

John M. Stropki, 45, †1972
Executive Vice President
President, North America

Richard C. Ulstad, 56, †1970
Senior Vice President,
Manufacturing

H. Jay Elliott, 54, †1993
Senior Vice President, Chief
Financial Officer and Treasurer

Frederick G. Stueber, 42, †1995
Senior Vice President,
General Counsel and Secretary

Frederick W. Anderson, 43,
†1978
Vice President,
Systems Engineering

Paul J. Beddia, 62, †1956
Vice President, Government and
Community Affairs

Dennis D. Crockett, 53, †1965
Vice President, Consumable
Research and Development

James R. Delaney, 47, †1987
Vice President
President, Lincoln Electric Latin
America

Joseph G. Doria, 46, †1972
Vice President
President and Chief Executive
Officer, Lincoln Electric Company
of Canada

Paul Fantelli, 51, †1970
Vice President,
Business Development

Ronald A. Nelson, 46, †1972
Vice President, Machine
Research and Development

Gary M. Schuster, 41, †1978
Vice President,
Motor Division

Richard J. Seif, 48, †1971
Vice President, Marketing

S. Peter Ullman, 46, †1971
Vice President
President and Chief Executive
Officer, Harris Calorific Division
of Lincoln Electric

Raymond S. Vogt, 54 †1996
Vice President, Human
Resources

John H. Weaver, 57, †1961
Vice President
President, Lincoln Africa, Middle
East and Russia

*Date elected as a Director
†Year joined the Company

Recruitment.   Every job opening at Lincoln was advertised internally on company bulletin boards and any employee could apply. In general, external hiring was permitted only for entry level positions. Often, applicants were relatives or friends of current employees. Selection for these jobs was based on personal interviews—there was no aptitude or psychological testing and no educational requirement—except for engineering and sales positions, which required a college degree. A committee consisting of vice presidents and supervisors interviewed candidates initially cleared by the Personnel Department. Final selection was made by the supervisor who had a job opening. Out of over 3,500 applicants interviewed by the Personnel Department in 1988, fewer than 300 were hired. The odds were somewhat better in 1995, as Lincoln scrambled to staff its new electric motor factory and to meet escalating demand for its welding products.

Training and Education.   New production workers were given a short period of on-the-job training and then placed on a piecework pay system. Lincoln did not pay for off-site education, unless specific company needs were identified. The idea behind this policy was that not everyone could take advantage of such a program, and it was unfair to spend company funds for a benefit to which there was unequal access. Recruits for sales jobs, already college graduates, were given an average of 6 months on-the-job training in a plant, followed by a period of work and training at a regional sales office.

Sam Evans, regional manager for international, described the training program when he joined Lincoln in 1953 as an electrical engineering graduate:

> A few months into the training, I decided to move to sales. During those days, the training program was about a year—several months learning to weld, several months on the factory floor, and in other departments. I got the MBA while I was working in Buffalo as a Sales Engineer.

Merit Rating.   Each manager formally evaluated subordinates twice a year using the cards shown in Exhibit 6. The employee performance criteria—"quality," "dependability," "ideas and cooperation," and "output"—were considered independent of each other. Marks on the cards were converted to numerical scores, which were forced to average 100 for each specified group, usually all the subordinates of one supervisor or other manager. Thus, any employee rated above 100 would have to be balanced off by another rated below 100. Individual merit rating scores normally ranged from 80 to 100. Any score over 110 required a special letter to top management. These scores (over 110) were not considered in computing the required 100 point average for each evaluator. Point scores were directly proportional to the individual's year-end bonus.

Welder Scott Skrjanc seemed typical in his view of the system. "You know, everybody perceives they should get more. That's natural. But I think it's done fairly."

Under Lincoln's early suggestion program, employees were given monetary awards of one-half of the first year's savings attributable to their suggestions. Later, however, the value of suggestions was reflected in merit rating scores. Supervisors were required to discuss performance marks with the employees concerned. Each warranty claim was traced to the individual employee whose work caused the defect, if possible. The employee's performance score was reduced, or the worker could repay the cost of servicing the warranty claim by working without pay.

EXHIBIT 6
Lincoln's Merit Rating Cards

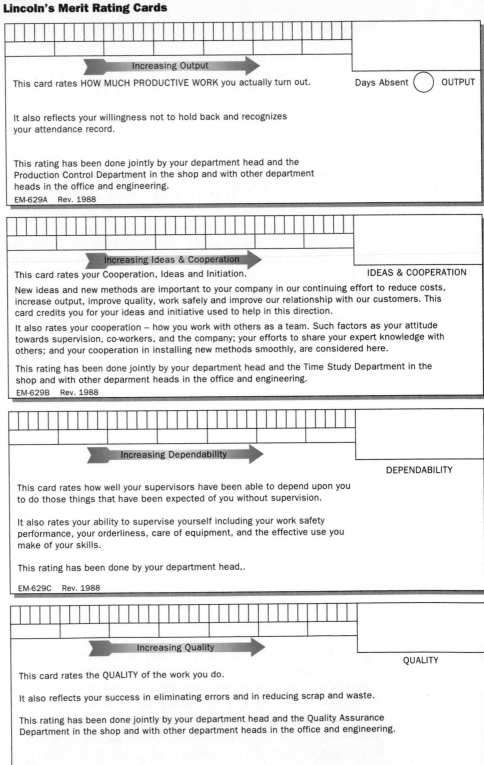

Increasing Output

This card rates HOW MUCH PRODUCTIVE WORK you actually turn out.

Days Absent ◯ OUTPUT

It also reflects your willingness not to hold back and recognizes your attendance record.

This rating has been done jointly by your department head and the Production Control Department in the shop and with other department heads in the office and engineering.

EM-629A   Rev. 1988

Increasing Ideas & Cooperation

This card rates your Cooperation, Ideas and Initiation.

IDEAS & COOPERATION

New ideas and new methods are important to your company in our continuing effort to reduce costs, increase output, improve quality, work safely and improve our relationship with our customers. This card credits you for your ideas and initiative used to help in this direction.

It also rates your cooperation – how you work with others as a team. Such factors as your attitude towards supervision, co-workers, and the company; your efforts to share your expert knowledge with others; and your cooperation in installing new methods smoothly, are considered here.

This rating has been done jointly by your department head and the Time Study Department in the shop and with other deparment heads in the office and engineering.

EM-629B   Rev. 1988

Increasing Dependability

DEPENDABILITY

This card rates how well your supervisors have been able to depend upon you to do those things that have been expected of you without supervision.

It also rates your ability to supervise yourself including your work safety performance, your orderliness, care of equipment, and the effective use you make of your skills.

This rating has been done by your department head,.

EM-629C   Rev. 1988

Increasing Quality

QUALITY

This card rates the QUALITY of the work you do.

It also reflects your success in eliminating errors and in reducing scrap and waste.

This rating has been done jointly by your department head and the Quality Assurance Department in the shop and with other department heads in the office and engineering.

EM-629D   Rev. 1988

Compensation.   Basic wage levels for jobs at Lincoln were determined by a wage survey of similar jobs in the Cleveland area. These rates were adjusted quarterly in response to changes in the Cleveland Area Wage Index, compiled by the U.S. Department of Labor. Wherever possible, base wage rates were translated into piece rates. Practically all production workers—even some fork truck operators—were paid by the piece. Once established, piece rates were changed only if there was a change in the methods, materials, or machinery used in the job. Each individual's pay was calculated from a daily Piecework Report, filled out by the employee. The payroll department, responsible for paying 3,000 employees, consisted of four people; there was no formal control system for checking employee's reports of work done.

In December of each year, bonuses were distributed to employees. Incentive bonuses from 1934 to 1994 averaged about 90 percent of annual wages, company managers said; the total bonus pool typically exceeded after-tax (and after-bonus) profits. Individual bonuses were determined by merit rating scores. For example, if the Board of Directors authorized a bonus equal to 80 percent of total base wages paid, a person whose performance score averaged 95 in the two previous evaluation periods received a bonus of 76 percent (0.80×0.95) of base wages.

Because of company losses in 1992 and 1993, the bonus was about 60 percent of base wages and management was forced to borrow $100 million to pay it. After Lincoln's turnaround in 1994, the 60 percent bonus rate was continued.

Continuous Employment.   In 1958 Lincoln formalized its guaranteed continuous employment policy, which had already been in effect for many years. Starting in 1958, every worker with over 2 years' longevity was guaranteed at least 30 hours per week, 49 weeks per year. The requirement was changed to 3 years' longevity in the recession year of 1982, when the policy was severely tested. In previous recessions the company had been able to avoid major sales declines. However, sales plummeted 32 percent in 1982 and another 16 percent the next year. Management cut most of the nonsalaried workers back to 30 hours a week for varying periods of time. Many employees were reassigned and the total workforce was slightly reduced through normal attrition and restricted hiring. The previous year had set records, and some employees grumbled at their unexpected misfortune, to the surprise and dismay of some Lincoln managers.

Among employees with a year or more of service, employee turnover ran only 4 percent at Lincoln Electric. Absenteeism, too, was extremely low; critics in the press noted this was understandable, since workers were not paid for sick days. They noted, too, that 25 to 30 percent of new hires quit in their first 6 months of work, in spite of Lincoln's intensive interview process. In 1995, Lincoln's Cleveland workers were averaging over 45 hours a week on the job. Employee turnover after the first year was under 1 percent per year, excluding retirements. "The vast majority that quit do so before their first bonus," said Dick Sabo, director of corporate communications. "Once they see the dollars, they realize they are extremely well paid for their efforts." The average length of service of Lincoln's Cleveland workers in 1995 was about 14 years.

Stock Ownership by Employees.   James Lincoln said that financing for company growth should come from within the company—through initial cash investment by the founders, through reinvestment of earnings, and through stock purchases by those who work in the business. He claimed this approach gave the following advantages:

1. Ownership of stock by employees strengthens team spirit. "If they are mutually anxious to make it succeed, the future of the company is bright."

2. Ownership of stock provides individual incentive because employees feel that they will benefit from company profitability.

3. "Ownership is educational." Owner-employees "will know how profits are made and lost; how success is won and lost."

4. "Capital available from within controls expansion." Unwarranted expansion would not occur, Lincoln believed, under his financing plan (which did not allow for borrowing capital for growth).

5. "The greatest advantage would be the development of the individual worker. Under the incentive of ownership, he would become a greater man."

6. "Stock ownership is one of the steps that can be taken that will make the worker feel that there is less of a gulf between him and the boss."

Under Lincoln's Employees' Stock Purchase Plan, each employee could buy a specified number of shares of restricted common stock from the company each year, with company financing. The stock was priced at "estimated fair value" (taken to be book value) and the company had an option to repurchase it. Lincoln had always exercised its option to repurchase shares tendered by employees and many employees felt it was obligated to do so. In 1992, approximately 75 percent of the employees owned over 40 percent of the total stock of the company. Lincoln family members and former Lincoln executives owned about half the remainder.

As Lincoln was preparing to report its first quarterly loss in August 1992 the directors voted to suspend repurchases under the Stock Purchase Plan, in order to prevent wholesale tendering of shares by employees at a time when Lincoln was short of cash. The change in policy meant that employees could sell their stock in the open market as unrestricted stock if they wished to convert it to cash. At that time, book value (and therefore market value) was about $19 per share. As it turned out, only 11 percent of the unrestricted shares were converted.

In preparation for the public issue of stock in 1995, the Employees' Stock Purchase Plan was terminated on March 30, automatically converting all shares issued under it to unrestricted stock. Market value of the shares at that time was about $40. After the public issue, shareholders approved a new stock purchase plan permitting employees to purchase up to $10,000 per year in open-market shares without brokers' commissions.

Vacations.   Lincoln's plants were shut down for 2 weeks in August and 2 weeks during the Christmas season for vacations, which were unpaid. For employees with over 25 years of service, a fifth week of vacation was allowed at a time acceptable to superiors. When Lincoln was unable to meet its customers' orders in 1994, most employees agreed to work overtime through the August vacation period. Some of these employees were given vacation at alternate times.

Fringe Benefits.   Lincoln sponsored a medical plan (whose cost was deducted from the annual bonus pool) and a company-paid retirement program. At the main plant, a cafeteria operated on a break-even basis serving meals at about 60 percent of outside prices. The Employee Association, to which the company did not contribute, provided disability insurance and social and athletic activities. Dick Sabo commented,

> The company maintains traditional fringe benefits which include life insurance, health care, paid vacations, an annuity program (401K), and a variety of employee participation activities. All of these programs, of course, reduce the amount of money which otherwise could be received by the employees as bonus. Each employee is, therefore, acutely aware of the impact of such benefit items on their overall earnings in each year.

He also cautioned,

> When you use "participation," put quotes around it. Because we believe that each person should participate only in those decisions he is most knowledgeable about. I don't think production employees should control the decisions of the Chairman. They don't know as much as he does about the decisions he is involved in.

The primary means of employee participation beyond an employee's immediate work environment were the suggestion program and the Advisory Board. Members of the Advisory Board were elected by employees and met with President Fred Mackenbach every 2 weeks. Unlike James Lincoln and Bill Irrgang, CEOs Willis and Hastings did not regularly attend these meetings. Responses to all Advisory Board items were promised by the following meeting. Exhibit 7 provides excerpts from minutes of the Advisory Board meeting of March 14, 1995 (generally typical of the group's deliberations).

The Advisory Board could only advise, not direct, although its recommendations were taken seriously. Its influence was shown on December 1, 1995, when Lincoln reversed a 2-year-old policy of paying lower wages to new hires. Veteran workers had complained loudly. *Business Week* quoted Joseph Tuck, an inspector with 18 years' service: "If an individual shows he can handle the workload, he should be rewarded" with full pay.[5]

INTERNATIONAL EXPANSION

Internationally, the welding equipment industry was highly fragmented but consolidating. No global statistics reported total economic activity or companies' market shares in various countries, but many developed economies had local suppliers. Two U.S. producers—Lincoln and Miller Electric—and one European firm, ESAB (the largest welding firm in the world by 1996), were present in most markets. (Exhibit 8 shows Lincoln's recent sales by region.)

Until 1986, Lincoln Electric held to James Lincoln's original policy toward international ventures, according to Sam Evans, Regional Manager of International and a 40-year Lincoln veteran. James Lincoln felt his company could manufacture in any

---

EXHIBIT 7
Excerpts from Advisory Board Minutes, March 14, 1995

Mr. Mackenbach opened the meeting by welcoming three new members to the Board. He called on Mr. Beddia to inform the Board about the Harvest for Hunger food drive.

Prior Items
1. Could all air-cooled engines be covered when we receive them? Answer: The Material Handling Department will cover the top pallet of each stack when the engines are unloaded.
2. Could the 401K contributions from bonus be included in the year-to-date totals on the remaining regular December pay stubs? Answer: Yes, it will be.
3. An employee was almost hit by a speeding electric cart in Bay 16. Could a slow speed sign be posted? Answer: Signs cautioning pedestrians regarding Towmotor traffic have been installed. Additional changes are being reviewed.

New Business
1. Why was an employee of the Motor Division penalized for a safety issue when he performed his job as instructed? Answer: Referred to Mr. Beddia.
2. Has our total percent of market share increased? Answer: In the past, we could provide a precise answer. Some of our competitors no longer provide the required information to NEMA. However, in our judgment, we are increasing our percent of market share in both consumables and equipment.
3. Could an additional microwave unit be installed in Bay 24 vending area? Answer: Referred to Mr. Crissey.
4. Could we consider buying an emergency vehicle instead of paying between $300 and $500 per ambulance run to the hospital? Answer: When we use the services of the Euclid Fire and Rescue Squad, there is a charge of approximately $350. While in general this charge is covered by hospitalization insurance, we will ask Mr. Trivisonno to review this with city officials.
5. When will the softball field be completed? Answer: A recreational area on the EP-3 site will become a reality, although certain issues with the city must be resolved first. We will show the preliminary layout at the next meeting.
6. Is a member of the Board of Directors being investigated for fraud? Answer: We are not aware of any investigation of this type.
7. Is our investment in Mexico losing value? Could we have an update as to how our Mexican operation is doing? Answer: Yes. An update will be provided at the next meeting.
8. Could something be done to eliminate the odor created when the septic tank is cleaned? Answer: Referred to Mr. Hellings.

English-speaking country. Otherwise, he let others promote Lincoln products internationally. Evans described the approach:

> We dealt with Armco International, which was a division of Armco Steel. Lincoln licensed Armco to manufacture and market our products in Mexico, Uruguay, Brazil, Argentina, and in France. It was electrodes, but included assembly of machines in Mexico. Armco also marketed Lincoln products along the Pacific Rim and in a few other areas of the world. At one point, we also had a joint venture with Big Three Corporation in Scotland.

In 1986, Lincoln Electric faced a newly aggressive Scandinavian competitor, ESAB Corporation, part of the Swiss-Swedish engineering/energy group Asea Brown Boveri. ESAB had bought up welding products manufacturers throughout the world during the industry downturn of 1982–1985. Starting in 1986, ESAB began to penetrate the U.S. market, buying several U.S. welding products companies (trade names acquired by ESAB included Oxweld, Genuine Heliarc, Plasmarc, Allstate Welding Products, Alloy Rods, and the former Lindy Division of Union Carbide). ESAB opened an electrode plant less than a mile from Lincoln's Cleveland headquarters.

EXHIBIT 8
Financial Results by Geographic Sector, 1993–1995
(in thousands of dollars)

	United States	Europe	Other Countries	Total*
1995:				
Net sales to unaffiliated customers†	$711,940	$201,672	$118,786	$1,032,398
Pre-tax profit (loss)	79,737	10,171	10,956	99,584
Identifiable assets	404,972	194,319	80,921	617,760
1994:				
Net sales to unaffiliated customers	$641,607	$156,803	$108,194	$906,604
Pre-tax profit (loss)	68,316	7,891	4,062	80,168
Identifiable assets	350,012	165,722	76,129	556,857
1993:				
Net sales to unaffiliated customers	$543,458	$211,268	$91,273	$845,999
Pre-tax profit (loss)	42,570	(68,865)	(22,903)	(46,950)
Identifiable assets	389,247	172,136	69,871	559,543

*Totals for profit/loss and identifiable assets will not cross-add due to elimination of intercompany transactions.
†Net sales reported for the United States include materials exported to unaffiliated customers, amounting to $81,770 in 1995; $64,400 in 1994; and $58,100 in 1993. Net sales excludes intracompany sales to Lincoln's overseas branches.

In the global recession of the early 1980s, ESAB's movement toward consolidation threatened to give the firm a volume base large enough to provide economies of scale for research and development programs. Dick Sabo said Lincoln's CEO, Ted Willis, was concerned and met with the Chairman of ESAB in 1986, hoping "that we could work together." The relationship soon soured, however, and Willis decided to challenge ESAB internationally.

From 1986 to 1992, Lincoln purchased controlling interests in manufacturing and marketing operations in 16 countries. It took over most of the operations previously licensed to Armco and Big Three. It put a factory in Brazil, where ESAB had an estimated 70 percent market share. Lincoln expanded into gas welding and cutting by buying Harris Calorific Corporation, which made oxyacetylene cutting and welding equipment in the U.S., Italy, and Ireland. Lincoln's largest new investment was purchase of Messer Griesheim's welding products business in Germany, considered ESAB's most profitable territory. Altogether, Lincoln opened or expanded plants in England, France, the Netherlands, Spain, Norway, Mexico, Venezuela, and Japan. The expansion required heavy borrowing; for the first time, James Lincoln's conservative financial policies were discarded. Long-term debt rose from zero in 1986 to over $220 million in 1992. (Exhibit 9 summarizes Lincoln financial statements for 1986–1994.)

Separate Lincoln-type incentive management plans remained in place at the company's factories in Australia, Mexico, and the United States, but attempts to implement such plans in other countries were largely unsuccessful. Sabo said the main problem was that Europe lapsed into recession. He added, "Germany started to fail

EXHIBIT 9
Summaries of Lincoln Financial Statements, 1986–1994
(in millions of dollars)

Balance Sheet

	12/86	12/87	12/88	12/89	12/90	12/91	12/92	12/93	12/94
Assets:									
Cash and equivalents	$ 47.0	$ 61.0	$ 23.9	$ 19.5	$ 15.5	$ 20.3	$ 20.6	$ 20.4	$ 10.4
Receivables	46.0	61.7	90.9	100.8	127.3	118.0	111.3	110.5	126.0
Inventories	52.3	74.7	116.3	120.5	164.4	206.3	171.3	143.7	155.3
Other current assets	9.4	9.1	12.0	14.4	14.5	17.5	18.0	51.1	21.7
Total current assets	$154.7	$206.5	$243.1	$255.1	$321.7	$362.1	$321.2	$325.7	$313.4
Gross plant	$153.2	$195.7	$274.8	$328.2	$387.7	$422.9	$435.2	$406.7	$444.5
Accumulated depreciation	93.4	121.2	148.6	170.2	193.1	213.3	226.8	237.0	260.3
Net plant	$ 59.8	$ 74.5	$126.3	$158.0	$194.7	$209.6	$208.4	$169.7	$184.2
Long-term investments	11.5	0.3	0.0	0.0	0.0	0.0	0.0	0.0	0.0
Intangible and other assets	13.1	13.4	33.8	42.6	55.9	68.6	73.7	64.1	59.2
Total assets	$239.2	$294.7	$403.2	$455.8	$572.2	$640.3	$603.3	$559.5	$556.9
Liabilities and equity:									
Short-term debt	$ 4.6	$ 6.6	$ 39.2	$ 41.6	$ 40.6	$ 50.7	$ 27.1	$ 33.4	$ 18.1
Accounts payable	11.2	23.4	36.8	40.0	44.3	46.6	44.2	43.5	54.8
Other current liabilities	25.1	32.7	38.1	41.0	52.4	61.3	77.2	99.0	71.2
Total current liabilities	$ 40.9	$ 62.7	$114.1	$122.6	$137.3	$158.6	$148.5	$175.9	$144.1
Long-term debt	$ 0.0	$ 5.7	$ 17.5	$ 30.2	$109.2	$155.5	$221.5	$216.9	$194.8
Other long-term liabilities	11.7	9.7	15.3	16.6	24.0	20.3	17.8	15.3	17.0
Minority interests	4.0	11.9	31.4	42.6	47.4	41.7	16.8	7.9	6.8
Total liabilities	$ 56.6	$ 90.0	$178.4	$211.9	$317.9	$376.1	$404.6	$416.0	$218.6
Common equity	$182.6	$204.7	$224.8	$243.8	$254.3	$264.1	$198.7	$143.5	$194.1
Total equity capital	$182.6	$204.7	$224.8	$243.8	$254.3	$264.1	$198.7	$143.5	$194.1
Total liabilities and capital	$239.2	$294.7	$403.2	$455.8	$572.2	$640.3	$603.3	$559.5	$556.9

EXHIBIT 9 (continued)

	12/86	12/87	12/88	12/89	12/90	12/91	12/92	12/93	12/94
				Income Statement					
Net sales	$370.2	$443.2	$570.2	$692.8	$796.7	$833.9	$853.0	$846.0	$906.6
Cost of goods sold	245.4	279.4	361.0	441.3	510.5	521.8	553.1	532.8	556.3
Gross profit	$124.8	$163.8	$209.2	$251.5	$286.2	$312.1	$299.9	$313.2	$350.3
SG&A expense	100.3	119.7	165.2	211.1	259.2	270.5	280.3	273.3	261.7
Operating profit	$ 24.5	$ 44.1	$ 44.0	$ 40.4	$ 27.0	$ 41.6	$ 19.6	$ 39.9	$ 88.6
Restructuring charge	—	—	—	—	—	—	−23.9	−70.1	2.7
Non-recurring operating expense	—	—	—	—	—	—	−18.9	−3.7	—
Other income	6.1	7.1	14.4	15.7	14.4	8.5	7.5	4.5	4.5
EBIT	$ 30.6	$ 51.2	$ 58.4	$ 56.1	$ 41.4	$ 50.1	$−15.7	$−29.4	$ 95.9
Interest expense	1.0	1.3	2.6	7.6	11.1	15.7	18.7	17.6	15.7
Pretax earnings	$ 29.6	$ 49.9	$ 55.9	$ 48.5	$ 30.4	$ 34.4	$−34.4	$−47.0	$ 80.2
Income taxes	13.7	22.3	21.5	21.0	19.3	20.0	11.4	−6.4	32.2
Accounting change	—	—	—	—	—	—	—	2.5	—
Net income	$ 15.9	$ 27.6	$ 34.4	$ 27.6	$ 11.1	$ 14.4	$−45.8	$−38.1	$ 48.0

Source of data: McDonald anc Company and SEC reports.

within two months after we purchased Griesheim. The country had 27% unemployment. So we didn't implement the system at all. We didn't get a chance to." In Brazil, Willis learned that regulations defined incentive bonuses to be part of base salaries, which could not be reduced during downturns, so the Lincoln system was not installed there.

Welder Scott Skrjanc, a 17-year veteran of the production force, had another idea about why the system did not work out overseas:

> Their culture, as I understand it, was so much different from ours. Their work ethic and work habits, I guess, aren't like the United States. They have a saying in German that means, "slowly, slowly, but good." And I guess that's how they perceive it. Here, we do high quality work, but we work fast—and smart. As you get older, you get wiser and work smarter.

Sam Evans, who had run Lincoln's operations in Eastern Europe until cancer forced his return to Cleveland for successful treatment, gave his view of CEO Willis's performance in the international expansion:

> Ted Willis's belief—and I think it was a very good belief, although he is often criticized by Lincoln people—was that we needed a stronger world organization. The welding industry was consolidating in the world market, much like the steel industry did in the 1930s. He felt we needed this larger sales base so that we could invest in the research and development to maintain our position in the industry. I think that has succeeded. Even though we have had failures internationally, we have grown with our base.
>
> We are coming out with a lot of new items—the new square-wave machines, which control the actual wave form, the new stainless products, the inverter technology in motors and machines. We are moving rapidly ahead of the industry. That was Mr. Willis's vision, and it was a good one. His financial vision wasn't so good—perhaps.

Retrenchment and Turnaround under Hastings

Willis retired in 1992 and Don Hastings became Chief Executive Officer. Hastings set about "consolidating and reorganizing" the foreign operations. He agreed with ESAB to close the Lincoln factory in Brazil and to license ESAB to make Lincoln products there. Similarly, ESAB closed its Spanish electrode plant and Lincoln used its excess capacity in that country to supply ESAB's needs. Lincoln mothballed its German plant, losing an estimated $100 million there. It also shut down factories in Venezuela and Japan. Practically all Lincoln's international operations which were not closed were scaled back. By 1996 ESAB, now owned by Britain's Charter Group, was recognized as the largest welding vendor in the world, with key markets in Eastern and Western Europe, South America, and the Far East; it had the "leading position in stick electrodes (a declining market) and an even bigger position in fluxed core wires (a rapidly growing market)."[6]

In 1992 and 1993, Lincoln wrote off about $130 million of its assets and reported its first-ever net losses—$46 million and $38 million, respectively. Citing the performance of the firm's U.S. workers, Hastings convinced the Board of Directors to give them incentive bonuses of 60 percent of wages each year in spite of the losses. Dividends were cut by nearly 40 percent from the 1991 level. In 1994, Hastings told the

U.S. employees, "We went from five plants in four countries in 1986 to 21 plants in 15 countries in 1992. We did it too fast, we paid too much, we didn't understand the international markets or cultures, and then we got hit by a tremendous global recession." By mid-1995, Lincoln was down to 16 plants in 11 countries. Dick Sabo described the company's new relationship with ESAB:

> So the animosity has ended. We're still competitors, but we are more like the U.S. competitors. In the U.S., we've always had a competitive situation, but we're friendly competitors. So, overall, the strategy that Ted Willis originated was good. The implementation was poor. That's where the problem was.

Rank and file employees commented on the results of the attempt at international expansion. Stenographer Dee Chesko, a 27-year employee, said she had heard no bitterness voiced about the losses:

> What I was hearing was people were disappointed—that they felt upper management should know, per se, what they're doing. You know, how could this happen? Not bitterness . . . a little frustration. But, if companies are to expand and be global, this has to be expected.

Assembler Kathleen Hoenigman, hired in 1977, added:

> They say, "We want to be number one. We want to be number one." So we are going to keep buying and buying and buying. I think we will be investing more overseas. And I think we are going to be number one internationally, not just in the United States, but the manufacturing will be done here. The expansion helped. We lost money, but I think it helped. You know what, if we didn't do as we did, we wouldn't be known as well as we are right now. Because we were staying just like a little . . . a little pea, while everybody was building up around us.

Sabo said Lincoln expected to continue expanding internationally, "But we're going at it a little differently." He explained,

> Under Willis, we bought a manufacturing site with the intent of creating the marketing demand. Under Hastings, we're developing the marketing demand with the anticipation that we'll build the manufacturing site to meet the demand. So what we're trying to do is take the existing facilities that we have and sell a lot of product and create enough demand so that we have to buy—or build—more facilities to service that demand.
>
> We're just getting there in terms of being global. We're global to the extent that we market in 123 countries. We're global to the extent that we have distributors in 86 different countries. We're global because we have manufacturing sites in ten countries. Are we global in our management style? No. We're just starting to develop that.

THE U.S. WELDING PRODUCTS INDUSTRY IN 1995

The welding products market of the mid-1990s was classified as "mature and cyclical." In the United States, annual sales volume had ranged between $2.5 and $2.7 billion since 1988 (see Exhibit 10). The main arc welding products were power sources

EXHIBIT 10
Trends and Forecasts: Welding Apparatus (SIC 3548)
(in millions of dollars except as noted)

	1987	1988	1989	1990	1991	1992*	1993†	1994‡
Industry data:								
Value of shipments §	$2,105	$2,498	$2,521	$2,684	$2,651	$2,604	$2,576	
Total employment (000)	18.7	19.7	19.0	19.2	19.5	19.4	19.5	
Production workers (000)	11.5	12.3	11.6	12.0	11.8	11.7	11.7	
Average hourly earnings (in dollars)	$12.10	$12.45	$12.67	$13.15	$13.07			
Capital expenditures	$ 45.4	$ 49.3	$ 59.1	$ 67.7	$ 50.5			
Product data:								
Value of shipments¶	$1,918	$2,263	$2,298	$2,475	$2,434	$2,374	$2,340	
Value of shipments (1987 $)	1,918	2,135	2,077	2,154	2,034	1,935	1,874	1,954
Trade data:								
Value of imports	—	—	480	365	478	381	458	458
Value of exports	—	—	491	566	597	621	661	671

	Percent Change (1989–1994)					
	88–89	89–90	90–91	91–92	92–93	93–94
Industry data:						
Value of shipments §	0.9%	6.5%	−1.2%	−1.8%	−1.1%	
Value of shipments (1987 $)	−3.3	2.5	−5.2	−4.1	−3.0	3.9%
Total employment (000)	−3.6	1.1	1.6	−0.5	0.5	
Production workers (000)	−5.7	3.4	−1.7	−0.8	0.0	
Average hourly earnings ($)	1.8	3.8	−0.6			
Capital expenditures	19.9	14.6	−25.4			
Product data:						
Value of shipments¶	1.5%	7.7%	−1.7%	−2.5%	−1.4%	
Value of shipments (1987 $)	−2.7	3.7	−5.6	−4.9	−3.2	4.3%
Value of exports	747	15.3	5.5	4.0	8.1	11.3

*Estimate, except exports and imports.
†Estimate.
‡Forecast.
§Value of all products and services sold by establishments in the welding apparatus industry.
¶Value of products classified in the welding apparatus industry.
Source: U.S. Department of Commerce: Bureau of the Census; *International U.S. Industrial Outlook*, January, 1994.

and welding machines, consumable items such as welding electrodes, accessories such as protective clothing, automated wire feeding systems, and devices to manipulate or position the electrodes, such as robots.

After the downturn in 1982–1983, when industry sales fell 30–40 percent, the U.S. welding products industry consolidated. By 1995, at least 75 percent of machine and consumables sales could be attributed to just four companies: Lincoln, Miller Electric Company (which did not sell consumables), ESAB Corporation, and Hobart Brothers, Inc. ESAB was now owned by Britain's Charter Group; both Miller and

Hobart had recently been acquired by Illinois Tool Works, Inc. Lincoln and Miller were thought to have about equal unit sales of machines and power supplies, about double Hobart's volume. Hundreds of smaller companies marketed various niche products and several international firms sold limited lines of transformer- and inverter-based machines in the United States and elsewhere. Over 600 exhibitors were registered to show their wares at the 1996 annual Welding Show in Chicago, where 25,000 potential customers would attend.

Starting in the early 1990s, Lincoln, Miller, and Hobart each began buying similar articulated-arm robots and adapting them to welding applications. The size of the robotics segment of the welding products market was unclear in 1995, but Chet Woodman, head of Lincoln Automation, said his unit had robotics sales of about $7 million in 1994 and predicted $50 million annual revenue by the year 2000.

ESAB, Lincoln, and Hobart each marketed a wide range of continuous-wire and stick electrodes for welding mild steel, aluminum, cast iron, and stainless and special steels. Most electrodes were designed to meet the standards of the American Welding Society (AWS) and were thus essentially the same as to size and composition from one manufacturer to another. Price differences for similar products among the three companies amounted to only a percent or two. Low-price competitors were well represented in the market, however, as imported consumables that purported to meet AWS standards were commonly available. There was no testing system to confirm a product's conformance to the standards.

Every electrode manufacturer had a limited number of unique products, which typically constituted only a small percentage of its total sales. There were also many producers of specialized electrodes for limited applications, such as welding under water and welding space-age alloys, and several international companies marketed general-purpose electrodes. Wire for gas-shielded (MIG) welding was thought to be the biggest-selling welding consumable. ESAB claimed to have the largest share of the global welding consumables and materials market.

LINCOLN'S MANUFACTURING PROCESSES

Lincoln made about twice as many different products in 1995 as it had 10 years earlier. Its net sales per employee in 1994 were $159,248. For U.S. employees only, the number was about $225,000. About 2/3 of net sales was represented by products made in the Cleveland area.

Fortune magazine declared Lincoln's Euclid operation one of America's ten best-managed factories, and compared it to a General Electric plant also on the list:

> Stepping into GE's spanking new dishwasher plant, an awed supplier said, is like stepping "into the Hyatt Regency." By comparison, stepping into Lincoln Electric's 33 year-old, cavernous, dimly lit factory is like stumbling into a dingy big-city YMCA. It's only when one starts looking at how these factories do things that similarities become apparent. They have found ways to merge design with manufacturing, build in quality, make wise choices about automation, get close to customers, and handle their work forces.[7]

As it had for decades, Lincoln required most suppliers to deliver raw materials just as needed in production. James Lincoln had counseled producing for stock when necessary to maintain employment. For many years after his death, however, the firm manufactured only to customer order. In the late 1980s, Hastings decided to resume maintaining substantial finished goods inventories. Lincoln then purchased its finished goods warehouse.

Outsourcing

It was James Lincoln's policy to keep Lincoln as insulated as possible from work stoppages in supplier plants, especially unionized ones. He also felt Lincoln quality was higher than that most suppliers could provide. So instead of purchasing most components from outsiders, Lincoln made them from basic industrial raw materials such as coils of steel sheet and bar, pieces of metal plate, spools of copper and aluminum wire, and pallets of paints and varnishes. Lincoln even made its own electronic circuit boards, to assure their performance in outdoor, cold, dirty conditions; commercial suppliers were accustomed to making circuits boards for warm, clean computers. At one point the firm had contemplated buying its own steel rolling mill. President Ted Willis, however, was concerned over the mill's union affiliation, and the purchase was not completed.

As an exception to on-site manufacture of components, gasoline and diesel engines for the engine-driven machines were purchased. Like its main competitors, Lincoln used Wisconsin-Continental, Perkins, and Deutz engines in 1995.

Welding Machine Manufacture

In the Machines area, most engine-driven welders, power supplies, wire feeders, and so forth were assembled, tested, and packaged on conveyor lines. Almost all components were made by numerous small "factories within a factory." Various of these small factories—mostly open work areas—made gasoline tanks, steel shafts, wiring harnesses, and even switches, rheostats, and transformers. The shaft for a certain generator, for example, was made from round steel bar by two men who used five machines. A saw cut the bar to length, a digital lathe machined differed sections to varying diameters, a special milling machine cut a slot for the keyway, and so forth, until a finished shaft was produced. The operators moved the shafts from machine to machine and made necessary adjustments and tool changes. Nearby, a man punched, shaped and painted sheet metal cowling parts. In another area, a woman and a man put steel laminations onto rotor shafts, then wound, insulated, and tested the rotors. Many machines in the factory appeared old, even obsolete; James Lincoln had always insisted on a 1-year payback period for new investments, and it appeared the policy was still in effect.

Consumables Manufacture

The company was secretive about its consumables production and outsiders were barred from the Mentor, Ohio, plant (which made only electrodes) and from the electrode area of the main plant. Electrode manufacture was highly capital intensive and teams of Lincoln workers who made electrodes shared group piece rates. To make electrodes, rod purchased from metals producers, usually in coils, was drawn down to make wire of various diameters. For stick electrodes, the wire was cut into pieces, most commonly 14" long, and coated with pressed-powder "flux." Dick Sabo commented,

> The actual production of a stick electrode has not changed for at least forty years. Bill Irrgang designed that equipment. As to the constituents which make up the electrodes, that may change almost daily. There are changes in design from time to time. And every new batch of raw material has a little different consistency, and we have to adjust for that. We make our own iron oxide [a main ingredient of many fluxes]. We have had that powder kiln in operation since about the 1930s. We may have the largest production facility for iron oxide pellets in the world. At first, we contemplated selling the pellets. But we decided not to give our competition an edge.

Stick electrodes were packaged in boxes weighing 2 to 50 pounds. Continuous-wire electrode, generally smaller in diameter, was packaged in coils and spools, also 2 to 50 pounds each, and drums weighing up to half a ton. Some wire electrode was coated with copper to improve conductivity. Lincoln's Innershield wire, like the "cored" wire of other manufacturers, was hollow and filled with a material similar to that used to coat stick electrodes.

The New Electric Motor Factory

In 1992, Lincoln saw an opportunity to become a major factor in the electric motor business by purchasing the assets of General Motors' AC-Delco plant in Dayton, Ohio. New government regulations on motors' energy efficiency made it necessary to re-design whole product lines; GM decided instead to exit the industry. Lincoln's intent was to combine AC-Delco's technology and product line with Lincoln's manufacturing expertise and cost structure in the Dayton plant. Don Hastings offered to involve the existing union in its operation of the plant if it were retained. Dick Sabo described the implementation efforts:

> We asked the AC-Delco employees if they wanted to adopt the Lincoln Incentive System and keep their plant open—and their jobs. They voted overwhelmingly not to adopt the system. And they knew all about us. We put a lot of effort into telling them about Lincoln, even brought some employees up here to tour our plant and talk to Lincoln people. What struck Mr. Hastings as odd was that people would vote themselves out of work rather than knuckle down and put in the effort that it takes to be in the motor business. That was sort of an eye opener for Lincoln Electric.

In mid-1995, Lincoln's new electric motor factory, close to the main plant, was near completion and in partial operation. The plant was designed to make motors from 1/3 to 1,250 horsepower, in custom configurations as well as standard specifications, with shipment 6 days after customer orders. Lincoln's net sales of electric motors in 1994 totalled about $50 million, and the goal was $100 million in sales by the year 2000.

Robotics

Adjacent to the electric motor factory was a smaller building housing Lincoln's Automation unit. There, work teams of two or three put together robotic welding units that combined Fanuc (Japanese) articulated arms with Lincoln automatic welders. In operation, the robot arm manipulated the wire electrode much as a human operator would, but faster and more accurately. The system, priced at about $100,000, could be purchased with a laser "eye," to track irregular seams and could be programmed to follow any three-dimensional path within the arm's reach. Chet Woodman, head of Lincoln Automation, was a former Hobart executive with over a decade of experience in robotics manufacturing and marketing.

MANAGEMENT ORGANIZATION

James Lincoln stressed the need to protect management's authority. "Management in all successful departments of industry must have complete power," he said. "Management is the coach who must be obeyed. The men, however, are the players who alone can win the game." Examples of management's authority were the right to transfer workers among jobs, to switch between overtime and short time as required, and to assign specific parts to individual workers. As to executive perquisites, there were few—crowded, austere offices, no executive washrooms or lunchrooms or automobiles, and no reserved parking spaces, except for visitors. Even CEO Hastings and President Mackenbach paid for their own meals, normally in the employee cafeteria.

James Lincoln never allowed preparation of a formal organization chart, saying this might limit flexibility. Irrgang and Willis continued that policy. During the 1970s, Harvard Business School researchers prepared a chart reflecting the implied management relationships at Lincoln. It became available within the company, and Irrgang felt this had a disruptive effect. Only after Hastings became CEO was a formal chart prepared. (Exhibit 11 shows the official chart in 1995 and Exhibit 5 lists officers and directors.) Two levels of management, at most, existed between supervisors and Mackenbach. Production supervisors at Lincoln typically were responsible for 60 to over 100 workers. Hastings, who was 67, had recruited experienced managers from outside the company and appointed a number of new, young vice presidents, mainly from the field, so they could compete for the top jobs.

Promotion from Within

Until the 1990s, Lincoln had a firm policy of promotion from within and claimed to hire above the entry level "only when there are no suitable internal applicants." In 1990, all senior managers at Lincoln were career Lincoln employees—and all directors were present or former employees or Lincoln family members. However, when Lincoln purchased Harris Calorific in 1992, its CEO, Paul F. Fantelli, was retained and later became Vice President, Business Development of Lincoln. A number of

EXHIBIT 11
Lincoln Organizational Chart, 1995

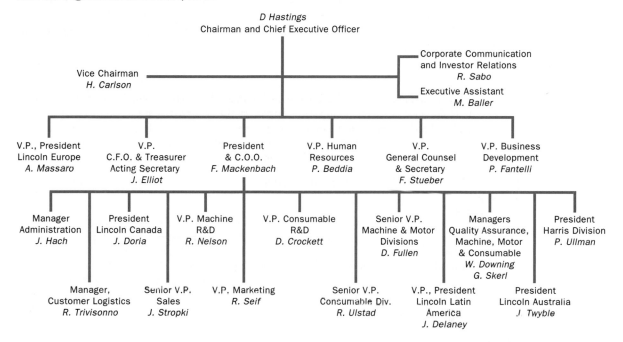

other acquired company officials were integrated into Lincoln's management structure.

Lincoln's CFO in 1996, H. Jay Elliott, came from Goodyear in 1993; General Counsel Frederick Stueber came from a private law firm in 1995; and Anthony Massaro, the nominated successor to Fred Mackenbach as President, joined Lincoln from his position as Group President of Westinghouse Electric Co. in 1993. Several outside directors were also elected, including the CEO of Capital American Financial Corporation, a former Vice Chairman of General Electric, a former CEO of Westinghouse, and the CEO of Libby Corporation. Still, there were no announced plans to hire more managers from outside. And insiders and Lincoln family members retained a clear majority on the board.

Lincoln managers received a base salary plus an incentive bonus. The bonus was calculated in the same way as for workers. The only exceptions were the three outsiders Hastings hired as managers in 1993–1995 and the Chairman and Chief Executive Officer. The former outsiders had special employment contracts. Sabo explained how the CEO was compensated:

> James Lincoln set the Chairman's salary at $50,000 plus 0.1% of sales. After Willis became Chairman, it was based on a percentage of sales plus a percentage of profit. It became apparent that when the company started losing money it was difficult to pay someone based on losses. So they changed the approach for Don Hastings. [Through the lean years] Don has somewhere around $600,000 base salary plus incentives.

For 1995, Hastings was paid $1,003,901.[8]

LOOKING TO THE FUTURE

When Lincoln in the spring of 1995 announced plans to raise capital with a public issue of stock, Dick Sabo said, certain Lincoln family members were afraid the family would lose control of the company. "Paranoid, I guess, is the proper term," he remarked. Sam Evans added,

> I hope the public issue is handled in such a manner that those public owners understand that the success of this company is based on the incentive system. For sixty or seventy years, that has been our success—through the contribution of the employees. We have succeeded because he had a good product, good R and D, and excellent management for most of that period. But we've also had great contribution from the employees.

With the public issue accomplished and a record year in the books, noted *Business Week,*

> . . . executives are now considering ways to move toward a more traditional pay scheme and away from the flat percentage-bonus formula. "The bonus is a good program, and it has worked well, but it's got to be modified some," says Director David C. Lincoln, whose father John C. Lincoln founded the company in 1895. Adds Edward E. Lawler, who heads the University of Southern California's Center for Effective Organizations: "One of the issues with Lincoln is how [its pay plan] can survive rapid growth and globalization."

References

1. Barnaby J. Feder, "Rethinking a Model Incentive Plan," *The New York Times*, September 5, 1994, Section 1, p. 23.
2. Thomas W. Gerdel, "Lincoln Electric Experiences Season of Worker Discontent," Cleveland *Plain Dealer*, December 10, 1995.
3. Zachary Schiller, "A Model Incentive Plan Gets Caught in a Vise," *Business Week*, January 22, 1996, p. 89.
4. F. C. Eiselen, E. Lewis, and D. G. Downey, eds., *The Abingdon Bible Commentary*, Nashville, TN: The Abingdon Press, 1929, pp. 960–69.
5. Schiller, op. cit.
6. N. Utley et al., Grieg Middleton & Co., Ltd. Company report number 1674211, Charter 12/12/95. Investext 02/23.
7. Gene Bylinsky, "America's Best-Managed Factories," *Fortune*, May 28, 1984, p. 16.
8. Baltimore, MD, Disclosures, Inc. (via Dow Jones News Service).

http://www.lincolnelectric.com/

STRATEGY IMPLEMENTATION

CASE 34

The Snowflake Potato Division*

The Snowflake Potato Division is a major division of a large national and international food products company. Snowflake manufactures a variety of processed potato products, but its two principal products are frozen french fries and instant whipped potatoes. French fries make up about 50 percent of sales while the whipped potatoes account for approximately 30 percent of sales. The remainder of sales are divided among several other processed potato products.

Sales are primarily to the consumer market under its own brand. A small part of the division's sales are in the institutional market (hospitals, schools, etc.) and to other businesses for sale under private labels (such as a private grocery chain label). The Snowflake label is generally regarded as one of the high quality products in the market, and the division's products have always excelled in consumer preference tests. Costs that are somewhat higher than competitors' prevent Snowflake products from taking a larger share of the institutional and private label markets.

The management style or culture of the firm is to give division managers broad discretion in decision making with the headquarters monitoring bottom line performance (profits and return on investment) and market share very closely. The public image presented by the company is that of a socially responsible firm.

The company has a formal code of ethics that explicitly calls for management not to engage in unethical business practices; however, the sanctions that would be imposed on a manager who violates the code are unclear. The internal environment is made more ambiguous because considerable pressure is placed on division managers to improve performance each year. Failure to meet performance goals reduces a manager's overall compensation and most certainly damages a division manager's career opportunities within the company. Consistent failure to meet performance goals will likely lead to outright dismissal.

Ed Smith, division manager for the Snowflake division, is confronted with a major problem. A primary competitor in the instant whipped potato market (also a division of a large food company) has made a significant technical breakthrough in

*This case was prepared by Gamewell Gantt, George Johnson, and John Kilpatrick of the College of Business, Idaho State University, and is intended to be used as a basis for class discussion rather than to illustrate either effective or ineffective handling of the situation. The names of the organization, individual, and location and/or financial information have been disguised to preserve the organization's desire for anonymity. Presented to and accepted by the refereed Society for Case Research. All rights reserved to the author(s), and the SCR. Copyright © 1995 by Gamewell Gantt, George Johnson, and John Kilpatrick.

process technology that will result in a dramatic improvement in the quality of its whipped potatoes. Market research has indicated that consumers feel that instant whipped potatoes lack the texture and flavor of real mashed potatoes. This factor, more than any other, influences consumer purchases. The competitor has perfected changes in its manufacturing processes that have yielded a whipped potato product that is better in both taste and texture than current products on the market. This breakthrough appears to solve one of the principal problems in marketing whipped potatoes and will have a major impact on sales for the Snowflake division. Unfortunately for Snowflake, the competitor's process changes are protected by a patent.

Ed hired a consulting firm to monitor the test marketing of the new product by his competitor, and the results are not good for his division. The consultant concluded that when the new product is introduced, market share for the Snowflake division will decrease from about 30 percent of the current market to less than 5 percent.

In response to queries from Ed, the division's R&D people indicated that to develop a comparable product and bring it to the market would take at least two years. Regaining significant market share at that time would be difficult and expensive, if not impossible. Snowflake's researchers understand the process changes instituted by their competitor, and these could be replicated quickly and easily. The problem is to develop changes that will not infringe upon the competitor's patent and to do this in a timely fashion.

In a nutshell, Ed's division is going to take a major hit in sales and profits over the next several years unless something is done now. Ed feels the net effect of this threat is that his division would be forced to withdraw from the instant mashed potato market. Without question, there would be major layoffs in the division, and even possibly plant closures, and his job would likely be on the line as well.

The management consultants have recommended a course of action to counter the adverse effects of the new product on Ed's division. Their recommendation is to go ahead and infringe upon the competitor's patent while Snowflake's R&D department develops an alternative process that would yield the same quality product but would not infringe upon the patent. The competitor would undoubtedly bring a lawsuit, but the suit could easily be delayed for the two years that Snowflake needs to develop its own process. Settlement of the suit would be expensive but not anything close to the damages the company will incur if it does not undertake this action. This course of action would also protect Snowflake's market share and allow the division to continue operations with little disruption. Even better is the fact that the cost of the legal action would be charged to Snowflake's corporate headquarters since that group would handle the defense of the lawsuit.

Ed has stalled making this decision as long as he can. If he goes ahead with the course of action recommended by the consultant and chooses to infringe upon the patent, then he needs to give his R&D people the authority to proceed. He also needs to decide whether to tell corporate management about his plan of action. Should he inform them immediately or delay any such communication, assuming that they would be just as happy not knowing until after the fact? Last, he must deal with his own conscience. What should Ed do?

http://www5.fullerton.edu/les/ethics_list.html

STRATEGY IMPLEMENTATION

CASE 35

Robin Hood*

It was in the spring of the second year of his insurrection against the High Sheriff of Nottingham that Robin Hood took a walk in Sherwood Forest. As he walked he pondered the progress of the campaign, the disposition of his forces, the Sheriff's recent moves, and the options that confronted him.

The revolt against the Sheriff had begun as a personal crusade. It erupted out of Robin's conflict with the Sheriff and his administration. However, alone Robin Hood could do little. He therefore sought allies, men with grievances and a deep sense of justice. Later he welcomed all who came, asking few questions and demanding only a willingness to serve. Strength, he believed, lay in numbers.

He spent the first year forging the group into a disciplined band, united in enmity against the Sheriff, and willing to live outside the law. The band's organization was simple. Robin ruled supreme, making all important decisions. He delegated specific tasks to his lieutenants. Will Scarlett was in charge of intelligence and scouting. His main job was to shadow the Sheriff and his men, always alert to their next move. He also collected information on the travel plans of rich merchants and tax collectors. Little John kept discipline among the men and saw to it that their archery was at the high peak that their profession demanded. Scarlock took care of the finances, converting loot to cash, paying shares of the take, and finding suitable hiding places for the surplus. Finally, Much the Miller's son had the difficult task of provisioning the ever-increasing band of Merrymen.

The increasing size of the band was a source of satisfaction for Robin, but also a source of concern. The fame of his Merrymen was spreading, and new recruits poured in from every corner of England. As the band grew larger, their small bivouac became a major encampment. Between raids the men milled about, talking and playing games. Vigilance was in decline, and discipline was becoming harder to enforce. "Why," Robin reflected, "I don't know half the men I run into these days."

The growing band was also beginning to exceed the food capacity of the forest. Game was becoming scarce, and supplies had to be obtained from outlying villages. The cost of buying food was beginning to drain the band's financial reserves at the very moment when revenues were in decline. Travelers, especially those with the most to lose, were now giving the forest a wide berth. This was costly and inconvenient to them, but it was preferable to having all their goods confiscated.

---

*Joseph Lampel, New York University. Copyright © 1991, by Joseph Lampel.

Robin believed that the time had come for the Merrymen to change their policy of outright confiscation of goods to one of a fixed transit tax. His lieutenants strongly resisted this idea. They were proud of the Merrymen's famous motto: "Rob the rich to give to the poor." "The farmers and the townspeople," they argued, "are our most important allies." "How can we tax them, and still hope for their help in our fight against the Sheriff?"

Robin wondered how long the Merrymen could keep to the ways and methods of their early days. The Sheriff was growing stronger and becoming better organized. He now had the money and the men and was beginning to harass the band, probing for its weaknesses. The tide of events was beginning to turn against the Merrymen. Robin felt the campaign must be decisively concluded before the Sheriff had a chance to deliver a mortal blow. "But how," he wondered, "could this be done?"

Robin had often entertained the possibility of killing the Sheriff, but the chances for this seemed increasingly remote. Besides, killing the Sheriff might satisfy his personal thirst for revenge, but it would not improve the situation. Robin had hoped that the perpetual state of unrest, and the Sheriff's failure to collect taxes, would lead to his removal from office. Instead, the Sheriff used his political connections to obtain reinforcement. He had powerful friends at court and was well regarded by the regent, Prince John.

Prince John was vicious and volatile. He was consumed by his unpopularity among the people, who wanted the imprisoned King Richard back. He also lived in constant fear of the barons, who had first given him the regency but were now beginning to dispute his claim to the throne. Several of these barons had set out to collect the ransom that would release King Richard the Lionheart from his jail in Austria. Robin was invited to join the conspiracy in return for future amnesty. It was a dangerous proposition. Provincial banditry was one thing, court intrigue another. Prince John had spies everywhere, and he was known for his vindictiveness. If the conspirators' plan failed, the pursuit would be relentless and retributions swift.

The sound of the supper horn startled Robin from his thoughts. There was the smell of roasting venison in the air. Nothing was resolved or settled. Robin headed for camp promising himself that he would give these problems his utmost attention after tomorrow's raid.

http://rodent.lib.rochester.edu/Camelot/rhbib.htm

STRATEGY IMPLEMENTATION

CASE 36

Dennis Hightower: Walt Disney's Transnational Manager*

Dennis Hightower settled into his airplane seat on a transatlantic flight from Paris to Disney Consumer Products' worldwide head office in Burbank, California. (Exhibit 1 presents revenues and operating income for Walt Disney company's three divisions.) It was August 1994. Hightower was pondering over how to organize Disney Consumer Products' apparel business in Europe and the Middle East.

CRAFTING A EUROPEAN STRATEGY

Named vice president of Disney Consumer Products–Europe in 1987, Hightower had taken charge of eight disparate country operations with a diverse composition of businesses engaged primarily in the licensing of merchandise, books, magazines, and children's music.[1]

Taking Publishing Beyond Licensing

Starting with Italian operations in July 1988, Hightower had begun to move beyond pure licensing into the publishing business. A country manager explained why Hightower was taking greater control of downstream operations, "As a licensor, you earn regular royalty but you are never a core business to your licensee. Your licensee will

---

*Professor Ashish Nanda prepared this case as the basis for class discussion rather than to illustrate either effective or ineffective handling of an administrative situation. Copyright © 1994 by the President and Fellows of Harvard College. To order copies or request permission to reproduce materials, call 1-800-545-7685 or write Harvard Business School Publishing, Boston, MA 02163. No part of this publication may be reproduced, stored in a retrieval system, used in a spreadsheet, or transmitted in any form or by any means—electronic, mechanical, photocopying, recording, or otherwise—without the permission of Harvard Business School.

[1]See "Walt Disney's Dennis Hightower: Taking Charge" (HBS No. 395-055) for a description of the DCP–Europe's evolution until 1987. The Middle East was added to Hightower's responsibilities in July 1988, when he was promoted to senior vice president in charge of Disney Consumer Products–Europe and the Middle East (DCP–EME).

EXHIBIT 1

Walt Disney Company: Divisional Revenues and Operating Income, 1987–1994
(all figures are in millions of dollars)

	1987	*1988*	*1989*	*1990*	*1991*	*1992*	*1993*	*1994*
Filmed entertainment:								
Sales	$ 876	$1,149	$1,588	$2,250	$2,594	$3,115	$3,673	$4,793
Operating income	131	186	257	313	318	508	622	856
Theme parks and resorts:								
Sales	$1,834	$2,042	$2,595	$2,933	$2,794	$3,307	$3,441	$3,464
Operating income	549	565	785	803	547	644	747	684
Consumer products:								
Sales	$ 167	$ 247	$ 411	$ 574	$ 724	$1,082	$1,415	$1,798
Operating income	97	134	187	223	230	283	355	426

Source: Refer to Exhibit 2 of HBS case No. 395-055 for the 1987 organization chart of the Walt Disney Company.

use your name to open doors with other principals, but he may invest too little in your products. Dennis feels that the time is ripe for Disney to take greater responsibility and risk."

Over time, Disney's European publishing operations became a mosaic of licensing in the United Kingdom, Germany, and the Nordic countries, joint venturing in France and the Middle East, and vertical integration in Italy.[2]

Integrating European Operations

In 1988, Hightower centralized European contract administration and auditing. "I told my country managers to focus on the revenue-production side of their business," he recalled, "and let me worry about the back office." Scale economies and elimination of redundancy yielded immediate savings.

Hightower also established marketing and creative services divisions in the regional office to offer common resources and coordinate activities of the countries and licensees. The marketing division supported merchandise licensing, the creative services division of the publishing and music businesses. He began to recruit from consumer products and creative companies experienced MBAs to staff the regional office.

Pan-European Licenses

With the regional office administering contracts, Hightower realized that DCP–EME could begin to enter into "mega-deals" with selected partner companies spanning multiple countries. In 1988, Hightower rolled out to the whole of Europe what had previously been a U.S.–wide deal with Mattel for toys, eliminating 68 local

---

[2]Because it was not yielding expected results, Disney unwound in 1991 a joint venture established in Spain in 1989 and reverted to licensing there.

toy licensees in the process. Next, he negotiated with Nestlé a comprehensive deal covering food products that eliminated 57 local licensees. The Nestlé deal was subsequently rolled out worldwide. These first two deals in place, Hightower picked up the pace, negotiating broad, transnational deals with Kodak, Sega, Nintendo, Coca Cola, IBM, Johnson & Johnson, and Seiko.

Notwithstanding the accelerated growth they offered, these mega-deals garnered mixed support from the country offices. "When regional office people start talking with someone for a pan-European license," a country manager remarked, "they expect the countries to stop talking with everyone else. It takes six months to two years for their negotiations to bear fruit and, even then, in the end they may not have any deal. Meanwhile, we are simply losing business in the countries. In any case, the mega-deal mentality of 'one size fits all,' which may work in the United States, is doomed to failure in Europe, given our diverse cultures."

Hightower was undeterred by such reservations. "I do empathize with the country managers who feel in their guts that such deals are proscribing their authority," he acknowledged, "but they need to appreciate that these deals have given them 'air cover.' The studio is leaning on all of us to reach our corporate target of 20% growth every year, and if pan-European deals get the whole of Europe there faster, we will take the pan-European deals route."[3]

Worldwide Operations

After consolidating European operations into a single region in 1987, worldwide head of DCP Barton K. ("Bo") Boyd had established three other regions worldwide—Asia Pacific, United States–Canada, and Latin America. Boyd took a hands-off approach towards his regional offices. "The studio has always had the philosophy of letting the operators operate," Hightower observed. "I talk with Bo three to four times a month at most."

HIGHTOWER'S MANAGEMENT APPROACH

"My role is to step back, take a global view, and evaluate tradeoffs," Hightower remarked of his role in the organization. "Once I have reached a decision, I try to make my country managers respond to my ideas in order to ensure that the entire region moves in concert. I believe not in ordering, but in persuading people to go along because they see the logic of what I want to do and how they fit into that, especially since I am leading a team of sophisticated marketing people who know their markets better than I will ever know them."

Boyd reflected on Hightower's management style:

Dennis carefully evaluates a situation, puts a plan together spelling out what he needs to accomplish, and then sets out to attain those goals. In the process, he is very fair and hon-

---

[3]Disney's worldwide head office at Burbank was called "the studio" inside the company.

est with his troops, and they in turn are very loyal to him. This combination of strategic thinking and organizational skills gives Dennis the rare ability to lead a diverse cultural group such that they all pull together in the same direction. However, in his urge to be close to the field, Dennis travels so much that he is probably not as accessible to his subordinates as they would like him to be.

"Dennis works on the squeaky-wheelchair theory: get involved only when you hear a squeak," observed an executive in the regional office. "He trusts people, but they must deliver. Since he is also running all the time trying to grow business, he isn't always easily reachable. Many decisions end up getting delegated down. Having so much authority can get uncomfortable, but I guess it is part of being treated as a grownup; personally, I find it very motivating."

Hightower spent considerable time on personnel issues. "Numbers don't get things done, people do," he remarked.

> It may not be the only concept of effective management, but it has worked for me. And there is great value in knowing who gets tweaked in what way. One of my key responsibilities is to know who to push and who to pull back, when to push and when to pull back, and how to push and how to pull back. I use a combination of personal persuasion, and financial and non-financial incentives. Then, if anybody chooses to ignore me, that person does so only at considerable career risk. I have to have the hammer in one hand and the velvet glove on the other and know when to use which, with whom to use which, and to what extent.

A country manager described the management approach that Hightower had inculcated in DCP–EME:

> Dennis often remarks that we are not brain surgeons out doing our own things, but a marketing team working with a network of people. The critical requirement is that we build working partnerships with others. Talented, motivated people sometimes fail on this front because they step on each other's toes. We have had some bright but inexperienced disasters who, two years out of their MBAs, felt that they should be running Europe.

RENEWING THE ORGANIZATION

"Dennis has achieved all his plan targets," Boyd had remarked upon naming Hightower president of DCP–EME in 1991. "More important, Europe is marching to the beat of one drummer." Vertical integration had dramatically raised revenues and increased operating profits, albeit at lower margins (see Exhibit 2).

On the horizon was a host of promising opportunities and new challenges. European unification seemed to be a distant dream at best, but the demise of communism had opened new market opportunities in Eastern Europe. EuroDisney was about to open. Hightower began initiating further changes in 1992 in order to build on the momentum DCP–EME had established over the past four years.

EXHIBIT 2
DCP–EME: Performance and Business Composition

				DCP–EME Growth Trend: 1988–1995					
	1988	1989	1990	1991	1992	1993	1994	1995e	CAGR(%)
Revenue (in millions of dollars)	$ 56	$108	$131	$143	$231	$279	$308	$351	30.0%
Operating income (in millions of dollars)	$ 36	$ 58	$ 66	$ 68	$ 92	$101	$115	$142	21.7%
Profitability (%)	65%	53%	50%	48%	40%	36%	37%	40%	
Human resources:									
Regional office	4	11	26	43	62	97	112	114	
Subsidiaries	124	169	186	238	282	329	354	371	

	DCP–EME Revenue and Income: 1994*				
			Product Line		
	Merchandise Licensing	Publishing	Music	Others	Total
Revenue:					
France	$14.6	$ 69.8	$12.0	$0.9	$ 97.3
Germany and Eastern Europe	22.8	14.5	2.5	0.6	40.4
U.K.	16.1	3.2	2.9	0.9	23.1
Italy	6.9	93.0	5.2	0.8	105.9
Others	21.1	12.8	2.7	4.8	41.4
Total revenue	$81.5	$193.3	$25.3	$ 8.0	$308.1
Operating income	$55.8	$ 49.0	$ 7.3	$ 2.9	$115.1

e: Expected.
*In millions of dollars.
Source: Refer to Exhibit 4 of HBS case No. 395-055 for DCP–EME's revenue and income in 1987.

Reorganizing the Regional Office

In the space of a few months in 1992, Hightower made several organizational and personnel changes at the regional office. (Exhibit 3 presents an organization chart for DCP–EME.) Over its four-year life, the creative division at the regional office had been operating uneconomically. Rather than prune its operations, Hightower split the division. He attracted a highly respected artist and designer from Disney U.S.A to head creative services, which would provide central creative resources to European publishers, and named Marie-France Garros, an experienced publishing industry insider who had been looking after publishing within creative services, head of the newly independent publishing division responsible for coordinating business with the country publishing operations.

Hightower moved the Finance head, who had been wanting to shift into an operating role, to head the Middle East subregion, and dismissed the head of Marketing, who, he observed, "had a divisive approach of pitting one country manager against another." Both positions were filled by internal promotions of European executives.

EXHIBIT 3
DCP-EME Organization Chart, 1994

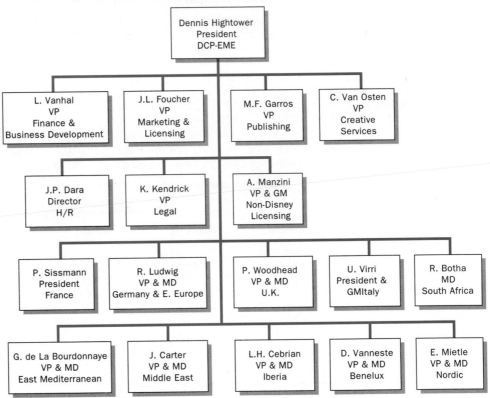

One of the newly appointed division heads commented on the working atmosphere at the regional office:

> The strategies of the earlier heads weren't too bad; they just had no patience or persuasion. When I became head of my group, I was amazed by the tension that existed between the different divisions. Members of our new regional office team, who had all been understudies to the departing managers, had learned from their mistakes. We chose to operate as a more integrated group. We knew Dennis wouldn't dictate to us how to operate, but he would not be very happy otherwise.

The 22-person marketing staff at the regional office continued to lead the effort to identify and initiate pan-European contracts. The 21-person publishing group took a different approach. "We offer our country offices a central facility for quality control and coordination, and expose them to new ideas through regular meetings, newsletters, and updates," Garros explained. "Besides, we conduct monthly reviews of all the magazines in our region and send our comments to the local offices, who very much appreciate them. On most issues, we offer suggestions. When we do have to mandate something, we try to be as precise and objective as possible."

Knitting the Country Operations Together

Hightower believed that bringing the country operations closer together had generated enormous synergies. "One legacy that I will be proud to leave behind," he remarked, "will be of far greater interplay among the countries on a positive collegial basis than when I had arrived." An operating council established by Hightower, comprising himself, the then eight country managers, and four executives from the regional office, met every quarter, and occasionally designated special teams to look into specific issues.

In 1992, the fiercely independent U.K. country manager was replaced by an outsider. "She took a strictly British perspective," explained an executive in the U.K. subsidiary. "Whenever a pan-European deal was struck, she had to be brought into it kicking and screaming."

Even as Hightower was weaving operations together, some country managers expressed their concern at losing autonomy to the regional office. Remarked one country manager:

> I am responsible for my budgets and performance, but I have to countenance the regional office people meddling in my business, pushing needless deals or doing country office jobs. I am not even sure whether current trends point toward harmonization of local environments in Europe. It is quite likely that people will identify even more fiercely with their local identities. Having effective local offices will continue to be critical.

Evolving Relations with the Rest of Disney

Hightower had been fairly successful in the ambassadorial task of building awareness of DCP–EME in Burbank. "Before Dennis, people in the studio would refer to the United States and the rest of the world," remarked a country manager. "Dennis has made them realize the richness, complexity, and potential of Europe."

Performance has yielded relative independence. "Chances are," reflected Hightower, "as long as we continue to deliver we'll continue to get autonomy."

Success had brought its own problems, however. Garros explained, "Some of our U.S. colleagues, whose operation is incidentally much smaller than ours, unilaterally enter worldwide agreements that can have huge consequences in our area."

LOOKING AHEAD

Looking out on the Atlantic, Hightower reflected with considerable satisfaction on his seven years with DCP–EME. He had overseen growth in the retail value of Disney business from $650 million in 1987 to $3.5 billion in 1993. Now he foresaw a number of organizational and strategic challenges.

Planning for Succession

Disney's president and COO Frank Wells died in a helicopter accident in April 1994. Three months later, Disney's chairman and CEO Michael Esner underwent quadruple bypass heart surgery. In August, chairman of Walt Disney Studios Jeffrey Katzenberg announced that he was leaving the company. Newspapers and magazines were suddenly filled with rumors and articles debating management depth within Disney. Such speculation was particularly unsettling for a company that had for years prided itself on its stable management.

It was in this context that Hightower perceived that one of his greatest challenges in the coming years was to be planning his succession. "I have been in this position for several years now," he remarked. "I want to have an organization in place that allows someone from Europe to take my place. The question I am increasingly asking myself is what should be the profile of the person who will replace me."

Reaching for the Sky

Having witnessed Disney's success in Europe, Warner Brothers had begun to move in with licensing deals and company-owned stores. Yet the Disney label continued to be extremely powerful: of the ten most popular characters in Europe, nine belonged to Disney.

More than competitive challenges, the issue facing DCP–EME was how to maintain its frenetic pace of organizational growth as business-mix changed and operations expanded. Business was growing at 30% per year in Eastern Europe, but at 11% per annum in the Nordic region, in which the company enjoyed more than 90% market penetration. The publishing business continued to contribute 63% of DCP–EME's revenues, but merchandise licensing was becoming an increasingly larger part of the business (see Exhibit 2). Observed marketing head Jean Luc Foucher:

> Eisner has made a commitment to the stock market to deliver 20% growth per annum over any five-year period. We have to constantly reinvent our business in order to continue growing at that pace. We are a big operation, and rapid growth on such a large base is very difficult. For example, generating such growth in publishing—a mature and stable business in which we have a 70% share of the market—is a huge challenge. In trying to reach for the sky, we have to be careful that we don't lose our soul by diluting our characters' images too much.

Hightower remained optimistic. "Our main lines are healthy, our structure is well established, we have a team of motivated and talented people," he remarked. "Several businesses are going in or coming out of our portfolio. Leveraging off our strengths helps us reach the 20% target without having to go back to Michael and ask for relief."

Besides pushing for sustained performance in existing businesses and territories, Hightower was looking at geographical expansion in Eastern Europe and the Middle East and growth options such as catalog selling, electronic publishing, comics syndication, and third-party licensing. However, a senior executive voiced a common concern within DCP–EME when he remarked:

Some people at the studio say that our job is just licensing. Others see our job in a broader way, as providing entertainment products and services. How the company eventually defines the scope of our activities will determine how we grow.

The Apparel Business

Regional office and country subsidiary views differed on the usefulness of almost all pan-European alliances, but in no category did they diverge as much as in apparel. Apparel was the company's largest merchandise category in revenue terms, contributing more than 30% to the retail sales of all Disney-licensed products. "It is a business close to everyone's heart," Hightower quipped, "since everyone thinks that he or she is the world's greatest fashion critic and designer."

Before Hightower's arrival, anybody could sell Disney apparel by paying the company a fee for a nonexclusive license. Distribution was spotty and product quality often shoddy. Hightower charged a regional office team to rectify this situation by developing an apparel strategy. A regional office marketing executive recalled how the team's strategy played out:

> The apparel team came up with a list of four manufacturers who could be developed into pan-European licensees. Weeding out the marginal licensees dramatically raised our designs and product quality. Europe-wide sales of apparel have gone up 24% since introduction of the pan-European policy. But the four manufacturers have preferred mutual exclusivity to vigorous competition; instead of jumping into the new opened markets, they have retreated into their home bases. Now we have several underexploited territories.

The German country manager described the consequences:

> My textile sales are down 30% this year. Germany has very structured retailing with big department stores and mail-order houses. It requires sustained relationship building. None of the pan-European licensees is German. As a result, none of our pan-European licensees was able to win the big accounts, despite intense efforts. In contrast, Italy is made up of small retailers. None of the licensees effectively penetrated Italy. Now I am unhappy since my market is underexploited and the Italian country manager is unhappy since his market is not being served. Incidentally, apparel is not the only category in which we have been hurt by the regional office taking control over some of these issues.

These different perspectives had given Hightower pause. "Do we need to move from where we stand on this issue today?" he wondered, "and, if so, where should we be heading and by what route?"

http://www.disney.com/

Name Index

Note: Italic page numbers refer to exhibits and applications. References to notes are indicated by italic *n*.

Subject Index

Note: Italic page numbers refer to exhibits and applications. References to notes are indicated by italic *n*. plus the note number appended to the page number (e.g. 447*n.24*)